FOR REFERENCE

Twentieth-Century
Literary Criticism

Guide to Gale Literary Criticism Series

For criticism on	Consult these Gale series
Authors now living or who died after December 31, 1959	*CONTEMPORARY LITERARY CRITICISM (CLC)*
Authors who died between 1900 and 1959	*TWENTIETH-CENTURY LITERARY CRITICISM (TCLC)*
Authors who died between 1800 and 1899	*NINETEENTH-CENTURY LITERATURE CRITICISM (NCLC)*
Authors who died between 1400 and 1799	*LITERATURE CRITICISM FROM 1400 TO 1800 (LC)* *SHAKESPEAREAN CRITICISM (SC)*
Authors who died before 1400	*CLASSICAL AND MEDIEVAL LITERATURE CRITICISM (CMLC)*
Black writers of the past two hundred years	*BLACK LITERATURE CRITICISM (BLC)*
Authors of books for children and young adults	*CHILDREN'S LITERATURE REVIEW (CLR)*
Dramatists	*DRAMA CRITICISM (DC)*
Hispanic writers of the late nineteenth and twentieth centuries	*HISPANIC LITERATURE CRITICISM (HLC)*
Native North American writers and orators of the eighteenth, nineteenth, and twentieth centuries	*NATIVE NORTH AMERICAN LITERATURE (NNAL)*
Poets	*POETRY CRITICISM (PC)*
Short story writers	*SHORT STORY CRITICISM (SSC)*
Major authors from the Renaissance to the present	*WORLD LITERATURE CRITICISM, 1500 TO THE PRESENT (WLC)*

ISSN 0276-8178

Volume 71

Twentieth-Century Literary Criticism

**Excerpts from Criticism of the
Works of Novelists, Poets, Playwrights,
Short Story Writers, and Other Creative Writers
Who Lived between 1900 and 1960,
from the First Published Critical
Appraisals to Current Evaluations**

Jennifer Gariepy
Editor

Thomas Ligotti
Associate Editor

GALE

DETROIT • NEW YORK • TORONTO • LONDON

STAFF

Jennifer Gariepy, *Editor*

Thomas Ligotti, *Associate Editor*

Susan Trosky, *Permissions Manager*
Kimberly F. Smilay, *Permissions Specialist*
Sarah R. Chesney, *Permissions Associate*
Steve Cusack, Kelly A. Quin, *Permissions Assistants*

Victoria B. Cariappa, *Research Manager*
Michele P. LaMeau, Andrew Guy Malonis, Barbara McNeil, Gary J. Oudersluys, Maureen Richards, *Research Specialists*
Julia C. Daniel, Tamara C. Nott, Tracie A. Richardson, Norma Sawaya, Cheryl L. Warnock, *Research Associates*

Mary Beth Trimper, *Production Director*
Deborah L. Milliken, *Production Assistant*

Christi Fuson, *Macintosh Artist*
Randy Bassett, *Image Database Supervisor*
Robert Duncan, Michael Logusz, *Imaging Specialists*
Pamela Reed, *Photography Coordinator*

Library of Congress Catalog Card Number 76-46132
ISBN 0-7876-1172-7
ISSN 0276-8178

Printed in the United States of America
10 9 8 7 6 5 4 3 2 1

Contents

Preface vii

Acknowledgments xi

Preface

Since its inception more than fifteen years ago, *Twentieth-Century Literary Criticism* has been purchased and used by nearly 10,000 school, public, and college or university libraries. *TCLC* has covered more than 500 authors, representing 58 nationalities, and over 25,000 titles. No other reference source has surveyed the critical response to twentieth-century authors and literature as thoroughly as *TCLC*. In the words of one reviewer, "there is nothing comparable available." *TCLC* "is a gold mine of information—dates, pseudonyms, biographical information, and criticism from books and periodicals—which many libraries would have difficulty assembling on their own."

Scope of the Series

TCLC is designed to serve as an introduction to authors who died between 1900 and 1960 and to the most significant interpretations of these author's works. The great poets, novelists, short story writers, playwrights, and philosophers of this period are frequently studied in high school and college literature courses. In organizing and excerpting the vast amount of critical material written on these authors, *TCLC* helps students develop valuable insight into literary history, promotes a better understanding of the texts, and sparks ideas for papers and assignments. Each entry in *TCLC* presents a comprehensive survey of an author's career or an individual work of literature and provides the user with a multiplicity of interpretations and assessments. Such variety allows students to pursue their own interests; furthermore, it fosters an awareness that literature is dynamic and responsive to many different opinions.

Every fourth volume of *TCLC* is devoted to literary topics. These topic entries widen the focus of the series from individual authors to such broader subjects as literary movements, prominent themes in twentieth-century literature, literary reaction to political and historical events, significant eras in literary history, prominent literary anniversaries, and the literatures of cultures that are often overlooked by English-speaking readers.

TCLC is designed as a companion series to Gale's *Contemporary Literary Criticism,* which reprints commentary on authors now living or who have died since 1960. Because of the different periods under consideration, there is no duplication of material between *CLC* and *TCLC*. For additional information about *CLC* and Gale's other criticism titles, users should consult the Guide to Gale Literary Criticism Series preceding the title page in this volume.

Coverage

Each volume of *TCLC* is carefully compiled to present:

- criticism of authors, or literary topics, representing a variety of genres and nationalities

- both major and lesser-known writers and literary works of the period

- 6-12 authors or 3-6 topics per volume

- individual entries that survey critical response to each author's work or each topic in literary history, including early criticism to reflect initial reactions; later criticism to represent any rise or decline in reputation; and current retrospective analyses.

Organization of This Book

An author entry consists of the following elements: author heading, biographical and critical introduction, list of principal works, excerpts of criticism (each preceded by an annotation and a bibliographic citation), and a bibliography of further reading.

- The **Author Heading** consists of the name under which the author most commonly wrote, followed by birth and death dates. If an author wrote consistently under a pseudonym, the pseudonym will be listed in the author heading and the real name given in parentheses on the first line of the biographical and critical introduction. Also located at the beginning of the introduction to the author entry are any name variations under which an author wrote, including transliterated forms for authors whose languages use nonroman alphabets.

- The **Biographical and Critical Introduction** outlines the author's life and career, as well as the critical issues surrounding his or her work. References to past volumes of *TCLC* are provided at the beginning of the introduction. Additional sources of information in other biographical and critical reference series published by Gale, including *Short Story Criticism, Children's Literature Review, Contemporary Authors, Dictionary of Literary Biography,* and *Something about the Author,* are listed in a box at the end of the entry.

- Some *TCLC* entries include **Portraits** of the author. Entries also may contain reproductions of materials pertinent to an author's career, including manuscript pages, title pages, dust jackets, letters, and drawings, as well as photographs of important people, places, and events in an author's life.

- The **List of Principal Works** is chronological by date of first book publication and identifies the genre of each work. In the case of foreign authors with both foreign-language publications and English translations, the title and date of the first English-language edition are given in brackets. Unless otherwise indicated, dramas are dated by first performance, not first publication.

- Critical excerpts are prefaced by **Annotations** providing the reader with information about both the critic and the criticism that follows. Included are the critic's reputation, individual approach to literary criticism, and particular expertise in an author's works. Also noted are the relative importance of a work of criticism, the scope of the excerpt, and the growth of critical controversy or changes in critical trends regarding an author. In some cases, these annotations cross-reference excerpts by critics who discuss each other's commentary.

- A complete **Bibliographic Citation** designed to facilitate location of the original essay or book precedes each piece of criticism.

- **Criticism** is arranged chronologically in each author entry to provide a perspective on changes in critical evaluation over the years. All titles of works by the author featured in the entry are printed in boldface type to enable the user to easily locate discussion of particular works. Also for purposes of easier identification, the critic's name and the publication date of the essay are given at the beginning of each piece of criticism. Unsigned criticism is preceded by the title of the journal in which it appeared. Some of the excerpts in *TCLC* also contain translated material. Unless otherwise noted, translations in brackets are by the editors; translations in parentheses or continuous with the text are by the critic. Publication information (such as footnotes or page and line references to specific editions of works) have been deleted at the editor's discretion to provide smoother reading of the text.

- An annotated list of **Further Reading** appearing at the end of each author entry suggests secondary sources on the author. In some cases it includes essays for which the editors could not obtain reprint rights.

Cumulative Indexes

- Each volume of *TCLC* contains a cumulative **Author Index** listing all authors who have appeared in Gale's Literary Criticism Series, along with cross references to such biographical series as *Contemporary Authors* and *Dictionary of Literary Biography*. For readers' convenience, a complete list of Gale titles included appears on the first page of the author index. Useful for locating authors within the various series, this index is particularly valuable for those authors who are identified by a certain period but who, because of their death dates, are placed in another, or for those authors whose careers span two periods. For example, F. Scott Fitzgerald is found in *TCLC,* yet a writer often associated with him, Ernest Hemingway, is found in *CLC.*

- Each *TCLC* volume includes a cumulative **Nationality Index** which lists all authors who have appeared in *TCLC* volumes, arranged alphabetically under their respective nationalities, as well as Topics volume entries devoted to particular national literatures.

- Each new volume in Gale's Literary Criticism Series includes a cumulative **Topic Index,** which lists all literary topics treated in *NCLC, TCLC, LC 1400-1800,* and the *CLC* yearbook.

- Each new volume of *TCLC,* with the exception of the Topics volumes, includes a **Title Index** listing the titles of all literary works discussed in the volume. In response to numerous suggestions from librarians, Gale has also produced a **Special Paperbound Edition** of the *TCLC* title index. This annual cumulation lists all titles discussed in the series since its inception and is issued with the first volume of *TCLC* published each year. Additional copies of the index are available on request. Librarians and patrons will welcome this separate index; it saves shelf space, is easy to use, and is recyclable upon receipt of the following year's cumulation. Titles discussed in the Topics volume entries are not included *TCLC* cumulative index.

Citing *Twentieth-Century Literary Criticism*

When writing papers, students who quote directly from any volume in Gale's literary Criticism Series may use the following general forms to footnote reprinted criticism. The first example pertains to materials drawn from periodicals, the second to material reprinted from books.

[1]William H. Slavick, "Going to School to DuBose Heyward," *The Harlem Renaissance Re-examined,* (AMS Press, 1987); excerpted and reprinted in *Twentieth-Century Literary Criticism,* Vol. 59, ed. Jennifer Gariepy (Detroit: Gale Research, 1995), pp. 94-105.

[2]George Orwell, "Reflections on Gandhi," *Partisan Review,* 6 (Winter 1949), pp. 85-92; excerpted and reprinted in *Twentieth-Century Literary Criticism,* Vol. 59, ed. Jennifer Gariepy (Detroit: Gale Research, 1995), pp. 40-3.

Suggestions Are Welcome

In response to suggestions, several features have been added to *TCLC* since the series began, including annotations to excerpted criticism, a cumulative index to authors in all Gale literary criticism series, entries devoted to criticism on a single work by a major author, more extensive illustrations, and a title index listing all literary works discussed in the series since its inception.

Readers who wish to suggest authors or topics to appear in future volumes, or who have other suggestions, are cordially invited to write the editors.

Acknowledgments

The editors wish to thank the copyright holders of the excerpted criticism included in this volume and the permissions managers of many book and magazine publishing companies for assisting us in securing reproduction rights. We are also grateful to the staffs of the Detroit Public Library, the Library of Congress, the University of Detroit Mercy Library, Wayne State University Purdy/Kresge Library Complex, and the University of Michigan Libraries for making their resources available to us. Following is a list of the copyright holders who have granted us permission to reproduce material in this volume of *TCLC*. Every effort has been made to trace copyright, but if omissions have been made, please let us know.

COPYRIGHTED EXCERPTS IN *TCLC*, VOLUME 71, WERE REPRODUCED FROM THE FOLLOWING PERIODICALS:

—*The American Journal of Psychoanalysis,* v. 14, 1954; v. 42, Spring, 1982. Copyright 1954, © 1982 Association for the Advancement of Psychoanalysis. Both reproduced by permission of the publisher.—*The American Journal of Psychoanalysis,* v. 42, Spring, 1982 for "Bargains with Fate: The Case of Macbeth" by Bernard J. Paris; v. 42, Spring, 1982 for "Karen Horney on 'The Value of Vindictiveness'" by Harry Keyishian. Copyright © 1982 Association for the Advancement of Psychoanalysis. Both reproduced by permission of the publisher and the author. —*American Literature,* v. 5, May, 1982. Copyright © 1982 by Duke University Press, Durham, NC. Reproduced with permission. —*American Quarterly,* v. 19, Winter, 1967; v. 19, Winter, 1968. Copyright 1967, 1968 by American Studies Association. Reproduced by permission of The Johns Hopkins University Press. —*Ball State University Forum,* v. XIV, Summer, 1973. Copyright © 1973 Ball State University. Reproduced by permission. —*The Christian Century,* v. 108, 1991. Reproduced by permission. —*Comparative Drama,* v. 28, Winter, 1994/1995. © copyright 1994/1995, by the Editors of Comparative Drama. Reproduced by permission. —*Contemporary Review,* v. 220, June, 1972. Reproduced by permission. —*Film Comment,* v. 10, 1974 for "Second Thoughts on Stroheim" by Jonathan Rosenbaum. Copyright © 1974 by the Film Society of Lincoln Center. All rights reserved. Reproduced by permission of the publisher and the author. —*Harvard Theological Review,* v. 75, January, 1982; v. 84, July, 1991. Copyright © 1982, 1991 by the President and Fellows of Havard College. Both reproduced by permission. —*International Journal of Women's Studies,* v. 1, July/August, 1978. —*Journal of American Culture,* v. 14, 1991. Reproduced by permission. —*Journal of Popular Culture,* v. 9, 1976. Reproduced by permission. —*The Journal of Religion,* v. 64, July, 1984 for "The Ambiguous Feminism of Mary Baker Eddy" by Susan Hill Lindley. Reproduced by permission of the publisher, University of Chicago Press and the author. —*Judaism: A Quarterly Journal,* v. 22, Summer, 1973. Copyright © 1973 by the American Jewish Congress. Reproduced by permission. —*Literature Film Quarterly,* v. 18, 1990. Copyright © 1990 Salisbury State College. Reproduced by permission. —*London Magazine,* v. 18, February, 1979. Reproduced by permission. —*London Mercury,* v. 16, August, 1927. —*The New England Quarterly,* v. XLIII, March, 1970 for "Mary Baker Eddy and Sentimental Womanhood" by Gail Parker. Copyright © 1970 by The New England Quarterly. Reproduced by permission of the publisher and the author. —*The New Republic,* v. 183, November, 1980. Copyright © 1980 The New Republic, Inc. Reproduced by permission of The New Republic. —*Sight & Sound,* v. 54, 1985. Copyright © 1985 by The British Film Institute. Reproduced by permission. —*Studies in American Jewish Literature,* v. 2, 1982; v. 3, 1983. Both reproduced by permission. —*Texas Studies in Literature & Language,* v. 36, Spring, 1994 for "What Blood Will Tell: Hereditary Determinism in McTeague & Greed" by Jared Gardner. Copyright © 1994 by the University of Texas Press. Reproduced by permission of the author and the University of Texas Press. —*TSE: TULANE STUDIES IN ENGLISH,* v. 23, 1978. Copyright © 1978 by Tulane University. All rights reserved. Reproduced by permission. —*The University of Windsor Review,* v. 21, 1988 for "Gurdjieff and the Literary Cult" by B. A. St. Andrews. Reproduced by permission of the publisher and the author. —*Yiddish,* v. 2, Fall, 1975 for "Abraham Cahan: Realism and the Early Stories" by Daniel Walden; v. 2, Fall, 1975 for "The Yiddish Fiction of Abraham Cahan" by Jules Chametzky. Copyright © 1975 by Joseph C. Landis. All rights reserved. Both reproduced by permission of the publisher and the respective authors.

Reproduced by permission. —Yagoda, Ben. From **Will Rogers: A Biography.** Alfred A. Knopf, 1993. Copyright © 1993 by Ben Yagoda. All rights reserved. Reproduced by permission of Random House, Inc. —Yates, Norris W. From **The American Humorist: Conscience of the Twentieth Century.** Iowa State University Press, 1964. Copyright © 1964 by The Iowa State University Press. All rights reserved. Reproduced by permission.

PHOTOGRAPHS AND ILLUSTRATIONS APPEARING IN *TCLC*, VOLUME 71, WERE RECEIVED FROM THE FOLLOWING SOURCES:

—**p. 1:** Cahan, Abraham, photograph. Jewish Daily Forward. Reproduced by permission. —**p. 90:** Eddy, Mary Baker (sitting in chair with hands crossed in lap), photograph. The Library of Congress. —**p. 174:** Gurdjieff, Georgei Ivanovitch, photograph. Archive Photos, Inc. Reproduced by permission. —**p. 207:** Horney, Karen, photograph. UPI/Corbis-Bettmann. Reproduced by permission. —**p. 275:** Rogers, Will, photograph. The Library of Congress. —**p. 327:** Stroheim, Erich von (wearing dark suit, holding eyepiece), photograph. The Kobal Collection. Reproduced by permission. —**p. 379:** Tomlinson, H. M., photograph. UPI/Corbis-Bettmann. Reproduced by permission.

Abraham Cahan

1860-1951

(Also wrote under the pseudonyms Sotius and David Bernstein) Lithuanian-born American novelist.

INTRODUCTION

Through his accomplishments as a newspaper editor and journalist, Cahan became a highly influential figure in early twentieth-century Jewish-American letters. His innovative editorship of the *Jewish Daily Forward* made it a major cultural force in the Yiddish-speaking American community. Writing in both English and Yiddish, Cahan also produced novels and short stories that were among the first to realistically depict the experiences of his fellow Russian Jewish immigrants in the United States.

Biographical Information

Cahan was raised in the lower-class Yiddish-speaking Jewish subculture of Vilna, Lithuania. As a young student, he taught himself Russian in order to gain access to the Gentile-dominated public schools and library in Vilna. He attended college, preparing for a career as a teacher, but involvement in a radical socialist group at the time of the unsuccessful 1881 revolution made it dangerous for him to remain in Russia, so he emigrated to the United States in 1882. He took up residence in a poverty-plagued, overcrowded section of New York City's Lower East Side that was populated predominantly by Jewish immigrants. While working in a cigar factory Cahan experienced firsthand the deprivations and exploitation suffered by many immigrant workers. Cahan became a successful union organizer and pro-labor orator. He also learned his trade as a journalist, serving as a correspondent for Russian newspapers and contributing to both Yiddish and English-language American publications, notably under editor Lincoln Steffens at the *New York Commercial Advertiser*. His work as a reporter brought him into daily contact with people of all classes in the Jewish and Gentile communities, and in his articles Cahan demonstrated skill as a canny social observer. Adapting the market-driven editorial strategies of mainstream American newspapers to the needs of America's new Jewish immigrants, Cahan built the *Jewish Daily Forward*, which he cofounded in 1897, into the most widely read Yiddish-language daily newspaper of its era. The *Forward*, which he edited until just before his death in 1951, championed socialist and progressive political causes, provided its readers with a forum for expressing their views and learning about American culture, and served as a showcase for fiction in Yiddish by such authors as Sholem Aleichem and Isaac Bashevis Singer. While engaged in his groundbreaking work as a journalist and social activist, Cahan also produced a number of novels, short stories, and nonfiction

books in Yiddish and English, most of which expanded on themes of the Russian Jewish immigrant experience.

Major Works

Cahan's first published short story, "Motke Arbel un zayn shiddokh" (1892; "A Providential Match"), introduced the topic that would typify his fiction: the struggles of Russian Jews to assimilate into American culture, and the moral, social, and psychological effects of this cultural change. The story's protagonist, a poor peasant who has made his fortune in America, sends for the daughter of his former employer in Russia, intending to marry her; however, his intended bride takes advantage of her newfound American freedom to choose her own mate. With the enthusiastic encouragement of one of his mentors, the novelist and critic William Dean Howells, Cahan expanded on this theme in his novella *Yekl: A Tale of the New York Ghetto* (1896), about an ambitious young immigrant who rejects his devoted Orthodox Jewish wife for a flashier, more Americanized young woman. In such stories as "The Imported Bridegroom" and "Rabbi Eliezer's

Christmas," Cahan further explored this theme of the clash of cultures experienced by new Americans. The novel *The Rise of David Levinsky* (1917), Cahan's most highly regarded work of fiction, evolved from a series of magazine articles he was commissioned to write about Jewish-American entrepreneurs. Cahan chose to tell this story as the personal history of one fictional representative of this type of man, an impoverished Russian yeshiva student who becomes a millionaire in America, but in the process loses his religious values, his respect for himself and his fellow human beings, and his ability to love.

Critical Reception

During his lifetime, Cahan's work as a newspaper editor and journalist overshadowed his career as a creative writer. Reviewers, tending to view him primarily as a reporter rather than literary artist, praised his novels and short stories for their accurate depiction of social conditions while downgrading their stylistic merits. With the emergence of interest in ethnic literature in the decades following Cahan's death, scholars have favorably reevaluated his fiction, particularly *The Rise of David Levinsky*. Critics have compared his experiments in social realism to those of his contemporaries Stephen Crane and Theodore Dreiser, and have observed that his frank, unromanticized treatment of the Jewish- American experience prefigured the work of later writers, including Irving Howe, Philip Roth, and Saul Bellow.

PRINCIPAL WORKS

Yekl: A Tale of the New York Ghetto (novel) 1896

The Imported Bridegroom, and Other Stories of the New York Ghetto (short stories) 1898

The White Terror and the Red: A Novel of Revolutionary Russia (novel) 1905

Rafael Naarizokh: An Erzaylung Vegin a Stolyer Vos Iz Gekommen Zum Saykhl [*Rafael Naarizokh: A Story of a Carpenter Who Came to His Senses*] (novel) 1907

Historia fun di Fareingte Shtaaten. 2 vols. [*History of the United States*] (history) 1910-1912

The Rise of David Levinsky (novel) 1917

Bleter fun Mayn Leben. 5 vols. [*Leaves from My Life*] (autobiography) 1926-31; Vols. 1 and 2 also published as *The Education of Abraham Cahan*, 1969

Palestina [*Palestine*] (nonfiction) 1934

Rashel: A Biografia [*Raschell: A Biography*] (biography) 1938

Grandma Never Lived in America: The New Journalism of Abraham Cahan (journalism) 1986

CRITICISM

Isaac Rosenfeld (essay date 1952)

SOURCE: "The Fall of David Levinsky," in *Preserving the Hunger,* edited and introduced by Mark Shechner, Wayne State University Press,1988, pp. 152-89.

[*In the following essay, originally published in 1952, Rosenfeld reviews* The Rise of David Levinsky, *noting the novel's study of "Jewish character" and its examination of American business culture.*]

I had long avoided **The Rise of David Levinsky** because I imagined it was a badly written account of immigrants and sweatshops in a genre which—though this novel had practically established it—was intolerably stale by now. It is nothing of the kind. To be sure, it is a genre piece, and excellence of diction and sentence structure are not among its strong points; but it is one of the best fictional studies of Jewish character available in English, and at the same time an intimate and sophisticated account of American business culture, and it ought to be celebrated as such.

The story is a simple one and fundamentally Jewish in conception, as it consists of an extended commentary on a single text, somewhat in the manner of Talmud. This text is presented in the opening paragraph:

> Sometimes, when I think of my past . . . the metamorphosis I have gone through strikes me as nothing short of a miracle. I was born and reared in the lowest depths of poverty and I arrived in America—in 1885—with four cents in my pocket. I am now worth more than two million dollars and recognized as one of the two or three leading men in the cloak-and-suit trade in the United States. *And yet . . . my inner identity . . . impresses me as being precisely the same as it was thirty or forty years ago. My present station, power, the amount of worldly happiness at my command, and the rest of it, seem to be devoid of significance.*

I have set in italics what I take to be the key sentences. These express Levinsky's uniquely Jewish character, as they refer to the poor days of his childhood and early youth ("my inner identity") when, supported by his mother, he devoted himself to the study of the Jewish Law. Nothing in a man's life could be more purely Jewish, and his constant longing, through all his later years, for the conditions of his past confirms him in an unchanging spirit. But the remarkable thing about this theme, as the late Abraham Cahan developed it, is that it is, at the same time, an exemplary treatment of one of the dominant myths of American capitalism—that the millionaire finds nothing but emptiness at the top of the heap. It is not by accident that Cahan, for forty years and until his death the editor of the *Jewish Daily Forward,* and identified all his life with Jewish affairs and the Yiddish language, wrote this novel in English (it has only recently been translated into Yiddish). He was writing an American novel par excellence in the very center of the Jewish genre.

It seems to me that certain conclusions about the relation between Jewish and American character should be implicit in the fact that so singularly Jewish a theme can so readily be assimilated to an American one. I am not suggesting that Jewish and American character are identical, for the Levinsky who arrived in New York with four cents in his pocket was as unlike an American as anyone could possibly be; but there is a complementary relation between the two which, so far as I know, no other novel has brought out so clearly.

David Levinsky was born in the Russian town of Antomir in 1865. His father died when David was three, and he lived with his mother in one corner of a basement room that was occupied by three other families. "The bulk of the population [of Antomir]," writes Cahan, "lived on less than . . . twenty-five cents . . . a day, and that was difficult to earn. A hunk of rye bread and a bit of herring or cheese constituted a meal. [With] a quarter of a copeck (an eighth of a cent) . . . one purchased a few crumbs of pot cheese or some boiled water for tea. . . . Children had to nag their mothers for a piece of bread." But Levinsky's mother, who "peddled pea mush [and did] odds and ends of jobs," was kind to him and indulgent, "because God has punished you hard enough as it is, poor orphan mine."

At the usual early age, Levinsky was sent to *cheder,* where he was made to feel very keenly the disadvantages of poverty, as his teachers risked nothing in punishing a poor boy. His mother would intervene for him (this impulse was to prove fatal) and fought with many a *melamed* for laying hands on her David. In spite of the humiliations and hardships, she maintained him in *cheder,* and after his Bar Mitzvah sent him to Yeshiva (Talmudic seminary) at an even greater sacrifice, as it meant he would not be in a position to relieve her distress by learning a trade. She was determined that he devote his life to God, and he showed great aptitude for holy study. He soon distinguished himself as a student, but his sexual instincts began to distract his mind. His contacts with women, as was the case with all Yeshiva students, were extremely limited. It was considered "an offense to good Judaism" for a pious man to seek feminine company, attend dances, dress in worldly fashion, or in any other way to behave as a "Gentile." Naturally, these restraints only multiplied Levinsky's temptations. He would do penance, undergo a period of religious exaltation, and again fall into sin (in his mind).

The next great event in his life was the death of his mother. Levinsky, in earlocks and black caftan, was attacked by Gentile boys on his way from Yeshiva. When he came home bruised and bleeding, his mother, against his entreaties and those of their friends and neighbors, ran to the Gentile quarter to avenge him. This was the

last time he saw her alive. She was brought back with a broken head.

It is a credit to Cahan's economy as a writer and to his grasp of character that at this point, in the sixty-odd pages which I have summarized, he has already drawn so convincing a picture of Levinsky, including all essential details, that Levinsky's subsequent adventures in the old country and America, his further encounters with poverty and with women, the rest of his intellectual development, and his ultimate transformation into a millionaire, have all been fully prepared. I will therefore cut off the exposition and attempt some generalizations which may serve the understanding of the whole of Levinsky's character and perhaps help explain how the old-world Yeshiva student is essentially an American in ethos.

Levinsky's character was formed by hunger. The individual experiences of his life—poverty, squalor, orphanage, years of religious study and sexual restraint, the self-sacrificing love of his mother and her violent death—all these experiences contain, as their common element, a core of permanent dissatisfaction. This dissatisfaction expresses itself in two ways: first, as a yearning for fulfillment, where it operates to win for him all the goods and values he has been deprived of—wealth, dignity, a "father principle" as well as a substitute for his father (as shown in his passionate attachment to Red Sender, with whom he studied at the Yeshiva), the pleasures of intellectual liberty that attend his break with Orthodoxy, the pleasures of sex, and unrestrained access to the society of women, though he goes among them mainly to find a substitute for his mother. (These are the positive "Americanizing" tendencies of his discontent.) At the same time, dissatisfaction has become an organic habit, a form which determines his apprehension of experience in general, and actually directs the flow of experience his way, so that he is not merely the result of what has happened to him, but on the contrary, the events in his life are predetermined, in large measure, by what he has already become. In the second sense, dissatisfaction is unending; instead of providing the urge to overcome privation, it returns every fulfillment, by a way no matter how roundabout, to the original tension, so that no satisfaction is possible.

Thus Levinsky is a man who cannot feel at home with his desires. Because hunger is strong in him, he must always strive to relieve it; but precisely because it is strong, it has to be preserved. It owes its strength to the fact that for so many years everything that influenced Levinsky most deeply—say, piety and mother love—was inseparable from it. For hunger, in this broader, rather metaphysical sense of the term that I have been using, is not only the state of tension out of which the desires for relief and betterment spring; precisely because the desires are formed under its sign, they become assimilated to it, and convert it into the prime source of all value, so that the man, in his pursuit of whatever he considers pleasurable and good, seeks to return to his yearning as much as he does to escape it.

Levinsky's entire behavior is characterized by this duality. In love, he is drawn to women he cannot have. They are either hopelessly above his rank in wealth, sophistication, and culture, or married and faithful mother-surrogates, or simply not interested. The women who do find him attractive fail to move him. He goes to prostitutes, one frustration feeding the other.

His accumulation of wealth, which he wins through perseverance, ingenuity, and luck, is also of this pattern—it, too, represents a loss, a virtual impoverishment. Before he turned to business enterprise, Levinsky had entertained serious academic ambitions. Though he had broken away from Orthodoxy, shaved his beard, adopted American dress, and gone to night school to learn English, he had retained his Talmudic intellectuality and love of scholarship. He took a job in the garment industry only as a means of sending himself through college. The event to which he attributes his becoming a businessman fell on a day when he was having his lunch in the factory. A bottle of milk slipped out of his hands as he was trying to open it and spilled on some silks. His employer, Jeff Manheimer, who witnessed the accident, broadly made fun of his clumsiness and called him a lobster. The humiliation festered and that very day Levinsky decided to steal the boss's designer and go into business for himself. This is the reason he gives, but it is a rationalization. He would never have entered business and gone on to wealth had it not been necessary to sacrifice something—in this case his desire for learning. And when he obtains great wealth, it makes a circle, joining the pattern of his love life by condemning him to loneliness, as he suspects all women who smile on him want only his money.

So with everything. All things in Levinsky's life are divided, alienated from themselves, and simplicity is impossible. But no matter how many transformations it undergoes, his hunger remains constant. He longs for his wretched boyhood (which appeals to him "as a sick child does to its mother") from which, were he able to re-enter it, he would again be driven in an endless yearning after yearning.

Now this is a profoundly Jewish trait, our whole history is marked by this twist. The significant thing about the structure I have been describing is that it is not confined to single personalities like Levinsky, but is exactly repeated on an impersonal and much larger scale in Jewish history, religion, culture—wherever our tradition and its spirit find expression. Consider *Galut*, the Diaspora, through the centuries in which it has dominated Jewish life: the theme of the Return, of yearning for Eretz Israel, to which are linked Cabala and Messianism, modes of prayer and worship as well as modern political and social movements, so that the whole becomes a compendium of Jewish activity per se—the yearning for Israel runs through the Diaspora in no simple sense, as of a fixed desire for a fixed object. It is a reflexive desire, turning on itself and becoming its own object. This is the meaning of the passage: "If I forget Thee O Jerusalem. . . ." The yearning is itself Jerusalem, as in the words ". . . if

I prefer not Jerusalem above my chief joy," and it is to this yearning that the good Jew remains faithful. Otherwise, why the proscription of temporizing in *Galut,* of making any compromise with desire, no matter how small, even down to the obdurate and seemingly ridiculous prohibition of shaving the beard? The hunger must be preserved at all cost. This theme is taken up and elaborated all through Yiddish literature, receiving its ultimate ironic sanctification in the work of Sholom Aleichem, where squalor, suffering, and persecution become the "blessings of poverty," signs and stigmata of the condition of being Chosen, "for which the whole world envies us." The character of David Levinsky, therefore, does not stand alone, nor does he come, with his four cents, unattended to the American shore. He drags the whole past after him, being himself the Diaspora Man.

But what is so American about this? Nothing directly, especially if I am right in calling Levinsky the essential Jewish type of the Dispersion. And yet in the character of the American businessman and in the surrounding culture that his figure dominates, there is also such a twist, a similar play on striving and fulfillment. We worship success; all the same it is on process and origin that we place the emphasis of gratification, seldom on the attainment as such. The value of the successful man's career lies in "rags to riches," it is defined in our saying, "He worked himself up." Of those who are born to wealth we say, "Poor little rich boy." Now this, I am aware, is folklore, and there is a great deal of irony in it, too. Nevertheless, our favorite representation of the rich is of a class that doesn't know what to do with its money. It has brought them no real accretion of happiness, and the process of accumulation, on which the emphasis falls, is manifestly a self-destructive one, as it never can be stopped in time: the successful man faces the futility of retirement. He, too, loves to dream about his boyhood in an unreal *askesis,* having for the most part been ashamed of the ascetic impulse (poverty, we protest too much, is no disgrace) which he has concealed under a conspicuous acquisition; and yet he is not enough a materialist to enjoy his goods as they come to him and welcome the spiritual consolations that worldly pleasures bestow. "Money isn't everything," he will say, making more, and he says this to preserve an air of disconsolateness, as though virtue were impossible without a sour face. He does all this for show, but unconsciously his affections hit upon the truth. All his life he is at loose ends, and expert only in ennui, which Tolstoy defined as the desire for desire, cousin to Levinsky's yearning. And even if none if this is true, and there is (as I strongly suspect) a direct gratification in wealth as such, it is still significant that most of us profess it to be true, clinging to a protective disenchantment.

Whatever the case with our much disputed and still, I suppose, amorphous American character, Levinsky, the Diaspora Man, had relatively little to overcome (speaking inwardly) to grow into the typical American of fortune. Only the environment was alien to him, but its inner loneliness was anticipated in his own, for one loneliness is much like another; and the very fact that the American environment was alien, and would remain so, to his Jewishness, enabled him to make good in it on his own peculiar terms—to satisfy everything but hunger. To be sure, his is only a single career, a single example of the Jew as American, but it draws our attention to the considerable structural congruity that must underlie the character and culture of the two peoples. And if Levinsky's career is understood in its essentially Jewish aspect, it may explain why the Jews, as an immigrant group, were among the first to achieve a virtually flawless Americanization.

I have purposely refrained from treating David Levinsky as a fictional character and have spoken of the novel as though it were the actual memoir of an American Jew, in tribute to Cahan's power of characterization. Such immediacy of revelation is the novel's strongest quality, and Levinsky is made to talk about himself not only with an authentic accent, but with a motive in disclosure verging on something sly—precisely as such a man would talk. This well known and widely respected businessman tells the truth about himself, his love affairs, his efforts to outsmart the unions, the way other men tell lies—to see if he can get away with it! But as fiction, Cahan's writing lacks continuity: his transitions from subjects tend to be abrupt, with a perseveration in the linking of sex and economics. Thus when he describes Levinsky's broken engagement (the cause was his falling in love with another woman), Cahan devotes less than twenty lines to the scene, and opens his very next paragraph (after a line space, but this may have been the typographer's doing) with the words, "Our rush season had passed. . . ." Often the trains of thought collide within the single paragraph, business plowing into everything else. True, Levinsky's mind would work this way, and the habit would also serve him the purpose of saying, "I may not be doing so well with the girls—but think of the money I'm making." (Though business is meaningless to Levinsky, one of the most touching insights of the novel is provided by Cahan's showing how he succumbs to a businessman's vulgarity of tone and manner, and berates himself for the weakness.) Yet it is not always possible to distinguish character from author, and this failure in detachment, the consequence of an imperfectly developed ear for nuances in language, becomes noticeable and sometimes quite confusing when there is no lucky congruity to justify it, as in the matter of the abrupt transitions from pleasure to business.

But these flaws, as I have already indicated, are of minor account. So much so, that I wonder what the critical reception and, no doubt, misunderstanding, of *The Rise of David Levinsky* must have been, that it should languish in the status of an "undiscovered" book, a standard footnote or paragraph in surveys of American Jewish literature, and not be known for the remarkable novel it is.

David Singer (essay date 1967)

SOURCE: "David Levinsky's Fall: A Note on the Liebman Thesis," in *American Quarterly*, Vol. 19, No. 4, Winter, 1967, pp. 696-706.

[*In the following essay, Singer examines* The Rise of David Levinsky *in light of Charles Liebman's thesis that most Jews who emigrated to the United States were shaped more by cultural and social mores than by religious orthodoxy.*]

The notion that the overwhelming majority of East European Jews who came to the United States between 1880 and 1915 were Orthodox has assumed a central position in the popular mythology of American-Jewish life. On a more scholarly level, this same idea has established itself in the canon of American-Jewish historiography. The standard works on American Jewry have, in varying degrees, accepted this premise, and their interpretations have been fashioned accordingly. Even Moses Rischin, whose *The Promised City* is perhaps the most sophisticated achievement to date in the reconstruction of the American-Jewish experience, seems for the most part to have accepted the prevailing thesis of the Orthodoxy of the East European masses. In part, this view follows from the tendency of historians to construct a rather stereotyped portrait of East European Jewish life, in which the Orthodox shtetl completely dominates the scene. On the other hand, the Orthodoxy of the immigrant masses would appear to be confirmed by every shred of evidence accumulated thus far by students of the period. Virtually everybody, including the immigrants themselves, has accepted the Orthodoxy of the "first generation" as an unquestionable fact.

Recently, however, this generally prevailing view has come under direct assault in the work of Professor Charles Liebman, whose illuminating studies of American Orthodoxy are setting in its proper historical perspective a subject long neglected. In essence, Liebman has argued that most of the nominally Orthodox immigrants who came to the United States were bound by commitments that were ethnic rather than religious. Because they often outwardly conformed to many traditional religious norms, they were regarded as Orthodox by their more acculturated coreligionists. At best, however, their residual piety was what Leo Baeck has called *Milieu-Frommigkeit.*

In support of his thesis, Liebman has compiled a body of evidence which, while it is often rather fragmentary, does raise serious doubts about the generally accepted view. In dealing with the European setting of the exodus to America, Liebman correctly asserts that historians have not paid sufficient attention to the forces of secularism which were shattering the Orthodox consensus of the East European Jewish communities. At the very time when large groups of Jews were emigrating to the United States, traditional Judaism was facing the challenge of such movements as the *Haskalah,* political Zionism and Marxist socialism.

Turning specifically to those Jews who came to these shores, Liebman argues that it can be expected that those who emigrated first would be the least traditional, since they were willing to uproot themselves from home and family. Among the evidence that Liebman cites in support of this contention is the significant fact that leading Rabbinic authorities such as the *Hafetz Hayyim,* warned their fellow Jews not to endanger their Judaism by leaving home. The Rabbi of Slutsk, on a visit to the United States, castigated those Jews who had emigrated to a *trefa* (impure) land.

Liebman's strongest argument, however, is the evidence he cites to show that the East European Jews failed to create those institutions which were necessary for the maintenance of an Orthodox community. The very multiplicity of synagogues which were established far exceeding the number necessary for the purposes of worship, Liebman argues, indicates that their primary purpose was cultural and social, rather than religious. While there was a superabundant proliferation of synagogues, there is evidence to indicate that there was a serious shortage of *mikvaot* (ritual baths). The most serious failure of the East European Jewish community in the United States, however, was in the area of Jewish education. A New York survey taken in 1908 produced the remarkable information that only 28 per cent of the Jewish children between the ages of six and sixteen were receiving any Jewish education at all. Until 1915, there were only two Jewish day schools in the whole country. America also suffered from a paucity of distinguished rabbinic scholars among the immigrants. When the New York Orthodox community began to search for a rabbinic leader, no American rabbi was even considered. Rabbi Jacob Joseph of Vilna was finally selected in 1887.

The implications of Liebman's thesis are, of course, revolutionary. If he is, in fact, correct, his arguments necessitate a radical reconstruction of our understanding of the American-Jewish experience. No longer will it be tenable to view Jewish history in the United States as a simplistic conflict between religious orthodoxy and secularism. Historians will have to refine their conceptual apparatus to deal with more subtle categories. The popular notion of the development of the Conservative movement will also have to be drastically revised. The rise of Conservative Judaism and secularism, according to Professor Liebman, "did not entail a decision to opt out of traditional religion. It was, rather, a decision to substitute new social and cultural mores for the older ones, which had been intermingled with certain ritual manifestations."

It should be emphasized that Liebman has presented his thesis in a rather tentative manner. In his writings thus far, the question of the Orthodoxy of the East European immigrants has been marginal to his primary concerns. Obviously, a great deal of basic research will have to be done before the issue can be considered with any kind of finality. To illustrate, however, how fruitful Liebman's thesis can be as an analytical tool in American-Jewish historiography, I would like to turn to an examination of Abraham Cahan's *The Rise of David Levinsky*.

Published in 1917, *The Rise of David Levinsky* was the foremost literary achievement of the man who, more than

any other individual, helped shape the cultural pattern of New York's Jewish community. As the editor of the *Jewish Daily Forward,* Cahan, who arrived in the United States in 1882, served for many years as the central mediating force between the Jewish immigrant masses and the great metropolis. *The Rise of David Levinsky,* which was hailed by many at the time of its publication as a masterpiece of realistic fiction, and which served to introduce New York's East Side to the American reading public, has continued to evoke high praise from discerning readers. The novel has been acclaimed by Saul Bellow, Isaac Rosenfeld and Nathan Glazer. John Higham has lauded the novel as a "unique masterpiece of social criticism," and as "the unrivaled record of a great historical experience."

While *The Rise of David Levinsky* has been praised both in terms of its literary merits and as a document of social history, it has been, I would contend, often misunderstood, because it has been analyzed from the perspective of the prevailing thesis of the Orthodoxy of the East European immigrants. To illustrate the standard interpretation of the novel, let me quote Nathan Glazer:

> We read in *The Rise of David Levinsky* of how a young Russian Jewish yeshiva student, learned and pious, emigrates to this country. On the boat he eats no forbidden food and prays daily. In America he seeks out and finds solace in the synagogue established by people from his home town. But he also moves inevitably from one transgression to the next. First his earlocks are cut off, then he shaves, soon he abandons the synagogue in favor of night school and English studies. And soon nothing is left—and with practically no soul searching.

To the casual reader of the novel this summary may well appear as quite accurate. A closer examination of Glazer's analysis, however, raises a serious problem. Glazer is certainly correct in placing great emphasis on the two dramatic scenes in the early part of the book, where Levinsky cuts off his earlocks and then his beard, for the loss of these two symbols does, in fact, immediately open the floodgates to a host of transgressions, and to Levinsky's complete abandonment of Jewish religious law. To the modern reader, however, these happenings can only be viewed with bewilderment. Why should a beard and earlocks, which are only customs, play such a pivotal role in Levinsky's religious development? Are we to believe that a "learned and pious" yeshiva student is so unable to distinguish between the essentials and nonessentials of Judaism, that the surrender of these customs becomes the decisive factor in his complete alienation from traditional norms? Yet Glazer has not erred in viewing Levinsky's loss of his earlocks and beard as a dramatic turning point in his life. The fundamental weakness of his argument is that Glaser views Levinsky's abandonment of these customs as the *beginning* of a process of alienation, when in fact, a close reading of the novel reveals that Levinsky's surrendering of his earlocks and beard is the *culmination* of an estrangement from his traditional roots that had begun much earlier, while he was still in Europe.

The society into which David Levinsky was born, and in which he remained firmly rooted until his eighteenth year, Cahan makes it abundantly clear, was one that would do justice to the most unsophisticated popular stereotype of the shtetl. Cahan was able to draw upon his own experience in sketching the background milieu of Levinsky's early years, since he was the scion of a rabbinical line and had lived for many years in Vilna, a city renowned for its Jewish learning. In *The Rise of David Levinsky,* however, the features of East European Jewish life often appear in an extreme form, since the scene is set in Antomir, a small backwater town.

In Antomir, where the "bulk of the population lived on less than fifty copecks (twenty-five cents) a day, and that was difficult to earn," grinding poverty was a lot shared by most of its inhabitants. The Levinsky home was a room in a basement, which David and his mother shared with three other families. The spiritual life of the community also testified to the influence of a small-town atmosphere in that it was characterized by an intense but simple piety. Thus, in speaking of his relationship with God, Levinsky tells us that it was "of a personal and of a rather familiar character. He was interested in everything I did or said; He watched my every move or thought; He was always in heaven, yet, somehow, He was always near me, and I often spoke to Him." David's description of his mother's piety is even more revealing: "She was passionately devout. . . . Being absolutely illiterate, she would murmur meaningless words, in the singsong of a prayer, pretending to herself that she was performing her devotions. This, however, she would do with absolute earnestness and fervor, often with tears of ecstasy coming to her eyes."

Together with piety, the central value in Antomir's ethos was learning, and particularly the study of Talmud. It was taken for granted by the inhabitants of the town that "the highest mathematics taught in the Gentile universities were child's play as compared to the Talmud," and parents were prepared to "starve themselves to keep their sons studying the Word of God." For the first eighteen years of life, the portals of the yeshiva constituted David's world, a world inhabited by the rabbis of the Talmud. "I could almost see them," Levinsky later recalled, "each of them individualized in my mind by some of his sayings, by his manner of debate, by some particular word he used, or by some particular incident in which he figured. I pictured their faces, their beards, their voices." It was, however, a world that was fated to disappear quickly under a succession of painful experiences.

It is rather remarkable that so many readers of the novel have assumed that when David Levinsky arrived in the United States he was a "pious" Jew, for in terms of the literary handling of the problem, Cahan is rather heavy-handed in delineating Levinsky's estrangement from the life and ethos of Antomir well before he came to America. This transformation, dealt with in two short chapters, comes about all too abruptly. In terms of its causes, Cahan makes it clear that three factors operated together to uproot David from his former way of life. Let us examine each of these.

A central motif running through *The Rise of David Levinsky,* as Leslie Fiedler has pointed out, is that of Levinsky (the Jew) as lover. While the sexual theme of the novel becomes increasingly important as Levinsky grows older, it is of major importance even in the earliest stage of the plot, for, at a moment of crisis in his life, Levinsky was in the midst of a sexual awakening that was shaking his psychological balance. One of the children who lived in the same apartment as the Levinskys was Red Esther, with whom David had often fought as a young child. Suddenly, however, Red Esther began to appear to him in a new light. "I still hated her," he later remembered, "but, somehow, she did not seem to be the same as she had been before. The new lines that were developing in her growing little figure, and more particularly her own consciousness of them, were not lost upon me. A new element was stealing into my rancor for her—a feeling of forbidden curiosity." In Antomir the relations between the sexes were "largely a case of forbidden fruit and the mystery of distance." This, however, only served to intensify David's curiosity and the anguish of the guilt feelings that followed. The psychological havoc wrought by his emotional maturation is made abundantly clear by Cahan: "The worst of it was that these images often visited my brain while I was reading the holy book. . . . in addition to the wickedness of my indulging in salacious thoughts, there was the offense of desecrating the holy book by them." That Cahan entitled the chapter dealing with Levinsky's sexual awakening "Enter Satan" was therefore an augury for the future, for it was indeed the opening wedge of a new life that awaited him.

Levinsky's emotional balance, already strained by the anxieties and uncertainties of growing up, suffered its most severe blow when his mother was murdered by a group of Russian peasants. It was, in fact, a blow that shook the very foundations of his world. David had lost his father when he was an infant, and had since then centered all his emotional life around his mother, whom Cahan portrays in the classical image of the saintly, self-sacrificing Jewish woman. The thought that his mother was dead smote Levinsky with "crushing violence." He was obsessed with the thought that "mother was no more, that I was alone in the world." Levinsky's incessant brooding over his "irreparable loss" made him a "nervous, listless wreck," a "mere shadow" of his former self.

The third blow to Levinsky's world-view, coming fast upon the death of his mother, was the painful discovery that his closest friend had become an atheist. David had always admired Naphtali, both for his piety as well as for his learning. With the loss of his mother, David, out of a need for both consolation and companionship, drew even closer to his friend. Therefore, when Naphtali one day proclaimed, in the most matter-of-fact way, that there was no God, that it was "all bosh," Levinsky was "hurt and horrified." His friend's words continued to haunt him. What was most painful, however, was David's discovery that while he yearned to smash his friend's atheism, he had "nothing clear or definite to put forth" in reply.

The cumulative effect of the events examined above was to break the bonds that tied Levinsky to the life of his community. Cahan was quite careful to underline David's alienation from the ethos to which he had been tenaciously loyal for his first eighteen years. "The shock of the catastrophe," we are told, "had produced a striking effect" on him. Levinsky now found that he "was incapable of sustained thinking," and that his "communions with God were quite rare. . . . " Though he tried, he was "powerless to restore . . . [his] former feeling for the Talmud." He was conscious of the fact that "the spell was broken irretrievably." David was restless and "coveted diversions." His surroundings had "somehow lost their former meaning. Life was devoid of savor, and . . . [he] . . . was thirsting for an appetizer . . . for some violent change, for piquant sensations."

A thirst for violent change! Here indeed is the key to Levinsky's growing desire to emigrate to America. It was neither economic privation nor religious persecution that first aroused in David the thought of leaving his home, but rather his own estrangement from his former way of life. America appealed to him precisely because it was not Antomir, because in his mind it represented an entirely different pattern of existence. It was while David was in the state of anomie described above, we are specifically told, that "the word America first caught my fancy." To Levinsky, America was a land of "mystery," a realm of "fantastic experiences," a place of "marvelous transformations." To seek his fortune in "that distant, weird world" seemed to him "just the kind of sensational adventure my heart was hankering for."

The fundamental link between Levinsky's alienation and his desire to emigrate to the United States is also underscored by Cahan through his emphasis on the antithetical ways of life represented by Antomir and America. On four separate occasions Cahan has David's friends and advisers make the point that America is indeed a *trefa* land. In his search for money to purchase a steamship ticket, Levinsky first thought of turning to a wealthy woman who had befriended him. He quickly realized, however, that she would never consider helping him in his plan to "abandon my Talmud, and go to live in a godless country. . . ." More significantly, the same point is made twice by Reb Sender, who functions in the novel as the pious Jew par excellence. He was absolutely thunderstruck to hear that David could even contemplate going to the United States. "Lord of the World," he is made to say, "one becomes a Gentile there." When Levinsky was about to board ship, Reb Sender made a final plea that David "not forget that there is a God in heaven in America as well as here [Antomir]." It is thus clear that when David spoke of America as a "far-away

land" he had something much more profound in mind than mere distance.

Our analysis thus far has been focused upon the course of Levinsky's estrangement from the traditional pattern of East European life, a process which, as we have seen, was virtually complete before David sailed for the United States. As for the new values and the new life-style that were to fill the void created by his alienation from his former way of life, these were, for the greater part, the result of Levinsky's later assimilation to the American environment. It is important to note, however, that David's initiation into the new life that awaited him in America began while he was still in Europe, for in the very heart of traditional Antomir, he was able to discover an island of modernism.

While in the state of emotional upheaval which followed upon the death of his mother, David, as was mentioned above, had been befriended by a wealthy woman, Shiphrah Minsker, who out of pity had taken him into her home. The Minsker family was one of the oldest in town, but its mode of existence differed drastically from that of the vast majority of Antomir's inhabitants. For the Minskers were, as Cahan informs us, a "modern" family, which prided itself on being enlightened. The younger members of the household had been educated at Russian schools, and in general "behaved like Gentiles." It was in the Minsker home that David first encountered the modern world and absorbed many of its values. Here he met Matilda, Shiphrah's oldest daughter, with whom he fell in love, and indulged in romantic behavior certainly not becoming a pious yeshiva student. As the most assimilated member of her family, Matilda demanded of David that he give up the "idiotic Talmud," and study at a university. At an earlier time, such a suggestion would have appeared to Levinsky as sacrilegious, but now Matilda's ideas seemed perfectly reasonable. He confessed that they "did not shock me in the least." Levinsky was determined to be "no more slouch of a Talmud student," and he faithfully promised to implement Matilda's proposals as soon as he arrived in America. Is it then any wonder that when David visited a synagogue before he sailed to the United States, "everybody and everything in it looked strange" to him?

Given the above analysis, there is little cause for surprise over the fact that shortly after Levinsky's arrival in the United States his Orthodoxy completely disintegrated with "practically no soul searching." Levinsky's transformation proceeded so swiftly and so smoothly precisely because there was so little left of his former piety by the time he reached these shores. The nontraditional atmosphere of New York merely served to precipitate a cultural change that had long been in the making. It is to this culminating process that we shall now turn.

From Cahan's literary handling of the problem, it would appear that two factors worked together to bring about the final collapse of Levinsky's Orthodoxy. The first of these was the trauma inherent in the ocean voyage to

America. Stanley Elkins, in his brilliant institutional study of slavery, has attempted to account for the Sambo image by arguing that it was the result of an actual transformation of the slaves' personalty structure. Drawing upon the literature of the concentration camps, he has contended that through the uprooting process of the trip from Africa to the United States, and the introduction of the slave into a tightly regimented system, the Negro adopted a new identity. Without attempting to carry the analogy too far, since Cahan's description of Levinsky's voyage is rather sketchy, we can, I think, see much the same process at work in the novel. It is significant that the chapter dealing with the ocean crossing focuses exclusively upon David's sense of "desolation, homesickness, uncertainty, and anxiety." This sense of terror is underlined by Cahan, when he informs us that Levinsky felt as one "abandoned in the midst of a jungle," and that he was caught "in the embrace of a vast uncanny force." David's "peculiar state of mind" during the trip is further underscored by Cahan's use of hallucinatory imagery. Levinsky thought himself to be in a "trance," a state of "ecstasy" in which America appeared as an "enchanted" land, the likes of which he had never "dream[t] of before." The new world, he tells us, unfolded itself to him like a "divine revelation." The implication of all of this for Levinsky's final estrangement from Orthodoxy is made strikingly clear, when Cahan states that David arrived in this country like a "new-born babe." The trip had, in fact, been a "second birth" for him!

If Levinsky's journey from Antomir to the United States had a corrosive effect on his psyche, the New York environment offered him little emotional relief. Having undergone the anguish of the ocean voyage, Levinsky was now forced to cope with the sense of isolation and inferiority that resulted from his being a "green horn" in the New World. Here, indeed, is the final factor in David's alienation from Orthodoxy. It was his intense discomfort at being called a "green one," and his frantic desire to blend into the American milieu that impelled Levinsky to discard the last vestiges of his former way of life. What is at work here is, of course, the process of *social* adjustment to American mores which Liebman has emphasized. This in turn serves to explain why David's earlocks and beard assumed such a central position in his personal development. For, though merely social customs, they stood out as the most tangible symbols of the life-style he was feverishly attempting to shed.

Again and again, Cahan stresses Levinsky's feelings of pain and frustration at his being a "newly arrived, inexperienced immigrant." "It stung me cruelly," he tells us, to be called a greenhorn. If he did not actually hear the term, he "saw it in the eyes of the people who passed [him]." Levinsky found himself "shuddering at the prospect" of his being singled out for comment. The relationship between Levinsky's sense of isolation and his surrendering of his earlocks and beard is, in fact, explicitly underscored by Cahan. The elderly gentleman who gave David the money to have his earlocks cropped told him that "now you won't look green." As for Levinsky's cut-

ting off his beard, he confessed that it was the result of "a remark dropped by one of the peddlers that my down-covered face made me look like a 'green one'." The pressure of events had simply proven too powerful for Levinsky to resist.

That David's loss of his earlocks and beard was not, as Glazer has argued, the beginning but rather the culmination of his alienation from Orthodoxy is made quite clear by Cahan. After cropping his earlocks, we are informed, Levinsky "scarcely recognized [him]self." Most significantly, Levinsky himself realized that "the hair-cut and the American clothes had changed my identity." This new identity, however, did not become completely manifest until David had made his final break with the past by cutting off his beard. The very next chapter, symbolically entitled, "A Green Horn No Longer," describes Levinsky's attempt to seduce two married women. It was, in fact, the "beginning of a period of unrestrained misconduct." The "last thread [had] snapped" and David Levinsky's new life had begun.

Given the present state of our knowledge, it would, I think, be presumptuous to attempt to generalize from David Levinsky's experiences. Cahan's novel is, after all, only a single, if quite significant, piece of a complex picture that can be clarified only through further research. It may safely be stated, however, that Professor Liebman's thesis will prove to be of invaluable aid in that process of clarification.

Sanford E. Marovitz (essay date 1968)

SOURCE: "The Lonely New Americans of Abraham Cahan," in *American Quarterly,* Vol. 20, No. 2, Part 1, Summer, 1968, pp. 196-210.

[*In the following essay, Marovitz argues that Cahan's characters fail to achieve healthy personal relationships because they abandon their faith for materialism.*]

William Dean Howells, impressed with a short story which his wife had pointed out to him, called on its author in the bustling ghetto district of New York's Lower East Side. Abraham Cahan was not home, but Howells left his card, and not long afterward his call was returned. The result of this interview in 1895 was Cahan's first novel, *Yekl; A Tale of the New York Ghetto,* which was published the following year, and which drew from Howells a very favorable review. In 1898 Cahan brought out his second book, *The Imported Bridegroom and Other Tales of the New York Ghetto,* a collection of five stories which Howells also greeted warmly. "No American fiction of the year," Howells wrote, "merits recognition more than this Russian's stories of Yiddish life"; and elsewhere he pointed out with confidence: "I cannot help thinking that in [Abraham Cahan] we have a writer of foreign birth who will do honour to American letters." Howells was right. When *The Rise of David Levinsky* was published in 1917 Cahan established himself firmly as an important American author, for since that time *David Levinsky* has become a minor classic in our national literature.

Yekl, a small and not particularly well-written book, nevertheless marks a noteworthy stage in Cahan's literary development. This is true not only because *Yekl* happened to be the author's first novel to appear in America, but more significantly because it provided the immigrant Russian Jew with the experience of writing in a language other than his native one; many of the stylistic errors which the author committed in *Yekl* are no longer apparent in his later work—not even in the short stories written immediately afterward. Furthermore, *Yekl* anticipates the two central elements of Cahan's later fiction: the realistic portrayal of ruthless sweatshop labor and the spiritual hunger of the estranged immigrant Jew in America.

These two primary ideas lead to the dual purpose of this essay: first, to explore the element of the "Americanized," secularized Jew in Cahan's ghetto fiction by tracing it throughout his novels and tales; and secondly, to prove thereby that it was neither America nor the sweatshop that defeated Cahan's soul-racked immigrants but an essential weakness, or flaw, in the characters themselves. Those who traded their faith for the gospel of materialism suffered the pangs of loneliness regardless of their wealth, prestige or position; those, however, who clung to their heritage, despite poverty and hard work, avoided the constant sting of isolation, disillusion and despair. Abraham Cahan was, indeed, more than simply a Jewish author writing a "Jewish" novel about a ghetto. In his fiction he accomplished what he advocated elsewhere by focusing on "human nature" as he perceived it operating among individuals, rather than by more broadly scanning social conditions and deducing from those what any specific Jewish ghetto-dweller's problems and reactions might be. Primarily concerned with delving into the plight of the alienated Jew, Cahan nevertheless was able to depict, with a selective eye for detail, the sordid state of existence suffered by the garment workers and peddlers of New York's teeming Lower East Side—an area where the author himself struggled to bring modernity into the lives of his immigrant neighbors through the medium of an oft-foundering Yiddish daily, *The Jewish Daily Forward,* of which he was editor for more than half a century.

Sweatshop clothing manufacturing was the most prominent and lucrative industry of the ghetto at the turn of the century, and it was only natural that the fiery young Socialist should devote particular attention to that trade in order to realistically depict the Lower East Side. Cahan, like Howells and James, whose work had inspired him, continually stressed the need to present real life in literature:

> Would that the public could gain a deeper insight into these [sweatshop] struggles than is afforded by [scornful] newspaper reports! Hidden under an uncouth surface would be found a great deal of

what constitutes the true poetry of modern life,—tragedy more heart-rending, examples of a heroism more touching, more noble, and more thrilling, than anything that the richest imagination of the romanticist can invent. While to the outside observer the struggles may appear a fruitless repetition of meaningless conflicts, they are, like the great labor movement of which they are a part, ever marching onward, ever advancing.

Cahan censured the gross sentimentalism that pervaded the novels and periodicals of the day, manifest particularly in the affected writing of multitudinous popular authoresses. Most American novels "smell of rouge and powder," Cahan sarcastically wrote; "they are a lot of stunts and phrasemongery." American businessmen, he continued, are

> the shrewdest men on earth, with a deep, keen understanding of human nature *as it is.* . . . [But they] delight in plays and novels whose authors apparently have not the slightest idea of human nature. They give you cant and cheap sentimentality, burlesque and the most ridiculous plots. This is not fiction: it is mere fake! . . . Is it not a time for sincerity here? Will it not be well for this Nation if strong, new, American writers arise who will give us life—real life, with its comedy and its tragedy mingled—give us what in my Russian day we called the *thrill of truth?*

Cahan's *"thrill of truth,"* however, had to include not only the accurate depiction of sweatshop struggles but also the immigrant Russian Jew's estrangement in the New World. Alienated from his homeland by increasing waves of anti-Semitism, with no money to live and work outside the ghetto, the immigrant Jew, like Cahan himself, either quickly became secularized and attempted to escape from his East Side tenement, or he turned inward to the faith of his fathers. About these more pious individuals, mostly of the older generation, Cahan wrote: "Their religion is to many of them the only thing which makes life worth living. In the fervor of prayer or the abandon of religious study they forget the grinding poverty of their homes." Their diverse Hebrew festivities "pervade the atmosphere of the Ghetto with a beauty and a charm without which the life of its older residents would often be one of unrelieved misery."

Yet in Cahan's fiction it is ironically not the pious Jew who suffers the pangs of longing and loneliness, but the secularized individual, the Jew who sloughed off his Judaism as though it were an old coat and thus left himself bare to face the world alone—as "an American feller, a Yankee." The Orthodox people of the ghetto celebrated and suffered together; each had his place in the common faith, and each drew his strength from this commonality. Hence they stood upon an adamant yet spiritual foundation of faith paradoxically strengthened by years of suffering and persecution. It is this solidity and tradition that Cahan's secularized Jew lacks, often unwittingly longs for, and needs. It is he who cannot satisfy the agony of loneliness, the "twinges" of his "stretching heart."

Yekl, egotistical and unsympathetic, was the first of Cahan's woebegone victims of alienation. After emigrating to America from Russia, Yekl changes his name to Jake and takes a job in a sweatshop; he rapidly becomes secularized and detached from his homeland and family. By the end of his third year in the New World, everything and everyone in Russia seem nothing more to Jake than parts of "a charming tale, which he [is] neither willing to banish from his memory nor able to reconcile with the actualities of his American present." But the reconciliation has to be attempted. When his penniless wife, Gitl, comes to America with their child, Jake sees immediately that he no longer has anything in common with the typically disheveled, uneducated and unsophisticated immigrant who has just stepped off the boat. "For a moment the sight of her . . . precipitated a wave of thrilling memories on Jake and made him feel in his old environment. Presently, however, the illusion took wing and here he was, Jake the Yankee, with this bonnetless, wigged, dowdyish little greenhorn by his side." Compatibility with her is impossible, and Jake—proud, arrogant and secularized—continues to sink further and further into a well of despair until he begins to wish for her death. Finally he turns for divorce money to a pretentious and passionate Jewess, who drags from him a promise to wed her in exchange for the necessary funds. He learns too late that it is a bad bargain.

Though Gitl tries gamely to become a "Yankee," her first efforts are vain; but the experience she undergoes during the lengthy process of alienation from her husband nevertheless has its effects on her. Jake offers her "cash"— a new Americanism in his vocabulary—for a divorce, and she is forced to accept it as a settlement. Yet at the divorce proceedings she is not the same immigrant Gitl who met her husband at the wharf. "The rustic, 'greenhornlike,' expression was completely gone from her face and manner, and . . . there was noticeable about her a suggestion of that peculiar air of self-confidence with which a few months life in America is sure to stamp the looks and bearing of every immigrant." Gitl, too, though she does not turn aside from Judaism, is quickly Americanized.

The novel concludes less unhappily for Gitl, who is given an almost immediate opportunity for a successful second marriage, than for Jake, who despondently looks forward to the end of his short-lived freedom. Anticipating David Levinsky, Jake sees no possibility of bringing together the charming dream of the past with the painful and banal activities of the present.

This hunger for reconciliation causes his most intense suffering, although he is seldom aware that his yearning is the real basis for his unhappiness. When the news comes to him of his father's death, however, Jake remembers—and forgets too soon:

> Suddenly he felt himself a child, the only and pampered son of a doting mother. He was overcome with a heart wringing consciousness of being an orphan, and his soul was filled with a keen sense of desolation and self-pity. And thereupon everything around him—the rows of gigantic tenement houses, the hum and buzz of the scurrying pedestrians, the jingling horse cars—all suddenly grew alien and incomprehensible to Jake. Ah, if he could return to his old days.

Jake's pride and his hard American shell do not leave him suffering for very long in a state of nostalgia. Nevertheless, this "heart wringing consciousness of being an orphan," this "keen sense of desolation," is the real root of Jake's emotional instability.

Abraham Cahan's short fiction reveals a notable consistency. As in *Yekl,* desolation and spiritual hunger are central in nearly all of the short stories; the one exception is **"Rabbi Eliezer's Christmas,"** Cahan's only thoroughly humorous tale, though even here one finds a note of resentment aimed at the dehumanizing effect of America's industrialized culture. "I make every letter with my own hands," Eliezer, an aging craftsman complains in despair to a businessman, "and my words are full of life." "'Bother your hands and your words!' said the merchant. 'This isn't Russia,' says he [*sic*]. 'It's America, the land of machines and of "hurry up,"'" says he." How obvious it is: where mechanical efficiency is dominant there is no room for an artisan's pride in his craft. And it is this "hurry-up" America, "the land of machines," that is to become central in *The Rise of David Levinsky*.

Other than **"Rabbi Eliezer's Christmas,"** all of Cahan's short stories are imbued with pathos, and nearly all of his fiction ends on a pessimistic, or even tragic, chord. Although in **"A Ghetto Wedding"** the conclusion is something brighter than unhappy, its optimism is but a tint of color amid varying shades of gray. Nathan and Goldie want to marry, but in order to provide themselves with a "respectable wedding," they attempt to save their scant earnings and therefore postpone the ceremony for years on end. Finally, still poor, they spend their few gleaned dollars on an immense wedding reception and banquet, anticipating a bountiful return of extravagant presents. But the wedding is held at an unfortunate time; no one has much money, few people send gifts, and, ashamed to arrive empty-handed, fewer still come to the celebration. Nathan and Goldie married are poorer than they were before. After the festivities the forlorn newlyweds walk through the darkness to their tenement. "When they found themselves alone in the deserted street, they were so overcome by a sense of loneliness, of a kind of portentous, haunting emptiness, that they could not speak, so on they trudged in dismal silence." Before they arrive home a group of Gentile rowdies shout and throw vegetables at them, and Goldie clings to her protective husband in the darkness. "The very notion of a relentless void abruptly turned to a beatific sense of their own seclusion, of there being only themselves in the universe, to live and to delight in each other." Here, then, Nathan and Goldie can be taken to represent historic Judaism, with their devotion to each other, their sense of exile and seclusion, and their persecution by the Gentile world that surrounds them. Isolated, perhaps, but not alone, they prevail together.

The title story of his collection, **"The Imported Bridegroom,"** clearly anticipates the major themes of Cahan's later fiction. The traditional past of the European ghetto is brought into touch with the Americanized, younger-generation present of the Lower East Side through the medium of Asriel, the "boor," a retired man of relative wealth and leisure who yearns nostalgically for his religion and the "old country." He travels to Pravly, the Russian city of his birth, and flashes his wealth in the synagogue; by offering an immense dowry, he literally purchases Shaya, a brilliant young Talmudist whom he brings back to America as the providential groom for his daughter, Flora. The secular American girl refuses to wed the old-fashioned, unsophisticated, ultra-pious Talmudic scholar. Soon, however, Shaya's earlocks and beard disappear, and the youth commences to study the "Gentile" books of learning with which Flora provides him; the two youngsters fall in love, and Shaya turns aside completely from his religion. "Bedeviled America" has made him "an appikoros," an atheist, Asriel moans. "America has done it all."

But it is Asriel who is really at fault and not America. Shaya has changed as Asriel himself had been transformed thirty-five years earlier. Moreover, Flora, whom he has raised with little or no concern for religion, is the direct cause of Shaya's abrupt westernization; she indoctrinates her brilliant fiancé so rapidly into secularity that he is soon far beyond her in the "Gentile" knowledge of mathematics and natural philosophy to which she has introduced him. The story ends as Flora sits in a garret, ignored and despondent, vaguely hearing the animated discussion of a group of Bohemian intellectuals, among whom is her new husband. "A nightmare of desolation and jealousy choked her, . . . jealousy of the whole excited crowd, and of Shaya's entire future, from which she seemed excluded." Here again is the dominant note of loneliness and estrangement, of despair and anguish that can be recognized in all of Cahan's American fiction.

The leading figures in nearly all of his stories are carried around and around a continual cycle of intense desire and foredoomed disappointment. The freedom of America paradoxically gives them nothing to be free *for*. They yearn for something to which they can bind themselves, something to replace the protective religious shawl which they have left behind. When Judaism and piety no longer provide Cahan's figures with the means by which to live, with the single guiding light of their behavior and existence, then their stretching hearts begin to twinge.

Nor can anything satisfy the pangs of spiritual hunger suffered by most of these people except maintaining the faith of tradition. Shaya, to be sure, has no time for yearning and suffering; his transformation from a pious Jew to a fervent Socialist is almost immediate; his change is not effected through the need of a substitute stabilizing force to compensate for spiritual loss, but more simply through a new and broader awareness. Shaya is a brilliant young man in a closed society; transplanted into a completely new and considerably more open environment, he reacts to it much as any vigorous and intelligent youth probably would: he rebels against the confining old-fashioned traditions which have held him unwittingly in check and opens himself wide to the secular world around him. Unlike Cahan himself, who was driven from his motherland for his socialistic views, Shaya is not converted, or westernized, until shortly after he sets foot in America. Because he is secularized without being tormented by his loss of faith, Shaya can be compared with few other figures in Cahan's American fiction, nearly all of whom suffer constant "twinges" of pain and remorse as the barrier between themselves and their heritage becomes almost impregnable.

Aaron Zalkin, for example, suffers intensely in **"The Daughter of Reb Avrom Leib"** until he manages to leap back over the barrier into restored faith and a happy life; he has been separated from his religion for more than fifteen years "when a great feeling of loneliness [takes] hold of him." He begins to attend a small synagogue, where he meets his "predestined one," and the story ends with his imminent marriage. Usually in Cahan's stories, however, there is no return to the faith.

More typical of his fiction was **"A Providential Match,"** Cahan's first published American tale, the one which had elicited Howells' initial encouragement; it was later included in *The Imported Bridegroom*. In this story Rouvke Arbel comes to America and is soon earning a moderate income; but he is a single man, does not attend synagogue, and "his heart was stretching and stretching" for someone to love. At last, after several lonely years, the *shadchen* (marriage-broker) arranges a match for him; but Rouvke loses his bethrothed to a scholar during her passage to the United States. Embittered, he is again left in desolation.

"So this is America and I am a Jewess no longer," are Michalina's first words in **"The Apostate of Chego-Chegg."** She is a *meshumedeste,* a convert, scorned by Gentiles for her Jewishness, and by Jews for her conversion. She longs to return to her Hebraic faith, but she is also devoted to her Catholic husband. In the same tale, Nehemiah the Rabbi cuts off his traditional earlocks and beard and becomes an atheist. "Religion is all humbug. There are no Jews and Gentiles," he tells Michalina. "This is America. All are noblemen here, and all are brothers—children of one mother—nature. But he fails to convince her. Michalina still yearns to return to Europe and to Judaism, but she loves her husband too much to leave him. So she must live under a curse and with the hunger of unsatisfied spiritual desire always within her.

In **"Dumitru and Sigrid,"** a well-educated Roumanian officer meets a beautiful Swedish girl. Both are immigrants, and they converse haltingly in English through their bilingual dictionaries. After they separate, Dumitru finds a pleasant job in New York, but still "his desolation grew and grew upon him. . . . Could it be that he was doomed to life-long exile? . . . He felt lonely, gnawingly lonely." When he meets Sigrid again, she is already a domesticated wife and mother, no longer the embodiment of the dream which she had become in his imagination; hence even the pleasure of illusive hope abruptly disintegrates, and another immigrant is lost through alienation in America.

"A Sweat-Shop Romance" displays a conflict of personalities among workers in a tenement garment factory; Heyman loses his sweetheart to David because he has not the courage to assert himself. He is thus left stunned and in wretched loneliness. In **"Circumstances,"** Boris and Tanya are a well-educated immigrant couple whose home life steadily deteriorates because of the low wages in the ghetto. Finally their relationship breaks completely; Tanya takes a job, and Boris breaks out in tears over his lost wife and bleak future. Both stories are included in *The Imported Bridegroom;* and, again, in both of them the emphasis is on desolation and despair in the New World.

"Tzinchadzi of the Catskills" is not as successful artistically as the other tales, but through Tzinchadzi, an alienated Russian nobleman, Cahan expresses his own understanding of the elemental paradox in the Jewish psyche—and ironically Tzinchadzi is one of Cahan's few non-Jewish protagonists. The Russian has explained how he lost his sweet-heart, Zelaya, through his vanity, and how he had yearned both for his homeland and for the girl herself before he became prosperous and apathetic:

> "I have money and I have friends, but . . . I am [not] happy. . . . I yearn neither for my country nor for Zelaya, nor for anything. . . . A man's heart cannot be happy unless it has somebody or something to yearn for. . . . [In the Catskills] my heart ached, but its pain was pleasure, whereas now—alas! The pain is gone, and with it my happiness. I have nothing, nothing! . . . I do enjoy life; only I am yearning for—what shall I call it? . . . I can't tell you what I feel. . . . Maybe if I could I shouldn't feel it, and there would be nothing to tell, so that the telling of it would be a lie."

The feeling cannot be explained, but it is nevertheless present in many of Cahan's characters, most particularly in David Levinsky, the multimillionaire.

The Rise of David Levinsky is Cahan's chef-d'oeuvre. Although autobiographical elements are pervasive in the novel, Levinsky and his creator are thoroughly different individuals, for the two men diverged in thought with their arrivals in America. However, there are inherent Judaic characteristics in each of them which can be extirpated neither by time nor by experience. If Levinsky is not the spokesman for Cahan's social and political views, he serves nevertheless as a persona through which the author can express the innate Jewish feeling common to the secularized people in his fiction—the craving for relief from spiritual vacuity.

David Levinsky flees from the poverty and persecution in his homeland to America, where within a few decades he becomes a multimillionaire. Levinsky's real story, however, lies in his character: how it is affected by his circumstances, by his ambition and by his success. It is a tale of industrial America, true, but even more, it is the psychological portrait of Levinsky himself.

In 1865 David Levinsky was born in Antomir, Russia, and raised by his mother in poverty; his father died before he was three. His early schooling was sporadic because of insufficient funds, but he learned to study the Talmud and was on his way to becoming an adept and devoted Talmudic scholar. During a wave of anti-Semitism his mother was beaten to death by a mob of Gentiles, and Levinsky was suddenly an orphan. His loneliness and poverty rendered him apathetic:

> Nothing really interested me except the fact that I had not enough to eat, that mother was no more, that I was all alone in the world. . . . My communions with God were quite rare now. Nor did He take as much interest in my studies as He used to. . . . I said prayers for [my mother] three times a day with great devotion, with a deep yearning. But this piety was powerless to restore me to my former feeling for the Talmud.

As Ranga observes in Aldous Huxley's final novel, *Island:* "Without bread . . . there is no mind, no spirit, no inner light, no Father in Heaven. There is only hunger, . . . despair, . . . apathy, . . . death." The young Levinsky's reaction to sustained physical hunger is a natural one.

It is not America, then, that turns Levinsky from Judaism, but the adverse circumstances of his situation in Russia. His secularization, or, as John Higham has suggested, his "Americanization," begins to lead him toward spiritual insecurity even before he commences his actual journey to the New World. In his excellent analysis of the novel, Isaac Rosenfeld has explained that Levinsky's "character was formed by hunger"; he lacked a father, and he therefore fastened himself spiritually to Reb Sender, a pious old Talmudist in young David's synagogue; he lacked normal sexual relationships because of his narrow religious training, and as a result the only women he desired were those beyond his reach; he lacked material comfort, and thus when the opportunity to acquire wealth arose, he reacted almost violently to it and became insatiable in his demands. Hence, like Clyde Griffiths in Dreiser's *An American Tragedy,* David Levinsky's future was predetermined in the "old country," before he ever set out on his journey to the Promised Land.

Once in the New World, Levinsky quickly throws off the mantle of tradition. It is his "second birth," and he intends to lose his status of "greenhornship" as soon as possible. Homesick and alone, he buys a peddler's stand and goes into business; and although he continues to study the Talmud during the evenings, he does so not as much for the sake of piety as to mollify his twinges of nostalgia:

> But many of the other peddlers made fun of my piety and it could not last long. Moreover, I was in contact with life now, and the daily surprises it had in store for me dealt my former ideas of the world blow after blow. I saw the cunning and meanness of some of my customers, of the trades-people, . . . and of the peddlers. . . . Nor was I unaware of certain unlovable traits that were un-avoidably developing in my own self under these influences. And while human nature was thus growing smaller, the human world as a whole was growing larger, more complex, more heartless, and more interesting.

In order to justify his own loss of piety, Levinsky criti-cizes the adamantine traditionalism of the Jewish faith. It must "learn the art of trimming its sails to suit new winds," he says; "it is absolutely inflexible":

> If you are a Jew of the type to which I belonged when I came to New York and you attempt to bend your religion to the spirit of your new surroundings, it breaks. It falls to pieces. The very clothes I wore and the very food I ate had a fatal effect on my religious habits.

Levinsky's self-vindication is almost convincing, but it must be regarded in the light of his past; for it was in Antomir that he lost his faith, not in America. Moreover, the first girl whom he loves is a westernized divorcée in Russia. By the time he arrives in the United States, Levinsky's psychological state is one in which he is try-ing to talk himself into being pious. He attempts to de-lude himself, and when he realizes that this condition is an impossible one to maintain for long, his pride leads him to excuse his action on the basis of a flaw in the religion itself—its inflexibility. Ironically, it is exactly this fundamental stability of the religion that has been its salvation.

During his rise from a street peddler to a ladies' garment manufacturer worth more than two million dollars, Levinsky steadily loses his soul to his desire for material gain. He becomes "Americanized," yes, but he becomes dehumanized as well. Levinsky is neither avaricious nor cruel. But he is an exploiter. He is shrewd and cold. He lives and operates his business solely according to the principles of Social Darwinism—"the survival of the fit-test." Once he becomes aware of Spencer's writings, he reads them through several times:

> I sat up nights reading these books. Apart from the peculiar intellectual intoxication they gave me, they flattered my vanity as one of the "fittest." It was as though all the wonders of learning, acumen, ingenuity, and assiduity displayed in these works had been intended, among other purposes, to establish my title as one of the victors of existence.
>
> A working-man and everyone else who was poor,

was an object of contempt to me—a misfit, a weakling, a failure, one of the ruck.

A contemptible, contemptuous—and yet pathetic—indi-vidual, it is no wonder that he can coldly regard Lucy, the daughter of a married woman with whom he falls in love, as "an interesting study."

At times David Levinsky appears to be nothing but a machine, requiring and exploiting all of humanity to keep himself well oiled and completely in tune. His capacity for spiritual fulfillment and affection seems to have con-tracted and disappeared, and therefore the industrialist should be considered a deviation from Cahan's proto-typal secularized Jew. But he is not essentially different, after all. Levinsky yearns for a wife and family, but it is an ideal woman whom he craves and not a real one. She is a shadowy figure whose picture has been compounded in his mind partially from his imagination and partially from the women in his past: his mother, who doted on him; Red Esther, who introduced him to the charms of femininity; Matilda, his first love; Bertha, the prostitute, who was "at heart . . . better than some of the most respectable people I had met"; and Dora, a friend's wife, whom he "loves" with "a blend of animal selfishness and spiritual sublimity." Of course, the matchmakers find him "a hard man to suit."

It is clear, then, that David Levinsky is not simply an-other face of S. Behrman or Flem Snopes, the economic "monsters" of Norris and Faulkner, for he is a much more elaborate and broadly conceived figure than they. John Higham recognizes him as "not a universal man or a wholly representative figure. He was partly an individual, partly a specific type." To be sure, Levinsky is an ex-tremely complex man—the embodied dichotomy of mind and soul in conflict.

Cahan clearly reveals this duality in Levinsky's character through the extensive use of self-contradiction. The two conflicting elements inside of him are constantly at war with each other; he is the employer who sympathizes with the strikers, and the presence of his name in a derogatory newspaper editorial "flattered [his] vanity." His attitude toward the Socialists is remarkably inconsistent; it varies radically according to circumstantial change. When he begins to work steadily for the first time, Levinsky ad-mits: "Had I then chanced to hear a Socialist speech I might have become an ardent follower of Karl Marx." Later, after he has become a wealthy manufacturer, he says that the "Jewish Socialist leaders . . . seemed to me to be the most repulsive hypocrites of all. I loathed them." And still later, during a major strike in his own factory, he recalls: "For all my theorizing about 'the sur-vival of the fittest' and the 'dying off of the weaklings,' I could not help feeling that, in an abstract way, the Socialists were not altogether wrong. The case was dif-ferent, however, when I considered it . . . concrete[ly]."

Irrational as it may seem, Levinsky truly suffers from this continual conflict within himself. It has become a part of his nature; both elements react against each other, thus keeping themselves insatiable and rendering the conflict itself irreconcilable. Shortly before his betrothal, Levinsky clearly but unwittingly gives voice to this contrariety in a single brief paragraph:

> I had no creed. I knew of no ideals. The only thing I believed in was the cold, drab theory of the struggle for existence and the survival of the fittest. This could not satisfy a heart that was hungry for enthusiasm and affection, so dreams of family life became my religion. Self-sacrificing devotion to one's family was the only kind of altruism and idealism I did not flout.

Levinsky's dream of a satisfactory family life cannot come true. The women he can have, he does not want; the few women whom he loves "to insanity" will not, *cannot,* have him. Anna Tevkin, who, because of an incident in his childhood, comes nearest to approaching his ideal woman, refuses to consider him a candidate for marriage. Shocked with his proposal, she turns him down and weds a high-school teacher. His dreams become his religion, but this kind of rootless faith cannot require anything of him. It is a whimsical, bloodless, unreal religion of the fancy, and therefore does nothing to fill the spiritual hiatus within him. His heart is stretching, but his hardened exterior confines it, and nothing is there for it to grasp.

Levinsky's paradox rests upon the circumstances of his past; despite his increasing material wealth, they continue to operate against him. He has won his struggle for survival, but in the process of doing so he has relinquished his kinship with humanity and has thus become, in a variation of the American success story, a "sad millionaire." "When I take a look at my inner identity," Levinsky meditates, "it impresses me as being precisely the same as it was thirty or forty years ago. My present station, power, the amount of worldly happiness at my command, and the rest of it, seem to be devoid of significance." Isaac Rosenfeld considers these lines the key to the novel, for they reveal Levinsky's fundamental Jewishness, his "uniquely Jewish character." They express the hunger that can be neither stifled nor satisfied. Again, Levinsky's statements are simply reiterations of Tzinchadzi's lamentations of apathy, and they also recall the despondency of Rouvke Arbel, Flora and divers other figures in Cahan's earlier fiction.

Moreover, the traditional Jewish emphasis on education strengthens the paradox. Levinsky's business acumen develops rapidly in America as a direct result of his intense study of Talmudic law and commentary. These studies sharpened his wit and memory, and because in his early years they were a mark of religious piety, they satisfied his spiritual and intellectual requirements simultaneously. During his process of secularization in America, Levinsky's wit and piety are transmogrified into shrewdness and longing. It is at this point that the two sides of the psychic conflict entrench themselves firmly in his nature, and with the passage of time each of the opposing elements strengthens proportionately.

Ronald Sanders has suggested that the most significant problem in the novel is an obtrusive flaw in American society. The spiritual life is lost, he says, from "a society that was in some ways built too fast." Certainly this is an important factor in Levinsky's unhappy situation, but it is not the decisive one. The freedom of America allows room for the pious Jew and the materialistic atheist. The question is one of self-discipline and desire. Levinsky's poverty as a youth induced him to sacrifice his religious devotion for the sake of wealth. Such was his wish; such was his achievement. But the choice was Levinsky's, and America's only "fault" was leaving him at liberty to make it. Inevitably reminding one of Yekl's enigma, Levinsky concludes: "I cannot escape from my old self"; and this is his tragic limitation—his inability to release himself from his fundamental Jewishness.

Although few people in Cahan's fiction amass great stores of wealth, most of them suffer from the same ironic duality that destroys all possibility of Levinsky's ever attaining spiritual fulfillment. The difference between their condition and his, however, is that Levinsky's financial success has all but atrophied his soul, whereas most of the lesser characters retain their elemental sense of kinship with humanity. Perhaps they have been forced to the fringes of society, perhaps into years of loneliness; but this alienation is usually unsought and unwanted; they consistently attempt to escape it. Levinsky, however, holds himself aloof from nearly all of society—he thinks of himself as one of the chosen "fittest."

But the failure of so many of Cahan's heroes is definitely not the failure of America. To assert that one's country is at fault on the basis of its allowing too much freedom of worship is absurd. If the immigrants and citizens of a nation wish to adore an economic god rather than a heavenly one, it is hardly advisable that government policy regulate these desires—unless, of course, too many innocent victims are sacrificed by exploitation to their voracious *deus auri.* Even then, however, it is the economic laws and principles that are at fault and certainly not religious liberty.

In *Yekl,* many of the short stories, and particularly in *The Rise of David Levinsky,* Cahan explored both of these elemental social factors—economics and religion—and the difficulties that derive from them—exploitation and secularization. Like Norris and Dreiser, Cahan realistically depicted a portion of industrial America; though his descriptions at times become sordid, they are never anything but convincing. But Cahan has given the Lower East Side of New York City a pervasive aura of warmth and charm that does not glow from the cold, amoral and indifferent visage of Dreiser's Chicago. For Abraham Cahan, religion tempers circumstance—simply because a strong sense of faith is a circumstance in itself. If religion is not the decisive factor in the lives of Cahan's immigrants, it is always one of the most influential, for few of his people are able to alienate themselves from it completely.

Hence a generation of lonely new Americans.

Dan Vogel (essay date 1973)

SOURCE: "Cahan's *Rise of David Levinsky*: Archetype of American Jewish Fiction," in *Judaism: A Quarterly Journal,* Vol. 22, No. 3, Summer, 1973, pp. 278-87.

[*In the following essay, Vogel contends that* The Rise of David Levinsky *became the archetype for later fiction in the same genre.*]

Some years ago, in a reconsideration of Abraham Cahan's 1917 novel, ***The Rise of David Levinsky,*** Isaac Rosenfeld declared, "Levinsky [is] the essential Jewish type of the Dispersion." The truth of this assertion is underlined, it seems to me, by the rehearsal of some essential elements of theme, characterization, and method in later American Jewish fiction. My purpose here is to explore the ways in which ***The Rise of David Levinsky*** is archetypal—archetypal, not in the sense of racial memory, but in the sense of community experience during the three generations since the flood of East European Jewish immigration in the 1880's. Nor do I mean that Cahan's hero is the ideal Jewish type of the Dispersion. Rather, he is the prototype whose features of personality and career, whether for ill or for good, are reborn in later protagonists of this genre.

The origin of the type is in the closed, theocratic world of the *shtetl* in Russia. In his sustained reminiscence, which makes up the entire novel, David recalls his early Gorky-an circumstances in Antomir, a *shtetl* somewhere in the Russian Pale. His father, it should be noted for later discussion, is dead; his mother, who scrimps in order to send David to *heder,* the religious school, dies in an altercation with anti-Semites, and it is of her only that the orphan dreams. Shifting for himself, David joins the round of his fellow-students in going from house to house for meals. Thus he grows into adolescence, a time which marks his discovery of girls and the concomitant neglect of Talmud study. In time, David joins the migration to America. He arrives poor and ignorant, garbed and hirsute in the manner of the greenhorn Talmudic student. The remainder of Levinsky's tale is about his peddling, his drift from Orthodox Judaism, his sexual debauchery, his acquisition of two million dollars, his loneliness, his futile attempts to marry and, finally, his total dissatisfaction with his life. He is still diffident in the presence of women, fearful in the presence of waiters, and indecisive in the presence of his workers. Though Cahan has not made David Levinsky into a *shlemiel,* he portrays him as a *nebbich* with a veneer.

Thus, Abraham Cahan formulated the first two archetypal characteristics of American-Jewish literature: the theme of the consequences of the collision of old world Orthodoxy with new world materialistic emancipation, and the anti-hero as the central character of this drama.

I think we can better appreciate Cahan's achievement in ***The Rise of David Levinsky*** by noticing that this protagonist of 1917 is, himself, the end-product of two ear-lier major efforts by Cahan to depict the new Jewish immigrant to America. Before publishing that novel, Cahan wrote, in English, ***Yekl: A Tale of the New York Ghetto*** (1896) and **"The Imported Bridegroom"** (1898). *Yekl* anticipates the later works negatively: that is to say, it is important in hindsight to see how different Cahan's emphasis is in this novella. The chief figure is Yekl, or Jake in English, whom we meet on the Lower East Side three years after his arrival in America. He had landed in Boston, sojourned there for a time, and now is living in the New York ghetto. He has emigrated alone, leaving aged parents, a young wife, and an infant son back home in Russia. Jake has long since given up his quaint religious upbringing: he is a modern American sweatshop worker, and a devil with the dance hall girls, for he had kept his married state a secret.

In time, he brings over his wife and son. But Gitl proves to be old fashioned, dowdy, and unexciting—unfit to be the consort of the new "Yenkee," as Jake sees himself. (Henry Roth, almost 40 years later, will exploit a similar situation.) Certainly, Gitl is not like the sharp, vulgarly Americanized girls with whom Jake has been making his mark. So, with some intermittent misgivings, Jake slides apart from her, and they are finally divorced, he about to marry the sharpest of the dance hall beauties, Gitl about to be courted by a scholarly, gentle, less Americanized sewing-machine operator. At the end, Jake is disquieted; he fears that he has been cheated, somehow, of the sense of freedom, superiority, and ebullience that his Americanized conduct should have given him.

This feeling of dissatisfaction, rising at the moment of seeming triumph, will become a Cahan hallmark. But here, in this early story, it is significant to note that Jake's disillusionment has nothing to do with the classic attempt at upward mobility nor with the loss of religious tradition, for Cahan does not deal with either theme here. The loss of tradition is only passingly dealt with in the story. There is no pain upon its loss; no substitute, like materialistic striving, in place of the Judaism that is rejected; no feeling of emancipation is suggested. We get the feeling that Jake's restlessness is inborn and that the ghetto served, not as the cause, but as the catalyst of his marital drift, divorce, and discontent. Cahan does not offer his tale as typical or universal among East Side Jews. Certainly, Jake is no hero of the Americanizing process. As Howells noted in his review, this is but a realistic story, perhaps reminding him of the tone and manner of Stephen Crane's *Maggie* (1893).

Two years later, in **"The Imported Bridegroom,"** which Cahan wrote as the lead story for a collection of his already published magazine stories, we begin to see a greater universalization of the ghetto experience. Reb Asriel Stroon, a widower, who had played loose with *halakhic* laws in order to amass his real estate fortune, now fanatically returns to religion. In fact, he goes back to his *shtetl* in Russia to find a bridegroom for his daughter, Flora. On her part, Flora is horrified, for she dreams of marrying a Jewish doctor, clean-shaven, American, modern, educated. Reb Asriel, in his hometown, discovers that you can't really go home again, but stays long enough to buy at auction a brilliant, shy Talmudic genius. He imports him for Flora.

At first, to Asriel's frustration, the wishfully emancipated Flora and the bewildered Shaya do not hit it off. Then Flora begins to teach him English. From that point on, the way to hell is opened. Shaya learns to read Socialist theory, which leads to the neglect of his Talmud studies, then to the abandonment of religious scruples and, finally, to outright atheism. He and Flora marry civilly only, and Flora dutifully accompanies her bridegroom to a free-thinking soirée, where Swedes, Englishmen, Russians, and Scots read and discuss the texts of utopian theory. At the end, Cahan pictures Shaya listening raptly to the new revelation, and Flora, unable to compete in this deeply intellectual discussion, feeling cheated and excluded from "Shaya's entire future."

Again disappointment at the moment of triumph. But now Cahan's attention has shifted. First of all, the chief character is the father. Significantly, the mother in this story is dead. The father dominates his daughter, who feels smothered by the weight of this dominance, desires to get out from under, and does. Of course, it will be recognized that the same story is told over and over again later in American-Jewish fiction, but with the sexes reversed.

It is no accident, I think, that Cahan does it this way in **"The Imported Bridegroom."** After all, immersed as he was in contemporary fiction, he had Henry James and W. D. Howells to point the way to him about how mothers dominated daughters in genteel American society. How a transplanted Jewish mother might have dealt with Flora might have made an interesting story, but Cahan did not write it. His interest here is the father, and presently I shall suggest why.

Secondly, the major theme of this novella is how an innocent refugee from the *shtetl* loses his Jewishness because of his exposure to America—a more pointed theme than the one in *Yekl*. To fill the vacuum created by the loss, Cahan offers one of the two religions prevalent at the turn of the century—Socialism. (The other, economic mobility, will be David Levinsky's.) But the handling of the theme is strange for Cahan. He himself was an old *yeshivah bohur* who became devoted to free-thinking socialism, and the last scene of **"The Imported Bridegroom,"** says Ronald Sanders, in *The Downtown Jews*, was drawn from an incident in his own life. But Cahan does not make Shaya the new immigrant intellectual hero, passionately embracing the dogma of progress. Indeed, he makes Shaya a source of disappointment and pain to his benefactor and his beloved. Cahan forces our sympathy upon Asriel and Flora, the woebegone greenhorns who simply are not with it. And the way Cahan describes the brilliant Shaya's participation in the avant-garde group restrains our admiration for his intellectual courage. **"The Imported Bridegroom"** is a story in which the rejection of tradition is depicted as an unretrieved

loss and a betrayal, rather than as a triumph over provinciality; and there is nothing—neither new doctrine nor economic ascendancy—to take its place.

When Cahan turned his attention entirely to the Shaya-figure, whom he renamed David Levinsky—he has his hero try the other religion that was touted at the turn of the century: financial success. However, the acquisition of money and position as the compensation for the loss of Jewishness, fails the test. And, in depicting the failure, Cahan concomitantly perceives that the East European heritage offers a glimmering of hope in the midst of despair. In the final paragraphs of his confessional, Levinsky says:

> When I think of these things, when I am in this sort of mood, I pity myself for a victim of circumstances. At the height of my business success I feel that if I had my life to live over again I should never think of a business career.
>
> I don't seem to be able to get accustomed to my luxurious life. I am always more or less conscious of my good clothes, of the high quality of my office furniture, of the power I wield over the men in my pay. As I have said in another connection, I still have a lurking fear of restaurant waiters.
>
> I can never forget the days of my misery. I cannot escape from my old self. My past and my present do not comport well. David, the poor lad swinging over the Talmud volume at the Preacher's Synagogue [in Antomir] seems to have more in common with my inner identity than David Levinsky, the well-known cloak-manufacturer.

"I cannot escape from my old self." In one sentence, Cahan announces a major theme of future American Jewish fiction: the attempt to escape Jewishness and the continual (though not invariable) realization that there is no escape. It is the attempt to escape Jewish identity and the consequent realization that the search for inner identity demands some sort of return. Cahan contains this theme in the story that has since become typical: the East European Jew confronting the freedoms of an emancipated America. He describes the competing attractions of piety, or at least of a Jewish ethos, on one side, and economic materialism and social belonging on the other, together with the almost inevitable drift from Judaism toward a vestigial Jewishness. Later writers, like Jerome Weidman and Philip Roth, will carry the story even further, to the point where their protagonists simply ignore their Jewish origins or embrace outright assimilation. Sanford Marovitz has called this theme the central one:

> The spiritual hunger of the immigrant Jew in America. . . . Those who traded their faith for the gospel of materialism suffered the pangs of loneliness regardless of their wealth, prestige, or position. . . .

In post-Cahan American Jewish fiction, the story of competing codes of thought and conduct is told over and over again. Never mind that Augie March, Marjorie

Morningstar, Alexander Portnoy, Eli Peck, Moses Elkanah Herzog, Stern, and a host of others were not born in the *shtetl*. The *shtetl* ethos has filtered into their consciousness, as it never left Levinsky's, and forces them to evaluate, and in many cases to decry, their slipping into the slough of despond of American social and philosophical emancipation. What Cahan did right at the beginning was to anticipate the tendency of American Jewish fiction—for all its claims of universality—to be inspirited with parochial introspection. And this parochialism often results in some kind of re-integration with the old time-value system: rarely halakhic (although it does occur in Blankfort's *The Strong Hand*, [1951], or Potok's three novels, [1967, 1969, 1972]); sometimes merely habitual (as in Wouk's novel, [1955]); perhaps psychological (like Eli Peck's moment of epiphany in Roth's story, "Eli, the Fanatic," [1957]); at best, spiritual (as in Bellow's *Herzog*, [1964]).

Cahan emphasizes this theme by reprising a motif from **"The Imported Bridegroom"**—the transference of the traditional faith in learning from religious to secular matters:

> My old religion had gradually fallen to pieces [recollects David Levinsky], and if its place was taken by something else, if there was something that appealed to the better man in me, to what was purest in my thought, and most sacred in my emotions, that something was the red, church-like structure on the southeast corner of Lexington Avenue and Twenty-third Street [the City College of New York].
>
> It was the synagogue of my new life. Nor is this merely a figure of speech: the building really appealed to me as a temple, as a House of Sanctity, as we call the ancient Temple of Jerusalem. At least that was the term I would fondly apply to it, years later, in my retrospective broodings upon the first few years of my life in America.

Though he never could drag himself away from making money to enroll, Levinsky did find the time to read Herbert Spencer.

Well, the genre-children of David Levinsky did go to college. Nonetheless, the new American Haskalah, when taken in place of, not as complementary to, the heritage of the Temple in Jerusalem, landed them in the same alienated corner in which Cahan placed Levinsky.

Through the theme of alienation, Cahan introduced into American Jewish literature the anti-hero as protagonist. Let us understand the nature of David's anti-heroism. No doubt, in a sense, Cahan saw the "yeshivah to penthouse" progression as but a variation of America's heroic myth of "rags to riches" or "log cabin to White House." No doubt he took pride in the kind of person that Levinsky represents—the greenhorn who meets the challenges of a totally new way of life and overcomes them in terms of the host society. In this sense, the old role of hero, as representative of his community in a confrontation with the Other and in the ultimate rush to victory, can still be discerned in David Levinsky.

But Cahan perceived that the nascent Jewish hero in America would find no satisfaction in his heroism. Much of the novel is given over to portraying the erosion of self-confidence and of any sense of accomplishment in success or sacrifice. Cahan's intent is not to delineate a romantic hero, who scores a victory over the odds of life; nor a realistic hero, who accommodates himself to defeat with dignity; nor a tragic hero, whose catastrophe is his victory. Whatever heroism lies in the character of David Levinsky lies in the recognition that his strengths and persistence have led him only to spiritual dissatisfaction and misery, and that all along he has avoided making the truly hard decisions. In the welter of these anti-heroic emotions, however, David Levinsky retains an important trait of the ancient heroes: he still represents his community, then and since.

In his portrayal of the anti-hero, Cahan considers two forms of spiritual weakness: the arguments of determinism and of self-pity. His rejection of the first presages the rejection of it by later writers in his genre. As for the second, however, Cahan's theme of self-pity can now be seen as an early symptom of a syndrome in American-Jewish literature that will be climaxed by the hatred of the Jewish self and of the Jewish mother.

Desperate, in his alienation, for a modicum of self-esteem, David Levinsky cries out, "I pity myself for a victim of circumstances." Quite candidly, the plea that he is a victim of circumstances sounds convincing to our generation, disposed as we are to find existential or Freudian or sociological justification to replace the old idea of guilt. Indeed, even Mr. Marovitz is persuaded, going so far as to compare David with Clyde Griffiths, the predestinated hero of Theodore Dreiser's *An American Tragedy* (1925), and to assert that David's future was predetermined in the old country before he ever started on his way to America. It seems to me, however, that Cahan's whole point in this novel is thus turned around.

The very title of the novel shows its affinity to the story of the successful rags-to-riches paint manufacturer in Howells' *Rise of Silas Lapham* (1885), rather than to the story of the bewildered, unsuccessful youth from the Middle West. American literary history records the warm friendship of Howells and Cahan, and, as John Higham points out in his introduction to the Torchbook edition, the novel is written in the tradition of Howells as well as of Dreiser, but the earlier Dreiser of *Sister Carrie* (1900, 1911). Dreiser's point in that novel is that success and social acceptance lead but to inner dissatisfaction and misery, precisely the *donnée* of **The Rise of David Levinsky**. And Howells means to tell us, as Cahan does, that success in business is not the true rise for a man. He must re-evaluate himself in terms of a traditional ethos—Christian and Yankee in the one, Jewish in the other—which in the last paragraph of Cahan's novel is hinted at.

There is, then, in Cahan's work, as in its literary progeny, a retreat from the logical finality of naturalism. Immediately after Levinsky utters his claim of victimization, he says that, were he able to do it all over again, he would have done something else. So he did have a choice, didn't he? The power to choose is Moses Herzog's discovery in Bellow's novel, and, indeed, is the climax of it. When Herzog rises above the feeling of victimization, then he decides to begin a new life. In almost all of American-Jewish fiction, the power of the Other—whether object, circumstance, or person—wields tremendous influence, but rarely to the point of total enervation. There is, at the very least, a confessional and, therefore, a ray of hope.

More important than the theme of determinism in the confessional is the strain of self-pity that begins in *The Rise of David Levinsky* and permeates much of future American Jewish writing. Already in Cahan's novel, self-pity develops into a lack of self-confidence and positive self-dislike. In time, this feeling will be developed into a castigation and denigration of the Jewish ego—in short, into self-hatred, which so disturbed the readers of *Commentary* magazine when it published a few of Philip Roth's stories in this vein.

Out of the *sturm und drang* of this process, the anti-hero emerges as an "I" persona that is solipsistic in its view of the world. I refer, not only to the predilection in American Jewish fiction toward the method of first-person narration but, also, to the way the psyche of the "I" persona has developed. *The Rise of David Levinsky* is in the first-person, but it is not a first-person narrative in the tradition of Conrad and James—the dispassionate development of moral perception and judgment in the narrator. Rather, Cahan's tone is in the line of Poe and Joyce—the passionate self-revelation of despair, stress, pain, and spiritual nakedness. Since then, with whatever variations of first-person method—*Portnoy's Complaint* (1969) is entirely so; *Herzog* weaves it in with agility; Markfield's *Teitelbaum's Window* (1970) in sections harks back to the epistolary variation—this psychological catharsis has become a feature of recent fiction in this genre.

It is the solipsistic "I," the extremity of anti-heroism, that has disfigured the Jewish mother in American Jewish literature and created a popular, if notorious, caricature. In Cahan's book, the pattern is quite innocently established: the father is dead and the mother becomes the center of the son's psyche. This situation, a generation later, becomes typical: the father is physically or symbolically dead; the mother survives to become her son's hang-up. But her role has been reevaluated since Cahan's time. Once she was praised for her influence upon her son's life. Now the solipsistic "I," casting about for a villain that has caused the hatred of self, accuses her of smothering her son's ego and freedom. She is the Freudian bogey of those who try to get out from under the accident or divine plan of their being born Jewish.

Because American-Jewish fiction since the second World War has become so popular and, along with it, the theme of the withdrawn papa, the *yiddishe mama,* and the choked son, this Oedipal-looking trinity has been thought of as uniquely Jewish. Lately, Professor Harold Fisch has argued that it is not Jewish at all, but is a by-product of the French Revolution's intellectual emancipation. In literature, Professor Fisch finds, the most blatant non-Jewish example of it is D. H. Lawrence's *Sons and Lovers* (1913), four years before the appearance of *The Rise of David Levinsky,* in which Mrs. Morel is a Gentile *yiddishe mama.* But this, for American-Jewish literature, smacks too much of the sexual and not enough of the cultural—too much Freud, as it were, and not enough Jung.

For Abraham Cahan and his heirs, the father symbolizes tradition, like Reb Asriel in **"The Imported Bridegroom."** When, in the story, tradition has been lost, the father is sick, dead, or a non-entity, as in so many stories from *David Levinsky* right up to Friedman's *A Mother's Kisses* (1964) and Roth's *Portnoy's Complaint.* This plot dominates our fiction because it is the reflection of the American-Jewish experience—the rejection of Orthodoxy. This is the theme, amply supported, of Professor Allen Guttmann's recent study.

There is, however, a sporadic, but definite, parallel line of stories in which tradition is seen as strong and viable, and in these the mother is cast in a distinctly lesser role. Thus, in **"The Imported Bridegroom"** and in Chaim Potok's first two novels, where tradition plays a central role, the mothers are absent and the fathers dominate. Even Philip Roth, perhaps instinctively, pays obeisance to the power of tradition as embodied in the father. Eli Peck, the fanatic, bursting out from under the smothering weight of his super-sophisticated, assimilated wife and of his own guilt feelings, dons the smelly garb of the young hasid. But the gesture is not yet a complete assuagement. He must run to confront his new-born son, brought before him in the hospital nursery; and, promising himself that his son will one day wear these gabardines, he cries out, *"I'm the father!"* Though Eli is mad, we are left with the feeling that he has reached a spiritual insight not vouchsafed his assimilated neighbors. He has fallen into what Melville called "the madness of vital truth."

Indeed, cued once more by Cahan, we may be on the verge of witnessing the restoration of the mother to a more healthy place in the triangle of the Jewish family. Henry Roth's *Call It Sleep* may be read as such a story. Though first published in 1941, it was reprinted just a few years ago to popular and critical acclaim. In *Herzog,* Bellow has Moses' mother remain in his memory as the paragon to which he hopes his daughter will aspire; and she is part of that poignant memory that includes his ineffectual but wonderful bootlegger father, his compassionate mother, and the bootlegger's sons saying ancient Hebrew prayers. And Chaim Potok, after two novels in which the mothers of his heroes are either literally or figuratively dead, resurrects the true *yiddishe mama* in Rivkeh Lev in *My Name is Asher Lev* (1972), a story about a God-endowed artist growing up in a Brooklyn hasidic community. It is significant, I think, that Asher's father is continually traveling, but leaves behind him the power of his personality and his traditional role which his wife must interpret for this son during his absences. This is precisely the role that fate and tradition devolved upon the mother of David Levinsky, to whom David's memory returns time and again later in life, a factor in his spiritually fructive dissatisfaction. Rivkeh Lev's presence in her son's psyche is what frees his artistic soul from the misunderstanding of his community, and yet prevents his drift into non-Orthodoxy.

These novels exemplify one of my emphases in this essay. Cahan insists that neither the theme of escape from Jewishness nor the self-hating nature of the American-Jewish anti-hero sentences him to a spiritual demise. Many critics of American literature have pointed to the theme of the self's spiritual death and rebirth. I suggest that, in the last chapter, David Levinsky's summation of his life implies such an awakening. But do not mistake me. The evidence in our fiction since Cahan does not reflect a religious revival and Cahan writes no portrayal of such. The competition between the *shtetl* ethos and the attractions of a materialistic haskalah society still goes on. Nostalgia for a lost, if seamy, Jewish paradise is not rebirth. And yet it was mainly emotion, not doctrine, that distracted our American Jewish heroes from their grandfathers' path. It may yet be the factor that will bring them to the threshold of spiritual peace. David Levinsky, of course, has no guarantee, but his suffering does lead to possibility.

Professor Guttmann thinks otherwise. He argues that American-Jewish fiction is the record of a generation of Jews that refuses to go on being Jews or to transmit Jewishness. Certainly, there is much sociological evidence to support his reading of the literature. Yet his study shows also that assimilation leads but to a crisis of identity. There is no epiphany or fulfillment depicted in stories that describe the adoption of a non-Jewish way of life. Consequently, even at the moment when he thinks he has successfully escaped, the straggler is still beckoned back, just as Cahan perceived more than half-a-century ago. I submit that there are too many marranos among our assimilated anti-heroes to permit total acceptance of Guttmann's bleak conclusion. Such are the heroes of some of the best old and new writers, like Lewisohn, Bellow, Philip Roth, Malamud, Wallant. All of them are heirs of Abraham Cahan.

Apparently then, in theme and vision, in method and thought, Abe Cahan blazed a trail for later American-Jewish fiction. Certainly, this trail has been broadened and strengthened so that stories of American Jews reflect, not only the experience of the East European immigrant community for three generations, but the general condition of mankind. This is an attempt by our authors to declassify this fiction as ethnic, and to incorporate it as characteristic of American literature in its totality. I refer the reader to an interview with Saul Bellow, in May 1971, in the *New York Times Book Review* for the expression of this sentiment. But the attempt is doomed to fail-

ure. Cahan's story—of one who tried to get out from under his Jewishness and learned that he could not—is archetypal of a specific genre of fiction, expressing a specific communal experience in America.

Louis Harap (essay date 1974)

SOURCE: "Fiction in English by Abraham Cahan," in *The Image of the Jew in American Literature,* The Jewish Publication Society of America, 1974, pp. 485-524.

[*In the following essay, Harap surveys Cahan's influence on American literature.*]

Abraham Cahan began to publish short stories, novellas, and novels in the 1890s. The themes and character types adumbrated through Cahan's fiction reached their mature development in 1917 in *The Rise of David Levinsky,* the most important fictional work about American Jewry up to that time by any American writer, Jewish or non-Jewish.

The depth of Cahan's fiction, both as social drama and as a personal statement, raises complex questions and invites interpretation on several levels. Part of these complexities and subtleties arise from the fact that Cahan was personally involved in and helped effect the transformation of the immigrant Jewish community from a poverty-stricken, densely packed mass in the ghetto to a highly significant force in much of American life. The fact that this milieu was Yiddish has made the materials for a thorough and comprehensive interpretation of Cahan's life and work almost inaccessible to most English-speaking critics and biographers. An adequately analytical biography of Cahan and a just evaluation of the positive and negative aspects of his life and work remain to be written. His work, indeed his life, was tied up with the Yiddish language and culture of the American ghetto, a culture from which virtually all writers in English were sealed off. Such a work would require an immersion in the passionately lived Yiddish milieu, which lasted from the 1880s to the 1940s—and in the Yiddish language.

Most critical writing on Cahan has been distorted by political or personal predisposition. The changes that occurred in both the Jewish community and Cahan's response to these changes, from the radicalism of his earliest years to his abandonment of socialism and the obsessive anticommunism of his last years, render it exceedingly hard to make a just evaluation. He has been considered as a central positive influence in the acculturation of the Jewish mass immigration and as a "misfortune" (*umglik*) for the Jewish people. Whatever judgment history may make on Cahan, it seems likely that his *David Levinsky* will be deemed a permanent contribution to American literature and will continue to be read as a social novel of permanent interest.

The essential facts of Cahan's life convey the remarkable scope of his activity and influence. He was born in a

Lithuanian shtetl in 1860, and his father began to give him instruction in Hebrew when he was four. The family moved to Vilna when he was six and he continued his education at a yeshiva, until he persuaded his parents to allow him to go to a government school at thirteen. He began to read Russian writers and lost his faith in Judaism. He went on to the free government Jewish teachers college at seventeen, and was attracted to and joined the peasant-oriented, nihilist Narodnaya Volya movement when he was nineteen. Following graduation in 1881 he taught at a Jewish school in Velizh, where he joined a local revolutionary circle. During the ensuing repression after the assassination of Alexander II, Cahan narrowly eluded arrest, and fled to the United States in June 1882. After several months of work in a cigar factory and a tin shop in New York, he had learned English sufficiently well to earn a living by giving private English lessons to immigrants.

Cahan became deeply involved in socialist activity soon after his arrival in the United States and quickly became a noted speaker, especially in Yiddish. He had his first article in English published in the New York *World* only six months after his entry into this country, and within two years was writing regularly for the New York *Sun* and other papers. He edited and wrote for the Yiddish socialist press until 1897, when he participated in the founding of the socialist *Forward (Forverts)*, a paper which he edited for a few months until a dispute about his journalistic methods caused him to resign. For five years thereafter he worked wholly in English as a reporter for the New York press and wrote articles and short stories for national magazines. During this period he was not only a colleague of Lincoln Steffens and Norman and Hutchins Hapgood on the daily New York *Commercial Advertiser,* but also published two volumes of fiction, *Yekl* (1896) and *The Imported Bridegroom and Other Stories of the New York Ghetto* (1898), as well as short stories in magazines.

In 1902 he returned to the editorship of the *Forward,* and, except for a few months, ruled that daily with absolute, dictatorial authority until his late years. When he took over the *Forward* in 1902 its circulation was about six thousand: at its height in the late 1920s circulation was said to be almost a quarter of a million. In its earlier years especially, it was the organizing center of union and socialist activity and was a driving force for the organization of the Socialist party and Jewish unions and the propagation of labor fraternalism. Cahan himself was at the center of this activity, and there can be no doubt that he was personally a significant influence in all aspects of the acculturation of the immigrant masses in their earliest years. A properly balanced, comprehensive judgment of the precise nature of this influence, it seems to me, has yet to be made.

Interpretation of Cahan's fiction can contribute substantially to an understanding of the man. At the core of his personality was a set of contradictions, a conflict, hints of which are discernible in his fiction and appear most clearly in *David Levinsky*. The central conflict was between fidelity to his intellectual, social, and esthetic convictions and his capitulation to expedience and the lure of success. At one pole was his fiction, in which his esthetic taste, founded on the realism of Turgenev and Tolstoy, and his social and intellectual integrity are expressed. At the opposite pole was the *Forward,* through which he carried on a campaign of vulgarized "Americanization" of the immigrant masses and the vulgarization and finally abandonment of socialism. Cahan's career as a fiction writer in English and as the journalist who dominated the *Forward* are distinct, and indeed opposite, because each was a path antagonistic to the other.

What were the sources of the contradictions within Cahan?

He had extraordinary talent. This was recognized early, when Lincoln Steffens hired him as a reporter for the New York *Commercial Advertiser* in 1897. Steffens had just taken over this stodgy daily, dismissed most of the staff, and hired a group of young writers fresh out of college—among them Norman and Hutchins Hapgood—to present the news in terms of its warm human significance, rather than as dry fact or sensationalism. He wanted, Steffens writes, "writers," men who "could see and express the beauty in the mean streets of a hard, beautiful city." He was interested in the motives behind deeds. A murder, he thought, should not be reported as a "bloody hoked-up crime," but rather "as a tragedy," and he instructed Cahan to write in this way. Steffens was himself deeply interested in the ghetto, and at that time, as he writes, he was himself "almost a Jew, . . . and nailed a mezuza to my office door. I went to the synagogue on all the great Jewish holy days." He reports that Cahan was the catalyst of much serious discussion in the paper's editorial rooms on the nature of art and realism, and under Cahan's influence the paper reported on the Yiddish theater of the time. "Whether it was Cahan and the Ghetto or my encouragement," Steffens concludes, "the *Commercial* city room had ideals and flaunted them openly." Cahan's full-time occupation as a journalist in English ended in 1901, when he resigned from the *Commercial* after Steffens left for *McClure's* and muckraking.

When Cahan was asked to become editor of the *Forward* in 1902, he agreed on the condition that he be given absolute editorial control. He differed from colleagues like Morris Winchevsky and Michael Zametkin in his conception of a socialist paper for the immigrant masses, and in some respects he was probably right in trying to make the paper more palatable to the nonsocialists in order to bring them closer to socialism. We can perceive from our present perspective that he was right in eschewing the open and offensive flouting of Orthodox Judaism that was then common among socialists. Although it is generally acknowledged that theoretical analysis was not among his talents, he had a great talent for popularization. However, he carried a sound approach too far, from popular journalism to vulgarized journalism.

He undertook to publish material new to the *Forward*—stressing a vulgarized lower-middle-class view of women and marriage that verged on sensationalism. The classic instance is the *Forward*'s method of promoting the Yiddish translation of August Bebel's *Woman and Socialism* in 1912 by advertising that it would throw light on "Why Were Women in the Past More Beautiful Than Today?"; tell why "Moslem Women Are Not Allowed to See a Doctor"; reveal that "Solomon Had a Thousand Wives and That Was No Sin"—all ending, "Read August Bebel's Book." It was said at the time that this type of advertising was stopped by the intervention of Bebel himself.

From the start Cahan rejected *"Daitchmerish,"* a stilted Germanified form of Yiddish, and supervised the use of "Yiddish Yiddish" in a simple, *"pleiner"* (plain) Yiddish easily understandable by the immigrant masses. At the same time, he followed the current usage of incorporating incorrectly pronounced English words into Yiddish. Cahan composed a sentence to illustrate this, as he notes in his autobiography, ending "Ich vel scrobbin dem floor, klinen die vindes, un polishen dem stov." Those who loved the Yiddish language charged him with vulgarizing and corrupting it. Cahan was a popularizer in the negative sense; he pandered to the inferior tastes of the uneducated, instead of combining simplicity with linguistic and literary integrity. The noted Yiddish writer Joseph Opatashu says of Cahan that he "spit on our language." Cahan was the promoter of *shund,* an untranslatable Yiddish word whose approximate meaning is a fusion of vulgarity, sentimentality, and banality, in language and literature. After Cahan assumed his dictatorial editorship of the *Forward,* there were vain protests by some of his socialist colleagues against the vulgarization of socialism, which the paper was perpetuating, and many left the newspaper and Cahan's wing of the movement. Cahan notes in his autobiography that his "intelligent *chaverim*" charged him with "cheapening the Jewish word." To such complaints, Cahan made the telling reply: "My policies don't please you. But the circulation which they bring is welcome. I used to say this in a joking tone. But in my heart I knew it was really so."

The rising circulation and the profit-making that came with it did indeed induce a toleration of whatever Cahan did. When it was charged in debates over the paper's policies that he stooped to the masses instead of raising them up, he replied: "If you want to lift up a child from the ground, you must first bend down to him. If not, how will you reach him?" The trouble was, however, that he did not lift the child.

The fact was that in the end Cahan was closer to the Hearst press than to the more responsible wing of the American daily press. Moses Rischin leaves an erroneous impression in his article on Cahan's apprenticeship in journalism at the *Commercial Advertiser.* In a fully documented account of Cahan's relationship with the paper, Rischin concludes that his employment there was "a seminal period in his journalistic apprenticeship," and asserts at the end that Cahan "carried back with him to the *Forward* the refreshing liberal American spirit that

animated that paper." One would never guess from Rischin's article that the *Forward* approximated the Hearst press more nearly than the *Commercial.* Several other writers with a more personal, intimate working knowledge of the *Forward* do not make this mistake. Melech Epstein, who worked for the *Forward,* observes that Steffens's training "stood Cahan in good stead [in] building the *Forward* into a powerful medium. It must also be noted that Joseph Pulitzer and William R. Hearst shared with Steffens in guiding the course of editor Cahan."

Cahan's *Forward* differed in essential respects from the *Commercial.* While Steffens sought writers and individuality of writing, Cahan expected something quite different from his staff. Lamed Shapiro, who worked on the *Forward* in 1907, has written that Cahan considered the editorial room his "shop," and used to say to his staff men: "I don't need any writers here, only 'hands.'" (David Levinsky, in the novel, several times alludes to the workers in his shop as "hands.") Cahan succeeded in alienating many, if not most, of the leading Yiddish writers of his time by his insulting behavior and insistence on promoting *shund.* Even a partial list of the men whom Cahan offended or forced out of the *Forward* reads like a roster of the outstanding figures of the East Side: Jacob Gordin, Michael Zametkin, Morris Winchevsky, Abraham Liessin, Isaac Hourwich, Morris Rosenfeld, Lamed Shapiro, Leon Kobrin, and Sh. Niger. So passionately did some Yiddish writers feel the culture-corrupting influence of Cahan to be that one of them, David Pinski, was led to exclaim that "the *Forward* is the greatest misfortune to befall the Jewish people since the destruction of Jerusalem."

Cahan exercised arbitrary personal judgment by simply excluding from mention, let alone review, certain Yiddish writers and intellectuals, so that a reader of the *Forward* alone would be unacquainted with leading figures and writers and movements in the Yiddish-speaking community. He did not tolerate dissent in the paper.

Furthermore, nothing could be farther from the "refreshing liberal American spirit" of the *Commercial* than the obsessive anticommunism that gripped Cahan and the *Forward* after 1922, and especially during the McCarthy period. Melech Epstein relates one reason why Cahan refused to employ him during the early years of World War II: Epstein, who had recently broken with the Communist party and the *Morgen Freiheit,* refused "to write pieces of 'inside information' on the workings of the Communist Party" and refused "to appear before the Committee on Un-American Activities, headed by Congressman Dies." On the other hand, Cahan readily employed informers against the Left.

Another phase of Cahan's inner conflict resulted in his gradual abandonment of socialism. In organizing and propagandizing for socialism in the earlier years of his career, his contributions to the unionization of the Yiddish-speaking workers were such that even his severest critics acknowledge that he was among the "pioneers." Paul Novick writes that "Ab. Cahan was one of the pioneers of the Jewish worker-movement in America. He took part in the founding of unions, socialist organizations and was a leader in the movement to found the *Forward*." Novick adds that, because the *Forward* was the sole labor daily in Yiddish until 1922 (when the *Freiheit* was established), it was indispensable for the labor and socialist movement; but Cahan converted it into a "necessary evil."

It is probable that Cahan's contributions were more positive in his earlier days, for it should be recalled that his participation in the socialist movement dates from shortly after his arrival in this country in 1882. But with the success of the *Forward* came the degeneration of his social thought. His socialism was so watered down in the last few decades of his life that it became imperceptible. Furthermore, his affinities in the labor movement early proved to be with the labor bureaucrats, just as was the case with Samuel Gompers, who was his ally. When the rank and file of the United Garment Workers refused to follow their leaders' settlement of a strike in 1913, the *Forward* supported the settlement, and irate workers broke windows at the *Forward*. In 1905 the typesetters on the *Forward* struck, and the impartial arbitrators concluded that the *Forward* used "capitalist methods" in fighting the strike. In 1909, 1917, and 1946 the staff writers of the *Forward* struck. There were occasions when a strike was reported on page one and an advertisement for scabs to break the same strike appeared on another page.

Philip Foner has succinctly stated the relation of the *Forward* to the labor movement:

> In the opening years of the twentieth century the *Forward* had helped the Jewish workers in their struggles to organize unions and conduct strikes for better conditions. As a result, the majority of Jewish immigrants read the paper. Before many years had passed, however, the character of the *Forward* changed sharply. As its circulation soared and its revenue from advertisements increased, the *Forward* became a wealthy and powerful organization. The interests of the *Forward* were paramount to any consideration. Those trade unionists who "played ball" with the paper were assured of its powerful support. Those who dared to take issue with Abraham Cahan, head of the Forward Association, and editor of the paper, would be attacked as enemies of the labor movement.

Cahan's promotion of the Americanization of his readers was another source of inner conflict. His notion of the function of the *Forward* was to speed the Americanization of the uneducated Jewish immigrant masses. But his concept lacked perspective and was limited to striving toward the prevailing code of manners and Anglo-Saxon mores—the use of a handkerchief instead of the sleeve, proper table etiquette—and minimizing external differences from the "Americans," like not using hand gestures while talking.

That Cahan's actual communication through the *Forward* did not exceed this elementary level of acculturation is indicated by Bezalel Sherman. One year before Cahan died, Sherman wrote an article for the *Yiddisher Kemfer* on the occasion of Cahan's ninetieth birthday in which he says that Cahan taught the largely uneducated masses of the pre-1905 immigration their ABC's, but never carried them further once they learned the elements. Thus, Sherman continues, Cahan did not respond to the needs of the more highly educated, liberal, and revolutionary immigrants who came after the 1905 revolution. Cahan was in error, says Sherman, when he tried to dictate the taste and social attitudes of these newer but more sophisticated Yiddish-speaking immigrants, as he had done for the earlier immigration.

Cahan's efforts to Americanize these Jewish masses were replete with personal contradictions. On one hand, Cahan was convinced that Yiddish was a dying language. He repeatedly prophesied that it had five or ten years more to live. Furthermore, he opposed efforts at Jewish education because he was an assimilationist, believing that the best course for the Jews was to become indistinguishable from their non-Jewish fellow Americans. At the same time, hardly any Jewish leader of his time was more deeply rooted in Yiddish and Jewish life than Cahan. Considering Cahan's well-known contempt for the immigrant masses, it is not surprising that his method of weaning them away from Yiddish and Jewishness was to exploit the less admirable potentialities of the masses of men in the Hearstian manner of the yellow press, through its Yiddish counterpart, *shund*. There was an inner conflict between the Cahan who was most at home in the Yiddish-speaking milieu and the Cahan who willed himself to live on the conscious level as closely as possible to the Anglo-Saxon American ideal. The mass of contradictions that we have tried to set forth provides the key to the meaning of Cahan's fiction. In these stories he writes out a kind of spiritual autobiography, whose fullest expression comes in ***David Levinsky***. These unresolved conflicts largely explain the pervasive tone of dissatisfaction, longing, "yearning" (a recurring word in his fiction), and frustration of his main characters.

Cahan quite consciously adopted a different attitude toward the literary and journalistic work written before he took over the *Forward* and his work on the *Forward* itself. He was a socialist and an artist of integrity in the former, and in the latter he was essentially an opportunist whose objective was to increase circulation. He subordinated his ambitions to his socialist conscience in his early years, as he explains in his autobiography. In those pre-*Forward* days, he writes, he "felt that there were limitations to what a socialist could write in the capitalist press. Frequently I would refuse to write on subjects editors tried to assign to me . . . because I thought it improper." He later realized that he was "naïve" in turning these down, but his scruples indicate the strength of his integrity in those early years.

Moreover, he was uncompromising in his condemnation of the new sensational journalism—which he was later to emulate—of Pulitzer's New York *World*. He relates how in 1898 the Sunday editor of the *World* asked if he could reprint several chapters of his novel *Yekl* with a sensational layout, and Cahan refused on the advice of his literary mentor, W. D. Howells. When the *World's* managing editor asked Cahan to write regular feuilletons about life in the various New York immigrant sections, Cahan refused the flattering and lucrative offer. For it appeared, writes Cahan, "that he meant them to be cheap, sentimental stories, fancied up with 'local color.'" Cahan's attitude toward his literary work was similarly austere, and it persisted, but his journalistic standards deteriorated steadily. "I expected," he writes, "no financial rewards [*gliken*] from my literary career. One could earn money from writing stories, romances, or pieces of the cheaper sort, and that kind of literature I could not think of doing." And, he added, "today, only *shund*-writers are rich." Although he promoted *shund* in the *Forward*, he was not himself a "*shund*-writer" in his own fiction.

Cahan's activity as a literary figure in English was largely concentrated in the decade between 1895 and 1905. In addition to several novels and short stories, his articles on Russian literary figures, on Zangwill, on Russian revolutionary politics, and on Russian Jews in this country appeared in leading national magazines. As a youth in Vilna, Cahan had started to read the great Russian authors of the century with enthusiasm and adopted their literary creed, as he understood it, in his theory of realism. He particularly admired Turgenev and Tolstoy, and delivered a lecture on **"Realism"** in 1889 that was published in the *Workman's Advocate*, the Socialist Labor party weekly, on April 6 of that year. Cahan had read Herbert Spencer, and he attempted to give his literary theory of realism a Spencerian philosophical foundation. More concretely, he discussed realism in terms of the socialist-oriented painting of Vassily Vereshchagin, a contemporary Russian who had exhibited in New York a year earlier, and most particularly in terms of the work of Leo Tolstoy, whom Cahan regarded as "the greatest of realists." Cahan looked upon Henry James as a realist, and evidence that he had read James is found rather quaintly in his repeated use in *David Levinsky* of James's revival of the Elizabethan phrase "as who should say."

But it was Howells to whom Cahan looked as the prime American advocate and exemplar of realism, as indeed he was. Because of Howells's devotion to the American reality, writes Cahan, his "pen makes a more dangerous assault on the present system than the most eloquent speeches of the most rabid 'foreign socialist.'" Cahan criticizes the then current view that "the beautiful" is the sole aim of art. An honest depiction of human reality is also art, and hence inevitably leads to social criticism. "The rottenness of capitalist society," he writes, "inevitably lends color to every work of realistic fiction."

Cahan was a devoted reader of Howells's work even before they became acquainted. Cahan was thrilled when Howells sought him out in 1892 as a union activist, a

"walking delegate," and Howells was amazed and pleased to learn that Cahan had read his novels.

When Howells read Cahan's first published short story in English, **"A Providential Match,"** in *Short Stories* for February 1895, he invited Cahan for a talk. Howells did not think the story was a "serious thing," he added, "but it convinces me that you can write. It is your duty to write," The story is a harsh depiction of Rouvke, an ignorant immigrant who works his way up from nothing to prosperity as a peddler, and thinks it time he enhanced his social position with marriage. After communication with his shtetl, a match is arranged with the daughter of his former wealthy employer, who is now bankrupt and accedes to the match out of desperation. Money for Hannah's journey to America is sent. When Rouvke and the shadchen (matchmaker) meet her boat on arrival, they learn to their fury and frustration that Hannah is engaged to a young student she met on the boat. The plot is amply filled with East Side lore.

One can understand why Howells urged Cahan to write: as a first effort the story is remarkably good. From the perspective of his entire work several features stand out. Already he has sounded the note of yearning, a theme that was to pervade his fiction. In his first few months in America, Rouvke yearns after his shtetl; after Hannah's father loses his money, the unmarried girl's "soul would be yearning and longing, she knew not after what." The syndrome of yearning and longing was in one form or another to afflict many of Cahan's fictional creations. Another recurrent feature is frustrated relations with women, as in Hannah's rejection of Rouvke.

One feature of this story he was to drop shortly afterward from his literary arsenal—his use of dialect. American literature is strewn with the Jewish stereotype who speaks a heavily accented, ungrammatical English, and the use of dialect in Cahan's story awakens the feelings aroused by the stereotype. Set in the context of Rouvke's vulgar ignorance and Cahan's palpable contempt for this type of character, some phrases attributed to Rouvke—"bishness is bishness"; "buy a teecket for a ball, veel you? A ball fi'sht clesh"; "I vant my hoondered an fifty dollar!"—verge on the anti-Semitic.

Cahan obeyed Howells's injunction to write, and after he finished a novel Howells read it and offered to see to its publication. *Harper's Weekly* rejected the manuscript because, the editor wrote, "the life of the Jewish East Side would not interest the American reader." Another rejection, Cahan recalls, offered the opinion that the magazine's men and women readers wanted romances about "richly-clothed cavaliers and women, about love that unfolds on the playing fields of golf. How then can they be interested in a story about a Jewish immigrant blacksmith who became a tailor here and his ignorant wife?" In a conversation, the editor of *McClure's*, who also rejected the novel, recommended that Cahan use his talent "to create art, by which he meant that I should write about 'beautiful things.'" Discouraged by these rejections, Cahan published his Yiddish translation of the novel in the *Arbeiter Zeitung,* which he was editing at the time (1895). However. Howells could finally report that Appleton and Company would publish the book, which appeared in 1896.

As in **"A Providential Match,"** Cahan had not yet achieved a tone that would carry his fiction beyond the thin line that separates the anti-Semitic from the naturalistic in fiction about Jews. His as yet insecure taste emerges from his discussion with Howells about the title of the book, as he recalls in his autobiography. Cahan suggested "Yankel the Yankee." Howells gently chided Cahan with the comment that such a title "would be appropriate for a vaudeville, but not for such a story as yours," and they finally agreed on *Yekl.*

Cahan's taste was insecure in another important respect: he makes Yekl talk in an extremely ugly dialect throughout the story, and, as was the case with the earlier Rouvke, Cahan's contempt for his character is patent. Leon Kobrin, the Yiddish short-story writer, who was working with Cahan on the *Arbeiter Zeitung* at the time, reports that Cahan would read the Yiddish translation of *Yekl* to him. Kobrin once remarked that the Jewish character was "a little caricatured," a criticism Cahan made Kobrin suffer for and for which he never forgave him. Cahan reports that while some reviewers praised his use of dialect because, they said, it reflected real life, the reviewer in the *Commerical Advertiser* expressed some impatience with the addition of Yiddish dialect to the already existing Irish and Negro dialects; he felt that though dialect may be necessary on occasion, it was not needed so constantly. Cahan then realized that the frequent use of dialect is "no more than a cheap bit of comedy." He then and there determined that he would "henceforth avoid such 'dialect' in my subsequent English stories."

As with other contemporary followers of Howells's realism, like Stephen Crane, the quality of much of Cahan's fiction—and this is especially true of *Yekl*—is naturalistic. Unlike Frank Norris, who was a devoted disciple of Zola's, Cahan did not read Zola or other naturalists, as far as we know. Perhaps Cahan's tough-minded attitude toward the ignorance and squalor and unpleasing realities of East Side life, together with his low opinion of the immigrant masses, led him by a logical process to naturalism. Yekl has been a blacksmith in the shtetl, but becomes a sweatshop worker in New York who emulates the "Yankees" by displaying his knowledge of boxing and baseball in conversation with his shopmates. Three years earlier he has left his wife, Gitl, and their six-month-old son in Povodye, expecting to send them their steamship tickets when he has saved enough. Yekl, or Jake, as he now calls himself, lives the free life of the single man, associates with several women without letting them know he is married and without being especially attached to one, and loses his incentive to bring over his wife and child, though he sends them a monthly allowance. Cahan describes Yekl's visit to a dance hall on

Suffolk Street and the several women who figure in his life; the story is replete with authentic details of ghetto life.

Yekl's course takes a sudden turn when he learns that his father has died. He borrows money for steamship tickets, and Gitl and his son arrive several weeks later. When they meet, Jake's "swell attire" makes him look to Gitl like a *poritz,* or nobleman, while Jake's "heart sank at the sight of his wife's uncouth and un-American appearance." Jake is ashamed of his wife's Old World manners and Orthodoxy, her appearance, and her lack of English. The couple follow the East Side practice of taking in a boarder, Bernstein, Jake's shopmate, "a rabbinical-looking man" and a reader of English books, to help pay the rent. Jake has not told his several girl friends that he is married, but when one of them, the perfumed Mamie Fein, comes to visit him after his long absence, she discovers this fact. Gitl is thrown into doubt about her husband's fidelity. For his part, Jake finds Gitl less and less tolerable, and Mamie more attractive. In a fit of jealousy another former girl friend of Jake's informs Gitl of her husband's infatuation with Mamie.

Gitl and Jake are divorced. Gitl marries the quiet Bernstein, and they open a grocery story with the divorce settlement from Jake. On his way to City Hall to marry Mamie, Jake feels that "he had emerged, after the rabbinical divorce, from the rabbi's house the victim of an ignominious defeat." His own future now "loomed dark and impenetrable." Life with Mamie is not really what he wants. "Each time the car came to a halt he wished the pause could be prolonged indefinitely; and when it resumed its progress, the violent lurch it gave was accompanied by a corresponding sensation in his heart."

The central character's frustrating relation with women and his vulgarized Americanization that results in unhappiness for him—Cahan was setting forth themes here that were to become more and more pronounced as his work matured. And herein lies one of the main contradictions of Cahan's life and work: Cahan, the Americanizer of the ghetto, projected the frustrations and unhappiness that issue from Americanization.

Although *Yekl* earned little money for Cahan, it did immediately project him onto the American literary scene. While it was generally reviewed favorably, the positive response was not unanimous. Nancy Huston Banks's review in *The Bookman* notes that the book has been "unreservedly praised" by the best critics, but she is dubious about the wisdom of publishing such a work. While granting that the story is "realism in the narrowest sense of the term," the book reveals "not a gleam of spirituality, unselfishness, or nobility. . . . It is a hideous showing, and repels the reader." Does Cahan wish the reader to believe, she asks, that the characters and ghetto mode of life depicted in the work "are truly representative of his race?" If this is so, "was it wise to develop the pictures? . . . Are such books ever worth while? . . . *are* they literature?" This reviewer was no doubt reflecting the conventional genteel conception of literature that led to rejection of the manuscript by several editors. But not entirely. For as we have seen, Cahan later realized that his taste was not yet secure, and the reviewer's observations were therefore not altogether lacking in penetration.

But Howells's review jointly of Cahan's *Yekl* and Stephen Crane's *George's Mother* in the Sunday, July 26, 1896, edition of the New York *World,* under the title "NEW YORK LOW LIFE IN FICTION," literally catapulted Cahan into public attention, for the review appeared on posters all over the city, advertising in its text that Howells had discovered a great new writer. The headline over the reat Novelist Hails Abraham Cahan, the Author of 'Yekl' as a New Star of Realism, and Says That He and Stephen Crane Have Drawn the Truest Pictures of East Side Life." Howells calls the story "intensely realistic." Cahan's "sense of character is as broad as his sense of human nature is subtle and deep," and he will "do honor to American letters. . . . He sees things with American eyes, and he brings in aid of his vision the far and rich perceptions of his Hebraic race." Howells sees in the book "its promise of future work."

The review stimulated great interest in Cahan on the part of the public and the press. A long biographical article was published in the *Boston Sunday Post* on September 27, 1896. In addition, Cahan came to know Stephen Crane. On September 22, 1896, a dinner in honor of three young "realists," Hamlin Garland, Stephen Crane, and Abraham Cahan, was given at the Lanthorn Club, a Bohemian group of artists and writers.

The temptation for Cahan to adopt the vocation of American writer must have been very strong. But his roots in the Jewish community were too deep and his devotion to socialism too intense at the time to permit him to sever his ties with Yiddish journalism. As we have mentioned, in 1897 he was one of the founders and an editor of the *Forward (Forverts),* but he resigned a few months later because his colleagues would not accept his proposals for popularization of the paper. The next five years, until he assumed the autocratic editorship of the paper, were consumed in writing essays and short stories in English. He continued to write short stories until 1901, and in 1905 he published a long novel, *The White Terror and the Red*.

By 1898 Cahan had five more short stories, several already published, for a second volume of fiction, *The Imported Bridegroom and Other Stories of the New York Ghetto*. In addition to **"A Providential Match,"** the group included **"A Sweatshop Romance,"** which the eager editor of *Short Stories* published in the June 1895 issue. The scene is a vividly etched picture of a subcontractor's sweatshop in his tenement apartment. Typical immigrants people the scene: Leizer Lipman, the ruthlessly aspiring boss subcontractor; his wife, Zlate, shrewish and ridiculously pretentious; the operator Heyman, miserly, clinging to his job in fear of his boss's displeasure; the girl he loves, Beile, the young finisher who awaits his proposal of marriage; David, the baster,

also in love with Beile. When Zlate orders Beile to go to the store for soda for some visitors Zlate wishes to impress, David urges Beile not to do the personal errand. Zlate fires Beile without demur from Heyman, who is loath to risk his job; and David walks out with Beile. Heyman is ashamed and does not attempt to see Beile for two weeks. When he does approach her house, he hears a wedding celebration in progress—the wedding of Beile and David. The story serves to highlight the dehumanizing and oppressive sweatshop conditions. But the stamp of the Cahan outlook is on Heyman's frustrated love for Beile.

The milieu of the immigrant Russian Jewish intellectual in which Cahan moved was first put in his fiction in **"Circumstances,"** which *Cosmopolitan* published in April 1897. Tanya, the daughter of a Jewish merchant and Hebrew writer from Kiev, and her husband, Boris, who has studied law at a Russian university, live in hardship because Boris earns a pittance in a button factory and refuses to allow Tanya to work. To make ends meet, especially during the dreaded "slack season," Tanya reluctantly agrees to take in their mutual friend Dalsky, a medical student and English teacher, as a boarder. After a few months Tanya becomes increasingly wearied of her work-sodden husband and attracted to the lively young student, until she succumbs to love for Dalsky. First the atmosphere of irritation between husband and wife, and then small hints in her behavior lead Dalsky to realize her feelings for him, and he invents a reason to move. Tanya, finding life with Boris intolerable, leaves him and takes a job as a sewing-machine operator. Boris is heartbroken, and everything ends quite unhappily. Once more, frustrated love is the theme, and the hard life of intellectual immigrants unable to pursue their professions in the new land is depicted.

Cahan returned to the life of the uneducated immigrant workers in **"A Ghetto Wedding,"** which appeared in the *Atlantic* in February 1898. Goldy and Nathan, living in the Grand Street area, wish to marry, but have not saved enough out of their pitiably meager earnings in the shop for the "respectable wedding" Goldy insists upon. After many delays, Goldy suggests that they spend all their money on a "respectable wedding" as a device to get an appropriately rich return in presents which will furnish them with money for their married life. Unfortunately the wedding occurs during a period of severe unemployment. Very few of the invited guests come because they cannot afford presents, and very few presents arrive. Goldy and Nathan walk home to their barren rooms. On the way home they are harassed by anti-Semitic hooligans; Goldy restrains Nathan from fighting back and they go home, drawn more closely together by the event, and warmly happy in each other. While love itself is not frustrated in this story, Cahan cannot avoid the element of frustration, which applies in this instance to their wedding plans.

The story was so well liked by Walter H. Page, editor of the *Atlantic,* that he asked Cahan for another story. The novella that Cahan submitted, **"The Imported Bride-**

groom," was too long for the magazine, but was published as the title story of a collection of his short stories. This novella was Cahan's most mature work so far. The range of material was broader, and the contradictions in Cahan's views and feelings were becoming more distinct. His themes exhibit how with seeming inevitability desired aims are frustrated.

Asriel Stroon has amassed a fortune in bakeries and real estate. Now in retirement thirty-five years after his arrival in this country from the shtetl of Pravly, he yearns to see the old home again and experiences a religious reawakening, partly out of fear of retribution for his sins after death. He goes to Europe to renew the link with his old home. His daughter, Flora, is a superficially educated, Americanized girl who aspires to marry a doctor, an alliance most desired by socially ambitious girls. In his hometown, which has changed little in the interim, Asriel refreshes his memories of people and the old life, and he realizes that he could buy up the town. In the synagogue he outbids Reb Lippe, the richest man in town, in the auction for the reading of the Peutateuch, but Reb Lippe is called nevertheless. Asriel makes a shocking scene in the synagogue to claim his right to the reading, but is prevailed upon to yield and apologize. That evening, Shaya, a talmudic prodigy, is to be claimed by Rep Lippe for his daughter, but Asriel's far more alluring bid, including an income for life in America, wins Shaya for Asriel's daughter, Flora.

Before presenting Shaya to Flora, Asriel bedecks Shaya in elegant American clothes. But Flora will not hear of accepting Shaya, brilliant as he may be in talmudic learning. She is determined to marry a doctor, certainly not an Orthodox rabbi. She consents to tolerate Shaya's presence in the household, however, and Asriel does not give up hope. After a few months Flora discovers that Shaya has been bootlegging secular learning at the Astor Library, thanks to the stimulus of the English teacher hired by Asriel. She proposes to Shaya that if he will study medicine and become a doctor, she will marry him, to which he agrees.

Asriel is overjoyed that Flora will have Shaya, but of course he is ignorant of the real state of affairs. Shaya not only studies profane subjects, but abandons his faith and violates the dietary laws—he is an *appikoros*, a nonbeliever. When Asriel learns the truth he forbids Flora to marry Shaya. But she now cannot live without him. They are married in a civil marriage; then Asriel capitulates and the pair are married in a Jewish wedding ceremony. Asriel gives Flora half his property and sells the rest, marries his housekeeper, and goes to Jerusalem to end his days.

But Flora soon faces an unhappy truth. Her husband is completely absorbed in his intellectual activities. He is now a member of a discussion group that is studying Auguste Comte. Flora accompanies him, but comes to realize that she is alien to these men and their interests. The scene

impressed her as the haunt of queer individuals, meeting for some sinister purpose. It was anything but the world of intellectual and physical elegance into which she had dreamed to be introduced by marriage to a doctor. Any society of "custom peddlers" was better dressed than these men. . . . She had a sense of having been kidnapped into the den of some terrible creatures, and felt like crying for help. . . . A nightmare of desolation and jealousy choked her . . . of the whole excited crowd, and of Shaya's entire future from which she seemed excluded.

Cahan's basic themes are developed in the story. Asriel's yearning and longing for the familiar and essentially congenial life of the old country reflect one form of Cahan's perpetual dissatisfaction with the present, and were probably experienced also by the author. The theme of frustration takes several forms in this story, in which Americanization turns out to be a disillusioning experience. Asriel's desire to unite his daughter to a learned talmudist and to have a son-in-law to say kaddish for his memory are frustrated by Shaya's Americanization. And Flora's Americanized longings for a doctor husband, and the respectable, exalted life she envisions as its concomitant, are thwarted by her own actions. Despite Cahan's own efforts in behalf of Americanization of the immigrant masses, his own deep roots in Yiddish life and his Russian childhood aroused in him ambivalent feelings toward Americanization, and all that it implied. In "**The Imported Bridegroom**," both the results of Americanization as they affect Asriel and Flora and the tribulations entailed by the transition are exposed.

Between publication of "**The Imported Bridegroom**" and 1901 Cahan published half a dozen stories which have not been reprinted or collected. In "**The Apostate of Chego-Chegg**," (*Century,* November 1899) Cahan continues to explore the theme of apostasy that was opened in the earlier story. The Jewish woman Michalina is married to a Polish Christian immigrant, Wincas, and is a *meshumedeste,* a convert to her husband's faith. Cahan describes the horror with which the Jews traditionally look upon apostasy: "Years of religious persecution and enforced clannishness had taught them to look upon the Jew who deserts his faith with a horror and loathing which the Gentile brain could not conceive." It was even worse than atheism: "Atheism would have been a malady; *shmad* (conversion to a Gentile creed) was far worse than death."

Michalina and her husband live in a Long Island village whose name, "Chego-Chegg," was bestowed by a politician as the closest approximation he could make to the Polish name of the village. Michalina expresses various forms of yearning: "She was yearning for her Gentile husband, and their common birthplace, and she was yearning for her father's house and her Jewish past." In the opening of the story Cahan thus enunciates the contradictions by which his characters (and he himself?) are riven, longing for the old home while in America, longing for the Jewish traditional past while repudiating it in practice. Near Michalina is a Jewish town, which her longing directs her to despite its rejection of her. She bears a daughter, but she is mocked by her Gentile townswomen as the "Jew woman."

Rabbi Nehemiah of the Jewish town had been horrified by Michalina's conversion earlier, but he is now a peddler, an atheist "cured of my idiocy." They now share contempt for the Jewish community. Nehemiah complains: "The one thing that gives me pain is this: The same fellows who used to break my bones for preaching religion now beat me because I expose its idiocies." America, he adds, wipes out all distinctions: "All are noblemen here, and all are brothers." Michalina longs for the devout Jewish world that he brings close to her, and clings to him as a "fellow-outcast"—she cannot resolve her contradictory longings. She persuades her husband to give up his farm and move closer to the Jewish town; she does her shopping there. Nehemiah agitates in the town for assimilation, while Michalina condemns herself for her doomed soul and for her apostasy.

Nehemiah tells her that in the eyes of the Talmud her marriage to a non-Jew is nonexistent. A venerable rabbi on the East Side whom she consults advises her that if she is genuinely repentant and properly marries a Jew, she will be that man's wife. The reformed Michalina, now called by the Jewish name of Rieva, is welcomed in the Jewish town; she goes through the Jewish marriage ceremony with Nehemiah, and they are about to leave for New York and the boat to Europe when Wincas appears. Michalina is torn between her Jewish roots and her love for Wincas, and she chooses the latter. "I know that I am doomed to have no rest," she cries, "either in this world or the other, but I cannot leave him—I cannot." Is Cahan torn between his Jewish roots and his American assimilationism, unsettled by his unquiet, unresolved acceptance of the latter?

His next story was free of these concerns. **"Rabbi Eliezer's Christmas,"** published in the December 1899 issue of *Scribner's,* is, as Cahan said, "a light, humorous story." Pious old Eliezer had been a sopher (a Pentateuch scribe) in the old country, but has had to resort to pushcart peddling in New York. During the pre-Christmas period, Miss Bemis, headworker of the College Settlement, and the philanthropic Miss Colton notice Eliezer during their tour of "deserving cases," and learn from him that with a few dollars he could bring his stock up to standard. Miss Bemis gives him a twenty-dollar bill. His neighboring peddlers tease and terrify him by suggesting that the money is a Christmas gift. After much soul-searching, Eliezer decides to return the money to the settlement worker. Miss Bemis assures him that the money was not a Christmas present, suggesting that he return the money to her for presentation to him later as "a fresh present." While he is reassured that he has not sinned, he is torn with anxiety as to whether Miss Bemis will really give him the money. Cahan exhibits considerable depth of sympathy for the displaced, lonely, unhappy old man, whose skill in fine lettering is obsolete in

technologically advanced America. The pathos of the story gives it deeper meaning than Cahan's characterization of it as "light, humorous" would indicate.

Perhaps it was in response to Howells's remark in his review of *The Imported Bridegroom*—"It will be interesting to see whether Mr. Cahan will pass beyond his present environment into a larger American world"—that Cahan attempted several non-Jewish stories in the next few years. As if to proceed by gradual steps, these stories deal with the life of non-Jewish immigrants. But after this first step he did not explore the American non-Jewish milieu any further. These short stories are less interesting than his others, and it is apparent that he was at his best in writing of the world that he knew to the marrow.

Frustrated love continues to play its part in the non-Jewish stories. **"A Marriage by Proxy,"** perhaps the least interesting of his tales, published in *Everybody's Magazine* for December 1900, is concerned with Italian immigrant life. An immigrant Italian barber sends his brother to Italy to marry a girl by proxy and to bring her to New York. The girl, Philomena, finds the barber not to her liking and wants to return to Italy, but her landlady advises her to go to the "wine-lady" for advice. The "wine-lady" shrewdly awakens jealousy in Philomena by making her believe that her husband will marry another girl, and Philomena returns to her husband and is contented.

In a second story, **"Dumitru and Sigrid,"** published in *Cosmopolitan* in March 1901, Romanian Dumitru and Swedish Sigrid are immigrants awaiting clearance at Castle Garden, the admissions depot at that time. Neither knows the other's language, but they communicate through dictionaries, and Dumitru falls in love with Sigrid. She is taken away by a relative, and for several years, while he gains a foothold in American life, Dumitru nurses his love for her. Walking in the uptown East Side one day, he sees Sigrid on the steps of a tenement building with a baby in her lap. "Her maidenly comeliness of yore was gone only to make room for the good looks and the ripe loveliness of young motherhood." As they converse, her husband comes out. She introduces him to Dumitru and says: "'Dis is de gentleman vat mashed me in Castle Garden.' . . . Husband and wife smiled as at a good joke." Dumitru finds the little family of three "equally uninteresting and incomprehensible to him, and he hastened to take his departure." The long-held illusion is shattered.

The third story with a non-Jewish background, **"Tzinchadzi of the Catskills,"** published in the *Atlantic* for August 1901, is important in Cahan's development because it brings into explicit focus the connection between his perpetual yearning and the failure of Americanization to set his mind at peace. The first-person narrator encounters a Circassian nobleman in the Catskills, and they chat in Russian. Tzinchadzi, the Georgian nobleman, still wears his native dress. He tells his story: after he lost his beloved to a rival in the Caucasus, he was persuaded by the American consul at Batum to ride a horse at the

World's Fair in Chicago. Later he sold Caucasian goods, and "a Jew" had suggested selling them in the Catskills. He is unhappy; he makes plenty of money, but that cannot bring back his lost beloved or the Caucasus.

Six years later the narrator meets him in New York. He is dressed in the American style; his name is now Jones; he has a good business and owns real estate. Then follows a passage that casts revealing light on Cahan and his work:

> "Shall I tell you the real truth?" he asked. . . . "I have money and I have friends, but you want to know whether I am happy, and that I am not, sir. Why? Because I yearn neither for my country nor for Zelaya, nor for anything else. I have thought it all out, and I have come to the conclusion that a man's heart cannot be happy unless it has somebody or something to yearn for. Do you remember how my soul was while we were in the Catskills? Well, there was a wound in me at that time, and the wound rankled with bitters mixed with sweets. Yes, sir. My heart ached, but its pain was pleasure, whereas now—alas! I have nothing, nothing! . . . It amounts to this: I do enjoy life; only I am yearning for—what shall I call it?" "For your old yearnings," I was tempted to prompt him. . . . He finally said, . . . "if you want to think of a happy man, think of Tzinchadzi of the Catskills, not of Jones of New York."

In other words, the desired mode of life for Cahan does not consist in a settled contentment, but rather in unresolved conflict. His ambivalence toward traditional Jewish life, assimilation, and Americanization would thus appear to be what at bottom he desired. A decisive break with one or the other would render life stale and unprofitable. For him, the essence of life was indeed this tension.

The successful but lonely and yearning manufacturer, who was to receive fullest treatment in *David Levinsky,* is prefigured by Aaron Zalkin in **"The Daughter of Reb Avrom Leib,"** published in *Cosmopolitan* in May 1900. After twenty years in business, the prosperous, nonreligious, unmarried Zalkin has "a great feeling of loneliness" and begins to "yearn for the Jewish quarter, his old home." He goes to an East Side synagogue, where his attention is caught by Sophie, the daughter of the cantor Reb Avrom Leib; Leib is also a composer whose work consists of "Hebraized snatches of popular operas and recent street music." Drawn by Sophie, Zalkin comes often to the synagogue and finally sends a shadchen to Reb Avrom. Zalkin impresses Reb Avrom with his talmudic learning and wins him over. Sophie and Zalkin are betrothed, but she is unresponsive and confesses that she is ambivalent about the marriage. He breaks off the engagement, but after a time he renews his suit and they are engaged again. Sophie is still indifferent, and again the engagement is broken.

Meanwhile, Reb Avrom dies; his final wish is that Sophie be reunited with Zalkin, who returns to the synagogue on Yom Kippur in longing for her. In common sorrow at the death of Reb Avrom, whom Zalkin has loved, Sophie gladly agrees to marry him. Yes, she will love Zalkin—and, "as if afraid lest morning might bring better counsel, she hastened to find herself by adding, with a tremor in her voice: 'I swear by my father I will.'" Ever distrustful of a satisfactory outcome for a love relationship, Cahan cannot help but introduce a nagging element of doubt in this "happy ending."

Cahan's fiction met with a mixed reception. W. D. Howells continued to welcome Cahan's work as it appeared. In a review of **The Imported Bridegroom,** Howells places Cahan among the regional realists, like Mary E. Wilkins Freeman of New England. "No American fiction of the year," writes Howells, "merits recognition more than this Russian's stories of Yiddish life, which are so entirely of our time and place, and so foreign to our race and civilization." Howells seems to me to be stretching the point when he calls Cahan a "humourist"; "ironist" would perhaps be closer. Cahan, he continues, "does not spare the sordid and uncouth aspects of the character whose pathos he so tenderly reveals. . . . Of a Jew, who is also a Russian, what artistic triumph may not we expect?" The severest criticism, however, issued from the American Jewish press. Cahan reports in his autobiography how the *American Israelite* was indignant at **"The Apostate of Chego-Chegg"** because, they held, the story was mistaken in asserting that marriage with a non-Jew is not recognized by Judaism. The paper asserts that Jewish law does not teach one to violate the law of the land, and says that "Cahan is prepared to sell the Jews for the price given him for a story." Cahan notes that "the 'Yahudim' are forever afraid that one might say they were not loyal Americans." He insists that his story is accurate, for he has conferred with two Orthodox rabbis. The established German Jews, the "Yahudim," he concludes, have "denied the law "in the interests of Judaism.'"

Complaints by the Yahudim against both fiction and descriptive stories about immigrant East Side life were frequent. They were embarrassed and even a little apprehensive that the emphatic differences between the Jewish immigrants and the Americans, of whom they considered themselves an inseparable part, might jeopardize their status and might even arouse anti-Semitism. The Reverend Rudolph Grossman, a Reform rabbi, charges in the *American Hebrew* of March 18, 1892, that "nothing has contributed so much toward keeping alive the old prejudices against the Jew, as these productions of fiction that place them before the reader, not only in the most unfavorable but in the most ludicrous and false light." It turns out, however, that the author includes among these "caricatures" articles "that represent the Jews of New York as observing the ceremonies and superstitions of the ghetto. . . . These garbled and misleading accounts of the Jew and Judaism . . . foster not only ignorance but prejudice and hatred." Apparently wishing the East Side ghetto out of existence, or else believing it only decent that one should be quiet about it, the rabbi points out that the Jew—that is, the assimilated German Jew—is different "in one respect only . . . from the generality of men—in his religion." To him, and to so many German Jews, the East European Jew of the ghetto was no more a valid subject for literature than the caricature and stereotype.

Displeasure of the Yahudim at Lincoln Steffens's feature stories in the New York *Post* about Orthodox East Side Jews was so great that in a letter to the editor one indignant "socially prominent Jewish lady" decried the great amount of space given "to the ridiculous performances of the ignorant, foreign East Side Jews and none to the uptown Hebrews." After Steffens called on her and defended his stories, she tried to get him fired. Since the paper was at the time campaigning against exclusion of Jews from clubs, the Jews could hardly insist on the firing.

Cahan's stories especially drew protest from the Yahudim. *The Bookman* came to Cahan's defense editorially: "To judge from the attitudes assumed by some of the Jewish newspapers, any attempt by a member of that race to depict the life of the Ghetto in a frankly realistic manner constitutes an offence only slightly less heinous than treason." Zangwill's and Cahan's work were targets of this protest, and a boycott of their works was threatened. The *American Israelite* is quoted as being

> convinced that this fellow Cahan has intentionally exaggerated what is worst among his own class of people. A man who is capable of painting the people from whom he comes in such vile colours would be enough of a scoundrel to lie about them for the sake of a few dollars. . . . It is infinitely better for Jews to buy books and other publications which advocate their cause, than to give through vulgar curiosity financial support and encouragement to writers and publishers who do harm to the cause of Judaism and to the Jews.

The Bookman editorially replies that such criticism increases the market value of Cahan's work and observes that Cahan is far too much the genuine artist and student of human life to allow such criticisms to inhibit him from further work.

These comments prompted one daughter of the Sephardic aristocracy, Annie Nathan Meyer, a cousin of Emma Lazarus's and a founder of Barnard College, to write her views; while rejecting the threat of boycott and personal abuse, she complains that "the Americanized Hebrew is denied *in toto* the luxury of pointing to any literature that pretends to describe him seriously." The exotic ghetto Jew is more interesting to the non-Jewish reader "than the Talmudically ignorant Americanized Hebrew," who is in turn getting tired of seeing these exotic Jews in print. She notes that in a world of discrimination, persecution, and anti-Semitism, "the Jew is asking himself is it wise, is it expedient, to hold up in literature all that is foreign, all that is strange, all that is exceptional in the Jew?" Is it any wonder that the Jew has a thin skin, she concludes?

In the same issue Martin B. Ellis replies to the Jews who threaten to boycott Cahan's stories, relating that he himself sees much beauty in the religious observances and way of life in the ghetto, while the uptown Jews seem not unlike the Christians. "The rich, Philistine, semi-Christianized Jews of the uptown or Golden Ghetto," he writes,"—I believed they are ashamed of Israel. . . . He is trying to become just like everybody else."

The bitter attacks by the Yahudim must have reinforced Cahan's intention to write a novel about a Russian immigrant that would, for one thing, show the deep gulf between the East Side Jews and their prosperous uptown German Jewish brethren. The theme he chose was the barriers placed in the way of intermarriage between children of the two groups. Cahan must have discussed this novel, *The Chasm,* at some length with *The Bookman*'s editor, who mentions that it is "nearly finished." *The Chasm* promised to be an epic of the post-1882 Russian immigration: it would show how the immigrant life of the time was a superimposition of second-century life on the nineteenth; would maintain that the struggle to abolish the sweatshop was an internal Jewish class struggle between the Jewish workers and Jewish bosses; and would point out the deep incompatibility between the two Jewish communities of New York. The editor notes that although Cahan grants the material aid bestowed upon the immigrants by the uptown Jews, their cultural differences "explained the half-veiled superciliousness, the unspoken animosity" of the uptown Jews. The irony of this is that Cahan himself was guilty of a like condescension toward the immigrant masses whom he was ostensibly raising up.

As it turned out, *The Chasm* was never finished. Instead, Cahan published a long novel, *The White Terror and the Red* (1905), which does not deal with the subjective themes that run through his other fiction. There is not yearning love—only militant revolutionary activity. The novel is, in fact, a fictionalized account of the related themes of the revolutionary movement in Russia, Jewish participation in it, and the counterrevolutionary pogroms that figured in Cahan's article **"Jewish Massacres and the Revolutionary Movement in Russia,"** in the *North American Review* for July 1903.

> The bulk of the revolutionary army is made up of Gentiles [he writes], not of Jews. . . . But it is true that the Jews have more than their quota among the men and women who defy the isolated prison-cell and the gallows in their devotion to the cause of liberty; . . . they take an exceptionally active part in the dissemination of Western ideas; and this is another reason why an anti-Jewish outbreak, on the eve of the proposed May demonstrations, would have been an advantage to the government in troublesome times like those. When the news of the Kishineff horrors spread, and the panic-stricken Jews of other towns begged the authorities to protect them in case of an anti-Semitic attack, they were given to understand, through their "official" rabbis, that full protection would be guaranteed to them provided they undertook to prevail upon the

revolutionists of their faith to stay away from the prospective demonstration. The result was that in several cities the May parade was abandoned.

While the novel dramatizes these themes, as well as the revolutionary movement in general, it also adds in analytic detail attitudes of the Jews to the revolutionary movement and to their Jewish identity, and those of the revolutionaries to the Jews. The writing, though competent, is uninspired and lacks the vitality of his other fiction. It is not surprising that the book has almost completely dropped from attention. From the historical point of view, however, it is of interest in its depiction of the nihilistic attitude of the Jewish revolutionaries to their Jewishness and to their fellow Jews.

Cahan had experienced some of these attitudes in 1891, when he went to Zurich as delegate from the United Hebrew Trades to the Second Congress of the Second International. He insisted upon placing a resolution about anti-Semitism on the agenda. He discovered considerable antagonism to his proposal, for the current agitation against Jewish bankers—especially the Rothschilds—was popular on class grounds and was reinforced by traditional anti-Semitism. Furthermore, there was a disproportion of Jews among the socialist leaders. An unqualified condemnation of anti-Semitism, it was feared, might tend to confirm the identification of Jews and socialists that anti-Semites insisted upon (as Chief Rabbi Dreyfus of Brussels tried without success to convince Cahan). Austrian socialist leader Viktor Adler tried to dissuade Cahan from pressing the resolution with the argument that it would lead the anti-Semites to call the congress a Jewish affair. But Cahan was adamant, and was shocked when the best that the congress could come up with was a condemnation of *both* anti-Semitism and philo-Semitism; then it passed on to the next order of business because the congress was not considered to be the proper place for consideration of the question. The ambiguous attitude toward anti-Semites in the context of the Russian revolutionary movement among both Jews and non-Jews is brought out in the novel in connection with the pogroms.

The locus of the novel is Russia of the 1870s and early 1880s. The activity centers about the love story of a young nobleman, Pavel Boulatoff, a leader of the revolutionary movement, and Clara Yavner, a Jew and leading revolutionary activist. Other significant Jewish figures are Clara's cousin, Volodia, an educated assimilationist; Elkins, "an underfed Jewish youth, with an anaemic chalky face and a cold intelligent look," a revolutionary who finally becomes a Jewish nationalist after disillusionment with his comrades' attitude toward the Jews; Makar, a brilliant medical student and talmudic scholar who is a revolutionary. The plot carries these characters through their interactions in revolutionary activity. At the end Pavel and Clara are married, and all but Volodia are thrown in the tsarist jail during the repression that follows the assassination of the tsar, Alexander II, in 1881.

Clara moves from an initial indifference to the Jewish question, to a disturbed feeling that all is not well with her comrades' attitude after she experiences a pogrom. Early in the story Cahan shows that her conceptions about the peasants are "so many literary images" and are quite distinct from the world of "Jewish realities." Thus when she discusses the hanging of four Jewish revolutionaries with her educated, assimilated, bourgeois cousin, Volodia, he complains that the execution does the Jewish people no good. Clara replies: "What else would you have Jews do? Roll on feather-beds and collect usury? Would that do 'the Jewish people' good?" Volodia replies: "You talk like an anti-Semite, Clara." Clara answers that she is proud of the four and then challenges him: "Since when have *you* been a champion of 'the Jewish people'—you who have taught me to keep away from everything Jewish, you who are shocked by the very sound of Yiddish, by the very sight of a wig or a pair of sidelocks; you who are continually boasting of the Gentiles you are chumming with; you who would give all the Jews in the world for one handshake of a Christian?" Volodia replies that his attitude toward Yiddish and earlocks harms no one. "If all Jews dropped their antediluvian ways and became assimilated with the Russian population half of the unfortunate Jewish question would be solved."

Clara chides Volodia for "worrying over the Jewish question" at a time when the "whole country is choking for breath." She further taunts him, as an assimilationist, on his interest in the question. Volodia insists that Jews have a right to protest because they are the target of "unnatural oppression." Clara replies that Jews should participate in the struggle, since they will participate in the ensuing freedom from *all* oppression. The argument goes back and forth, Clara charging Volodia with total indifference to the Jews and insisting that, when the revolutionaries have succeeded, "there won't be any such thing as a Jewish, Polish or Hottentot question." Volodia replies that Clara's "golden mist of that glorious future" does not negate enforcement of equal rights in the present. The argument ends in an unfriendly impasse.

This exchange has a certain irony, for each represents one side of Cahan's own views: he was both an assimilationist and a socialist. His assimilationism, though, was troubled by his actual immersion in the Yiddish-speaking community, and his socialism included a specific concern for the Jewish question (although many of his comrades, both nationally and internationally, believed with Clara that Jewish issues would automatically be resolved with the victory of socialism).

Volodia's dilemma is carried further. When he visits a Russian princess, he manifests great love for Russia and its literature. She is both surprised and bored—"I had an idea," she says, "Hebrews were only interested in money matters"—and dismisses him. He agonizes over this rebuff and this challenge to his "right" to love "Gogol, Turgeneff, Dostoyevski." Volodia's father, an enlightened Jew who is learned in both secular and talmudic thought, calms him with the thought that the princess, a "penniless spendthrift," is like a pig who knows only the backyard of a mansion: it is quite natural that "she should mistake a handful of usurers for the whole Jewish population." A "Gentile reprobate" would have no occasion to go to any other kind of Jew because the latter has no money to lend.

As for Clara, she comes to the realization at last—after the pogroms have begun, and her party shows insensitivity at best and anti-Semitism to the slaughter and persecution of the Jews at worst—that all is not well on the Jewish issue among her comrades. She is now married to Pavel. An issue of the *Will of the People,* the organ of the Narodnaya Volya (People's Will party), comments on the anti-Jewish riots in a manner "as puerile as it was heartless." Clara resents this position. "As long as it does not concern the Jews they have all the human sympathy and tact in the world. . . . The moment there is a Jew in the case they become cruel, short-sighted and stupid—everything that is bad and ridiculous." Even of her husband, she thinks to herself that "he is a Gentile after all. . . . There is a strain of anti-Semitism in the best of them." Her conclusion is that she must endure.

For Pavel, his love for Clara has given the problem immediacy. On one hand, he shares the view of his party that if the peasants "can attack Jewish usurers, I don't see why they could not turn upon the government some day." But he feels uneasy and guilty about his view in relation to Clara, for he knows on reflection that the Jewish poor and workers are the targets of the pogroms at the hands of those whom his party aims to liberate. At the same time, the cult of the Russian peasant projects him under a "golden halo," so that "if the Russian masses were rioting, could there be a better indication of a revolutionary awakening? And if the victims of these riots happened to be Jews, then the Jews were evidently enemies of the people."

In a proclamation the revolutionary party has at first joined the Jews with the tsar and landlords as enemies of the people, but protests by both Jews and non-Jews have forced withdrawal of the proclamation. Despite the generally unsympathetic attitude of the nihilists toward the Jews, writes Cahan, "so far as the higher strata of the movement were concerned, the personal relations between Jew and Gentile were not affected by this circumstance in the slightest degree." Most Jewish comrades, moreover, greet the pogroms as "a popular revolutionary protest." Makar, the gifted student and erstwhile talmudic scholar, sees nothing new in persecution of the Jews: "One might as well stay away from the *Will of the People*" he says, "because, forsooth, Jews were burned by Gentiles in the 15th century." Clara is not at this stage occupied with the threat to Jews in general, but concerned for the safety of her parents in Miroslav, her hometown. She has gone there to be with them, and the loving Pavel ardently hopes for her sake that the Jews of Miroslav will be spared. Moreover, Pavel realizes that his uncle, who is governor of the province, might be able to stop the pogrom if he wishes, and since "he is in league with his fellow-fleecers, the Jewish usurers, . . . he simply cannot afford an anti-Jewish demonstration, the old bribe-taker."

The pogrom does take place after the peasants are incited by false rumors. Pavel, now in Miroslav, observes the whipping up of a pogrom spirit, and he is inspired by the thought of the French Revolution. "So our people are *not* incapable of rising!" he thinks to himself. The nihilists decide that during the riots they will try to divert the mob away from the Jews and aim their fury at the tsar and his officials. One revolutionary shouts to the pogromists: "Don't drink too much boys! Don't befog your minds! For this is a great historical moment! Only why attack the Jews alone? Behold, the Czar is at the head of all the blood-suckers of the land!" The crowd accuses him of having been sent by the Jews with such talk, and they rush at him. After it is all over, the revolutionaries still do not understand the counterrevolutionary nature of the pogroms. They are mesmerized by the prospect of an actual mass rising, mistaken by them for a sign of revolutionary awakening against economic oppression, which the masses identifies with the Jews. Even Clara finally works herself into approval of this view of the matter, regarding her earlier doubts as a relapse into "racial predilections."

The effect of the pogroms on Elkins, who has become a revolutionary earlier than Clara or Pavel and is the original organizer of the Miroslav group, is different. He now decides that his loyalty to the Jewish people transcends the claim of Russia upon him. He still believes in socialism, but his tactic now is to organize communistic colonies and to emigrate to the United States with them. In a conversation with Elkins Pavel is angered by what he conceives to be Elkins's attempt "to mix socialism with Jewish chauvinism." Elkins's retort is: "Can socialism be mixed with . . . the welfare of the Russian people with a pailful or two of Jewish blood thrown in; in plainer language, socialism can only be mixed with anti-Semitism. Is that it?"

Pavel's reply is that there are other Jews in the movement on whom the pogrom does not have the same effect that it does on Elkins. The feeling on both sides grows bitter, and Elkins leaves. The gist of the conversation is that "no effort should be spared to keep the mob from attacking the Jewish poor," but that an attempt should be made to divert the pogromists to attack the tsar, "to lend the disturbance a revolutionary character." Elkins and Volodia are in the Jewish defense force, and during the pogrom the nihilists and Elkins are on opposite sides. After the pogrom, Clara's efforts to win Elkins back to the revolutionaries are unsuccessful, nor does he convince her to join his emigrating colonists. Before he can leave, however, the repression has imprisoned him, Clara, Pavel, and their other comrades. At the novel's end they communicate with one another by a wall-tapping code.

What makes *The White Terror and the Red* distinctive from the rest of Cahan's English fiction is that it is his most objective work, in which typical attitudes toward the Jews, especially among revolutionaries, are set forth. His purpose in the novel, as in the *North American Review* article, is to convey the truth about the Russian revolutionary movement, especially as regards Jews in general and Jews within the movement in particular. No single character represents his own view, but each of them manifests what he considers valid or invalid aspects of the movement. The characters are treated very sympathetically, with less sense of personal tragedy than in his other works. In sum, the novel is virtually his sole effort at socio-political realism in fiction divorced from his personal ambivalences.

. . . . .

When Cahan was again offered the editorship of the *Forward* in 1902, he faced a dilemma. The reception his fiction had received forecast a promising career as an American writer in English. At the same time, he was assured absolute control of the *Forward,* subject only to confirmation each year by the Forward Association. At first Cahan thought that he could pursue both his writing career and his editorship by leaving the paper at two o'clock each day and returning home to write. But the press of editorial work was too heavy to allow for afternoon writing sessions. Nevertheless, for a few years Cahan did turn out fiction in English, as we have seen. After *The White Terror* was published in 1905 no more fiction in English appeared until 1913, and this at a significant point in his life which helps account, at least in a symbolic sense, for the underlying meaning of *David Levinsky*. Since Cahan had taken over the *Forward* a decade earlier the paper had prospered mightily: its circulation had risen to over a hundred thousand, and in 1910 the *Forward* started to build a ten-story building that towered over the Lower East Side. As the sole Yiddish labor paper it was looked to by the Jewish workers for support of their trade union struggles.

In 1912 the United Garment Workers, with a membership of only about five thousand, struck against oppressive conditions, but about fifty thousand workers followed the strike call. By this time the *Forward* had developed vested interests in certain unions and union leaders, and Tom Rickert, president of the UGW was one of these. After nine weeks of a bitter strike, Rickert reached an agreement with the bosses and settled the strike without consulting the workers. On March 1, 1913, the workers read the banner headline in the *Forward:* "THE STRIKE IS SETTLED—BRAVO, CUTTERS!" The workers were enraged at what they regarded as a sellout. They stormed the *Forward* building in protest and broke its windows. When Cahan came out to address them, he collapsed and was rushed to the hospital for an emergency abdominal operation. As a result of this strike and its settlement, the union was weakened and its leaders were rejected. A few years later the Amalgamated Clothing Workers of America was formed.

This incident is a striking manifestation of one of the central contradictions within Cahan—between his labor socialist convictions, and his vested interest in a successful newspaper and socio-political expendence. By 1913 Cahan not only had absolute authority over the *Forward,* he exercised this power tyrannically. He had already established himself as the enemy of Yiddish culture, language, and literature, and as the foremost exponent of *shund* in Yiddish journalism and literature. He had employed and then alienated, as he was to continue to do, outstanding Yiddish writers. As Bezalel Sherman has written, while one must recognize Cahan's early pioneering work for socialism among the masses, one cannot deny "his dilution and vulgarization of socialism." The contradictions in Cahan's life and career form the basis for his culminating work in English, *David Levinsky*.

The first form of this story was published in 1913. Cahan was asked by *McClure's* to write some articles on the sensational successes in the economic world achieved by erstwhile Jewish immigrants. Cahan responded with two articles in the form of a fictional autobiography of a successful garment manufacturer. *McClure's* was delighted with them and asked for more. Before Cahan could comply he was involved in the United Garment Workers strike, which as we have seen ended in collapse for him. During his convalescence he supplied two more parts, and the whole was published serially in *McClure's* from April to July 1913. This early version was amplified in the novel published four years later as *The Rise of David Levinsky*.

Like all his English fiction, Cahan's novel is a vivid, perceptive document of aspects of Jewish life on the East Side between the 1880s and World War I, the heyday of Yiddish-speaking immigrant life in New York. No single work of fiction can capture all the features of the richly varied life of that community. Later works of permanent value like Mike Gold's *Jews without Money* and Henry Roth's *Call It Sleep* provide different angles of vision on East Side life. But Cahan's sensitive, tough-minded rendering of that life preserves for posterity a vision by one who was himself immersed in the community. By placing his central character in the garment industry, in which the largest portion of the Jewish immigrants were engaged as boss or worker—a sector of economic life Cahan was intimately familiar with, both as observer and labor organizer—Cahan was able to picture the growth of that industry.

It is a matter of history that the garment manufacturers in the 1870s and 1880s were mainly German Jews, and that they were pushed out by the newer East European immigrants. This process is portrayed by Cahan though his depiction of the "rise" of Levinsky as garment manufacturer. John Higham has observed that *David Levinsky* is "among the best novels of American business." He further notes that other novelists of the period, like Dreiser and Frank Norris, present business tycoons and show, as Cahan does, "the conquests of the market-place as morally debasing." But Cahan does more. "Whereas Dreiser and others concentrated on the businessman's personal style of life, Cahan also wrote, in the guise of fiction, a critically important chapter in American social history."

Cahan himself writes in *David Levinsky:*

> The time I speak of, the late 80's and the early 90's, is connected with an important and interesting chapter in the history of the American cloak business. Hitherto in control of German Jews, it is now beginning to pass into the hands of their Russian co-religionists, the change being effected under peculiar conditions that were destined to lead to a stupendous development of the industry. If the average American woman is today dressed infinitely better than she was a quarter of a century ago, and if she is now easily the best-dressed average woman in the world, the fact is due, in large measure, to the change I refer to.

The talent of the pioneer German manufacturers in an industry "scarcely twenty years old" was primarily mercantile, while the workers in the shops, the East European immigrants, knew tailoring and practiced better product control. As he is trying to obtain an order from an influential non-Jewish Chicago buyer, Levinsky explains the reasons why the rising Russian Jewish manufacturers were displacing the German Jewish ones:

> The Russian cloak-manufacturers operated on a basis of much lower profits and figured down expenses to a point never dreamed of before; . . . the German American cloak-manufacturer was primarily a merchant, not a tailor; . . . he was compelled to leave things to his designer and foreman, whereas his Russian competitor was a tailor or cloak-operator himself, and was, therefore, able to economize in ways that never occurred to the heads of the old houses.

Levinsky's ascent of the economic ladder is pictured in detail. Beginning on a shoestring as a shopworker, he parlays his small capital into success as a small manufacturer. Finally, through skillful manipulation and good luck, he works his way up and uptown from the sweatshops of Division Street, via Broadway, to the pinnacle of Twenty-third Street and Fifth Avenue. It is obvious from Cahan's account that the survival and growth of Levinsky's business would never have occurred without his resorting to a series of deceptions and to antiunion manipulation of his workers. These were the classical business methods of the laissez-faire age, as the histories of the great corporations attest, and Levinsky is an astute practitioner of them. He is able to get started in business by deceiving his designer as to the extent of his capital. When he is in dire need of capital, he proposes marriage to a fellow worker, a "homely" girl who has saved money to attract a prospective husband in lieu of physical beauty. Possessed of great common sense, she rejects his offer.

But his greatest resource for undercutting his competitors is to employ cheap nonunion labor. This did not mean inferior workers. Levinsky runs an informal shop in which the workers feel at home, and he permits them to observe the Saturday Sabbath and work on Sunday instead. Although his piecework rates are low, his workers operate at greater speed and work longer hours than in other shops, so that they draw more pay. Furthermore, Levinsky cuts his profit margins below those of established firms. When the union is strong enough to require his shop to become a union shop, his workers still continue to work on a nonunion basis. He betrays not only the union, but his fellow manufacturers. When they lock out the workers, he formally agrees to follow suit but clandestinely continues to operate his shop. He even subcontracts to established firms during the lockout. His deception is exposed, and the labor paper calls him a "cockroach manufacturer." When the strike is won, his workers receive the union wage but are forced to kick back the difference between the union and his own scale of wages. "The lockout and the absolute triumph of the union," he says, "was practically the making of me."

The designer who has made possible the beginning of Levinsky's business has continued in his old job with the understanding that he is to become Levinsky's partner when the firm is established. But when his business expands, Levinsky gets rid of the talented designer: why share his profits when he can hire a designer? Another reason he no longer needs the designer is because he knows an employee of a large shop who agrees to let him steal the designs of the shop. This practice of copying designs from the big firms soon becomes a regular practice in the trade.

In addition to his antiunion practices, the shrewd Levinsky helps form a "Levinsky Antomir Benefit Society," composed of immigrants from Levinsky's hometown. Most of his workers are members of the society, thus affording him a cosy personal connection with them that virtually assures him of freedom from "labor troubles." Levinsky uses a "shadchen," a bought shop chairman who cheats the union in the employer's favor, and stool pigeons to report any union agitation.

Levinsky has come to the United States with four cents in his pocket; thirty years later he is worth several millions. Cahan shows how this was done by what is in essence a vivid case history. Along the way Cahan depicts many East Side characters: Anna Tevkin, the young woman with whom Levinsky is desperately in love at the novel's end, her socialist sisters and brothers, and her father, a Hebrew poet of declining reputation who is employed as a real estate broker. Tevkin and other characters participate in the speculative real estate boom in the first decade of the century, in which many Jews lost or gained a fortune. Various types of workers and employees are encountered. The kind of Americanization that Cahan tried to teach the Yiddish masses is illustrated, both in its more admirable aspects as a road to a cultured and useful life, and as a vulgarized emulation of the dominant culture. We meet once again the themes and types of characters that Cahan had broached in the short stories. The novel is, in objective terms, a remarkable microcosm of the East Side.

But these objective features do not at all exhaust the content of the novel. For it is also Cahan's personal testament, and thus derives added interest and significance, in light of the important role played by Cahan in the life of the Jewish immigrant community for more than three decades. The dominant mood of the novel is one of melancholy and yearning. Besides occurring in so many of Cahan's stories, this word itself is used more than two dozen times in the course of the novel. What is David Levinsky to Cahan? Above all, Cahan was a realist and Levinsky, the enemy of the socialists, is the ruthless capitalist boss worshiping at the shrine of the bitch goddess Success. The evidence points to this: Levinsky is a thinly disguised Abraham Cahan.

The import of this first-person novel is announced in its first paragraph, and reiterated in the final paragraphs.

> Sometimes, when I think of my past in a superficial, casual way, the metamorphosis I have gone through strikes me as nothing short of a miracle. I was born and reared in the lowest depths of poverty and I arrived in America—in 1885—with four cents in my pocket. I am now worth more than two million dollars and recognized as one of the two or three leading men in the cloak-and-suit trade in the United States. And yet when I take a look at my inner identity it impresses me as being precisely the same as it was thirty or forty years ago. My present station, power, the amount of worldly happiness at my command, and the rest of it, seem void of significance.

At the end of the novel, as he contemplates his lonely, luxurious mode of life, he says to himself: "There are cases when success is a tragedy." He was born to live the life of the mind; he would have preferred to gain distinction in the professions or sciences instead of business, where many successful men "have no brains."

How did Levinsky happen to traduce his own best instincts? In the novel Cahan improbably attributes the choice to an "accident." In his first few years in this country Levinsky determines to save enough money by working in a shop to take him through college, and thence to the intellectual life. He is working in the shop of Jeff Manheimer, a native American of German Jewish origin, who treats his immigrant workers with contempt. One day a bottle of milk slips out of Levinsky's hands onto the floor and spills on some silk coats. Manheimer rages against him and says that the cost of the soiled garments will be charged against Levinsky, who then "became breathless with hate." He will get revenge by inducing Ansel Chaikin, Manheimer's talented designer and the soul of the business, to enter a partnership with Levinsky himself. The more he thinks of the scheme the less revenge figures in it, and the more the vision of himself as a rich man challenges him. From these beginnings develop the structure of his power and wealth. So Levinsky's manufacturing career has not been wholly an accident after all, but more deeply an expression of a commanding strain of his character.

How, then, can we demonstrate the essential identicalness of Levinsky with Cahan himself? In writing the original sketches that resulted in this novel, Cahan was fulfilling the *McClure* editorial request to present the success story of Jewish business. But Cahan himself represented one such success story, with his conversion of a socialist paper of limited circulation into a popular Yiddish paper with the highest circulation of any Yiddish paper in the world. What Cahan did (with what degree of awareness we do not know) was to invest his own qualities, minus his socialist convictions, in Levinsky, as if Cahan had been himself in Levinsky's situation. There is some truth in H. W. Boynton's observation: "The disconcerting thing is that we cannot make out whether Mr. Cahan appreciates the spiritual obscenity of the creature he has made; embodiment of all the contemptible qualities an enemy of the Yiddish Jew could charge him with." If Boynton implies that Levinsky is a stereotype, he seems to me mistaken, since Levinsky is a complex individual and a credible character. But it is true that in a subtle way Levinsky and his deceptions are presented so sympathetically as to justify Boynton's perception of an ambiguity in Cahan's own feeling toward Levinsky.

Like Levinsky, Cahan went through a critical period of deciding which course to follow: that of his higher inclination or the one which promised personal power and success. For Cahan, the choice was between continuing as a man of letters in English ("the ideal of my personal life") or being a journalist in Yiddish. In his autobiography he records his internal debate as to whether to reassume the editorial post of the *Forward* in 1902. One could make money as a writer only by writing "pieces of the cheaper sort." While *shund*-writers were rich, a real writer like Theodore Dreiser earned very little in the first few decades of his writing—only with *An American Tragedy* in 1925 did he achieve financial success. Life as a writer could yield deep spiritual satisfaction but a meager livelihood. At the same time, the prospect of building the *Forward* attracted him.

Cahan's decision was—as Levinsky told himself when he decided to plunge into manufacturing, and at the same time to continue his college education—"again performing the trick of eating the cake and having it. I would picture myself building up a great cloak business and somehow contriving, at the same time, to go to college." Although when he resumed the editorship it was understood that Cahan would be free after two o'clock to work on his writing, he was no more able to pursue both careers—except, of course, to write the masterpiece that gave expression to his lifelong dilemma—than Levinsky was able both to be a manufacturer and to pursue a college career. That this conflict was one source of Cahan's yearning is attested to by a comment made by Hillel Rogoff, who succeeded Cahan on the *Forward*. Rogoff was reported in an obituary article to have said that "Cahan did not follow the profession of his choice. He wanted, and in all probability was intended to be, a novelist and a writer of short stories." And Cahan has Levinsky muse at the end of the novel: "I think that I should be much happier as a scientist or writer, perhaps. I should then be in my natural element."

Furthermore, there is a similarity, within limits, between the actual careers of Cahan and Levinsky and their desired vocations: writer and college-educated man (a doctor, perhaps.) Both Cahan and and his fictional hero are huge successes in their chosen work. When Levinsky moves into his Fifth Avenue establishment occupying five floors of a great building, he is aware of how he is regarded. "Success! Success! Success! It was the almighty goddess of the hour. Thousands of new fortunes were advertising her gaudy splendors. Newspapers, magazines, and public speeches were full of her glory, and he who found favor in her eyes found favor in the eyes of man." At about the same time that Cahan reached a peak of success with the *Forward* he moved into the new ten-story building, and was the object of interviews and magazine articles in recognition of his success.

By this time, too, the dilution and vulgarization of his socialist views were apparent in the *Forward,* as we have indicated, and the decades that followed saw the end of even any pretense of a socialist approach and the adoption of some of the worst features of yellow journalism. When Cahan came to write **David Levinsky,** the contrast between the intellectual and personal integrity of himself as writer, on one hand, and as master journalist who stooped to the level of the uneducated and unenlightened masses and, so to speak, held them down at that level, on the other, must have been one source of the dissatisfaction he felt and transferred to his fictional hero.

In his personal life, too, Levinsky is unhappy, full of yearning and frustration, especially in his relations with women. Of Levinsky's relationships with five women with whom he is in love or who wish to marry him, none is stable or satisfactory. From beginning to end, Levinsky courts only women whom he cannot marry for one reason or other. I do not know to what extent this frustration reflects Cahan's life, since I know of no biography that conveys such intimate information about him. However, it is known that he was an unhappy man and that his marriage in 1885 to Anna Bronstein (Levinsky's last love in the novel is also called Anna), an intellectual Russian, was not altogether satisfactory. The obituary article cited earlier states that "in his personal life Cahan was a lonely and unhappy man. He had few friends and many enemies. He was respected by almost all, but loved by few." This real-life statement is close to Levinsky's lament at the end of the novel: "Am I happy? . . . I am lonely. Amid the pandemonium of my six hundred sewing machines and the jingle of gold which they pour into my lap I feel the deadly silence of solitude." What Cahan himself would have said about the circumstances and meaning of **David Levinsky,** as he promised to do in volume 5 of the *Bleter* (page 288), might have proved revealing, but Cahan never completed his autobiography.

The reception of **David Levinsky** was mixed. W. D. Howells, now eighty years old, was repelled by the love scenes, which he thought "too sensual." In a letter on September 20, 1917, he wrote: "Abraham Cahan has done a pretty good autobiographical novel, but it is too sensual in its facts, though he is a good man." Some assimilationists among the Jews were unhappy with the novel because they regarded an American Jewish novel as an invalid concept altogether. As one said of the early version of the novel in *McClure's:* "There is no more reason for Abraham Cahan to write the autobiography of an American Jew [the title of the series in *McClure's*] than there would be in Domenick Petro writing an autobiography of an American Catholic, or of Tommy Atkins writing of an American Anglican. There ought to be organized a society among the Jews . . . to compel both Jews and Christians to look upon the Jew as a human being and full grown." In this passage the assimilationist's insistence that the Jew is, or should be, regarded as different from all others *only* in religion, arising from the wish to obliterate differences he disapproves of or fears, is exposed in all its blindness to actual distinctions. On the other hand, the critic and scholar Isaac Goldberg, writing in *The Call,* the Socialist party organ, on September 23, 1917, hails the book as being "unique among the books published not only this year, but during the past decade. . . . This book is more than a literary event; it is a permanent addition to American letters."

Howells's genteel revulsion from the naturalism of the novel was shared by Kate Holladay Claghorn in *The Survey.* The novel, she writes, "reveals with crude and unashamed realism the growing ascendancy of the sensual over the spiritual, the material over the ideal, in the narrator's own life. . . . The people we are introduced to are in varying combinations crude, selfish, sensual, tasteless—above all, tasteless!—foolish, ignorant, ambitious and egotistical." The rendering of the Jews in the novel is so utterly negative, she believes, that if a Jewish author had not written it, if it had been published anonymously, "we might have taken if for a cruel caricature of a hated race by some anti-Semite." She exposes her limited comprehension of the book by calling it a "campaign poster," calling on the "non-socialist, non-union sinners of the household to repent." She assures her readers that this novel is not "a picture of Jewish life in general. There are some admirable traits in the character of even the business Jew."

She was not alone in warning of the anti-Semitic effect of the book. Cahan's own colleague on the *Forward,* Hillel Rogoff, reviewing the book in that paper on September 28, 1917, is unhappy with the naturalistic rendering of Jews in the novel. He says he wishes that Cahan had omitted some chapters "which portray the swamps of the former East Side and vulgarities and superficialities of the 'allrightniks.' First, these aspects are superfluous; secondly, they make a bad impression on the non-Jewish readers because the portrayals are one-sided and sometimes over-spiced. The East Side of the 90's had a lofty, beautiful, idealistic spiritual life, which the book does not mention."

The charge that the novel, and specifically the portrait of Levinsky, damages "the public concept" of the Jew has been maintained in recent years by Morris U. Schappes.

He does not challenge the portrait of Levinsky as such, but he maintains that "more of the truth is required." The piratical business ethics of Levinsky are not peculiarly Jewish but those of American free enterprise. Therefore, Schappes holds, by isolating Levinsky and his fellow Russian Jewish clothing manufacturers and by not depicting "elements of the Jewish working class, that idealistic, militant, heroic and often noble working class," and the "non-Jewish rapacious American business man, alongside of and in contact with and in fact 'inspiring' the Levinskys," he has left the reader with "a partial truth." Such partial truths are dangerous for the Jews because "anti-Semitism is a staple in the system in which we live."

Had Cahan indeed done what John Macy in a review in *The Dial* claims for the novel, the hazards would have been avoided. "The portrait of David Levinsky," writes Macy, "is a portrait of a society, not simply of the Jewish section of it, or of New York, but of American business. And business is business, whether done by Jew or Gentile. If Levinsky is a triumphant failure, he is so because American business, which shaped him to its ends, is, viewed from any decent regard for humanity, a miserable monster of success." As Schappes notes, "the few non-Jewish business men who appear in the volume fleetingly are all paragons of business virtue, of etiquette, of manners, of personal morality and of English speech." Only the Jewish businessmen in the book are represented as less than scrupulous in both business and their private lives. It is apparent to the reader that Cahan was like Levinsky in his awe and emulation of "American" status and manners; his chary, almost reverent treatment of the non-Jewish businessmen in the novel is a manifestation of Cahan's contempt for the immigrant.

It will not do to dismiss these considerations. When the book was first published, there remained a huge mass of recently arrived shtetl Jews living in the teeming tenements. Racist theories of Anglo-Saxon or Teutonic superiority were quite respectable and the movement for immigration restriction was strong, so that the apprehensions of some Jews and non-Jewish liberals were not groundless. It should be recalled that the anti-Semitic atmosphere in 1915 permitted Leo Frank to be lynched in Georgia after conviction on a false charge of murdering a Christian girl. Under such conditions, a candid portrayal of ruthless pursuit of profit by a Jew in a totally Jewish milieu, as *David Levinsky* is, might readily serve to reinforce prejudiced attitudes. Since the end of World War II, however, the Jew has become such an accepted and familiar figure of American literature that Cahan's novel may be grasped as a trenchant depiction of a talented, conflicted Jew who succumbs to the lure of money and power at a given juncture in the development of industry in the United States. The hazards to the "public image" of the Jew may perhaps always be present in some degree, but the novel must be recognized as the most talented contribution by a Jew to American literature up to that time, a work of permanent interest.

A large degree of truth inheres in the judgment of Cahan's fiction made in 1900 by Leo Stein, the brother of Gertrude Stein and a student of esthetics. While Stein may have somewhat exaggerated Cahan's "disinterested" attitude toward the fictional Jew, on the whole his statement is precise.

> In the work of an American writer, Abraham Cahan [writes Stein] we have finally what we may call the disinterested attitude toward the Jew in fiction. By this I mean that the author writes about the Jew not because the Jew is more admirable than others or more interesting, but because the writer is interested in the delineation of human character in imaginative form, and deals with the Jew because, having been born and bred in the ghetto, he knows the Jew better than he knows other kinds of men.

This is, at the least, an objective judgment. But the novel is more: it is Cahan's fictionalized evaluation of himself as a conflicted person who chose success over integrity, a career as an exploiter and reinforcer of inferior journalism over a career as a writer devoted to maintaining human dignity and integrity. It must be remembered by those who would rush to his defense that this is Cahan's own judgment as revealed in the novel. But all was not lost—the best part of Cahan must have derived great artistic satisfaction and comfort from the awareness that he had produced the finest American Jewish novel of the first century and a half of the American nation.

Jules Chametzky (essay date 1975)

SOURCE: "The Yiddish Fiction of Abraham Cahan," in *Yiddish,* Vol. 2, No. 1, Fall, 1975, pp. 7-22.

[*In the following essay, Chametzky provides an overview of Cahan's writings in Yiddish.*]

Cahan began to write fiction cautiously—that is, in Yiddish, in the pages of the *Arbeiter Zeitung,* where critical tastes in literature were as yet largely unformed. Nevertheless, his first story, **"Motke Arbel and His Romance"** (1892), was a more than respectable performance, embodying a new literary voice and sensibility. The story tells of a low-bred fellow whose modest business success in America enables him to contract to marry the daughter of his former employer and social superior in Russia, but who is frustrated in the end because the young woman becomes engaged to another man on the journey to America. Even this cursory summary shows the undercutting of "romance" suggested in the title; **"Motke Arbel"** displays a sure sense of the Jewish immigrant experience and a lively feeling for real character, dialogue, situation. It was a great success with Cahan's readers.

Cahan's first English story was a translation and version of this one. As **"A Providential Match"** (1895), the story was to have fateful consequences for Cahan's career when it attracted the attention of William Dean Howells. On the basis of that story Howells urged Cahan to attempt a longer work on the experiences of the ghetto—the genesis of *Yekl*.

Encouraged by the reception of his first story, Cahan undertook a longer work in Yiddish, which went on for many issues in the *Arbeiter Zeitung* in 1894 and which had an even greater impact on his readers than the earlier effort. Called ***Rafoel Naarizokh iz gevorn a sotsialist (Rafael Narizokh Becomes a Socialist)***—and subtitled in its book version. "The Story of a Carpenter Who Came to His Senses"—it was a didactic tale about a simple immigrant's awakening class-consciousness in America and his conversion to socialism. Largely a vehicle for transmitting Socialist ideas to the readers of the journal, the story avoids aridity by its concrete details of street, shop, and cafe and its overall wit and good humor. The real strength of the story as it drags on (occasionally) through many episodes and twenty-one chapters is the sympathetically conceived and presented character of the naive Rafael.

A carpenter in his native village of Kriletz, Rafael Radetsky is extremely honest, speaks his mind, hates lies—and so is thought something of a fool. He is a gifted artisan who likes good work, a good bean stew, the singing of a good cantor. His nickname "Naarizokh" comes from the name of a portion of the sabbath service that he continually hums and sings while engrossed in his work. Above all, although without education, Rafael likes to think and reflect on just about everything. A letter from his brother in America describing glowing conditions (he could make $10 a week as a carpenter in America, besides there being no Czar and tax assessor) induces him and his Sara Gitl to emigrate. They sell all that they own for $45 and go to New York.

He soon discovers that the New World is no golden land. Almost immediately he learns that the many "machines"—a word that in Kriletz referred only to locomotives—employed in America's shops mean amazing productivity, but not, to his surprise, more rewards for those who work the machines. As a countryman tells him, he is truly a "greenhorn" to possess such a simple idea. Factory work and mass-production techniques are entirely new and alienating to Rafael. In his first job he is whacked on the back by the foreman and told to shut up ("Sharrup!") or be fired when he starts singing his familiar "naarizokh" He stops singing, feels defeated and shamed, no longer the man he was formerly; his wife, too, is lonely and forlorn as she sits in her dreary East Side apartment—both regret leaving Kriletz.

Within six months, Rafael has aged ten years. But in his thoughts he has also lived ten years. He reflects continually on his situation—a boss who is more concerned with his machine (which Rafael is expected to attend like a robot) than with him, the disparity between East Side ghetto streets and Fifth Avenue, the existence of rich and poor. At first he blames the machines for all his and other workers' troubles, but in an argument with his wife he talks himself into a new idea: machines themselves are not the cause of misfortune—in fact, they ease his work—but rather it is the ownership of them that is the root problem. He pursues this insight with great excitement—if only he owned the machines . . . but one man alone cannot run a factory . . . so if many workers got together and bought a factory they could then be the bosses and live well! But where to get the money?

As he continues to work in different furniture factories these ideas are further refined and he gains new insights into the system. He learns that bosses are not necessarily enviable—they are caught in a savagely competitive situation and can be ruined at any time: the big fish eat the little fish. When he learns about monopolies and their control of prices, he concludes that a single cooperatively run factory could not succeed. He arrives at the notion that a supermachine, above all the others, that would make them all work rationally is really needed. This he calls his "song of songs," which would make the workers rejoice. The more he thinks about the world, the more it seems a prison to him and that he needs a plan of escape to a wider, more beautiful world.

In a conversation about the new technology, he realizes that the achievement of such a plan is not impossible: surely a "song of songs" should not be more difficult to invent than the telephone, telegraph or horseless carriage! One day, short two cents for his fare on an elevated train, he walks across the bridge from Brooklyn to New York. Once there had been a charge for this walk, but it had been dropped as soon as the cost of building the bridge was repaid. The bridge now belonged to the community, the train to a private owner. Suddenly all becomes clear to Rafael. The answer is community-owned trains and then why not community-owned bread and clothing factories? In the idea of public ownership of *everything* he has discovered his "song of songs."

Immensely excited, Rafael wants to bring this idea to the whole world, which he feels sure will accept it and put it into effect at once. What he needs, he believes in his innocence, is to take out a patent on the idea. He gets a lawyer, who quickly sizes him up as a "damn fool" and obligingly agrees to get him a patent in three days for twenty-five dollars. The days and the fees stretch on, but of course Rafael receives no patent, and is ultimately thrown out by the lawyer.

Still bemused by his dream, Rafael responds to a leaflet that announces a meeting promising to explain why the workers are miserable and what they can do to make their existence a paradise. In great anticipation he attends the meeting and discovers, much to his surprise, that his "song of songs" has a name—Socialism—and that he is, in fact, a Socialist. This knowledge comes in a strange new language, in many long speeches, frequently too abstract for his simple, concrete turn of mind (when Rafael decides to speak his full mind from the floor it causes much good-natured laughter at the meeting). But it does come, and he soon becomes a passionate convert to Socialism. The goals of liberty, equality, and fraternity which the Socialists claim as their own enrapture him and the "Marseillaise," he himself reflects, replaces the "Naarizokh."

His transformation is completed through a relationship with a cafe intellectual and Socialist named Vicker. From him Rafael learns about Science and Nature (which brings him out of the darkness of his religious superstitions), dialectics (as difficult for him, and as intellectually tempting, as Gemorrah), political and economic class war, the history of social organization, and, finally, the need to remove from love and marriage any trace of economic interest. In becoming a Socialist, Rafael has become a new man—he has shaved his beard (with mixed feelings), taken pains with his wardrobe and personal hygiene, looks and acts younger (as does his wife, prodded by his example), is capable of abstract discourse—in short, he has become, as one of the chapter headings affirms, "Not richer, not more pious, but more of a mentsh (more of a person)."

As can be seen from this summary, there are long stretches of theorizing in *Rafoel Naarizokh*—several chapters are devoted to the speeches at the crucial meeting attended by Rafael, others to Vicker's patient exposition of the Socialist line on everything. Yet the book does not quite sink under this weight, or survive merely as an extended pamphlet. Action and development are minimal, to be sure, in any traditional fictional sense—it is episodic, and the characteristic "action" is a speech conversation, or inner reflection on a social idea. But as all of it serves to illuminate the straightforwardness and wonder of Rafael's consciousness, it can be read sympathetically. The vernacular, too, works to take the curse off arid theory—in Rafael's homey translations of abstruse matters, in Sara Gitl's crusty responses to his efforts to enlighten her, in the American-English learned and needed by the characters (a glossary of 145 such terms is appended to the volume: among them "barber," "boss," "furniture," "party," "wages"). All in all, *Rafoel Naarizokh* displays the developed skill of Cahan as the old Proletarian Maggid and Hester Street Reporter, who can take a small concrete incident or insight—no charge for walking across a bridge, let us say—and develop it into a larger general idea. The overall achievement of this book lies in its coherence, deriving from the socialist spirit informing it, and the charm of its central character.

Cahan published one other story in the *Arbeiter zeitung*—**"Di tsvey shidukhim"** ("The Two Matches")—which he later thought the best short story he wrote in the early period in either language.

The story concerns Harris and his friend Jake and their marriages to Becky and her aunt. Harris is an installment agent, lively and good-looking, who woos Becky too ardently. She allows him to kiss her, but then regrets it, thinking he may consider her "cheap." Although she likes Harris, she refuses to marry him. She almost immediately

regrets *that* decision, but it is too late to rectify it. A few weeks afterward, Harris marries Mrs. Zager, Becky's widowed aunt. Jake meanwhile consoles Becky. He is aroused by her, and though Jake seems less attractive than Harris, Becky marries him. At the story's end, both marriages have foundered—Jake abandons Becky after a few months; Harris is revealed to be a lazy and worthless charmer.

Slight as the tale may seem, the situation and characters are unforced and credible, and Cahan reveals a fine sensitivity toward psychological states of mind and the subtlety, new in his work, of awakening sexuality. This element in the work may account for Cahan's decision not to convert the story into English for an American audience. In matters of social theory and sex he seems less restrained with his Jewish audience. On the other hand, he published the story under one of his two *Arbeiter zeitung* pseudonyms, Sotsius (the other, David Bernstein, was used for his Tolstoy translation), which indicates an attitude not without ambiguity toward them or toward his emerging identity as a writer. It was the last story he wrote in the Yiddish language for several years.

Cahan's first stories in English, **"A Providential Match,"** and **"A Sweatshop Romance,"** were included in *The Imported Bridegroom,* a collection of five stories published in 1898, two years after the success of *Yekl.* But they appeared first in the magazine *Short Story* in 1895, so it will be useful to focus upon them at this point as forerunners of the more significant *Yekl.*

They may both be considered somewhat slight stories, but **"A Providential Match"** shows real talent, and even the less interesting and successful one, **"A Sweatshop Romance,"** flashes to life occasionally as it depicts a locale new to American fiction, the tenement sweat-shop. Cahan later preferred **"Di tsvey shidukhim"** because he thought the people in that story, their speech, relationships, spirit, were (despite a bad ending), more natural and full of life than the others; but this kind of judgment only points to the difficulty of Cahan's often ambiguous relation to the languages he worked in.

The original Yiddish title of **"A Providential Match,"** it will be remembered, was **"Motke Arbel and His Romance."** To the Yiddish audience, the title reveals the coarse, somewhat comic nature of the story's central character. Motke is a familiar diminutive that can be slightly patronizing, while "arbel" is Yiddish for "sleeve." In the opening paragraph of the English version, the narrator explains the significance of the hero's curious nickname, "Rouvke Arbel" (his American name is Robert Friedman): "Before he came to America, and when he still drove horses and did all sorts of work for Peretz the distiller, he was in the habit of assigning to the sleeves of his sheepskin coat such duties as generally devolve upon a pocket handkerchief." Cahan changed the name Motke to Rouvke, the diminutive of Rouven, because it seemed more understandable to the audience in English. That audience might lose the significance of his former occupation, as well—the word for a drayman in Yiddish ("balegole") is the word for a coarse, low-bred type of person. After four years in America, the narrator tells us, Rouven is "now quite a different young man in a different coat and with a handkerchief in its side-pocket." He is also the proud possessor of a business card in English ("his diploma"): "Robert Friedman, Dealer in Furniture, Carpets, Jewelry, Clothing, Ladies' Dress Goods, etc. Weekly Payments Taken." He took the name Robert instead of Reuben because he thought it had a more "tzibilized" sound to it.

The basic elements of many Cahan stories can already be discerned: the superior narrator explaining to a reader, whose values he presumably shares, some inside information about the Jewish immigrant culture in America. The emphasis will be on the effects of the culture-clash upon the immigrant. In this case, the protagonist is faintly comic, although a success (on some level) in business, and "Americanized" in his name, dress, and on the crudest level of deportment. He is a "freed man" in America, but, as the story shows, he is not fully liberated. Much of his old character and ethos remain, while his grasp of the new ethos is partial, crude, superficial. New coat and business card notwithstanding, the laugh finally *is* on him.

The story is as follows: Rouvke has done relatively well in America, but despite his efforts at self-improvement and meeting "young laddas," he is still a bachelor. Reb Feive, a *shadkhn* (marriage broker) enters the picture. He convinces Rouvke that he can negotiate a match with Hanele, the previously inaccessible daughter of Peretz, Rouvke's former employer and the first citizen of Kropovetz in Russia. Rouvke always felt great tenderness for the lovely Hanele, but such a match would have been unthinkable in the old village. He wonders, too, if he wouldn't be better off in a business way to marry a merchant's daughter who could bring him a dowry. Feive prevails, however, and letters sail back and forth between New York and Kropovetz. At first Peretz is outraged at the suggestion that his former *balegole* aspires to wed his refined and accomplished daughter. Gradually, however, Peretz comes to reflect that she is in her twenty-fifth year and no new suitors have recently appeared, and that America does indeed make new men. The glowing account of the *shadkhn* about Rouvke's piety, success, education, and general excellence (all wild exaggerations) take effect and Peretz consents to the match. Hanele, being a "true daughter of Israel," soon acquiesces in her father's decision. Rouvke is delighted and sends enough money (to Rouvke the "only fly in the ointment") for her clothes and transportation. When the times comes for her to arrive, Rouvke waits excitedly at Castle Garden with carriages and in the company of friends. Hanele arrives, charming and beautiful, but on the arm of a young man in the seedy uniform of a Russian collegian. She and this man, called Levinsky (how curious that this name appears in Cahan's first and last fiction—probably an echo of Levin from *Anna Karenina,* the work that meant so much to Cahan), have met on shipboard, where the moon was the best *shadkhn*—they have fallen in love, in a true

"Providential Match." Rouvke is stunned, but cannot do anything except exclaim, in Yiddish, "I want my hundred and fifty dollars back!" and then in English, "I call a politzman. I vant my hoonred an' fifty dollar." Rouvke is brushed aside by a burly employee of an immigrant hotel who takes Hanele and Levinsky away. Rouvke is speechless, Reb Feive wrings his hands, and the young peddlers Rouvke has brought along to show his triumph now bandy "whispered jokes."

Despite its apparent simplicity and the O. Henry quality of the ending, Cahan gets a good deal into his story. He tells the American reader many things about Jewish life and customs, about the new immigrant's experience in America, and Rouvke's climb in business. But what marks the story off is Cahan's sensitivity to character and theme. He presents a careful analysis of motive and behavior in Rouvke and Peretz, shrewdly showing the interplay of each as they realistically appraise their situations. An earthy material incentive is shown to combine with the longing in their hearts about Hanele. The laugh is certainly on Rouvke at the end, but it is somewhat chilling. That Rouvke is left speechless is a fine touch. There is a real sense of loss, but he is incapable of expressing precisely the nature of his loss. Shylock had cried "My ducats! My daughter!" when he lost Jessica, placing money before the human relationship. That seems to be Rouvke's first, almost instinctual cry ("My hundred and fifty dollars!"), but that is clearly a displacement, not the real or central loss he feels. There is a poignant note in his inability, in a new language and in a hostile environment (the burly runner who pushes him aside, his unsympathetic colleagues), to express his innermost feelings. Cahan strikes this note—a theme of longing, unfulfillment, and essential loneliness—early, continues it through many stories in various guises, until its culmination in the complicated and final statement of *The Rise of David Levinsky.*

In a story like **"A Providential Match"** we are aware of several verbal structures, languages, operating simultaneously. There is the immigrant's English—crude, to a native speaker often comic; there is the language of low-life America, both directly and indirectly coming through in the immigrant—in other stories there may be other, more ordinary or even refined American speech; there is Yiddish in translation by the narrator, usually as simple as the characters, but nevertheless more supple and resonant than any ostentatiously sophisticated English, which tends to be lifeless, although acceptable to the best literary taste of the time. This pattern, with variations, of course, will appear in most of Cahan's work.

Upon the success of **"A Providential Match,"** Cahan quickly wrote **"A Sweatshop Romance."** This is less complicated in almost every respect than the first story, but not without some characteristic and interesting touches.

The sweatshop of the title is the three-room tenement apartment of Leizer Lipman, a "contract tailor." Besides

Leizer and his wife Zlate, there are four workers in the shop: Meyer the presser, Heyman the operator, Beile the finisher, David the baster. Beile and Heyman are interested in each other, although Heyman is too timid to propose to her. All the relationships are transformed suddenly when Zlate, trying to impress some visitors, tries to treat Beile like a domestic, ordering her to go out to buy some soda pop. David, the shop joker, urges Beile to refuse to go. Zlate is angered; Beile and David quit their jobs. Heyman had sat silently throughout the altercation, too intimidated to speak out. For two weeks following the incident, Heyman can not screw up the courage necessary to visit Beile and commiserate with her. When he finally does go to her apartment, he is in time to overhear the conclusion of David and Beile's wedding ceremony.

The story is obviously slight—the ending especially caused Cahan distress when he later reflected on it ("how on earth did it pop into my head?"), although he explained it away on the grounds that it was the sort of thing American audiences at the time expected. With all its faults and inconsequentiality, the story does provide a good picture of a shop, the crowding, the scramble for work when the boss entered with his "bundles"; more than anything else there is the retained and recognizable humanity of the people, however crudely presented or however crudely they presented themselves (Zlate is a bit of a ranting hysteric, not a person). The portrayal of the sweatshop was not as stark as Jacob Riis's account, but Cahan was making an effort to show his characters as rounded people, not merely victims of a system. He erred in ending his small tale in a romantic glow, although even in this regard, because his characters did not really possess the vocabulary of love (it was something Beile had only *heard* of), there is authenticity in the flat-footed exposition and dialogue. This story should be seen as essentially transitional and experimental. *Yekl* would provide a greater challenge and achievement.

Cahan was restlessly moving between various worlds during the years of his earliest literary ventures, and to some extent this uneasiness shows in them, although not necessarily in obvious and literal ways. In addition to his immense activity in these years as editor, translator, journalist, he made three trips to Europe as a Socialist delegate to international congresses. On his last trip in 1894 he went as a companion to an American friend, James K. Paulding, who was eager to have Cahan's running commentary and impressions of the scenes, events, personalities they encountered. This role may have kindled in Cahan a perception of his great potential as an interpreter to the broader English-reading public of the materials of his radical, Russian-Jewish world. The medium of this interpretation, obviously, would have to be the English language.

Despite the success of *Rafoel Naarizokh,* or his own high regard for **"Di tsvey shidykhim,"** a literary career in the conditions of the 1890s meant, for Cahan, writing in English. The prevailing attitude among Jewish intellectuals and much of the middle-class toward Yiddish was

that it was a sub-literary jargon, incapable of a rich and subtle literature. As we have seen, this was a view that Cahan certainly did not wholly share. He was sympathetic to the substantial development of the Yiddish stage and was aware of and appreciated the birth of serious Yiddish literature then taking place. In the year he reread *Anna Karenina* for the third time he also published and wrote enthusiastically about the first stories to appear in America by I. L. Peretz, and in the year of *Yekl* he was writing appreciatively and shrewdly about Sholem Aleichem. Nevertheless, the Yiddish audience in America was small and relatively unsophisticated, and the term "Yiddish Literature" was then something of a joke (*Bleter fun mayn leben,* IV, 20).

In his memoirs Cahan tells of an experience that crystallized for him his feelings about the language he would have to write in if he was to have a serious literary career. At the Zurich Socialist Congress he encountered several sympathetic Bulgarian and Romanian delegates, Jews and writers. Their situations seemed to parallel and illuminate his own. These writers knew they were cut off from readers outside their native countries (few of whom could be expected to learn Bulgarian or Romanian), so that if they wanted to reach a significant audience that would take their work seriously, they would have to write in one of the great languages of the world. Cahan believed that his situation as a Yiddish writer in America was analogous to theirs.

The question came down to one of an audience, therefore, and the inevitable writer's problem of relationship to that audience. For Cahan, Socialist, Jew, Realist, immigrant, the problem of the right balance to be struck with a potential American reading public was an acute one.

Cahan was uniquely qualified to render the subject of his fiction, although he did not always resolve satisfactorily the complicated pull of subject, audience, vision. He had sympathy for the Jews, his people, but as a Realist he eschewed mere advocacy and tendentiousness He understood the limitation of the Jewish immigrant—indeed, one of his self-proclaimed tasks for more than a dozen years had been to help bring a semi-literate, largely uneducated and backward people (despite the high value placed on learning in the Jewish ethos, this was the truth about the masses) into the contemporary and enlightened world. On the other hand, a feeling of gross superiority would be offensive and, indeed, un-Socialist (although elitism was embodied in some of the offshoots of Socialism). Modulating this tension was the pity and compassion for the human condition that he absorbed from the Russian writers. As we have seen, Cahan asked for truth in dealing with Jewish life, despising "shund" (pulp) literature or its counterpart in inflated rhetoric and historical melodrama. He knew that the "greenhorn" and what was happening to him was an important subject and that it should be presented without ridicule or romance. It cannot be said that Cahan always achieved equilibrium amidst the contending forces; the balance was always perilous. That he achieved it at all, as I think he does in *Yekl* and with far more complex material in *Levinsky,* is remarkable.

For obvious reasons, Cahan was fascinated by the differences among languages as well as the class and character differentiations within a language. For him, Russain was the embodiment of his intellectual life, Yiddish of the emotional, English of the fascinating and rich "other" world, the mastery of which was a measure of one's sophistication and status. Language, of course, is the embodiment of culture, and everywhere in Cahan's work we see his attention to linguistic expressions of the clashes between and within cultures.

Cahan's stories in English combine, as we have seen, the elements of his Russian and Jewish experience within an American framework—bringing news of other worlds, other sensibilities, to his American readers. During the years as a reporter on the *Commercial Advertiser,* his essays in American periodicals, as well, inform an English-reading public about Jewish and Russian life, Jewish and Russian authors. Toward the end of this period, Cahan was induced to write in Yiddish again for the audience of the *Forward,* to help articulate for those readers some qualities of their American experience. The most notable difference from his English stories is that the Yiddish work was scarcely to be considered "fiction" and that in it Cahan was overtly the teacher and Socialist.

Between November 1900 and January 1901 Cahan produced a series of "articles" in Yiddish, later published in book form as *Neshomeh yesere,* that tells a good deal about Cahan's feelings about Socialism at the time and about his more casual attitude toward writing in Yiddish than in English. The series was only undertaken after much imploring by the editor of the *Forward,* the busy Cahan hoping to find something in his notes that would not take much effort to work up. Among his notes for **"The Imported Bridegroom"** he found such an idea—a sketch for a story that would involve a disappointment like Asriel Stroon's, but whose central character would be a Socialist worker, not a successful and religious businessman.

An honest Socialist worker, Cutler, has a daughter, Rachel, who marries another Socialist (Harry). Cutler also has a son named Muzi whom he brings up in the true faith from childhood on. Harry and Rachel have a cheerful household—many guests come there, all Socialists. The careers of Cutler and his family and some of their acquaintances are followed over many years. Harry owns a store that thrives; he becomes rich and abandons Socialism. He and Rachel now see only two of the former comrades, both doctors and utterly in the grips of money-making. The old *neshome yesere* (the transcendant spirit of idealism) is gone from them all. The Socialist Party itself is in the control of less admirable types than formerly and so has lost the respect of the masses. Muzi has gone to City College and grown away from his father. Cutler has kept the faith, but wanders about like a lost soul. His final tragedy occurs when he sneaks into a Tammany beef-steak party and hears his son make a speech for the local boss. Cutler shouts a protest and is thrown out. Ultimately, he becomes ill and dies. His name is not even commemorated in his comrades' newspaper, since he has not been a well-known writer or speaker. His survivors continue to ride in their carriages and to play poker.

Another story of the death of the spirit is told about a once virtuous man who became an important and corrupt saloon owner. America had made him a worse man than he had been formerly; of course there are instances of the opposite occurring. Circumstances can occasionally improve people whose inner spirit enables them to act humanely.

The narrator recalls that in the first group of immigrants all were poor, all lived in one world, all were Socialists. Now at New Year's, two parties are held on the East Side: a Socialist one at which beer is drunk, and one at which full-dress suits are worn, champagne is drunk, and Socialist ideals are held in contempt. There are now two worlds where formerly there was one.

Finally, the narrator notes that the *neshome yesere* does not discriminate between Jews and Christians. There can be an aristocracy of the spirit. The largest number of great men in the world are, after all, not Jews; but still, for their small numbers, Jews do have the greatest proportion of poets, singers, martyrs (he had spoken earlier of the Russians, especially the nihilists), good heads, and good hearts. The time will come when we will all be united and the result will be a stronger and better mankind. On this note the story ends.

The work runs to over eighty pages, in nine sections, and betrays, even in the summary above, the makeshift and structurally awkward quality to be expected from the circumstances of its composition. Cahan fleshed out his idea about the honest Socialist worker—a later, sadder version of Rafael Naarizokh—with several other case histories and much commentary. Cutler does stand out, and the theme of disappointed expectations, paralleling the Asriel-Shaya story in **"The Imported Bridegroom"** is nicely handled, but even more than in the earlier story characterization is overwhelmed by narrative comment and moralizing.

Cahan knew his audience, however, and the series was a great success. *Neshome yesere* is a Hebrew phrase, referring to the second soul that is supposed to descend on Jewish households on the Sabbath. It is a concept that has a great appeal for Cahan. Towards the end of the series he defines it as being like Emerson's "oversoul," so that a good translation of the phrase would be "The Transcendent Spirit." That spirit should inform all idealist aspirations and deeply humane relations. It is the spirit which should inform true Socialism. Cahan's ethical idealism, the spiritual nature of his Socialist commitment—and the rueful sense of its precariousness in the American reality—has rarely been better or more directly conveyed than in this work. *Neshome yesere* was even praised by his then great adversary Jacob Gordin; but the best comment reported by Cahan was that "In the several years in which Cahan has been writing only English, his Yiddish has become better." (*Bleter,* IV, 251-54).

The relation of the two languages and the different parts of his sensibility Cahan explored in each is vividly demonstrated in another work he undertook at this time. Cahan wrote an English draft of a long story called "Fanny and Her Suitors," which he hoped some day to polish and make the basis of a book. But he never found time to fulfill the plan. Instead, several years later he reworked it, translated it into Yiddish and published it as *Fanny's khasonim* in a volume along with *Neshome yesere,* where it appeared for the first time 1913.

Fanny's khasonim is a third longer and is more unified than *Neshome yesere,* but shows even more clearly the split between Cahan's Yiddish didacticism and his less tendentious English literary work. The novella of seven chapters that originally composed "Fanny and Her Suitors" is included within a Prologue and Epilogue that are added for the Yiddish version. The additions introduce a Socialist editor given to long speeches presenting the Socialist line on love, marriage, the family, whereas the body of the tale allows Fanny, an ordinary shop worker, to tell her story in her own words.

The Prologue sketches an encounter in a park where Cahan (or, rather, an unnamed "I"—and an editor) and several friends are having a discussion that draws a crowd around them. Among the listeners is a middle-aged woman who involves him in an intense conversation, wanting to know his—and generally the Socialist—view of love, marriage, and related questions. She poses good questions and interests him. She reveals that she has a manuscript at home, and though she is an uneducated and ordinary woman, a shop worker, it might be of some interest to others. She would like him to read it and then do what he pleased with it—throw it out, revise it, publish it. She brings it to him the next day. The editor reads it and decides it should be published just as she wrote it. The tale that follows purports to be this story in her own words, only slightly edited.

Fanny tells about a series of suitors she has had who have ultimately turned away from her, and about twice being in love. Through her tale she sprinkles reflections on being an "old maid," one who was "left," and upon men and women's relations—love and marriage—generally. Marriage has been urged upon her for many years, largely by her younger sister (who ran off in the old country with a deserting Jewish soldier) and her old mother—although the mother is in conflict, since Fanny is her breadwinner. All of her popular sister's friends also enter into the sport of finding appropriate suitors for her. Fanny is under a great deal of pressure from them all, as she sees it, and from the community at large.

Fanny cannot hold any suitor's interest for long. Even one who admires her good sense and steadiness and

thinks he is beyond romance finally seeks out someone who can touch his heart. She believes that the root of her problem is, vicariously, that unlike her sister she simply does not radiate feminity that she is only ordinary in appearance—neither beautiful nor ugly; she simply cannot attract attention to herself—or that she does not have a large enough dowry (from which she concludes that money in itself is the source of all evil). The men she meets are not always entirely attractive types, either. But the double standard of morality places them under less pressure to marry and, in any case, they are always the choosers, not the chosen.

When she finally does fall in love, where for the first time in her life her heart impels her to behavior her intellect recognizes as absurd, the man she loves rejects her. When she presses him for a reason, he succumbs to her importuning and blurts out the truth: she *bores* him. This revelation is the most insupportable blow yet to her self-esteem. When she rallies and falls in love once more—the greatest love of her life—she is thwarted again. This time it is by her lover's selfish children. She has met a man at last who fully reciprocates her feelings, but he is much older than she (in his 50s—she is in her 30s) and his children break up the affair. Fanny believes that they are afraid he will leave her money when he dies, and so for the sake of a few dollars they sacrifice his hopes of peace and love in his late years. An ugly world.

In the Epilogue, the editor meets her again and they have a long discussion of some of the issues raised in the story. During this talk the editor gets a less sympathetic impression of her than he received through the tale. Her reiterated claim to being merely an ignorant, humble and uneducated woman he perceives as a cloak for her narrowness and self-righteousness. She now looks to him "as hard as an old bagel." Despite her claim to an interest in Socialist ideas, he finds her obsessed with one subject only: love and marriage, and the relations between men and women. She displays an uneasy mixture of extraordinary knowledge—in her subject she reads everything she can get her hands on—and the coarsest ignorance. The editor lectures her at length, simply and clearly, but she never really accepts what he says. She does not seem to understand the implications of the Socialist solution to society's problems, including family relations and aspects of the woman question. He explains that morality is always relative to the class or group in power, so that if she was puzzled at the double standard, she should see it as made by and benefiting men, who had the power to impose their morality because they were the breadwinners in family relations. When women are equal, they will share in creating a new, more equitable morality. Of course Socialism did not pretend to have answers for everything—it could no more relieve the pain of unrequited love than it could that of a toothache. The editor continues with disquisitions on the history of the rise of a money economy, the inevitable combination of workers in the era of industrial production as the instruments for the overthrow of capitalism, and other Marxist ideas, but anything not bearing directly upon her obsession glances off her consciousness. Basically, she refuses to be broadened. Her portrait, and that of the didactic editor, are lightened somewhat in the last line of the novella, when she asks, all too humanly, "When were you planning to publish my piece?" She is a writer after all.

The work is written in Cahan's usual plain Yiddish, and is full of familiar Jewish types drawn from his vast experience. On the whole it seems unnecessarily drawn out and, except for discussions on the power of sex, not as subtle as some of his earlier English efforts. Fanny is interesting as a case study, and her unconscious self-revelation is nicely presented, but the reader may find himself too close to the view taken by one of her lovers and the editor: boredom and irritation. That Cahan thought the book good enough for Yiddish publication as late as 1913, but never for English publication, reveals again the somewhat lower status he accorded Yiddish as a literary vehicle—at least in his own work.

One measure of the lack of literary sophistication Cahan assumed in his Yiddish audience may be his attitude toward narrative point-of-view. *Fanny's khasonim* appeared in the same year he was publishing **"The Autobiography of an American Jew"** in *McClure's Magazine,* his most extensive attempt to write a fiction wholly in the first person. In the Yiddish story, the first-person technique is attempted only within a protective Prologue and Epilogue—assurance, almost, to the reader that the worthy editor was different from and wiser than the narrator. No such assurance, apparently, would be offered to the reader of **"The Autobiography of an American Jew"** or *The Rise of David Levinsky,* the complex novel that was to grow from the *McClure's* story.

But *Fanny's khasonim* cannot be dismissed altogether lightly. The focus on the woman question and on the Socialist attitudes suggested as the answer to it is intelligently double-edged, sophisticated. There is a dramatically effective opposition set up between the editor and Fanny. Hers is a good persona, since a more rigorously intellectual woman might not have been as accessible to the average reader. Self-taught, dogmatic, slightly ridiculous, Fanny is nevertheless very present and alive in the story. Cahan's—or the editor's—wrestling with this intractable woman brings the issues into bold relief.

What is salutary about Cahan's treatment of women in all of his work generally is the absence of the stereotypic Yiddishe Mamma. There are no sentimentalized, heroic kinds like Michael Gold's mother in *Jews Without Money,* nor the nagging, cloying types like Sophie Portnoy in *Portnoy's Complaint.* Cahan's women are by and large individualized; most of them *do* things, have separate and recognizable consciousnesses, and strengths outside the traditional wife-mother roles. Of the three women we will see in David Levinsky's life, two are intellectuals while only one chooses the traditional role. Even she displays a strength of personality larger than the role she chooses, and when she realizes at the end that the daughter for whom she makes the choice is unworthy, she bears her disappointment with pride and dignity.

Many of the women in Cahan's stories may indeed marry or, like Fanny, want to, but they do not lose themselves in the role. Tanya in **"Circumstances"** remains a pure intellectual; Sophie Lieb is enigmatic still; Flora may be an allrightnik, but her ambition raises her above the girls of her set; Clara Yavner in *The White Terror and the Red* remains impossibly idealistic. Whatever one may say of any of them there is not an earth-mother among them. Even in *Yekl,* the traditional Gitl starts as child-and-kitchen-centered, but soon learns the limitations of that world and ends by dreaming of the grocery store she will own with Bernstein. Cahan the Socialist seems more aware of the realities and potentialities of women's lives than are provided in more sentimental versions of Jewish women locked happily into traditional roles. His women toil, think, hold firm to ideals, or have none, act well or badly, suffer, and communicate independent spirits. As the didactic Yiddish editor he may lecture (perhaps ineffectually) the exasperating Fanny; but this unenlightened woman communicates a stubborn and even admirable sense of self when she speaks in her own voice. On his literary side, which is most often English, and not explicitly Socialist, Cahan tends to allow that voice.

Bonnie Lyons (essay date 1978)

SOURCE: "David Levinsky: Modern Man as Orphan," in *TSE: Tulane Studies in English,* Vol. 23, 1978, pp. 85-93.

[*In the following essay, Lyons examines* The Rise of David Levinsky*'s broader impact as a novel of modern alienation.*]

Those who have acclaimed Abraham Cahan's last novel, *The Rise of David Levinsky,* as a great immigrant novel, as an exemplary business novel, or as the novel of the Diaspora Jew have all stressed single, usually parochial aspects of the novel and thus pigeon-holed it within a limited genre. Indeed, the novel is deeply grounded in realistic specifics about typical greenhorn experiences, coat manufacturing, and Jewish rituals—about pirated cloak designs, steerage passage to America, and Talmud scholars. But this first person confession of a wealthy unhappy Jewish businessman transcends these specifics; the various strands are united and subsumed in a more universal theme: modern man as spiritual "orphan" in search of his parents, of legitimate authority.

In spite of the obvious differences in fictional technique, Cahan's *David Levinsky* resembles that central exploration of the modern condition: the story of Stephen Dedalus wandering through Dublin looking for his father. And as Joyce uses Bloom's Jewishness as a metaphor for alienation as well as a literal fact, so Cahan organizes his complex narrative around the multiple meanings and implications of Levinsky's orphaned state: as a man without parents (literally), home, God, or any satisfactory center to give meaning to his life. Reading the novel in light of this central, unifying theme has two important results. First, it gives focus and coherence to the disparate and superficially disconnected aspects, particularly the seemingly unrelated business pursuits and abortive love life. Second, it clarifies the novel's genuine significance for the modern reader by allowing us to see the novel as more than a dusty rambling period piece interesting only in terms of literary history or nostalgia. *David Levinsky* is a surprisingly modern parable.

Orphanhood was clearly a resonant theme for Cahan. In his other major narrative, *Yekl; A Tale of the New York Ghetto,* the main character Jake experiences his first sharp spiritual awakening when he learns of his father's death. "Desolation and self-pity" and a shortlived resolve to live a better life mark his powerful reaction to his orphaned state. In *Levinsky* the orphan theme is announced early in the narrative, for after the death of David's father, his mother calls the boy "'My poor little orphan'" and "'my orphan mine.'" And Levinsky's sadness, self-pity, and curious pleasure in the misery of his orphaned state are adumbrated in the first pages when he kisses his mother passionately and enquires, "'Are people sorry for us, Momma . . . because I have no papa and we have no money?'." Here at the very beginning of the novel Levinsky's orphaned state is linked to the lack of money—the pursuit of which provides a major strand of the novel's structure.

Actually before his mother's death Levinsky is orphaned only in the sense of having no father; he is spiritually and psychologically secure: beloved by his mother, in harmony with his religion, and a member of a cohesive people. Cahan does not sentimentalize David's native Antomir in the novel; it is an impoverished, desperate place inhabited by imperfect, complex people. Nonetheless, it offers a life with coherence, meaning, and values.

David's mother is adoring and protective; as in many subsequent American Jewish novels including the strikingly opposite *Call It Sleep* and *Portnoy's Complaint,* the mother/son relationship is central. Here the relationship is unashamedly tender. David's mother is also his spiritual and emotional guide. Although completely illiterate, she is passionately devout; she prays with "absolute earnestness and fervor, often with tears of ecstasy coming to her eyes." She feels communal ties to her neighbors, gives alms regularly despite her poverty, acts as a defender of religious morals, and has an acute sense of justice. In spite of her extreme poverty and overwhelming work, the impossibly cramped and horrible living conditions, Levinsky's mother feels moments of transcendent joy: "The sight of me learning the Word of God so diligently was a source of indescribable joy to my mother. She struggled to suppress her feeling, but from time to time a sigh would escape her as though the rush of happiness was too much for her heart." And Mrs. Levinsky is no rare exception: "there were hundreds of other poor families in our town who would starve themselves to

keep their sons studying the Word of God." In such a community where the aim of being a good, learned Jew was a clear and unequivocal goal, poverty was bearable and self-sacrifice, nobilizing.

In addition to his mother, in his youth David temporarily possesses a satisfactory "spiritual" father in Reb Sender. "A dreamer with a noble imagination, with a soul full of beauty," Reb Sender is one of the "quick-witted, nimble-minded scholars in town," full of gentleness and religious fervor. For Sender life is ordered and meaningful; he knows that "only good deeds and holy learning have tangible worth."

And within this paradoxically "secure" world, Levinsky as a young boy experiences the deepest happiness he is ever to know in his life: he feels a "veritable delirium of religious infatuation" and an occasional "fit of happiness." But the security and authority are transitory; in a section (or book) called "Enter Satan," Levinsky describes his dual temptations: sexual desire and envy. Levinsky's growing adolescent sexuality has no sanctioned outlet; orthodox Judaism allows no expression of sexuality outside of marriage, considers even looking upon a strange woman a sin, and has no concept of romantic love. The envy Levinsky feels for a pampered, glib Talmudic student is even more immediately destructive: Levinsky begins to use his studies as a way to outshine the other boy and thus perverts his entire religious orientation.

When his mother is murdered, Levinsky's whole structure of authority crumbles. Deprived of his mother's meager financial support, he is acutely hungry. But this hunger is more than physical. The rent in the fabric of his belief widens, and his "communions with God" become rare. Where before Levinsky saw the "Divine Presence shining down" on him, now the face of his martyred mother looms. Levinsky is now a "famished orphan . . . all alone in the world," for he has neither mother, nor father, nor God as heavenly Father.

His spiritually orphaned condition is underscored by the fact that the same friend Naphtali introduces him to both sex and agnosticism. In both cases, his reaction is a sense of loss. When Levinsky first sees a Jewish wedding, he is "in a trance"—he sees the ceremony as "a poem," as "something inexpressably beautiful and sacred." When Naphtali tells him about the relation between sex and marriage, the beauty of the wedding Levinsky had witnessed and of weddings in general seems to be "irretrievably desecrated." Later when Naphtali calls reading Talmud "all bosh," Levinsky has "nothing clear or definite to put forth."

Thus by the time Levinsky leaves for America at age twenty he is truly orphaned—without God, without biological or spiritual parents, and in fact without a true home as well, because local pogroms force the Jews of Eastern Europe to realize that their "birthplace was not their home." The enclosed, self-sustaining Antomir is itself passing even before Levinsky departs for America. As David Singer has noted, the forces of secularism which overwhelm Levinsky upon his arrival in America were, to a lesser extent, at work in Europe too. The Minsker family who virtually arrange for Levinsky's passage to this country are themselves symbols of the break-up of the cohesive, orthodox ghetto and mark the entrance of Jews into modern, secular society. Which is to say that the self-contained *shtetl* with its poverty and piety was disintegrating before the seemingly benign forces of modernity as well as the clearly malevolent forces of physical destruction.

In this last meaning of orphanhood, homelessness, Levinsky is truly the archetypal immigrant. His yearning parallels the yearning of the immigrant everyman. The hunger at the heart of the immigrant experience is well-captured in the memoirs of a self-educated worker quoted in Irving Howe's *World of Our Fathers:*

> While I was growing up in Russia, I developed a tremendous hunger for learning . . . since I had also gone a little to Russian school, I began to swallow—I mean really swallow—Russian books. How can I describe to you, you who live with a mountain of books, the hunger that I and my friends felt? . . . I went to lectures. God, those lectures of ours! The socialists, by the dozens, the anarchists, the schools, everybody. . . . And I thought to myself, maybe next time I can swallow it all!

The unnamed worker's hunger is for learning—a phenomenon which frequently suggested the Jewish immigrant's transference of devotion from Talmud to secular sources. But to Levinsky America's meaning is not the possibility of enlightenment or worldly wisdom, rather the United States appeals to him as a land of "mystery, of fantastic experiences, and marvelous transformations." His eventual spiritual emptiness, loneliness, and purposelessness are suggested by the fact that he conceives of his journey in naive and shallow terms as a "sensational adventure." Levinsky sees his immigration as a picaresque journey toward new experiences, adventure, personal freedom, possibility. What he finds is that while this new experience is more exciting and complex than the narrow, closed world of Antomir, it is empty, valueless, and he remains in every sense an orphan.

That Cahan did not believe that the American experience was devoid of meaningful possibility is clear from his depiction of other characters in the novel who sustain themselves through religious faith, political activity, art, workers' associations, family and social ties. Moreover, Cahan's own rich, full life in America is in fact almost a paradigm of the American immigrant dream. Within a few years after his arrival in this country in 1882, Cahan was becoming known as a socialist, political speaker, writer, and editor in Yiddish, English and Russian. Cahan participated actively in union activities and wrote articles, stories, and novels praised by William Dean Howells and Stephen Crane. Cahan had a major impact on the entire American Jewish community as the editor of the *Jewish Daily Forward,* the largest Yiddish newspaper in the world. Cahan's life in this country was marked by devotion to trade unionism and socialism, by identification with the Jewish masses, and by a Tolstoyan sense of literature as embodying the highest moral and artistic value.

Cahan himself experienced a complex relationship to his dual identity as Jew and American. It is generally accepted that through his influence as editor of the *Forward,* he was the most influential Americanizing force in the lives of the Eastern European immigrants. Enlightened, secular, and, particularly in his early years, politically radical, Cahan clearly did not argue for a return to Old World values and Talmudic devotion. His years of writing in Yiddish—a procedure adopted in order to serve the masses—forced upon Cahan "his own ineluctable Jewishness." Moreover, as Sanford E. Marovitz has observed, in much of Cahan's fiction the immigrants "who clung to their heritage, despite poverty and hard work, avoided the constant sting of isolation, disillusion and despair." In the same way that Cahan believed that literary realism and socialism "must ultimately work toward the same end," so he assumed that Judaism could be expressed without orthodoxy and that assimilation to American values and style was possible without loss of Jewishness. In short, Cahan avoided the dilemma of assimilation by a faith that commitments to Judaism and to American life were totally compatible.

In contrast to Cahan's complex involvements and commitments, Levinsky achieves only wealth and the specious "authority" of being the boss of his own business, which bring him no happiness, and in fact estrange him further from everyone around him. Having lost all bearings and ties, the orphan continually seeks to feed his insatiable, nameless hunger.

Satan first appeared in the dual forms of unsanctioned sexual appetite and envy—or in the more abstract sense of unsatisfactory relations with women and negative relations with his fellow men: Levinsky's later career recapitulates these same patterns. His sexual encounters with women remain unsatisfying, transitory. Outside the sanctity of Jewish marriage, women become "quarry." He never achieves any lasting or satisfying connection between sex, love, and marriage, as he compulsively visits prostitutes, tries to seduce his landladies, and falls in love with his friend's wife. Levinsky's three most significant love affairs reveal his main motive: to escape his orphaned state. With Dora, his friend's wife, the appeal is that of refuge, home. As a boarder in their house, Levinsky experiences a sense of belonging—and immediately falls in love: "my lonely soul had a sense of home and domestic comfort that all but overpowered me."

Indeed even Levinsky's conscious plan to seek a wife is announced in terms of an escape from orphanhood. Meyer Nodelman, the closest approximation to a friend Levinsky ever achieves, tells him, "'You are an orphan . . . you're still a child. You need a mother . . . get married and you will have a mother—for your children. It isn't the same kind, but you won't feel lonesome any longer'."

And in his two subsequent serious love affairs, the orphan Levinsky seems in search of a mother as wife—and a father as father-in-law. He decides that marrying into a well-to-do orthodox family would mean respectability and solidity and seems more attracted to his prospective father-in-law than to Fanny, his bride-to-be: "It was sweet to hear myself called 'as good as a son' by this man of Talmudic education who was at the same time a man of substance and of excellent family."

After breaking off this engagement, perhaps unconsciously realizing that he "can't go home again"—home being Old World orthodoxy—Levinsky then falls in love with Anna, the socialist daughter of a once-famous Hebrew poet with Zionist leanings. Once again, much of the woman's appeal is her father's spiritual claims.

Significantly, all three women and their families represent viable alternatives to Levinsky's selfish, soulless, endless money-getting. Dora represents sacrifice for one's family: she stays with her boorish husband so that her daughter will have a freer, more meaningful life. Fanny and her family represent traditional religion and Old World authority. Anna and her family stand for artistic endeavor, Zionism, socialism—the whole intellectual Lower East Side.

That Levinsky fails to marry is particularly poignant because he comes to think that the family is the only possible source of value. As Levinsky becomes more enamored of Spencer and social Darwinism, he learns to look at a working man or poor man as an object of contempt: "a misfit, a weakling, a failure." He believes that outside the family "the human world was as brutally selfish as the jungle"—a conclusion which justifies his own exploitative treatment of others.

It is telling that education, the only value Levinsky holds with any assurance when he arrives in America, is forsaken for his business career. During his early years as a garment worker, Levinsky feels the satisfaction of physical work: "I was in an uplifted state of mind. No one seemed to be honorable who did not earn his bread in the sweat of his brow as I did." Moreover, in those early days he regards his work as a "stepping stone to a life of intellectual interests." City College becomes the nexus of values, the "synagogue of my new life." Paradoxically, Levinsky loses his dream of an intellectual life not during his physically taxing life as a worker, but when he becomes a businessman. And, ironically, he gives up his dream in a moment of business failure, not success. His first efforts as an independent cloak manufacturer having apparently failed, Levinsky finds that instead of thinking about a college career, he now cannot "resist the temptation" of dreaming of recouping enough money to go on manufacturing. The reason for this decision is the same one that brought Levinsky to America—adventure. He is

taken by the "venture of the thing" and the "great, daring game of life." And once again his journey has no real destination, the apparent means become ends; the same hungry orphan gobbles experiences, relentlessly makes more and more money.

Despite his financial success, the sadness of Levinsky's later life is underscored in several ways. Tellingly, the penultimate chapter, about Levinsky's courtship of Anna Tevkin, is entitled "At Her Father's House." In addition to suggesting that Levinsky is searching for a father as well as for a wife, the title signifies Levinsky's separation from God: he no longer has a place in his Father's house. Unable to answer the real question—what are you living for?—he broods over his inability to fulfill the lesser substitute: "Who are you living for?". In the last pages of the novel, Levinsky bemoans the fact that he pursued business instead of art, science, or music. Even these last words reveal his old pattern: he envies those who achieve in intellectual fields. He has no sense of the value of these endeavors in themselves, outside of personal aggrandizement. Rather, envy and success-worshiping mark his spiritual emptiness.

In total Levinsky fails both of Reb Sender's injunctions: "'Be a good Jew and a good man'." Later American Jewish novels like *The Assistant* explore what it means to be a good Jew and what, if anything, must be added to the general requirements of a good man. In *Levinsky* the character's lack of any values obviates the subsequently haunting problem. The fact that at the end of the novel Levinsky is unmarried, childless—without descendents—serves three related symbolic functions: 1) Levinsky is thus deprived of the traditional, limited Jewish immortality: a child to say Kaddish over his grave 2) the sense that there is literally no future for Levinsky is stressed and 3) Levinsky remains defined by his primary role as orphan.

Ironically, at the time that Cahan published *The Rise of David Levinsky* in 1917, the novel was realistic but probably not representative. The novel rings with "the thrill of truth" Cahan and the American realists desired, but it was not the story of the usual or general American Jewish immigrant. For Levinsky, unlike the majority of immigrants including Cahan himself, did not genuinely participate in the experience of *Yiddishkeit,* which Howe called a "way of life, a shared experience, which goes beyond opinion or ideology." While the orphan Levinsky sheds Yiddish as well as all visible signs of his Jewishness and then tries to fill the bottomless hole of spiritual vacuity, most American Jewish immigrants shared the *Yiddishkeit* which thrived precariously in the early years of this century as it rested on the unresolved tensions of faith and skepticism, of the alien world (representing both high culture and revolutionary movements) and the native tradition. Unlike the countless unknown "little" Jews, Levinsky finds no real authority or home in any of these possibilities—high culture, revolutionary movements, or native traditions.

Levinsky is, ironically, more the spiritual prototype of the immigrants' descendents. *David Levinsky* is peculiarly prescient in its prediction of the malaise of the post-immigrant generations: the loss of values that accompanied the normalization and *embourgeoisement* in suburban America. In this connection the metaphor of orphan is particularly apt in that the *raison d'être,* the hope, and justification of the difficult immigrant life was often the children—both literal offspring and, in a general sense, the next generation.

But in the largest sense, Cahan's novel explores more than the world of the modern American Jew; *David Levinsky* probes the condition of modern man in a world where God is dead, where homes are transitory or absent, where authority is specious or at best dubious. Levinsky was an orphan before his time; he is, alas, a more modern man.

Sanford E. Marovitz (essay date 1982)

SOURCE: "The Secular Trinity of a Lonely Millionaire: Language, Sex, and Power in 'The Rise of David Levinsky,'" in *Studies in American Jewish Literature,* edited by Daniel Walden, Vol. 2, 1982, pp. 20-35.

[*In the following essay, Marovitz examines what he considers Cahan's major themes in* The Rise of David Levinsky.]

When Abraham Cahan sailed from Liverpool in late May 1882, his knowledge of English was yet to be acquired, but by the time he had docked in Philadelphia less than two weeks later, he was already acting as translator, dictionary in hand, for other European immigrants like himself. Cahan quickly learned the value of linguistic facility, not in one language and not in two but in as many tongues as were useful in promoting his aims. When still an eight-year-old child in Vilna, he tells us in *Bleter fun Mein Leben (Leaves from My Life),* he paid a little gentile boy two pennies to purchase a Russian grammar for him and a few more pennies to give him weekly lessons in the language; forbidden to learn Russian by his parents, who insisted that he use only his native Yiddish, Cahan independently set out to acquire it without their help. Although this first attempt was quickly thwarted, he soon found other ways of achieving his goal, and eventually he attended the secular Russian school. Language, Cahan knew, was power; the lack of it, veritable impotence.

One might expect, them, to find in Cahan's vaguely autobiographical *magnum opus, The Rise of David Levinsky* (1917), that the thematic tie of language to power would be crucial—and indeed it is. Less predictable, however, is the intricate enfolding of a third central motif—sexuality—with the other two. Further, the linguistic theme itself is twofold: on the surface Levinsky, as the principal actor in his narrative, is anxious to become totally fluent in American English and its accompanying mannerisms. Equally important but far more subtly incorporated is the occasionally suggestive language of Levinsky's "autobi-

ography" particularly his extraordinary application of sexual imagery in seemingly incompatible contexts. What Levinsky tells us of himself directly is easily comprehensible though not always credible, for he is at times a most unreliable narrator. What he implies about himself, on the other hand, through his unexpected choice of terminology is quite another. The overt and covert together lead the reader of Cahan's novel to see Levinsky in a new light. Although he remains, of course, as has often been noted, a secularized and alienated multi-millionaire whose life, he alleges, is "devoid of significance," he also reveals an heretofore neglected cause of his unremitting frustration—repressed sexual conflict induced by a complex fear, erotic desire, and Oedipal longing. Converting the many women in his life into a single composite ideal, an unattainable phantom, Levinsky confronts the problem on a bias, exacerbating it and rebounding from it with both an increased sense of frustration and another shadowy feature assimilated onto his visionary uxorial princess or queen with every new and never permanent encounter.

I.

Levinsky is at once attracted to women and repulsed by them, an ambivalence which first emerges in his early childhood. His father dies when the boy is not yet three, a circumstance that inevitably pushes him into a faster, more tender relationship with his mother than is normal. Although she is seldom effusive in her endearing remarks to him, he recalls that he was never beaten as the other children in the neighborhood were. He remembers using his father's old coat as a quilt and dreaming of "bizarre visions, which at times seemed to have something to do with [his] father's spirit." These dreams come when he has grown too old to sleep any longer with his mother. After his father's death, he—young boy that he is—becomes the man of the family; for a time he sleeps in his father's place, uses his father's coat, dreams strangely of his father. His relationship with his mother is warm, intimate, ideal. She warns him against walking on "that street" where the "half naked women and soldiers" can be seen together and where one of the women gave him a piece of cake. His mother's admonition confirms his repugnance toward sexual play, an experience he first endures when Red Esther, a little red-headed girl living nearby, forces kisses upon him. The result is mockery. "There were some other things that she or some of the other little girls of our courtyard would do to make an involuntary 'sinner' of me," he recalls, "but these had better be left out." Attraction/Repulsion. Mother/Prostitute/Playmate. LOVE and SEX and SIN.

These experiences constitute Levinsky's polarized introduction to womanhood, femity and sex. From the time of childhood, his encounters with women in native Russia and more often in the New World lead to a series of attempted seductions, brothel visits, and infatuations. He learns that he can satisfy his physiological and perhaps psychological hunger for erotic activity, but his emotional and spiritual needs remain unfulfilled. By the time he takes it upon himself to tell the story of his life, Levinsky has left a long string of female companions, professional and otherwise, behind him. In fact, it is remarkably iluminating to trace his sexual encounters in this naturalistic novel that is usually analyzed for its social and religious themes. Even a brief account of the individual women in Levinsky's past clearly indicates that amour is as important to him as business, though it is much underplayed. (In order to comprehend the pervasiveness of Levinsky's sexuality, one must carefully examine his choice of language as both narrator and confessor, a major point which will be developed later.)

While living with his mother in Antomir, Russia, Levinsky meets Red Esther and sees prostitutes. His first childhood romance is with an eleven-year-old neighbor, Sarah-Leah. From his closest friend, Naphtali, he hears a moving tale about the in-laws of Abraham Tevkin, the Hebrew poet: this romantic story of their courtship eventuates in his ardent pursuit of Anna many years later. Shortly before emigrating, Levinsky fervently kisses Matilda, the sophisticated young Russian divorcee who gives him money for his ticket to America; she laughs at the young Talmudist for his hypocrisy—professing orthodoxy and succumbing to passion—but despite her mockery, she becomes the subject of his dreamy infatuation for five years in the New World. (As a successful industrialist long afterward, he wonders when he meets her again in New York if she remembers him "with a gleam of romantic interest." Homesick almost immediately upon setting foot in the United States, Levinsky thinks longingly of his "poor dead mother": "I thought of her . . . , and my pangs of yearing for her were tinged with pangs of my unrequited love for Matilda." Already, prominent elements of the composite ideal Woman have begun to merge.

Uncommitted for the time to anything but becoming Americanized as quickly as possible Levinsky lapses temporarily into self-indulgence and debauchery. Paradoxically, he learns from the very man he later cuckolds, Max Margoils, a pushcart peddler like himself, that "Every woman can be won, absolutely every one, provided a fellow knows how to go about it." Levinsky applies this street wisdom immediately, though he bungles at first when he clumsily attempts to seduce his landladies, one of whom bears his own surname—an unmistakable manifestation of Oedipal longing. He frequents brothels, accepting and rationalizing the sham love offered by prostitutes, fully aware that their artifices reflect his own deceptions as a peddler in everyday dealings with his customers. Bertha, with her ten-year-child, subject to the taunts of men awaiting their turns; Argentine Rachael from Antomir, who at once repulses Levinsky and attracts him as "a good girl," "truthful and affectionate," and who is yet "as repellent to [him] as the rest of her class": these and others of their trade teach Levinsky that the true moral worth of a person is not determinable by surfaces and that "the average man or woman was full of all sorts of false notions." And yet it is obviously not for lessons in morality that Levinsky sees the prostitutes

occasionally twice in the same evening, finally spending more than he can afford. At this stage of his life there seems to be a decided streak of satyriasis in Levinsky's drive. The faces, behavior, and backgrounds of the prostitutes are assimilated into the ungraspable, ever-evasive ideal Woman for whom Levinsky yearns.

His erotic fancy is constantly working. Fully cognizant of the difference between reality and hazy romantic suggestiveness, he is nevertheless inclined to daydream and poeticize when in the presence of women—regardless of their beauty or lack of it. What comeliness the shopgirls do not have is compensated for by Levinsky's active imagination. Individually uninteresting to him, collectively they cast a spell over the workroom "as though the workaday atmosphere were scented with the breath of a delicate perfume—a pefume that was tainted with the tang of my earning for Matilda." Two "homely girls, with pinched faces," giggling and whispering nearby, lead Levinsky to believe that they are attentive to him, and he finds it difficult to keep his mind on his work. Later he convinces himself that one of these girls, Gussie, is worthy of his affection, though he is more concerned with her savings then herself. Sober and unattractive, she partially succumbs to his appeals on a starry spring evening near the river, but only for a few hours; the illiterate but astute shopgirl breaks the illusory romance with a letter she has paid a man to write for her. Upon reading the short, sensitive missive, Levinsky feels ashamed and "badly out of spirits" until the following noon. Then, presumably, the episode is forgotten.

Shortly before this transitory experience with Gussie, Levinsky passes through a most peculiar stage of his sexual growth when he is suddenly starstruck over a Madam Klesmer, "the leading Jewish actress of that period, . . . a tragedienne and a prima donna at once." Surely, it cannot be considered extraordinary that a young man is overwhelmed by the magnetic charm and beauty of a popular actress. The paradox for Levinsky is not that it does not happen, however, but the way it does; for he is provoked into the infatuation by an unwitting third party, Jake Mindels, the younger brother of an avid devotee of the Yiddish theater. Levinsky characterizes Mindels as a fascinating androgyne:

> He was the handsomest fellow I had ever-seen, with a fine head of dark-brown hair, classic features, and large, soft-blue eyes; too soft and too blue, perhaps. His was a manly face and figure, and his voice was a manly, a beautiful basso; but this masculine exterior contained an effeminate psychology. In my heart I pronounced him "a calf," and when I had discovered the English word "sissy," I thought that it just fitted him. Yet I adored him, and even looked up to him, all because of his good looks.

Mindels is thoroughly bewitched by Madame Klesmer, about whom Levinsky has never expressed a feeling one way or the other. He does not mention her name until he recounts the episode initiated by Mindels' infatuation.

When the two young men attend a "historical opera" in which she is performing as a Biblical princess, Levinsky (as far as we know) is seeing her for the first time, but Mindels cannot take his eyes from her; he applauds vigorously and shouts her name. To Levinsky he admits that he loves her and would "go crazy" to kiss even her little finger. Levinsky, amused, teases his friend with a variety of taunting remarks. Nevertheless that night he has a "chain of dreams" in all of which Madame Klesmer appears; when he awakens the next morning in love with her himself he is overjoyed (yet he also confesses that this new love does not interfere with his lingering thoughts of Matilda). Levinsky soon tells Mindels of his devotion, and their resultant community of feeling excites no envy but cements their friendship. Jointly, they write her a long impassioned letter filled with "Biblical and homespun poetry," the language of which is absurdly unrestrained and artificial, and they converse at length about both their affection for her and love in general.

What is happening here to this budding industrialist and millionaire? Levinsky suddenly and with no apparent motivation falls in "love" with a stage queen as a direct result of his friendship with an effeminate young man whose own devotion to the same actress has kindled the passion. This osmotic affection further intensifies their fellowship, and they begin to talk intimately of love. Clearly, Levinsky finds immense satisfaction through this intercourse: by way of discussing Madame Klesmer, who is the next step down from an ideal image but equally unattainable, this intimate chatter enables him to court, as it were, an effeminate male companion. His collaborative writing, singing, and dreaming of her constitute his share of the courtship in which Mandels is the real if subliminal object of his attention and Madame Klesmer only the ostensible one.

Indeed, when he learns of Mindels' chastity, Levinsky ridicules him only momentarily and then finds his friend "more attractive than ever." Yet he is "bothered" by the youth's virginity, which, as is characteristic of any infatuated suitor with strong erotic urges, he considers a challenge: "The idea of breaking it down became an irresistible temptation." He futilely strives to implement Max's lesson that any woman can be "won"—i.e., *conquered*—though in this case an effeminate male companion rather than a woman is the object of his quest for power: "I would ridicule him for a sissy, appeal to him in the name of his health, beg him as one does for a personal favor, all in vain." Levinsky's desire to dominate his friend as he would a paramour is unmistakable. Although his attempted "seduction" does not succeed, the friendship remains firm. "By his cleanliness and tidiness," Levinsky acknowledges, Mindels "reminded me of Naphtali." (Many years later, Levinsky sees Mindels walking along Broadway "handsomer than ever."

Although Mindels significantly abets Levinsky's rapid acculturation, the ambitious young immigrant is still desperately in need of cash. He goes to Max Margolis and meets Max's wife, Dora, whom he begins to pursue with

Max's own "all-women-can-be-won" advice in mind. Like a suitor courting a wedded noblewoman—and Dora is without a doubt the most attractive, sympathetic, indeed noble figure in the novel—Levinsky woos her with a combination of tenderness and circumspect deviousness, intending soon after their introduction to take her as his mistress. Despite his impassioned avowals of love, however, Levinsky succumbs to his unsatisfied lust and takes once again to the streets, frequently to the apartment of a Hungarian prostitute. Though he claims to respect Dora, he brazenly acknowledges his illicit intentions: "I never ceased to dream of and seek her moral downfall." Obviously his desire here echoes his craving to lure Mindels from chastity. But unlike Mindels, Dora eventually yields to Levinsky's persistence, though by the next morning she suffers overwhelming remorse; and in a short but brilliantly Jamesian scene in Stuyvesant Park, she abruptly ends their relationship. Then she, like the many girls and women who have preceded her, becomes a part of the ideal image glowing deep in the back of his psyche, an image that finally will make normal love impossible.

As he continues to prosper with age, Levinsky's loneliness and despondency become more acute. Dora remains in his mind, "an image of an enshrined past." He enters the "marriage market" to meet the eligible daughters of Jewish couples anxious to provide a good match for their offspring. The first attempt, Miss Kalmanovitch, is a disaster: "large and plump, with full ivory-hued cheeks, . . . a dimple in her fleshy chin," and large, round, black eyes, Miss Kalmanovitch also possesses a double chin, seems to exude oil, and shakes hands with a palm that is "fat and damp with perspiration." The proposed match goes no further than an introduction, and Levinsky is subject to the complaints of well-wishing friends that he is "too particular."

But Levinsky himself knows basically where the problem lies. His desire cannot be achieved because it is at once ambiguous and ideal: "The vague portrait of a woman in the abstract seemed never to be absent from my mind. Coupled with that portrait was a similarly vague image of a window and a table set for dinner. That, somehow, was my symbol of home. Home and woman were one, a complex charm joining them into an inseparable force. There was the glamour of sex, shelter, and companionship in that charm" as well as the alluring anticipation of progeny. He is homesick for the past and ensconced in the present. His values clash; his aims are uncertain; his ambivalent attitudes fluctuate. He is, in a word, insatiable.

At the age of about forty, Levinsky suddenly announces his engagement to Fanny Kaplan, the "self-satisfied" daughter of "a fine Jew, a man of substance and Talmud," native to a village near Antomir, strongly attached to the synagogue and yet thoroughly assimilated into the American way of life. Prosperous and respectable himself, Levinsky is considered a superb match even by the uptown Jews who would have scorned him only a few years before. He admits that although he is not in love with the girl, "she certainly was not repulsive," either; and he looks toward marriage as a means to end his root-less, homeless, alien existence.

But unfortuitous circumstances intervene. On his way to the Kaplans' cottage in the Catskills, Levinsky stops for a day at a resort in order to commence his visit on a Sunday rather than chance offending the religious sensi-bilities of his future family by riding on the Sabbath (a practice forbidden by Orthodox Jewish law). Teeming with wealthy Jewish women, the wives and eligible daughters of businessmen and professionals who flock to the hotel to spend weekends with their families, the Rigi Kulm House is a Vanity Fair of the Catskills, exposing a grossly ostentatious, materialistic, and acquisitive femi-ninity at its lavish worst: "The crowd was ablaze with diamonds, painted cheeks, and bright-colored silks. It was a babel of blatant self-consciousness," epitomizing the garish smugness of the *nouveaux riches* on show. Though not seriously tempted to flirt with the bejeweled and extravagantly gowned young ladies and heiresses, Levinsky nevertheless momentarily considers taking a sensual Miss Lazar "out into the night [to] hug and kiss her and tell her that she [is] a nuisance." He rationalizes away the twinges of guilt and doubt which remind him that he ought to mention his engagement; but saying nothing about it, he is considered by the anxious maidens to be an available and very desirable bachelor.

The Catskill surroundings create an aura of romance and lassitude that captivates Levinsky. Not long after his ar-rival, he sees Anna Tevkin for the first time, on the tennis court. He is enchanted; his immediate recollection of her father's courtship of her mother through a series of deeply moving love letters automatically lifts Anna from the plain of reality into the ether of ideality, and by evening, he confesses, "the prospect of seeing Fanny had lost its attraction" for him. Again he loses touch in order to follow the gleam with a "love-maddened brain"; and, of course, he breaks his engagement upon returning to the city. Nevertheless, his ardent appeals and manifold at-tempts notwithstanding, Anna refuses to think seriously of him as either suitor or husband, and sometime later he learns that she has married a high-school teacher. His money could not tempt her.

Before concluding his "autobiography," Levinsky indi-cates that he has continued to seek an acceptable mar-riage. But to succeed would be impossible, for in his search he turns only to women who for one reason or another will not and cannot satisfy his need. It is as though he pulls with one hand only to push with the other. At times he suffers from "morbid amativeness and seem[s] to be falling in love with woman after woman." Seeing shopgirls walking together appeals to him, for they appear to be vaguely distant, in a world of their own. He falls in love with a wealthy Jewish girl whom he meets in Florida, but she has "the bashfulness of sin," he complains; her "guilty looks" disturb him, so their rela-tionship ends. He considers marrying a gentile woman of "high character," but despite his declaration of atheism, he finds the "chasm of race" unbridgeable; the possibility of marriage is modulated to the reality of a continuing friendship, and Levinsky remains a lonely man, dreaming of Anna as he once did of Dora, of Matilda, and of his mother before them. Moreover, what is true with Anna is equally true with the rest: distance increases their power of fascination and their desirability. His ideal Woman, a union of Mother, Wife, Harlot, and Princess, is the subject of his fancy; colored by wishful thinking, beshadowed by ambivalence, the image floats ever-present in the recesses of his mind, an impossible dream that can nowhere find substantiation in the light of com-mon day.

II

Levinsky becomes aware of the relation between power and sex while still a boy in an Antomir *cheder* (Hebrew school). One of his Hebrew teachers is named Shmerl but called by the pupils "Shmerl the Pincher" because of his method of inflicting punishment: "He seemed to prefer the flesh of plump, well-fed boys, but as these were usu-ally the sons of prosperous parents, he often had to forego the pleasure and to gratify his appetite on me. There was something morbid in his cruel passion for young flesh, something perversely related to sex, per-haps." Levinsky recalls childhood dreams of "becoming a great man some day, rich and mighty, and avenging [my] self on him. Behold! Shmerl the Pincher is running after me, cringingly begging my pardon, and I, omnipotent and formidable [will be merciless]." Thus early Levinsky perceives, though he may still be too young to understand the implications of what he observes, the unholy linkage of knowledge (language), power (domination), and sex (perversity, in this case).

Hence for Levinsky, as was true for Cahan himself, the acquisition of fluent English is a prerequisite for success: language leads to power, power to domination; and domi-nation in Levinsky's order of being is a thoroughly mas-culine principle. Women, on the other hand, are associ-ated with subordination, sexual relief, beauty, perfume, and poetry. Pointing out that love affairs among the male and female employees in the same ghetto factories are relatively uncommon, Levinsky explains: "The factory is scarcely a proper setting for romance. It is one of the battlefields in our struggle for existence, where we treat women as an inferior being, whereas in civilized love-making we prefer to keep up the chivalrous fiction that she is our superior." Although the hard-working shopgirls arouse his sympathy, they do not stimulate enduring ro-mantic interests. Clearly, Levinsky here implies that the male role is dominant in work and love ("*we* treat woman, . . ." and "*we* keep up the chivalrous fiction that she is our superior"), thus exposing an attitude that rein-forces his preoccupation with personal sexual conquest. The result of this constant "sex-consciousness" but-tressed by the intense drive to prevail over all competi-tors is manifold and highly paradoxical: first, Levinsky generates and continually augments a composite image of his ideal Woman; second, unable to attain this ideal, for even as a young man he makes his quest impossible to fulfill, he looks toward masculine companionship for quasi-sexual gratification, not through homosexual activities but by attempting to impose his will upon weaker, less able, and more effeminate males than himself (hence his paternalistic method of running his factory and sales); and finally he impregnates his narrative with terminology that exposes the sexual frustrations he constantly endures.

Throughout his account Levinsky pays particular heed to nuances and varieties of language used among associates and on the streets. Like Cahan in *Bleter fun Mein Leben,* Levinsky recalls from his early Antomir years that the "'modern' young Jews" who speak Russian instead of Yiddish alone "belonged to a world far removed" from his own. These are the young men who walk, talk, and dance with the local girls as Levinsky, with his knowledge of language limited to Yiddish, cannot do; instead, he can only look on with "envy" and an intense if unspoken desire to emulate them. The rigid restrictions against women in Judaic law convince the young Levinsky that members of the opposite sex serve only to propagate the species and to tempt man toward sin as agents of Satan. Love can exist only among the family, not between strangers, and therefore marriages are "arranged"; falling in love is for "modern Jews" and gentiles only. Levinsky accepts these views as a boy and seems to hold to them later as a man, a narrator of his life story; but he confesses, too, that the hard, misogynic laws "merely deepened the bewitching mystery of the forbidden sex in [his] young blood." Although he continues his religious studies, he realizes even thus early that the knowledge of a new language will make him a part of the contemporary secular world, and once in the United States his Americanization is rapidly effected chiefly as a result of his quickly achieved and consistently improved fluency in English.

Perhaps it is Cahan himself rather than Levinsky who is carried away by an encyclopedic tendency to tell his readers more than necessary about his East Side milieu simply because of his own fascination with the subject. Be that as it may, Levinsky's persistent attentiveness to the English language per se and its value to the immigrants in terms of growth, achievement, and power cannot be dismissed merely as a realistic quirk on the part of either author or narrator. Levinsky's discussion of the term "greenhorn," for example, covering nearly half a page, permits him to admit that he is "stung . . . cruelly" when it is used in reference to himself, though the passage is also an item of socially informative linguistic data.

How profoundly the newcomers could be affected emotionally and psychologically by the transition from their native to American Yiddish and finally to English is illustrated in Levinsky's account of an immigrant child's education in the public school. Lucy, Dora's young daughter, has begun learning to read and write English;

within weeks she shows "signs of estrangement from her mother-tongue. Her Yiddish was rapidly becoming clogged with queer-sounding 'r's' and with quaintly twisted idioms. Yiddish words came less and less readily to her tongue, and the tendency to replace them with the English equivalents grew in persistence." Dora begins taunting her, albeit with no little pride, on her "Gentile Yiddish." The effect on Dora is twofold: at first she despises herself "for her inferiority to [Lucy]"; then she decides that Lucy must teach her how to read and write. The daughter of seven becomes the instructor; the mother, her pupil. Their roles are reversed, manifesting the power that language alone can bring. At times bitter over her recognizable inferiority to Lucy in her knowledge of English, Dora commences to react violently, to beat the child furiously in retaliation for knowing more than she. Having lost to Lucy in a spelling match, Dora "took her defeat so hard that she was dejected all that evening." After her irritability has passed, she is remorseful, suffering, of course, from guilt over blaming her little daughter for her own inadequacies. Levinsky's witnessing such events on many occasions over an extended period of time only confirms his earlier observations that linguistic fluency provides the rungs upon which one must step on his climb to the top. Dora's domination of her daughter would remain physical and temporary were she not to acquire a correspondent knowledge of English, which she does, though ultimately, to her dismay, Lucy's American education leads the girl to wed for money rather than love—a reflection of Levinsky's own selling of his soul for gold.

As he approaches the apex of power and prosperity, Levinsky exudes self-assurance; he egotistically assesses himself in Spencerian terms as "one of the fittest," a select man of the business world. By chance he encounters his former English teacher, Bender, who congratulates him on his success and his excellent English. In obvious financial difficulties, Bender still teaches part-time but has no other work. Levinsky condescendingly offers him a job as a salesman with the factory, and he obsequiously accepts. Bender, Levinsky muses, "was a singular surprise to me. Formerly I had looked up to him as infinitely my superior, whereas now he struck me as being piteously beneath me." Bender has the linguistic facility but lacks the acumen and ambition to put his knowledge to effective use; Levinsky and he, in a reversal paralleling that of Dora and Lucy, are transposed, and the erstwhile pupil becomes the paternal provider for his former teacher, a transposition that could not have been made—as Levinsky himself well knows—without the English fluency which Bender once helped him to achieve.

Furthermore, he is shrewd enough to realize that having so articulate a salesman as Bender in his employ bodes well for the business. Linguistic accuracy and polish impress his clientele, a factor which Levinsky keeps in mind when hiring models; he knows that personal attractiveness alone is not qualification enough. The girls must also have, "if possible, good grammar," for "refinement in a model was helpful in making a sale, even in the case of the least refined of customers. Indeed, often it is even more effectual than a tempting complexion." In his careful selection of models, then, to enhance his ready-made ladies' ware, Levinsky conjoins for a clear and practical purpose all three of his major preoccupations: language, sex, and power (through capital). The implication is immediately apparent: by the end of the narrative and his rise to economic supremacy, he controls what he has been seeking throughout his life—words, women, and wealth.

Levinsky's deliberations over choosing his models are carried on with specific criteria—attractive appearance, good manners, and correct grammar—in mind; but long before he is in a position even to dream of hiring such employees, when he is still but a seasonal wage-earner in a sweatshop, the intimate association of these three ostensibly independent factors is evident just below the surface of Levinsky's consciousness. Recalling his habit of stopping to listen intently to lecturers, "street fakers," and any other Americans speaking their native tongue, Levinsky concludes that "[p]eople who were born to speak English were superior beings. Even among fallen women I would seek those who were real Americans." The juxtaposition of these two short sentences at the close of a chapter is too thematically pertinent to be mere coincidence; for here, as in his selection of models much later, the relation of sex, language, and the acquisition of wealth and power is overt.

Elsewhere in his narrative, similar associations among the three are equally significant, but their implications are considerably less distinct. Several examples appear in Levinsky's references to the "obscene story-telling" he overhears in the streets and shops; although he alleges that he is disgusted with the lewd jests when they are offered obliquely in the presence of shopgirls, he is notably impressed with the "passionate" phrase-making of a vain if haggard violinist, who "was as sensual as Maximum Max [Dora's husband], only his voluptuous talks of women were far more offensive in form. But then his lewd drivel was apt to glitter with flashes of imagination." No less telling are several unexpected and remarkable sexual images which manifest Levinsky's subliminal preoccupation with sex. He informs us, for example, that as a child he "loved [God] as one does a woman," a clear association of eroticism and power at a very early age. In America he studies "with a passion amounting to a frenzy" as he looks upon the college building of CCNY as "a bride-elect" of his own. Like the gradually developing ideal Woman in his imagination, college for him is and will remain chaste, a profound dream beyond experience. Intellectualism, like domestic happiness, is but a rosy illusion to which he pays homage with words alone, whereas practical power and self-gratification are Levinsky's real concerns; to these ends he dedicates himself through rapid Americanization and what seems at times to be an almost compulsive drive toward sexual conquest. He looks ambivalently toward Dora, for example, who inspires him "with something like reverence"

but who nevertheless becomes the willing if cautious object of his seductive intentions: "we often held converse in that . . . gesture language of sex across the barrier of decorum." Much later, attempting to court Anna Tevkin, Levinsky is again beguiled through his romanticized association of language and sex, for he is aware that "the glow of her nimbus" is intensified for him by the fact that her father is the author of several moving volumes of Hebrew poetry. Nor does he overlook the idea that his appreciation for Tevkin's verse is at least in part attributable to the poet's being the father of this hagiologized Jewish Beatrice who eludes him. The powers of language and sensual magnetism are mutually reinforcing. Together they generate a romantic ideal that no real woman—not even Anna—could ever sustain.

Levinsky is doomed to incessant frustration, for although his basic dedication is to vanity, self-indulgence, and domination of the world around him, he tries to convince himself as well as his readers that he yearns for the mundane comforts of love and domesticity. His language becomes a cover, a facade. His rhapsodizing over a Catskills sunset, for example, is a mawkish contrivance that exposes his artificial sentiments in a miasma of purple prose and inane imagery. Readers may well be moved to laugh aloud over grandiloquent passages containing such factitious descriptions as: "The edge of the sun, a vivid red, was peeping out of a gray patch of cloud that looked like a sack, the sack hanging with its mouth downward and the red disk slowly emerging from it"; and such lamentations as: "The rebuff I had received at [Anna's] hands in the afternoon of that storm lay like a mosquito in my soul." To be sure, Levinsky is no more a poet than was Cahan himself, but both author and narrator are meticulous observers of the appropriate—and inappropriate—use of language. The "note of consciousness" that Levinsky discovers in Anna's praise of the same sunset only heightens the grotesqueness of his own.

Indeed, Levinsky's misuse of language here betrays his disingenuousness in much the same way as his apparently unconscious application of sexual imagery elsewhere reveals the underlying sensuality of his character. Incapable of choosing between idealization and self-gratification, between love and lust, between compatibility and conquest, between virtuous domesticity and sin, Levinsky wishes for the one element of each pair while he invariably and inexorably works toward the other; as a result he is necessarily frustrated. Hence it is no wonder that at middle age he finds his life "devoid of significance" despite his wealth. Often his confessions are deceptive and unreliable, but this one is not. With neither love nor faith as a motivating force, he is dominated by ego alone, and his life is without meaning. If fluency in English has been instrumental in Levinsky's rise to economic power on an outer level, it has also been subtle means of suggestively and ambiguously conveying the extent of his ambivalence, frustration, and alienation on an inner one. His indirect use of implicatory language is as revealing to us as his hypocrisy is at times deceiving to himself, and the ultimate result is that we can accurately observe

Levinsky's true identity only by retaining a double perspective and adjusting the focus as necessary. Even so, self-contradictory and self-deceiving, he will continue to remain a paradoxical figure as complex as the composite ideal Woman who tantalizes him in the depths of his delusive and highly romantic imagination.

David Engel (essay date 1982)

SOURCE: "The 'Discrepancies' of the Modern: Towards a Revaluation of Abraham Cahan's *The Rise of David Levinsky,*" in *Studies in American Jewish Literature,* edited by Daniel Walden, Vol. 2, 1982, pp. 36-60.

[*In the following essay, Engel interprets Levinsky's inability to integrate the dichotomies in his life—including the differing cultures of Europe and America—as his greatest flaw.*]

The life of Abraham Cahan bears witness to a significant chapter in modern history, the massive immigration of the east European Jews to the United States in the years between the Russian pogroms (1882) and the start of World War I. Born in a Lithuanian *shtetl* and raised for the most part in Vilna, Cahan himself immigrated in 1882. In his long and protean American career Cahan distinguished himself as a journalist and writer of fiction (in Yiddish and English), translator, Socialist, and union organizer. Above all, his reputation in American Jewish culture rests, of course, on his work as founder and editor for fifty years of the largest Yiddish newspaper in the world, *The Jewish Daily Forward.* Under Cahan's editorship *The Forward* served uniquely as counsellor, mentor, and consoler to the Jewish population of that crucible of acculturation, the Lower East Side.

Insofar as Cahan may be said to have secured a place in American letters it is thanks to his novel **The Rise of David Levinsky,** written in English and serialized by *McClure's Magazine* in 1913, expanded and published in hardback in 1917. In the first words of Cahan's novel, David Levinsky straightforwardly summarizes his story:

> Sometimes, when I think of my past in a superficial, casual way, the metamorphosis I have gone through strikes me as nothing short of a miracle. I was born and reared in the lowest depths of poverty and I arrived in America—in 1885—with four cents in my pocket. I am now worth more than two million dollars and recognized as one of the two or three leading men in the cloak-and-suit trade in the United States. And yet when I take a look at my inner identity it impresses me as being precisely the same as it was thirty or forty years ago. My present station, power, the amount of worldly happiness at my command, and the rest of it, seem devoid of significance.

And the last words of the novel repeat the first, reiterating the theme of Levinsky's spiritual failure:

> I can never forget the days of my misery. I cannot escape from my old self. My past and my present

do not comport well. David, the poor lad swinging over a Talmud volume at the Preacher's Synagogue, seems to have more in common with my inner identity than David Levinsky, the well-known cloak-manufacturer.

The halves of David's life "do not comport well." This is the *discrepancy* (the word must occur two-dozen times in the novel) which makes his rise a fall, and which describes the peculiar nature of Levinsky's unhappiness: his inability to make some inner, unifying sense of a life that has been European and American, traditional and modern, faithful and apostate. This failure of wholeness, which Levinsky can describe but neither fully understand nor remedy, creates the disturbing impression of Levinsky as a man somehow absent from his own life, self-estranged, and this is Cahan's greatest success in his novel.

Although **David Levinsky** has had its admirers, it has rarely been praised strictly on its own merits as a novel. Claimed as an ancestor, the first American Jewish novel of consequence, **David Levinsky** has more often had the equivocal honor of being bathed in the reflected glory of the later generation of Bellow, Malamud, and Roth.

The same sort of oblique compliment has been paid **David Levinsky** by those readers who have identified it as primarily a document of cultural history, largely sociological in its methods and achievements. In an important article, David Singer made use of the novel to confirm a historian's thesis on the process of Jewish secularization. Cushing Strout has suggested the value of **David Levinsky** as a historically dense account of identity under the pressure of "cultural strain" and recommended it to sociologists as a valuable source on this subject.

Other readers have highlighted the novel as a genre piece, a fine example of, variously, realism, "ghetto realism," or naturalism. When mentioned in some academic context other than a course in Yiddish or a survey of American Jewish literature, Cahan is most likely to appear as an epigone of his sometime patron William Dean Howells and a lesser light among the realists. So far as I know, the only mainstream American literary journal that has published more than a single item on Cahan is *American Literary Realism, 1870-1910,* to whose lot he falls willy-nilly. Even so sympathetic a reader as Irving Howe, although according **David Levinsky** a fair measure of praise, has brought the novel up short by labelling it, finally, "a minor masterpiece of genre realism." This emphasis on the novel's realism, while not inappropriate, has too often tended to draw attention to the novel as a specimen of the genre while obscuring its more distinctive merits.

Finally, **David Levinsky**'s themes have been applauded, in a way that Cahan's assimilationist hero would have envied, as "real Yankee," that is, characteristically American. Although the distinctive life of the Jewish Lower East Side began to wane in the Twenties with the fixing of immigration quotas, it left a legacy which includes patterns of experience that do seem typcially American. The lost home, the cost of success: these alone locate the immigrant adventure in the thick of or imaginative preoccupations. In his excellent introduction to the recent reprint of *David Levinsky* John Higham has suggested that the novel's theme of success derives from American literature, from Howells, Norris, and Dreiser. Isaac Rosenfeld has called *David Levinsky* "an American novel *par excellence* . . . and exemplary treatment of one of the dominant myths of American capitalism, that the millionaire finds nothing but emptiness at the top of the heap."

It is this emptiness, the all too familiar canker at the heart of the American dream, that *The Rise of David Levinsky* is about. But it is about more than that. The pluralism of Cahan's experience, his outsider's perspective coupled with his intimate participation in an important historical occasion, expands the novel so that it is more than the chronicle of a place in time (the ghetto, turn-of-the-century America); it is, I would argue, a novel richly descriptive of that situation of history and feeling we call modernity. And I believe that we may gain a more accurate appreciation of Cahan's achievement in *David Levinsky* by coming to see it as a novel absorbed with the issue of what it means to be modern.

The modernity of Cahan's writing in *David Levinsky,* as in virtually all his fiction, begins in his customary historical subject, which is an episode in that epochal process that is often called "modernization": the transition of the east European Jews from the traditional world of *shtetl* and ghetto to the new world of open society, city life, and industrial labor. Cahan contributes as few other American writers have to our understanding of that constellation of decisive historical turnings—secularization, urbanization, proletarization—which has enacted the transformation of traditional into moderen society, and which finds its classic treatments in European social thought and literature. In a briefer, more abruptly violent arc, Cahan's Jews travel the same historical distance as the English of Cobbett and Carlyle. The violence of this journey lies not only in its ability to alter the tangible life of a people, providing new opportunities and new manners, but in its power to reshape the intimate life of feeling and belief. We can see the full reach of this transformative process, as it typically asserts itself in Cahan's fiction, in *Yekl,* the 1896 novella which brought Cahan to the attention of Howells.

Cahan begins his story with the palpable trappings of the new life—the sweat shop and dancing academy, the half mastered idioms and proudly displayed slang of newly acquired English, excited talk about boxing and baseball—the circumstances among which the old country's "Yekl" becomes America's "Jake." Jake is enthusiastic for everything in his experience that strikes him as American and modern, and Cahan develops and deepens his story by showing, through Jake's growing disgust with his too old-fashioned, "dowdy little greenhorn wife"

and their eventual divorce, how a man can come to decide *against* the past and try to kick free of it. The story concludes with Jake half-reluctantly on his way to take a new, more Americanized wife. At the close of *Yekl,* Cahan succeeds impressively in suggesting what is truly unprecedented in Jake's feelings: not only regret, but a confused sense of new possibility and freedom which Jake doesn't know how to act on but which he feels he mustn't lose, a new uncertainty which colors all his perceptions.

The subject of *Yekl* and the essential subject of all Cahan's fiction is the impact of historical change on culture, that region of experience where private and collective meaning merge to set the limits on what possibilities we can imagine for ourselves in such things as marriage, livelihood, the fundamental matters of a life. And the power of Cahan's stories derives in large part from our assumption that this base of unexamined, everyday belief is *immune* to history and change. Culture, as we unreflectingly participate in it, is the natural, timeless, and true. Intruded upon by history, it is none of these things. The effect of historical change on those significances which are cultural can accurately be called radical, because change reminds culture of what it has forgotten, that it too is history, not "the way things are" but merely "the way things are now." What felt secure now seems impermanent. The sense of unspecifiable possibility which troubles Jake at the close of *Yekl* is due not only to the specific changes in his life but to the fact that change itself, the possibility of possibilities, has entered permanently into his life.

The modernity of Cahan's fiction lies in his depiction of this radical process whereby new experiences are compounded to alter the boundaries of a life, changing the fundamental feeling of experience itself. His writing is of more than documentary value because it expresses this process, as few documents can, as it is enacted in consciousness. Cahan's stories are less interested in directly representing the large, collective dimension of historical events than they are in intuiting history as an event for consciousness.

Yekl ends inconclusively, with Jake's own uncertainty and a more general uncertainty about the questions his experience poses: Can a man walk unencumbered, as Jake hopes, from the past into the future? Is it possible to simply decide against the past and for the future? Or are the consequences of such a choice so ramified and unpredictable that inevitably one chooses blindly, and choice is no choice at all? To claim that Cahan's attention to these questions, which are the same questions posed by *David Levinsky,* provides a vision of the modern, is to assert something about Cahan's understanding of the exigencies of experience in time. And it is Cahan's imagination of history, as the individual experiences it, which, I should like to argue, makes *David Levinsky* a novel of modernity.

To be sure, the idea of modernity seems to introduce more problems than it solves. Like its famously difficult kin, *romantic, modern* eludes definition. Its range of reference—which can include any manner of event in time, along with any kind of art and matters of subject, style, and form—is immense, and its boundaries are unclear and flexible. In addition, it presents the special problems of those terms whose reference is temporal. Our attempts to apply the word "modern" to a text or an occasion are liable to end up meaning it in that weak sense whereby it serves as merely a marker for the contemporaneous; and if, as the joke on the historians' cliche goes, every age is an age of transition, it's equally true that it's always modern times. But, on the other hand, if we try to define the modern as something more than the fashion of the day, by specifying certain traits of spirit or style as definitively modern 'for all time,' we quickly find that such definitions are helpless against shifts in taste and opinion. The modernism of one age is notoriously the classicism of the next.

Those accounts of the modern which try to evade the temporality of the concept inevitably fall victim to it. A more adequate understanding of the modern must, instead, *account for* its temporality by recognizing that modernity as such is a mode of historicity, an attitude toward experience in time. The modern comes after. It begins in an awareness of change and develops into a sense of discontinuity. The past seems to have receded faster than before and left the present stranded, cut off from tradition, radically free but also uncomforted by any faith in history. In literature, those texts are modern which, through subject, style, or form, raise the issue of change, discontinuity, novation. Modernity can be claimed, then, for any text of any period that raises in this way the issue of modernity. This is not to say that the texts we generally recognize as modern need to be redefined and reclassified on these terms—this essay will continue to use *modernism* in its common acceptation, which clusters together certain familiar texts, authors, and issues of nineteenth and twentieth century literature—but only to suggest that what our modernist texts most fundamentally share may be an attitude toward history. So many of modernism's characteristic griefs, its feeling of loss and homelessness, as well as its brighter moments of radical liberation and invention, seem implicated in its loss of faith in teleology and its sense of discontinuity.

A useful account of the modern in its relation to history and, at the same time, an excellent standpoint from which to consider the modernity of *David Levinsky,* is Paul de Man's essay "Literary History and Literary Modernity," which I'd like to consider briefly before turning more directly to Cahan's novel. De Man has fittingly chosen to center his discussion on that paradigmatic modern, Nietzsche. And equally appropriate is his emphasis on Nietzsche's 1874 essay "The Use and Disadvantage of History for Life," which stands, if any single text can, at that point which is both culmination and crisis of the nineteenth century historicist tradition. The special authority of Nietzsche's text derives from his own participation, through his philological training and scholarship, in this tradition, which he here turns so violently against.

Nietzsche's essay begins in his recognition that his age has seen the triumph of history as the sole category for the understanding of man, and he seconds historicism's anti-metaphysical tendency to reduce man to his history and history to man. However, Nietzsche attacks what he calls the "historical sickness" of the age: this is the excessive admiration for the past which amounts, he feels, to a weak-willed escape from the present. All historical thought which is merely comtemplative, which does not explicitly serve the present, enfeebles it, inhibiting action, spontanaiety and change. Nietzsche calls instead for a "critical" historical consciousness willing to "judge and condemn the past" in order to free the present generation from its encumbering weight.

As de Man points out, history and modernity relate to each other as antonyms in Nietzsche's essay. History oppresses modernity's desire for originality and change, and modernity must, in order to come into being, assert itself against the historical past. In this opposition de Man recognizes the "radical impulse that stands behind all genuine modernity." "Modernity," de Man writes, "exists in the form of a desire to wipe out whatever came earlier, in the hope of reaching at last a point of origin that marks a new departure. This combined interplay of deliberate forgetting with an action that is also a new origin reaches the full power of the idea of modernity."

However, as de Man also recognizes, Nietzsche is too subtle a thinker to really believe in a present entirely cleansed of any past. Only in desire or abstraction are past and present, history and modernity, fully separable from each other. The image of the chain, firmly linking past, present, and future, and the image of the growing tree, affirming the continuity of identity through time, run throughout Nietzsche's essay. Not only is the past linked to the present, it is, moreover, constitutive of the present. Given this fact, the destruction of the past that is the precondition of modernity is bound to be, as Nietzsche admits, "a dangerous process, dangerous for life itself. Men and eras that serve life in this manner, by judging and destroying the past, are always dangerous and endangered. For we are inevitably the result of earlier generations. . . . It is not possible to loosen ourselves from this chain." The destruction of the past is dangerous because the past inheres in the present and in ourselves.

It should be clear that Nietzsche is not writing about history considered only as the collective or national past, but equally about the individual's attitude to his experience in time, his relationship to his own past, the power of his memory and his desire to forget. Nietzsche's essay isn't so much a philosophy of history as it is a phenomenological and psychological account of history and modernity as elements in individual consciousness. And it is Nietzsche's ability to bring these issues to a focus in individual consciousness which makes his essay useful to our understanding of Cahan's unhappy hero.

If modernity's murder of the past is parricide, de Man writes, making explicit the psychological current in

Nietzsche's essay, it is also suicide, since the son who turns his hand against his father also strikes at whatever of his father there is in himself. Equally paradoxical is modernity's leap forward toward some absolute origin, since the new can only originate a new history, becoming itself the past from which it had hoped to escape. This turbulent but unbreakable relationship between history and modernity is endlessly *ironic:* its individual ironies born at those moments when the implacable opposition of history and modernity suddenly shifts to reveal the mutual constitution of each by the other, and then again when this new vision of interpellency, continuity, and renewal shifts once more, revealing opposition. De Man captures this irony and also says something marvellously suggestive about this day's modernism—its familiar subject, failure, and its own habitually ironic tone—when he observes that "the modernity of a literary period [may lie in] the manner in which it discovers the impossibility of being modern." We can overhear the modern in the act of uttering its own impossibility when Stephen Dedalus, in that quintessentially modern novel made from cliches and twice-told tales, proclaims: "History is the nightmare from which I am trying to awaken." This is no more than the sleeper's dream talk, not loud enough to awaken him, borne back into the dream.

In David Levinsky, Cahan has imagined a man tempted by the essential modern possibility, which is at the same time the eternal American promise: the fresh start. Levinsky's life in America is dominated by his strenuous efforts to remake himself in some ideal image which combines the immunity of an aristocrat with the power of a magnate. Although he denominates this fantasy self "American," it really stands as a general wish for invulnerability, a desire to escape whatever is conditioning and constraining in experience. Levinsky wishes to escape, most of all, from the past, that portion of experience which insists that identity is not only something to be willed, originated, but something to which one must also submit. Levinsky's denial of his past, his Jewish identity, and his European experience, amounts finally to a disabling self betrayal, an unmaking of the self. Levinsky finds that the past can indeed be destroyed, but it is this destruction which then becomes his inaugurating act: ironically, Levinsky finds his future determined, not only by the past, but by his vehement denial of it. This irony, whereby his denial of his past becomes his past, dogs Levinsky at every turn: we see it clearly in the way his immigrant awkwardness and his self consciousness are compounded by his frantic efforts to appear a real American, supremely at ease in the world. Cruelly, it is Levinsky's exaggerated conformity which, more than anything else, marks him as ineradicably an outsider. A fellow immigrant acknowledges this, in his taunt, "You're awful*ly* grammatical, Levinsky."

The trajectory of Levinsky's American experience describes, then, that double movement of radical aspiration and necessary failure, which in de Man's account is the process whereby the modern discovers its own impossibility. As it takes place in ***David Levinsky*** this process is

at once: concrete, in its treatment of Levinsky's unhappy life history; representative, in the relevance that Levinsky's experience has to the collective history of Jewish immigration (compare the structure of Levinsky's experience in time, his self-making as unmaking, to the structure of this statement by Irving Howe: "The dispersion of the immigrant Jews began the very day they started shaping themselves into a community."); and paradigmatic, in its description of what we might call the phenomenology of being modern and, also, in its depiction of the final effect of this experience on Levinsky's identity, his self-estrangement, a condition of spirit which we recognize as modern in an exemplary way. It is with an eye to each of these aspects of the novel that we can turn now to pursue a reacquaintance with ***David Levinsky***.

The first sixth of the novel is comprised of David Levinsky's reminiscent account of his childhood and adolescence in the provincial Russian city of Antomir. From the death of his father when he is three, David, an only child, is raised by his devoted and strong-minded mother. Her single ambition is that her son become a Talmudic scholar. David undertakes the life of a young Talmudist, spending his days in the synagogue and, as a charity scholar, at religious schools. Ghetto life, impoverished though it is, makes sense to David, the unexamined sense of tradition seen through a child's eyes. Piety, learning, and loyalty to faith and family, are the transcendent values of the community.

Although Cahan does not idealize this traditional life, it clearly manifests the unity of experience which Levinsky's American experience so damagingly lacks. The same values, or at least the imperatives to them, are reiterated at each level of experience: individual, familial, communal, and in the religious institutions of the community. The unity of this culture is preserved by its resistance to change, its orientation toward mythical rather than historical time. The unworldliness of a people in daily contact, through its holy texts, with a mythical past and aspiring to a millenial future is captured in Reb Sender's words to David: "What is this world? A mere curl of smoke for the wind to scatter. Only the other world has substance and reality." Weighed against the other world and eternity, this world and its history are as nothing.

The surrounding Russian state also contributes, in its exclusion and confinement of Jews, to the integrity of the Jewish community and its insulation from history. But at the time of David's young manhood this is changing. A program of russification is in effect. Jewish students are being admitted to Russian schools and being taught, by Gentiles, Russian language and culture. Although David attends no such school this wedge of modernity penetrates the community and touches him. His friend Napthali, a devoted Talmudist, develops a passion for Russian literature and becomes apostate. After the death of David's mother at the hands of a Gentile mob it is a modernized Jewish family, the Minskers, which takes him in. Matilda Minsker, the daughter, is the typical *barishnaya,* the new Jewish woman who speaks Russian, plays the piano, and keeps company with the young *gymnasists*. It is Matilda who gives David his fare to America; but just as important, it is she who introduces David to new standards of love and sex which depend upon the canons of neither the Talmud nor the community nor the family. Even before David arrives in America he is caught between the wheels of contrasting ways of life.

From the moment of Levinsky's departure for America his experience is shaped by the persistence of the past, which he is eager to leave behind, *in* the present. Although by this point an unbeliever, Levinsky is unable to keep from reading psalms and benedictions for his ship's safety. Similarly, on his arrival Levinsky lags oddly behind himself, unable to catch up with and assimilate his new experiences. Of his landing, he writes stiffly, "I am at a loss to convey the peculiar state of mind the experience created in me." As Jules Chametzky has pointed out, Levinsky's account of his first American impressions suffers from a dull, over-literary quality which fails to capture them in their immediacy or take their measure in retrospect. Levinsky offers a static, pictorializing description—"The magnificent verdure of Staten Island, the tender blue of sea and sky, the dignified bustle of passing craft"—which replaces perception with cliche, demonstrating Levinsky's failure to fully grasp his own experience.

In a famous sentence, Marx has written that history is the formation of the five senses down to the present. But the possibility remains that the senses will not keep pace with history, that perception may not be adequate to the moment. Levinsky's summary metaphor for the spectacle of the new world, "It unfolded itself like a divine revelation"—shows that he still sees with old world eyes.

Cahan's writing here seems entirely right, true to the difficulty of any attempt to grasp powerful, unprecedented experience and true, no doubt, to the real disorientations of the immigrant's arrival. However, Levinsky's failure at this moment to comprehend his experience exemplifies a defining element in his character, his persistent distance from himself, from his true feelings and ambitions. This passage prefigures the alienation that characterizes his entire life, the hyperconsciousness which inhibits some truer self-understanding, his perverse success in pursuit of his own unhappiness. In addition, this passage, showing as it does how the past inheres in and shapes the present—something Levinsky vigorously denies until his unhappiness forces him to admit it—suggests that Levinsky participates in that typical self-estrangement of the modern will to self-origination, whereby "in separating itself from the past, it has at the same time severed itself from the present."

Levinsky marks the self-originating quality of his enterprises by referring to his arrival as a "second birth," and to himself as "a new born babe." From the first, he does all he can to abet the transformation from "greenhorn," a word that rings cruelly and contemptuously in his ears, to

"real Yankee." He goes about memorizing Americanisms ("Good looks aren't everything. Beauty is skin deep, and handsome is as handsome does;"), trying to eradicate his "Talmudic gestures," and dressing in the bowler-hatted American style of the day. He attends night school with "religious devotion," straining to emulate the *th* of his teacher's born-in-America diction. Despite his aversion to their sound, he masters the difficult *satisfaction, think,* and *because* but learns from Bender (a pun here), his teacher, that the real American bywords are "Dil-i-gence, perr-severance, tenacity!"

Levinsky's frantic self-acculturation amounts to a wholesale assault on the integrity of his European experience and identity. Even the organism is open to the prospect of americanization: "That I was not born in America was something like a physical defect that asserted itself in many disagreeable ways—a physical defect which, alas! no surgeon in the world was capable of removing." In shaving his beard and his earlocks, Levinsky removes as much as he can.

Only when David Levinsky can look at himself and finally say "I scarcely recognized myself," does he feel truly American. But with the new man comes a new life. Levinsky has kept some tally of his experience; he knows that the glory of his new clothes has been paid for with his brutalization as a peddler: "Nor was I unaware of certain unlovable traits that were unavoidably developing in my own self under these influences. And while human nature was thus growing smaller, the human world was growing larger, more complex, more heartless, and more interesting." As the world expands in interest, in possibility—for money, for sexual adventure, for personal aggrandizement—something valuable is diminished. The bargain of modern life counters the promise of religion, the things of the flesh or those of the spirit. In choosing the former, Levinsky denies the Old World and the values which are still deeply his own, and so denies a part of himself.

Even before leaving Russia, Levinsky had thought of himself as no longer a believer. However, in America certain elements of his orthodox faith persist, transformed. The sixth chapter of the novel is entitled "My Temple." Levinsky's new temple is the house of man, CCNY. The College's buildings and students become objects of religious veneration: "I would pause and gaze at its red, ivy-clad walls, mysterious high windows, humble spires; I would stand watching the students on the campus and around the great doors, and go my way, with a heart full of reverence, envy and hope, with a heart full of quiet ecstasy." The word rings with cabalistic significance: "College! The sound was forever buzzing in my ear. The seven letters were forever floating before my eyes. They were a magic group, a magic whisper." Although Cahan intends some irony at the expense of Cahan's displaced piety for profane knowledge, this is Levinsky's one chance to be true, in some form, to his mother's hope that he become a man of learning, and to be true to himself, to "the better man in me, to what was purest in my thoughts and most sacred in my emotions." But in point of these aspirations, Levinsky is destined to become a Jude, and what is worse, a Jewish Babbitt. *Destined,* is the wrong word, though. Although Levinsky blames his fall (recorded in "The Destruction of My Temple") on a single fatal accident, the point at which he abandons his plan of working just long enough to earn his tuition is characterized by decision as well as destiny.

While working at the stitching machine of his employer, Jeff Mannheimer, a German Jew (and so a rival), of American birth (and so envied), Levinsky accidentally spills a bottle of milk on some coats. Mannheimer flies at him, chastises him, and embarrasses him in front of his shopmates. Burning with humiliation and desire for revenge, he decides to steal the designer who has made Mannheimer's fortune and enter the "great, daring game of life" (business) on his own. In later years, Levinsky is to blame his disappointments as well as his riches on the fall of a bottle of milk.

Here is one of the trademarks of naturalism, the tiny event whose *raison d'être* is cosmic but whose repercussions are all too human—the click of the safe door in *Sister Carrie,* for example. However, those readers who have imagined that Cahan is writing as a naturalist here have overlooked his rather broad joke on Levinsky, crying over spilt milk. It is only Levinsky's cowardly desire to deny responsibility for his own actions which leads him to blame Fate. Cahan is far too attuned to the contingencies of character, circumstance, and history, and far too interested in his character's psychology to take very seriously the determinist explanations and facile pessimism of naturalism. It is not Cahan, but Levinsky who chooses an oversimplified and inadequate explanation of his own behavior. In this incident, Levinsky acts with his typical perversity, first deciding against his own best hopes for himself and then rationalizing and mystifying his own action. In this way, Levinsky proceeds to make a life which, despite his success, seems not so much lived as inflicted upon him and an identity which meets itself as a stranger.

As Cahan makes plentifully clear, Levinsky's fate is not determined by a single slip, but multiply determined by his own character. Even in his Antomir childhood, Levinsky's emotional life has been characterized by proud self-pity, envy, and vengefulness. In one of his juvenile daydreams David plans the comeuppance of a cruel school master:

> In my helplessness I would seek comfort in dreams of becoming a great man some day, rich and mighty, and avenging myself on him. Behold! Shmerl the Pincher is running after me, cringingly begging my pardon, and I, omnipotent and formidable, say to him: "Do you remember how you pinched the life out of me for nothing? Away with you, you cruel beast!"

With its exaggeration and magical transformations, this rings true as child's fantasy; yet, the fantasy comes true.

David's mother is his avenging angel and, sure enough, discovering her son black and blue, she lights out after the villianous Shmerl. Even with his mother's death, David's pity is reserved for himself, his mother again expected to play the role of intercessor:

> I would shut my eyes and vision my mother looking at me from her grave, her heart contracted with anguish and pity for her famished orphan. . . . It would give me satisfaction to denounce the whole town to her. "Ah, I have got you!" I seemed to say to the people of Antomir. "The ghost of my mother and the whole Other World see you in all your heartlessness. You can't wriggle out of it." This was my refuge. I reveled in it.

Perpetuated into adulthood, these feelings constitute a deep vein of childishness in Levinsky's character. Levinsky is dominated by those reactive emotions which express a desire to annul the slights and wounds of the past, to reach back and punish one's first enemies. However, Levinsky's resentful animus against the past binds him to it, brings it into the present and, with cruel irony, determines his future. As Levinsky admits, of the Mannheimer episode, "I was bound to make good, 'just for spite.'" Of course, Levinsky's unhappy success spites no one but himself. His inability to place himself in some adequate relation to the past, neither denying it nor wholly submitting to it, contributes to his failure of adulthood. In his complaint, at the end of his autobiography— "I pity myself for a victim of circumstances"—it is hard not to hear the whine of a disappointed child.

Levinsky's passivity before his own childishness and pettiness, his failure to win through to the best in himself, rather than circumstance, destroys his temple. The special pathos of his life is that as David Levinsky watches with regret he becomes exactly what he hoped not to be—a man of business, not letters, a parvenu boor.

Once in the world of business all questions of ideals and ethics are subjugated to the ethos of Success. For the businessman with an intellectual bent the age supplies a practical philosophy, Social Darwinism. The factory is "one of the battlefields in our struggle for existence." A Rivington Street sage offers a counterpart to Dreiser's lobster and squid: "The world is not a wedding-feast, Levinsky. It is a big barn-yard full of chickens and they are scratching one another, and scrambling over one another. Why? Because there are little heaps of grain in the yard and each chicken wants to get as much of it as possible." Levinsky reads Spencer and Darwin and chooses his theories according to his needs. "It was as though all the wonders of learning, acumen, ingenuity, and assiduity displayed in these works had been intended to establish my title as one of the victors of Existence." One of Nature's elect, Levinsky is not above employing scabs, stealing designs, and spying on the unions. His fortune is raised on a foundation of cheap labor.

Levinsky's education in the American ethos is an education in cynicism and deceit, and the discrepancy between

American ideal and American reality contributes some leavening ironies to the novel. In his "greenhornhood," exposed for the first time to the machinations of ward politics, Levinsky "formed a conception of political parties as of a kind of competing business companies whose specialty was to make millions by ruling some big city, levying tribute on fallen women, thieves and liquor dealers, doing favors to friends and meting out punishment to foes." In his American maturity, Levinsky himself adopts this too-shrewd Yankee apothegm: "If you have his confidence, you have him by the throat." He conforms to the type of the two-faced businessman, the "cheerful competitor" who is as much back-stabber as back-slapper. He learns to smoke "the cigar of peace and goodwill" with a rival salesman, all the while gauging their shared duplicity: "He seemed to like me. But then he hated me, too. As for me, I reciprocated both feelings."

Levinsky's final initiation into Babbittry occurs, appropriately, in the dining-car of a west-bound train. After contributing his share of shop talk and dirty stories in conversation with some Gentile salesmen, he joins them for dinner. He steers the conversation to politics and receives their attention and, it seems, their acceptance. But even in his joy Levinsky must struggle to restrain his European gesticulations. He is all the while "aware that it was 'aristocratic American' food, that I was in the company of well-dressed American Gentiles, eating and conversing with them, a nobleman among noblemen." With this, the epiphany of his acculturation, Levinsky is taken to the cold steel heart of a new, faintly inhuman world: "I throbbed with love for America . . . The electric lights, the soft red glint of the mahogany walls, the whiteness of the table linen, the silent efficiency of the colored waiters, coupled with the fact that all was speeding onward through the night, made me feel as though I were partaking of a repast in an enchanted palace."

If Levinsky could disappear into this wonderland all would, I suppose, be well. But he is still David of Antomir, the Talmud student, his mother's son. The self-consciousness which he cannot banish is the warning "You do not belong." Flushed with his companions' acceptance of Mr. Levinsky the American businessman, he asks himself, "Can it be that I am I?". Walking away from the table he wonders, "Had I talked too much? Had I made a nuisance of myself?"

The way in which Levinsky courts acceptance is slavish and unsavory. Through his life he broods on some unknown inner world and finds only the half-solace of position and prestige. But even though his emotional defeats are clumsy and the saddened tenderness with which he regards himself is often repellent, his unhappiness speaks of genuine pain and truly regretted loss. He writes, "My wretched boyhood appeals to me as a sick child does to its mother." David Levinsky's appeal, to the Gentile "noblemen," to those whose respect he tries to buy, is for love. His real affliction is lovelessness. He makes no true friend, has no family, and is welcome in no home. He arrived in America homesick and lovesick

(over the loss of Matilda Minsker) and this, in a sense, is his condition throughout his American life. Leslie Fiedler has recognized this, calling *David Levinsky*'s theme "the failure of love." He says of Levinsky, "some deep impotence dogs him . . . he is somehow sexually or affectively incapacitated." Isaac Rosenfeld suggests the same when he writes, of Levinsky's women, "He goes among them mainly to find a substitute for his mother."

In his childhood, as an adored son, David learned that the place for love was in the home. The orthodox law of the community supports this: "To be 'in love' with a girl who was an utter stranger to you was something which only Gentiles or 'modern' Jews might indulge in." Even through the changes of David's adolescence, sexuality remains associated only with the family and marriage: "the word 'girl' had acquired a novel sound to me, one full of disquieting charm. The same was true of such words as 'sister,' 'niece,' or 'bride,' but not of 'woman'." This pushes David toward a not unusual adolescent meditation, but one which seems crucial in terms of his later life:

> Kissing meant being fond of one. I enjoyed kissing my mother, for instance. Now I certainly was not fond of Esther [a neighbor, his own age]. I was sure that I hated her. Why, then, was I impelled to kiss her? How could I hate and be fond of her at once? I went on reasoning it out, Talmud fashion, till I arrived at the conclusion that there were two kinds of kisses: the kiss of affection and the kiss of Satan.

Levinsky's failure to integrate the sexual and the affective, the failure that Freud called "the most prevalent form of degradation in erotic life," makes a shambles of his love life. He visits prostitutes but, even though he feels he is being unreasonable, despises both himself and them. He pursues women he abhors and women he cannot have: older women when he is young, young women when he is old, a Socialist when he is rich, married women, and, at the last, a Gentile. The family is the one ideal that he has clung to through his life. And his inability to find love and a home is the final measure of his spiritual failure and sterility. When Levinsky reaches his fortieth year, despairing—"without knowing who I worked for"—he looks, desperately now, to find a meaning for his life in love. He writes:

> The vague portrait of a woman in the abstract seemed never to be absent from my mind. Coupled with that portrait was a similarly vague image of a window and a table set for dinner. That, somehow, was my symbol of a home. Home and women were one, a complex charm joining them into an inseparable force.

This picture of nurturance and security suggests that Levinsky's longed-for home is not really a hope for the future but a recollection. When he plans a honeymoon that never happens he imagines a trip to Antomir and thinks to name his daughter after his mother. Despite his changes in worldly circumstance, Levinsky's past, his motherland, remains hugely important to his inner life.

However, when Levinsky, sick of his barren life, tries to return in feeling and imagination to the past, he bathes it in a falsifying nostalgia. He writes, "My heart was still in Antomir, in the good old Antomir of synagogues and Talmud scholars and old fashioned marriages, not," he adds, "of college students, revolutionaries, and Matildas." Levinsky idealizes and simplifies, redrawing the past to suit his present needs. But he can't even be true to this idealization; he contributes to the Sons of Antomir Benefit Society only to secure a supply of non-union labor, compounding his sentimentality with hypocrisy.

During the last third of the novel nearly every figure from Levinsky's early days reappears, but each reunion, instead of restoring the past, deprives Levinsky of the satisfactions of memory and mocks his nostalgia. Shmerl the Pincher reappears, a ragged and puny Lower East Side peddler, hardly a fitting object for the spite which has helped goad Levinsky to success. Levinsky reencounters his night school teacher, his first partner, and his first business rival, but instead of establishing some more feeling relationship with these men who had been so important to him, Levinsky can only think to hire them, humiliating them and widening the distance he had hoped to close. When Matilda Minsker, a socialist now, arrives in New York, it is inevitable that Levinsky should visit her dressed in his most opulent fur coat and win her disdain as a bourgeois exploiter of labor.

The reunion Levinsky arranges with Gitelson, a "ship brother" who shared the crossing twenty-five years earlier, is marred by the awkwardness of the two men, one a success and one a failure. Levinsky looks at Gitelson, giddy on a single glass of champagne, and thinks that the Waldorf is no place for such a man; but he also admits to himself his own discomfort: "At the bottom of my heart I cow before waiters to this day. . . . They make me feel as if my expensive clothes and ways ill become me." Both men are marked by a new gracelessness, and their attempt to commemorate the past seems instead to prove its annihilation.

Levinsky finds that the past, having been denied, cannot be willed back into existence, anymore than faith once lost can be reclaimed. What remains of his past is blighted by sentiment or simply false or trivial. He savors matzo balls with "the genuine Antomir taste;" a way of life has become a fragment of ethnicity, and ethnicity is reduced to a gustatory phenomenon—a matter of what you eat, not who you are.

Estranged from his past, as choice and circumstance have made him, Levinsky is estranged from himself. With the loss of Levinsky's real feelings there comes in place of them a crowd of ersatz emotions. In this passage Levinsky woos a shopgirl to whom he has already proposed; they are both aware that he is attracted only by her savings, which he hopes will start him on a career:

> Poor Gussie! She was not a pretty girl, and she did not interest me in the least. Yet at this moment I was drawn to her. The brooding, plaintive tones which resounded around us had a bewitching effect on me. [They are on an East River dock.] It filled me with love. Gussie was a woman to me now. My hand sought hers. It was a proffer of endearment, for my soul was praying for communion with her.
>
> She withdrew her hand. "This should not be done in a hurry either," she explained, pensively.
>
> "Gussie! I swear to you you're dear to me. Can't you believe me?"
>
> The singing night was too much for her. She yielded to my arms. Urged on by the chill air, we clung together in a delirium of lovemaking. There were passionate embraces and kisses. I felt that her thin, dried up lips were not to my taste, but I went on kissing them with unfeigned fervor.
>
> As I trudged along through the swarming streets on my way home the predominant feeling in my heart was one of physical distaste. Poor thing! I felt that marrying her was out of the question.

Besides the duplicity caused by sexual urgency, Levinsky's feelings are further confused by the attraction of Gussie's money and the persistence of his old-fashioned standards of sexual behavior. His attempt at cold-hearted, modern indulgence is subverted and muddled by the traditional beliefs which are still stubbornly his. Ultimately, Levinsky is left without any solid ground for his feelings, which are all, his warmth and his coolness alike, equally inauthentic. But the unsettling thing is that it's Levinsky himself who is telling this all to us. His lies are conscious ones and his inauthenticity is, exactly, a matter of his exaggerated consciousness. Levinsky's lying confessions, and much of his memoir could be considered just that, make him a character not out of Tolstoy or Chekhov, those fellow realists with whom Cahan is so often compared, but out of Dostoevsky. Lionel Trilling's description of Dostoevskian man rings true to a great deal of Levinsky's behavior: "stronger than his desire for respect is his appetite for demonstrative self-abasement; his ego, betraying its proper function, turns on itself . . . at once inviting shame and achieving shamelessness."

At one moment Levinsky repudiates the insincerities he finds all around him, "sham ecstasy, sham sympathy, sham smiles, sham laughter." But it is just these falsehoods which infest his life, and Cahan, with a skill that has been little noticed, uses the first-person narrative to emphasize this fact. Levinsky's "autobiobiography" is dotted with the tag-lines of bogus emotion: "———, I said feelingly"; "———, I added mournfully";"———, I exclaimed, with a thrill of genuine pity";"———, I cooed." He becomes expert in the gestures he hates, "the unsmiling smile."

When Dora, the one woman in his life whom Levinsky feels he genuinely loves, professes her love for him, he is "somewhat bored" by her earnestness and put off by her diction. Although Levinsky threatens suicide when she ends their affair, he is distracted by trifles from her grief; they are walking in Stuyvesant Park: "The revolting sight of the dog-faced fellow who was ogling Dora so fascinated me that it interfered with my listening to Dora." In his hero, "distracted from distraction by distraction," Cahan anticipates no less a modernist than Eliot.

The quality missing from Levinsky's feelings is what Erik Erikson has called "actualness," and what replaces it is a self-consciousness which not only signals the absence of real emotion but which prevents it. There is, of course, the self-consciousness ("I am always more or less conscious of my good clothes") of the poor Jewish boy who is anxious to be taken for something he's not. This is Levinsky in the dining car. Yet, beyond this, Levinsky comes to display a new and pernicious self-consciousness without immediate cause. In this passage, Levinsky is in the Catskills pursuing the much younger Anna Tevkin. There is a magnificent sunset which she comments on appreciatively. Levinsky writes:

> I discovered a note of consciousness in her rapture, something like a patronizing approval of the sky by one who looked at it with a professional eye. Nevertheless, I felt that my soul was cringing before her.
>
> An epigram occured to me, something about the discrepancy between the spiritual quality of the sunset and the after-supper satisfaction of the onlookers. I essayed to express it, but was so embarrassed that I made a muddle of my English. Miss Tevkin took no notice of the remark.
>
> The sunset was transformed into a thousand lumps of pearl, here and there edged with flame. In some places the pearl thinned away, dissolving into the color of the sky, while the outline of the lump remained—a map of glowing tracery on a ground of the subtlest blue. Drifts of gold were gleaming, blazing, going out. A vast heap of silver caught fire. The outlined map disappeared, its place being taken by a raised one, with continents, islands, mountains, and seas of ravishing azure.
>
> What was the power behind this sublime spectacle? Where did it come from? What did it all mean?

What Levinsky sees as Anna's "consciousness" is equally his own. Not only is he estranged from the girl, but from Creation, which he watches dissolving and reforming before him. Whereas formerly his "relations with God were of a personal and rather familiar character," he is now confronted by a Creator of unfathomable dimension. The many dislocations of Levinsky's life have been compounded until he is now out of sympathy with the universe, with some first principle of life.

At this moment Levinsky suffers what can only be called *alienation,* that compound condition of consciousness, identity, and the self in relation to others which, as melancholia was the typical ailment of the Elizabethans, is the classic affliction of our times. Apart from the notable confusions that surround the word, it can be agreed that,

as Istvan Meszaros has noted, "'Alienation' is an eminently historical concept." Although there does not seem to be any reason why alienation, as a condition, could not be suffered in any age, as a *concept* it belongs distinctively to the post-nineteenth century world that has radically historized its understanding of man and experience. Alienation is a condition of historical man; it measures the discrepancies between the past and what has been lost of it, between the present and what can be hoped for it. And Levinsky here experiences one of those characteristic moments of modern consciousness—exemplary recognitions by Nietzsche and Virginia Woolf immediately come to mind—in which the death of the old, the fact of irreversible change, has been categorically realized. Gone so long, there is no longer any way home.

It's difficult to think of Levinsky standing embarrassed before the sunset as a World Historical figure, but I don't think it would be a mistake to think of this as a World Historical moment; Levinsky stands at a crux of history—the end of the old dispensation and the beginning of purely secular life. I use these grandiose phrases premeditatedly, since it is Hegel, the "historian" of such crises, who is particularly apposite here. At this moment Levinsky experiences alienation in one of Hegel's primary senses: he feels man and his world to be external to Spirit. Spirit appears to Levinsky precisely as what Hegel calls, in the *Phenomenology of Spirit,* "picture thinking," thinking that registers only objectivity and estrangement, the same sort of perception that characterized Levinsky's stilted description of his landing. Furthermore, Levinsky's behavior throughout his life identifies him as what Ilegel calls a "hero of flattery," whose peculiar heroism (in Hegel's special sense of that word) it is to face society in a posture which combines fawning complicity and secret antagonism. The hero of flattery is the discrepant middle term, the man who is no longer loyal to the old "noble" life of obedience and servitude (David's life in Antomir) but who has not found it possible to become the man suitable for the new "base" life of bold opposition and autonomy. In this connection, it may be of more than passing interest that Levinsky calls the gods of his new life, the gentile travelling salesmen, "noblemen."

There is no need to suggest that Cahan's novel is directly indebted to Hegel. Although Cahan assuredly came into contact with Hegel in some form, at least through Marx, any certainty on this point will have to await Moses Rischin's forthcoming biography of Cahan. In any case, the abstruse, systematic quality of Hegel's thought seems foreign to Cahan the realist. What should be stressed, however, is **David Levinsky**'s kinship with a tradition, a *particular* analysis of modernity which does owe a debt to Hegel. This is the tradition of secularized Jewish writers who, building on a rich German canon, raised a virtual ontology of estrangement on the historical fact of their own marginality. This tradition includes not only Marx, but Georg Simmel, the German sociologist who, himself forced by anti-semitism to work on the peripheries of his profession, established a sociology of the marginal in essays on "The Stranger" and "Secrecy in Social Life."

Here we can turn to Georg Lukacs, a late member of this tradition. Compare the famous opening passage of *The Theory of the Novel*, Lukacs' paean to the lost "integrated civilisations" and lament for our fall into philosophy, with Levinsky's disintegrated consciousness at sunset:

> Happy are those ages when the starry sky is the map of all possible paths—ages whose paths are illuminated by the light of the stars. Everything in such ages is new and yet familiar, full of adventure and yet their own. The world is wide and yet it is like home, for the fire that burns in the soul is of the same essential nature as the stars; the world and the self, the light and the fire, are sharply distinct, yet they never become permanent strangers to one another, for the fire is the soul of all light and all fire clothes itself in light. Thus each action of the soul becomes meaningful and rounded in this duality: complete in meaning—in *sense*—and complete for the senses; rounded because its action separates itself from it and, having become itself, finds a centre of its own and draws a closed circumference round itself. "Philosophy is really homesickness," says Novalis: "it is the urge to be at home everywhere."

In his Preface to *The Theory of the Novel,* added nearly fifty years after writing this remarkable passage, which dreams of healing discrepancies like those which fracture Levinsky's experience, Lukacs confessed that in his youthful work he "was not looking for a new literary form but, quite explicitly, for a 'new world.'" Although none of Lukacs' various national and intellectual immigrations took him to David Levinsky's new world, Levinsky's experiences can, I think, augment our sense of Lukacs' thought in its historical situation. Lukacs and Levinsky share a common "structure of feeling" in which American experience and European thought meet, and seeing what is shared between them allows us to recognize *David Levinsky* as a novel that has a place in one of the main traditions of modern imagination.

However, the differences between Lukacs' essay and Cahan's novel are equally instructive. Lukacs wrote at the start of World War I, which seemed to him the final catastrophe of bourgeois civilization. At this moment, Lukacs turned to the vision of a lost ideal, the "integrated civilisation" of Greece and its epic, the form adequate to totality. What is weakest in Lukacs' essay is his nostalgia and, his "hunger for wholeness," which Peter Gay has described as a wish common to Lukacs' intellectual kin in the anxious society of late Wilhelmian Germany. As Lukacs very nearly admits in the 1962 Preface, the elements of idealism in his essay, especially his neo-Kantian attempt to discover the super-historical essences of genres, amount to a desire to escape from "concrete socio-historical realities."

Like Lukacs, Cahan wrote in response to a historical crisis, the entry of east European Jewry into modern, bourgeois society. However, the lyrical, elegiac mood in which Lukacs contemplates the lost past, what Nietzsche would call Lukacs' commitment to "monumental" history, is absent from Cahan's novel. The only nostalgia in Cahan's novel is Levinsky's, and Cahan is unsparing in his mockery of it. Such nostalgia is dishonest, Cahan seems to say, when it denies the hard fact that for Levinsky's generation there is simply no viable world to which one can return. On the other hand, Cahan offers no easy faith in progress. Cahan does nothing to suggest that any law of history compels the future to compensate Levinsky for the loss of his past or the emptiness of his present. In *David Levinsky* the facile optimism which would view Levinsky as a member of a "transitional generation"—that first generation whose sacrifices are to be redeemed by the advances of the next—is refuted by the fact that Levinsky is most damaged in his ability to feel, to love, to marry and father a successor.

Cahan's imagination of the immigrant experience accommodates its ironies: the way in which a boldly conceived new life can be molded by the past it has denied, and the way in which the past, when frantically clutched at, can recede out of reach. For Cahan, unlike Lukacs, past and present are not so easily separable from one another nor so confidently judged. In his own tough mindedness about "concrete sociohistorical realities," the skepticism which allows him to include, without either despairing or offering any easy solace, all the discrepancies of Levinsky's experience, Cahan achieves a negativity which, especially in comparison with Lukacs' uncritical longing for a mythical past, seems characteristically modern.

The issues raised by *David Levinsky* expand beyond the rich historical particularity in which the novel is rooted and beyond the literary labels—naturalism, regionalism, sociological realism—that have too often confined it. The question *David Levinsky* builds to is a canonical American question. Levinsky finally asks himself "Am I happy?" But with his answer, "No," America fails on its own terms. With this completed catastrophe, the loss of the old and the failure of the new, come the perenially open questions, not only of the immigrant experience, but of "homeless" modernity.

Susan Kress (essay date 1983)

SOURCE: "Women and Marriage in Abraham Cahan's Fiction," in Studies in *American Jewish Literature,* edited by Daniel Walden, Vol. 3, 1983, pp. 26-39.

[*In the following essay, Kress discusses Cahan's portrayal of women and marriage, arguing that his characters' ambivalence about marriage parallels their ambivalence about assimilation in America.*]

Much of Abraham Cahan's fiction reflects upon the institution of marriage in the lives of his Jewish immigrant characters at the turn of the century. Unlike writers of sentimental fiction, Cahan does not focus exclusively on the vicissitudes of courtship prior to a happily-ever-after marriage presumably to be enjoyed by the characters after the book is closed; rather, as the realist praised by William Dean Howells, he shows us glimpses of courtship in a sweatshop, of difficult married life, of the pain of adjustment to life in the new world. In Cahan's fiction, the terrors of being unmarried are balanced against the claustrophobia of the married condition, and it is possible to see the immigrants' ambivalence about assimilation mirrored in the individual's—and especially the woman's—attitude toward marriage.

While Cahan does not create the strikingly bold women protagonists that we find in, say, Ibsen, he nevertheless avoids stereotyped portraits, frequently expresses the woman's perspective, and creates a series of memorable female characters. In the following essay, I hope to show that, throughout his work, Cahan presents a thorough analysis of the limitations of the institution of marriage, with particular emphasis on the point of view of women. I have chosen to deal primarily with those short stories written in English which treat marriage directly and avoid chronological order, because, in my view, Cahan's treatment of this subject does not change significantly during the course of his fictional career. Cahan's portrayal of character, his choice of interior settings, his depiction of enclosed city space, indeed the very shape of his narratives, compel attention to the constrictions of life for the immigrant woman; moreover, Cahan the realist not only challenges the assumptions and conventions of romantic fiction but also tests and defines the limits of the kind of realism advocated by Howells.

"The Imported Bridegroom" (1898) demonstrates the typical contours of a Cahan story about marriage. There are three major characters in the story and it will be helpful for our present purposes to tell the story from the point of view of each of them in turn. First the father. Asriel Stroon, a devoted father and successful businessman, suffers, as the story opens, from spiritual emptiness. He goes back to his home town in Russia, and is impressed by the brilliance of Shaya, a young Talmudic scholar. In the traditional way, he wants to choose the bridegroom for his daughter, and, spending a good deal of money to settle the competition for the scholar, he imports him to America, as a husband for his daughter and as spiritual insurance for himself in the hereafter. The daughter, Flora, is initially unwilling to accept Shaya, but then seems satisfied to marry him, and all goes well until Stroon discovers Shaya forsaking his spiritual heritage by entering libraries and eating unkosher food in a restaurant. Stroon denounces both Flora and Shaya, but Flora manages to bring about a reconciliation. The father then decides he will be "born again" by marrying his housekeeper, Tamara, and living in Israel, thus enacting in his own life the resolution he has wanted to control for his daughter, and ensuring his spiritual life, not by importing a bridegroom but by exporting himself and his new devout wife. Thus, at this level, all ends happily

What about the bridegroom? We know less of him since we are rarely granted access to his consciousness; he is

an *illoui,* a prodigy of deep learning and spirituality, but also fond of a certain kind of mischievous fun ("he was detected giving snuff to a pig, and then participating with much younger boys in a race over the bridge." He comes to America with Stroon, allows his clothes to be exchanged for those of American fashion, meets Flora, and suffers her obvious distaste and distress. Nevertheless, in pursuing a secular education, he wins her love and prepares to become the doctor of her (and now his) dreams. All this must, of course, be kept secret from the father, but Stroon discovers the truth and then the guilty pair wed hastily. At the end of the story, when Flora tells him she has won her father's grudging approval, Shaya is delighted, but yet more interested in a meeting of his intellectual discussion group to whom he introduces Flora, and whose company he is most reluctant to leave even though Flora feels they should be celebrating their new union. Thus, for Shaya, too, the end is a happy one: he has a wife who pleases him, a handsome marriage settlement, and the opportunity to pursue his newly chosen studies.

Now for Flora's perspective. The story begins with a brief closeup of a young girl sitting comfortably before a parlor stove "enveloped in a kindly warmth." The imagery of dusk, however, creeping into the room "in almost visible waves" prefigures the enclosure and envelopment of the story's formal closure. The narrative situation is a familiar one: a young woman, unmarried, is thinking about the sort of husband she wants—in this case a successful young doctor who will provide a life for her that will be very different, in her mind, from those of the other Mott or Bayard Street girls who marry businessmen. Within the terms of the social world she knows, her script is both predictable and acceptable, and, despite her father's opposition, she will succeed, for "when she took a resolve she could not imagine herself otherwise than carrying it out, sooner or later." But the imported bridegroom produced by her father is a blow to all these ambitions: a throwback to a Russian/Jewish past and not a passport to an American future, he fails to claim her interest. By a witty twist, however, the young man turns out to be not only handsome and appealing but also willing, in spite of the father's wishes, to educate himself in the values of secular American society, according to the daughter's desires. All seems to go well. Flora even manages to win her father's consent to the union. So far, she has managed to manipulate both men she has Shaya; Shaya will become a doctor; her father approves the marriage. All should end happily for Flora, too, but the final scene shows Flora, now tied to Shaya by marriage, but shut out of his life. He introduces her to his discussion group, and she feels "overcome by the stuffy, overheated atmosphere of the misshapen apartment," and as if she has been "kidnaped into the den of some terrible creatures." She is devastated by feelings of "desolation and jealousy . . . of the whole excited crowd, and of Shaya's entire future, from which she seemed excluded."

The story enacts conflict on a number of levels. The father's desire to import the values of his Russian/Jewish background into secular American life, his wish to recapture his past (underlined by the shift to the present tense when he visits his home town, Pravly), his conflict with the changing values and aspirations of the younger generation, and, finally, the opposing needs of Shaya and Flora are never resolved. The conventional solution to fictional plot complication is, of course, marriage, and so all these tensions build about and within the institution of marriage. But this story, while it ends in two marriages, is not fully resolved: the father's marriage, seen as it is from his point of view, promises resolution, the daughter's marriage, seen from hers, is a dead end, a stifling and suffocating conclusion that foreshadows the exclusions and constrictions of the life to come.

From this analysis, we can begin to appreciate the radical differences between the lives of men and women in this story. For the men, there is space and movement across continents; for the woman, enclosure, stasis. Shaya quickly masters the geography of the city ("in less than six months he knew the city and its suburbs much better than Flora"), and investigates the Astor Library ("the 'holy soul' was clearly forging ahead of her in a world which she considered all her own"); Flora is almost always pictured in interiors, protected and confined. When Stroon's first plan for spiritual regeneration fails, he has other options; when Shaya comes to America, the whole world of secular knowledge and attainment is open to him; Flora's imagination is, however, controlled by a vision of the kind of husband she can marry and her future is a blank. Yet Cahan chooses to give great weight to Flora's point of view. The story begins and ends with her, and the final shape of the story is determined by Flora's sense of the limitations of her future. But there is irony in the form, too; for if Flora's opportunities are circumscribed, so, too, are the freedoms of Asriel Stroon and Shaya enclosed by the nature of the fictional form, the enveloping perspective of Flora.

"The Apostate of Chego-Chegg" (1899) also emphasizes the woman's point of view, and recounts the tale of two recent immigrants from Poland settled in a Long Island village. The protagonist is Michalina who, married to a Catholic, has renounced her Jewish religion and been baptized as a Catholic. The story explores the conflicts suffered by Michalina, married to a Gentile yet still attached to her Jewish faith and the tradition of her father. Complication is introduced in the character of Nehemiah, a rabbi, who subsequently gives up his faith, falls in love with Michalina, and offers to marry her. Michalina discovers that, according to Jewish law, her marriage to a Catholic is invalid and exists only in American secular law as well as, presumably, in Catholic law, and she decides to marry Nehemiah and return to her Jewish faith. Accordingly, the women of the Jewish community collect the money for a passage to England for Michalina, Nehemiah, and her baby daughter. But, while the secret preparations are going forward, Wincas, the husband, returns early from work, and Michalina realizes, amidst the curses of the community, that she cannot leave him.

The first thing to note about the story is that there are two apostates, Nehemiah and Michalina, but only Michalina is accounted as such:

> Disclaim Judaism as Nehemiah would, he could not get the Jews to disclaim him; while Michalina was more alien to the Mosaic community than any of its Christian neighbors.

Of course, Michalina's outcast status is a result of the fact that she has not only renounced her faith as Nehemiah has, but also converted to another; this makes him an *appikoros* and her a *meshumedeste*. But if we think further about Nehemiah and Michalina, we see that Cahan has made clear the difference between not only an atheist and a convert but also a man and a woman. At one point in the story, Nehemiah attempts to rouse Michalina from her despair by claiming, "'There are no Jews and no Gentiles, missus. This is America. All are noblemen here, and all are brothers'." Indeed, the words are telling, but he might have added that all women are daughters and wives. Nehemiah has given up his faith as a result of his own choice, his own spiritual development, an inner conviction that it is right and necessary for him to do so. Michalina has relinquished her faith because she has married Wincas and must take on the faith of her Gentile husband; it is unlikely that a man would convert for reasons of marriage—his wife would normally take his faith.

Indeed, the tale as a whole, while it seems to be the particular story of a woman conflicted in her loyalty among two faiths and three men—her father, Wincas, and Nehemiah—is rather a representative story of the social control of women by the patriarchy. Michalina is born with one name, Rivka (or Rebecca), assigned to her by her father, and when she gives up that identity, he mourns her as if she were dead, as if she *were* not. When she marries Wincas, she takes the name of her husband, converts to his faith, and is baptized with a new "christian" name. The conversion is a rich, suggestive metaphor for a woman's marriage in that the wife, like the convert, takes on the man's name, faith, community, his very identity. Michalina is treated as an outcast by her Jewish community, but, ironically she is only doing what every married woman must do. Her only way of resolving her conflicts is to marry again, this time the Jew, Nehemiah, which act will serve to "reconvert" her to the faith of her father. Now some aspects of this analysis would hold if Michalina were male, but the point is that the story illustrates supremely well a woman's lack of individual identity and autonomy in marriage, her constant reference to her father, her husband, her community, and her denial of self.

When Michalina decides to return to Wincas, the act is presented as a gesture of love, compassion, and loyalty. Surely it is; but surely, too, it is partly a recognition that to turn to another man in order to return to the faith of her father (and let us note that Michalina has no mother, that she married Wincas not so much for himself but in "revenge," against her stepmother, for in this world women are enemies in their competition for the favors of men) will bring her no closer to understanding and achieving her own identity and her own needs, no closer to any genuine resolution of her internal conflict. Since the woman's conversion takes place for the sake of another, she cannot solve the confusion between what she wants for herself and what she wants because she is, or must be, devoted to another. Hence, again, the marriage is a dead end. In the last paragraph of the story, Michalina runs to her husband and "the door closed upon the apostate." The words have an ironic double meaning; the door has closed behind her, but it has also closed in her face.

The claims of a father, the relation of a father to the daughter's choice of husband—these are motifs that run through both stories just analyzed. In both cases, the daughter seems to make a choice, seems to defy her father, but in both cases, she discovers that in making her choice, she dooms herself to choicelessness. The influence of the father is extremely important, as the title reveals, in **"The Daughter of Reb Avrom Leib"** (1900), which has as its background the festivals and holy days of the Jewish religion. Indeed, the story is formally divided into parts according to certain holy days, and most of the story's scenes are set in the Synagogue where Reb Avrom Leib is the cantor, or official singer. Aaron Zalkin, a businessman, entering the Synagogue after many years of absence, sees the cantor's daughter and is attracted. A visit "'to view the bride'" is arranged, and, after some Talmudic exchanges between suitor and father, we learn that, with all due irony, it will be a love match, for "Reb Avrom Leib fell in love with his daughter's suitor on the spot." Sophie, the daughter, is much less sure of her feelings and, once again, like the other daughters examined, is torn between pleasing her father and pleasing herself. The engagement is made, broken, made, broken again, until, after the death of her father, Sophie seeks out the one man who also loves her father as a "father." The last paragraph sounds with all the foreboding we have come to expect from references to marriage in Cahan's work:

> "Will you marry me?"

> "Yes, yes," she answered, impetuously. The street was dark. From the Synagogue came the hum of muffled merriment. It sounded like a wail. "Yes, yes," she repeated in a whisper. And, as if afraid lest morning might bring better counsel, she hastened to bind herself by adding with a tremor in her voice: "I swear by my father that I will."

The setting of the story and the final "wail" from the Synagogue underline the fact that patriarchal Jewish law and convention "bind" the woman into a marriage and her devotion to her father (or husband, or lover, as is the case in some stories) seals the trap. The conventions, the ritual, the commemoration of festival, the very use of language like "predestined one" to describe the suitor suggest the inevitability of a woman's destiny, the weight of tradition that works to suppress her individual identity.

The funereal "wail" sounded in the last paragraph of **"The Daughter of Reb Avrom Leib"** is echoed in **"A Ghetto Wedding"** (1898). Goldy and Nathan are making wedding plans, and Goldy wants to save enough money to carry the event off in style. But times are difficult and their money is shrinking, and so Goldy hits upon the plan of using what money they have for an extravagant wedding and relying on their guests to furnish them with sufficiently generous gifts to set up house. This is realistic fiction, however, and many guests cannot afford to accept the invitation to the wedding; those who do come give only meager presents.

Before the wedding, Goldy spends many days in her new apartment waiting in vain for gifts to arrive, and Cahan emphasizes through repetition the "vacuity" of the "empty little rooms," a theme which recurs in the somber description of the wedding celebration: "the few waltzers looked as if they were scared by the ringing echoes of their own footsteps amid the austere solemnity of the surrounding void and the depressing sheen of the dim expanse of floor." Yet the imagery becomes even more dismal in reference to Goldy. As the ritual of veiling the bride commences, Goldy is "pale as death" and looks "as if the bard were an executioner come to lead her to the scaffold." The traditional song of the bard. "'Wail, bride, wail! / This is a time of tears,'" has a ghastly effect, causing the bride to faint and the bard to earn the name "'murderer.'" During the wedding supper itself, Goldy tries "to imagine herself dead."

At the end of the story, walking home from the wedding, the couple's spirits are higher: "they felt a stream of happiness uniting them" and "the very notion of a relentless void abruptly turned to a beatific sense of their own seclusion." Most critics, focusing on this language, read the story as uncharacteristically optimistic or even "sentimental," and see the married couple as united in their Judaism against a hostile world. But Cahan is not sentimental or inconsistent; even in the midst of describing the couple's bliss, his use of somber "d" sounds in the following sentence belies the seeming romance of the ending: "they dived into the denser gloom of a sidestreet." It is true enough that Goldy and Nathan have been disappointed by their lack of wedding gifts and will have a difficult time struggling against poverty, nor is this romantic fiction where the ordinary facts of material life are unimportant; nevertheless, the pervasive language of emptiness, death, and darkness seems out of proportion to the material hardship and is not cancelled out by the momentary happiness described at the end. We can only assume that Cahan is telling us something not only about Jews in a Gentile world but about marriage itself, and we should note that, clearly here, the imagery of death and murder of self is associated with the woman, and recall, too, that the daughter of Reb Avrom Leib called her father "'murderer,'" when he was pushing her, unwilling, into the arms of Zalkin.

One of Cahan's most interesting stories dealing with the poverty of immigrant life is **"Circumstances"** (1897) which explores the marriage of an immigrant couple, Boris and Tanya, who come to America as a land of freedom from prejudice but who find their lives depressed by poverty and Boris forced to work in a button factory. Boris will not allow Tanya to work and so, in order to improve their finances, they take in (much against Tanya's will) a boarder, Dalsky, who is studying to be a doctor. Given the close living quarters, Tanya's lack of consuming interests, Dalsky's fresh appearance, his success at pursuing his studies in the face of Boris' failure to find the money and energy to pursue his, the inevitable happens. Circumstances press, and Tanya falls in love with Dalsky.

Tanya is presented as an intelligent, educated woman. She graduated from a Russian gymnasium, and when the story opens, she is excited about receiving the latest issue of *Russian Thought* (we recall Flora reading Dickens at the beginning of **"The Imported Bridegroom,"** though Flora's cultivation is clearly much shallower). The heightened language used to describe Tanya's avid interest in the journal is usually reserved for sexual passion: she was in a "flurry" of enthusiasm, "feverishly" reading, "burning to glance over the beginning, the middle, and the end of the article simultaneously." True, Tanya's intellectual attainments are treated with some irony by her husband, and, indeed, the narrator, but nevertheless, these genuine interests must be set against the actual details of her life which she spends housekeeping, making soup, and waiting, waiting for her husband: "'The whole day I am all alone, and when he comes he plunges into some book or other or falls asleep like a murdered man.'"

But given the circumstances and limitations of Tanya's life, she can only measure options in terms of the available men. The passion she directs at *Russian Thought,* thwarted, must be turned to another object: Dalsky—seemingly more intellectual, more interesting, more appealing than the abject Boris. When Tanya realizes her plight (and, significantly, she realizes it through comparing herself with Anna Karenina), she immediately has a confrontation with Boris. Interestingly, she cannot speak to him of her changed feelings, but she can write them down. What she writes is clearly melodramatic and derivative, borrowed from second-rate literary models, but the very act reflects a need on the part of a woman who, though educated, is deprived of work, choice, and—as an immigrant—of language, to write her own text, assert herself, take charge of her story in her own words. It is worth recalling that, at the beginning of the story, Tanya lights on an idea, expressed in *Russian Thought,* which Boris had disputed "with a patronizing and slightly ironical tone," when she had voiced it herself. She eagerly reads him the passage, and, when he accedes without a battle, she retorts: "Of course, once it is printed in *Russian Thought,* it is 'rather an interesting point,' but when it was only Tanya who made it, why then it was mere rubbish." The published word, then, has an authority, a power which is denied her speech, and her written words to Boris are a pathetic attempt to be taken seriously—not

to suffer patronage or condescension. Additionally, the letter reveals her moral clarity: since she no longer loves Boris, she cannot live with his. She does not, however, flee to Dalsky, but has the courage to eke out a wretched life in a sweatshop. The story ends with Tanya struggling over a machine and recalling the promise of her graduation from the gymnasium; meanwhile, Boris weeps out his despair in the "dead emptiness," of their now deserted rooms.

The stories analyzed so far reveal the woman's point of view in detail. Others do present primarily the man's perspective—but that is almost always conveyed with much less compassion by Cahan. Typical is the story of Yekl, or Jake, to give him the American name he prefers, in the short novel, *Yekl* (1896); Jake comes to America with the promise that he will shortly send for his wife and young child. The freedom of American life intoxicates him, and he postpones sending for them until his father's death forces his hand. The sight of his wife, who clings to all the old ways of his home town, disgusts him and their relationship deteriorates to the point of divorce. Meanwhile, Jake, who has been much taken with the American women of the dance halls, decides he will marry Mamie, not unaware that she probably has a respectable bank balance. In this realistic fiction, their moment of passion takes place on the roof of a tenement building, with washing flapping round their ears—again that imagery of envelopment and enclosure. Further, the escape from one wife to another is signalled by images of claustrophobia and suffocation. Confined in a Third Avenue cable car, Jake is on his way to marry Mamie while feeling "painfully reluctant to part with his long-coveted freedom so soon after it had at last been attained," and conscious that his future "loomed dark and impenetrable." But Jake, through his double-dealing and dishonesty, has forfeited our sympathy which is deflected to his first wife, the woman who arrived in America without possessions, without language, whose entire life was directed toward pleasing Jake.

Other men suffer (though they, too, fail to win our compassion as the women do) not because they marry, but because, like David Levinsky in Cahan's novel *The Rise of David Levinsky* (1917), they fail to. In **"A Providential Match"** (1895), Cahan paints an ironic portrait of a man who has bought the passage of his future wife from Russia. He is devastated on her arrival to discover that she has met her "Providential" husband on the boat, and he must watch the two of them walk away. In **"A Sweatshop Romance"** (1895), a man who is too timid to support his woman friend when she is insulted by the wife of their mutual employer, finds himself standing outside her door listening to the sounds of her engagement to another.

The imagery of restriction and constriction, then, is prevalent in Cahan's work. In Cahan's city, one is always coming up against walls or closed doors; whether the focus is on the one outside the door, wanting to beat it down, or the one inside, suffering enclosure, the pressures of isolation and suffocation are similar. The city seems to promise expansion, space, opportunity but the reality is, invariably, a sweatshop, a small suite of empty—or near empty—rooms, and a street which is not a passage through but a *cul-de-sac.* At the beginning of **"A Ghetto Wedding,"** Grand Street seems to be buzzing with crowded life and energy, but the bright display of material goods is set against the "empty purse," the "empty" rooms of Goldy and Nathan, and the dark "sidestreet." Most of the immigrant dwellers view the city's goods only from the outside, faces pressed against the glass. David Levinsky, whose "rise" is measured by the frequency with which he changes and improves his places of business, finds the changes merely superficial and his emotional life blocked off. Further, few of the stories convey any sense that the characters have a future, indeed, in this regard, David Levinsky explicitly bemoans his lack of progeny but none of the couples discussed has a child except for Michalina whose daughter will surely inherit a legacy of conflict and alienation. Many of the characters believe that they have free will, that they can control the life of a future husband, shape the course of a wedding, take revenge on a stepmother, and leave a husband, but they inevitably find themselves hemmed in by economic reality, the past, fate, circumstances, conventions, and traditions. The new world only seems to be new; the old traps merely appear in different disguises.

The institutional trap which most frequently absorbs Cahan's imagination is marriage—and Cahan's fiction presents us with a full indictment of marriage, beginning with the courtship. In *The Rise of David Levinsky,* we recall the scene in the Catskills where men look over the "merchandise" and assess "matrimonial possibilities" in terms of flesh and diamonds. In **"A Providential Match,"** we learn that the woman has never spoken to the suitors who "sought her hand and her marriage portion." **"A Marriage by Proxy"** offers a more satirical view of marriage, suggesting the absurdity of an institution where couples who do not even know each other contract to marry. Marriage in this world is an arrangement, usually negotiated by the father, for virtual strangers to live together for economic reasons: the bridegroom is bought in **"The Imported Bridegroom"** and the bride in **"A Providential Match."** Those women who resist being married for their money, like Gussie in *The Rise of David Levinsky,* cannot expect happiness either, for, as we have seen, marriage is the primary option for women in Cahan's society. Moreover, the women are more or less friendless; the only bonding between women such as that in **"The Apostate of Chego-Chegg"** or the friendship between Mrs. Kavarsky and Gitl in *Yekl* is directed toward helping the woman either make the best of her current marriage or settle in another.

Woman's role is defined and limited by marriage, and her life is spent living through or supporting fathers, husbands, children. In *The Rise of David Levinsky,* we learn that the greatest honor for a man is the privilege of passing his days in studying the Torah; the greatest honor for a woman, therefore, since she is excluded from full par-

ticipation in religious life, is the privilege of supporting him in this occupation. David Levinsky's mother, in effect, dies for her son, attempting retaliation against some Gentiles who have harmed him, and Dora, one of the women to whom Levinsky is drawn, lives for her children, for the day when her daughter, Lucy, will be "both educated and happy." And when Lucy marries for safety, for money, Dora can only wonder hopelessly, as she contemplates the waste of her daughter's life and her own, "Of what good is education, then?" Life is hard for all the immigrants, and Cahan certainly does not simplify the problems of maintaining integrity and identity in the new world, but it is especially hard for women whose identity must be submerged in that of others. Women have marriage and marriage means conversion to the life of the husband and death of the self. It is always risky to speculate on what has formed the imagination of the artist, but it is tempting to claim that the imagery of death, conversion, and exclusion might readily inform the vision of an immigrant who feels excluded from a culture and wants desperately to be assimilated or "married." But to assimilate means not only conversion, or the renunciation of language, customs, dress, beliefs, but the death of the individual autonomous self. Moreover, as an immigrant, an outsider shut out from the centers of influence and with no voice in the official culture, Cahan must have had a special sensitivity for the woman's peripheral role in society and for her irresolvable conflict: to marry is to risk absorption in the identity of another; not to marry is to risk displacement. Many critics have pointed out Cahan's ambivalence about assimilation, but it is worth emphasizing how skillfully Cahan conveys this anxiety through his treatment of the woman's attitude toward marriage. And if the irresolution of his endings serves to raise questions about assimilation, it also surely raises questions about marriage.

Cahan's fiction offers poignant, compassionate portraits of women; and while these women are often morally superior, they are not particularly outstanding, and not capable of transcending circumstances and convention. And perhaps this has, in part, to do with the problems of writing realistic fiction. As we know, W. D. Howells was advocating that American writers reject romantic and sentimental models; for the influential Howells and his growing body of disciples in the late nineteenth century, realism was the new unorthodoxy which would challenge received ideas about art. Cahan wrote of ordinary immigrant people in ordinary working class situations for the most part, and many students of Cahan's work have pointed out that his socialism and his commitment to literary realism are linked, that the critical realism encouraged by Howells would show things as they are and thus provoke social change. Nonetheless, by exchanging romantic fictional conventions for realistic ones, Cahan is forced to confront the limitations of that mode and to demonstrate that Howellsian realism is by no means revolutionary; for in depicting life as the Howellsian realist says it is, Cahan must only show the ordinary person, the typical situation, the predictable outcome. Thus art, imitating life in accordance with the particular principles of realist selectivity and reacting against romanticism, must itself come up against dead ends. Cahan's fiction presents us with a compelling set of reasons for changing the world, but, at the same time, both formally and thematically, his art demonstrates the extraordinary difficulty of personal or political transformation.

Sam B. Girgus (essay date 1984)

SOURCE: "A Convert to America: Sex, Self, and Ideology in Abraham Cahan," in *The New Covenant: Jewish Writers and the American Idea,* The University of North Carolina Press, 1984, pp. 64-91.

[*In the following essay, Girgus examines Cahan's portrayal of the perversion of the American ideal in* The Rise of David Levinsky.]

The world of European Jewry that sent forth waves of mass immigration to America has been described and dramatized in many tales and stories. This is the world of Heinrich Heine, Sholem Aleichem, and Isaac Bashevis Singer. It is a world of the ghetto and the schlemiel and of emancipation movements that had to look to the New World for examples of how to treat Jews with freedom and equality. With all its mystery, vitality, and richness, it is also a world of terror and ambiguity, of the loveless Jew, and of the wasted pariah who existed on the margins of society Who better tells the story than the baptized Heine in "The Rabbi of Bacherach"? In this story Heine summarizes the history of the oppression of Jews in Europe: the Great Persecutions during the Crusades, the catastrophes at the time of the Great Plague, the rage of the rabble, the Flagellants, the blood libels, and the wafer desecration charges. Thus he weaves history into the story with a detailed account of a Passover service that devotedly renders the beauty of Jewish religious practice, customs, and belief. Throughout the story runs an ambivalence toward the culture of Germany and Europe. This ambivalence is seen in the image of "old, kind-hearted Father Rhine" who "cannot bear to see his children weep." For the culture of the Rhine is also terrifying as it stands ready at any moment to change its mood and devastate its Jews. The unfinished novella by Heine trails off almost as though history must fill the silence and complete the story with our knowledge of the fate of European Jewry in our century. Heine's tale implies a catastrophe that only modern history could create.

To some Jewish historians, however, the disabilities of medieval and preemancipation Jewry were exaggerated by reform-oriented scholars and writers. Such reformers, it is argued, saw the preemancipation era in Europe in completely negative terms because they desired the Jews to modernize and sacrifice their ethnic and national identity for an exclusively religious affiliation that would allow them to be total citizens of the modern nation state. Thus, Salo W. Baron wrote in 1925, "Ardent advocates of liberalism and democracy, visioning a reformed society guided by beneficent rationalism, believing reli-

giously that the world in general and the Jews particularly could be improved by an extension of rights, it is easy to see how they found it useful to take as black a view as possible of the pre-Revolutionary treatment of the Jews." In a sense, according to Baron, such reformers were apologizing for Jewish "peculiarities" by seeing them as scars of oppression that should be healed through emancipation so that Jews could become like everyone else. In so doing, Baron felt, reformers also were ready to cast aside significant aspects of modern Diaspora Jewish character and culture. Baron's interest in correcting this historical view of the ghetto was based in part upon his uncertainty about the quality and the depth of emancipation for Jews in Europe. As it turned out, Jews who staked their security and identity upon their full emancipation in Europe built their futures upon quicksand. In Baron's later estimation, they mistook the visible signs of emancipation for solid and deep-based support from within European culture. The roots into Europe that seemingly nurtured their freedom were extirpated in modern times. Following the Holocaust and the war, Baron wrote that a major test for the reality of emancipation for Jews is the viability and endurance of the social and cultural structures upon which that emancipation is based. "On my part, I have long come to the conclusion," he writes, "that one cannot hope to understand the development of legal and political emancipation without a careful review of the basic social forces which brought them about. That is why one must deal at the same time with the impact of both the economic and cultural emancipation which had preceded the legal emancipation by several generations." In America Baron felt emancipation was built upon custom, belief, and opinion. His analysis of "long-range socioeconomic and cultural factors" as opposed to dramatic historic events indicated a long tradition of emancipation for Jews in America that provides a contrast with the more superficial emancipation movements in European countries.

Emancipation in America in the context of continuing efforts to develop political, economic, and cultural democracy proved irresistible to many Jews, including, as I have already noted, many radical socialists who often were critical of American culture and politics while adhering to the principles of the American idea. The accommodation of these socialists to America anticipates the later movement of intellectuals who became what Alfred Kazin terms with apparent sarcasm *"converts to America."* These intellectuals, he says, grew inclined to view "America as an ideology." This shift toward America can be seen symbolically on the cover of Irving Howe's collection of radical and socialistic pieces drawn from the journal *Dissent.* The title of the book, *Twenty-Five Years of Dissent: An American Tradition,* demonstrates how even the opponents of so-called dominant political beliefs and values still see themselves as modern Jeremiahs working within an American tradition that makes them part of the American Way in its broadest and most meaningful sense. One of the first and most important examples of this phenomenon can be found in the life and career of Abraham Cahan. As a writer, intellectual, and activist, Cahan represents something of a paradigm for the Jewish man of ideas and letters whose original opposition to American culture evolves into a more complicated prophetic position of advocacy for the ideals of the American Way and of criticism for the failure to live up to them. In many ways, Cahan provides a model for the Jewish intellectual who begins as an alien to America but turns into a convert while even being a critic. The great depth and breadth to Cahan's understanding of the American experience can be found in his novel *The Rise of David Levinsky*. A classic study of immigration and success, the novel dramatizes the meaning to a generation and a culture of the myth of America as the new promised land. It shows the shift from European experiences and ways of thought to the adoption of the American way of life. The novel further dramatizes the psychological, sexual, sociological, and intellectual roots within both American and Jewish culture of the corruption of the American idea. Thus, Cahan uses the persona of David Levinsky in order to take the traditional stance of a modern-day Jeremiah attacking those who have lost their faith or cheat in their proper observance of the ideals of the American idea. As such the novel is more than an important literary work and cultural document. It forms part of the traditional ritual of renewal of the American Way.

Abraham Cahan was a man of many conflicts and aspects. As Louis Harap says, "at the core his personality was a set of contradictions." Indeed, he was born into a world of cultural contradictions on July 6, 1860, in the town of Podberezy, situated about twenty miles from Vilna, the city Napoleon called the "Jerusalem of Lithuania." This was also Cahan's Jerusalem under siege by new ideas, institutions, and philosophies that reflected the enormous social and economic forces changing modern Jewish life. As the grandson of a famous rabbi, Cahan was expected to maintain that tradition. However, by the time he arrived in Philadelphia in early June of 1882, socialism had for several years become a new religion to him. His flight to America as a revolutionary was made to avoid arrest by czarist police. In his later years, Cahan recalled the confidence with which he and his friends in Europe emphasized socialism over Judaism, even in the wake of the pogroms that followed the assassination of Alexander II in 1881. He writes, "Even though the pogrom brought dread into the heart of every Jew, I must admit that the members of my group were not disturbed by it. We regarded ourselves as human beings, not as Jews. There was only one remedy for the world's ills and that was socialism." In spite of such youthful bravado, Cahan never actually lost his concern as a Jew over matters relating to Jewish welfare, although there remained a lingering tension between his religious roots and his belief in a universal socialism. Thus Ronald Sanders notes that in his fiction "Cahan seems to have been unable to find the proper control of his own ambivalences about Jewishness." Almost immediately upon his arrival in America this conflict between religion and politics was compounded by another conflict of loyalties between the revolutionary cause in Russia and political

realities in America. In his first speech to Jews and Socialists that made him by his own account "the hero of the day," Cahan said: "'We have come to seek a home in a land that is relatively free,' I began. 'But we must not forget the great struggle for freedom that continues in our old homeland. While we are concerned with our own problems, our comrades, our heroes, our martyrs are carrying on the struggle, languishing in Russian prisons, suffering at hard labor in Siberia. There is little we can do from this distance,' I continued. 'We can raise money to aid the sacred cause. And we must keep the memory of that struggle fresh in our minds'." Throughout his life, attitudes and policies toward Russia were to consume a considerable amount of Cahan's attention.

In America there also developed a split between Cahan's work in Yiddish and his writings in English. Indeed, Cahan the Yiddish journalist and socialist leader at times seems to be a different person from the Cahan who wrote both fiction and journalism in English. From his first days in America, Cahan became a force within the Jewish community. Throughout the 1880s and 1890s, he wrote for the Yiddish journals, *Di Neie Tseit,* the *Arbeiter Tseitung,* the Yiddish weekly of the Socialist Labor party, and *Di Tsukunft.* In 1897, however, in helping to form the *Jewish Daily Forward,* Cahan took the most important step in his journalistic career. After heated dealings with other editors and managers that caused him on various occasions to leave the paper, Cahan finally returned in 1903 as editor with unqualified authority. Editing the *Forward* became his major work. "Cahan's greatest achievement," writes Leon Stein, "was the *Jewish Daily Forward,*" while Jules Chametzky says that "Cahan's life-work was the great Yiddish newspaper, the *Jewish Daily Forward.*" The newspaper was a leading force in the Yiddish community in shaping political attitudes, supporting socialism and social welfare measures, and establishing and maintaining the garment unions. It also participated in the daily life and activities of the Jewish community through its editorial features such as the *Bintel Brief* (a "Bundle of Letters" section that created a dialogue with the people of the ghetto about the most intimate and personal of problems) and its political and social commentary. In this paper Cahan exercised a direct influence on the daily customs, habits, and attitudes of Jews in the community.

However, his progress as a writer in English seems no less remarkable than his success as a Yiddish writer. He moved quickly from using *Appleton's English Grammar* to teaching himself English to writing sketches and pieces in English for various papers and journals. His most important experience on an English language newspaper occurred from 1897 to 1901 when he worked on the *Commercial Advertiser.* Lincoln Steffens was the editor, and the staff consisted of talented writers such as Hutchins Hapgood. On the newspaper he learned the basics of modern journalism that helped him so much in his later work as the editor of the *Forward.* Around this time he also began to write fiction in English, publishing his first story, **"A Providential Match"** in 1895 and his first novel, *Yekl: A Tale of the Ghetto,* in 1896. The latter provided the basis for the contemporary movie *Hester Street.* Cahan was encouraged to pursue his work in fiction by William Dean Howells, who was interested in Cahan both as a young realistic writer and as an expert on the Jewish Lower East Side. For his part, Cahan, according to Ronald Sanders, "still considered Howells to be the greatest living American author, but he had never met him, nor did he ever dream that he would." Cahan also ranked Howells with Henry James as a leader in the "avant-garde." Howells had first heard of Cahan's work as editor of the *Arbeiter Tseitung* and paid a surprise visit to Cahan's office. Not finding him there, Howells also missed Cahan at a neighborhood café called Sussman and Goldstein's that Jewish intellectuals frequented. He followed this excursion with an invitation to Cahan to visit him at home on East 17th Street and Second Avenue. "Cahan's visit here," writes Sanders, "provided him with his first glimpse of the upper-class life of an established American writer." Howells tried to help Cahan in important ways, including finding a publisher for the English version of *Yekl.* He then favorably reviewed the book along with Stephen Crane's *George's Mother* on the front page of the literary section of the *New York World* of July 26, 1896.

As a socialist critic of both European and American literature who had his own literary ambitions, Cahan developed a theory of realism that attempts to establish a connection between his work as a writer of fiction and his experiences as a journalist and active socialist. This theory of literary criticism and social values was presented first as a lecture before a cultural group of the Socialist Labor party. It was printed later on March 15, 1889, in the *Workmen's Advocate* as an article entitled "**Realism.**" The article reflects Cahan's devoted readings of Howells as well as his admiration for Tolstoy. In this piece Cahan advocates a literature of realism on the grounds that the accurate portrayal of social conditions inevitably would lead to social change and revolution. Writing retrospectively in his autobiography, Cahan admitted the naiveté of some of his ideas about art as expressed in "**Realism.**" He also described his confusion between art and propaganda. "In the portion of the article dealing with the social question," he writes, "much of the language is straight propaganda and creates an impression that undermines my own integrity. Now, it is easy for me to separate the passages that were written from the heart, with conviction, from those which were written as propaganda, from a sense of duty. We used propaganda for an honest purpose, and there are still socialists who feel that this should be done. Almost all that I wrote at that time suffered from this fault."

Cahan's literary production in English constitutes a measure of his success in overcoming his initial tendency to confuse propaganda with art. After writing *Yekl,* his stories such as "**The Imported Bridegroom,**" "**A Providential Match,**" "**Circumstances,**" "**A Sweat Shop Romance,**" "**A Ghetto Wedding,**" and "**Tzinchadzi of the Catskills**" appeared in the *Atlantic, Cosmopolitan,*

Short Stories, Century, and *Scribner's.* Thus, by 1913 when *McClure's Magazine* asked him to write an article about the economic success of American Jews, he already was an important figure both in the Jewish community and in New York literary and intellectual circles. Just three years before the request from *McClure's,* the celebration of his fiftieth birthday filled Carnegie Hall. The work he produced for *McClure's* was a four-part series entitled "**The Autobiography of an American Jew.**" Described sensationalistically on the cover as "The Confessions of a Jew," the articles were written in the form of fiction but really were more on the order of a modern "documentary." The series provided the basis for his novel *The Rise of David Levinsky*.

Cahan's willingness to see himself as a writer rather than as a propagandist for socialism follows his critical reexamination upon reaching America of the political ideology that inspired his early years of intellectual development. Almost immediately the experience of America and the American ideology tended to challenge the rigid socialism that Cahan like others brought from Russia. Thus, Cahan states that "for the first four or five years of my life in America I had no answers—only perplexities." Among the greatest perplexities was his immediate impression that America was a new kind of political and cultural enterprise. He writes, "The anarchists and even the socialists argued that there was no more freedom in America than in Russia. But that was just talk, I concluded. After all, in America there was no Czar, there were no gendarmes, no political spies. You could speak and write what you wanted! The President was elected, the governor was elected, even the congressmen who made the laws were elected." At the same time he also could perceive that "some things were strange, ridiculous, wild, sometimes even disgusting." The imbroglio of conflicting beliefs and perceptions that Cahan faced led him to feel that "what I considered to be my convictions were in truth a mishmash of ideas." Out of this percolation of new ideas and impressions emerged a fresh analysis from Cahan of European political philosophers and thinkers such as Proudhon, Johann Most, William Frey, Bakunin, Kropotkin, and Herbert Spencer.

Cahan's sense of the importance of America to the future of the Jews helped him ultimately to moderate his socialism and to give priority to the American ideology over other systems of belief. Thus, upon seeing America as a real refuge for the world's Jews, he reversed his early inclination to prefer socialism over Judaism. By converting to Americanism, Jews could survive as a people and as free individuals. As early as 1890, he understood that "we have no Jewish question in America. The only question we recognize is the question of how to prevent the emergence of 'Jewish questions' here." In addition, Cahan saw that America offered the average Jew a way of life that seemed inconceivable in Europe. "The life of the Jewish sweatshop worker was hard," he writes. "Still the average Jewish immigrant felt that in comparison with what he had suffered in the old country, America was paradise. The worker ate better and was better clothed than in the old country." The benefits of this life, according to Cahan, were apparent even in the physiques of the younger generation. He writes, "The immigrant family began to understand the difference between the old and new lands when it looked upon its children, who grew tall and strong and were better built than their parents. It was not uncommon to see a sixteen-year-old boy towering over his father." To Cahan, however, it was freedom in America that was of the greatest importance to the American Jew. "And what value there was in political freedom!," writes Cahan. "Here, one was a human being. My friend Alter, who always worked hard but barely made a living and considered himself to be a failure, once said to me with a resigned smile, 'Never mind. In the old country I kept my head bowed and my back bent. Here I keep my head high and my back is straight'." Cahan was especially impressed by the fact that Jews could participate so freely in the political process in contrast to Russia where "Jews were denied even the small rights granted to their gentile neighbors. But here in America all enjoyed the same rights, whether Jew or gentile. And for us the right to vote should have been even more precious than for our Christian fellow Americans."

In assuming this commitment to the American ideology, Cahan in effect was accepting the inevitable. He recognized that the mass movement of Jews from the oppression of Europe to the freedom and opportunity of America dramatized an inexorable shift in the direction and meaning of modern Jewish history There is a touching moment in his autobiography when Cahan discovers that he is part of forces larger than himself. During his escape from Russia, he realizes that on roads all over Eastern Europe other Jews also are on the move toward America. This happens to him as he boards a train at the Kiev station and sees how many other Jews are also traveling. "On that Saturday night there began the broad stream of Jewish migration that was to continue for almost two generations," he writes. "It was to make America the major center of Jewish population. The course of Jewish history would be changed by it." He notes that "soon every emigrating Jew moving westward realized he was involved in something more than a personal expedition. Every Jew, even the most ignorant emigrant, came to feel that he was part of a historic event in the life of the Jewish people. Ordinary, common Jews became as idealistic and enthusiastic as the intellectuals. Even Jewish workers and small tradesmen who had managed fairly well sold their belongings and joined the exodus from Russia and the move westward to start a new Jewish life in America. They did so with religious fervor and often with inspiring self-sacrifice."

Cahan realized that the socialism in which he believed so strongly would not be as acceptable to many of his fellow immigrants. He saw that even before arriving in America many Jews forgot their radicalism as their expectations about America grew. Thus, while still in the European phase of his journey to America, Cahan remembers that he was "bitterly disappointed at not finding more social-ists. In fact, in the seething tumult of Brody [the first city on the Austro-Galician side of the Russian border] even some who had considered themselves socialists in their hometowns began to have doubts about the political meaning of their journey to America."

However, even while criticizing the abandonment of radical doctrine, Cahan himself fell victim to the excitement of going to America. He felt the enthusiasm for achieving a new life and identity in accordance with the myth of America. In spite of his radicalism, Cahan, like so many others, saw himself as a new man in the new American garden. Cahan writes, "America! To go to America! To re-establish the Garden of Eden in that distant land. My spirit soared. All my other plans dissolved. I was for America!" It is this mythic sense of America as a new land that dominates Cahan's novel *The Rise of David Levinsky*. The idea of America as a unique culture offering a new way of life constitutes the book's central concern; it is not a discussion of political principles and ideologies disguised as a novel.

The story of America in *The Rise of David Levinsky* can be compared with that in F. Scott Fitzgerald's *The Great Gatsby*. Fitzgerald writes, "And as the moon rose higher the inessential houses began to melt away until gradually I became aware of the old island here that flowered once for Dutch sailors' eyes—a fresh, green breast of the new world. Its vanished trees, the trees that had made way for Gatsby's house, had once pandered in whispers to the last and greatest of all human dreams; for a transitory enchanted moment man must have held his breath in the presence of this continent, compelled into an aesthetic contemplation he neither understood nor desired, face to face for the last time in history with something commensurate to his capacity for wonder." Years before Fitzgerald, Cahan describes the same kind of experience for Levinsky. Cahan's language is far more literal than Fitzgerald's. Indeed, his language at times approaches sociology. Nevertheless, like Fitzgerald, Cahan attempts to relate fact to symbol as they merge in the psychology of one individual who comes to represent a people, a generation, and a culture in one moment in history. Both Fitzgerald and Cahan dramatize the myth of America through their portrayals of men who are propelled by their "vision" of what America could mean to them. And like Fitzgerald, Cahan shows how the concept of America translates itself into perceptions of the landscape. This projection of the self onto the landscape in turn reflects back onto the self with a force that inspires a belief in self-transformation.

Accordingly, to Levinsky America is a place of awe and wonder. "The United States lured me not merely as a land of milk and honey," he says, "but also, and perhaps chiefly, as one of mystery, of fantastic experiences, of marvelous transformations. To leave my native place and to seek my fortune in that distant, weird world seemed to be just the kind of sensational adventure my heart was hankering for." Based on his own first view as an immigrant of New York, Cahan describes David Levinsky's vision of the city "as something not of this earth" until he glimpses a cat. The reality of the cat brings America back to earth—somewhat. "For a moment," Levinsky says, "the little animal made America real to me." The wonder of America creates a physical and psychological reaction in Levinsky. Levinsky, Cahan notes, "was in a trance or in something closely resembling one" upon actually seeing "the hostile glamour of America." His feelings of "ecstasy" and "transport" contribute to his "sense of helplessness and awe." Such emotions result in the immigrant's belief in his own rebirth. "The immigrant's arrival in his new home," writes Cahan, "is like a second birth to him. Imagine a new-born babe in possession of a fully developed intellect. Would it ever forget its entry into the world? Neither does the immigrant ever forget its entry into a country which is, to him, a new world in the profoundest sense of the term and in which he expects to pass the rest of his life." For Levinsky, the transformation is so complete that he thinks of it as a metamorphosis. "Sometimes," he says, "when I think of my past in a superficial, casual way, the metamorphosis I have gone through strikes me as nothing short of a miracle." A similar change seems to occur for the Jewish people as a whole as they participate in "the great New Exodus" to America.

Although the novel focuses on graphic and momentous transformations, it also dramatizes the significance of the idea of regeneration through a woman who denies herself the opportunity to achieve a new life because of fear and inexperience. In some ways, the meaning of the chance for a new life becomes most palpable in this woman who seems compelled to suffer the constraints of the life she has but wants to change. The misery and self-sacrifice of Dora Margolis emphasize the importance of giving people the opportunity to create their own futures. In love with David but unable to escape from her marriage, she feels "'buried alive'" and decides that her only alternative is to live vicariously through her daughter "'I want to know everything about her. Everything. I wish I could get right into her. I wish I could be a child like her.'" Mostly she wishes that life would give her the opportunity for a second chance. "'Oh,'" she asks Levinsky, "'why can't a person be born over again?'". The intensity of her lament greatens by contrast the dimensions of Levinsky's own rebirth in America.

Unfortunately, Levinsky's transformation in the New World garden seems more diabolical than miraculous. He becomes The Great Levinsky, a grotesque perversion of the American dream whose enormous economic success leaves him feeling homeless. Like Gatsby, he is without any real sense of identity or place as he comes to embody the corruption of the myth that brought him to America in the first place. As Levinsky the immigrant is transformed into The Great Levinsky the giant of the cloak and suit trade, we see the myth of regeneration and new life transmogrified into the "gospel of success." Levinsky represents a Jewish version of the rags-to-riches myth in America in which success and power are values in and of themselves. Thus, Levinsky notes how people who con-

gratulate him on his achievements "were inspired by genuine admiration for my enterprise and energy." He goes on to say, "All of them had genuine admiration for my success. Success! Success! Success! It was the almighty goddess of the hour. Thousands of new fortunes were advertising her gaudy splendors. Newspapers, magazines, and public speeches were full of her glory, and he who found favor in her eyes found favor in the eyes of man." The deification of success for Levinsky into what William James called "the bitch goddess" indicates his ready adaptability to a world in which there are no greater ideals than power over others. Students of American culture such as John Cawelti and Moses Rischin have pointed out how the myth of success reaches far back into our history. Originally, success in the form of wealth and power often were considered symbolic of righteousness and strong character. In this novel, however, success becomes its own justification and establishes a new ideology that counters the more traditional democratic values of the ideology of the American Way. As a member of this new ideology, Levinsky finds himself with the rest of American culture on the brink of an abyss from which no higher values and beliefs can be seen. In the novel Tevkin the old poet summarizes this situation by condemning America as a cage of the spirit. Levinsky, who admires the poet, is shocked by "'the idea of America being likened to a prison.'" The poet, however, tells him that Russia is a "'freer country, too—for the spirit, at least'." Levinsky's own values seem to prove the poet's point. For Levinsky develops a world view based on his business experience in the garment industry and his reading of Darwin and Spencer. His philosophy goes back to a comment made by a friend who compares the world to "'a big barn-yard full of chickens'" in which all the chickens are "'scratching one another, and scrambling over one another'" in their greed for shares of "'little heaps of grain'" scattered in the yard. Levinsky identifies himself with the fittest and develops a concomitant contempt for workers and the poor. He says, "A working-man, and every one else who was poor, was an object of contempt to me—a misfit, a weakling, a failure, one of the ruck." His experience in business teaches him that life is a jungle. "My business life had fostered the conviction in me that, outside of the family, the human world was as brutally selfish as the jungle, and that it was worm eaten with hypocrisy into the bargain." With faith only in success and power, Levinsky espouses a philosophy of nihilism that starkly contrasts with the idealism and wonder of his original idea of America. "I had no creed," he says. "I knew of no ideals. The only thing I believed in was the cold, drab theory of the struggle for existence and the survival of the fittest."

The ideology of success changes the emphasis in the idea of being American from a question of inner values, ideals, and strengths to a matter of images. However, because appearances are inherently ephemeral and contingent upon others' perceptions, it condemns one to continual frustration. Thus, success, as Levinsky perceives it, is simply a part of never-ending failure. In the novel, the road becomes an important metaphor for this aspect of American life. It dramatizes how American mobility and change inspire both alienation and adventure. As noted earlier in this study, on the road Levinsky learns how to disguise his shame and uncertainty about being Jewish through his adoption of the style and manners of the dominant culture. Thus, he sees the road as a "great school of business and life" that brings out and develops "the 'real American' quality" in him as opposed to New York, which he comes to see as "not an American city at all." He becomes self-conscious about his mannerisms, "trying to make them as 'American' as possible," and attempts to overcome his "Talmudic gesticulations, a habit that worried me like a physical defect." Instead of simply seeing himself as different from others, he feels deformed because such Jewish gestures were "so distressingly un-American." He says, "I struggled hard against it. I had made efforts to speak with my hands in my pockets; I had devised other means for keeping them from participating in my speech. All of no avail. I still gesticulate a great deal, though much less than I used to." Thus, attempts to literally shackle himself and to stifle the Jewish self within him fail, leaving him feeling always out of place and inferior. Guilt over such reactions compounds the complexity of his feelings. Literally a man divided against himself, he laughs publicly over another Jew's jokes about Jews. "I laughed with the others," he says, "but I felt like a cripple who is forced to make fun of his own deformity. It seemed to me as though Loeb, who was a Jew, was holding up our whole race to the ridicule of Gentiles."

However, the contrast between the appearance of being American and the inner reality of the values below the surface startles Levinsky when he realizes that one of the most American-looking travelers is in fact a butcher, a gentile who undoubtedly deals in unkosher meat, which is an abomination to orthodox Jews. Levinsky says, "He fascinated me. His cultured English and ways conflicted in my mind with the character of his business. I could not help thinking of raw beef, bones, and congested blood. I said to myself, 'It takes a country like America to produce butchers who look and speak like noblemen.' The United States was still full of surprises for me. I was still discovering America." Thus, the road teaches him about the brutality of shaping and turning people into a single definition of what it takes to be an American. On the road with strangers Levinsky comes to feel at war with himself and devoid of any reality or sense of self beyond what others see in him. "'Can it be that I am I?'" he asks himself. In the end he is alone and miserable. "After dinner, when we were in the smoking-room again, it seemed to me that the three Gentiles were tired of me. Had I talked too much? Had I made a nuisance of myself? I was wretched."

Levinsky's response to such insecurity is to fight even harder for success. One of the novel's frequently heralded achievements is Cahan's method of relating the psychology of the individual immigrant, as seen through Levinsky's drive to success, to the rise of the Jews as a group in the clothing and other industries. In the novel, the Jews take the lead in the national anxiety to shed one identity and assume a new one by putting on a new fashion of clothes. Through the Jewish experience in this industry, the novel documents the growing national obsession with looking a particular way labeled "American" at a time when there was a growing uncertainty over what such an identity entailed. This was, after all, the eve of the twenties when, as Robert Sklar notes, "careful self-schooling in the mass technological norms of dress, habits, manner and language" could enable the individual, especially a minority member, to establish a new identity, even if that identity made the person like everyone else. "You could change your name, ignore your religion, leave your background a thousand miles behind," writes Sklar. "But you could never afford to neglect your appearance. In the twenties Americans began their grand obsession with cosmetics. The absence of body odor mattered more than the lack of a family tree." Ironically, the Jews, as Moses Rischin indicates, achieved dominance in the clothing and such other industries related to taste and style as communications, films, and media because they were so systematically excluded from participating significantly in more basic American industries. Such dominance in these industries helped create a myth of Jewish power. However, there is another irony in the prominence of Jews in relatively marginal enterprises that depend so much upon public taste and fashion. Rather than setting or establishing tastes, styles, and trends, the leaders in these kinds of industries often resemble slaves to the publics they serve. This can be especially true for minority or ethnic leaders whose own self-image and ambition compel them to anticipate the desires and standards of the dominant culture. Moreover, progress in such areas often can undermine individual power because success requires participation in mass markets that tend to redefine the whole concept of taste and fashion to mean only the average, the mediocre, and the marketable. Cahan's novel dramatizes these kinds of weaknesses that lurk beneath the cover of success in America.

Levinsky becomes a perfect model of impotence masking itself as power as we get beneath the surface of his claims concerning his business success. The contrast between visible success and inner weakness grows apparent as we see that his reputed influence over fashion really reflects a demeaning readiness to trade his own sense of self for a system that imposes one standard of beauty and style upon the new market of women buyers. At one point in the novel Levinsky in a reportial voice boasts of "the advent of the Russian Jew as the head of one of the largest industries in the United States," which can, because of the Jew's leadership, provide "clothes for the American woman of moderate or humble means." Proud of this visible success he maintains that "the average American woman is the best-dressed average woman in the world, and the Russian Jew has had a good deal to do with making her one." "Indeed," says Levinsky, "the Russian Jew had made the average American girl a 'tailor-made' girl." However, the diminution of individuality implied by such appeals to the "average" have their impact upon Levinsky himself. While Levinsky does exert power over women by averaging their tastes and influencing them to tailor their buying habits and expectations, he also must place his own mind in a kind of straitjacket that will enable him to exert such leadership. To become a success, he totally accepts an external—in a sense, a foreign—set of values and standards.

With all his supposed influence over taste and standards. Levinsky finds only one ideal for beauty and charm—the Anglo-Saxon—in a way that clearly demonstrates his deep sense of ethnic inferiority. Thus, of his models he writes, "These models were all American girls of Anglo-Saxon origin, since a young woman of other stock is not likely to be built on American lines—with the exception of Scandinavian and Irish girls, who have the American figure." Of course, the idea of women as "stock" built according to certain "lines" fuses racist and sexist ways of thinking with the steady movement of American culture toward a uniformity of style and taste that fits the needs of a mass-market industry and economy. The conformity sought by Levinsky extends to more than looks. His models have to be the "right" examples of accepted and standard American behavior and thought. Thus, Levinsky, who is only too ready to sell himself for success in the system, learns how to expect others as well to sacrifice their ways of thought and patterns of behavior in order to satisfy a model created for them. Levinsky says, "But the figure alone was not enough, I thought. In selecting my model-girls, I preferred a good-looking face and good manners, and, if possible, good grammar. Experience had taught me that refinement in a model was helpful in making a sale, even in the case of the least refined of customers. Indeed, often it is even more effectual than a tempting complexion." Besides an obvious disdain for his own people and other non-Anglo-Saxons, the language of this paragraph shows Levinsky's strong animosity toward women. The man who clothes women and brags about taking care of them in fact talks about them as though they were merchandise and hates them.

Levinsky's hatred of women signals a deep sexual neurosis. Cahan connects this psychic phenomenon in Levinsky to the attitude toward clothing in both Jews and other Americans. For Cahan, the obsession with style and the need to dress up the self and the body dramatize a problematic attitude toward sexuality. The neurosis vitiates the opportunity within both cultures to achieve autonomy and individually. Moreover, each culture in its own way nurtures the psychic causes for the individual's ambivalence toward women. Accordingly, Cahan couples this basic psychic discontent toward women with institutions and behavioral patterns in both cultures that tend to turn Levinsky into a psychic and social outcast. Aspects of Levinsky's life as both a Jew and an American, some of which already have been described, interiorize a sense of inferiority and inadequacy in him that strengthens the immutability of his alienation. Thus, both cultures contribute to Levinsky's misery and unhappiness. Both share responsibility for the corruption of his character and for

his unrealized regeneration. This attempt to demonstrate partial responsibility within Jewish culture itself for Levinsky's suffering and moral failure is contrary to most interpretations of the novel. While Irving Howe notes that Cahan was concerned about Jewish "*alrightniks,*" or parvenus, other critics tend to place the burden of the blame for Levinsky's problems and unhappiness upon materialistic America. These critics believe that American values encouraged Levinsky to abandon more spiritual Talmudic and intellectual pursuits. Thus, John Higham says, "But David Levinsky's 'rise' is simultaneously a fall, and the reader participates in both. . . . In any case, the American experience, so stimulating and manifold in its possibilities, coarsened Levinsky's character in the very process of liberating it. Since he could not forget what he had betrayed, the path of commercial achievement ended in spiritual loss and emptiness." In an indispensable study of Cahan and his fiction, Jules Chametzky writes, "Rich in the things of this world, he [Levinsky] finds at last that he has purchased them at the expense of his inner spirit. At the end Levinsky yearns for more spiritually satisfying fare than business and the success ethic. He envies those of his brethren who have distinguished themselves in science, music, art, and he says that if he had it to do all over again, he would *not* think of a business career. At the heart of whatever is self-serving rationalization in that statement, we must discern a legitimate and despairing hope for an elusive center that would stabilize and legitimate his American life."

Aspects of the novel certainly support Chametzky's interpretation. For example, in the last paragraph Levinsky says, "I cannot escape from my old self. My past and my present do not comport well. David, the poor lad swinging over a Talmud volume at the Preacher's Synagogue, seems to have more in common with my inner identity than David Levinsky, the well-known cloak-manufacturer." This paragraph repeats an important theme of yearning for the past that appears throughout Cahan's writings. It also suggests, as Chametzky notes, a longing for the kind of center Levinsky thinks once existed in his life. However, this interpretation also exaggerates the significance and solidity of Levinsky's earlier identity and implies too great a discontinuity between the old David of Europe and The Great Levinsky of America. In fact they are, as Isaac Rosenfeld and David Engel suggest, very much the same person. Both have the same roots in a diminished and miserable sense of self, a self that derives from Levinsky's cultural origins as a poor Jew in Russia, which in turn involve his ambivalent psychosexual relationship to his mother.

However, before describing one basic source of his misery in his pathological relationship to his mother, I wish to discuss how his origins in Russia helped to make Levinsky a man of great loneliness and despair. Levinsky grew up in an atmosphere of poverty, misery, and worldly ignorance that cultivates the psychic insecurity and ambivalence of his relationship with his mother. Born in northwest Russia, David becomes the archetypal

Jew: an alien among aliens, an outcast among a dispersed nation of pariahs. He yearns for the past because in sentimentally recalling the circumstances of his youth he can explain his current state of despair without accepting responsibility for it. "I love," he says, "to brood over my youth. The dearest days in one's life are those that seem very far and very near at once." The very next line, however, indicates that beneath this sentiment are feelings that associate his youth with a form of sickness. He says, "My wretched boyhood appeals to me as a sick child does to its mother." Throughout the novel, he describes this inner identity, this center of his existence, in images of sickness and desolation. His mother also saw his situation in pathetic terms, at least since his second year when his father died. From that moment his mother regarded him as an orphan. "Sometimes," he remembers, "when she seemed to be crushed by the miseries of her life, she would call me, 'My poor little orphan'." In fact, the absence of a father creates a vacuum in his life that helps to shape his view of the world. "I scarcely remembered my father, yet I missed him keenly," he says. "I was ever awake to the fact that other little boys had fathers and that I was a melancholy exception; that most married women had husbands, while my mother had to bear her burden unaided. In my dim childish way I knew that there was a great blank in our family nest, that it was a widow's nest; and the feeling of it seemed to color all my other feelings."

Thus, the key to Levinsky's character lies not in his solid sense of belonging and identity during his youth in Europe but in the exact opposite—a pervading sense of destitution and deprivation. Moreover, because of their poverty David and his mother are made to feel like the black sheep of the community. Unable to pay as much as others for his Hebrew education, his mother perennially fights to give him opportunities they cannot afford. At school the teachers vent their frustrations on David so that at one point he compares himself to a friend who is always abused at home. He says, "She was the outcast of the family just as I was the outcast of her father's school." The event that turns Levinsky into a permanent outcast with a deprived and inferior sense of self is the violent death of his mother at the hands of neighborhood bullies. This occurs when Levinsky is attacked and beaten by a group of gentiles who are amused at his Orthodox style of dressing in a "long-skirted coat" and his Orthodox appearance with his hair grown out into "side-locks" over his ears. Upon seeing her son bloodied and disheveled, the mother races out of the house to attack the bullies and is killed by them. Since he is in his late teens at this time, her overly protective reaction indicates his prolonged adolescence.

His mother's death reduces David to a condition of mendicancy and despair. The impact of her death and the horrible manner in which it occurred together with the resulting state of isolation, insecurity, and misery mark the climax of the processes that shaped his character from the beginning. Describing his situation after her death, he says, "Nothing really interested me except the fact that I had not enough to eat, that mother was no more, that I was all alone in the world." He notes how the "shock of the catastrophe" had altered his outlook and way of relating to people. "My incessant broodings," he says, "and the corroding sense of my great irreparable loss and of my desolation had made a nerveless, listless wreck of me, a mere shadow of my former self. I was incapable of sustained thinking." Throughout the rest of the novel, Levinsky continues to feel essentially the same way.

American conditions nurture the insecurity of Levinsky's youth. "'You are all alone in the world!,'" he says to himself in the midst of his rise to success in the clothing industry. He also describes himself as "a lonely man." A friend says to him, "'You feel more alone than any bachelor I ever knew. You're an orphan, poor thing. You have a fine business and plenty of money and all sorts of nice times, but you are an orphan, just the same. You're still a child. You need a mother'." By the end of the novel, he still says of himself, "I am lonely," and he adds that, even after having a good time, "I suffer a gnawing aftermath of loneliness and desolation." As a permanent pariah and outsider, Levinsky's relationships with people always awaken his feelings of inadequacy and misery. Thus, he feels sure that a condescending gentile merchant believes him to be "his inferior, all the same—a Jew, a social pariah. At the bottom of my heart I considered myself his superior, finding an amusing discrepancy between his professional face and the crudity of his intellectual interests; but he was a Gentile, and an American, and a much wealthier man than I, so I looked up to him." He fails to see the contradiction of "looking up" to a man whose condescension amuses him. Similar feelings occur even in his dealings with other Jews. A Jewish sculptor doing a head of Levinsky arouses a comparable sense of inadequacy in him. Levinsky says of the sculptor, "His demeanor toward me was all that could have been desired. We even cracked Yiddish jokes together and he hummed bits of synagogue music over his work, but I never left his studio without feeling cheap and wretched." The problem obviously resides more in Levinsky's head than in the sculptor's.

Given his background and the nature of his developing values, The Great Levinsky can only feel "cheap and wretched." His debilitated sense of self makes it impossible for Levinsky ever to consider himself worthy of love or able to love successfully. Although he has a long series of infatuations and affairs, he can neither establish a solid and permanent relationship nor find a real home for himself. As David Engel says in his brilliant study of the novel, Levinsky "is nowhere at home." Levinsky's "real affliction," writes Engel, "is lovelessness. He makes no true friend, has no family, and is welcome in no home." Thus, as a boarder during the early days of immigration, Levinsky pursues the married woman from whom he rents. After years of infatuations, he becomes engaged to a woman he does not love but who promises him a Jewish home. However, he falls in love with another woman so intellectually and emotionally removed from him that the lesson of this unhappy relationship can clearly be attributed to his penchant for hurting and punishing himself.

At the core of Levinsky's diminished sense of self is a pathological attitude toward women that goes back to his relationship to his mother. In what has been a neglected aspect of this novel, Cahan shows how family and culture prime Levinsky for an ambivalence toward women and sexuality that receives added reenforcement in his life in America. In her provocative discussion of the role of mothers in shaping attitudes toward life and sexuality, Dorothy Dinnerstein uses Freud and Norman O. Brown to provide an important model for gaining insight into the formation of Levinsky's character. She argues that the mother as the "first parent" receives the first love of the child but also the burden of the first hatred for being the apparent cause of life's initial pain of separation. The mother, therefore, also introduces the first intimation of death. Dinnerstein writes, "As Brown, following Freud, maintains, the adult's grief at mortality is preceded and preformed by the infant's grief at its lost sense of oneness with the first parent: The later knowledge that we will die resonates with the pain of our earliest discovery of helplessness, vulnerability, isolation; with the terrified sorrow of the first, and worst, separation." The logical extension of this fear of death and separation is the denial of the vulnerability of the flesh that in turn requires a denial of the flesh itself. The mother as the first parent operates at the center of these drives. "Freud has pointed out," Dinnerstein argues, "how the child tries to console itself for the first great loss by mastery, by the exercise of competence and will: Torn from what he calls the 'oceanic feeling' that it enjoyed at the outset, from the passive infinite power that lay in unity with the all-providing mother, it explores the active, the finite but steadily growing, powers of its newly isolated self." In order to gain a sense of "control" over the ineluctable forces of separation, the child and then the adult renounce "the fundamental, primitive joy of the body." Dinnerstein maintains that this revolt against the flesh to achieve through denial control over death also amounts to a revolt against women because the entire process occurs "under all-female auspices." "The relation," she writes, "between our sexual arrangements and our unresolved carnal ambivalence begins with this fact: when the child first discovers the mystical joys and the humiliating constraints of carnality, it makes this discovery in contact with a woman. The mix of feelings toward the body that forms at this early stage, under female auspices, merges with our later-acquired knowledge of the body's transience and the flavor of this early mix remains the most vivid ingredient of that unassimilable eventual knowledge." This ambivalence turns woman into a magical goddess with both a life-giving power and a shame-ridden carnal body that invites death. "Woman, by and large," writes Dinnerstein, "meekly carries this burden of shame and sacredness, relying on man to represent matter-of-fact spiritual self-respect, clean, world-conquering humanity."

Dinnerstein's analysis of Freud and Brown describes very well the psychology of Levinsky's attitude toward women and sexuality. Without the influence of a strong father, caught in a culture of poverty and alienation, characterized almost from birth as an orphan, Levinsky develops an abnormal dependence upon his mother. The heightened intensity of the relationship demonstrates contradictory feelings of both love and hate. In Levinsky's case, the initial feeling of death associated with the first separation from the mother merges psychologically with the physical death first of the father and then of the mother. In spite of the separation in time of these events, the second death confirms the domination of death and isolation in his childhood. Moreover, the manner of the mother's death on the son's behalf and the guilt it engenders further intensify their love-hate relationship. She died for him. Therefore, she not only acts as the vehicle for his knowledge of separation and death but she also helps to make him feel responsible for her death. Thus, he shares death with her. So while Levinsky throughout the novel indicates his love and grief for his mother, he also demonstrates a calculating ability to exploit her in a manner that implies deep-seated hostility toward her. In a scene suggesting true grief immediately after her death Levinsky says, "I had been in an excited, hazy state of mind, more conscious of being the central figure of a great sensation than of my loss. As I went to bed on the synagogue bench, however, instead of in my old bunk at what had been my home, the fact that my mother was dead and would never be alive again smote me with crushing violence. It was as though I had just discovered it. I shall never forget that terrible night. At the end of the first thirty days of mourning I visited mother's grave. 'Mamma! Mamma!' I shrieked, throwing myself upon the mound in a wild paroxysm of grief."

Later in his life, however, the authentic quality of his grief seems to change. The artificiality of his emotions—what Engel characterizes as his penchant for "bogus emotion"—dramatizes Levinsky's ambivalence toward his mother as he lights a memorial candle for her. He remembers that "as I gazed at that huge candle commemorating the day when my mother gave her life for me, I felt as though its light was part of her spirit. The gentle flutter of its flame seemed to be speaking in the sacred whisper of a graveyard. 'Mother dear! Mother dear!' my heart was saying." This, of course is the language of sentimental popular music and the stage. It is filled with stock images and emotions. Such language and thought patterns enable Levinsky to avoid confronting his complex and contradictory feelings toward his mother. However, his actions in other parts of the book also demonstrate his confused emotions. Levinsky exploits the drama of his mother's death to gain the attention and favor of his first benefactor in America. The man offers to take Levinsky to a restaurant for a meal. Levinsky says, "On our way there I told him of my mother's violent death, vaguely hoping that it would add to his interest in me. It did—even more than I had expected. To my pleasant surprise, he proved to be familiar with the incident. It appeared that because our section lay far outside the region of pogroms, or anti-Jewish riots, the killing of my mother by a Gentile mob had attracted considerable attention. I was thrilled to find myself in the lime-light of world-wide publicity. I almost felt like a hero." Calling him "'My poor orphan boy!,'" the man asks for additional details about the incident. Levinsky says, "I made it as appallingly vivid as I knew how. He was so absorbed and moved that he repeatedly made me stop in the middle of the sidewalk so as to look me in the face as he listened." Transparent exploitation of his mother's death, however, does not always work for Levinsky. To his great dismay, he learns that not everyone knows of her or cares. There was only a murmur of curiosity and sympathy" among worshipers in a synagogue when he identifies himself and tells the story of his mother. The congregation is interested in other things and Levinsky must operate on his own.

Levinsky's contradictory feelings toward his mother dramatize the pattern of ambivalence that Dinnerstein delineates. Moreover, the drive that Dinnerstein describes which denies the flesh as a response to the mother and to death finds significant reenforcement in the Orthodox religion and culture of Levinsky's background. In fact, the theme of God, sex, and women dominates an early chapter of the novel. As a Talmudic student prior to his mother's death in Antomir, Levinsky receives instruction in the absolute opposition of sex and religion. He says, "In the relations between men and women it is largely a case of forbidden fruit and the mystery of distance. The great barrier that religion, law, and convention have placed between the sexes adds to the joys and poetry of love, but it is responsible also for much of the suffering, degradation, and crime that spring from it." Levinsky adds that in his case "this barrier was of special magnitude." Levinsky is taught about women in a way that guarantees his perpetual distrust of them. "In the eye of the spiritual law that governed my life women were intended for two purposes only: for the continuation of the human species and to serve as an instrument in the hands of Satan for tempting the stronger sex to sin." This attack on women as instruments of sin and the embodiment of evil ultimately constitutes an attack on masculine flesh as well. When Levinsky's teacher, Reb Sender, catches him eyeing an attractive woman, he tells him about Satan and refers him to a lesson in the Talmud of Rabbi Mathia. The rabbi "'had nails and fire brought him and gouged out his own eyes'" because of Satan's effort to tempt him with the image of a naked woman. The vision of the rabbi "gouging out his eyes supplanted the nude figure" that had been in Levinsky's mind. An ideology that places women in an inferior status and a religious orthodoxy that preaches self-mutilation to suppress sexuality intensify Levinsky's ambivalence toward sex and women. Both ideological and religious restrictions tend to intensify his confusion and curiosity concerning sex and the flesh. "But at present," he says, "all this merely deepened the bewitching of the forbidden sex in my young blood. And Satan, wide awake and sharp-eyed as ever, was not slow to perceive the change that had come over me and made the most of it."

A girl from Levinsky's youth serves as a symbol throughout the novel of his uncertainty about sexuality, women, and the body. Her family is one of four that crowd into the basement in which the Levinskys live. Her name of Red Esther refers not only to the color of her hair but also suggests his fear of sexuality and the female body. Throughout his life, female sexuality arouses in him the feelings and associations he had toward Red Esther. This is true of his relationship with Matilda Shiphrah, the daughter of a woman who adopts him for a brief time following the death of his mother. Matilda's situation as a divorcée and her name fascinate him. "Her Gentile name had a world of charm for my ear," he says. These factors give her a quality of forbidden experience that tantalizes him. Her flirtations and teasings remind him of Red Esther and conjure up an aura of Eve. "A thought of little Red Esther of my childhood days flashed through my brain, of the way she would force me to 'sin' and then gloat over my 'fall,'" he says.

All of the sexual images and contradictions that operate in Levinsky's mind come together in the American landlady who serves as his surrogate mother. As though to drive home the point of Levinsky's lingering sexual obsession with his mother, Cahan awkwardly names this woman Mrs. Levinsky. Levinsky takes his room and board with her and notes, "The curious thing about her was that her name was Mrs. Levinsky, though we were not related in the remotest degree." Of course, a relationship does exist but on a deep psychological level that indicates how well Dinnerstein's theory explains Levinsky's condition. The relationship with the landlady dramatizes his neurosis as a pattern of contradictory attitudes that dehumanizes women by turning them into either whores or goddesses. Subconscious drives propel him toward this woman while hidden needs to overcome the flesh and sensuality cause him to hate her. He manifests a self destructive cycle with her that typifies his relationships with all women. Thus, while observing Mrs. Levinsky one morning, he thinks: "'I don't like this woman at all,' I said to myself, looking at her. 'In fact, I abhor her. Why, then, am I so crazy to carry on with her?'" Levinsky follows this question about his compulsion with a statement that indicates a continuity of contradiction in his relationships that begins with his mother and carries forward to all future experiences with women. "It was the same question that I had once asked myself concerning my contradictory feelings for Red Esther, but my knowledge of life had grown considerably since then." The irony, of course, of this increased knowledge is that it simply adds more female names to the same pattern of love and hate, a pattern he is never able to break and which keeps him so unhappy. Thus, while dealing with Mrs. Levinsky, he thinks of Matilda in a way that seems new to him. In reality, however, his thoughts of Matilda as having fallen from a pedestal only reflect the same pattern of his relationships with other women who as goddesses must fall because they cannot escape their flesh. Accordingly, in the midst of his flirtations with the innocent Mrs. Levinsky he thinks, "I saw Matilda from a new angle. It was as if she had suddenly slipped off her pedestal. Instead of lamenting my fallen idol, however, I gloated over her fall. And, instead of growing cold to her I felt that she was nearer to me than ever, nearer and dearer." Levinsky gloats because her imagined fall helps to justify his own sexuality. At one point Matilda had called him a "'devil with side-locks'," but Levinsky never learns to confront and cope with that devil within himself and the flesh of the women he wants to both possess and idolize.

Levinsky's neurosis becomes a social pathology when he moves into the clothing industry. The Great Levinsky's personal problem achieves institutionalization in this business. His rise documents the growing dominance of a special social phenomenon of outward success based on self-deprecation, mass conformity, and the values of prejudice. Levinsky's story indicates that such success sustains the denigration of women, the debasement of the body, and the dehumanization of the spirit. Cahan's social criticism and his lines of attack anticipate by several decades the arguments and theories of many later social theorists. There is a direct link, for example, between his understanding of the social significance of the clothing industry and Marshall McLuhan's analysis much later of modern advertising. For McLuhan, the world of advertising constitutes another layer of signs and symbols that reenforce the messages of the world of fashion as rendered by Cahan. McLuhan's interpretation of advertising demonstrates the continued relevance and significance of Cahan's portrait of modern American character. McLuhan believes that advertising turns women into "mannequins" of "competitive display" as opposed to real persons of "spontaneous sensuality." He argues that advertisements demonstrate that men are threatened by the power women exercise in order to move between the contradictory images of whore and goddess. Such power heightens masculine hostility and suspicion and arouses feelings of violent detachment. This situation, according to McLuhan, creates "the view of the human body as a sort of love-machine capable merely of specific thrills." Levinsky's sexual life with women, who do not even rate a name, exemplifies such mechanical sexuality. For McLuhan, these values further debilitate the qualities of inner character and strength that are necessary for democracy. Thus, he suggests, "we would do well to strengthen those inner resources, which we still undoubtedly exert, to resist the mechanism of mass delirium and collective irrationalism."

Precisely such "inner resources" are dissipated in Levinsky. In addition, the inner weakness that Cahan's novel describes goes beyond simply constituting an attack on business and commercialism. The character of David Levinsky, who feels himself to be of little worth in a world that defiles man's greatest dreams and ideals, finds duplication in other characters far removed from the garment industry. In other words, Levinsky's belief that he would be a happier man in a more established and prestigious intellectual, professional, or academic position seems to be another example of self-deception and rationalization. Levinsky's character and background, his

sexual pathology, his place in both Jewish and American culture suggest that he would feel unhappy, insecure, and unworthy in any situation in contemporary American culture. Moreover, if we accept Isaac Rosenfeld's insight that *The Rise of David Levinsky* "consists of an extended commentary . . . somewhat in the manner of Talmud" from the opening paragraph of the novel, we can say that many Jewish writers since Cahan continue that Talmudic commentary.

Like Cahan himself, David Levinsky became a convert to the American Way. However, in his search for the "real" America, he turned to the artificial and superficial as substitutes for values of independence and inner strength. This amounted to a turn against himself and his potential. As the story of a Jewish immigrant's journey on the wrong road to the "real" America, *The Rise of David Levinsky* serves as Cahan's vehicle for an attack against those social, ideological, and psychological factors undermining the promise of America. Cahan viewed the corruption and perversion of the American idea from the vantage point of his own culture of Yiddish life and thought. To such Jews there seemed a possibility of losing two cultures at once. As their own world of Yiddish changed and moved more into the mainstream of American life, they also could imagine the America of their hopes losing its way in a world of reactionary and violent totalitarian "isms." At the same time, the belief in the importance of America to the future welfare and survival of the Jews added to the sense of Jewish investment in the idea of America. Rather than opposition to American politics and alienation from American life, Cahan's public career as a political leader and editor increasingly demonstrated a growing commitment to and participation in the American Way. Along with union leaders Sidney Hillman and David Dubinsky, he was instrumental in putting Jews at the center of the liberal consensus of the New Deal in the mid-1930s. However, examples of such personal achievement and national consensus are generally missing from *The Rise of David Levinsky*. The novel intends, instead, to uncover the other side of the American dream, to expose the nightmare of conformity, materialism, and dehumanization that corrupts the idea of America. In effect, Cahan gives us this story of America to help revivify the moral imagination of all the people. Like the traditional jeremiad, the story functions as a warning and an attack. Moreover, this jeremiad achieves special immediacy and intensity because it is rendered through the perspective of a lost generation. Engel correctly articulates Levinsky's dual tragedy by claiming that "there is simply no viable world to which one can return" and that there can be "no easy faith in progress." The moral rhetoric of the story, however, mitigates such pessimism by insisting that "modernity" may complicate but does not automatically eliminate the moral vision of America. A myth of regeneration and a rhetoric of moral responsibility in Cahan's novel suggest the possibility of a future of choices that were unavailable to the oppressed cultures of the past.

L. S. Dembo (essay date 1988)

SOURCE: "Levinsky and the Language of Acquisition," in *The Monological Jew: A Literary Study,* The University of Wisconsin Press, 1988, pp. 84-92.

[*In the following essay, Dembo discusses Cahan's use of language and dialogue in* The Rise of David Levinsky.]

What does the rise in *The Rise of David Levinsky* actually mean? We know what it means in *The Rise of Silas Lapham* by that author whom Abraham Cahan admired as a realist, William Dean Howells, but the question of Cahan's attitude toward his hero is more complex and more fraught with ambiguity. Even though Levinsky is in many ways a projection of his creator and often serves as his spokesman, the novel is far from being autobiographical. For one thing, the author was a life-long socialist, the character a business tycoon, portrayed as having, whatever his faults, a great deal of sensitivity and insight.

Why has Cahan chosen, in his one important novel, to omit the struggles of the Jewish socialist movement in America, in which he himself played no mean part, and instead to concentrate on the personal problems of a single, bourgeois man—to take as his central concern not the class struggle in the period of rapid industrialization after the Civil War but the vicissitudes in the life of an ambitious but essentially nonpolitical Russian immigrant? His reading of Plekhanov, Marx, and Engels, not to mention his personal experiences as a propagandist and agitator, does not shape with any real consistency Cahan's conception of the virtues and flaws of American society or his view of the life of the Jewish immigrant.

Atheistic socialism and monotheistic Judaism have, perhaps, a common denominator in the belief that self-fulfillment is possible only in social terms, in contrast with individualistically centered theories, which state that perfectability lies only with the single man and that self-fulfillment cannot be transcended. David Levinsky is neither a socialist nor, in his adulthood, a Torah-reading Jew; he is philosophically, as well as literally, on his own. He must, in essence, create his own values or at least act without any sanction of authority or possibility of confirmation. His values and ideals are therefore an assemblage drawn from the various layers of his experience and they ultimately satisfy psychic needs rather than claim universality.

It is precisely the preoccupation with language—with the perpetual confrontation encounter, or meeting expressed in and by dialogue—that makes the theories of Martin Buber so valuable as a perspective on Cahan's novel. The world of individuality—the existential world in which the predatory Other and the I-It relations among men prevail—appears here in sharp definition. It is a world that Cahan cannot condemn or exonerate, neither rebel against as militant socialist or disillusioned Jew nor wholly embrace.

Whatever its defects, America is the Golden Land and that faith underlies and is expressed in this outburst in a Catskill resort during a dinner concert (Levinsky is caught up in the emotion and so, we can assume from the absence of irony, is Cahan, himself):

> [The audience has joined in with the playing of the "Star Spangled Banner"] Men and women were offering thanks-giving to the flag under which they were eating this good dinner, wearing these expensive clothes. There was the jingle of newly-acquired dollars in our applause. But there was something else in it as well. . . . It was as if they were saying: "We are not persecuted under this flag. At last we have found a home."
>
> Love for America blazed up in my soul. . . . we all sang the anthem from the bottom of our souls.

I do not think it is coincidental that Thackeray should be mentioned as one of Levinsky's favorite writers, for Levinsky's world, if not one of upheaval in the socialist sense, is a Vanity Fair in which the struggle for survival is carried out with chiefly verbal weapons and nothing succeeds like eloquence.

Now, Buber classifies dialogue into three forms, the last of which is of particular interest to us here. I shall not insist that the description is applicable in all its technical details to Cahan's novel, but it does give us an insight into the relation between speech and character when the ideal cannot be reached. Buber calls the first variant *debate* and says that in this form,

> thoughts are not expressed as they existed in the mind but in speaking are so pointed that they may strike home in the sharpest way and moreover *without the men that are spoken to being regarded in any way present as persons;* [then there is] *conversation* characterized by the need neither to communicate something, nor to learn something, nor to influence someone, nor to come into connexion with someone, but solely by the desire to have one's self-reliance confirmed by marking the impression that is made, or if it has become unsteady to have it strengthened. (my italics)

Buber concludes the list with "friendly chat," in which each speaker regards himself as an absolute and the other as relative, and lovers' talk, in which each partner enjoys only his own soul and "precious experience." I do not propose, at this point, to seek out passages in the novel that best illustrate these categories. I'm sure very few would exist in the pure state. They are most useful when taken suggestively rather than literally. Monologue disguised as dialogue is, I daresay, the primary expression of the moral vulnerability of the fictive America that Cahan has created and peopled.

"We are all actors, more or less," says Levinsky. "The question is only what our aim is, and whether we are capable of a 'convincing personation'." This principle underlies social discourse in a culture founded upon competition, and competition not just for material gain or "success" but for psychological and spiritual fulfillment as well. The real crisis of dialogue in Levinsky's America does not stem from the simple antagonism of material and spiritual values; it stems from bringing spiritual values under the aegis of the principles of acquisition. Thus Levinsky is neither morally nor culturally insensitive; he fully recognizes the values of education, family life, religion, art—indeed, without them, he has found that, despite all his commercial success, his life is empty and lonely. His yearning for love and a family eventually outweighs his financial ambition, though he never captures the happiness he so avidly pursues. Like the pursuit of love or God, the pursuit of happiness is fraught with deception and contradiction. Manifested in dialogue, it reveals or yields nothing more than the vanity of the speaker, his inability to transcend the logic and rhetoric of materialism, and thereby his definitive failure to attain the wholeness and communion with another that he seeks throughout a lifetime.

Consider the episode in which, desperate for cash to hire a talented designer that can make his cloak factory prosper, Levinsky approaches an old girl friend, Gussie, to ask for a loan. The conversation, held in a quiet place in a park, rapidly turns into a "fencing contest" in which Gussie, stung before by Levinsky, smartly counters all his arguments. Midway through, Levinsky finds himself being carried away by the beauty of the spring night and the sounds of a nearby band:

> We fell silent, both of us, listening to the singing. Poor Gussie! She was not a pretty girl, and she did not interest me in the least. Yet at this moment I was drawn to her. The brooding plaintive tones. . . . filled me with yearning . . . filled me with love. Gussie was a woman to me now. My hand sought hers. It was an honest proffer of endearment, for my soul was praying for communion with hers.

"An honest proffer of endearment"—as though endearment were a commodity over which one entered into negotiations. And although the religious rhetoric of "My soul was praying . . . " is sincere, its very sincerity betrays a shallow idea about the true meanings of "soul," "praying," and "communion," all of which Levinsky has trivialized by associating them with what he admits are "temporary" feelings. "I swear to you you're dear to me," he argues, forgetting that if she really were dear to him, he wouldn't have to "swear" to the fact. But the lady yields and there follows, sure enough, a "delirium of love-making" (passionate embraces and kisses) at the conclusion of which both are left sober and depressed. That Levinsky had at one point been ready to marry Gussie all the more underscores his confusion of motives. Whether spiritual or material, all things are to be attained by the techniques of acquisition. Even the genuine intimacy of an I-Thou relation is diluted by exploitation as the it, to which the Thou is more and more reduced, begins to emerge. The subject is no longer regarded as a whole human being and a "partner-in-dialogue" but as an object to be pursued and acquired.

Levinsky's real attitude toward Gussie is one of condescension and pity, and there is little room left for genuine love or even romance. His relation with Dora Margolis, wife of his friend Max, is another matter. Whatever the sincerity of his love—indeed all the more so because of it—Levinsky never stops calculating. Attempting to seduce Dora, he slips into Yiddish, a language regarded as being suitable only for personal or family matters. It's not that he is fundamentally apathetic toward her as he was to Gussie; we can believe him when he says, "I really loved her." On the other hand, he knows all too well exactly what he is doing:

> "Dearest, I whispered.
>
> "I must go out," she said. . . .
>
> "Don't. Don't go away from me, Dora. Please don't," I said in Yiddish, with the least bit of authority. "I love thee. I love thee, Dora," I raved, for the first time addressing her in the familiar pronoun. . . . "Dost thou love me Dora? Tell me. I want to hear it from thine own lips."

This appeal ends in a kiss that sends Levinsky into ecstasy. But is it physical or spiritual ecstasy—lust or love, thrill of conquest or intimacy, egocentricity or genuine sharing with another? These are the very questions that Levinsky was capable of asking himself:

> My heart was dancing for joy over my conquest of her, and at the same time I felt that I was almost ready to lay down my life for her. It was a blend of animal selfishness and spiritual sublimity. I really loved her.

It will remain a "blend" until Levinsky is able to give himself without there being anything for him to pursue and acquire—until no longer wanting anything, he ceases "personation," and speaks to the lady in his own voice and in his wholeness as a human being. Circumstances, however, will not let him break the pattern. In regard to Max Margolis, Dora's husband, with whom he wishes to keep cordial relations, he tells us:

> I consulted Max, as I did quite often now. Not that I thought myself in need of his advice, or anyone else's, for that matter. . . . I played the intimate and ardent friend, and this was simply part of my personation.

Levinsky may seem close to entering into a "dialogical event" with Meyer Nodelman, who, he says,

> was a most attractive man to talk to, especially when the conversation dealt with one's intimate life. With all his illiteracy and crudity of language he had rare insight into the human heart and was full of subtle sympathy. He was the only person in America with whom I often indulged in a heart-to-heart confab.

It is to his credit that Levinsky recognizes that "crudity of language" can be as valuable as, if not more than, the eloquence with which he himself invariably speaks. Ironically, Nodelman, recognizing Levinsky's loneliness, tries unsuccessfully to act as a marriage broker for him and leaves Levinsky no better off than he was. The more he seeks an escape from the materialist and philistine world, the more confirmed he becomes in his acquisitive habits: "I had no creed, I knew of no ideals. The only thing I believed in was the cold, drab theory of the struggle for existence and the survival of the fittest."

This is, of course, not enough for Levinsky (we have heard him say things like this before) and he tells us: "This could not satisfy a heart that was hungry for enthusiasm and affection, so dreams of family life became my religion. Self-sacrificing devotion to one's family was the only kind of altruism and idealism I did not flout." If we are suspicious of such a declaration, it is with good reason, for Levinsky continues.

> I was worth over a million, and my profits had reached enormous dimensions, so I was regarded as a most desirable match, and match-makers pestered me as much as I would let them, but they found me a hard man to suit.

The assumption here is simply that old cliché that money can buy anything, a family no less than a factory—and that money coupled with eloquence are the main implements for acquiring whatever one yearns for or dreams of. Levinsky tries to perform his "public duty" in the same way and describes his philanthropic activity, proudly citing that he gave so much that they put his picture in the newspaper. Vanity is so obviously mixed with altruism here, we don't know whether to praise his efforts or decry their motives.

Levinsky's narration reveals that his rise was to wealth and a greater awareness of the refinements of American civilization and human nature, in general. It also reveals that the very elements that gave him his wealth and led to a certain sophistication are the ones that kept that sophistication limited and subverted his sense of values. Wooing Anna Tevkin, the daughter of a well-known but now neglected poet, he shows us how little he has learned about the love and family life that he has never stopped pursuing:

> I loved her to insanity. She was the supreme desire of my being. [This does not assure us of Levinsky's maturity, nor, considering his expectations, does it bode well for the lady who is the object of all this supercharged feeling.] I knew that she was weaker in character and mind than Elsie, for example, but that seemed to be a point in her favor. [A point in her favor to be of weaker character and mind? This is not the case of man and woman entering into an I-Thou relation as partners-in-dialogue and other, more physical, forms of communication; it is the precondition of an I-It relation, in which the woman tries to be whatever her husband's values dictate that she should be.] "She is a good girl," I would muse, "mild, kindly, girlish." As for her 'radical' notions, "they really don't matter much.

> I could easily knock them out of her. I should be happy with her. Oh, how happy!" [Is comment necessary?]

Levinsky's assumptions about marital relations, about women as a whole, and about Anna Tevkin in particular are perfectly in keeping with his assumptions about the way of life in America. His egoism, his chauvinism, the materialism by which he measures all things are not an eccentricity but representative of an entire society. In his own way Levinsky has succeeded in assimilating where so many others (like Stern, for example) have failed.

His is not a story of the contradictions of being a Jew in America. True, Levinsky clings to Judaism and from time to time goes to temple. He longs for the old days when he read Talmud, but this is mere nostalgia, for his actual practice of Judaism is a matter of philanthropy and has little to do with any spiritual belief. He suffers no crisis of faith on his way to becoming an American and experiences very little anti-Semitism to test his belief. Here is how he resolves the age-old problem:

> [The cloth merchant] was well disposed toward me. . . . he addressed me as Dave. (There was a note of condescension as well as of admiration in this "Dave" of his. It implied that I was a shrewd fellow and an excellent customer, singularly successful and reliable, but that I was his inferior, all the same— a Jew, a social pariah. At the bottom of my heart I considered myself his superior, finding an amusing discrepancy between his professorial face and the crudity of his intellectual interests; *but he was a Gentile and an American, and a much wealthier man than I, so I looked up to him.*) (my italics)

Thus, after scoffing at the cloth merchant for thinking him inferior, Levinsky reverts to the same anti-Semitic logic and ends up agreeing with him. And he can agree with him precisely because anti-Semitism is not an important factor in his life. It enters the narration only once again—in the episode in which Levinsky gives up any idea of marrying a gentile woman with whom he has much in common, because he is frightened by that "medieval prejudice against our people which makes so many marriages between Jew and Gentile a failure." But Levinsky gets over this loss with little grief just as he gets over the loss of all the Jewish women with whom he sought matrimony. His real agony comes from "loneliness" and that is a hazard of individualism in general and not an evil experienced just by exiled Jews.

In other words, Levinsky is not alone in his loneliness; he is lonely because he lives by the values of a society atomized by competition—a society oriented to the marketplace and not the hearth. His tragedy is that, though desperate in his loneliness to enter the hearth, he cannot do so without bringing the values of the marketplace with him.

Daniel Walden (essay date 1990)

SOURCE: "Abraham Cahan: Realism and the Early Stories," in *MJS: Annual VII*, edited by Joseph C. Landis, Vol. 7, No. 4, 1990, pp. 5-18.

[*In the following essay, Walden discusses Cahan's influence on Jewish-American culture in the early twentieth century and its reflection in his early stories.*]

Almost from his first days in America, Abraham Cahan was determined to be a man of letters. He had been influenced by pre-Marxian socialists, by Chernyshevsky's *What Is to Be Done?* and by Nekrassov's *Who Lives Well in Russia?*, so it's not surprising that he was concerned at first solely with the social component of literature. Literature had to be didactic, it had to point a lesson, it had to instruct. Thus when he discovered Herbert Spencer, and when he translated Marx, Darwin, and Spencer for *Di Zukunft,* he felt he had stumbled on a key to the philosophical materialism that gripped him.

Gradually, turning from politics and social behavior to literature, Cahan had to move from a literary understanding of sciences toward an aesthetics theory and then work out a philosophical synthesis of Marxism and Darwinism. The values of socialism for Cahan were becoming ethical and philosophical-spiritual, rather than programmatic. As part of the Yiddish-language radical press corps, Cahan had become an integral part of the cultural, social, and moral leadership of the East-European Jewish community. Ideologically, in Russia he had been committed to so-called universals, to mankind; in the United States he came to see himself as an American Jew, not a Vilna or Galician or Litvak Jew, and a Jew committed to the American Jewish culture. Deeply held elements in the work of all Yiddish, radical, cosmopolitan writers now came to the fore in an unparalleled way.

Yet there was a paradox in that the result of the work of the Jewish press—of which Cahan was the leading spirit—was to increase and deepen the group consciousness of East-European Jews in America at the same time that it Americanized them. In this context, as Irving Howe concluded, "Cahan stands out overwhelmingly" as the "most lucid intelligence in the early Jewish labor movement." He was, according to French Strother in 1913, "the one who taught hundreds and thousands of immigrants what America means, what their duties to it are, and how they can become worthy citizens of this country."

In an essay titled **"Realism"** in the March 15, 1889, issue of the *Workmen's Advocate,* the socialist Labor Party's English language weekly, Cahan defined man as "an inquiring, social, imitating creature." Showing the influence of Social Darwinism (which was to figure prominently in *The Rise of David Levinsky*), he wrote that "the inquiring impulse springs from thought" while "sociality" [sic] is due to the instinct of self-preservation, which causes us to unite with our fellow men in joint war upon the rest of creation and which grows, according to Herbert Spencer, into hereditary habit, increasing through the survival of the fittest. As to the sources of art, "The imitating activity seems to me to be stimulated by the reflective or imitative character of our sensations. . . . For sensation is nothing else than the mental counterpart of our nature." That is, if one extends his argument, Cahan was arguing for the severance of literary and artistic realism from what was commonly understood as photographic realism. The sole end of art was *not* to afford pleasure, nor should it be limited to the province of the beautiful. His arguments proceeded from the proposition that the word was not as important as the content. This is why he preferred William Dean Howells' social consciousness to Henry James' verbiage, and the Russian scenes of battles, of gibbets and hospitals, to the beautiful, fashionable landscapes so dear to the New York bourgeoisie. That Cahan was ultimately predisposed to some form of photographic realism in the arts will be developed later. The "thrill of truth" was what he was after.

The term "Realism" was first used in France in the 1820s to describe the literary process of imitating originals from nature as opposed to imitating art, the older method. Though "Reality" differed from writer to writer, what remained constant was that it would be found in commonplace things, in average lives and events, in the great undergirding truths of humankind, and in the recognition that Romance and Ideality had been giving way to the new world of science, technology, and fact, Balzac, Stendhal, and Flaubert were the earliest French Realists; Jane Austen, George Eliot, Thackeray, and Trollope were among the earliest English Realists, while Tolstoy, Chekhov, and Gorki were considered the leading Russian Realists (Cahan thought Tolstoy the greatest of the Realists). In the United States after the Civil War, Twain, DeForest, James, and Howells were the major proponents of Realism; they proposed honesty to life as the standard against which all literary output was to be measured.

In the 1890s, as Larzar Ziff has pointed out, the continuity of the Realists' careers was interrupted. With the onset of Naturalism (an excessive form of realism in which the forces of nature and the city encroached on individuals, deterministically and pessimistically), there was an unsettling pause, a temporary state of confusion. At the same time, Romance and Ideality appeared to be making a comeback. It is in this context that Howells, as an editor and critic, looked to the young Realists who he felt would continue the struggle. Cahan, along with Stephen Crane, Hamlin Garland, Paul Lawrence Dunbar, and Charles Chesnutt, was one of the young, promising Realists.

After reading Chekhov, Cahan had recently rediscovered Tolstoy, mainly through his wife Anna Bronstein's efforts. Tolstoy, he believed, understood the Russians; Chekhov, Cahan wrote (*Bookman*, December 1902), was the Tolstoy of the Russian short story, as realistic in character portrayal as in detail and motive, and with a mature humor. Now, Cahan believed, he was beginning to know his people, in America. Tolstoy was a realist whose pedantic truthfulness he appreciated. In Tolstoy, "the power of realistic art arises from the pleasure which derives from recognizing the truth as it is mirrored by art." In his eyes, these writers led inevitably to social protest or socialism, in large part because their work was in a tradition parallel to that of Howells, the great American Realist, "whose pen makes a more dangerous assault on the present system than the most rabid 'foreign socialist.'" Cahan, without saying so, had come to appreciate the American brand of socialism. He decided to compromise his own formerly rigid ideological Marxist positions in order to accommodate socialism to the dynamic character of American society.

As early as 1883 Cahan had achieved some recognition with an English article in the *New York World* critical of the coronation of Alexander III. Soon he was able to make his living by teaching English to Russians on the East Side. Every moment he could spare from working he devoted to learning about America. One day he heard that the political leaders Evarts and Blaine were to speak at the Grand Opera House in New York. He badly wanted to hear them. Realizing that he could not understand even a little of what they said unless he heard every word distinctly (he was still unsure of his command of the language), he went to the stage entrance, mingled with the guests of honor, and was invited to sit on the platform. Not sure that he had understood their speeches, he looked at the morning paper and found that Evarts had made a dull speech. Now he was satisfied, because he had concluded that Evarts had been a poor speaker.

Within the next few years the *New York Sun* published a series of Cahan's sketches on life on the Lower East Side. Through such work, along with articles on American politics that he wrote in Russian for Russian magazines, Cahan made enough money to give up his evening school teaching. He had acquired this mastery of English in an incredibly short time. When he arrived in New York in 1882, he had known almost no English. With Appleton's *Grammar*, some amateur tutelage, and dedication, he began to learn the language. Deciding that he must really learn English, he bought a copy of Eliot's *The Mill on the Floss*, in the old Seaside edition for twenty cents. At night in his room on Clinton Street he read the book, underscoring every word he did not understand and copying it into a pocket notebook along with the definition. The first page of the novel was black with scorings. The last page was clean except for one underlining.

In those days Cahan breakfasted on stale bread at two loaves for five cents, both because it was cheap and because by putting it in his pockets he was able to study and eat at the same time. Gradually he was being introduced to what Louis Wirth called "urbanism as a way of life." Through the use of his mind, the use and command of Russian, Yiddish, and then English, and the intensity of his motivation, Cahan moved into his proper place in society. His work tested modernity in terms of an urban

vision of human freedom, taking its place among the efforts of the liberating imagination in reminding us that tradition is recursive, a dominant presence within and despite the overwhelming power of the modern. "Even here in this rich country," wrote Louis Simpson, "scripture enters." The fact is that in America only those things are real whose strength is not impaired but confirmed by thinking. "Neither the freedom of the schlemiel and poet nor the innocence of the suspect nor the escape into nature and art, but thinking," says Hannah Arendt "is the new weapon—the only one with which . . . the pariah is endowed . . . in his vital struggle."

Cahan had entered the United States as a pariah from Russia. He learned to adapt, not to become subservient, but to allow his own personality, talent, and individualism to emerge. As Ralph Ellison's Invisible Man learned, gradually, and then all in a rush, the world was full of possibility if one knew how to use the past to move into the future. As the protagonist in Isaac Rosenfeld's *Passage from Home*, defines the problem,

> as a Jew I was acquainted as perhaps a Negro might be, with the alien and the divided aspect of life. . . . I had come to know a certain homelessness in the world, and took it for granted as a part of nature; had seen in the family, and myself acquired, a sense of sadness from which both assurance and violence had forever vanished.

A *zwischenmensch* (a between person), he understood that, just as a black person pondered his skin and body, asking himself why it differed so much from others when inside he felt his common humanity, "so I would consider my skin, my eyes, my hair, and wonder why I should feel an inner difference when outwardly I was the same as other men." Rosenfeld's hero learned as did Cahan, that if our lives contain a secret, the recognition of our failing, then to discover that failing and to speak of it is "the whole truth."

When he wrote for the *Arbeiter Tzeitung*, in **"Two Worlds in One World,"** Cahan used a Yiddish deliberately geared to the general reader. In the first issue he wrote, "alts geyt vi geshmirt," that is, "Everything goes smoothly," or, literally, "Everything goes as if it were greased," a prelude to contrasting wealth and poverty in the salons and parlors of New York's Fifth Avenue, that he would use so often. In January 1891 "Sidra" (Bible Portion of the Week), as the Proletarian Traveling Preacher, *Der Proletarisher Maggid*, he began "I am Joseph your brother, whom ye sold unto Egypt," but the meat of his article dealt with the fact that rich and poor, masters and slaves, all existed at the same time in the same place, as is true still. Cahan was telling a story, though didactically. Already, he was evoking plot and character, as a realist would do.

There is no doubt that Cahan's years as a Yiddish journalist were all-important to his career. As editor of the *Arbeiter Tzeitung* he created a weekly column called the "Sidra," because he had to turn out a class-conscious, proletarian interpretation of a biblical story, precisely because, though he was a socialist, he was also convinced that tradition and religion could not be ignored. Week after week he used a biblical episode, such as Moses protecting a Jewish worker from a cruel Egyptian overseer, or Joseph and his brothers, to accomplish his purpose. In this column he began his first proper story in Yiddish, **"Motke Arbl and His Romance,"** and it was here that *Rafoyel Naarizokh* was serialized a few years later. It was also here, as "The Hester Street Reporter," that he wrote a column titled "Fun a Vort a Kvort" (From a Word a Quart), a column that forced him into imaginative and literary directions, that gave him the opportunity (*Bleter,* III, 409) to invent "half-belletristic thoughts and expressions" and pile them on people's lives or include them in his stories.

"Motke Arbl and His Romance" appeared in Yiddish in 1891. Displaying a fairly sure grasp of the Jewish immigrant experience and a good feel for character, dialogue, and situation, the story related Motke's attempts to contract a marriage to Hannah, the daughter of his former employer in the old country. Unfortunately for him, on the boat his intended falls in love with another young man on his way to America. Motke, a cartdriver-peddler, who had just begun to succeed in America, had made his arrangements through a matchmaker. After learning that Hannah had fallen in love "under the moon," all he could do was lament the money spent and demand his money back. Motke, who used his sleeve (Arbl) for a handkerchief, is to be pitied. Meanwhile, in spite of the bathos, one has to admire Cahan's early sensitivity to the early Lower East Side; his scenes are memorable.

Cahan had been learning rapidly and well. His objective reporting for the *New York Sun* as early as 1888, despite a penchant for sentimentality, made a solid base for his later work as a writer of realistic fiction. **"Hebrews in Summer Hotels—How They are Treated—A Strange But Strictly True Illustration"** (September 2, 1888) is an illuminating description of discrimination against Jews in summer hotels and the ruses used to deal with the problem. The use of Anglo-Saxon sounding names to get reservations, for example, was one way Jews tried to get around anti-Semitism. **"Mothers of Immigrants—Unofficial Function of the Barge Office Matron"** (July 9, 1898) was another piece of realistic fiction as journalism, the story of a young mail-order bride's problems upon arriving at the barge office and the help she received. In **"Imagined America—How a Young Russian Pictured It"** (also 1898) the sub-headings almost tell the story: "A many-colored meadow with tall, young beardless men in Grey Overcoats—Women Had Been Forgotten—The Language—The Twittering of Birds Trying to Speak French—The Immigrant's Discovery—A Live Cat, A Blue-Coated Customs Official and a Frog-Like Preacher with a Bandaged Hand." It was on the basis of sketches like these and dozens more than Cahan wrote his stories, novellas, and novels. It was already clear certain themes would appear: Cahan's recognition that friends (especially *Landslayt,* countrymen) were always around, that

men had to contend with disappointments with women, that women were often abandoned, that many people would yearn for the Old Country, that success was a complex and perhaps costly quest.

Cahan's conception of art was being worked out in those first decades. After attending an exhibit in 1888 of the Russian artist Vereschagin's paintings Cahan was enraged that the critics praised Vereschagin's talent but decried his subject, the Russian-Turkish War of 1877. According to Cahan in his essay on **"Realism,"** art flows from man's imitative nature; the "end of imitative activity," he wrote, "is not so much to copy the outside nature as to stimulate the sensation which it evokes in us." Concerned with the "thrill of truth," he praised Tolstoy's "pedantic truthfulness," even as he complimented Howells for his vision as a Realist. In Cahan's mind, literary Realism and Socialism led to the same end. Interestingly, when he reread the essay many years later he quoted the words he still thought of as central: that "the power of realistic art arises from the pleasure which derives from recognizing the truth as it is mirrored by art." He added, in 1926, that he realized the propagandistic bent of his essay but that he still retained a "degree of satisfaction from the thought."

Of course, what he believed down deep, as he put it in *The Education,* was that "It is truth that we admire and that is the source of our artistic delight. The heart experiences a thrill in recognizing a friend in a faithful portrait. Yet capitalist critics don't want the truth. It disturbs the class they serve." That is to say, as he put it in **"The Yiddish Theatre & American Novels"** (*Arbeiter Tzeitung,* April 29, 1892).

> True literature mirrors life—including relations between men and women. . . . The French are proceeding to reveal the truth of things [about sexual relations and close relationships]. American literature and Yiddish could both improve in the direction of Realism.

When Cahan referred to the "Thrill of Truth," when he referred to realism, he referred to the relationship between literature and ethnic problems that he took for granted in the first decades of his years in America. Chekhov, for example, reminded him of Tolstoy, he wrote in the *Forum* in 1899, because his characters were "irresistibly real," and because of his grasp of the "evanescent detail of life and his incisive sense of motive." Art for art's sake he rejected, of course; and propaganda held little attraction for him. Rather, what he looked for was that a story must be artistic and through illusion provide a faithful transcript of life. For the same reasons he admired the English-Jewish novelist and playwright, Israel Zangwill, because Zangwill's work exuded sadness and tragedy colored by a sense of fun and the ludicrous. In the same way he wrote glowingly of the new Yiddish writers in America. Although uneducated in the ways of the world, they were religiously, traditionally educated, and able somehow to sense human motive and character. Whether they wrote of the issue that separated the immigrant from Americanness or depicted scenes of the pathetic and extraordinary, they proved capable of handling everything. His admiration stemmed from his sympathy for the writer's love for "the little man," the figure immortalized by the great Yiddish writers Mendele, Perets, and Sholem Aleikhem. Far from being alienated by these Russian and Yiddish characteristics, Cahan thought them central to his definition of literature, and they account for his approval of William Dean Howells, Frank Norris, and Theodore Dreiser. His search for and love of "the thrill of truth" motivated him in almost everything he wrote and explains whom he was drawn to and why.

His next story in Yiddish, *Rafoyel Naarizokh Iz Gevoren a Sotsialist* (*Rafael Naarizokh Becomes a Socialist*), published also in the *Arbeiter Tzeitung,* was about an immigrant who slowly becomes aware of class differences and turns to socialism. Rafoyel, a carpenter from a small town in Russia, is a talented worker but is so honest that he's considered almost a wimp His last name, Naarizokh, actually a nickname, comes from a part of the Sabbath service that he constantly hums. Induced to go to America by his brother's promise of $10 a week without a Czar or tax assessor, he and his wife soon learn that America's "machines" lead to greater productivity for the employers and owners, nothing for the workers. A greenhorn, having learned that America is not necessarily a golden land, Rafoyel cannot forget the contrast between the rich and the poor, and the emphasis on machines, not people. True, he recognizes that the fault doesn't lie with the machines but with those who own them. At the same time he learns of the problems of ownership, of the nature of predatory capitalism, of the need for a more beautiful world. His vision is his "song of songs"; given the state of technology, it should be possible. Then suddenly it occurs to him that the answer is in community-owned factories, corporations, everything. When he discovers at a meeting that his idea is called "socialism," his "song of songs," he realizes that he is a socialist—not richer, not more pious, but more of a *mentsch.*" In the American vernacular, he has become a new man. As Cahan recalled in 1911, "If as a socialist you want to influence real live men, you must first be a real live man yourself."

Finally, **"Di Tsvey Shidukhim"** ("The Two Matches"), which appeared in the *Arbeiter Tzeitung,* describes the marriage of Harris and his friend Jake. After Harris kisses Becky, whom he likes, she rejects him, mistakenly feeling that she's been too forward. A few weeks later, on the rebound, Harris marries Becky's aunt, Mrs. Zager. Meanwhile, a distraught Becky marries Jake. Both marriages, needless to say, are failures. The point of the story, going beyond the bare outline, lies in Becky's awakening sexuality and in the conflict-laden social situation. Probably because of the daring nature of the theme for the 1890s, this story was never translated.

Cahan's first story in English, a translation and variant of **"Motke Arbl,"** was published in *The Imported Bridegroom and Other Stories* in 1898. **"A Providential Match"** begins with an explanation of the nickname of the hero, Rouvke Arbl, now Robert Freedman (Freed—man). In Russia, Rouvke used the sleeve of his coat as a handkerchief. Rouvke—thought to be a more familiar, understandable name than Motke to an American audience—drove carts and was a man-Friday for Peretz the distiller. In America, with four years of experience, he's a different young man with an imposing business card: "Robert Freedman; Dealer in Furniture, Carpets, Jewelry, Clothing, Ladies Dress Goods, etc. Weekly Payment Taken." A modest success, Americanized to the extent that he is called Robert instead of Rouvke, he dresses appropriately and watches his manners (as far as he can); he is free but the Old World clings to him. Rouvke is convinced by Reb Fayve, a melamed who was a shadkhen (marriage broker), that a match could be arranged with Hanele, the refined daughter of his former employer Peretz. Peretz's initial revulsion changes when he realizes that Hanele, at twenty-five, is unlikely to marry in the near future. Fayve's letters stress that "America makes a new man of every young fellow." On the trip across, Hanele falls in love with a young man with spectacles wearing the seedy gray uniform overcoat of a young Russian collegian.

On his arrival at Castle Garden, where Rouvke has gone to meet Hanele, she introduces him to "Gospodin Levinsky, my chosen," and told that, "it is my Providential Match." Rouvke can only sputter, in Yiddish, "I want my hundred and fifty dollars back." Although Levinsky promises to pay him back, as Hanele and Levinsky sweep past him and as the marriage broker stands wringing his hands, Rouvke is left staring, at a loss to explain the situation; too late, ruefully, he realizes that in America he doesn't need a marriage broker, a shadkhen, and that "the soothing smiles of the moon—that skillfulest of shadkhens," had proved most potent of all.

"A Providential Match" foreshadows later stories as well as *The Rise of David Levinsky,* where we learn of the fabric of the immigrants' life and experiences, the clash of values, and the nature of the interaction of the immigrant and the factory and business world. What makes the story appealing is Cahan's ability to show us full-dimensioned characters, especially Rouvke-Robert and Reb Fayve, as they struggle with the confusing mores of America and are unable to define and express their feelings, their disappointment, and their sense of loss at the end.

What Robert learned immediately was that a matchmaker cannot guarantee the results of his work. The more important lesson was that he now had to recognize that he was still a kind of greenhorn. Though his four years in America had earned him a measure of success, he had to take account of the intangible and irrational. A balegole, a drayman, in Russia, nicknamed "Arbl," he hadn't really changed; although he had convinced himself that he had, "the face was precisely the same." Understandably he had deluded himself. Mixed with his feeling that he had succeeded was his yearning for his native Kropovetz. Simultaneously attracted to and repelled by American-born girls, he couldn't quite grasp the fact that he couldn't fulfill their expectations. Even if they were Jewish they appeared "Christian," and they would expect to be on a level with him, perhaps to dominate him. No wonder he decided to try to contract for Hande.

The title **"A Providential Match"** is a delicious irony, even comical. Obviously the match was made by Robert and the matchmaker, and Peretz and his daughter, all human beings operating without heaven's assistance. That Robert's face is pockmarked is unfortunate, but Cahan allows the hero to overhear others speaking of his face and that he is no "catch." That Cahan's comic language goes too far, and may be seen as caricature, is also true. Comic language is a valid comic form. Unkind references to dialect or too many gross malapropisms reduce the language to bad taste, ugly dialect. Perhaps, as Louis Harap writes, Cahan had not yet achieved a tone that would carry his fiction beyond the thin line that separates the anti-Semitic from the naturalistic in fiction about Jews. Whichever interpretation one accepts, the fact is that **"A Providential Match"** was a successful story, the one that drew Howells to contact him and led to their longlasting relationship.

Howells first met Cahan in 1892. While doing research for the opening section of *A Traveler from Altruria,* in which he was to write about union organizers, Howells sought out Cahan at an East Side cafe but missed him. He left his card asking Cahan to come see him. Much to Howells' amazement, when they met, Cahan told the senior writer that he had read everything he had written, and that he admired him very much. As was to be expected, they talked about writers in general and then about Russian writers. Although Howells had invented a likable socialist, Lindau, in *A Hazard of New Fortunes,* he could not have imagined an Abraham Cahan. Nothing prepared him for this intelligent, intellectual, passionate socialist. They met again, in 1895, after Mrs. Howells had picked up a copy of *Short Stories* on a newstand and, recognizing Cahan's name, brought it home. On this occasion Howells, convinced that Cahan must continue to write, although he had some reservations about **"A Providential Match,"** noting that the story was not "really a serious thing," encouraged him to work up something more substantial on ghetto life. This impelled Cahan to begin work on *Yekl.* It was Howells' interest and support that would find a publisher for *Yekl.* As would be evident in both *Yekl* and *The Rise of David Levinsky,* what stood out were the yearning to be someone, to be recognized as a Yankee or an American, the terrible longing to become a success, and the loneliness of "pecuniary emulation" and achievement, words soon to be popularized by Thorstein Veblen. Along the way, Cahan manipulated language, as Henry Roth and Bernard Malamud would decades later, albeit at times awkwardly. When the characters spoke in English, accents abounded; when they spoke in Yiddish, there was fluency. That the English tended to the heavy, ponderous Victorian tones of the day was expected. Drawing upon Russian, Jewish, and American sources, Cahan's English vacillated from

cliches to subtitles, from obvious influences of the Old World to the nuances of the New Cahan remembered:

> Between the walls of the synagogues, on the top floor of some ramshackle tenement house, they sing beautiful melodies, some of them composed in the caves and forests of Spain, and these and the sighs and sobs of the Days of Awe, the thrill that passes through the heartbroken *talith*-covered congregation when the *shofar* blows, the mirth which fills the house of God and the tenements upon the Rejoicing of the Law. . . . all these pervade the atmosphere of the ghetto with a beauty and charm.

Immediately following the success of **"A Providential Match,"** Cahan wrote **"A Sweat-Shop Romance"** (originally titled **"In the Seventh Shop,"** and published in *Short Stories* (XIX June 1895, 129-43), the story of the courtship and marriage of Beyle, a finisher in Leyzer Lipman's shop. Leyzer Lipman was one of the contract tailors (called "cockroaches," that is, they ran small "cockroach-shops") on the third floor of a rickety tenement on Essex Street. In great detail, Cahan described the sweatshop:

> Dangling against the door or scattered among the bundles, there were cooking utensils, dirty linens, Lipman's velvet skullcap, hats, shoes, shears, cotton-spools, and whatnot. A red-hot kitchen stove and a blazing grate full of glowing flatirons combined to keep up the overpowering temperature of the room, and helped to justify its nickname of sweatshop in the literal sense of the epithet.

Beyle loved her coworker Hyman even though she was aware that he was very stingy. She kept wondering when he would propose marriage. One day Zlate, Leyzer's wife, asked her in an imperious tone to get two bottles of soda to impress Old Country visitors. When Beyle refused, egged on by another hand, David (while Hyman remained silent), she and David were fired. A week later, after Hyman finally got up enough courage to visit Beyle he arrived in time to hear, through her door, the unmistakable sounds of a party celebrating the engagement of Beyle and David. While Hyman had been tied to his machine, tongue tied, David had acted. David found work for himself and Beyle, saw her home every night, and treated her to candy and to a coffee saloon.

Although Cahan regretted the pat ending, the romantic finish, explaining lamely that it appeared right for an American audience, the story succeeded in picturing the lives and problems of the garment hands and the bosses and their cockroach shops, so common then, and the human dimension of the Jewish immigrants in the 1890s. Contrasted with the realistic description of the sweatshops was the limited but real emotional stress of the lovers, the would-be lover, and the boss and his wife. At first, Beyle wondered whether she was really in love, because she "never feels anything melting, nor can she keep disliking certain things about Hyman" Later, it was David's image that overwhelmed her, "the image of a pluckier fellow than Hyman, or one with whom there was more protection."

In spite of its weaknesses, the story was memorable for it was a transitional phase on the way to *Yekl* the later stories, and *David Levinsky.*

The sweatshop, in which many Jews were employed, was the most prominent and lucrative industry of the ghetto at the turn of the century. The shop, the Lipmans' apartment after hours, had three rooms; the hot stove served to keep the flatirons hot. Beyle was a finisher, David was a baster, and Hyman (whose name has sexual connotations), the sewing machine operator. Piece-work ruled, for, as Cahan put it, "the sweatshop day will not coincide with the solar day unless a great amount of work be accomplished in its course." As Cahan contended, the Russian Jewish immigrant entrepreneur was not responsible for the sweating system; it was the inevitable outgrowth of mass production industrialism, and unregulated capitalism in America. The Jewish immigrants learned America's values and the rules for success and practiced them well. That, along the way, they exchanged their Old World values for those of the New World, was not unexpected; however, it was an event of importance to Cahan and to several generations of Jewish American writers.

The Yiddish word "roman" in the original title means "romance" and "novel." The "sweatshop romance" that we read implies growth, and suggests characters larger than life. Perhaps Cahan meant to see Beyle and David grow, but his inability to make them full-dimensional is a disappointment. Hyman is obviously disapproved of: he failed as a man when he silently watched his beloved humbled and fired, and again when it takes him a week to get up enough nerve to see her. Similarly Beyle, an innocent, appears out of place as the prize over which two men fight, while David, for all his earnestness, is sticklike, a serious but pontificating suitor. Yet, withal, **"A Sweatshop Romance"** succeeds because of its vivid descriptions of a tenement sweatshop and its delineation of a widespread immigrant problem, consisting of adaptability, loneliness, love, and the dynamics of mobility in sweatshop capitalism. The conditions that surround them are harsh, but their failures are due to their inability to retain their old values in the new context, not to their being ground down by the system. As for Cahan, as Ronald Sanders so eloquently put it, he "seems to have been unable to find the proper control of his own ambivalences about Jewishness." Perhaps because he was in transition from being a Socialist in Russia to being an American Socialist, his discussions of immigrant dislocation and trauma, of rising from greenhorn to "Yankee" to American Jew, were affected by his biases. He forced his point, which was not needed; his impatience and lack of compassion detracted from his artistry and realism. Pushing heavy-handed irony into the realm of anti-Semitic caricature, in **"A Providential Match,"** interfered with the local-color of the Lower East Side; similarly, his socialist didacticism, in **"In the Sweatshop,"** combined with a persistent account of unhappy love, continued his

use of themes that he would rely on throughout his career, though more skillfully later on.

FURTHER READING

Bibliography

Marovitz, Sanford E., and Lewis Fried. "Abraham Cahan (1860-1951): An Annotated Bibliography." *American Literary Realism* 3, No. 3 (Summer 1970): 197-224.
> Works by and about Cahan in English, with author index.

Richards, Bernard G. "Introduction: Abraham Cahan Cast in a New Role." In *Yekl and the Imported Bridegroom and Other Stories of the New York Ghetto*, by Abraham Cahan, pp. iii-viii. New York: Dover Publications, 1970.
> Short survey of Cahan's literary career.

Biography

Sanders, Ronald. *The Downtown Jews: Portraits of an Immigrant Generation.* New York: Harper and Row, 1969, 477 p.
> Discusses Cahan's activities as a writer, editor, and political activist.

Criticism

Carlin, M. M. *"The Rise of David Levinsky." UCT Studies in English*, No. 9 (September 1979): 54-70.
> Praises the stylistic and thematic strengths of Cahan's novel.

Fine, David M. "Abraham Cahan, Stephen Crane, and the Romantic Tenement Tale of the Nineties." *American Studies* 14, No. 1 (Spring 1973): 94-107.
> Discusses Cahan's novels and stories of Jewish ghetto life in the context of turn-of-the-century American literary realism.

Greenspan, Ezra. "Westward the Course of History." In *The "Schlemiel" Comes to America*, pp. 30-43. Metuchen, N.J.: Scarecrow Press, 1983.
> Notes Cahan's use of the traditional Jewish "schlemiel" archetype.

Guttmann, Allen. "The Rise of a Lucky Few: Mary Antin and Abraham Cahan." In *The Jewish Writer in America: Assimilation and the Crisis of Identity*, pp. 25-33. New York: Oxford University Press, 1971.
> Highlights the clash-of-cultures theme in Cahan's fiction.

Higham, John. Introduction to *The Rise of David Levinsky*, by Abraham Cahan, pp. v-xii. New York: Harper Torchbooks, 1960.

Presents Cahan's novel in the context of its author's life and times.

Howells, W. D. "American Literary Centres." In *Literature and Life*, p. 178. New York: Harper and Brothers, 1902.
  Brief appreciation of Cahan's contribution to American ethnic literature.

Kahn, Lothar. *"The Rise of David Levinsky:* Fifty Years After." *Chicago Jewish Forum* 26, No. 1 (Fall 1967): 2-5.
  Examines themes of morality and cultural dislocation in Cahan's novel.

Levenberg, Diane. "David Levinsky and His Women." *Midstream: A Monthly Jewish Review* 26, No. 7 (August-September 1980): 51-53.
  Discusses the subconscious motivations of the protagonist of *The Rise of David Levinsky*.

Marovitz, Sanford E. *"Yekl*: The Ghetto Realism of Abraham Cahan." *American Literary Realism* 2, No. 3 (Fall 1969): 271-73.
  Underlines *Yekl*'s significance as an unusually realistic depiction of the Lower East Side slum life of its era.

"Glimpses of Reality." *Nation* 105, No. 2729 (18 October 1917): 431-32.
  Brief review of *The Rise of David Levinsky*, noting its harsh realism.

Pinsker, Sanford. "Sixty Years of David Levinsky: An Abiding Presence." *Reconstructionist* 43, No. 8 (November 1977): 13-20.
  An appreciation of Cahan's novel.

Rosenfeld, Isaac. "America, Land of the Sad Millionaire: Abraham Cahan's Legend Succeeds Horatio Alger's." *Commentary* 14, No. 1 (July 1952): 131-35.
  Commends *The Rise of David Levinsky* as a neglected classic.

Weinstein, Bernard. "Cahan's David Levinsky: An Inner Profile." *Melus: The Journal of the Society for the Study of the Multi-Ethnic Literature of the United States* 10, No. 3 (Fall 1983): 47-53.
  Perspectives on Levinsky's character and motivations.

Zanger, Jules. "David Levinsky: Master of Pulpil." *Papers on Language and Literature* 13, No. 3 (Summer 1977): 283-94.
  Relates Levinsky's behavior and psychology to his Orthodox Jewish origins.

Zlotnick, Joan. "Abraham Cahan, A Neglected Realist." *American Jewish Archives* 23, No. 1 (April 1971): 33-46.
  Surveys Cahan's achievements as a social realist.

Additional coverage of Cahan's life and career is contained in the following sources published by Gale Research: Contemporary Authors, Vols 108 and 154; *Dictionary of Literary Biography*, Vols. 9, 25, and 28.

Mary Baker Eddy

1821-1910

(Full name Mary Ann Morse Baker Glover Patterson Eddy)
American nonfiction writer, autobiographer, editor, poet,
and songwriter.

INTRODUCTION

Eddy was the founder and controversial figurehead of
Christian Science, a religion based on spiritual healing.
Through her writings and public promotion of Christian
Science, as well as careful management of the church that
evolved from her teachings, Eddy established the basis for
an international religious organization that would remain
viable after her death.

Biographical Information

Born in Bow, New Hampshire, Eddy never attended school
but read extensively on her own. At the age of sixteen she
began contributing prose and poems, usually of a religious
nature, to various publications. Widowed shortly after her
first marriage and abandoned by her second husband, she
lived for many years in genteel poverty and obscurity. She
became interested in mental healing as an alternative to
conventional medicine in 1862 after a consultation with
Phineas Parkhurst Quimby, a specialist in animal magnetism. In 1866 she injured her spine in a slip-and-fall accident, but recovered within a few days without medical help.
She experienced this cure as a revelation that spiritual
power was the only true way to alleviate human suffering.
As she formulated this insight into a new system of religious
belief, she began to attract followers with her teachings and
worked on the book that would prove to be the primary text
in Christian Science theology, *Science and Health with Key
to the Scriptures* (1875). The Church of Christ, Scientist,
was chartered in 1879, with Eddy later ordained as its pastor, and the Massachusetts Metaphysical College was established in 1881 to train Christian Science practitioners. Eddy
also founded and edited the *Christian Science Journal*, one
of several periodicals that would be instrumental in publi-
cizing the new religion. When Eddy died in 1910, there
were over 600 Christian Science places of worship, with
central authority resting in the Mother Church in Boston. As
a result of Eddy's sustained efforts to promote her ideas
through books and periodicals, the church has maintained a
lasting influence through such venues as the Christian Science
Reading Rooms, which make writings by Eddy and other
church-issued publications available to the general public, and
the highly respected newspaper *The Christian Science Monitor*.

Major Works

Eddy established *Science and Health* and the Bible as
the key texts of Christian Science, and readings from

both books are central to the Christian Science religious ceremony. *Science and Health* underwent several revisions during
Eddy's lifetime, once reportedly under the editorship of the
Unitarian minister James Henry Wiggin. The principles of
Christian Science set forth in *Science and Health* were inspired
by the descriptions of Christ's restoration of the sick and dead
in the Bible, which Eddy believed demonstrated that divine
healing power is available to ordinary human beings. The material world is an illusion, and so sin, physical infirmity, and
mortality can be conquered by methodically focusing on the
reality of God's spiritual realm. Eddy published a number of
inspirational books under the auspices of the Christian Science
Church, including *The People's Idea of God* (1883), *Christian
Science: No and Yes* (1887), and *Christian Science versus
Pantheism* (1898). She also wrote an autobiography, *Retrospection and Introspection* (1891), as well as hymns, poems, and
articles for Christian Science newspapers and magazines.

Critical Reception

As a powerful religious leader who advocated faith healing over conventional medical treatment, Eddy became a

target of intense media attention, much of it negative. Since Eddy relied on her publications to promote Christian Science and to shape her own public image, these were closely scrutinized by her critics. She was accused of falsifying aspects of her life in her autobiographical writings and plagiarizing her ideas about mental healing from Quimby and other sources. In 1907 and 1908, the magazine *McClure's* published a series of articles profiling Eddy, written by Georgine Milmine and edited by Willa Cather, that revealed unflattering facts about her life and dealings with the church. Concerned that Christian Science might become a dominant American religion, Mark Twain published *Christian Science* (1907), which used Eddy's writings as the basis for a rationalist argument against her teachings.

PRINCIPAL WORKS

The Science of Man (nonfiction) 1870
Science and Health with Key to the Scriptures (nonfiction) 1875
Christian Healing (nonfiction) 1880
The People's Idea of God (nonfiction) 1883
Historical Sketch of Metaphysical Healing (nonfiction) 1885
Defence of Christian Science (nonfiction) 1885
Christian Science: No and Yes (nonfiction) 1887
Rudiments and Rules of Divine Science (nonfiction) 1887
Unity of Good and Unreality of Evil (nonfiction) 1888
Retrospection and Introspection (autobiography) 1891
Rudimental Divine Science (nonfiction) 1891
The Manual of the Mother Church (nonfiction) 1895
Miscellaneous Writings (nonfiction) 1896
Christian Science versus Pantheism (nonfiction) 1898
Messages to the Mother Church (nonfiction) 1900-02
The First Church of Christ, Scientist, and Miscellany (nonfiction) 1913

CRITICISM

Arthur James Todd (essay date 1948)

SOURCE: "Christian Science," in *Religion in the Twentieth Century,* edited by Vergillius Ferm, The Philosophical Library, 1948, pp. 357-78.

[*In the following essay, Todd provides an overview of Christian Science and of the principal tenets of Eddy's writings.*]

Christian Science is the system of religious thought and the denomination founded by Mary Baker Eddy in 1879

as the outcome of her discovery of this religious truth at Swampscott, Massachusetts, in 1866, and her publication of the first edition of its basic textbook, *Science and Health with Key to the Scriptures,* in 1875. From childhood Mrs. Eddy had been deeply religious and a profound student of the Bible, and had long been inclined to attribute all causation to God, and to regard Him as infinitely good, and the Soul and source of all reality. But in 1866 a lifetime of ill-health was climaxed by what was regarded as a fatal injury from which she recovered almost instantaneously after reading an account of healing in Matthew's Gospel. That seeming miracle set her mind to work. It appeared to her as a divine revelation, the prophecy of a revolution in human thinking, and an inspired call to action. She describes (in her brief autobiography *Retrospection and Introspection*) how she withdrew from society for about three years "to ponder [her] mission, to search the Scriptures, to find the Science of Mind that should take the things of God and show them to the creature, and reveal the great curative Principle,—Deity." In this process of seeking for a solution of the problem of Mind-healing she readily grasped (as recorded in her textbook) "the Principle of all harmonious Mind-action to be God, and that cures were produced in primitive Christian healing by holy, uplifting faith." But that was not enough. She insisted on knowing the process, the method, the rationale, the Science of such healing, and finally reached absolute conclusions. But again mere theory, however well-founded and consistent, did not satisfy her. Hence for several years she put her discovery and conclusions to practical test by healing many sorts of disease and human disorders, both organic and functional, and by teaching students to heal. This experience led her to write and publish her basic book. It had been her earnest expectation that her discovery would be welcomed as a fresh spiritual dynamic by all religious denominations of those who professed belief in the Bible and in the word and works of Jesus the Christ. But it soon became evident that her discovery was ahead of the general frontage of contemporary Christianity; therefore it appeared necessary to found a separate church to preserve the purity of the teachings and practice of Christian Science and to more effectively present it to the world. Accordingly in 1879 she and her small band of followers organized the Church of Christ, Scientist, in Boston for the avowed purpose, as expressed by her, "to commemorate the word and works of our Master, which should reinstate primitive Christianity and its lost element of healing." Ten years later this Church was dissolved, and in 1892 the present Church, The First Church of Christ, Scientist, in Boston, Massachusetts, known as The Mother Church, was organized. At present there are approximately 3,000 authorized branches of this Church established throughout the world. It is contrary to the basic governing Manual of The Mother Church, written by Mrs. Eddy, to give out statistics of membership, but authoritative newspaper accounts of the dedication of the Extension of the Original Mother Church in 1906 expressed astonishment at a movement which in thirty years had grown from a "mere handful of members" to a body of adherents numbering probably a million. Mrs. Eddy in a Message to her Church in 1901 answering a critic of her work, challenged him to match a record which "could start thirty years ago without a Christian Scientist on earth, and in this interval number one million." It may be asserted with confidence that the number of adherents has rapidly increased in the forty-five years since that challenge was issued.

Such in brief is the outline of the first eighty years of Christian Science history. Against this background certain significant details may now be presented. First, how does the Discoverer and Founder of Christian Science define it?

In her little volume **Rudimental Divine Science,** she defines Christian Science as "the law of God, the law of good, interpreting and demonstrating the divine Principle and rule of universal harmony." Any work of scholarship is primarily an extended definition of its primary concept or theme; hence it is not surprising to find on nearly every page of Mrs. Eddy's writings some new turn of thought, some phrase or term which adds a new flash of meaning to the expression Christian Science. Perhaps the most compact summary of her revelation opens the chapter on Science, Theology, and Medicine in her textbook: "In the year 1866, I discovered the Christ Science or divine laws of Life, Truth, and Love, and named my discovery Christian Science." But elsewhere occur such revealing synonyms as Science of Mind, Mental Science, Science of Mind-healing, Science of mental healing, Divine Science, Science of Christianity, Science of God, Science of good, Science of Life, Science of being, Science of man and the universe, etc. The purpose of Christian Science is to correct wrong human thinking and to replace it with Godlike understanding. Indeed on the very first page of the Preface to **Science and Health** Mrs. Eddy sounds the trumpet call: "The time for thinkers has come." In so far as clarifying terms or phrases will wing their way to the target of human consciousness she utilizes them to the utmost.

Through Christian Science the redoubtable term "metaphysics" takes on new significance. In the correction of false human thinking Christian metaphysics is the essential tool. Mrs. Eddy posits mental causation as primary by saying, "Christian Science explains all cause and effect as mental, not physical," and at once relates causation to divinity by declaring that "God is the Principle of divine metaphysics."

At this point it should be stressed that Christian Science is not, as many have supposed, just a recrudescence of deistic philosophy, nor primarily a method of healing. It is a philosophy of God, man, the inter-relationship of God to man, and man to man, and of the universe of which God is the sole creator and man His indispensable expression. It is a system of healing, but as its Discoverer clearly pointed out, "the mission of Christian Science now, as in the time of its earlier demonstration, is not primarily one of physical healing. Now, as then, signs and wonders are wrought in the metaphysical healing of physical disease; but these signs are only to demonstrate its divine origin,—to attest the reality of the higher mission of the Christ-power to take away the sins of the world."

Hence Christian Science is a religion based upon a specific content of spiritual truth. It has a literature, an organization, a basic Manual and a varied pattern of activities. But have Christian Scientists any religious "creed"? Mrs. Eddy squarely anticipated this question and answered it in her text book: "They have not, if by that term is meant doctrinal beliefs. The following is a brief exposition of the important points, or religious tenets, of Christian Science:—

> 1. As adherents of Truth, we take the inspired Word of the Bible as our sufficient guide to eternal Life.
>
> 2. We acknowledge and adore one supreme and infinite God. We acknowledge His Son, one Christ; the Holy Ghost or divine Comforter; and man in God's image and likeness.
>
> 3. We acknowledge God's forgiveness of sin in the destruction of sin and the spiritual understanding that casts out evil as unreal. But the belief in sin is punished so long as the belief lasts.
>
> 4. We acknowledge Jesus' atonement as the evidence of divine, efficacious Love, unfolding man's unity with God through Christ Jesus the Way-shower; and we acknowledge that man is saved through Christ, through Truth, Life, and Love as demonstrated by the Galilean Prophet in healing the sick and overcoming sin and death.
>
> 5. We acknowledge that the crucifixion of Jesus and his resurrection served to uplift faith to understand eternal Life, even the allness of Soul, Spirit, and the nothingness of matter.
>
> 6. And we solemnly promise to watch, and pray for that Mind to be in us which was also in Christ Jesus; to do unto others as we would have them do unto us; and to be merciful, just and pure."

Christian Science is in the line of Christian tradition, indeed of Protestant tradition, but is not to be considered as merely another Protestant sect or denomination. Current practice in radio circles and elsewhere is to set up four major religious classifications in the United States, namely, Protestant, Catholic, Jewish, and Christian Scientist. The Discoverer and Founder of Christian Science was brought up in the atmosphere of New England Protestantism, and was for nearly forty years a member of the Congregational church, taught in Sunday School, and participated actively in current theological discussions. Only when it became necessary to establish her own church did she sever the link to the church which had nourished her. But her own church in no wise disavowed historic Christianity. Mrs. Eddy never claimed to have invented any new doctrine, invoked any new powers, nor introduced any new healing methods. She did claim that Christian Science is the Comforter promised by the Master in John's Gospel. She did claim that her discovery is the answer to prophecy as recorded in both the Old and the New Testament. She did claim that her method of healing was that of Jesus and his students, disciples, apostles. Thus she traces Christian Science practice directly to Christ Jesus.

Christian Science is not new: it is as ancient as God-like thinking and spiritual perception. Why then did it need to be "discovered"? Mrs. Eddy replies: "Our Master healed the sick, practised Christian healing, and taught the generalities of its divine Principle to his students; but he left no definite rule for demonstrating this Principle of healing and preventing disease. This rule remained to be discovered in Christian Science."

Hence the ideal set forth by Mrs. Eddy is to make every Christian Scientist his own practitioner. Is not that the significance of her prophecy: "When the Science of being is universally understood, every man will be his own physician, and Truth will be the universal panacea"?

Let it be reiterated that Christian Science does not actually claim nor enjoy a monopoly on spiritual healing. Some two score religious denominations listed by the United States Census indicate that "divine healing" occupies some place more or less significant in their systems of belief. It remained, however, for Christian Science to bring out into the foreground what the other sectors of Christendom had allowed to lapse, become obsolescent, or be relegated to back stage as peculiar to some remote "apostolic age."

Enough has been said now to warrant turning to answer certain inevitable questions. For example, how can Christian Science reject the idea and the fact of evil, since it is so obvious, so universal, so persistent, so powerful? First, let it be clear that to deny the reality or power of evil is not to ignore it. Hundreds of references to evil in Mrs. Eddy's writings prove keen awareness of the problem. In both the teaching and practice of Christian Science students are warned to detect, recognize, uncover, handle and destroy the claim of any particular form of error or evil to existence, reality, or power to injure. This rejection of evil is fundamental to Science: to admit it would nullify spiritual healing from the outset.

It is obvious that, as Mrs. Eddy declares, the "foundation of evil is laid on a belief in something besides God." That something is matter. Reject that belief, and error disappears with its suppositional origin, history, and effects. After such heroic surgery the world is welcome to whatever seems to remain of evil's claim to be. Thus Christian Science offers not merely an authoritative religion and a demonstrable system of healing, but also a sound and coherent philosophy of life. Indeed on this account many have accepted it who had no immediate need of its healing ministry.

But what of the demand of Christian Science to be rated as not only *a* Science but *the* Science? Certainly Christian Science claims not only to have searched for truth, but to have found Truth, to have reduced this basic knowledge of Truth to a system which is eminently communicable; to have brought to light general or fundamental laws, and to have made this organized system of knowledge available in work, life and the search for truth.

It declares that this Truth includes all known or knowable fact, phenomenon, or action. What other knowledge remains to be apprehended or organized? What becomes of physical science, so-called? How does Christian Science regard the apparent sweeping domination of contemporary thought by the physical sciences? To the extent that they base themselves upon a concept of elementary material substance or force, it rejects them as a valid statement of ultimate truth. In short, Science rejects matter as without existence, reality, actuality, substance, or power. As put in the Scientific Statement of Being, quoted from *Science and Health,* which climaxes every Christian Science Sunday church service, "There is no life, truth, intelligence, nor substance in matter. All is infinite Mind and its infinite manifestation, for God is All-in-all."

In this rejection of matter as a reality and the basis for true knowledge, Mrs. Eddy anticipated by half a century such philosophers as Whitehead, who complain that for three hundred years human science has limited itself by its assumption of basic materiality. She puts the whole trouble in a nutshell: "Matter is an error of statement. This error in the premise leads to errors in the conclusion in every statement into which it enters."

When Mrs. Eddy wrote, "We tread on forces . . . Divine Science, rising above physical theories, excludes matter, resolves things into thoughts, and replaces the objects of material sense with spiritual ideas . . . Material so-called gases and forces are counterfeits of the spiritual forces of divine Mind," such bold challenges shocked and even amused the academic world and scientific orthodoxy. But the past quarter century witnesses a steady albeit cautious approach of many of the world's leading physical scientists to a not dissimilar ideology.

For example, Sir James Jeans speaks of annihilating matter, and frankly confesses that "the universe begins to look more like a great thought than like a great machine." Professor Eddington also speaks of matter as "an imaginary something," and concludes that "the physical world is entirely abstract and without 'actuality' apart from its linkage to consciousness." Dampier in the 3rd edition of his *History of Science* devotes a whole section to the "Evanescence of Matter," and likewise speaks of annihilating matter.

Christian Science does not, however, derive its validity from such corroborative testimony of physical scientists. It maintains hold on its status as Science by its utilization of accepted scientific methods and procedures, notably revelation (spiritual enlightenment); reason (gathering of factual data and utilization of inductive logic); demonstration (practical proofs).

Christian Science is an eminently practical way of life. Its Founder and Leader had an enormous fund of common sense and a lively wit along with the deepest grasp of spiritual truth since the days of Christ Jesus the Way-shower. Hence her constant urging to beware of running ahead of one's power to demonstrate one's spiritual attainments, and her insistent injunction not to ignore evil or erroneous material beliefs. For contrary to common apprehension, as we have already pointed out, Christian Science does not ignore what it regards as unreal. This religion teaches its adherents to forsake and overcome every form of error or evil on the basis of its unreality; that is, by demonstrating the true idea and fact of reality. This it teaches them to do by means of spiritual law and spiritual power. Thus the practice of Christian Science is not merely mental; it must be also spiritual. Indeed, it is truly mental only as it is absolutely spiritual.

Christian Scientists on this present plane of existence do not claim to have realized or manifested fully the spiritual perfection which the Bible teaches from the first chapter of Genesis, through the teachings of Jesus and the apostolic doctrine, to the final scene of St. John's apocalyptic revelation. Their more modest claim derives from their Leader's teaching that perfection must be won, and that "earth's preparatory school" becomes an instrument to this end. Human experience is the arena for the regeneration of the fleshly mind through Truth and for the substitution of better for poorer beliefs until absolute Truth is reached.

We have now set forth the justification of the term Christian Science as both Christian and scientific. Moreover it ascribes to itself nothing short of being the only true and valid science, Mind-science, the revelation of the infinite divinity in all His "nature, essence, and wholeness"; and it posits the unity, indeed the identity of Science and Christianity. Hence it cannot be classified as merely a Christian sect or another denomination, for it permeates and must eventually transform every other statement of the Christian message to mankind.

Such declarations will continue to provoke in the serious inquirer's mind a flock of questions, just as they did when the Discoverer of Christian Science first issued her challenge. Topping the list would probably stand this one: Do Christian Scientists believe in God? In her Message to The Mother Church for 1901, Mrs. Eddy gave a full and direct answer: "We hear it said the Christian Scientists have no God because their God is not a person. . . . The loyal Christian Scientists absolutely adopt Webster's definition of God, 'A Supreme Being,' and the Standard dictionary's definition of God, 'The one Supreme Being, self-existent and eternal.'"

Is Christian Science, then, a rather thin modern broth of Deism? When Mrs. Eddy was asked directly, Do you believe in God?, she replied: "I believe more in Him than do most Christians, for I have no faith in any other thing or being. . . . To me God is All. He is best understood as Supreme Being, as infinite and conscious Life, as the affectionate Father and Mother of all He creates."

The concordances to Mrs. Eddy's writings reveal how the allness of God permeates Christian Science, and how it derives not from Platonic, Hegelian, or any other philosophy, but directly from the Scriptures. And yet it does not indulge in mere Bible-worship. As noted in the Tenets already quoted, it accepts the "inspired Word of the Bible." Thus the Bible is a source, a guide, but not a fetish. God alone is to be adored, worshiped, and obeyed. Hundreds of references might be cited from the approximately 2,500 which appear in *Science and Health* and the 4,000 in Mrs. Eddy's other writings. Only the ill-informed person or the most bigoted critic could claim that Christian Science is "godless."

Next in order, Do Christian Scientists believe in man, and what do they believe about man? Mrs. Eddy considered the term Christian Science as related especially to this truth as "applied to humanity." Hence the need for a clear concept of man. This she supplies in a three-page definition in *Science and Health,* making clear the distinction between mortal, corporeal, physical human kind, and spiritual, real, immortal man, the son of God. It is just at this point that Science parts company with traditional theology and accepts the spiritual record of man's creation in God's image and likeness described in the first chapter of Genesis and in the first five verses of the second chapter. In other words, Science rejects in toto the dustman theory and all it implies as primitive allegory and folk-belief. Mrs. Eddy epitomizes the issue in two brief sentences: "Human philosophy [and she might have included traditional theology] has made God manlike. Christian Science makes man Godlike."

Human consciousness becomes the arena in which Science, the revelation of divinity, battles with, displaces, and finally extirpates the mesmeric belief of man as material, as separated from his Father-Mother, creator and sustainer, God. That battle is the practice of Christian Science.

It is impossible in Science to mix material medicine and spiritual healing. You cannot work from two opposite standpoints and succeed. Hence a patient may not at the same time invoke both material remedies and scientific prayer. This does not mean discourtesy nor antagonism toward medical doctors or surgeons. Indeed Mrs. Eddy frequently paid high tribute to the better representatives of the medical profession.

But how can a Christian Scientist speak of healing unless he believes in a human material body which seems to demand healing? Of course man has a body. But that body is not material or physical. Human body and human mind are merely two aspects, outer and inner, of the same appearance. Human belief constructs this human body, controls it, afflicts it, and finally destroys it. Never was that body material; it was always a mortally mental concept,—although appearing to the human senses as an aggregation of organic cells. Hence the possibility of utilizing spiritual power, right thinking, spiritual prayer, to heal what appears to the corporeal senses as a sick, diseased, broken body, but which must be conceived as a sick, disordered, lawless, and fearful human mind.

Christian Science teaches further that in the so-called "experience of death," there is no interruption of life, continuity, or activity, no cessation of being, no dissipation of being into some pool of Nirvana, no absorption of individual identity into Deity; therefore body continues. Mrs. Eddy unequivocally declares: "Mortals waken from the dream of death with bodies unseen by those who think that they bury the body."

Now let us turn to certain other theological concepts and indicate the teaching of Christian Science regarding them. First, do Scientists accept immortality? Indeed they must, for they utterly reject the idea of mortality as part of the whole texture of belief in matter. Life, continuous life, is the reality, death the illusion. Man is immortal, cannot help being so, since God is Life itself and man lives in God. He is immortal and harmonious now and does not have to achieve immortality by dying. This very inextinguishable continuity of being, infinite, uninterrupted, and eternal connotes pre-existence as well as "future life." Life is not chopped into little segments by some mythical Lachesis and Atropos, is not limited by any so-called "natural lease on life," nor contingent on a mortal physical body. But this teaching does not in any way involve the complicated oriental beliefs in transmigration or reincarnation.

So large a role does this idea of immortality play in Christian Science that at least four Lesson-Sermons out of the twenty-six in the semi-annual cycle constituting the basis of church services are devoted to aspects of this subject. And this immortality is not conceived as a gray static condition in limbo, but as a continuous growth which all must experience until conscious perfection is attained.

Since all sin or sickness derives from a belief of separation from God, salvation is conscious at-one-ment with Him. And this at-one-ment is achieved by divine aid and encouragement to human effort, not by a substitutionary sacrifice or vicarious atonement by Jesus on the Cross. Jesus' life, not the belief in his death, is the important fact in Science.

One of the commonest questions addressed to Christian Science betrays a hang-over from primitive oriental beliefs about cosmology and the future life, namely: Do you believe in heaven and hell? The answer is unreservedly, yes,—but without any reference to a geographical location or to material conditions. After declaring that all is Mind and that metaphysics reduces things to thoughts, heaven and hell must be conceived as mental states. Indeed Mrs. Eddy tells us plainly that "heaven is not a locality, but a divine state of Mind in which all the manifestations of Mind are harmonious and immortal." As for hell, she says, "The sinner makes his own hell by doing evil, and the saint his own heaven by doing right."

Sin which is violation of divine law, brings inevitable penalty. Mrs. Eddy assures us that the heavenly Father who is Love and Truth, is not at war with His own image and likeness, man. Therefore the atonement of the Christ achieves the reconciliation of man to God, not vice versa. In this process of self-discovery and attainment of unity with God, the sin of belief in separation from God, of idolatrous acceptance of other gods, notably matter, must in some way be purged out of human thinking. Hence there must be active cooperation on the individual's part; he cannot merely manifest sorrow for wrongdoing, but must become convinced that sin confers no real satisfaction, must reform, and make restitution. Following St. Paul's injunction Christian Science requires that "the old man with his deeds must be put off," if man would avoid penalty, achieve spiritual maturity, and win heaven.

In this process of attaining daily *rapport* with divinity and ultimate unity or salvation, prayer is a method recognized by most of the great religions. Curiously enough, however, some uninformed critics have charged that Christian Science dispenses with prayer. Indeed, besides being called an infidel, an atheist, a spiritualist, a medium, a drug-addict, the Discoverer of Christian Science was referred to by a clergyman as "the pantheistic and prayerless Mrs. Eddy of Boston!" She promptly but lovingly gave him her answer which may be found in her volume of **Miscellaneous Writings:** "Three times a day, I retire to seek the divine blessing on the sick and sorrowing, with my face toward the Jerusalem of Love and Truth, in silent prayer to the Father which 'seeth in secret,' and with childlike confidence that He will reward 'openly.' In the midst of depressing care and labor I turn constantly to divine Love for guidance, and find rest." It was no mere accident which led the author to place the chapter on prayer at the very beginning of **Science and Health**. Nor did mere casual concern dictate in that same chapter the characterization of the Lord's Prayer as the "prayer which covers all human needs," and follow it with the inspired recognition that "only as we rise above all material sensuousness and sin, can we reach the heaven-born aspiration and spiritual consciousness, which is indicated in the Lord's Prayer and which instantaneously heals the sick."

No prayerless religion would provide that every church service must include a period for silent prayer and the audible repetition of the Lord's Prayer. Note further that Mrs. Eddy directs in the Church Manual that members of her Church should "daily watch and pray to be delivered from all evil, from prophesying, judging, condemning, counseling, influencing or being influenced erroneously." Moreover, in that same Manual she enjoins that it shall be the duty of every member of this Church to pray each day the prayer which now has attained wide acceptance: "'Thy kingdom come;' let the reign of divine Truth, Life, and Love be established in me, and rule out of me all sin; and may Thy Word enrich the affections of all mankind, and govern them!"

How does Christian Science view the traditional sacraments of the Christian church? It does not engage in controversy nor take sides with either those who accept the whole seven or only the two commonly adopted by Protestantism. But from the beginning Mrs. Eddy's followers retained the sacramental concept but without material expression. Thus baptism, for example, becomes not a single rite or ceremony but a continuing spiritual purifying process. Mrs. Eddy devotes to marriage a whole vigorous chapter in her textbook, which sets forth the highest ideals of chastity, purity, and stability in the marriage bond.

Communion, the Eucharist, plays an important role in Christian Science thinking and church services. Twice a year, Sacrament appears in the cycle of Lesson-Sermons. A modification of the regular order of services permits featuring a period of special communion through reading the Church Tenets and silent prayer.

Here and there we have made passing reference to such terms as spiritualism, pantheism, hypnotism, mesmerism, faith cure. Has Christian Science any kinship with them? Mrs. Eddy answered categorically in her textbook: "No analogy exists between the vague hypotheses of agnosticism, pantheism, theosophy, spiritualism, or millenarianism and the demonstrable truths of Christian Science." Chapter IV of *Science and Health* bears the title "Christian Science versus Spiritualism," and in it while displaying great courtesy and charity towards spiritualists, she leaves no doubt as to her own position. As to pantheism, Mrs. Eddy in two score passages refutes it as utterly inconsistent with Science. The reason is surely obvious, for pantheism accepts the reality of matter which Science utterly rejects.

As to hypnotism, mesmerism, or the older term animal magnetism, she devotes a brief but unequivocal chapter, "Animal Magnetism Unmasked," in her textbook. Neither in theory nor in practise can the slightest relationship be established between Christian Science and hypnotism, since Science depends upon and utilizes the divine Mind, whereas hypnotism or suggestion uses the human mind for its manipulative purposes.

How about faith cure? Since an individual seeking to be healed must start somewhere and with some inclination towards belief in the healing agency, that point of departure may be called faith. But this is faith in God, not in the healer. And many people have been healed who started with little or no faith at all. Note that faith is the first step, but even that faith in God is insufficient. Blind faith in God is limited and soon exhausted because it savors of emotionalism.

From the foregoing it must be clear that Christian Science is a universal gospel, designed to meet every human need and for the benefit of all mankind. It has already in less than eighty years spread to every part of the globe. It has permeated religious and philosophic thinking, medicine and literature, wherever such exist. Its terminology has been widely even if unconsciously accepted. State laws and courts of justice almost everywhere accept Christian Science as a recognized method of healing. In her book *Pulpit and Press,* Mrs. Eddy set down this prophecy: "If the lives of Christian Scientists attest their fidelity to Truth, I predict that in the twentieth century every Christian church in our land, and a few in far-off lands, will approximate the understanding of Christian Science sufficiently to heal the sick in his name."

The Christian Science denomination cooperates in many ways with other denominations including foreign war relief, disaster relief, and in weekday religious education (where that plan is in vogue). It is represented on the General Commission for Army and Navy Chaplains. Its members as individuals participate energetically in national and local movements for civic and moral welfare.

This admittedly cursory and inadequate doctrinal summary must suffice, although naturally a full understanding could be secured only by studying the basic source book, *Science and Health.* We must now turn to the organization or institutional aspects of Christian Science. In 1875 a few of Mrs. Eddy's students arranged with her for weekly Sabbath meetings to be conducted by her in Lynn, as their teacher or instructor, and the following year organized the Christian Scientist Association. This germinal organization continued until its dissolution in 1889, after which time it functioned merely as an alumni group of the Massachusetts Metaphysical College founded by Mrs. Eddy in 1881. Meanwhile in 1879, after a few months of preliminary discussion and counselling together, she and twenty-six of her followers organized the Church of Christ, Scientist. For a while the church did little beside hold Sunday services. Other agencies such as the pioneer Christian Scientist Association, carried on most of the distinctive activities later concentrated in the Church. The need for simplification, co-ordination, and for a focal point of administration and responsibility became increasingly clear during the ten years after the first church was formally launched. Mrs. Eddy's students had established centers of healing and teaching (sometimes called "Institutes") all over the United States; churches had been organized in several localities and even in Europe. Yet the major problem which confronted Mrs. Eddy was the need for an adequate agency to be the central administrative and executive body of the Christian Science movement. Characteristically enough, Mrs. Eddy then recommended that the Boston church organization be dissolved. This was done in December 1889. For three years the Church carried on its work in an informal way, its affairs being managed by a Board of Directors. During this time of somewhat informal conduct of church affairs the Directors were encouraged to greater assumption of responsibility. But by 1892 Mrs. Eddy had matured the plan which still remains the organizational pattern of this denomination. This plan culminated in the organization of the present Church, The First Church of Christ, Scientist, in Boston, Massachusetts. Since 1892, the denomination has consisted of The Mother Church in Boston, Massachusetts, and branch churches or branch societies wherever adherents number enough to warrant founding local organizations.

Branch churches or societies are entirely self-governing, have their own corporate existence, their own by-laws; set up their own membership qualifications; elect their own officers and Readers. They must, however, conform to certain requirements laid down in the Church Manual. The Manual requires that branches must be "distinctly democratic" in government. The form and order of exercises for Sunday, Wednesday, Thanksgiving, and Communion services, and for the Sunday Schools are prescribed in the Manual as uniform for all churches. Each branch church maintains or cooperates in maintaining a Reading Room, and calls upon the Board of Lectureship annually for one or more lectures: a branch society, being only an incipient church, may but need not do either.

The officers of The Mother Church consist of The Christian Science Board of Directors, a President, the First and Second Readers, a Clerk, and a Treasurer. The governing body of the denomination is the Board of Directors. While each branch church has its own self-government, its roster of officers patterns that of The Mother Church. The Directors of The Mother Church are self-perpetuating, elect the President, Clerk, Treasurer, Readers, Superintendent of Sunday School, editors of publications, Board of Lectureship, Committee on Publication, and other executives. In branch churches members elect Readers, also Directors, who may or may not name the other church administrative officers.

The income of The Mother Church derives from a per capita tax provided in the Church Manual, from bequests, donations by branch churches, contributions from the field for war relief, disaster relief, or other special needs, payment by guests of the benevolent institutions, and profits from church publications.

From what has been said, quite evidently Christian Science is a "laymen's movement," in the sense that it permits no professional clergy or priesthood. Each member is his own priest. Each is eligible for election to any and all church offices. Rotation in office assures democracy and participation by members in all church activities. No titles are permitted except those conferred under laws of state or nation.

What then are the specific "activities" of the Christian Science movement? First, as might be expected, church services,—public worship. In the beginning these services included preaching of the traditional type. Mrs. Eddy herself preached sermons for several years by invitation in churches of other denominations and in the meeting halls where Christian Science services were held. As she gradually withdrew from this phase of directing her movement, other preachers took over, some of them

regularly ordained ministers formerly serving other denominations. The momentous year 1895 records two significant steps in preserving and consolidating the outward aspects of Christian Science, namely, dedication of the Original Mother Church Edifice, and ordination of the Bible and *Science and Health* as the only preachers henceforth for both Mother Church and all branches.

Accordingly, reading from the King James version of the Bible and from *Science and Health* became the new order in January, 1895, for The Mother Church; and in April of the same year the branch churches followed suit. The order of services thus instituted became fixed by appropriate rules in the Church Manual.

The Wednesday testimonial meetings offer opportunity not only to hear selections from the Bible and *Science and Health,* but also testimonies of healing through application of Christian Science.

Each church may, and most do, conduct a Sunday School to which pupils up to the age of twenty may be admitted. Adult classes are no longer permitted, since the church service offers the same Lesson-Sermon for daily study, which is the basis of teaching for all but the younger Sunday School pupils.

Each branch church is required to establish and maintain a Reading Room, either on its own premises or in other quarters. Here the public may read, consult, borrow, or purchase the Bible, the writings of Mary Baker Eddy and other authorized literature published or sold by The Christian Science Publishing Society.

Since on the very first page of the Preface to *Science and Health* its author has challenged, "The time for thinkers has come," Christian Science is fundamentally committed to education. Not mere intellectual, nor cultural, nor vocational education, but education in its broadest, most regenerative sense. Mary Baker Eddy was not only well educated herself, but prized and fostered education. The nobility of her English and the originality of her style indicate an outstanding cultivated mind. But she warned against the limited knowledge gained through material senses alone, and foresaw precisely how such knowledge could be turned against its possessors and bring on disaster.

The wide circulation of the periodicals issued by The Christian Science Publishing Society offers a great variety of educational content. Of these periodicals public opinion would probably rate *The Christian Science Monitor* as the most unique educational contribution of its founder, Mrs. Eddy. For almost forty years this international daily newspaper has been setting a standard of decent journalism, authentic news, and truth in advertising; hence its wide use by classes in public schools, colleges and universities.

The Christian Science church as such maintains no denominational school or college, but several private schools and one college are operated by Christian Scientists. Christian Science Organizations may now be found in over seventy colleges and universities in the United States, Canada, and England.

We have repeatedly emphasized that Christian Science is a religion, and not just a new-fangled form of medicine or faith healing. Yet healing is the irrefutable witness that Science does embody the word and works of Christ Jesus the Way-shower and is thus able to "reinstate primitive Christianity and its lost element of healing." Hence every genuine Christian Scientist is expected to be a healer. But it was entirely natural that certain among them should feel the special qualifications for and an urge to devote their time and energies to healing on a full-time basis. *The Christian Science Journal* at present lists over 10,000 such practitioners serving throughout the world. In most localities Christian Science practice is recognized by statute or court decision as a legal method of healing, and practitioners are permitted to charge for their services. Mrs. Eddy approved such charges.

Because of persistent misapprehension the question, What is Mrs. Eddy's relation to the Christian Science movement? must be squarely faced and answered. She is known as the Discoverer, Founder and Leader of Christian Science. She wrote its basic textbook, *Science and Health,* the **Church Manual,** and a half score of other volumes large and small. She established the first Church of Christ, Scientist, and was its first pastor. After the dissolution of this Church she organized the present church, The First Church of Christ, Scientist, in Boston, of which she became Pastor Emeritus. She also provided for the establishment of its branches. She founded the Massachusetts Metaphysical College and taught classes in it for nearly ten years. She set the pattern for metaphysical healings as witnessed by many so-called miraculous cures, including cancer, insanity, deformity, tuberculosis, enteritis, "brain fever," deafness, dumbness, stomach ulcers, ankylosed joints; and was able to restore both children and adults who manifested the common evidences and appearance of death. Pressure of other leadership activities led her to publicly decline further patients after 1885, but her healing work continued on occasion directly, and also on ever increasing scale, indirectly through inspiration and continued teaching of her students. She set up all the various boards and activities of her church, including lecturers, Reading Rooms, benevolences, publications. She launched *The Christian Science Journal* (of which she served as first editor and publisher) and every successive periodical including *The Christian Science Monitor,* which was the crowning achievement of her eighty-eighth year.

Small wonder then that Christian Scientists revere and love Mrs. Eddy, consider her as divinely inspired and guided, and pay grateful tribute to her at Wednesday testimonial meetings and in the denominational periodicals. But do they identify her *as* Christian Science? Do they worship her? Do they consider her as another Christ? The answer is an emphatic NO! The growth of Christian Sci-

ence since Mrs. Eddy's passing on in 1910, however shocking to the soothsayers who predicted its immediate collapse after removal of her personality, witnesses to her genius as an organizer and to the inherent truth of her message. Mrs. Eddy never exalted her own personality, nor exacted personal homage, following, or adulation. To the contrary she constantly urged that her students follow her, their Leader, "only so far as she follows Christ." She begged them not to lean too much on her, but trust God to direct their steps. Again and again she warned her followers to beware of personalizing Christian Science or of worshiping her own personality. It was partly to avoid just this tendency of human nature to lionize and exploit personality that she withdrew from Boston and removed to Concord, New Hampshire, seventy miles away: and this at the very time her college was enjoying its highest prosperity and her fame widespread.

She never manifested false modesty as to the value and God-inspired quality of *Science and Health,* but likewise never plumed her own vanity as its author. She never considered her textbook as a substitute for the Bible, but as a scientific explanation and key to it. Hence the "only preachers" at a Christian Science church service, as she directed, are the Bible *and* the textbook.

In view of these facts one can easily comprehend Mrs. Eddy's reaction to the question of whether she was Christ. In a letter to the *New York Herald* just after the original Mother Church Edifice was dedicated, she wrote: "A despatch is given me, calling for an interview to answer for myself, 'Am I the second Christ?' Even the question shocks me. What I am is for God to declare in His infinite mercy. As it is, I claim nothing more than what I am, the Discoverer and Founder of Christian Science, and the blessing it has been to mankind which eternity enfolds. . . . There was, is, and never can be but one God, one Christ, one Jesus of Nazareth. . . ."

So Mary Baker Eddy stands as the messenger to this age of the same truth glimpsed by the prophets, taught and exemplified in its acme by Christ Jesus, practised for three centuries by the early Christian Church, overlaid by materialism and ecclesiasticism and dormant for over a millennium, again discovered, organized, and put into such form as to be available for all mankind henceforward and forever. The Christian Science Board of Directors in a public statement concerning "Mrs. Eddy's Place" which appeared in the *Christian Science Sentinel* for June 5, 1943, states in part: "she (Mrs. Eddy) represents in this age the spiritual idea of God typified by the woman in the Apocalypse." Concerning this "spiritual idea" Mrs. Eddy writes in *Science and Health*: "The impersonation of the spiritual idea had a brief history in the earthly life of our Master; but 'of his kingdom there shall be no end,' for Christ, God's idea, will eventually rule all nations and peoples—imperatively, absolutely, finally—with divine Science."

What now may be said as to the fruitage of Mrs. Eddy's leadership, the organization she founded, the church activities, the practitioners' services, and the publications? The important consideration is not the number of church members, nor church edifices, nor money value of properties, but does Christian Science maintain the healing mission its Discoverer and Leader conceived? It does. The demand for its textbook increases steadily. Many hundreds of editions of it have been issued. Dr. Lyman Powell writing in 1930 declared that *Science and Health* had become, next to the Bible, the "best seller" among serious books. But its sales have leaped to new heights since that date. It has been translated into German and French, and other translations are under consideration. This textbook contains a hundred pages of "Fruitage,"—testimonials of persons healed of desperate organic as well as functional ailments, through study of the book. The last chapter of Mrs. Eddy's *Miscellaneous Writings* consists of seventy pages of similar testimonials. Every issue of *The Christian Science Journal* (monthly now in its 64th volume) contains several pages of authenticated testimonials of healing. An almost equal number appear in the weekly *Christian Science Sentinel.* The various *Heralds* (monthly in German, French, Dutch, Scandinavian, and Spanish languages) likewise include such testimonies. One may hear oral testimonies at any Wednesday church meeting or at Thanksgiving services. Practitioners offer healing help in every state in the Union, in Alaska, Hawaii, the Philippines, Puerto Rico, Canada, Egypt, South Africa, India, Java, Australia, New Zealand, most European countries, Argentina, Brazil, and before the recent World War, in China and Japan. Christian Science nurses are available, though in much fewer numbers, in nearly two-thirds of the United States and in Australia, Great Britain and Ireland, Netherlands, Switzerland, and British Columbia. The current issues of the *Journal* and *Sentinel* record healings of such physical and mental troubles as sprained ankle, ivy poisoning, pernicious anemia, tuberculosis, blood poisoning, nervous breakdown, broken bones (including hips and pelvis), measles, whooping cough, influenza, chicken pox, ringworm, goiter, appendicitis, chronic indigestion, grief, smoking, drinking. An analytical listing of disorders healed as published in these two periodicals for the five years 1940-45 brings together not less than 250 physical ailments both organic and functional, such as acne, Addison's disease, adenoids, angina pectoris, apoplexy, arthritis, astigmatism, blindness, Bright's disease, cancer, chorea, colitis, deafness, dementia praecox, diabetes, dysentery, encephalitis, epilepsy, gangrene, hay fever, hernia, jaundice, locomotor ataxia, malaria, neuritis, osteomelitis, paralysis, pneumonia, pyorrhea, shingles, sciatica, smallpox, St. Vitus' dance and stuttering. Note that this list includes the most inveterate and dreaded organic diseases as well as functional disorders.

Hence it is no exaggeration to assert that countless thousands in this world today are "living witnesses" and monuments to the power of Christian Science to meet every human need, to heal every type of sickness and disease, and to rescue untold numbers from a premature grave to which earnest but baffled doctors and their own fears had consigned them.

The whole field of medicine and surgery has felt the impact of Christian Science. The "mental factor in disease" receives more and more attention from medical schools and practitioners. Mental traumatism now occupies a fixed place in medical and surgical parlance. In polite circles discussion of one's diseases and ailments tends to become "bad form." Even language reflects Science terminology: for example, the now common usage of "passed on" for died.

Not unnaturally the dramatic emergence and spread of Christian Science as a major religious phenomenon of the last eighty years finds expression in a multifarious literature. Books, pamphlets, and periodical articles abound,—some ignorantly hostile, some malicious, some well intentioned but inaccurate. Hence it has become necessary to set up in library cataloguing two categories, "authorized" (i. e. Mrs. Eddy's own writings or publications of The Christian Science Publishing Society) and "unauthorized" (miscellaneous publications of varied derivation and content).

Gail Parker (essay date 1970)

SOURCE: "Mary Baker Eddy and Sentimental Womanhood," in *The New England Quarterly,* Vol. XLIII, No. 1, March, 1970, pp. 3-18.

[*In the following essay, Parker discusses Mary Baker Eddy and the Victorian notion of women as purely moral beings.*]

As Mark Twain described her, Mary Baker Eddy was the very type of the American businessman, with a mouth full of moral phrases, and a totally unscrupulous head for profit. "She was always in the front seat when there was business to be done; in the front seat, with both eyes open, and looking out for Number One; in the front seat, working Mortal Mind with fine effectiveness and giving Immortal Mind a rest for Sunday." For Twain, Mrs. Eddy's hypocrisy reached a peak in her denial of the existence of matter. "From end to end of the Christian-Science literature not a single (material) thing is conceded to be real, except the Dollar," and the dollar was hunted down in a dazzling variety of ways. The "Mother-Church and Bargain Counter in Boston peddles all kinds of spiritual wares to the faithful, and always on the one condition—*cash,* cash in advance. The Angel of the Apocalypse could not go there and get a copy of his own pirated book on credit."

Twain's characterization reveals a great deal about Mrs. Eddy, and about Twain, but not if it is accepted as literal truth. Twain was outspoken in his repugnance for sentimentalism in all its forms, and felt particularly uncomfortable about the notion that women were the conscience of the nation. Preternaturally alert to the emasculating implications involved in equating the female of the species with what we would now call the superego, he was able to deal directly with the fakery of Walter Scott and the Southern Female Academy, but was profoundly uneasy about opening fire on the formidable Mary Baker Eddy. Only after turning her in his own mind into a masculine type of the Gilded Age could he vent his hostility freely. Twain's nightmare vision of a nation of superwomen concealing their lust for power behind claims to a monopoly on virtue seemed to him to have come to life in Mrs. Eddy.

Always strong-minded and histrionic, Mary Baker at the age of ten kept her family in an uproar with her tantrums and was known around the neighborhood as the spitting image of her irascible father. However, with the approach of adolescence she suddenly changed her tactics. Many years later she attributed this change of heart to an overwhelming religious experience in which she overcame in a moment the horrible decrees of both disease and predestination. Mark Baker's "relentless theology emphasized belief in a final judgment-day, in the danger of endless punishment, and in a Jehovah merciless toward unbelievers; and of these things he now spoke, hoping to win me from dreaded heresy." But her mother, as she bathed Mary's "burning temples," bade her "lean on God's love, which would" rest her if she "went to him in prayer." And as she prayed, "a soft glow of ineffable joy came over" her. The fever was gone. Her mother "was glad. The physician marvelled. . . . "Mary Baker had discovered a way to rebel against her father and a masculine Jehovah without leaving herself open to punishment. She would no longer play the dangerous game of childish willfulness; she would become a woman, and thus so spiritually perfect that man and God together could pose no threat. Sublimation, not screaming, was the secret of power.

This is not to imply that Twain's dream come true had a rare talent for hypocrisy. The inherent logic of her relationship with her father, the physiological and psychological imperatives of puberty, all those pressures upon her to become more womanly, all were strongly reinforced by certain cultural assumptions about what being a woman really meant. And these assumptions, synthesized in what Leslie Fiedler has called the Sentimental Heresy, taught that women, woman in general and some women in particular, were absolutely pure and could themselves do Christ's work in this world. Mrs. Eddy represents to Fiedler the fulfillment of his own vision of American history. It seems peculiarly fitting to him that a country in which national and individual life has been dominated by first rejecting the (European) father and then filling the symbolic vacuum left by his deposition with a composite Maiden-Mother image should be "the only Christian country in which a major religious denomination was founded by a woman."

Where Twain made Mrs. Eddy into a monster of American success, Fiedler sees her as a kind of culture hero; neither of these interpreters of her career was intrigued by the possible meanings of her failure. In fact, the combination pope and holy mother of Christian Science consolidated an empire and healed thousands without ever really integrating her own conflicted personality. At the end of a long life Mrs. Eddy fell prey to kidney stones and paranoia, proving just how vulnerable she had always been despite her energetic role-playing. Fearing the very ambitions that would have made her a superb captain of industry, she had sought the safety and sanctity of sentimental womanhood. But her naked urge to dominate could never be fully clothed in a garment of spiritual superiority tailored for the average American woman, and Mrs. Eddy was fatally tempted to try divinity on for size. What she continually sought was a way of life in which she could sublimate her drives so completely that she never really had to acknowledge them; what she found was that sublimation quickly became indistinguishable from exploitation, and that the role of Mother Mary that had once seemed so fitting was somehow sullied by contact with her own willful personality.

Mary Baker's first hope after her conversion to the Sentimental Love Religion was to carve a niche for herself in the temple of art. And although she eventually chose enshrinement in the First Church of Christ Scientist, Boston, she never really gave up the idea that her genre was inspired verse. The very real differences between Mrs. Eddy's poems, at least her mature poems, and the effusions of more typical sentimental poetesses, provide a good way to begin to see the difficulties she faced when she attempted to take female divinity literally. Women such as Lydia Huntley Sigourney who were never tempted to stray from sentimental stereotypes into religious typology never had to confront their exploitation of female spirituality—at least within the context of their verse. Sentimental formulas could contain and channel these women's ambitions; no one, and particularly not the poetesses themselves, was moved to ask whether they were secretly usurping masculine prerogatives, either in their careers or their art.

Mrs. Sigourney's muse was so methodical that she could, on request, write tributes to dead people she had never met. Even when she did draw from personal experience she never really lost herself in emotion, but moved, sometimes with almost indecent haste, from grief to Christian triumph. In "'Twas But a Babe," for example, she spoke first as a kindly passerby who comes upon a new grave and asks, "Who goeth to his rest in yon damp couch? / The tearless crowds pass on— ''twas but a babe.'" Appalled by their callousness, she cries, what of a mother's love, a mother's woe; what of the father whose agonized prayer is heard only by God? This is her cue, and quietly, between stanzas, the motherly stranger is transformed into the Great Sympathizer, and Mrs. Sigourney speaks, if not precisely with the voice of God, with all the assurance of an experienced clergyman. "Trust to Him," she calls, "whose changeless care. . . . / Passeth a mother's love." The child is with cherubim and seraphim; "Can ye not hope? When a few hasting years their course have run, / To go to him, though he no more on earth / Returns to you?"

Mrs. Sigourney had lost her first three children in infancy and undoubtedly found personal comfort as well as a ready market when she wrote her poems of consolation. Mrs. Eddy was unable to care for her only child, and eventually allowed his nurse to adopt him, while she spent the months immediately following parturition being rocked by an attendant in an adult-sized cradle she insisted her father build for her. When she pictured glad reunion in the skies it was not between mother and child, but in one curious poem at least, the "Meeting of My Departed Mother and Husband." The poem begins with her mother's welcoming Mr. Eddy; "Joy for thee happy friend! thy bark is past / The dangerous sea, and safely moored at last— / Beyond rough foam." Only the title at this point gives the reader any clue as to who is speaking, the tone is one of perfect omniscience from the beginning; there is no emotional arousal; there is no universal consolation. Instead the poem spirals around to end on a note of megalomania. When Mr. Eddy finally interrupts his mother-in-law it is not to talk of heavenly bliss, but of Mary, the girl they left behind. "She that has wept o'er thee, kissed my cold brow, / Rears the sad marble to our memory now, / In lone retreat." Yet in the end it is not Mary but her loved ones who are bereaved, and we see them trying to keep each other's spirits up by envisioning that time when she "shall mount upward into purer skies" and at last make heaven seem like home.

The ineffable joy in God's love that Mary Baker Eddy had experienced as a girl, that passive satisfaction in the arms of a maternal deity, was no longer hers. Instead, the full responsibilities of divinity were on her shoulders— she had to stand everything for everyone and always stand alone. Once she had gone beyond the limits of sentimental womanhood to explore the possibilities of a more than mortal purity, she had forever left behind the traditional consolations of the sentimental genre—the pleasures of dependency.

If it is easy enough in retrospect to see that Mrs. Eddy's solipsistic mentality was not to be the source of great cathartic art, the limits of the divine role were only finally brought home to her in terms of religious typology. In 1938 the Board of Directors of the Christian Science Church officially announced what Mrs. Eddy had hinted years before—she had been the spiritual idea of God, typified by the woman in the Apocalypse, and at last made flesh. It is only too easy to understand the appeal that this kind of typological play had for Mrs. Eddy; if she were the fulfillment of prophecy and in the direct line of Holy Mothers, she could hardly be accused (or accuse herself) of a lust for notoriety. The apotheosis of the Sentimental Love Religion need never fear Mark Twain's perceptions. Sometime in her adolescence, if her memory can be trusted, Mary Baker first seized upon the strategy that so appalled Twain; she could rebel against the authority of her father and Jehovah without laying herself open to their wrath if she but sided once and for all with her mother and the God of Love. Ironically, the problem with this logic lay in its very success. The allegiance of her most devoted disciples to her typologically proven

divinity was what finally revealed to Mrs. Eddy how the passive Holy Mother image had been permanently tainted by contact with her own will-to-power.

Mrs. Eddy, like Mrs. Sigourney before her, had seen in sentimentalism not only a literary technique by which an all-male ministerial corps might be deprived of its copyright on publishing the word of God, but, in plain terms, a job opportunity. And once Mrs. Eddy switched her energies from poetry to Christian Science, other women were quick to perceive the possibility of new careers for themselves. Augusta Stetson was easily Mrs. Eddy's most devoted follower, and necessarily, in a hierarchical organization such as the early Christian Science Church, her greatest rival. No one could have hewed more closely to the party line in believing women the chosen of God.

> It was a woman who put the leaven into the meal which leavened the whole lump. It was a woman who poured the precious ointment, an offering to the divine inspiration. A woman knelt at the foot of the cross when all the terrified men, save one, forsook Jesus in self-protection. To a woman Jesus first revealed himself after the resurrection. It was the woman in Revelation who was to be clothed in light to interpret the Word of God. Woman's spirituality first discerned Truth, and she will finally lead to spiritual heights all who have heretofore failed to discern the immutable things of the Spirit.

Despite her doctrinal purity, however, Augusta Stetson had an unparalleled ability to embarrass Mrs. Eddy by making the inconsistencies in Christian Science (and in the life of its founder) glaringly obvious. It was impossible, for example, to pass off the diamond brooch she gave "Mother Mary" as a fit emblem of disdain for material concerns simply because the diamonds were set in the shape of a cross. Before the outbreak of World War I, Mrs. Stetson had become even more notorious for taking it upon herself to hand out peace flags to "deserving" nations. Mrs. Eddy eventually found it necessary to rebuke her for this particular bit of public relations. To a sharply worded command to stop giving symbols and reflect upon spiritual substance which alone brings true peace, Mrs. Stetson replied contritely. "When I received your loving warning . . . I was *aroused,* and had the nations been a unit in demanding a peace flag to be presented by me, or take the consequences of universal war, I should have said, 'Go and destroy yourselves.'"

When the redoubtable sensitivity of women was raised to a supernatural pitch it was not a viable basis for widespread feminism. Significantly, a number of the most powerful women affiliated with Christian Science during Mrs. Eddy's lifetime quit to find room to express their own personalities. But Mrs. Stetson was not a quitter. Instead she hung on until she was excommunicated, reaffirming the glory of "Mother Mine," "My Precious Leader," and raising vast sums of money to build churches in New York. Mrs. Eddy, like Mrs. Sigourney before her and Mrs. Stetson after, was fairly candidly interested in parlaying female spirituality into upward mobility, and each of these women managed through her own efforts to rise to the ranks of the upper-middle class. Still, when Augusta Stetson passed the hat in her own inimitable style it was difficult for Mrs. Eddy to ignore certain anomalies at the heart of Christian Science. How could Scientists simultaneously deny the existence of matter and pride themselves on becoming the new success heroes in the field of church finance?

It was perhaps inevitable that Mrs. Stetson would rely more and more on typology to disguise her personal triumphs as impersonal victories for the spirit; Mrs. Eddy had after all pioneered in turning sentimental stereotypes into justification for a whole way of life. In a letter to Mrs. Eddy dated March 12, 1909, Mrs. Stetson wrote: "I think it is needless to tell you that during the twenty-three years of my work in this city, I have never attended places of amusement nor participated in social functions." However, she went on to qualify this statement, confessing that she *had* heard one opera, witnessed two plays, and attended several oratorios and symphony concerts. But that was all long ago. More recently she had accepted the invitation of a "dear student" to attend a private rehearsal of his orchestra. "I was greatly impressed with the object lesson and its application to Christian Scientists; and may I tell you, dearest, how I read it? If I am trespassing on your time, just forgive me and put this letter out of mind." The relationship of the orchestra to the conductor, Mrs. Stetson began, showed the necessity for obedience so indispensable for Scientists. Even the first violinist had to bend to the leader's will. Then, turning from the baton to the tuning fork, she observed that like true pitch, the Scientific Principle of Being was never affected by mortal opinions. Thus in a stroke she had defied Mrs. Eddy's censure of any and all amusements and used the sacred instrument—the type—to justify her rebellion. With another twist she managed to read the lesson of obedience into forbidden experience, and finally, to assert that truth had been revealed once and for all.

The subversiveness of Augusta Stetson's reasoning here seems at first almost too thorough not to have been malicious. Yet given Mrs. Eddy's unwittingly fertile suggestion that the way to excuse your own willfulness lay in typology, it is not unreasonable to suppose that Mrs. Stetson was no more than a second-rate artist in an already orthodox art form. By pushing that strategy to its logical limits, she made it perfectly clear even to her "Great Teacher" that types at best were a dangerous business, and that any claims to divine inspiration based on a typological reading of the Bible could be devastatingly twisted by the most devoted follower. If lavish temples and costly jewelry could be written off as testimony to spiritual values, what was the meaning of radical idealism, and, even more important, where was its comfort?

Twain read Mrs. Eddy's denial of matter as the strategy of a master hypocrite. It would be fairer to see it as her last, most desperate tactic to avoid any confrontation between the two halves of her profoundly divided personality. For most of her mature life Mrs. Eddy hoped that by selling her own patented brand of mariolatry she might find psychological as well as physical comfort. However, once she reduced divinity to a commodity (no matter how unconsciously) the law of diminishing returns set in. The vision of loving passivity she had had at the moment of conversion was progressively tarnished by experience. And she began to resort more and more to denying the existence not only of her own willfulness, but of anything and everything that might arouse her will. As the role of Maiden-Mother became more unsatisfactory, and the dangers of sublimation clearer, Mrs. Eddy sought refuge with increasing frequency in that fatherless vacuum that Leslie Fiedler has described.

One of the easiest ways today to see just how Mrs. Eddy transformed her fear of impulse into repugnance for the object that aroused it is to examine her curiously consistent relationships with younger men. In a post-Freudian age it is difficult not to read her mistrust of her own will wholly in these sexual terms; that is, to see in her fervent denials of heterosexual attraction the source of her determination to thwart all impulses. Freud's insight, that there is a dynamic congruence between the way an individual channels his energies and the expression-repression pattern he has developed for handling his sexuality, is illustrated in a classic way by the case of Mary Baker Eddy. Nevertheless, to take her concern with the freedom of the human will and translate it into a recognizable paranoia-with-delusions-of-grandeur syndrome is to make little progress. It is one thing to try to understand the internal connections between, say, her rejection of her own sexual nature and her radical idealism, and quite another to debate whether or not she was insane.

In a book entitled *Mental Healers* (1932), Stefan Zweig was confident that "the modern psychologist can see plainly enough what was amiss with her. . . ." After abandoning her own infant son, she devoted herself to compensatory endeavors, alternately trying to marry and adopt young men. In almost every case, her tyrannical ways alienated those she courted. Yet instead of grieving over her losses—which would have entailed confessing her own initial feelings of attraction—she turned on these wretches, complaining that they had let their minds prey upon her. To one of her ex-favorites she wrote a confused letter which seems "to the psychiatrist [Zweig here], remembering the writer's sex and age, a plain indication of sexual repression."

> Now, Dr. Spofford, won't you exercise reason and let me live, or will you kill me? Your mind is just what brought on my relapse and I shall never recover if you do not govern yourself and turn your thoughts wholly away from me. Do not think of returning to me again. I shall never again trust a man. They know not what manner temptations assail.

The letter was dated December 30, 1876. Less than twenty-four hours later Spofford received a second letter informing him that Mary Baker Glover Patterson was about to marry Asa Gilbert Eddy.

Despite her intimations that even the marriage bed was ungodly, Mrs. Eddy was drawn into marriage three times. Despite her longing for a universe that snuffed out will in a vacuum, she exaggerated the powers of mortal mind into a demonology of mental influence. What might crudely be phrased as her inability to keep her hands off young men was translated by Mrs. Eddy into their inability to get their minds off her. In later years she kept a rotating staff of students in residence at her Brookline mansion whose major responsibility was to ward off the Malicious Animal Magnetism (M.A.M.) generated by her enemies.

Edward Dakin in his *Biography of a Virginal Mind* (1929) read Mrs. Eddy's early interest in mesmerism and spiritualism, like her diligence in elegiac verse, as simple manifestations of her lust for notoriety. To be sure, all three were art forms which offered untrained girls an opportunity to gain considerable local reputation. Still, the fact that Mrs. Eddy continued to believe in mesmeric and spiritualistic phenomena throughout her life suggests that she was never simply using them as a means to success. What, after all, could have been more fascinating to a woman obsessed by the problem of willfulness-versus-submission than the spectacle of possession, whether by the mesmerist or the legions of an invisible spirit world. To be mesmerized or controlled by spirits might easily seem a perfect way to become the center of attention without having to take personal responsibility for self-assertiveness. Once in a trance it was possible to be as dictatorial as you wished while attributing your revelations to some higher power. The gap between Mary Baker local mesmeric performer, and Mother Mary the fulfillment of Biblical prophecy, was really not so very great. To give orders while feeling perfectly passive, to be the boss and yet still profoundly obedient, was the dream of her life.

However, long before Mrs. Eddy discovered the drawbacks of mariolatry, she began to discern the dangers of yielding to either mesmerizers or the suasions of spirits. To be susceptible to their influence was in some sense to be susceptible to your own impulse to be mastered. Before 1870 Mrs. Eddy had recognized the phenomenon that Freud would call patient transference. Yet, unlike Freud, she did not welcome it as a vital part of the therapeutic process, for it seemed a fundamental denial of all that she had sought in giving herself up to the ministrations of the healer. After years spent cultivating a safe invalidism, she had ventured to hope that cure was possible in submission to an ex-hypnotist turned healer named Phineas P. Quimby. Passivity might not entail taking to your bed, but might instead be found in perfect receptivity to Quimby's healing message. It took Mrs. Eddy a decade to realize that what she had been yielding to was the irresistible attraction she felt for the person of Quimby himself.

No one can compare Quimby's writings with those of Mrs. Eddy and doubt that at the very least Mrs. Eddy had

lusted after her healer's manuscripts. Mrs. Sigourney's insistence that her verses were inspired and not formulaic was of a piece with Mrs. Eddy's protests that God, not Mary Baker Eddy (or Phineas Quimby), had written *Science and Health*. This was one sentimental strategy that never lost its charms. But Mrs. Sigourney had never pushed the Sentimental Heresy to the point of megalomania and always had the satisfactions of male impersonation open to her in her poetry. Mrs. Eddy, in contrast, could never come to any terms with either a masculine God or the fact of heterosexuality.

Sexual relations, which did violence to her ideal of a perfectly passive self, were always abhorrent—at least in theory. It is not surprising, therefore, to find one of her followers lining her room with pictures of madonnas, instructing her students to live in nun-like cells, and finally taking quite seriously the hints in *Science and Health* that someday the propagation of the species would be insured without copulation. In June, 1890, this literalist, Mrs. Woodbury, produced a son whom she named The Prince of Peace and for whom she claimed immaculate conception. The publicity surrounding this incident should perhaps have forewarned Mrs. Eddy about the dangers of reading metaphor as prophecy. But there is no real evidence that Mrs. Woodbury prepared her for Mrs. Stetson. Nor did she drive Mrs. Eddy to abandon the hope that sexual differences and thus sexuality would some day be eliminated, although she was careful not to phrase this hope in terms of parthenogenesis again. Fifteen years after the Woodbury incident, Mrs. Eddy wrote a letter to the *Boston Herald* to suggest that the abolition of sex was the divine solution to the divorce question.

> Look long enough, and you see male and female one—sex or gender eliminated; you see the designation *man* meaning woman as well, and you see the whole universe included in one infinite Mind and reflected in the intelligent compound idea, image or likeness, called man, showing faith in the infinite divine Principle, Love, called God— man wedded to the Lamb, pledged to innocence, purity, perfection. Then shall humanity have learned that "they which shall be accounted worthy to obtain that world, and the resurrection from the dead, neither marry nor are given in marriage; neither can they die any more; for they are equal unto the angels; and are the children of God." (Luke 20:35, 36) This therefore is Christ's plan of salvation from divorce.

For a self-avowed gentlewoman living at the end of the nineteenth century, Mrs. Eddy's marital history was complicated, to say the least. She had married three times, and actually divorced her second husband, when he, unlike the others, did not have the tact to die. Perhaps only George Eliot of the notable women of the period had lived a more irregular life. Nor do the parallels between these two stop here, for George Eliot had gone through a distressing experience with an overzealous disciple who insisted on calling her "Mother," an experience that finally forced her to reevaluate the satisfactions of maternal role-playing, and in the process to make some very provocative remarks about heterosexuality in the divine economy.

Unlike Mrs. Eddy, George Eliot did not have the voice of All-Truth in which to rebuke her followers, and when Edith Simcox's devotion grew oppressive she simply told the infatuated younger woman, "She did not like for me to call her 'Mother.' . . . Not with her own mother, but her associations otherwise with the name were as of a task." Three months later in an even more revealing interview, George Eliot again bade Edith not to exaggerate as she

> murmured broken words of love. . . . I said I didn't—nor could, and then scolded her for not being satisfied with letting me love her as I did—as in present reality—and proposing instead that I should save my love for some imaginary he. She said—expressly what she has often before implied to my distress—that the love of men and women for each other must always be more and better than any other and bade me not wish to be wiser than "God who made me"—in pious phrase. . . . Then she said—perhaps it would shock me—she had never in all her life cared very much for women— . . . she cared for the womanly ideal, sympathized with women and liked for them to come to her in their troubles, but while feeling near to them in one way, she felt far off in another; the friendship and intimacy of men was more to her.

For Mrs. Eddy whose fears about openly challenging (and perhaps capturing) traditionally male prerogatives were transformed into a fanatic insistence on the perfect spirituality of the female, frank heterosexuality was unthinkable. George Eliot could speak of her initial willingness to serve as Edith Simcox's "mother" as an impulse; "she was apt to be rash and commit herself in one mood to what was irksome to her in another." Mrs. Eddy's inconsistencies were never the result of rashness; impulse in any form was anathema to her. The way to fulfillment as she saw it lay through rigidly categorizing sensations—will and passivity, manipulation and inspiration, male and female, and firmly subordinating the first set of these categories to the second.

George Eliot celebrated heterosexuality as a way of exploring and valuing the widest possible range of human experience. Sentimentalists like Mrs. Sigourney were staunch advocates of a single standard that covered not only sexual behavior but included all morality as the special province of women. Yet this ethic of female superiority would have been meaningless without the existence of a lower order of humanity. Civilizing efforts could not be carried on in a vacuum; every would-be feminine missionary needed a Twain to focus her energies on. In her determination to be perfectly self-reliant Mrs. Eddy went beyond the single standard, all the way to a radical idealism. Still, she ventured into the vacuum only in desperation. During most of her long life she directed her energies into playing the role of sentimental heroine become divine. But by the time she had turned from writing the literature of revelation to addressing

letters to the *Boston Herald* she had abandoned her dreams of glory for the prospect of anesthesia.

Once Mrs. Eddy stopped talking about female superiority and a maternal God and turned to imagine "sex or gender eliminated . . . the designation *man* meaning woman as well . . . the whole universe included in one infinite Mind and reflected in the intelligent compound idea, image or likeness, called man, showing faith in the infinite divine Principle," she had given up the only terms she had for describing, and handling, the tensions she felt in her own personality. Hostile biographers have suggested that in her declining years Mrs. Eddy became a morphine addict; her kidney stones proved what these critics knew all along—mental healing was a humbug. However, it is necessary to assume that Mrs. Eddy seized on Christian Science primarily as a means to physical health if this kind of debunking is to be taken very seriously. Where Christian Science really failed was not in preserving her life, but in preserving her will to live (and to dominate) intact.

Just as it was more than coincidence that Mrs. Eddy chose to side with her mother and a maternal God at puberty when her body was making the fact of her own womanhood unmistakably clear, a certain congruence can be seen between her growing age and infirmity and her longing for anesthesia. But this simple-minded psychodynamism has to be supplemented by an understanding of cultural givens. Everything in Mrs. Eddy's upbringing reinforced the idea that males were to be dominant, manipulative, and even brutal, while females were to be passively receptive and perfectly virtuous. Christian Science was the Sentimental Heresy institutionalized. The holiness of motherhood evolved into a species of mariolatry; the fear of playing any role too actively was exorcised by radical idealism. But in the end Mrs. Eddy found that in a world divided into mutually exclusive categories you ultimately could not have things both ways. In her poetry, her correspondence with Mrs. Stetson, her mature thoughts on divorce, she again and again confronted the truth that she could not go home again. But where else did a woman belong? Enshrinement in the Mother Church was no substitute for a sense of being fulfilled, of being at one with yourself. Christian Science provided no final answers for Mrs. Eddy; its consolations were as limited as her own imagination, and once she had explored the universe of sentimental womanhood she was really left with nothing.

Robert B. Downs (essay date 1971)

SOURCE: "Mental Healer," in *Famous American Books,* McGraw-Hill Book Company, 1971, pp. 147-54.

[*In the following essay, Downs discusses* Science and Health *and Eddy's career.*]

America has given the world two major religions—the Church of Jesus Christ of Latter-day Saints, or Mormonism, and the Church of Christ, Scientist, or Christian

Science. The latter has the distinction of being the only religion founded by a woman.

Throughout the nineteenth century, during which both the Mormon and Christian Science churches were established, occult philosophies flourished. Nonconformist and utopian movements attracted numerous adherents. Particularly appealing in the latter part of the century were such Oriental faiths as Vedanta, Baha'ism, Rosicrucianism, Theosophy, and Yoga, and there were churches of Divine Science, Religious Science, the Science of Mind, and New Thought.

In this highly charged atmosphere, so preoccupied with the supernatural and theological disputation, a new faith was born, Christian Science, destined for a permanence, vitality, and wide acceptance denied a majority of other sects of the era.

The founder of the Christian Science movement, Mary Baker Eddy, was a controversial figure for a major portion of her nearly ninety years of life and remained so after her death. From infancy she was an odd child, given to "fits," temper tantrums, and hysteria. Because of delicate health, she remained out of school for long periods, and thus most of what she learned was absorbed from books at home. Her mind was filled with religion at an unusually early age, and she could hear voices calling her name. At the age of twenty-two, Mary acquired the first of three husbands. None of the marriages was happy or successful, and Mary's poor health continued. When her spells of depression were most profound, and morphine failed to relieve pain, the family called in a local mesmerist, "Boston John" Clark. Mary, who was peculiarly suggestible, became fascinated with mesmerism—an omen of things to come—developed a habit of falling into trances, and began to receive messages from the dead.

The turning point in Mary Baker Eddy's life came at the age of forty, when she heard of Phineas P. Quimby, of Portland, Maine, a man who was reputed to effect miraculous cures through the use of hypnotism or mesmerism, rather than through orthodox medicine. Mary resolved at once to visit the new wonder worker, and secretly and alone she set off for Maine. Three weeks later, in a letter to the local Portland newspaper, she declared that through the great principle discovered by Dr. Quimby, who "speaks as never man spoke and heals as never man healed since Christ," she was well on the way to complete recovery of her health. Thereafter for the next several years she was an ardent disciple of Quimby. She read all his writings and continued to write letters to the newspapers extolling his work. The Quimby method, Mrs. Eddy insisted, did not resort to "animal magnetism," "electro-magnetism," or hypnotism, but was based on a "science not understood." "I can see dimly the great principle which underlies Dr. Quimby's faith and works," she wrote, "the truth which he opposed to the error of giving intelligence to matter."

The essence of Quimby's teaching was to deny all evil and to affirm the reality and possession of all good. His system of mental suggestion is in accord with modern psychiatry. Quimby's fundamental premise was that suggestion would cure disease, and further, that all states of either health or disease were created solely by the mind. Carrying the idea further, it was held that a person would be affected physically by his own mind or by other minds; that is, that one mind could affect the life of another even from a remote distance. Finally, the theory is advanced that the mind creates all objective reality.

In later years violent controversy was to rage concerning Mrs. Eddy's debt to her teacher. At first she remained deeply loyal to Quimby and made extensive use in her own teaching of a Quimby manuscript entitled "The Science of Man." Gradually she lost her sense of dependence upon her tutor and convinced herself that the doctrines developed by him were original with herself. Most non-Christian Science writers believe that Mrs. Eddy derived at least the beginnings of her system of healing from Quimby, though all agree that she added significantly to his thought and even modified it substantially. The official Christian Science view, however, is that Quimby was merely a hypnotist, a mesmerist, making use of animal magnetism, and perhaps something of a charlatan, to whom Mrs. Eddy gave more than she received. If this were true, it is hardly probable that when Quimby died in 1866 Mary Baker Eddy would have written a commemorative poem, **"Lines on the Death of Dr. P. P. Quimby, Who Healed with the Truth that Christ Taught in Contradistinction to All Isms."**

Another turning point in Mrs. Eddy's career came a few weeks after Quimby's death. The event, generally recognized as marking the actual beginning of Christian Science, is thus described in the Lynn (Massachusetts) *Reporter:*

> Mrs. Mary Patterson [later Mrs. Eddy], fell upon the ice near the corner of Market and Oxford Streets on Thursday evening and was severely injured. She was taken up in an insensible condition and carried into the residence of S. M. Bubier, Esq., near by, where she was kindly cared for during the night. Dr. Cushing who was called, found her injuries to be internal and of a severe nature, inducing spasms and internal suffering. She was removed to her home in Swampscott yesterday afternoon, though in a very critical condition.

The attending physician believed that his patient would never walk again, and possibly her injuries would prove fatal. It was then, Mrs. Eddy wrote, that "I discovered the science of divine metaphysical healing, which I named Christian Science." Opening a Bible by her bedside, her eyes chanced to fall upon an account of the healing of the palsied man by Jesus. The passage became a revelation to her, she arose from her bed, dressed, and walked into the parlor, to the astonishment of a group of friends gathered there. The marvelous experience of healing herself, of recovering from "an injury that neither medicine nor surgery could reach," according to Mrs. Eddy's autobiography published twenty-five years afterward, "was the falling apple that led me to the discovery how to be well myself and how to make others so." "During twenty years prior to my discovery," she continued, "I had been trying to trace all physical effects to a mental cause; and . . . I gained the scientific certainty that all causation was Mind, and every effect a mental phenomenon."

Mrs. Eddy was in her fiftieth year when the first draft was completed of the book which was to bring her fame and fortune. Three more years were spent in revisions before the volume appeared in print in 1875, a 456-page work. Quimby had called his method the "Science of Health;" Mrs. Eddy entitled her book *Science and Health,* later adding a subtitle, *With Key to the Scriptures.* Two devoted students agreed to provide a subsidy of 1,500 dollars demanded by the publisher.

The first edition of *Science and Health* consisted of 1,000 copies, cheaply bound, crudely printed, and full of typographical errors. Today it is one of the rarest books in the world, for only a handful of copies survive; the remainder have been systematically destroyed. In his *Mental Healers,* Stefan Zweig suggests that "this almost unobtainable version, the only one that was exclusively Mary Baker's work and was untouched by any editorial hand, is essential to the psychological understanding of the book and its author, for none of the very numerous subsequent editions have more than a trace of the primitive and barbaric charm of the original. In later editions many of the wildest tilts against reason, many of the crudest historical and philosophical blunders, have been expunged by better-educated advisers." The text was completely reworked by a retired minister, James Henry Wiggin, who turned out to be an excellent editor.

Successive editions of *Science and Health* were subjected by Mrs. Eddy to rearrangements of chapters, partly in a search for some logical order in the text and in part for financial reasons, since members of the church were expected to purchase the latest edition. The headings in the first edition read as follows: "Natural Science," "Imposition and Demonstration," "Spirit and Matter," "Creation," "Prayer and Atonement," "Marriage," "Physiology," and "Healing the Sick." The last edition is arranged under these chapter titles: "Prayer," "Atonement and Eucharist," "Marriage," "Christian Science versus Spiritualism," "Animal Magnetism Unmasked," "Science," "Theology," "Medicine," "Physiology," "Footsteps of Truth," "Creation," "Science of Being," "Some Objections Answered," "Christian Science Practice," "Teaching Christian Science," and "Recapitulation." Two Eddy biographers, Bates and Dittemore, conclude that after all Mrs. Eddy's efforts, "the arrangement of chapters in the last edition is less logical than that of the first," since in its original form the book began with an exposition of general metaphysical principles, followed later by specific application, whereas the final version scatters the discussion of general principles among a number of chapters near the end.

Christian Science as a system of healing had one great improvement over Quimby's doctrine—it was a theology, not merely a method of healing. As stated by Mrs. Eddy's biographer, Dakin,

> The main thesis of *Science and Health,* stripped of its contradictions, develops the conviction that Christ came to redeem men not merely from sin but also from sickness and death; that his methods are applicable to a modern age; that all men can heal both themselves and others if they develop the correct Christ consciousness, and this long lost Christ-art was again revealed to mankind in the instruction from Mary Baker Eddy.

The one basic thought is the "unity of God and unreality of evil." In brief, nothing exists but God, and if God is good there can be no evil. Therefore pain and illness may appear to exist, but in reality are due entirely to the "error" of the human senses.

In further elucidation of the doctrine, Mrs. Eddy declares, "The chief stones in the temple of Christian Science are to be found in the following postulates: that Life is God, good, and not evil; that Soul is sinless, not to be found in the body; that Spirit is not, and cannot be, materialized; that life is not subject to death; that the spiritual real man has no birth, no material life, and no death." In making theology serve as a therapy, Mrs. Eddy was convinced that she had discovered and revealed a hitherto-unknown means of divine healing. Man can be troubled by illness, old age, and infirmity only so long as he remains under the delusion that illness and old age exist. The idea that man may be attacked by physical infirmities is rejected by Mrs. Eddy with the declaration that "God never made a man sick."

Mrs. Eddy's adamant belief in the unreality of matter is difficult for those not philosophically inclined to grasp. In this concept, she departed radically from such predecessors as Mesmer and Quimby, who accepted the fact that they were treating material human bodies and attempted to relieve the suffering of their patients by animal magnetism, hypnosis, mental suggestion, or similar devices. But Mrs. Eddy insisted that "man is not matter, he is the composed idea of God"; we merely dream that we have bodies, and man's earthly existence is nothing more than a "dream of life in matter." Though there seems to be no evidence that she was a student of Hinduism or ever read the basic Hindu sacred texts, the whole idea of the unreality of matter could have been taken directly from those sources. As Charles S. Braden, in *These Also Believe,* observes:

> The closest approximation to the thought of Mrs. Eddy is to be found in the Hindu concept of the one Real, and the illusory character of all else. So, also, her fundamental denial of the reality of evil and suffering is an almost exact restatement of one phase of Hindu thought.

The prevention and cure of illness are only one side of Christian Science, but they are the aspect that looms largest in public consciousness. How authentic are the claims of the Christian Science practitioners to having been responsible for innumerable miraculous recoveries? Braden, a nonmember, concedes: "There can be no doubt that myriads of people have been healed and have stayed well, thanks to the help of Christian Science." Mrs. Eddy herself maintained that she had cured consumption, cancer, and diphtheria, restored sight to the blind, hearing to the deaf, speech to the dumb, made the lame walk, and caused an eighty-five-year-old woman to grow new teeth. In an appendix to the version of *Science and Health* in current use, entitled "Fruitage," 100 pages are devoted to letters testifying to cures wrought through Christian Science for rheumatism, hernia, tumors, cataracts, heart disease, cancer, Bright's disease, dyspepsia, deafness, rupture, dropsy, kidney disease, eczema, asthma, and a variety of other ailments.

In few instances where remarkable cures have been claimed were there any expert diagnoses of the diseases or objective reports on the results of the treatments. It is also certain that delays among Christian Scientists in seeking medical advice in the early stages of diseases have not infrequently proved fatal. But in situations where applicable, the combination of religious emotionalism and applied psychology in Christian Science have achieved near miracles, especially in mentally disturbed patients. As Dakin points out in his biography of Mrs. Eddy:

> Human experience has tended to indicate, over a long period of years, that the force called suggestion is particularly effective when a state of high religious exaltation can be induced in the subject. Healing through suggestion has been associated with religious ecstasy as far back as there is a record of human history; and modern psychologists and psychiatrists have not been slow to recognize evidence of some important relationship between these two forces.

Christian Scientists are quick to deny, however, that their doctrine is based on mental healing, as practiced by others. "On the contrary," in Mrs. Eddy's words, "the physical healing of Christian Science results now, as in Jesus' time, from the operation of divine Principle, before which sin and disease lose their reality in human consciousness and disappear as naturally and as necessarily as darkness gives place to light and sin to reformation."

In *The Doctors' Dilemmas,* Louis Lasagna reports on a twenty-year study of deaths of Christian Scientists in the Pacific Northwest area. The average age at death was found to be slightly below the average for the state of Washington; no deaths from homicide or suicide occurred; the incidence of pneumonia did not differ from non-Christian Scientists, but malignant disease was much more common among Christian Scientists; diabetes as a cause of death in Christian Scientists was in excess of the national average, and the incidence of tuberculosis was significantly higher; deaths from automobile accidents and accidental falls,

however, were almost nonexistent in the Christian Science group.

A phase of Christian Science not mentioned in the first edition of *Science and Health,* but featured forcefully in the second and later versions, was a belief in mental malpractice, identified as "malicious animal magnetism," a mental influence which evil-minded persons could exert, to produce disease or misfortune in others. Such absent mesmerism could make another person sick, if the mesmerist so desired. Mrs. Eddy attributed the ills and difficulties in her own career to "M.A.M.," or the mental malpractice of some of her enemies, and in her writings and in several lawsuits she repeatedly demanded that the courts take cognizance of the crime of mesmeric influence. The death of her third husband in 1882 was blamed by Mrs. Eddy on malicious magnetism. To counteract this baleful influence a method of treatment was devised whereby a group of Mrs. Eddy's friends would gather around and set their minds to warding off the evil feared or anticipated.

The first organization to support the new faith, established in 1876 by an informal group of students, was "The Christian Scientists' Association." Three years later a charter was obtained for "The Church of Christ, Scientist." It is contrary to the church's rules to publish statistics of membership, though in 1901 Mrs. Eddy challenged a critic of her work to match a record which "could start thirty years without a Christian Scientist on earth, and in this interval number one million." On the other hand, writing as late as 1949, Braden concluded that "the total world membership would be certainly not more than 375,000." According to the most recent statistics available, there are more than 3,200 branches of the Mother Church in Boston in some forty-five countries, as well as 278 Christian Science organizations at colleges and universities. In any case, the doctrine that traces physical effect to a mental cause and asserts that the power of prayer and belief will deliver one from sickness has had an influence out of all proportion to the church's actual membership. The whole field of medicine and surgery has felt its impact, as the mental factor in disease receives increased attention from medical schools and practitioners.

An excellent summation of Mary Baker Eddy's extraordinary career appears in Zweig's *Mental Healers:*

> In twenty years out of a maze of metaphysical confusion she created a new method of healing; established a doctrine counting its adherents by the myriad, with colleges and periodicals of its own, and promulgated in textbooks credited with inspiration; established a Church and built numerous churches; appointed a sanhedrin of preachers and priests; and won for herself private wealth amounting to three million dollars. Over and above all this, by her very exaggerations she gave contemporary psychology a vigorous forward thrust, and ensured for herself a special page in the history of mental science.

Mason Olds (essay date 1972)

SOURCE: "Mary Baker Eddy: A Sesquicentennial Acknowledgement," in *Contemporary Review,* Vol. 220, No. 1277, June, 1972, pp. 294-300.

[*In the following essay, Olds discusses Eddy's life and religious beliefs.*]

Today, most moderns view the real world as the world of sense experience. In this world there is flesh which we enjoy both seeing and touching. In this world there is also war, poverty, sickness, suffering and death. Because the world of the five senses has such a strong hold on us, many are driven to doubt the existence of a Supreme Being and the possibilities of immortality. Many feel that they have been cast into a world they did not create, and so they must make the best of a bad situation.

Yet in this crazy mixed-up world which we both love and hate there is a small religious group which claims to hear the sound of a different drummer. In fact this drummer is a female, who made music on her drum before it was popular for women to play more than a piano or flute. This woman is Mary Baker Eddy, the founder of that little known American religious denomination which goes under the heading of Christian Science.

The writings of Mrs. Eddy inform us that we are greatly mistaken when we think that we experience the empirical world, for the natural world of matter, sickness, suffering and death are not real but an illusion. They are the results of erroneous thinking. If we straightened out our crooked thinking we would discover much to our surprise that men neither get sick nor die. Although it might seem strange to the average modern, there are those who view the world through Mrs. Eddy's nineteenth century rose coloured spectacles and claim that if one would only make the effort, one could discover the Truth also.

Like her movement Mrs. Eddy, as a woman, is a controversial figure. Some of her non-critical followers view her as one notch above the Virgin Mary, whereas her more severe critics claim that she was a charlatan. Perhaps the truth lies somewhere between these extremes.

The general facts of Mrs. Eddy's life are readily available. She was born on July 16, 1821, on a farm near Bow, not far from Concord, New Hampshire. Being both the youngest of six children and delicate from an early age, she received special attention from her parents and siblings alike. Often her education was interrupted because of her various illnesses, and her older brother, Albert, with whom she was very close, tutored her when he was home on vacation from college. Albert, however, died in 1841 when a brilliant young lawyer running for Congress. Of course, this affected her deeply. Also, Mrs. Eddy recalled that at the age of eight she thought that she heard a voice call to her as it had to Samuel in the Bible, but when her mother suggested that she respond with Samuel's reply: 'Speak, Lord, for thy servant heareth';

she never heard the voice again. Moreover, she argued theology with her father who was a strict Calvinist, rebelling especially against the doctrines of predestination, hell and election. At the age of fifteen her family moved to Tilton, where she met the Reverend Enoch Corser, the Congregational minister, who apparently encouraged her intellectual interest in religious questions and who later performed the marriage ceremony for her and her first husband.

In 1843, at the age of twenty-two, Mrs. Eddy married George Washington Glover who was a contractor and builder from Charleston, South Carolina. Glover was also a slave holder and once his new wife was exposed to the institution she pleaded with him to free his slaves, but to no avail. Only seven months after their marriage, while they were on a trip to Wilmington, North Carolina, Glover contracted yellow fever and tragically died. His young wife returned to New Hampshire, giving birth to George Jr. three months later. Being in poor health, the young widow was forced to place her son in a foster home, while she lived with her sister Abigail, whose health also was not very good. For various reasons Mrs. Eddy was never able to take her son back.

Ten years after her first marriage, Mrs. Eddy married Daniel Patterson, a dentist, who apparently was more successful with the ladies than with his profession. In time Patterson went to Washington to enlist in the Union army but was captured watching the battle of Bull Run. However, through the efforts of his wife, the governor of New Hampshire intervened and Patterson was released from prison. Upon his return Patterson established a dental practice in Lynn, Massachusetts, but shortly eloped with the wife of a wealthy patient. When the elopers returned, Mrs. Eddy persuaded the offended husband to take his wife back, but she divorced her husband in 1873.

However, it was a hand bill that Patterson had given his wife before leaving for Washington to enlist in the army that proved most decisive. The advertisement told of a Dr. Phineas P. Quimby of Portland, Maine, who had great success in healing without the use of surgery or drugs. With great hopes for a cure from Quimby, Mrs. Eddy went to him in October of 1862, and after several treatments her health was greatly improved. She also discussed with Quimby, at some length, his theory of healing and in time she both lectured and wrote about his theories. Mrs. Eddy's relationship to Quimby is most controversial, with her critics maintaining that she plagiarised Quimby's theories, whereas her supporters argue there are fundamental differences between the two methods.

Nevertheless, on February 1, 1866, Mrs. Eddy fell on an icy street in Lynn, hurting herself 'severely'. Many of her friends had doubts about her recovery. However, she read the story in the Bible of Jesus' healing of the man with palsy and as a result had a great 'spiritual awakening'. She heard a voice say: 'Daughter arise!' and got out of bed, dressed herself, and went downstairs, much to everyone's amazement. It was from this healing experience that Christian Scientists date the beginning of their movement and sometimes refer to it as 'the Great Revelation'.

From 1866-1875 Mrs. Eddy lived in various towns of eastern Massachusetts, where she lectured on the new science of healing and even did some cures herself. In 1870 she conducted classes in mental science while her colleague, Richard Kennedy, was a practitioner. In 1875 she published the first edition of *Science and Health* which she revised numerous times before her death. This work is viewed as being divinely inspired by her followers and the views expressed in it are seen as a recovery of the authentic Christian gospel. Hence, in the Christian Science worship service, the first reader reads selections from this book while the second reader reads from the Bible. Since *Science and Health* is alleged to contain the revealed interpretation of the Christian gospel, Christian Scientists feel no need for preaching. Their church services consist only of readings from the Bible and *Science and Health*. Each Sunday throughout the world the same selections are read in each church so there is uniformity throughout the denomination.

When Mrs. Eddy first wrote *Science and Health* it was sold from door to door without great success, but in 1877 she married one of her followers, Asa G. Eddy, a capable businessman. Through his knowledge of marketing techniques the book began to sell. It was also during this period that Mrs. Eddy held public meetings in Lynn, Roxbury and Boston. In 1879 steps were taken to organise the First Church, Christ Scientist, in Boston, and in 1881 Mrs. Eddy became the pastor. In 1895 the first structure of the Mother Church was dedicated, and in 1906 the church was completely renovated and enlarged at the cost of $2,000,000, which was subscribed before the work was begun, becoming one of the landmarks of Boston. In 1881 she founded the Massachusetts Metaphysical College, where she taught until she closed it in 1889 at the 'height of its success'. She contends that she taught over four thousand students during this period and closed the school to devote her time to revising *Science and Health*. After the closing of the institution the Board of Education of the denomination took over the functions of the college. Through the years Mrs. Eddy founded a number of publications such as *The Christian Science Journal* (1883), *The Christian Science Sentinel* (1898), and the well-known daily, *The Christian Science Monitor* (1908).

Mary Baker Eddy, the woman who dared to deny the reality of death, died on December 3, 1910, at the age of 89. Her critics point out that although she attributed the validity of sense experience to the error of mortal mind, she wore eye-glasses and false teeth and that she was attended by physicians and took drugs to relieve the suffering brought on by kidney stones while her close associates attempted to ward off the effects of 'animal magnetism' (the power of evil thought) which she believed was causing her to suffer. Moreover, they point out that

since the age of forty-five Mrs. Eddy had amassed a personal fortune of over two million dollars.

Mrs. Eddy grew up in a time in which the tides of Protestant liberalism were beginning to rise in the eastern part of the United States. Within the Congregational church of her youth there was the debate between the unitarians and trinitarians, as well as between the revivalists and anti-revivalists. It was only four years after her birth that the American Unitarian Association, a liberal denomination, was founded in Boston. Hence, her denial of such Calvinistic doctrines as hell and double predestination were in line with many of those of the middle and upper middle classes of eastern Massachusetts.

The emphasis on mind and rationality and the playing down of the emotions was in part one of the sides taken by the anti-revivalists against the advocates of revival. Even her philosophy of absolute idealism was in the background of both Continental and American liberalism. In fact, idealism in the west has a distinguished tradition reaching back to Plato, coming into Christianity as it branched out into the Greco-Roman world in the fourth and fifth centuries, and dominating Christian thought until St. Thomas introduced Aristotle into western thought in the thirteenth century. In the nineteenth century Hegelian idealism had a great influence on both Continental and American philosophy and theology. With the doctrine of creation, Christians have generally emphasised the primacy of the spiritual over the material as the former existed before the latter. Furthermore, with the advent of Darwin's theory of evolution later in the century many liberals repudiated the traditional doctrine of original sin, maintaining instead that man was evolving from his animal past and that the evil existing in the world was the result of the residual animality which ultimately will be overcome.

To point out that many of the ideas held by Mrs. Eddy were in line with much of the thinking of eastern Massachusetts at her time is not to maintain that she was merely reflecting her culture, for there is no doubt that she put her own unique stamp on the doctrines. To deny completely the existence of matter was going much further than those liberals who spoke of a dualism. Obviously, Mrs. Eddy was convinced that she was divinely inspired, that she was presenting the authentic interpretation of Christianity which Jesus himself had taught but which had been distorted through the centuries and that the key doctrine which had been neglected was that of healing. Healing does mean the healing of sickness but it means much more. It also refers to the solving of interpersonal problems that exist between people. It has a personal aspect, but more recent Christian Scientists have become aware of its social dimension. In this concern they claim to find support in the thought of Mrs. Eddy.

Mrs. Eddy called her faith 'Christian Science'. Generally the word science is used to refer to the natural or material world. It is a method that is used to determine the truth or falsity of statements about this world of the senses. In contrast to this commonsense understanding, Christian Science teaches that the material world is an illusion; it only appears to be real because of erroneous thinking. Christian Scientists then try to teach men to think correctly. For them, the real is the spiritual, and there are certain laws that govern it. Christian Scientists believe that these laws or principles were revealed to Mrs. Eddy and that they have been passed on to them through her writings, through Christian Science practitioners and teachers. They maintain that they have received results from following Christian Science, and that anyone who follows it, will receive similar benefits. So we see that in the term Christian *Science* Mrs. Eddy took a word with great prestige and applied it to her teachings, thus appealing to a latent pragmatism that lies deep in every American if not in every occidental.

In referring to God Mrs. Eddy says: 'God is incorporeal, divine, supreme, infinite Mind, Spirit, Soul, Principle, Life, Truth, Love'. To maintain that He is infinite is to say that He always has been and always will be, for He is without beginning and end. Later, she speaks of man and his relationship to God in the following way: 'God is the Principle of man, and man is the idea of God'. Man and God go together, for man is 'created' in God's image. He mirrors or reflects God; he is a 'tributary to God'. In this sense man always has and always will be, and hence it is impossible to speak literally of creation, as this would imply a time when God's image was not reflected. It would seem that since God does not come into being and cease to be, man does not come into being and cease to be. The divine image (man) then is co-eternal with the infinite Mind.

With respect to the thorny problem of theodicy, Mrs. Eddy deals with it in a most unusual way. Since God is both infinite and good, He can only create what is good, and as God makes all that is made, he must make it good; therefore, there can be no evil. As man is created in the divine image, he reflects the divine goodness. If man were evil or a sinner, then the origin for evil would have to be in something other than God, which in turn would imply a denial of either God's infinitude or His goodness. Thus, to solve the problem of God as being both infinite and good with the presence of evil, Mrs. Eddy denied the presence of evil, for she maintains '. . . evil is but an illusion, and it has no real basis. Evil is false belief.' She then goes on to say 'In reality man never dies . . . Death is not the result of Truth but of error . . . .'

The problem then is to teach men how to look at life from the metaphysical position of Mrs. Eddy's idealism. If they will but learn to view life from her perspective, they will discover that the path of the Christian Scientist is the path of Truth.

The question then arises: what kind of people are Christian Scientists? Although the directors are very parsimonious in realising figures and profiles, some sociological studies have been made. Professor R. W. England studied the testimonies of some five hundred Christian Scientists as contained in the *Christian Science Journal* and concluded: (1) The largest single group of converts to Christian Science are 'urban, middle-class, married females who are suffering from bodily disorders of physical or emotional origin'. (2) Over 50 per cent of those coming to Christian Science 'are motivated by specific troubles, with problems of health predominating'. (3) Affiliating with Christian Science because of specific difficulties is 'more characteristic of women than men'. (4) The greatest benefit offered by the religion is the 'alleged' power of the religion to cure bodily disorders. (5) The role of the Christian Science practitioner is similar to that of a psychologist or psychiatrist to his patient, with good rapport between practitioner and sufferer being essential for results.

Christian Science has a proportionately much larger female following than male. It has been estimated that for every 100 female members there are only 31.3 males. Furthermore, in 1953, approximately 77 per cent of all full-time practitioners were married women; another 11 per cent were single women, giving a total of 88 per cent. Also, unlike the beginnings of many sects. Christian Science originally appealed to the middle class with a few coming from the upper middle class. Being a religion which places great stress on reading and denying the existence of the physical world, which only one whose basic physical needs have been securely satisfied has the luxury to deny, the middle class appeal is understandable. This of course implies that in the United States few blacks are drawn to the religion.

If the present status of Christian Science can be judged by the establishment of churches and societies the situation is somewhat as follows: there are now 2,405 churches and societies in the United States and 838 in other parts of the world. In fact, there are now churches and societies throughout the United States. Although England has the second largest number it is believed that the membership there has reached a standstill, if not a decline. In the United States during the early part of the present century Christian Science growth was almost phenomenal but more recently the rate of growth has dropped considerably. For instance, in 1906, there were about 635 churches in the United States and in 1926 there were 1,913, a growth rate of over 200 per cent. However, in 1953 there were 2,284 churches and societies and when this number is compared with the present number of 2,405, the growth rate is less than 8 per cent in the past 18 years.

As Bryan Wilson has pointed out, the evidence seems to be that Christian Science has reached its high tide. There are probably a number of good reasons for this levelling off. First, the movement did not revolutionise the practice of medicine as many of the pioneers, including Mrs. Eddy, thought it would. In fact, medicine has increased in the popular esteem and people are living longer today than in any other period of man's history. This longevity is generally attributed to the efforts of modern medicine. Second, Mrs. Eddy cast her organisation and thought in her own nineteenth century mould and then claimed that it was divinely inspired, which has put her denomination in a straitjacket which makes it difficult for it to adjust to the rapidly changing world of the last quarter of the twentieth century. Thirdly, in the nineteenth century, Christian Science provided many women with a creative outlet, but today women seem to have found more creative outlets so that there is little, if any, connection between Christian Science and such movements as women's liberation. Finally, Christian Science has ceased to be a novelty.

Christian Scientists believe that they have been grossly misunderstood, and they are willing to assume some responsibility for this problem. Believing that this has been their greatest failure, they are now making efforts to rectify it. As to its greatest success, Christian Science believes that it has brought health, healing and happiness to thousands of people who were suffering. It is here that it feels that it has made a lasting contribution.

As to Mary Baker Eddy, one may or may not accept her claims to divine inspiration, and yet one can still believe that here was a woman with a charismatic personality, who obviously was an effective speaker and who had a genius for administration. She left a religious movement, at least a monument to herself, that has outlasted her death by sixty years, but all indications are that although the movement is firmly established, the next sixty years will be more difficult than the past.

David Sowd (essay date 1973)

SOURCE: "The Dusky Genius of Mary Baker Eddy," in *Ball State University Forum,* Vol. XIV, No. 3, Summer, 1973, pp. 38-43.

[*In the following essay, Sowd examines the culture and theoretical background from which Christian Science came.*]

For Mark Twain, Mary Baker Eddy was "the most daring and masculine and masterful woman that has appeared on the earth in centuries," and he wrote of her: "Closely examined, painstakingly studied, she is easily the most interesting person on the planet, and in several ways as easily the most extraordinary woman that was ever born upon it."

But, contrary to what is most often asserted by her biographers, Mrs. Eddy did not operate in some sort of cultural vacuum; like Thoreau, she was truly "born in the nick of time," and if she was extraordinary, it is precisely because she managed so perfectly to embody the peculiar concerns of the age and place in which she found herself.

"The dusky genius of Mrs. Eddy was," according to Van Wyck Brooks, "a sign of the times, a portent of the race, the place, the moment; for only a time of declining vital-

ity, only a region at ebb-tide could have given birth to the cult of Christian Science."

"In the year 1866," Mary Baker Eddy reflects in her religious textbook, *Science and Health with Key to the Scriptures,* "I discovered the Christ Science or divine laws of Life, Truth, and Love, and named my discovery Christian Science." The date is not without significance: the doctrines of Transcendentalism which, greatly exaggerated, were to form the basis of Mrs. Eddy's theology, had been formally introduced exactly thirty years earlier with the publication of Emerson's *Nature* in 1836; and, perhaps more important, the Civil War had just ended and much of the brightness of that hopeful current of idealism which the Transcendentalists had tried to channel into the mainstream of American life had been sadly tarnished in its sudden and awful confrontation with the realities of war.

In his study of the culture from which Christian Science emerged, Robert Peel makes this analysis:

> There was little in the world of 1866 to suggest that Transcendentalism's failures were really successes. More and more, during two decades, that early idealism had been gathered into a single channel, the antislavery crusade; and when the Civil War was over and freedom's battle was won, men saw what base and sordid purposes their idealism had led to. The cynical reaction that always follows war set in. A sort of moral exhaustion marked the postwar years. Materialism roared ahead. Ostentation and bad taste were rampant.

The old ideals, the old myths, somehow just did not fit the new realities of postwar America. There were, in effect, *two* Americas: the one existing in the mind, made up of preconceived notions of what should be, and the other evident in the everyday experience of practical life—the reality that actually was. "Just as Sunday was divided from the days of the week," explains Malcolm Cowley, American practical life was divorced from the life of the mind:

> Practical life . . . had become a hard, dirty scramble in which the only justifiable aim was to get ahead, be successful, make money, but meanwhile the life of the mind was supposed to be kept as spotless and fragrant with lavender as a white Sunday dress.

This tendency to keep the life of the mind aloof and innocent, "spotless and fragrant," was termed by George Santayana the "Genteel Tradition": "The American Will," he said, "inhabits the sky-scraper; the American Intellect inhabits the colonial mansion. The one is the sphere of the American man; the other, at least predominantly, of the American woman. The one is all aggressive enterprise; the other is all genteel tradition."

While the American Will was settling the West and building cities, political machines, and industrial empires, the American Intellect was still back in New England, detached and going nowhere. "Boston could still fancy itself the Hub of the Universe, though its culture grew increasingly genteel and bloodless and unrelated to the vulgar vitality of the age." It was in the stale atmosphere of this "region at ebb-tide," this "sphere of the American woman," that Mary Baker Eddy found comfort and created the religion that would make the life of the mind sacred and insure the preservation of its innocence.

"The connection may have been tenuous," writes Van Wyck Brooks, "but still it existed between this new religion and Emerson's doctrines, which denied the reality of matter, or seemed to deny it, while they taught the omnipotence of mind:"

> Had not Emerson said, "Never name sickness"? Was it not his idea that, since man was divine, evil could scarcely have any real existence? Alcott had shown an active interest in Mary Baker Glover—Mrs. Eddy, as she was known in Boston,—for whom pain, disease, old age and death were "errors." Alcott had been struck by her **Science and Health** and had visited her classes in Lynn and lectured before them. There was a deep relation between the Concord point of view and the mind-cure that was raging through New England. . . .

This is Brook's perceptive analysis of the lineage from which Christian Science was evolved; and in his *American Renaissance,* F. O. Matthiessen similarly observes that "From the weaker aspects of Emerson's thought, the rocking chair of Mrs. Eddy . . . is only just around the corner."

Mrs. Eddy seems to have been clearly aware of an affinity between her religion and what she termed "the philosophy of a great and good man, for such was Ralph Waldo Emerson." Shortly before his death, "she realized her long-held desire to meet the Sage of Concord." Emerson had been ailing and Mrs. Eddy, though uninvited, felt certain that he would receive her warmly as a kindred spirit, recognizing his own early ideas mirrored in her theology and, probably, humbly thanking her for reworking, perfecting, and attempting to popularize them. "I saw Emerson," she writes, "some months before his demise; went for the purpose of *healing* him." A noble purpose indeed, but the Sage would have nothing to do with the seeress. His flat rejection, however, was not to discourage Mrs. Eddy; undaunted, she later attributed her failure to his lack of vision: " . . . he was as far from accepting Christian Science," she says, "as a man can be who is a strict moralist."

She also decided that "Bronson Alcott is far in advance of him,"—a judgment prompted no doubt by Alcott's greater tolerance of her. Alcott, the dreamer's dreamer, whom Thoreau had apostrophized as "Great Thinker! Great Expecter!" had offered sympathy and encouragement to both Emerson and Thoreau when they had needed it most, and similarly he had tried to cheer up Mrs. Eddy. Just as she had gone to Emerson, Mrs. Eddy had taken it upon herself to mail a copy of her newly-published **Science and Health** to Alcott; these overtures

would seem to suggest that she was trying to become accepted by the Transcendentalists who, she knew, would be at least somewhat familiar with her ideas.

Alcott graciously read the book and, in a letter reminiscent of Emerson's memorable greeting to Whitman upon the appearance of *Leaves of Grass,* he wrote to her in 1876:

> In times like ours, so sunk in sensualism, I hail with joy any voice speaking an assured word for God and Immortality. And my joy is heightened the more when I find the blessed words are of woman's divinings.

He offered further encouragement by visiting her at her home in nearby Lynn and attending several of her classes in Christian Science (mainly, it seems, to voice his own opinions). Alcott's interest was just what Mrs. Eddy needed; she later wrote of him:

> After the publication of **Science and Health with Key to the Scriptures,** his athletic mind, scholarly and serene, was the first to bedew my hope with a drop of humanity. When the press and pulpit cannonaded this book, he introduced himself to the author by saying, "I have come to comfort you." Then eloquently paraphrasing it, and prophesying its prosperity, his conversation with a beauty all its own reassured me.

Yet Alcott, like Emerson, remained unconverted; Mary Baker Eddy began to realize that perhaps he was not so far in advance of Emerson after all! In the absence of any disparaging final estimate of Alcott's shortsightedness as Mrs. Eddy had made of Emerson's, Robert Peel (himself a Christian Scientist and former editorial writer for the *Christian Science Monitor*) has provided his own:

> Mrs. Eddy's attempt to reach through to Alcott at a point of crucial understanding had met with placid incomprehension. . . . For all his open-mindedness, this was too bold a leap for Alcott to take. . . . It was evident, by the time he had paid his last visit to Mrs. Eddy, that Alcott has missed the essential logic of her position.

Peel does admit that when they finally severed their relationship Mrs. Eddy "had now faded in Alcott's eyes to a genial fanatic" (the implication being of course, that there was something wrong with Alcott's eyes!). "Perhaps," he concludes, "Alcott may safely be left halfway between Emerson and Mrs. Eddy."

But while Mrs. Eddy's personal relations with the Transcendentalists were rather pathetic and unfruitful, the ideological parallel between her religion and their philosophy is a more serious matter. Paul Elmer More characterizes Christian Science as "a diluted and stale product of Emersonianism:" "There is a story," he says, "that when Emerson was visiting Carlyle, the gruff Scotchman, who certainly believed heartily in evil and damnation, carried his guest to the slums of London and pointed out to him one horrible sight after another:"

"And do you believe in the deil, noo?" he would say; and always Emerson would shake his head in gentle denial.

"The story," More concludes, "is at least *ben trovato;* it sets forth clearly the facile optimism out of which Christian Science was to spring:"

> Such a creed, when professed by one who spoke with the noble accent and from the deep insight of an Emerson, was a radiant possession for seeking humanity forever; it is folly and inner deception when repeated parrot-like by men and women with no mental training and, visibly to all the world, with no warrant of spiritual experience.

Although optimism was an attitude expressed by Transcendentalists and Christian Scientists alike, the optimism of Mrs. Eddy and her followers was basically shallow and desperate—if for no other reason than simply that, immediately after the Civil War, there was just not much to be optimistic about. In Malcolm Cowley's view, high optimism was one of the chief characteristics of the Genteel Tradition into which Christian Science emerged; and in an apt description of the period, Robert Peel writes: "The wrong people were optimistic for the wrong reasons." Where Emerson had denied evil and had been optimistic that men could perfect their souls, Mary Baker Eddy denied sickness and was optimistic that she and her disciples might get through life with no pain or discomfort whatsoever. (Mrs. Eddy's emphasis is suggested by the title she chose for her textbook: *Science and Health.*) Christian Science offered an escape, with all the solemnity of a religion, from the insecurity and chaos of post-war America. "The prevailing religion," according to Van Wyck Brooks, "was comfort, with accessories . . . mind-cure and easygoing optimism. . . . Mrs. Eddy's world was a world of lonely people who had lost their vital interests and were bored and ailing." The religion she offered them "presupposed hysteria as the normal condition; for health," says Brooks, "is the centre of religion only for the sick." Christian Science indeed "answered a deep, insistent need of the population." The answer it provided was a sort of cure by denial: the world and all its problems, the evils engendered by a rapidly-growing industrial society, all sin and sickness, all nastiness, ultimately even all death (it was piously believed), could be overcome—i.e., made to go away—by simply pretending that these things were nonexistent; and in this hope was the essence of Christian Science optimism.

Christian Science was the product of a proximity to Transcendentalism that was both ideological and geographical. Yet while both movements originated in New England, what really separated them was the passage of time; the post-war New England of Mary Baker Eddy was a far cry from what it had been in the early days of Transcendentalism. "In nineteenth-century New England," writes Robert Peel, "the brief flare of Transcendentalism seemed to promise the advent of a new Golden Age. Instead it was succeeded by a tawdry Gilded Age in which idealism appeared to be swallowed up by materialism." Christian Science was, essentially, a form of Transcendentalism ready-made for this Gilded Age. To keep from being swallowed up it had to stick its neck out farther than Emerson's doctrines had gone—so far, indeed, that it appeared not a little ridiculous: in desperation, it denied everything material, from the existence of the human body to the hallowed Nature of the Transcendentalists. But if Mrs. Eddy's ideals seemed to be higher up in the clouds, her practical vision remained very much fixed on goals that were less lofty. She offered, not to all men a key to their souls, as Emerson had tried to do, but to her followers alone a means for escaping discomfort. "In religion," says Van Wyck Brooks, the "springtime faith" of Transcendentalism, "with its feeling of a world to create and redeem, yields to the conception of religion as hygiene in the valetudinarian Mrs. Eddy."

Because she aimed lower, she naturally managed to hit the target more often: her religious enterprise was popularly received and became immensely successful. By 1903, Paul Elmer More was able to report that "Mrs. Eddy now numbers her disciples by the million—many of them educated and thoughtful people," and Mrs. Eddy herself could boast in a press release that her *Science and Health,* which sold for three dollars (out of which—according to Mark Twain—"the average profit to her on these books, above cost of manufacture, is all of seven hundred per cent!"), "is already in its two hundred and seventy-fourth edition of one thousand copies each. I am rated," she said, "in the *National Magazine* (1903) as 'standing the eighth in a list of twenty-two of the foremost living authors.'" As Van Wyck Brooks notes in his discussion of this phenomenal success: "The faith-healer had won the day, and invalids frequented practitioners who silently thought benevolent things about them. The miracles of mind-cure were naturally numerous. . . ."

They were not, however, free of charge; Mrs. Eddy's was truly a gilded rather than golden idealism, and she and her practitioners made a handsome living on their income from patients. Mark Twain describes a fictional encounter with a Christian Science practitioner:

> Mrs. Fuller brought in an itemized bill for a crate of broken bones mended in two hundred and thirty-four places—one dollar per fracture.
>
> "Nothing exists but Mind?"
>
> "Nothing," she answered. "All else is substanceless, all else is imaginary."
>
> I gave her an imaginary check, and now she is suing me for substantial dollars. It looks inconsistent.

The practice was indeed inconsistent, and this inconsistency is indicative of what had happened to idealism in post-war America; it had tainted, gone sour and become commercialized, so that now it was a highly profitable business. Mrs. Eddy was able to charge $300 for a series of twelve lectures at her Massachusetts Metaphysical

College, with none but the slightest misgivings: "When God impelled me to set a price on my instruction in Christian Science Mind-healing," she later reflected, "I shrank from asking it, but was finally led, by a strange providence, to accept this fee. . . ." "Mrs. Eddy's rising fortunes showed," according to Brooks, "how far these border-line activities, which were neither religion nor science but partook of both, answered a deep, insistent need of the population. It was riddled with nervous disorders. It was also bored."

While Mrs. Eddy was able to infuse some novelty into that bored life of the mind which New Englanders cherished so much, at the same time she pulled those who followed her even farther away from their practical lives and left them more detached from reality than ever. In the midst of the Genteel Tradition, Mrs. Eddy's religion was ultra-genteel—not merely putting the life of the mind first, but actually denying the existence of any other life.

Today Mrs. Eddy's church is governed by the same set of thirty-five "Church By-Laws" she concocted and published as the *Manual of the Mother Church* in 1895. These "Laws" are final and absolutely unamendable; the organization of the Christian Science Church exists for the sole purpose of carrying them out to the letter. In an accurate description of this institution, Mark Twain lists what he calls the "Main Parts of the Machine:"

> *A Supreme Church.* At Boston.
>
> *Branch Churches.* All over the world.
>
> *One Pastor for the whole of them:* to wit, her book, *Science and Health.* Term of the book's office—*forever.*
>
> In every C. S. pulpit, two "Readers," a man and a woman. *No talkers, no preachers, in any Church—readers only. Readers of the Bible and her books—*no others. No commentators allowed to write or print.
>
> *A Church Service.* She has framed it—for all the C. S. Churches—selected its readings, its prayers, and the hymns to be used, and has appointed the order of procedure. No changes permitted.
>
> *A C. S. Book-Publishing House.* For books approved by her. No others permitted.

Twain was not exaggerating; all of this exists today in exactly the same form in which Mrs. Eddy created it (and as he described it—with the exception that since she is no longer alive, books published by the Publishing Society are now approved by Trustees who pass judgment strictly according to the explicit terms of her will). It is a rigid, authoritarian, conservative structure, which bears witness to Mrs. Eddy's dusky genius as Founder and Leader. Like some sort of inviolable time capsule, it stands today as a living monument to the extraordinary woman Mark

Twain loved to hate, and—perhaps more important—to the Genteel Tradition that she so perfectly represented.

Stephen Gottschalk (essay date 1973)

SOURCE: "Conclusion: Christian Science and the American Pragmatic Orientation," in *The Emergence of Christian Science in American Religious Life,* University of California Press, 1973, pp. 275-93.

[*In the following essay, Gottschalk examines the continuing influence of Christian Science.*]

Christian Science can be best understood as a *pragmatic interpretation of Christian revelation.* It is the pragmatic character of Christian Science which most adequately conveys its distinctiveness as a religious teaching, most clearly illumines its relations with the patterns of American culture, and most fully explains the source of its appeal. To have used the term *pragmatic* in connection with Christian Science before this point would have been ahistorical, since the term never occurs in Mrs. Eddy's writings and, to my knowledge, was not used by Christian Scientists nor by others in reference to her teaching during the period with which we are concerned. Despite William James' passing interest in Christian Science, there were no direct links between Christian Science and the pragmatic movement in American philosophy.

Yet the emergence of both within roughly the same period is far from fortuitous. Certainly it was not just a coincidence that the development of an indigenous American philosophy should have taken place in the decades following the Civil War when the United States was emerging into modern industrial nationhood and world power. Nor should it be surprising that the pragmatic direction of American culture and thought should have been given expression in the only major religious movement to have originated in the United States after the Civil War—Christian Science. Indeed, since Christian Science was formulated a decade or more before the emergence of pragmatism, Mrs. Eddy's teaching may be said in a limited sense to have anticipated its development.

Pragmatism is a term susceptible to many definitions, and it is important at this point to indicate the range of meanings with which it will be employed here. It can, of course, be used as a term for expediency and uncritical adaptability to conditions; but pragmatism in this sense is a distortion and vulgarization of its genuine philosophic content. In its basic philosophical sense, pragmatism is an attitude which insists that coherent theory must be related to practice, that the meaning of a concept is to be found in its bearing upon experience, and that the truth of an idea is to be tested by the actual consequences of believing in it. Whatever their differences in other respects, the major American pragmatic philosophers Charles Sanders Peirce, William James, and John Dewey, were united in their emphasis upon these points. In its larger aspects, pragmatism can be understood as the philosophic expression of a much broader orientation toward experience than is embraced in traditional philosophic categories. John Dewey pointed out that philosophy is "the conversion of such culture as exists into consciousness"; and it is no original observation to say that pragmatism converted the open, fluid patterns of the American experience into philosophic consciousness.

Yet to understand pragmatism in its ultimate meaning, we must relate it to a tradition in American thought that can only be defined in religious terms. This tradition centers in New England, reaches back to American Puritanism, through Jonathan Edwards to Transcendentalism, and from Transcendentalism to pragmatism. It is unified by the tendency to define the content of religion in terms of the immediate possibilities of experience rather than with reference to a future realm of experience. In the broadest sense, this tradition can be called a religious naturalism, if that term is carefully understood. In this context, it refers to the disposition to think in terms of one order of experience, rather than in terms of two opposing orders of experience. In this sense it constitutes a rejection of the dualism of the secular and the sacred, earthly and heavenly, natural and supernatural and approaches the understanding of that which is ultimate in terms of that which is immediate—experienceable in man's present life-situation.

This naturalistic tendency becomes more and more conspicuous with each phase of the development of this tradition. Its first manifestation is in the eschatology of New England Puritanism, which was dominated by the concept of the Kingdom of God. Puritanism held as man's central duty, not the vision or contemplation of God, which is the basic ideal of Medieval Catholicism, but the actual living under the sovereignty or Kingdom of God, in obedience to Him in this present experience. Whatever the supernatural elements in Puritanism, the dominance of this tendency gave a distinctly ethical, this-worldly caste to American religious thought. Jonathan Edwards' powerful restatement of Calvinism in the American context in the mid-eighteenth century, though rejecting the Puritan scheme of the covenant, intensified the naturalistic tendency implicit in Puritanism. For Edwards saw the process of regeneration in radically experiential and non-legalistic terms as involving the new sense of God and nature entertained by the newly born. It remained for Transcendentalism to entirely discard the theological framework of both Puritanism and Edwardsian theology, and to identify the religious experience with the illumined perception of nature. John Dewey made this line of development explicit when he rejected the concept of religious experience as such, and understood the term *religious* to apply to the ideal potentials of experience itself.

Christian Science is congruent with this tradition as briefly sketched, and is to a certain extent explicable in terms of it. Mrs. Eddy's background lay in New England Puritanism. She was schooled in the New England The-

ology that stemmed from Edwards, and adopted the term *spiritual sense,* so fundamental to Edwardsian theology, as one of the rubrics of her teaching. The immediate religious background of Christian Science, moreover, lay in New England Transcendentalism, and the development of American pragmatism was contemporaneous with the emergence of Christian Science. It is not difficult, of course, to see profound differences between Mrs. Eddy's teaching and all these other forms of thought. But the continuities are real and are essential to an understanding of the meaning of Christian Science in American religious life. For Christian Science reflects—indeed, in a radically intensified form—this disposition to see religious experience in terms of immediate possibilities.

Relating Christian Science to the pragmatic strain in American culture generally and to the pragmatic movement in philosophy specifically may run counter to the convictions of both scholars and Christian Scientists, though for very different reasons. In general, academic scholars have not taken Christian Science seriously enough to warrant relating it to so prestigious an intellectual movement as pragmatism, while Christian Scientists, holding that their faith is not culture-derived but issues from revelation, often dismiss any effort to relate Christian Science to its cultural context on religious grounds. Still, the relationship developed here is not imposed upon the materials of this study but emerges naturally from them, and tracing it can scarcely be avoided by the intellectual historian who wants to assess the meaning of the emergence of Christian Science when and where it emerged.

My conclusions, then, are as follows: (1) that Christian Science as a religious teaching is best understood as a pragmatic interpretation of Christian revelation; (2) that as such it is Christian, but definitely not Protestant; (3) and that in the pragmatic character of Christian Science one can most clearly see the source of its appeal as well as the greatest potential danger to its correct practice.

In characterizing Christian Science as pragmatic, it is necessary to emphasize at the outset that it is a pragmatic grasp of *Christian revelation.* Mrs. Eddy never claimed to have discovered a truth that had not been objectified before her time. She claimed, rather, that through her discovery the full practical implications of Biblical revelation, most particularly the Gospel narratives, had been made clear. Underlying everything Mrs. Eddy said was the fact that she *accepted Biblical revelation as given.* Her interpretation of its meaning, of course, is widely at variance with that of traditional Christianity; but she never claimed to have set forth any truth that had not been experimentally lived by Biblical figures, most particularly Christ Jesus.

Moreover, Mrs. Eddy held that the discovery through which she understood the full meaning of the Scriptures was in itself a spiritually empowered revelatory event. Perhaps her most succinct statement of the spiritual fact which she claimed to have envisioned in the discovery of

Christian Science was her declaration that she then gained the sense of "Life in and of Spirit, this Life being the sole reality of existence." Mrs. Eddy did say that the healing work she pursued in the years prior to her discovery confirmed the truth of what she envisioned. But her conviction of the reality of this spiritual fact was not, for her, just a warranted conclusion drawn from experimental inquiry, and it obviously could not be substantiated on the basis of human rationality resting on material sense testimony. However great the emphasis upon the practical demonstration of Christian Science in her teaching, demonstration does not make truth true. Mrs. Eddy taught, rather, that basic truth is apprehended only through spiritual sense receptive to revelation. Demonstration confirms only that revealed truth has been understood.

To say that Mrs. Eddy predicates her teaching upon revelation, however, is not to say that she takes the revelation in its ordinary theological sense. She does so only in the sense that spiritual truth must come to human thought from a source absolutely outside itself. But the character and significance of revelation is for her a wholly practical affair. She interprets the revelatory event of the life of Jesus as a demonstration of divine manhood which when correctly understood discloses man's *present* possibilities. And she sees Christian Science as providing the understanding through which these possibilities can be realized in practice. There is, then, no split in Mrs. Eddy's teaching between that which is revealed to be true and that which can be demonstrated as truth. And if demonstration must be based on revelation, it remains true that for her revelation without demonstration is incomplete. Indeed, in **Science and Health** she cites the proof by demonstration of the truth of her discovery as one aspect of the revelation of Christian Science itself.

Christian Science is, therefore, understood by its adherents as a revelation, not of a dogma, but of demonstrable religious truth. In this sense it may be said to be a spiritually scientific discovery, and Mrs. Eddy's role as a revelator may be defined as essentially that of a discoverer. She claimed to have discovered a truth objective to herself, and sought to focus her followers' attention on her discovery and not on her person. Her active role as the founder of the movement made her its leader, a position which is permanently hers in the Christian Science church. But even in the extensive prerogatives which Mrs. Eddy claimed as leader of the movement, her main interest was in the promulgation in pure form of teachings which she held to be objectively and demonstrably true. Mrs. Eddy did claim that she could not ultimately be separated from her discovery, and that a correct understanding of her mission was crucial to an understanding of her teaching. But ultimately her personality, complex and controversial as it was, cannot be the main issue in any assessment of Christian Science. For granting the radical character of what Mrs. Eddy claimed to have discovered, her claims were in one respect similar to those of any scientific discoverer: to have set forth objective truths the validity of which is entirely independent of the personality of the discoverer, and which are demonstrable by anyone who understands them.

The scientific character that Mrs. Eddy claimed for her teaching might easily be dismissed as rhetoric used with the intent to gain prestige for a religious teaching in an age that to a large extent took material science as its standard for knowledge. But considered as a manifestation of an insistence upon rigor of method, the claim that Christian Science is scientific takes on real and illuminating meaning. Pragmatic thought is, after all, an expression of a scientific world view in the sense that though it upholds the view that experience is an open-ended affair, it is committed to rigorous subjection of claims of experience to the test of provability. Much of Mrs. Eddy's much vaunted rigidity in insisting that Christian Science be practiced without admixture just as she taught it can be understood as an expression of a devotion to scientific rigor rather than religious dogmatism. It is this insistence in part that accounts for her disdain for the free-roving mysticism and eclectic spirituality of the mind-cure movement. Mrs. Eddy's writings are permeated by an insistence upon the right use of method in healing and practice generally. For in the largest sense, the scientific character of Christian Science is its claim to *be* method—the method for the demonstration of the spiritual fact in practice. It is this pragmatic-scientific aspect of Christian Science which—whatever one thinks of the truth or untruth of the possibilities it claims are present to man—most decisively separates it from the mystical mood and temper.

Christian Science, therefore, is best understood, not as an abstract metaphysical or theological system, but with reference to *what it claims to make possible*. Mrs. Eddy's most metaphysical statements are intended to be understood as pointing to demonstrable conditions of experience. Actually, she never intended to construct a metaphysical system as such. Rather, metaphysics for her was a mode of communication by which the practical significance of Christian revelation could be pointed out. In her own way, Mrs. Eddy voiced a very pragmatic concept of meaning when she spoke of her metaphysics as meaningful only when put into practice. And in one of her most frequently quoted characterizations of Christian Science she speaks of it in pragmatic terms as making something possible, for she refers to it as "that through which can be discerned the spiritual fact of whatever the material senses behold."

At the heart of Christian Science, therefore, is the claim that it is possible for man now to inwardly and subjectively know the spiritual fact of being even before it is objectified in the human situation. For Mrs. Eddy, this process of inner knowing is not just "taking thought" but is truly prayer. And throughout her writings she uses such terms as *know, realize, apprehend, discern, behold, affirm, become conscious, understand, etc.,* to indicate the *active* nature of this process through which alone spiritual healing can be wrought. Prayer in this sense is, for her, communion with God, in that it is spiritual receptivity to divine Truth. But it is a comprehensible process which, though not humanly visible, makes a difference in actual experience. Mrs. Eddy speaks of it as an *act* which is spiritually substantive, and to which rules and laws (though not formulas) do apply. To be sure, this act is in the first instance inward and subjective. But Mrs. Eddy claims that through the discernment of the spiritual fact the energies of Truth are released into the individual consciousness of the one being treated and act as healing power in the specific situation at hand. The healing power in Christian Science, it should be emphasized, is the power of Truth itself, not of the individual thought that beholds it. But the act of discerning the spiritual fact in Science is central as far as the practitioner of Christian Science is concerned.

Spiritual reality in Christian Science, of course, wholly transcends common sense testimony. But Mrs. Eddy does not conceive of the term *reality* as appertaining to a transcendental realm wholly uncognizable by human consciousness. For the implicit claim of Christian Science is that men can achieve some grasp of basic reality in their present situation, and that the understanding of true being releases spiritual power into their present experience. In this sense, the meaning of reality in Christian Science is far different from its ordinary meaning in traditional metaphysics in the Platonic tradition. It is to this more traditional concept that John Dewey refers when he writes of reality as "the most obnoxious of all metaphysical words in the most obnoxious sense of metaphysics; for it purports to speak of that which underlies all but which is incapable of being known in fact and as fact." Mrs. Eddy, of course, claims that reality *is* capable of being known and demonstrated "in fact and as fact"; that what the human mind calls reality is not the fact of being, but merely a limited percept treated as fact; and that the percept will change as more of the fact is understood.

Christian Science stands, therefore, for the idea of an experienceable absolute. The Godhead—Life, Truth, and Love—is to the degree of one's spiritual apprehension knowable as the actual condition of being. Since Mrs. Eddy understands God ontologically as the "source and condition of all existence," her assertions about His nature are in the final analysis claims about the nature of experience. And since she understands man as the expression of God's being, these theistic assertions are likewise claims for what is divinely and demonstrably true about man. Thus when Mrs. Eddy states that God is Life, she is asserting as the spiritual fact that man is in no sense dependent upon material organization for life. In the same sense, when she declares that God is Mind, she is proclaiming the possibility that one can demonstrate the infinite intelligence of which truly understood He is the expression. And when she claims that God is All, she is affirming that the true understanding of Him dispels belief in an opposite power and demonstrates His supremacy.

Correlatively, her assertion of the nothingness of evil amounts pragmatically to the claim that the conditions of experience make it possible to actually reduce evil to nothingness in specific situations. Mrs. Eddy's definition of matter is also wholly pragmatic in character, for she treats it, not as an actual substance which is in some metaphysical sense unreal, but as a name for limitation. When Mrs. Eddy declares that there is no matter, she is claiming that limitation is not in any sense inherent in being and in man. The problem of the origin of evil or of the belief in matter is not a question which Mrs. Eddy even tries to answer satisfactorily at an intellectual level. Her basic concern is with what can be experienced, not with answering questions which contain, from her viewpoint, false premises to begin with; and her ontological claims regarding the non-existence of evil and matter must be understood entirely in this light.

Since Mrs. Eddy's claims concern the actual conditions of experience and therefore are oriented to what can be experienced, she is obviously not offering a philosophical interpretation of the nature of reality. The only real continuity between Christian Science and philosophic idealism lies in the fact that Mrs. Eddy at points found it helpful to use an idealistic vocabulary to communicate her concept of the potentials of experience. Her denial of the reality of matter is in abstract terms reminiscent of philosophic idealism. But in Mrs. Eddy's teaching this claim is made on a theological rather than a philosophical basis. And Mrs. Eddy holds, moreover, that it is a claim which can be progressively validated in practice. The so-called idealistic element in Christian Science, therefore, is actually the engine of its pragmatic thrust. And the locus of Mrs. Eddy's efforts lay not in offering a philosophic conception of the nature of existence, but a practical understanding of regeneration and its requirements.

The process of regeneration in Christian Science is the demonstration, or pragmatic living out, of what Mrs. Eddy declares as the spiritual fact of being. For her, it is not something to be sought and accomplished in another realm of being, since there is but one actual realm of experience. The basic reference point in her thinking is not a future life for which this is a preparation but one order of experience correctly or incorrectly discerned. Nor is Mrs. Eddy's teaching really oriented to any antecedent order of experience or realm of being in which all spiritual facts are presumed to be wholly demonstrated in final form. Mrs. Eddy does not posit some other worldly Platonic realm in which man's perfection is already wrought out, but claims that perfection as the *basis* for demonstrating in practice. She always insists that the reality of Life obtains now and that man's perfection is structurally and essentially his. Were this not the case demonstration would be impossible. But without demonstration, the assertion of the reality of perfect God and perfect man points only to what can and must be tangibly manifest in life-practice, not to a condition which is already objectified in experience. Mrs. Eddy's eschatology, therefore, does not point so much to the disruption of a material order (though to mortals that will appear to occur), as the consummate demonstration of the divine order, already established as the reality of being.

Christian Science, it has been claimed, can be best seen as a pragmatic grasp of Christianity. But in view of its radical departure from orthodoxy, its connection with traditional Christianity becomes problematic. Mrs. Eddy claimed to have cut behind historical Christianity to grasp the full significance of Biblical revelation. And the elements which define Christian Science as a distinctive religious teaching definitely do mark a departure from the theology of historical Christianity. But at the same time, Mrs. Eddy always claimed that her teaching was thoroughly Christian. And most of the elements of traditional Christian teaching are present in Christian Science, even though the radicalism of Mrs. Eddy's vision drastically alters their customary meaning.

Perhaps the clearest way of establishing this point is through a contrast between Christian Science and New Thought with respect to the basic Christianity of each. For it is in Mrs. Eddy's differences with New Thought and the variant forms of mind-cure which antedated it that one sees most clearly the essentially Christian nature of her teaching. The New Thought and mind-cure movements (with the exception of Unity) did not claim to be specifically Christian and drew inspiration from a variety of religious sources, among which the Bible was far from the most important. Mrs. Eddy, on the other hand, claimed most emphatically that her teaching was Christian, that it was founded squarely upon the Scriptures, and that it was in fact continuous with Biblical revelation. It was not because of personal rivalry that she so vehemently opposed these movements, which were so often confused with hers in the public mind and which recruited much of their membership from the Christian Science movement. It was, rather, because they negated those very elements in her teaching which most clearly identify it as Christian.

More specifically, the contrast between Christian Science and New Thought highlights those elements in Mrs. Eddy's teaching which link it with her Calvinist background. Unlike New Thought, Christian Science claims to be a redemptive religion. It holds that men need to be radically saved from the flesh, that "mortal mind" has within itself no resources on the basis of which to work out this salvation, and that men are thus wholly reliant upon divine revelation for an understanding of the way that leads to salvation. Mrs. Eddy speaks of mortal mind in very much the same way as did Paul when he referred to the carnal mind. To her mortal mind was not the subject of the healing wrought by Christian Science, but rather the object of this healing. Mind-cure, on the other hand, sought, as its name suggests, not the regeneration of mortals but the amelioration of human ills through the exercise of the benevolent powers of thought. In almost all of its forms, it rejected the radical distinction made by Mrs. Eddy between mortal mind and the divine Mind, and elevated the human mentality to virtually deific status. Thus it held that revelation is unnecessary, since the mind is capable of discerning religious truth through its own enlightened intuitions, and that man requires, therefore, not radical regeneration, but moral and physical improvement through the beneficent exercise of his latent powers.

A more pointed contrast lies in the fact that mind-cure, unlike Christian Science, has no doctrine of radical evil. Mrs. Eddy, of course, did maintain that evil was unreal to God and has no foundation in true being. But she insisted also that evil was completely real to mortals and had to be recognized and dealt with as a mortal belief. Indeed, she claimed that Christian Science revealed as had no other religious teaching the nature and operations of evil. The term *animal magnetism* in her teaching indicates the operation of the radical evil of the belief in a mind apart from God. The most conspicuous manifestation of animal magnetism Mrs. Eddy termed *mental malpractice,* the injurious effect of one human mind upon another. It is important that where mind-curers had no room for this concept in their teachings and for the most part dismissed it as nonsense, Mrs. Eddy identified their very practice as in large part a form of malpractice and the rise of the mind-cure movement itself as the effect of animal magnetism.

Similarly, it is the Christian character of Christian Science which most decisively differentiates it from Oriental religion. The limited congruence between Christian Science on the one hand and Buddhism and Hinduism on the other, lies in their rejection of the belief in the objective reality of a physical universe. But the differences between the two are of much greater ultimate consequence than the similarities, and even the limited area of congruence that they share leads to different attitudes in practice. For if the material picture of man and the universe in Christian Science is false, it is a false sense of a spiritual reality which Mrs. Eddy insists must be demonstrated as the fact of being. Christian Science, therefore, can be said to be a redemptive religion in a way that is uncharacteristic of either Buddhism or Hinduism, for it insists upon the thorough-going practical regeneration of mortals from all phases of the flesh through the demonstration of the spiritual fact. It insists, moreover, that this regeneration is wrought through the Christ, the objective healing power of divine Truth acting on mortal thought. Mrs. Eddy, then, rejects the strongly subjective, mystical quality characteristic of Indian religious thought. For her, God in no sense indwells mortal consciousness, but rather, His power acts upon it to dissolve human error and elevate men to the demonstration of divine manhood. Where Buddhism and Hinduism, particularly as popularized in America, tend to negate man's individuality through absorption into the divine, Mrs. Eddy always maintains that God and man are distinct as Principle and idea.

These defining features, then, constitute the Christian core of Mrs. Eddy's teaching: reliance upon Biblical revelation, specifically the life and work of Christ Jesus; belief in a God absolutely transcendent to mortal thought and wholly distinct from man; and the insistence upon the requirement of the radical regeneration of mortals from the flesh. Certainly some of the critics of Christian Science both in the period of our study and since would have been loathe to identify Christian Science as Christian. And whether one chooses to so designate it remains, of course, a matter of individual definition. But the presence of these distinctively Christian elements as essential aspects of Mrs. Eddy's teaching is good warrant theologically for so doing.

The crucial point here, however, is that *Christian Science, while Christian, is definitely not Protestant*. It is possible to speak of Christian Science as Protestant, in the sense that the religious and social background of Mrs. Eddy and most of her followers was Protestant. Further, in a sermon Mrs. Eddy once counseled them to display a Protestant spirit in these words, "Intrepid, self-oblivious Protestants in a higher sense than ever before, let us meet and defeat the claims of sense and sin, regardless of the bans or clans pouring in their fire upon us . . ." Yet she also wrote that Christian Scientists "have no quarrel with Protestants, Catholics, or any other sect," implying a clear distinction between her teaching and other religious positions. There are, of course, some important continuities between Christian Science and various forms of Protestantism, particularly the New England Puritanism in which Mrs. Eddy was raised. Yet when one identifies the *distinguishing* elements of Christian Science as a religious teaching, it is difficult to see how it can be classed as Protestant. For Mrs. Eddy asserted that man and creation understood in Science are the expression of God, hence that the belief in a God-created material universe and man are the products of a radical misconception of true being. Salvation in Christian Science, therefore, means the full demonstration of the spiritual fact and is predicated upon the understanding of the truth of being in Science as differentiated from the mortal picture of being as presented to the physical senses. Protestantism, however, accepts as true that very picture of man and the universe which Mrs. Eddy declares is a misconception of being, understands man's materiality as natural to him in his creaturely estate, and conceives of salvation as the moral transformation of a fallen man rather than the demonstration of man's inherent perfection as the son of God. Underlying the specific attacks of Mrs. Eddy's theological opponents upon Christian Science was this basic area of radical disagreement; and whatever the shades of theological difference among them, they agreed with each other in these basic points in which they all disagreed with her. The continuities that do exist between Christian Science and Protestantism are real and important. But they indicate only that both partake of a Christian base. The teaching of Christian Science, however, cannot be located on the spectrum of Protestant theology and should not really be referred to as Protestant at all.

Of course, Protestantism in the late nineteenth century was not untouched by the pragmatic, anti-formalist strain of thought that was also objectified in Christian Science. Though the liberalism of the New Theology and the Social Gospel have analogues in European movements, their character as they emerged in America was decisively influenced by indigenous cultural tendencies.

These movements, however, are best understood as *pragmatic reinterpretations of Protestantism* rather than radically new appraisals of Christian revelation. They were in essentials modifications of orthodox Protestantism intended to reconcile it with modernity in an age where the traditional symbols of orthodoxy were undergoing collapse.

The difference between liberal Protestantism and Christian Science can be seen particularly in their Christology. The Christology of liberal Protestantism is in some respect on the surface at least quite similar to that of Christian Science. Jesus is regarded more as an exemplar than as a supernatural mediator, the older Protestant concept of the vicarious atonement is rejected, and the Christly nature of Jesus is understood as embodying an ideal manhood to which all men should aspire and which they are capable of achieving. But here the resemblance ends. For Christian Science emphasizes the works of Jesus over his ethical example, which is generally stressed in Protestant liberalism to the detriment of concern for the miracles and the resurrection. In Christian Science, the miracle is understood as a natural demonstration of divine power, this view being predicated on the fact that the true condition of being is spiritual—wholly unfettered by material limitation. The significance of Jesus' lifework lies in the fact that he demonstrated that the ideal man is not subject to material limitation in any form. He is, therefore, an exemplar of a far more radical truth in Christian Science than in liberal Protestantism, though he is an exemplar in both. Liberalism, then, modified the Protestant tradition by emphasizing the moral aspects of Jesus' teaching, but maintained its continuity with the Protestant tradition. Mrs. Eddy claimed to offer an understanding of Jesus' life and works on a basis which departed radically from the Protestant ontology.

An even more telling contrast can be drawn between Christian Science and the Social Gospel. The two movements, the developments of which ran almost parallel, have certain pragmatic elements in common but point in completely different directions. Both did express a certain anti-formalism and offered alternatives to orthodoxy. But the Social Gospel, theologically reliant upon liberalism, stressed the ethical component of Protestantism in conjunction with a rejection of laissez-faire, thus giving rise to the idea that the Christian's ultimate commitment is to the amelioration of the social order. In this sense, traditional Protestant beliefs were radically immanentized and the supernaturalistic elements of orthodoxy were slighted or rejected outright. But the Social Gospel operated well within the world view or cosmology of Protestantism generally. It challenged traditional social ethics and doctrinal interpretations, but it did not in any sense challenge the basic ontology of Protestantism, as did Christian Science. Indeed, on the basis of the belief that social problems like all others flowed from a radical misconception of the nature of being, Mrs. Eddy developed a wholly different approach to the resolution of social problems than that of the Social Gospel. And whatever congruence there might be in the anti-formalism that both represent, they are wholly irreconcilable as religious orientations.

A final point here is that the institutional character of the Christian Science movement puts it well outside the framework of American denominational life. For The Mother Church cannot be understood along the lines of the ordinary sacramental or liturgical idea of church as an institution. In its ultimate spiritual signification, Mrs. Eddy defined church in such a way that it is inseparable from the structure of reality itself. As a human institution, church for her had an entirely instrumental character: it was designed to carry out certain essential purposes necessary to the growth of the Christian Science movement and the dissemination and protection of its teachings. Overall, the Christian Science church may be said to have an educational function. Its mission, as Mrs. Eddy defined it, is to bless the race through the promulgation of demonstrable truth. The end of the church, therefore, is not to exist as a church—indeed, Mrs. Eddy in the first years after her discovery of Christian Science did not want to found a church, and when she did so it was only as a concession to necessity. Thus the character of The Mother Church, as it took shape in the 1890s was as streamlined as possible to fulfill its intended function. Similarly, its services are designed to inspire through the communication of truth rather than through participation in symbolic rites. And its governing law, the *Manual,* is a skeletal system of providing the bare necessities of church government while allowing a good deal of flexibility in the day-to-day administration of church affairs.

How then are we to account for the emergence of Christian Science in American religious life? What made it a religious movement of significant proportions rather than just a minor sect? We have to account for this phenomenon in the first instance in terms of the religious situation into which Christian Science was projected. For the emergence of Christian Science coincided with a particularly crucial stage in American religious development. All the major mutations in American religious life before the late nineteenth century had transpired within the framework of Protestant supernaturalism. In the late nineteenth century, however, the very structure of Protestant supernaturalism itself began to give way, not just for a few intellectuals but for the laity in general. To a large extent, the dilemmas of present day Christianity can be traced back to the profound religious reorientation that began to assume major proportions in the period in which Christian Science first emerged on the American scene. Of course, Mrs. Eddy's teaching had been formulated just after the Civil War, a decade or more before this reorientation began to become apparent. Yet the significant fact here is that Christian Science gained a following and came to prominence in the midst of a period of profound spiritual turmoil.

The character of this orientation was marked by a rejection of the dualistic supernaturalism of orthodoxy and a longing, expressed in different ways, for religious experience which was vital, immediate, and comprehensible in practical terms. By the late nineteenth century, it was becoming increasingly impossible for the modern mind to accept a religious orientation which divided man's experience into the natural and supernatural, the here and the hereafter, the sacred and the secular. Progress, industrialization, the impact of science—indeed, almost all the elements characteristic of modern life—conspired to render increasingly meaningless the symbols, doctrines, and promises of orthodoxy. If religion were couched in terms of an apposition of the life to come to this life, then men were increasingly willing to let go any concern with the life to come and live in terms of the present alone. Correlatively, their institutionalized professions of faith tended to devolve into a meaningless conventionalism that masked the increasing secularism of the culture. This process had reached such a point in Europe by this period that Friedrich Nietzsche could declare the death of God, not as a theological pronouncement, but as a cultural diagnosis of the decline of the whole scheme of supernatural transcendence in the modern mind. The significant point for our purpose was that this decline in America was just becoming apparent in the period when Christian Science emerged in American religious life, though it was not to become generally characteristic of the culture until nearly a century later.

In the light of these points it should not be surprising that the main direction of religious innovation in this period was toward a more pragmatic conception of what religion includes. Whether we are speaking of the advent of the New Theology, the development of the Social Gospel, or even the popularity of variant forms of mysticism, the tendency was the same: toward a conception of religious experience in more pragmatic—more immediate, experienceable, and vital—terms. The New Theology verbalized this tendency in terms of an identification of God's kingdom with the progress of human culture. The Social Gospel expressed it by urging upon Christians the uplifting work of living the Gospel through aiding in the efforts at social amelioration. The Pentecostal movement reflected this trend through emphasizing speaking in different tongues and other manifestations of religious immediacy. William James spoke for a generalized mood among many of the religiously concerned of his day when he attempted, in his *Varieties of Religious Experience,* to adduce the meaning of religion in terms of concrete experiences rather than abstract formulations of theology. James approached religion through the analysis of mystical experience, but in mysticism he saw a strongly pragmatic element: for it was what seemed to him and to others as well most immediate and vital in religious life. This same concern for immediacy and vitality was voiced in a variety of ways in religious thought at that time and since in a renewed interest in the idea of Holy Spirit, God's operative and sustaining power. And it was, of course, the Holy Spirit that Christian Science claimed to reduce to human understanding and demonstration.

Those who embraced Christian Science as a religious teaching had in almost all cases in some way experienced the devitalization of orthodoxy that was so much a part of the inner history of Protestantism in their age. For in a variety of ways they had come to feel that orthodox doctrines and symbols, together with the institutions which perpetuated them, had lost whatever meaning and comprehensibility and vitality they once might have had. Some could no longer accept belief in a God who, as the Creator of a universe in which suffering and death seemed constant, appeared to be morally inferior to His worshipers. Others had lost faith in the doctrines of orthodoxy through the influence of scientific materialism or the higher criticism. For still others, the experiential immediacy of religion simply seemed to evaporate and its symbols became hollow shells. And many of those who turned to Christian Science found welcome surcease from the prevalent Protestant belief that in the face of suffering one must resign oneself to the will of a God who in some sense decreed it as a necessity. In any case, the doctrines, institutions, and symbols of orthodoxy seemed to converts to Christian Science quite remote from the felt realities of experience. Hence they were receptive to a religion which claimed that Christian promises were to be realized in the present; which offered demonstration instead of doctrine; and which taught that symbols of religious truth could be replaced by the discernment and demonstration of the spiritual fact of being.

To Christian Scientists, Mrs. Eddy's teaching constituted a revelation of spiritual power far beyond what they found in either liberal or orthodox Protestantism. To them, its glory lay in its promise that *now* men could begin the demonstration of eternal life. It lay in the conviction that men could be fully delivered from sickness, sin, and death, and that these forms of evil were neither necessary to being nor spiritually legitimate. Glowingly, Christian Scientists spoke of the release they had found through the study of Mrs. Eddy's teachings from physical suffering, the fear of death, the bondage to sin, and the dreariness of meaningless lives. And often they contrasted the spiritual power which they felt Christian Science had brought into their experience with the ineffectiveness of the orthodoxies they had left behind.

For such people, Christian Science healing was indeed a crucial religious experience, but not because of the material change it effected in their physical well-being. For healing validated the claim that spiritual power was presently effective in experience—that religion, therefore, was a matter of immediate experience and not just of ultimate assurance. The experience of healing was, therefore, not so much a matter of a physical change as a religious awakening. And in Christian Scientists' testimonies of healing, particularly those which involved a conversion experience, the really crucial factor is the religious awakening which accompanied and gave ultimate significance to the healing experience. Mrs. Eddy's claims for the efficacy of spiritual healing power were indeed radical, for they extended to the healing of virtually every disease on record. But the ultimate radicalism of her claims was for the immediacy and *experience-ability* of spiritual power through which these diseases were healed. And to her followers, the practice of Christian

Science in individual instances seemed to make good these claims in an overwhelming way.

It was, therefore, the pragmatic quality of Christian Science that accounted for its religious appeal. But it must be carefully understood here that this defining element in the character of Christian Science made it if anything more demanding as a religious teaching than the orthodoxies which it claimed to supersede. Though Mrs. Eddy did define the meaning of salvation in radically experiential terms, salvation is in the final analysis the only thing she claims to offer. And there is no denying the fact that her demands on those who would practice Christian Science according to her standards were rigorous in the extreme. Christian Scientists often testified that the practical requirements of being a follower of Mrs. Eddy were difficult indeed. They found that they were required to put off old ways of thinking, to commit themselves to reliance upon spiritual power for healing, and in many cases to endure the bitter reproaches of those who could only see her teaching as dangerous heresy or quackery. But to devoted Christian Scientists, the effort expended in the study of Mrs. Eddy's teaching and the personal sacrifices entailed in its practice seemed well worthwhile.

To the degree that Christian Science was secularized in practice—and there is some evidence that it was—its character as a pragmatic grasp of Christian revelation was vitiated. The point can be stated in terms of two ways in which the term *pragmatic* may be used. In its larger and more philosophic sense, *pragmatic* signifies a quality of being experientially meaningful. But in its lesser and more popular usage, it connotes convenience and mere expediency. The secularized practice of Christian Science amounts to the reduction of a pragmatic religious teaching in the larger sense to a pragmatic problem-solver in the lesser sense. The teachings that inspire any movement that gains some widespread popularity are, of course, subject to being distorted in practice. But the particular *character* of this distortion in the case of Christian Science can only be understood as an inversion of its basic strength.

The process by which the pragmatic character of Christian Science was inverted into a narrow utilitarianism should be familiar to students of American religion. For it is essentially the same process that was at work in the secularization of Puritanism in the seventeenth and eighteenth centuries. Puritanism was characterized especially by a strongly activist thrust which bade men obey the divine will in all phases of their lives. Through a subtle, long-term process, this activist tendency in Puritanism was channeled into the secularism of the "gospel of wealth" and cult of success. Obedience to the divine Word was subverted into moralism, the establishment of God's Kingdom on earth was identified with the attainment of the good life in purely human terms, and the religious impetus of original Puritanism was cooled into a form of rationalism. Christian Science shares with Puritanism the activist tendency which commits its adherents to seek to extend their religion into all phases of daily activity. Indeed, the pragmatic character of Christian Science, and in part the origins of pragmatism itself, are to some degree traceable to the activist thrust of New England Puritanism. Little wonder, then, that the practice of Christian Science should have been subject to the same distortions which plagued the development of Puritanism and impels the misinterpretation of Pragmatism as a philosophy of mere expediency. The secularized practice of Christian Science bears very much the same relationship to Mrs. Eddy's teaching as does the cult of success to original Puritanism and the ethic of expediency to Jamesian or Deweyan Pragmatism. Christian Science, in its more secularized form, becomes a kind of rationalistic neo-Protestantism which must be distinguished from Mrs. Eddy's basic vision. . . .

Margery Fox (essay date 1978)

SOURCE: "Protest in Piety: Christian Science Revisited," in *International Journal of Women's Studies,* Vol. 1, No. 4, July/August, 1978, pp. 401-16.

[*In the following essay, Fox offers an interdisciplinary interpretation of Christian Science, concluding that many Victorian women found social and intellectual freedom in the religion.*]

INTRODUCTION

This paper re-examines Christian Science, a 19th century American religious sect, in its sociohistorical setting using interdisciplinary sources and methods to develop a new interpretation of the movement's original social function. In giving historiography an anthropological reading, this work underscores the complementary relationship of anthropology and history that prompted Claude Levi-Strauss to assert in *The Savage Mind* that the study of history over time and the study of anthropology in space are alternative ways of doing the same thing. Beyond its relation to history, this kind of interdisciplinary effort reveals the synthesizing potential of anthropology.

Christian Science was founded in New England c. 1875 by Mary Baker Eddy at a time when a number of metaphysical healing cults arose that were known collectively as the Mind Cure movement. William James, who was trained in both medicine and philosophy, noted in *The Varieties of Religious Experience* the broad resemblances between Christian Science and other Mind Cure groups such as New Thought. In both, the philosophy promoted social equality between the sexes; similar theological tenets held that reality existed only in an all-encompassing divine mind; and in both, physical and mental health were bound up with a particular belief system.

The doctrine of Christian Science represents a syncretism of Mrs. Eddy's interpretation of primitive Christianity, which emphasizes the healing mission of Jesus, and a metaphysical philosophy that scholars have linked with various 19th century American intellectual currents, from a backwoods Transcendentalism to expansionist optimism and a general belief in human perfectability. The doctrine is based on the opposition of spirit and matter, spirit being of god and the one mind (god's) that governs the universe, therefore good; matter being not of god, therefore evil and false. In this system, the individual is wholly spiritual and perfect, like his creator, therefore incapable of suffering, sickness, sin, or death. It is only the counterfeit, material self that experiences those illusions of evil as false claims of the senses.

The therapeutic system, an integral part of Christian Science, is directly related to Mrs. Eddy's interpretation of Jesus. The orthodox Christian concept of a suffering divinity gives way in Christian Science to the image of an earthly individual so suffused with the divine spirit that he could become, in Mrs. Eddy's terms, the most scientific man the world has ever known, therefore able to gain mastery over natural phenomena. Healing in Christian Science rests on the belief that through prayer the believer may acquire a spark of the divine mind that Jesus possessed and become similarly empowered to break through the material world of pain and suffering. Mastery over the world is strongly emphasized in Christian Science. Healing work is performed with the help of practitioners whose training is supervised by the Christian Science organization.

To live in the world and cope with workaday situations, however, Christian Scientists mitigate their perfectionist ideology by recognizing two levels of existence: an absolute, spiritual level which is the sacred world, and a relative level which is the mundane world. While their ideology sanctions mastering the mundane world, which means succeeding in it, good Christian Scientists work spiritually toward the absolute level of consciousness at which the Christian Science beliefs are exclusively in force. The social implications of these religious attitudes and objectives involve self-isolating mechanisms. Christian Scientists occupy themselves with a fairly continuous round of rituals, lectures, films, meetings and informal social gatherings that accentuate group boundaries and insulate individual members from outside influences.

In its near-simultaneous acceptance and rejection of the world, Christian Science has been cited as an example of ascetic Protestantism. British sociologist Bryan Wilson in his book *Religious Sects* analyzed the movement as a sectarian phenomenon appealing to middle-class urban sectors of the population because of its highly individualistic, manipulative philosophy. These are stimulating interpretations which have contributed much to our understanding of Christian Science.

This paper proposes an entirely different interpretation, arguing that Christian Science assumed a historical role often seen in new religions, that of an unconscious protest movement. In this case, protest was directed specifically against women's social disabilities in the latter part of the 19th century. Robert Merton's term latent function applies, inasmuch as Christian Scientists failed to recognize the underlying character of protest in their religion and outside observers as well have consistently overlooked the movement's historical role in relation to women.

To develop the theory, I will delineate the 19th century social stereotype for women and its medical underpinnings, describing role conflicts and discontinuities that caused many women to eschew the traditional female role through hysteria, a typical women's illness of this period. I will then suggest that Mary Baker Eddy, founder of Christian Science, was a classic female hysteric who resolved her personal conflicts by developing Christian Science and assuming an extraordinary power role. Finally, it will be shown that Christian Science initially attracted women like Mrs. Eddy who wanted to be healed, but who also wanted to enact dominance roles that society denied them access to by becoming healers themselves. Christian Science thus cured both the physical symptoms of illness in its recruits as well as attacked the contributory social causes of illness.

Ethnographic data richly affirm that religious roles have often served women with channels of escape from their low social status *vis a vis* men. However, the roles women have assumed—whether of soothsayer, nun, shaman, deaconess or abbess—have historically been subjected to masculine authority and control. Women have risen above secondary status in religion in none but the most favorable and/or special circumstances, usually as saints and prophets. In Christian Science, we find an example of the latter.

WOMEN IN NINETEENTH-CENTURY AMERICA

A rampant biological determinism helped to create the personality stereotype of the 19th century American woman. The ideal female character as one given over entirely to nurturance, intuitive morality, domesticity, passivity, and affection rested in part on then-current medical and scientific views of female physiology. Medical opinion held that women were physically frailer than men, with smaller skulls and more delicate muscles. The female nervous system was thought to be more susceptible to irritation and prone to overstimulation and exhaustion. In men, by contrast, the brain (and presumably the intellect) ruled, whereas women were dominated by the nervous system and the emotions.

Medical men believed that women's weaknesses were rooted in their reproductive system which controlled their behavior. To buttress this view, doctors posited a hypothetical connection between the uterus and the central nervous system which became the logical basis for "reflex irritations." The prevailing theory of disease was based on the notion that any imbalance, exhaustion, or infection of the reproductive organs could cause pathological reactions in other parts of a woman's body, however remote from the source.

Woman's physiology and anatomy oriented her toward an "inner" view of herself and her worldly sphere. In 1869, W.H. Holcombe, a Philadelphia doctor, wrote:

> Mentally, socially, spiritually, she is more interior than man, . . . Woman is to deal with domestic affections and uses, not with philosophies and sciences . . . She is priest, not king.

Their limited social sphere, lifelong dependence on, and submission to male protectors, and their educational bias against so-called male traits of curiosity, self-assertion, and aggression prevented American girls from developing adult skills and strengths and doomed them to remain forever child-women.

The social role assigned to women, although consistent with popular biological credos, embodied a functional ambiguity which ultimately made the female body appear confining and degrading:

> While the sentimental poets placed woman among the angels and doctors praised the transcendent calling of her reproductive system, social taboos made woman ashamed of menstruation, embarrassed and withdrawn during pregnancy, self-conscious and purposeless during and after menopause.

Women who tried to live in opposition to their physiology, and one could do this either by reading or studying too much, wearing "improper" clothing, working in factories, or living overly luxurious or sendentary lives, risked the stiff penalty of producing weak or degenerate offspring. Medical men believed that education was dangerous for women at puberty, because the brain and the ovaries could not develop at the same time. The effect on some educators was to lighten women's courseloads or prohibit them from taking the regular degree programs in colleges and universities. Not all women tolerated the stereotypic role, however, and protests rose in diverse quarters and in various forms. By the 1870's and 80's a good education was becoming available to those who had the courage, the money, and the cultural impetus to pursue it; women were themselves founding the great women's colleges at this time: Mount Holyoke, Smith, Wellesley, and Vassar.

Although the Women's Rights Movement, launched at Seneca Falls, New York, in 1848, stalled after the Civil War when Northern Abolitionist support evaporated, the movement's principal leaders, Elizabeth Cady Stanton and Susan B. Anthony, never abandoned the cause of universal suffrage; with Stanton supplying the ideas and written material, Anthony traveled and lectured across the country for nearly 40 tireless years after 1865 to rally new followers.

The dress reform movement pioneered by Sally Bloomer and others had important sociological implications because clothing was part and parcel of women's role. Women physicians struck out against fashionable modes of dress, blaming female weakness and poor health on compressed viscera. Wrote Dr. Sarah Stevenson, "Looks, not books, are the murderers of American women."

Women began to treat other women's illnesses in various medical and quasi-medical capacities. Professional medicine was in a rudimentary state until Pasteur's ideas were introduced in the 1880's, for, lacking a germ theory of disease, no unified theoretical approach to the study of illness had developed, nor were there uniform standards of training and practice for physicians. In an atmosphere of medical heterodoxy, lay people experimented with all manner of cures, remedies and irregular health beliefs.

The career of Mary Nichols (1810-1884), a self-educated health reformer, is illustrative of medical practice in the 19th century. Raised in a small Vermont town, a girlhood convert to Quakerism, she was teaching school at 18, contributing poems and stories to local newspapers, and studying medical textbooks in secret. (She married Hiram Gove, a hatter, and bore five children, only one of whom lived beyond infancy.) About 1832, she became interested in the therapeutic virtues of water and began giving cold water treatments to women. In 1837 she opened a girls' school in Lynn, Massachusetts and was the first to lecture local women on anatomy, hygiene, and physiology. Her health reform was founded on the belief that women's physical and mental sufferings were largely due to their ignorance about sex. She recommended a regimen of fresh air, plain food, exercise, and daily cold baths. The Ladies Physiological Society of Boston invited her to give a series of lectures, which she published in 1842 under the title of *Lectures to Ladies on Anatomy and Physiology*. Breaking off with Hiram Gove, she established her own water cure house in New York City in 1845. Besides her therapeutic activities, she published a novel and several short stories, and her house became a literary salon frequented by men like Edgar Allan Poe and Arthur Brisbane. In 1848, she married Thomas Nichols who afterward obtained a degree in medicine and joined her in the water cure establishment. Together they planned a Utopian community that never opened. She went through several religious conversions, and claimed for her last curing method a gift of healing by the laying on of hands.

Mary Nichols' life and work exemplify the eclectic approach to illness so characteristic of the period, in which the supernatural and the merely faddish mingled indiscriminately with good sense. She is an interesting precursor of Mary Baker Eddy, but sharp personality differences between the two women probably account for their disparate styles in rejecting the female role.

In all cultures, certain individuals experience role conflict, but most societies provide alternative roles to accommodate the variant personalities. Religious roles often satisfy this function in simpler societies; in late 19th century America, a common role alternative for women was illness. Talcott Parsons' construct of the sick role has some relevance to the historical phenomenon. Parsons conceptualizes the sick role as a non-deliberate form of social deviance for which the individual ought not to be blamed. In this formulation, persons in the sick role should be excused from normative social duties and obligations, but are expected to take the necessary steps to get well so that the social system can return to normal. Victorian women on the whole did not comply with the last stricture, the obligation to assist in their own recovery.

HYSTERIA

Hysteria has a centuries-long clinical history in Western culture that identifies it as a characteristically female disorder. Translated from the Greek, the word hysteria means wandering womb. Physicians and psychologists have traditionally defined it from the standpoint of individual psychodynamics as a neurosis. More recently, hysteria has been seen as a form of behavior closely related to social and cultural values and role expectations.

Hysteria was prevalent in the 19th century during a time when social upheaval created stress in the Victorian family structure and few domestic role alternatives were available. According to Carroll Smith-Rosenberg, who has documented this period and its pathologies, hysteria became "an alternative role option for particular women incapable of accepting their life situation." While hysteria could afflict both sexes, all ages and classes, physicians reported its highest incidence among middle and upper middle class urban women between the ages of 15 and 40; women in their childbearing years whose cultural training as delicate, passive creatures prepared them neither for the physical rigors of childbirth and childbearing nor for the fortitude and authority they were expected to display as co-heads of families.

Hysteria had variable and complex symptoms; nervousness, depression, crying spells, chronic fatigue, disabling pain. The most characteristic of them, however, was the hysterical "fit," which resembled an epileptic seizure, sometimes coming on suddenly, at other times occurring in the wake of depression, nervousness, or crying. Thought by physicians to have been precipitated by intense emotion or physical trauma, these seizures could cause the sufferer alternate laughter and sobbing, heart palpitations, feelings of strangulation, and loss of speech and hearing. A prolonged trance lasting even days might follow, or perhaps violent convulsions, sometimes accompanied by hallucinations. Such seizures were believed also to cause more permanent symptoms of paralysis and contracture.

MARY BAKER EDDY

Considered against this background of role dis-continuities, cultural pathology, and the general health problems of women, Mary Baker Eddy's life history assumes an archetypal significance.

Most individuals routinely learn and transmit their culture to the next generation with few modifications. Others, perhaps more sensitive and unstable, embody in their personalities the salient conflicts of their time. Often these latter become maladjusted—society's deviants. Certain ones, however, are exceptional in possessing the capacity for resolution of these conflicts, for themselves and for others like them: these people may become prophets, as Mrs. Eddy did.

She was born Mary Morse Baker on July 16, 1821 in the small village of Bow, New Hampshire, the youngest of six children. The family were orthodox Calvinist farmers and landowners. A gentle and pious mother, cast in the prevailing 19th century mold, tried to buffer the friction between Mary, who was a strong-willed young girl, and a stern, authoritarian father. Biographers theorize that fear of her father's punishments may have induced Mary's frequent tantrums, which were so severe that the family physician often had to be summoned to subdue her. Neighbors called them Mary's "fits." E. F. Dakin, in his biography of Mrs. Eddy, diagnosed them as unmistakable hysterical seizures. The symptoms included screaming and crying, lying on the floor and pounding her heels against the floor, sometimes passing into unconsciousness. These attacks recurred at stressful periods throughout Mary's early life, leaving her with a chronically weak back that could become disabling, especially at those times when the role of wife and mother was thrust upon her.

To illustrate, when Mary returned to her family in New Hampshire from Wilmington, Virginia in 1844 at 23 years of age after the premature death of her first husband, she bore a son whom she was never "well" enough to care for. At birth the boy was entrusted to a wet nurse and as he grew older the local blacksmith's daughter virtually brought him up. During these years Mary's seizures grew more terrible; she lived alternately with her father and her sister and brother-in-law, who devised a special cradle in which she had to be rocked to quiet her. A swing was put in her room, also to soothe her with its movement. On her good days when she was not having physical symptoms, Mary remained nervous and excitable.

Fond of being the center of attention, she played the raconteur at the ladies' sewing circle, and also submitted poetry and articles for publication in New England journals. This aspect of her behavior fits the hysterical female character Smith-Rosenberg describes that emerged gradually in the 19th century medical literature as based increasingly on mood and personality rather than on strictly physical symptoms.

> Doctors commonly described hysterical women as highly impressionistic, suggestible and narcissistic. Highly labile, their moods changed suddenly, dramatically, and for seemingly inconsequential reasons. Doctors complained that the hysterical woman was egocentric in the extreme, her involvement with others consistently superficial and tangential.

Taken together with Dakin's picture of Mary as unstable and suggestible, the foregoing may explain why she failed in two attempts to support herself by teaching, and also explain her reported interest in the spiritualist and mesmerist crazes of the late 1840's.

Despite illnesses, affectations, and egocentricity, Mary had a string of suitors. Smith-Rosenberg states:

> While the hysterical woman might appear to physicians and relatives as quite sexually aroused or attractive, she was, doctors cautioned, essentially asexual and not uncommonly frigid.

A second marriage to the itinerant dentist Daniel Patterson in 1853, which continued her pattern of marrying men who were not her intellectual equals, was accompanied by a renewal of seizures, uncontrollable outbursts of temper, and frequent periods when she was bedridden. She had to be carried downstairs to Patterson's carriage on their wedding day. Their years together in the several drab towns where Patterson tried to establish a practice were marked by both financial and intellectual poverty, her husband's frequent absences and infidelities, and what seemed for Mary a downhill life of chronic invalidism.

Her behavior was entirely consistent with Smith-Rosenberg's interpretation of hysteria, for consciously or not, through hysteria she avoided the traditional woman's role. Her illness with its dramatic symptoms forced others to assume the domestic responsibilities (poor as he was, Patterson hired a servant to take care of her), and in taking to her bed she continued to dominate the household in a way not possible for a healthy woman. Patterson's worry and concern, however, eventually dwindled into disaffection, and in the spring of 1866 he deserted his wife.

The next four years were for Mary Patterson, penniless and practically homeless, a mental wilderness of ineptitude, irresolution, and failure. She moved from house to house, either as a boarder or a guest, often getting herself evicted by hosts who turned intemperate in the face of her "spells," her affectations, unpaid bills, and occasional viciousness.

Her biographers speculate that only a sense of religious mission could have carried Mary through this difficult period. The source and inspiration for that mission was Phineas Quimby, the Portland healer whose treatments had helped to relieve Mary's back troubles from time to time. During her visits to Portland, Mary became attached to the "doctor," as he styled himself, and he in turn was pleased to share with so quick and willing a pupil the principles of his therapy. Then in 1866, some months before Patterson left her, Mary received word of Quimby's death.

The decision to continue her mentor's work may date from that winter of 1866, which was noteworthy in her life as the season she fell on the ice in Lynn, Massachusetts, and injured her back. In her autobiography written

25 years later, she claimed to have cured herself metaphysically from the ill effects of that fall:

> My immediate recovery from the effects of an injury caused by an accident, an injury that neither medicine nor surgery could reach, was the falling apple that led me to the discovery how to be well myself, and how to make others so.

Mary's determination to become Quimby's successor was evidenced, between 1866 and 1870, in her continuous lectures to anyone who would listen on the merits of Quimby's ideas. She also spent a good part of each day writing her "book"—known as The Bible to her hosts. She resumed the name of Glover about 1867, tried her hand at healing the sick, crediting herself with a number of cures, and began to attract pupils whom she taught from a copy of a Quimby manuscript entitled *Questions and Answers*.

Curiously, but significantly, biographical references to Mary's physical disabilities, which seemed so severe a few years earlier, cease altogether at this time and do not reappear in the literature. Catching sight of a larger goal and channeling her talents and energy into achieving it seem to have improved Mary's health. At the very least, poor health presented no obstacles to her ambition.

In 1870 Mary emerged from her wilderness, the prophet of a new faith. That year she formed a business partnership with an affable young man, Richard Kennedy, whom she had met two years before. They opened offices in Lynn with "Dr. Kennedy" in charge of the actual healing, while Mrs. Glover kept discreetly in the background, writing. Those patients who voiced curiosity about the rationale of their treatment were sent to Mary for instruction, and in this way she was able to form classes. Initially each student agreed to pay $100 in advance for a course of 12 lectures, and either 10% of her income from practicing or $1000 in case the student did not go into practice. Within a few weeks the tuition jumped to $300, equal to half the yearly wages of a Lynn shoeworker, but they paid the price.

A small manufacturing city of 30,000, Lynn furnished a fertile social setting for the Kennedy-Glover enterprise, for it had been the site of labor strife primarily involving women workers in the local shoe factories. Kennedy and Glover offered these exploited, discouraged women (and a few similarly disadvantaged men) an opportunity to advance themselves socially in the respectable profession of healing.

Although their practice flourished, Richard Kennedy terminated the partnership in 1872 over ideological arguments concerning healing techniques, money matters, and personality conflicts. The break, though it earned Richard her undying enmity, left Mary Glover with about $6,000 as her share, more capital than she had ever seen in her life.

According to Dakin, Mary's release from poverty had salutary effects on both her personality and physical appearance.

> Month by month and year by year she became a more commanding, more dominating figure. . . . No longer forced to constant scheming how she might live on the charities of her acquaintances, she gradually dropped many of those little oddities in speech, clothes, and manner which she had unconsciously adopted as a sort of psychological barricade. Her nervous and scrawny figure developed some curves, her carriage became erect, her gaze turned steady and piercing.

It can be argued that Mary's discovery of a new power role for herself that repudiated the traditional 19th century female stereotype, a role that enabled her to express the extraordinary person she felt herself to be, was, more than money *per se,* responsible for her changed appearance and behavior. A parallel can be seen in the career of Mary Wollstonecraft, the 18th century British feminist, whose latest biographer remarks on her increasingly attractive appearance after she published *A Vindication of the Rights of Women* (1792) and received recognition and acclaim for her work.

CHRISTIAN SCIENCE

With the publication of **Science and Health** in 1875 as a doctrinal foundation and the support of a fiercely loyal group of students, Mary Glover was able to institute the Christian Science Association in 1876. Her efforts during this formative period were greatly facilitated by the cooperation and probably even the devotion of a series of men. Favorites rose and fell among male students, reflecting her emotionalism on the one hand, and equally perhaps, her special appeal for suggestible and highly strung people like herself. It was something of a surprise, therefore, when in 1877, having divorced Patterson some years before, she married Asa Gilbert Eddy, a mild-mannered student and former sewing machine salesman who thereafter adopted the title of doctor and worked closely with Mary until his death in 1882.

Nevertheless, however strongly Mrs. Eddy may have depended on masculine assistance in starting Christian Science, the majority of her students were always women. No feminist, she actively tried to prevent Christian Science from becoming a "women's religion," exhorting her female followers to bring their husbands. Many did, but she could never stem the tide of women and balance the sex ratio. Her first class at the Massachusetts Metaphysical College (she originally founded this institution in Lynn in 1881 with herself as president and sole faculty member) numbered six women and one man, and that sex ratio remained fairly constant. Today the sex ratio among Christian Science practitioners is about eight women to one man.

Who were these women? At the beginning they consisted of factory workers and shop girls from Lynn and the surrounding community: also widows and spinsters seeking a way of earning a living by becoming healers; as the movement grew, numbers of middle-class women who inhabited an occupational and educational desert between the fortunate few who went to college and an enlarging class of menial workers. With Mrs. Eddy's increasing fame, women of a higher socioeconomic class came to Christian Science. At every stage of the movement's development, there seemed to be a good fit between the prophet and her public; as Mrs. Eddy matured in wisdom, her adherents, too, became more sophisticated.

Mrs. Eddy's influence as a role model cannot be overestimated, for in her followers' eyes she was both divinely inspired prophet and charismatic leader, part of a cosmology and head of an organization. (She formally adopted the title of Leader in 1894, in preference to Mother.) Such were her entrepreneurial skills that between 1884 and 1888 she master-minded Christian Science from a struggling, insignificant sect to an institution of national prominence. Biographers Bates and Dittemore assert that:

> It was not until this, her seventh decade, that Mrs. Eddy reached the height of her powers. She had at last found the field in which lay her real strength, which was that of an organizer and promoter.

While furthering her own objectives, Mrs. Eddy was at the same time giving other women opportunities to realize their ambitions in leadership roles which were not available outside the movement. To spread Christian Science, she forged a series of networks radiating outward from Boston, the movement's dynamic center. Systematically she dispatched her favorites—talented, eloquent women like herself—to the major cities: Augusta Stetson, whom many considered Mrs. Eddy's logical successor at the time, went to New York and founded the spectacularly successful First Church of Christ, Scientist; Sue Bradshaw became known as "the Christian Science boss of San Francisco"; Josephine Woodbury is reported to have swept Denver off its feet in 1887. Mrs. Eddy personally directed her forces via a vast correspondence, bolstering the down-hearted, if needed, with terse notes of advice and encouragement.

Men were not absent, but Mrs. Eddy placed them in business-like, administrative roles, while she reserved for women the tasks that demanded persuasive communication. It should be emphasized that her emissaries traveled across the country not as mere ordinary women but as women in formally established religious roles that elevated their status and endowed their missions with a high holy purpose. The major Protestant churches would wait another 75 years to confer similar statuses on women.

Elements that were inherent in the ideology of Christian Science probably attracted women; for example, the androgynous nature of the deity. The concept of a father-mother god, like the Unitarian god which preceded it some 40 years earlier in Boston, was an abstraction that contained both feminine and masculine principles. The egalitarian image of the deity was refracted into the social sphere where, to qualify as complete persons, men and women were expected to possess a harmonious balance of masculine and feminine traits. The Christian Science Sunday Service expressed equality between the sexes in dispensing with a minister and having the ritual led by two Readers, almost always a woman and a man who were elected from the congregation.

Another possible factor in attracting women was the metaphysical doctrine of denial. We have seen that women's lives in the 19th century were often full of pain and frustration for which the social system provided few compensations. A set of beliefs that declared sin, suffering and evil illusory and affirmed the sole reality of a spiritual existence could have considerable appeal to women. Denial, was, of course, a principal technique of the therapeutics, which rested on the claim that all ills could be healed metaphysically.

Healing was certainly an important factor in the overall success of Christian Science. Taking it in the literal sense alone, healing had a special significance for women who for decades had been afraid to talk to male doctors about their problems. Mary Nichols' popular anatomy lectures, even though they were based on incomplete knowledge, were an indication of that need. Christian Science provided women with practitioners of their own sex, sometimes gifted healers to whom patients could confide a whole range of problems that medical doctors either failed to recognize as problems or condescendingly ignored. The ties between practitioner and patient went beyond the purely professional since the practitioner was the spiritual advisor and often the close friend of her patients. It is not an exaggeration to describe Christian Science in the early years as largely a religion in which women helped other women overcome suffering.

SOCIAL HEALING

In studying a healing religion one almost inevitably confronts the larger theoretical issue of the relationship between individual illness and disturbed social relations. The anthropological literature contains some interesting examples for comparison in which healing becomes a metaphor for curing social ills. Robin Horton, a British social anthropologist, observes that in traditional African cultures which assign all causation to individual agents, there is a predisposition to see a connection between social disturbance and individual affliction. An outstanding ethnographic example can be found in the Ndembu of Central Africa. Victor Turner's analysis in *The Forest of Symbols* shows how the Ndembu diviner, diagnosing illness, relates his patients' symptoms to a whole chain of disturbances in his social field. Turner uses the term "social analysis" to describe divination. The patient is cured only when the social tensions are repaired.

These ethnographic sources referring to the social causes of individual illness are analogous to Smith-Rosenberg's delineation of the social causes of hysteria in 19th century American women. In each instance, amelioration of the offending social conditions contributes to the cure. Hardly a better example exists than the case of Mary Baker Eddy, in which the hysteria subsided, she claimed, after she discovered a healing method in Christain Science; but I contend, and more importantly, because she assumed a power role contrary to the 19th century stereotype.

Further associations between women, illness, and social dysfunction appear in I. M. Lewis' work with Somali possession cults. The cults are concerned with illness and curing and have disproportionately large numbers of women members. Lewis states:

> For all their concern with disease and its treatment . . . women's possession cults are also, I argue, thinly disguised protest movements against the dominant sex. They thus play a significant part in the sex-war in traditional societies and cultures where women lack more obvious and direct means for forwarding their aims.

Lewis' interpretation of the cults is very similar to mine regarding Christian Science, and some of his arguments apply quite precisely to Christian Science's early history. For example, although women dominate in the possession cults, socially subordinate men are also involved. We may recall that in the factory town of Lynn, birthplace of Christian Science, young men like Richard Kennedy were menial shoe workers, socially disadvantaged and ambitious for new careers in a "respectable" profession.

Lewis views possession itself as an "oblique aggressive strategy" that gives an afflicted person privileges and liberties he/she is not normally entitled to. Possession works in the interests of the downtrodden who have few other effective means of getting attention and respect. Horton goes further, stating that under possession, African women frequently act out dominance roles.

Substituting hysteria for possession will approximate fairly closely the picture in 19th century America; women who were discontented and whose domestic roles were devalued often adopted the hysterical role as an escape and used illness to gain attention, if not always to secure power. Vittorio Lanternari, writing of prophetic religions in developing nations, updates and enlarges the ethnographic parallel:

> The voice of these countless prophets reminds us of the boundaries we have imposed on our own civilization. The cry for freedom . . . inherently denounces the contradictions within our own culture, as they appear to the new worlds now beginning to take shape.

These similarities aside, Christian Science operated very differently from the possession cults in regard to the conscious motives of its women members. Women did not convert to Christian Science to wage war on the opposite sex. In general, women came into Christian Science for no other purposes than to be healed of whatever was bothering them, and to heal others. Christian Science was never a "thinly disguised" protest; it was a wholly unconscious one, which makes it so preeminently a case of latent function.

In a symbolic sense, the metaphysics of Christian Science gave women an otherworldly bastion from which to conduct an "argument" against "Illness." Substantively, by becoming a large, successful organization, Christian Science gave a real place in the world to women in the 19th century who had been considered out of place, with all the stigma that phrase implies, if they ventured away from hearth and home. Through Christian Science, women obtained legitimate power and leadership roles, becoming practitioners, nurses, teachers, readers in their churches.

This interpretation transforms Christian Science into a religion of the disadvantaged, a position that may astonish its present-day affluent members. But perhaps today's prosperous, middle class membership had tended to obscure from scholarly view the movement's original social function of mobilizing an unconscious protest against 19th century America's unequal treatment of approximately half its population.

CONCLUSIONS

A religious movement appearing at a stressful period in history in regard to the social position of women, Christian Science invites comment about the capacity of social systems in general for stability and change. To maintain themselves and to function efficiently, all social systems, regardless of their degree of complexity, must provide regular, orderly means of dealing with dissident and innovative elements in the population and to enable numerous personality types to navigate in society. In periods of social upheaval, new religions frequently serve either as instruments or mediators of change. The major evangelical movements of the 18th and 19th centuries in the U.S. are cases in point.

However, formal church attitudes vary toward social change. The noted scholar Ernst Troeltsch constructed a typology that recognizes two fundamentally different religious approaches to the dynamics of change. Troeltsch termed those sects aggressive which play an active part in attempting to radically reform society here and now in harmony with the will of god. On the other hand, he designated as passive sects those which can endure contempt and even persecution because they are largely indifferent to the world.

Christian Science touched on elements of each type. Arriving in the wake on a post Civil War turmoil which also saw the Women's Rights movement foundering, Christian Science advocated no programs for social improvement. On the contrary, the doctrine denied social reality altogether, conforming to the character of a passive sect. But within its sectarian boundaries, Christian Science corrected for flaws in the wider society by building an enclave in which female and male sex roles were less rigidly defined and more egalitarian than in the outside world.

In this sense, Christian Science assumed the role of an aggressive sect, which created a separate organizational world for women and rapidly changed the lives of its women followers. At the same time, it is important to note that the social system itself was scarcely if at all disrupted; hence it is somewhat ironic that in "containing" a portion of the dissident and discontented elements of society, Christian Science may have contributed to the equilibrium of the very same social order that gave the movement its initial impetus and latent function.

Stephen J. Stein (essay date 1982)

SOURCE: "Retrospection and Introspection: The Gospel According to Mary Baker Eddy," in *Harvard Theological Review,* Vol. 75, No. 1, January, 1982, pp. 97-116.

[*In the following essay, Stein explores Eddy's autobiography* Retrospection and Introspection.]

In 1891 Mary Baker Eddy (1821-1910) opened her autobiography, *Retrospection and Introspection,* with a romanticized account of her family tree entitled "Ancestral Shadows." Little more than one hundred pages later she closed her presentation with a confident prediction that in future centuries the "Tree of Life" would "blossom" under the influence of "Divine Science," benefiting all the nations. Between these extremities of genealogy and eschatology she grouped a potpourri of reflections—personal, historical, literary, and theological—which defy easy categorization and lack apparent organization. To this day her self-portrait remains a puzzle, a resource often ignored by those struggling to understand this "remarkable" woman. This essay is an attempt to unlock the enigma of *Retrospection and Introspection* by examining the content and the structure of the text itself, thereby shedding light on Mary Baker Eddy's self-conception as the discoverer and founder of Christian Science.

Even the most distinguished biographer of Mary Baker Eddy has only modest insight to offer concerning this unusual document. Robert Peel suggests that *Retrospection and Introspection* is properly divided into two parts with chapter 10 detailing Eddy's discovery of the principles of Christian Science serving as the point of division. The retrospective portion which precedes the account of her healing in 1866 Peel describes as partaking of a romantic quality. Factuality was not her primary concern, according to him. The second and introspective part of the autobiography, he declares, focuses on the author's "vision of reality," a topic with which she was more at home. It is this portion that is highly representative of Mary Baker Eddy's manifold other writings on the Science of being. The volume is not traditional autobiography, in Peel's view, for "it is clear that her real interest

is in the spiritual ancestry and destiny of her child, Christian Science."

As useful as Peel's statement concerning Eddy's primary interest may be, it is difficult, if not impossible, to reconcile fully his assessment of her intention in the autobiography with an analysis of its content and structure. Peel's position leads logically to the conclusion that Mary Baker Eddy was not interested in telling her own story, a rather unusual state of mind to ascribe to one who writes an autobiography. It is particularly improbable to attribute such lack of interest to the founder of Christian Science who was careful about most things she wrote, and who in 1891 had a variety of reasons why she wanted to portray her life to the public. A fuller explanation of the autobiography is needed which will take into account Eddy's obvious interest in self-revelation and which will reflect more consistency between the content and the structure of the final product.

One element in Peel's assessment is especially significant, namely, his judgment that Mary Baker Eddy was vitally concerned with the "destiny of her child, Christian Science"—a fact that must be integrated into any interpretation of *Retrospection and Introspection*. Eddy herself offers valuable assistance in this task. In chapter 8, entitled "Marriage and Parentage," among a series of comments related to the years of her unfortunate second marriage, she interjected an excursus on the subject of history. "It is well to know, dear reader," she counseled, "that our material, mortal history is but the record of dreams, not of man's real existence, and the dream has no place in the Science of being. It is 'as a tale that is told,' and 'as the shadow when it declineth.'" According to Eddy, "earth's shadows" are designed to turn human consciousness "from a material, false sense of life and happiness, to spiritual joy and true estimate of being." Divine Science seeks this "awakening," she wrote. "Mere historic incidents and personal events are frivolous and of no moment, unless they illustrate the ethics of Truth." The only acceptable reason for "such narrations" is that they work toward "spiritual conclusions." If such is not the case, then "human history needs to be revised, and the material record expunged." All biography, accordingly, must serve spiritual ends.

But has such biography ever been written? Has history ever met the demands of the Science of being? If so, when? Mary Baker Eddy answered these questions in the same chapter. According to her, spiritual history was written on one occasion in a form familiar to all Christians. "The Gospel narratives bear brief testimony even to the life of our great Master," wrote Eddy. "His spiritual noumenon and phenomenon silenced portraiture." The scriptural lives of Jesus written by the hands of the apostles under the direction of God's Spirit were successful biography. When others "less wise than the apostles" tried to formulate "a legendary and traditional history of the early life of Jesus," their apocryphal gospels were unsuccessful because they focused on the material plane of his existence. The goal of biography remains the vanquishment of errors "by victory-bringing Science." When it is understood that "real man is not of the dust, nor is he ever created through the flesh; for his father and mother are the one Spirit, and his brethren are all the children of one parent, the eternal good," then the true nature of history and biography will be realized. When it is affirmed that God "alone is our origin, aim, and being," then proper biography can be written. In *Retrospection and Introspection* Mary Baker Eddy set out to write spiritual biography in a form similar to the gospel narratives of the New Testament.

There is a broad resemblance between the general scheme of events in the canonical accounts of the life and teachings of Jesus and the materials in *Retrospection and Introspection*. The parallel is most striking in the retrospective portion of the autobiography (here, in contrast to Peel, defined as the first twenty chapters) which tells of Mary Baker Eddy's life and work, of her discovery of the Science of being and of her founding of the Christian Science community. The several stages in her experience—spiritual childhood, religious maturation, public ministry, and the final establishment of the church—follow in some measure the accounts of the activities of Jesus recorded in the gospels. The introspective portion of the autobiography, which embraces the last ten chapters, is an extended theological reflection on Christian Science as the way of truth and life. Included in these last chapters are a "sermon on a mount" by Mary Baker Eddy and a farewell discourse by her. In combination, the retrospective and the introspective portions of the autobiography present the author's understanding of herself.

. . . . .

The opening stage in the retrospective section of Mary Baker Eddy's autobiography (chaps. 1-7), an account of her spiritual childhood, resembles the birth narratives in the canonical gospels and the story of Jesus' youth. Eddy begins with a series of stylized observations concerning her "ancestors, according to the flesh," who were characterized by their piety, nobility, patriotism, gallantry, and poetic accomplishments (Matt 1:1-17; Luke 3:23-38). Following these genealogical glosses, she supplies the recollection of an almost idyllic birthplace in Bow, New Hampshire, with its "green pastures bright with berries, singing brooklets, beautiful wild flowers, and flecked with large flocks and herds" (Luke 2:6-20). She also records fond memories of the members of her family. About her father she recalled only his "strong intellect" and "iron will" (Matt 1:19). By contrast, Eddy spoke about the difficulty of doing justice to the memory of her "sainted mother" whose eulogy she echoed: "Her life was a living illustration of Christian faith" (Luke 1:28). Eddy also noted the "calamity" of the early death of her brother Albert, who, next to her mother, was "the very dearest" of her "kindred," a death which destroyed a promising public career (Matt 14:10).

Mary Baker Eddy continues the account of her childhood with the story of her calling at the age of eight, an episode singled out from a multitude of "peculiar circumstances and events" that thronged the "chambers of memory." For the period of a year, young Mary "repeatedly heard a voice," calling her "distinctly by name, three times, in an ascending scale." Others heard it also. After months of perplexity and anxiety, her mother read to her "the Scriptural narrative of little Samuel" and told her to respond "as he did, 'Speak Lord; for Thy servant heareth'" (1 Sam 3:9). Subsequently, she wrote, when "the call came again I did answer, in the words of Samuel, but never again to the material senses was that mysterious call repeated." Eddy closed the chapter entitled "Voices Not Our Own" with a poem containing musings about the presence of God discerned in the roll of thunder and about the joy of recognizing his "voice"— a note reminiscent of the prophetic call sounded at the beginning of the gospel accounts: "The voice of one crying in the wilderness, Prepare ye the way of the Lord" (Matt 3:3).

Four subsequent chapters of *Retrospection and Introspection* underscore the spiritual precocity of young Mary by evoking images of the twelve-year-old Jesus in the temple. Nevertheless, a subtle inversion occurs on the theme of the "Father's business" (Luke 2:49). These chapters portray Eddy's father, Mark Baker, in a poor light. According to her, his misguided judgment was responsible for Mary's extended absences from school as a child. Furthermore, at an early age she rejected his "relentless theology," a form of Calvinism, and instead chose to "lean on God's love," a position her mother urged upon her. Eddy asserted that as a child she was able to learn from books easily, but most of that knowledge "vanished like a dream" after her discovery of Christian Science. "Learning was so illumined," she wrote, "that grammar was eclipsed. Etymology was divine history, voicing the idea of God in man's origin and signification. Syntax was spiritual order and unity. Prosody, the song of angels, and no earthly or inglorious theme." Mary Baker Eddy left no uncertainty about the superiority of spiritual knowledge and the divine origins of her insights into the Science of being.

The most explicit demonstration of Mary's spiritual precocity occurred at "the age of twelve" when, Eddy stated, she was formally received into membership in the Congregational Church. (In fact, she joined the Congregational Church at Sanbornton Bridge in 1838 at the age of seventeen.) On that occasion she instructed her minister, "an old-school expounder of the strictest Presbyterian doctrines," concerning the unacceptability of the concepts of "unconditional election, or predestination" (Luke 2:46-47). Despite his unbending theological position, her protest melted the hearts of the minister and of others at the meeting, and she was accepted into the congregation. These same years established that poetry rather than prose was more "suited" to Mary's needs and emotions (Luke 1:46-55). In *Retrospection and Introspection* she included two examples of her early verse. One is a youthful effort that celebrates knowledge and science. The other speaks of the superiority of the spiritual over the earthly: "hope," she wrote, "as the eaglet that spurneth the sod, / May soar above matter, to fasten on God, / And freely adore all His spirit hath made, / Where rapture and radiance and glory ne'er fade." The poem concludes, "This life is a shadow, and hastens away." Young Mary is thus portrayed in these chapters of the autobiography as already understanding her "Father's business" (Luke 2:49).

The second stage of the retrospective portion (chaps. 8-10), which describes Eddy's spiritual coming of age and the maturation of her own distinctive religious ideas, recalls events surrounding the transition from private to public activity in the life of Jesus. This section contains chapters on "Marriage and Parentage," "Emergence into Light," and "The Great Discovery"—the last identified as pivotal in Robert Peel's analysis. In the autobiography Mary Baker Eddy signaled her abrupt entry into the adult world by brief mention of her marriage to George Washington Glover on whose death, within a year, she was left pregnant and impoverished. The birth of a son and his subsequent removal from her added a new "trial" to her "terrible bereavement." Eddy spoke of this "separation" as living death. According to her brief account, a second marriage was intended to provide a means to regain the child, but her plans were thwarted by a "plot" to keep mother and child apart. (More than thirty years passed before Eddy was reunited with her son.) At this point in the text she reflects upon the "frivolous" quality of "mere historic incidents," contrasting them with the spiritual realities embodied in the canonical gospels.

Then follows the description of Mary Baker Eddy's greatest temptation, a temptation that came in the form of "the illusion that this so-called life could be a real and abiding rest" (Matt 4:1-3). During these years she clung to the hope that her son could have a home with her again and that happiness could be restored. These circumstances prevailed before she began to see the light, before the "character of the Christ was illuminated by the midnight torches of Spirit." Then a new marriage was consummated, one superior to those she had known, promising new fulfillment as a mother. "Thus it was when the moment arrived of the heart's bridal to more spiritual existence. When the door opened, I was waiting and watching; and, lo, the bridegroom came!" (Matt 25:6). Sorrow and heartache were destroyed. "My heart knew its Redeemer. He whom my affections had diligently sought was as the One 'altogether lovely,' as 'the chiefest,' the only, 'among ten thousand'" (Cant 5:10). Eddy now realized, according to the autobiography, that the "substance, cause, and currents" of being were "God and His idea." She had "touched the hem of Christian Science" and for a first time had felt its power in her life (Matt 9:20). Never again would the force of "mortal mind" exercise dominion over her as in the past.

By her own statement, 1866 was the *annus mirabilis,* the year in which she came to full recognition of "the Science of divine metaphysical healing." This discovery, Mary Baker Eddy was careful to point out in 1891, followed the death of the mental healer, Phineas Parkhurst Quimby, whose patient and student she had been in earlier years. Eddy came to the "certainty" that "all causation was Mind, and every effect a mental phenomenon" following recovery from an injury for which "neither medicine nor surgery" had been of any effect. After this "miracle," she "withdrew from society about three years" in order, she wrote, "to ponder my mission, to search the Scriptures, to find the Science of Mind that should take the things of God and show them to the creature, and reveal the great curative Principle—Deity" (Matt 4:1-2). During these times her "textbook" was the Bible, and from it she derived the insight which allowed her "for the first time" to understand the "spiritual meaning" of the teachings and activities of Jesus (Matt 4:4). Eddy was to "bear witness" to a new gospel—named by her "Christian Science" (John 5:31-32). Christian Science affirmed the reality and immortality of God as well as the unreality of the physical senses and all that they "testify falsely." Jesus of Nazareth, the "Way-shower," taught and demonstrated the same truth; he was "a natural and divine Scientist," one born of the spirit (John 3:8). But to a person born of the flesh, "divine Science must be a discovery" (John 3:6). "Woman must give it birth. It must be begotten of spirituality, since none but the pure in heart can see God, . . . and none but the 'poor in spirit' could first state this Principle" (Matt 5:3, 8).

For Mary Baker Eddy the discovery of Christian Science was a birthing process. The new child brought great joy to its mother; it was the sound of "sweet music" to her (Luke 2:51). Yet during these same years the mother was herself as a "little one" (Matt 18:4). Her earliest efforts to speak the truth were faltering. Only gradually did she gain the "experience and confidence" necessary to express adequately "the harmony of divine Science." During these maternal years the "great Master" led her like a child into "a fresh universe." Guided by an apprehension of the Spirit, she grew in wisdom and understanding (Luke 2:40). As the "mystery" of Divine Science was revealed to her, Eddy discovered that "reliance upon material things must be transferred to a perception of and dependence on spiritual things." Like Jesus of Nazareth, she committed herself to the task of proclaiming the good news of a new age (Matt 4:17). In the face of rising opposition, she determined to love her enemies and to do good to those that despitefully used her and persecuted her (Matt 5:44).

The third stage of Eddy's retrospection (chaps. 11-15), an account of her efforts at preaching, healing, and publishing the good news of Divine Science, is reminiscent of the descriptions of the public ministry of Jesus of Nazareth. As with Jesus, Mary Baker Eddy's task was not easy, for at this point in her career she "stood alone" in the attempt "to smite error with the falchion of Truth" (Matt 10:34). Toil, suffering, and conflict filled her life. Even internal struggles occurred, for passage through "the mazes of divine metaphysics" was an arduous undertaking, as Eddy acknowledged when she wrote, "No one else can drain the cup which I have drunk to the dregs as the Discoverer and teacher of Christian Science; neither can its inspiration be gained without tasting this cup" (Matt 26:39). Recognizing that "Bethlehem and Bethany" had led Jesus to "Gethsemane and Calvary," she nevertheless set out on her "divinely appointed human mission" to proclaim "the gospel of healing" and "the possibilities of spiritual insight, knowledge, and being." Self-sacrifice in the service of love, according to the autobiography, became the theme of her ministry; she reminded herself of the words of Jesus: "For whosoever will save his life shall lose it" (Matt 16:25).

The good news preached by Mary Baker Eddy—the power of the "immortal Mind, the curative Principle"—challenged the claims of the "different schools" of her day (Matt 16:1). Competition was fierce from "allopathy, homeopathy, hydropathy, electricity, and from various humbugs," all of which Eddy knew firsthand because she had once "wandered through the dim mazes of *materia medica*." Nevertheless, Christian Science prevailed over the other views because it demonstrated its truthfulness. The manifold "advantages" of the Science of mind were evident in that a "person healed by Christian Science is not only healed of his disease," she contended, "but he is advanced morally and spiritually" (Luke 5:24).

Time after time during her ministry, according to *Retrospection and Introspection,* Mary Baker Eddy healed "desperate cases," never once taking pay, healing "without money and without price" (Isa 55:1). One remarkable instance recounted in the text is that of an "invalid" whose "physicians had given up the case and retired." The woman, whose condition stemmed from an injury related to childbirth, was expected to die, and in fact, "the clothes [were] already prepared for her burial." Eddy noted, "I had stood by her side about fifteen minutes when the sick woman rose from her bed, dressed herself, and was well" (Matt 9:25). Unfortunately, this "scientific demonstration" did not persuade the "doctors and clergy" who increased their opposition to her teachings (Luke 6:11).

Mary Baker Eddy also "published" the good news of "spiritual, scientific Mind-healing" during the years of her public ministry. A first "little book" she copyrighted on the topic in 1870 was not published, however, because the times were not right for its reception (Matt 16:20). In a chapter on that "First Publication," she spoke of her new truths as "spiritual interpretations" of the Bible. The "gospel according to Jesus," she wrote, was the message that Christ is "the Truth and the Life" (John 14:6). It was this same affirmation, according to the autobiography, that she set out to publish in obedience to the command of Jesus. Yet certain "evil-minded" persons opposed her effort, charging that her "manuscripts" were not original (Luke 5:21).

As the years passed, the opposition to Mary Baker Eddy's publications increased. When *Science and Health* first appeared 1875, critics denounced it as "foolish and eccentric." Again the issue of originality surfaced, and her defense in *Retrospection and Introspection* was to declare that the "mystery of Godliness" was for the first time revealed in her "textbook" (1 Tim 3:16). She regarded the entire process leading to publication as under the direction of the "heavenly Father." According to her, "divine purpose" guided every step in the development of the "Precious Volume," as she entitled the chapter. "Whosoever learns the letter of this book," she wrote, "must also gain its spiritual significance, in order to demonstrate Christian Science" (2 Cor 3:6). Eddy's claims may have seemed high for her volume, but no higher than her representation that all of her teaching, healing, and publishing had the same objective, namely, revelation of a new truth.

The final stage in the retrospective portion of Eddy's autobiography (chaps. 16-20), a narrative of the culmination of her public ministry in the establishment of the Church of Christ, Scientist, brings to mind the post-resurrection activities of Jesus of Nazareth. The canonical gospels feature the themes of true discipleship, the pastoral role of Jesus, and the steps taken by him to establish the continuity of the Christian community on earth. One brief chapter in this section of *Retrospection and Introspection* describes the exemplary discipleship of a Gilbert Eddy, Eddy's third husband and namesake, a man with whom she had "a blessed and spiritual union." He was the first student to declare himself a "Christian Scientist." "He forsook all to follow in this line of light" (Luke 5:11), wrote Eddy. Asa Eddy was tireless in devotion to his calling, and though he "passed away" after only five years of marriage, his widow was certain that he embodied the character of the "perfect *man*" Ps 37:37). Her husband was joined by other faithful disciples who eventually organized themselves to undertake a new apostolic mission (Luke 9:1-2). In 1879 these organizational efforts led the formation of the Church of Christ, Scientist, and to the selection of Mary Baker Eddy as "pastor." She carried out the functions of shepherd, feeding and leading her followers. She committed herself to protecting the church from "envy and molestation" and from other dangers which threatened. Her poem entitled **"Feed My Sheep,"** written during these years, gives voice to her sense of pastoral responsibility (John 21:17). The concluding stanza reads:

> So, when day grows dark and cold,
> Tear or triumph harms,
> Lead Thy lambkins to the fold,
> Take them in Thine arms;
> Feed the hungry, heal the heart,
> Till the morning's beam;
> White as wool, ere they depart,
> Shepherd, wash them clean.

Under Mary Baker Eddy's pastorate the young church prospered.

The autobiography tells of the provisions Eddy made for the continuity of the community. In the 1880s she took a series of steps to solidify the future prospects of the church, measures she regarded as consistent with the principle that "Christian Science shuns whatever involves material means for the promotion of spiritual ends." By this point in her life Mary Baker Eddy was also "yearning for retirement" from her work (Luke 23:46). Her last years of public activity were dominated by the dual concerns to expand the impact of Christian Science and to protect it from a variety of "contaminating influences." In 1883, for example, she began the first official publication of the community, a monthly periodical subsequently known as *The Christian Science Journal,* which was used to disseminate and defend the Science of being. In 1886 she formed a national association for Christian Scientists in order to "meet the broader wants of humanity, and provide folds for the sheep that were without shepherds" (Mark 6:34). In 1889, despite its great success as an instructional agency, Mary Baker Eddy closed the Massachusetts Metaphysical College which had provided her a major platform for teaching. All of these changes she justified as necessary to prepare for "a new rule of order in divine Science." And on this note of shepherding she closed the retrospection in her autobiography.

Mary Baker Eddy opened the introspective portion of the autobiography on a similar note (chaps 21-30), effecting at the same time the transition to a different view of her role as the discoverer and founder of Christian Science. The last ten chapters of *Retrospection and Introspection* do not concern themselves with her life and work but rather with her teaching and ideas. These chapters depict the Science of being as the way of truth and life.

Eddy opens her "sermon on a mount" (chaps. 21-24) with encouragement for her disciples to "follow the example of Jesus, the master Metaphysician, and gain sufficient knowledge of error to destroy it with Truth." She evoked for them the image of Jesus as the Good Shepherd (John 10:11). The pursuit of life, she wrote, demands that the Christian Scientist enter a "strait and narrow path" (Matt 7:14). The way of truth also necessarily involves the recognition of error. For example, she counseled, her disciples will discover that faith healing rests on a false principle by contrast with the divine healing that stems from the Science of Mind.

Mary Baker Eddy subsequently spells out more fully the nature of truth by reflecting upon the "Foundation-Stones" of Christian Science, the "ideas of Deity" which include the "omnipotence and omnipresence of God, or divine good" (1 Cor 3:11). This "divine Principle," she explained, Jesus taught "as one having authority, and not as the scribes" (Matt 7:29). He affirmed the spiritual, not the material quality of life. Christian Science, according to Eddy, teaches that it is error to believe that man has "a mortal mind and soul and life," for it contradicts the "grand verity" of the Science of being. The "Great Revelation" states that God is life. Everything that coincides with life is compatible with the Science of Mind; everything that conflicts with the principle of life arises from the "fallibility" of "mortal man's ignorance."

Christian Science, wrote Mary Baker Eddy, proclaims that God is all and that evil—the opposite of God and life—is unreal. Sin and the sinner alike are destroyed by recognition of the illusory nature of their existence. They rest on false claims, "on the evidences of the physical senses" instead of on the spiritual perception of the Science of Mind (John 6:63). Unfortunately, Eddy contended, the ecclesiastical communities have not understood or proclaimed the truth. "Pharisaism killeth; Spirit giveth Life," she wrote (2 Cor 3:6). For this reason Jesus attacked the Jewish establishment in his day because it was not "spiritual" (Matt 23:13-39). By contrast, she affirmed, Christian Science proclaims "the pure evangelic truth. It accords with the trend and tenor of Christ's teaching and example, while it demonstrates the power of Christ as taught in the four Gospels." Christian Scientists have no use for creeds, rituals, or dogmas because their goals are "spiritual understanding and scientific demonstration of God" (Matt 6:7).

Nevertheless, Eddy recognized the power of the "false claim" of the "human concept" (Matt 7:15). Therefore she endeavored to identify as fully as possible the nature and origin of sin. Sin was and is a lie, according to her; the idea of man's mortality is also a product of deception. "In the words of our Master," wrote Eddy, "it, the 'devil' (*alias* evil), was a liar, and the father of it" (John 8:44). True disciples, she admonished, are instructed by the Master to call the Father in heaven their only father (Matt 23:9). The notion of Adam as the mortal parent of mankind must be condemned.

At this point in the autobiography (chap. 25), Mary Baker Eddy's self-identification becomes increasingly explicit. "The second appearing of Jesus is, unquestionably," she affirmed, "the spiritual advent of the advancing idea of God, as in Christian Science" (Matt 24:3). For her the theological claims of the Christian Scientists and the self-conception of the founder are inextricably bound together as are the respective roles of Jesus of Nazareth and the Virgin Mary as well as the functions of Jesus and the agent of his "second appearing," namely, Mary Baker Eddy herself. Eddy wrote, "We do not question the authenticity of the Scriptural narrative of the Virgin-mother and Bethlehem babe, and the Messianic mission of Christ Jesus; but in our time no Christian Scientist will give chimerical wings to his imagination, or advance speculative theories as to the recurrence of such events." Although Mary Baker Eddy discourages wild speculation, at the same time she invites continuing conjecture concerning her role as the founder. "No person can take the individual place of the Virgin Mary," she adds. "No person can compass or fulfil the individual mission of Jesus of Nazareth." But in like manner, she writes, "No person can take the place of the author of *Science and Health,* the Discoverer and Founder of Christian Science. Each individual must fill his own niche in time and eternity."

At the same time that Eddy warns against casual misunderstanding of her role, she leaves little doubt about her own self-conception. In *Retrospection and Introspection* she affirms that the arrival of Christian Science was a moment of equal importance with the first advent and that she—author, discoverer, and founder—has equivalent responsibilities to those of the Virgin Mary and Jesus of Nazareth because, on the one hand, the revelation of the true idea of God has been a birthing process and, on the other, she too has suffered for the sake of truth and has established a community of disciples. The form of the autobiography follows her understanding of her functions and proclamation. The truth of Christian Science dictates that immortal men put off the things of the flesh, materiality, "physical personality, or selfhood in matter" (Col 2:11). Accordingly, Eddy's autobiography takes on an impersonal and abstract character. She writes, "My own corporeal personality afflicteth me not wittingly; for I desire never to think of it, and it cannot think of me" (John 6:63). For this reason in *Retrospection and Introspection* she rejected ordinary models. The truth of Christian Science demands biography of a spiritual variety.

Mary Baker Eddy's exalted self-conception led her to attack the borrowing of her ideas without proper acknowledgment. For her the problem of plagiarism was tied to the question raised by the disciples of Jesus, "Who shall be greatest?" (Matt 18:1). Eddy reaffirmed the principle of Jesus that a student cannot speak evil lightly of the master (Mark 9:39). There is no ground in law nor "permission in the gospel," she pointed out, for uncredited borrowing; it violates the principles of the Sermon on the Mount. The teachers of Christian Science are obliged to give full due to the source of their truth, thereby rendering appropriate tribute to both God and to the discoverer of Christian Science (Matt 22:21) whose mind "must have risen to the altitude which perceived a light beyond what others saw." True disciples will acknowledge the source of their ideas, for "life and its ideals," affirmed Eddy, "are inseparable" as a mother and a child. Furthermore, when disciples feel "spiritual love" for their master, such "affection" is not "personal worship" but simply an expression of the "unity of good and bond of perfectness." The same force bound together the disciples of Jesus on the day of Pentecost (Acts 2). Spiritual love between teacher and students will cure the "growing evil" of plagiarism.

The closing section (chaps. 28-30) of *Retrospection and Introspection* constitutes a farewell discourse similar to that of Jesus in the gospel of John (John 14-17). Eddy offers parting words of counsel and encouragement to her followers. She urged her students, for example, not to read "so-called scientific works, antagonistic to Christian Science" because they distort the truth. The faithful disciple, she advised, guided by the "spirit of Truth" (John 16:13), will be meek, unselfish, temperate, and patient, even though the "kingdom of heaven suffereth violence" (Matt 11:12). If truth does not prevail, then mankind sinks into greater darkness, as Jesus stated: "If the light that is in thee be darkness, how great is that darkness!" (Matt 6:23). Eddy urged her followers to locate in "large cities" because there they would be able to do the great-

est good. They should also use the latest edition of *Science and Health* because it is "clearer than any previous edition." That textbook should be employed regularly in their classrooms. Her disciples must keep their lamps "trimmed and burning" (Matt 25:7), confident of the significance of their work and knowing that the cause of Christian Science "is highly prosperous, rapidly spreading over the globe; and the morrow will crown the effort of to-day with a diadem of gems from the New Jerusalem" (Rev 2:10).

It is the nature of the faithful disciple, wrote Eddy, to "take up his cross" and follow truth (Matt 16:24). Jesus commanded, "Follow me; and let the dead bury their dead" (Matt 8:22). He also directed his disciples to heal the sick (Matt 10:8), to treat others as they would be treated (Matt 7:12), and to bear one another's burdens (Gal 6:2). In the days of Jesus, "preaching and teaching were substantially one"; the "precedent" of "the four Gospels" remains. Christian Scientists are also to "raise the dead" (Matt 10:8) and to "preach the gospel" (Mark 16:15). Jesus' "method" was to "instruct" his disciples; "he watched and guarded them unto the end, even according to his promise, 'Lo, I am with you alway'!" (Matt 28:20). Similar responsibilities are laid upon the teachers of Christian Science. They must not forsake their flocks; they must not itinerate (John 10:11-13). "The true mother never willingly neglects her children in their early and sacred hours, consigning them to the care of nurse or stranger" (John 10:5). The "ardent mother," wrote Eddy, is solicitous for the welfare of her children. So Jesus ministered to the "spiritual needs" of his disciples. His teachings were the "bread of Life" (John 6:35). The most exalted of his discourses, the Sermon on the Mount, was a "series of great lessons" addressed to the concerns of his followers. His classroom was wherever he taught; nature was his "university." The legacy of his teaching and action is preserved by Christian Scientists who are the recipients of his promises, "If ye abide in me, and my words abide in you, ye shall ask what ye will, and it shall be done unto you" (John 15:7).

The final paragraphs of *Retrospection and Introspection* underscore once again the link between the experience of Jesus and his disciples and the activities of Christian Scientists. In the first century, Mary Baker Eddy wrote, the spiritual idea of Christ "appeared to human consciousness as the man Jesus." At that time both Jesus and the disciples wandered about. Now, however, Christian Science has elevated the ideal of God in fulfillment of the saying of Jesus, "And I, if I be lifted up from the earth, will draw all men unto me" (John 12:32). No longer is truth a "wanderer," nor "fragmentary, disconnected [or] unsystematic." Now it is a "stationary power" and has become a "model for human action" (John 16:13). According to Eddy, the statement of the apostle Paul—"For in Him we live, and move, and have our being" (Acts 17:28)—is "in substance identical" to her own manifesto, "There is no life, truth, substance, nor intelligence in matter." Christian Science must demonstrate "to the world convincing proof of the validity of this scientific statement of being." When this principle is fully ac-knowledged, when all error is destroyed, all matter purged from "mental consciousness" and "every spot and blemish on the disk of consciousness is removed, then, and not until then, will immortal Truth be found true, and scientific teaching, preaching, and practice be essentially one." Then the new heaven and new earth will be estab-lished (Rev 21:1). Divine Science, wrote Eddy, is "the same yesterday, and to-day, and forever" (Heb 13:8). The first and the nineteenth centuries are joined in common cause. Christian Science, Eddy stated, must "aid the es-tablishment of Christ's kingdom on the earth." In concert the two ages have revealed the way of truth and life by bringing the gospel to the nations. "In the first century of the Christian era Jesus' teachings bore much fruit, and the Father was glorified therein" (John 15:8), she wrote, "In this period and the forthcoming centuries, watered by the dews of divine Science, this 'tree of life' will blossom into greater freedom, and its leaves will be 'for the heal-ing of the nations'" (Rev 22:2).

· · · · ·

Retrospection and Introspection is less of an enigma when the thematic and structural parallels with the ca-nonical gospels are identified. The self-conception of Eddy as the discoverer and founder of Christian Science is also clarified in the process as is the methodological advantage of examining an old source from a new van-tage point.

For more than one hundred years a heated debate about the character, contributions, and self-conception of Mary Baker Eddy has been in progress, a debate that extends from the first days of her public ministry until the present. Although the terms of the controversy have shifted somewhat with the passage of years, nevertheless, nearly all parties involved concede that Eddy rarely did anything without specific objectives. Critics and defend-ers alike have detected a strong sense of self-direction in her. There is no reason to quarrel with that consensus or to suggest that she was any less clear about her intentions in the formation of her autobiography.

Nonetheless, it is impossible to establish beyond debate that the gospel character of *Retrospection and Introspec-tion* was a matter of conscious design by Mary Baker Eddy. Barring additional testimony from her hand, one must rest content with the supposition that the canonical narratives may have been an informing factor in the con-struction of the autobiography. There is sufficient evi-dence to support this judgment. Eddy prided herself on her years of preoccupation with biblical studies and inter-pretation. As knowledgeable as she was about the Bible and as explicit as she became with scriptural references in the autobiography, it is unreasonable to suggest that the biblical parallels could have been lost on her. That she avoided public comment on them was strategically a sound decision. The fact that the autobiography does not follow the paradigm rigidly and uses biblical citations and themes from other sections of the Bible does not detract from the argument, but rather underscores Eddy's subtle use of the gospel pattern by which she avoided the additional charge of blasphemy. It is significant that, unlike her fixation with editing new editions of *Science and Health,* she did not alter the autobiography during the remaining twenty years of her life.

The publication of *Retrospection and Introspection* ac-complished several things for Mary Baker Eddy. First and most importantly, it allowed her to tell her own story in 1891 in a way that had not been done prior to that date. That she chose to avoid the distressing side of her earlier years by focusing upon her religious development is understandable. Her decision shaped a long tradition of sympathetic biography. That Eddy placed her life within a scriptural framework is also understandable, for her world view was essentially biblical despite [commenta-tors who] attacked this biblical character of her work with special vehemence. That the autobiography of the founder of Christian Science bears striking resemblance to the accounts of the life of Jesus has never before been described. If the parallels were at all of conscious design, then *Retrospection and Introspection* was an ingenious device for affirming her own sense of identity and signifi-cance. If not intentional, then the autobiography was a coincidental but fascinating by-product of the biblical world view of Mary Baker Eddy.

Second, the publication of the volume provided Eddy another means to affirm anew her view that life and truth cannot be separated from one another. The account of her own life and the statement of the truth she had discovered joined to establish the origins of Christian Science and to demonstrate its special theological character. The narra-tive and the discourse together—somewhat like synoptic and Johannine counterparts—documented her view of the reality of the spiritual and the insignificance of the mate-rial. The canonical pattern proved an appropriate vehicle for the religious message of Christian Science, a message which stated that all of existence is divine and that evil in its various manifestations has no reality.

Retrospection and Introspection also had a practical side for Mary Baker Eddy. The volume contributed to the consolidation of her position as the leader of the Chris-tian Science community at a time when her authority was not fully secure. It became an instrument whereby she was able to bolster her leadership among a sometimes defiant and often undisciplined group of disciples. The autobiographical statement of her function was a power-ful weapon against internal and external opposition. The comparison with Jesus and the Virgin Mary had the effect of exalting her person within the community and raising her above criticism. *Retrospection and Introspection* played a role in the consolidation and institutionalization of Christian Science by strengthening the ecclesiastical position of the founder.

Finally, *Retrospection and Introspection* functioned for Mary Baker Eddy in another way. She was able to use her autobiography to "impose a pattern" on her life, to find meaning in it as "a coherent story." The passage from childhood to adulthood, from private to public ministry, from persecuted to established community, culminated appropriately in a coherent body of teachings. The autobiography, in effect, provided Eddy a superb opportunity to discover herself as she defended her ideas against her opponents and proclaimed a new gospel.

L. Brent Bohlke (essay date 1982)

SOURCE: Willa Cather and *The Life of Mary Baker G. Eddy,*" in *American Literature,* Vol. 54, No. 2, May, 1982, pp. 288-94.

[*In the following essay, Bohlke explores Willa Cather's connection to Eddy and Christian Science.*]

As with many other writers of fiction whose foundations were laid in journalism, the total number of words which came from the pen of Willa Cather will never be known. Besides the great number of unsigned articles which appeared in numerous newspapers and other publications, Cather also published several stories, articles and reviews under pseudonyms. John P. Hinz, Bernice Slote, Mildred R. Bennett, Virginia Faulkner, William M. Curtin and others have done prodigious work in the identification and publication of several such works. Even so, there remain in the archives of *The Home Monthly, McClure's Magazine* and other publications several likely candidates for Catherian ascription.

It is well known that Cather herself wished to suppress much of her early writing and on several occasions refused permission to have it reprinted: " . . . in her later years Willa Cather closed the door firmly on all but a fraction of the work that had preceded *O Pioneers!* and did her best to discourage inquiry concerning it." Cather held the copyright on many of her early stories and was able to prevent republication. "She compared her attitude to that of an apple-grower careful of his reputation: the fruit that was below standard must be left forgotten on the ground; only the sound apples should be collected." Only since the early works have come into the public domain have they been generally available to Cather scholarship. Gradually, we have come to know and appreciate the breadth and scope of the Cather canon as far greater and richer than had been suspected.

A major work with which Cather has always been identified, but in a tentative and limited way, is *The Life of Mary Baker G. Eddy and the History of Christian Science.* When Cather first went to work for S. S. McClure on the staff of *McClure's Magazine,* he was in possession of a manuscript which he felt had many possibilities. Georgine Milmine, then the wife of a journalist in Rochester, New York, had submitted a large amount of interesting and revealing material concerning Mrs. Eddy and the Christian Science Church. McClure wanted to use the material, but it was poorly organized and needed much reworking, as well as verification. "He had different

people in the office try their hand [sic] at it, but finally turned the whole thing over to Willa Cather." Most biographers tell us that Mark Sullivan was the first staff member to work on the material and that he spent much time in New England attempting to verify some of the astonishing facts about Mrs. Eddy's early life. Cather was sent to Boston in 1907, to complete the project. "The assignment involved interviewing many of Mrs. Baker's early associates, looking up records, working over the manuscript with Mrs. Milmine." The final version was published in fourteen installments, at intervals, ending in the June, 1908, issue. It was then revised and published in book form by Doubleday, Page & Co., in 1909. Elizabeth Shepley Sergeant says:

> But the book that ensued was largely written in the *McClure's* office, and was a composite, not Willa Cather's personal work. It bears little mark of her own style, but it "stood up" as a dramatic and frank controversial biography, chiefly remarkable for the unique story it tells. With its serial publication *McClure's* announced that it was "as close to truth as history ever gets." The book that followed the magazine serial disappeared almost immediately from circulation—the Christian Scientists are said to have bought the copies. It is hard to find one nowadays, even in a big library, and the reader is likely to have to borrow the only copy from the chief librarian's safe, and be watched by a detective while reading it.

E. K. Brown says that Cather had "chief responsibility for preparing the remainder of the long manuscript for publication." But it has been generally held that Sergeant's evaluation of Cather's involvement was the correct one. As Stewart Hudson states in his introduction to the second edition of the book:

> . . . it will probably never be possible to determine exactly which passages are primarily the work of Miss Cather, those which remain substantially the work of Mrs. Milmine, or even those portions which are the work of other editorial writers in the New York offices of *McClure's.* However, we do have the emphatic testimony of one knowledgeable inside observer of the operations at *McClure's* as to Willa Cather's dominant role in the final production of the series. Witter Bynner, who was later to attain distinction as a poet, was an assistant editor (and, indeed, managing editor for a five-day period) of *McClure's* in 1906. He later inscribed this notation in a copy of the Eddy biography: "The material was brought to *McClure's* by Miss [sic] Milmine, but was put into the painstaking hands of Willa Cather for proper presentation, so that a great part of it is her work. Witter Bynner, February 12, 1934."

Cather was unwilling to have any such credit given to her. Her correspondence contains many vehement denials of having much of a role in the Eddy biography at all. As late as 1934, she wrote to Harold Goddard Rugg that she was in charge of the publishing of the material supplied by Mrs. Milmine, that she did a large amount of cutting and some rewriting, but that she would in no way claim credit for authoring the book, which she considered to be written very poorly. In fact, it annoyed her greatly that people were trying to attribute the book to her, but she said that she found that the more she denied authorship the more others tried to credit (or discredit) her with it.

The book is very uneven, and one can see, upon reading it, why Cather would not have wished to claim responsibility for its final form. Despite some isolated passages of superior writing, fine character analysis and graceful dealings with rather weighty philosophical questions, the book as a whole does not hang together well. Part of this is, no doubt, largely due to the nature of the writing and publishing itself—installments, and a less than comprehensive revision when the pieces were put into book form to rid the articles of their serial nature, which of necessity involved some redundancy and often had to keep the reader hanging: in order that he might buy the next issue.

Nevertheless, a re-evaluation of Cather's involvement is due. Although in interviews and correspondence with those who were not close to the work's inception Cather denied much involvement, in other correspondence with those who would know (and those she trusted) she painted quite a different picture. Shortly after resigning from the staff of *McClure's* she was requested by her former employer to assist him in writing his autobiography. In June of 1912, she wrote to S. S. McClure from Red Cloud saying that she would be glad to assist him in any way that she could and that since she had neither money nor influence to give him she would be glad to lend her wits. However, she feared that she might not be able to do the writing in a way that would be entirely satisfactory to McClure. She says that there were chapters of the Mary Baker Eddy work which she simply could not write in a manner that would please McClure. The general tone of the letter and the person to whom it was written would lead one to suspect that indeed Cather did have a considerable hand in writing the biography.

Any remaining doubts are resolved by a letter written ten years later to an old friend from Cather's Pittsburgh days, Edwin H. Anderson. Mr. Anderson (1861-1947) was one of the organizers and the first director of the Carnegie Library on Forbes Avenue in Pittsburgh. "He resigned the position in 1904 and two years later went to New York City where he eventually became director of the New York Public Library. He retired in 1936 and died just five days after Cather." Cather had met and become friends with Anderson and his wife in Pittsburgh and was frequently a guest in their home. That their friendship continued in New York is evident from the correspondence between them in the Manuscript and Archives Division of the New York Public Library. On one occasion Anderson had written to her asking about the details concerning the Christian Science articles, and in an unusual burst of candor about the event, Cather wrote a letter on 24 November 1922, just before leaving New York for Red Cloud to celebrate Thanksgiving with her family. In a very orderly fashion, even using numbered paragraphs, Cather outlines the development of the entire

matter. She says that Mrs. Milmine had spent a great deal of time collecting material regarding the subject. S. S. McClure purchased all the memorabilia and notes, which included news clippings from newspapers in the 1880's, records from court cases, first editions of Mrs. Eddy's writings and other material that was simply not available elsewhere. She says that after the magazine was sold, the new publisher discarded the entire collection—including some valuable books. Mrs. Milmine never claimed to have the expertise to utilize her material in writing a biographical work, so McClure organized a sort of contest at the magazine, trying out several staff members on the writing. He favored Cather's initial attempts and selected her to do what she felt was her first notable magazine writing. On the strength of that work she was promoted to Managing Editor.

Cather goes on to say that no expense was spared in documenting the material obtained from Mrs. Milmine, except for that in the first chapter. Cather says that she did not write the initial installment, which was done by Burton J. Hendrick, and was based on rumor and popular myth more than anything else. Hendrick was irritated at not being allowed to finish the project and held a grudge against McClure for some time.

In the fifth and crucial paragraph of the letter Cather says that the publishers probably have valid commercial considerations in mind in not reprinting the book, even though there was a consistent public clamor for it. Cather claimed that the writing of the book was a kind of training for her and that it was not really the kind of work in which she was interested or which she was willing to champion. Mrs. Milmine, who since had remarried a Mr. Benjamin Wells of Aubrey, New York, was in the interesting and rather embarrassing situation of being listed as author of a book of which she did not write a single word!

Cather concludes by emphasizing the personal and confidential nature of the letter and by admitting that she has not related the truth about it previously, either orally or in print. She does say that she feels the true story should be known by someone and that since she trusts Mr. Anderson she will request him to be the keeper of that truth.

The letter is a remarkable one for Cather and tells us as much, perhaps, about her regard for Edwin Anderson as it does about the writing of the Eddy biography. Rarely does Cather write with such disarming honesty about her involvement in a project which she at other times sought to denounce. This single piece of correspondence does give us the first reliable account in Cather's own words of the writing of *The Life of Mary Baker G. Eddy and the History of Christian Science*. It necessitates the inclusion of that book within the Cather canon. Stewart Hudson has already pointed out the interesting influences that her research into Mrs. Eddy's life and Christian Science undoubtedly had on many later fictional characters, as well as showing persistent thematic interests that Cather developed while working on the book. However, in light of Cather's own admission, a more comprehensive and systematic study of the entire work is now called for.

It has often been noted that the real value of Cather's assignment to the Eddy study was her meeting with Mrs. James T. Fields, widow of the great publisher, and her subsequent introduction to Sarah Orne Jewett, whose advice about writing eventually led to *O Pioneers!* and Cather's other early midwest writings. But the assignment had other value as well. It resulted in Cather's first book-length writing, after a collection of poetry and one of short stories. It may have given Cather the confidence she needed to tackle a novel, for *Alexander's Bridge* followed shortly. It certainly must be included as an important step in Willa Cather's apprenticeship. She herself wrote, "The novelist must learn to write, and then he must unlearn it; just as the modern painter learns to draw, and then learns when utterly to disregard his accomplishment, when to subordinate it to a higher and truer effect." In writing *The Life of Mary Baker G. Eddy and the History of Christian Science* Willa Cather was still learning to write—then she went on to unlearn it, to disregard her accomplishment and to subordinate it to the higher and truer effect in the novels for which she is famed.

R. Laurence Moore (essay date 1983)

SOURCE: "Mormonism, Christian Science, and Spiritualism," in *The Occult in America: New Historical Perspectives,* edited by Howard Kerr and Charles L. Crow, University of Illinois Press, 1983, pp. 135-61.

[*In the following essay, Moore examines the connection between Christian Science and the occult.*]

Mary Baker Eddy's first husband happened to be a Mason. Briefly but happily married to George Glover, she remained forever grateful for the help she received from his brother Masons when Glover died. Later, membership in a Masonic lodge was the single organizational affiliation that was not ruled incompatible with membership in the Christian Science mother church. However, Eddy's gratitude toward the Masons never prompted her to imitate their ritual. Although some links to occult sciences were strikingly present in the church she founded, those links had nothing to do with Masonry. Rather, it was the peculiarities of her extreme version of philosophical idealism that allowed Eddy's critics to charge her with occultism.

Mary Baker Eddy must have thought it uncommonly bad luck that *Science and Health* was published in the same year, 1875, that Madame Blavatsky founded the Theosophical Society. Thereafter, she was never able to change the minds of her critics who thought that the two women had a great deal in common. She wanted no association with Blavatsky, who returned the favor by calling Christian Science a form of crude occultism similar to spiritualism. Nonetheless, the fact that some of Eddy's

followers became Theosophists (and vice versa) was sufficient evidence to many that a common appeal joined Christian Science not only to Theosophy but also to spiritualism, Rosicrucianism, Mormonism, and the "fantastic and crude dogmas savoring of . . . the mystic East." The intent in suggesting these connections was not always hostile. To Eddy's dismay, some Hindu swamis, who began to tour America after the Chicago World Parliament of Religions in 1893 (a parliament that accorded a great deal of attention both to Christian Science and to Eastern mysticism), attested to startling similarities "that exist between the fundamental principles of modern Christian Science and those of that ancient system of philosophy known in India as Vedanta."

These were not the only associations that Eddy denied. Throughout her long career as a religious leader, she adamantly refused to acknowledge an intellectual debt to anyone. When she described herself as the "discoverer of Christian Science," she allowed a certain ambiguity to cloud the issue of whether divine inspiration had aided her. Her doctrine, as she put it, was "hopelessly original."

It was not, of course. The most important debt Eddy owed, a debt clear even in her denials, was to her teacher, Phineas Parkhurst Quimby. Quimby's ideas can in turn be related to the intellectual universe of Andrew Jackson Davis and his version of Harmonial Philosophy. On a more sophisticated intellectual plane, one might even suggest parallels that connect Eddy to the metaphysical assumptions of the transcendentalists and especially to the philosophy of Emanuel Swedenborg. No scholar has yet adequately examined the impact of the Swedish philosopher upon popular versions of philosophical idealism in nineteenth-century America. But doubtless his American followers helped prepare the way for the reception of Christian Science. Swedenborg's theories about the mystical interconnections of all things and his Doctrine of Correspondence, ideas suggestive of Renaissance magic and alchemy, were related to an idea, found in Davis, Quimby, and Eddy, that physical illnesses are reflections merely of discord in man's spiritual force or principle. A spiritual disturbance causes a corresponding material imbalance to appear as disease, which can be cured by mind. Eddy built a church organization that was distinctly her own. But her version of the idea that sin and evil are illusions cannot be set down as an original contribution to philosophy.

In her teachings Eddy attempted to undermine our usual reliance on ordinary sense perception to receive truth and on ordinary language to communicate it. Eddy followed Quimby, who followed Swedenborg, in teaching that biblical words had a spiritual interpretation differing from their literal meaning. She wrote: "We have learned in Christian Science that when reading the Scriptures if you substitute the spiritual significance of a term for its material definition, or the bare word, it will elucidate the meaning of the inspired writer." "I read the inspired page," she added elsewhere, "through a higher than mortal sense." To make plain the hitherto unknown "inner" sense of the words of the Bible, Eddy added a glossary of spiritual meanings (a Key to the Scripture) to the sixth and subsequent editions of *Science and Health*. The connection between her glossary and Swedenborg's *A Dictionary of Correspondences, Representatives and Significatives Derived from the Word of the Lord* (first printed in Boston in 1847) is clear enough.

Unlocking the spiritual significance of a word did not, of course, wholly solve the problem of communicating a nonobvious truth. Whatever care Eddy took in revising and perfecting each edition of *Science and Health* ("a misplaced preposition would change the sense and misstates the science of the Scriptures"), she believed that the printed word could never seem spiritual to the uninitiated reader. "The English language," Eddy regretted, "or any other language with which we are familiar, is inadequate to fully convey a spiritual meaning with material terms." Seekers who wanted to progress in the wisdom of Christian Science had to pay for a series of lessons taught by an authorized instructor.

All of these points suggest that Eddy's early followers were attracted to a style of thought that Edward Tiryakian has identified with "esoteric culture." According to Tiryakian, such a culture relies on commonly available religious texts—the Bible, the Torah, *Science and Health*—but insists that the meaning of these is not exhausted by an ordinary reading. Furthermore, the esoteric group advertises itself as possessing a unique understanding of the secret and real meaning in the text and adopts a parlance that to the outside world must necessarily seem obscure. Eddy prided herself in thinking that Christian Science healing could be both logically and practically demonstrated. In contrast, she said, Theosophical mysteries were like the excavated cindered human bodies of Pompeii—they fell into dust the moment that air touched them. But whatever she said, her epistemological views were not unlike those of P. D. Ouspensky, a twentieth-century occultist. He said: "The idea of a knowledge which surpasses all ordinary human knowledge, and is inaccessible to ordinary people, but which exists somewhere and belongs to somebody, permeates the whole history of the thought of mankind. . . . Magical or occult knowledge is knowledge based upon senses which surpass our five senses and upon a capacity for thinking which surpasses ordinary thinking but it is knowledge translated into ordinary logical language, if that is possible or in so far as it is possible."

The parallel between occultism and Eddy's church goes beyond a shared attitude toward the limitations of ordinary sense perception and language. Eddy maintained around herself an inner circle of trusted students who often met in secret. Her enemies insisted that she obtained money for Christian Science lessons "by pretending that she had important secrets relating to healing the sick which she had not theretofore imparted." She in turn replied much like the early Mormon leaders: the early private sessions of the church were necessary to protect her followers from persecution and ridicule. Only "ad-

vanced Scientific students" were ready for some of the truths she had to impart. Whatever the justification, the hierarchical nature of Christian Science wisdom set novices apart from adepts. And Eddy not only maintained strict control over who was authorized to teach Christian Science lessons but forbade any of her teachers from trying to convey the contents of those lessons to the general public.

If Eddy had been worried merely about the confusion and misunderstanding that her teaching could arouse in inadequately prepared students, she might have avoided some of the portrayals of herself as a dangerously superstitious woman. But Eddy made the explicit claim that the end result of Christian Science teaching was power—indeed, the shamanistic power to heal, which Mircea Eliade has called "the most archaic and most widely distributed occult tradition." Where there was power to do good, there was power to do evil. "Why we take so few students," Eddy wrote, "is because of the great danger there is in promiscuously teaching metaphysics, or the power of mind to do good, lest it abuse that trust, forsake metaphysics, and this developed mental power becomes the . . . extracts and essences of evil." To the newspaper editorialists who were hostile to Eddy, this statement clearly implicated her in an attempt to devise a system of black and white magic.

Such criticism grew particularly strong because of Eddy's obsessive concern with what she called "malicious animal magnetism," the use of mental powers to cause disease and illness in others rather than to heal. Eddy always argued that malicious animal magnetism was the opposite of Christian Science and was part of the illusion her philosophy wished to dispel. Nonetheless, the behavior that resulted from her belief in malicious animal magnetism contributed with legitimate reason to her reputation as an occultist. For example, in the spring of 1878 a suit was filed in Salem against Daniel Spofford, a former student of Eddy who was bitterly estranged from her. The charge against him was that he had practiced harmful mesmerism against a Christian Scientist, Lucretia L. S. Brown. The charge was dismissed, but not before the press had branded it an attempt to resurrect the Salem witchcraft trials. Eddy's chapters on "Demonology" in the early editions of *Science and Health* indeed warned that "the peril of Salem witchcraft is not past, until that error be met by Truth and Science."

The summary dismissal of the case did not discourage Eddy from continuing to make strong public warnings. In 1882, when her third and last husband died, Eddy told a *Boston Globe* reporter that he had been the victim of mental malpractice. The activators of the fatal poison, which she claimed was applied mentally without any physical contact with Dr. Eddy, were again alleged to be former Eddy students. In Eddy's mind, largely because of the growing popularity of her doctrines, the dangers of mental malpractice never thereafter slackened. Quite the contrary: "The mild forms of animal magnetism are disappearing, and its aggressive features are coming to the front. The looms of crime, hidden in the dark recesses of mortal thought, are every hour weaving webs more complicated and subtle. So secret are its present methods, that they ensnare the age into indolence, and produce the very apathy on this subject which the criminal desires."

Eddy's personal sufferings from malicious animal magnetism became well known. She publicly maintained that her crusade for Truth made her the brunt of mental attacks from those who had vested interests in the continued domination of Error. However, she and her followers tried to keep secret the steps that they took to ward off the effects of malicious mental malpractice. According to one unfriendly reporter, Eddy organized "watches" to turn the effects of evil thoughts back upon particular enemies. She would gather students in a room and have them "treat in thought" someone she suspected of causing harm to herself. "Say to him," she instructed, "your sins have found you out. You are affected as you wish to affect me. Your evil thought reacts upon you. You are bilious, you are consumptive, you have liver trouble, you have been poisoned by arsenic, etc."

Somewhat startling confirmation of these practices was provided in a memoir written by Adam H. Dickey, Eddy's private secretary during the last three years of her life and for a time chairman of the board of directors of the mother church. The memoir was a considerable embarrassment to the church, but for Dickey it fulfilled his promise to Eddy that he would prove after her death that she was "mentally murdered." Her failure to prevent the occurrence was not, by Dickey's account, for want of trying. She turned her household into a mental fortress, dividing the night into four mental watches. Each was assigned to different mental workers, all residents of the house, who had specific instructions about how to counteract the "evil influence of mental mind directed against our Leader and her establishment during their hours." The typewritten instructions designated in numerical order which phases of error they were supposed to combat. Since Eddy had a horror of excessive snowfall, she even directed her watchers one winter to "make a law that there shall be no more snow this season." After Eddy experienced one particularly severe mental attack, Dickey reports that she told her staff: "You don't any of you realize what is going on. This is a dark hour for the Cause and you do not seem to be awake to it . . . I am now working on a plane that would mean instantaneous death to any of you."

In view of such words and practices, critics of Christian Science understandably doubted whether the movement reduced demonology, as it claimed, to "a record of dreams." In a telling sentence Eddy wrote, "Let the age that sits in judgment on the occult methods of her period sanction only such as are demonstratable on a scientific principle, and productive of the greatest good to the greatest number." Eddy obviously considered the "occult methods" of Christian Science worthy of sanction. Surprisingly, however, in view of her implied distinctions, Eddy's publications often advertised competing "occult

methods." When Warren Felt Evans published *Esoteric Christianity and Mental Therapeutics* in 1886, Christian Scientists attacked it. Ignoring its claim to have stripped the veil from the "ancient mystic brotherhoods," they accused Evans of forcing Christianity "into the farcical grooves of Occultism." They reproached him for saying that he gave readers only the principles "which it may be proper openly to promulgate to the world at large in the present state of the mind of man." Yet throughout the 1890s the book was prominently advertised in Christian Science publications as being available from the Christian Science Publishing House. Other recommended titles included J. H. Dewey's *Christian Theosophy*, Swedenborg's *Correspondences*, and the *Bhagavad-Gita*. If the intellectual connection suggested by these advertisements was a mistake, someone within the Christian Science empire was ready to capitalize on it.

Susan Hill Lindley (essay date 1984)

SOURCE: "The Ambiguous Feminism of Mary Baker Eddy," in *The Journal of Religion*, Vol. 64, No. 3, July, 1984, pp. 318-31.

[*In the following essay, Lindley discusses Eddy's feminist principles.*]

Among women who have achieved recognition in the field of religion, Mary Baker Eddy frequently appears as a pioneer, a woman who founded and led a major religious movement and who used feminine imagery for the divine. During and since her lifetime, biographers and historians have presented portraits of the founder of Christian Science of an almost dizzying variety, from unadulterated adulation to devastating attack.

More recently, Mary Baker Eddy as woman has been the focus of scholarly analysis, with mixed conclusions as to her place in the women's movement of nineteenth-century America and her heritage for contemporary feminism. Gail Parker's study stresses psychological analysis, seeing in Eddy's denial of the material an attempt "to avoid any confrontation between the two halves of her profoundly divided personality"—that is, willfulness and submission, the appropriate masculine and feminine identities of nineteenth-century America. According to Parker, Eddy tried to use the "Sentimental Womanhood" ideal of her time to overcome masculine dominance but was ultimately unsuccessful, in part because of her claims to divinity and her method of exercising power, in part because "when the redoubtable sensitivity of women was raised to a supernatural pitch, it was not a viable basis for widespread feminism."

Susan Setta argues that in Mary Baker Eddy's thought is to be found "an early attempt to achieve this goal [of incorporating feminine and masculine qualities into one's life] by integrating the masculine and the feminine in her image of God and in her theology of Mind Heal." Like Parker, Setta sees in Eddy a rebel against the dominant masculine culture of her time, but unlike Parker, Setta sees her endeavor as at least partially successful. But to achieve this goal of affirming the feminine, Eddy had to deny "her womanhood, as the nineteenth century defined it, through the negation of her body." If there is no matter, there can be no restrictive sex roles based on the body; if God is both masculine and feminine (in a spiritual sense, of course), men have no advantage over women of closer identification with the divine.

Mary Farrell Bednarowski includes Christian Science as one of four examples of religious movements "outside the mainstream" in nineteenth-century America which, because of their theological positions, were able to allow women greater freedom and power than the orthodox Protestant churches of the time. Bednarowski, too, sees a key to Christian Science's greater openness to women in Eddy's denial of the material and her insistence on an androgynous God. "Two aspects, particularly, of the Christian Science concept of deity have significance for women. First, Eddy stressed that God is non-anthropomorphic, but nonetheless incorporates the feminine as well as the masculine. Second, Eddy divorced God from responsibility for the world's ills: God is not the creator of the material world—that is the work of mortal mind." Thus Bednarowski concludes, "Christian Science demanded of women that they give up the claim of reality for their material bodies, but in return it gave them a connection to the numinous in the Father-Mother God, and it promised them power over their own lives as well as equal participation in the religion they had chosen."

Thus all three authors see Christian Science, the child of Mary Baker Eddy, as at least partially rooted in and rebelling against the restricted roles permitted to women in nineteenth-century America; yet they disagree on the success or failure of Eddy's solution—that is, denial of the material—and none deals fully with the consequences and implications of that solution. Such diversity of opinion is not surprising, for Eddy's ideas about women and religion are complex, even ambiguous, both in the context of her own time and in light of contemporary feminist theology.

The purpose of this essay, then, is to survey briefly Mary Baker Eddy's ideas about women and religion, set in a context of nineteenth-century American views of women and religion, and to compare them with contemporary feminist theology. To do so, however, one needs to suggest something of the nineteenth century and the contemporary contexts. Nineteenth-century American feminism, broadly and in its religious manifestation, saw two streams: a more "radical" wing based on a firm premise of human equality of men and women and typified in a figure such as Elizabeth Cady Stanton; and a more "conservative" stream which tacitly accepted differentiation of nature and roles by sex, along the lines of the "cult of true womanhood" but then argued, first, that the peculiar female nature and role was not inferior but equally as or more important and valuable than the male nature and role, and second, that it was just because of woman's

superior moral sensitivity that her influence should be felt more in the public sphere. Frances Willard is a prominent example of the second type.

To define "contemporary feminist theology" is no easy task, in light of the diversity which has emerged in the field in recent years. To use the typology suggested by Judith Plaskow and Carol Christ, there are the revolutionaries and the reformists. The former argue that Christianity and Judaism are so pervasively sexist and patriarchal that a new religion for women is needed, while the latter believe that the patriarchy of Judaism and Christianity is not so essential that it cannot be overcome; one can work from within. There are those feminist theologians who deny any peculiarly "feminine" nature beyond cultural conditioning and those who argue for a distinctive female perspective or psychology, but one which should be valued and celebrated rather than denigrated. There are disagreements among feminists about the kind of female experience to be considered and the weight to be placed on it. Christ and Plaskow distinguish between "woman's *feminist* experience and . . . woman's *traditional* experience, which includes, but is not limited to, woman's body experience." Such differences are real and important; feminist theology today is no monolith. Nevertheless, one can identify some common, if not universal, themes which characterize the religious concerns of contemporary feminists.

First, there is the basic agreement that women are not naturally inferior to men and that God is not male. Such assertions may sound so elementary as to be gratuitous, but they run counter to the vast majority of Western religious tradition, and their implications include criticism of exclusively male language and imagery of God and humanity and of the exclusion of women from ordination and religious leadership.

Second, virtually all contemporary religious feminists would agree that marriage and motherhood (or, in the Roman Catholic tradition, a religious vocation) are not the only proper and fulfilling spheres—the "natural" roles—for a woman. Again, this assertion only seems obvious if one ignores the overwhelming weight of Western tradition in the past and, in some quarters, even today.

Third, most religious feminists would affirm the goodness of the material, rejecting any dualistic philosophy which identifies the spirit with "good" (and usually male) and the body with "evil" or, at best, "inferior" (and usually female). One might argue that such an affirmation is simply a recovery of a genuine Hebraic and biblical understanding, for Jews and Christians, or of the value system of a Great Goddess religion, for the revolutionary feminist. True—but nonetheless, that understanding has been obscured for much of Western history to the particular detriment of women, and it is a typical and central theme of religious feminism.

Fourth, most contemporary religious feminists prefer an egalitarian model to a hierarchical one for personal and social relationships and for institutional structures. An authoritarian church receives no more approval than an authoritarian, patriarchal family. Similarly, they express a strong preference for cooperation rather than patterns of dominance and submission.

This list is by no means comprehensive, but it does suggest areas of agreement within the diversity of contemporary religious feminism and hence a basis for comparison with the ideas of Mary Baker Eddy.

Mary Baker Eddy has been praised for a number of ideas in her religion favorable to women. Most obvious is her description of the Deity as "Father-Mother God." The concept as well as the title is pervasive in her writings. Images of Father and Mother present different aspects of the divine, and the feminine is at least as important as the masculine. "The ideal man corresponds to creation, to intelligence, and to Truth. The ideal woman corresponds to Life and to Love. In divine Science, we have not as much authority for considering God masculine, as we have for considering Him [*sic*] feminine, for Love imparts the clearest idea of Deity." If then, God is both masculine and feminine, men and women are equally in the image of God. "Man and woman as coexistent and eternal with God forever reflect, in glorified quality, the infinite Father-Mother God." Such nontraditional female imagery for God distinguished Mary Baker Eddy in her own time and has been one of the most remarked qualities of Christian Science in contemporary feminist scholarship; it was not, however, necessarily unique or original. The most obvious American predecessors with a Mother element in the Godhead were the Shakers. There is some confusion as to the degree to which Eddy picked up the idea from the Shakers: she was exposed to a Shaker community in her youth, but there is question about how influential that exposure was.

Mary Baker Eddy apparently considered it no accident that the revelation of God's female nature should come by a woman. As one author writes, "Mrs. Eddy felt that her womanhood was essential to the very nature of her mission; for she and her followers believed that it had been given to her to reveal the Motherhood of God." Eddy herself believed in "woman's special adaptability to lead on Christian Science," and she spoke at an 1888 address in Chicago of the unique role of woman "to awaken the dull senses, intoxicated with pleasure or pain, to the infinite meaning of [Christ's] words [of Truth and Love]." In sum, from a contemporary perspective, among the most significant characteristics of Christian Science was not only the fact that it was a major religion founded by a woman but also its belief that a woman, specifically, had to perform the task of revealing the fullness of a Mother-Father God.

What does Christian Science have to say about equality between the sexes? Mary Baker Eddy could be bitingly critical of the male power structures of her day, particularly the church and the medical profession, and she did advocate equal rights for women. She endorsed especially equal legal and economic rights for men and women and praised women for their activity in reforms of her era, although her commitment to woman's suffrage was qualified. "If the elective franchise for women will remedy the evil [of discrimination] without encouraging difficulties of greater magnitude, let us hope it will be granted." While Eddy supported major issues of feminism of her day, women's rights were, for her, a subordinate interest. Perhaps more significant than her statements on theoretical equality was the practical opportunity Eddy allowed in Christian Science for women to become religious leaders and healers, and to support themselves thereby.

The central text of Christian Science is *Science and Health with Key to the Scriptures*, and Mary Baker Eddy's "spiritual" interpretation of the Bible was a foundation of her theology. Here, too, one can trace Eddy's positive view of women in her comments on famous women of the Bible. Hers was not the typical interpretation of the role of Eve in the Fall; she argued that the woman was

> the first to confess her fault. She says, "The serpent beguiled me, and I did eat"; as much as to say in meek penitence, "Neither man nor God shall father my fault." She has already learned that corporeal sense is the serpent. Hence she is first to abandon the belief in the material origin of man and to discern spiritual creation. This hereafter enabled woman to be the mother of Jesus and to behold at the sepulchre the risen Saviour, who was soon to manifest the deathless man of God's creating. This enabled woman to be first to interpret the Scriptures in their true sense, which reveals the spiritual origin of man.

One can see even in this brief passage the way Eddy traced her central theological assertion, the nonreality of matter, through the women of biblical history. Eve begins the rejection of the material for the spiritual, but other women of the Bible follow her lead. "The masculine belief called Isaac cherished the spoils of error or Esau, 'but feminine belief named Rebekah was drawn to the more spiritual Jacob.'" Mary was important particularly for her virgin conception of Jesus, which signified spirituality. But the biblical female figure which appears to have held the most fascination for Eddy was the woman of the Apocalypse, Rev. 12:1 ff. In *Science and Health*, she wrote, "The woman in the Apocalypse symbolizes generic man, the spiritual idea of God; she illustrates the coincidence of God and man as the divine Principle and divine idea." Later in a long section of interpretation on the passage, she asserts that the woman also typifies "the spiritual idea of God's motherhood." In Eddy's interpretation, the woman, or Spirit, stands against the dragon, symbolizing the evil and lie of "materiality." Toward the end of the discussion, Eddy implies—but only implies, there is no direct claim—that she is the woman of the Apocalypse. When pressed, Mary Baker Eddy specifically denied such a literal identification; nevertheless, the hint is obvious in *Science and Health*, and clearly some of her followers made that identification.

Similarly, many Christian Scientists saw in Mrs. Eddy a kind of second incarnation, this time in the form of a woman. Again, she made no clear, direct claim to divinity, but there are passages in her writings which suggest that conclusion. For example, having suggested that the meaning of the parable of the woman hiding leaven in three measures of meal "signifies the Science of Christ and its spiritual interpretation," she asks, "Did not this parable point a moral with a prophecy, foretelling the second appearing in the flesh of the Christ . . . ?" Moreover, given the theme of the motherhood of God, now revealed in Christian Science, Mary Baker Eddy's preference of the title "Mother" is suggestive, although it was a title she later repudiated, "owing to the public misunderstanding of this name. . . ." In view of the apparent conflict over Eddy's claims, the conclusion of John Dittemore, a former director of the Mother Church, is worth nothing: "Despite public disclaimers of equality with Christ, Frye's diary makes it clear that Mrs. Eddy privately regarded herself in that light."

Whether or not Mary Baker Eddy's exposition of the "true" meaning of Scripture or claims about her own position are found to be convincing may well depend on one's agreement or disagreement with Christian Science as a faith. But beyond such questions, Eddy offered reinterpretation of some traditional views of biblical women and emphasized their importance in the divine scheme of redemption, thus contributing to a positive view of women in Christianity. Women were not, to her, in any sense second-class citizens of the religious world. In sum, she projected an equal feminine nature and image for God; she encouraged equality of the sexes; she offered a religion in nineteenth-century America in which a woman, and women, played leading roles.

Yet, at least from the perspective of twentieth-century feminism, Mary Baker Eddy's ideas are ambiguous. In her own time, she avoided clear identification with the woman's movement. If she, too, suffered from the limitations her age put on women, she was no self-conscious feminist. Her poem, **"Woman's Rights,"** called for no radical shifts in society and indeed might well have drawn praise from the most conservative defenders of "true womanhood."

Grave on her monumental pile:
She won from vice, by virtue's smile,
Her dazzling crown, her sceptred throne,
Affection's wreath, a happy home;

The right to worship deep and pure,
To bless the orphan, feed the poor;
Last at the cross to mourn her Lord,
First at the tomb to hear his word:

To fold an angel's wings below;
And hover o'er the couch of woe;
To nurse the Bethlehem babe so sweet,
The right to sit at Jesus' feet;

To form the bud for bursting bloom,
The hoary head with joy to crown;

In short, the right to work and pray,
"To point to heaven and lead the way."

A major recommendation of Christian Science, as presented by Mary Baker Eddy, was its morality. But what was the content of that morality? Its central thrust was, as she put it in *Science and Health*, the promotion of "chastity and purity" over "sensualism and impurity." "Christian Science despoils the kingdom of evil, and pre-eminently promotes affection and virtue in families and therefore in the community."

Beyond the unorthodox nature of some of her religious ideas, Mary Baker Eddy posed few challenges to reigning nineteenth-century American morality. Chapter 3 of *Science and Health* discusses marriage, and while Eddy suggests that this mundane institution will have no place in the final spiritual Kingdom, she is absolute in her endorsement of conventional marital morality for this age. "Chastity is the cement of civilization and progress. Without it there is no stability in society, and without it one cannot attain the Science of Life." "Man should not be required to participate in all the annoyances and cares of domestic economy, nor should woman be expected to understand political economy." No challenge to traditional sex roles or to the sacred institution of the family, so dear to nineteenth-century moralists, would be raised by Mary Baker Eddy. Though she herself took virtually no part in the raising of her son, she seemed to have had no quarrel with the prevalent ideals of motherhood for most women, writing, "A mother is the strongest educator, either for or against crime." And "Mothers should be able to produce perfect health and perfect morals in their children . . . by studying this scientific method of practising Christianity." The home was "woman's world" and on the female guardian of that world rested the responsibility for the virtue and nurture of future American citizens.

Christian Science endorsed values of purity and temperance in other ways. High on Mary Baker Eddy's list of sins or errors was the use of alcohol and tobacco, and many of the testimonials which fill the last one hundred pages of *Science and Health* report the efficacy of Christian Science in enabling the writer to overcome the liquor and tobacco habits. Perhaps it was the very conventionality of her moral statements which led outsiders to commend Christian Science and Mary Baker Eddy, despite what they regarded as the heresy of her religious beliefs. A reviewer from the *Springfield Republican* includes the revealing judgment that the doctrines of Christian Science are "high and pure, wholly free from those vile theories about love and marriage which have been so prevalent among the spiritualists."

It has frequently been observed, and rightly, that the majority of Mary Baker Eddy's followers were women and that Christian Science offered them a position of religious independence and leadership unavailable in most mainline Christian churches of the time. Nor was the significance of Eddy's sex as founder of Christian Science lost on her followers. As one female lecturer on

Christian Science commented "No women had ever founded a Church before, far less had any woman been the inspired leader of a scientific and religious movement. In achieving this she lifted all womankind forever." In her own person, Eddy set an example for other women of one who had broken with cultural limitations on female achievement.

Yet generalizations about the religious leadership of women in Christian Science must be qualified: the supreme leader was a woman, yet men filled the great majority of prestigious and responsible places below her in the church structure. As Peel notes, women did the "pioneer work in far-off areas" and were active in healing, but men filled the executive positions. Women who became too strong or too prominent—most notably, Augusta Stetson—and thus might rival Mary Baker Eddy were not tolerated, and Eddy's closest support came from a succession of men. It is true that the *Manual of the Mother Church,* with its absolute authority for Christian Scientists, specifies that "the Readers for the Mother Church shall be a man and a woman, one to read the *Bible,* and one to read *Science and Health with Key to the Scriptures*"; yet the same *Manual,* in its section on Committees on Publication, states, "The Committee on Publication shall consist of men generally. . . . If a suitable man is not obtainable for the Committee on Publication, a suitable woman shall be elected."

How, then, did Mary Baker Eddy fit into the context of nineteenth-century American feminism? On the one hand, some of her ideas might be identified as religiously radical: her dual image of God; her own role as a religious founder; the possibilities she opened for other women, both in terms of religious leadership and of an alternative spirituality; her break with much of traditional—and patriarchal—Christianity. On the other hand, Eddy could be aligned with the "conservative" wing of nineteenth-century religious feminism, insofar as she seems to have endorsed a peculiar (and superior) nature and role for women, just as she raised few questions of the prevailing moral patterns and assumptions of her day. Yet although she argued for a broad and positive impact on society at large from the emergence of women and the feminine, her primary concern and vision were personal, even individualistic, and spiritual. Despite a secondary concern with issues like suffrage and economic rights for women, it is striking how limited were the practical and political implications of her form of conservative feminism, particularly if one compares her to a contemporary like Frances Willard.

Finally, there are two points on which Christian Science and contemporary religious feminism are in great contrast. The first is the matter of power and structures. Where contemporary religious feminism generally criticizes hierarchical systems in favor of egalitarianism and cooperation, Christian Science under Mary Baker Eddy was extremely authoritarian. She was *the* authority, whose word was never to be questioned. Those who disagreed with her were simply in error. "Diverse opinions in Science are stultifying. All must have *one* Principle and the same rule; and all *who follow the Principle and rule* have but one opinion of it." The absolute nature of her authority included the institutional as well as the theological aspects of Christian Science. On any matter of policy or government, her word was final. This authority extended to Christian Science worship: she was the only pastor. Services, according, to the *Manual,* were to consist primarily of readings from the Bible and from *Science and Health,* and readers were forbidden to comment on those passages. Supporters of Mary Baker Eddy defended her actions, seeing her as possessed of a unique revelation and beset continually by those whose ignorance or malice would distort the truth. Critics, on the other hand, decried Eddy's unquestioned and arbitrary authority, and none was more biting than Mark Twain. Whatever its justification, the fact of the hierarchical and authoritarian structure of Christian Science, as decreed by Eddy, is clear.

The second area of contrast between Mary Baker Eddy and contemporary religious feminism lies in their views of the material. Eddy inherited a Christian tradition which was basically dualistic in its preference for the "spiritual" realm and its suspicion, if not outright rejection, of the worth of the material, which was seen as transitory, or a source of temptation, or, at best, of secondary importance. Yet that tradition also decreed that men were more closely identified with the spiritual (hence superior) and women with the material (hence inferior—a concept which fit neatly with the traditional legacy of Eve as bringer of sin and temptress of men). The nineteenth-century American "cult of true womanhood" dealt with the problem by having women switch sides: women are naturally pure, virtuous, and pious. Mary Baker Eddy resolved the dualistic tension, and the identification of women with its inferior half, by simply denying the material altogether. If matter does not exist, there is no dualism, only a monism of Spirit, shared equally by men and women. But Eddy achieved this resolution at a price: not only of her own female body, as Setta and Bednarowski have argued, but of the entire world of the material, not to mention a significant core of Hebraic faith, of God as creator of a heaven and an earth which were pronounced "good." In denying the value and even the existence of the material, Mary Baker Eddy implicitly accepted, in a more drastic way, the very evaluation which had imprisoned her sex for centuries.

Yet contemporary religious feminism, faced with the same dualistic problem, responds not by denying the reality on worth of the material but by affirming its goodness, including the worth and goodness of the female body. Not only is the old "inferior" half of the equation to be raised to worth, but the sex-related division along spirit-matter lines is rejected as well. Woman is not defined by the body any more than man is; man is no more naturally spiritual than woman. Finally, the very world view that insists on such dualistic division and categorizing is rejected and a more holistic vision advanced.

Thus the feminism of Mary Baker Eddy is ambiguous, both in her own time and in its legacy. She, as a woman, founded a religion and gave women a significant place in it; she pressed for feminine imagery of God and insisted that women shared equally with men in the divine image; she defended equal rights for women; she presented positive pictures of biblical women, even the much-maligned Eve. Yet her conscious identification with the woman's movement of her own day was minimal; she raised few questions of the conventional morality and sex roles of her time beyond the matter of formal religious activity; she gave no quarter to potential female rivals and restricted the power just beneath her own to men. Finally, the authoritarian model she endorsed is uncongenial to contemporary religious feminism, and her resolution of a dualism which denigrated women and the material was no real solution to the tension, for it denied rather than redeemed the "lost half."

David L. Weddle (essay date 1991)

SOURCE: "Christian Science Textbook: An Analysis of the Religious Authority of *Science and Health* by Mary Baker Eddy," in *Harvard Theological Review*, Vol. 84, No. 3, July, 1991, pp. 273-97.

[*In the following essay, Weddle argues that Christian Science is based on a "mythic vision of Christian history."*]

> A holy book arouses the greatest respect even among those (indeed, most of all among those) who do not read it . . . and the most sophistical reasoning avails nothing in the face of the decisive assertion, which beats down every objection: *Thus it is written.* It is for this reason that the passages in it which are to lay down an article of faith are called simply *texts.* The appointed expositors of such a scripture are themselves, by virtue of their occupation, like unto consecrated persons; and history proves that it has never been possible to destroy a faith grounded in scripture. [Immanuel Kant, *Religion Within the Limits of Reason Alone*]
>
> If there is a supernatural realm, the "science" of this realm is sheerly verbal. [Kenneth Burke, *Language as Symbolic Action*]

One of the more curious proclamations in the history of American religion is found in the ***Manual of the Mother Church*** of Christian Science:

> I, Mary Baker Eddy, ordain the BIBLE, and ***SCIENCE AND HEALTH WITH KEY TO THE SCRIPTURES,*** Pastor over the Mother Church,— The First Church of Christ, Scientist, in Boston, Mass.,—and they will continue to preach for this Church and the world.

In a letter to the Board of Directors of the church she had founded, Mary Baker Eddy explained the benefits of installing these two texts as the "Pastor" of Christian Sci-

ence churches: "This will tend to spiritualize thought. Personal preaching has more or less of human views grafted into it. Whereas the pure Word contains only the living, health-giving Truth."

Later, when admiring visitors to the grand Mother Church in Boston were disappointed by the infrequency of her personal appearances there, she offered the comfort of the constant presence of "your dual and impersonal pastor." In the explanatory note now republished in every issue of the *Christian Science Quarterly* Eddy wrote,

> The canonical writings, together with the word of our textbook, corroborating and explaining the Bible texts in their spiritual import and application to all ages, past, present, and future, constitute a sermon undivorced from truth, uncontaminated and unfettered by human hypotheses, and divinely authorized.

As such, the combined readings constitute a "text" in Kant's sense of the term: *Sprüche,* words as such, intended as unconditioned speech, sounded in our world but not bounded by it.

Yet this "holy book" does not derive its authority from "sheerly" (or "merely") verbal assertions either, but from the concrete demonstration of its role as the founding revelation for a new age in Christian history. Many studies have been made of the claims of Christian Science practitioners to effect that "demonstration" in healings. This article focuses rather on the way in which Mary Baker Eddy established the authority of ***Science and Health*** by interpreting its teachings as the fulfillment of the biblical drama of salvation and comparing the experiences of her early followers with those of the first Christians. Eddy consistently sought in the Bible what Mircea Eliade calls "paradigmatic models" for her exercise of religious leadership. These biblical models were the means by which she and her students could participate in the "sacred world," the world that is founded by God and therefore cannot deteriorate or pass away. It is the world of the divine mind to which Eddy's teachings give access, and that is the world in which actions are "*real* and *significant*" because they are founded on mythic archetypes.

This article begins with a brief examination of the fundamental claims about reality made in the text, followed by an analysis of Eddy's own healing experience and initial vision of Christian Science. I shall then consider the ways in which Eddy interpreted the teaching she discovered and the church she founded as the fulfillment of biblical models. The conclusion I shall reach is that the usual claims for the authority of ***Science and Health*** based on the coherence of its metaphysics and the efficacy of its healing practice are fully intelligible only when placed in the wider context of the mythic vision of Christian history, shared by Eddy and her students in a community of interpretation.

EDDY AND KANT ON "HOLY BOOKS"

Among his many other reservations regarding religion, Kant considered belief in "a holy book" as the mark of an immature mind, the result of the "self-incurred tutelage" of the unenlightened. The only true holiness for Kant is pure moral will. Thus he proposed that even the Bible deserves our admiration only insofar as it meets the criterion by which practical reason tests claims to divine revelation: "[since] the moral improvement of men constitutes the real end of all religion of reason, it will comprise the highest principle of all scriptural exegesis." Only what promotes consistent obedience to the moral law can be regarded by a rational mind as having divine authority.

Mary Baker Eddy, acting almost exactly a century after Kant published his critique of religion, set out to establish the authority of her book by the "demonstration" of its power to improve the human condition in ways that surpassed what Kant thought possible. She claimed that her text contained not only the means of achieving moral perfection, but also the knowledge that could heal the sick and raise the dead. Kant would have been as fascinated, scandalized, or amused as most of Mrs. Eddy's contemporaries were by her writings. Mark Twain lavished vitriolic wit and grudging admiration on her; Longfellow commended *Science and Health* to the public, even though he admitted he had "not found time" to read it; Bronson Alcott was "almost persuaded" by her logical extension of transcendentalist notions; Emerson received her in his declining years. Many were intrigued by her writings, but few would follow her extreme idealism all the way into "Divine Science."

In part this reluctance was due to the influence of Kant whose radical philosophical revolution had become, by the mid-nineteenth century, the established view. A strict dualism between the external world and the inner realm of human freedom was accepted by nearly everyone, from the Transcendentalist holdouts to the Pragmatists and the new advocates of theological Liberalism. After all, Kant's basic distinction made sense to most people: the material world of objects in motion seems to operate according to its own natural laws, and there seems to be little that the best intentions of human reason and the noblest aspirations of human freedom can do to change them.

It was also apparent to most people, religious or not, that no supernatural agent intervenes in nature. The standard theological explanation was that the age of miracles was confined to the time of the apostles, and that humans must now take responsibility for maintaining faith and good morals without such spectacular displays of divine power. While several explanations, of varying degrees of consolation, were offered for the disappointment, all sides in the discussion were convinced that neither human nor divine spirits act directly on the material world.

Against this conventional wisdom of metaphysical dualism, Eddy insisted on a radical monism of spirit and matter, of God and world, of divine and human. She drew upon an esoteric tradition (whose best-known representative in her day was Emmanuel Swedenborg); some notes from her teacher and pioneer in the "mind-cure" movement, Phineas Quimby; a work or two by Jonathan Edwards (with whose Calvinist idealism she had a love-hate relationship); and her own well-read King James Version of the Bible.

Over a span of forty years, the last half of her life, she wrote and revised *Science and Health* until—regardless of how much the first edition borrowed the phrases and ideas of others—it was unquestionably her own. What she finally constructed is an original synthesis of biblical piety and metaphysical speculation, expressed in an amazingly plastic vocabulary molded by the consistent application of a few general principles. The most startling of these is found among the "reversible propositions" she offered as the fundamental and self-evident basis of Christian Science: "God, Spirit, being all, nothing is matter."

Eddy undertook to establish the authority of her "holy book" by demonstrating the utter sovereignty of divine mind over the world of perception created by human, or "mortal," mind. Her radical conclusion is that the material world is not simply unknown to us, it is in fact nonexistent. The phenomenal world of Kant, the vale of tears of traditional theology, the self-contained system of nature of the scientist, the diseased and dying body that is the frustrating object of the physician's attention—all are illusions, cruel jokes that our fears and false beliefs play upon our true selves.

Further, she claimed that humans are capable of participating in the divine mind whose ideas alone are real. "By this reflection, man becomes the partaker of that Mind whence sprang the universe." Such participation brings us into conformity with God's original idea of perfect humanity, morally pure and exempt from the imperfections that haunt our anxious imaginations. Eddy writes that, as the image of God, "Man is incapable of sin, sickness, and death" (*Science and Health*) That is a text with which to reckon—or conjure. It suggests a vision of human possibilities untrammeled by material limits, an ideal nothing less than "man's perfectibility and the establishment of the kingdom of heaven on earth" (*Science and Health*). Because she believed that "suffering, sinning, dying beliefs are unreal," it was her hope that "when divine Science is universally understood, they will have no power" over humanity (*Science and Health*).

Thus, Eddy's "holy book," unlike the heteronomous "texts" that Kant feared, does not appeal to social approval, but to the consistency of its ideas ("Science") and the power of its teachings ("and Health"). The title corresponds to a phrase in Wycliffe's translation of the Gospel of Luke, in a passage where the King James Version reads "knowledge of salvation." The parallel is significant, not only as an indication of the dual focus of the text on knowledge and practice, but also for placing the book in the context of a messianic interpretation of history. The phrase "to gyve science & helthe to his puple" (Luke 1:77) occurs in the inspired speech of the father of John the Baptist, describing the blessing of the Messiah. Although Eddy decided on her title before learning of its correspondence to this biblical passage, the parallel strengthens the identification of her work with the primordial authority of the founding events of the Christian church.

THREE GROUNDS OF AUTHORITY

The discovery of Christian Science began for Eddy in the winter of 1866, when the world literally slipped away from her and she fell on the ice. The extent of her injuries has been extensively debated, and the accounts of her contemporaries are contradictory. Julius Silberger speculates that the fall was a symbol of her loss of support after Phineas P. Quimby died and that her trauma was more emotional than physical. Regardless of the medical diagnosis, for both Eddy and her followers, the event became the turning point of history. Or perhaps we should say, "the re-turning point" because her experience opened the way to recover the sacred time of Jesus and to participate in the eternal power of "Christ-Science." She writes, "When I discovered the power of Spirit to break the cords of matter . . . I discerned the last Adam," that is, Christ.

Eddy later testified that "an injury that neither medicine nor surgery could reach, was the falling apple that led me to the discovery how to be well myself, and how to make others so." As Newton was jolted into the awareness of a physical law, so Eddy was shocked into the recognition of a spiritual law. Thus she insisted that her recovery was no miracle, but like the healings of Jesus, it occurred by "the operation of divine Principle . . . these mighty works are not supernatural, but supremely natural" (*Science and Health*). It follows that "miracles are impossible in Science," since there is no set of material laws that God chooses on occasion to violate, but only the laws of God's own mind which necessarily produce health and life (*Science and Health*).

For three years afterwards she reports that she "sought the solution of this problem of mind-healing, searched the Scriptures and read little else." What impelled her was not the knowledge she (and every other reader of the Bible) already possessed, namely, that "cures were produced in primitive Christian healing," but the desire to know *how* such cures were achieved. She recalled her passion in these words: "I must know the Science of this healing, and I won my way to absolute conclusions through divine revelation, reason, and demonstration" (*Science and Health*).

In the last clause Eddy identifies three grounds of the authority of her text: religious, rational, and empirical. Her "absolute conclusions" are based on the certainty of

divine revelation, the coherence and consistency of her conceptual system, and the confirming evidence that Christian Science practice produces healings. These three grounds of authority are interdependent, inasmuch as both the metaphysics and the demonstration of Christian Science are persuasive only in the interpretive context of the religious community. This analysis is supported by Robert Peel's insistence that Christian Science practitioners cannot carry out healings in "the sort of experimental, laboratory atmosphere which the scientific investigator demands." The attempt to measure or test the healing by material means is inappropriate for two reasons. First, it would contradict the basis for the whole process by assuming that the healing occurred according to natural laws. Second, it would focus attention on the result rather than the increased spiritual understanding that produced the healing. So the healings are "facts" offered as evidence that Christian Science is true, but they cannot be confirmed as such by conventional scientific means. It is not surprising, then, that despite the thousands of confirmed testimonies to physical healings in Christian Science literature, there is continuing skepticism about their validity outside the Christian Science church.

One might say that the main difference is that the "demonstration" of healing in Christian Science is an interpretation of experience formed by the community of faith in the reality of spiritual restoration—faith in the biblical sense of "the evidence of things not seen" (Heb 11:1). Insofar as the faith that informs the scientific community is in the reality of sense perception, Eddy claimed that it is misled into "the first idolatry": faith in matter (*Science and Health*). Sense perceptions are merely projections of ideas. "Mortal mind," she wrote, "constructs a machine, manages it, then calls it material" (*Science and Health*). It follows that "disease is an image of thought externalized" (*Science and Health*), even bones "have only the substance of thought" (*Science and Health*). The best advice to any patient, then, is to "tell him that he suffers only as the insane suffer, from false beliefs" (*Science and Health*). Accordingly, the evidence of healing is to be found more in changed minds than in altered bodies. That is, the "evidence" of healing requires for its persuasive interpretation commitment to the metaphysical vision shared by the Christian Science community. And that vision is informed throughout by biblical paradigms.

EDDY AS INTERPRETER

The earliest followers of Mary Baker Eddy comprised a "community of interpretation," to borrow a phrase from Josiah Royce, organized by her teachings and marked by unconditional loyalty to her as the "leader" of the "cause." Royce's analysis of the power of interpretation to create community applies directly to the formation of the Christian Science movement. Eddy provided her followers with a new understanding of themselves drawn from her "spiritual interpretation" of the Bible, and they responded with "the will to be interpreted." The terms of that interpretation were the creative blend of biblical images and idealist philosophy contained in *Science and Health*.

Eddy regarded her book, written as a magnificent obsession during nine years of difficult and nomadic existence (1866-75), as the dawning of the messianic age: the second advent of Jesus. In her autobiography, she declared that "the second appearing of Jesus is, unquestionably, the spiritual advent of the advancing idea of God, as in Christian Science." On the first page of *Science and Health,* the publication of her "new thoughts" is placed parallel to the birth of "the Bethlehem babe," illuminated by the "daystar of divine Science." Just as the "Virgin-mother conceived this idea of God, and gave to her ideal the name of Jesus," so the latter-day Mary has given birth to the first complete written statement of the divine knowledge of which Jesus was "the highest human corporeal concept" (*Science and Health*). One of her students recalled Eddy's direct statement that "Christian Science is indeed 'the Christ, the Saviour of the world.'"

In the section of the book called "Key to the Scriptures," Eddy identified the woman "clothed with the sun" in Revelation 12 as "generic man," yet she established a parallel between Jesus as "the masculine representative of the spiritual idea" and the woman who bears the "Christ-idea" in the last days as "the spiritual idea of God's Motherhood" (*Science and Health*). Eddy's interpretation of this maternal revealer inspired one member of an early class on the Apocalypse to exclaim, "Thou art the woman." It was a symbolic correlation kept before the eyes of the congregation in the original Mother Church by a stained-glass window of the Woman of the Apocalypse, looking a bit like the Queen of Heaven, over which is depicted a copy of *Science and Health* open to "Key to the Scriptures."

The first issues of the *Journal of Christian Science,* published in 1883, also contained enthusiastic testimonials to Eddy's teachings as the fulfillment of biblical promises of salvation. One student of the Massachusetts Metaphysical College (which Eddy established in 1881) wrote an open letter to her skeptical brother in which she referred to her own healings, which "prove this Science divine, and none other than the Holy Ghost." Then she added, "To all who gain the spirit of Divine Science in the study and practice of it, Christ is revealed to their spiritual understanding as already come 'the second time,' and without sin unto salvation." One of Eddy's household staff recounted that under her tutelage, "we felt very much as I believe the disciples felt when being taught by the Master." Present-day members of the Church use similar language in referring to the significance of Eddy's work.

> As one sits quietly in the Original Edifice of The Mother Church today and sees as through the eyes of those who first attended services the inscriptions on the walls from the Bible and Mrs. Eddy's writings, one can easily experience again the impact of the coming of Christian Science. The healing touch of the Christ was being felt as in the time of the Master.

By accepting Eddy's own interpretation of her teachings, her students provide the necessary condition for the formation of a community of interpretation. Moreover, as Royce pointed out, "in a community thus defined, the interpreter obviously assumes, in a highly significant sense, the chief place." Mary Baker Eddy knew her place, and her students marked it with biblical signifiers.

For example, in an early issue of the *Journal of Christian Science* Eddy declared that *Science and Health* is

> a complete textbook of Christian Science. . . . There is no additional secret outside of its teachings that gives one the power to heal. But it is very essential that the student gains the spiritual understanding of the contents of that book, which none but its Author is able to impart at this period.

In the same issue a student urged readers to seek Eddy's own instruction as the only way to grasp "the *spirit* of that Word" in *Science and Health*.

> Only one of all the earth hath mastered it, and only one of all the earth can teach it. . . . If you are seeking Truth go where it is taught—to the fountain head—to "the seed of the woman," which in these latter days, is bruising the head of the wily serpent error, and and [sic] bringing Love and Good home to the nations.

Another student defended Eddy as "the teacher chosen of God to whom the light of this great truth has been revealed as to no one else since the early Christian period." Under her personal instruction, these students thought of themselves as participating in an event so momentous that the only adequate parallel was to the time of Jesus and his original disciples. In describing the circumstances of the congregation who met in Boston before the construction of the Mother Church, Annie Robertson writes, "When Mrs. Eddy talked about the Cause, which she invariably did, it was easy to realize that we were living in a time like that of the early Christians."

The authority of Eddy's teachings for these first followers derived in part from the power to represent the "sacred time" of the founding events of Christianity. As Mircea Eliade argued, the experience of the sacred in historical religions is made possible by the belief that the sacred time of divine activity in the world can be recovered through reliving myths. In the specific case of Christianity, he wrote,

> The *illud tempus* evoked by the Gospels is a clearly defined historical time—the time in which Pontius Pilate was Governor of Judaea—but it was sanctified by the presence of Christ. When a Christian of our day participates in liturgical time, he recovers the *illud tempus* in which Christ lived, suffered and rose again.

For Eddy's first students the functional equivalent of "liturgical time" was those liminal evenings when she initiated them by the power of her language into a new world of ideal reality. One of those students described the effect of her teaching in terms that dramatically illustrate

Eliade's words. Emma Easton Newman recalled that "when [Mrs. Eddy] spoke of Jesus Christ, it seemed as if time and space, the barrier of two millenniums and two hemispheres, were swept away."

The sense of contemporaneity with the originating events of the Christian church is particularly evoked by the experience of healing. Indeed, for Eddy the healing efficacy of Christian Science was another parallel between her teachings and the presence of Christ.

> Christ, as the spiritual or true idea of God, comes now as of old, preaching the gospel to the poor, healing the sick, and casting out evils. Is it error which is restoring an essential element of Christianity,—namely, apostolic, divine healing? No; it is the Science of Christianity which is restoring it, and is the light shining in darkness, which the darkness comprehends not. (*Science and Health*)

The reference to John 1:5 leaves no doubt that Eddy considered her book to be the incarnation of Christ, the same Word that was with God "in the beginning" and had now been discovered in its fullness. Elsewhere she made the identification explicit: "the true Logos is demonstrably Christian Science, the natural law of harmony which overcomes discord" (*Science and Health*). Further, just as in orthodox theology Christ is the eternal Son of God, the preexistent Logos, so the "healing power of Truth must have been far anterior to the period in which Jesus lived. It is as ancient as the 'Ancient of days.' It lives through all Life, and extends throughout all space." The marginal notation for this passage reads: "Christian Science as old as God" (*Science and Health*).

Eddy also emphasized the confirming evidence of healings in her interpretation of Christ as the "three-fold Messiah [who] reveals the self-destroying ways of error and the life-giving way of Truth." The "three-fold Messiah" is not Jesus himself, but his teaching; and "it is his theology in this book and the spiritual meaning of this theology, which heals the sick and causes the wicked to forsake his way" (*Science and Health*). Again drawing from biblical archetypes, Eddy cited the Christian reading of Isa 9:6 as a prophecy of the healing power of Christ. She then claimed its fulfillment in the teaching of Christian Science: God "loves them from whom divine Science removes human weakness by divine strength, and who unveil the Messiah, whose name is Wonderful." The pattern of interpretation is clear: Eddy presents her teaching as the representation of Christ, the principle of divine Truth, Love, and Life manifested in the Jesus of history and active in the present experience of the Christian Science community.

The traditional Christian symbol of God's continuing presence with the Church is the Holy Spirit, who Jesus promised would guide his disciples "into all truth" (John 16:13). Eddy's first students readily accepted that association with Christian Science as well. Annie Knott, who later became the first woman to sit on the Board of Di-

rectors of the Mother Church, testified that by following the teaching of *Science and Health* she had proven that "Christian Science is indeed the promised Comforter, and that the healing work practiced by Jesus and taught to his disciples had become a present reality." Another student, Daisette McKensie, exhorted others in the community in these terms: "Let us hold in our forever consciousness that Christian Science is the Comforter promised by the Founder of Christianity, and that it is the complete and final revelation of absolute Principle." The identification of the teachings of *Science and Health* with the Holy Spirit is consistent throughout Christian Science literature. For example, one writer traces the "thread of prophecy" to the "revelation" to Eddy and reiterates that "she recognized this Science as the second coming of Christ, the Comforter foretold by Jesus."

It should be clear by now that Eddy did not make messianic claims for herself, but for her text. While Eddy is intensely jealous of her position as the discoverer of the teaching in the text, she consistently subordinates herself to it. How else, apart from unjustifiable cynicism, can one interpret her withdrawing from publication the booklet *Christ and Christmas*? In the infamous 1893 edition, published during the holiday season in gift book form, there is an illustration of a woman, resembling Eddy, standing hand-in-hand with Jesus and holding a scroll on which is inscribed "Christian Science." Some of her followers were moved to embrace the illustrations as icons; one of those summoned to attend her final class recalled that all the participants acknowledged Eddy as the "highest visible idea of divine mind." Another early follower called her "the highest manifestation of Love" since Christ.

Eddy, however, was embarrassed by the charge of her critics that the book was blasphemous self-deification. Her response was to warn her students sternly against "idolatry": "Whoever looks to me personally for his health or holiness, mistakes. . . . The Scriptures and Christian Science reveal 'the way,' and personal revelators will take their proper place in history, but will not be deified." There is no question that Eddy insisted on her "proper place in history," along with the Virgin Mary and Jesus, but her place is that of "the author of *Science and Health,* the Discoverer and Founder of Christian Science."

Nevertheless, Eddy did draw parallels between her experiences and those of biblical archetypes, especially heroes who bravely confronted the enemies of God. As "the herald of this new crusade," she must confront the "educational systems of the Pharaohs, who to-day, as of yore, hold the children of Israel in bondage" (*Science and Health*). Engaged in combat with materialism, "in this revolutionary period, like the shepherd-boy with his sling, woman goes forth to battle with Goliath" (*Science and Health*). As one who destroyed the original illusion that disrupted the paradise of Eden, she fulfilled the responsibility of Eve and challenged her readers to share her struggle: "Bruise the head of this serpent, as Truth and 'the woman' are doing in Christian Science."

Finally, as one who endured vilification for her message, Eddy identified with the apostle Paul. "Abuse of the motives and religion of St. Paul hid from view the apostle's character, which made him equal to his great mission. . . . To misunderstand Paul, was to be ignorant of the divine truth he taught" (*Science and Health*). This last parallel provides a clue for understanding the intensity with which Eddy protected her teaching from variations introduced even by her own brightest and most enthusiastic students: like Paul she made no real distinction between the message and the messenger. That is why it is as important to her, as it was to Paul, to vindicate herself of any charges injurious to the progress of her mission. Her letters, like his, contain passages of clarification, rebuke, warning of deviation from the true way. As he rejected any other "gospel," even if revealed by an angel from heaven (Gal 1:8), so she rejected any version of Christian Science other than the one in her book, *Science and Health*.

TEXT AS REVELATION

Although Eddy insisted that her text be regarded as "revelation," she continued to craft the language of the book, through seven major revisions, until her death. How can such editorial labor on her part be reconciled with the claim that the book is divinely inspired? If Eddy spoke with the authority of a biblical prophet, why was it necessary that she tirelessly revise her language? Thus far, we have seen that Eddy assimilated her own experiences, as well as her teachings and healing practice, to biblical archetypes. But at the point of *identifying* her text with biblical revelation did her own language prove too imprecise even for her to maintain the parallel?

To test the consistency of Eddy's views on this point we must briefly investigate her understanding of revelation. Gottschalk suggests that, since Eddy did not think of God as a personal being, she did not understand "revelation" in the orthodox Christian sense of "the conscious self-disclosure of a personal God in time." Eddy thought rather of revelation as the process by which humans discover the truth that is eternally known by divine mind. But eternal truth can be known only in a formal sense because every particular expression of it, in the concrete terms of a specific culture and language, is limited by the material means of its articulation. Therefore, all statements of "divine truth" are open to improvement, as are all things human.

The necessity of critical revision is also clear from a consideration of the manner in which Eddy received inspiration. Daisette McKenzie records Eddy's own description of the experience:

> When the ideas of Truth poured into my thought, I was so careful not to miss anything, that I let my papers fall to the floor. When the moment of revelation passed, I gathered them up and arranged them. . . . It was not myself, but the divine power of Truth and Love, infinitely above me, which dictated *Science and Health with Key to the Scriptures.*

The process of revelation was like both *possession* (in which sheets of paper were no sooner covered with ink than they were crowded off the desk to make room for more with an intensity akin to "automatic writing") and *composition* (in which sections were ordered and words meticulously chosen). Thus, unlike "revelations" to biblical apostles and prophets, the text of *Science and Health* was not given to Eddy in a fixed or final form. She had to struggle to clarify "its grand facts" in appropriate language. "As former beliefs were gradually expelled from her thought, the teaching became clearer, until finally the shadow of old errors was no longer cast upon divine Science" (*Science and Health*). She later declared, "I have been learning the higher meaning of this book since writing it." Her gift, as revealer, was to receive inspired ideas, but her task as interpreter was to find the right words to express their meaning.

Thus the language must be both historical and eschatological, and for the model of such transformative discourse Eddy again turned to a biblical archetype. Recognizing that, "like all other languages, English is inadequate to the expression of spiritual conceptions," Eddy urged her students to struggle to master her vocabulary for it represented the "new tongues" with which the first apostles gave voice to Christian truth (*Science and Health*). She assimilated her message to the original gospel preached on the first Pentecost, insisting that her peculiar language is the fulfillment of millennial prophecy. "The spiritual sense of the Scriptures brings out the scientific sense, and is the new tongue referred to in the last chapter of Mark's Gospel" (*Science and Health*). The text of *Science and Health,* then, carries the eschatological authority of the "signs" promised to Jesus' followers. For her students, Eddy's interpretation of the Bible itself is the "gift" of the divine Spirit, the inspired speech of the "last days" uttered now; the basis of its authority is that it "works." Like the charismata of the early church, the text has the power to effect what the Bible promises, that is, the "transformation of the body by the renewal of Spirit" (*Science and Health*).

What, then, is the precise relation between *Science and Health* and the Bible? In a recent essay on that topic, Robert Peel likened Eddy's book to the historic creeds of the Christian church in that "it claims only to be making explicit what is inherent in the Scriptures." Yet *Science and Health* is more than another commentary on the Bible. Eddy also regarded her writing as a clarification, and even an extension, of biblical revelation. As one example, let us consider Eddy's interpretation of the theology of Paul. While Paul reached what she called an "intermediate line of thought," Eddy "continues the explanation of the power of Spirit up to its infinite meaning, its allness." Paul understood the spiritual influence of Truth upon the material world, but he did not carry the insight to its logical end: "If Spirit is *all* and everywhere, what and where is matter?" (*Science and Health*). In fact, once this higher insight given to Eddy is attained,

Paul's emphasis on suffering as the emblem of Christian discipleship can also be transcended.

> St. Paul said: "For I determined not to know any-thing among you, save Jesus Christ, and him crucified." (I Cor. ii.2). Christian Science says: I am determined not to know anything among you, save Jesus Christ, and him glorified. (*Science and Health*)

Eddy thus exchanges Paul's "theology of the cross" for a "theology of glory" on exactly the basis that Paul himself thought premature, namely, that the kingdom of heaven has already come on earth. Here is the point of most radical departure from Pauline theology: the daring declaration that what the apostle hoped for Eddy had discovered. She believed that "millennial glory" had been realized in her teaching. "This Science of being obtains not alone hereafter in what men call Paradise, but here and now" (*Science and Health*).

Her early followers also shared Eddy's self-understanding as a revealer of new truth, the last in the biblical line of divinely inspired teachers. One wrote that

> Moses gave us the moral law. Elias exemplified prophecy. Christ Jesus demonstrated the divine law in the destruction of sin, disease, and death. Mrs. Eddy gave us the Science of Christianity which forever reveals to all mankind the practical application of the divine law.

The last phrase echoes Eddy's own description of Christian Science as "more than a prophet or a prophecy; it presents not words alone, but works." Another student went so far as to claim that all of Eddy's works constituted divine instruction "on practically every subject and situation in life," so that "we are not limited as were the early Christians in the possession of the written word." The advantage Christian Scientists had over the original Christians was the extent of authoritative writings made available through continuing revelation to Eddy. The student continued, "The other writings of Mary Baker Eddy, which she describes as 'indispensable to the . . . student,' seem to me to be . . . the breaking of the Bread of Life contained in the textbook, and are inspired by the same divine Spirit." Following the logic of progressive revelation, her students came to regard Eddy's other prose works as the "key" to *Science and Health,* as it is the "key" to the Bible.

Yet it was to her demanding textbook that she continued to return, seeking an elusive perfection of language to match its divine ideas. It was not until 1895, twenty years after its initial publication, that Eddy was sufficiently satisfied to install her book, along with the Bible, as the "pastor, on this planet, of all the churches of the Christian Science denomination."

THE MOTHER CHURCH AS RESTORATION

The installation of the textual pastor, or pastoral text, was made official in another book that Eddy labored to per-fect, her *Manual of the Mother Church*. This text, too, she revised repeatedly, until she found the form of organization that was as appropriate to her vision as the language of *Science and Health* was to her teaching. Further, she regarded this text also as divinely inspired and unalterable because its provisions "sprang from necessity, the logic of events" (*Manual*). Thus, Eddy understood the founding of the Mother Church as a decisive event in the biblical history of salvation, understood as the inexorable unfolding of the mind of God.

It followed that the authority of her teachings was based not only on assimilation of her texts to the incarnation of the Word and to messianic prophecies, but also by the identification of her revelation with the descent of the Holy Spirit on the day of Pentecost:

> The advent of this understanding is what is meant by the descent of the Holy Ghost,—that influx of divine Science which so illuminated the Pentecostal Day and is now repeating its ancient history. (*Science and Health*)

The full repetition of sacred history required that the students of the Word become the members of the church. The transition was easily made by one of Eddy's secretaries, who recalled that when Eddy read one of her hymns to the assembled staff, "we felt we had had a baptism in Spirit."

The charter for the First Church of Christ, Scientist was granted on 23 August 1879. The congregation had no regular meeting place, however, until the legal way was cleared in 1892 for incorporation and the construction of an edifice on land Eddy gave to the Board of Directors. The stated purpose of the Mother Church was "to commemorate the words and works of our Master, which should reinstate primitive Christianity and its lost element of healing" (*Manual*). Here sounds the familiar note of the repristination of the Church, which "restores the lost Israel." In her own version of the Christian appropriation of Jewish symbolism, Eddy wrote that the children of Israel were so called only "until the Messiah should rename them," and they were brought back from apostasy in the material world in order "to be renamed in Christian Science" (*Science and Health*).

The organizing of the Mother Church of Christian Science signified something more than mere repetition of the past: "for 'the stone which the builders rejected, the same is become the head of the corner'" (*Manual*). By this reference to Ps 118:22 Eddy links the hope of ancient Israel for the eventual vindication of their sufferings to the construction of her church in which all suffering would be overcome. In early Christian tradition, the verse was interpreted as a prediction of Christ's rejection by Israel, followed by his death and resurrection (Acts 4:10-11). In Matt 21:42-44 the prophecy is cited as an interpretation of Jesus' parable of the unfaithful tenants, turning it into a direct warning to those who reject him. In this reading of the gospel, Christ is the stone on which some will fall and be broken and which will fall upon others and crush them.

This is a curious prophecy, yet Eddy evokes by its quotation a cluster of associations with Jesus, who suffered opposition yet was triumphant. It is a text of the reversal of fortunes and the dawning of new light. As the passage continues: "This is the day which the Lord hath made: we will rejoice and be glad in it" (Ps 118:24). Such imagery of creation renewed each morning is appropriate here. The discovery of Christian Science is for Mary Baker Eddy the dawning of the messianic age: the rebirth of moribund Christianity, a decisive return to original and originating authority.

The means of that return is through replication of the founding of the Church, a drama in which Eddy serves as the bearer of the eternal truth and her small band of followers constitutes the faithful disciples. It is significant that in her "historical sketch" of this event, Eddy records that there were "twelve" who formed the nucleus (*Manual*). Appropriately, these few were then called "First Members." In 1903, when the transition from tiny beleaguered community to thriving new organization was complete, their title was changed to "Executive Members." Their mission as witnesses to the founding event and guarantors of the authority of the founder was completed, and they were assigned administrative posts. In Eddy's final revision of the bylaws in 1908, the special status of the original company was revoked altogether.

Thus in less than two decades these loyal students had traced backward the traditional hierarchy of ecclesiastical authority: from apostles to elders to ordinary members. The sequence of their demotion corresponds to the consolidation of authority in the institution of the Mother Church. The First Members had no other authority than the grace of their title, bestowed upon them by Eddy herself. She entitled them and by that action gave them their roles in the drama of reactualizing the sacred time of Jesus and his disciples. By her naming the First Members they were called to play apostles to Christian Science as Christ, "the stone which the builders rejected [and] is now become head of the corner."

If Christian Science is Christ, then Mary Baker Eddy is the mother of the Messiah, the woman through whose suffering labor the truth is born and through whose faithful teaching the Church is born. She names her students, as a mother names her children. In the drama of reenactment they are "First Members" and she is "Mother." Although the creative moment of participation in the primal myth initiates historical process, it cannot sustain it. Once the crisis of repristination passes, the reborn must assume more adult roles. Accordingly, the First Members become executives and finally have the maturity to relinquish all special claims for themselves (*Manual*).

It is entirely consistent with this reading of events that Eddy later prohibited her students from calling her "Mother." Her stated reason for this public taboo on her primal name was that the practice was creating the wrong impression among those outside the movement. The change was appropriate moreover to her vision of Christian Science as recapitulating the history of the early church. As the events that originally covered two centuries were compressed into two decades, the community underwent frequent and sudden transitions. Old familiarities gave way in the process of the "routinization of charisma"; henceforth, "Mother" was to be called "Leader" (*Manual*).

The provisions in the *Manual of the Mother Church* maintain the authority of the community personally led by Eddy. For example, the church in Boston has exclusive claim to the definite article "the" before its name (*Manual*). All branch churches derive their authority from that of "The First Church of Christ, Scientist," just as it in turn derives authority from the paradigm of the church Christ founded. Further, other churches can be organized only by members of the Mother Church. Eddy may here be thinking of the biblical pattern of authority in which the mother church in Jerusalem sent apostles to sanction Christian experience elsewhere (Acts 8).

Further, the *Manual* gives ultimate control to Eddy in her new role as "Pastor Emeritus." She is given veto power over all elective processes, and all officers are required "promptly to comply with any written order" from her regarding their duties on pain of removal from office (*Manual*). Individual members are required to spend three years in Eddy's personal service if so summoned (*Manual*). Any donations from the church require "written consent of the Pastor Emeritus" (*Manual*). Also, the reappointment of the officers of the Christian Science Publishing Society requires her written consent, and she has veto power over works proposed for publication (*Manual*). On her testimony alone a member may be "excommunicated" for "mental malpractice" (*Manual*).

The section on teaching Christian Science, the analogue to missionary activity in the early church, is also designed to insure tightly regulated propagation of Eddy's system of "mind-healing." Thus, teachers are limited to one class a year, of not more than thirty pupils; and the "normal classes" at the Mother Church for training teachers are held only once every three years and are limited to thirty students. Yearly associations of pupils of particular teachers are allowed, but more frequent gatherings are forbidden, as are special meetings of selected pupils (*Manual*).

Whether one regards these provisions as expressions of profound paranoia or justifiable safeguards against unscrupulous former students, they are effective means of discouraging dissension and fragmentation within the growing Christian Science movement. The specific conflicts with competitors and entrepreneurial students were painstakingly detailed by Robert Peel and provided Eddy with what she regarded as sufficient ground to be wary of any Christian Science teacher who seemed to be building a potentially fractious following. Thus, she reaffirmed the textual basis of authority in Christian Science: "The pupils shall be guided by the BIBLE, and SCIENCE AND HEALTH, not by their teachers' personal views" (*Manual*).

The parallel to the development of early Christian orthodoxy is clear: the establishment of one right teaching and the exclusion of all variations as heresies. Are we then only hearing another verse of the old song that power once gained takes power to maintain? Are these suspicious denials of the rights of free speech and voluntary association merely the autocratic impulses of an aging woman who cannot stand the competition and who is fighting a desperate defense against the inevitable loss of health and life itself?

Such psychoanalytic interpretation has much to commend it. During most of her life, Eddy was weak, vulnerable, and dependent. She suffered and overcame fierce opposition to establish her movement in Boston and, even in 1879, the future was by no means guaranteed. There was every reason for her to feel threatened and to respond by tightening her grip on the control of power. Her very language invites analysis in psychoanalytic categories: she described herself as the pastor of "the Mother Church," at first she encouraged her students to call her "Mother," she accepted male protegees, and she disciplined female students who began to teach on their own. It requires little imagination to suggest that she had begun to resent her "daughters" and to fear the "mental malpractice" of these metaphysical Electras.

As with most psychoanalytic interpretations, however, so with this one we are left with the truly interesting questions still unanswered. Whatever her motivation, what in fact did Eddy achieve in this detailed church constitution? How did she translate her personal authority into institutional form? Although Mary Baker's relationship with her parents is classic material for Freudian analysis, it does not help us much in understanding the woman who wrote this manual. At age fifty-nine, a time when most people are worn out and ready to slide into retirement, she was poised to enter three decades of rising power and accomplishment. The *Manual of the Mother Church* is her manifesto, her aggressive claim on the future. There is little in the document to suggest that the "Pastor Emeritus" is anticipating a time when authority will be transferred from her to her church.

Yet she is not immune from the problem of how to transfer authority in the future. It is the same problem faced by other movements of the time. The Mormons divided on the question. The main body followed the new president, Brigham Young into Utah, while a small band of dissidents, insisting on the principle of familial descent, remained in Missouri under the leadership of Joseph Smith's son. The issue of transference had been anticipated by Joseph Smith, one of whose revelations designates the office of "First Presidency" as the heir of his mantle of prophetic authority. Thus the locus of revelation shifted from the person of the prophet to the office of the "First Presidency."

Eddy followed a different route. She designated neither a successor nor an office as the means of maintaining the continuity of authority: she ordained the compound text of the Bible and *Science and Health* as the normative and unalterable source of understanding and guidance. Further, the *Manual of the Mother Church* is "adapted to form the budding thought" and cannot be amended without "written consent of Mary Baker Eddy, the author of our textbook, SCIENCE AND HEALTH" (*Manual*, 104-5). Accordingly the *Manual* ends with a reminder of Eddy's title most relevant for the task of organizing the church: "author of our textbook." It is under the instruction of that authorship that Christian Scientists continue to gather as a "community of interpretation."

I conclude that Mary Baker Eddy intended Christian Science to be the movement that would both restore primitive Christianity and also advance Christian understanding into the promised age of redemption. To accomplish this epochal task she wrote her "textbook," laboring over its birth and development for three decades, and she authorized a polity for the Mother Church designed to preserve the integrity of her "miraculous vision." In fulfilling both tasks she followed models from the story of the early Christian church. These biblical archetypes provide the context of mythic drama in which her "textbook" can be seen as the reenactment of the advent of Christ, and her church as the new Pentecost opening the age of the kingdom of heaven. Only in this light does the religious authority of *Science and Health* as a holy book become clear.

Stephen Gottschalk (essay date 1991)

SOURCE: "Honesty, Blasphemy and *The Destiny of the Mother Church*," in *The Christian Century*, Vol. 108, No. 32, 1991, pp. 1028-1031.

[*In the following essay, Gottschalk explores the controversial reception of Bliss Knapp's biography of Mary Baker Eddy.*]

A book and an endowment have thrown the Church of Christ, Scientist, into its most significant controversy of the past 70 years. The dispute erupted after the church announced it would publish a book it had rejected over four decades ago, Bliss Knapp's *The Destiny of the Mother Church*, as part of a new biography series on church founder Mary Baker Eddy. Then in early September former church archivist Lee Z. Johnson sent a letter to librarians of the denomination's more than 2,300 reading rooms, as well as to the executive boards of churches. The letter quietly and knowledgeably set forth six specific points—expressed to the church's board of directors three weeks before—for these "branch" churches to consider before selling *Destiny* in their reading rooms. As democratically self-governed institutions they are under no compulsion to carry it.

Publication of this book has drawn protest from Christian Scientists because it asserts that Eddy was more than human, a counterpart to and equivalent of Jesus Christ. Its publication also appears to compromise principle for financial gain: $92 million from the Knapp estates, which the church badly needs to fund its media operations and which it will receive if it fulfills conditions of the Knapp wills. The entire controversy illustrates how churches are tempted to abandon their deepest convictions for a mess of pottage—to cave in to secularizing pressures rather than maintain with quiet integrity the spirituality that is what they really have to offer.

Extensive press coverage predictably has focused on the element of controversy. But as a recent Boston news report put it, "One of the beliefs of Christian Scientists is the process of healing. It seems now that the church may have to do some self-healing of its own" (WBZ-TV Evening News, October 16). More than a few Christian Scientists involved in the dispute feel the need to point out how the church, rather than focusing solely on conflict, might find renewal and wholeness—though not without clarifying the serious issues at stake.

Since these issues go to the very heart of what Christian Science stands for, the controversy is even more serious than the crisis of November 1988, when *Christian Science Monitor* editor Katherine Fanning and two top editors resigned in protest over the downgrading of the *Monitor* to make way for the church's expanding media ventures.

Eddy claimed to have discovered the continuing power and truth underlying Jesus' life and works. But for her, Jesus remained unique and incomparable, humanity's master and savior. So when the *New York Herald* in 1895 asked her if she thought she was the second Christ, she responded, "Even the question shocks me . . . to think or speak of me in any manner as a Christ, is sacrilegious. Such a statement would not only be false, but the absolute antipode of Christian Science."

Imagine how dismayed she would be to find her own church publishing a book that speaks of her in just such ways. *Destiny* argues in strongly cultic accents that both Eddy and Jesus were "Incarnations of Truth," she being God's "original woman" just as Jesus was God's "original man." Created with him prior to all others as one of the "two great lights" that "appeared on the fourth day of creation," she and Jesus "occupy a position that is above their fellows" and were prophetically hailed as "the two great rulers in the heavenly kingdom." Jesus, says Knapp, is "ruler over the foundations and Mrs. Eddy ruler over the gates, by which we enter the Holy City," for "she was invested with deific power to make laws as a ruler in the heavenly Kingdom." Knapp further argues that God revealed Eddy's exalted status through Jesus to John as the "specific woman" spoken of in Revelation 12—a view Eddy explicitly disavowed in her textbook *Science and Health* as well as in unpublished writings.

Far from being taken out of context, these are the very points around which the labyrinthine arguments of the last third of Knapp's 300-page book revolve. Knapp, a Christian Science teacher and lecturer, was undoubtedly sincere in these beliefs, vastly distant as they are from Christian Science teaching and the Christian tradition as a whole. Helmut Koester of Harvard Divinity School observes that Knapp's view of Eddy as God's "original woman" is reminiscent of "Gnostic speculation that parallels Eve and Jesus," though in Gnostic texts one almost never finds a "specific human being identified with the primordial female principle." And as religious historian Lex Hixon comments, "Not even the most extreme veneration of the virgin Mary elevates her metaphysically, as Knapp does Eddy, to a par with Christ."

Eddy so strongly opposed the sacrilege of comparing her—or anyone—to Jesus that she included in the church's governing *Manual* provisions forbidding "careless comparison or irreverent reference to Christ Jesus" and a warning against believing or signifying belief in "more than one Christ." Other bylaws proscribe members' buying, selling and circulating "literature which is not correct in its statement" of Christian Science and stipulate that the Publishing Society will not sell "books or literature" of which Eddy disapproved.

Why, then, would the present board depart from the spirit and letter of these bylaws? Why would it reverse the 1948 board's unanimous decision, expressed in a letter to Knapp, that the book is unsound on a number of specified points? Why publish the book now, after more than 40 years during which its predecessors have rejected it, despite the lure of a growing trust dangling before it?

As a Christian Scientist, it gives me no joy to say this, but the answer comes down to money. If branch churches do not fulfill the conditions of the wills left by Knapp, his wife and sister-in-law—that *Destiny* be displayed and sold in "substantially all" Christian Science reading rooms indefinitely as "authorized literature" of the church—the Knapp trust funds will revert in 1993 to Stanford University and the Museum Associates of the Los Angeles County Art Museum. Using the wedge of their huge fortune, the Knapps in this way sought to impose the views expressed in *Destiny* on the church as accepted and acceptable teaching.

The church's need to sustain its media operations is what led it to capitulate. By the church's own figures, these operations have cost over $400 million since 1986 and depend substantially on subsidies from the church. Last spring, as a result of media expenses now running $90 million per year or more, the funds available for the subsidies probably would have been nearly exhausted except for an infusion of $40 million over a two-year period from the pension account.

The justifications church leaders have cited for publishing the Knapp book have been somewhat embarrassing excursions into "official truth." Treasurer Donald Bowersock, for example, acknowledged to the *Philadelphia*

Inquirer that "from a fundraising standpoint, the directors have to ask themselves whether to forgo the income. It was reasonable to proceed in such a way that the bequest came to us" (October 14). Yet in a television interview two days later he declared that "if there was no money associated with the Bliss Knapp book, we would have published it" (WBZ-TV Evening News).

Not publishing the book, church officials say, would have left a conspicuous omission in the projected new 15-volume series on Eddy. Knapp's book, according to church spokesman Nathan Talbot's monumental understatement, simply presents "a little more visionary sense of her" (*Boston Globe,* October 13). Yet the book itself contains relatively little biographical material on Eddy in contrast to what it provides about Knapp's parents.

Including the book in a biographical series, however, has given church officials a way to dodge the question of whether *Destiny* qualifies as "correct" literature. As a biographical reminiscence, they say, *Destiny* simply isn't "literature" in the sense of being a direct statement of Christian Science. But this assertion ignores the fact that the last third of *Destiny* consists of 100 pages of almost nothing but Knapp's personal teaching, repeating his exaltation of Eddy in the final three chapters. It also amounts, in the words of one unconvinced church member, "to an attempt to reinvent the English language by saying that a book somehow isn't literature."

Policy also has been reinvented for the occasion. An October 3 church mailing to members maintains, against all historical evidence, that Eddy's standards for church publications applied only to church periodicals and not to other Publishing Society books, even when they discuss Christian Science. The same mailing paints Knapp as a "trusted associate" of Eddy, whereas he met her only on a few occasions during his adult years; asserts that his views were well known to Christian Scientists, though none of his available writings contain views as extreme and aberrant as *Destiny;* and omits mentioning that after the 1948 board rejected the book he agreed not to teach and did not do so for the rest of his life.

Indeed, John Hoagland of the Publishing Society's board of trustees has argued that it would have been illiberal and repressive *not* to publish *Destiny,* since the church "has always respected the intellectual integrity and freedom of its authors" (*New York Times,* September 30). Intellectual integrity is hardly the term that springs to mind when one considers Knapp's fast-and-loose use of biblical prophecy to "prove" Eddy's quasi-divine status. The church has respected the intellectual freedom of a scholar such as Robert Peel, whose biographical trilogy on Eddy, though controversial among some church members, commands wide academic respect. But there is a world of difference between Peel's serious scholarship on Eddy's life and Knapp's personal views about her place in biblical prophecy—views as offensive to her as to other Christians, and thoroughly uninformed by anything resembling biblical scholarship.

Their defense of publishing *Destiny*'s aberrant views as part of a new-found pluralism puts church officials at cross purposes with the Knapp wills' clear stipulation that *Destiny* must be published as "authorized" literature. "Authorized literature" in the Christian Science tradition has always meant genuine, responsible and correct. If this standard sounds illiberal, it reflects Eddy's clearly stated and understandable view that, given widespread misrepresentation of Christian Science, the public should at least be able to look to the church for a responsible expression of what she taught.

The church has not used this term officially since the 1970s, when it concluded that it sounded censorious. But its substantive meaning is very much the same for today's Christian Scientists as it was for the Knapps. As a practitioner expressed it to a reporter recently, "What comes from the Mother Church is true" (*Miami Herald,* October 11). In effect, the church is now caught in the dilemma of on the one hand saying that the book is authorized, but on the other hand denying everything that word means. Board chairman Harvey Wood has already publicly disavowed that the book is "authorized" in the familiar sense when he said to the *New York Times* that publishing it was "not an official embrace of Mr. Knapp's conclusions"—which is exactly what "authorized" would have meant, in the sense in which the Knapp wills use the term.

Church officials have also tried to downplay the controversy by maintaining, as did Hoagland in *Time* (October 14), that "the commotion is not about the Bliss Knapp book. It's about our move into television." But the publication of *Destiny* would have aroused just as much opposition had no money been involved. What links the furor over *Destiny* to the media effort is that money needed to fund that effort was so obviously a factor in the decision to publish the book.

The media issue is, in fact, something of a red herring. Most of those who question the publication of *Destiny* as well as the church's recent media ventures have no quarrel with the legitimate use of television and radio to further Christian Science. They generally support, for example, shortwave religious programs, though these constitute only a small element of the media program as a whole. What does concern many members is that the mass communications program seems to have almost no religious content. As Harvey Wood, who more than anyone has spearheaded the secular media effort, described its purpose to the *New York Times,* "I'm not talking about religion. I'm talking about ethics, standards and values."

Eddy, however, was talking about a great deal more than "ethics, standards and values" even when she founded the *Monitor* as a link between her church and the world. As part of the church, the paper was to give evidence of Christian Science's constructive realism. But Eddy never wanted it to supplant the church's religious purpose, to overshadow its activities, or to be the primary means through which Christian Science reached the world.

While *Monitor*-style journalism can be applied to other media, Eddy did not intend the *Monitor* in any form to expand to the point that it would virtually cannibalize the church.

The only faintly plausible reason for the church greatly to expand its media effort is, according to Wood's views as reported in the *New York Times,* "that high-quality news and public affairs programming will also attract interest in the church's spiritual side." Yet for Eddy the church didn't have separate spiritual and secular sides. She taught that spirituality and the spiritual healing that results from it is not only intrinsically interesting but radical and radically needed by humanity. And that kind of spirituality is, in the final analysis, the only thing the church she founded has to offer.

Over the past decade, however, the church has increasingly replaced its foundational purpose of spiritual healing with a secular public service mission, drastically subordinating the spiritual nurturing of members to secular modes of outreach and use of marketing techniques. This is happening just when Christian Scientists' practice of spiritual healing is under intense public scrutiny and when disciplined commitment to that practice most needs deepening. The church's administration has not made this change explicit to a trusting membership, who have been pressed to contribute the staggering sums necessary to fund the church's media empire. But only the shift in the church's priorities can explain the events of the past decade, including the publication of *Destiny.*

The controversy over that book, however, appears to be drawing members as never before into the affairs of the Mother Church and awakening them to their responsibilities under the *Manual*. To a large extent, members have assumed that the board of directors functions as Eddy's successor. But the board's only function is to administer the church's affairs according to the *Manual,* to which they and all members remain subject. Indeed, a key element in the current crisis is that by sanctioning the publication of *Destiny,* the board is encouraging members to violate the key bylaw on "incorrect literature" in the very *Manual* the board is charged with upholding.

This bylaw, however, is directed to members as members, a fact that Johnson's letter brought directly to their doorsteps in an unavoidable way. Until that point some members' deepening concern about the direction the church was taking had not significantly penetrated into local congregations' everyday life. Now members have been awakened to their responsibilities under the *Manual* to think for themselves and make independent, informed judgments—not only about *Destiny,* but about other aspects of their church and how it is being administered.

Church officials have called Christian Scientists to break out of their shells and become more aware of the world about them. But these same officials are apparently balking at members' increased interest in the affairs of the Mother Church itself. Even in the face of a rising chorus of dissent over the last five years, the administration has argued in the media and in mailings to church members that the current stir is simply the work of "mischief makers," "disgruntled former employees" and "dissidents"—dismissive epithets that do little to further reconciliation and hardly reflect liberal tolerance of divergent views.

They also argue, plausibly, that one of the church's basic problems is its adherence to traditions that have no real basis in Eddy's teaching or the *Manual*. One of these traditions, however, is the Christian Scientists' passive resignation of all responsibility to the Mother Church in Boston. Ironically, church officials have traded on that very passivity by treating branch churches as little more than adjuncts to "progressive" Boston-based media initiatives, whereas Eddy believed that the real locus of the movement had always been with members "in the field."

The dust hasn't settled in branch-church debates over whether to sell *Destiny*. But fragmentary reports make it dubious that "substantially all" reading rooms will be carrying the book. Whether or not the church ultimately receives the Knapp bequest, it has already undergone a fundamental and irreversible shift. As one teacher remarked, "Members who are actually reading the book are finding its viewpoint preposterous and outrageous. An awakening of individual responsibility to hold the directors to the church *Manual* and to make their own thinking felt is catching on. This exercise of individual responsibility can heal and unify the church."

Paradoxically, a new unity may be forged through what has appeared to be a searing controversy. Despite divergent opinions on a number of questions about the destiny of the Mother Church, members are becoming far more than ever before thinking participants in shaping this destiny. They are finding that in the Christian Science church as in any religious tradition, true unity cannot be imposed from above any more than renewal can be manufactured. Rather, both come from returning to the original sources of the church's strength and moving forward on the basis of loyalties that members already share.

Glen W. Gadberry (essay date 1994)

SOURCE: "Lost American Opportunity: Two 1931 German Plays about Mary Baker Eddy," in *Comparative Drama,* Vol. 28, No. 4, Winter, 1994/1995, pp. 486-509.

[*In the following essay, Gadberry discusses two little-known German dramas about Eddy.*]

> My personal interpretation is that Germany has such a wealth of love, mercy, and other virtues found in the Christian faiths that we do not need an American sect, which in my opinion, does not teach humility, but strives for business success in addition to religious goals.—Ilse Langner (1931)

In 1930 and 1931, a critical biography and two plays about Mary Baker Glover Patterson Eddy appeared in Germany, and a third was announced. They were but part of the Euro-American revival of interest in the problematic founder of Christian Science, who had died in 1910. "Mother Mary," as she came to be called, remains a fascinating and outrageous character. Mark Twain, her contemporary, found much to ridicule and fear in her despotic irrationality, yet he could conclude, "Closely examined, painstakingly studied, she is easily the most interesting woman on the planet, and in several ways, as easily the most extraordinary woman that was ever born upon it." His various satires on Christian Science, combined into a 1907 book, helped publicize the scandals, principally plagiarism, greed, and drug use, that kept Eddy in the public view even years after her death. If religion is the opiate of the masses, morphine was the crutch of Mary Baker Eddy. Her chronic use of the then legal drug and her probable addiction were more a scandal of hypocrisy than narcotic abuse itself: Christian Science forbade the use of any medicine, even to ease pain.

While charges of plagiarism would occupy her ideological descendants, it was her greed which most outraged her critics. She denied the material but actively sought, acquired, and held material wealth. After starting her own academy, she charged exorbitant amounts for healing lessons and claimed that God set her fee structure; she demanded kick-back percentages from her graduates and sued if any fell behind; she also sued for full royalties on her publications, even though, as Mark Twain sardonically observed, she claimed they were divinely written. The faithful saw her as God's incarnation; her American critics as an ignorant and money-loving huckster; the Germans as an American capitalist, preying upon a simple land's unbounded naiveté. The Eddy phenomenon, so wrote a Berlin critic, "was only possible in America, whose people in their constant search for business are more receptive for superstitions and sects than any other people on earth." Although this kind of religion-money combination is all too familiar in the American religious marketplace, it was incomprehensible for Germans, in part because the country's two authorized Christian faiths, Roman Catholic and Lutheran, enjoyed the benefits of a legislated church tax.

In America, the Eddy debate was played out in print and pulpits, but in Germany it was also treated in the theater: *Wunder in Amerika* (*Miracle in America*) by Ernst Toller and Hermann Kesten premiered at the Mannheim Nationaltheater on 17 October 1931, and three weeks later, on 4 November, Ilse Langner's *Die Heilige aus USA* (*The Saint from the USA*) opened at Reinhardt's Theater am Kurfürstendamm in Berlin. Written independently, the plays cover the last forty-five years of Eddy's life: her miracle cure, the founding of a Christian Science empire, subsequent physical decline and death at age eighty-nine. Written and staged with epic and expressionist embellishment, Langner's version is the more inventive and significant as both text and performance. It will be the principal focus, but paired with Toller-Kesten the Eddy texts

and performances allow us to imagine a portion of the complex mosaic that is German theater history and at the same time to infer the limits of the American theater.

A major impetus and source for these concurrent plays was the essay "Das Leben und die Lehre der Mary Baker-Eddy" ("The Life and Teachings of Mary Baker Eddy") by Austrian cultural critic and author Stefan Zweig (1881-1942). It was initially published in the Berlin journal *Neue Rundschau* in three installments in May, June, and July 1930. The essay was subsequently repackaged early in 1931 in Zweig's three-part *Heilung durch den Geist* (*Healing Through the Spirit,* subsequently translated as *Mental Healers,* 1932). In this final version, Eddy was positioned chronologically and ideologically between Anton Mesmer and Sigmund Freud, the whole introduced by an essay on the origins and development of "organic and mental therapy." The placement was to her advantage on a continuum of mental and physical health through suggestion. Like Mark Twain, Zweig found her a fascinating study as founder of a new illusion, with implications for social and personal psychology; accordingly, she deserved a "permanent place among the pioneers of psychology, of the science of the soul." And he also found much to censure, for the love of money compromised religious integrity. This "founder of the new American religion, was the first of the great prophets who had no objection to a fat banking account, and who found it easy to combine faith in Christ with faith in the dollar." But there were deeper causes of rejection: he uses the words "absurd," "impossibility," "delusion," and "insanity" regularly in his narrative to characterize Eddy and her arcane theology. The faith required a blind "credo quia absurdum [est]."

Zweig also positioned Eddy in the Euro-centric spiritual and historical context of his readership by citing other "theological outsiders" such as Agrippa of Nettesheim (1486-1535) and Jakob Böhme (1575-1624)—or the Nancy apothecary who popularized healing through suggestion in the twentieth century, Emile Coué (1857-1926). The playwrights embraced Zweig's skeptical fascination but left cultural parallels to audience imagination. By and large they were content to keep Eddy an American phenomenon, a New World problem.

It might seem curious that there would be any German interest in the founder of a nineteenth-century New England quasi-Christian faith-healing "religion," "sect," or "cult" (the designation depends upon viewpoint, and also the term "cult" represents current popular usage). Yet Christian Science had crossed into Germany: its first church was built in Hanover in 1899; by 1931, despite opposition from the German religious and medical establishments, there were six churches and an inflated claim of 80,000 members. It was, at most, a little more than one percent of the population, but, as Mark Twain had predicted, Christian Science growth patterns, financial manipulations, autocratic structure, and questionable ideology were to be seen as threats to democracy, not only as a cause for laughter. The faith was a challenge to the

Lutheran and Catholic monopoly on German Christianity, certainly if taken in conjunction with the migration of other neo-Christian ideologies such as Jehovah's Witnesses, Mormons, Salvation Army, and other sects, most of which would dead-end in the Third Reich. That Christian Science might actually threaten the political and religious structures of Weimar Germany was not developed by the authors except by implication: the plays document the dangerous growth of an anti-democratic, irrational power system. Spectators in 1931 Mannheim and Berlin may have thought such an ideology would never take root in an enlightened German republic.

One appeal of the Eddy plays was interest in the rebirth and variety of American religious fundamentalism. Central Europe had watched a coalition of arcane religious sects emerge to help promote prohibition in 1919 and to challenge the teaching of evolution, culminating in the highly publicized 1925 Scopes trial. Germans welcomed the 1928 translation of *Elmer Gantry,* Sinclair Lewis' 1927 satire of evangelical hypocrisy. And there was Aimee Semple McPherson, charismatic "radievangelist" of Los Angeles, who was cashing in on America's continued weakness for religious revival and instant salvation. McPherson's 1930 Easter road show to the Holy Land, with conversions of Moslem Arabs, gave dramatic exposés of Mary Baker Eddy their contemporary cultural context. Two of the principals had direct knowledge of McPherson in California: Ernst Toller, who visited in 1929, and Langner's director, Ludwig Berger, who had made a career in Hollywood. The McPherson persona supposedly shaped the writing of one play and the staging of the other. Yet it was the deceased Eddy, with German branch churches, not the living McPherson and her newly formed International Church of the Foursquare Gospel (1927), who was the focus of Zweig, Toller-Kesten, and Langner.

As with any powerful figure, there were contradictory biographies available. Zweig and, through him, the playwrights favored Twain's satires and a pair of "hostile" biographies. In a series of articles in *McClure's Magazine* in 1907 and 1908, expanded into her *Life of Mary Baker G. Eddy and the History of Christian Science* (1909), Georgine Milmine diligently set about to locate and publish every damning piece of evidence against Eddy. Accordingly, she preserved a wealth of nineteenth-century documents, interviews, and affidavits. Her book became rare as Christian Scientists not only bought and destroyed copies of the text but also even the printer's plates. But her documentation survived in the most widely-read, objective, and damaging biography, Edwin Franden Dakin's *Mrs. Eddy: The Biography of a Virginal Mind* (1929). Zweig's essay brought much of Dakin and Milmine's evidence and conclusions into German. Dakin seems also to have been used directly by Langner.

None of the German writers embraced the official biography written from within: Sybil Wilbur's *Life of Mary Baker Eddy* (1907). Translated in 1926, it was the most readily available biography in German. It was seriously flawed by adoration, and Zweig dismissed it as "a truly Byzantine example of literary embroidery," composed in the "style of the Gospel of St. Mark." Wilbur revered Eddy and thought Christian Science to be the true religion. Dramatization from her hagiographic perspective might have produced a modern miracle or passion play, but the playwrights were not among the faithful. They also dismissed the validity of Eddy's own texts, or, rather, they adopted Zweig's critique of the Christian Science bible *Science and Health* (1875, repeatedly revised and reissued): "Bearing unmistakable marks of genius and at the same time absurd in its fierce disregard of all the accepted canons of knowledge, at once ludicrously childish and illogical, amazing, quasi-maniacal, simple and direct, this codex has a thoroughly medieval flavour [of] religious fanaticism."

Whether "black" (Zweig's term for Milmine and Dakin) or "rose-coloured" (Wilbur), the Eddy biographies interweave themes of feminism, psychology, medicine, religion, money, and (American) society. Each comes into the Eddy plays, but none is the sole focus, except perhaps the definition of New World naiveté. Some themes might be of more interest now, such as the extent of female empowerment. Eddy could be viewed as a paradigm of the independent and successful woman eclipsing the restrictions of nineteenth-century American and, because of the time and place of composition and production, twentieth-century German patriarchy. Her feminist theology alone is of interest: apparently appropriating the central ideas of Anne Lee's New York Shakers, Eddy advocated the dogma of "Our Father-Mother God" with His-Her incarnations in Bethlehem, Palestine (Jesus Christ, sometime B.C.E.), and Bow, New Hampshire (Mary Baker, 1821). A feminist dimension is frequently suggested in relation to Langner because "one of [her] primary concerns" was "the right of women to participate on equal terms in every form of social intercourse." Her Eddy play accordingly should chart "the spectacular success of a woman during an age in which women were typically denied all opportunities (and the religious establishment was, of course, patriarchal to an exceptional degree)," yet the feminist dimension seems ill-applied to *Heilige aus USA* (or to *Wunder in Amerika*). Although she is certainly independent and successful, someone who does "participate on equal terms" in her fight for the religious dollar and church power, Langner's Mary is also a manipulative hysteric, sexual predator, abandoning mother, and greedy demagogue, independent of the pressures of patriarchy. And, more importantly, no one opposes her as a woman who has exceeded her social standing or her gender role; instead, she is critiqued as a hypocrite who advocated an absurd but lucrative religio-medical ideology.

Another inherent theme is Christian Science and medicine: Eddy and her followers were programmatically hostile to the medical profession and to the use of medicines, while at the same time they touted miraculous cures of their own. In 1872, Mother Mary was claiming she could raise the dead, walk on water, restore sight when the optic nerve was destroyed, set and heal broken bones without artificial means, live twenty-four hours without air and twenty-four days without food. Such claims did not go unchallenged, but criticism was offset by sporadic "cures" and by the chronic hope of the terminally ill. Twain observed that Christian Science did, in fact, have an impressive record of healing because most disease was imaginary and therefore quite treatable through psychic suggestion. But it tended to fail against "real" disease, and its record overcoming the "illusion" of death was extraordinarily dismal. Although provocative, the medical questions are marginal to the plays. The success of some cures, most notably Mary's in 1865, reinforces the stage efficacy of mental healing, but its power is offset when "cured" blindness returns a day later, as dramatized by Toller-Kesten, or when Mary is unable to cure third husband Asa Gilbert Eddy of his fatal illness, as shown in both plays.

The most intriguing issue then and now, with implications for German and American theater and social history, is Christian Science as "cult," in the current popular definition of the term. Intervening experience with groups like the Reunification Church of the Rev. Moon and with such episodes as those that occurred at Jonestown and Waco, Texas, have also made this issue timely, but even in 1931 it was appropriate to ask at what point should a religious group be treated as a destructive cult? Central Europe had traditionally ridiculed, suppressed, or exterminated splinter faiths as abberations or heresies, while America (but obviously not all Americans) tended to embrace them as long as they were Eurocentric and quasi-Christian. With smug irony, Zweig wrote that Christian Science was particularly attractive to the "American mind, which had not, like the European mind, been burdened with skepticism by the weary experiences of two millennia;" it was a sentiment altogether absent from the American biographers. But Germany was being tested by new religious imports, and plays about Eddy could strengthen a presumably healthy skepticism. Is it ironic or merely typical that the only plays about this religious leader are German? Are they renewed examples of European intolerance, or does it merely seem so because America has no critical standards for its tolerance? These questions will reemerge at the close of the present paper.

Each play is grounded in documents, dates, facts, and anecdotes which authenticate Eddy's strange life, yet each, especially Langner's, embellishes the strange truth of Christian Science with fiction. The Toller-Kesten text (commentators note that it is impossible to discover what parts of the play were written by each of the authors) is a more conventional five-act drama, nine scenes in nine settings. By 1931, Toller (1893-1939) had abandoned or outgrown the avant-garde techniques of his youth, although he could not resist giving a fictional banker the English name "William Money." In general, there is little in the text to suggest his expressionist past; Hermann Kesten (1900-) was already a leading representative of the more sober *Neue Sachlichkeit*. Their play calls for

forty-five characters (plus extras) grouped around Eddy as dominant character. Despite the large number of characters, the typical stage picture is an indoor room, of increased lavishness as Eddy becomes one of America's most successful entrepreneurs.

Their most theatrical and inventive scene comes in the fourth act (IV.3); the playwrights call for a deep three-part stage, well suited to the old Mannheim theater (and to most German theaters of 1931, which were equipped with deep-stage prosceniums). Closest to the audience is a Boston street with newsboys hawking *Christian Science Monitor* headlines; in the middle is the lavish Mother Mary sanctuary within her new five-thousand-seat church; furthest to the rear are the nave and chancel of the church itself, wrapped in organ music and the hushed voices of thousands. Action is not simultaneous in the three settings; we are moved from street to sanctuary, to chancel, and then back again. The up-and-down-stage spaces are public venues of controlled knowledge, of Christian Science propaganda—church-filtered news hawked to the people of Boston and Mary's lecture to the faithful. Each is a frame to the sanctuary, where, relieved of holy image, she strips her wealthiest patron of her estate, expels her adopted heir because of sexual jealousy, and purchases the silence and exile of her only child, an adult son, abandoned in his infancy. The triple scene accentuates some of the hypocrisies surrounding Eddy: the last two charges were true, the first only probable.

Die Heilige aus USA by Ilse Langner (1899-1987) is also grand scale, with twenty-nine characters (plus extras). It is arranged in thirteen *"Bilder"* in twelve separate settings. It is not surprising that six scenes correspond to the Toller-Kesten text since the playwrights sought dramatic turning points in the Eddy biography, but each is combined with other material and written in different styles. Langner's twelfth scene, for example, corresponds to Toller-Kesten's triple scene, but the actual overlap is only one speech, one important event of 1896. In that year Eddy surprised the faithful by withdrawing from all duties and positions; her "retirement" was in fact a calculated act to deflect criticism of her penchant for power and wealth and, more importantly, a way to reclaim personal control over a too dispersed structure. In Toller-Kesten the announcement is the climax of Eddy's sermon; in Langner it comes as a quiet close to a riotous stage debate, pitting Christian Science apologists against medical doctors, philosophers, main-stream churchmen, Mark Twain, and Berlin's Court and Cathedral Pastor, Adolf Stöcker, who resisted the coming of Christian Science to Germany. Langner goes beyond the merely biographical to create an international docu-debate which never happened but which allows her to present the breadth and intensity of the "Christian Science question" in an economical and theatrical way.

In three statements made immediately before and after the premiere, Langner speculated on her approach. Three days prior to the opening she wrote, "Mary Baker-Eddy, not [Herbert] Hoover, is the true founder and promoter of PROSPERITY; it was not chance that Eddy triumphed at the same time as the mercantile and industrial upswing of this land of unlimited possibility. She preached success and proved there was no stopping the strong personality. Her own career demonstrates the fantastic path of a superhuman energy, to go from a beggar to a millionaire, from a nameless farmer's daughter to the idol of a huge religious community." This pre-production commentary positioned expectations about the possibly unfamiliar American faith-healer, dead for twenty years, within the development of American capitalism and perhaps also within the struggle for women's rights. Here might be a Horatio Alger heroine, who actually achieved success and wealth, who lived "the American dream." The historic parameters of American capitalism, two years after the 1929 Stock Market Crash, were of considerable interest. Langner's original title, *Manhattans grosse Mutter* (*Manhattan's Great Mother*), reflected this economic dimension.

On the day before the premiere she talked about Eddy's life, with some editorializing, drawing upon Zweig and Dakin. She introduced her narrative with the following statement: "The life of the sect founder Mary Baker-Eddy, on whom America manifested its unlimited possibility in the most crass manner, is full of such fantastic contradictions, deep defeats, and arcs of success that the mere telling of the basic facts would shame the creator of an adventure novel." The would-be spectator was thus prepared for a fabulous stage biography built out of the facts Langner subsequently recounted. *Die Heilige* would present a truth stranger than fiction which might also reveal the functioning of American capitalism.

A few days after the premiere as Berlin's score of reviewers wrestled with the play in performance, Langner again addressed her creation in her most provocative and engaging statement: "Fascinated by a woman's act of will and fantastic rise, I have extracted and crystallized the life of the American sect founder Mary Baker-Eddy in its points of development, defeat, and moments of success so that it rolls forth as a history before the eyes of the spectators: Saint From USA." What had been presented as a kind of accurate reportage for all its fantastic quality was now revealed as a different kind of historic record, one that had been concentrated and "crystallized." Because in spite of Zweig's essay few Germans were familiar with Eddy or with Langner's biographical sketch published days earlier, there was some danger the "crystallized" play would be seen as "straight history," especially when the text called for projections of newspaper headlines to reinforce the impression of being a documentary. Fortunately, interventions of director, designer, and star actress reinforced the abstractions in Langner's text.

Langner, throughout seeking and developing the inner meaning and larger context of the Eddy material, transcends the merely biographical and realistic. She aims at a stage-effective image of the essence rather than the appearance of reality but from her own perspective—i.e.,

at times she will be an expressionist, redoubling the grotesque in the life of Eddy. She will be an active member in the communication from stage to audience, thought-provoking and didactic: "I intend to interest [the spectator] and chain him and teach him something new."

> I will be involved, not shoved off to the side; that first powerful moment is mine, the EFFECT upon the spectator. I will seize him, throw him around, present him with the harsh moments and the mad reversals of life, show him the tragic next to the grotesque, and how they impact each other with force and without nuance. The spectator should come along and learn new views of the world, rich in its forms, and that beyond his narrow circle of consciousness the world takes pleasure in its mad rotation, enjoys remarkable and deeply affecting fates. This was the sense of my history.

A few examples, with correspondences to Toller-Kesten and the sources, will provide a sampling of her stage-conscious technique.

The first relates to Mary's 1862 cure, the Quimby Scene (Bild 2, comparable to Toller-Kesten Act I). Historically, after twenty years of debilitating agony and gradual paralysis which had no physical cause and proved un-treatable by conventional medicine, Mary Baker acquired enough money to travel to the up-and-coming hypnotic healer Dr. Phineas Quimby. How she wins her travel funds is "crystallized" as invented "history" in Langner's first scene: Mary badgers her sister Abagail for the gold cross and chain left to her by their mother, and both will be pawned to finance another attempt at physical cure. The episode is artfully created "essence," for Mary was always selfish, manipulative, unsentimental, and dependent upon the kindness of her sister or indeed on anyone who could endure her character flaws. The use of the gold cross is a perfect touch to establish Mary's hypocrisy. The real Abagail, incidentally, was only too happy to rid herself of the burden of her younger sister; she even forbade Mary to attend her funeral. It is a grotesque detail out of a most remarkable life.

The trip to consult Dr. Quimby was historically a painful journey. Because of exhaustion and chronic paralysis Mary had to be carried physically into his presence. And then, in but one treatment session, twenty years of agony were eliminated by the laying on of Quimby's skilled hands and by his hypnotic presence. She thereafter proclaimed that a divine miracle had occurred, but in the meantime she carefully learned Quimby's technique. Christian Science was born when she took his method as her own, allegedly through God; when accused of plagiarism, she first denied any connection but then countered that Quimby had in fact learned his methods from her! The "facts" of that cure are essentially the same in Zweig, Toller-Kesten, and Langner and make for a powerful scene of on-stage psychic healing. Toller and Kesten do, however, provide one dramatic invention of their own at this point: when Mary leaves to proclaim Quimby's genius, she swears, "Let me for ever be damned from the day when I deny that all that I have and am belongs to you." The irony is blatant and even comic when she makes a grand exit without paying Quimby his ten dollar fee.

Langner takes Quimby out of what passed for a sober medical setting (an office in the International Hotel in Portland, Maine, where we find him in Zweig, the earlier play, and history) and puts him into the flashy milieu of a country carnival medicine tent, competing with a noisy carousel and exotic dancer Suleika. The real Dr. Phineas Quimby was not a con-man or quack, although his title was purely honorary. He had learned Anton Mesmer's technique through the 1838 lectures and training offered by French immigrant Charles Poyen Saint Sauveur, an expert on "animal magnetism." Quimby subsequently discovered he could in fact heal a great number of apparently seriously ill people. It was a measure of the man that he was perfectly willing to share his discoveries with anyone who was interested, and no one showed more interest in his ten volumes of hand-written "medical" notes than Mary Baker, who recognized their financial potential. By putting Quimby into a side-show, Langner expresses her subjective and expressionist reaction to all such healers. The change is especially effective if the spectator knows the Quimby biography or if the production further abstracts the scene design or performance style. Otherwise the fair setting could be mistaken as realism: Quimby is another nineteenth-century American carnival charlatan who might also deal in snake oil. In other plays and films, the effective expressionist technique distorts or exaggerates some part of a reality that is understood by the audience; faced with a new or extreme image, the spectator recognizes and feels the artist's intense emotional response to the original. In the film *Metropolis,* for example, the image of the factory as Moloch is properly powerful but only if we know what a factory is. On the page, for the typical German reader, Langner's Quimby is not sufficiently abstract, but fortunately his expressionist essence can be saved by acting style and scene design.

Another useful example involves the "crown" as it appears in Bild 9. Here Eddy is presented to us as divine monarch, in her own lavish chapel, the "Mother's Room" of the Boston church. (It is the same room at the center of the Toller-Kesten triple stage.) Here she is enthroned with ermine cloak, diamond-studded cross, and jeweled crown. The royal paraphernalia, like the stage space, is historic: "Mother Mary" had been presented these regalia of cloak, cross, and crown by Auguste Stetson, the head of the New York Church of Christ Scientist. But Langner makes a typical artistic change: the Stetson "crown" was not a tiara but a brooch in the shape of a crown, embellished with diamonds. Langner enlarges the icon to correspond to the ermine and Eddy's pretension. She probably found the information in Dakin (it is not in Zweig or Toller-Kesten) and misread, or more likely she elected to transform the brooch into the larger and stageworthy symbol. As with the side-show Quimby, unless the spectator is aware of the source, or unless the designer further

exaggerates the regalia, the spectator might think it realistic, appropriate to Langner's commentary on the Eddy biography's fantastic truth.

As might be expected with such subject matter, the plays revealed their strengths and weaknesses in performance. Reviews are enlightening with regard to production and reception, at least for their premiere performances; for all their methodological failings, they nevertheless can provide insight into theater history. The Toller-Kesten Mannheim premiere was directed by Richard Dornseiff and starred Ellen Widman; neither had a noteworthy record before or after 1931. The reviewer for the national *Frankfurter Zeitung* thought the text interesting enough, as "a cold *Lehrstück,* to cure [us] of these remarkably dark and irrational movements which have today seized people so powerfully and inexplicably." Like Zweig, he felt the biography spoke to contemporary psychology, "spiritual fanaticism," and the "net of mercantile, yes of Mammonistic greed." But the production merely emphasized what he thought was a mechanical structure. His objections suggest that there was an expressionist interpretation, which he took as weakness. The designer (Eduard Löffler), for example, used minimal light so that the play remained in "dusky/dim relief." Dialogue was clipped and "nervous," like a caricature. And as Mary Baker Eddy, Ellen Widman began at an ecstatic (i.e., expressionist) level and could not grow during the course of the performance. The Frankfurt reviewer felt her strongest scene was the last, when ecstasy finally succumbed to a realistic portrayal of the dying octogenarian, with her unsteady gait, grotesque rouged cheeks, and morphine-induced calm. Toller and Kesten were in Mannheim and joined director and cast for "heartfelt" applause, but it had not been a "pervasive success." Local critics, Stefan Kayser in the *Neue Mannheimer Zeitung* and Fritz Droop in the *Mannheimer Tageblatt,* were more favorable and do not suggest the expressionist overlay. Droop agreed that the play concerned "deceptions which we call [religious] belief," but it was otherwise "pure reportage of America." Certainly more familiar with Mannheim style, they thought it "well above average": it won strong applause, with an obligatory mix of boos.

Langner's *Heilige* was a greater success, in part because of publicity: German Christian Scientists agitated for a suit against all parties on a charge of blasphemy, the same paragraph No. 165 used against Georg Grosz for his sketches for Piscator's production of *Der gute Soldat Schwejk* (November 1928). A week after the premiere, the publicist of the German Church of Christ Scientist, Count Helmuth von Moltke, the grand-nephew of the field marshall, complained about the production. He objected to Langner's use of Zweig, who had no real knowledge of the movement and avoided sanctioned biographies in favor of the hostile Milmine and Mark Twain (he does not mention Dakin). A week later, an open letter to the producer Max Reinhardt complained of an assault on a "beautiful and distinguished religious movement" and on its deceased founder, who could not answer the charges herself. Indeed, many Christian Scientists were incensed by the play. Although the Boston Mother Church declined a request to proceed legally, Christian Scientist Fritz Seeberg, Ph.D., brought suit against the Reinhardt theater, the playwright, director, and star actress for blasphemy and "contemptuous treatment of religious practices."

That evening, 20 November 1931, prominent jurists, theologians, writers, and actors held a post-performance meeting. Herbert Ihering found it "interesting" that this West-End theater, accustomed to "elegant social plays or demi-monde revue and operetta," was embroiled in such a serious matter. Since there were no Christian Scientists present or at least any who chose to reveal themselves, there was no debate or discussion but rather a series of speeches. It was chaired by Heinrich Mann, President of the Prussian Writers' Academy, who alluded to the Georg Grosz fiasco and commented, in effect, that "Those portrayed, not the portrayers are guilty"; the audience responded with "bravo" and "quite right." Langner said her play came from historic sources and personal knowledge of Christian Science. Although she had little sympathy for the movement and its founder, which should have been clear from the play, she had not intended an "insult to religious feelings." The director defended Zweig and his actors, who should not be held responsible for the opinions of the roles they play. He also berated the mixing of money and Christianity as it was continuing in the alleged heirs of Mary Baker Eddy—e.g., Aimee Semple McPherson. Bertolt Brecht, not surprisingly, found no blasphemy in the play, and most theater people agreed. Two legal councilors with experience in such cases (there had been 206 prosecutions in recent years) felt there was no case: there had been no blasphemy, and according to German law there had been no assault on Christian Science as religion because it was not "a recognized Christian church, or a church with corporate status within an existing religious community recognized by the German state." The German Church of Christ Scientist was merely an association serving religious ends.

Albert Schweitzer commiserated that Christian Scientists could be upset by the portrait of Eddy and "the cult of their science"; he advocated compromise, with some textual cuts. But "whether blasphemous or not, the play had the same tendency to sensation attributed to Mary Baker." Berlin Pastor Koch did not find the work censorable except in the matter of "good taste"; "But in my opinion, the cultic, even the cult-like, does not belong on stage as a matter of human tact, neither Parsifal nor representation of a howling dervish." In her account, Berlin freelance author Doris Wittner brought the issue back to the play itself: if Langner's *Heilige* offered offense, it was the "sin against the Holy Ghost of art. . . . To our eyes, nonetheless unforgivable." The highly publicized evening event bolstered theater and cast and reinforced the arts in their stand against censorship. See-berg's case never developed, in part because the Boston Mother Church was not interested in endorsing the suit. The play continued nightly for twenty-two performances.

The production itself was a more significant artistic success than Wittner would allow because of the combined talents of seasoned ensemble, star actress, and experienced director. The Reinhardt theaters had acquired the fashionable west Berlin Theater am Kurfürstendamm at the start of 1931. *Heilige* was the third production in the 750-seat space and, more importantly, the third premiere of the multi-theater Reinhardt company in less than two weeks. It followed Ferenc Molnár's *Jemand* (*Someone,* which opened 26 October at the Komödie, directed by Gustav Gründgens, with Albert Bassermann) and Ödön von Horváth's *Geschichten aus dem Wiener Wald* (*Tales from the Vienna Woods,* 2 November at the Deutsches Theater, directed by Heinz Hilpert, with Peter Lorre and Lucie Höflich). Berlin critic Franz Koeppen thought *Heilige* the most successful of the three because the Molnár was "flat" and the Horváth "problematic." In all the production used fifty-six actors, all but one drawn from the Reinhardt company; they included Else Bassermann (Abagail), Brigitte Horney (Auguste), Hans Halden (Quimby), and Egon Fridell as Mark Twain. As a guest performer, Agnes Straub created Mary Baker Eddy. Unlike Ellen Widman in Mannheim, Straub was a major actress. By 1931 she was an independent star and had completed a particularly stellar year: she had created Ferdinand Bruckner's *Elisabeth von England* for a 122-performance run at the Berlin Deutsches Theater, and had played Kate in *The Taming of the Shrew* in Munich, Goethe's suffering Cäcilie in a revival of Reinhardt's famed production of *Stella* in Salzburg and Munich, and the avenging Kriemhild in the Hebbel *Nibelungen* trilogy in Munich while alternating as Schiller's Maria Stuart. And now for this, her thirtieth and last production for the Reinhardt theaters, she created a woman as strong, vengeful, capricious, passionate, and hysterical as any of her heroines of the past year.

Straub was forty-one, roughly the same age as Eddy at the start of the play; photographs suggest that little effort was made to age the actress to correspond to the next forty years of Eddy's life except to whiten her hair. Physically, Straub was tall, blond, robust, a powerful stage presence, with "Teutonic features" and "Slavic cheekbones and eyes," while Eddy was frail, diminutive, intense. Eddy's "wizened and bony figure with its masculine lines," Zweig wrote, "recalls that of another strong-willed woman of our time, Cosima Wagner," the composer's imperial widow. To heighten the difference between actress and historic character, a picture of Eddy was printed in the program, and to place her in European context it was paired with that of another muddled mental mystic, Grigori Rasputin. The program left little doubt about production sympathy for Eddy or Christian Science.

Most critics agreed with Herbert Ihering that it was Straub who, "at the peak of her ability," held the play's scenes together. Her Eddy grew from the "lame hysteric, from an evil female Rasputin into a calculated propagandist of her sect. . . . She was at home as Mary Baker, in each witch-like detail as in her narrow-minded, shrewd spirituality." Bernhard Diebold was in a novel minority: for all her virtuosity, Straub was unable to unite the forces combined in Baker, the love of God and the dollar. But, he added smugly, she could not, because she was European: "The true actress for this role must come from abroad." Diebold reinforced German incredulity at America's gullibility; several critics agreed that Straub was unable to show how such a religious leader could have succeeded and advanced into the twentieth century. They expected much more spiritual truth from Eddy and Christian Science when actually there was even less than Langner (or Toller-Kesten, or Zweig) had presented.

Director and designer were brothers Ludwig Berger (born Bamberger) and Rudolf Bamberger. Berger had playwriting credits (*Griseldis* 1921, *Kronprinzessin von Preussen* 1925, *Die Rosenbraut* 1931, among others) and had directed for Reinhardt and Jessner. He had made a reputation for his "anti-Reinhardt" stage simplicity, particularly in his productions of Shakespeare. After 1920, he was principally a film director (with nine German films up to the Langner premiere, most recently *Meistersinger von Nürnberg* [1926-27] and *Liebe, Liebe* [1928]). From 1928 to 1930 he directed five films in Hollywood, including *Sins of the Fathers* (1929) with Emil Jannings and Zasu Pitts, *The Vagabond King* (1930) with Dennis King and Jeannette MacDonald, and *Playboy of Paris* (1930) with Maurice Chevalier and Duke Ellington and his Cotton Club Orchestra. His German and American film experience helped shape his multi-media production style.

Hollywood also shaped his attitude towards Langner's central character, for it was in California that Berger had come into contact with Aimee Semple McPherson, her evangelical power, and personal scandals. Following the premiere he commented in a Berlin newspaper that he did not take Eddy's situation "as a unique case, but as a typical example for a kind of enterprising spirit" which seeks to "make capital, plus interest, out of basic religious necessity, an enterprising spirit, which I had ample opportunity to study during my sojourn in Hollywood." For there was another "evangelist in Los Angeles, perhaps less brilliant than Mary Baker, but both have become quite rich." C. Hooper Trask, European theater reporter for the *New York Times,* was also reminded of "Sister Aimee": Langner had "touched up her protagonist with some of the traits of Aimee McPherson," particularly in the scene of her dedication of her Boston church. Those additions, in terms of gesture and speech patterns, may have come from Berger, who had been an eyewitness.

Langner advocated stage "movement, flashing lights, sharply rising and falling fortunes, and a figure who rushes through it all like a flame" under the dictum that the only "killing bacillus in theater is boredom." Although the Kurfürstendamm Theater was not equipped with the revolving stage for which Langner's text called, Bamberger and Berger did use her filmic, agit-prop, and epic embellishments to enliven the production. Reviewers were reminded of Erwin Piscator's epic productions or Erik Charell's garish revues, depending upon point of view. A running advertising line was used in Bild 7, while projections of American newspaper headlines appeared in Bild 12 (presumably rendered in German, as they are in Langner's text). A trick film sequence merged dollar signs into Eddy's Boston Mother Church. The cathedral scene, with Eddy in white silk and diadem standing at a gold cloth-covered pulpit in a glowing cathedral-style interior, above which loomed impressions of stained-glass windows, recalled Reinhardt's production of *Das Mirakel.* A spirited revival march wound from the audience up onto the stage. Because the theater was not outfitted with banks of boxes, Langner's use of actors planted in a front box had to be restaged, probably using the orchestra section. And Berger brought Eddy into 1931 experience by incorporating the dissonant jazz compositions of Ernst Toch (1887-1965) for incidental and scene music. Toch's typical style, "light, gracious, lean, was hardly recognizable here, with the heavy horns, grating woodwinds, hard percussion." He succeeded in "converting reportage into a fantastic event," filling out what was thought a too sparsely-written text. It "didn't sound pleasant, but it was excellent music" which sought "the tone of the age, of history." Berger had overseen a tumultuous theater event which to be sure did not have universal appeal. C. Hooper Trask thought Berger "did the whole in too lurid a style. It was as flat and glaring as a poster."

A common critique of both plays and productions was related to the dominance of the central character. Writing about the Toller-Kesten play in the Berlin journal *Die Literatur,* Paula Scheidweiler noted, "All light and all power are so concentrated on this one figure that there is hardly space or air to breathe left for the others around her. The masses stand opposite her, without so much as a profile"; a month later Ernst Heilborn, essentially writing the same thing about the Langner drama, complained that the "subsidiary characters" were reduced to mere types. A more serious and recurring objection was that neither play had a real opponent for Eddy and hence no essential dramatic conflict. The playwrights could not find an active antagonist in Zweig, Dakin, or Wilbur or even in Eddy's life. The biographies and plays record Eddy's series of triumphs and setbacks, significant and petty, over relatives, acquaintances, disciples, competitors, the courts, and so on. (By most accounts, Eddy never got along with anyone, after an initial period where she would be fascinating and even charming.) There were always scoffers, of course, but, like Mark Twain, they were little more than momentary irritants: they had no real power over Eddy while she lived and had no power over Christian Science after her death.

The enemies most feared by Eddy were three apostates who supposedly turned Christian Science teachings against her as "malicious animal magnetism." She was assured that every setback or recurring symptom of illness came from the distant mind waves of three one-time favorites (Kennedy, Arens, and Spofford) who had deserted because of her material or personal demands. When she felt under attack—she believed she could tell which of the three had turned his evil mind against her—she would array her disciples in psychic assault circles or round-the-clock defense teams to focus their thoughts to block those malicious mind waves. Those testaments to her mental instability and cult power, in the modern sense of the term, are wonderfully bizarre but did not provide active antagonists suitable to 1931 dramaturgy. The supposed malefactors were unaware of their evil ways, at least until Eddy tried to get an injunction to block the assaults.

The only sustained conflict Eddy ever lost was to reality, to the material world. She denied its existence, and she denied death. Despite her claims of divinity and despite prayer, faith-healing, and positive thought, she was defeated by Death, that dart-throwing realist and bane to human pretension. Each play ends with Eddy dying but without surrendering her illusions. In Toller-Kesten, the ideologically embarrassing news of her death is momentarily suppressed; in Langner, a character steps to the curtain to announce: "The Holy Mother has altered her form of appearance." The holy business of Christian Science will continue, without its colorful founder and leader.

The Eddy plays help establish the rich diversity of Weimar theater but also speak to American theater and society. There have been no American plays about Mary Baker Eddy, but America does now have some three thousand cults and scores of "legitimate" sects currently agitating for millenarian miracle. Skeptics might suggest there has been too much emphasis upon uncritical religious freedom in the theater and perhaps in society. To see the mundane and familiar in a new way (the basic artistic and critical principle of Mark Twain, Brecht, expressionists, post-modernists, and other skeptics), perhaps America's "virtue" of tolerance was not such a virtue after all, especially if it left such fascinating figures as Mary Baker Eddy to foreign playwrights. Berlin critic Emil Fechter observed that *Heilige aus USA,* and he would probably add *Wunder in Amerika,* would not increase the love of Germany in many parts of the Anglo-Saxon world. He was right not only as far as the Christian Scientists were concerned but also for theater history: America should have brought its Mother Mary and Tammy Faye Bakkers, its Sister Aimee McPhersons, Father Coughlins, Jimmy Swaggarts, and Pat Robertsons *et al.* to a skeptical stage of material reality. Little would have changed, of course: those who believe that some American Founding Fathers wisely defined a freedom from religion would attend the theater to reinforce that belief; the faithful would be offended and stay away, as Christian Scientists did in Mannheim and Berlin while they plotted ways to close the theater. But at least history could have documented a free American theater.

Robert David Thomas (essay date 1994)

SOURCE: "With Banners Still Flying: Christian Science and American Culture," in *With Bleeding Footsteps: Mary Baker Eddy's Path to Religious Leadership,* Alfred A. Knopf, 1994, pp. 291-310.

[*In the following essay, Thomas surveys Eddy's impact on modern American social and religious thought.*]

Mary Baker Eddy's death in 1910 was not the passing of an ordinary woman. Obituaries appeared in big-city tabloids and small-town weeklies across the country. Thumbing through a sample of these editorial comments today, one is struck by their lack of neutrality. Even when progressive America admired her accomplishments, it was uncomfortable with her, not knowing where to fit her into its notions of authority, leadership, and gender.

The *Rochester Times* observed that Mrs. Eddy's death marked the passing of a woman who was "probably the most notable of this generation; certainly none other has had more widespread influence or is regarded with greater reverence by more people." Indulging in hyperbole, the paper noted that "millions of followers" flocked to fill the pews of her worldwide church. The *Chicago Tribune* reflected the same sentiments: with her death, "there passes from this world's activities one of the most remarkable women of her time."

The *Chicago Post* accurately summed up the meaning of Christian Science to Mrs. Eddy's followers. "Without humbug or sentimentalism, any outsider can and must admit that Christian Science people are good people. They not only believe in their church and attend its meetings with a passionate faithfulness that other churches envy, but they also carry their faith with them into their daily lives." Other newspapers were not as perceptive or careful in their assessments of Mrs. Eddy's contributions. A North Carolina paper stated that "her gospel was largely one of sunshine and mental uplift," while a Michigan daily thought that if Mrs. Eddy was remembered for anything, it would be for the "optimism" that she taught. "Christian Scientists are sunny, hopeful, cheerful."

Even before Mrs. Eddy died, Georgine Milmine was evaluating Christian Science in terms that made her sound like a precursor of such positive thinkers as Norman Vincent Peale. "Mrs. Eddy's teachings," said Milmine, "brought the promise of material benefits to a practical people. . . . In the West, especially, where every one was absorbed in a new and hard-won material prosperity, the healer . . . met with an immediate response. This religion had a message of cheer for the rugged materialist as well as for the morbid invalid. It exalted health and self-satisfaction and material prosperity high among the moral virtues." Mrs. Eddy would have grumbled at these words, because she saw her ideas as radical rather than assimilative, and she pushed for religious rigor rather than comfortable accommodation. Christian

Science went against the grain; it demanded a spiritual inner-directedness that withstood the whims and fancies of others.

In life, Mrs. Eddy's rigorous spiritual demands and her Christian Science doctrines had the capacity to disturb the wider culture. The *Springfield Union* captured the flavor of Mrs. Eddy's unsettling influence. "About no personage of her generation has so much and such bitter controversy raged as around the Founder and Leader of the organization and doctrines known as Christian Science." The *Concord Monitor* skated delicately around this issue by noting that whether one was an admirer of Mrs. Eddy or not, an "impartial pose toward her seems to have been very difficult to maintain." Both of these papers were ostensibly referring to Mrs. Eddy's radical idealism regarding the meaning of reality and how man could overcome disease and death. Her theology sounded strange and threatening to secular ears. Though Mrs. Eddy and her doctrines repelled some people, the papers indicate that she appealed to others, and hint that she and her Christian Science touched the core of American society in diverse, fundamental ways.

One might be hard-pressed to see much of cultural connection in the early years of the movement. From the time when she lived in her modest, nondescript home at 8 Broad Street in Lynn, Massachusetts, to her final days in her tasteful, twenty-five-room gray stone mansion in Chestnut Hill, Mrs. Eddy—as much as was humanly possible—kept her movement enveloped in the spiritual realm. This was especially true for the first decades, when she struggled to keep her fledgling movement alive. Even in its early days, Lynn reflected the disruptive changes of the nineteenth century. As she walked the streets, Mrs. Eddy easily could have brushed shoulders with Quaker and Methodist dissenters, vocal temperance advocates, and disgruntled shoe workers. Indeed, the Lynn of Mrs. Eddy's day was "notorious as a hotbed of radicalism," according to one historian.

But as Mrs. Eddy took those walks along Lynn's streets, it was as if she and many of her early followers, who came from the city's shoe factories, had spiritual blinders on. They simply did not become involved in the social discontents of the day, and often when they did acknowledge them in *The Christian Science Journal,* they were quickly subsumed under the teachings and meaning of Christian Science. And yet, despite Mrs. Eddy's focus on spiritual matters, the world and its diversity did filter into her movement. A full exploration of this diversity is beyond the scope of this book. The demographic data for any future study of her students would be exceptionally difficult to accumulate; the Mother Church did not keep these kinds of records. Nevertheless, we can make hypotheses based upon some fragmentary, impressionistic evidence about Mrs. Eddy's appeal to the wider culture.

In the late 1890s, Alfred Farlow was asked where Christian Science students came from, and he replied that there was no single type. They came from all kinds of

churches; some did not even have an official church affiliation, and they stood on all rungs of the social ladder. There were hints of this diversity even in the early days of the movement, although most of Mrs. Eddy's students clustered around the lower end of the social scale. Mrs. Eddy attracted a number of men and women in their mid- to late twenties from Lynn's shoe factories. Until he devoted himself to the practice of Christian Science, Samuel Bancroft was a worker in a shoe factory. So were Richard Kennedy and Miss Dorcas Rawson, a member of one of Mrs. Eddy's first classes and one of the eight defectors in 1881. Daniel Spofford worked in a shoe trade in Tennessee, while his wife was a Christian Science practitioner. Others among Mrs. Eddy's early followers came from equally modest beginnings. Delia Manley grew up in Tiverton, Rhode Island; her father was a farmer and made shoes during the winter. Walter Watson came out of the New Hampshire Hills as a house painter, and his wife worked in a glove factory.

Stephen Gottschalk, a close student of Christian Science, noted that until the early 1880s a "significant proportion" of Mrs. Eddy's students came from spiritualism or had some spiritualism in their backgrounds. Indeed, many of Mrs. Eddy's students came from a patchwork quilt of religious backgrounds. Dorcas Rawson, for example, was a "Holiness Methodist," while Laura C. Nourse was raised in a more regular Methodist church. Wallace Wright was a Universalist; so was Mary Godfrey Parker, whose mother was an "ardent Universalist," and her husband was of a similar persuasion. Delia Manley was a churchgoing Baptist; Walter Watson was raised by "good, staunch, New England parents of the Unitarian faith." In looking over her 1880s class, Jennie Sawyer found it remarkable that people representing so many different denominations could find a consensus on such a critical issue as "one's Christian faith."

It is understandable that other Protestants might find Christian Science attractive in the late nineteenth and early twentieth centuries. While Mrs. Eddy's Christian Science may have been cut out of new cloth, in her public writings, and sometimes in her interviews, she wove the threads of the Puritan past into the fabric of her appeal. In *No and Yes,* for example, Mrs. Eddy linked herself and her Christian Science to many of America's cherished values. Her ancestors, she proudly noted, were among the first to settle in New Hampshire, where they raised "the Puritan standard of undefiled religion. As dutiful descendants of Puritans, let us lift their standard higher, rejoicing as Paul did, that we are *free born.*"

On many occasions in *Science and Health* Mrs. Eddy spelled out the duty and destiny of her movement. In one instance, her words harked back to John Winthrop's charge to his small band of Puritan followers. In the current age, Christian Scientists occupied the same position that the disciples did when Jesus confirmed the uniqueness of their mission. They were special, and to convey this Mrs. Eddy repeated the biblical phrase that has come to mean so much to America's special mission:

"Ye are the light of the world. A city that is set on a hill cannot be hid." Then, much like Winthrop, Mrs. Eddy urged her students to be fully dedicated to their calling so that "this light be not hid, but radiate and glow into noontide glory."

Mrs. Eddy was also forging stronger links between her Christian Science and other Protestant traditions in America. As far back as the Genesis manuscript she hinted at this when she equated the importance of her discovery to Robert Fulton's. In an 1893 article in *The Christian Science Journal,* her movement was linked to two of America's most resourceful and innovative men, Benjamin Franklin and Thomas Edison. Until Franklin, the article noted, there was no real knowledge of electricity, and until Edison no one realized its potential. The analogy was self-evident: Mrs. Eddy was just as innovative in her spiritual work.

In another article in the *Journal,* not only were Mrs. Eddy's Protestant roots stressed—she was a New England girl raised by "God-fearing parents"—but it was also emphasized that her parents were middle-class. And Mrs. Eddy tried to convince her readers that Christian Science's spiritual rigor was not out of step with the postmillennial secularism in American society after the Civil War. The current age appeared to be moving toward perfectibility on a number of cultural levels, Mrs. Eddy noted in an 1884 article. Why, then, she questioned, should religion not also strive for "a more perfect and practical Christianity?"

By invoking the Puritan past, Mrs. Eddy appealed to those who wished to cling to cherished values and ideals in a rapidly changing America. The intellectual historian Michael Kammen has recently shown that the Puritan past served late-Victorian Americans in a number of ways. At one end of the spectrum, a number of nineteenth-century Americans used it to attack religious bigotry and intolerance, while in the bulging middle were those who saw the Puritan past as "a mixed blessing." "Moving from the center of the spectrum to the end," writes Kammen, "there remained a considerable number of vocal and perfectly sensible individuals who between 1880 and 1910 not only retained an extremely positive view of the Puritans but felt nostalgia for the qualities of intense faith, imagination, and courage that seemed to be in short supply in late Victorian America."

Mrs. Eddy could be counted among those "perfectly sensible individuals" described by Kammen. For her the Puritans came to represent not only a step back into an ideal past, but also a step forward into the future. Evolutionary ideas and a secular optimism helped to reshape the image of the Puritans; increasingly they were seen as having cut the umbilical cord to England. Having thus broken from a confining, immoral past, they were free to invent their own tradition. In the 1884 article, Mrs. Eddy tapped into this radical tradition; thus, her link to the Puritans is much more complicated than it first looks. She was, in effect, allowing people to acknowledge their roots and to break from them, to be conservative and radical simultaneously.

Puritan roots, Benjamin Franklin, science and manufacturing, perfectibility; no wonder Christian Science began to appeal to more and more middle-class people as the nineteenth century gave way to the twentieth. Businessmen, clergymen, doctors, lawyers, clerks sought out Christian Science. (And it is no wonder that by the turn of the century this connection to basic American values appealed to a number of ethnic minorities such as European Jews who converted to Christian Science as a way of assimilating into American society.) Though Christian Science made headway in small Midwestern towns in this same period, and though Alfred Farlow was probably right in contending that Christian Science drew from all ranks of society, by the late nineteenth century the tone, the attitude, and the language in many of the articles in *The Christian Science Journal* and the *Christian Science Weekly* seemed slanted to a middle-class audience's hopes and fears about life in an urban, increasingly bureaucratized, corporate America.

The historian George Cotkin has characterized the intellectuals of the late nineteenth century as "reluctant modernists." This is an apt phrase, for it could easily apply to a large segment of middle-class men and women. In the case of men, for example, though they made their accommodations to the emerging bureaucratized world of corporate America, and seemed to enjoy the growing leisure time and the cornucopia offered by the emerging consumer culture, this acceptance of the new did not come without serious strain and hesitancy. Christian Science addressed its message to those middle-class men who were highly sensitive to these kinds of tensions.

William Rathvon, a prominent Christian Scientist in Mrs. Eddy's last years, wrote a 1903 article extolling the benefits of the religion, and his language reflected this strong middle-class bent. Nineteenth-century Victorians were obsessed with the meaning of character, as if somehow a person's inner qualities would buttress him or her against the onslaughts of modern life. Christian Science, said Rathvon, stood for a special kind of power and permanence. The mental attitude of every person should be "active, alert, and assiduous." The particular kind of fitness in Christian Science was not limited to any one kind of culture or any one kind of person; it applied to all men in all cultures. Though Christian Science "declares daily dividends, its capital is never impaired." By infusing Christian Science thought into daily business activities, one would begin to guarantee higher returns "than any investment that lies within the scope of our modern man of affairs."

Rathvon was comfortable employing the secular idioms of his day; in this essay he even sounded a bit like William James, who, in his quest for security in a pluralistic world, often combined metaphors from the sacred and the profane. Christian Science, however, was never sanguine about the individual's place in the ever-changing secular world. Psychologically, life was not simple for many well-educated middle-class Americans during the late nineteenth and early twentieth centuries. Many of them were "battling a dread of unreality." These feelings, according to T. J. Jackson Lears, "stemmed from urbanization and technological development; from the rise of an increasingly interdependent market economy; and from the secularization of liberal Protestantism among its educated and affluent devotees."

For many in an emerging consumer culture it felt as if the core meaning of self had been lost. Now the self was nothing more than a mask, a false self a person constructed to "sell" others. As this sense of alienation grew at the end of the nineteenth century and into the next, and as it became increasingly possible to define the self through the desire and enjoyment of things, many middle-class Americans increasingly yearned to rediscover "the real thing" in virtually all aspects of their lives. As Miles Orvell has recently noted:

> Again and again, around the turn of the century, as the saturation of *things* reached the limit of containing space, the social and spiritual grace afforded by material objects was put to the question. And Nietzsche's observation on the European bourgeoisie would apply to America as well: "Men of the seventies and eighties . . . were filled with a devouring hunger for reality, but they had the misfortune to confuse this with matter—which is but the hollow and deceptive wrapping of it. Thus they lived perpetually in a wretched, padded, puffed-out world of cotton-wool, cardboard, and tissue-paper."

Mrs. Eddy never confused matter with reality; in Christian Science, the spiritual core of the self was the "real thing." Some Christian Scientists were lured down the path of material comfort, but Mrs. Eddy always accepted the things of the real world for what they were: illusions, sometimes destructive ones. She held out a warning, for example, that imperialism, monopoly, and a decline in religion posed real threats to the moral fiber of the nation. Yet she also held out a hope for the future if people would only accept "a true Science and Christianity."

A number of Christian Science writers did not sugar-coat their concern that America was deeply divided between the haves and the have-nots. For self-satisfied Americans basking in the sunlight of American prosperity, one writer saw dark clouds gathering, harbingers of a potentially destructive storm that would "threaten our civil institutions, producing universal distrust among all classes." The massive corporations had "grown wealthy and arrogant," and in their rapid growth they had lost sight of the larger community and the meaning of justice. Officeholders were no better. They violated the public trust, lining their own pockets at the public's expense. No matter where one looked, civil and religious institutions had compromised their principles.

What to do about these social ills? By the turn of the century, Americans were offered a variety of social plans

that promised a more efficient, equitable world, whether it was from the blueprint of a progressive or a socialist. According to one Christian Scientist writer, socialism, because it aimed at the betterment of all, was an improvement over the "selfish individualism" of capitalism, but like all other "isms" it had a fatal flaw: it mistook institutions and social conditions as "the real and ultimate conditions of earthly existence." From this erroneous assumption emerged a faulty conclusion: if these institutions could be changed and improved, then mankind could attain an earthly paradise. From the Christian Science perspective, this was an illusion.

To achieve true social harmony one had to penetrate beneath the surface of things to get in touch with the spiritual reality. The recognition that what most people took to be real and concrete was actually erroneous belief and illusion is what separated Christian Science reform from "ordinary social reforms." The socialist erred when he or she believed "all discord to be material inequality and individualism." Other reformers were equally mistaken when they considered "competition and private, unchecked capitalism" the major cause of social disharmony.

Christian Science plainly revealed that these causes were not really causes after all; they were effects "of a false sense of Life as material, a false sense of Mind as plural, a false sense of substance as matter, a false sense of existence as temporal." It stood to reason, therefore, that "an entire readjustment of the constituent relations of man to man must be reached and reorganized before we can hope for ultimate harmony." But this could only be accomplished when man understood true spiritual individuality and a true relationship to God. With these understandings, a person could then adjust his or her life to the spiritual reality rather than the material illusion. In *Science and Health,* Mrs. Eddy held out the hope that Christian Science was slowly, inch by inch, leading the way toward a morally reformed society:

> I have never supposed this century would witness the full fruitage of Christian Science, or that sin, disease, and death would not continue for centuries to come; but this I do aver, that, as a result of Christian Science, ethics and temperance have received an impulse, health has been restored, and longevity increased. If such are the present fruits, what may not the harvest be, when this Science is more generally understood?

Christian Science's spiritual radicalism was clothed in a gray flannel suit; it promised a transvaluation, but it would not lead an assault on America's corporate walls. Change, when it came, would be evolutionary, not revolutionary. This was a comforting message to an anxious, if not increasingly neurasthenic, middle class that craved order and stability and yearned for verities. While Christian Science produced testimony after testimony confirming its healings of broken bones and major illnesses from tuberculosis to cancer, its healings were also attractive to people suffering from psychosomatic illnesses like neurasthenia. In the late-Victorian era this was a catchall psychological disorder whose long list of symptoms ranged from depression, to male hysteria, to stress, to chronic fatigue. Though neurasthenia crossed class and gender lines, it seemed to find a welcome home among middle- and upper-middle-class men—the very people supposedly adapting the best and making the most out of a rapidly changing social world.

Ironically, as these men exerted themselves to climb economic and social ladders, they suffered a paralysis of will; seemingly the faster they scrambled to get to the top, the further they fell away from old-fashioned values and from a sense of who and what they were. Indeed, it seemed as though they had lost contact with any kind of emotional center, as though they had become detached from "real things." When Christian Science turned its penetrating look into the workplace of middle-class America, it identified the secularization process as a major source of the middle class's ills. Most businessmen kept their Christian ideals separated from their work, content to devote one hour on Sundays to God and to spiritual concerns.

This was an artificial separation that produced a deep alienation. Indeed, Christian Science made it eminently clear that "a business based on Principle" and governed by Christian values was impervious to the wild fluctuations in the marketplace, where today's success was tomorrow's failure. A host of middle-class professionals—"merchants, bankers, traveling salesmen, railroad officials, and busy people in all aspects of industry"—were turning to Christian Science with spectacular results in their businesses and in their private lives, one writer tooted.

Another writer addressed his article to the rising middle-class businessman, encouraging him never to think about "danger, disaster, failure, limitation, discord, confusion," unless he wanted to have these unnerving thoughts "manifested on your body or in your business." Once a businessman fully accepted the principles of Christian Science; once every act he performed and every relationship he entered into were governed and directed by God, then the vicissitudes of business life could never make him a helpless victim.

Interestingly enough, when Mrs. Eddy died a newspaper in Spokane, Washington, listed Christian Science's spiritual help to the businessman as one of her real contributions. The typical businessman, the paper remarked, was overworked, overanxious, and overwrought. There seemed no place for religion in his practical world, which left him empty and adrift. Above all else the emotionally battered businessman needed a "mental anchorage that . . . maintains and buoys," that allowed him the freedom to move in the world while at the same time he was firmly anchored in "absolute certainty." This is what Christian Science provided.

A number of newspapers turned Mrs. Eddy's life into a reaffirmation of America's most cherished middle-class values and myths. America was the land of unlimited opportunity; like Horatio Alger, Mrs. Eddy had risen from rags to riches; she had moved from a New England saltbox to a Chestnut Hill mansion. A Milwaukee paper pointedly observed that history was full of women who had made their mark in a world dominated by men, but most of those women had to exercise their power indirectly through "their feminine charms." If it was true that behind every great man stood a woman, then it seemed as if Mrs. Eddy had stepped from the shadows and created a niche all her own.

This was quite a niche. By 1906, Mrs. Eddy's **Science and Health** had sold 400,000 copies. In the brief span from 1882 to 1890, Christian Science had grown from a paltry group of fifty to a burgeoning organization of "twenty churches, ninety societies, at least 250 practitioners, and 33 teaching centers scattered across the country." *The Christian Science Monitor* had a healthy daily circulation of 50,000. These accomplishments in corporate America did not escape the eye of the Cleveland *Plain Dealer* and the *Baltimore Sun*. In their evaluations of Mrs. Eddy's achievements they used words and phrases commonly reserved for the careers of powerful men like Andrew Carnegie, John D. Rockefeller, and Teddy Roosevelt. The Ohio paper described her as "virile and vigorous," a "natural commander," a "natural organizer" who possessed "intellectual qualities of the highest order." The *Sun* chipped in by noting that Mrs. Eddy exhibited a "fine business acumen" in managing her church; she had a "tremendous capacity for work" that was coupled to "a great executive ability and penetrating judgment."

Other newspapers, however, had difficulty accepting Mrs. Eddy as a symbol of authority and success in America. They recognized her achievements, but it was as if Mrs. Eddy had crossed gender lines and the newspapers wanted to nudge her back to her proper, feminine side. One newspaper from the West, for instance, lauded her for bringing Christian Science into the crass, materialistic world where success "was the fetish men were worshipping." Even when it praised her, however, the paper did not link her to the great male discoverers and inventors as she and *The Christian Science Journal* had, but to Joan of Arc. A Philadelphia newspaper duly noted that many women had made their marks as humanitarian reformers in a variety of fields where the moral purity of women was permitted active expression. The paper bemoaned the fact that recently Julia Ward Howe and Florence Nightingale had died. Mrs. Eddy, "the leading woman of her time, and among the greatest in history," achieved her status in religion, a field segregated from the economic and political corridors of power, and she chose not to challenge men from her bastion of strength.

As excerpts from these editorial comments reveal, outsiders found much to admire in Mrs. Eddy, but her success and authority made a number of people—especially men—nervous. We earlier saw that James Henry Wiggin gave a flattering assessment of Mrs. Eddy's power and effectiveness as a teacher. Wiggin, we recall, was the ex-Unitarian minister whom Mrs. Eddy hired to help her smooth out the rough edges of her 1886 revision of *Science and Health*. Like any demanding executive, she had high standards, knew what she wanted, and would settle for nothing less. When it came to the publication of her book, Mrs. Eddy would not tolerate shoddiness, and she could be exasperating as she fought over the meaning of a word or phrase. Still, Wiggin had a healthy respect for her—or at least that is the impression he gave in his correspondence with her.

But working with a dynamic religious leader who happened to be a woman pricked the masculine pride of this lapsed Unitarian minister. In 1889 he wrote a college friend, mocking Mrs. Eddy's theology as muddled and as "an ignorant revival of one form of gnosticism." As for Mrs. Eddy herself, well, what he really wanted to say would have to wait until he saw his friend, because it was too hot and damning to put in writing. What he did say was damaging enough. "An awfully (I use the word advisedly) smart woman, acute, shrewd, but not well read, nor in any way learned." Apparently this smart, acute, shrewd woman did not have the ability to create, for as Wiggin saw it, she had borrowed all of her ideas from Quimby. In one fell swoop, Wiggin demeaned Mrs. Eddy, her accomplishments, and her Christian Science.

By the turn of the century, when she was becoming something of a household name, Wiggin was not the only man whose gender anxieties were aroused by Mrs. Eddy, and increasingly these men treated her as an aberration. Sometimes these fears of an assertive woman were masked in wider cultural concerns; for some men Mrs. Eddy became a cultural symbol for all that ailed America. No one manipulated this multilayered symbol better than Mark Twain.

In a provocative analysis of Twain and other male writers in the nineteenth century such as Emerson, Thoreau, Melville, and Cooper, Joyce Warren argues that Twain, like the others, accepted assertive individualism and the American dream of success for men, but when it came to women in his life and fiction, he treated them as "abstract symbols of purity and selflessness." Twain, furthermore, could not conceive of a woman as an independent person. "For Twain, woman existed only as imaged by and in relation to the male self." As Warren notes in a sentence or two, Mrs. Eddy was "the ultimate example of the woman who did not fit the image." In 1899 Twain fired his first salvo at Mrs. Eddy in *Cosmopolitan,* and three years later his sardonic articles on her and Christian Science began to appear in the *North American Review*. In 1907 he wove his articles into an even nastier attack in his book *Christian Science.*

In the early twentieth century, Protestant America was bewildered by the forces that it suspected were invading it. The millions of immigrants from Southern and Eastern Europe not only brought their Catholicism along with their trunks and suitcases, but they also packed their threatening ideologies of anarchism and socialism. Once settled in their urban tenements, these Catholic ethnic groups, it was feared, would breed and overrun the WASPs of America. And for many Americans the threats did not emanate only from without. The changes in urban living and the growth of the large corporations challenged accepted beliefs about the meaning of American individualism and freedom.

Twain adeptly wedded Mrs. Eddy and Christian Science to those forces that were conspiring to undermine traditional American morality. Twain knew precisely what kind of response he would evoke when he asserted that Mrs. Eddy and her Christian Science church were no better than any other monopoly or trust. She was as power-hungry and money-hungry as any grasping business titan, and the authority of her organization constricted liberty and individualism as effectively as any trust did.

To a Protestant nation beset by fears of being smashed in a tidal wave of Catholic immigrants, Twain's symbolic linking of Mrs. Eddy to the Pope and religious authoritarianism was well calculated to stimulate anxieties and inveterate prejudices. The way Twain pictured it, Mrs. Eddy and the Pope, her Christian Science and his Catholicism, were two unnatural peas in a rotten pod. In the preceding ten or fifteen years, as Protestantism had relaxed its guard, Catholicism had slipped in and taken over the public schools, contaminating America's youth and its future. Christian Science was just as invasive a threat as Catholicism. The Scientists, who looked like your everyday Protestants, were already here; they had already invaded the community. "There are families of Christian Scientists in every community in America," Twain warned, "and each family is a factory; each family turns out a Christian Science product at the customary intervals, and contributes to the Cause. . . . Each family is an agency for the Cause, and makes converts among the neighbors, and starts some more factories."

Guiding this far-flung empire, this monster with its tentacles reaching into every American community, was the authoritarian Mrs. Eddy. Like the Pope, she did not run a democratic organization. To the contrary, she, too, claimed infallibility; she, too, governed with an iron hand. If one looked closely one could see that in her tight-fisted feminine hand she held more power than the Pope. "A marvellous woman; with a hunger for power such as has never been seen in the world before," wrote Twain. He pounded away at Mrs. Eddy's insatiable need for power and dominance:

> No thing, little or big, that contains any seed or suggestion of power escapes her avaricious eye; and when once she gets that eye on it, her remorseless grip follows. There isn't a Christian Scientist who isn't ecclesiastically as much her property as if she had bought him and paid for him, and copyrighted him and got a charter. She cannot be satisfied when she has handcuffed a

member, and put a leg-chain and ball on him and plugged his ears and removed his thinker, she goes on wrapping needless chains round and round him, just as a spider would. For she trusts no one, believes in no one's honesty, judges every one by herself.

She is not merely an autocratic leader; she has become a primitive, terrifying creature. And when she was not enslaving her followers this way, her powerful grip was castrating them.

Twain was not the only man to use primitive imagery to convey vividly her threat to the stability of the social world. As Mrs. Eddy went about God's business and her movement grew, she began to unnerve men in the healing professions, particularly the doctors and the clergymen of the conservative Protestant denominations. In a recent article, Jean A. McDonald waded through the periodicals and books of the period and uncovered the primitive fantasies and exaggerated fears that Mrs. Eddy's success stirred in some doctors and ministers. Feeling threatened by the appearance of a strong woman on the public stage, they transmogrified Mrs. Eddy into a witch, a spider, a worm, and an anaconda. As the giant spider, she lured unsuspecting souls into her web in order to "devour" them, while as the giant snake she "coiled herself around the Christian system, breaking all the doctrinal bones of Christianity," and then "slimed it over" so that she could swallow it easily. Like the witch, Mrs. Eddy could change her form, and in one writer's imagination she had taken the "slimy, repulsive worm" of her teachings and transformed them into a beautifully seductive butterfly that would entrap innocent, simple souls.

To one minister she was "the modern witch of Concord," brewing God-knew-what in her cauldron. Another distressed minister envisioned Mrs. Eddy as a seductress enticing young people with "the sweet cup of her sorcery." Moreover, if Mrs. Eddy denied the literal truth of the Adam and Eve story, as she wrote in *Science and Health,* then she was like Satan's serpent in the garden. Her beguiling interpretations could not hide the fact that in her words there "lurks always the face of that Evil One who can hiss through a serpent, sin through a woman, shine in an angel, be a harlequin in logic, and a devil behind it all." For another anxious clergyman, Mrs. Eddy was Satan disguised as a woman; she was "the woman who introduced the corrupting leaven into the pure meal in the Gospel and leavened the whole lump." How could any man or woman digest what Mrs. Eddy had concocted?

Doctors were not much kinder to Mrs. Eddy. As was to be expected, they used their science to attack hers. Hysteria was one of their old standbys, but sometimes they could be more inventive: "neurotic," "psychotic," "paranoid," and "manic" were some of the terms they used to label and categorize her. No matter which label of pathology one chose to use, Mrs. Eddy clearly had a degenerate mind that employed "morbid symbolism."

These male professionals saw Mrs. Eddy as abnormal. She had surrendered her femininity when she became a strong, competent leader—in short, when she became a man. Mrs. Eddy was not blind to the gender issues her leadership provoked. She knew the risks of being an outspoken woman in late-Victorian America; she knew that for her Christian Science organization to gain a foothold in American culture, she would have to accept some of its expectations regarding gender roles.

An 1895 article in *The Christian Science Journal* again linked Mrs. Eddy to the basic values and ideals of American culture. From her Puritan past she inherited the innate "love of freedom" that was prominent in all she did. The article also praised Mrs. Eddy's work for what it meant for women. Within Christian Science she had opened to women "the two noblest of all avocations, philanthropy and medicine." Her work had "placed women by the side of men in the pulpit." In *No and Yes* Mrs. Eddy championed the role of women as spiritual reformers. Let no one say in Boston, she declared, that a woman had no rights that man had to respect. Natural law and religion both established woman's inalienable right to be educated and to hold important governmental jobs. These rights, moreover, were ably supported by the best people of both genders. As she drew this essay to a close, Mrs. Eddy foresaw a religious change coming to America; she knew that both Christian Science and women would be at the forefront as America began to fulfill its spiritual destiny. America, yearning for health and spiritual rebirth, must accept Christ, whose life and teachings were imparted by Christian Science. In its march toward its destiny, America should not relegate women to the rear. And in a jab at traditional ministers, she said in words that still have a ring of truth today: "Theologians descant pleasantly upon free moral agency; but they should begin by admitting individual rights."

Clearly representative of Mrs. Eddy's thinking about gender roles were her notes **"Man and Woman,"** which she wrote in December 1900 and which Calvin Frye transcribed about five years after her death. She acknowledged that her organization seemed to favor men in positions of influence and power. There was, for example, only one woman compared to three men on the Board of Education. The Board of Trustees, the Board of Directors of the Mother Church, and the Publication Committee were all male. Out of thirteen members on the Board of Lectureship, only two were women.

To some this may have looked hypocritical. After all, this was a church headed by a woman, a church whose healing practitioners were predominantly female. Why did the men in the church—especially this church—control virtually all the positions of influence and power? From Mrs. Eddy's perspective, there was no real inconsistency or hypocrisy. In terms of gender, God was feminine, masculine, even neuter. God was everything; He was the Mother and Father of the entire universe. As such, man, created in His image, reflected both of His qualities, not simply one or the other. It was this unity that Christian Science aspired to recognize in both men and women.

Although the direction that Mrs. Eddy's argument took next has a remarkably modern ring, we must be careful not to read too much of the present into it. She clearly had her own late-Victorian culture in mind when she said that if at any period of history the reflection of God's masculine side seemed ascendant and more dominant than His feminine side, then it was because human perception and understanding had not fully grasped the true meaning of God's dual nature.

One could not deny that men had predominated in positions of power and influence in history, but history was temporal. "The divine data," on the other hand, was spiritual and infinite. It stood to reason, therefore, that men should not complain if in some future period the balance of power shifted to women. Society would then have to recognize that God's feminine nature had come to the forefront. Mrs. Eddy felt that in the eyes of God men and women were equal. In the divine order, man and woman began "in One and as one." There was no artificial sexual division to mar this unity and harmony. Unfortunately, in the world of material beliefs this inherent unity of God was sundered, split into two artificial halves instead of a seamless whole. However, this did not mean that she capitulated to convention regarding gender issues and role relationships. From the day she fell on the ice to the day she died, Mrs. Eddy saw herself and her movement not in terms of gender, but in spiritual terms: they were all reflections of God. From the early days of the Genesis manuscript, through the 1881 revision of *Science and Health,* in which she employed feminine pronouns in referring to God, to her notes on **"Man and Woman,"** Mrs. Eddy wrestled with the issues of gender and the gap between man's personal sense and spiritual reality. It would have taken a Solomon to avoid the psychosocial implications of the Bible's account of Adam and Eve and the secondary status of women. It was also impossible to use gender pronouns and nouns in a spiritual sense without people assuming a social-psychological meaning and thus missing the heart of her message.

Most of the full-time practitioners in Christian Science were women. According to one historian they outnumbered men "five to one by the 1890s and eight to one by the early 1970s." In the late 1880s, a *Chicago Times* reporter was sent to cover a Christian Science meeting. He noted the preponderance of women in the audience and was not too far off the mark when he wrote, "Grammatically viewed, Christian Science is a noun in the feminine gender."

It is clear that no matter how imperfect Mrs. Eddy might have been in reconciling the gender issue (Mary Collson, for one, found that Christian Science fell short of the feminist expectations she carried into the movement), she provided an arena in which women could demonstrate intellectual, organizational, and publicity skills, a sphere of power in which they could demonstrate moral superiority, a sphere prepared by the culture of domesticity but outside the home on a public scale.

The resistance to Mrs. Eddy's leadership on the grounds of gender was confronted in an article in *The Christian Science Journal* in the spring of 1899. The article hailed Mrs. Eddy as a forceful, active leader whose long years of service had earned her the respect of her followers, much like "a commander whom every private soldier loves and honors." Of course, Mother Eddy was a woman, "and so too is your mother." Was it not obvious that in charitable work and in religion the brunt of the work was borne by women? Was it not also true that "in spiritual perception and intuitive power" women were at least the equal of men?

This was an ingenious argument, for the author placated fears of Mrs. Eddy's strong leadership by claiming that she had not breached the sphere of domesticity; she was merely extending it into the outside world, and, after all, who could deny that a moral woman's place was in religion? But this justification of Mrs. Eddy was also a bit disingenuous, because Mrs. Eddy was being more than a good girl who knew her proper place. She was not merely enlarging a separate sphere for women; other women had been doing this for some time. In terms of gender, she went a long way toward creating interlocking circles rather than separate spheres for the men and women in Christian Science. Women, like men, could exercise a dependent autonomy—as paradoxical as that might sound—within the world shaped by Mrs. Eddy's religious ideology.

It was this kind of feminism and autonomy that Mary Collson measured against the kind she had known at Hull House, and she found it wanting. But it was this kind that allowed Caroline Noyes and Edward Kimball to work side by side despite their disagreements (although Mary Collson and Alfred Farlow could not). As one Christian Science writer put it, "Through the understanding of Christian Science men and women, by one and the same method, can reform the sinner and heal the sick." Throughout the world Mrs. Eddy had "placed woman by the side of man in the pulpit as co-worker and co-equal."

From these pieces of impressionistic evidence, one can also see that Mrs. Eddy provided an arena for men who were looking for nurturing consolation but who for cultural reasons could not find it in Catholicism (here the Mother Mary connection is striking). We recall that Alfred Farlow discovered Christian Science to be a fertile ground for his skills and competence, but he also sought something more than autonomy. As he once put it, "Indeed, we seek [Mrs. Eddy's] advice as a child would seek the advice of its mother, and because of her peculiar relationship to us in this work, we have learned to call her 'Mother.'"

Yet gender stereotypes simply are not adequate to convey the reality of what Mrs. Eddy provided men and women in Christian Science. One crucial aspect of what she did through her connections to a Puritan past and Protestant values was to synthesize Protestant and Catholic images. She legitimated for Protestants the idea of a nurturant-maternal-consoling figure in terms that they could live with and in terms she preferred, as an ideal figure, a vessel for God's intentions, a denial of corporeality, which is consistent with the kind of disciplined rationalization they were learning. As a woman she could not have had such an appeal, especially for men in the nineteenth century, but as an idealized, spiritual figure she could.

In many respects Mrs. Eddy hit the right note at the right time; she synthesized "science" and nurturance, and she contained the anxiety by taking the process out of the body. She emphasized what many wanted to believe anyway: if they were able to couple the will, belief, and discipline to the true spiritual reality, then they could purge from their spirit the kinds of strivings and feelings the capitalist society was imposing. In one of its appeals, at least, Christian Science was a Protestant-capitalist version of nurturance, but precisely for whom will have to await a demographic study, if the data exists. For now, however, we can say that Mrs. Eddy and Christian Science were multivocal symbols. She succeeded in part because of the strength of her religious truth and because she provided an opportunity for different kinds of people. Putting the issue of Christian Science's radical idealism to one side, one can see that her success and the movement's were limited, at the same time, because of their maternal-nurturant-female quality.

Mrs. Eddy's followers, of course, were not swept up in these sociological abstractions; they responded to her in a more immediate, heartfelt way, which was poignantly demonstrated at her funeral. While most of her followers accepted her passing with a sadness moderated by restraint, John Salchow, her "Johnnie," more openly expressed a deep sense of loss. Just as her casket was being placed in the vault at Mount Auburn Cemetery and the door was being closed, Salchow looked at his watch, which read two o'clock. This was the exact time at which Mrs. Eddy used to take her daily drive, and this association had a profound effect upon the grief-stricken Salchow. The emotional pain was too much for him, and he had a brief out-of-body experience. To him it suddenly seemed as if he had become detached from reality. He then felt as if he were "suspended far above the earth," completely unaware of the other mourners. He had a single desire; he wanted to be with his beloved Mother. "I began to separate from myself," he wrote, "rising at an angle of about forty-five degrees and seemed to become two distinct persons, both dressed alike." When he had arisen about a foot or more from what appeared to be his other self, another Christian Science student, sensing his distress, approached him and, gently laying her hand on him, said, "John, she loved you." These comforting words brought Salchow down to earth and slowly he "was again one person." In an exaggerated way, he was expressing what all of the mourners—these children of Christian Science—felt at the loss of their Mother. She

had guided them, and especially in "Johnnie's" case, shown them a great deal of love. Now she was gone. Yet as Salchow and the others would rediscover in the days ahead, she still lived through her words: *Science and Health with Key to the Scriptures,* along with her other writings, would continue to guide man into the path of spiritual reality.

FURTHER READING

Biography

Milmine, Georgine. *The Life of Mary Baker G. Eddy and the History of Christian Science.* Grand Rapids, MI: Baker Book House, 1971, 495 p.
    First major exposé of Eddy, based on series of articles in *McClure's;* originally published in 1909.

Peel, Robert. *Mary Baker Eddy: The Years of Discovery.* New York: Holt, Rinehart, and Winston, 1966, 372 p.

_____. *Mary Baker Eddy: The Years of Trial.* New York: Holt, Rinehart, and Winston, 1971, 391 p.

_____. *Mary Baker Eddy: The Years of Authority.* New York: Holt, Rinehart, and Winston, 1977, 528 p.
    Three-part biography written by a member of the Mother Church's Committee on Publications.

Silberger, Julius, Jr. *Mary Baker Eddy: An Interpretive Biography of the Founder of Christian Science.* Boston: Little, Brown, 1980, 274 p.
    Psychologically oriented study of Eddy.

Smith, Louise A. *Mary Baker Eddy: Discoverer and Founder of Christian Science.* Boston: The Christian Science Publishing Society, 1991, 142 p.
    Part of a series of biographical works about Eddy published by the church.

Criticism

Gardner, Martin. *The Healing Revelations of Mary Baker Eddy: The Rise and Fall of Christian Science.* Buffalo, NY: Prometheus Books, 1993, 255 p.
    Skeptical analysis of Eddy's life and doctrines.

Johnsen, Thomas C. "Historical Consensus and Christian Science: The Career of a Manuscript Controversy." *The New England Quarterly* 53, No. 1 (March 1980): 3-22.
    Case history of a forged document that was used to falsely accuse Eddy of plagiarism.

Knapp, Bliss. *The Destiny of the Mother Church.* Boston: The Christian Science Publishing Society, 1947, 306 p.
    Discussion of the development of the church by one of Eddy's protégés.

Knee, Stuart E. *Christian Science in the Age of Mary Baker Eddy*. Westport, CT: Greenwood Press, 1994, 158 p.
　　Analyzes the rise of Christian Science as an American cultural phenomenon.

Lasagna, Louis. "The Professional Layman." In *The Doctors' Dilemmas*, pp. 64-80. Freeport, NY: Books for Libraries Press, 1962.
　　Derisive account of Eddy's career and the possible health benefits of Christian Science.

Morris, Lloyd. "The Mysticism of the Middle Classes." In *Postscript to Yesterday: America: The Last Fifty Years*, pp. 422-43.
　　Focuses on Eddy's declining years and her attempts to defend herself and Christian Science against their detractors.

Simmons, Thomas. *The Unseen Shore: Memories of a Christian Science Childhood*. Boston: Beacon Press, 1991, 173 p.
　　Traumatic experiences of a former Christian Scientist.

Twain, Mark. *Christian Science*. Buffalo, NY: Prometheus Books, 1986, 196 p.
　　Humorous, highly critical dissection of Eddy and Christian Science, first published in 1907.

Untermeyer, Louis. "Mary Baker Eddy." In *Makers of the Modern World: The Lives of Ninety-Two Writers, Artists, Scientists, Statesmen, Inventors, Philosophers, Composers, and Other Creators Who Formed the Pattern of Our Century*, pp. 73-81. New York: Simon and Schuster, 1955.
　　Biographical sketch of Eddy, portraying her as a flawed, shrewd individual.

Additional coverage of Eddy's life and career may be found in the following sources published by Gale Research: *Contemporary Authors*, Vol. 113

G. I. Gurdjieff

1877-1949

(Full name Georgei Ivanovich Gurdjieff) Russian philosopher and occultist.

INTRODUCTION

Eclectically educated, widely traveled, and uninterested in perpetuating established forms of religious and mystic experience, Gurdjieff emerged as one of the most colorful and prominent figures in the occult explosion at the turn of the twentieth century. Although he published only one book during his lifetime, his hermetic communes attracted international attention. His many disciples, most notably fellow Russian Pyotr Demianovich Ouspensky, circulated his writings during his lifetime and saw to their publication and propagation after his death.

Biographical Information

Gurdjieff's birth-date, as with many other details of his early life, is a matter of debate. Most sources conclude that, as Gurdjieff once said, he was born in 1877, although his students and biographers variously date his birth as much as eleven years earlier. The site of his birth, however, is known: Alexandropol, now Leninakan, located in southwest Russia, near the Turkish-Armenian border. His family was of Greek origin. Initially, his father had been a prosperous cattle rancher, until plague wiped out his herds. Financially ruined, he changed trades and became a carpenter, moving his family to the nearby citadel city of Kars. Gurdjieff's father was also an "ashokh," or bard, who kept the oral tradition of the region alive in his memory, performing songs and traditional narratives, including the entire epic of Gilgamesh, on Sundays and holidays. Gurdjieff was educated first at a Greek school in Kars, and then at the local Russian municipal school, supplementing his education with tutorials arranged for him by the Dean of the Cathedral, who prepared him for a career in either medicine or the clergy. Then, in 1896, Gurdjieff left Kars and began a journey that would last roughly nine years. Specific information about this period of Gurdjieff's life is sketchy, and his travel-stories, most of which appear in his posthumously published *Meetings with Remarkable Men* (1963), are difficult or impossible to corroborate. He claims to have joined a group known as the "Seekers of Truth," and to have traveled extensively with them, visiting the Mongol cities of Tashkent, Bokhara, and Samarkand, and a number of highly obscure and exclusive Tibetan lamaseries. He also claimed to have spent long periods of time in Turkish and Central Asian Sufi monasteries. Gurdjieff returned to the Caucasus in 1905, where he set himself up as a mystic, healer, and hypnotist, and gathered a number of followers. Then, in 1912,

he bought an estate just outside Moscow, endeavoring to establish there an "Institute for the Harmonious Development of Man." He married one of the Tsarina's ladies-in-waiting, the Countess Ostrowska, that same year, and they remained together until her death in 1927. In 1915, Gurdjieff met Pyotr Ouspensky, occultist and author of the *Tertium Organum*, in a Moscow cafe. Ouspensky was fascinated by Gurdjieff and became his chief pupil and chronicler. In 1917, during the Russian Revolution, Gurdjieff fled Moscow, going first to Essentuki, in the Caucasus, where he continued working to establish his Institute. From there, he and some of his students escaped to Tiflis, and then to Constantinople, where he carried on the work of the Institute until 1921. At that point, Gurdjieff saw fit to move his operation to Berlin for a time, and then to England. When London authorities refused him permission to set up his Institute in the England, Gurdjieff moved again, this time to a French manor, Le Prieure, in Fontainebleau. He would reside there from 1922 to 1933. Wherever the Institute went, Gurdjieff's method of spiritual instruction remained the same: students lived in spartan conditions at the compound and engaged in a regimen of demanding physical labor, Gurdjieff's occasional lectures, and the regular practice of a series of physical movements designed by Gurdjieff, with Gurdjieff providing musical accompaniment. His students gave a performance of these movements in Paris in 1923, and toured the United States the following year, attracting the attention of poet Hart Crane, among others. In addition to these methods, Gurdjieff would also try to shock students out of accustomed patterns of thought by intentionally placing them under great stress, or otherwise demanding that they behave in ways contrary to their previous character. His intention throughout was to "awaken" the sleeping spiritual self. Shortly after his return to France from the United States, Gurdjieff was seriously injured in a car crash. During his convalescence, activity at the Institute was suspended, and he dedicated his energies to writing. These writings were not generally submitted for publication, with the exception of one volume, *The Herald of Coming Good* (1933), which was the only book Gurdjieff published during his lifetime. His other writings were circulated privately among his students. However, as the Institute remained in abeyance, his following at Fountainebleau fell off, and in 1933, Gurdjieff was compelled to close it and move to Paris, where he lived the rest of his life. He continued to teach, to write, and to compose music. He weathered the Nazi occupation, making frequent visits to the United States until 1939, and, after the war, resumed his teaching as well. He died in 1949.

Major Works

The only account of Gurdjieff's life from his departure from Kars in 1896 to his reappearance in the Caucasus in 1905 is contained in his *Meetings with Remarkable Men*, which most of his students and readers concur is not entirely true, while at the same time maintaining that this in no way detracts from the value of the work. As with all of Gurdjieff's writings, it has an entirely enigmatic complexion, and therefore takes a variety of interpretations. Ouspensky and other disciples throughout the world have found that this narrative corresponds to a higher type of truth and is a more accurate picture of Gurdjieff in his essence than would be a strictly factual autobiography. Gurdjieff summed up his teachings in two other works, *All and Everything: Beelzebub's Tales to His Grandson* (1950), and *Life Is Real Only Then, When 'I Am'* (1975), both of which are characterized by Gurdjieff's challengingly opaque prose. In these volumes he stresses a distinction between being and knowledge, and the importance of balancing the two; the way that the inflexibility of personality blocks mankind from awakening spiritually, and the necessity of shocking and destabilizing that personality as a means of effecting an awakened state; and the need for self-discipline as the key to acquiring and maintaining lucidity in one's daily routine and spiritual life.

Critical Reception

As a figure of public scrutiny, Gurdjieff has elicited extreme reactions. He has been both revered as a true mystic and reviled as a fraud. Gurdjieff met and fascinated a great many prominent persons of his time, from the Russian composer Thomas de Hartmann to American avant-garde magazine publisher Margaret Anderson. Biographies and interpretive works, often written by Gurdjieff's disciples or followers of his methods, continue to appear with regularity.

PRINCIPAL WORKS

The Herald of Coming Good (nonfiction) 1933
All and Everything: Beelzebub's Tales to His Grandson (nonficiton) 1950
Meetings with Remarkable Men (nonfiction) 1963
Life Is Only Real Then, When 'I Am' (nonfiction) 1975

CRITICISM

Kenneth Walker (essay date 1951)

SOURCE: "The Greatness of Gurdjieff," in *The Saturday Book,* Vol. 10, 1951, pp. 86-91.

[*In the following essay, Walker provides an appreciation of Gurdjieff.*]

What constitutes a great man? In the past I have often asked my friends this question and none of them have ever been able to give me a satisfactory answer. It is a searching question because actually we know far less about the nature of man than about anything else. It is easy to describe the good points of a horse, but we can only define the qualities of a great man if we know the direction in which it is possible for man to evolve, and there is no agreement on this subject.

Because they have no clear ideas about it, novelists come badly to grief whenever they attempt to describe the superman or the more highly evolved human being. After James Hilton, in *Lost Horizon,* had deposited his party of Europeans at the doors of the monastery in a remote valley of the Himalayas, he was quite unable to describe the more highly evolved monks who inhabited it. All that he could say about them was that they were learned and very polite and that they contrived to live far longer than other men. Even Bernard Shaw is unable to paint a satisfactory picture of the superman. Nietzsche was more successful, but his *Thus Spake Zarathustra* has been so grossly misinterpreted and his ideals so badly misused that it would perhaps have been better if this book had never been written.

It is not altogether surprising, therefore, that my friends have never been able to tell me the hallmark of a great man. I recall a conversation with the late H. G. Wells on this subject. 'You have met a number of important people in your lifetime,' I said. 'Tell me whether amongst them you ever met a man who could be called truly great?' After a moment or two's thought he replied, 'Lenin.' On being pressed to name the qualities that rendered Lenin great he answered, 'Well, look at all he managed to do'—but this, of course, was no answer. There is a difference between *doing* and *being*, and it was with the latter alone that I was concerned. Men may be borne aloft on the forward surge of great events and may appear to be in control of them, whereas they are actually only men who happen to have been born at the right historical moment. Hitler was one of these mascots of history, and to my way of thinking Lenin, though a far greater man than Hitler, was another.

And now the Editor of *The Saturday Book* has neatly turned the tables on me. With a disarming smile—a perquisite of all successful editors—he has invited me to contribute again to his well-known annual volume, and having received my enthusiastic assent, he has sprung his mine. 'Answer your own question' he said, quietly, 'and write about "A Great Man".' I had been hoist with my own petard. But I enjoy the great advantage of having met a man whose greatness lay in what he was rather than in what he managed to achieve. I refer to the late Mr G. Gurdjieff, a man known only to a comparative few. It is he who will serve me as a model of human greatness, but as he was not well known something must first be said of his life.

He was born in 1877 in the Caucasus and was of Ionian Greek lineage. His father made his living as a carpenter but also practised the profession of bard, for at that time there still survived in Asia men who travelled from village to village reciting by heart the ancient Asiatic legends that had been handed down by word of mouth from an incredibly distant past.

These old myths and stories fascinated his young son, and when he grew older the young Gurdjieff became convinced that these old allegories were fraught with meanings which had now been lost. He came to the opinion that they were fragments of some ancient system of knowledge which had all but disappeared from the world, but which might still survive in some remote spot in Asia. The determination to search for this ancient wisdom grew in him and a few years later we find the young Gurdjieff acting as the leader of a group of like-minded companions who called themselves 'Seekers of the Truth.' He and his companions made more and more ambitious journeys into the neighbouring countries, penetrating into the lesser known regions of Persia, Afghanistan, Baluchistan, Turkestan, China, and Tibet. They talked to wandering dervishes and religious hermits, stayed in old monasteries, were admitted to ancient world brotherhoods and followed up every clue that seemed to lead them towards the object of their search. Later they were joined by older men with greater experience and better endowed with worldly goods. Gurdjieff would only talk in general terms of these difficult and often perilous journeys that he had

formerly made and he would never reveal to anyone the exact source of the knowledge which he taught. His answers suggested that it had come from various sources and had later been put together.

He brought back from his travels not only the knowledge he had long been looking for, but also some very ancient music, a number of temple dances, and a set of very complicated movements. These last-named exercises enabled those who practised them to gain greater and greater control over their bodily movements, and they took a very important place in the system of development he taught in his later years.

By 1910 'The Seekers of the Truth' had completed their work and Gurdjieff returned to Russia to teach what he had learnt; in 1915 he founded in Moscow what he called the 'Institute for the Harmonious Development of Man.' But the first World War prevented the carrying out of his plans and in 1917 he and his followers were forced to flee from Russia and to seek refuge in Constantinople. This period of Gurdjieff's life history has been fully described by Ouspensky in his recently published book, *A Search for the Miraculous.* In 1921 Gurdjieff purchased a chateau at Fontainebleau and opened there the institute which he had formerly planned to develop in Moscow. The principle on which everything was based was that the further evolution of man could only be brought about by man's own individual efforts. He could no longer rely on Nature to give him all that at present he lacked, namely, inner unity, a permanent controlling self, and a higher level of consciousness. These could never be developed mechanically but must be evolved by man's own struggles, guided by the special knowledge which Gurdjieff believed himself to possess. But before these new qualities could be evolved in man much that was wrong in his thinking and in his mode of living must first be destroyed. Gurdjieff taught that man is controlled by his 'ego,' or 'personality,' that is to say, by his many and often conflicting desires, and by his imagination about himself.

Although his 'Institute for the Harmonious Development of Man' had been closed down for many years when I first met him, Gurdjieff had numerous followers, not only in Europe, but also in America. A constant stream of visitors arrived from all over the world in Paris for the purpose of visiting him in his small flat in the rue des Colonels Rénard. There he would entertain as many as forty guests to lunch or dinner in a dining-room which had been designed for the accommodation of a small family only. He not only entertained them but he often cooked the meals himself in a still smaller kitchen. He was a generous host, yet it was not for the sake of his excellent lunches and dinners, but to talk to him, that people made their way down the avenue Carnot towards his flat. They had been struggling to live in accordance with the principles he had taught them and they had come to Paris for further instructions and more help.

This they always received provided that Gurdjieff believed them to be sincere and felt that they were making real efforts. It was sincerity that Gurdjieff demanded above everything else; he was utterly ruthless whenever he discovered in his followers any form of pretence. He had an uncanny gift for detecting everything that was fraudulent or artificial, however carefully it was covered up. 'You may be a very clever person,' he would say, 'but you are also a very big fool. I have no time to waste on stupid and worthless people.' It was useless to attempt to deceive him or to pretend that things were different from what they were, for he could see the character of his pupils far more clearly than they could see it themselves. A visit to Gurdjieff was therefore not to be lightly undertaken, for at any moment one might have one's inner weaknesses revealed, not comfortably in a private talk, but to all the assembled company.

And what a varied company it was that sat down to a meal at his table: the widow of a world-famous tenor, a wealthy supporter from America, a sprinkling of British and French doctors, a British peer, typists from London offices, business men, lawyers and scientists, Americans, British, French, Germans, and Russians, people of many different types, of different classes, of different upbringing and education, all held together in a single group by the immense respect they shared for this wise and truly remarkable man. Although he was in the late seventies when I first knew him, he seemed to radiate force from his person, so much so that one felt that strength had been gained by coming into contact with him even when no words had been interchanged.

But it may still be asked: 'What were the qualities in him that entitle him to be used as an example of greatness?' This question can best be answered by saying that he exemplified in his own person the truth of his teaching. He taught that by the adoption of certain measures a man can become other than he has been born; he can achieve inner unity; he can become more conscious; he can develop new powers. Here in Gurdjieff one saw a man who by ceaseless struggle with the mechanical parts of his nature had brought about this change. It is true that consciousness admits of no objective measurement, but consciousness confers on its possessor both greater knowledge and more control and these results of consciousness can be seen. I have never met anyone who possessed more of that knowledge which cannot be found in books but can only come from experience than did Gurdjieff. There are men with encyclopaedic minds, so well furnished with facts that they are able to talk on almost any subject, but far from being wise, such men are often fools. They possess a mass of information, but little understanding of it, and are singularly lacking in wisdom. The knowledge of Gurdjieff was of an utterly different kind; it was knowledge that conferred on its possessor understanding and power. His ability to control himself and others was as obvious as was his knowledge. Gurdjieff never fumbled; everything he did, he did with the strictest economy of effort.

What was true of his movements seemed to be equally true of his emotions. When he displayed anger, as he not

infrequently did, the anger served some definite purpose, and when this purpose had been achieved it was immediately laid on one side. It was ended as abruptly as it has begun and the talk that had been suddenly interrupted was quietly resumed. And Gurdjieff had conquered man's two worst enemies, anxiety and fear. He appeared to be fearless.

No man can act so differently from his fellows as did Gurdjieff without arousing suspicion, and it is not surprising that he excited enmity as well as devotion. It was said by some that he was a black magician who cast a spell over his followers, so that they were quite unable to tear themselves away from him. Others stated that he gained his power over people by means of hypnotism, and yet others that he was a completely amoral, irreligious, and in every way a dangerous man. He cared far less about these accusations than his followers did and snapped his fingers at public opinion. What did it matter what people thought of him? His whole attention was concentrated on his work and on what he had planned to do ever since he had returned from the East with his system of knowledge.

Yet there is always some fire where one sees smoke and undoubtedly there was some reason for the hostility he often evoked. He was utterly ruthless in the carrying out of his mission to attack what stood in the way of human development. As has previously been said, he had to destroy before he could build and in his opinion there was much to be destroyed in modern civilization if men were ever to evolve. During the last ten years of his life he was forced, much against his personal inclinations, to make some change in the character of his activities. He had no desire for authorship, but he saw clearly that it was essential that he should leave behind him when he died some record of all that he taught.

With characteristic energy he set about this new task and wrote not one but three whole series of books. The first of these *All and Everything* has now been published. His object in writing it is clearly set out on the fly-leaf; 'To destroy, mercilessly, without any compromise whatsoever, in the mentation and feelings of the reader, the beliefs and views by centuries rooted in him about everything existing in the world.' It is not to be wondered at that a man with such an extensive programme of destruction as this, a man moreover who refused any compromise with what he regarded as being false, should have excited opposition. It was his function to disturb and to destroy complacency wherever he found it, and disturb he did, in no mean fashion. Nobody ever came into contact with him without being in some way ruffled. Sometimes the upheaval he produced was too strong even for his followers and they left him, disgruntled by what he had done to them. And judged by ordinary standards his behaviour was often callous in the extreme, as unkind as the treatment meted out by surgeons must often have seemed to their patients in pre-anaesthetic days. The explanation in both cases was the same. False ideas had to be destroyed in a man before he could develop, and few things can be more painful than the rooting out of fond illusions about oneself. Yet ruthless though he often was, I personally have never met a man who showed more clearly than did Gurdjieff a deep compassion and love for humanity. He was a mixture of devil and angel but the angel was paramount in him.

He died in the American Hospital in Paris in October 1949, and was buried in accordance with the rites of the Orthodox Greek Church. He carried on his work right up to the end, compelling his body, as he had always compelled it, to carry out his will. He was never an ascetic but lived life to its fullest, looking upon his body as his servant, and never allowing it to be his master. In teaching, he often made use of the ancient allegory of man which likened him to a carriage, horse, and driver. The body was the carriage, the emotions the horse which drew the carriage, and the mind the driver who controlled the horse. But, he said, in ordinary men it was the body and the body's desires which really took charge of everything. Only in the more fully developed man was the driver in control of his horse, and seated by his side was an entirely new figure. This was the master who gave orders where the driver was to go, and the driver understood and obeyed him. Gurdjieff was such a man as this, a man who had developed qualities which others do not possess.

Kenneth Walker (essay date 1957)

SOURCE: "Gurdjieff and Ouspensky," in *A Study of Gurdjieff's Teaching,* Jonathan Cape, 1957, pp. 11-18.

[*In the following essay, Walker recounts the development of Gurdjieff's major theories.*]

GURDJIEFF AND OUSPENSKY

It is fascinating, and at the same time rather alarming, to look back along the line of the past and to note how thin was the thread which the Fates spun and how easily it could have been broken—and if it had been broken, then one's life would, of course, have been quite different. How little I guessed that when a young Russian journalist on the night staff of a St. Petersburg newspaper made a journey to Moscow in the spring of 1915 he was initiating a sequence of events which was eventually to be of the utmost importance to me also. 'What,' I should have protested, had a clairvoyant gipsy drawn my attention to this—'what on earth have a St. Petersburg journalist's movements got to do with me, the resident surgeon to the British Hospital in Buenos Aires?' There seemed to be no connection at all between myself and any events occurring in Russia, and many things had to happen and many years had to flow past before the path of the stocky young Russian journalist with the cropped hair and the strong glasses crossed that of the Buenos Aires surgeon.

Ouspensky tells us in his book, *In Search of the Miraculous,* that during this said visit of his to Moscow in the spring of 1915 two friends, a sculptor and a musician, spoke of a small group in Moscow which was engaged in certain investigations and experiments which were difficult to describe. They worked under the direction of a Caucasian Greek and, rather against his will, he agreed to be introduced to their Caucasian teacher. The meeting took place at a small café, and Ouspensky gives the following description of his first encounter with Gurdjieff— 'I saw a man of an Oriental type, no longer young, with a black moustache and piercing eyes, who astonished me first of all because he seemed to be disguised and completely out of keeping with the place and its atmosphere. I was still full of impressions of the East. And this man with the face of an Indian raja or an Arab sheik . . . seated here in this little café . . . in a black overcoat and a velvet collar and a black bowler hat produced this strange, unexpected and almost alarming impression of a man poorly disguised, the sight of whom embarrasses you because you see he is not what he pretends to be and yet you have to speak and behave as though you did not see it.' (P. D. Ouspensky, *In Search of the Miraculous.*)

They met together several times at the same café, and Ouspensky began to realize more and more that the man to whom he was talking here in Moscow, this man who spoke incorrect Russian with a strong Caucasian accent, was possessed of the kind of knowledge for which he, Ouspensky, had recently been seeking without success in India and Ceylon. It was the beginning of a seven years close association between the two men of great importance to them both.

Then came the War and the Revolution, which brought to an end not only the old Czarist régime but also all thought and culture in Russia. In 1917 Gurdjieff and Ouspensky, with several other members of Gurdjieff's group, were refugees in Constantinople, but they were as far from being any concern of the writer of this book as they had always been. Then the thin thread of events began to draw them nearer to me. There were influential people in England who had read Ouspensky's book, *Tertium Organum,* and who, on hearing that its author was one of the many Russian refugees stranded in Constantinople, invited him to come to London.

The next significant event took place right on my doorstep at 86, Harley Street. 'We have been granted an interview with the Home Secretary in twenty minutes' time and I want you to be a member of the deputation.' It was my friend Dr. Maurice Nicoll who said this and, without giving me time to answer him, he bundled me into a waiting taxi.

'But what's it all about?' I inquired, after having been introduced to the other members of the deputation.

'About Gurdjieff. We have to get a permit for him to come to London. Ouspensky is already here, and we want Gurdjieff as well. You are to represent orthodox medicine and to say how important it is that Gurdjieff should be allowed to come here.'

Half an hour later I found myself explaining to a bored Home Secretary how essential it was to the welfare of British Medicine that Gurdjieff (who was only a name to me) should be granted permission to settle in London. But the Home Office explained next day that it had already granted so many permits to White Russian officers that it was unable to issue one to Gurdjieff.

So Ouspensky settled down in London and began holding meetings there, whilst Gurdjieff remained where he was in Paris, and eventually established in a Fontainebleau château what had for so long been only a project in his mind, the Institute for the Harmonious Development of Man.

Maurice Nicoll was responsible for the forging of the last link in the long chain of events which had started, eight years previously, with Ouspensky's fateful expedition to Moscow and his meeting with Gurdjieff. He buttonholed me one day at the corner of Weymouth Street and Harley Street and told me that Ouspensky was now holding very interesting meetings in Kensington and that he had obtained permission for me to attend. He explained that it was by private invitation only that people were allowed to come, and left me with the impression that I could consider myself very fortunate to have received an invitation. 'Wednesday next at eight o'clock in Warwick Gardens,' he concluded, and disappeared.

I have told the story of my meeting Ouspensky, of my close association with him for over thirty years and of my subsequent encounters in Paris with that still more remarkable man George Ivanovitch Gurdjieff in a previous book. All of these events, of great concern to me and of sufficient general interest to warrant their being put on record, were recounted in *Venture with Ideas,* but little was said in that book about the ideas taught by these two men, and it was the unique quality of their teaching even more than their characters which bound me to them for so many years. Ideas are not always passive, submissive things which we can lay aside when we have no further use for them, and this was particularly true of the ideas which I obtained either from Gurdjieff directly or else by way of Ouspensky. They were ideas heavily charged with energy and they soon began to work in me like some powerful ferment. Attracted to them originally on the grounds that they were unlike anything that I had previously come across, they gradually took possession of me and propelled me in a direction in which at first I had no desire to go. Unlike Ouspensky, who had deliberately abandoned his work in 1914 in order to search in the East for what he called 'Esoteric schools', I was, or believed myself to be, content with things as they were. In short, I had no need for a philosophy of life. Yet here was I being jerked out of my usual rut of living and my customary channels of thought and feeling, not so much by the impact of two powerful men—remarkable though they both were—but by the sheer weight of their teaching. All these things are explained in *Venture with Ideas.*

Gurdjieff was in Paris and Ouspensky in London, so it was from the latter that I learnt the system of knowledge which Gurdjieff had brought back to Russia from his years of wandering in the East. And it was perhaps as well that the Fates who were responsible for all that was now happening to me arranged it thus. Gurdjieff used strong medicine, and I doubt whether I should have stomached his very drastic treatment had I met him at the beginning. I owe a great deal to Ouspensky for all he did for me during those earlier years, and I am deeply grateful to him for his patient and clear-headed interpretation of Gurdjieff's teaching. He had a much better command of English than had Gurdjieff and a methodical and tidy mind which imposed order on the latter's less systematized method of teaching. His patience was remarkable. From 1917 onwards he sought clearer and yet clearer formulations for the ideas he had received from Gurdjieff, with the intention, possibly—for he never spoke with certainty about this—of publishing them in the form of a book after the latter's death. But he died before his teacher, and it was upon Gurdjieff that the responsibility then lay of deciding whether or not Ouspensky's much-revised typescript should be sent to a publisher. Gurdjieff had a Russian rendering of it read to him, declared it to be an accurate account of his own teaching and gave instructions that it should be published forthwith.

Gurdjieff and Ouspensky are now dead and, if I am ever to put on printed record what I learnt from them, it must be now. I have hesitated for a very long time before embarking on this task, and for a great many reasons. An important one was that I was well aware of the difficulty of putting into a book a teaching so individual as that of Gurdjieff, a teaching which, to be effective, cannot be read, but must be imparted to individuals by word of mouth. Gurdjieff believed that men and women are divisible into a comparatively small number of types, and that what is applicable to one type is not necessarily applicable to another. This being so, instruction has to be given individually, and it is obvious that this cannot be done in a book. I also foresaw the difficulty of presenting ideas, first in the raw as I received them from Ouspensky, and of then showing the gradual deepening of my understanding of them as the years passed. This slow growth of understanding could only be suggested in a book by telescoping time, and the result of this might be confusing, so that the reader would often be left in doubt whether I was describing ideas as I had first received them from Ouspensky, or as I understood them much later on. This method of presentation might also require that I should sometimes have to put into Ouspensky's mouth words which he had never uttered, even although they were completely in keeping with his teaching. All this made it clear to me that I should encounter many difficulties in writing about Gurdjieff's ideas.

Gurdjieff once said: 'I have very good leather to sell to those who want to make shoes out of it', and when these words came into my mind they immediately gave me the right plan for the book. No better description than this could be given of Gurdjieff's role as a teacher. He was a man who had ideas of an extraordinarily high quality to sell to those who required ideas of this kind. Moreover, he had used the word 'sell' deliberately because he always maintained that men never appreciated anything which they had not paid for; the payment need not necessarily be in terms of money, but something had to have been sacrificed if the leather they had acquired was to be properly appreciated. Another important point he made in this short sentence of his was that the leather was for those who intended to put it to a practical use and not for dilettantes or exhibitionists who required it merely for display. The buyer would have to make something out of the leather he had bought, and nothing could be more serviceable than a strong pair of shoes for life's difficult journey. I saw that the aim I should have to keep in view whilst writing the projected book was that of showing the reader the excellence of Gurdjieff's leather, and of then displaying the shoes I had made out of it. The workmanship and design of my new shoes could, of course, have been much better, but they have this at any rate to be said in their favour, that they are handmade and my own work.

As will later be seen, having given an account of Gurdjieff's ideas, I often compare them with kindred ideas obtained from scientific, philosophical and religious sources. These comparisons have been made because it has long been of great interest to me personally to compare and to contrast Gurdjieff's ideas with those I have come across in a somewhat varied reading during the course of the past thirty years. Many striking similarities have been discovered in this way, but what I want to emphasize here is that nowhere else can so many ideas of this nature be found welded together into such a self-consistent and coherent whole. Or it would perhaps be better to use an entirely different simile and to liken Gurdjieff's system of knowledge to a living organism, in which every part is related to and dependent on everything else.

It is because Gurdjieff's teaching possesses the qualities of coherence, integration and growth, characteristic of life, that I am attempting to bring it to the notice of other people, so far as it is possible to do this in a book. This last conditional clause is necessary, for formulation and printing squeeze out of the spoken word almost all of its vitality, as pressing deprives a flower of nearly all its beauty. The great religions have all been subjected to this devitalizing process. As taught by their great founders they were beautiful, living things, but as later set down in books and scrolls by the scribes, the Pharisees and lawyers, they become as forlorn and as desiccated as are the Thirty-Nine Articles of the Anglican Church.

Unfortunately there is no way of avoiding the devitalizing effect of books on oral teaching, and all that can be done in the present instance is to warn the reader that it is bound to happen. He must be put on his guard on another score also, to wit, on the use of the word 'system' in connection with Gurdjieff's teaching. It is a term which should have been avoided, had it not been sanctioned by long use. The reason for its being objectionable is that the term 'system' is closely linked in our minds with such qualifying adjectives as correct and incorrect,

orthodox and heterodox, and these are words to which Gurdjieff would have taken strong exception.

They are words to which another modern teacher of spiritual truths also takes exception: Krishnamurti deplores our tendency to organize and systematize wisdom and illustrates this with a parable. He recounts how one day the devil and a friend of his were out for a walk on the earth when they noticed a man suddenly bend down and pick up something from the ground. The devil's friend said: 'You had better be on your guard, for that man over there has picked up a particle of Truth.' The devil smiled and was not in the least disturbed. 'It will make no difference,' he replied; 'they will organize and systematize it. There is no cause for worry.'

The Zen Buddhist Master likens all teaching to the pointing of a finger at the moon, and his disciple is very severely reprimanded if he places emphasis on the finger instead of the object at which the finger is pointing. So also must Gurdjieff's teaching be looked upon as a finger which directs attention to certain principles and methods which, properly used, lead to certain results. All that this book can do is to give the reader a notion of some of the methods and principles Gurdjieff used. To imagine that any book could achieve more than this would obviously be absurd. Gurdjieff did not draw diagrams on a board and teach from these. His method of instruction was far less comfortable to his class than this. He carved out from us living chunks of experience and taught from these. One found one's own petty vanities and follies being used as the specimens on which Gurdjieff was able to demonstrate to his class the mechanical nature of human life. A book is but a poor substitute for such vital and direct teaching as this.

MAN'S SEVERAL MINDS

To maintain a group's interest in an organism of ideas, to bring something for discussion every week, to guide people through their private confusions, stupidities and difficulties for over a quarter of a century, was no mean achievement, and this is what Ouspensky did for his followers. And we, for the most part, gave him our staunch support. We were a motley crowd held together almost entirely by the teaching. There were also people who came and went—the floating population of the work; there were its beachcombers who wandered about on the edge of things picking up odd trifles but making no real efforts; there was the stranger who would turn up for a single meeting and then, not getting the answer he required of Ouspensky, would come no more; and there were visitors who were already encumbered with so much mental and emotional luggage in the way of immovable convictions, theories and firm beliefs that it was quite impossible for them to find room for anything new. There were all these and many other types of people who came to a few of Ouspensky's meetings, manifested signs of disapproval and then disappeared for good. But all the time there remained a solid core of followers who rarely missed a meeting.

Ouspensky was holding his meetings, at the time at which I joined his group, in a house in Warwick Gardens. In the large ground-floor room in which we met there was a blackboard, some forty straight-backed, hard-seated, wooden chairs, and a small table on which had been placed a carafe of water, a tumbler, a brass ashtray, a duster and a box of coloured chalks. At the table sat Ouspensky, a thick-set man with closely cropped grey hair, a man whom, judging by appearances, I should have taken to be a scientist, a lawyer or a schoolmaster, but certainly not the exponent of what I understood to be a mystical form of philosophy. At first I found him very difficult to understand, chiefly because he spoke with such a marked Russian intonation that I had the impression that I was listening to a foreign tongue. But very soon I became accustomed to his Slavonic diction and discovered to my surprise that he possessed a very large English vocabulary. When talking to us he made little use of gestures or of the other aids employed by experienced lecturers, and this absence of art seemed to add weight to his statements. One felt that he had no desire to persuade one—as indeed he had not—and that what he said was sincere, reliable and likely to be true.

The bare room, the blackboard, duster and chalks, the hard chairs, Ouspensky's appearance, the way he peered at his notes through and sometimes over his strong glasses, his dogmatic statements, his 'let's have no nonsense' manner of conducting his meetings and his curt dismissal of many questions as too long or useless—all these things transported me straight back to the schoolroom. I was a small boy again, listening to a kindly but rather severe headmaster delivering a talk to one of the lower forms. And although I was associated with Ouspensky for nearly a quarter of a century, our relationship remained as it had begun, that of a pupil—a prefect perhaps in later years—and his headmaster. I was never completely at my ease with him and I never met or talked with him as one human should meet and talk with another human being, openly and without fear. Nevertheless I am deeply conscious of indebtedness to him, and feel that I owe to him almost as much as I owe to Gurdjieff, for without Ouspensky's help I doubt whether I should ever have understood Gurdjieff. Not that I claim, even now, to understand fully that truly astonishing man.

Ouspensky's starting point for the study of G's system—he always referred to his teacher in this way—was that which G himself had selected as a starting point in Moscow, namely, the study of the nature of man. He used as his text the words usually ascribed to Socrates but which are actually much older than the age of Socrates, the statement that self-knowledge is the beginning of all wisdom. He then went on to say that we had an immense amount to learn concerning ourselves, for it was a subject about which everybody was abysmally ignorant. We were, in fact, very different from what we imagined ourselves to be, and attributed to ourselves all sorts of qualities, such as inner unity, control and will, which we did not, in fact, possess. Our work must begin, therefore, with giving up the idea that we knew ourselves and with

discovering what we were really like. This was a necessary preliminary to becoming something else if, after knowing ourselves a little better, we disliked some of the things we had seen and wanted to change them.

Then, without any more introductory remarks or conditional clauses or mention of extenuating circumstances, Ouspensky plunged abruptly into G's system of thought. 'Man', he said, 'is a machine which reacts blindly to external forces and, this being so, he has no will, and very little control of himself, if any at all. What we have to study, therefore, is not psychology—for that applies only to a developed man—but mechanics.'

Ouspensky said that he would begin the study of man the machine with an investigation of his mind, and G's teaching on this subject differed from all other Western teachings. It proclaimed that man possessed not just one mind but seven different kinds of mind, each of which could make its contribution to the sum total of his knowledge. The first of these minds of man was his intellectual mind, an instrument which was occupied with constructing theories and with comparing one thing with another. Man's second mind was his emotional mind, which was concerned with feelings instead of with ideas; his third mind was the mind controlling his movements, and to his fourth mind G had given the name 'instinctive mind'. This fourth mind supervised all the physiological functions of his body, such as the processes of digestion and respiration. There was also the mind of man's sex life, and, in addition to these ordinary minds, two higher varieties of mind, the Higher Emotional and the Higher Intellectual. These Higher minds did not work in ordinary people like ourselves but were active only in fully developed men. Yet they existed in ordinary people and sometimes, through some accident, for a moment or two became active in them.

The members of Ouspensky's audience who had been brought up on the Cartesian idea that the mind was a kind of ghostly presence that made use of the central nervous system much as a householder uses a telephone, that is to say, as an instrument for receiving messages from the outside world and for issuing orders to the body, found this idea that the body possessed so many minds a little confusing. I personally was not of the Cartesian persuasion and I was particularly interested in the idea that there existed a special mind for co-ordinating the various physiological processes in the body. For how, otherwise than by attributing to the body its own native intelligence, was it possible to explain the marvellous work the body did, the complicated chemical processes which it carried out so rapidly in its laboratories, the astonishing cleverness it displayed in the regulation of its growth, the wonderful way in which it accomplished its own repair work and the promptness with which it mobilized its defences against the attack of hostile micro-organisms? These physiological marvels had always astonished me, and they suggested very strongly that intelligence resided not only in the brain, but in all the living tissues of the body. Philosophically speaking, I had already come to the conclusion that mind and body had to be regarded as co-existent and interdependent, each being a condition of the other's existence, and, as will later be seen, this philosophy is in harmony with G's teaching on this subject. I accepted very readily, therefore, this preliminary report that there were several kinds of mind in man and that the body possessed its own physiological variety of it.

Ouspensky made free use of diagrams when teaching us, and a diagram which was frequently drawn on the blackboard was the one showing man's several minds. He said that in this diagram man was regarded as a three-storied being, in the top story of which there resided the intellectual mind or, as Ouspensky now preferred to call it, the Intellectual Centre. In the middle story was man's emotional mind or centre, and in the lower story both his moving and his instinctive minds or centres.

When asked where, anatomically speaking, these minds or co-ordinating centres of man were situated, he answered that they were widespread throughout the whole body, but that the maximum concentration of the intellectual centre, or what could be called its centre of gravity, lay in the head. The centre of gravity of the emotional centre was in the solar plexus, that of the moving centre in the spinal cord and that of the instinctive centre within the abdomen. Ouspensky advised that those of us who found this widespread diffusion of the various centres difficult to visualize should think of man's minds in terms of functions or activities rather than in terms of centres and anatomical structures. Instead of talking about the four lower centres, they could say that there were four different functions in a man: those of thinking, feeling and moving, and that of regulating the various physiological needs of his body. In addition to these, there were the sexual functions and the functions of higher thought and higher feeling which were only latent in us and unable to manifest themselves.

According to G, all living creatures on the earth could be classified in accordance with the number of minds or centres which they possessed, and man was the only creature on this planet equipped with an intellectual centre. The higher animals possessed emotional, moving, instinctive and sexual centres, but such lowly things as worms were devoid even of emotional centres and managed to get along with moving and instinctive centres alone.

The relative activity of the three chief centres in man (intellectual, emotional and moving-instinctive) was different in different individuals, and this provided us with a means of classifying men under three or four headings. There were men who did everything by imitating the behaviour of those around them, and who thought, felt, moved and reacted much as everybody else thought, felt, moved and reacted. Such people were controlled almost entirely by their moving centres, which possessed a special gift for imitation, and a man of this type would henceforth be referred to as man number one. There were other people in whose lives the emotions played a leading part, people who were guided by what they felt and by what they liked and disliked rather than by what they thought. Such people spent their lives in seeking what was pleasant and in avoiding what was unpleasant, but sometimes they reacted pathologically in the reverse way, extracting a perverted pleasure from fear and suffering and converting what was distressing into a horrid form of voluptuousness. An emotionally controlled person of this kind would be spoken of in future as man number two. Finally there was man number three, the man who was swayed by theories and by what he called his reason, a man whose knowledge was based on logical thinking and who understood everything in a literal sense. A man of this third kind would be called man number three.

Ouspensky made it clear to us that no one of these three types of men was superior to any other one and that all three stood together on the same level, equally at the mercy of their psychological machinery and without any will. All that this classification was meant to show us was that the individual behaviour and decisions of one kind of man could often be explained by the predominance in him of one kind of function, and the behaviour and decisions of another kind of man by the predominance in him of another kind of function. This method of classifying people was possible because human development was usually lopsided and it was much less serviceable when a man's development had proceeded in a more balanced way.

A properly balanced man, working as he should work, resembled a well-trained orchestra, in which one kind of instrument took the lead at one moment of the performance and another instrument at another, each making its contribution to the symphony being played. Unfortunately it rarely happened that our centres worked harmoniously, for not only was one centre liable to interfere with the work of another centre, but it often attempted to do the work of another centre. There were occasions, for example, when our actions should be based on feeling rather than on thought, and other occasions when feelings should yield precedence to thought. But arguments often replaced feeling in the first instance, and emotions were liable to interfere with thought in the second instance. As the result of these disagreements between centres, and of the absence of any conductor of the orchestra, discords were frequently sounded, our feelings contradicting our thoughts, and our actions being at loggerheads with both our thoughts and our feelings. We resembled, therefore, orchestras which not only lacked conductors but which were composed of musicians who had quarrelled with one another. The players of the stringed instruments were no longer on speaking terms with the players of the wind instruments, and nobody in the least cared what the rest of the orchestra was doing. In short, each member of it did what he deemed to be right in his own eyes without any regard for anybody else.

Ouspensky said that to know oneself meant many years of self-study and that we must first understand the correct way of doing this. He explained that he had started by giving us G's account of the different centres because we should find it of use to us in the work we were about to undertake, that of self-observation. What was now required of us was that we should begin to observe the working of the various centres in ourselves, as they were functioning, and should assign to the appropriate centre each activity as we saw it. By obtaining our own examples of the working of these centres within ourselves we should become more and more familiar with the working of our machinery. As G had long ago remarked, the study of man began with the study of mechanics and not of psychology, for psychology was applicable only to more fully developed people. To know ourselves in the way in which it was necessary for us eventually to know ourselves was a very ambitious aim, which could only be realized after many years of patient and painstaking self-study. He warned us against confusing self-observation as it should be carried out with that highly unprofitable occupation known by the term introspection. Introspection was very different from self-observation. What was required of us was that we should register or take note of our thoughts, emotions and sensations at the moment of their occurrence, and introspection usually meant only thinking and dreaming about ourselves. Introspection also entailed analysis and speculating about the motives behind our behaviour, but as our pictures of ourselves were to a great extent imaginary pictures, all this speculating and probing about in the darkness was of very little profit to anybody, so far as real self-knowledge was concerned.

In observing ourselves we must look at ourselves with detachment and as though we were looking at another person about whom we knew very little. At first we might find difficulty in assigning our activities to the right centres, but with experience this would gradually become easier. For example, at first some of us would confuse thinking and feeling, and feeling and sensing, and it would be helpful to us to remember that intellectual centre worked by comparing one thing with another thing, and by making subsequent statements on the basis of this comparison, whereas emotional centre worked by recording its native likes and dislikes and acting directly on this basis. Instinctive centre was similarly occupied with deciding whether the sensations it was receiving were of a pleasant or of an unpleasant nature. We should bear in mind the fact that neither emotional nor instinctive centre ever argued or reasoned concerning anything, but because they perceived everything *directly* they returned to the perception an equally direct response. We should look upon these psychic functions of ours as being different kinds of instrument, each variety of which made its characteristic contributions to the sum total of our knowledge.

There were different ways of knowing a thing and to know it completely was to know it simultaneously with our thinking, our emotional, and even with our moving and instinctive minds. Ouspensky warned us that whilst studying ourselves in this manner we should come across many things which we disliked in ourselves, as well as many things of which we approved. But for the time

being we must be content only to note our likes and dislikes without attempting to bring about any change in ourselves. It would be a grave mistake, he said, and fortunately a mistake almost impossible to make, for us to alter anything in ourselves at this very early stage of our work.

To change something in oneself without running the risk of losing something else of value required a knowledge of the whole which we were very far from possessing. In our present state of ignorance of the whole we might struggle to get rid of some personal quality which, properly handled, might at a later date become an asset to us, or else we might strengthen some other feature in ourselves which we happened to admire, but which would be a hindrance to our future development. Moreover, if a man were able to destroy some feature in himself which he happened to dislike, he would at the same time alter the whole balance of his machinery, and thus bring about a number of unexpected changes in other parts of himself. It was fortunate, therefore, that it was beyond our present powers to tamper with ourselves, but possible only for us to see ourselves a little more clearly than we had formerly done.

Ouspensky advised us to put all activities of a doubtful character aside until we had gained greater skill in the work of sorting them out. For the present we should concentrate our attention on the classification of activities of a clear-cut nature. Then, after we had gained skill in observing the working of our various centres, we could begin the more difficult job of looking for examples of the wrong working of centres, due either to one centre attempting to perform the work of another centre, or else to one centre interfering with the functioning of another centre. He gave, as examples of a centre doing the work of another centre, intellectual centre pretending that it 'felt', whereas it was quite incapable of feeling anything, or emotional centre coming to a decision which it was not within its province to make. He described the moving centre as a very clever mimic and said that it often imitated other centres working, making it appear outwardly that real thinking or feeling was going on, whereas in actual fact nothing of a genuine nature was happening at all. For example, a person might read out loud from a book or talk to somebody quite impressively, yet he might be only uttering words without any more meaning for him as he uttered them than the words spoken by a parrot had any meaning for the parrot. Reading, speaking and so-called thinking on this very low level often occurred and they were all imitations of other activities concocted by moving centre.

Ouspensky pointed out that the ability of one centre to work for another could often be very useful, in that it allowed of continuity of action, but he warned us that if it occurred too often it might become a habit and thus be harmful. There were occasions, for example, when clear thinking was of vital importance, and if at a particular moment of clearer thought emotional centre intervened through sheer force of habit and took it upon itself to pass judgement on a situation for which the reason was required, the result of its untimely interference would be extremely unsatisfactory. Man, he said, was a highly complicated and delicately adjusted piece of mechanism and, if the balance between the various parts of it were upset, the whole of the machinery began to work very badly. This sort of thing happened frequently in psychotic and neurotic individuals, that each centre was continually interfering with the activity of another centre or else was attempting to do its work for it, and failing badly to accomplish it. As a result of all this interference and wrong functioning, everything in the machinery of the neurotic person was at sixes and sevens.

But badly working machinery was by no means confined to the people we labelled neurotic. Ouspensky said that although Western psychologists had recognized that wrong inner work and the interference of one psychic function with another psychic function were responsible for many nervous diseases, they had not yet realized how much faulty work went on in ordinary and supposedly healthy people. Wrong work of centres occurred in us all. It accounted for the dullness of the sensory impressions we received from the outside world, for our apathy and lack of understanding, for our inability to see things vividly and directly as a child sees them, and for the general drabness of our lives. 'Man', continued Ouspensky, 'is not only a machine but a machine which works very much below the standard it would be capable of maintaining if it were working properly. It is necessary for us, therefore, to observe ourselves very closely, not only in order to obtain knowledge of our mechanism, but also in order that we may realize how much better our machinery might be made to work. There are many defects which are common to us all as ordinary human beings, and there are also forms of bad working which are peculiar to ourselves individually. In this preliminary stage of self-study it is necessary that we should become thoroughly familiar with our own particular failings.'

As I have said earlier in this chapter, the idea that man has other minds than the single mind which the physiologists have linked with his brain and central nervous system made a strong appeal to me. Moreover, all that Ouspensky was now saying about the ability of one centre to take on the work of another centre was fully in accord with my personal experience. I could recall how long ago in learning to ride a bicycle my moving centre had, at a certain moment, taken over the work which had been performed up till then by my intellectual centre. At the beginning of the lessons an immense amount of thought had had to be directed to the way in which body-weight was distributed and, if my attention had been allowed to stray for a moment from this task of balancing myself and of turning the handlebars in the right direction, I promptly tumbled over. Then, quite suddenly, all this thinking and scheming became unnecessary and I found myself riding a bicycle and balancing myself as though to the manner born. Something within me had suddenly assumed responsibility for the whole business of riding a bicycle, and the 'something' which had re-

lieved the head of its previous work was clearly my moving centre. I could recall, also, the abrupt change which had taken place in my mode of speaking Spanish, when I was living in Buenos Aires. Up till a certain dramatic moment much thinking had been required for talking in Spanish, and what I had really been doing all the time was translating painfully from English into Spanish. Then, within the space of a week, a marked change occurred, and I found myself thinking and dreaming in Spanish. All need for translating had gone, and my moving centre was mimicking everybody around me and doing much of the work previously performed by my intellectual centre.

Like other people, I had some difficulty at first in distinguishing between instinctive movements and movements carried out by moving centre, but Ouspensky had helped us greatly by saying that instinctive movements were inborn, whilst moving centre movements had to be learnt. For example, the new-born infant knew how to breathe from the very start and quickly learned to suck and to swallow, but the art of walking had to be acquired painfully at a later date. Ouspensky also said that each centre possessed its own form of memory, and I recalled the surprise which I had felt on discovering that, although I had not ridden a bicycle for over twenty years, I was still able to leap on to a machine and to pedal off without thought or difficulty. My moving centre had remembered the technique of bicycle-riding all that time. Bicycle-riding also illustrated what Ouspensky had said about one centre interfering with another. If after moving centre had taken over the responsibility for bicycle-riding, one started to think about it and to work out intellectually how the weight should be distributed and in which direction the handlebars should be turned, one was likely to have a spill, and this was a clear instance of intellectual centre interfering with moving centre.

There was an interesting connection also between G's idea of memory in instinctive centre and Samuel Butler's view that instinct in animals, and even heredity as a whole, are the result of inherited memories. Samuel Butler protested against what he called 'shearing the thread of life, and hence of memory between one generation and its successor'. According to him, our bodies inherit memories from a long line of ancestors, memories which are carried across the gap between successive generations by the ovum and the spermatozoon. He gave, as an example of inherited memory, the fact that at a certain stage of its development within the egg the chick 'remembered' that it had to tap with its beak on the inner side of the eggshell in order to break out into the world. Not only did the chick remember how to do this, but at a still earlier stage of its development its instinctive centre had recalled in time the need for developing certain very hard cells at the tip of its beak, in order that it might be able to break the shell, and, having remembered this, it had promptly proceeded to do what was required of it. Heredity, therefore, was for Samuel Butler a manifestation of racial memory, a theory of his which had always fascinated me. And here was G supporting Samuel Butler by speaking of a memory in instinctive centre which regulated all physiological and growth processes. It was true that since the days of Weismann scientists have been of the opinion that characteristics acquired by the parents are never handed down to the offspring, but I had always been sceptical of Weismann's arguments. At heart I had always remained a heretic, a Lamarckian and an admirer of Butler.

I was surprised at the richness of the haul of observations I made during the next few weeks by observing myself in the way Ouspensky had advised, as though taking stock of some other person with whom I was only slightly acquainted. Perhaps the earliest and most disquieting of the findings made in this way was that I was never the same for more than a few minutes, and yet I had the effrontery to preface many of my remarks with such misleading phrases as 'I always think that . . . ' or 'I am convinced that . . . ' or 'I feel strongly that . . . ' What nonsense! I realized now that frequently I had thought and felt quite differently from the way in which I was thinking and feeling at that particular moment. And who was it that was making this dogmatic statement about his own thoughts and his feelings? Who, in short, was 'I'? Here was a problem of the first magnitude to be faced. Self-observation gave rise to a host of new questions.

Over two thousand years ago Heraclitus proclaimed that 'everything flowed', and up till that moment I had imagined that in uttering these well-known words he was referring only to the world outside ourselves. Now, as the result of only three months' self-observation, I realized that what was undoubtedly true of the world outside myself was equally true of the world within me. Everything 'flowed' within me as it flowed without me; one inner state quickly followed another, a feeling of pleasure being quickly replaced by one of displeasure, so that, when I looked within, it seemed to me that my various emotions were playing a game of family coach, all changing places. A study of these two flowings—the inner and the outer—soon convinced me that the inner was of far greater importance to me than the outer, so far as the business of living was concerned. Yet it was the instability of the outer world that I always blamed whenever anything went wrong with my life, and never the instability within me.

It was the same with other people. They were always struggling to alter things outside themselves without ever realizing the much more urgent need to change the world within. All would be well if only A, B and C would behave differently, if the law were altered, if people were not such fools, if certain things were done which ought to be done—but they never stopped for a moment to look within at the great current of life, partly conscious, but still more unconscious, which was carrying them along as an incoming tide sweeps in on its surface fragments of wreckage and seaweed.

According to Freud, what we do, what we feel and what we think, are but the by-products of those dark and dy-namic regions of the mind in which lie all our primitive animal instincts, and Freud gives us quite a good account of the subconscious mind responsible for all these activities in us. But the best descriptions of this great underground river of desires, thoughts and feelings, are to be found in the much earlier works of the Cambridge neo-Platonists written about a century ago. In 1866 E. S. Dallas gave the following dramatic description of the surge of life in the poorly lit caverns of the mind: 'In the dark recesses of memory, in unbidden suggestions, in trains of thought unwittingly pursued, in multiplied waves and currents all at once flashing and rushing, in dreams that cannot be laid . . . in the force of instinct . . . we have glimpses of a great tide of life ebbing and flowing, rippling and rolling and beating about where we cannot see it.' (Quoted by Michael Roberts in *The Modern Mind*.) No better description could be given of the force which carries us along with it, a force of life of whose existence I was now becoming dimly aware.

J. G. Bennett (essay date 1973)

SOURCE: "Is There an 'Inner Circle' of Humanity?," in *Gurdjieff: Making a New World*, Bennett Books, 1973, pp. 38-60.

[*In the following essay, Bennett discusses Gurdjieff's theory of the "inner circle of humanity."*]

Reports of brotherhoods whose members possess wisdom and powers that are different from and more significant than those of ordinary people suggest that they may be founded in fact and should be taken seriously. The supposition that such people have existed in the past, and that they decisively influenced human life in ways that ordinary people cannot understand, is the hypothesis that an Inner Circle of Humanity existed in the past. If we extend the idea to include the present and the foreseeable future, we have the hypothesis in the form of a perpetual hierarchy. This tradition is common to most Sufi teachings, and it was affirmed by Gurdjieff himself. He associates it with the idea of esoteric schools. He defined "schools" as organizations that exist for the purpose of transmitting to the Outer Circle—that is, ordinary people—the knowledge and powers that originate in the Inner Circle.

The conclusion that schools do exist is by no means the same as a belief in the existence of an Inner Circle of Humanity. The latter can be regarded either as a dogma to be believed or as hypothesis to be tested. We shall follow the second line. The hypothesis can be understood in a "strong" sense or in a "weak" one. The strong sense holds that there are people who possess incomparably greater knowledge and powers than ordinary men and women, including those who occupy positions of authority in church, state, and centers of learning. These people constitute a hierarchy at the head of which are superhuman beings who may or may not live in human form, but who, in any case, have a direct insight into cosmic purposes and processes, and who can exercise powers that are entirely beyond the reach of ordinary mortals. Such are, for example, the Masters described by the theosophists, anthroposophists, and other arcane schools. These are, as we saw in the last chapter, very different from the historical Masters in central Asia, the Khwajagan, who were not at all mysterious. In recent years, the strong hypothesis has been extended to include visitors from extraterrestrial regions who visit the earth in "flying saucers" as part of a plan to "save" mankind.

The strong view is very attractive to writers of fiction, and it has been debased to such an extent that few people would be inclined to think it worth serious examination unless they were already convinced that superhuman beings do exist and take an interest in our welfare. A trite objection to the belief in supernatural beings who are responsible for the welfare of humanity is that they do not seem to be doing their job very well. A more serious difficulty is that we should expect such a significant factor in human history to be better known. There is no obvious reason why the Inner Circle of Humanity—if it is as powerful as the strong view suggests—should hide itself. Presumably, it requires cooperation from the uninitiated, and one would expect that this cooperation would readily be forthcoming if only people were made aware of the help offered them and told what was required of them.

The objection "if they existed, we should know them" conceals the fallacy that they must be "knowable" to us. We can picture wise men exercising extraordinary powers and being able to influence the immediate course of events. It must be conceded that human history as we know it during the past seven to ten thousand years is quite incompatible with this interpretation of the strong view. In any case, the strong view would violate the law of probability, which asserts that the time required for a change to occur is a parabolic function of the number of interacting factors that require to be changed. We cannot, however, exclude a different interpretation according to which the Inner Circle is not concerned with short-term events but surveys human affairs on a time scale of centuries or even millennia.

In several passages in *Beelzebub's Tales,* Gurdjieff made it clear that "care for one's remote descendants" is one of the obligations of a man who has attained "objective reason." He also refers to the errors made by individuals of high reason that resulted in misfortunes that afflicted mankind for thousands of years. Nevertheless, it must be said that there is no hint in *Beelzebub's Tales* of a permanent hierarchy that has influenced history. I myself have suggested in *The Dramatic Universe* (vol. 4:360, 413) that influences guiding human affairs may intervene directly in the form of a hidden directorate, surveying the human scene from epoch to epoch. Now, ten years later, in light of my subsequent work, I regard it as more likely that the method of intervention is indirect. Though more than ever convinced that there is a conscious guidance in human affairs, I believe that this comes from a level of being quite unlike that of people as we know them. It

does not seem at all probable that there is a group of living people who have the power to influence human affairs on a grand scale. There is a certain naiveté in the strong view that a higher level of being is describable in the language of the everyday world. If we accept Gurdjieff's dictum that ordinary man "perceives reality in his attention upside down," it may well be that the characteristics of a true Inner Circle would be exactly the opposite of what we should expect. I will return to this suggestion after considering the "weak" view. We need not examine the "strong" view of the Inner Circle in terms of visible history.

The weak view attributes superior wisdom and powers to the Inner Circle but does not regard it as all-powerful. This weaker view might take various forms, ranging from simple confidence that there are good and wise people who are working in some kind of concert for the welfare of mankind, to belief in a traditional teaching transmitted by people who have attained a higher level of being by their own efforts and who use their knowledge and powers to the extent that world conditions permit. The second version corresponds to the picture of the Khwajagan as it emerged in the last chapter. Virtually any form of belief in the possibility of man attaining higher levels of being implies acceptance that such men have lived in the past and may be living in the present and have, because of their transformation, a clearer understanding of human destiny and a greater capacity for concerted action than ordinary people. If there are people on a higher level of being, we could reasonably expect that they would recognize one another and share between them the burden of helping the world. The objection to this supposition is that it appears to lead back to the strong view that we have rejected.

The objection rests on the assumption that the way in which higher beings work can be deduced from the methods that are adopted by ordinary people and their societies. Now, a most striking feature of all ordinary human activity is its shortsightedness. Crisis government—one that stumbles from one awkward situation to another—characterizes all the political systems of the world. There are very few departments of human life in which decisions are made with regard to the foreseeable but remote future. It is the immediate present that dominates. We never catch up with ourselves, because our activity is so often directed toward targets that are no longer there when we reach them. Furthermore, our decision making is always too narrowly based. We evaluate situations in terms of the factors that we believe we understand, and disregard those that are outside our competence. We do not see that events are governed by laws that are quite different from "causality" as we suppose it to operate. These observations will be examined in depth when we come to study Gurdjieff's cosmology. The point to be made here is that we have no means of evaluating an activity that uses techniques of which we are totally ignorant. We can "judge by results" only if we know how to recognize what results were aimed at. A townsman sees a farmer plowing a field and concludes that his aim is to destroy vegetation. Six months later, he sees that the result is a crop of wheat. The next year, he sees the farmer leaving the field unplowed and accuses him of negligence, never having heard of the need from time to time to let land lie fallow. We suffer from a far deeper disability than the townsman on his first visit to the country. We look at events in the wrong time scale, but we do not even recognize the processes that must be set in motion if mankind is to go forward along the path of creative evolution.

In order to put the notion of an Inner Circle into perspective, we need to introduce categories that are foreign to ordinary thinking. Three areas of human experience may be distinguished:

The Area of Fact: This comprises all that is in communication with our bodies by sense perception and mechanical interaction. This is preeminently the domain in which science, technology, and economics operate. For materialistic and mechanistic theories of the world, it is the sole reality.

The Area of Value: This includes all those intangible influences that determine our judgments and our motives. This is preeminently the domain of morality, aesthetics, and jurisprudence. Its content is all that ought to be. Usually "values" are regarded as ideas or attitudes held by human beings. We should treat them as having their own reality, independent of our experience. The domain of value is the "ideal world," and for the idealist who regards mere fact as illusion, the domain of values is the "real" world.

The Area of Realization: The notion of a nonfactual domain in which reality is constantly being created is foreign to ordinary thinking, but it is implicit in all that Gurdjieff taught and did. It is indeed the central concept of all work that, by definition, proceeds exclusively by creative activity that cannot be reduced to fact and value or even to a combination of the two.

Two great illusions by which mankind is enslaved are the belief that the domain of fact is real and the belief that values can exist without being realized. We have sense experience and we have emotional impulses from which we construct in our "minds" pictures of the world. We take these pictures for representations of reality. Gurdjieff was never tired of denouncing as self-deception such attitudes that effectively block the way to self-realization. "Real" men are those who can create their own "reality," but this takes them into a domain that is incomprehensible for those who believe in facts and values as "real" in themselves.

The hypothesis of an Inner Circle can now be stated as the supposition that there are people who have discovered the secret of realization. Since we do not look upon these as incarnations from another world, they must have attained their place by their own efforts. But, since they also have access to supernatural knowledge, they must have been chosen and given special help. They are the "elect" upon whom the destiny of the world depends.

Such people, if they do indeed exist, must be able to see more deeply into the way the world works than ordinary people. Among ordinary people in this sense we include philosophers, scientists, sociologists, historians, economists, and the leaders of church and state whose perceptions and powers have been exercised solely in the domains of fact and value. In principle, artists and religious people should be creating values, but for the most part they are content to base their vocations upon acts of faith. Because they do not know how to change their perceptions, they are obliged in their conduct of practical affairs to rely upon the same methods as everyone else. They claim to rely upon the inspiration and guidance of the spirit, but they seldom have the courage to throw away the calculations of human reason that cannot transcend the domain of fact.

By eliminating what would not qualify as the Inner Circle of Humanity, we have come a little closer to answering the question of whether such groups of people have existed in the past and do exist today. A fairly strong version of the hypothesis must be considered if we are to reach significant conclusions. This can now be expressed as the presence on earth of self-realized people who are working in the domain of realization in order to redeem humanity from the consequences of excessive reliance upon the power to manipulate facts. Such people are strong, but not in the sense of being powerful or influential. They are also wise, but not in the sense of being learned. They are, therefore, likely to attract little attention from those who assess their fellow men in terms of their visible attainments.

It is probable that Gurdjieff's searches convinced him that people with such higher powers have lived on the earth and that they are active in our day. But, apart from what he told Ouspensky in 1916, he does not seem to have made this a central feature of his teaching. Various explanations for this have been given. Some people say that he was never admitted to the innermost groups and was obliged to put together, as best he could, fragments collected from a variety of sources. Others believe that he was accepted as a missionary or messenger to prepare the way for a more decisive entry of the guardians of the tradition into the life of the West. We should certainly expect that he would have left sufficiently clear indications to enable us to reconstruct the true position. The purpose of the present book is to examine this expectation. . . . [In] none of his own writings does Gurdjieff explicitly assert that there is an Inner Circle or that he met with any evidence of it. It is true that he refers to "world brotherhoods" particularly in *Meetings with Remarkable Men*—but he presents them as closed orders, withdrawn from the world and concerned with the personal salvation of the few fortunate souls who happen to find their way to them. It is, however, possible to put together a more encouraging picture if we follow some clues he left in various places.

One such clue given by Gurdjieff is his mention in several passages of the Sarmoun or Sarman Society. The pronunciation is the same for either spelling, and the word can be assigned to Old Persian. It does, in fact, appear in some of the Pahlawi texts to designate those who preserved the doctrines of Zoroaster. The word can be interpreted in three ways. First, is the word for "bee," which has always been a symbol of those who collect the precious "honey" of traditional wisdom and preserve it for future generations. A collection of legends, well known in Armenian and Syrian circles with the title *The Bees,* was revised by Mar Salamon, a Nestorian Archimandrite in the thirteenth century—about the time of Jenghis Khan. *The Bees* refers to a mysterious power transmitted from the time of Zoroaster and made manifest in the time of Christ.

A more obvious interpretation of the word is to take *man* in its Persian meaning as "the quality transmitted by heredity" and hence a "distinguished family or race." It can also refer to the repository of an heirloom or tradition. The word *sar* means "head," both literally and in the sense of principal or chief. The combination of *sarman* would thus mean "the chief repository of the tradition," which has been called "the perennial philosophy" passed down from generation to generation by "initiated beings," to use Gurdjieff's description.

Still another possible meaning of the word *sarman* is "those who have been enlightened"; literally, "those whose heads have been purified." This gives us a possible clue to Gurdjieff's intention. In the chapter "Beelzebub's Opinion of War," he refers to a fraternity existing in central Asia under the name of the Assembly of the Enlightened. He adds that in those days the brothers of this fraternity were very much venerated by other three-brained beings around them, and hence their brotherhood was sometimes called The Assembly of All the Living Saints of the Earth. This is the nearest Gurdjieff comes to specific mention in his own writing of a group that could correspond to the Inner Circle of Humanity.

Gurdjieff says that this brotherhood had already been formed long before by a group of beings who had noticed in themselves the properties of the organ kundabuffer and had banded together to work collectively for their deliverance from these properties. The narrative goes on to describe the initiative taken by the Assembly to set up a society to prevent war. Gurdjieff carefully places this event by referring to the center of the society as Mosul, which is across the River Tigris from the ruins of Numrud and Nineveh. He says it occurred several centuries ago, and fixes the date by saying that the society included the personal representatives of the famous conqueror Tamerlane. Tamerlane certainly passed through Mosul and, as we saw in the last chapter, he was a patron of the Sufis and a devotee of Khwaja Ahmed Yesevi of Tashkent.

The reader can reasonably infer that Gurdjieff is referring to historical events of special importance. This is confirmed by the surprising list of communities represented in the society: Mongols, Arabs, Kirghizes, Georgians,

Little Russians, and Tamils. These cover most of the main religious groups—shamans, Muslims, Buddhists, Christians, and Hindus—with the notable exception of Zoroastrians and Jews.

Now, it is a historical fact that, after two centuries of wars and civil wars, Asia had a period of relative peace in the fifteenth and sixteenth centuries. I suggested in the last chapter that the Khwajagan may have played some part in this. It does not seem in the least likely that the Assembly of the Enlightened can be identified with the Khwajagan, for the simple reason that there is no evidence that the latter ever assembled to act in concert. The Masters were highly independent individuals who accepted and supported one another but did not form a society until the dervish brotherhoods, such as the Naq'shbandis, began to be organized in the sixteenth century.

Even if the Khwajagan and the Sarman were not identical, it is possible that individual Khwajas were associated with the Sarman Brotherhood. This is suggested by Gurdjieff, and by comparing dates and activities, we may identify his Brother Olmantaboor as Ubeydullah Ahrar. Ahrar's biographer, Mevlana Djami, the greatest literary figure of central Asia, was evidently aware that Ahrar's influence went far beyond his immediate environment. It will be remembered that he made a strong point of his concern with the prevention of war. This was something of a departure for the Sufis, who had until that time tended to regard the world and its wickedness as an evil to be avoided rather than a field of beneficent activity.

It is likely that the original custodians of the traditions were the Sarman Brotherhood, and we must find out all that we can about their origins and activities. Gurdjieff provides here another astonishing clue. He says that the society entitled. The Earth is Equally Free for All set out to establish in Asia a single religion, a single language, and a single central authority. The religion they selected was "to be based on that of the Parsis, only changing it a little." The language was to be Turkmen, the Turkish dialect spoken in Turkmenistan from Samarkand to Balkh. The central authority was to be established at Margelan, the capital of the Ferghanian Khanate. No reference to the Parsis, the religion founded by Zoroaster, appears elsewhere in Gurdjieff's writings. It is particularly remarkable that there is no reference to Zoroaster in the chapter on religion; nor does his name appear among the wise men who assembled in Babylon and formed the Society of Adherents of Legominism. The date of the latter is easily fixed at 510BC because Cambyses is known at that date to have brought learned men from Egypt to Babylon. According to Iamblichus, Pythagoras was one of them. This agrees with Beelzebub's tale.

Gurdjieff must have known the Greek traditions referring to Zoroaster or Zaratas. Apuleius refers to Zoroaster as the spiritual guide of Cyrus the Great and the teacher of Pythagoras, and there are many similar references in Greek literature. Iamblichus, in his *Life of Pythagoras* (chapter 4), states that Pythagoras spent twelve years in Babylon consorting with the Magi. These are passages remarkably reminiscent of Gurdjieff's description of the Society of Adherents of Legominism (*Beelzebub's Tales,* chapter 30). Gurdjieff certainly had read his Iamblichus and to some extent modeled his Institute upon the Pythagorean schools. Unless Zoroaster is to be identified with Ashiata Shiemash, he does not appear in Beelzebub's tales of the Babylonian period. Why, then, should this religion be referred to—in a much later chapter describing events two thousand years after the time of Zoroaster—as the best foundation for a creed in which all Asiatic communities could share?

We should note here that in 1911 Rudolf Steiner wrote a book called *The Spiritual Guidance of Mankind* in which he claims that, by clairvoyant insight, he was able to reconstruct the history of the Zoroastrian influence in human life over a period of eight thousand years, or from the origins of the Aryan culture. As Gurdjieff makes several references to anthroposophy in *Beelzebub's Tales,* we may assume that he was aware of the importance that Steiner attached to the Zoroastrian traditions. Gurdjieff invariably refers to anthroposophy in slighting terms as an aberration of the same order as theosophy and spiritualism. It does not, by any means, follow that he rejected all the conclusions reached by Rudolf Steiner. From his attitude in conversation, I would surmise that he objected to the uncritical acceptance of statements that were unsupported by historical evidence.

It has been suggested that the "cosmic individual incarnated from Above," who is called Ashiata Shiemash in *Beelzebub's Tales,* is Zarathustra (Zoroaster). Gurdjieff certainly spoke of Ashiata Shiemash in three different ways. He was a historical character who had lived in Asia thousands of years ago. He is also the prophet of the New Epoch who is still to come, and he is also Gurdjieff himself. Gurdjieff said more than once, "I am Ashiata Shiemash." It has also been asserted that these chapters are purely allegorical and refer to no historical situation past, present, or future. In my opinion, all four interpretations are valid, and we should therefore examine the first to see if it helps us with the search for an Inner Circle.

After his enlightenment, Ashiata is said to have gone to "the capital city Djoolfapal of the country then called Kurlandtech, which was situated in the middle of the continent of Asia." If this refers to Zarathustra's journey in his thirtieth year, after receiving enlightenment, the city must have been Balkh, where Kave Gushtaspa was king. Here Zarathustra found two men, counselors of the king, Jamaspa and Frashaostra, who were seeking wisdom. He enlightened them and initiated the king. There is a remarkable verse in the Avesta, fifth Gatha, verse 16 that says:

> The leadership of the Maga mysteries has been
> bestowed on Kave Gushtaspa.
> At the same time he has been initiated into the

> path of Vohu Manah by inner-vision.
> This is the way that Ahura Mazda has decreed according to Asha.

In later Persian sacred literature, Asha becomes Ashtvahasht, which is strangely suggestive of Ashiata Shiemash.

According to the legend, Kave Gushtaspa placed himself entirely under the direction of Zarathustra, and this inaugurated the reign of the "good law". It is obviously possible that Gurdjieff had all this in mind, but he left no clear indication. The name Ashiata Shiemash could have been derived from the Turkish word *ash,* meaning "food," and the words *iat* and *iem,* which refer to eating. According to this interpretation, Ashiata Shiemash personifies the principle of reciprocal feeding. This is very interesting because of the conclusion I reached on other grounds that the principle had a Zoroastrian origin.

The nearest Gurdjieff comes to describing a society that influenced history is in the "Organization for Man's Existence Created by the Very Saintly Ashiata Shiemash." The society, called the Brotherhood Heechtvori, developed from the society he found in Djoolfapal (Balkh?). He interprets the name to mean "only he will be called and will become the son of God who acquires in himself conscience." This society was not occupied with social organization and reform nor with the exercise of power. It was a training establishment to which people went to have their "reason enlightened": first as to the real presence of conscience in man, and, second as to the means whereby it can be "manifested in order that a man may respond to the real sense and aim of his existence." The external, social consequences of the training are depicted as deep and far reaching. New kinds of relationships came into being; men looked for guidance rather than for authority. Social and political conflicts disappeared. This was not the result of reform or reorganization, but solely of a change in people. I think Gurdjieff uses the story of Ashiata Shiemash not only to underline the central significance of conscience in his message to humanity but also to suggest that he has no confidence in any kind of occult "action at a distance." People are to be helped by actions that they can understand and, in due course, produce for themselves.

Zoroaster was associated in the minds of central Asian communities with the struggle that endured for thousands of years between the Turanian nomads and the Aryan settlers. The Avestan Gathas often identify the Turanians with evil spirits in spite of the fact that more than one Turanian prince became a follower of Zoroaster. The society mentioned by Gurdjieff, The Earth is Equally Free for All, was to adopt the ancient Turanian language, and combine it with the Aryan religion of the Parsis, and establish its main center in Ferghana. The only possible interpretation of such a combination is that it refers to a society that was on such a high level that the conflicts that divide religions and peoples did not touch it. No higher society could be imagined than the Assembly of All the Living Saints of the Earth.

The connection between this society and the Sarman Brotherhood is given both by the name and by the location, first in Mosul and then in Bokhara. In *Meetings with Remarkable Men,* Gurdjieff describes how he and his Armenian friend, Pogossian, found ancient Armenian texts, including the book *Merkhavat,* that referred to the "Sarmoung" society as a famous esoteric school. According to tradition, this school had been founded in Babylon as far back as 2500 BC and was known to have existed in Mesopotamia up to the sixth or seventh century of the Christian era. The school was said to have possessed great knowledge containing the key to many secret mysteries. The date of 2500 BC would put the founding of this school several centuries before the time of Hammurabi, the greatest lawgiver of antiquity, but this is not impossible. It is an interesting date, because it coincides with the migration that brought together a Semitic people, the Akkadians, and the older Indo-European race of the Sumerians. It is quite plausible to suppose that a school of wisdom could then have been established that guided the course of events toward the wonderful achievements of Sargon I and Hammurabi. If such a school existed, it would have abandoned Babylon after the time of Darius II, about 400 BC, and could very well have moved north into the upper valley of the Tigris where the Parthians were about to begin their long period of dominance in the mountains of Kurdistan and the Caucasus. The Parthians brought with them a pure Zoroastrian tradition. The Armenian hegemony bridged the gap until the arrival of the Seljuks at the end of the first millennium AD. This was a time when caravan routes in all directions passed through the upper valleys, and it was possible to collect and concentrate traditions from China to Egypt.

This leads us to the next phase of Gurdjieff's contact with the Sarman Brotherhood. He reports that in the course of a sojourn at Ani, one of the capitals of the Bagratid Armenian kingdom, he and Pogossian found a collection of letters written on parchment some time in the seventh century AD. One of these letters contained a reference to the Sarman Brotherhood as having one of their main centers near the town of Siranush. They had migrated to the northeast and settled in the valley of Izrumin, three days' journey from Nivssi. Gurdjieff goes on to say that their further research led them to identify Nivssi with Mosul, which was already connected with the Society of the Enlightened. By the date mentioned, Nineveh had ceased to be inhabited, but Nimrud, the ancient capital of the Assyrian king, Assurbanipal, was still a great trading center due to its location at a point where the Tigris begins to be navigable all year round.

Three days' journey by camel from Nimrud through almost desert country leads to a valley green with trees, in the midst of which is Sheikh Adi—the chief sanctuary of the Yezidi Brotherhood. Now, the Yezidis are certainly inheritors of the old Zoroastrian tradition, and Gurdjieff specifically refers to them among the groups of Assyrians he found in the region surrounding Mosul, which was the heart of the old Assyrian Empire. I visited Sheikh Adi in 1952 and was convinced that the Yezidis possessed secrets unsuspected by Orientalists, who classify their faith as a relic of paganism. Their connection with the Mithraic tradition is generally accepted because of their chief festival of the white bull, which takes place at Sheikh Adi in October every year. They are even more directly descended from the followers of Manes, whose influence spread very widely all through Asia in the third and fourth centuries of our era, only two hundred years before the Sarman Brotherhood was reported as having its headquarters at Izrumin.

It seems probable that a very strong tradition did exist in Chaldaea from very early times. Gurdjieff, both in his writings and in his conversations with his pupils, constantly referred to this ancient tradition. We can assume that, during the great upheavals of history, the guardians of the tradition responded in the way described in the last chapter: it divided into three branches, one of which migrated, one of which was assimilated into the new regime, and one of which went into hiding.

At the time of the Muslim conquests in the seventh and eighth centuries, groups like the Yezidis and the Ahl-i-Haqq were formed. They presented more or less acceptable doctrines to the Arabs, who could not understand the subtleties of Persian spirituality. There was relatively little forced conversion of Nestorian Christians, whose beliefs were substantially compatible with the teaching of the Qur'an. Our main concern is with the third group, who withdrew into central Asia. This is the group that corresponds to Gurdjieff's account of the Sarman Brotherhood.

Gurdjieff himself makes no attempt to explain the migration. In writings of his adventures with Pogossian, the "Sarmoung" Brotherhood is located in Chaldaea. In the story of Prince Yuri Lubovedsky, they have moved to central Asia, twenty days' journey from Kabul and twelve days' journey from Bokhara. He refers to the valleys of the Pyandje and the Syr Darya, which suggest an area in the mountains southeast of Tashkent. He discloses at the end of this chapter that this particular brotherhood had another center in the Olman monastery on the northern slopes of the Himalayas. The word Olman is a link with Olmantaboor, who was the head of the Assembly of the Enlightened. The northern slopes of the Himalayas connect with the Amu Darya and Syr Darya rivers.

We must now closely examine the slender clues that Gurdjieff has left us to reconstruct the teaching that he found at the monastery between the Amu and Syr Darya rivers and that was described both directly and obliquely in *Meetings with Remarkable Men.*

Gurdjieff provides us with no direct information about what he learned during his three-month stay at the Sarman monastery. For a man as quick in perception as Gurdjieff, three months is a long time, and he could have acquired all that the sheikh chose to make available, once he was accepted there. He does not make it clear, by the way, how long he remained after the departure of Prince

Yuri. Reference in another place to a two years' stay at a sanctuary in central Asia may refer to the same place. In any case, he leaves the reader in no doubt that his contact was of the greatest importance to him and that he learned secrets of a different order of significance from those he found in the various Sufi communities he visited.

By drawing attention to the "apparatuses" used to train priestesses, Gurdjieff fixes in the mind of the reader the central importance occupied by the "Law of Sevenfoldness." These apparatuses were of very ancient workmanship, made of ebony and inlaid with ivory and mother-of-pearl. Since ebony was brought from Africa and mother-of-pearl from India, this suggests that such an apparatus represented a synthesis of Semitic and Aryan teachings. Associated with the apparatus were plates carrying the pattern of the message to be conveyed. The plates were of gold, and they and the apparatus were of great antiquity. They had a vertical column to which were fitted seven movable arms, and each of these arms was provided with seven universal joints similar to those of the human shoulder. Each of the forty-nine joints and the ends carried a sign. The positions were read from the plates and were interpreted in the postures and gestures of the dancers. The dance thus became an utterance, the language of which was known to the brethren and enabled them to read truths placed there thousands of years before. There is no indication that the dances served any other purpose than the transmission of truths and Gurdjieff underlines this by comparing them to our books.

According to Gurdjieff, experts had determined that the plates were at least forty-five hundred years old. This corresponds to the date 2600 BC given in the Pogossian chapter for the founding of the Sarman Brotherhood in Babylon. It also agrees with the date given in *Beelzebub's Tales* for the Tikliamishian Civilization, which refers to the kingdoms of Sumer and Akkad in Mesopotamia prior to the Hittite invasions at the end of the second millennium BC. The dating would suggest the time of Sargon I, the first Semitic ruler. He did much to promote intercourse with other countries and, in his time, Kish, only thirty miles from Babylon, became one of the first centers of culture. Although Gurdjieff specifically associates Tikliamish with the Sumerians, he distinguishes between a legendary period—before the destruction of cultures by the dry sandstorms of the fourth millennium BC—and the historical period of the third and second millennia. The word Tikliamish, as so many others in *Beelzebub's Tales,* must be read both in an allegorical and historical sense. When definite dates are given and means of relating to known historical events are inserted, I assume that Gurdjieff intends the reader to undertake the historical research needed to elaborate the meager details he provides.

I asked Gurdjieff in 1949 whether some of the stories in *Beelzebub's Tales* were to be taken in a strict historical sense. He was most emphatic in his affirmation, saying, "Everything in *Beelzebub* is historical." He added that it

is indispensable to seek for reliable knowledge of long-past events, not only to help us to understand the present, but because we are connected with the past and must learn to make use of this connection.

In all his descriptions of what he found in this and other monasteries, Gurdjieff makes no reference to any higher powers or to the control of energies that could produce external results in the world. It seems likely that if Gurdjieff had regarded the Sarman Brotherhood as the Inner Circle in the strong sense discussed at the beginning of this chapter, he would have said so or at least left some hint to this effect.

The episode that suggests a widely spread influence is the story of Prince Yuri's invitation. He meets an old man in the house of the Aga Khan whom he suspects of being connected with a visitor who came to him in Russia many years earlier and set him upon the path of his subsequent search. The Ishmailis, of whom the Aga Khan is the hereditary spiritual leader, were then a widely spread brotherhood with remarkable influence in all parts of the world. Gurdjieff never mentions them by name, but he must certainly have met many Ishmailis in the course of his travels.

It seems to me that Gurdjieff neither expected to find nor looked for an Inner Circle of Humanity in the strong sense. He did, however, unquestionably believe in a traditional wisdom that is not preserved in books but in the experience of people. Indeed, the collection, preservation, and transmission of "higher knowledge" occupies such a central position in all Gurdjieff's writings and in his conversations with his pupils and friends that it would be absurd to suggest that he did not take it seriously.

What did Gurdjieff mean by "truths" transmitted from the past? He sometimes refers to true information about past events and the difficulty of finding it except through legominisms, to be interpreted by initiates. This information is necessary for subsequent generations to enable them to meet the difficulties that arise in the rise and fall of cultures, difficulties that people never believe will occur again because "the world is now different." Gurdjieff, on the contrary, believed that there is a pattern of events that is destined to lead man along the path of evolution but is constantly disrupted by our own egoistic foolishness and "unbecoming conditions of existence."

In order to understand what is required of us, we must not only know ourselves, but also the "laws of world creation and world maintenance." Ashiata Shiemash is said to have given his disciples five principles of right life. They should strive:

> To have in their ordinary being-existence
>   everything satisfying and really necessary for
>   their planetary body.
> To have a constant and unflagging instinctive
>   need for self-perfection in the sense of being.
> To know ever more and more concerning the laws
>   of world creation and world maintenance.

> To pay for their arising and their individuality as
> quickly as possible, in order afterwards to be
> free to lighten as much as possible the sorrow
> of our Common Father.
> Always to assist the most rapid perfecting of other
> beings, up to the degree of self-individuality.

The third principle was certainly manifested in Gurdjieff's own life's search. From childhood, he had reached the conviction that, at different times in the past, men had made significant discoveries about the way the world works, and that these discoveries were subsequently, for the most part, lost or distorted. Since knowledge of man and the world is necessary for right living, a part of our own effort should be directed to rediscovering these laws.

I think it is fair to suppose that during his stay at the Sarman monastery Gurdjieff was brought into contact with the extraordinary system of thought that he represents with the aid of the enneagram symbol. I shall discuss the symbol and its significance in a later chapter, but here will only say that it makes use of the properties of the numbers three, seven, and ten in a way that makes its Chaldean origin almost certain. The Sumerians, or possibly their Semitic neighbors, the Akkadians, were the first to use an arithmetic based on the first six numbers, with sixty as the base, and to observe that the number seven would not fit into it. We are then taken back to the period forty-five hundred years before the present to which Gurdjieff attributes the formation of the Sarman Society. The science of numbers, in the widest sense, originated in Mesopotamia and developed over a period of four thousand years, from 2500 BC to 1500 AD. By this time, it had moved north into Sogdiana, that is, the region of Samarkand and Bokhara. We should have no difficulty in accepting the suggestion that the Sarman were founded in Kish by agreement between the guardians of the Aryan (Sumerian) and Semitic (Akkadian) traditions about 2400 BC, at the time of Sargon I. They moved to Babylon a few centuries later and became active during the most glorious, if not the most magnificent, period of Babylonian history, which was crowned by the reign of Hammurabi.

This period has remained in Middle Eastern tradition as the Golden Age of Peace and Justice. When it ended, the Sarman Brotherhood moved north to Khorsabad and only later returned to Babylon. The strange powers exercised by Nebuchadnezzar and his final breakdown may have been associated with a period of contact with the Brotherhood that was broken by the jealousy of the regular priests of Ishtar. The Sarmani may have, during this time, retired into the mountains and come forward much later when Cyrus the Great destroyed the Assyrian power and inaugurated a rare period of spiritual activity. This period included the return of the Israelites from the Babylonian captivity, the promulgation of the "new law" (Deuteronomy), and probably the incorporation into the beliefs of the Israelites the Babylonian account of the creation of the world and man. It included the time that Pythagoras and Epaminondas, two of the founders of Greek phi-

losophy, spent in Babylon. The Achemenean Dynasty, founded by Cyrus, was the first since Hammurabi, thirteen hundred years earlier, to have a genuine spiritual basis, although unfortunately after a few generations very little remained. When Cyrus's grandson Cambyses conquered Egypt in 524BC and destroyed the center of culture that had existed there for thousands of years, he took into captivity all the technicians and artists who could serve to enrich and beautify Babylon.

Cambyses also took the priests and scientists—in those days the two were the same—whom Gurdjieff describes in Chapters 24 and 30 of *Beelzebub's Tales*. One very significant hint is dropped where it is said that "the highest school existing on earth at that time was found in Egypt and was called the School of Materializing Thought. Materializing of thought, or the creation of thought forms, is one of the principal techniques whereby events can be influenced and forces transmitted from one place and time to another. Gurdjieff refers to it in an earlier chapter in connection with the Society Akhaldan, which migrated to Egypt. The "sympathetic Assyrian," Hamolinadir, who discourses on the instability of human reason, was trained in the "school of materializing thought," but evidently recognized the uselessness of the acquisition of mental powers in the absence of an established set of convictions. This indirectly suggests that the Sarman Brotherhood had a more practical understanding of human needs than the Egyptian sages. This agrees with an often-quoted statement of Gurdjieff's that different kinds of schools have, from very early times, existed in different regions. "In India, philosophy; in Egypt, theory; in central Asia and the Middle East, practice."

This is not to say that the interaction of different cultural streams in Babylon, in the middle of the first millennium BC, was not highly significant. On the contrary, it was one of the turning points of human history, and its effects are still with us. Babylon continued to be the headquarters of the Sarman Brotherhood until the dispersal of 320BC. They then moved north again to avoid contact with Alexander of Macedon—that "vainglorious Greek" as Gurdjieff calls him—and the degrading Hellenistic period that preceded the time of Christ. Their role in the gospel drama is an unrevealed mystery, unless we associate them with the "wise men from the East" of St. Matthew's Gospel.

It seems that Manes, that remarkable prophet of the third century AD (born 216, martyred 276), was in some way associated with the Sarman Brotherhood, for, at that time, according to Gurdjieff's account, the Brotherhood was at Nivssi, which corresponds roughly to the ancient Nimrud, the modern Mosul. Manes was such an important figure in the transmission of the traditional wisdom that we must ask why Gurdjieff never mentions him by name. The Manichean teaching was upon all levels. Manes was the first to bring art and music fully into the service of sacramental religion. The liturgy of the Christian church created by Gregory and his school in Cappadocia was taken directly from the form of worship that comes from the Aryan tradition and is found with its fourfold ritual in the Avestan Gathas. It is probable that Manes drew upon Mithraic and Christian sources for his own liturgy. His ideas had a powerful influence in spite of his premature death.

All over Europe, including Britain, we can find evidence of the widespread penetration of Manichean ideas between the third and fifth centuries of our era. His influence spread northward across the Oxus into central Asia. When Gurdjieff was traveling in those regions in 1907, a Russian expedition to the center of the Gobi Desert discovered at Turfan a collection of manuscripts attributed to Manes himself and certainly emanating directly from his school. I have not been able to trace the translation of these manuscripts, which were published in Russia, but they must have been known to Gurdjieff, as they were highly relevant to his own research. According to the extracts I have seen, they contain teachings about world creation that have significant points in common with what we find in *Beelzebub's Tales,* particularly the doctrine of reciprocal maintenance. Now, Gurdjieff writes that this latter doctrine was rediscovered by a Kurdish philosopher in the fifteenth century. It was in an ancient manuscript, written by "some ancient learned being," which contained the hypothesis that "in all probability there exists in the world some law of the reciprocal maintenance of all that exists" Since this discovery is directly connected with the Assembly of the Enlightened, which I have suggested may stand for the Sarman Brotherhood, we have a possible link with Manes, who had lived twelve hundred years earlier in the region of the upper Tigris where Kurd Atarnakh is said to have been born. One could follow up such clues by the legion; they cannot be called evidence, and it was not Gurdjieff's purpose to "prove" anything, but rather to make the reader search and think for himself.

The conundrum Gurdjieff sets before us here is to account for the place of Manes in the esoteric tradition and to see if he was likely to be connected with the Sarman Brotherhood. Manes declared that, in two spiritual experiences at the ages of sixteen and thirty, he had been called to be the prophet of Christ sent into the world to bring about the unity of religions. He accepted the Pauline doctrine of the redemption, but he saw that much that was of vital importance to mankind in the teaching of Zoroaster had been left out of Christianity. In particular, the dualism of the worlds of matter and spirit—the idea that they have nothing in common—had entered Greek thought and been taken over by Christian theologians, and was evidently leading to the eventual collapse of religion. Manes saw that the Israelites, in taking over the doctrine of the *Saoshyant* or Divine Savior, had converted it into a quasi-political expectation of the Messiah who was to restore the kingdom of Judah. The more serious error has been that of dividing man on the same dualistic basis into an immortal, spiritual soul and a mortal, physical body. This false dualism, in spite of its obvious absurdity, has never been eradicated from Christian doctrine.

All this was clear to Manes, who seized the essence of the Zoroastrian and Mithraic psychology and succeeded in converting a very large following. Gurdjieff castigates the "Babylonian dualism" in terms reminiscent of Manes. An even closer correspondence is to be found between Gurdjieff's teaching of conscience and Manes' "call from Above," described in a manuscript discovered in Egypt and reputedly from his own hand. The "call of conscience" is the message sent by the good spirit, Ahura Mazda, to awaken man from his prevailing state of delusion.

Some connection between Manes and the Sarman is suggested by his life story, his teaching, the geographical location, and by the indication given by Gurdjieff that the society existed in Nivssi from the fourth to the tenth century. During the early period, Manicheanism was the accepted religion of the region between Mesopotamia, Iran, and the Caucasus until the rise of the Armenian power that dominated from the eighth to the twelfth centuries. Once again, we have the phenomenon of threefold preservation. One part of the Manichean heritage was directly assimilated into Armenian Christianity, which made it so distinctively different from that of the west. A second part migrated to the north. A third part went underground and reappeared later in the form of the Yezidi community and other sects that persist to this day as a spiritual force in the region. The interest taken in the Brotherhood by the Armenian monk whose letters were discovered by Gurdjieff and Pogossian in the ruins of Ani is a good indication that the Sarmani were not regarded as alien by the Armenian Christians as late as the twelfth or thirteenth century. They were, however, driven out by the "Byzantines" who, during the time of Paleologue II, erupted into Assyria and drove Assyrian Christianity into the mountains.

It is probable that the Sarman Brotherhood went across the Amu Darya in the twelfth century, at the time of the rise of the Khwajagan, with whom they must have had some link. They are not likely to have settled in the troubled region of Transoxiana, which was for two centuries to be ravaged by war, but further north on the Syr Darya, where the almost limitless limestone caverns have been inhabited for the past ten thousand years. It is quite possible that the legend brought back by Helen Blavatsky of the hidden Masters living in the great caves of central Asia may have originated in stories of the Sarman Brotherhood. Gurdjieff (*Meetings with Remarkable Men,* p. 148) says that a brotherhood was "known among the dervishes by the name of Sarmoun." I should here mention a clue given in the name of the dervish Bogga Eddin, through whom Gurdjieff learned in Bokhara of the Sarman monastery. Gurdjieff invariably rendered the letter *h* as a *g,* for there is no appropriate *h* in Russian, Armenian, or Greek. Bogga Eddin would, therefore, have been Bahauddin; the founder of the Naq'shbandi dervishes was also a native of Bokhara. In *Beelzebub's Tales,* another dervish with the name Hodje Zaphir Bogga Eddin appears. Hence, the name is evidently derived from familiar Muslim names and should read Hodje

Zafer Bahauddin. The combination of Hodje, which derives from Khwaja, and Zafer, which means conqueror, suggests that Gurdjieff wishes to contrast the outwardly successful Khwajagan with the hidden Sarman. The "caves" in which Beelzebub meets the "last really great terrestrial sage," Khwaja Asvatz Troov, are probably the caves of the Syr Darya, which runs about two hundred miles to the north of the Amu Darya and is a part of Turkestan, with which Gurdjieff was personally familiar. The caves were accessible, as he describes them himself, by horse from Bokhara.

I think we should accept that Gurdjieff himself does wish to convey, in his chapter "The Bokharian Dervish," something of his own personal experience of contact with a source of knowledge. He disguises this source in various ways: first of all, in this Bokharian dervish chapter, by making the source an individual who was living in caves to the northwest of Bokhara; and, in the chapter on Prince Lubovedsky in *Meetings with Remarkable Men,* where he makes it a monastery to the southeast of Bokhara in the regions of the Pyandje River, which is one of the tributaries of the Amu Darya. The whole of that extraordinary country, which lies above the central plateau where Bokhara, Samarkand, and Tashkent are situated, is and has been for a very long time the home of a number of remarkable communities. There was a town called Sarmanjan or Sarmanjin, between Tirmidh and Balkh, which flourished from the eighth to the fourteenth centuries AD. This is the only reference I have been able to find to a place containing the name Sarman. It was visited by Chinese and Indian travelers, and it is just possible that it was the place of one of the Sarman monasteries at that time (W. Barthold, *Turkestan Down to the Mongol Invasion,* 1958, pp. 73-4). In the midst of these communities, there are also monasteries of brotherhoods who occupy favorable situations so remote from the general movement of trade and travel that they may very well have remained undisturbed to this day. Reviewing the evidence I have been able to collect, I must admit that the very existence of a brotherhood with the name Sarman or Sarmoun remains speculative; but this does not invalidate the belief that there has been a very ancient tradition linking many different teachings, and that this tradition has, for more than a thousand years, been situated in Turkestan.

If we now proceed on the assumption that there has been a tradition that was for a very long time associated with central Asia, and that from time to time has spread outward into different parts of the world—north, south, east, and west, and that at other times has drawn back again toward the source, we have to ask ourselves the questions, What is this tradition? and What part has this tradition played in the general history of mankind? There are two points to be made: first, the generation of ideas, and, second, the generation of energy.

I will illustrate the generation of ideas by looking at the period of about 500 or 600 BC, when there was a profound change introduced into the thinking of people about the significance of the human individual. It had previously been held that immortality, giving unique significance to the individual human soul, was the privilege of the few, and that the many did not participate in this. This concept was clearly held in Egypt; it belonged also to the earlier Sumerian teachings. This is what I call the Heroic or Hemitheandric Age, when it was believed that there were beings on earth who were already half-divine and whose destiny was totally different from that of ordinary people. This, on the one hand, created a sense of security that there were such people who had higher powers, who had the ability to communicate directly with the gods, and that this was their chief privilege. In that sense, they were the descendants of the magicians or the shamans who were able right through that period to communicate with the higher or spiritual powers. But, on the other hand, this idea was capable of terrible abuse, as occurred when the privileged spiritual position was associated with despotic political power in the external sense. It reached the height of its wickedness with the Assyrian kings who dominated southwest Asia, and finally with Nebuchadnezzar and his immediate successors until they were overthrown by the Persians when a different regime was inaugurated.

It is true that in much earlier periods, for example in the time of Hammurabi the lawgiver, or in Sumeria, or in the time of the great Egyptian reformers, there were edicts protecting and safeguarding the welfare of the individual; but it still remained true that these privileges were conceded by the favor of the king or pharaoh or the representative of the gods, who alone had rights. No rights inhered in the people; but, chiefly because they were helpless, and were an inferior race, there was an obligation to protect them and see that they were not unjustly treated. So long, however, as it was believed that this was a grace conceded by the semidivine rules, there was always the possibility of its being revoked; the semidivine ruler himself could then become a ruthless despot, as happened a number of times in all parts of the world.

The new idea referred to arose in China, India, Mesopotamia, Egypt, Greece, and Rome about the sixth century BC, with such names as Lao Tzu, Confucius, Gautama the Buddha, the Mahavira, the Jain, Zoroaster, the Hebrew prophets of the Exile, Solon, Pythagoras, and other Greek philosophers. This extraordinary set of men preached the right of every man to find his own salvation, to look directly for his own completion. It was implied that the possibility of completion and liberation was inherent in every human soul. Hence arose the idea of the sacredness of the individual, which gradually emerged and has dominated the last two thousand years. However often we depart from it, and however much brutality and savagery there is in the world, we now have an attitude which is totally different from that which existed before about 600 BC.

We saw earlier that there was a contact between all these prophets and founders of the new religions, taking place, according to some, in Babylon, and according to others, in the city of Balkh in northern Afghanistan. At any rate, there was some kind of concerted action by men of wisdom and foresight to introduce a new mode of thinking into the world. Whether or not we accept this as historical fact, it does represent a way in which we can look at the working of the Inner Circle of Humanity. If there is an Inner Circle of Humanity, this is how we should expect it to operate. The point here is that, at the time these events occurred, they were insignificant as compared with the greater political events that were taking place in the realms of conquest, and of opening up of trade routes, of the scientific and technical progress that so marked the period between the twelfth and seventh centuries BC. These new ideas that were injected into the world were, at first, accepted only by small groups, but they gradually began to spread, partly by force of the ideas themselves and partly by the strength conveyed by the transformation of the people who were responsible for spreading them. This is why the entry of new ideas has always been accompanied by a religious and spiritual revival.

Those who study the origins of the great religions generally direct their attention primarily to the message and manifestation of the founder, to the activity of the apostles who were left behind to spread the message, and to the subsequent social and political activities that made the message effective. Conventional history regards the takeover of Christianity by the Roman Empire, the launching of Buddhism by King Asoka in India, and the success of the Abassid caliphs in establishing Islam as a world power with its center in Baghdad as the important milestones in religious thought.

But these accounts of the origin of religions miss one essential point: that the transition from the activity of a small, esoteric group to that of a great public organization, a church, is made possible because a certain kind of energy is at work. This energy is required to be concentrated, and must be controlled by those who understand how it is to be channeled. This we dimly suspect when we see the martyrs and early apostles of the great religions—when we see what they were able to do and how they were ready to suffer for the cause for which they stood. However, we tend to regard this as a personal matter, something which they did because of their own faith and integrity. There was more to it than this, for they became centers for the production of energy of a very high level. Gurdjieff understood this very well. It is inherent in his approach to the problem of human transformation and of human history that there is an invisible action of the higher energies that makes the work of evolution possible.

Here we have to look again at this concept of an Inner Circle, not only as a source of new and powerful ideas that will eventually change the course of human thinking, but also as the generator of high-level energy. Gurdjieff, in *Beelzebub's Tales,* and particularly in the first book, says categorically that the role of man on earth is to be an apparatus for transformation of energy; that certain energies that man has to produce are required for cosmic purposes, and that those who understand how these energies are produced are the ones who truly fulfill the purpose of human life.

This brings us back again to the question of whether Gurdjieff himself was in contact with people who not only understood energy transformation but practiced it at a high intensity. Everything he has written in his books indicates that he not only believed this to be man's destiny but also that he had learned a great deal about the practical methods and the practical significance of this energy transformation. If this is so, it is probably the most convincing evidence that Gurdjieff did come, during his travels in the East, in contact with a higher source. We can identify this source with what we may call either the Masters of Wisdom or the Inner Circle of Humanity. It does not mean, of course, that he reached the innermost circle of this source; but it shows that he had access to the essential teaching and was able to draw upon the methods emanating from it. We must ask whether the belief in energy transformation is something characteristic of Gurdjieff's system or whether it has a wider range, for example, in the great religions of the world.

There is an old Christian doctrine of the transfer of merits. According to this, an individual who has already reached a certain degree of sanctification can, either by his or her prayers and austerities, or by the purity of his or her life, be a means for helping those who cannot help themselves. In the first method, the monk or nun can help sinners toward repentance even without their knowledge and perhaps even without their own wish. The second method is a means of transferring effectual grace, by which the work of sanctification is possible to those who are at an earlier stage in their spiritual evolution. Similar beliefs are held in India and in Buddhism, where it is particularly taught that it is sufficient to enter into the *darshan* of a sanctified individual to receive permanent and enduring help in one's own spiritual progress. Similarly, in Islam, there is the doctrine that the simple contact, *sohbat,* with a man of a high level of spiritual development is sufficient to bring about a transformation of the fortunate person.

These doctrines, however, do not give the same interpretation as Gurdjieff gives to the mechanism by which this help is transferred. As taught by Gurdjieff, the transfer is by a particular substance or combination of substances that are generated by the being who is already more fully developed and can be transmitted to others. In *Beelzebub's Tales to His Grandson,* this substance is liberated by the work of conscious labor and intentional suffering; these are the same qualities taught in religion: work, austerity, sacrifice, and prayer.

The question is whether Gurdjieff himself had access to a source or generating center for such energies. About this he says nothing very specific, but he told me in 1923 about those who were able to produce a certain substance that could help individuals accomplish in their work what they could never accomplish by their own unaided efforts. He said that those who had this power were regarded as "a special caste of the Inner Circle of Humanity." It is interesting to compare this with the belief of Christian Monasticism that it is possible under certain circumstances for this transfer of merits to take place. Again, particular monasteries or orders exist whose work is directed specially to praying for others, and particularly for those who recognize and know themselves to be sinners.

Similar doctrines are present in different traditions throughout the world. The difference is that Gurdjieff appears to have come across some concrete evidence of the way in which this process works, and even to have learned himself how to generate such energy. He used to speak himself, for example, about what he called *hanbledzoin,* or the life energy of the second body, the *kesdjan* body of man. He also called it the blood of the *kesdjan* body. He referred to himself as being able to produce this *hanbledzoin* in quantities that were in excess of his own needs for his own spiritual development. It could, therefore, be lent to others. Sometimes, when people could not perform the difficult tasks he set them, he would tell them to "draw on my *hanbledzoin* and you will be able to do this work." In that sense, Gurdjieff held himself out to be a source of higher energy upon which people could draw. He also, though not so specifically, referred to himself as being in contact with a higher source, and said that by drawing upon this higher source, the work for which he was responsible would be able to spread and gain strength in the world.

In one very remarkable conversation, a few months before he died, he referred to this in a cryptic but unmistakable manner. He said that at this time an organization of a higher order was being established in the world that would be able to accept only those who had reached such a stage of spiritual development that they were able to generate higher energies. Those who were able to communicate with and draw upon this organization would themselves have to be able to participate in this work of generating and transmitting higher energies. He certainly did not refer to this organization as being of his own creation. He spoke of it in an objective way, as something that was being done of which he was aware and with which he was associated, but not in a central capacity—not as the leader or originator. I think he wished to convey to us that we should, after his death, have the opportunity, if we were prepared and able to work as required, to become connected ourselves with this source and in turn to become a means for the transmission of this higher energy to those who require it.

I have left to the end of this survey the most significant reference to the way in which the Inner Circle is said to operate. This is by the Fourth Way, mentioned many times in Ouspensky's book but not once in any of Gurdjieff's own writings. Gurdjieff gave a special meaning to the word "way": namely, the transformation that leads a man from the Outer Circle to the Inner Circle. Most people are familiar with the Buddhist *marga,* which

is the path of liberation, but the Noble Eightfold Path is entirely different from Gurdjieff's Fourth Way. The contrast lies precisely in the absence in Buddhism of an Inner Circle of Humanity doctrine. The Fourth Way would have no meaning if there were not an Inner Circle to which it leads. Even more important is the reverse notion that the Fourth Way alternates between activity and repose according to the decision of the Inner Circle as to the needs of mankind. If this is accepted, we are involved in a fairly strong version of the Inner Circle hypothesis. Those of us who in the early 1920s accepted Gurdjieff and Ouspensky as our teachers had no doubt that we were entering a Fourth Way school. Our only doubt was whether we were sufficiently prepared for the opportunity.

Michel Waldberg (essay date 1973)

SOURCE: "Reflections on the 'Inhumanity' of Gurdjieff," in *Gurdjieff: An Approach to His Ideas,* translated by Steve Cox, Arkana, 1973, pp. 1-31.

[*In the following essay, Waldberg examines Gurdjieff's major works.*]

REFLECTIONS ON THE 'INHUMANITY' OF GURDJIEFF

The name of Gurdjieff almost always arouses suspicion or hostility. The man is usually described as a kind of werewolf or cynical tyrant, demanding much from others and little from himself, making use of his disciples for mysterious ends, seeking powers rather than virtue, and with an absolute contempt for the whole of humanity.

As for his teaching, it is supposed to be impenetrable, arid and deadening, because it contains a ruthless, 'objectively impartial' critique of human life. Because that critique is ferociously funny; because it is radical, and nothing which constitutes the human treasure escapes it; because in an allegedly Christian civilization Gurdjieff condemns the sophism whereby inconsistency is forgiven in the name of mercy; because he reminds us, as do all the great masters, of primary truths, and tells us that a Christian 'is not a man who calls himself a Christian or whom others call a Christian—Christian is one who lives in accordance with Christ's precepts'; because the way he proposes, which is the way of *consciousness,* appears arrogant to the ordinary eye, and because he is blamed for not giving love its place.

So Gurdjieff is seen as an 'inhuman' figure, demonstrating what he calls 'the Terror of the Situation', and offering a 'dry' path to his disciples. Whereas the humane master is supposed to be understanding and compassionate, gentle and benevolent.

But it must be emphasized that ordinary language is quite mistaken when it associates the notions of benevolence or compassion with the notion of sweetness. Gurdjieff is less isolated than is commonly believed when he rejects common paths, received ideas, and morality in the ordinary sense of the word; when he rails against men; and when, in order to work on men's minds effectively, he employs humour and bad taste, the 'way of blame'. No matter what has been said about him, benevolence, compassion and—above all—goodness are qualities which he developed in himself to the highest degree, while never allowing them to be associated with any useless and harmful gentleness.

It is in the apparently brutal relationship with a disciple that these qualities are manifested. For to love the disciple means not to console but to heal him. And the more serious the disease, the more violent the cure. Sometimes, in fact, amputation is necessary. 'If thy right eye offend thee,' said Christ, 'pluck it out, and cast it from thee.'

But Gurdjieff is not only a doctor, or a surgeon. He also points men towards paths to wisdom and happiness. Painful paths, often arduous, barren paths in the eyes of those whose 'personality' (that rigid monster) lacks the necessary flexibility to overcome obstacles; but they are also straighter ways, for those whose hearts are not yet hardened, for those 'common men' who have not systematically 'wiseacred', but have listened humbly and attentively to the 'inner voice'. For apart from the rugged path of the School, there exists the way of life, of 'popular' wisdom whose importance Gurdjieff always stressed. Thus in the first chapter of *Beelzebub's Tales* he writes: 'I [am] a follower in general not only of the theoretical—as contemporary people have become—but also of the practical sayings of popular wisdom which have become fixed by the centuries.'

This special way is the way of the *obyvatel*. '*Obyvatel* is a strange word in the Russian language,' Gurdjieff said. 'It is used in the sense of "inhabitant", without any particular shade. At the same time it is used to express contempt or derision—"*obyvatel*"—as though there could be nothing worse. But those who speak in this way do not understand that the *obyvatel* is the healthy kernel of life.'

It is also along the way of the *obyvatel* that the traveller encounters the legendary Persian master Mullah Nassr Eddin (Nasrudin), whom Gurdjieff constantly mentions in his books, ascribing to him most popular aphorisms and the most baffling and the wisest of his commentaries.

There exists in the Islamic world a legend of Mullah Nassr Eddin, a body of anecdotes whose hero is a master of paradox. For the Mullah is both the wisest of initiates and, apparently, the most stupid of yokels. Whether the Mullah really existed does not matter. He is the hero of hundreds of good stories which are also superb fables, some of which can rival the best of the many Zen stories collected by D. T. Suzuki in his *Essays*.

Several of these stories appear, with shrewd commentaries by Idries Shah, in his book *The Sufis*. The following is among the most typical:

The Mullah was thinking aloud.

'How do I know whether I am dead or alive?'

'Don't be such a fool,' his wife said; 'if you were dead your limbs would be cold.'

Shortly afterwards Nasrudin was in the forest cutting wood. It was midwinter. Suddenly he realized that his hands and feet were cold.

'I am undoubtedly dead,' he thought; 'so I must stop working, because corpses do not work.'

And, because corpses do not walk about, he lay down on the grass.

Soon a pack of wolves appeared and started to attack Nasrudin's donkey, which was tethered to a tree.

'Yes, carry on, take advantage of a dead man,' said Nasrudin from his prone position; 'but if I had been alive I would not have allowed you to take liberties with my donkey.'

In *Beelzebub's Tales,* as well as in *Meetings With Remarkable Men,* Mullah Nassr Eddin is constantly intervening, either to pronounce one of those 'true and scathing' sentences from his inexhaustible store, or to comment in a few words on a situation which Gurdjieff sees as characteristic of the inconsistency of human beings.

Mullah Nassr Eddin makes his appearance in order to remind us of the limits of the intellect; unless the whole being is involved, experience is in vain, and knowledge evanescent. The Mullah reaches his ends by apparently improbable means. He is the master of the way of blame, where the initiator takes on the role of the fool, the idiot, or the madman. But predicaments, however tricky they may be, always turn to his advantage.

Another master of the way of blame was Christ. Now we live in a society which is dominated, consciously or unconsciously, by the image of 'gentle Jesus'. When Gurdjieff affirms that we are suffering from 'the crystallization of the consequences of the properties of the maleficent organ Kundabuffer', an organ which causes us to perceive reality upside-down, I can think of no better justification of this admirable myth than the expression 'gentle Jesus' applied to the man who said: 'Think not that I am come to send peace on earth: I came not to send peace, but a sword. Nobody would dream of calling Christ inhuman.

Gurdjieff is often reproached for the way he rebuffed the curious and refused to answer any of their questions. But this same 'gentle Jesus' said: 'Give not that which is holy unto the dogs, neither cast ye your pearls before swine, lest they trample them under their feet, and turn again and rend you.'

Something else needs pointing out here, and that is that we find Gurdjieff all the harder to swallow because he addresses us in our own language, tells us in our own language: Become aware of your own nothingness. If he had been a Zen master, for instance, we would find him infinitely easier to accept. Yet anyone who has read Suzuki's *Essays in Zen Buddhism* knows how much violence may enter into the relations between master and disciple at the very core of Zen. But Zen is fashionable. Hence it is acceptable for a master to call his disciple a 'rice-bag', or take a stick to him, or slap him: it's exotic. Or else, worse still, Zen is watered down as Christianity has been watered down. The only thing that matters in Zen is the bliss of *satori*. The incredible efforts made by disciples to attain it are forgotten. In the end we come to confuse this or that rare emotion with true *satori*.

Gurdjieff, knowing the way people's minds work, protected himself against such abuses. He piled up the obstacles, highlighted the difficulties, demanded much of those who wanted to follow him. He spewed out the lukewarm, and for this they never forgave him.

NOTES ON *BEELZEBUB'S TALES*

One of the obstacles encountered by the student of Gurdjieff's teaching is created by the very style of writing that he uses both in *Beelzebub's Tales to His Grandson* and in *Meetings With Remarkable Men*. Yet these works are not at all alike. One is extraordinarily complex and hard to approach; the other is written more simply, almost in a strictly narrative style. But what they both have in common is that Gurdjieff introduces fantastic elements: in the former, extraterrestrial myths and fictions; in the latter, improbably marvellous events, such as the crossing of the Gobi desert on stilts.

The two books were written in Russian. But what is most remarkable is that the translations made of them both in English and in French have such quality that they stand up as exemplary literary creations in both languages. (There are also German translations of these works, but I shall leave it to German speakers to point out their quality.) How is it that these texts never give a hint of translation? It is because they were undertaken by Gurdjieff's very own disciples, and under his direction; they are the work of a *group* which was not in the least pressed for time, and whose sole concern was to communicate to the reader the special quality of a style unmatched, to my knowledge, in this century.

It has often been said that the style of *Beelzebub's Tales* is awkward. That is because we are not accustomed to it, because it runs counter to all the fashions and all the researches outside of which the iron rule holds that there is no possible salvation for a writer.

The essayist Jorge Luis Borges, well known for his paradoxes and fertile and individual ideas, in an essay entitled 'On the superstitious ethic of the reader' written in 1930 and reprinted in French in the collection *Discussion* (Paris, Gallimard, 1966), also stressed what he called 'the indigent condition of our literature, its inability to attract', which underlie what he considers to be a 'superstition about style':

> Those who are affected by this superstition understand by style not the effectiveness or lack of effectiveness of a page but the apparent successes of the writer— his comparisons, his harmony, the episodes of his punctuation and syntax. They are indifferent to personal conviction or emotion; they look for 'techniqueries' (the word is Unamuno's) which will tell them whether or not what is written has the right to please them.

Here we undoubtedly touch upon the most important problem in present-day literature. Form is no longer the servant of the idea (this statement is not to be taken as a profession of faith in classicism: in Lautréamont, for example, there is nothing gratuitous about the extreme 'baroquery' of the form). On the contrary, form exists, so to speak, in and for itself. And the author will reach the point of seeking to achieve nothing less than the dislocation of language, because he no longer has anything more to communicate than his own confusion, when it is not simply the arrogant affirmation of a pernicious capacity for constant so-called 'innovation'. What Mallarmé unquestionably suffered as a kind of martyrdom, the inability to write, which emerges in his work in the double dead-end of unintelligibility and affectation, most of today's writers experience through their own conformism, because it has become 'good taste' to hold forth incessantly about the celebrated 'incommunicability' of just about everything.

Hence the 'superstition about style' so roundly condemned by Borges when he says of writers,

> They have heard it said that close repetition of certain syllables is cacophonous, and they will pretend to be put out by it in prose, even if in poetry it brings them a particular—and in my opinion equally pretended—pleasure. *In other words they are looking not at the efficiency of the machinery but the arrangement of its parts.* They are subordinating emotion to ethic, or rather to good form [my italics].

Writers nearly always look for the 'page of perfection', but, as Borges emphasizes,

> The page of perfection, the page where not a word can be altered without damage, is the most precarious of all. . . . Conversely, the page which is destined for immortality can go through the furnace of errata, rough versions, careless readings and lack of understanding without losing its soul in the ordeal.

This is the case with the translations we have of the work of Gurdjieff, apart from the fact that they are quite untouched by the 'furnace of errata'. What Gurdjieff aims for is efficiency, which is why he has to create an utterly personal language able to convey both 'personal conviction' and 'emotion'.

The language of *Beelzebub's Tales to His Grandson* has as yet received very little worthwhile attention. I believe that Charles Duits's as yet unpublished study—not an exhaustive study, but rather thoughts which someone might confide, with no literary intention, to his diary, or to a friend—is worth quoting at length:

> The great qualities of the introduction to the *Tales* need not be emphasized. That introduction unarguably constitutes, in its own right, one of the most striking works of its era, and André Breton considered printing extracts from it in his *Anthology of Black Humour.*
>
> But the main text of the book is, to say the least, not easy to approach. Since it so happens that I have been studying it for years, it seemed that the best means available to me for honouring Gurdjieff's memory was to make it easier for the reader to approach this apparently forbidding text, in so far as this is possible.
>
> In fact it belongs, as the very title indicates, to one of the best-known of literary genres, the genre of Montesquieu's *Lettres persanes* and Voltaire's *L'Ingénu.* Beelzebub, a very kindly old man, has devoted the greater part of his existence to the inhabitants of the earth. He has tried his hardest to cure them of the terrible disease which afflicts them because of the "lack of foresight on the part of certain Most High, Most Very Saintly Cosmic Individuals". So we already see the "catch", because this being whose behaviour has obviously been nothing less than "angelic" is considered by human beings to be the devil in person. Thus, right from the start, we have a key: men see the world upside-down—that is their disease. They take Angels for Devils, and Devils for Angels.
>
> Clearly, if the genre to which *Beelzebub's Tales* belongs is a classic one, its teaching—or at any rate one of the teachings expressed in it—is also thoroughly traditional. Beneath the humorous surface of the fable we again meet the doctrine of illusion, of *Maya,* of the famous "sleep" which all the masters speak off, a sleep which must be broken and, from which the sleeper must "awaken".
>
> It will also be seen that Gurdjieff is seeking nothing less than to do something "new"—in which respect he certainly distinguishes himself from most professional writers. What is new—and prodigiously so—is the *form:* we have already seen enough to show that the content is ancient, classical and traditional.
>
> Having said that, it must also be said that no matter how apparently strange, baroque and even preposterous is the form adopted by Gurdjieff to express this traditional thinking, it too belongs to a very old tradition, that of the *Thousand and One Nights.* It seems to me very important to underline this point, because it is indisputable that only a reader capable of taking a *childish* pleasure from listening to stories can appreciate such a work. The gravest problems are at issue, yet Beelzebub is addressing a child, his grandson Hassein, and he narrates the cosmic adventure in the oriental style, that is to say, according to a certain rhythm which has admittedly become quite foreign to the modern Western mind. It is obvious that Homer's listeners enjoyed hearing the same epithets and the same phrases repeated again and again. The same goes for the Sultan listening to Scheherazade, and certainly too for the troubadours' listeners as they learned, for the thousandth time, that Charlemagne had a "flowing beard".
>
> Here we may be touching on what most deters the modern reader. What for a "childish" mind constitutes the charm and strength of the *Tales*— as of the *Iliad,* the *Chanson de Roland* and the *Thousand and One Nights*—namely the constant harping on the same images, the same expressions, and that tide-like ebb and flow—is just what the "intellectualized" reader finds hardest to take.
>
> We have to make up our minds here: this is a "process", very different from current practice, and like any other process it has its pros and cons. The use of a "primitive technique" in the twentieth century is obviously a gamble. Most readers will undoubtedly be put off. But some may find something of the fairy tale in them, and also—why mince words?—an inspiration which will carry them along in the end, if they can get over their initial bias.
>
> The process in question—as anyone soon realizes who has the patience to read a work like the *Tales*—in fact has a very special quality. Certainly a fearsome dragon stands on the threshold of such a book, a dragon which can only be called boredom. But whoever crosses the threshold discovers little by little that the repetitions and so on produce an altogether different effect. They take hold of the reader, create an "atmosphere"; he wants to go further, and like Hassein he asks for more. . . .
>
> I have mentioned the *Iliad* and the *Thousand and One Nights;* in many ways the *Tales* are also reminiscent of Rabelais, who, like Gurdjieff, takes his time and presents the modern reader with what is at first a hard surface to penetrate, but eventually gains a lasting hold on him. One returns to these books again and again, reading a page, or a chapter, stopping and then starting again, so that their quintessence penetrates without being noticed.
>
> I have dwelt on the Gurdjieffian process at some length, because it seems to me that what matters most is to prepare the possible reader. Misunderstanding is inevitable if you try to read the *Tales* as you read a novel. There is another way of reading, and therefore another way of considering literature (Joyce also tried to retrieve it in *Ulysses,* and above all in *Finnegans Wake*). A work which has no beginning and no end, which speaks of "all and everything", refuses to make any haste at all, and imposes its own pace on the reader.
>
> Having said this, we can now tackle the modern and even ultra-modern aspect of the book, Gurdjieff's great comic innovation, an invention which to my

mind makes him one of the literary geniuses of the century, and from which he draws an infinite variety of effects whose humour is sometimes disquieting. The entire book is written in a pseudo-scientific jargon whose cumulative effect—but with Gurdjieff all the effects are cumulative—is in my opinion utterly irresistible.

In some respects the *Tales* are nothing other than a marvellously extended satire on modern science, or to be more precise, on the scientific mind. Certainly Gurdjieff sees the extraordinary vanity of scholars as one of the most perfect illustrations of universal folly. This vanity goes hand in hand with pedantry, and is principally manifested in the continual use of a Greco-Latin jargon which enables the pundits to conceal the ordinariness of what they are saying, exactly like Molière's doctors, and to impose on everyone's credulity. Thus "saliakooríapa" is used for "water", "teskooano" for telescope, etc. I must add straight away that this jargon also has another totally serious purpose: there is in Gurdjieff a "verbal cabbala" which calls for an extremely meticulous and careful examination. But what concerns us here is to see how, with the help of this very simple means, Gurdjieff achieves an effect of absolute disorientation. Beelzebub talks to his grandson Hassein, and of course he talks in his grandson's language. They live on a planet unknown to the men of earth, called Karatas. So that in order to make himself understood by human beings Beelzebub has to *translate* certain of the words he uses. He gravely teaches Hassein the earth-men's word for "saliakooríapa", "teskooano", etc. The reader quickly reaches the point of considering the earth words from the viewpoint of the inhabitants of Karatas, and seriously follows such remarks as:

'And thus the three-brained beings breeding on the planet Earth call the greatest period of the flow of time "century," and this "century" of theirs consists of a hundred "years."

'A "year" has twelve "months."

'A "month" has an average of thirty "days," that is, diurnities.

'Further, they divide their diurnity into twenty-four "hours" and an "hour" into sixty "minutes."

'And a "minute" they divide into sixty "seconds."'

. . . only to suddenly be brought up short and then to roar with laughter. For actually he has just learned . . . nothing whatsoever.

And yet he has after all learned something, for he has begun to consider mankind from outside, and from much further outside than when he slipped into the skin of Montesquieu's Persians or Voltaire's Ingénu. It is our whole language, and hence our whole world, which loses its familiarity, and no longer just various manners, customs, laws and conventions. Like Montesquieu, and like Voltaire, Gurdjieff interposes a distance between the reader and mankind. But here the process is radicalized to the utmost. It is not our society which is made foreign, but the whole Earth, its history and geography, the most common and ordinary things. One is quite surprised to learn that human beings also practise "Elmooarno" (make love) and at the end of their lives undergo "Rascooarno" (die).

Thus the book is presented in the form of a comic ethnology—which takes the wind out of many sails. Just as ethnologists enjoy larding their writings with words borrowed from the peoples they study, so Gurdjieff manages to thoroughly "exoticize" us, so that our lives and our most everyday activities display their underlying structure. Life could be different: things are not simply "as they are".

And of course other fields are involved, as well as ethnology. Through this infinitely simple and infinitely effective process, Gurdjieff perfidiously incites us to ask questions: first, of course, to question the authority of science. But also—and even more disconcerting—to question the very reality of its findings. Everything is affected—physics, chemistry, biology. For it goes without saying that Gurdjieff is not satisfied only to substitute words of his own devising for those we use in everyday life. Generalizing the process, he replaces our entire science with another, and our "laws of nature"—as we call them—with a whole other system, described, of course, in a pompous, rebarbative language. Never mind the value of this system for the moment. The important thing here is once again the disorienting and "diabolic" effect, for in "explaining" all phenomena by laws unknown to Earth science, Gurdjieff insinuates a fundamental doubt. Is Einstein right? But what is there in Einstein which is not in the law of Triamazikamno or of Heptaparaparshinokh? Perhaps we do obtain some results, but not because we know the laws, rather because we have glimpsed certain aspects of much more general laws which we do not know. To tell the truth, here one tends to forget that the *Tales* are, after all, a work of fiction. Thoroughly bewildered, we are ready to admit that the sun gives neither heat nor light, that the moon is a nascent planet, not a dead one, and so on. Without realizing it we reach the point of *taking Gurdjieff at his word,* so that we have to make a certain effort to *wake up,* to understand the game we have just been taken in by, and also to see that in life we are perhaps taken in by just such a game.

I hasten to add that Gurdjieff's "laws" are definitely not as fantastic as one might think, and that his cosmology may be less absurd than it seems. For the moment, though, this is not what matters: the important thing is to see the process through which Gurdjieff, so to speak, disabuses his reader, forces him to question what he never questions and—last but not least—makes him grasp at first hand what it is that produces that dismal mechanization of thought which lies at the root of so many of our troubles.'

GURDJIEFF AND 'WORD PROSTITUTION'

Gurdjieff went at some length into his literary project, and into the means chosen to implement it, in the first chapter of *Beelzebub's Tales* and the introduction to *Meetings With Remarkable Men.*

First, he writes because he is compelled to do so. No one cared less for 'fame' than Gurdjieff, and for some time his writings were available only to the members of the groups he guided. He insists that his work is not essentially 'literary' in the usual sense of the word. Writing is above all a religious act, as the first paragraph of the *Tales* makes eminently clear;

> Among other convictions formed in my common presence during my responsible, peculiarly composed life, there is one such also—an indubitable conviction—that always and everywhere on the earth, among people of every degree of development of understanding and of every form of manifestation of the factors which engender in their individuality all kinds of ideals, there is acquired the tendency, when beginning anything new, unfailingly to pronounce aloud or, if not aloud, at least mentally, that definite utterance understandable to every even quite illiterate person, which in different epochs has been formulated variously and in our day is formulated in the following words: 'In the name of the Father and of the Son and in the name of the Holy Ghost. Amen.'

> That is why I now, also, setting forth on this venture quite new for me, namely, authorship, begin by pronouncing this utterance and moreover pronounce it not only aloud, but even very distinctly and with a full, as the ancient Toulousites defined it, 'wholly-manifested-intonation.'

Gurdjieff's intention is nothing less than to reach the reader in his deepest being, and in all the regions of his being, mental, emotional and corporeal. In this respect Gurdjieff's books stand utterly distinct from the works of someone like Ouspensky, remarkable as they are, whose scope is necessarily reduced by their overly intellectual character.

Gurdjieff has been much talked about but very little read, and when read, rarely appreciated. The fact is that he is an anomaly. His work cannot be compared with anything else written in this century, nor classified in any precise genre. Hence the disaffection of those head-hunters of the mind, the critics: finding themselves unable to reduce what is so vast that they cannot even grasp it, they ignore or despise it—this is proved, I think, by those critical commonplaces to the effect that Balzac wrote badly, and Victor Hugo was stupid. Nowadays one hears that Gurdjieff was dangerous, dishonest. People steered clear of him, and after his death they steer clear of his work, which is simultaneously fiction, epic poem, satire and autobiography—as well as constituting a world-view unknown to those who claim that thinking is their calling. The perfection of Gurdjieff's work has seldom been recognized.

Yet as far back as 1956 a writer like Manuel Rainoird was praising 'his literary mastery, so clearly displayed (the genres he calls into play leave our elegant efforts far behind)'. Rainoird adds:

> I feel the strong necessity, once having read *Beelzebub's Tales to His Grandson: An Objectively Impartial Criticism of the Life of Man*—if I say 'read' it is for want of a better word, for the work is much more than that suggests, like an infinitely testing trial, a substance both assimilable and unassimilable by every organ—to pronounce in the midst of my stunned astonishment the words 'great' and 'new'. But as I also run my eye through the library of contemporary fiction, I realize that here there is no possible term of comparison, and that when it comes to 'great' and 'new' there is no book to approach it—what work of philosophy, science, legend or history? And yet it is our history which is in question, yours and mine, universal and personal.

The greatness lies in the undertaking, the total novelty in the *tone,* that particular tone (as Rimbaud's dawns are 'particular') which makes a major work, and which has never been heard or conveyed by those whom Gurdjieff calls 'ordinary patented-writers'.

The *Tales* begin with a reiterated profession of faith:

> In any case I again repeat—in order that you should well remember it, but not as you are in the habit of remembering other things and on the basis of which are accustomed to keeping your word of honor to others or to yourself—that no matter what language I shall use, always and in everything, I shall avoid what I have called the 'bon ton literary language.'

'Bon ton' was undoubtedly what he ridiculed the most; and education, as we understand it, was what he saw as the most grievous problem of all. Literature seemed to him to be one of the noblest of disciplines, sorrily reduced in this century to what he harshly describes as 'the development of "word prostitution".' Read the introduction to *Meetings With Remarkable Men,* with its merciless speech by the elderly cultured Persian. Anyone who has prided himself on his skill with the pen, and anybody who dips complacently into the stagnant water of contemporary prose and cadences—when these amount to nothing more than futile yet injurious linguistic manipulations—if there is a jot of honesty left in him, will not be able to read that speech without being overwhelmed by the power of those *basic truths* which are the common province of the masters, and which in their apparent triteness we tend to bypass, to our own detriment, when instead we should pay them the closest attention.

The journalism whose faults are condemned by the genius of Balzac in *Illusions perdues* rots language and rots thought. With trivial games on the one hand, and continual lying on the other, the spirit becomes irretrievably corrupted:

'According to my conviction, which has finally become as firm as a rock—and anyone thinking more or less impartially will come to the same conclusion—it is chiefly owing to this journalistic literature that any man who tries to develop by the means available in contemporary civilization acquires a thinking faculty adequate, at the very most, for "the first invention of Edison", and in respect of emotionality develops in himself, as Mullah Nassr Eddin would say, "the fineness of feeling of a cow".'

Consequently, one can only turn to those ancient methods some of which Charles Duits elicits in the essay quoted above, if one wishes not only to communicate essential information to the reader but also to act, as Gurdjieff sets out to act, on the reader's entire being.

The dramatic question which today faces the writer who cares about truth, namely how can sublime words still be uttered without being misunderstood, Gurdjieff settles in an exemplary manner. Just as the sacred *wonder* of the heroes of tragedy metamorphoses into the mere raising of a blasé eyebrow, so, day after day, the holy words love, hope and freedom are watered down; these words, among others, have been tainted and weakened every time they have fallen from the mouths of fanatics and tyrants. How is the original strength of these words to be restored? Gurdjieff either translates them into the language of Karatas or else uses the same unchanging method to clarify their meaning: when he means the vague idea he will say 'love', in inverted commas, and when he means the idea in its fullest sense he will say 'sacred being-impulse of genuine Love'. And this insistence on repeating the words of Karatas, and on solemnly defining ideas, is to my mind one of the strengths of his language, even though it has often been felt as unnecessary emphasis.

What should the reader of the *Tales* guard against, above all? To find that out, all it takes is to read through the familiar expressions which are put between inverted commas in the first pages of the book: the fatal ability to put off anything we wish to do 'till tomorrow', all the 'wealth' people have, the 'professional writers', and their 'instructive-articles', 'patented-writers', 'bon ton literary language' and so on. But the inverted commas may also highlight some just expression used by Beelzebub and his kind: 'active being-mentation', for example, or 'higher being-bodies' or 'being-Partkdolg-duty'.

Thus there is nothing fortuitous in Gurdjieff's style. The *Tales* are a book of initiation, with numerous facets. Again I am obliged to turn to a writer who will illuminate certain aspects of the diverse body of Gurdjieff's work better than I can:

So here is a book which cannot be read as we read our books—which simultaneously attracts and repels us. A book of a stature and inspiration which, although it entirely contains us, bag and baggage, is manifestly far above our heads! It is as if, caught up in that inspiration, engulfed in it and exhorted along the way to behave as something

other than children, we were being urged to want what is wanted without our participation. It is like the implacable guard who chivvies and rouses the passengers before the train reaches some frontier, out of sheer kind-heartedness (since he is not involved), so that they will be ready and things will go smoothly.

Here man is seen from above, as he had never previously been seen. This vision from a very great distance—Beelzebub the narrator is the inhabitant of worlds like our own, only far removed, and as an envoy from above he has sometimes had occasion to make flights to the planet Earth—this overview on the scale of our Great Universe engulfs any reader and bathes him in an extraordinarily clear light, so that far from blurring the details, the hidden springs of the human mechanism, it has the effect of revealing them all the more. The more the view embraces, the better it explains by analogy the function and meaning of the creature made in the image of God. Here, distance has a twofold and quite astonishing effect. The greater the height to which Beelzebub goes, the more the confusion of our usual jumble of ideas is dispelled. What emerges is the opposite—we see in high relief what was previously screened and misunderstood. The high has illuminated the low. Infinite spaces have ceased to frighten us. They no longer appear in the void of a bleak futility, produced by the musings of the top mathematician in the open examinations; instead, now that they are peopled—revealing themselves in their tangible aspect as emanations of the affliction of Our deeply-Loving and infinitely patient eternal Creator—they become living, transmitting matter, creative of a new language, matter of which Beelzebub is a more and more conscious emanation, through his merits and his efforts.

Now in spite of this grandeur Beelzebub still remains a kind of standard or model, all other things being equal. His personality is attractive. Deprived of his horns, Beelzebub, devil though he is, has not been exempt from the process of expiation. This was his exile in the solar system Ors, to which our own planet belongs—exile for errors made in his youth, and which greatly resemble our familiar *sins*, with the corollary they imply, the forgetting of man's cosmic functions in the universe, and the concomitant unhappy effects which are impartially noted by Beelzebub, who would like to see them rooted out from inside the three-centred beings of the planet Earth.

What do we know of the meaning of our life on Earth? If G. I. Gurdjieff works within a literary form so that this question may some day occur to us, under certain conditions, he does it like no one else. All commentaries past, present and future, even *In Search of the Miraculous,* are mere pools compared with his ocean. If Gurdjieff tackles his task in one manner only, he has available an arsenal of ways to arouse our interest. Although it is impossible to follow the usual practice of giving a glimpse of what is named or described, it would be an act of charity at least to point out to the dear public, fond of philosophico-literary tracts, that we are actually dealing here with the disconcerting question: 'Who are we, where are we going?', but strongly flavoured, according to a recipe it will not find familiar, with an accompaniment of cymbals and the use of other sonorous and percussive instruments. In this recipe, iced water and itching powder are also involved.

But let me repeat that the reader is not simply *defeated*. He is reading the kind of *roman-fleuve* which, in the long run, will sweep him along with it. The work of demolishing received ideas is not undertaken with the aim of imposing a knowledge which we have not drawn in through our own roots, or which, taken literally, and without genuine links with the inner world, would tend to generate grave misapprehensions. With our minds under such fiendish attack, we give way to the following mental gymnastics: we defend ourselves, we surrender. And if we surrender it is because somewhere around the plexus a warmth may develop—like the air filling in our lungs—by virtue of the representations which have been aroused, as if all at once there had been correspondences established between the superb obscurities of this book and unknown areas of ourselves. In simpler terms, let us recall that certain writings, such as the Song of Solomon, or the Gospel According to St John, were designed to rouse our emotions. The *Tales* are of this nature. There is nothing in them for rigid minds.

This uncommonly accurate account comes from the article quoted at the beginning of this chapter, by the writer Manuel Rainoird.

As that other spiritual master, Georges Saint-Bonnet, would have said, a plague on all 'verbal felicities'. Writing only has meaning when it describes genuine—'being', as Gurdjieff would say—experience, and the writer is the repository of a teaching worthy of the name. 'The favourite error of present-day literature is emphasis,' said Borges. 'Definitive words, words postulating the wisdoms of soothsayers or angels, or the resolves of a more than human firmness—"unique, never, always, altogether, perfection, complete"—are common currency with *every* writer. They do not think that saying a thing too much is just as clumsy a thing for a writer to do as not saying it at all, that generalization and intensification due to negligence are signs of poverty, and that the reader feels this. Their thoughtlessness is the cause of a depreciation of language.'

Gurdjieff is formidably well armed against any such depreciation. The methods he develops to counter it may be surprising, but they are particularly effective. I feel that it is by success on such a scale that genius is measured. As for his thinking, its originality, at least in this century, and its remarkable cohesion are proof enough of its importance. Add to this that his speech is a *speech of life,* and that once it is taken really seriously it has the power to break down the solid walls of unawareness and indifference, and you have measure enough of its range, when you consider that ours is essentially a day of error and delusion.

B. A. St. Andrews (essay date 1988)

SOURCE: "Gurdjieff and the Literary Cult," in *The University of Windsor Review,* Vol. 21, No. 2, 1988, pp. 46-51.

[*In the following essay, St. Andrews examines the group of literary figures, including Katherine Mansfield and Jean Toomer, that followed Gurdjieff's teachings.*]

Many and strange are the tales from the literary crypt. As any quick look at James Sutherland's fascinating *Oxford Book of Literary Anecdotes* or Donald Hall's American corollary proves, writers seek the ever-elusive Muse in some strange places. Almost with abandon, they delve into cults and the occult; they pursue spiritualists and mystics, sometimes finding inspiration, often times not. But the quest seems a worthy one, no matter how questionable the result.

Not one of the movers and shakers (or the preachers and fakirs) who have created popular cults in our century is more controversial than one George Ivanovich Gurdjieff, an Armenian mystic. Nor has any cult figure, with the possible exception of one Madame Helena Petrovna Blavatsky of the still flourishing Theosophical Movement, maintained a greater influence over literary seekers.

Yet while Madame Blavatsky's influence may seem to have influenced, in positive ways, the mature consciousness and, in turn, poetry of such notables as W. B. Yeats, the influence of Gurdjieff on major writers is roundly proclaimed a negative one. And, students of both British and American letters might insist, for a multitude of reasons. Gurdjieff, in fact, as Antony Alpers recalls is his engaging study, *The Life of Katherine Mansfield,* is still widely considered to be "the man who killed Katherine Mansfield."

Not that she would have thus accused him; indeed, Mansfield sought Gurdjieff out as a healer and lifegiver. With her fear of tuberculosis a confirmed reality, she began a frenzied search for a miracle; she needed to believe that Gurdjieff held some power, some secret for her physical restoration. Mansfield willingly accepted that her spiritual health, too, needed regeneration. So, in 1922, having attended a lecture by Gurdjieff's most eloquent disciple, P. D. Ouspensky, Mansfield committed herself to Gurdjieff's "Institute for the Harmonious Development of Man" which, she apparently believed, could as harmoniously develop Woman. In a chateau in Fontainebleau, France, Mansfield lived with "the Master" and his devotees.

There, according to her own correspondence, Mansfield shared the chores and the cold. Despite sometimes scant foodstuffs and rigorous schedules, she foreswore any other form of treatment than that prescribed by the Gurdjieff encampment: work, dancing, and "balancing the centers." Gurdjieff defined these 'centres' as the intellectual, the emotional, and the moving; he later added, according to Ouspensky's voluminous study, *In Search of the Miraculous,* the instinctive centre and the sexual centre.

Mansfield did indeed find some balance at Fontainebleau, spiritually if not physically. She quieted her life-long friend, Leslie Moore's fears about Fontainebleau, asserting on December 22, 1922: "My existence here is not meagre or miserable. Nothing is done by accident." So, it was surely not by accident that, on the evening of January 9, 1923, Katherine Mansfield enjoyed the music, the dancing, the good company at Fontainebleau; her guest and husband, J. Middleton Murry, was among that company, as was one Olga Ivanovna. Ivanovna later married the eminently 'balanced' architect, Frank Lloyd Wright, but, more to the point, Ivanovna befriended Mansfield at the Institute and rendered one of the most moving accounts of the writer's last evening.

Mansfield was "transformed" by a spirit of love: "Her face was shining with inexpressible beauty, and when she left the party in the great hall she was so full of joy that she must have forgotton her physical weaknesses and she ran . . . up the stair." Within half an hour of her joy, Mansfield suffered a massive and fatal hemorrhage. None of this was caused by "the Master;" Gurdjieff neither killed nor cured Mansfield. He extended to her, by her own accounts, both courtesy and kindness. Yet he became the center of recriminations and anger as the literary community reacted to the loss of a considerable young talent: a writer compared favorably with the great Chekhov. Nor was this the last of Gurdjieff's supposed sins against the literary cult.

His unpopularity in British literary circles was easily matched by American disfavor when Jean Toomer, the brief, bright light of the Harlem Renaissance defected, to join Gurdjieff's band the following year. That year, 1923, was monumental for Toomer; he met Gurdjieff and published his own masterwork, *Cane.* Most critics of the Harlem Renaissance, from Charles Davis to Arna Bontemps, consider Toomer's book the trumpet fanfare of the literary period. As Darwin T. Turner puts it in his introduction to the novel, *Cane* was both "a harbinger" of the renaissance and "an illumination of significant psychological and moral concerns of the early '20's."

Among these concerns was the great spiritual longing of that time, reflected in works by T. S. Eliot, Toomer, and others. Little wonder that their generation sought out— much as the cult generation of the 1960's later would— the spiritual wisdom of the East. The unsettling pronouncements of Darwin and Nietzsche, as well as the turbulence of World War I, had considerably depleted the spiritual stockpile of the West. This longing for harmony filled many Americans and Europeans in the time between two wars; into this partial vacuum walked George Ivanovich Gurdjieff with his system of cosmic and earthly order. Looking himself like "something between a carpet dealer and a spy," Gurdjieff invited these, the spiritually beleagured, into his system.

Toomer entered. He, too, joined the Institute for the Harmonious Development of Man, leaving behind a burgeoning literary career where he had been embraced by such established notables as Sherwood Anderson and Langston Hughes. Toomer took a leap of faith, one might say, from literary fame to spiritual obscurity. Gurdjieff— that harmless mystic, that dismissible cult figure—had struck again; he had disrupted the literary community a second, unforgiveable time. Toomer's essays, poems and plays, which never again received the acclaim of his first work, have been collected by Darwin T. Turner under the title *The Wayward and the Seeking;* one nearly epic poem called "The Blue Meridian" offers an image appropriate to Toomer's quest: despite losing literary fame he "found / A river flowing backward to its source."

Yet, while Toomer declared his profound conviction that he had, thanks to Gurdjieff's system, gained a balanced center, Gurdjieff again appeared to be more spiritual culprit than spiritual guide. Condemned by some, extolled by others, Gurdjieff remains enigmatic; the stories about him provide a portrait of a pompous man, an independent one; an inspiring personality, an insulting one. Gurdjieff is charlatan and saint, shyster and sage.

Perhaps Katherine Mansfield best characterized Gurdjieff as being "not the least what I expected. He's what one wants to find him, really." This odd notion of the plastic personality may best suit Gurdjieff, the man. The confounding facts of his life enhance this enigmatic image. His obituary in the London *Times* (November 12, 1949) lists his birth in 1872; his passport declares him born in 1877, yet he insisted on having been born in 1869. As Kathleen Speeth and Ira Friedlander note in their almost devout study, *Gurdjieff: Seeker of the Truth,* a series of such confounded facts make Gurdjieff's life read like holy runes. The conflicting details invite, that is, apocryphal interpretations which becloud yet enlarge the man himself.

For example, Gurdjieff was born at the foot of fabled Mt. Ararat; as a boy, he responded whole-heartedly to tales of adventure and mystery which filled his native Armenia. Chief among these stories, according to Speeth and Friedlander, were tales of the "Imastun," a society of initiates who wandered the planet after the disappearance of Atlantis. Gurdjieff, inspired by the arcane tales, undertook religious study with a group of like-minded adventurers. In the major religious centers of the world, he studied Buddhist, Hindu, Christian, Islamic, and Lamaist thought, integrating these many systems into one of his own.

Gurdjieff created, in doing so, a personality loaded with practical insights about people, on the one hand, and impudent repudiations of established religious orders, on the other. Emblematic of his growing confidence is one story involving Gurdjieff's saving of a Yezidi boy which is recorded by Speeth and Friedlander. At the center of this possibly apocryphal tale is the idea of the "sacred circle" which is complete and inviolable. Within such a circle drawn by the Yezidi tribe of Iran sat a boy who could starve there or await religious enlightenment forever, according to the will of those who drew the circle. In a brazen act, a spiritual correlative to Alexander's handling of the famed Gordian knot, Gurdjieff erased part of that circle and led the boy to freedom. That he did this with impunity added to his growing reputation as a holy man of irresistible force.

As controversial as his violations of sacred ritual were Gurdjieff's abilities to manipulate people, either singly or in groups. He could deliver a verbal insult the equal of Dorothy Parker, destroying even the strongest facade of self control or self delusion with a single phrase. An example of this odd ability to humiliate others yet prove himself indispensable at the same time is recounted in a lively and highly amusing way by Arthur "Fritz" Peters in *Gurdjieff Remembered*. Greeting a collection of wealthy and influential New Yorkers, Gurdjieff acted the harmless, humble foreigner. Having put them at their ease, he quite deliberately turned the dinner conversation to sex, rousing them to a frenzy by recounting, in detail, the sexual customs of cultures both familiar and exotic.

As Peters recalls, "after about two hours of unadulterated four-letter word conversation, their behavior became completely uninhibited." An orgy ensued, after which Gurdjieff insisted that "he deserved to be paid for this lesson." He promptly collected several thousand dollars from his already spent guests.

New Yorkers and other species of Americans rarely encourage those who abuse, chastise, or mock them. Yet, far and wide, Americans found this strange man fascinating and, often, inspiring, Despite their lavish monetary contributions to his cause, however, Gurdjieff maintained a low opinion of his American followers. He considered Americans to be, as the tale of the party-goers sufficiently suggests, genitally insecure. He warned, as early as the Thirties, that the "new American gods" of psychiatry and medicine would further dupe and divide the American psyche. He considered, quite simply, that none of these scientists understood the balances in Nature and in human nature. He—George Ivanovich Gurdjieff—did. He offered into the criticism the one element which has proved alluring since Dante and Blake and Yeats and, for that matter, Christ: a formulated system of cosmic order.

Ironically, the best written presentation of this system may well have been written not by "the Master" himself but by his talented and intelligent disciple, P. D. Ouspensky. Gurdjieff did write, however, and the stories surrounding his compositions and their sales invite affirming sighs from the true believers and rueful glances from everyone else. Many people familiar with book publication and promotion might well find his methods direct, honest, and innovative. Consider his pitch for *An Objectively Impartial Criticism of the Life of Man* or its alternative title, *Beelzebub's Tales to His Grandson*, gleaned from fifty years of thought. He gathered together his followers from many different nations, classes and

professions. He urged those who had "gained personal help from contact with (his) ideas" to buy a copy of his book for the tidy sum of one hundred pounds, the equivalent of four hundred American dollars, at that time.

Those not under the influence of "the Master" might find either this approach to advanced sales or the price quite unacceptable. In any case, such were the book parties of George Ivanovich Gurdjieff and his disciples. This anecdote comes from a memoir containing a guileless and therefore complicated portrait of Gurdjieff as writer and as spiritual leader. Best known as the writer of *A Nun's Story* Kathryn Hulme composed a book entitled *Undiscovered Country* which should be better known not only because of its study of a spiritual quest but also because of Hulme's talent for bringing an historical moment alive.

Her recollections begin with meeting Gurdjieff, but she also recreates the Paris of the Thirties and Forties. She includes fascinating accounts of her patriotic service welding ships as a "Rosie the Riveter" as well as of her administrative service to the European relief efforts after the war. These facts and impressions about the millions of "D.P.'s"—displaced persons—from Poland and the Nazi concentration camps prove to be as compelling as her recollections about "the Master."

Yet her details about Gurdjieff and his only occasionally merry band bring up, quite unintentionally, serious questions about the nature of discipleship. Any reader not under the spell of "the Master," that is, might find some of her precise recollections somewhat disturbing. Her records even make Gurdjieff's followers seem somewhat dim-witted, yet she recounts these incidents with neither resentment nor embarrassment. For example, Gurdjieff liked to propose toasts to "the diverse categories of 'idiots' in which he classified his guests." These gatherings were always dramatic, well-staged, and eventful: Gurdjieff at his theatrical best. Even those "idiots" who felt disillusioned by Gurdjieff's personal behavior and performances—Toomer, for example, experienced this negative conversion from "the Master,"—still praised Gurdjieff's ideas and influence.

To study this attitude of "true believers" is to examine something as complex as "the Master" himself. Certainly, as Eric Hoffer noted long ago, the disciple is aware of moving against the mainstream of orthodoxy and fervently fights upstream anyway. The choice of spiritual guide or guru or confessor rarely makes serene good sense to anyone other than a fellow "true believer." The "idiots"—from Toomer to Mansfield to Ouspensky to Hulme—were simply too talented and intelligent to be conveniently dismissed. They each found spiritual well-being within Gurdjieff's system. For these diverse people, the quest led them to an American mystic with a cunning sense of physics and metaphysics. To dismiss him merely as "the man who killed Katherine Mansfield" or as the man who robbed the Harlem Renaissance of its crown jewel seems to avoid the deeper issue.

Gurdjieff is, rather, a figure emblematic of the baffling and endless quest for the spiritual certainty; many seekers are drawn magnetically to those who proclaim, "This is the way." Further, this search seems absolutely endemic to the creative life; whether this trait is considered foolish, tragic, or transcendent is, of course, significant. Cults can create or destroy personalities and, as the story of Jesus and his cult of followers rather convincingly attests, transform culture, as well.

In his astute article for *Nation* entitled "Skepticism and the True Believer," Theodore Roszak remarked that the issue of spiritual seeking remains one of monumental import in a world where "conducting autopsies on dead gods is a Freshman philosophy assignment." The writer is always, consciously or unconsciously, searching for the Muse; this fusion of the mystical and practical sources of writing has an age-old credibility still. That such a sacred Source might find embodiment—for Mansfield, Toomer, Hulme, and other writers—in one George Ivanovich Gurdjieff may seem lamentable to the literary cult but perfectly lucid to his devoted defectors.

FURTHER READING

Bibliography

Driscoll, J. Walter. *Gurdjieff: An Annotated Bibliography.* New York: Garland, 1985, 363 p.
   Comprehensive bibliography of secondary sources.

Biography

Bennett, John G., *Gurdjieff—A Very Great Enigma: Three Lectures.* Reprint. York Beach, ME: Samuel Weiser, 1973, 96 p.
   Discusses "the incredible environment of Gurdjieff's boyhood," the eclectic influences on his occult beliefs, and the major concepts on which his teachings are based.

De Hartmann, Thomas, and De Hartmann, Olga. *Our Life with Mr. Gurdjieff.* New York: Viking Penguin, 1992, 304 p.
   Divided into three sections: the first, a brief introduction to the book, written by Thomas de Hartmann and later expanded by Olga de Hartmann; the second, a biographical sketch of Gurdjieff; the third, a biographical sketch of the de Hartmanns.

Moore, James. *Gurdjieff—The Anatomy of a Myth: A Biography.* Rockport, MA: Element Books, 1993, 415 p.
   A defense of Gurdjieff against allegations of fraudulence.

Nott, C. S. *Teachings of Gurdjieff: A Pupil's Journal.* New York: Viking Penguin, 1991, 256 p.
   A day-to-day account of studies with Gurdjieff and

A. R. Orage. "The first part of the present book consists chiefly of accounts of work with Gurdjieff; the second of Orage's commentary in the New York group; while the third is a kind of sequel to and result of the first two."

Criticism

Anderson, Margaret. *The Unknowable Gurdjieff.* London: Arkana (Penguin), 1962, 212 p.
   A firsthand account of Gurdjieff's teachings, and ". . . a rectification—which will prevent anyone from ever again having the hardihood to call Gurdjieff an impostor."

Hough, Graham. "The Shaman of Fontainebleau." *The Times Literary Supplement* (13 June 1980): 665-666.
   A review of three memoirs of Gurdjieff. Hough concludes that "looked at in the right context Gurdjieff appears as merely one in the long line of mystagogues, masters, gurus and shamans whose operations have been a constantly recurrent feature of our world, and remain an eternal puzzle to those who are constitutionally immune to their influence."

Lefort, Rafael. *The Teachers of Gurdjieff.* New York: Samuel Weiser, 1966, 157 p.
   Sketches of fifteen Sufi mystics known to have encountered and influenced Gurdjieff during his travels.

Ouspensky, P. D. "Food for Transformation." *Parabola* XVII, No. 4 (Winter 1992): 16-19.
   Recalls one of Gurdjieff's talks.

Speeth, Kathleen Riordan. "Gurdjieff." In *Transpersonal Psychologies*, edited by Charles T. Tart, pp. 281-328. New York: Harper & Row, 1975.
   An introduction to Gurdjieff in the context of psychological behaviorism and Gestalt psychotherapy.

——, and Friedlander, Ira. *Gurdjieff: Seeker of the Truth.* New York: Harper Colophon Books, 1980, 175 p.
   A series of essays about Gurdjieff and his teachings.

——. *The Gurdjieff Work.* Los Angeles: Jeremy P. Archer, 1989, 144 p.
   Chapters: Who Was Gurdjieff?, The Philosophical Basis of Gurdjieff's System, The Psychology of Ordinary Human Beings, Human Possibilities, The Gurdjieff Work, and The Living Tradition.

Vaysse, Jean. *Toward Awakening: An Approach to the Teaching Left by Gurdjieff.* London: Routledge & Kegan Paul, 1980, 170 p.
   Analysis of Gurdjieff's ideas, which constitute "the truest answer to the questions raised by the tremendous material power now in the hands of modern man as he questions himself in front of the so-called 'options' which its use obliges him to face."

Karen Horney

1885-1952

(Born Karen Clementine Theodore Danielsen) German-born American psychiatrist and nonfiction writer.

INTRODUCTION

Horney is best known as a trenchant critic of orthodox Freudian psychoanalysis and as a founding theorist of humanistic psychology. Countering the biological determinism she found integral to Sigmund Freud's theories, she emphasized the importance of social, cultural, and interpersonal factors in the formation of personality. Horney argued that the underlying causes of neurosis and anxiety are the same for men and women, and thus corrected what she saw as Freud's overemphasis on instinctual drives and his "male bias" in regard to feminine psychology.

Biographical Information

Horney was born near Hamburg, Germany. Her father, a naturalized German citizen from Norway, was a sea captain and, by her own accounts, an intimidating and emotionally repressive figure. Her mother, who had ancestors in the German and Dutch nobility, was roughly twenty years younger than Horney's father and a much more nurturing presence in her life. While she excelled in school and was encouraged in intellectual pursuits by her mother, Horney attended college only after promising her father—who did not believe in education for women—that she would never again ask him for anything else. She graduated in 1906 and entered the University of Freiburg Medical School; she was one of fifty-eight women enrolled with well over two thousand men. In 1909 she married Oskar Horney, a lawyer. Two years later, after having studied at Freiburg, Göttingen, and Berlin, she was graduated from medical school. She was awarded her medical degree in 1915 after completing her dissertation entitled "A Casuistic [Clinical] Contribution to the Question of Traumatic Psychoses." While working at various hospitals and institutions in Germany, Horney met and received psychoanalytic therapy from Karl Abraham, a well-known psychiatrist and colleague of Freud. In 1917 she presented her first professional paper, "The Technique of Psychoanalytic Therapy," in which she argued for the individual's potential for lifelong emotional growth. This view was at odds with Freud's, who soon after pointedly ridiculed and refuted her work. Horney entered into private practice in 1919, which she continued—along with teaching at the Berlin Psychoanalytic Institute—until 1932, when the rise of Adolf Hitler and the Nazi party impelled her to emigrate to the United States. First at the Chicago Institute of Psychoanalysis, then in New York at the New School for Social Research

and the New York Psychoanalytic Institute, Horney practiced psychiatry, taught, and wrote many influential papers, essays, and books.

Major Works

Critics note that Horney's first important works were fourteen papers she delivered at conferences between 1922 and 1937. In these works, collected posthumously in *Feminine Psychology* (1967), she laid out her primary objections to Freudian psychoanalysis and outlined the ways in which she felt women should be treated in psychiatric theory and practice. In "On the Genesis of the Castration Complex in Women" and "The Flight from Womanhood," for example, Horney took issue with, among other things, Freud's concept of "penis envy." Freud argued that early in their development girls regard their genital difference from boys as a "lack," as castration. Consequently, their "envy" of boys is manifested in feelings of inferiority and subservience. For Horney, this represented Freud's chauvinistic tendency to view the male as the measure of the female. She proposed that there are social, cultural, and ideological factors responsible for women's anxieties regarding their adequacy and potency, and that, as Agnes N. O'Connell summarized, "what women envy is not the penis but the superior position of men in society." Freud also held that, because of the "castration complex," women are inherently masochistic, or given to seeking situations—not necessarily sexual in nature—in which they assume roles of dependence and victimization. In "The Problem of Feminine Masochism" Horney again argued that there are compelling social, cultural, and economic factors to which one should attribute women's reliance upon men for love, security, etc. Arguing against Freud's "instinct-based metapsychology," Horney's works from this period and after increasingly view the causes of neurosis and anxiety—for both men and women—as stemming from social forces and damaged personal relationships. In her fullest examination of these causes, *The Neurotic Personality of Our Time* (1937), she concluded that basic anxiety is not the result of unavoidable and gender-specific psychosexual traumas, but rather is the manifestation of repressed hostility generated in a disturbed relationship with one or both parents. Furthermore, as R. N. Iyer noted, for Horney "neuroses have a power of continuous growth that cannot be explained exclusively in terms of past experiences. . . ." Elaborating on these ideas in *Our Inner Conflicts* (1945) and *Neuroses and Human Growth* (1950), she posited that there are three predominant "neurotic trends," or ways in which individuals cope with potentially overwhelming anxiety. She described the first as "moving toward others"; through this process, the neurotic individual ingratiates him- or herself with others seeking affection and acceptance. In the second, "moving against others," the individual tries to dominate and manipulate people in order to express aggression and experience a sense of control. "Moving away from others," the third major "neurotic trend," involves both a protective attempt to isolate oneself and an obsessive concern with one's own perfection. Horney believed that an individual could manifest elements of all three tendencies, the mutual incompatibility of which could itself produce further neurosis. In the neurotic or "alienated" personality, Horney argued, there is a discrepancy between what she called the "Real Self" and the idealized self the individual constructs in order to deal with inner conflicts. As she conceived it, the goal of psychiatric therapy is to reconcile this discrepancy, to bring about integration and "self-realization." Iyer noted that in Horney's approach, "[g]enerating spontaneity of feeling is requisite for authentic expression. . . . The most comprehensive therapeutic goal is wholeheartedness, living without pretence, wholly sincere and fully engaged." In his eulogy for her, the existential theologian Paul Tillich said of Horney: "She knew the darkness of the human soul, and the darkness of the world, but believed that what giveth light to any one suffering human being will finally give light to the world. The light she gave was not a cold light of passionless intellect, it was the light of passion and love. She wrote books but loved human beings. She helped them by insights into themselves which had healing power."

PRINCIPAL WORKS

The Neurotic Personality of Our Time (nonfiction) 1937
New Ways in Psychoanalysis (nonfiction) 1939
Self-Analysis (nonfiction) 1942
Our Inner Conflicts: A Constructive Theory of Neurosis (nonfiction) 1945
Are You Considering Psychoanalysis? (nonfiction) 1946
Neurosis and Human Growth: The Struggle Toward Self-Realization (nonfiction) 1950
Feminine Psychology (nonfiction) 1967; also published as *Feminine Papers*, 1967
The Adolescent Diaries of Karen Horney (diaries) 1980
†*Final Lectures* (lectures) 1987

*This work was edited by Harold Kelman.

†This work was edited by Douglas H. Ingram.

CRITICISM

Cyril Connolly (essay date 1940)

SOURCE: "Psycho-analysis," in *The Condemned Playground: Essays, 1927-1944*, New York: Macmillan, 1946, pp. 227-30.

[*Connolly was a very influential English critic, nonfiction writer, and literary journal editor. In the following review, originally published in 1940, he praises the accessibility of Horney's prose in* New Ways in Psychoanalysis *and the humanity of her approach to psychotherapy.*]

Psycho-analysis leads to the most profound discoveries man has made about himself. Yet most people would agree that its results have been disappointing. The cures are few, and seem confined to certain extreme cases, while the neurotic infirmities of human beings increase out of all proportion. Of the two or three hundred Londoners I know, almost all between the ages of twenty-five and forty would be improved by analysis in so far as they are neurotic cases. But many border-liners are in a state of flux. When they are absorbed in work or living in the country or with one type of friend they get better; when they are lonely, poor, or tired they get worse. In fact, they react to environment, and are therefore capable of improving themselves. The tragedies of infancy do not seem to remain ever present, ever re-enacted by the inconsolable ego, or the ineluctable id. Dr. Horney records fifteen years of relative therapeutic failure as a pure Freudian, and has written a book [*New Ways in Psycho-analysis*] in which she takes his theories one by one and gives her verdict on them. Some she finds unsubstantiated, others too limited in their refusal to allow validity to cultural background. In fact, the gist of her book is that education and environment do count, that the battle of life and the part we are to play in it is not decided at the breast or on the pot, but is fought out with constant reinforcements and changes of plan, many of which repeat the infantile pattern, but are not for that reason strategically useless. The trouble is that Freud, like all great geniuses, created his universe: his theories dovetail together; it is impossible to accept two or three without accepting them all. So beautifully do they fit in and so magnificently are they presented to us that we are slow to detect certain man-made aspects. That lecture on the psychology of women—how Victorian! That worship of science at the expense of all other methods not strictly scientific—how nineteenth-century! That contempt for rivals and that extreme pleasure in making his audience defy common sense, in getting them to swallow the most improbable explanation, on the slenderest evidence—how typical of the great artist! Yet his world is so incredible and so complete that when an Adler substitutes a banal desire for power or a Dr. Horney adds a craving for security to the basic instincts, we have a sense of disappointment, and we return to the preposterous claims of the great seducer himself, or to those of an orthodox disciple like Groddeck.

Yet Dr. Horney, though lacking in the graces and the art of surprise, may well be right. Psycho-analysis is in its infancy. It sets out to study the Nature of Mind with rudimentary instruments, it makes certain inferences as to that nature which seem to work—but the bits of the jig-saw puzzle which have been fitted together may not be arranged in the right way; it may still be necessary to try many combinations. The only favour psycho-analysis must demand is that we believe that the puzzle and its solution exist, that we realize that the mental is more powerful than the physical, that against the small amount of psycho-analytical cures must be set the enormous improvement in our dealings with each other which a general acquaintance with such ideas as the Oedipus complex, masochism, or the death-wish affords. Normalcy does exist and is desirable, and in proportion as we deviate from it we are unhappy and a cause of unhappiness; the abnormal remain abnormal because all the defences which they can erect, narcissism, masochism, perfectionism, etc., are sufficiently adequate for their normal needs. This does not mean however, that such defences may not prove quite useless when an unforeseen danger arrives, and then the débâcle is all the more terrible. And the abnormal are not the neurotic few but the majority of the human race, all those who are unhappier than they need be, the discontented women and the defeated men, the faces in the tube, the sheep with the nasty side. It is a consolation of human life that the sick forget what it is like to feel well, or the miserable to be happy. They jog along. But, nevertheless, health and happiness exist, and may tend to grow identical, and it is a disaster that they seem to be outside the range of more than a few people and that anxiety, relieved only by cruelty or the opiate of indifference, is the lot of the rest. Even the masochist does not like being unhappy, and since he cannot make the efforts necessary for happiness he has to intensify his

misery till it generates a stimulus—at the cost of getting farther and farther away from reality, where alone happiness is to be found.

Dr. Horney has some interesting things to say about masochism, which she is inclined to dissociate from the sexual basis insisted on by Freud. "Masochistic strivings are ultimately directed towards satisfaction, namely, towards the goal of oblivion, of getting rid of self with all its conflicts and limitations." As an amateur psychologist I would like to add that I have observed masochism in animals, who seem to be trying to avoid punishment by a kind of anticipatory acceptance of it, and that I believe masochism to be a process of ridding oneself of the fear of death by counterfeiting that sensation. In fact, there is an element of masochism in all acceptance of death, in fatalism, in many religions. This acceptance may be partly sexual, but it is also—since death must happen—the only logical strategy to adopt in face of it. For this reason most human beings are masochists and it would be a good thing if the word were freed from its connotation with sexual perversion and given a fuller meaning. There is even an element of courage in masochism, which we see in the tendency to embrace the fear of destruction in the hope that destruction thus will be evaded. The masochist is often one who was exposed to too many dangers in childhood, such as loneliness and the dark, and who, unable to defend himself, made use of others to protect him. Since then he retains both the anxiety and the need for protection, and as Dr. Horney points out, "relationships built on masochistic dependency are replete with hostility towards the partner." Often both partners are masochists, and hence the spectacle, which has done so much to discredit marriage, and indeed the whole system of the human couple, of the Babes in the Wood, escaping from their pursuers and clinging helplessly to each other in the bracken—by the throat.

Dr. Horney's book is easily read by the unscientific. In spite of her attrition the tremendous statue of Freud remains with only a few chips taken off it, but it is clear that she shows the trend of future investigation, which will be in the direction of helping patients to help themselves through an altogether thorough and complete analysis, rather than concentrating, fatalistically, on the therapeutic effects of the discovery of the initial error. We cannot be happy until we can love ourselves without egotism or our friends without tyranny. The issue, even in war-time, cannot be avoided, so any attempt to cast new light on the problem, especially from such a patient and humane angle, is to be encouraged and to be read.

Lionel Trilling (essay date 1942)

SOURCE: "The Progressive Psyche," in *The Nation* (New York), Vol. 155, No. 11, September 12, 1942, pp. 215-17.

[*Trilling was one of the most respected literary critics in the United States. Among his most significant works are*

The Liberal Imagination: Essays on Literature and Society *(1950) and* Freud and the Crisis of Our Culture *(1956). In the following largely negative review of* Self-Analysis, *he argues that Horney's criticisms of Sigmund Freud's theories represent a politically and ideologically liberal desire to view the psyche in hopeful and flattering terms. Trilling states that while Freud's view is darker than Horney's, it more adequately addresses "the savage difficulties of life."*]

Readers of this review, like its writer, will be diffident of judging the technical grounds on which Dr. Karen Horney has forced a schism in the ranks of American psychoanalysis. But Dr. Horney is not only a clinical physician; one of the few psychoanalytical writers of recent years to capture the imagination of the general public, she has established a philosophy of human nature and society on the basis of her divergence from Freud and has become, not one of the seminal, but surely one of the symptomatic minds of our time. Her work, therefore, may be judged not merely in a professional but also in a cultural context.

In her latest book [*Self-Analysis*] Dr. Horney carries her rejection of Freud's theories about as far as it can go short of an explicit denial of the unconscious mind; she propounds the belief that by adapting the techniques of regular analysis a neurotic person can effectually psychoanalyze himself. Judging by the criteria available to a layman, it seems to me that Dr. Horney makes but a weak case for her belief. The evidence she adduces is, in point of quantity, not adequate; in all propriety, so important an idea—important because it controverts one of Freud's fundamental concepts but important too because it is sure to raise hope in so many hearts—should be advanced on a wider and firmer ground of fact. Dr. Horney cites but four illustrative cases of "occasional self-analysis"—that is, of people who, equipped with some degree of psychoanalytical knowledge, were able by their own efforts to gain insight into and relief from some simply motivated psychic disturbance. Of systematic self-analysis she gives but a single example, and the case of Clare, a young woman who ventured into self-analysis after a year and a half of analysis with Dr. Horney, is possibly suggestive but not convincing. This patient no doubt advanced her understanding of her unconscious motives and thereby won a measure of emotional freedom; yet it is not entirely clear why her discoveries about herself—they are not remarkably deep—were not in large part her belated, developing realization of insights to which she had been helped by Dr. Horney in the course of her regular analysis.

In place of evidence Dr. Horney gives us argument and moral exhortation. The argument is dashing but verbalistic and prestidigitary; I shall touch on some of its assumptions below, but I cannot help feeling that, in a popular book like this, exhortation is even more important than argument and that the exhortation is a little irresponsible. When Dr. Horney suggests that one of the advantages of self-analysis is the pride that comes from

getting out of neurotic difficulties all by oneself, she implies assent to the popular feeling that there is something "humiliating" about psychoanalysis; and it is hard not to contemplate the even greater pride we might get from bringing ourselves up. When she tells us that, after all, a neurotic lives with himself all the time and therefore knows himself better than anyone else can, I do not understand her. When she tells us that "life itself is the best therapist," I find her trivial.

Then, too, I am disturbed by Dr. Horney's inconsistency in her own statements of the scope and value of self-analysis; she insists on its feasibility, says that some self-analysts have "dealt with problems that are generally deemed inaccessible even with the help of an analyst" and that some have succeeded where analysts have failed, questions whether self-analysis may not be conducted even without the occasional help and supervision which, as a general rule, she feels to be necessary; but when she commits herself to a summation of the possible effectiveness of self-analysis, she is far from sanguine: "Therefore after a period of common work with an analyst even patients who started with severe neurotic difficulties may in some cases be able to continue on their own, if necessary." I feel that a conclusion so tentative on a matter so important should have been confined to a scientific paper, not communicated with enthusiasm and more than a hint of promise to a general public always avid for new ways of psychic self-help.

For psychoanalytical theory the crucial point of *Self-Analysis* is its substantial denial of Freud's theory of "resistance." According to Freud, the neurosis, however painful, serves a certain purpose; the very symptoms which are so painful cloak impulses which the patient fears and cannot cope with. Even when they are pointed out to him by the analyst, the patient is likely to deny their existence because they are repulsive to his morals and pride; indeed, for a long time he will not even perceive them, for, perverse as the idea may seem, there are powerful forces in the unconscious mind which desire the unhappy neurotic status quo. Dr. Horney does not, to be sure, explicitly reject the theory of resistance which is so basic to the theory of the unconscious, but she does everything possible to minimize the fierce stubbornness Freud attributes to it. She insists that with the right spirit and a sufficient will (knowledge is of far less importance), the patient will be able to bring to light the hidden elements which the unconscious is at such pains to hide. No doubt it is the easier for Dr. Horney to maintain this because in her present book there is no slightest mention of those unconscious drives which are so horrifying to our conscious minds, such as homosexuality, sadism, masochism, Oedipus feelings. (Of course, many educated persons nowadays are willing to admit finding these elements in themselves, but their perception is at most a "novelistic" one, far short in intensity of a psychoanalytical realization.) The effect of Dr. Horney's position is that, though she continues to affirm her belief in the unconscious, she actually denies it by making it an unconscious so easily accessible to an untrained person working on himself; she seems to be talking rather of an "unawareness" or of what, by popular habit, is so often and so significantly substituted for unconscious, a "subconscious."

I have spoken of Dr. Horney as one of the symptomatic minds of our time; she is symptomatic—and most notably in her latest book—of one of the great inadequacies of liberal thought, the need for optimism. It seems to me that her denial or attenuation of most of Freud's concepts is the response to the wishes of an intellectual class which has always found Freud's ideas cogent but too stringent and too dark. They have always wanted a less tragic and strenuous psychology, a more reasonable, decent, and cooperative psyche, and Dr. Horney, in all her three books, has given them what they want.

The basis of Dr. Horney's divergence from Freud is an emotional one; her protest is always that Freud sets gloomy bounds to man's nature, that he is negative, cynical, without "faith." In her present book she quotes with approval a passage from Max Otto: "The deepest source of man's philosophy, the one that shapes and nourishes it, is faith or lack of faith in mankind." But there is no such simple alternative and it is dangerous to suppose there is—as we see when we understand what "faith in mankind" means for Dr. Horney. It means the belief that man is "free" and "good"—she has revived those old, absolute simplicities of eighteenth-century liberalism. To assert man's "freedom" she attacks Freud for finding man's psyche biologically determined; she often speaks of Freud as an old-fashioned dualist (it is clear that he is quite the opposite), but actually her own passionate rejection of the biological determination of mind constitutes a dualism of the most sterile sort and puts the attributes of body in a "lower" place. Further, in attacking Freud for his biological orientation, she makes the tiresome old mistake of confusing mind with the determinants of mind. Then, in the place of Freud's biological determination she puts a determination by culture: there can be no doubt that Dr. Horney has done psychoanalysis a service by forcing the cultural issue; Freud's views of culture, though suggestive, are surely not adequate. But Dr. Horney's view of culture is both vague and formalistic. Sometimes culture is a norm by which we judge whether or not a certain way of action is neurotic, but then again a culture may itself be neurotic, though by what norm we judge the culture (possibly a biological one?) we are not told. In Dr. Horney's hands culture becomes as much an absolute as she claims biology is in Freud's; but Freud saw a complex and passionate interplay betwen biology and culture, whereas Dr. Horney sees the individual infant as a kind of box into which culture drops this trend or that. The Freudian man may not be as free as we should like, but at least he has insides.

Then, in order to affirm that man is "good," Dr. Horney, like Erich Fromm, attacks Freud's theory of morals for representing morals as arising from forces themselves not virtuous. This Dr. Horney calls a fallacy of genesis,

which of course it is not. She represents Freud as implying that virtue is not virtue because it springs from destructive or anarchic origins, but this Freud never does imply—Dr. Horney, by the way, is not the most reliable expositor of Freud; indeed, if anyone has committed the genetic fallacy, Dr. Horney has done so by implying that virtue can only be virtue if it springs from innate (biological?) virtue.

If we are to talk of faith in man, in the realistic rather than the sentimental sense of that phrase, it seems to me that of the two psychologies it is Freud's that demonstrates faith by daring to present man with the terrible truth of his own nature. When Dr. Horney speaks of faith, she does not mean faith so much as optimism, that emptiest of words. The psyche she has described has won wide assent in liberal, progressive circles exactly because it is a progressive psyche, a kind of New Deal agency which truly intends to do good but cannot always cope with certain reactionary forces. It is a flattering view of the mind and Freud's is not, but Freud's has the advantage of suggesting the savage difficulties of life.

Francis Bartlett (essay date 1945)

SOURCE: "Recent Trends in Psychoanalysis," in *Science and Society,* Vol. IX, No. 3, Summer, 1945, pp. 214-31.

[*In the following essay, Bartlett discusses Horney's revisions and criticisms of Freudian psychoanalysis, discussing in particular her focus on the importance of social influences on the psyche.*]

In recent years, the writings of Dr. Karen Horney have become very popular. Socially minded psychoanalysts and social workers who previously relied on Freudian theories which they could never quite believe, are exceedingly enthusiastic about Horney's work. They find in it a useful theory of neuroses which includes Freud's valid observations but eliminates the fantastic distortions and reactionary implications. Horney is one of the first psychoanalysts to contend that the "neurotic personality of our time" is at bottom the product of capitalism. Erich Fromm, Reich and other analysts have also opposed Freud's biologism with a social emphasis, but do not have as wide a following as she in progressive circles. Because of this especial significance and influence the present article will, therefore, be devoted to the views of Karen Horney.

I. THE DEPRESSION AND THE "NEED FOR SAFETY"

Dr. Horney worked out her revision of Freud mainly during the decade of the economic depression, and it bears the stamp of that period. Already the naive assumptions of Freud—instincts, emphasis on heredity and the conception of social man as an isolated atom—were being discredited by the progress of science. The depression struck such complacent principles a further severe blow. Influential psychoanalysts, social workers and teachers swung to the left, and a new generation of radical youth entered these professions. Psychological views which merely reflected conservative political opinion were roundly attacked. There was a renewal of interest in the role which the social environment plays in the development of personality and the production of neuroses. The focus was shifted from sexual processes and supposedly instinctive aggression to social insecurity and its effect upon individuals.

How deeply Horney was influenced by the chaotic events of the depression is to be seen in her description of capitalism. Anarchic competition of each against all, in which the success of one is achieved only through the failure of others and in which antagonistic interests isolate and alienate everyone from everyone else, are, in her view, the chief features of the economic system. Penetrating into all other social relations, these characteristics create in individuals distrust, animosity, fear of failure and a sense of having no control over their own destiny. The only aspects of our culture which might tend to offset these realities, she holds, do not exist within the practical life of economic organizations. They exist only as ideals and standards of goodness, Christian principles and humanitarian sentiments.

During the years of the depression, it might have seemed that there was nothing to add to such an unflattering picture. Our entrance into a new period, however, in the war against fascism, has illuminated the one-sidedness of Horney's description. One of the outstanding facts in the present war is the enormous productive power of the United States, its ability to organize despite the obstacles and divisions which stem from the individual ownership of industry. Individualistic competition is only one side of capitalism. The other is the increasingly social nature of production. To describe the economic system as Horney does, entirely in terms of competition, means to ignore the working class and the conditions which tend more and more to cement the interests of the entire working population. It means, in fact, to leave out what is most essential: the contradiction between the individualistic productive relations and the social form of production.

The inadequacy of Horney's economic analysis is important because it is inextricably bound up with a corresponding analysis of the neurotic personality. She sees in the individual primarily the isolation and alienation which reflect the competitive nature of capitalism.

Competition, planlessness and insecurity bear upon individuals from birth to the grave and in particularly unfavorable circumstances give rise to a profound sense of being alone and helpless in a potentially hostile world. This sense is called "basic anxiety." It is the "soil out of which neuroses grow," the dynamic force at the root of neurotic trends. The neurotic trends are ways of coping with the world and relating oneself to others as a protection against basic anxiety. A person may seek security in power, prestige or possessions, or in scrupulous adherence to current rules and regulations. He may seek safety in excessive dependence upon the help or approval of others or in obscurity and withdrawal from competition. If the person develops a pattern of mutually incompatible neurotic trends, a conflict ensues which gives rise to further anxiety and a neurosis.

Such interpretations, one-sided as they may be, represent an undeniable advance over Freud. They avoid absurd and reactionary sociological conclusions and distorted emphasis upon infantile physiological processes, and they open up a perspective in which the individual can be understood as an active participant in social life. By employing these concepts Horney is able to refute the Freudian instinct hypothesis in each particular instance by showing that the compulsive power of neurotic strivings is due, not to their derivation from alleged biological instincts, but rather to the underlying basic anxiety which in turn is the outcome of our social relations. The trends motivated by the need for safety and security can be shown to be preponderant over all other values. The conclusion which Horney draws is that man is governed by two principles: satisfaction, which Freud emphasizes; and safety, which is the key to her own system.

Satisfaction and safety are important human needs that seemed momentously significant during the years of the depression. They merit analysis now when the world has become far more dangerous and hostile than it ever was in the darkest years of the crisis. Individual careers, personal plans, and life itself are at the mercy of destructive powers against which the individual cannot wholly protect himself. He is called upon to run the risk of losing not merely his income, nor his social position, but his irreplaceable existence. Surely anxiety is increased by this insecurity. Yet the outstanding fact about people in this war is precisely the sacrifice of their personal satisfactions and safety for values involved in the destruction of fascism. These sacrifices have nothing in common with masochistic perversion or *hara-kiri* nor do they involve any dehumanization. They go along with an increase in the love of life, a deepened conviction of the worthwhileness of threatened human values, and a sense of closer connections with other people, even those yet unborn. The individualistic needs of satisfaction and safety are, on a gigantic scale, thrust into the background by other motivations; love and appreciation of others, the desire to do one's part regardless of personal consequences, and the identification, however in articulate, with those values of human decency and equality which fascism destroys. Admitting that these motivations exist in various degrees, that full consciousness of them is relatively rare and that they are mingled with doubts and cynicism and many other less admirable motives, yet it is impossible to deny that this war shows us on an immense scale expressions of a sound vital solidarity between people quite as fundamental and powerful as isolating individualism.

In fairness to Horney, it must be said that she herself has criticized Freud for excluding healthy, progressive motivations. "In Freud," she remarks in *Self-Analysis,* "not much if any space is left in human nature for constructive forces which might strive toward growth and development." Freudism involves the systematic reduction of the specifically human to the purely animal. There exists no self-sacrificing, constructive, responsible action which can not be "reduced" to the infantile satisfactions involved in sucking, eating, biting, defecating or some other bodily process. This type of thinking is so deeply embedded in psychoanalytic literature that when Horney first begins to speak of genuine concern for others or real respect, she actually puts "genuine" and "real" in quotation marks as if she were afraid of being laughed at by case-hardened Freudians. She has become more and more convinced of the importance of these constructive forces, for it is they, she says, which "constitute the dynamic counterpole to the forces producing resistance."

Despite her repeated statements to this effect and her undoubted attention to healthy strivings in practice, one cannot help being impressed that her analysis of constructive forces is perfunctory and abstract compared with the richness of her analysis of neurotic trends. Even in practice, it is the negative side which receives the greatest attention. Horney schematizes the steps of analysis as follows: To discover a neurotic trend, to work out its full implication in the patient's life and finally to understand the relation of this neurotic trend to other neurotic trends in order to get a synthetic picture. As so conceived, neither the patient's nor the analyst's attention is constructively directed toward the healthy strivings. The main focus, the direction and movement, remain negative. The preoccupation with one's weaknesses is only partially offset by the analyst's continued acceptance of the patient through all vicissitudes. No matter what he thinks, feels or does, the orientation leads directly to the question whether it may not be a manifestation of a neurotic trend and ultimately of anxiety. It is a common criticism of analysis that such preoccupation has a demoralizing effect. Certainly periods of depression if not despair over one's character are regarded as normal phases of analysis. Whether this is avoidable in any case, the criticism strikes at one of the weakest points of analytic theory and practice.

It might be thought that since Horney is dealing with neurotics, her attention must necessarily be drawn mainly to neurotic trends, to the comparative neglect of constructive motivations. Horney herself would not hide behind such an explanation. She asserts that a fully rounded analysis requires an understanding of constructive qualities. Yet we can find in her writings hardly more assistance toward such an understanding than their bare suggestion. The constructive forces are not in any way related to the economic order, they are described simply as forces "striving toward growth and development" and Horney does not undertake a further analysis. They are regarded as existing apart from the neurotic structure instead of being, as I hope to indicate, essential to the formation of the basic conflicts. Horney simply acknowledges their importance in carrying through what is still

regarded as the main task, the analysis of the patient's defects.

A complete emancipation from Freudism requires more than this. Analysts must turn their eyes not only from the past to the present, as Horney has already done, but from the weaknesses which have been diligently explored to the constructive qualities which have been relatively neglected. However frail and entangled in the neurosis such trends may be, it is necessary to focus attention upon them and find ways of developing them to full strength. Such a break with the Freudian tradition is not easy to accomplish. Psychoanalysis has not even yet raised the question of methods for strengthening the patient's healthy potentialities except negatively, through the understanding of his defects. The development of such methods implies a radical break with present psychoanalytic treatment.

II. SOCIAL CONTRADICTIONS AND MENTAL CONFLICT

We have noted a one-sidedness in Horney's description of capitalism and a comparable one-sidedness in her account of the neurotic personality. Corresponding to an economic system in which she sees little but individualistic competition is her conception of the individual who springs from these social conditions. In both cases, she fails to analyze such social and constructive factors as the growth of trade unionism and the development of science and technology. I would like to pursue further the relation between the neurotic personality and the contradiction within our economic life.

Describing the "middle-class neurotic of western civilization" (from which class the overwhelming majority of analytic patients come), Horney says: "This type is characterized by a great potential hostility, by more readiness and capacity for hate than for love, by emotional isolation, by a tendency to be egocentric, ready to withdraw, acquisitive, entangled in problems concerning possessions and prestige." All of these trends, she adds, are brought about by "the conditions of a specific culture." They are trends, we must now remark, very closely related to the one side of capitalism which Horney sees clearly.

No doubt the middle-class neurotic does possess these qualities. But there is a conspicuous and indeed astonishing omission in the list. Horney has failed to bring to light the real structure of the conflict which is the central feature of every neurosis and also the most obvious predisposition of the middle class generally.

The existence of diametrically opposed strivings in the middle class has long been observed by political and economic writers who were not concerned with neurotic conflicts. Both the "old" middle class consisting of small property owners and the "new" middle class which is more heterogeneous have been marked by the conflict which grows out of their intermediary social position. They are transitional between the two main classes of capitalism and have no independent interests apart from these polar classes. Historically their political role has been ambiguous and unstable.

Individuals of this class were described by Lenin as having "two souls." If they are part of the working population, they are also potential capitalists. Their interests are linked to the working class yet they are isolated and strive to "get ahead" in an individualistic way and are averse to organization. They feel sympathy with the mass of workers, but tend to set themselves apart and fear nothing so much as being forced into that level themselves. They strive to be cooperative and friendly, but are involved in fierce competition which alienates them and makes them indifferent to others. Toward big capital, their relations are equally ambiguous. They are hostile and fearful, yet they admire it, seek to emulate it, and hope for its small favors and protection. They are at once rebellious and submissive.

In short, their practical interests, habitual attitudes, their loyalties and their aspirations draw them in opposite directions. Decisive action in either direction appears to threaten their interests in the other. Hence, as Marx said, "their will is blunted," and under conditions of stress they have tended to indecision and instability.

Such conflicting trends are, of course, not confined to members of the middle class. The opposing features of capitalism, individualistic ownership and socialized production, reach into every corner of the social life. Individualistic competition and ambitions penetrate into the activities of even the most democratic working-class organization. The cooperativeness, mutual dependence and democratic relations affect even the upper classes.

However that may be, a psychology which purports to analyze the "neurotic personality of our time" should, for example, attempt to show the connection between the conflicts of the "middle-class neurotic" and the contradictory social position of the middle class. One can hardly doubt, on Horney's own showing, that the middle-class neurotic is prone to suffer from precisely the same conflicts which characterize the middle class generally.

Horney, however, has very little to say about these fundamental conflicts or the contradictory social relations out of which they grow. These conflicts are, as I shall indicate presently, somehow hidden away in the concept of basic anxiety. The conflicts with which Horney is chiefly concerned are secondary conflicts between neurotic trends which arise out of basic anxiety. They are conflicts between incompatible individualistic trends or are strivings for appearances such as the neurotic may need to appear perfect. Horney is most interested, one might say, in the secondary conflicts which appear when a middle-class person becomes a middle-class neurotic. But instead of a concrete analysis of the relationship between the secondary conflicts and the social contradiction, Horney refers us to an abstraction—basic anxiety.

I would like to illustrate this point with a schematic example. Imagine that toward the end of the depression an auto worker gets a job as foreman in a plant. He identifies himself with his men, works side by side with them from time to time, knows some of them socially and treats them as equals. At the same time, he has a new authority over them, must order them to do what the employer requires and can fire them if they refuse. He begins to find that the exertion of his authority in the employer's interests threatens his friendships. And his identification with the interests of his men threatens his ambition to get ahead and might cost him his job. Here is a simple case of the contradictions inherent in a middle-class position. It is an unstable situation. The foremen have not yet organized their own union, and a fraternal bond with the U.A.W. has not been established. Our foreman may in time begin to develop the feeling that the other men are not his equals, partly because he attributes his advancement to his own superiority and partly because the men, whose interests are no longer identical with his, may behave in what seems to him a most unreasonable manner. His relations to the men are impaired. While still regarding himself as one of the gang, he develops feelings of contempt and tendencies to disparage them. He still wants them to like him, but he no longer does like them, at least as formerly, as equals. His friendliness becomes more and more a cloak for exerting his authority. He thinks that a pat on the back and a smile make up for real injuries. At the same time, he becomes hesitant about exerting his authority or administering rebukes. He conceals his disparaging tendencies, his instability and his ambition behind a façade of irreproachability and imperturbable calm. He may even refrain from reasonable and necessary criticism, only to burst out with tangential criticism which may then have an irrational quality. With the further impairment of his relations to the men and his failure to get ahead with the employer, he develops an increasing need for affection which he seeks from one woman or another.

At this point, our imaginary individual is hardly distinguishable from a neurotic personality. An analyst might well be able to ferret out his neurotic trends; his striving for power, his need for affection, his disparaging tendencies and his perfectionism. He would probably attribute these trends to a "basic anxiety." If so, is it not clear that he has substituted a convenient abstraction for a concrete analysis of the primary conflicts and the social situation underlying them? This hypothetical illustration shows how necessary it is to understand the relation between the conflicts which appear in a neurosis and the contradictions which inhere in the practical everyday life of our society. The concept of basic anxiety seems to do away with this requirement.

In its simplest form, the conception is that the frustration of man's need for safety by anarchic social conditions, produces basic anxiety. But, as we know, economic insecurity does not in itself produce basic anxiety. The behavior of individuals in this war is evidence. Even in peacetime during economic crises the people who characteristically suffer from neurotic conflicts are those whose problems of actual livelihood are overshadowed by other problems which Horney describes.

Anxiety in general differs from ordinary fear in several important respects. It is disproportionate to the external danger because part of the danger comes from within. One fears the consequences of his own strivings or impulses. There is an inner paralysis which precludes taking steps to cope with the danger and produces a feeling of helplessness.

It seems clear from Horney's own writings that anxiety is the expression of inner conflict. She asserts this unequivocally when she discusses the secondary anxiety which arises from the conflict of incompatible neurotic trends. She also recognizes that basic anxiety in its childhood origins arises out of a contradictory situation. It is the outcome of the child's hostility to his parents and his exclusive dependence upon them. It is only when she tries to relate basic anxiety to the broader underlying economic situation that this insistence on conflict disappears and we get the introduction of an abstract principle of safety.

This abstraction is necessitated only by her one-sided analysis of the social relations in which she sees only isolation and competition apart from mutual dependence and cooperation. If an individual is sufficiently integrated with others, even catastrophic social events may not produce anxiety, but rather joint action against the danger. On the other hand, an individual utterly isolated, individualistic and alienated might react with fear, but not with the special feeling of anxiety. It is only a conflict between these opposing tendencies which produces the conditions characteristic of basic anxiety. This is the case with the basic social conflicts which we have considered. Incompatible interests produce under stress an indecision which may amount to paralysis. Action in either direction threatens equally important interests so that the strivings themselves are a danger. It should be added that organization and joint action which lie so close to hand for the working class are not so easy for the middle class. They are more likely to feel themselves alone and powerless in a potentially hostile world.

To sum up, the concept of basic anxiety, as used by Horney, appears to be a substitute for a concrete analysis of the social position of neurotics, in relation to the conflicts they experience. Our contention is that the soil out of which neuroses grow is not an abstract emotion produced by the frustration of an equally abstract need for safety; that neuroses grow out of the basic conflicts which reflect the basic contradictions of economic life.

It is important theoretically, and will become more so practically, to understand just how fundamental conflicts in the mind reflect objective contradictions in practical life. Unprecedented class alignments are taking place and new objective conditions of life are coming into existence which will increasingly reflect themselves in the minds and characters of those who grow up and participate in this world. We cannot continue to base our understanding upon psychological abstractions which fail to keep pace with these developments.

III. EMOTIONS AND PRACTICAL LIFE

"Basic anxiety" is Horney's particular variation of the Freudian dictum that human behavior is ultimately the outcome of emotional drives, one of the Freudian theories which Horney believes worth salvaging. To Freud, biologically given emotional drives were deeper than any convictions, beliefs or standards taken over from the surrounding culture. Ideas, according to him, have power and vitality only when they express an emotion or serve some emotional function. While Horney decisively rejects the instinct theory, she does assert that a theory of emotional motivations is more satisfactory than a psychology of conditioned reflexes or one which attempts to explain human behavior as the outcome of reason. She believes that she has separated this kernal of truth from its husk of instinctivism.

The neurotic trends which govern to such a degree the behavior of neurotics are not themselves emotional forces. They are rather unconscious principles. One may live according to the principle that safety lies in obscurity, or in compliance with rules and regulations, or in the appearance of perfection or in universal admiration. The individual does not necessarily formulate these principles. He may not be aware of their existence or of the extent to which they govern his behavior. They are, in Shaw's phrase, the principles upon which he acts habitually. These neurotic trends may give rise to emotions; they may, in conflict, give rise to neurotic anxiety. But they are not themselves emotional forces. They are unconscious *ideas*. Therefore, they have no urgency or power except as they stem from basic anxiety which is considered an emotion.

But is basic anxiety an emotion? At first glance it appears to have in common with fear certain physiological concomitants. An increment of adrenalin is added to the blood stream when it comes into play; there are changes in pulse and respiration, increased blood supply to the muscles, familiar visceral sensations and perhaps sweating and frequent desire to urinate. Such physiological reactions are generally considered an essential aspect of an emotion. James went so far as to say that the emotion *is* the bodily response.

But according to Horney, anxiety may be unconscious. This may occur in a limited sense, as when the only physiological sign of anxiety is the frequent desire to urinate, a sign which the individual may not recognize as conected with anxiety. It may happen that a person will be unconsciously anxious without any physiological response at all. Horney therefore concludes that James was wrong. The emotion is not the bodily response. On the contrary, if there is any physiological response at all, it is caused by anxiety. But what then is this anxiety?

Freud was faced with precisely the same problem in accounting for the assumed operation of sexual drives even in the absence of physiological processes characteristic of sex. He solved it by assuming the operation of an unconscious instinct which was, in itself, unknowable. It could not be perceived directly, but only through its "mental representatives," i.e., ideas and emotions. The instinct could be presumed to operate twenty-four hours a day whether appropriate bodily processes occurred or not.

This is a mystical theory, but it is at least a consistent one. Horney will have nothing to do with such an unknowable instinct, yet she wishes to retain a force which, like Freud's, is independent of physiological processes. She discards the name of instinct, but wishes to retain its content. Actually the rejection of the instinct theory involves also the rejection of the theory that emotional drives are more basic than ideas.

Basic anxiety, as Horney herself tells us, is the outcome of particularly unfavorable experiences which give rise to a deep sense of being alone and powerless in a potentially hostile world. It is obvious that such a deeply engrained attitude to the world may easily, under conditions of stress, give rise to emotions of anxiety and hostility. But it does not itself have the attributes of an emotion. It is a deep-seated conviction perhaps, an unformulated world-view, an habitual attitude toward society, but no more an emotion than the neurotic trends which are said to arise from it. In what essential respect does the sense of being alone and powerless in a potentially hostile world differ from a sense of being superior in a stupid world or deeply distrustful of an unreliable world? All of these are formulated convictions or prejudices which have grown out of the experience of life. They are all principles upon which we habitually act. They are not emotions at all; they are ideas.

What is basic in personality is not an abstract emotional force, but the totality of conflicting attitudes, convictions, prejudices and deeply rooted principles which have grown out of habitual participation in social life. The particular conflicting attitudes which reflect the contradictions of capitalism easily lend themselves to inner paralysis, the blunting of spontaneity and the reduction of maneuverability, all of which form a rich soil for the development of anxiety. But the emotion itself does not exist apart from this basic character structure.

Since we have noted that the basic character structure is closely akin to ideas, it is necessary to distinguish between these ideas and intellectual processes in the narrow sense. Theories which divided personality into basic emotions and superficial ideas may not be valid, but the theoretical distinction reflects an actual distinction with a long and honorable history. Instinct vs. reason, unconscious vs. conscious, biological vs. cultural—all of these antitheses are, roughly speaking, attempts to formulate the same important difference. In saying that ideas are basic, I do not wish to gloss over this difference.

To begin with a simple example, a person reared in a family where there is prejudice against Negroes may discover through study that this attitude is not based upon any biological inferiority, and he may come to believe in social equality for Negroes. But it is not so simple for him to rid himself of his deep-seated racial chauvinism of which he may no longer be aware. We might say that intellectually he is convinced of racial equality but that emotionally he retains his prejudice.

Such an expression, however, would be inaccurate and misleading. The real difference is between his theory and his practice. Theoretically, in terms of conceptual knowledge acquired from the conversation and writings of others, he has come to believe in equality. But such a belief may not yet be sufficient to outweigh or transform attitudes and convictions which have grown out of the contacts of a lifetime.

The "ideas," then, of the character structure are the profound convictions of personal experience in contrast to ideas which are passively taken over from others and which may not correspond to the individual's practical experience. They are the reflection of the individual's actual mode of life. The organic body, participating in the life of its time, coping with necessities, entering into practical relations to others, develops, through its own actions, a governing pattern of living. A pattern of inarticulate attitudes and unformulated convictions, of habitual modes of reacting which is a reflection and synthesis of his living relationships. It is the outcome of his class position and resulting action in contrast to the beliefs and ideas which he passively receives from his "culture."

The distinction between the embodied convictions of practice and the intellectual conceptions of theory is far from absolute. But in our society, there is a separation of theory from practice which appears in the individual as a separation between his "emotions" and his intellect. There is an exaggerated gap between the person as he really is because of his life experience and the person he imagines himself to be, thinks he should be and earnestly strives to be. From earliest infancy the individual is impressed with ideas and values which do not correspond to his actual experience. Ideals whose function it is to mask and sentimentalize the harsh and often irrational realities of people's actual relationships constitute a great part of our education. It is these ideals which are usually treated in Freudian literature as the social or cultural influence in opposition to the biological impulses. These are, however, but the trappings, not the actualities of society. The effect of this separation of theory and practice is that individuals may be unable to distinguish between their "real selves," the outcome of experience, and the notions which come from outside. They become afflicted by a subtle hypocrisy which deceives even themselves. Many intelligent people have spent the greater part of their later lives divesting themselves of what they acquired with so much trouble in youth.

Even so, there is no impermeable barrier between the convictions of experience and ideas which come from outside. The attitudes of the basic character structure may be and generally are unformulated, unconscious. A person may never be aware of his most fundamental convictions. His actual relationships as they have developed through life are never completely known to him. He is wiser and also more foolish than he knows. He is more complex than he is aware. On the other hand, the convictions of experience can be verbalized. A person may and does to some degree become conscious of his actual relationships. In an analysis a great part of what is called making the unconscious conscious is the process of cutting through appearances and formulating the hitherto unspoken attitudes and convictions.

Conversely, "mere ideas" or theories can and do become a part of the individual's spontaneous response, not directly, but by guiding his action. Through practice, ideas become more than merely theories. They become embodied, part of the character pattern. They become, as Marx said, a "material force."

The distinction is often made between the emotions and the intellect that the former are irrational. But this distinction will not hold. Men are certainly capable of irrationality, but there is quite as much irrationality in their theories as in their spontaneous actions. Experience, when it is guided by false ideas or none at all, can certainly give rise to distorted convictions which we call irrational. Individual experience is limited and partial, the realities of life are complex and themselves distorted. Attitudes growing out of these experiences are invariably one-sided and sometimes fantastic. It is this fact which gives rise to many of the irrational ideas uncovered by psychoanalysis. On the other hand, the spontaneous responses of an individual whose practical life has been guided by correct theories are perfectly rational. Such a person may react directly to the most complex social situations without deviating a hair's breadth from what is reasonable.

To sum up, it is not valid to oppose a theory of emotional motivations to one of conditioned reflexes or even to one which explains men's actions as the outcome of reason. While in human beings the processes are infinitely more complicated and in some degree different in character from those in Pavlov's dogs, the development of conflicts through habitual participation in contradictory social relations does bear a recognizable relation to Pavlov's laboratory neuroses. And while attempts to explain human behavior as the outcome of reason are shallow, the basic character structure is by no means inherently unreasonable. On the other hand, a theory which refers all complexities to an unanalyzed emotional force cannot entirely escape the mysticism of the instinct theory. Emotions as bodily responses are, to be sure, closely tied in with the practical life and the character which evolves in practical life. But emotions do not and cannot exist apart from that character as abstract forces.

IV. THE ROLE OF UNDERSTANDING

The principles just put forward have a bearing on treatment. With Horney a point has been reached at which psychoanalysis is ready to become something quite different from the analysis of the past. The differences from Freud in theory appear to be fundamental; but in practice much persists from the earlier school. There is a significant difference in the way in which the analysis is conducted, the direction of associations and the interpretations rendered. There is a salutary shift of emphasis away from infantile memories toward the everyday life of the patient's present. Nevertheless, an agreement remains which overshadows all these differences. It is the common reliance upon *understanding* as that which changes a person.

Despite Horney's continual attempt to get beyond this principle, she seems unable to do so. She points out time and again that understanding is not enough. Yet it is dismaying to see how one phase of understanding leads only to further and endless phases of understanding. Certainly it is necessary to understand your relations to others in order consciously to change them. But what is the process by which these changes occur? One can hardly avoid the impression that the analysts themselves do not know. They only know that the more the patient understands, the more likely it is that he will begin to get better.

How does a person change himself? According to Freud the therapeutic process takes place within the analyst's office. It is there that the patient associates, the unconscious becomes conscious and the transference exerts its curative powers. But with astonishing regularity it is found that during long interruptions or after termination of a period of analysis in which no substantial improvement takes place, the patient will proceed to make considerable gains. There is no doubt of their genuineness, depth and lasting quality. These "delayed" improvements have always been a puzzle and something of an annoyance to analysts who have tended to attribute them to the patient's ingratitude. Horney lists the factors which she believes might be responsible. They may be summarized by saying, as she does in *Self-Analysis,* that "some mental activity must have gone on in the patient without his being aware of it, or at least without his consciously determined efforts."

Indicative of the tenacity of Freudian theories is the fact that Horney does not so much as hint at the part played by the activity which she herself regards as the prime therapeutic agent. "Life itself," she says in another place, "is the best therapist. What analysis can do is to make one able to accept the help that life offers, and to profit from it." It is not mental activity alone, but practical activity—life itself—which accounts for these "delayed" improvements.

"Life itself is the best therapist." This is, for psychoanalysis, a really revolutionary idea. I think that perhaps Horney's failure to give it proper weight in her theory is due to her continued adherence to the supposed primacy of emotional drives. The attempt to change emotions, without dealing with their specific social sources and objects, is unavailing. The terms aggression and anxiety become stereotypes, therapeutically useless, if they are not articulated in terms of current economic and political trends. If, however, we recognize that the underlying "emotional" structure does not consist of abstract drives but of the totality of the attitudes, convictions and valuations developed primarily through life's practice, then the mystery of further change disappears. It does not seem at all strange that deep-going and permanent changes should occur during interruptions or after termination of the analysis. Nor is there any mystery in the patient's unawareness or lack of consciously determined efforts. These may or may not play a part in practical day-to-day living. Even *during* the analysis it would be wrong to believe that the change is taking place largely within the analyst's office. The mental activities of the analytic sessions serve as a guide not only to further understanding, but to action where the attitudes are fundamentally changed. The intellectual insights become embodied. A patient who has discovered in analysis that he does not assert his own wishes from fear that others will not like him, will learn in his daily life that he can assert his wishes without catastrophe. If he acquires an intellectual insight into his previously unconscious tendency to disparage other people, it is in his daily life that the insight will become a conviction—understood "emotionally." The relation to the analyst is of course a fraction of the patient's practical life and a great deal of its value lies in its practical rather than its theoretical character. But for the most part, the process of change takes place outside the analyst's office. Perhaps that is why they have not easily discovered what that process is.

Psychoanalysis prides itself that it deals not with superficial ideals and notions, but penetrates to the deepest realms of emotional life. Yet curiously, understanding, which is the strong point of psychoanalysis, cannot alone have any decisive effect on the underlying "emotional" structure. Changes in that structure are dependent upon action.

The unashamed free associations of psychoanalysis may enable both patient and analyst to peer through the superficial appearances to his actual relationships. They may help to understand the person as he really is and formulate the most profound and inarticulate convictions and attitudes of the character structure. Yet of itself understanding cannot change his character structure. To take the example given earlier, namely race prejudice, an analysis might expose the belief in the equality of races to be, for that person, a superficial and merely intellectual conviction. It might reveal his true attitude toward Negroes as one of contempt. Such an understanding would undoubtedly be of great importance to the patient. It might even give him a sense of liberation from hypocrisy and both a hope of changing his attitude and a resolution to do so. But the recognition of the contempt will not itself do away with it. To alter an epigram of Freud's,

the fact that such an attitude is recognized by your theory does not prevent it from existing. Theory alone cannot eradicate racial prejudice. It can be eradicated only by work and experience which will change the old convictions.

Understanding can lay bare the underlying emotional structure, but cannot alter it. What is necessary is action—the continuation of life in such a way and in such relationships as will change the deepest attitudes in the desired direction. This action must be guided and illuminated by understanding not only of the personality, but of the world in which the person lives.

The outlook implicit in Horney's statement that life is the best therapist cannot fail to result in the most radical changes in treatment methods. But as yet, traditional conceptions still weight heavily on our minds.

It means that the analyst is far from being, as he sometimes imagines himself, the prime mover in changing people. All people are changing and the movement of history is the mighty agent of that change. Analysts will find it necessary to understand the world, including contemporary political situations. They must be able to evaluate which activities further social progress and tend to strengthen an individual's connections with humanity. They must be sensitive to the social elements already in their patients and learn how to guide them back into life in such a way as to develop these healthy potentialities. The detailed working out of new treatment methods based on these principles is the difficult task of the growing number of psychotherapists who are becoming aware of them.

The outlook for the forward movement of humanity, the strengthening of connections between all peoples and classes is brighter than ever before. Millions of people are involved not only in changing the world but in changing themselves. If psychoanalysis in this changed world is to deal effectively with the 300,000 men who have been discharged from the services for psychiatric reasons, and the 30,000 more who are being discharged each month, and if it is to treat the civilian cases as well, there must be expansion and redirection. Therapy must become more responsive to change, and outworn ideas must be left behind.

Joseph Wortis, M. D. (essay date 1946)

SOURCE: "Freud, Horney, Fromm and Others," in *Science and Society*, Vol. X, No. 2, 1946, pp. 176-85.

[*In the following essay, written in response to Francis Bartlett's essay "Recent Trends in Psychoanalysis" (Science and Society, Vol. IX, No. 3, Summer, 1945), Wortis examines Horney's theories in relation to both the Freudian tradition she rejects and to more contemporary trends, of which she claimed to be part. Wortis argues that Horney's conception of psychiatry is not as "progressive" as she claimed it was.*]

Bartlett's critique of Horney in this magazine [*Science and Society*] (Summer, 1945) seems to me to be basically correct and very welcome. It is precisely because Horney cast off some of the more flagrant errors of Freudianism that she has led so many people into another blind alley, perhaps more attractive than Freud's, but also more deceptive. Bartlett, like Horney, relates neurotic conflicts to the real world of social relationships, but unlike Horney, sees that the emotional forces behind these conflicts are bound to ideas which can be isolated and described. Bartlett also parts company with Horney when he recognizes that the patient's present system of relationships supports and maintains his conflict of ideas. From this Bartlett draws the conclusion that the task of the analyst is to expose these ideas, relate them to real situations and experiences—present as well as past—and guide the patient toward action which will resolve the conflicts or lift them to a more productive level. All this involves more than a re-evaluation of analysis or mere shift of emphasis: it requires a fundamental change in the technique of analysis itself.

In a recent paper of mine ["Freudianism and The Psychoanalytic Tradition," *American Journal of Psychiatry*, Vol. XXV, May, 1945] I have attempted to show that the reactionary role of Freudianism consists essentially in the fact that it drives a wedge between the ideas of men and the material world which creates or maintains these ideas, and tries to split them apart. In spite of its materialist phraseology this is idealism, and psychoanalysis is a misguided contemporary form of idealism. Both Fromm and Horney form part of this tradition because their basic tendency is much the same, in spite of the fact that Fromm uses the language of Marxism and Horney the language of cultural anthropology.

How was it possible, we may ask, for both Freud and Horney to proceed from a position of professed materialism to an actually idealist position? Freud reached his idealist position by deriving ideas from biological experience—as instincts—instead of social experience. Horney achieves her idealist position by deriving ideas from childhood experience as opposed to adult experience. Fromm does the same. "There is no doubt whatever," wrote Horney in her *New Ways in Psychoanalysis* "that childhood experiences exert a decisive influence on development. . . ." Once the personality pattern congeals it is supposed to become more or less impervious to further influence from experience, unless an analysis effects an internal rearrangement of the parts. Idealism in one form or another is implicit in the whole concept of psychoanalytic therapy, which promises a man nothing less that the privilege of lifting himself by his boot-straps. For if it were conceded that neurotic conflicts are not only created, but also maintained or changed by experience, then the process of cure would have to take place out in the world of experience, away from the doctor's office.

There are many aspects to Freudianism and psychoanalysis and such is the complexity of the material that separate quotations in support of almost any point of view

could be found in the psychoanalytic literature. We shall have to satisfy ourselves here with a discussion of the prevailing tendencies and errors, and insist that these must be regarded mainly as errors of emphasis, without complete exclusion of their opposites. Freud and his followers have each emphasized different aspects of the psychoanalytic structure and are not always in agreement as to what is basic and what secondary. Freud himself was not consistent in his enumeration of the basic propositions of psychoanalysis, and at times he seemed to believe that it was all basic.

It should be noted that Bartlett in his latest essay is much sharper in his attitude toward psychoanalysis than he was in his earlier writings. In his first penetrating analysis of Freudianism (*Sigmund Freud: A Marxian Essay*) he declared, for example, that Luria's experiments confirmed "almost word for word the three main assumptions upon which the entire mass of psychoanalytic observations depends. They confirm the fact that unconscious and active mental processes do exist; that these processes remain unconscious due to an economic mechanism of repression which manifests itself as resistance in the conflicting nature of the cure; and finally, that the free flow of associations is determined and in part derived from the subject's secret complexes." In addition, Bartlett spoke approvingly of the psychoanalytic therapeutic procedure which uses free association to reconstruct these unconscious complexes in consciousness "and very often thereby succeeding in bringing about those more stable reactions to which Luria refers." Bartlett finally concluded: "considering these circumstances and the degree of agreement on essentials, it is highly probable that the observations made by psychoanalysts are substantially correct."

In this earlier essay Bartlett thus accepted the following Freudian principles: (1) the dynamic unconscious; (2) repression and resistance; (3) psychoanalytic therapy. His essay on Horney indicates a considerable development of his views on these topics.

Our own attitude toward these principles may be briefly stated. In relation to (1), the question may be posed: Do we believe that unconscious forces motivate and affect behavior? The answer is, we do. Under (2): Do we believe that disagreeable memories can be displaced and forgotten and that it takes an effort to recall them? Here again, we do. Under (3): Do we believe that presentation or restoration to consciousness of these unconscious forces is helpful? Once more the answer is affirmative.

Yet our point of view is fundamentally opposed to Freud's in the following important ways:

(1) Though we believe, with Freud, that neuroses develop from conflicts, we do not believe that the conflict necessarily involves the opposition of the individual's unconscious drives to his conscious needs. All other types of unresolved conflict, including fully conscious conflicts, can engender neurotic symptoms.

(2) Our concept of unconscious drives is quite different from Freud's, who pictured them as originating from innate instincts or early childhood experiences. We reject his instinct theory, reduce the importance of childhood experiences, and emphasize the factor of ignorance in considering a drive unconscious. This means that a patient must not only be made to recognize the presence of a certain drive but must learn its origin, implications, and consequences. We can agree with Horney's statement in *New Ways* that the "main objective in therapy is, after having recognized neurotic trends, to discover in detail the functions they serve and the consequences they have on the patient's personality and on his life." Unlike Horney, however, we would regard many neurotic drives as expressions of certain social or class functions; we would emphasize the social consequences of their full expression; and we would relate them to the actual conflicting material needs and circumstances of the patient.

(3) In emphasizing the role of ignorance on the one hand and of actual material circumstances on the other, in the development of neurotic drives, the role of repression becomes less important, though it may still play a role. In the same way the chief sources of resistance to the analytic process appear to us to be ideological and material—but basically material. Actually the patient's resistance to a cautious, sympathetic and correct scientific analysis of his problem has been generally overrated.

(4) Inasmuch as neurotic conflicts are basically due to conflicts in material circumstances or social relationships, the analytic therapy, as we have elsewhere indicated, has mainly a preliminary value to the real therapeutic process, which involves changes in material and social relationships.

It can thus be seen that an acceptance of certain of Freud's principles by no means necessarily involves an acceptance of the Freudian structure, for important changes in emphasis and in relationships between these principles can impart altogether new meanings to them, or rob them of their old significance.

What has Horney done with the Freudian inheritance? In her first book, *The Neurotic Personality of Our Time,* she made a number of real contributions and advances, not the least of which was a refreshing simplicity of language. Yet in spite of a wholesome shift of emphasis to problems of real life and conduct, she declared herself fundamentally a believer in psychoanalytic treatment. "If . . . one believes," she wrote, "that the essentials of psychoanalysis lie in certain basic trends of thought concerning the role of the unconscious processes and the ways in which they find expression, and in a form of therapeutic treatment that brings these processes to awareness then what I present is psychoanalysis." Of the instinct theory she retained the instincts of sex and hunger. Though she wavered in her emphasis on childhood experiences she regarded them as the chief determinants of neurotic development. "It seems," she wrote, "that the person who is likely to become neurotic is one who has experienced the culturally determined difficulties in an accentuated form, mostly through the medium of childhood experiences, and who has consequently been unable to solve them or has solved them only at great cost to his personality." The question then arises: What is it that distinguishes the childhood of the neurotic from that of normal people? Horney replies by saying that the basic evil in the childhood of the neurotic "is invariably a lack of genuine warmth and affection." This is her explanation of the cause: "The main reason why a child does not receive enough warmth and affection lies in the parents' incapacity to give it on account of their own neuroses." Thus the vicious circle is created, apparently to be broken only by psychoanalysis.

Horney correctly saw that symptoms must be regarded as the expressions of fundamental difficulties of the personality as a whole. Under the slogan, "every neurosis is a character neurosis," she loosened the psychoanalytic procedure from a tangle of luxuriant detail, and treated her patients as anxious, insecure individuals involved in one or another typical personality conflict of our time, without paying undue attention to the particular symptoms through which they expressed their anxiety.

But even Horney's emphasis on social factors is distinctly one-sided. It is, to put it simply, completely middle-class. This, for example, is her concept of the abnormal individual: "We should be inclined to consider neurotic, for example, a girl who prefers to remain in the rank and file, refuses to accept an increased salary and does not wish to be identified with her superiors. . . ." Again: "In an individualistic culture," she writes elsewhere [*New Ways in Psychoanalysis*], "the individual is expected to stand on his own feet, assert himself, and if necessary, fight his way." There is not the remotest suggestion that complete identification with the rank and file, even at a sacrifice of salary, might be wholesome even in our society. She obviously pictures our culture as homogeneous, and regards the middle class character as universal. She moreover presents this character as derivative from an abstract cultural tradition, quite independent of the individual's adult experience. A worker whose loyalty to his fellow workers and to his union has been burned into him by harsh experience would be regarded as abnormal by these standards, for according to Horney, "A neurosis is a psychic disturbance . . . which deviates from the pattern common to the particular culture" [*The Neurotic Personality of Our Time*]. Where Horney recognizes the presence of conflict in our society, she sees it operating mainly through the medium of family life. Following Fromm, she pictures a continuity in which competitive hostility in the family circle engenders anxiety in the growing child, who in turn imposes his own anxiety and hostility upon his children when he grows up, without regard to the contingencies of his own later experience. The actual social relationships engendering the anxiety, in other words, are everywhere except in the present, and are hence not amenable to change. And since nothing can be done to change these factors, there is nothing left to do but understand.

Thus it is that Horney places *understanding* in a central position in her analytic treatment, almost completely neglecting the role of the patient's actual social situation and his real mode of existence. Bartlett has dealt adequately with this aspect of Horney's work. If it is protested that a depreciation of the role of understanding robs psychoanalytic treatment of a most essential feature, it must be acknowledged that this is true. It should be added, however, that by giving insight its proper preliminary place, and emphasizing action, we are also depriving analysis of its chief reactionary tool, and making it an instrument of progress.

But it is not enough to break with the Freudian tradition; a body of scientific fact and theory is needed to supplant it. The appeal of psychoanalysis to many thoughtful people cannot be glossed over and is based on some real attractions. Psychoanalysis conferred the dignity of scientific rank on psychology at a time when mechanical materialists refused to take psychology seriously. Some of the opposition to analysis still comes from this source. It was dialectical in its emphasis on conflict and change, and it satisfied the craving for scientific realism at a time when the prim bourgeois hypocrisies of the period were no longer tenable. Its concept of the unconscious, above all, satisfied the need for an understanding of drives that seemed so often to make an individual act against his own best interests. We now know that these conflicting ideas and drives originate in social forces. Freud mistakenly related them to instincts, but the urge to explain these obscure forces in terms of an unconscious that did not derive from the individual's rational interest remains the chief attraction of Freudianism, and is its most valuable commodity. The details of a new psychology of the unconscious based on an understanding of the individual as a social product now need to be elaborated.

In this connection the role of insight must be carefully evaluated. It must be recognized that psychoanalysis not only makes the analysts feel good: it often has the same effect on troubled patients too. The perplexed neurotic individual in our society is often at a loss when he tries to understand his plight or tries to treat himself. He cherishes the illusion that he is free and independent. If he is employed and has a family he will insist there are no objective reasons for his discontent. A theory which tells him that vague aboriginal instincts are disturbing him sounds plausible, because he does not feel all in one piece: he knows that he is torn by conflict. If the development of these conflicts can be traced back to childhood—as they often can—there is a real thrill of discovery and the plausibility of the theory is enhanced. The relationships to the analyst itself is usually pleasant. It is relaxing to be so honest and the analyst is nearly always friendly. Such relationships are both valuable and rare. The self-knowledge achieved is by no means nonsensical: much of it is valid and beneficial. (The fact is that the patient often feels better and recommends analysis to his friends.) In apparent opposition to our theory, these benefits are often derived before any change has taken place in the patient's formal mode of existence. It seems to me

that Bartlett leaves himself open to misunderstanding by failing to concede this point. Let us, for the sake of clarity, assume that the analysis proceeds in a correct manner and gives the patient valid insights to his problem. We may list some of the immediate effects upon the patient as follows:

(1) Analytic insight tends to make neurotic problems more human. The neurotic patient is often possessed with the notion that his symptoms and problems are special and unique; they interfere with his capacity for social identification and tend therefore to discourage social activity. As the analysis reveals that fundamentally human drives lie at the basis of the symptoms, it becomes easier for the patient to see his resemblance to others and to recognize his identity of interests.

(2) Insight spares energy. Unresolved problems make constant demands on the patient's interest and attention, drain his energy, produce tension, and leave the patient with the constant dissatisfaction of a task undone. Correct insight allows the patient to clear the field for effective action and to turn his interest to other tasks. Mistaken insight gives temporary relief, but leads to extra trouble later on.

(3) Analytic work is an approximation to socially useful and socially acceptable work. Every analysis is an exercise in psychology. An interest in psychology—even though it be in one's own psychology—has a higher social value than an obsessive unproductive preoccupation with a personal problem. Analytic work thus facilitates the transition from mere personal preoccupation to social interests and activity.

(4) Analytic insight has educational and cultural value. Every analysis is bound to involve issues of general social and cultural interest. The analyst functions as a teacher and can exercise all the useful functions of a teacher in other spheres.

(5) Analytic insight is a social product. Analyst and patient work together to achieve it. Within its limits this is an important step toward socialization: The analyst is a valuable new and sympathetic friend—the relationship relieves the oppressive sense of loneliness felt by so many neurotics.

(6) Beyond the immediate benefits noted above, the analytic relationship has an important supportive function in the patient's transitional period. It affords encouragement, companionship, guidance, insight and fresh hope until the patient feels his strength emerging or reviving in the new situation created by his actions.

(7) Analytic insight prepares a program for action. This seems to me to be the main function of analytic insight. By understanding how his problem developed, the patient learns what line of action must be followed to relieve the problem. The prospect of useful action is as helpful to the neurotic as the promise of a good job to an unem-

ployed individual. It is not the real thing, but it is close to it.

In summary, we can say that there are some features essential to the analytic procedure and also some incidental features. The essential features involve the acquisition of scientific insight to be used for a plan of action. The incidental features are the reassurance, friendliness, occupational activity and general educational advantages involved in an analysis. But the reassurance and friendliness cannot and should not be a substitute for the strength that comes from a broad social integration on the outside. For that reason the very relief the patient derives from the analytic relationship can prove to be a snare and an illusion, especially if it is overvalued and becomes the model for narrow and exclusive personal relationships later on. The chief value of an analysis is and should be, the scientific insight it provides.

There are a number of helpful auxiliary techniques for retaining the neurotic as a patient, teaching him effectively, influencing him, and so on. One must not be rude, over-critical, too dogmatic, too forward or eager; one must not make all decisions for the patient, nor make explanations for which the patient is inadequately prepared. All these rules, dressed up in technical language, comprise part of the method of analysis. A knowledge of psychological mechanisms is also necessary, but all these have too often served to obscure basic misconceptions or even to create the illusion that these "inner laws of movement" in psychology operate, like some sort of perpetual motion, without important influences from outside.

Practical considerations, however, make it altogether unlikely that individual psychoanalytic treatment will ever be regarded as a satisfactory method for alleviating the widespread neurotic discontent in our culture. Its chief danger lies in the fact that mistaken theories developed from individual treatment will be applied to general policies affecting social welfare. This is already taking place in the fields of social work and welfare, and in the social sciences.

In these areas current psychoanalytic theories are exerting a wider and more harmful influence on progressive thought than is generally realized and have tended always to confuse or divert decisive action. Wherever a theory of social action is blended with psychoanalysis, it is to the detriment of action. In spite of Freud's sharp opposition to Marxism, attempts are made repeatedly to unite the two. Fromm, who moved in the Social Democratic circle of Horkheimer in Frankfort before coming here, spoke quite frankly in his German writings of the "enrichment" of historical materialism by psychoanalysis. Wilhelm Reich in that period also made an attempt to synthesize Freud and Marx, with unhappy results, and has since given himself up completely to a hodgepodge of mysticism called sexo-economics. Osborn made another attempt a few years ago in his *Freud and Marx,* which carried a laudatory introduction by John Strachey. It is instructive, in retrospect, to read Strachey's plea, "To-

day, however, an increased emphasis should, surely, be laid on the subjective, dynamic factors innate in men." In addition the review of Horney's *Self-Analysis* in this magazine gave it almost unqualified praise. "Dr. Horney," the reviewer wrote (*Science & Society,* VI [1942]), "has tackled the problem of what the individual can do about himself, for himself and by himself with that same courage and originality that distinguished her first two books . . . [The present volume] offers a methodological approach which diligently pursued under favorable conditions, promises to help develop one to the full of his potentialities."

It is no accident that psychoanalysis never attracted a following in Soviet Russia. Dmitri Mirsky ridicules the Bloomsbury intellectuals who become intrigued by their own minutest inner experiences, and record their dreams every night, in his *The Intelligentsia of Great Britain.* Soviet psychology is oriented around the unity of activity and consciousness. "In concrete activity, in work, in adult social practice, in child-training and education, mental characteristics do not only *appear,* but are *formed.*" This is the formulation of S. L. Rubinstein ["Soviet Psychology in War Time," *Philosophy and Phenomenological Research,* Vol. V, December, 1944].

Horney let the cat out of the bag when she declared in her *New Ways* that "analysis helps the patient to realize gradually that he is following the wrong path in expecting happiness to come to him from without, that the enjoyment of happiness is a faculty to be acquired from within. . . ." A progressive psychiatry, it seems to me, should teach on the contrary that the individual is nothing, and achieves nothing, by himself alone.

D. Ewen Cameron (essay date 1953)

SOURCE: "Karen Horney: A Pioneer in the Science of Human Relations," *American Journal of Psychoanalysis,* Vol. 14, No. 1, 1954, pp. 19-29.

[*In the following essay, which was originally presented at a psychiatric conference on 22 April 1953, Cameron addresses the main aspects of Horney's thought and lauds her ability to incorporate into her work the social and historical issues of her time.*]

Karen Horney was one of the children of her times. She walked among us distinguished by her originality of mind and by her leadership. Her life fell within a period of unusual turbulence and ferment in the world of thought. The long upward climb of humanism, which had started as far back as the time of the Renaissance and which was gathering strength to become one of the most important forces of our times, was met and vastly stimulated by another current having its origins very early in the modern period and already, as Karen Horney's life began, starting to impinge upon human affairs with gathering power. This was the scientific method—first applied only to material things and, at that, things remote from human life, such as astronomy and mathematics. Its increasing successes led us, somewhat timorously, to apply it to the affairs of everyday living and ultimately to man himself, beginning cautiously with biochemistry and physiology. But eventually, toward the latter part of the Nineteenth Century, it began to influence those thinking about the problems of human nature.

It is extraordinary to contemplate that it was only during the latter part of the Nineteenth Century that the great fact-finding sciences of human behavior—psychology, sociology and anthropology—began to be established. And so great was the change wrought in the whole field of psychiatry at that time that to many of those engaged in the field it has seemed as though psychiatry was a young science instead of one which dates back many centuries.

The intermingling of these powerful forces of humanism and of science applied to human behavior was rendered the more meaningful and vital by reason of the fact that the enormous progress of the industrial revolution was freeing more and more men and women from the immediate labor and preoccupation of winning their daily bread, freeing us in progressively greater numbers to think and to consider and to ponder upon our own nature.

This exploration of man's nature has gained power and impetus by the nature of our times, and an increasingly large number of able men and women, gravely concerned with the failures of our systems of social control to maintain an equable and strife-free world society, began to press forward studies of the nature of man. It was in this world of urgency and inquiry, this world of the exciting and sometimes almost explosive interlocking of great systems of thought, that Karen Horney came to work.

We must be forever indebted to her for her responsiveness to the world scene and for the extent to which her thinking about the problems of our field is set up with clear appreciation of the fact that we are essentially dynamic and reactive individuals, responding, and occasionally breaking down, in terms of the world in which we live.

At first, profoundly influenced by the new ideas being worked out by Sigmund Freud, Dr. Horney's career was absorbed in these early concepts. Later, however, she became progressively aware of the importance of ongoing events as factors causative of breakdown. This change in her thinking, which had long been germinating in her mind, was brought into particular clarity for her by her arrival in the United States in 1932—this allowing her to note the differences in the structure and manifestation of the neuroses in this country from those which she had observed in European countries. She also recorded the various differences in attitude toward life problems, and derived from this the fact that only differences in civilization could account for the variations in the neuroses.

As a further point of departure one may note her deep humanism and her optimism, as contrasted with Freud's

pessimism and his tendency to express human behavior in terms of a philosophy of science developed by the basic disciplines. While to Freud man seemed postulated to suffer or to destroy, Karen Horney believed in a limitless ability for man to develop his potentialities throughout his life.

CHALLENGE OF THE TIMES

These times offer a particular challenge to the inquiring and independent mind, a challenge which is essentially centered upon the problem of human nature itself. We have been a long time applying the scientific method to the study of human behavior, and a still longer time in coming to grips with some of the central and primary problems, particularly the matter of values. From this area—so explosive, so difficult, so deeply buried in the very heart of our societies, and therefore so profoundly imbedded in our own personality structure—Karen Horney did not shrink.

If Freud, who so greatly molded Karen Horney's earlier thinking, may be seen as having been much influenced by the premises of the basic sciences as applied to medicine (for instance, his insistence upon determinism as the primary type of causality; his anticipations that ultimately one would find a biological and, perhaps primarily, an endocrinological explanation for many of our problems; his insistence upon deviant behavior as the frequent outcome of a genetic unfolding of some primary or very early acquired damage) we must see Karen Horney, in contrast, as responding to her times in terms of another great trend in thinking about human behavior—the significance of on-going interpersonal relations. This premise, which is assuming dominance at the present time, is expressed in the vast range of manifestations of scientific humanism, in personnel work, in group dynamics, and increasingly in the trend toward what is termed "comprehensive medicine," which is the moving force in the great revisory experiments now going on with reference to the undergraduate curriculum in medicine.

In this lecture I should like to concern myself primarily with the matter of the influence exerted by basic premises upon scientific thinking. And I should like to take as the point of departure for these considerations the interesting and fruitful shift in basic premises which we can see in the work of the distinguished scientist whom we are memorializing.

As we have brought out earlier, there took place—presumably in mid-career—a progressive shift in Karen Horney's thinking, from an instinctual, genetic orientation toward neurotic illness to one which regarded the causes of such phenomena as arising primarily from relationships, and from on-going relationships at that.

As one studies the series of contributions which she made from the 1930's onward, one is left with the conviction that she was in the process of a further active shift in her thinking; she was still reorganizing and evolving her thinking in response to new premises.

It has been said that progress in human affairs is not made by the mere accumulation of more facts, but by the production of fruitful hypotheses. [J. B. Conant, *Education in a Divided World,* 1948]. In recognition of the fact that it is customary for us to think about a given matter in depth—to think not only of its visible manifestations but also about its roots and its ramifications—I should like to substitute the term "basic premise" for "hypothesis."

DEFINITION OF BASIC PREMISE

I define a basic premise as a constellation of action tendencies, usually having considerable inner consistency and endowed with a degree of intensification which results in the premise inhibiting all contradictory activity. I have used the term "action tendency" to designate both explicit and implicit behavioral patterns, to designate both thinking about doing something and actually carrying out motor activity with respect to something. I also view the action tendency as being either conscious or unconscious. Hence, when one talks about the premises of fundamentalism as a way of life, or of the heroic-romantic subcultural pattern of living, or when one talks about the premises of the basic sciences, one is talking about a very considerable constellation of behavioral patterns which reveals itself both in implicit and explicit behavior and in unconscious and conscious activity.

Having defined what is meant by the term "basic premise," let me now go on to explore its operation, to show how it may affect our thinking, how it determines what we are able to identify from among the things which pass before us, how it rules the kind of questions which we ask, and how it molds the methods we use to answer those questions. And, in doing so, I mean to use the premise that on-going human relations are a major factor in neurotic breakdown.

From time to time during the course of this discussion I hope to refer to, and illustrate, the extent to which these basic premises tend to inhibit alternative and, particularly, contradictory patterns of behavior. From our work, we are already aware how difficult it is for the fundamentalist, with his emphasis upon will power, upon absolutism of value and, indeed, upon the unchangeability of human nature, to accept the alternative but contradictory conceptions of the modifiability of human behavior, of the infinite variety of alternative ways of doing things, as long reported by the anthropologist [R. Benedict, *Patterns of Culture,* 1934].

Perhaps we are less clear about the limiting effects of the basic disciplines' philosophy of science upon progress in the field of the sciences of man. In Karen Horney's work one can see this admirably demonstrated. In accepting the relatively unlimited modifiability of human behavior in response to on-going experience, in her acceptance of the importance of interpersonal relations as producing changes in personality function, she came to develop a whole series of related concepts which stood in widening

contrast with those held by her earlier teacher, Sigmund Freud. In her own teachings she began to stress that the developing personality should not be seen merely as the unfolding of the already-given, but that new and unique constructs could be discerned. It is not altogether clear to me whether she recognized directly that the conception of causality which had been borrowed from Nineteenth Century science—namely, that of determinism—could not be maintained, and that different conceptions of causality would have to be elaborated to serve as explanations of the different ways in which event might be related to event under certain circumstances. It is clear, however, that she departed from the earlier conception voiced by Freud that the therapist should listen to the patient's associations with an "evenly hovering attention," avoiding deliberate attentiveness to certain details and avoiding conscious exertion.

In her *New Ways in Psychoanalysis,* she says specifically, "My view, on the other hand, is that the analyst should deliberately conduct the analysis." And later: "The analyst should exercise influence, not only in the direction of the patient's associations but also on those psychic forces which may help him eventually to overcome his neurosis."

I should like to suggest that, perhaps all unnoticed, these new premises which came to govern so much of Karen Horney's thinking have taken us considerably further than has hitherto been expressly stated. The premises drawn from the basic disciplines' philosophy of science and from Freud's conception of the instinctual nature of much of behavior have insensibly given place, progressively, to premises supporting the dominant importance of relationship as governing behavior.

These new conceptions have gathered force from many different sources: from the work of Adolf Meyer, who continually stressed the importance of the conception of the organism as being incomplete, as requiring relationship with other organisms in order to achieve full expression of many of its functions, including its sexual functions and its functions of communication; from the work of the anthropologists, who have shown repeatedly the enormous significance of child-parental relations in determining personality structure, and have revealed from material drawn from a great range of cultures what extraordinary diversities of subsequent personality structure may be produced by exposing the infant and child to a given set of interpersonal relations. Subsidiary support has also been derived from the study of group dynamics and from studies—both longitudinal and retrospective—of the development of the child.

EFFECT OF PREMISES

These new premises concerning the importance of relationship in determining, to a major though not exclusive extent, the personality structure and behavioral patterns of the individual are beginning to exert a profound effect upon our techniques of general psychotherapy. Karen

Horney has already indicated that the role of the therapist should be more active than that originally countenanced by Sigmund Freud. But many workers are now going far beyond this point, and it would seem probable that the future will see still greater changes in our conception of what occurs in the patient-therapist relationship. References are now being made to the growing importance of the therapist in identifying what is going on; and the phrase of the "resolving power" of the therapist has been coined. By this is meant the capacity of the therapist to respond to what the patient is saying and doing in terms of a series of problem-solving behaviors, which are in turn transmitted to the patient as he is ready to receive them and use them. I stress the latter phrase since, quite clearly, pattern of behavior transmitted to the patient before he is able to use them must by definition be useless.

In further pursuit of the ramifications of this premise concerning the importance of interpersonal relations in determining behavior, we begin to approach the fringes of its influence—the borderland between this premise and other great operational hypotheses of our society. For instance, it is not altogether clear whether it is this premise concerning the importance of interpersonal relations which is altering so much of our conceptions of science, or whether these have evolved in response to the need to work with ever more variable phenomena as science has been progressively applied to the understanding of sugar in the blood, of skin responses, of sexual guilt, and of social institutions. Whichever has taken the lead, it is nonetheless now certain that the emergence of our modern premises concerning interrelationships has required the abandonment of the old fundamentalist laws-of-nature idea. Men no longer set out to discover rules and regulations set up by nature and hitherto obscured by our own stupidity and dark ignorance. Rather, if we see ourselves setting out to find ways of controlling phenomena, I think those ways will depend upon our own perceptual and conceptual capacities.

As a very natural consequence of this we have abandoned the old idea of absolute truth and see, indeed, that what we call scientific truths are actually operational designs, the form of design depending, as indicated above, upon our own inherent and—perhaps more important—our acquired ways of thinking; and the validity of these designs being based solely on their effectiveness. We see, too, that the kind of facts which we discover are, for the most part, determined by the kind of questions we ask. Very little is known, as yet, about this missing half of science. Science, as you can see, is an asymmetrical body, exceedingly well developed with respect to procedures for the answering of questions, but with practically nothing to say about the most important thing of all—how we go about asking questions.

It does not seem unreasonable, however, to say that the kind of questions which we tend to ask are determined by our needs. And here we are confronted with the tempting hypothesis that one of the reasons for the emergence of the basic premise of the great importance of interpersonal relations in understanding human behavior is because of the needs of the times.

THREE SOCIAL SOLVENTS

Into our rural, largely hierarchical, societies of hardly three generations ago were poured three great social solvents. Not unreasonably, they may be described as mordants in many of their actions—excoriating and destroying, as well as building. These amazingly powerful forces are: industrialization, instant and universal communication, and general literacy. All three have had an extraordinary effect upon our social structure. And in almost all their actions they have served to lay bare the basic importance of human relationships. Masses of people uprooted from rural communities, transported into largely unstructured industrialized areas, have come to know this poignantly enough. Communication and transportation have shown us the myriad adaptations possible in some of those things which we have thought basic and absolute, such as our way of bringing up children, our way of living with women, our way of sharing goods. Hence, it is far from astonishing that this should have been a period during which keen attention came to be directed to problems in interpersonal relations.

In conformity with this basic hypothesis, then, we must see those people whom earlier times had conceived as primary originators of new ideas, as discoverers of fundamental facts, being more properly conceived of as individuals who are specially responsive to their times. Karen Horney, in her many works, has shown herself to be such. It would be doing her far less than justice to see her as having acted as a catalyst for the thinking of her times. I should rather coin a term and say that she was a crystallizer. Her sensitive and perceptive mind had remarkable capacities to free itself from the conceptions of an earlier period—a capacity which we know, to our sorrow, is by no means widespread. Her mind was able to respond to the emergent thinking of her times in the sense of giving form to the trends and forces which beat upon her. She was able to crystallize out, from the still amorphous movement of her period, those conceptions which have become rallying points, platforms and points of departure for others who did not have her special gift. And she did so with a clarity which, in itself, gives her clear title to the term crystallizer.

This at once brings us to the exceedingly important question of how basic premises are set up. To this we can only give partial answers. To say that they are culturally determined is not particularly exciting, since it immediately must bring us to the more pointed query: "How does a given premise become established in our culture in the first place? What determines how long it shall persist?" For instance, we have a record of the dichotomy as going back at least to the time of Aristotle.

We may perhaps get some leads as to how this happens by asking another question: "How do basic premises become modified?"

Somewhat earlier, in discussing the emergence of the premises concerning the influence exerted by relationships upon behavior, it was indicated that evolving needs of a society may determine shifts in basic premises. At the same time, we have to recognize that a given premise may be so highly sanctioned by a society—and, hence, so deeply and powerfully indoctrinated, so buttressed by taboos and other defenses—that it may be impossible to modify it at all freely. Hence the basic premise may persist long after the changing nature of the times has demanded its modification. In this lag in the shift in premises can be seen one of the most fruitful grounds of neurotic breakdown. We have only to point, for instance, to the considerable lag in our basic premises concerning the sexual life of the individual and, indeed, concerning the nature of his aggressive instincts.

In presenting this first general aspect of the basic premise, I have attempted to show (using as an illustration those premises concerning the significance of human relationships upon the genesis of behavior which have so profoundly influenced Karen Horney's earlier work) how such a premise can and does affect our thinking with respect to etiology, to practice and the direction of our research.

CONFLICT OF PREMISE AND REALITY

I should like now to pass on to another aspect: the role which a basic premise plays in producing behavioral breakdown as a result of conflict between itself and the reality situation, or between itself and other co-existing premises. Karen Horney's recognition of this is clear in two most illuminating books, *The Neurotic Personality of Our Time* and *Our Inner Conflicts*. And, indeed, she lays great stress upon the importance of the consistency of the personality.

There is now wide recognition of the fact that many of our behavioral difficulties, much social insecurity, and any number of anxieties, hostilities, and crippling guilt feelings, arise because our premises concerning living are at odds not only with reality but often with themselves. Sometimes that recognition is quite explicit, as it was in the 1951 panel discussion, organized by Karen Horney and held at the American Psychiatric Association's annual meeting, on the subject of "Moral Values in Therapy." For the vast mass of people, the recognition is implicit. There is a general and rising belief that men and women everywhere are being deprived of that well-being, that satisfaction in living, which can be theirs. There is a feeling that that deprivation is unnecessary, and there is a determination that it shall come to an end. There is a belief, slowly spreading through the minds of men and women—a belief passionately expressed in Karen Horney's life and works—that life is not necessarily a vale of tears, that our world does not have to be a place dark with passion and fury, hatred and death; that these come from our way of living, from our customs, from our conceptions of ourselves and of our fellows. In the most powerful of all, there is a belief that the remedy is in our hands, that we can remold and remodel ourselves and our world.

It is perhaps illuminating to make a comparison between what has happened in the economic field and what is now emerging in the field of individual welfare and social well-being. There was a time when there was a belief that poverty was part of man's destiny. In hierarchical societies, whole classes of human beings were seen as destined to live out their days and bring up their families in destitution. Nothing else was conceived as possible; such was man's lot. Whoever sought to defy this state of affairs or to change it was, at the least, presumptuous. But within the last half century, a series of entirely new concepts concerning the right of the individual man and his family to economic security and freedom from want has arisen. From these beliefs have flowed a great series of social services, of wise reforms, both in the economic and in the social field. The old poverty and destitution, so long felt to be inevitable, is rapidly disappearing.

There seems little doubt that the same process is being enacted with respect to our present deprivations which have been so crippling and so devastating with respect to our satisfaction in living.

It is against this background of forces now gathering up strength for another great forward movement in human affairs that I should like to discuss briefly the part played by conflicts between our basic premises and reality, and between the premises themselves as factors contributing seriously to present social insecurities, hostilities and the general neuroticism of our period.

CONTRASTING SANCTIONS

At the International Congress of Mental Health held in London in 1948, a series of most able reports was made upon the existence of certain great rifts within our cultural patterning. By rifts I mean basic contradictions between groups of premises, many of which have an equally high and extensive degree of acceptability within our culture. I should like to make reference, in the first instance, to the contrasting sanctions which exist relative to aggressiveness and acceptance. As we all know, there exist sanctions for the demand by the parent that the child be good, obedient and submissive. In a slightly earlier decade, there was prevalent the dictum that "Little children are to be seen and not heard." Other phrases from that time come readily to mind: "Little birds in their nest agree", "Let not the sun go down upon your anger."

As we all know from our retrospective psychotherapeutic studies, these premises concerning the behavior of children, if applied with full success, result in the development of some very good little boys and girls who, growing up and continuing to be good little boys and girls, are almost certain to meet major psychoneurotic disaster along life's road. When the child thus indoctrinated comes to adolescent years, he will find waiting for him a whole series of sanctions for the avoidance of strife, for walking humbly and meekly, for deferring to authority; great, solemn, stentorian voices are waiting to ask: "Who are you, little man, that you should question?"

But, alongside this sanction for submissiveness, acceptance and renunciation of individual decision in favor of the precepts of authority, there is another set of sanctions, also well supported throughout our society. These are the sanctions for vigor, for energy, for getting up and getting going, for working harder and longer and more shrewdly than one's neighbor, for getting to the top of the pile, for walking upward through the night while others sleep. Here, then, one sees the stage set for the genesis of an immense range of feelings of guilt, confusion, resentment. How often in our work have we heard the "good little girl," now grown up, saying, "I have done everything for my mother, devoted my whole life to her, and my sisters they have done nothing; and yet look how she loves them, and how she takes me utterly for granted." In her voice one hears the vicious impact of the counterbalancing guilt which this "good" girl feels whenever she ventures to criticize others.

DICHOTOMY THINKING

Still another great rift between opposing premises referred to at the International Congress was the great difficulties which arise in the lives of all of us through our ancient dichotomy thinking, which sees good men as people who do good things, and bad men as people who do bad things; this being in violent contrast to the reality situation which is that quite contradictory trends can coexist in the individual. In other words, our premises concerning our social relationships are at odds with the reality situation—namely, that our relationships with others are essentially ambivalent. Again, as we know from our daily work, one of the big forward steps in therapy is taken when the patient is able to recognize that he can love and hate the same person at the same time. But until he recognizes that there is likely to arise, from conflict between the realities and the current premise that one only loves or hates, a whole series of anxieties, guilt feelings and resentments.

This leads us, in natural sequence, to consideration of a still more pervasive conflict between our on-going premises—one which particularly concerns us as social scientists and which time and again concerned Karen Horney. This is the rift between the social imperatives of "should" and "ought" [*Neurosis and Human Growth*], and the whole framework of the scientific approach to human behavior, which may indeed be said to rest on one word: "is." "Why is this so?" "How is this so?" And sometimes, "What is this?"

As we are aware, one of our major problems is to enable the patient to see what *is* actually happening, rather than continuing to look at what he feels *should* be happening, what he feels he *ought* to be doing and thinking. The essence of this is the great on-going, and perhaps increasing, conflict between moralism and realism, between

authoritarianism and scientific humanism. This is not the occasion to explore this fascinating matter further, since my primary purpose is to look for a time at the work of Karen Horney and, in particular, to explore her response to a great, emerging, basic premise in our society. But I feel that I should not leave this densely conflicted area without suggesting that when we think about it, when we attempt to understand it, we are most likely to succeed if we do not ourselves moralize and say that realism obviously is destined to succeed where moralism has failed. Rather, one hopes that the approach would be through a continuation of our scientific way of thinking about things, that we would ask more and more searching questions as to how moralism operates, what are the forces which brought it into being, and to what extent is it continuing to add to the measure of individual and collective satisfaction in life.

The conflict between great contending premises are numerous and I shall attempt to examine only one or two in passing. Margaret Mead, in her book, *Male and Female,* has outlined in her fascinating way the confusing sanctions which govern the young girl in her pre-courtship sexual patterns on the North American continent. On the one hand she must be as attractive and enticing as possible, she must show every evidence of lively responsiveness to sexual cues put forward by her partner, but she must do so only to a point. There is no generally accepted social sanction for the complete playing out of the pattern, and Margaret Mead has suggested that for many women this results in finding complete response impossible after marriage. They have been so conditioned to be completely responsive in the early stages of the sexual pattern, so completely conditioned to absolute avoidance of the final stages of that pattern, that in full marital relationship they remain, with quite unconscious willingness, completely inhibited.

From another field I should like to draw still another interesting and fascinating illustration, not so much of conflict between basic premises but, rather, of conflict between a basic premise and the on-going reality situation.

Before industrialization brought its many and mixed changes to our society, there existed a social stereotype of the master craftsman. He was someone—perhaps a builder of boats, perhaps a blacksmith—who by the very excellence of his work had achieved a reputation and had become known as a master in his field. Men came from far and wide to seek his services. With industrialization, however, handiwork and the long and patiently acquired skills became of less account. Men, if they showed special competence, were given special rewards in the way of increased pay or promotion.

LIMITED VALIDITY OF SOCIAL DICTA

The old idea of the master craftsman has disappeared in favor of the idea that if you are good you will get ahead; if you are smart, able and efficient, you will be promoted.

It is a widely held conception, especially among middle-class social strata. But, like all social dicta, in practice it has only limited validity. There are many places in many industries where no matter how efficient and able a man is, it may not be possible for him to be promoted. There may be no place for him to go to, or it may be that the boss's nephew is the next person to be elevated. But such is the strength of the belief that there are, everywhere, overmotivated white-collar workers, living like mindless salmon striving to spring up over an impassable waterfall and injuring and exhausting themselves in consequence.

I cannot leave this most intriguing area of the basic premise as a factor in the production of breakdown without making brief reference to the extremely interesting work which has been done in so many centers, and which has been so ably compiled by Bowlby [*Maternal Care and Mental Health,* 1952], upon the effects of maternal deprivation. Here one sees a whole series of basic premises concerning the management of the child, so seriously at variance with the realities of child care as to have produced the utmost damage, and even death, in countless children. Beliefs that children could be managed almost equally well in foster homes and in orphanages, beliefs that mere physical cleanliness and sufficiency of food were all that the child required, have had most tragic consequences.

A last illustration I will draw from a field in which we have ourselves been much interested: attempts to delineate subcultural ways of life learned by the individual in his childhood and dominating his later life. Among these is the heroic-romantic conception of life, one of whose precepts is a belief in the unlimited capacities of will power: "You must never give up", "You must do it yourself", "You can do anything on earth if you simply will it strongly enough." The tragic conflict between this unrealistic premise and the facts of alcoholism are so well known that I do not think that I need to underscore it.

DISSOLVING THE DICHOTOMY

A third general aspect of the basic premise is the modifying influence which one basic premise may exert upon others. Earlier I indicated that a basic premise should be seen as a constellation of action tendencies, both implicit and explicit in their manifestations and operating both consciously and unconsciously. Here would seem to me to be a convenient place to stress the growing interest in seeking some means of dissolving this dichotomy of conscious and unconscious, and to see the phenomena which we have grouped under these headings as actually lying in a continuum. This step would seem to me to follow naturally and almost inevitably upon what I have already outlined earlier on the recognition of the importance of relationships as determining behavior.

No one can question the enormous importance of our discoveries about what has been hitherto designated as "unconscious activity." Without them, many of the most dynamic conceptions concerning human behavior would be lacking. There can, however, be little doubt that, again, the inhibitory powers of basic premises have been at work here, and the very intensity of our absorption in the phenomena of unconscious activity has served to block off work which should have been done during these last several decades upon the no less important activities being carried on within the field of awareness.

CONSCIOUSNESS

Recently I have had occasion to discuss the emerging importance of consciousness. It seems almost absurd to have to stress this fact, but it is only in the area of awareness that our major adjustments are made, that the major reconceptualizations take place, that new and original syntheses of behavior take form. Hence, passing forward as we are into a period in which we seem destined to carry out intense work on the importance of the interpersonal relationship as determining behavior, we must clearly recognize that much of the import of relationship takes place at the level of awareness. Moreover, if we are going to see the therapist as playing a more active part in psychotherapy—or, to put it perhaps more realistically, if we are going to recognize more clearly the active part that the therapist does play in psychotherapy—we are going to have to understand more clearly the phenomena of consciousness.

It would, however, seem a very great pity indeed if, in swinging our attention from unconscious activities to conscious ones, we perpetuated the old dichotomy error of paying attention to one thing by neglecting the other. I should hope that we would see determined efforts to produce a synthesis, perhaps, as I have already suggested, in the form of seeing the phenomena occurring in both areas in terms of a continuum.

I have indicated that the basic premise concerning the effects of relationships upon behavior is already exerting an influence upon this ancient dichotomy of consciousness-unconsciousness. Of the various components of our basic premises concerning the importance of relationships, no part seems more likely to bring about a breakdown in this dichotomy than that comprised by communication. Communication has come to constitute a whole field of inquiry on its own, and the aspects to which I refer are the non-verbal communications. Here it can be demonstrated that a whole series of activities and attitudes on the part of one person can be picked up without being consciously perceived, and reacted to by another, although possibly without the fine discrimination of response which occurs when perception is carried out with full awareness. Nonetheless, the fact that perception does occur in both instances again advocates strongly the desirability of seeing these activities in the form of a continuum.

COMMUNICATION

When we come to the matter of communication to our introjected stereotype of the other person, and particularly to the matter of communication to the self, the need for a revision of our consciousness-unconsciousness dichotomy becomes the more apparent. To see what limited exploratory value our present conceptual framework possesses, it is only necessary to consider such phenomena as the dynamics of the playback. This is a psychotherapeutic technique which has been increasingly used with the rapid postwar improvements in recording devices. It has been used particularly to facilitate identification by the patient of his own aberrant behavior. In other words, it facilitates the communication by the patient to himself concerning some of his own difficulties. It seems to do so by reason of two things: 1) the greatly decreased work involved in listening to what one has said as contrasted with listening to what one is saying, since the latter activity has to be carried on coincidentally with the formation of what one has to say, putting it into suitable grammatical form, holding to the goal idea, considering the other individual's capacity to receive what is being said, and checking on how he is reacting. And 2), the fact that when we hear the playback our voice does not sound the way it ordinarily does. Customarily we hear our own voice—at least in part—transmitted through the bones of the skull; when we listen to the playback, it comes through the air. This permits some degree of separation from ourselves and, apparently, evasion of defenses we have established to block out the recognition of neurotic content, inconsistencies, hostilities and anxieties in tone and expression when we listen to our voice conducted in the ordinary way.

Still another aspect of the playback which, if it does not offer a solution of the consciousness-unconsciousness dichotomy at least adds to its general untenability, is the curious phenomenon evoked by repeated playbacks of some significant sentence. While the inner meaning of this sentence may be far from apparent either to the patient or to the therapist, it is curious to note how repetition—say, ten, twenty, thirty or forty times—will first of all make the inner meaning progressively clearer, as though from the summation of stimuli, and then almost inevitably make the patient acutely uncomfortable, to the point of refusing to listen to it further.

I would now like to explore a fourth, aspect of basic premises to which I made reference earlier—namely, their inhibitory capacities. I have already indicated the fact that basic premises are comprised of a constellation of action tendencies which are commonly endowed with sufficient intensity to inhibit all contradictory and antagonistic action tendencies. I would like to suggest to you that it is in actuality this inhibitory power of basic premises which, in large measure, is responsible for the maintenance of a separation between those happenings which can come into awareness and those which remain unconscious. One can say that there is something of a natural selection in basic premises and that those which are effective tend to have reasonably ready access to awareness, whereas those which are less effective are inhibited under most circumstances. It will be understood, of course, that the social sanctions of the period will determine, in a measure, whether or not a set of basic premises is going to operate effectively for the individual.

Passing from this, I would like to put before you a possible fifth aspect: that these basic premises are set up in some measure by trial and error, that those essays which are not accepted are then inhibited and, therefore, kept in the area of awareness. So that one may see as part of any basic premise a series of shadow premises usually made up of variant and sometimes completely contradictory action tendencies. Under certain circumstances, there may be a complete swing-over as has been described by William James in his studies on religious experience [*The Varieties of Religious Experience,* 1908], and more recently refered to by Sargant ["The Mechanism of Conversion," *B.M.J.,* Vol. 11, No. 311, August 11, 1951].

HORNEY'S DIRECTNESS AND SIMPLICITY

Finally, I should like to make reference to an important characteristic of Karen Horney's work: her essential directness and simplicity of approach to the problems on which she worked. One may attribute this to two things. First, she was not trapped, as so many others are and have been, in the theoretic superstructure of her teachers. It is one of the unhappier aspects of the development of a new field that so much becomes institutionalized so soon, and that so many of the students and disciples of the outstanding leader apparently are quite unable to distinguish the living substance of what that leader has developed from the forms in which he cast it. It is quite tragic to see what a vast amount of labor has been spent in endlessly turning over and exchanging, with wearisome repetition, the thought forms of the original mind—thought forms from which the vitality has now departed as certainly as it has from an empty seashell. And secondly, we must attribute Karen Horney's essential directness and simplicity of approach to the fact that she herself did not seem to require the successive development of theoretic structure which has been so much of an inpediment to the communication of the work of others.

In this review—limited and rapid as it must be—of the response of this able and gifted mind to the rapidly changing and crucial demands of one of the great pivotal periods in the history of humanity, we have glimpsed something of the leadership exerted by a sensitive, perceptive and highly gifted person. We have seen how, time and again, she served to crystallize from the amorphous strivings of her day conceptions destined to be built into areas of strength for others. The number of those others, in our society and in the world of thought that knew her, is a continually growing multitude.

Frederick A. Weiss (essay date 1954)

SOURCE: "Karen Horney: Her Early Papers," in *American Journal of Psychoanalysis,* Vol. 14, No. 1, 1954, pp. 55-64.

[*In the following essay, Weiss examines some of the central ideas in Horney's thought, focusing on their expression in some of her early writings and comparing these with her later works.*]

"Science has often found it fruitful to look at long-familiar facts from a fresh point of view. Otherwise there is a danger that we shall involuntarily continue to classify all new observations amongst the same clearly defined group of ideas" [**"The Flight From Womanhood: The Masculinity Complex in Women, as Viewed by Men and by Women,"** *International Journal of Psychoanalysis,* Vol. VII, 1926]. This statement by Karen Horney expresses the spirit of sincere acceptance and creative reevaluation of previous observations which have characterized her work from the beginning. The study of her early papers provides a fascinating experience. It means participating in that process of constructive questioning which is the *status nascendi* of any pioneering step in the development of science.

Looking back on her very first paper, **"The Technique of Psychoanalytic Therapy,"** written in 1917, we can already discern beginnings of the new ways which in the subsequent thirty-five years led her, step by step, to a creative reformulation of the meaning and structure of psychoanalysis.

UNITY OF THEORY AND THERAPY

"The analytical theories," Horney states, "have grown out of observations and experiences which were made in applying this method. The theories, in turn, later exerted their influence on the practice."

This emphasis on the basic unity of theory and practice prevented Horney's work from getting lost in ideological speculations and always kept her close to the fertile soil of human experience. At the time this paper was written the evolution of psychoanalysis had led to the abandonment of three earlier concepts:

1. Psychoanalysis was no longer a merely symptomatic theory concerned mainly with searching for the emotional trauma in the past.

2. In contrast to its earlier stage, still influenced by having derived from hypnosis, psychoanalysis abolished the use of suggestion, including any kind of do's or don'ts.

3. Its indications were constantly growing broader.

Horney reviews the main roads that lead to the unconscious motivation: following the "basic rule," using free associations, dream interpretation, symbolism, slips, and the observation of psychosomatic symptoms which occur during the analytical hour. But she immediately emphasizes that discovering the unconscious motivation represents neither the main difficulty nor the main task of therapy. "Even presuming that I could completely interpret the patient's entire emotional life," she writes, "that

in itself would not help him one step forward. This may be imagined as though the patient had locked up his unconscious drives like strange animals, behind a high wall, beyond which he can no longer look. He no longer knows these animals, but their noise disturbs and frightens him." What the patient needs is help in gradually breaking down this wall. Then he can grow aware of these drives, up to now unknown to him, and can consciously face them, accept or reject them.

"BLOCKAGES FIRST"

Horney considered the breaking down of this wall a main task of therapy, just as thirty years later she emphasized in her lectures on psychoanalytic therapy: "Blockages first!" Blockages include anything that interferes with the progress of analysis, such as coming late, missing sessions for insufficient reasons, complete lack of associations or dreams, or such an over-abundance of dreams that reporting them takes up the whole hour. Or, the patient may use half of the hour for complaints that he is making no progress, instead of using the time for analytical work; or he may suddenly talk about the furniture of the office or may try to involve the doctor in critical discussions of psychoanalysis. The patient must be helped to become aware that a blockage exists, and it is necessary to uncover its cause which may be connected with the material that came up in the analytical hour, or with the development of the analytical relationship.

NOT ADVICE, BUT ANALYSIS

Often the patient asks for advice. The analyst, however, knows that conflicts cannot be understood without exposing the underlying unconscious drives. Horney stresses that the analyst renders a much greater service to the patient if he confines himself to clarifying the motivations that compel the patient to make this decision or that, thus enabling him to be the active agent in his own decisions. Among the therapeutic factors mentioned are: the analytical relationship, the gradually growing interest in the analytic process, and the wish to be relieved of the suffering caused by the neurosis. A retarding force may be the gain derived by the patient from his neurotic suffering, for example, in the case of a woman who uses her suffering to force her inconsiderate husband to treat her with greater consideration.

As for the timing of interpretations, Horney suggests waiting until a good analytical relationship is established and the patient has come close to the insight himself. The patient may respond to an accurate interpretation in very different ways. Immediate insight may take place, accompanied by a feeling of relief. A symptom may appear, change, or disappear during the hour. Or, the first reaction of the patient may consist of a conscious denial, while simultaneous associations might nevertheless lead him to the pertinent insight.

The analyst is in need of continuous self-analysis, particularly regarding counter-transference reactions which occur in him during the analytic hour.

POTENTIALITIES AND LIMITATIONS OF ANALYTIC THERAPY

The paper ends with reflections on the potentialities and limitations of analytic therapy: "Psychoanalysis can free a human being who was tied hands and feet. It cannot give him new arms or legs. Psychoanalysis, however, has shown us that much that we have regarded as constitutional merely represents a blockage of growth, a blockage which can be lifted."

This formulation reveals two basic attitudes which characterize Horney's approach to therapy: freedom from magic expectations, but faith in the constructive forces of man. She opposes an outdated, static concept of an unchangeable constitution from which so much therapeutic pessimism originates. Leaders of contemporary dynamic psychiatry reaffirm this view. Whitehorn, for example, states: "'Constitutional' consideration has sometimes been urged as an a priori reason why psychotherapy would be futile. On the other side . . . one finds evidences of assets and capacities constitutionally determined, which have remained unutilized or fallen into disuse until evoked by psychotherapy" [J.C. Whitehorn, "Psychotherapy," *Modern Trends in Psychological Medicine,* edited by N. G. Harris and Paul B. Hoeber, 1948].

ON COMPULSION NEUROSIS

"Research has at all times been greatly endangered by the tendency to cover up real gaps in knowledge by the suggestion of pseudo knowledge, thereby blocking the path to true insight." With this admonition Horney approaches the "specific problems of compulsion neurosis in the light of psychoanalysis" [**"The Specific Problems of Compulsion Neurosis in the Light of Psychoanalysis"**]. She rejects the then prevailing concept that the specific characteristics of compulsion neurosis consist of the compulsive repetition of certain thoughts or actions, since this symptom also occurs in many other conditions, for example, in the stereotype pattern of schizophrenics; and she rejects Freud's mechanism of repetition compulsion [*Beyond the Pleasure Principle,* 1922] as the explanation for its dynamics. The concept of repetition compulsion, characterized by Freud himself as hypothetical, must always be suspected as serving as a convenient substitute for a genuine explanation. The basic role of anxiety, while undeniable in compulsion neurosis, is by no means specific. It is rather surprising and significant, however, that anxiety here hardly appears in manifest form. More important is the existence of strong, aggressive, destructive impulses which here—in contrast to hysteria—are not accompanied by simultaneous love impulses. The hysteric can also discharge many of his forbidden impulses through sensory or motor pathways (hysterical fits, conversion phenomena) thereby finding, time and again, relief from the onrushing impulses. The compulsive neurotic, however, knows no such relief. The road which leads to motor discharge—impulse, thought of action, action—is, as a rule, cut off before the action. The compulsion neurotic gets stuck in thinking. The immense danger of the naked, unadulterated destructive impulses,

force him to restriction of all real activity. What is the result? The entire energy, which otherwise is transformed into action, is here thrown back to the preparatory stages: impulse and thought of action. The will and thought processes thereby become so greatly intensified that in the self-perception of the patient they acquire a magic power, in the face of which his intellectual insight proves powerless.

THE MAGIC OF THOUGHT

The magic of thought, co-existent with an otherwise sound intellect, is perhaps the most conspicuous feature of compulsion neurosis. Thoughts and impulses thus acquire the characteristics of reality. The blocking of action, therefore, proves to be an inadequate defense because in the subjective experience of the compulsion neurotic thinking itself generates dangerous magic effects. Rigid constraint alone, the patient feels, can prevent this threat which originates in himself. Thus compulsion, the mechanism which provided the name for this emotional disturbance, actually proves to be only a secondary reactive phenomenon. The patient apparently must fight on two fronts. On the external front he has to prevent destruction by counteracting in magic ways the magic effects caused by him. On the internal front he must fight his own guilt feelings.

The treatment is difficult. The hysteric patient takes his affects to the physician whose task is limited to interpreting them. The compulsive neurotic, however, refuses to let himself be driven out of the sanctuary of the merely rational. Horney considers it particularly characteristic that the compulsive ideas or impulses appear dissociated from emotional affect, so that it becomes possible for the patient to experience them as something alien which forms no part of him. The patient may tell you how he will poison, smash or choke you or others, but when you point to aggressive impulses in him he will assure you that he is not aware of them.

Horney's emphasis on the decisive role which the process of dissociation plays in compulsion neurosis is shared by contemporary authors such as Alexander and Shapiro who state: "The objectionable ideas are de-emotionalized; they appear disconnected and almost as abstractions, like foreign bodies for which the patient does not feel responsible" [F. Alexander and H. Shapiro, "Neuroses, Behavior Disorders and Perversions," *Dynamic Psychiatry,* edited by Alexander and H. Ross, 1952].

In her first paper on the psychology of women, **"On the Genesis of the Castration Complex in Women,"** which was delivered in 1922 at the Seventh International Psychoanalytical Congress in Berlin, Horney summarizes Abraham's view concerning penis envy and castration complex and challenges the underlying thesis.

"The assertion," she says, "that one-half of the human race is discontented with the sex assigned to it and can overcome this discontent only in favorable circumstances is decidedly unsatisfying not only to feminine narcissism but also to biological science."

ELEMENTS OF PENIS ENVY

While in this early paper penis envy and castration complex are still considered significant in the development of character and neurosis in women, Horney denies that penis envy is a primary phenomenon. "The little girl's sense of inferiority is . . . by no means primary but it seems to her that, in comparison with boys, she is subject to restrictions as regards the possibility of gratifying certain instinct-components which are of the greatest importance in the pregenital period."

From the point of view of a child at this stage of development, little girls are at a disadvantage, compared with boys, in respect of certain possibilities of gratification. Horney refers to the desire to urinate like a boy. Fantasies of omnipotence are more easily associated with the jet of urine passed by the male. Important, too, is the fact that "just in the act of urinating a boy can display his genital and look at himself and is even permitted to do so, and he can thus in a certain sense satisfy his sexual curiosity, at least as far as his own body is concerned." Finally, Horney believes that a third element in the so-called "penis envy" may be suppressed onanistic wishes connected with the mostly unconscious idea that the fact that "boys are permitted to take hold of their genital when urinating is construed as a permission to masturbate."

In the genesis of the castration complex in women, Horney considered more important than penis envy the "fantasy of having suffered castration through the love relation with the father . . . it is wounded womanhood which gives rise to the castration complex . . . a highly important piece of repressed womanhood is most intimately bound up with the castration fantasies."

THE INHERENT VALUE OF WOMANHOOD

This paper still reflects the full impact of the libido theory, but seen historically it is the first publication in which she rejects the concept of a primary penis envy and emphasizes the value inherent in womanhood itself. "When she reaches maturity, a great part in sexual life (as regards creative power, perhaps even a greater part than that of men) devolves upon a woman."

Using still the limited sex-centered symbols of penis envy and castration complex, this paper, translated into holistic terms, contains the beginnings of the dynamic concept: it is the rejection of her total self, her sexual role and her creative power which impede the healthy development of the woman.

During the following years the spirit of constructive and courageous questioning grew stronger in Karen Horney. She began to ask herself whether perhaps the source material on which psychoanalytic research had hitherto been based might have been not fully representative. "Till quite recently the mind of boys and men only was taken as the object of investigation." Might this fact not have led to a more or less masculine psychology and a one-sidedness in the analytical approach to the study of feminine development? With these questions in mind she writes her paper on "**The Flight from Womanhood.**"

A fresh point of view was needed. "The new point of view," Horney states, "came to me by way of philosophy in some essays by Georg Simmel." According to Simmel [in *Philosophische Kultur,* 1921], the very standards by which mankind has estimated the values of male and female nature are "not neutral, arising out of the difference of the sexes, but in themselves essentially masculine . . . We do not believe in a purely 'human' civilization, into which the question of sex does not enter, for the very reason that prevents any such civilization from in fact existing, namely the (so to speak) naive identification of the concept 'human being' (*Mensch*) and the concept 'man' (*Mann*), which in many languages even causes the same word to be used for the two concepts . . . This is the reason why in the most varying fields inadequate achievements are contemptuously called 'feminine,' while distinguished achievements on the part of women are called 'masculine' as an expression of praise." Could it be that the psychology of women hitherto was also influenced by male viewpoints and male wishes, wishes to which women adapted themselves "as if their adaptation were their true nature"? How far has the evolution of women, as depicted by analysis, been measured by masculine standards and how far therefore does the picture perhaps fail to present the real nature of women? "The present analytical picture of feminine development . . . differs in no case by a hair's breadth from the typical ideas which the boy has of the girl."

The existence of this over-exact agreement is certainly no criterion of its objective correctness or falseness. The analytical ideas of feminine development are derived from research and, Horney says, "analytical research has always been founded upon the sure ground of experience . . . but all experience by its very nature contains a subjective factor. Thus, even our analytic experience is derived from direct observation of the material which our patients bring to analysis in free associations, dreams, and symptoms, and from the interpretations which we make or the conclusions which we draw from this material. Therefore, even if the technique is correctly applied, there is in theory the possibility of variations in this experience."

Up to now, the genital difference between the sexes has been made the cardinal point in the analytic conception, but the other great biological difference has been left out, namely the different role in the function of reproduction. According to Ferenczi [in "Versuch einer Genitaltheorie," 1922] the woman lacks any real primal impulse to coitus, or at least she is debarred from all direct fulfillment. Only indirectly she obtains a certain fulfillment, partly by the roundabout way of masochistic conversion, and partly by identification with the child she may conceive. These, however, are considered "compensatory devices."

CREATIVE EXPERIENCE OF MOTHERHOOD

"At this point," Horney writes, "I, as a woman, ask in amazement, 'And what about motherhood? And the blissful consciousness of bearing a new life within oneself? And the ineffable happiness of the increasing expectation of the appearance of this new being? And the joy when it finally makes its appearance and one holds it for the first time in one's arms? And the deep pleasurable feeling of satisfaction in suckling it and the happiness of the whole period when the infant needs her care?'"

The desire to be a man, familiar from the analysis of adult women, has only very little to do with primary penis envy. "It is a secondary formation, embodying all that has miscarried in the development toward womanhood." In this statement Horney already indicates her basic concept that the capacity for growth and self-realization, which includes the acceptance and realization of the sexual role, is inherent in human beings and that only interference with this self-realization leads to neurotic disturbance.

In this paper Horney goes so far as to state: "From the biological point of view, woman has in motherhood, or in the capacity for motherhood, a quite indisputable and by no means negligible physiological superiority. . . . Masculine envy certainly serves as one, if not as the essential, driving force in the setting up of cultural values."

Similar views were recently expressed by anthropologists such as Margaret Mead [in *Male and Female,* 1949] who speaks of "womb-envying" patterns, and by analysts such as Gregory Zilboorg [in "Masculine and Feminine: Some Biological and Cultural Aspects," *Psychiatry,* Vol. 7, No. 3, 1944] who is "inclined to think that it is not penis envy on the part of women, but woman-envy on the part of men that is psychologically older and therefore more fundamental."

But in the perspective of Horney's total development these early views have to be considered as a kind of antithesis to Freud's thesis regarding penis envy and the "psychology of women." At the time when Horney wrote these early papers, other leading Freudian analysts also experienced healthy doubts concerning these concepts. Ernest Jones, for example, wrote: "There is a healthy suspicion growing that men analysts have been led to adopt an unduly phallocentric view of the problems in question, the importance of the female organs being correspondingly underestimated "["Early Development of Female Sexuality," *International Journal of Psychoanalysis,* Vol. VIII, 1927].

In her later work, and most clearly in her *Neurosis and Human Growth,* Horney achieved a constructive and holistic synthesis in which the problem of feminine ver-

sus masculine psychology becomes part of the basic total problem of healthy human growth. The goal of analytical therapy for women as well as for men is genuine self-acceptance, which includes the acceptance of one's sexual role, and the realization of the inherent potentialities of the real self, which also embodies the capacity for love and constructive interpersonal relationships.

PROBLEMS OF SEX AND MARRIAGE

From feminine psychology, Horney's analytical interest turned to problems of sex and marriage. She refuses to blame "biological" facts for the high frequency of conflicts in this area. Such an approach, followed by some psychoanalysts and philosophers at that time and even today, while ostensibly scientific, is in essence unscientific because it deals with only one factor in human nature and human relationships, neglecting the equally and often more significant psychological, social, and cultural factors. It leads, as I have expressed it, to the biologizing of psychological phenomena, which by necessity precludes consideration of human freedom and responsibility, concepts which have come to be basic in contemporary thought, and particularly in modern psychoanalysis.

There is no need to assume the existence of biological, innate hate between the sexes, as postulated, for example by Schopenhauer, Nietzsche, or Weininger. The **"Distrust Between the Sexes"** is a psychological phenomenon which, intensified by social and cultural factors, can be traced to conflicts caused by unconscious needs and fears. Magic expectations of which we are unaware, compel us to anticipate that the partner will fulfill all our needs and wishes, contradictory and limitless though they may be. "The partner should be strong and helpless, master and slave, ascetic and sensuous. He should rape us and be tender, devote all his time to us and yet be intensely creative." And as long as we believe in the possibility of fulfillment, we invest the partner with a halo of overestimation; we even consider the degree of this overestimation a yardstick of our love, whereas in reality it merely indicates the extent of our expectations.

This process, which Stendhal called "crystallization [*De l'amour,* 1826], reveals, in my opinion, not only the extent but the specific quality of these expectations. The color of the crystallization reflects the color of the neurotic needs. One partner endows the other with precisely those qualities he hopes to find in him. Any frustration is countered with hostility, which, however, is experienced as coming from the partner. *His* love, faithfulness or sincerity are doubted. It is this discrepancy between expectations and fulfillment which often threatens the marital and sexual relationship.

In **"The Problems of Marriage"** Horney continues this trend of thought. Once more she rejects the "biological" explanation that marriage is doomed to decay because living together with one and the same person is bound to lead to routine weariness and dullness in the human, and especially in the sexual, relationship. Those who, like

Van de Velde [in *Die vollkommene Ehe,* 1926], approach the problems of marriage on this level and offer as a solution multiple prescriptions regarding variations of sex technique, must fail because they deal with a symptom only and not with the basic process which produced it.

The emptiness of a marriage is not the inevitable outcome of biological laws, is not due to weariness, but is the result of unconscious forces which undermine its foundation. They are neurotic needs such as the compulsive need for triumph and conquest, or for vicarious glory, or for a maternal or paternal type of protection. Thus the "free" choice of the partner, so called, here becomes the automatic move of a puppet on strings. Sooner or later the frustration of these needs must lead to disappointment and resignation, or rejection.

INNER CONFLICT AND CONTRADICTORY EXPECTATIONS

The dilemma grows worse if needs and expectations are highly contradictory in themselves. Of such contradictions we are usually unaware. "As a rule, we consider ourselves more integrated in our strivings than we really are, because we are frightened of inner conflict and consider it dangerous to our personality or our life" ["**The Problems of Marriage**"]. The attempt to solve our conflict through the partner is, of course, doomed to failure.

The ambitious woman who lacks the assertiveness to pursue her dreams of glory on her own expects the fulfillment of her ambition from the husband. He should be more creative and famous than anyone else. But this same woman often cannot accept the fulfillment of her expectations because her own power drive makes it intolerable for her to stay in the shadow of her husband.

The opposite dynamics may lead to a similarly destructive result. The expansive woman, driven by a need for mastery, "chooses" a more gentle, weaker man. But, simultaneously, she feels the need for the strong, more brutal male who overwhelms her. Inwardly, she constantly reproaches him for failing to fulfill both needs, and secretly she has contempt for his weakness.

Similarly contradictory needs are reflected in the inhibited man who, on the one hand, wants the "good" woman—decent, respected, selfless, sacrificial, more or less asexual—symbolized most clearly in the cult of the madonna, but who simultaneously longs for the erotic, flirtatious, sensuous woman whom he can not only love and respect, but also desire and enjoy sexually.

Neither the dulling of emotions nor the interference of a third person causes the decay of a marriage. It is the result of the unsolved inner conflicts which the partners have brought to marriage with them. The chances for success in marriage depend on the degree of integration and of emotional maturity of husband and wife.

In these last two papers the following concepts are already discernible: inner conflicts and attempts at their solution; the process of externalization; the difference between neurotic pseudo-unity and genuine integration; and, though still only in outline, some of the character types which Horney ultimately developed fully more than a decade later [in *Our Inner Conflicts*].

DOUBTS ABOUT DEATH INSTINCT

When Freud published his pessimistic study, *Civilization and Its Discontents,* he stated that man has an innate trend toward evil, aggression, destruction, and cruelty. Horney writes that the manifold evidence of cruel and destructive acts in human history does not prove the innate quality of those tendencies. Accurate study, for instance, would be required to determine under what kind of psychological or social pressure they may have developed.

"I believe," Horney writes, "that the cardinal question is whether really everything that manifests itself as destructiveness, can be *essentially* derived from a drive to destroy. To clarify this point, we must, first of all, discuss the conceptual distinction between aggression and destruction. It is not by chance, nor looseness of expression, that Freud continuously couples these two concepts or equates them. The intimate relationship he intends to assign to them is made quite clear by the fact that he conceives of drives for domination, for power, for the mastery of nature, as 'modified and tamed, as it were, aim-inhibited expressions' of this drive for destruction."

"The constructive an aim-inhibited expression of the destructive?" Horney asks, fully aware that she is raising a question which is fundamental in modern psychoanalysis. And she proceeds to answer it: "To be sure, each step in our mastery of nature brings with it a gratification of our sense of power as well. However, aside from the fact that this sense of power might represent an intensified sense of living, the essential motivation for the mastery of nature would seem to originate in hunger, or, to define it more broadly, in those drives which impel us to preserve life and to improve its conditions. . . . Might not all these tendencies be seen as a vital need for expansion of life? Are they not all exquisitely life-affirmative? Are they not clearly precipitates of phylogenetic acquisitions needed for the pursuit and protection of food, of love objects, and defense of the young? It is true that the proverbial lioness turns savage, defending her cub; but are we faced here with malevolence, destruction, and the wish to kill—or with the wish to preserve life and to defend it? That which here leads to the actual annihilation of another living being is without a doubt determined by a drive to live. Moreover, when does an animal attack at all? When it is hungry or when it feels attacked; each time in the service of self-preservation."

PROOF THROUGH ANALYTIC EXPERIENCE

For further proof Horney turns to analytical experience: "It also appears to me that analyses, no matter how deep, do not reveal a different picture either. Certainly, a great amount of rage and many destructive impulses emerge from even the calmest and most 'decent' people. But why, then, do we not shy away from them in horror? Why, despite all this, does our empathy with the patients increase with our understanding? Surely, because we find that all this rage has, or once had, a real cause; that it stems from hurts, for example, from frustrations, and, above all, from anxiety. Our experience also shows us that once these causes are made inoperative, especially when the amount of unconscious anxiety has been reduced by the analysis, these same people cease to be malevolent. Not that they become particularly good, but their unconscious strivings no longer aim at destruction. They grow active, taking up the struggle for life. They are able to question, to demand, to work, and to defend themselves."

MAN INHERENTLY CONSTRUCTIVE

"We are not magicians. Freud himself has always stressed this. We cannot produce by magic constructive, life-affirmative forces that were not there from the beginning, having been merely distorted into rage, destructive impulses, sadism and cruelty under the pressure of anxiety. . . . " [**"The Role of Aggression in Civilization: Some Thoughts and Objections Regarding Freud's Death Instinct and Drive for Destruction"**]

It is this conviction of the existence and activity of life-affirmative forces inherent in human nature which makes Horney's approach to psychoanalytic theory and therapy essentially constructive. Twenty years later, in one of her last public lectures [**"Human Nature Can Change"**] she reformulated this same basic idea:

> If a tree, because of storms, too little sun or too poor soil, becomes warped and crooked, you would not call this its essential nature. . . . Our belief is that the constructive possibilities stem from man's essential nature, from the core of his being, from what he calls his real self. Conversely, we believe that man turns unconstructive or destructive only if he cannot fulfill himself.

Horney never denied the existence of destructive trends. Yet by taking them out of the realm of the more or less immutable, innate and constitutional, she paved the way for the therapeutically and prophylactically decisive question: which changeable, emotional factors in the early interpersonal (familial, social and cultural) environment of the growing child are likely to foster the development of destructive tendencies? Which intrapsychic factors later tend to perpetuate and intensify their power?

These questions Horney began to answer step by step in her later work by uncovering the dynamics of neurotic development. The self which develops in the poor soil of early emotional starvation is bound to be weak. Feeling helpless in a potentially hostile world, the child experiences basic anxiety and responds with compulsive strivings for safety. Lacking genuine acceptance by others, he rejects himself and, in his desperate search for acceptance, begins to form an idealized image of himself with which unconsciously he tries to identify. This neurotic process, set in motion as defense against anxiety and conflict, later proves destructive to the self and to others. Like a malignant tumor, it drains off the energies needed for healthy growth; and interference with self-realization and self-fulfillment also fosters sadistic trends which make others mere tools for the gratification of compulsive drives.

With each answer she gave, Karen Horney lessened the dehumanizing power which irrational drives exert on the individual and on mankind. She helped man to regain his self, his freedom and his responsibility.

Jack L. Rubins (essay date 1978)

SOURCE: "XXI: *Neurosis and Human Growth*," in *Karen Horney: Gentle Rebel of Psychoanalysis,* New York: The Dial Press, 1978, pp. 304-17.

[*In the following excerpt from his biography of Horney, Rubins discusses* Neurosis and Human Growth, *examining the ways in which this articulation of her psychiatric approach differs from earlier ones. Rubins also briefly addresses the extent of Horney's influence on world psychiatry.*]

Neurosis and Human Growth constituted the fourth and final version of Karen's psychoanalytic theory. It showed many changes from her earlier writings: in the style of writing, in emphasis and details of the theoretical structure and in the overall spirit of her thinking.

One modification was the different significance accorded to the idealized image of the self. Previously the creation of this irrational self-image had been seen as only one of four major defensive solutions to conflict. Now it became the nuclear process of neurotic development, a comprehensive solution that occurred in all neuroses regardless of their form. Spurred by the child's rich imagination, the process begins in early childhood as a reactive defense against basic anxiety. It has two stages. First is the creation of the fantastic idealized self image, starting in the child as a conscious process, later continuing in the adult as an unconscious one. It is derived from the person's special needs, abilities and experiences. In it, needed neurotic trends are idealized, contradictory attitudes isolated or transformed into positive traits so as to eliminate the conflicts. In the second stage, the person identifies with, actually becomes this image; it becomes an idealized self.

Several drives contribute to this self-idealization (otherwise known as actualization of the idealized image). These include the need for perfection, neurotic ambitiousness and the need for vindictive triumph. Such drives are compulsive, insatiable and absolute in their intensity.

Another new concept was self-realization. Growing in a healthy parental environment, the child would be able to develop his real native attributes, his given potentials. Such a milieu would require from parents a basic warmth, freedom of expression, encouragement and guidance, healthy friction and rational discipline. The child's positive qualities would include his spontaneous feelings, interests, wishes, personal abilities, will power and values. He can tap all his resources. Such a type and direction of growth is termed self-realization. The inner force which moves the person toward this end is the real self. It is not a specific form of personality or infantile homunculus; it refers to forces or energies, exerted in a certain direction, analogous perhaps to the Bergsonian "élan vital."

This healthy child can relate to others by pleasing, or drawing closer, by assertion or opposition, by withdrawal or being alone. As long as these attitudes are spontaneous, flexible and appropriate, they are complementary and easily integrated.

If, on the contrary, the child grows up in an atmosphere of neurotic attitudes in his parents, he can develop the feeling of insecurity, distrust and loneliness previously described as basic anxiety. His relations with his parents and others then become one-sided, rigid and compulsive, motivated by a need for safety and security. They become neurotic trends, in dynamic opposition with each other, therefore creating conflict. With each trend, particular needs, inhibitions, sensitivities and values also develop. The need to maintain such a defensive stance in the face of underlying conflicts and lack of self-confidence drives the neurotic toward actualization of an unreal façade, an artificial way of life and a false image of himself.

The neurotic expects to be treated by others as if he really were this grandiose self. His expectations and demands, unconsciously aggrandized, are endowed with feelings of entitlement, of being due him as if they were a right. They become claims on others or on the world and life. Their frustration brings an abused feeling, of being unfairly treated. Since demand is based on a neurotic need, its content varies with the predominant trend. It may be a claim for obedience or uncritical acceptance, for understanding, for happiness, for results without making any effort, for unconditional love, for immunity from aging or stressful events, for invulnerability to illness, suffering or change, for freedom from rules, problems, restrictions or limitations, for recognition of his superlative qualities, for special consideration or privilege.

All neurotic claims have several characteristics in common. They do not take into account the realistic possibilities of fulfillment. They are unreasonably egocentric and so do not allow for the needs of others. They should be satisfied without appropriate efforts. And as demands, they may include a feeling of vindictiveness. The degree of awareness of the entitled feeling can vary from conscious to completely unconscious.

But it is their effects that call attention to their presence. Frustration of a claim often leads to anger. If repressed, this feeling can be transformed into a psychosomatic symptom, a vindictive rage reaction, or a feeling of depression. The presence of chronic claims is often signaled by a chronic pessimism about life, an envy of others, or a general uncertainty about one's own rights.

The striving to maintain the idealized image is expressed differently toward oneself than toward others. Claims are directed toward others. The neurotic whips himself by a system of "shoulds" and "musts." These will also vary according to the major trend. As examples, he should be strong, stoic, enduring; loving, generous, self-sacrificing; omniscient, omnipotent; serene, tranquil, untouched by events; unemotional, in absolute control of feelings, or ultra-sensitive to emotions; wise, reasonable, understanding; infallible—the list is unending. And like claims, they ignore the reality of whether they can ever be achieved. Since they have an absolute quality, they do not represent attainable ideals or genuine moral standards.

Most important, shoulds have a coercive quality; operating from the unconscious, they exert a constant pressure. This attribute gives rise to their major symptomatic effects. Failure to measure up to them can produce a gamut of reactions: anxiety, self-criticism, self-hatred, depression, usually disproportionate to the apparent cause. Reactive feelings toward what is, in effect, an inner authority, can vary. One person may accept it, welcoming a system that checks disturbing feelings. Another may rebel against it passively, feeling only chronic strain, resentment or inertia. Or it may be an active rebellion, being "bad," acting out. If the inner authority is externalized on to others, he becomes hypersensitive to external authorities.

Finally, having to do, feel or be the way one *should* do, feel or be, results in a loss of spontaneous actions, emotions or attitudes. The neurotic's life becomes a spurious as-if façade or only a shallow unfulfilling existence.

What gives the idealized image its immense value and intense hold on the neurotic is that it becomes invested with pride. Such neurotic pride must be distinguished from a healthy form, real self-esteem. The latter is based on realistic factors: some true ability, a job well done, a real achievement, a sense of worth or self-confidence. Neurotic pride is based on the spurious, imagined irrational values of the idealized image. Therefore it is shaky, easily hurt, needed rather than appreciated for itself. Depending on his neurotic structure, the person will invest his pride in specific attributes. For instance, he may pride himself on his prestige, his intellectual functions like knowledge or reason, his ability to control through power or will, his lofty standards like wisdom, honesty, good judgment or rightness, his goodness, his lovability, his invulnerability, his capacity to get away with things. It is here that the transformation of imperfections into virtues is best seen.

While such pride is needed to deny unwanted negative qualities, it inevitably leads to even greater distress. It renders the neurotic vulnerable to hurt pride reactions. Two of the most typical emotional reactions are to feel shame and humiliation. The former is felt when one becomes aware that the prideful standard is being disproved from within; the latter when it is violated in or by others, from without.

However, these simple reactive emotions frequently do not even come into awareness. Pride in self-control may cause their immediate and automatic repression. Or they may be unconsciously transformed into some other emotion, like grief. Or finally, only a secondary reaction to the shame may be experienced, such as rage or fear. In fact, a humiliating situation need not even occur. Sometimes even the anticipation of such a situation can produce the reaction—anticipatory anxiety or fear. Finally, when this rage does occur, it too may be immediately repressed and changed into depression, psychosis or somatic symptoms.

Several typical dynamic responses to hurt pride can occur as defensive means of restoring pride. Taking revenge is one way of assuring a vindictive triumph. Another is to lose interest in the event. A third is by frank denial or by forms therof, like forgetfulness or evasiveness. Still another can be the self-conscious use of humor.

When the neurotic identifies with his pride-invested grandiose image, he views his actual self from that vantage point. What he actually is becomes the ever-present obstacle to being the godlike creature he imagines himself to be. How he actually functions always highlights the discrepancy. He then must inevitably hate himself as he really is. Pride and self-hate are two unavoidable sides of the same coin, both encompassed by the term "the pride system." The neurotic is rarely aware of his self-hate, at least in its true intensity and ramifications. He only experiences its effects.

The expressions of self-hate can be grossly categorized into six forms. First are the *coercive demands* on the self. Failure to fulfil or violation of shoulds calls down intense hatred upon the self. Second, *self-accusations* are directed at any faults, difficulties or pretenses that give evidence of weakness in attaining one's ultimate standards. They carry a tone of moral condemnation and give rise to guilt feelings. And they will be felt despite their obvious irrationality or even if the failure is beyond one's real control. They can also be externalized, and then experienced as accusations by others. Neurotic standards differ from healthy conscience, which is a reminder to the real self of realistic shortcomings.

Third, *self-contempt* (self-disparagement, self-belittling) is a way of negating any attempt at achievement or improvement. Its symptoms can be seen in the neurotic's constant comparison of himself with others and envy of those perceived as better. When externalized, it may be a hypersensitivity to criticism or rejection—real or misin-terpreted. Or it may exist as a constant need for the regard, admiration or recognition of others as a means of compensating for feelings of inferiority. Fourth, *self-frustration* inhibits hope, striving, choice, potential, enjoyment, inner freedom. Fifth, *self-torturing* attitudes go beyond even the torments of the other forms. These can include severe hypochondriacal fears and obsessions, masochistic fantasies or impulses. Sadistic urges may be active externalizations of these attitudes.

Lastly, direct *self-destructive* impulses may be acute or chronic, conscious or unconscious. They can consist of minor activities like nailbiting or scratching; transitory thoughts of harming oneself; reckless conduct in sports or driving or neglect of physical infirmities; drug or alcohol use; accident-proneness; and possibly chronic illnesses like cancer or tuberculosis. Often such attitudes will only be expressed in a disguised form in dreams.

Alienation from self is now seen as the core process of neurosis. It is defined as a remoteness from one's genuine, spontaneous feelings, wishes, energies, self-directedness, values—from the real self. It can also involve the body, manifesting itself as a numbing of sensations, loss of identity, or feelings of depersonalization, "like being in a fog."

The many processes occurring in every neurosis combine to produce this result. All compulsive drives remove a person from his real spontaneity and autonomy. The movement toward actualization of the idealized image, with all its shoulds, determines a mode of existence other than what one really is. Externalization further removes one from all inner phenomena; they are experienced from without. Self-hate is an attitude of active rejection of the self. When pride governs feelings, then true feelings are ignored. The inertia resulting from inner conflicts saps one's energies. Lastly, the need to maintain spurious values denies one's genuine values and responsibility for oneself.

And yet, however comprehensive a solution like self-idealization may be, the personality still remains poorly integrated, unstable, caught in conflicts and tensions. Five additional factors must also be present in order to relieve such tension, corresponding to the seven listed in her previous book as auxiliary measures or approaches to inner harmony.

One of these is alienation from self, which is thus not only a result of the neurotic process but an active defensive measure. By blurring all inner experiences, it lessens the intensity of inner conflicts. The second is externalization. Any inner quality, whether admired or despised, healthy or neurotic, can be seen in others. Compartmentalization (or psychic fragmentation) is another. Inner processes are experienced as disconnected and isolated rather than as parts of a whole, or contradictory or causally related, as the case might be. The fourth is automatic control of impulses, actions and feelings. This can take place at their unconscious source or as they emerge into consciousness. The fifth is supremacy of the mind or intellectualization. This refers to the use of the mind or knowledge to avoid participation in one's feelings and conflicts. The person becomes a disinterested spectator of his own experiences. He may believe that knowing in itself means changing.

All these various dynamic solutions to conflict, comprehensive and auxiliary, operate in all neurotics, but they will be expressed differently in each type of personality. The three initial ways of relating were described as "moving-against," "moving-toward" and "moving-away from others" in the previous version. Now they are termed "major solutions," and grouped into expansive, self-effacing and resigned orientations. They are seen to involve not only attitudes toward others, but toward the self as well.

The expansive personality identifies with his glorified self. He is bent on mastery and superiority; he despises self-effacement—helplessness, failure, timidity, weakness. Three subforms of this orientation are distinguished.

Narcissism is the psychic state of loving the attributes of one's idealized image. The narcissist believes in his greatness, uniqueness, omnipotence, infallibility and freedom from limitations. He must impress others and needs their admiration. He overlooks flaws or transforms them into virtues. But his relations with others are poor; he imagines criticism and becomes easily enraged by it. He disregards the needs and feelings of others. His work suffers from being too grandiose in its aims. So he often incurs failure through real limitations. He may seem optimistic and happy, but just underneath the surface are pessimism and despondency.

The perfectionist neurotic identifies with his demanding standards and feels superior to others because he alone carries them out. So he denigrates and despises others. He needs to be perfect in behavior, attitudes and values. The discrepancy between what he believes he is (and tries to be) and what he really is is blurred by his self-deception. Since he feels himself to be fair, dutiful, just, he feels entitled to fair treatment, fortune or success. But he can collapse with self-hate when misfortune contradicts this claim, or when he makes mistakes.

With the arrogant-vindictive solution, the neurotic has identified with his pride. The need for vindictive triumph makes him highly competitive. He cannot tolerate losing and when it threatens, he can be subject either to violent rage or to distrust of others; they are out to beat him. Therefore he is constantly scheming to frustrate others. These attitudes enter into his sexual relations also. He needs to dominate and exert power. On this basis he builds extreme claims: to be right, to be respected despite his disregard for others, to be invulnerable and immune. His pride in strength, power and control is so absolute that any "softer" feelings like love, compassion or sympathy are crushed. When they might emerge, his self-contempt is tremendous. When he perceives these traits in others, he may feel disposed to punish them.

The self-effacing neurotic identifies with his despised self. He shuns, even fears any expansive qualities. Suffering and helplessness in fact have a certain unconscious appeal for him. He craves the help and care they could procure for him. He can accept failure, inferiority, self-denial. If any self-contempt comes up, it is passively externalized; others are looking down on him. He fears hostility in himself and in others. Arguments must be avoided. He must be loving, giving, understanding, self-sacrificing. These attitudes are glorified into the "good," the lovable qualities in himself, even though it may mean completely eliminating his own interests. But intense self-hatred is generated when any awareness of his repressed hostility, pride or vindictiveness emerges. He needs others not only for love, but also to avoid being alone—proof of his being unwanted and unloved. When his claims for love or help are not met, he feels chronically abused. This can make for chronic resentment of others or for accusations against himself—often in the form of somatic symptoms and suffering.

Neurotic suffering serves several purposes. It acts as a justification for claims. It often is a means of being vindictive or exploitative without having to consciously admit it. One avoids accusing oneself by accusing others and suffering becomes an excuse for not making more of life. In extreme cases, helplessness, illness or even psychic suicide present themselves as the ultimate way out of difficulties. They can even be experienced as the final triumph over the world or fate.

Morbid dependency is an extreme form of this orientation, occurring mainly in erotic love relationships. The self-effacing person is often attracted to a dominating partner in whom he sees those traits that he misses in himself. These he admires in others, and concludes, consciously or unconsciously, that their absence in himself is responsible for his suffering. Besides, even though he wants to obtain love and sympathy, he can be repelled by another compliant person, who displays the same irritating weaknesses as himself. The need for surrender through self-degradation or self-elimination is compulsive. And once begun, the person is too fearful of asserting himself to take a stand—a situation that eventually makes for increased inner conflicts.

The third major solution, resignation, differs dynamically from the first two. Here the neurotic removes himself totally from all conflicts instead of simply repressing one contradictory side, as in the other solutions. It provides a freedom "from" the unpleasant rather than "for" something positive. Typically, he gives the impression of being an observer of himself and of life. This nonparticipation is much broader than the simple intellectualizing described previously. Here, the neurotic avoids being emotionally touched by anything that happens within himself. He eliminates awareness of painful conflicts by distancing himself from all feelings.

A second trait is the aversion to any serious striving toward a goal, to any effort or to any psychic movement.

To achieve peace and serenity may be a conscious aim, but at a deeper level this means an absolute freedom from change, an unrealistic nirvana-happiness. Detachment from others is a typical quality, especially insofar as relations will demand emotional involvement. Sex is usually only physical contact.

Characteristic, too, is a hypersensitivity to coercion, influence, obligation, restriction, limitation, pressure or intrusion. This occurs because one's pride is invested in stabilizing or immobilizing the dynamic forces of two repressed orientations, both of which are still compulsive. The person still identifies with the attributes of his idealized image but he has renounced the active drive to make it real in life. He therefore may show self-effacing or expansive attitudes at various times, but these are not compelling drives. Nevertheless, he still feels the shoulds from both sets of attitudes. In addition, newer shoulds express needs for independence, stoicism, privacy, freedom from want or desire, passionless and unruffled serenity. This combination accounts for his sensitivity to any coercion. Then by externalization, his own inner dictates will be experienced as coerciveness and authoritarianism in others.

Different inner reactions to this basic process can be observed clinically. Persistent resignation may be low-keyed and still permit some activities. Feelings of inertia and chronic strain then often accompany sustained effort and work. Inner feelings are restricted, including interest, curiosity and enjoyment. If any of these are felt, they quickly fade. A deadness or emptiness is sometimes experienced. However, since freedom is always sought, this inertia always contains an element of passive rebellion.

Another reactive type is the actively rebellious person, who may rebel against the external environment or his own inner restrictions. To a limited degree this can be a healthy movement.

Behavior of the third group is characterized by shallow living. Increasing emptiness, loss of feeling, futility and lack of direction can result in an attempt to fill one's life with meaningless distractions. Emphasis is then placed on having fun: on parties, sex, socializing, amusements; or on opportunistic success, on money, seizing the advantage—but solely for the freedom these offer from life's difficulties; or on automatic adaptation to the prevailing codes and habits of others.

In the last chapters of *Neurosis and Human Growth,* some of the therapeutic problems posed by this character analysis are discussed. Actually, to speak of a "cure" of neurosis is not appropriate. Psychoanalysis only helps the patient overcome his growth-obstructing needs and attitudes, thus relieving his conflicts and obviating the necessity for solutions. This includes dissipating his illusions about himself. Then, and then only, can he grow in a healthier direction and develop his potentials.

But this goal of the analyst is not the goal of the patient in therapy. He feels that analysis should help him retain—even strengthen and perfect—his neurotic solutions and values. To renounce them would endanger his psychic existence. It would be too dangerous to obtain real insight into what he feels to be his shortcomings. He wishes to remove only the disturbing situation, the immediate problems, the painful symptom. Furthermore, since his unconscious expectations of therapy depend on his particular neurotic solution, he seeks change through his own will power and control, or without effort and involvement, or through the analyst's magic wand. Each growing awareness will bring some blockage: evasiveness, argument, hostility, spurious agreement, apathy or forgetfulness, periods of self-hate, anxiety, etc. All the specific defenses must be understood and laid bare: needs, claims, shoulds, prides, solutions, values. In this process, intellectual knowledge is insufficient. There must occur an emotional experience of each specific defensive attitude as well. This aspect of the therapy constitutes a disillusioning process, occurring during the first phase of analysis. At the beginning, conflicts are still blurred. The second phase must consist of delineating and mobilizing constructive assets of the patient. Then a gradual moving forward will occur, with more spontaneity and vitality. But this, in turn, will bring repercussions in the form of periods of self-contempt, with rapid up-and-down shifts in mood and symptoms. Rapid changes later in the analysis are indicative of the *central conflict,* the struggle between all the obstructive, neurotic forces and the constructive, healthy forces. Passing through each of these phases will eventually result in a strengthening of self-confidence.

In this book, the final version of Karen's theory differs from the previous ones in several ways. In the first place, she modified the theoretical structure of the neurotic (and healthy) personality. The role and importance of the idealized self-image have been changed. From simply one tactic (out of four) of resolving inner conflicts, it became the crucial defensive move of neurosis. The relation between self-glorification and self-hate were clarified. The entire concept of self-hate assumed a greater significance. The new concepts of self-realization and real self were introduced. This led to an expansion of the notion of conflict. It occurred not only between opposing compulsive solutions, but also between the pride-system and the real self (central inner conflict). Alienation from self was now seen to constitute a key process of neurotic development. Yet with all these modifications, the theory remained a personology, a study of character structure.

In the second place, this work is much more sophisticated and complex, both theoretically and stylistically. In her previous books, Karen's view of personality was relatively simple—perhaps even deceptively oversimplified. Here one senses a much greater realization of the profundity of the human psyche and the complexity of human relations, whether healthy or disturbed. Even a well-demarcated symptom like anxiety cannot be ascribed to some limited conflict between basic drives. It can result from active opposition between more complex trends or their secondary and tertiary products, like claims, values or shoulds. Conflicts breed further conflicts; reactions to conflicts may create new reactions, and so forth. The degree to which the neurotic is enmeshed in his web of defensive devices becomes more evident here. The intensity of feelings (or lack of them) is conveyed much more dramatically here, whether it be despair, self-hate, pride or emptiness.

In the third place, the theory has evolved in terms of psychodynamics. The concepts of peremptory forces, psychic movement and directions have become as important as descriptive traits and behavior types. Consider the concept of direction. In the first version of the theory, emphasis was primarily placed on the influence of the culture on the individual personality. The direction was mostly from the outside inward. In this final version, the main focus is on the influence of intrapsychic forces on interpersonal relations. The direction is from within outward. Even within the self, growth is seen to occur in a healthy direction (self-realization) or neurotic direction (self-idealization). The neurotic rises above conflicts and then looks down on others.

Direction also implies movement, both microcosmic and macrocosmic. The child moves toward, against, away from parents; alienation is movement away from self. Movement is implicit in the very notion of dynamic, active conflict and active escape from it.

Lastly, a holistic spirit is now quite evident here. Despite her emphasis on intrapsychic phenomena, she makes clear that these only occur in a context. The cultural, the interpersonal and the intrapsychic, the mental, the emotional and the somatic, the past and the present are all closely in tertwined. Even though one aspect can be observed and studied, the other aspects of the individual are still very much present, and must be taken into account. In the first version of her theory, personal attitudes and inner conflicts were seen to be a reflection of similar factors in society. The two could nonetheless be easily differentiated. In this version, the distinction is not so clear. At numerous points we are told that what is described as past history may be a projection of one's present attitudes. What is seen as outside situations may really be an externalization of internal events. Subjective and objective are often difficult to separate. The individual produces his needs, claims, shoulds, conflicts at the same time that he directs their effects back upon himself; it is a reflexive influence, even though he may feel that he is being acted upon by "something" within himself. But hopefully, as therapy progresses, the person grows closer to his real self. Then he will come to feel active in his own being and life, responsible for himself and "the captain of his own ship."

This final version of her theory was to have many long-term effects that Horney neither intended nor would have completely wished, and in any event could not have foreseen. She was basically trying to systematize her con-

cepts of personality but was attempting to do so by extending and building only upon her previous ideas. The major exception to this was her introduction of the real self and the process of self-realization. She often stated that any one of her ideas could not be really understood if isolated, taken out of context of the whole framework. When she did discuss her ideas in her classes or her Academy lectures, she always linked them with their dynamic emotional causes and effects. Unfortunately, others who have followed her and who have borrowed or "rediscovered" ideas she enunciated have either changed their meaning or have failed to convey their scope. And this is usually done without giving credit to her.

A number of her ideas have become incorporated into the then new ego psychology begun by Freud and developed by his followers. For example, her notion of pride, transformed from healthy into an exaggerated neurotic form, was elaborated upon by Heinz Hartmann, a distinguished Freudian analyst. He called attention to the neglect of this emotion in classical analytic writing and the need to give it its rightful importance. Horney's concept of irrational self-idealization was further amplified by Annie Reich, Jeanne Lampl-de Groot and Samuel Novey. It was redefined much as Horney conceived it to be, as a narcissistic defensive operation against anxiety, rather than simply as part of the normal ego-ideal. These authors still linked it directly to traumatic experiences of the infant; grandiose fantasies would be a compensation for feelings of helplessness. More recently, younger Freudian analysts like Heinz Kohut and Otto Kernberg have extended and refined her concept of neurotic, defensive narcissism, especially in relation to the "borderline" personality. Their work is replete with terms introduced by Horney, such as the splitting of the self into omnipotent and self-devaluative attitudes, pathological self-esteem and integration of the self.

Karen's idea that the relationship between the patient and analyst consisted of more than the simple repetition of the infant's attitudes toward parents has also been confirmed in recent years. Many classical analysts now speak of the broader "therapeutic alliance" or the "working" or "real" relationship during psychoanalysis. Following Karen—and Franz Alexander, who also stressed this point at about the same time—they believe that healthy, later-developed, here-and-now aspects of both patient and analyst enter into the analysis as much if not more than infantile ones. Her insistence on the need to experience emotionally all on-going feelings, that is, on emotional instead of only intellectual awareness, has appeared in the so-called experiential schools of psychology. These include the client-centered therapy of Carl Rogers, the Gestalt-therapy of Fritz Perls and Whitaker and Malone's experiential therapy.

One of her most far-reaching contributions was the introduction of the concept of self-realization—the innate tendency of the individual to grow in a healthy direction—into her systematized theory of personality and neurosis. Following this principle, there have appeared several schools of "self-actualizing" psychotherapy, the so-called third force in psychology to counterbalance the Freudian biological views as well as the culturalist approach. Notable among these are Kurt Goldstein's organismic approach (although he also influenced Horney and was himself previously affected by Gestalt psychology), and especially Abraham Maslow's theories.

Aside from these specific derivations, Horney's theory presaged other more general currents in psychological thought that have become popular today. One has been the increasing emphasis on socio-cultural factors as the causes of emotional illness. She would have found this overall trend congenial. But not completely! She would have disagreed with the degree to which society is blamed for neurosis and the resulting attempts to treat neurosis by simply changing social conditions. In point of fact, even though she continues to be considered a "Neo-Freudian culturalist" psychoanalyst, this classification is misleading. It was based on her earlier work; she remained individual-oriented and in her later work focused almost exclusively on the inner structure of the psyche.

The second current popular today is related to this, namely her holistic emphasis on the dynamic, continuous interaction between external cultural conditions, interpersonal relations and inner emotional experiences. This view is described today as "systems-theory." Her contribution to this trend was significant, though, like so many of her other advances, it has been largely overlooked.

Patricia Meyer Spacks (essay date 1980)

SOURCE: "Fiery Giants and Icy Queens," in *The New Republic,* Vol. 183, No. 19, November 8, 1980, pp. 30-3.

[*In the following review of* The Adolescent Diaries of Karen Horney, *Spacks discusses Horney's early life and the ways in which her diaries shed light on her professional writings.*]

As an adolescent, Karen Horney argued with her parents, and condescended to them, worried whether anyone would ever love her, expressed her contempt for the older generation, had crushes on her teachers, overvalued the opinions of her peers, felt a horrified fascination with the idea of sexual activity: just like everyone else. Nevertheless, her diaries are remarkable.

Here she is at 15:

> Tomorrow we go to Frl. Banning. Of course, we are both awfully glad, but we try to persuade ourselves that it is all the same to us or even a bother. On that account I've just been up on the Heideberg alone, for Mother is awfully down again, and picked some flowers for her. Oh, it was so lovely up there, the beautiful landscape spread in a sweep at my feet. I love such a wide view because it brings peace to my heart, which, though only in

its *Backfisch* state, still is often quite sad and discouraged. For things are bad at home, and Mother, my all, is so ill and unhappy. Oh, how I would love to help her and cheer her up. If only she had, as I do, some sort of school or other means of distraction.

The banality of the experience and the prose may obscure at first the sensitivity of the response: the observer's capacity to understand her own emotion as a phenomenon of adolescence (the "*Backfisch* state") while indulging it, her ability to imagine that directed activity would alleviate her mother's depression, her willingness to comment on the discrepancy between genuine and enacted feeling as she prepares to visit the teacher on whom she has a crush. Even if Karen Horney were no one in particular, these diaries would offer material of compelling interest: the private reflections of a mind already intensely focused, at the age of 14 (when the diaries begin), on the ways and the reasons people act as they do. Since we read them with the advantage of hindsight, they sound prophetic in their effort to investigate the general truths implicit in the particularities of one girl's experience.

The girl Karen hated her father. Her diaries report her usually unsuccessful struggle to obey the fourth commandment. Sometimes she rages that no one should be expected to honor a man so insensitive and overbearing, sometimes she tells herself that she should respect the authority inherent in the idea of a parent rather than the qualities of the individual. Meanwhile the father, a pious man forever preaching to his children, opposes her continuing her education beyond the age of 15. She should stay home, he says, and save him the expense of a maid. Karen and her mother swear that he will never have to contribute to her support after she leaves the Gymnasium; apparently this argument persuades him. Strangely, when her parents separate, the diarist does not mention the event.

She saw in work—first in study, then in the career it would lead to—the hope of salvation from the inner chaos which terrified her. Work provided an ordering principle, a basis for hierarchy. For a time she felt unsure what career to follow (medicine? teaching?); at one point she triumphantly announces that she has obtained her mother's permission to be an actress. Her sense of the internal forces to be kept at bay, however, hardly varies, although she finds different formulations for what she sees as her problem. "There is such disordered turmoil within me," she writes at 17, "that I myself cannot burrow my way through the labyrinth." When she used to pray, she continues, "only the same 4 words passed my lips: 'Lord, give me truth.' Now I know that no one can give that to me, but only through my own work will I get a clear view, or perhaps not get it." She has asked, and been refused, permission to join a class in animal dissection. "*Et voilà* a substitute: I shall take myself to pieces. That will probably be more difficult, but also more interesting."

Although the impulse toward self-dissection—a way of using her intellect to contain turmoil—continued, elaborated, and intensified, conflict attended it. Two years before, on the brink of leaving school for the Gymnasium, she had reported telling herself stories "all the time, now more than ever." These stories, she explains, use what she has read and experienced, have herself and her "crushes" as central characters, and offer variations on a single theme: "what I would like to have." They embody wish-fulfillment fantasies and they multiply in response to stress. She describes such story-telling as one of her chief activities, then immediately deprecates it: "really awfully funny." More sophisticated at 17, she comments, "Only one half of my being lives, the other observes, criticizes, is given to irony." The antithesis between "living" and "observing" suggests her self-critical attitude toward her attempts to master experience by understanding it (or by narrating it, a form of understanding).

"Living," of course, implies sexuality. I say, of course, and Horney appears to think, of course. At other times, however, she expresses great anxiety over what she calls the "sensuality" of her nature. Shortly after writing the passage about self-dissection, she spends an evening with a friend who informs her that girls whom they both know go to bed with men. "No, Alice, it isn't possible," Karen responds. Alice, undaunted, reports that she herself has actually considered "doing it," and she goes on to instruct Karen in the nature of prostitution. Karen feels "very exhausted. The whole dreadful knowledge at once. It was too much." She longs for a chance to let "the storm within" subside. The storm, however, was only beginning. Soon her fantasies turn sexual: "In my own imagination there is no spot on me that has not been kissed by a burning mouth." She decides that "it is never immoral to give oneself to a man one really loves, if one is prepared to also bear all the consequences." She values sensuality—but it is "a *spiritualized great sensuality*" that marks the great soul, in her view. And as the expression of her own sensuality becomes an increasingly real possibility, it seems not so easy to spiritualize it. By the time she is 19, she has shifted ground. "To be free of sensuality means great power in a woman. Only in this way will she be independent of a man. . . . Otherwise eternal battling. And every victory of the senses a Pyrrhic victory, bought with loathing, ever deadly loathing afterwards." The battle is internal. The young woman confesses her longing vision of strong men and harmonious women, women "who know nothing of that war to the death in us between fiery giants and icy queens, between sensuality and intellect."

The dichotomy of living and observing has become heightened into this "war to the death"—the war which Horney's writing richly documents. The first four diaries here printed cover the years from 1899 to 1907, the year Karen turned 22. Then comes a series of revealing premarital letters to Oskar Horney, and finally a diary for 1910-11, after her marriage, recording the partial course of her analysis with Karl Abraham. All the diaries, as well as the letters, reveal the same conflict—sometimes open war, sometimes half-acknowledged struggle.

From the time she decided that a woman who loved should give herself to a man without caring for convention, Karen Horney wanted love affairs. The diary's meticulous accounts of her relationship with men, however, suggest different underlying wishes. Often tortured, often tortuous, her "friendships" with men, like her "loves," never work out satisfactorily. She declares herself in love with a man whom she has only known a few days, then is desolated when he goes away and fails to write. She loves Ernst, but he shilly-shallies, can't decide if he really loves her. She falls in love with Rolf, toward whom, she says, she feels powerful physical attraction. But when he tries to make love to her, "his amorous attentions were simply repugnant to me." On another occasion, "his passionate attentions again were repulsive to me. I found it crude of him to kiss me when he had a sore throat." Then she feels overcome with passion and goes to his room, where they sat on the couch and "chattered and kissed"—but very soon she must leave because her parents expect her.

At some point, the diary suggests, she manages to have sexual relations, but for all the extreme detail of such narratives as the story of Rolf, she fails to specify when or with whom. Meanwhile, she has met Oskar Horney, "the little Hornvieh," and begun a correspondence and what she calls a "friendship" with him. She emphasizes this fact at the end of her account of 1906, then concludes the narrative—which has dealt, for many pages, entirely with her male friends and lovers—in a rather unexpected fashion. "But, if I were to read this some day in later years, I would get no correct impression of the year 1906 if at least one more point were not mentioned: I am getting fonder and fonder of my studies and my working power is born[e] on the wings of joyousness in work."

The image of intellect as an icy queen in conflict with the fiery giant of sensuality by no means applies to Karen Horney: probably it never did. The language of passion attaches itself readily to her feelings about her work. (A few months later she would write to Horney, "I think I would die if I should now stop studying medicine.") Her intellectual activity, in other words, provided not so much a principle of containment as an alternate focus for passion: fiery intellectual desire "battling" its fiery physical counterpart. She sees it as relatively safe, a permissible intensity. Her relationship with Oskar, as far as one can understand it from the letters, emphasizes the intellectual far more than the physical, and thus seems to promise security.

At the beginning of 1906, Horney toys with suicide in case she fails an exam. She moves from the subject of death to her longing for a leader, a strong man who will guide her.

> I am clever enough to learn a great deal in life, but not to find my way out of the confusion of knowledge. Where is the person who is to lead me? Does no one hear how I cry out for him? . . .

Rolf understood it. He told me the last time in Berlin: 'You need someone to lead you now. Let me be the one!'—But Rolf was not strong enough to hold me. Was he perhaps—? No. The one who is to come is not Rolf.

Presumably she thought Oskar the person capable of leading her. Her letters often sound deferential, unsure; she tells him how much she has learned from his reflections on ego or offers him book reports on her reading. He appears to have firm convictions about moral matters (we do not have his side of the correspondence); she defers to him. Her letters hold less immediate interest than the diaries specifically because in them one can feel her adapting herself to another mind, writing with an eye to her reader. On the other hand, the hope and pathos of that effort at adaptation make the correspondence absorbing as part of the drama unfolding in this volume. "How do you manage to make me feel ashamed of playing tricks on you? I believe, because you are yourself so true and because you can understand and because you are good." It won't work, one wants to shout, you're making it up. Rarely have the dynamics of psychological projection been so clearly exposed.

Of course she goes ahead and marries Oskar, in 1910. The couple apparently have difficulty achieving sexual compatibility, but Karen declares herself sexually content in the final diary, dominated by her reflections of her work with Abraham, at the time the only practicing psychoanalyst in Berlin. The diary also reports her persistent prostitution fantasies, her doubts (during her first pregnancy) about her capacity for motherhood (she has a "masculine complex," she decides, and uses work to compensate for her feelings of inferiority as a woman), her recurrent longings to return to her unattached student days, and an episode in which Oskar tells her she has degraded herself by flirting so conspicuously with a man she has known in the past. Like the adolescent turmoil, these feelings sound universal (though no less painful for that): the extraordinary thing about this as about the other diaries is the absolute honesty with which they are exposed and examined. But the diary also reports something more ominous frequent incapacitating fits of fatigue which make work impossible and which the writer now identifies as her "illness."

As far back as 1901, not yet 16, she had recorded a similar difficulty ("In the condition I am in now, I am absolutely good for nothing.") and, characteristically, tried to comprehend its causes. A note of panic creeps into her tone every time she recounts such an episode. All she wants, she says, is to work, and she can't. Even after the analysis, she cannot count on continuing capacity. The book ends with a letter to Dr. Abraham, presumably never sent, asking to resume analysis specifically to concentrate on the work difficulty. It is a sad ending for the girl who had longed "to learn how to listen to the delicate vibrations of my soul." The listening had failed to reveal to her that the battle of fiery giants and icy queens could not be resolved by conscious commitment to the life of the mind.

One can only feel privileged at the opportunity to read these documents. Later in her life, Karen Horney wrote passionately (even in scientific papers) about the development of women, but she also revealed an intense desire for privacy: she would not have wanted us to see her diaries. On the other hand, if she could realize their power to clarify familiar conflicts, perhaps she wouldn't mind. The diaries and letters possess narrative force and interest, in their account of a young woman's development, but they also offer something far rarer: the unflinching insight of a mind insistently concerned "to be incorruptibly *true to myself.*"

Bernard J. Paris (essay date 1981)

SOURCE: "Bargains with Fate: The Case of *Macbeth*," in *The American Journal of Psychoanalysis,* Vol. 42, No. 1, Spring, 1982, pp. 7-20.

[*In the following essay, which was originally presented at a conference held in February of 1981, Paris offers an interpretation of William Shakespeare's drama* Macbeth *(1606) utilizing some key concepts from Horney's psychoanalytic theory.*]

According to Horney, each of the interpersonal strategies of defense involves a "bargain with fate" in which if a person lives up to his shoulds, his claims are supposed to be honored. The bargain of the self-effacing individual is that if he is a good, loving, noble person who shuns pride and does not seek private gain or glory, he will be well-treated by fate and by other people. The narcissistic person feels that if he holds onto his dreams and to his exaggerated claims for himself, life is bound to give him what he wants. The perfectionistic person believes that his own rectitude will insure fair treatment from others; through the height of his standards, he compels fate. The bargain of the arrogant-vindictive person is essentially with himself. He does not count on the world to give him anything, but he is convinced that he can reach his ambitious goals if he remains true to his vision of life as a battle and does not allow himself to be seduced by his softer feelings or the traditional morality. The detached person believes that if he asks nothing of others, they will not bother him; that if he tries for nothing, he will not fail, and that if he expects little of life, he will not be disappointed.

I have found Horney's concept to be of great help in understanding Shakespeare's four major tragedies—*Hamlet, Othello, King Lear,* and *Macbeth.* Each of these plays deals with characters who are in a state of psychological crisis resulting from threats to their bargains with fate. The failure of the bargain calls their whole strategy for living into question and generates rage, anxiety, and self-hate; and each behaves in a way that is destructive to himself and others in the course of his attempts to restore his pride, repair his defenses, and hold onto his idealized image of himself. Hamlet and Desdemona have a self-effacing bargain; Othello's bargain is predominantly perfectionistic; Iago has an arrogant-vindictive bargain; and Lear's bargain is narcissistic. All of these characters have their bargains violated by other people, by external events. The case of Macbeth is somewhat different. At the beginning of the play, Macbeth is a perfectionistic person whose solution has been highly successful. He precipitates his own psychological crisis by violating his dominant set of shoulds in order to act out the arrogant-vindictive trends which are reinforced by his wife. Once he violates his own bargain, he is overwhelmed by fear and self-hate. He tries to cope with his crisis by whole-heartedly embracing the arrogant-vindictive solution, but he cannot really do so, and the result is despair.

In her soliloquy upon the receipt of Macbeth's letter, Lady Macbeth provides some excellent insights into her husband's conflicts.

> Yet I do fear thy nature.
> It is too full o' th' milk of human kindness
> To catch the nearest way. Thou wouldst be great;
> Art not without ambition, but without
> The illness should attend it. What thou wouldst
>   highly,
> That wouldst thou holily; wouldst not play false,
> And yet wouldst wrongly win.
>
> (I, i)

Macbeth is an ambitious man who wants more than he can legitimately have, but who is prevented from going after it by powerful compliant and perfectionistic tendencies. His compliance is indicated by the milk imagery which is consistently used by aggressive characters in Western literature to describe self-effacing behavior, and his perfectionism is indicated by his need for righteousness. Macbeth is a man who is deeply committed to the values of his society and who has invested his pride in living up to them. He has a powerful need to be great but an even more powerful need to be good. His solution to his inner conflict has been to search for glory in acceptable ways, through loyal service to the state. He is a man of honor who exults, like Othello, in "the big wars that make ambition virtue." As the play opens, he is receiving all of the recognition that he can reasonably expect. In I, ii alone, he is described as "brave Macbeth," "valour's minion," "valiant cousin," "justice . . . with valour armed," "Bellona's bridegroom," and "noble Macbeth." These are the "golden opinions" (I, vii) which mean so much to him. He is named Thane of Cawdor and is promised an even "greater honour" (I, iii). The problem is that, whetted by his success and by his encounter with the witches, Macbeth's ambition and his sense of his deserts cannot be satisfied by anything which Duncan can do for him. His need for greatness threatens to get out of control and to violate his need to be good.

Macbeth's inner conflict is evident in his reaction to the witches' prophecy. He starts and is "rapt" because the witches have brought to the surface a fantasy which he has been trying to repress. He wants to believe that the supernatural soliciting is good, but he is afraid that it is not:

> If good, why do I yield to that suggestion
> Whose horrid image doth unfix my hair
> And make my seated heart knock at my ribs
> Against the use of nature?
>
> (I, ii)

Since he can imagine no honorable way to the throne, the thought of becoming king arouses in his mind images of himself murdering Duncan; and, since this is a violation of everything he believes in, he reacts to it with a feeling of horror. At the beginning of this speech, Macbeth is entranced by the prospect of his imperial destiny, but within a few moments he finds himself in the throes of an anxiety attack. He feels weak, he trembles, and he has palpitations of the heart. In effect, Macbeth's thoughts of murder activate all of his taboos against it. His anxiety attack is produced by his dread of the self-hate and retribution to which he would be exposed should he violate his own most sacred values. He defends himself against his feelings of terror by renouncing his criminal intentions: "If chance will have me King, why, chance may crown me,/ Without my stir." Having chance crown him is the perfect solution for Macbeth; it permits him to realize his dream of glory without having to sacrifice his rectitude.

Macbeth's inner conflict has only momentarily subsided, of course. When Duncan names Malcolm his successor, Macbeth feels that chance is not going to crown him; and his regicidal impulses rise once more to the surface. He swings back and forth between his compulsion to do the deed and his dread of its consequences. As the moment approaches when he must carry out his murderous intentions, he becomes prey once more to his fears and scruples; and he leaves the chamber in which he and Duncan are dining in order to reconsider his course. He seems to have gotten over one of the major obstacles to the crime, his fear of damnation. His desire for the crown is so great that he is willing to "jump the life to come" (I, vii) in order to obtain it. What torments him in this soliloquy is the fear that, after having made such a terrible sacrifice, he will still have to face the earthly consequences of his crime:

> But in these cases
> We still have judgment here, that we but teach
> Bloody instructions, which, being taught, return
> To plague th' inventor. This even-handed justice
> Commends th' ingredience of our poison'd chalice
> To our own lips.
>
> (I, vii)

Underlying this speech is Macbeth's deep belief that reality conforms to the traditional code of morality. He conceives of retribution as the result of a natural process. If he becomes King by murdering Duncan, he sets a bloody precedent which will return to plague him. His fears are in part reality based, but his sense of the inescapability of "this even-handed justice" derives very largely from a magical system of thought. The claims of the perfectionistic person are based, says Horney, "on a 'deal' he [has] secretly made with life. Because he is fair, just, dutiful, he is entitled to fair treatment by others and by life in general. This conviction of an infallible justice operating in life gives him a feeling of mastery. His own perfection therefore is . . . a means . . . to control life" [*Neurosis and Human Growth*]. Part of every bargain is a belief not only in the rewards of living up to one's shoulds but also in the penalties for violating them. Receiving "justice" means both having our claims honored when we have fulfilled the terms of our bargain and being punished when we have failed to do so. Macbeth's conviction of an infallible justice operating in life gives him a feeling of mastery when he is virtuous, but it fills him with dread when he contemplates committing a criminal act, and it is largely responsible for the intensity of his fears after the murder. It derives less from reality than from his own sense of what is fair. It is difficult to see this because his belief is borne out by the action of the play. It corresponds to the reality of the world of the play, the laws of which seem to be those of the perfectionistic solution.

Macbeth's sense of justice expresses itself not only in his fear of retribution, but also in his rehearsal of the moral objections to the murder. Activated by the imminence of their violation, both his perfectionistic and his self-effacing shoulds fill him with a sense of horror. He is Duncan's kinsman, his subject, and his host, "who should against his murder shut the door,/ Not bear the knife myself."

> Besides, this Duncan
> Hath borne his faculties so meek, hath been
> So clear in his great office, that his virtues
> Will plead like angels, trumpet-tongu'd, against
> The deep damnation of his taking-off . . .
>
> (I, vii)

We have here our first direct evidence of that softer side of Macbeth about which his wife was concerned when she received his letter. Duncan is a meek, mild, overtrusting, overgenerous person. A predominantly arrogant-vindictive person scorns men like Duncan and has no qualms about moving against them. Macbeth, however, honors Duncan for his self-effacing traits and feels that they add to the heinousness of the murder. The killing of so virtuous a man is an outrage against justice and will assure the murderer's damnation.

The soliloquy ends with Macbeth recoiling against his evil intentions. The only thing driving him is his ambition, which he now sees from the self-effacing point of view as an unholy overreaching which is bound to result in a fall. He defends himself against his anxieties as he had done earlier, by abandoning his murderous plans. He can quiet the clamor of his perfectionistic and self-effacing shoulds only by putting himself in harmony with them.

Macbeth announces his decision in the ensuing dialogue with his wife, telling her that he has "bought/Golden opinions from all sorts of people,/Which would be worn now in their newest gloss,/Not cast aside so soon" (I, vii). Macbeth is a man who has lived for recognition, and he is now receiving it in a greater degree than he has ever done before. He is a national hero whose exploits are being widely acclaimed. If he kills Duncan, he will be the national villain from whom everyone will shrink with moral aversion. The "golden opinions" which he has hardly begun to enjoy will be lost forever.

It is not surprising that people have had difficulty understanding how a man with so many powerful motives against it could actually have committed the murder. He would not have done it, I believe, if it had not been for the influence of his wife. After he tells her that he "will proceed no further" (I, vii), she literally badgers him into doing what she wants. It is important to see, however, that the outcome is the product of the *interaction* between these two people. She could not have affected him so powerfully if she had not struck a responsive chord in his nature.

Lady Macbeth is, like Iago, a great psychologist who understands other people's vulnerabilities and is a genius at exploiting them. She attacks her husband initially by trying to make him feel that he will be despicable if he allows his scruples to stand in his way. She portrays the situation as a test not only of his manliness, but also of his love; and she threatens the withdrawal of her own affection. If he is to have her love, he must prove his love for her; and he can do this only by killing Duncan. She is playing upon his softer side in order to get him to commit the murder. She is playing upon his aggressive side also. She is the voice of his arrogant-vindictive shoulds, which were drowned out in his soliloquy by his opposing trends. He is now caught in a crossfire of conflicting shoulds. He knows that he will hate himself if he violates his code of honor, but Lady Macbeth makes him see that he will also hate himself if he does not commit the murder: "Wouldst thou have that / Which thou esteem'st the ornament of life,/And live a coward in thine own esteem, / Letting 'I dare not' wait upon 'I would'"? His wife's contempt would not affect him as strongly as it does if he did not feel that he would, in fact, despise himself as a coward—not because he is a warrior, as many critics have said, but because part of him shares her arrogant-vindictive value system. He is profoundly uncomfortable about committing the murder, but he is also uneasy about being afraid to do so. She senses his ambivalence and tries to reinforce the shame which derives from the aggressive side of his personality.

The conclusion of Lady Macbeth's speech is brilliant, both rhetorically and psychologically:

> I have given suck, and know
> How tender 'tis to love the babe that milks me.
> I would, while it was smiling in my face,
> Have pluck'd my nipple from his boneless gums
> And dash'd the brains out, had I so sworn as you
> Have done to this.
>
> (I, vii)

She compares herself to Macbeth in a way which is extremely threatening to his pride. She presents herself as a woman engaged in the most womanly of all acts who has more guts and determination than he. Macbeth does not want to kill Duncan because of his innocence. Lady Macbeth parallels Duncan's innocence with that of the nursing babe, which she would kill while it was smiling in her face. She is asking him to do nothing more cruel than she is prepared to do herself. The image of milk reminds us of Lady Macbeth's fear that her husband is "too full o' th' milk of human kindness/To catch the nearest way." She is trying here to exorcise the softer feelings which are holding him back by pointing out that she, too, has such feelings, but that she would not let them stand in her way. The milk of human kindness is epitomized by a nursing mother. What more tender feelings, what more sacred bond could Macbeth cite as a reason for not proceeding?

Macbeth's resistance is swept away by the onslaught of his wife. The forces propelling him toward the murder are stronger now than those which have been holding him back. Although gaining the throne is what initially prompted him to think of killing the King, it is no longer his major motivation. He is driven less by his search for glory than by fear of his wife's rejection and of his own self-contempt. He is compelled to live up to the idealized image of a man which is dictated by Lady Macbeth and by his arrogant-vindictive shoulds.

Caught as he is in a crossfire of conflicting shoulds, Macbeth is bound to suffer no matter what he does. He is damned if he does not kill Duncan and damned if he does. He returns from the murder in a panic-stricken state. He could not say "Amen" when he "had most need of blessing," and he has heard a voice cry "Sleep no more./Macbeth does murder sleep" (II, ii). He has violated his need to be holy, and hence he cannot say "Amen." He had feared damnation before the murder, and now he is sure that he is lost. He had thought that he was ready to pay this price, but he finds that he is not. His auditory hallucination derives in part from his belief in an "even-handed justice." According to the *lex talionis,* if you murder a man in his sleep, then you may be murdered in yours. When we sleep we are most vulnerable, least in control of our fate. We are dependent upon other men, upon the protection of a stable order. It is not only Duncan, it is also this order which Macbeth has murdered. He fears that he will no longer feel safe enough to sleep, that he has deprived himself of the "chief nourisher in life's feast." His sleep does, in fact, become disturbed, as does that of his Lady.

Macbeth's transformation from a reluctant, conscience-ridden conspirator into a cunning and brutal murderer begins in the very next scene. Despite his panic immediately after the murder, he is remarkably self-possessed when Duncan's death is discovered. He eloquently expresses his sorrow, boldly kills the chamberlains, and effectively defends this precipitous action. When we next see him he is planning the murders of Banquo and Fleance; and after his encounter with Banquo's ghost, he immediately begins to plot against Macduff. By the end of the play he is a "butcher" (V, viii) who has turned Scotland into a slaughterhouse. Given his inner conflicts before the murder and his fear and revulsion after, how can we account for his growing brutality through the rest of the play? This may be the central puzzle of Macbeth's character.

Macbeth has a number of motives for wanting to kill Banquo. The chief of these are fear, feelings of inferiority, and anguish at the thought of Banquo's line succeeding to the throne. Macbeth's fear arises, I believe, less from any specific threat posed by Banquo than from profound feelings of anxiety with which Banquo has little to do. By his murder of Duncan, Macbeth has turned the world into a jungle in which no one can be trusted and no one is safe. In addition, he has violated his perfectionistic bargain, and he expects to be the object of retribution. His fears are widespread and overwhelming. He fears poison in his food and either lies awake in "restless ecstasy" or is visited by terrifying dreams. He is afraid of domestic malice and of foreign invasion. Why, then, does he say that "there is none but [Banquo]/Whose being I do fear" (III, i)? His fears are generated at this point less by external threats than by the violation of his shoulds, but for Macbeth to recognize the intra-psychic sources of his anxiety would leave him in despair. What steps could he take to find peace? He needs to believe that his fears have a tangible, specific, external source in order to feel that there is something he can do about them. He defends himself against his fears by attributing them to one person and then imagining that he can rid himself of them by disposing of their source. Banquo is a logical focus for his fears because he has good reason to suspect Macbeth's wrongdoing, and he is a formidable person.

Macbeth is psychologically oppressed by Banquo, who makes him feel inadequate, foolish, morally inferior. As G. Wilson Knight observes, "he fears, envies, hates Banquo who has the reality of honour whereas he has but a mockery, a ghoulish dream of royalty" [*The Imperial Theme,* 1951]. Macbeth sees Banquo as the opposite of himself: he had similar temptations but did not give way. Banquo represents to Macbeth his perfectionistic shoulds, his earlier self. He is what Macbeth wishes he were instead of what he has become. Comparing himself to Banquo fills Macbeth with self-hate. He externalizes this self-hate actively by hating Banquo and passively by imagining himself to be the object of Banquo's aggression. One of his reasons for killing Banquo is to alleviate his self-contempt and sense of inferiority by removing the person who triggers these feelings. It is part of his effort to escape the perfectionistic side of his own nature, which is largely responsible for his mental torment.

One of Macbeth's strongest reasons for wanting to kill Banquo and Fleance is his anguish at the thought of Banquo's line succeeding to the throne. When Macbeth contemplated violating his perfectionistic bargain, he knew that he would sacrifice his soul if he did so. He thought he was willing to pay this price if he could strike a new bargain in which he gained the earthly glory which he desired. He is now confronting the failure of his new bargain, and he turns to more violence in a desperate effort to make it work. Being king has turned out to be devoid of satisfaction. He now needs to found a dynasty in order to compensate for the emptiness of his triumph and the apparent meaninglessness of his sacrifice. Macbeth believes in the prophecies of the witches. His enemy is not simply Banquo; it is fate, which has ordained that Banquo's line shall be kings. For him to have sacrificed everything to make "the seeds of Banquo kings" is too unfair to be borne: "Rather than so, come, Fate, into the list, / And champion me to th' utterance!" (III, i).

By killing Banquo and Fleance, then, Macbeth is not only trying to assure his safety and to cut off a rival line; he is also trying to master fate, to force it to honor his bargain. The futility of this enterprise is brought home to him by the escape of Fleance: "Then comes my fit again" (III, iv). Macbeth would feel "Whole as the marble, founded as the rock" if both Banquo and Fleance had been killed because this would have established his independence of external ordinances. He is aspiring to the position of lawgiver, not merely in the state, but in the universe. If he can prove that he is above fate, then he may not be subject to the retribution which he fears. The escape of Fleance shows him that he is not a free agent but is "bound in" by an external order whose laws he has violated. As a result, his anxieties are intensified. His attempt to master fate leaves him more rather than less exposed to "saucy doubts and fears."

It is striking that after vacillating so much before the murder of Duncan, Macbeth moves against Banquo with an apparent absence of inner conflict. Consciously, he has adopted the value system of the arrogant-vindictive solution and is attempting to live up to the idealized image which it prescribes. His conscientious side is still present, producing his anxiety, but this is largely an unconscious process. Macbeth is aware of the effects, but not of the causes. His inner conflicts are brought to the surface by the appearance of Banquo's ghost. It is impossible to say whether Shakespeare meant for the ghost to be real or an hallucination. If it is the latter, then it is Macbeth's conscientious side emerging and haunting him with what he has done. If the ghost is real—and Macbeth at first thinks that it is—then its effect is to reaffirm the moral order and to exacerbate Macbeth's fear of retribution.

> It will have blood, they say; blood will have
>   blood.
> Stones have been known to move and trees to
>   speak;
> Augures and understood relations have
> By maggot-pies and choughs and rooks brought
>   forth
> The secret'st man of blood.
>
>   (III, iv)

Macbeth is in the grip here of a mystic belief that murder will out, that a supernatural order will see to his punishment. He is as panic-stricken as he was after the murder of Duncan. His arrogant-vindictive defense system has broken down, his suppressed trends have emerged, and he is experiencing great anxiety.

At this moment occurs a major turning point in Macbeth's development. He expresses resentment toward Macduff, who did not attend the feast, and determines to embark upon a course of reckless cruelty. The appearance of Banquo's ghost might, one would think, deter him from future crimes or at least make him more fearful of the consequences; but it seems to have the opposite effect. Instead of shrinking from further violence, he embraces it wholeheartedly. He has not been a bloody tyrant up to this point, but he becomes one now. Henceforth we see neither hesitation before nor moral discomfort after his crimes. His inner conflicts seem to disappear. How are we to account for this change?

The change in Macbeth is a direct reaction to the anxiety which he has just experienced. He defends himself against his fear of being punished by determining ruthlessly to eliminate anyone who threatens him: "For mine own good/ All causes shall give way." If he is not to succumb to his dread of the moral order, he must defy it. His idealized image of himself as a "man" has been undermined by his response to the ghost and by Lady Macbeth's mockery. He turns his anger at his own weakness onto Macduff and resolves to show both his wife and himself what kind of man he is by pursuing a course of unrestrained violence. Macbeth is defending himself most of all against the threat of psychological collapse which is posed by the emergence of his repressed trends. He senses that to think of "these deeds . . . after these ways" will make him mad. The emergence of his conscientious side can only fill Macbeth with self-hate and anxiety, for there is no longer any way in which he can put himself in harmony with it. Because Macbeth is more perfectionistic than self-effacing, repentance is not an option which he considers. Salvation for him comes from obeying the law; once he has broken it, he feels himself to be doomed. He has stepped in blood so far that there is nothing to be gained by going back and nothing to be lost by going forward. His only hope of avoiding a total breakdown is to rebuild his arrogant-vindictive defense system and to identify himself with it completely. If he is not to be destroyed by his conscientious side, he must destroy it first.

There are two major ways in which Macbeth hopes to accomplish this—by inuring himself to violence and by acting on impulse. He now sees the ghost as an hallucination which was caused by his inexperience, and he determines to harden himself by steady course of violence: "My strange and self-abuse / Is the initiate fear that wants hard use. / We are yet but young in deed." This is a way of dismissing what has just happened, as well as of assuring himself that he will be able to avoid such visitations in the future. Thinking about his murderous intentions has tended to fill him with horror. He will put an end to this by purposely acting on impulse: "Strange things I have in head, that will to hand,/ Which must be acted ere they may be scann'd." He wants to anesthetize himself so that he will be free of moral anxiety both before his crimes and after.

The first victims of Macbeth's impulsive violence are Macduff's wife and children. He moves against them for several reasons. One of the strange things which he had in mind was the murder of Macduff, but he put it off until he had visited the Weird Sisters. When Macduff escapes, Macbeth is angry with himself for having delayed and resolves never to do so again: "From this moment/ The very firstlings of my heart shall be/ The firstlings of my hand" (IV, ii). He had gone to the witches in order to learn "By the worst means the worst" (III, iv), but he still had hoped for a reversal of their earlier prophecy, and he is furious at hearing once again that Banquo's issue will be kings. He is full of rage at himself, at Macduff, and at destiny; and he takes out this rage on Macduff's wife and children. By murdering them, he will punish Macduff for his defection and will restore his sense of power. He needs to prove to himself that he can actually carry out the murderous impulses that flit through his mind: "No boasting like a fool!/ This deed I'll do before this purpose cool" (IV, ii). The murder of Lady Macduff and her children has little practical purpose, but it serves a multitude of psychological needs. It is the means by which Macbeth acts out his rage, relieves his feelings of impotence, and actualizes his idealized image of himself as a man who can commit the most heinous crimes without flinching. It is the first step in his effort to kill his conscience by accustoming himself to murder. Macbeth's further crimes are not presented in any detail but are conveyed to us in a general way through a series of laments for Scotland and denunciations of Macbeth and by Macbeth's own feeling that he has "supp'd full with horrors" (V, v).

As a number of critics have observed, Shakespeare has achieved a very complex effect in the last two acts of the play by making us shrink from Macbeth as a monster and side with those who are fighting against him while inducing us to retain our sympathy with Macbeth and even to feel some degree of admiration for him. He has kept his criminal a hero. Macbeth retains our sympathy partly because his effort to kill his conscience fails and he remains a suffering human being. Macbeth's feelings of guilt are too deeply repressed to be directly available to our observation, but Shakespeare makes us aware of them by having Angus and Menteith comment on Macbeth's psychological state:

> ANG.   Now does he feel
> His secret murders sticking on his hands.
> Now minutely revolts upbraid his faith-breach.
> Those he commands move only in command,
> Nothing in love. Now does he feel his title
> Hang loose about him, like a giant's robe
> Upon a dwarfish thief.
> MENT.   Who then shall blame
> His pester'd senses to recoil and start,

> When all that is within him does condemn
> Itself for being there?
>
>   (V, ii)

These speeches are given great weight by the following scene, in which Macbeth is trying to control the panic caused by the desertions of which Angus speaks. We do not see Macbeth condemning himself in the way that Menteith describes, but he displays the effects which Menteith attributes to his sense of guilt. Macbeth is struggling in this scene with the fear of retribution which derives from his self-condemnation and with despair. There is no way at this point in which he can succeed. Even if he were to repel the invaders, he would not really be cheered; for he has lost the things which he had always cherished most highly and which are still of great importance to him: "honour, love, obedience, troops of friends" (V, iii). Instead of having "Golden opinions from all sorts of people" (I, vii), he now has merely "mouth-honour" from people who are compelled to give him homage while hating him in their hearts. Since life has nothing to offer, Macbeth feels ready for death.

Macbeth's darkest expression of despair occurs in the speech which follows the death of his wife. Many critics feel that Macbeth reacts to the news with callousness or indifference, but the grimness of his reflections indicates that he finds it deeply disturbing:

> To-morrow, and to-morrow, and to-morrow
> Creeps in this petty pace from day to day
> To the last syllable of recorded time;
> And all our yesterdays have lighted fools
> The way to dusty death. Out, out, brief candle!
> Life's but a walking shadow, a poor player,
> That struts and frets his hour upon the stage
> And then is heard no more. It is a tale
> Told by an idiot, full of sound and fury,
> Signifying nothing.
>
>   (V, v)

The death of his wife fills Macbeth with a sense of the futility of all their striving. Life is so transitory and insubstantial that it is foolish to take anything seriously. We aspire to fame and glory, but after our brief hour upon the stage, we disappear and are forgotten. Viewed from the perspective of death, our hates and loves, agonies and triumphs have no ultimate meaning. They are but "sound and fury, / Signifying nothing." These are not Shakespeare's sentiments, of course, but Macbeth's, who is generalizing from the emptiness of his own existence to the absurdity of the human condition.

This speech is not only an expression of despair; it is also a defense against it. Lady Macbeth's death threatens Macbeth by making him feel the futility of his own life and by intensifying his own fear of dying. He defends himself by withdrawing to a detached perspective from which nothing matters. Life is meaningless because of death, and death has no significance because life is such a burden. Macbeth is looking at time from both a subjective and a cosmic perspective. From the subjective perspective, it moves with agonizing slowness through a series of empty tomorrows. From the cosmic perspective, life is so ridiculously short—an hour upon the stage, a brief candle—that it seems like "a walking shadow." Both perspectives make death more acceptable, the subjective because it makes death a release from the wearisome round of tomorrows, and the cosmic because it makes our lives seem unreal and their duration of little significance. If life is so empty, insubstantial, burdensome, and brief, what difference does it make whether we die now or a little later? Macbeth's sense of absurdity is a defense not only against his fear of death, but also against his frustration and self-hate. Despair about life in general is much easier for Macbeth to handle than is a sense of personal defeat. If all lives are futile, if all men are made fools of by fate, then his own life has not been such a tragic disaster. He can blame his suffering on the idiotic nature of existence rather than upon himself.

As the play draws to a close, Macbeth oscillates between fear, despair, hope, and courage. His hope is based upon the words of the apparitions, which give him a feeling of invulnerability until they prove to be equivocal. He is confident that his "castle's strength/ Will laugh a siege to scorn" (V, v) until he hears that Birnam wood has begun to move. With this blow to his hope in a magical protection from the retribution which he fears, Macbeth's death wish grows stronger: "I gin to be aweary of the sun,/ And wish th' estate o' th' world were now undone" (V, v). One of the reasons we admire Macbeth is that although he has received two terrible blows in this scene—his wife's death and the moving of Birnam wood—he does not, in fact, "pull in resolution," but determines to fight on in spite of everything: "Blow wind, come wrack,/ At least we'll die with harness on our back" (V, v). This pattern is repeated in his encounter with Macduff. He exults in his sense of invulnerability when he fights the young Siward, but his "better part of man" is "cow'd" when he learns that Macduff was ripped untimely from his mother's womb (V, viii). He knows that he is lost, but once again he rallies his spirit:

> Yet I will try the last. Before my body
> I throw my warlike shield. Lay on, Macduff,
> And damn'd be him that first cries, "hold,
>   enough!"
>
> (V, viii)

Macbeth still seems heroic because despite the hopelessness of his situation, his energy does not fail. He wavers again and again, but in the end he stands up to psychological pressures under which most men would collapse. Though his courage is not morally redemptive, it earns our respect. He maintains his expansive pride and dies in a way which fulfills his image of himself as a fearless warrior. The manner of his death not only earns our respect, it enables him to retain his own.

Though it has numerous affinities with the morality play, *Macbeth* also has much in common with a realistic novel like *Crime and Punishment*. Like Raskolnikov, Macbeth has inner conflicts before and after his crime; and it is his guilt and fear more than anything else which are responsible for his downfall. The compelling power of both works derives in large part from their brilliant portrayal of the effects of crime upon the psychology of the criminal. What Shakespeare and Dostoevsky are showing us is that men like Macbeth and Raskolnikov cannot commit such crimes without undergoing terrible inner torment and triggering self-defeating behavior. It is less the external consequences of the crimes than their internal deterioration which brings about their downfalls. If Macbeth had not been so afraid, he might have gotten away with his crime; and his fear, as we have seen, is largely psychological in origin. To cope with it, he embarks upon a series of actions which turns everyone against him and brings about the very thing which he dreads. *Macbeth* is the tragedy of a man who violates his own bargain with fate and then as a result of the psychological consequences compulsively destroys himself.

Harry Keyishian (essay date 1981)

SOURCE: "Karen Horney on 'The Value of Vindictiveness,'" in *The American Journal of Psychoanalysis*, Vol. 42, No. 1, Spring, 1982, pp. 21-6.

[*In the following essay, which was originally presented at a conference held in February of 1981, Keyishian discusses the ways in which Horney's essay "The Value of Vindictiveness" can be used to illuminate the natures of various literary characters.*]

I first came to appreciate the special value of Karen Horney's work while doing research for a study of revenge as a literary theme. Through an exploration of writings on power and punishment I progressed a certain distance with a general theory of revenge. I came to see that the main feelings underlying revengeful acts were shame, violation, and the sense of injustice. I concluded that revenge had three main aims, often intermixed, but each with its own strategies, satisfactions, and dangers.

First, revenge aims to restore personal integrity and self-esteem. The person who must accept injury or insult over a prolonged period without being able to retaliate may come to feel severe self-contempt, a loss of bearings, and crippling fearfulness; his intellectual and moral perceptions may become warped if he rationalizes the injustice perpetrated against him or overvalues his injurer. Such was often the case in German concentration camps, Bruno Bettelheim [in *Surviving, and Other Essays,* 1979] has reported; similar observations have been made about hostages and other victims of violent crimes. One aim of retaliation, then, is to stave off such reactions by proving one's strength to oneself; through striking back, we hope to restore the integrity—the sense of wholeness and unity—that may have been damaged through our injury.

However, a danger of revenge is that it may, in itself, cause a warping of integrity which may be more damaging than the original injury. The revenger may neglect his own legitimate interests to pursue revenge; he may feel himself to be—and may actually become—no better than his injurer.

The second aim of revenge is to change the perceptions and attitudes of the injurer. By committing deliberate harm, the aggressor has demonstrated contempt for his victim, a feeling that the victim is weak, inferior, or deserving of injury. The revenger acts to change that perception, both in the aggressor and in others. He aims to gain respect and to deter further injury. The dangers of revenge on this level include the possibility of counter-revenge or a loss of reputation if the revenge is perceived as excessive.

The third aim of revenge is to satisfy the desire for justice—or, to put it more accurately, to appease the pain of injustice. Legal philosophers like John Rawls [in *A Theory of Justice,* 1971] and Edmond Cahn [*The Sense of Injustice,* 1975] have argued that the desire for fairness and the tendency to fight injustice may be instinctual in the human species; and that they underlie the desire to "even the score" or "pay someone back," as we say, by acts of punishment. The desire for justice may motivate noble and heroic actions; dedicated individuals may work to change society for the better in the name of justice. We also know, however, that the cry for justice may be used to excuse despicable tyrannies and acts of great cruelty, as the restraints of sympathy, mercy, are overwhelmed and the conscience is enlisted in the service of revenge, to endorse the return of injury.

This analysis served me well enough in some respects. It gave me tools for the analysis of public attitudes on capital punishment; it helped disentangle the issues in the Iranian hostage crisis and gave me clues to the strategies of both sides; it helped me understand feuds, duels, and other forms of unregulated retaliation.

The trouble was that it didn't help me very much in thinking about the literary characters I wanted to discuss—Medea, Elektra, and Orestes; Richard III, Shylock, Hamlet, Iago, and Othello; Milton's Satan; Bronte's Heathcliff; Dr. Frankenstein and his creature; Von Kleist's Michael Kohlhass; Dumas' *Count of Monte Cristo;* numerous characters in the works of Dickens, Kipling, James, Faulkner, Nabokov, and others. It didn't help me confront either the psychological undercurrents revealed by the creators of these characters or the ways they work on our imaginations as readers. It wasn't that my categories were invalid; they just didn't tell me enough that was interesting about these figures.

It was at this point that I encountered Karen Horney's essay **"The Value of Vindictiveness,"** which first appeared in the *American Journal of Psychoanalysis* in 1949, rightly regarded as a classic by those who know it. This essay helped me distinguish between free acts of retaliation and acts of neurotic vindictiveness; it revealed, as well, the hidden strategies and the sources of vindictive behavior.

In her essay, Horney refers to a "rational anger, proportional to the provocation, that flares up and subsides with its expression"—an anger that might have been suppressed but which the individual chose freely to express; and she notes how vastly different is the quality of vindictiveness, a desire for retaliation which goes beyond what is appropriate. Horney contrasts the person displaying "rational anger" with the person in whom the "expression of . . . vindictiveness . . . pervades his whole personality." She adds, "In neuroses, vindictiveness can become a character trait; it can amount to vindictive attitude toward life; it can become a way of life."

She defines vindictiveness as a desire to subject others to "pain or indignity" with the aim of humiliating, frustrating, and exploiting them. She notes that vindictiveness can be expressed directly, through actions taken against individuals; it also can be expressed indirectly, through suffering which accuses others and makes them feel guilty; and it can also be expressed through detachment, by ignoring the needs and feelings of others.

This analysis came as a crucial and clarifying revelation. By isolating the quality of vindictiveness as it cropped up in various personality structures, it revealed hidden patterns among seemingly different types. It showed, for example, the speciousness of forgiveness granted in a vindictive spirit. I understood the strategy of the Apostle Paul when he wrote, "Dearly beloved, avenge not yourselves. . . . If thine enemy hunger, feed him; if he thirst, give him drink; for in so doing *thou shalt heap coals of fire on his head.*" I also understood the point of Oscar Wilde's advice: "Always forgive your enemies; nothing annoys them quite so much."

Whichever strategy he chooses, the vindictive individual is marked by the fact that his behavior is compulsive—that is, he acts in a manner that is rigid and mechanical, an expression of his neurotic structure rather than his spontaneous wishes or even his best interests. Horney notes that "often there is no more holding back a person driven toward revenge than an alcoholic determined to go on a binge. Any reasoning meets with cold disdain. Logic no longer prevails. Whether the situation is appropriate does not matter. . . . Consequences for himself and others are brushed aside." The drive can become "the governing passion of a life-time," as individuals search for the "one goal of vindictive triumph . . . [which becomes] the flame sustaining their lives." Frustration of revenge can cause deep physical and psychological distress. Horney mentions *Hamlet, Moby Dick,* and *Wuthering Heights* as literary works presenting valid portraits of vindictiveness.

Horney traces three main sources of hostile retaliatory impulses. The first is hurt pride—a neurotic pride "not built upon existing assets but upon an imaginary superiority." Such pride is, of course, easily offended, and every "slight" becomes fuel for increased vindictiveness. The second source is the externalization of self-hate, through which self-destructive impulses are perceived as coming from outside, causing the individual to think himself despised and unfairly treated by others. The third main source is *Lebensneid*—an envy of life based on the feeling that one is excluded from the joys felt by others. Ironically, the individual by his very actions and neurotic entanglements may cause the exclusion he feels.

As Horney points out, tendencies toward vindictiveness are strengthened by the fact that it seems to serve several useful functions. Some of these are defensive: because he has a grudge, the neurotic can make demands on the world—present a bill, as it were. Vindictiveness also protects him from external hostility (imagined or actual) and from unrecognized self-hate. It also helps restore injured pride.

And in addition to its defensive functions, vindictiveness also holds forth the tempting promise of triumph. Some forms are relatively benign—Horney cites the Cinderella story as one—but others are more destructive. The individual, perhaps because he has suffered from a history of humiliation, may develop a longing to reverse roles, to be the one with the power to exploit, frustrate, and inflict pain. The vindictive person may feel a great thrill from such actions: indeed, Horney says, "it often constitutes one of the rare alive feelings he is capable of having." As an example from literature, she cites the excitement Hedda Gabler feels in destroying the irreplaceable manuscript of Eilert Lovborg.

Unfortunately for the vindictive individual, the process is self-defeating. The search for triumph involves him in a vicious circle, as he searches for sharper stimuli to arouse him; furthermore, he is unable to value life's experiences for their own sakes: love, family, and work becomes merely means to achieve the true goal to which his life is dedicated—the goal of vindictive triumph.

Clearly, vindictiveness is not the solution to the individual's problem: in fact, it *is* the problem. It renders the individual "isolated [and] egocentric [; it] absorbs his energies, makes him psychically sterile, and, above all, closes the gate to his further growth." Horney concludes, "When we realize how deeply he is caught within the machinery of his pride system, when we realize the effort he must make not be crushed by self-hate, we see him as a harassed human being struggling for survival."

Is vindictiveness "curable"? Horney says the condition is difficult to treat because superficially it offers too much—defense, the thrill of triumph, self-respect, and a sense of identity. Horney reports that patients will often wish to defeat their analysts more than they desire to be cured. When a vindictive person does seek treatment, it is often in a search for ways to overcome his inhibitions and become more effectively vindictive.

The individual who wishes to rid himself of this trait must work at the whole range of personal relations and take the risk of "becoming more human," Horney writes. Recovery would necessitate his "giving up his isolated grandeur, his uniqueness, and becoming an ordinary human being like everyone else without any special privileges; becoming part of the swarming mass of humanity he so despises." He will have to learn sympathy, "not in the grand style of providence for others, but, to start with, just for his own life." In short, life itself must become more important than vindictive triumph.

Later, when I came to study **Neurosis and Human Growth,** I understood how vindictiveness fit into her larger system. The original article remains, however, a key work for me.

Reviewing other psychological literature, I found material of interest in the work of Fritz Heider, Gregory Rochlin, and Anthony Storr. A 1966 article by Charles Socarides usefully described vengefulness in a Freudian context ["On Vengeance: The Desire to 'Get Even,'" *The Journal of the American Psychoanalytic Association,* Vol. 14, 1966]. Heinz Kohut has written informatively about rage and revenge, and I have found interesting links between his views on "grandiosity" and Horney's concept of self-idealization. And a fine and sensitive article by Marvin Daniels ["Pathological Vindictiveness and the Vindictive Character," *Psycho-Analytic Review,* Vol. 56, 1969] explored the psychodynamics of revenge, offered a theory of the origins of vindictiveness, and suggested ways of approaching literary portrayals of vindictiveness.

Daniels suggests that the vindictive individual acts on the implicit assumption that "a principle of 'just deserts' operates inexorably in the universe. According to this principle, everything must be requited—not only injury for injury, but favor for favor." He traces the assumptions of vindictive persons back to childhood experiences with parents who related to them without intimacy, who treated them like mechanical objects in a universe of strict rewards and punishments. As a result, the child came to perceive himself as mechanical, as "a living fortress who walks around." For this reason, Daniels says, "the vindictive character comes to limit, as much as he is able, all intercourse with the rest of the world. He remains watchfully on guard. Little goes in and little goes out."

Daniels sees vindictiveness originating in the individual's "shattering" disappointment at the hands of a parent figure. And, like Horney, he points out that the vindictive person is doomed to fail in his search for contentment because he is unaware of the true cause of his misery— "of his agonizing yearning for reunion with the loved one he lost in the dark, forgotten past. Thus, any 'vindictive triumph' which comes to him is rarely an occasion for great rejoicing, and his pleasure is usually short-lived."

Daniels describes vindictiveness as an effort to "enter into a relationship with the envied person and make him miserable too." He cites the example of Milton's Satan, who plots the downfall of Adam and Eve in order to lessen his own loneliness. Daniels concludes, like

Horney, that "despite his hollow vindictive victories, life's real values continue to elude" the vindictive person.

The acute insights provided by these works have given me the tools for analysis of the characters I have sought to study and, perhaps more significantly, for the understanding of the general phenomenon of revenge. Like the instinct for self-defense, through which the individual is preserved, and the sexual instinct, through which the species is perpetuated, the desire for revenge has a deep hold on us and serves an important role in our lives. I have come to see both the constructive and destructive aspects of that desire; I have come to understand better the tangled aims and goals of revenge. A force so powerful cannot be ignored, nor should we expect to suppress or discard it from our lives easily. We must see it for what it is and understand what we expect it to do for us before we can find constructive ways to cope with it.

In achieving this understanding, Horney gives us much; but I also believe that the portraits of revengefulness and vindictiveness we find in literature—whether "great" or popular—reveals a congruence of insights which presents the hopeful possibility that our combined resources, we as literary analysts and you as psychoanalysts, will be most productive in developing and communicating an understanding of this complex phenomenon.

Karen Ann Butery (essay date 1981)

SOURCE: "The Contributions of Horneyan Psychology to the Study of Literature," in *The American Journal of Psychoanalysis,* Vol. 42, No. 1, Spring, 1982, pp. 39-50.

[*In the following essay, which was originally presented at a conference held in February of 1981, Butery demonstrates some of the ways in which applying Horney's theories to the study of literary characters reveals a fuller sense of their often self-contradictory natures.*]

When accepting the Nobel Prize for literature, William Faulkner said that the "only" things "worth writing about" are the "problems of the human heart in conflict with itself." He laments that too many young writers "labo[r] under a curse" because they have ignored these problems. Many literary critics also labor under this curse, for the new emphasis on structuralism, semiotics, linguistic typology, and sociopolitical theory has resulted in a disregard of the mimetic quality, which to a great extent gives literature its power and humanistic value.

Certainly, if literature is to be fully appreciated, neither its formal nor its mimetic dimensions can be slighted. However, I have discovered as a teacher and student of literature that often the predominant reason why I, my students, and more of my colleagues than will admit it have read and re-read the great masterpieces is that we identify with the intensity of the struggling human beings portrayed. Indeed, it might be concluded that the fundamental criterion by which a work's greatness is measured

is that it "speak[s] to our condition," striking some common chord in human experience [C. Heilbrun, *Toward a Recognition of Androgyny,* 1973]. This is the yardstick used by Karen Horney, when at the age of twenty-one she explored the question, "What does 'artistic value' mean?" [*The Adolescent Diaries of Karen Horney*]. She was certain that "it can't be purely formal—for with 'structure' or 'dialogue' alone it still isn't done." Although Horney discovered no definitive answer, her own interaction with literature corresponds to that of most readers: " . . . I must say, if I approach any literary creation it is with the question: what ideas has the poet or writer about people and human life, about this or that struggle which happens to preoccupy me? Or else I can find in the work some sort of tone that is sympathetic to me. . . . " Horney's career channeled her energies in another direction, and she does not address this issue in her professional writings; but her use of literature to illustrate her theory indicates one of the ways it became valuable to her. Her psychological theory reciprocates, as it were, by making literature more valuable to its readers. It contributes to literary criticism by enriching our understanding of the conflicts underlying the struggles of fictional characters and providing a terminology to talk about them. It contributes to the humanistic value of literature by helping the reader transfer to real life the deeper understanding of human nature gained through a Horneyan interpretation of these characters. Horney's theory, therefore, helps us experience literature more intensely, both intellectually and emotionally.

In order to demonstrate how Horneyan psychology can be used as a valuable tool in literary criticism, I shall refer to my psychological study of the Victorian heroine [an unpublished dissertation] which reinterprets the problem novels of *Jane Eyre, Daniel Deronda, Jude the Obscure,* and *The Portrait of a Lady.* The Horneyan approach used in this study sheds new light on both formal and mimetic problems and explains what aesthetic and thematic approaches often describe or only partially account for. It explains, for example, the tensions in these novels between characterization and theme by helping to show that structure and theme are primarily determined by the author's craftsmanship, whereas characterization often grows out of his psychological intuitions. What puts characterization and theme at odds is that the author's intuitions often surpass his conceptual powers so that characters escape thematic categories and become creations in their own right. Indeed, each of the authors of the above novels describes this phenomenon. Charlotte Brontë speaks of an "influence" which "seems to waken in [her], which becomes [her] master—which will have its own way—putting out of view all behests but its own . . . [as it] new-mould[s] characters. . . . " [letter to G. H. Hewes, 12 January 1848, in *Shakespeare Head Brontë*, edited by T. J. Wise and J. Alexander Symington, 1932]. Similarly, George Eliot describes a "'not herself' which took possession of her, and . . . [used] her own personality . . . [as] merely the instrument through which this spirit, as it were . . . act[ed]" [J. W. Cross, *George Eliot's Life as Related in Her Letters and Journals, Ar-*

ranged and Edited by Her Husband, J. W. Cross, Vol. 3, 1885]. Thomas Hardy admits that Jude Fawley and Sue Bridehead "take things into their own hands and . . . d[o] better work than he had anticipated" [letter to *Harpers Magazine,* April, 1894]. And Henry James emphasizes his conscious passivity, declaring that something "had extraordinarily happened" to his "imagination" when the full-blown character of Isabel Archer came to it "straight from life" ["Preface," *The Portrait of a Lady*].

The nature of the contradictions between the representation and interpretation of characters is described by Bernard J. Paris in *A Psychological Approach to Fiction:* "The implied authors glorify unhealthy attitudes which are close to their own, while at the same time *showing* their destructiveness." Brontë rewards Jane Eyre's adoption of a self-effacing solution by fulfilling Jane's dreams through the novel's fairy tale ending, but the maiming and blinding of Rochester necessary to Jane's "perfect concord" highlights the unhealthy nature of such a solution. Eliot and James each misinterprets as healthy growth Gwendolen Harleth's and Isabel Archer's relinquishment of expansive tendencies for an equally unhealthy self-effacement by the former and resignation by the latter. Because Hardy, as implied author, is himself torn by conflict, he vacillates between glorifying Sue Bridehead's defensive strategies as comprising a nobility which elicits her persecution by an ignoble world and pointing to them as the basis of a self-inflicted disintegration. All of these authors show some confusion about their own characters, the roots of which can be uncovered and the results explained by Horneyan psychology.

Significantly, there would be no formal tensions if these characters were streamlined to fit the novels' designs, but the price paid for structural balance would be the loss of the heroines' vitality and appeal. Thus, the aesthetic flaws in these novels attest to the intuitive powers and psychological brilliance of the authors. The weaknesses lie in the interpretation, not the representation of the remarkably accurate portraits. Since the greatest achievement of these novels is the mastery of their mimetic portraiture, the richest experience of them can be gained by focusing on the heroines; and because the disparity between characterization and formal design make it impossible for one critical approach to do justice to both aspects of the novels, a psychological approach is needed to understand fully the complex heroines. But literary criticism is dominated by formal and thematic approaches which interpret characters as illustrative rather than mimetic, and to this extent these approaches are severely handicapped. They often do an injustice to a heroine's intensity by reducing her multi-faceted personality to a one- or two-dimensional level. For example, Helene Moglen's study of Jane Eyre in terms of an "allegorical movement of self-discovery" fails to account for Jane's dynamism [*Charlotte Brontë: The Self Conceived,* 1976]; and R. W. Stallman strips Isabel Archer of vitality when he declares that she "is as predictable as the moon," for she has only "two extremes in her character" illustrating James' "theme of Illusions of Appearances

versus Reality" ["Some Rooms From The Houses that James Built," *Texas Quarterly,* No. 1, 1968]. One of the most common limitations of thematic analysis in the interpretation of these heroines is the unquestioned acceptance of the novel's rhetoric. Thus, John Halperin's study of the Victorian novel as *Bildungsroman* incorporates the blind spots of both authors and characters by crediting Jane Eyre with a "self-knowledge," Gwendolen Harleth with a "moral expansion," and Isabel Archer with a "moral education" which none of them demonstrates [*Egoism and Self Discovery in the Victorian Novel,* 1974]. Another danger of traditional approaches is that they may erroneously dismiss the complexity of a character as superfluous, as in itself comprising an aesthetic flaw. This happens when in spite of Henry James' assertion that the "subject" of *The Portrait of a Lady* is Isabel Archer's "own consciousness," Arnold Kettle insists [in *Introduction to The English Novel,* 1953] that the novel is impaired by the "depth of 'felt life,' that 'ado' which is the story of Isabel Archer, [because] all this . . . may easily distract our attention from the central theme." Even if, at best, these heroines are neither simplified nor underrated, they are still unexplained by formal criticism. Although Irving Howe points out [in *Thomas Hardy,* 1967] that Sue Bridehead's "human character" is "open to far-reaching speculative inquiry," he also warns that it is "perhaps beyond certain knowledge" because it is "an amorphous and ill-charted arena in which irrational impulses conflict with one another." In the same vein, Robert Heilman concludes that Sue "simply is," and that it is up to the reader "to sense the inner truth that creates multiple, lively, totally conflicting impressions" ["Hardy's Sue Bridehead," *NCF,* No. 20, 1966].

Horneyan psychology enables us to do much more than *sense* the inner truth of these complex heroines. Not hampered by a focus on theme and structure, a Horneyan approach allows us to analyze these heroines as creations in their own right. It shows us that although the novels are not harmoniously integrated, the heroines—as works of art in themselves—do pass the Coleridgean test for artistic unity by manifesting a "balance or reconciliation of opposite or discordant qualities. . . . into one graceful and intelligent whole" [Samuel Taylor Coleridge, *Biographia Literaria,* 1817]. By analyzing the heroines in the motivational terms used to understand human beings, a Horneyan approach helps us to piece together the character structures into which all the heroines' contradictory behavior fits and provides new insights into their conflicts and inconsistencies with a depth, precision, and attention to detail heretofore unrealized.

Although much space must be devoted to a full study of Jane Eyre, Gwendolen Harleth, Sue Bridehead, and Isabel Archer, I shall in a general way point to some of the new insights about them provided by Horneyan analysis. A fresh look at Jane Eyre shows us a young woman plagued by many more conflicts than the two most often discussed: passion versus morality, and independence versus a patriarchal society. For example, in addition to the opposition between Jane's feelings and her morality, her morality itself is burdened with a conflict between personal and traditional values. Furthermore, the genuineness of both sets of values is called into question when Jane emphasizes her love for Rochester by freely admitting that she has made him her "idol" and placed him "between [herself] and . . . God," while she proves that her love for Rochester is too weak to "transgress a mere human law" by refusing to live with him unmarried even though she agrees that no one would be hurt. An understanding of Jane's pride system clears up this confusion by making it apparent that it is neither personal nor traditional values but an idealized self-image entirely dependent upon the world's good opinion that accounts for Jane's horror of public adultery but complacency about private idolatry.

A full understanding of Jane also makes it evident that the conflict between her independence and a patriarchal world cannot be resolved, as it is often believed to be, by her running away from domineering men. Because Jane's need for independence is countered by her desire to be subsumed by a powerful male personality, it is precisely their expansiveness which both attracts Jane and repulses her. Running away cannot free her because she is *self-victimized*. At any rate, her running back and forth between two overbearing males like Rochester and St. John is jumping out of the frying pan into the fire and makes no sense at all in terms of asserting her independence.

The novel's ending cannot be attributed to what most critics view as Jane's choice between personal values and traditional morality or as the assertion of her independence. Jane's basic needs to be loved, to be good, and to be independent never change; and the conflicts among them are never resolved. Jane's and Rochester's initial relationship fulfills her need for love but threatens and, thus, intensifies her need for independence; and when her need to be good is thrown into jeopardy by the prospect of adultery, Jane must run away to escape the imminent danger. That she does not resolve her conflict is evidenced by her self-condemnation both before and after leaving Thornfield. Indeed, Jane's problem simply shifts into another gear, for the sacrifice of her love reactivates her need for it. This problem is exacerbated by Jane's relationship with St. John because he repeatedly frustrates her already intensified need for love. When he pushes her to the point of deciding to give up love forever in order to prove her goodness by marrying him and becoming a missionary, Jane grows so desperate that she runs back to Rochester. Just as she did before, Jane must escape in order to protect the need which is in immediate jeopardy and which is, therefore, momentarily the strongest. But Jane still has not resolved her conflict, as is evidenced by her rationalizations, which disguise her real reason for returning to Rochester. Indeed, her return would throw her back into the same dilemma which caused her to run away in the first place had Brontë not manipulated the plot so that all of Jane's needs are fulfilled and the bases of her conflicts eliminated. The removal of Bertha Mason makes it possible for Jane to be good, while the crippling and blinding of Rochester make

him dependent upon Jane's love and render him less threatening to her independence, which is also secured by her inherited fortune. Everything has been done for Jane by a seemingly "impossible change in circumstances." Her happiness is contingent upon her not having to make any choices.

A Horneyan interpretation gives us an equally fresh view of Gwendolen Harleth. It negates the accepted theory that Gwendolen's *volte-face* from egoist to martyr is a moral "conversion." By sensitizing us to how repetitive detail fits into the overall jigsaw puzzle of character structure, it alerts us to the significance of Gwendolen's vague fears and easy penances occasioned by her childhood misdemeanors. Contrary to what the novel's rhetoric calls the embryo of a moral conscience, this behavior is the beginning of an unhealthy pattern set into motion by Gwendolen's insatiable need for approval and her fear of losing it. Since her feelings of self-value depend upon her mother's praise, Gwendolen attempts to fulfill her mother's neurotic needs. To do so pulls her in contrary directions because the self-effacing Mrs. Davilow needs to live vicariously through an aggressive type, but also makes tacit claims on others to live up to her ideals of goodness, humility, and self-sacrifice. On the one hand, therefore, she encourages Gwendolen to be selfish and egotistical—a master of fate rather than a victim like herself—and on the other hand, she makes Gwendolen feel guilty and inferior for not being as loving as she. Mrs. Davilow sows the seeds of self-effacement in her twelve-year-old daughter by severely scolding Gwendolen—accusing her of "hav[ing] no feeling"—because Gwendolen criticizes her mother's martyrdom to a cruel husband. Gwendolen reacts by becoming unconsciously terrified lest she lose her mother's love, and therefore her own self-esteem, by proving her cold-heartedness. Her rejection of Rex Gascoigne, for example, elicits this unconscious fear in the form of hysteria, which Gwendolen cannot understand because the narcissistic side of her character forbids her awareness of any threat to her glorified self-image.

As Gwendolen grows older, her dependency upon her mother expands to include society, which also caters to Gwendolen's whims but expects her to be a proper lady. Thus, her conflicts and fears are reinforced, and earlier defensive strategies become established patterns. But there is no indication of moral growth. Gwendolen's remorse over her worst behavior, the betrayal of Lydia Glasher, is born of a fear that she herself will be scorned. Similarly, it is the preservation of her public image which enslaves Gwendolen to Grandcourt. What looks like moral growth is the reinforcement of Gwendolen's self-effacing solution and the steady undermining of her narcissism by the fears engendered by Lydia's curse and by the fact that Gwendolen's marriage proves to be a trap instead of a step on the ladder of social eminence and freedom.

It is Gwendolen's fears and desperate need for approval, intensified by her growing self-effacement, which bind her to Daniel Deronda. She attempts to mold herself to his ideal of "one of the best of women" for the same reason she had patterned herself after her mother's ideals: she needs love to reinforce her shaken sense of self-value. Gwendolen's change cannot be attributed to the emergence of a "better" self; even though her ideals are praiseworthy, they are not adopted for their own sake. Gwendolen's martyrdom at the end of the novel is simply another form of "the hunger of the inner self for supremacy"; the "only . . . difference" is "the way in which . . . supremacy is held attainable."

The deeper understanding of Sue Bridehead provided by Horneyan psychology reveals much more complicated problems than the perverse sexuality, which has claimed almost the exclusive attention of literary criticism. Indeed, it becomes evident that Sue's perversion is not the cause of all her other problems, as it is generally believed to be, but is itself a symptom of a complex network of unhealthy needs, values, and taboos arising from her self-alienation. She has compulsive needs to prove her power, independence, freedom, and unconventionality countered by an insatiable need to be loving and by exaggerated fears of rejection, contention, and reprisal. Sue is so embroiled in the conflicts caused by this network that everything she does triggers the opposite behavior. She runs away from Melchester Normal School because she hates conventions and is fiercely proud of her independence, but she humbly asks to be readmitted the very next morning out of her terror of retaliation, which is automatically set into operation whenever she acts rebelliously. Her relationships with men follow a rigid cycle of Sue's setting up barriers between herself and her lovers, frantically tearing them down, and immediately rebuilding them. It is both her fear of commitment and an indiscriminate craving for men's devotion which cause Sue to play the coquette with Jude while she is engaged to Phillotson; but her need for absolute self-sufficiency drives her away from both men as soon as she is certain of their vassalage; and then her compulsive fear of losing homage or inciting vengeance results in a mixture of penitence and renewed coquetry. Specifically, Sue's frigidity functions in contradictory ways; it is a means of maintaining her hold on men by tantalizing them, and it is also a means of maintaining her distance in order to protect her personal freedom.

Sue's growing dependency on Jude, because he helps her identify with her glorified self—a Shelleyan goddess, is tolerant to her only because she keeps up a semblance of self-sufficiency by refusing to marry him, to sleep with him regularly, or to avow her love for him. However, since living with Jude even under these conditions undercuts her independence, makes her feel guilty for torturing Jude, and results in hers and Jude's social ostracism, Sue is in a constant state of unconscious fear and self-hate. The horror of the children's deaths acts as a catalyst by releasing these repressed feelings which have grown to such fantastic proportions that Sue imagines the tragedy as a Nemesis inflicted by some supernatural agent whom she has antagonized by daring to be happy. Her religious

fanaticism culminating in self-immolation when she remarries and gives herself sexually to Phillotson is Sue's way of appeasing fate by attempting to backtrack and wipe out through self-effacement all the expansive behavior that elicited her retribution.

The new light shed on Isabel Archer's conflicts by a Horneyan approach shows us that her life is not ruined because a naïve romanticism led her to marry an ogre whom she cannot leave out of loyalty to her marriage vows or to her stepdaughter. First, although Isabel is young and romantic, she is not as naïve as most readers suppose. She is experienced enough to realize that should she "give her mind to it," she could "well . . . criticize" her own intended union. But Isabel's mind is taken up in justifying marriage to Osmond because it is tremendously attractive in many ways: it reinforces Isabel's pride in her uniqueness, in her search for knowledge, in her self-sacrifice for an ideal, and in her equality with a man; and it fulfills her needs to pass on the responsibility for using her fortune wisely and to escape the pressure of her friends' expectations that she embark on a glorious career. Isabel is compelled by her pride and inner dictates to magnify these attractions and ignore the drawbacks.

Second, Gilbert Osmond is not by any means a good person, but he is not the villain Isabel portrays. She exaggerates his negative characteristics after marriage in the same way that she had embellished his virtues during their engagement. Isabel needs to see herself as Osmond's helpless victim in order to blame him for the original mistake of their marriage, to justify her own inability to correct it, and to avoid recognizing her inner conflicts. Actually, Isabel's admitted "exultation" over deliberately humiliating Osmond proves that she herself is no saint and is more often Osmond's "match" than his victim. (Because Isabel's intelligence and idealism make her charming, the reader wants to view her in the best light. Therefore, the reader, no more guilty of naivete than Isabel, makes the same kind of mistake she does in accepting Isabel's indictment of Osmond but choosing to pass over the incriminating evidence against her.) Moreover, to a great extent, Isabel's unhappiness arises from her own inner conflicts, which would be exacerbated no matter whom she married. Her need to be independent and her desire for unlimited possibilities, for example, are threatened by any commitment; yet her narcissism compels her to make a grand marriage, for it is the only spectacular career through which she can prove her superiority without touching the "cup of [worldly] experience," "poisoned" by the chance of failure. Moreover, Isabel's pride is so exorbitant that no matter how "fabulous" her marriage might be, it would not be grand enough; while at the same time, any extraordinary marriage would threaten her puritanical perfectionism which puts a taboo on "separat[ing] [her]self from what most people know and suffer."

Finally, Isabel's decision to return to Osmond has little to do with loyalty to marriage vows or to Pansy. Isabel's vacillations between scorn for her marriage and awe for her vows and between compassion for Pansy and using Pansy to serve her own ends indicate a compulsiveness and absence of wholeheartedness which rule out loyalty to any cause as a primary motivating factor behind Isabel's behavior. Isabel simply resigns herself to a "horrible life" with Osmond, and in "default of a better" reason for doing so uses her marriage vows and promise to Pansy as rationalizations. She succumbs to this resignation because her pride has been so severely crushed by the failure to make a glorious marriage that would prove her perfection and she is so frightened of the self-hate another such failure would generate that she embraces a death-in-life rather than take the risk of starting over.

The Horneyan reinterpretations of these novels reveal that all of the heroines are as unhealthy at the end of the novels as at the beginning and, therefore, that all of them undercut the thematic idealization of self-effacement and resignation by demonstrating the destructiveness of these solutions. But are we to be disheartened by these revelations? Are we to lament Jane's failure to solve her own conflicts, Gwendolen's failure to become "one of the best of women who make others glad that they were born," Sue's failure to realize the virtues of a Shelleyan goddess, or Isabel's failure to play the role of "guardian angel"? Surely not. It is not Victorian morality or the expectation of a new version of the Saints' Lives which holds our attention to the very last page of the lengthy novels enlivened by these heroines. It is in the heroines themselves that we become absorbed because they are so very human, because we identify with them as fellow struggling creatures. Were they to succeed in becoming Madonnas, our identification would be lost in distanced awe. And if we are looking for spiritual elevation from literature, we might discover that the empathy we feel for another frail soul is ultimately more uplifting than the undersense of being cheated felt when we apotheosize human beings.

Because Horney's theory highlights the humanness of literary characters, its critical value to explain formal and mimetic problems is equalled by its humanistic value. A Horneyan approach counterbalances the tendency to apotheosize characters who exhibit defensive strategies favored by culture and to condemn those who hold opposite trends. Not only does this tendency discourage some neurotic attitudes by encouraging equally unhealthy trends, but also, by viewing characters as *super*human or *sub*human, it limits the deep insights into human nature which literature affords. Horneyan interpretations of character, on the contrary, promote neither a veneration of heroes nor an aversion for villains, but an empathy with *human beings* and an understanding of human problems which can help us to live better lives. This empathy and understanding can help us to become more tolerant, to distinguish between existential suffering and the needless pain people bring on themselves and cause others, and, of primary importance, to alleviate the latter.

We can overcome our prejudices against people with character structures different from our own when we re-alize that to some degree most of us are driven by compulsive inner dictates, harassed by conflicts, and plagued by fears and feelings of inferiority. Horneyan interpretations of characters promote this understanding, for they allow us to see from the inside personality types whose counterparts we would never get close to in real life. We can even begin to feel compassion toward destructive people and perhaps learn to help them when we understand that the hate and bitterness that drive a Joe Christmas to murder his stepfather and his mistress and, finally, to set up his own execution is generated by the same original search for glory in order to compensate for a lack of self-esteem which urges Daniel Deronda to found a Jewish nation and St. John Rivers to sacrifice himself as a missionary in India. We might reexamine our own motives, moreover, when we see that St. John's and Deronda's focus on the end result of glory causes them to make mistakes and spread suffering along the way which violate their ideals. Blinded by pride, St. John does not realize that making his own heart "no more than a sacrifice consumed" and attempting to persuade Jane to "wrench [her] heart from man" undercut the very essence of the Christian gospel he would propagate. His "insatiable" ambition destroys his own humanheartedness and makes him, no less than Captain Ahab, an "ungodly godlike man." Similarly, Deronda's pride in his "redeeming influence" causes him to encourage Gwendolen's morbid dependency on him and then to abandon her for the greater glory of saving a nation. He unwittingly sacrifices Gwendolen on the altar of his pride in an even more harmful way by creating a Madonna figure for Gwendolen to live up to which prevents her from realizing her own human potentialities and lays the groundwork for her self-hate when she inevitably fails to achieve perfection. St. John and Deronda are not bad men, but their pride causes them to do bad things. For that matter, Joe Christmas is not a bad *man;* it is his crushed pride transformed into self-hate which is responsible for the desolation he wreaks. The point is that none of these men are free; all of them are enslaved and tormented to a greater or lesser degree by pride and self-hate.

It might be feared that the dethroning of our literary heroes and heroines will have a deleterious effect by causing us to expect less of ourselves. On the contrary, we can expect much more of ourselves as human beings when we stop apotheosizing fictional characters and trying to emulate them. As humans, we can succeed; our failure to be gods is inevitable. When we learn to distinguish between the good qualities and the shortcomings of literary characters, they will no longer be stumbling blocks. Most of them fail to actualize their potentialities and to resolve their conflicts, because they are self-alienated—bound and blinded by compulsive and contradictory needs; but Horney enables us to see where they might have succeeded instead of failed and to use this knowledge for self-enlightenment so that we can improve our own chances of success. We can adopt their noble ideals without repeating their mistakes if, instead of blindly following their example, we refocus our attention from the glory to be gained by achieving ideals to the ideals themselves. When we learn to strive out of a genuine love for what is good instead of driving ourselves by pride and self-hate, we will not only accomplish more but also be happier. Certainly, we will have a better chance of avoiding the despair which led Quentin Compson to drown himself because he failed in his role as Sir Galahad to protect his sister's chastity. It is less likely that we will be victims of the self-hate which erupts in Jude Fawley's deathbed curse on his own conception because he could not be the University of Christminster's "beloved son" and because Sue could not be the "divinity" for whom he made his heart a shrine. Above all, we need not feel the desperate isolation of Meursault, the "Stranger," whose self-alienation, not his existential predicament, so thoroughly cut him off from everything, including his own inner being, that "for [him] to feel less lonely, all that remained to hope was that on the day of [his] execution there should be a huge crowd of spectators and that they should greet [him] with howls of execration" [Albert Camus, *The Stranger*, 1961]. These men enact what Horney calls "perhaps the greatest tragedy of the human mind. Man in reaching out for the Infinite and Absolute also starts destroying himself. When he makes a pact with the devil, who promises him glory, he has to go to hell—to the hell within himself' [*Neurosis and Human Growth*]. We can choose not to inflict this tragedy on ourselves by choosing to pursue reasonable goals, to enjoy the process itself of working toward them, and to learn from unavoidable errors and failures so that in lieu of punishing ourselves we can either continue toward our goals more efficiently or change them for ones commensurate with our capabilities.

The insights into human nature and the growth of charity attained by using Horneyan psychology to interpret literary characters can equip individuals for partaking of the richer life to which masters like William Faulkner wished to contribute by his portrayal of men and women as "immortal," " . . . not because [we] alone among creatures ha[ve] an inexhaustible voice but because [each of us] has a soul, a spirit capable of compassion and sacrifice and endurance." Karen Horney adds to this list "the capacity to change" [*Our Inner Conflicts*]. If we do not have the qualities Faulkner names, we *can* develop them. The understanding of others and self gained by Horneyan analyses of characters can help put into practice Horney's optimistic conviction that "all of us retain the capacity to change [for the better], even . . . in fundamental ways, as long as we live."

Marcia Westkott (essay date 1986)

SOURCE: "A Social Psychology of Women," in *The Feminist Legacy of Karen Horney*, Yale University Press, 1986, pp. 66-87.

[*In the following excerpt, Westkott offers a detailed examination of Horney's theory of neurosis, concluding that her "universalizing" of childhood experience—that is, Horney's view that the sources of neurosis are not*

gender-specific—is in fact a description of female psychology.]

In her later work Horney built on her critique of Freud to create an alternative explanation of character development and conflict. This was her theory of neurosis, which substituted experience for instinct in explaining psychology. But with this alternative foundation Horney did more than give primacy to cultural context and social relations; she feminized psychoanalysis. More specifically, she universalized female experience as the basis for understanding human development and conflict.

The Theory of Neurosis

For Horney neurosis is the consequence of cultural contradictions and constricting expectations that block the development of a whole self. All members of a culture, healthy and neurotic, experience these detours. In American culture, for example, a strong element of competitiveness, which promotes interpersonal hostilities and undermines self-esteem, creates fertile ground for the development of neurosis [*The Neurotic Personality of Our Time*]. Moreover, conflicting cultural values and social conditions—competition versus brotherly love, or conspicuous consumption versus the reality of limited economic resources—foster neurotic conflict. Thus the neurotic, "the stepchild of our culture," reflects culturally engendered problems in the extreme. The stepchild is in this sense the one who shows the most obvious resemblance to its cultural parent. The implication of this explanation is, of course, cultural criticism: some cultures are healthier than others.

Some people become neurotic because they experience the neurotic elements of society and culture more intensely than others. Their family settings transmit and replicate rather than mitigate the competition, hostility, and contradictions of the culture. A parent who is anxious about competing with others, who needs blind admiration as a bulwark against a hostile world, who has difficulty giving genuine warmth and nurturing to others passes these traits along to his or her child. The neurotic parent is too egocentric to cope with the normal egoism of a child. The child, in turn, develops neurotic defenses in response to the fear and hostility generated by inadequate parenting. The parent creates for the child the very conditions that the parent fears in the outside world, thus perpetuating the neurotic cycle [*Neurotic Personality*].

Horney also believed that our culture creates values which foster neurotic personalities. While she did not coin the concept of inadequate parenting as a mediation between culture and psyche, it is clearly implied in her analysis. Horney would have agreed that neurosis is produced not only by the child's embeddedness in neurotic culture but also—and especially—by the parents' continuing unsuccessful struggle with that culture, which leads to inadequate parenting and hence reinforces the child's neurosis.

The concept of inadequate parenting implied in Horney's analysis has been developed more fully by ego psychologists and theorists of object relations. The latter emphasize the mother-child relationship in the earliest months of life as the foundation for the child's psychological health. They claim that either too little or too much maternal involvement during various stages in infant and early childhood development can create serious personality disorders in the child. If the mother herself lacks ego strength, she will transmit these problems to her children.

From the perspective of Horney's analysis, the problem with these more recent works is that they treat the mother's mental health as a means to the health of the child, and they abstract the mother-child relationship from the contexts of family and culture in which they are embedded. Thus they make an independent variable of a factor that Horney implied was a mediator between culture and psyche. The notion that neurosis is perpetuated by transmission from a disturbed mother to her children, among whom the daughters ultimately become disturbed mothers themselves, ignores the cultural and social contexts of neurosis.

Horney's work asserts the contrary: a disturbance in particular social relations can never be abstracted from the cultural contexts in which they are embedded. "In fact the cultural conditions not only lend weight and color to individual experiences but in the last analysis determine their particular form. It is an individual fate, for example, to have a domineering or a self-sacrificing mother, but it is only under definite cultural conditions that we find domineering or self-sacrificing mothers, and it is also only because of these existing conditions that such experiences will have an influence on later life" [*Neurotic Personality*].

The key to Horney's linking of culture and psyche is her assumption that human beings are "ruled not by the pleasure principle alone but by two guiding principles: safety and satisfaction." Safety, because it is the condition for the realization of satisfaction, is the primary requirement. "People can renounce food, money, attention, affection so long as they are only renouncing satisfaction, but they cannot renounce these things if without them they would be or feel in danger of destitution or starvation or of being helplessly exposed to hostility, in other words, if they would lose their feeling of safety."

The concept of safety introduces social and ethical elements to Horney's theory of human development. Whereas satisfaction refers to the need for an object world—a world of people, and food and other things that are the objects of one's needs and desires—safety refers to conditions that others must create. From the perspective of the developing infant, safety implies caretakers and a human community. The theoretical primacy of safety suggests that the human infant is not simply—or even primarily—a bundle of desires but a being at risk, dependent upon the ethical conduct—the care—of others.

Only the individual can develop his given potentialities. But, like any other living organism, the human individual needs favorable conditions for growth "from acorn into oak tree"; he needs an atmosphere of warmth to give him both a feeling of inner security and the inner freedom enabling him to have his own feelings and thoughts and to express himself. He needs the good will of others, not only to help him in his many needs but to guide and encourage him to become a mature and fulfilled individual. He also needs healthy friction with the wishes and wills of others. If he can thus grow *with* others, in love and in friction, he will grow in accordance with his real self.

Foreshadowing Erikson's assumption that an infant needs first and foremost to experience "basic trust" in relation to his or her caretakers, Horney claimed that a child's fundamental need is for a loving and warm atmosphere that provides inner security [*Neurotic Personality*]. Inextricably linked to that inner security is inner freedom, the feeling that one is free to become oneself without risking the loss of parental love. Horney was not so naive as to believe that becoming oneself occurs without conflict. Echoing Freud's concept of the reality principle she suggested that in pursuing one's wishes one will inevitably clash with reality, which includes the wishes of others. But in calling for "healthy friction," she interjected a parental ethic into the conditions of reality. That ethical imperative is the parents' genuine care for the child as a unique human being. This permits friction to occur without fear and with the assurance that despite differences with the parent the child will continue to be loved and cared for, promoting, to use Horney's term, a feeling of "we."

Inner security is the condition necessary for the realization of inner freedom, which allows the development of the real self. The *real self* is Horney's concept of the ideal outcome of human development: a person who has been loved and is able to love and care for others in return, who has been free to develop his or her potentials without feeling compelled to live up to externally defined expectations. In the real self desire and judgment are not the functions of separate components (as in id and superego) but are integrated into a whole thinking, feeling, and judging being. Horney appears to have hedged on whether the real self is discovered or created, an essence to be uncovered or a product of human choice. On the one hand, she stated, "Whatever the conditions under which a child grows up, he will, if not mentally defective, learn to cope with others in one way or another and he will probably acquire some skills. But there are also forces in him which he cannot acquire or even develop by learning. You need not, and in fact cannot, teach an acorn to grow into an oak tree, but when given a chance, its intrinsic potentialities will develop. Similarly, the human individual, given a chance, tends to develop his particular human potentialities." This suggests an essentialist perspective: the core of the oak is determined by the acorn. Yet when describing the release of the real self from neurotic conflicts, Horney emphasized that the basis of the real self is choice. If so, the real self is created; and freedom to create oneself implies ethical responsibility for the choices one makes.

Horney's apparent vagueness on whether the real self is an essence to be discovered or a product of creative choice reflects, I think, her assumption that it is both. Individuals are born with unique physical and mental faculties that can be tapped and developed. These potentialities and limitations are not rigidly determined; what one does with them is a matter of choice and chance. "Under favorable conditions man's energies are put into the realization of his own potentialities. Such a development is far from uniform. According to his particular temperament, faculties, propensities, and the conditions of his earlier and later life, he may become softer or harder, more cautious or more trusting, more or less self-reliant, more contemplative or more outgoing; and he may develop his special gifts. But wherever his course takes him, it will be *his* given potentialities which he develops."

The concept of human growth captures both the discovered and the created components of the real self. By engaging with the world, one both discovers one's unique characteristics and creates one's future. From this perspective growth is self-directed life itself, and at its core is the central inner force that is the real self.

If safety and satisfaction, inner security and inner freedom form the conditions necessary for the growth of the real self, it was their absence that captured Horney's attention. Her concern with the conditions that foster neurotic conflict reflected both her therapeutic purpose and her criticism of culture.

Being abused, unloved, or treated solely as an object for parental satisfaction or control is both a personal fate and a circumstance that occurs within a wider cultural context. The cultural pattern that Horney critiqued most sharply was the rampant competitiveness that she associated with capitalist industrial societies:

> Modern culture is economically based on the principles of individual competition. The isolated individual has to fight with other individuals of the same group, has to surpass them and, frequently, thrust them aside. The advantage of the one is frequently the disadvantage of the other. The psychic result of this situation is a diffuse hostile tension between individuals. Everyone is the real or potential competitor of everyone else. This situation is clearly apparent among members of the same occupational group, regardless of strivings to be fair or of attempts to camouflage by polite considerateness. It must be emphasized, however, that competitiveness, and the potential hostility that accompanies it, pervades all human relationships. . . . It remains one of Freud's great achievements to have seen the role of rivalry in the family, as expressed in his concept of the Oedipus complex and in other hypotheses. It must be added, however, that this rivalry itself is not biologically conditioned but is a result of given cultural conditions and, furthermore, that the family situation is not the only one to stir up rivalry, but that the competitive stimuli are active from the cradle to the grave. [*Neurotic Personality*]

In Western society, pervasive competitiveness forms a normal cultural pattern of social relations. According to Horney, it generates psychic consequences in feelings of hostility and fear, which serve to undermine genuine self-confidence and self-esteem. Competitive culture also creates a paltry substitute for the self-esteem it destroys: the *image* of success, an other-directed emphasis upon valuing people for "what they appear to be [rather] than for what they are." Predominant cultural values of competition and success also foster an obsession with presenting the appearance of having socially valued qualities. Superficially cultivating the grandiose image of superiority constitutes the self-inflation that Horney associated with narcissism. "A striving for admiration may be a powerful motor toward achievement, or toward developing qualities which are socially desirable or which make a person lovable, but it involves the danger that everything will be done with both eyes on the effect it has on others. An individual of this type chooses a woman not for her own sake but because her conquest would flatter him or add to his prestige. A piece of work is done not for its own sake but for the impression it might make. Brilliancy becomes more important that substance."

The illusion of success belies its rickety basis in feelings of insecurity. Self-aggrandizement is a false substitute for genuine self-acceptance. Horney called it the *idealized self,* which is fundamentally alienated from the real self. An individual consumed with narcissistic self-inflation desires most of all the respect, admiration, and affection of others. "He loses any understanding of the fact that friendliness and love can include an objective or even a critical attitude. What falls short of blind adoration is to him no longer love; he will even suspect it of being hostility." Thus, the narcissist needs constant affirmation from others that the created illusion of desirable qualities—the idealized self—is admired. Consequently, this type "is incapable of loving either himself or anyone else."

Parents who are insecure, vulnerable to the ideals and stresses of a competitive society, and obsessed with an other-directed image of success reproduce these insecurities in their children by creating the same conditions within the family that they fear in the world outside. Their self-absorption interferes with their capacity to care. The danger to the child can take many forms; the most extreme is physical or sexual abuse [*Neurotic Personality*]. Less obvious but more pervasive, according to Horney, is the absence of genuine love and concern for the child. "People in the environment are too wrapped up in their own neuroses to be able to love the child, or even to conceive of him as the particular individual he is; their attitudes toward him are determined by their own neurotic needs and responses. In simple words, they may be dominating, overprotective, intimidating, irritable, overexacting, overindulgent, erratic, partial to other siblings, hypocritical, indifferent, etc. It is never a matter of just a single factor, but always the whole constellation that exerts the untoward influence on a child's growth."

Particularly destructive is the pattern of treating a child as a narcissistic extension of the parent's idealized self. In their desire to take on the image of success, they may use the child to achieve their own social aspirations. When treated in this way, "a child may be led to feel that his right to existence lies solely in . . . living up to the parents' expectations—measuring up to their standards or ambitions for him, enhancing their prestige, giving them blind devotion; in other words he may be prevented from realizing that he is an individual with his own rights and . . . responsibilities. The effectiveness of such influences is not diminished by the fact that they are often subtle and veiled" [*Self-Analysis*].

Abuse, disregard, or the more subtle self-absorbed use and control of a child form a pattern—particularly, in Horney's examples, among the middle class—of childhood danger in a competitive society. Horney did not equivocate about this source of neurosis: the danger in the home is a basic theme in her analysis of character development. The type and intensity of family danger can vary considerably; some of the children in a family may experience it more than others, and certain families may escape it altogether. For some its impact may be lessened through some mitigating circumstance such as a loving relative or friendly teacher [*Neurotic Personality*]. But, like the competitive, hostile world that it reflects and reproduces, the dangerous family was for Horney a fact of modern life.

In the face of such jeopardy, the child's response is fear and anger. Horney saw this fear as a realistic reaction to hostile conditions that the child cannot control. Powerless and devalued, he or she feels weak, helpless, and worthless. At the same time, the child feels hostile toward the devaluing or abusive parents. This, too, is a realistic response. Horney implied that the hostility is a healthy way of fighting back, an expression of self against feelings of worthlessness. The problem, she argued, is not in the protest but in its repression, which forces the child to repress his or her legitimate feelings [*Neurotic Personality*].

Unfortunately, the conditions that give rise to hostility also foster its repression. Neurotics cannot tolerate criticism or hostility, especially from those who are expected to be under their control. Criticism from people of lower status is the ultimate humiliation. The neurotic parent thus responds to a child's hostility by employing the same abusive or devaluing means against which the child is protesting. Expression of hostility thus intensifies the child's danger, while repression of his or her legitimate anger serves to diffuse it, creating the illusion of being protected, cared for, and loved as a "good" child. Fear, then, overpowers the assertion of hostility and becomes the foundation of repression. The consequence of this

repression is the development of basic anxiety [*Neurotic Personality*].

As mentioned, Horney considered fear a realistic reaction to parents' devaluing behavior rather than an inevitable response to biological helplessness. "In children growing up under adverse conditions helplessness is usually artificially reinforced by intimidation, by babying or by . . . keeping a child in a stage of emotional dependence" [*Neurotic Personality*]. Fear can also be aroused by "threats, prohibitions, and punishments, and by outbreaks of temper or violent scenes . . . ; it may be aroused also by indirect intimidation such as impressing the child with the great dangers of life—germs, street cars, strangers, uneducated children, climbing trees." In the face of parental hostility and fear of life's dangers, a child may also fear loss of the illusion of love and protection that the parent offers. "When genuine affection is absent there is often a great emphasis on how much the parent loves the child and how they would sacrifice for him up to the last drop of their blood. A child, particularly if otherwise intimidated, may cling to this substitute for love and fear to be rebellious lest it lose the reward for being docile."

Thus, out of fear of reprisal or loss of love, the child represses hostility; the feared and resented parent becomes admired and the child becomes the object of his or her own hostility. This "shift from true rebellion to untrue admiration" [*Self-Analysis*] is a solution to interpersonal danger. By admiring the powerful parent and accepting his or her devaluing judgment as true, the child eliminates interpersonal conflict and thus diffuses danger. Horney recorded this conversion in the patient Clare, who, as I have indicated, was probably a representation of Horney herself.

> This shift from essentially true and warranted accusations of others to essentially untrue and unwarranted self-accusations had far-reaching effects . . . [it] entailed more than an acceptance of the majority estimate of herself. . . . She repressed all grievances against the mother. If everything was her own fault the grounds for bearing a grudge against the mother were pulled away from under her . . . it was much safer to find shortcomings within herself than in the mother. [*Self-Analysis*]

By reversing hostility, the child loses touch with the real self, the locus of judgment and feeling. "Clare lost the feeble vestiges of self-confidence she had. To use a somewhat vague term, she lost herself. By admiring what in reality she resented, she became alienated from her own feelings. She no longer knew what she herself liked or wished or feared or resented" [*Self-Analysis*].

Repressing legitimate anger also intensifies fear. In rejecting protest, the child accepts his or her helplessness and dependency upon the gratuitous good will of others, in effect conceding his or her susceptibility to danger. "Repressing a hostility means 'pretending' that everything is all right and thus refraining from fighting when we ought to fight, or at least when we wish to fight. Hence the first unavoidable consequence of such a repression is that it generates a feeling of defenselessness" [**Neurotic Personality**].

The world is seen as a dangerous place and other people as intimidatingly powerful figures. These perceptions constitute *basic anxiety,* which "may be roughly described as feelings of being small, insignificant, helpless, deserted, endangered, in a world that is out to abuse, cheat, attack, humiliate, betray, envy."

Thus the neurotic character foundation is reproduced in basic anxiety. Realistic fear of a person is internalized as irrational fear of the world in general. Those who deserve hostile protest are, paradoxically, admired, and the repressed hostility is not only turned back on the self but also diffused and projected onto others. The neurotic feels threatened by a menacing environment, which in turn generates additional feelings of defensive hostility. A cycle is created: fear and anxiety lead to hostility, which is projected and experienced as an external threat. This heightens anxiety, provoking hostility in defense. "This effect of reciprocity between hostility and anxiety, one always generating and reenforcing the other," creates the underlying dynamic of the neurotic personality [**Neurotic Personality**].

THE NEUROTIC TYPES

Horney's best-known theoretical construct is most often identified with her typology of neurosis. The neurotic types are character strategies that individuals create to cope with the anxiety-hostility conflict. If anxiety predominates, the sense of helplessness and fear prevails. Like the child's admiration for what it fears, the solution for neurotic anxiety is self-effacement, compliance, and excessive admiration. This is the *compliant* or *dependent* type. Conversely, when hostility is employed defensively, aggression, power, and domination prevail. These are characteristics of the *hostile* or *domineering* type. Because anxiety and hostility are interlocking components of neurotic character structure, each type incorporates the other. Hence, beneath neurotic compliance and admiration smolders a rage for revenge, and beneath neurotic aggression and domination naked terror hides.

These two neurotic types represent logical solutions to the problem of feeling helpless in a hostile world: relying on others to protect one from hostility, or overpowering the aggression of others through one's own hostility. The third solution is flight from the problem, an attempt to quell anxiety and avoid hostility by withdrawing from social relations. Basic anxiety and hostility remain, but the social contexts that aggravate them are avoided. Like the other two, the *detached* type strives for safety in a dangerous environment.

Horney described four neurotic patterns in **The Neurotic Personality of Our Time** (1937): (1) seeking affection, (2) submissiveness, (3) gaining power over others, and

(4) withdrawal. Eventually, however, she came to understand the first two as aspects of a single type and collapsed them into a category of dependency [**Self-Analysis**]. She used this threefold typology throughout her subsequent work. In **Our Inner Conflicts** (1945) she termed the patterns (1) moving toward people (emphasizing helplessness), (2) moving against people (emphasizing hostility), and (3) moving away from people (emphasizing isolation). In her last book, **Neurosis and Human Growth** (1950), her terminology emphasized the intrapsychic over the interpersonal: (1) self-effacing, (2) expansive, and (3) resigned. Each book emphasizes different aspects of the neurotic types and her understanding of them became more complex, but the three types remained. For consistency, I shall call them *dependent, domineering,* and *detached,* terms that Horney herself used at various times.

The dependent type attempts to gain reassurance and protection against basic anxiety through the affection of others. Dependent types believe that others will protect them from the hostile world and make them feel safe [**Our Inner Conflicts**]. To attain this protection they adopt attitudes of helplessness, docility, and self-effacement. The behavior of the dependent type conveys the message, "if I give in, I shall not be hurt" [**Neurotic Personality**]. Various techniques—including belittling or denying oneself, living according to others' expectations, and being unassertive, placating, and self-effacing—comprise this defense. Dependent people learn to "like" others because they are essentially afraid of them. They are often naively accepting or enchanted by the goodness of everyone and are genuinely shocked to discover that people can hurt them, a denial of their own unconscious fears.

If dependent types subordinate themselves as protection against a hostile world, domineering types control and overpower others to protect themselves. While both types resort to egocentric use of other people, dependent individuals make themselves appealing so others will express protective affection rather than hostility, and domineering types intimidate others so they will not dare treat them badly. While both types fear their own weakness, dependent people become lovable as a reaction to fear and domineering ones elicit fear because they believe that love is impossible. Dependent types develop survival strategies around weakness, domineering types around aggression.

In contrast to the dependent types, who convert fear to love, the domineering ones protect themselves by overcompensating for their weakness, converting it to a semblance of strength. Thus behind the quest for power and prestige, the appearance of mastery and superiority, and the style of self-assured aggressiveness lies contempt for their own weakness. People of this type despise and feel humiliated by weakness and therefore demand that others unquestioningly accept their illusion of capability and strength. They must be admired as protection against their own feelings of insignificance; they must be obeyed as protection against their fear of being dominated. But, just as the dependent types deep down question the love that is their salvation, the domineering types are never fully convinced of the admiration and obedience they receive. This suspicion derives not only from the sense that their superiority is a bluff but also from a projection of their envy of others. They suspect that no one truly admires or submits to them and that expressions of admiration or subordination from others are simply masks for envy or hostility.

Horney regarded the conflicts of the dependent and domineering types to be the most central to modern neurosis. Especially as each represses the tendencies of the other, these types express what Horney called the central human conflict of the age: "the craving for affection and the craving for power and control" [*Neurotic Personality*].

The detached type attempts to evade the conflict between affection and ambition by withdrawing socially. Unlike the other two, this type is expressed primarily in negative terms as a desire to avoid, rather than to use, other people. The need is for utter independence, "not being influenced, coerced, tied, obligated" to others [*Our Inner Conflicts*]. Independence is expressed by piling up possessions as a safeguard against all eventualities, jealously guarding one's privacy, restricting one's needs, resisting advice, schedules, competition, obligation, and demands for compliance. Internal needs are repressed through emotional detachment, renunciation of desire ("wish-lessness"), an impersonal onlooker attitude toward oneself and others, a sense of one's superiority and unique significance in combination with a shrinking from and curtailing of life in resignation to the unalterable status quo. In seeking freedom from others, the detached individual attempts to evade the conflict between needing love and needing to dominate, between self-effacement and expansion. Physical and emotional isolation can create a sense that life is "easy, painless, and effortless" as well as a feeling of inner integrity and sincerity. Detached people keep themselves "unsoiled and untarnished" by avoiding others.

Horney saw these three neurotic "solutions" to basic anxiety and hostility as ideal types. As concepts, each one forms a pure configuration of motives, feelings, and behaviors uncontaminated by the others. The dependent and domineering types, for example, are diametric opposites, and the detached type opposes them both. As extremes they represent analytical concepts, not actual people, who display greater variety, complexity, and intermeshing of characteristics than the types suggest. But the analytic purity of the types permits greater theoretical insight and development.

Horney did not employ these types according to the methodology of classical sociological analysis. First, they are not used to build a theory of historical change. Her concern was rather with understanding intrapsychic and interpersonal processes for purposes of healing. Second, while the types display conceptual clarity and focus, they

are also extensively elaborated. This, too, is a reflection of Horney's clinical emphasis. A theorist concerned with economy and conceptual development would have pared down the details. As a therapist, however, Horney emphasized concrete examples. It is people's variety and complexity that makes them unique. Horney did not permit the theoretical imperative to overshadow human complexity.

Yet Horney's work does not lack theoretical depth or conceptual precision. Her writing is strong, clear, and straightforward, addressed to both the lay person and the expert. She introduced complexity and variation into her types in a way that was both cognizant of psychoanalytic tradition and committed to truth. Her attention to human reality lends her theoretical formulations verisimilitude and conceptual power. Consequently, her types suggest other possibilities for conceptual development. The varied applications of her types by scholars in fields from literary criticism to religious studies display this depth.

Most important for my purpose, the theory and its types provide a conceptual basis for developing a social psychology of women. This extension of Horney's work is not simply another application; it is the unfolding of a central meaning in her theory. The key to that meaning is the pattern of female experience that Horney associated with the development of neurosis.

GIRLHOOD EXPERIENCE

The two categories of danger to which Horney implied children are exposed are devaluation and sexualization. Devaluation refers to the parents' lack of respect for the child as a unique and worthwhile human being. Sexualization "may consist in a gross sexual approach to the child; it may arise from sexually tinged caresses, or from an emotional hothouse atmosphere surrounding all members of the family or including some members and excluding others." Sexualization is, in effect, a form of devaluation; the authentic needs of the child are subordinated to the self-absorbed purposes of the adult.

A child who is devalued may cling to a parent for reassurance. "Such a hanging on to a person out of sheer anxiety is easily confounded with love, and in the child's own mind seems like love. It does not necessarily take on sexual coloring, but may easily do so. . . . The resulting picture may look exactly like what Freud describes as the Oedipus complex: passionate clinging to one parent and jealousy toward the other." But the reason for this clinging, according to Horney, has nothing to do with so-called incestuous desire on the part of the child. Rather, it is his or her anxious response to the parents' sexualizing and devaluing treatment. "I know of no case in which it was not neurotic parents who by terror and tenderness forced the child into these passionate attachments, with all the implications of possessiveness and jealousy described by Freud" [*Neurotic Personality*]. The Oedipus complex is thus not the natural consequence of blocked instinct, but the neurotic outcome of the abuse of parental power.

While Horney assumed that these experiences affect children of both sexes, her discussions more often linked them to female socialization than to male. Horney repeatedly referred to the unfavored child, whose condition appears to encapsulate all the features of parental disregard and lack of affection. Being unfavored is not necessarily a result of being unwanted, although that too can be expressed and felt. It rather involves being considered less than valuable by parents. This may be expressed in outright abuse, but more often it is manifested more subtly. Many of Horney's examples describe a daughter who is less favored than her brother. Horney's adolescent diaries poignantly record her own response to feeling unloved and unappreciated: her anger and sense of rejection in response to her father's stern distance and control and her misery over her mother's preference for her older brother, Berndt [*The Adolescent Diaries of Karen Horney*]. As a young woman of twenty-two Horney described to her future husband her mother's favoritism as well as her own vulnerability to it: "she silently overlooks my brother's meannesses, while at an unfriendly word from me she loses her temper. Incidentally, I am *really not* of a lovable nature, I mean even where it is not just a matter of fighting for a principle. A lack I am trying to get over but am not yet finished with."

The experience of Horney's patient Clare, described in *Self-Analysis* (1942), exemplifies the subtle pattern of female devaluation. "She was not badly treated or neglected in any coarse sense: she was sent to schools as good as those her brother attended, she received as many gifts as he did, she had music lessons with the same teacher, and in all material ways was treated as well. But in less tangible matters she received less than the brother, less tenderness, less interest in school marks, and in the thousand little daily experiences of a child, less concern when she was ill, less solicitude to have her around, less willingness to treat her as a confidante, less admiration for looks and accomplishments."

Horney regarded the devaluation of the daughter as more than an incidental fate; she asserted that it reflected a general cultural pattern of female inferiorization. Echoing her earlier critique of masculine civilization, she attacked Freud for dismissing the importance of the typical parental preference for sons. "How little weight Freud ascribed to cultural factors is evident also in his inclination to regard certain environmental influences as the incidental fate of the individual instead of recognizing the whole strength of cultural influences behind them. Thus, for example, Freud regards it as incidental that a brother in the family is preferred to the sister, whereas a preference for male children belongs to the pattern of patriarchal society. Here the objection might be raised that for the individual analysis it is irrelevant whether the preference be regarded in one way or the other, but this is not quite so. In reality, the preference for the brother is one of many factors impressing on the female child the feeling that she is inferior or less desirable."

Horney's emphasis on the cultural pattern of preference for sons suggests that parents are disappointed with daughters whether or not there is an actual son who is favored in contrast. The family articulates broader cultural values, and daughters experience pervasive devaluation and a sense of inferiority. While individual cases indicate that parental devaluation is experienced by some males as well, that pattern of patriarchal society makes it a fundamentally female experience.

Horney's examples of the sexualization of children in families indicate that this too is a predominantly female experience. Sexualization includes brothers and fathers incestuously using their sisters and daughters or making sexual advances toward them, father flirtatiously treating a daughter and all other females as sexual playthings, or a mother whose identity derives from male admiration of her beauty. Horney's examples suggest that the pattern of family sexualization of females creates an atmosphere in which girls' sexuality is presumed to be the fundamental aspect of their identity and the basis for male exploitation.

Thus, I contend, Horney's discussion of the universal features of childhood that promote neurotic character structure is a presentation of predominantly female experience. Because that experience reflects generally accepted cultural values, the family devaluation and sexualization of daughters appear to be normal occurrences, independent of the intentions or foibles of particular parents. Individual parents may genuinely believe and report that they love their daughters at the same time that their behavior favors their sons. They may believe that in encouraging a daughter to see herself as a sex object they are treating her in a normal way. Indeed, by wanting "what is best" for their daughter, they may promote the very practices that devalue her. Individual circumstances may involve variation but not—except under unusual circumstances—reprieve. Thus, the implication of Horney's analysis is that to grow up female in this culture is to grow up neurotic.

But this is not exactly the intention of her analysis. Men are neurotic, too, as her discussions of the neurotic types indicate. Horney contended that each of the three types—domineering, dependent, and detached—can be found among men and women alike. Thus, her theory of development of the types should also reflect the childhood experience of both sexes. But on this point Horney was inconsistent. She employed the neurotic types as gender-neutral categories, yet she explained their development in terms of a predominantly female pattern of experience.

The contradiction between the typology and the theory is partially resolved by Horney's qualification of her claim that the neurotic types are gender-neutral. She conceded that the two primary types did tend to separate along gender lines: men tend more often to display the characteristics of the domineering type and women the dependent type. The detached type remains a secondary category, although Horney did link it more frequently to the drive for superiority, which she associated with the domineering type.

The gender pattern of the types links the female experience undergirding the theory of neurotic development and the female characteristics of the dependent type. This link is underscored by Horney's explanations of the child's response to danger. In reaction to parental devaluation, the child develops an essentially submissive solution. The power of the parent is not challenged; it is instead solicited as a protective rather than an abusive force through the child's emphasis on his or her own weakness and need. The child, in effect, learns to identify with the aggressor and becomes pleasing, compliant, and affectionate as a means of securing safety. Hence fear is allayed by acquiescing to power, and hostility is turned back on the self, a self defined as bad in contrast to the now-admired parent.

Thus the basic neurotic solution to the anxiety created by childhood danger is compliant affection and repressed hostility, the solution of the dependent type. The theory did not explain the development of domineering or detached neurotic patterns as primary solutions. While repressed aspects of the other types always exist, Horney argued that one type predominates in the neurotic character structure. Her theory explains how compliant dependency emerges as a core neurotic type. But for hostile-domineering or detached types to emerge, the child would have to assume or be given power to express its hostility or independence vis à vis the parents. The theory does not explain how this might happen. In her emphasis on the child's basic anxiety and the solution of repressed hostility, Horney permits only one core neurotic solution, that of her dependent type.

Horney therefore seems to have left unexplained the development of the neurotic types that she associated with masculinity. When these types are presented in male examples, the men attempt to overcome basic anxiety by overpowering others or separating from them. But Horney did not explain developmentally why these solutions are employed or encouraged. Her failure to describe male development leaves a gap in understanding: one may see what the domineering male does, but one does not completely understand why.

The domineering and detached types seem more intelligible when considered as secondary characteristics of the dependent type, Horney's concept of modern woman. Domination and detachment emerge in this type, as a protest against powerlessness, only after the core dependent character is formed. They are essentially attempts to claim power or establish restitution for past mistreatment. They remain repressed in the face of the dangerous parental power but appear later under social conditions in which the individual becomes able to exercise some power over others or independence from them.

My interpretation of Horney's theory of neurosis as a critical theory of female psychology is based on the idea that the dependent solution is the core neurotic pattern. The anger characteristic of the dominant type and the desire for social withdrawal common to the detached type are interpreted as repressed aspects of the core dependent character. This interpretive synthesis of Horney's three neurotic types elaborates her earlier concept of the feminine type as the sweetly compliant woman who brims with rage and longs for freedom from others' expectations. The feminine/dependent type is masculine civilization's stepchild; she has become the ideal object that her culture promotes. But the cost of her success in an inner conflict that alienates her from her real self.

Marjorie B. Haselswerdt (essay date 1986)

SOURCE: "'Keep Your Muck': A Horneyan Analysis of Joe Christmas and *Light in August*," in *Third Force Psychology and the Study of Literature,* edited by Bernard J. Paris, Associated University Presses, 1986, pp. 206-24.

[*In the following essay, Haselswerdt presents a detailed discussion of the character Joe Christmas from William Faulkner's novel* Light in August (*1932*), *analyzing his "arrogant-vindictive" personality based primarily on Horney's theories as she presented them in* Neurosis and Human Growth.]

1

When Alfred Kazin describes the "pinched rotted look" of Faulkner's *Light in August,* he is referring to the influence of the depression on the atmosphere of the novel ["The Stillness of *Light in August,* in *Faulkner,* edited by Robert Penn Warren, 1966]. But his words have a resonance for the story of Joe Christmas that goes far beyond the superficial. *Light in August* looks "pinched and rotted," it seems to me, not only because its characters live stark, luxuryless lives on a barren landscape but because it contains buried within it an aversion to life, a profound inability to confront human existence with openness and joy. Though Faulkner's public utterances on the novel give heavy emphasis to Lena Grove, her "courage and endurance" and her pagan joy in giving birth, the novel itself embodies a denial of those things that Lena represents which is only partly compensated for by her rather bewitching presence. In fact, it is Joe Christmas—cold, violent, driven—and not the gentle Lena who dominates *Light in August,* and he dominates it not only because his is the central story but because his personality finds striking parallels in the implied world view of the novel as a whole.

Joe Christmas is a highly complex and difficult fictional character. Though Faulkner has presented him in great detail, his motives and reactions often seem bizarre and puzzling. Before we can understand his relationship to the atmosphere and significance of *Light in August,* we must understand Joe himself in some systematic way. I propose to analyze his character from the point of view of the Third Force psychology of Karen Horney, and to move from this analysis to a consideration of the relationship between Joe and his creator, and the effect of this relationship on the novel itself. Wayne Booth [in *The Rhetoric of Fiction*, 1961] tells us that every novel implies an author, a guiding consciousness who is responsible for the "core of norms and choices" that shapes the novel, and who uses rhetorical devices to influence his readers to share his perspective on the world he has created. In the case of *Light in August,* as we shall see, this "implied author" gives evidence that his relationship to life is at times as troubled and contradictory as that of Joe Christmas, indeed that there is a kind of collusion between him and Joe that has a great deal to do with the vision of the world he ultimately portrays in the novel.

The detailed Horneyan analysis that follows indicates that Joe Christmas is a type of aggressive personality that Horney labels "arrogant-vindictive" [*Neurosis and Human Growth*]. A person afflicted with this kind of neurosis is consumed with the desire to seek vindictive triumph. His ideal self is immune to human attachments and needs and he seeks to quell his inner conflicts by focusing on his need to achieve revenge for the wrongs done him in childhood and since by a world he sees as hostile. He externalizes his own feelings of hostility and convinces himself that the world is hateful and mean—if he were not convinced of this, his solution would not "work" and he would be beset by the anxiety that accompanies inner conflict. Thus he sees all attempts by others to "move toward" their fellow man as hypocritical and revolting. In himself, self-effacing tendencies are deeply buried, and if he is threatened with their emergence he will feel intense shame and self-hate, perhaps in the form of rage. Self-effacing "shoulds" generally influence his behavior in a negative way. Whatever a loving or loyal or trusting person "should" do in a given situation is what he must avoid doing in order to avoid anxiety. Nevertheless, as we shall see, in a crisis his repressed desires to "move toward" others, to seek their acceptance and love, may emerge to haunt him, causing him to feel guilt for his aggressive behavior and motivating him to act in ways inconsistent with his dominant solution.

By analyzing Joe Christmas's nature and behavior in terms of Horney's theories about this particular type, we shall be able to understand much about him, and to appreciate Faulkner's artistry in creating a character of such vividness and coherence. And once we understand Joe's inner conflicts and the "solutions" that he brings to bear on them, we shall be able to study the conflicts present in *Light in August* itself, and thus to identify and analyze the bleakness that pervades it in spite of all that Lena's quiet cheerfulness can do and the energy that hums through its pages, holding the reader in thrall. While most of Faulkner's work ostensibly espouses "self-effacing" values, asking us to empathize with sensitive and/or helpless victims like Quentin Compson or Darl Bundren, and his public pronouncements on his work virtually always emphasize humanist themes such as the importance of love and of endurance in the face of trial, *Light in*

August is permeated with an aggressive attitude which resembles that of Joe himself.

2

Like Jason Compson's, Joe Christmas's adulthood is made up of attempts to achieve revenge against and mastery over those people and forces responsible for his mistreatment and frustration as a child. As Horney describes it, the arrogant-vindictive person's development

> started in childhood—with particularly bad human experiences and few, if any, redeeming factors. Sheer brutality, humiliations, derision, neglect, and flagrant hyprocrisy, all these assailed a child of especially great sensitivity. . . . He may make some pathetic and unsuccessful attempts to win sympathy, interest, or affection but finally chokes off all tender needs. He gradually "decides" that genuine affection is not only unattainable for him but that it does not exist at all. [*Neurosis and Human Growth*]

"Memory believes before knowing remembers," begins the chapter on Joe's childhood, indicating that Faulkner means to trace the unconscious legacy of the child to the man. And what a legacy it is. No child-victim of Victorian literature ever had a worse time of it than Joe. Imprisoned behind the bleak, soot-blackened walls of the orphanage, "small, still, round-headed, round-eyed," Joe grows to the age of reason without love, his only treat an occasional "pink work" of the dietitian's toothpaste. One older girl he likes "well enough to let her mother him a little," but she suddenly disappears (not t.b. or small pox, adoption). Like many another little victim he has someone assigned especially to hate him, Doc Hines, the racist lunatic who devotes his life to the destruction of the "abomination" that is Joe. In addition, he suffers the derision of his fellow inmates who, out of some natural but obscure evil impulse, since he does not then and never will look black at all, call him "nigger."

As the toothpaste episode unfolds, we see that Joe has very early (he is now five) come to see punishment and persecution as the central facts of his life. When the dietitian tries to bribe him instead of beating him, he becomes profoundly confused, and his mistrust of his fellow men increases. By the time he is adopted by the McEacherns he has taught himself not to expect anything good from life, in fact to defend himself from disappointment by hating, as Hyatt Waggoner says, "not *even* those who love him but *especially* those who love him" [*William Faulkner,* 1959]. He has learned to deny the very existence of the love that has been denied him, and seems not to hope for any positive results from the adoption. He does not reach out at all to McEachern during their long ride to his new home, sitting, a silent little bundle in the wagon, even more taciturn and unresponsive than McEachern himself. But it is Mrs. McEachern's welcome—the attempt to carry him to the house, the washing of his feet, the watching by his bedside—that is most wasted on him; he can only wait for "the part that would not be pleasant" to begin. Already he has taught himself not to believe in the genuineness of human affection, so her actions, the "trivial, clumsy, vain efforts," can only mystify and eventually disgust him.

His initial response to his foster mother is the first indication we have that Joe will make the transition from victim to victimizer typical of the arrogant-vindictive type. The real turning point occurs on a Sunday when the eight-year-old Joe is beaten and starved by his Calvinist foster father in an attempt to get him to learn his catechism. Unable to prevent the beatings, he accepts them without emotion, "with a rapt expression like a monk in a picture." He is calm because McEachern's treatment of him corresponds to his view that life consists of a series of punishments, and because by remaining "rapt" he can refuse McEachern mastery over him. After his inevitable collapse he awakens feeling "quite well," at peace, as if he has just made an important decision. Looking back on this day he thinks, "On this day I became a man," and it becomes apparent that at this moment, starved and aching from repeated beatings, he embarks on the search for vindictive triumph that will lead him to murder at least twice. Unable to revenge himself as yet on McEachern, he lashes out at his foster mother, violently rejecting her offer of love and comfort in the form of food by dumping the tray of secretly prepared dishes in the corner, only later, when it is just food and no longer a tangible symbol of the love in which he cannot believe, kneeling over it and eating, "like a savage, like a dog." The events of this day establish the pattern of Joe's life. He will for the rest of his days accept, and even seek out, punishment, taking his revenge where he can, and behaving with particular violence in response to offers of love or aid.

Once, however, taken off guard by the exigencies of adolescence, Joe displays the vulnerability to human feelings that his "solution" denies him. In his relationship with Bobbie Allen we find the lessons of his childhood confirmed, and the hardening process completed. Falling in love with a peculiarly stunted blonde waitress with oversized hands, Joe risks a partial abandonment of his drive for mastery and his need to deny and repress positive feelings, only to be taught again that there is not really any such thing as love. At first he is caught up in the mystery of Bobbie and of sexual love in general, but his belated discovery that Bobbie is a prostitute imported from Memphis (though, as the older blonde woman complains, in Joe's case she has brought "it" all the way down to Jefferson just to give it away) leads him to compensate for this vulnerability by aggressive behavior. Now he smokes and drinks and "in his loud drunken despairing young voice," calls Bobbie his whore.

It is in the midst of his sexual initiation into adulthood that Joe finds an opportunity for vindictive triumph. His murder, or attempted murder, of McEachern, and his brutal robbery of Mrs. McEachern free him from the role of victim and release him forever from the standards of behavior that govern mere mortals. On his way back to Bobbie, "The youth . . . rode lightly, balanced lightly,

leaning well forward, exulting perhaps at that moment as Faustus had, of having put behind now at once and for all the Shalt Not, of being free at last of honor and law." For the moment he is his idealized self, but, as his haste to return to Bobbie indicates, he is not yet completely hardened.

Bobbie takes care of that. In the scene that follows Joe's heroic journey to her house with Mrs. McEachern's egg money, Bobbie provides Joe with the experience that finally "choke[s] off all tender needs," and leads him to behave for the rest of his life as if "genuine affection is not only unattainable for him but . . . does not exist at all." Her feelings presumably wounded by McEachern's rather polite reference to her as a "harlot," Bobbie has exchanged her usual cowlike demeanor for that of a cornered rat. Her rejection of Joe's offer of matrimony is ugly and vicious: "'He told me himself he was a nigger! The son of a bitch! Me f—ing for nothin a nigger son of a bitch that would get me in a jam with clodhopper police. At a clodhopper dance!'" No, Bobbie does not want to get married, and Joe's last attempt to win affection is rewarded by several cruel blows to the face. Now, with the taste of bitter rejection mingling on his tongue with the flavor of vindictive triumph, Joe embarks on his adult journey, "the street which was to run for fifteen years," and then for three more before Percy Grimm's knife and gun bring it to a close. During these years he systematically denies his connection to men of any race, and searches out opportunities for reenacting the punishment and revenge pattern established in his childhood.

We get our closest look at the adult Christmas during the three years that the spends in Jefferson before the murder of Joanna Burden. During this time he exhibits virtually every personal quality ascribed by Horney to the arrogant-vindictive type: arrogance, envy, the need to frustrate others, the inability to feel sympathy, the inability to ask for or receive aid graciously, the tendency toward uncontrollable rage. His need to keep others at bay, or, when he has the chance, to make them the recipients of his contempt, to triumph over them with tongue or fist, governs his every action. He manages to repress thoroughly all self-effacing or loving tendencies, thus avoiding the intense self-hate that would accompany any violation of his solution.

Appearing on the Jefferson scene, Joe is "sullen and quiet and fatal as a snake." The men at the mill know him by his "darkly contemptuous expression," and the "silent and unflagging savageness" with which he shovels sawdust. These are apparently enough to keep them at bay, but with the arrival of Brown, made of denser stuff, Joe resorts to blows, curses, and murder threats.

But it is in the portrait of Joe's most "intimate" relationship that Faulkner shows most vividly the emotional paralysis and the compulsive need to deny others warmth that are the inevitable adjunct to the search for vindictive triumph. Joe first encounters Joanna Burden when she finds him standing in her kitchen, surreptitiously eating the food that he could have had for the asking. At first, their relationship is based on her supplying him with the food and shelter that he needs but will not ask for. It is not much of a connection, but it is enough to make Joe uncomfortable, especially when he realizes one day, "liplifted," that she has put herself above him by not inviting him into the "house proper." He revenges himself by raping her, unfeminine and unattractive as she is, but his triumph is rendered incomplete by her failure to disintegrate at his touch. Her surrender is "hard, untearful and unpitying and almost manlike," and thus he is compelled to try again. This time he approaches her "in a quiet rage," determined to "show the bitch," but he meets neither enthusiasm nor resistance, and so is, again, denied the triumph that would allow him to leave her alone. "It was as though some enemy upon whom he had wreaked his utmost violence and contumely stood, unscathed and unscarred, and contemplated him with a musing and insufferable contempt." Eventually he rids himself of this sense of her contempt in a scene reminiscent of Catechism Sunday. As he sniffs and audibly identifies each dish of food that has been left for him before he sends it crashing into the kitchen wall, he feels an exhilarating sense of vindictive triumph. It is no accident that this is one of the few times in the novel that Joe really seems to come alive, to do more than cast a baleful shadow on the page. These are the moments for which the arrogant-vindictive type lives: the moments that deny his dependency on others and establish his ascendancy over them, the glittering prizes that inspire his search for glory.

Now that he has caught on to the way to establish his ascendancy over Joanna, Joe can stay on at her place and wait for her complete surrender, a surrender that comes in the form of a grotesque middle-aged sexual awakening: "In this way the second phase began. It was as though he had fallen into a sewer." The words "fallen" and "sewer" are important here. What happens to Joe in his relationship with Joanna is that her "surrender" threatens to confine him. In the "sewer" of her sexuality he might be trapped, and as Horney observes [in *Neurosis and Human Growth*], "all human ties . . . are felt as restraints on the path to a sinister glory" by the arrogant-vindictive type. Joe is wary, and tries to preserve his distance by having no daytime contact with Joanna at all, scarcely, indeed, exchanging any words with her at any time except for the obscenities that she perversely demands. And he is able to resume his progress down the path toward aggressive triumph when, following Faulkner's rather bizarre notion of female sexuality, Joanna abruptly becomes asexual at the onset of menopause, and insists on praying over Joe and trying to reform him. Now she is vulnerable because she is asking for something that he is adept at denying, expressing a need that he is indeed compelled to frustrate, just as he was compelled to frustrate Mrs. McEachern's need for affection. Again the "need for triumph and the need to deny positive feelings" [*Neurosis*] come into play at the same time. Now Joe can taste his triumph over Joanna, thinking, "There is something I am going to do." Now he can deny her any feel-

ings of love or respect, "his lip lifted into the shape of a soundless and rigid snarl," saying, "'You just got old and it happened to you and now you are not any good any more.'"

He hates her now "with a fierce revulsion of dread and impotent rage" for threatening his solution by caring for him. His rage, maybe not really so impotent, leads him to tote his razor up her stairs and slit her throat so thoroughly that the country man who finds her body will be afraid to pick it up for fear that her head will stay behind. The intensity of his rage is partly a response to her determination to deny him mastery, but it is primarily his reply to her attempts to be a loving mother to him. *"All I wanted was peace,"* he thinks, "'She ought not to started praying over me.'" By praying over Joe, Joanna, like Mrs. McEachern before her, violates Joe's "peace," threatening his vindictive solution by implying that the world is not entirely hostile, and reviving suppressed conflicts between his hated and repressed self-effacing shoulds and his need for vindictive triumph. Like any other human being, Joe has a deep-seated need to give and receive love, but if he recognized this aspect of himself at this point in his life, it would lead to the disintegration of his neurotic personality—the "solution" that allows him to function (albeit on a pitifully restricted level) without the agony of inner conflict. His fear of such conflict is reflected in the intensity of his rage, an intensity that eventually makes murder inevitable.

In examining Joe's relationship with Joanna we have seen all of the elements of his disturbed personality revealed. But his neurosis is not confined to one relationship—all of his contacts with the people of Jefferson reflect his compulsive need to move against others. To begin with, there is his consistently arrogant and rude demeanor. This is the result of his need to externalize the self-hate that is the inevitable concomitant of the gap between his actual self (a two-bit drifter) and his idealized self (the young Faustus above honor and law). It also serves his needs to deny positive feelings, to reject the self-effacing strategies that his childhood taught him were ineffective, and his need to intimidate others into allowing him the vindictive triumph that is his only source of satisfaction. All who come in contact with him—the McEacherns, the mill workers, "Joe Brown"—are treated with the same distancing coldness and contempt. He establishes around himself an impenetrable aura of sullenness.

Then there is his tendency to respond violently to the friendly gesture, his inability to ask for or receive help graciously, because to do so would be to admit a failure of mastery and to recognize the existence of the humane values that he must deny in order to protect his neurosis. This is especially evident in his response to proferred food. We have seen what he does with Joanna's and Mrs. McEachern's carefully prepared meals, and when Byron Bunch offers his lunch pail, Joe's response is again violently negative. "I ain't hungry,'" he says, "'Keep your muck.'" This tendency also extends to money. He is careful to remind Mrs. McEachern as he steals her little hoard that he has not accepted it as a gift: "'I didn't ask, because I was afraid you would give it to me. I just took it. Dont forget that.'" It is important to note that this inability to take from others is compulsive, and not a healthy desire to "live on the terms of his own self-definition," as John Lewis Longley, Jr., describes it [in *The Tragic Mask: A Study of Faulkner's Heroes,* 1963]. Joe does not merely refuse aid, he responds with fury, with physical or verbal violence when it is offered. He does so because of a need to reassert the false feeling of superiority that is threatened when people behave as if they think he needs help, and because such offers of aid remind him of the despised and repressed part of himself that would depend on others for love, approval, or aid.

Joe's relationship with Joanna also brings into clear perspective another pattern of dealing with others typical of the arrogant-vindictive personality. As we have seen, his most common stance is that of a highly controlled sullenness. But in opposition to this guardedness we find a tendency toward violent and uncontrollable rage. The vindictive type, though he may be very unpleasant indeed, ordinarily does not express much of the hostility that he feels (this would be too dangerous). But on occasion his compulsions overwhelm him, and he feels rage as something impinging on him from outside, something over which he has no control, something which frightens even him. These occasions arise when there is a clear threat to his idealized image, when his mastery or his freedom from positive feelings is threatened. When Brown laughs at him and calls him "nigger," Joe comes close to killing him, seeing his actions as out of control, as coming from another source: *Something is going to happen to me. I am going to do something.* When he goes for a walk in Freedman Town and encounters some blacks talking and laughing, he almost cuts a man with his razor: "'What in hell is the matter with me?'" he wonders. Then, *Something is going to happen to me.* As they are throughout the book, blacks here are a reminder to Joe of his despised actual self, the self that he is afraid might be black, and thus, in his mind, inferior. As we have seen, Joe's murder of Joanna is also the result of vindictive rage, a rage so far out of control that he begins to think of the murder as past before it has even happened: "'Maybe I have already done it,'" he thinks. "'Maybe it is no longer now waiting to be done.'" Again we must note a flaw in Longley's argument that Joe is an existential hero. His acts of violence are not evidence of rebellion against a controlling society. They are evidence of a profound loss of choice emanating from an irrational rage at those who threatened his identification with his ideal self.

Faulkner's portrayal of Joe Christmas builds to a climax in the description of his relationship with Joanna, but the events following the murder are also of importance to our understanding of his character and its significance. Once "something" has indeed happened, and Joanna's throat is slit, Joe's revenge for the damage done him in childhood is almost, but not quite, complete. He has destroyed the punishing man (McEachern) and the confining women

(Joanna and Mrs. McEachern), but one more threat remains. He still has to triumph over the spectre of his weakness and inferiority, the "actual self" that he has come to associate with blacks. To this end, he bursts in upon a black church, cursing God, slapping the minister, knocking a seventy-year-old man "clean down into the mourner's pew," fracturing the skull of that man's six-foot grandson with a bench leg. "'I'll cut a notch in it tomorrow,'" he thinks and, close to laughter for the second time in the novel, says, "'Have a butt, boys,'" as he flicks his cigarette into the bushes where the mystified and frightened black men wait. The next time we see Joe it is at dawn, and he is feeling a sense of peace and exhilaration, the rewards of complete vindictive triumph. His dragons slain, Joe need fight no longer.

Joe's passive surrender to the law, and then to the gun and knife of Percy Grimm, may seem to be grossly inconsistent with his character as I have described it, but in fact his martyrdom is readily explicable in Horneyan terms. Every arrogant-vindictive type, as I have mentioned, harbors powerful self-effacing trends. They are part of the actual self that he is compelled to despise. They threaten him with helplessness, and they cast doubt on the "truth" of his solution, but they remain to tempt him with a means of obtaining the affection and acceptance that he was first denied and has since denied himself. Drawing on her psychoanalytic experience, Horney describes the frequent reaction of a patient whose vindictive trends are brought to light by analysis: "a period ensues when he feels altogether contemptible and helpless and tends to prostrate himself for the sake of being loved" [*Neurosis*]. This extreme response is, in a sense, paralleled by Joe's response to the fulfillment of his vindictive desires. Once he has succeeded in slaying all of his demons—the confining women, the threat of negritude, the spectre of his helplessness in a hostile world—Joe has carried his aggressive solution to its logical conclusion. He has achieved a palpable vindictive triumph, and like Horney's patients who suddenly turn against their own solutions, he now feels compelled to allow his submerged needs for love and approval to surface. The self-effacing shoulds that he has so brutally repressed and violated are now the source of a guilt that must be expiated. That Joe that we see shaving and combing his hair, preparing himself, the town says, like a bridegroom, for death, is a Joe who has satisfied his compulsion to make others suffer, and has been overcome by that hitherto submerged part of his personality that wishes suffering on itself and cannot allow itself to fight back. As we shall see, this sudden emergence of Joe's self-effacing trends is part of his creator's plan to elicit our sympathy for and identification with Joe, but first let us understand the psychological implications of his surrender.

The suffering that Joe undergoes during his "passion" and death is, it is clear, very real suffering indeed. Nevertheless, in the context of Faulkner's characterization, it is "neurotic" or "functional" suffering in that Joe seeks it out deliberately, and uses it with the apparent object of "dying on the doorstep" of the world that has abused him for so long. Functional suffering, a prominent aspect of self-effacing neurosis, has as its purpose the accusing of others and the excusing of oneself [*Neurosis*], and Joe's sudden switch from murderer to passive victim can be understood as a product of his need to do just that. He is reacting to the fulfillment of his drive for vindication in the same way that Horney's patients react to the vision of their own vindictiveness: by switching the emphasis onto himself as needy victim and sufferer in order to mollify those self-effacing shoulds that he has repressed for his entire adult life but never eradicated. Captured in Mottstown, Joe allows Halliday to hit him in the face, "acting like a nigger" (i.e., prostrating himself) for the first time, according to the town. He escapes, apparently only in order to increase his suffering, to hurry his martyrdom, and does not defend himself against Grimm even though he is carrying a loaded pistol. Faulkner describes his castration and death in a remarkable passage:

> For a long moment he looked up at them with peaceful and unfathomable and unbearable eyes. Then his face, body, all, seemed to collapse, to fall in upon itself, and from out the slashed garments about his hips and loins the pent black blood seemed to rush like a released breath. It seemed to rush out of his pale body like the rush of sparks from a rising rocket; upon that black blast the man seemed to rise soaring into their memories forever and ever. They are not to lose it, in whatever peaceful valleys, beside whatever placid and reassuring streams of old age, in the mirroring faces of whatever children they will contemplate old disasters and newer hopes. It will be there, musing, quiet, steadfast, not fading and not particularly threatful, but of itself alone serene, of itself alone triumphant.

Once again we are witness to the successful completion of the search for glory, but this time the reward is the crowning glory of martyrdom rather than vindictive triumph. This glory is bought with suffering rather than mastery, and it is shown to be a thing greatly to be desired. Those who have neglected and persecuted Joe, who have denied him love and understanding, are now never to lose the memory of his suffering, the image of his martyred face.

3

Thus far my analysis has been restricted to making psychological sense of Faulkner's portrait of Joe Christmas. It would appear that his character is psychologically explicable as that of a man whose horrendous childhood has caused him to behave in rigidly prescribed patterns—first as avenging angel, then as suffering martyr—patterns responsive not to objective reality, but to his unrealistic vision of his idealized self. But we are left with some questions. We have evaluated Joe's motives and behavior from an objective standpoint, but we have not evaluated them in the context of *Light in August* as a whole. How is the reader to view Joe's troubled life and ultimate martyrdom? With admiration, or sympathy, or with the amiable condescension of the sociologist? And what of the other characters in the novel, particularly what of Lena Grove and Byron Bunch? How does their story of birth and love and ongoing life relate to Joe's story of death and death-in-life? In other words, what does the guiding consciousness of *Light in August* want us to think about the characters and events of the novel?

As we shall see, this question is not easily answered. An analysis of the subtle rhetoric of *Light in August* reveals that the author that it implies is, like Joe Christmas, a being in conflict. Like the Joe we have observed, he is ultimately torn between a need to deny positive feelings and pursue triumph over the weak, and a need to compensate for this aggressive activity. In fact, we can find much rhetorical evidence for the theory that Joe's creator identifies with him and with his world view. *Light in August* is primarily an aggressive novel that seeks to compensate for its tendency to "move against" humanity by martyring its aggressive protagonist, and by making various mostly halfhearted and unsuccessful attempts to affirm the value of life and love.

We can begin our analysis of the implied author and his intentions by examining his relationship to his protagonist. As we have seen, he has painted in Joe a portrait of a very disturbed man. But instead of always seeing Joe for what he is, he seems at times to see him for what he would be, to mistake his idealized for his actual self, and particularly to overemphasize his role as victim and martyr as a way of excusing his aggression. As we shall see, this treatment of Joe is reflected in the thematic structure of *Light in August* as a whole.

Though it is quite rare in Faulkner's major works to encounter lines or descriptions that do not ring true to the characterizations of which they are a part, this does happen, it seems to me, in the case of Joe Christmas. Occasionally he is given a line to speak that strikes a false note in relation to the rest of his characterization. These lines seem designed to ask our participation in his irrational sense of injury, to encourage us to identify with him, and to prepare us to accept his "apotheosis" at the end.

For example, there is Joe's plaintive reaction to Bobbie's rejection of his proposal of marriage: *"Why, I committed murder for her. I even stole for her."* As Waggoner points out, the effect of this passage is sentimental because Faulkner seems to ask us to accept this assessment of the situation, to pity Joe for being betrayed, when, in fact, what he says is a lie. Joe killed McEachern, gleefully, for revenge, and he stole from Mrs. McEachern, not to get the money for Bobbie, because he could have had it for the asking, but to demonstrate his complete rejection of his foster mother and her way of being. But putting this unlikely line in Joe's mouth (his motives seem clear enough to him moments before), Joe's creator is asking us to play down Joe's victimization of others.

A similar situation occurs when Faulkner has Joe ask Joanna, after hearing the story of her ancestors, "'Just when do men that have different blood in them stop hating one another?'" Hitherto Joe's only contribution to brotherly love between the races has been to hate whites for being white and blacks for being black. And the Joe Christmas that Faulkner shows us would never have said those words—self-pity and humanism are most definitely not his style. Here, as in the jarring passage that describes Joe as being "sick for two years" after sleeping with an unsegregated prostitute, his creator is asking us to give more weight to Joe's distress over his racial ambiguity than it will bear. He does so, I think, in order to increase our sympathy for and involvement in Joe's plight.

This sentimentalization of Joe's role as victim culminates in his final martyrdom. As we have seen, Joe's "conversion" itself is psychologically explicable. He is driven from one neurotic solution to another by an overwhelming sense of guilt that is brought on by repeated and flagrant violations of his deeply buried but still active self-effacing trends. But in attempting to discover what the author of *Light in August* wants us to think of all this, we find that he seems to share in Joe's desires to accuse others and excuse himself through suffering, that he too sees Joe's life as justified by his end, that, in fact, he sometimes sees Joe as his idealized self, as a god.

There is much discussion among critics as to whether the parallels between Joe and Jesus Christ are meant to be ironic or not. It seems clear to me that they are not. The language used to describe Joe's death, the idiotic cruelty of Percy Grimm, the ugliness of the lynch mob, the sympathy due Mrs. Hines, the dignity of Joe: these are just a few of the things that encourage our positive identification of Joe with Jesus. The religious imagery surrounding Joe's death has been heavily documented. There are angels and halos; there are "slashed garments," and a wound to the body. The language used to describe Joe's death makes it obvious that he is to be identified with the Jesus who ascended into heaven to sit at the right hand of His Father. When, on the geyser of "pent black blood" from his loins, Joe seems to "rise soaring into [the] memories forever and ever" of the men who are watching him; when his face is immortalized, "of itself alone serene, of itself alone triumphant," it becomes clear that his death is meant by his creator to justify all that has gone before, in fact, to accuse others and excuse Joe. Like that of Jesus, Joe's martyrdom is seen as willed and redemptive. The compulsions shown to have been set in motion by his childhood are now forgotten as he soars into our memories, purified and glorified by his suffering. Critics have found this apotheosis difficult to account for, and no wonder. As our psychological analysis of Joe's character allows us to see, it is possible for a man like Joe to feel driven to martyrdom, but highly unlikely that he should achieve such glorious results (based on fantasy, like all other manifestations of the neurotic search for glory, such attempts at martyrdom are unlikely to buy one the kind of eternal life granted to Joe). Joe's soaring departure is made possible not by the realities of his characterization, but by the tendency of Joe's creator to mistake Joe's idealized self for reality, and to manipulate his fictional world to honor Joe's neurotic bargains with fate.

The emphasis on Joe's role as victim and martyr is evidence of the partial identification of Joe's creator with his creation, an identification the reader is invited to share. Though the implied author of *Light in August* never addresses the reader directly, an analysis of some of the patterns of imagery in the novel and of the treatment of some of the characters other than Joe will reveal that the novel often asks the reader to participate in the same denial of "weakness" and search for "triumph" that govern Joe's life until the bench leg comes in contact with Roz Thompson's head.

It has often been pointed out that for Faulkner women represent that aspect of humanity which is most basically human: physical as opposed to intellectual, realistic as opposed to idealistic, enduring as opposed to vengeful, accepting as opposed to aggressive. In Horneyan terms, women in his novels are ordinarily seen as superior to men because they tend to embody the self-effacing values espoused by his humanist themes. But if we look closely at the treatment of women in *Light in August,* we find that instead of representing the "weaker" (that is to say more human, more accepting, less aggressive) aspects of humanity in a positive sense, they are presented as by and large the objects of squeamishness and contempt. Their physical selves, accepting and giving rather than moving against, are either malfunctioning or nauseating; their attempts to love or to be kind are generally awkward, ridiculous, and unsuccessful. In other words, the novel as a whole tends to share Joe Christmas's perspective on women rather than the perspective of the public Faulkner. In the novel, as in Joe's mind, they are associated with "muck," this four letter word referring not only to their association with food but to their sexuality and to their tendency to try to make positive human connections.

Here is what happens to you if you are a female character in *Light in August.* If you are past menopause you are asexual; you are ugly; you dress funny; you wear your hair in an unattractive "tight screw" at the back of your head, and your gestures of kindness or affection are "savage," "clumsy," even ridiculous. If you are young and do not have sex then you look "frozen and skinny," are driven to run off to Memphis where you can get what you need, have a nervous breakdown in church, and finally feel so guilty that you jump out a hotel window. If you are young and do have sex then maybe you are the "prone and abject" recipient of organized fourteen-year-old lust, or maybe you are unnaturally short and have great big hands "dead and pale as a piece of cooking meat," the outer signs of your "inner corruption of the spirit." Or maybe you are a "pinksmelling" wild-eyed young woman willing to destroy a child's life to keep your activities secret. Or just maybe you can give off the air of an unravished bride of quietness even while eight months pregnant and demonstrate your "courage and endurance" by pursuing across three states a man who does not want you and would not be worth catching even if your "slow time" did not make it seem highly improbable that you would do any such thing. But if you are a middle-aged woman who has sex, then you are in real trouble, because while a man's "sin" can be "healthy and normal," making love with you is like falling into a sewer. You will try to draw a man into the "black thick pool" of your sexuality. You will be afflicted with that ghastliest of infirmities, nymphomania, and will cast yourself about in wild poses and shout obscenities. You too look funny in your clothes, but underneath is a "rotten richness ready to flow into putrefaction at a touch." Eventually you will reach menopause and make a fool of yourself by suddenly thinking you are pregnant. Then you will lose all interest in sex and absurdly transfer your energies to a scheme to send your ignorant millhand lover to law school, that is before you go completely nuts and try to shoot him with an old pistol that does not work. Then you will get your throat slit and look funny lying on the ground for all the world to see with your head turned around completely backwards (if you'd been able to do that before, they say, maybe you wouldn't be doing it now). As Albert J. Guerard points out [in *The Triumph of the Novel: Dickens, Dostoevsky, Faulkner,* 1972], "The misogynous imagination selects for its female victims appalling situations and punishments." These things do not happen to Joanna Burden by chance. They happen to her because her creator manipulates her world to make her appear ridiculous and contemptible. It would seem that the guiding consciousness of *Light in August,* far from setting himself to admire the "courage and endurance" of women, wishes to reject or deny or ridicule the messy humanity that they represent. Their sexuality in particular is shown to be the source of corruption, ugliness, stupidity, mean-spirited behavior, and bad smells.

To a lesser extent the blacks of the novel are also the objects of this compulsive rejection of all that is "weak" or "inferior" in humanity. It has not gone unnoticed that there are some blatantly racist descriptions in the novel, such as that which refers to the "vacuous idiocy" of "idle and illiterate" Negro nursemaids, or the "fumbling and timeless Negro fashion" of a black expectant father. But there is also a consistent pattern of imagery that places blacks in the messily human, and thus despicable, category of women; their alleged inferiority and tendency to connect with others (they seem to crowd together and are over and over again described as "fecund") qualifying them to be the recipients of the implied author's contempt. Like women, blacks are associated with smells and unpleasant enclosure. Freedman Town is like "the bottom of a thick black pit." This echo of the description of Joanna's sexuality is no accident; a walk here is like a return to "the lightless hot wet primogenitive Female" and, as we have seen, that is like a stroll through the sewer. Joe can hardly breathe lying next to his ebony carving of a common-law wife, and blacks are smelled before they are seen. The air around whites is "cold and hard," and, if they are male, presumably odor-free.

Just as Faulkner's public statements ask us to see *Light in August* as a celebration of womanhood, however, some elements of the novel ask us to see it as a sympathetic tract on the race question. The novel seems at times to ask the question so improbably attributed to Joe, "'Just when do men that have different blood in them stop hating one another?'" As we have seen, Faulkner's portrayal of Joe asks for our sympathy for the outsider, the "nigger," the victim of the lynch mob, the man unjustly hated because of the "curse" of his alleged black blood. But at the same time we are subtly asked to despise all those who do not pursue mastery and deny positive feelings, and thus the black race, condemned to an inferior position and prone to close associations, is seen as fumbling, stupid, and smelly.

A look at the positive imagery associated with aggression in the novel confirms our theory that it tends to encourage aggressive fantasy. When Samuel A. Yorks points out that in the world of *Light in August* it seems "better to be castrated than seduced" ["Faulkner's Women; The Peril of Mankind," *Arizona Quarterly,* No. 17, 1961], he is obliquely referring to the way the novel continually contrasts the admirably "clean" tendency to move against people or things, or to separate oneself from them, as opposed to the "messy" tendency to move toward them, to make physical or emotional connections.

When Joe violently removes his undergarment in a bizarre "streaking" episode, his right hand slides "fast and smooth," striking the remaining button a "light, swift blow." Then the dark air breathes "smoothly" around his male nakedness: it is "soft" and "cool." This is his answer to the "thick still black pool of more than water" that is the image for Joanna's frantic attempts to move toward him. This same contrast of phallic with womb-sewer imagery is encountered in the description of Joe's trip through the black section of town. Here Joe is the "lone telephone pole," connoting something "clean, hard, and dry," as Yorks points out, while, as we have seen, the black area where people are gathered closely together, presumably in the process of being "fecund," is like the womb, "lightless, hot, wet," like "the bottom of a thick black pit." The contrast also appears in the description of Joe's response to Bobbie's explanation of menstruation. Nauseated, he runs to the woods where he takes brief solace in the "hard trunks" of the trees, "branch shadowed, quiet, hardfeeling, hardsmelling, invisible," and then seems to see a row of misshapen urns (the shape of the womb, the functions of which are to give and receive rather than move against): "Each one was cracked and from each crack there issued something liquid, deathcolored, and foul." Naturally, Joe vomits. But then he buys a nice new rope with which to escape from the house at night, and the next time he sees Bobbie manfully hauls her off to the woods with no preliminaries.

In the description of Joe's childhood the imagery used in connection with McEachern and his cruelty towards Joe tends to be more positive than that connected with Mrs.

McEachern's ineffective attempts to move toward him. Mr. McEachern is frequently described by terms like "hard" and "vigorous." He is "rocklike," indomitable. He smells of the "clean hard virile living leather" with which he beats Joe coolly, without heat or anger. Mrs. McEachern, on the other hand, is a "stiff caricature" when she reaches out her hand to Joe. She is "shapeless, a little hunched." She hovers, she fumbles, and she huddles, like some unattractive little bird. This imagery is not wasted on Longley, who refers to her "sickening attempts to make [Joe] as cringing as herself." It is Joe, of course, who accepts and models himself after his foster father and despises his foster mother because he cannot understand or believe in love, but the novel seems to lend some support to his choice.

Even in Percy Grimm's final pursuit of Joe we see that the imagery gives a positive connotation to aggression and a negative connotation to its opposite. Grimm's face is "rocklike," "bright." It has "that serene, unearthly luminousness of angels in church windows." The rest of the community, on the other hand, huddled together, look at "his tense hard young face," their own faces "blanched and gaped with round, toothed orifices." And Hightower, who frantically and ineffectively tries to give Joe aid, has "[a] bald head and [a] big pale face."

Light in August presents a world where the warm gesture, the act of giving or physical union, and the source of life itself are seen as unbeautiful, awkward, even "foul," while the tendency to move against others, or at least to maintain a "clean" and "hard" separateness, is invested over and over again with a certain beauty. Like Joe Christmas, the consciousness that has created this world seems to have a compulsive need to deny the reality and efficacy of human bonds, and to indulge in pleasurable fantasies of triumph and separation. The novel also presents a world where human physical and emotional ties are warmly, if a bit condescendingly, accepted, but though this seems designed to compensate for the strain of aggression that we have been observing, it is undercut in various ways and does not do so effectively.

I am not the first to notice that the thematic impact of Byron and Lena is reduced by their creator's tendency to make light of their crises and motivations, to place himself and the reader at a distance from them for the sake of comic effect. Though Lena, for example, seems to be presented as an important thematic force when she draws Hightower into life through the birth of her baby, this impression is undercut when we see her reduced to a comic figure (in the Bergsonian as well as the conventional sense) as she mechanically resumes her pursuit of Lucas after he jumps out the window. "'Now I got to get up again,'" she says out loud to herself. And in the scenes that portray a Lena who could not resist the callow Burch rejecting the advances of Byron, her devoted protector, it is obvious that the implied author is more concerned with humor than with theme. The humor is very good, and Lord knows it is welcome, but it has a rather negative effect on Lena's status as a redeemer. The qualities that she represents—loyalty, endurance, an accepting spirit— are a little hard to take seriously. Her loyalty is misplaced, her endurance seems to be the result of a one-track mind, and her accepting spirit begins to seem primarily comic and mechanical, as she continues to ignore the negative aspects of her situation and extol the virtues of traveling. There is much to be said for Lena's enjoyment of her situation, and much to be appreciated in her characterization, but there is also in the novel at least a partial denial of the positive feelings that she represents, a denial which coincides with the strain of aggression that we have been tracing. Her creator is obviously smitten with her, but he demonstrates a certain contempt for her as well. Her femininity and fertility are the source of jokes, and her treatment of Byron puts her in a category with other women of loose morals and bad taste in men.

The strain of aggression is even more clearly at work in the novel's treatment of Byron Bunch. The original description of Byron is flavored with sentimentality. He works six days a week, not for money or pleasure, but because working is somehow the thing to do, and because it keeps him out of "trouble." On the seventh day, not content to go to the local church of his choice, or even to ride two hours to a different one like McEachern, he rides *all night* Saturday and *all night* Sunday in order to lead the choir at an *all day* country church service, only to be on hand with "clean overalls and shirt" when the mill whistle blows Monday morning. He eschews "meanness" to the extent that he does not even know who the local moonshiner is, and his only friend is an ex-minister who is neglected and persecuted by the rest of the town. He stumbles on this man's doorstep every time he goes to visit him until, transformed by love and a newly found decision-making ability, he is able on one occasion to stride right in. This portrait is sentimental because it is based on exaggeration and cliche. Unlike the Faulkner of *Snopes* who was able to create in V. K. Ratliff a "good" man of many dimensions, a character who gets right up and walks off the page, the implied author of *Light in August* seems only able to define a healthy lack of aggression in a character by relying on stereotype.

As Slatoff points out [in *Quest For Failure: A Study of Faulkner,* 1960], Faulkner allows Byron a brief gain in stature (as he arranges for Lena's lying-in and defies the Mrs. Grundies of Jefferson, he stands up straight and has a "new air born somewhere between assurance and defiance"). But in the final chapter he is greatly reduced. The furniture dealer, rather a wonderful narrator, describes Byron as "the kind of fellow you wouldn't see at first glance if he was alone by himself in the bottom of a empty concrete swimming pool," and says it is impossible to imagine "any woman knowing that they had ever slept with him, let alone having anything to show folks to prove it." He "trots" into the store and, over-eager, comes out with so many bags that, little as he is, he can hardly see over them. He is a "durn little cuss" about to "burst out crying" because of sexual frustration. He is not only rejected by Lena, but is hoisted out of the truck by her as if he were a six year old. I submit that in these scenes Byron's creator has castrated him just about as effectively as Percy Grimm castrates Joe Christmas. His thematic role as a man who accepts and involves himself in humanity is seriously undercut. He becomes first and foremost a "little" man, cute and amusing, but eunuchlike and ineffective.

We have seen that the desire for aggressive triumph and the need to deny positive feelings play important roles in the guiding consciousness of *Light in August.* But we have also seen that the canonization of the aggressive protagonist (with whom the implied author seems to identify) is bought with his suffering, with his ultimate assumption of the role of passive victim. And we have seen that various attempts (mostly half-hearted or unsuccessful) are made throughout the novel to portray the importance of positive feelings. What can we hypothesize about the implied author in relation to these conflicting aspects of the novel?

It seems to me that the occasional attempts to espouse nonaggressive values in *Light in August* are meant to serve the same purpose for the novel as a whole as Joe's "passion" and death serve in relation to his character. By showing Joe's assumption of a self-effacing value system at the end, and by closing the book with Hightower's conversion and the coziness of the furniture dealer's narration, the implied author is attempting to compensate for the intense aggressiveness of the novel. Guerard attributes much of the appeal of Faulkner's work to "highly liberated fantasy." It is my view that the central fact about *Light in August,* its source of appeal, the quality that makes it fairly hum with forbidden energy, is its "highly liberated" use of aggressive fantasy. Joe may be made to wonder why the blacks in the cabin are "of their brother afraid;" Hightower may come to see that he was wrong to neglect his wife; Mrs. Armstid may demonstrate the fundamental generosity of her kind by giving away her egg money; but these moments do not define the essence of *Light in August.* It would be more accurate to say that they seek to compensate for it. The essence of the novel is found in the disturbing and vicious chapters on Joe's affair with Joanna Burden, in the portrayal of his stand-off with McEachern and his cruel treatment of Mrs. McEachern, in Doc Hines's excruciating narration of his attempts to destroy "God's abomination," in the image of the bloody butcher knife in Percy Grimm's hand. These passages, permeated with a consciousness that is drawn again and again to the aggressive vision, appeal not to our reason, our social conscience, or our admiration for Nobel-Prize-speech sentiment, but to our less wholesome impulses.

FURTHER READING

Biography

Quinn, Susan. *A Mind of Her Own: The Life of Karen Horney.* New York: Addison-Wesley, 1988, 479 p.
  Overview of Horney's life and career, with particular emphasis on her role in various debates and controversies within the psychoanalytic community.

Rubins, Jack L. *Karen Horney: Gentle Rebel of Psychoanalysis.* New York: The Dial Press, 1978, 362 p.
  Examines Horney's life and career.

Criticism

The American Journal of Psychoanalysis: Special Issue on Interdisciplinary Applications of Horney 49, No. 3 (September 1989): 181-341.
  Includes several essays that investigate the works of such authors as Mary Shelley, Doris Lessing, and William Shakespeare in light of Horney's psychoanalytic theories.

The American Journal of Psychoanalysis 51, No. 3 (September 1991): 191-291.
  Special issue devoted to Horney's life and work, including reminiscences by friends and colleagues, letters to Horney, comparative and interdisciplinary studies relating to Horney's psychoanalytic theories, retrospectives of her accomplishments in the field of psychoanalysis, and a bibliography.

Burgum, Mildred. Review of *Our Inner Conflicts: A Constructive Theory of Neurosis,* by Karen Horney. *Science and Society* X (1946): 96-102.
  Discussed with Wilhelm Reich's *Character-Analysis* (1945), lauds Horney's theories and methods but suggests that she does not fully address the ways in which "social, economic and cultural factors combine with the biological and the personal to form the life conditions under which specific personalities develop."

Kelman, Harold, M. D. *Helping People: Karen Horney's Psychoanalytic Approach.* New York: Science House, 1971, 621 p.
  Analysis of numerous case studies using Horney's psychoanalytic theories.

———, ed. *New Perspectives in Psychoanalysis: Contributions to Karen Horney's Holistic Approach.* New York: W. W. Norton and Company, 1965, 249 p.
  Includes essays on various aspects of Horney's clinical psychoanalytic methods. This volume also includes Horney's essay "The Value of Vindictiveness."

Paris, Bernard J., ed. *Third Force Psychology and the Study of Literature.* Cranbury, N.J.: Associated University Presses, 1986, 338 p.
  Compilation of essays that apply the psychoanalytic theories of Horney, Abraham Maslow, and other "humanistic psychologists" to the study of various literary works.

Rubins, Jack L., M. D. "Karen Horney." In *Comprehensive Textbook of Psychiatry,* edited by Alfred M. Freedman and Harold I. Kaplan, pp. 327-38. Baltimore: The Williams and Wilkins Company, 1967.

  Detailed introduction to the main tenets of Horney's psychoanalytic theory, "as it is elaborated in her last published volume, *Neurosis and Human Growth.*"

Sayers, Janet. "Karen Horney." In *Mothers of Psychoanalysis: Helene Deutsch, Karen Horney, Anna Freud, Melanie Klein,* pp. 85-140. New York: W. W. Norton and Company, 1991.

  Overview of Horney's life and works.

Additional coverage of Horney's life and career is contained in the following source published by Gale Research: *Contemporary Authors*, Vol. 114.

Will Rogers

1879-1935

(Full name William Penn Adair Rogers) American humorist and journalist.

For additional discussion of Rogers's life and career, see *TCLC,* Volume 8.

INTRODUCTION

Rogers was an American "cracker-barrel philosopher" and one of the most celebrated and beloved public figures of his day. Like his predecessor Artemus Ward, and to a certain degree Mark Twain, he offered dry, whimsical commentaries on numerous political, social, and economic issues. Rogers's aphoristic, satirical observations, which he voiced in magazine articles and nationally syndicated newspaper columns, revealed the foibles and injustices of society and earned him the role of the voice of the "average" American.

Biographical Information

Born in Claremore, Oklahoma, into a wealthy ranching family, Rogers, who was one-quarter Cherokee Indian, never graduated from high school and ran away from the military school his father sent him to. After briefly managing his father's ranch, he sailed to South America and worked a variety of jobs that eventually took him to South Africa, where he joined Texas Jack's Wild West Show as a trick rider. After touring Australia and New Zealand, Rogers returned to the United States, where he began performing his roping tricks on vaudeville stages in New York City. From 1905 to 1916 he perfected his performance, adding jokes and stories to his repertoire, and became popular enough for Florenz Ziegfeld to hire him as part of the Ziegfeld Follies in 1916, which he stayed with for eleven years. In addition to his theatrical performances, Rogers appeared in the movie *Laughing Bill Hyde* (1918) and wrote articles for many newspapers and magazines. In 1930 he began a series of highly popular weekly radio broadcasts, which, like his columns and articles, consisted of witty comments on contemporary issues. Rogers died in a plane crash in 1935; killed with him was the pilot, his friend and famed aviator Wiley Post.

Major Works

Rogers's first two books, *The Cowboy Philosopher on the Peace Conference* (1919) and *The Cowboy Philosopher on Prohibition* (1919), were drawn from his Ziegfeld Follies monologues. His subsequent works, such as *The Illiterate Digest* (1924), *Letters of a Self-Made Diplomat to His President* (1926), and *There's Not a*

Bathing Suit in Russia (1927), were culled from the newspaper columns "Will Rogers Says," "The Worst Story I Ever Heard," "The Daily Telegram," as well as from his serialized correspondences from abroad that appeared in *The Saturday Evening Post*. In his writings, as on the stage, Rogers affected a pose of ignorance, emphasizing his simple, rural background and lack of formal education. In fact he was a shrewd, well-informed, and thoughtful commentator, skilled in the use of the pun, metaphor, and hyperbole. By assuming the stance of a good-natured and somewhat naive country boy, Rogers was able to lampoon Congress, presidents, and foreign heads of state without engendering offense or indignation. For example, in *The Cowboy Philosopher on the Peace Conference* he mocks the diplomatic machinations of the leaders involved in the Versailles talks that took place after the First World War; in *The Cowboy Philosopher on Prohibition* he skewers the futility and hypocrisy of the Volstead Act that outlawed the sale of alcohol. Rogers's canny and fundamentally pessimistic point of view has been compared to Twain's, as has his distrust of the motives and objectives of those in power. Unlike Twain, however, whose *The Adventures of Huckleberry Finn (Tom Sawyer's Comrade)* (1884) is one of the master-works of American literature, Rogers was incapable of sustaining an idea at length. Rogers's talent was for the pithy sentence—the short but highly suggestive statement calculated to effect an immediate response.

Critical Reception

Today, Rogers's work is generally regarded as rather dated. His topical humor is no longer relevant, and the intentional misspellings and grammatical errors he employed to construct his literary persona seem excessive and forced. Nevertheless, his writings are valued for the insight they provide into the concerns and opinions of the country during the tumultuous decades of the 1920s and 1930s. Damon Runyon wrote: "Will Rogers was America's most complete human document. He reflected in many ways the heartbeat of America. In thought and manner of appearance and in his daily life he was probably our most typical native born, the closest living approach to what we like to call the true American."

PRINCIPAL WORKS

The Cowboy Philosopher on the Peace Conference (aphorisms) 1919
The Cowboy Philosopher on Prohibition (aphorisms) 1919
The Illiterate Digest (sketches) 1924
Letters of a Self-Made Diplomat to His President (fictional letters) 1926
There's Not a Bathing Suit in Russia (sketches) 1927
Ether and Me (nonfiction) 1929
Twelve Radio Talks Delivered by Will Rogers during the Spring of 1930 (radio speeches) 1930
The Autobiography of Will Rogers (sketches and aphorisms) 1949
The Will Rogers Book (sketches and aphorisms) 1961
The Best of Will Rogers (sketches and aphorisms) 1979
Will Rogers at the Ziegfeld Follies (sketches and aphorisms) 1992

CRITICISM

Henry Seidel Canby (essay date 1936)

SOURCE: "Estimates of the Dead," in *Seven Years' Harvest: Notes on Contemporary Literature*, Farrar & Rinehart, 1936, pp. 49-53.

[*In the following essay, Canby discusses Rogers in the context of other "homespun philosophers."*]

Will Rogers was a fellow of infinite jest, a true Shakespearian clown, who used clowning to savor his philosophy. Yet it was not what he said, or did, but what he stood for in the American scene that seems most interesting.

We Americans have had a long tradition of philosophers in homespun, so long considering the little age of the Republic, and so notable in their day and sometimes after it, as to ask for comment. Homespun in mind they have all been, which means, that whatever the source of their wisdom, its form and pressure were distinctively local to this continent, and many of them have been homely also in speech, self-made in knowledge, and blatantly provincial. Franklin's Poor Richard was our first of note, a small-town sage who repeated the commonplaces of the eighteenth century with a difference that came from shrewd experience in a struggling community. Irving, I have always believed, was satirizing the village wiseacre and know-it-all in his Dutchmen who puffed smoke instead of thinking. But it was Petroleum V. Naseby, Artemus Ward, Mark Twain, and "Hosea Biglow" in which the type finally realized itself, and took on an originality which must be credited to America.

Artemus Ward was certainly the Will Rogers of his day. He had not been a cowboy, was not semi-literate, could not use by nature a dialect so colloquial that the native American recognized in him the fellow who sat every Saturday night on the cracker barrel. And so Artemus hit upon the device of bad spelling to make himself homely. His spellings are often funny, but often absurd, with no possible relation to mispronounciation. Nevertheless they accomplished what he wished, which was to wrap up his quite serious political and social philosophy in wit and humor. If what he said was not funny, the way it was spelled made it seem to be, and so he got readers who never would have been trapped by an English above their own, or ideas that were not offered as a joke.

Mark Twain learned much from him, but did not change the principle, or when he did, lost his audience. "Huckleberry Finn" is a masterpiece of irony in which a ragamuffin says things which the low-brow American audience would never have taken so readily if spoken with authority and by an educated man. He was addressing a nation with little intellectual self-confidence although a vast certainty in its own judgment. It was a practical nation that had succeeded by rule-of-thumb where every scholar had said that it would fail, and that was terribly shy of abstract ideas except such religious notions as were insulated from direct contact with the ordinary business of living. If you wished to get it, you had to bait your hook with something homely, familiar, and attractive, that sounded like Saturday-night story telling. And, even more important, you yourself had to be a little homely and a little gun-shy of learning and everything not practical. If in addition you could make a good story out of it, you were on the home trail where thousands of Americans had eased the weary legs of their horses or their own tired feet while they passed on the latest wisecrack from the settlements.

The type has varied since, although Will Rogers bred true, and was the perfect up-country philosopher who would have been at home in Lincoln's law shop, or Red Gulch, or Down East on a Gloucester wharf. To the last dash and comma his tricks were the same, and his mind was the same—that combination of a shrewd human philosophy as broad as human nature with a fundamental distrust of everything not made in America which has made us a trial to Europe and sometimes to ourselves. The first great variant was Mr. Dooley. It was not by chance that Dunne chose his spokesman from an immigrant race with a Catholic philosophy. His United States of the 1890s was getting cock-sure on a large scale. Our boys were in big cities now and playing big-boy tricks in world politics and economics. No one listened to the anti-Imperialists, but they did listen to the Irish bar-keeper who saw that the winners of the Spanish War of '98 were only a row of thirsty drinkers, a little tipsy with success, a little boastful.

And one should add to this gallery of homespun satirists another variant with a different weapon but of the same steel—Robert Frost, the Yankee poet, whose simple language of New Hampshire farmers is so racy and so deceptive in its homely provincialism. It took the English to see that here was another of the well-known American breed. We laughed at him in the beginning as a vain fellow who tried to make hired men pathetic and stone walls a subject for wit.

Note well that some of these writers have nothing to do with literature, and some have everything to do with literature. Viewed nationally they all belong together, a phenomenon of American self-criticism, historically very important for anyone who would understand Americanism from the pioneers to the comics. But regarded as artists, which means as makers of something that stays good beyond their own lifetime, they live in different wards. The divergence begins with skill. Ward is clumsy and banal, even in his best pieces. Twain never, except in potboilers and seat-fillers. Thoreau, who may be described as always wearing Yankee underclothes under his robe of an Oriental sage, could make a sentence that would last. Will Rogers wrote good paragraphs but did not have that steady power over his mind or his words which makes a book. He was a drug-store talker who never went home to write.

The real difference between the humorous men-of-letters and the humorist wisecrackers was, of course, in their mental furniture. It takes more than a character and a shrewd philosophy to make a writer. Rogers could spot a fool or a foolishness, but when he had turned his joke he was through. Whitman, another homespun philosopher, lacked his wit and his healthy back-country skepticism, but he knew, what Rogers never realized, that the plain man's ribald jesting is good as a purge, but poor stuff to grow on. Yet we shall always need Will Rogerses. There is something in the American temperament that is sure to produce an Emerson who keeps zooming skyward because there is too little dirt in his ballast, or a Woodrow

Wilson whose heroic moralities lack just that indispensable streak of homely cynicism that any cowboy philosopher could give him; and there are always stuffed shirts in office who can be deflated only by a kick on their own level.

The chair—it is really a stool—is vacant. Who comes next?

Walter Blair (essay date 1942)

SOURCE: "Abe Martin and Will Rogers," in *Horse Sense in American Humor: From Benjamin Franklin to Ogden Nash,* The University of Chicago Press, 1942, pp. 256-73.

[*In the following essay, Blair surveys early humorists who influenced Rogers.*]

I

Plenty of people in 1930 were ready to swear that, in Kin Hubbard and Will Rogers, the twentieth century had produced two figures the like of which America had not seen in the past. But anyone who looks back through the years at the scores of homespun philosophers who said things as Americans liked to have them said will see that the resemblances between these writers of our own day and the men who went before them are much more important than the differences—that a good old pattern in humor is often better than a new one and the popular literary memory is short.

Kin Hubbard, born in Bellefontaine, Ohio, in 1868, went for a short time to public school and then broke into writing just as Artemus Ward, Petroleum V. Nasby, and Mark Twain had done—taking off as a typesetter on a country newspaper. In 1891 he began working for the *Indianapolis News* as a cub reporter who illustrated many of his news stories. He took about fourteen years, after that, to find himself as a humorist. It was in 1905 that, making use of some of the rural local color he had picked up while covering Indiana political campaigns, he began to phrase his ideas in the words of a Hoosier bumpkin, Abe Martin.

The formula he used then and for about a quarter of a century thereafter was a simple enough one. In the part of the paper assigned to Hubbard, there would be a picture of the musing Abe, perhaps working away at some farm chore or, perhaps, sitting or standing and thinking. The old farmer, with his floppy hat, his old shirt, his striped pants, and his old boots, had a scarecrow-like figure. His face had the button eyes, the one-line mouth, and the careless nose of a cartoon, and he had the chin whiskers of a low-comedy farmer. James Whitcomb Riley did some verse which captured very well the spirit of the drawing:

The artist, Kin Hubbard,'s so keerless

He draws Abe 'most eyeless and earless;
But he's never yit pictured him cheerless
  Er with fun 'at he tries to conceal—
Whuther onto the fence er clean over
A-rootin' up ragweeds er clover,
Skeert stiff at some "Rambler" er "Rover"
  Er new fangled automobeel.

Underneath such a picture would be written, as a rule, two sentences, usually sentences which had no connection except that they happened, both of them, to have been said by Abe in his Brown County dialect. Thus:

> There was a ole fashioned one-ring weddin' at th' Tilford Moots home t'day. Some folks git credit fer havin' hoss sense that haint ever had enough money t' make fools o' themselves.

At the end of every year a collection of these sayings would be made in a little book sometimes called *Abe Martin's Almanack* and decked out with monthly calendars, but usually given a title like *Abe Martin's Back Country Sayings* or *Abe Martin's Home-cured Philosophy*. In such a book the previously wedded sentences would be divorced—separated by spaces between them. In addition to these daily skits, Hubbard now and then wrote an essay, usually in language rather like that which Abe used but as a rule signed by one of Abe's Brown County neighbors.

No one who knows the humor of Josh Billings can fail to see that, whether Abe Martin knew it or not, he had in Josh his nineteenth-century prototype. The strange spelling had given away to a more restrained dialect, and many of the topics—automobiles, fashions in dress and entertainment, farm woes and city woes—were not of the nineteenth century but of the twentieth. But the appeal was to lovers of the aphorism phrased in homely rural language, and when a longer passage of humor was written it was an old-fashioned essay, with aphorisms playing the chief part in causing laughter. Even the "almanacks" remind one of Billings. The character back of the talk is just as sketchy as Billings was, an embodiment simply of good horse sense with a vague quirk or two. Many of his sayings might easily have been written by Josh Billings—sayings such as these:

> Don't be fooled on purrin'. A cat would attack us in a second if it wuzn' afraid.

> Christmas jewelry often turns green in the spring.

> Lots o' people insist on eatin' with a knife that wuz born with a silver spoon in their mouth.

> Ther's somebody at ever' dinner party that eats all th' celery.

> Of all th' home remedies a good wife is th' best.

But, of course, the fact that the author belonged to this century rather than to the last one makes him appeal more strongly to readers of today. Many of his sayings, even those written many years ago, have point today; for example:

> I wish somebuddy would make a new Republican speech.

> Ther's some folks standin' behind th' President that ought t' git around where he kin watch 'em.

> Our unemployment parade yisterday wuz a big success, some three hundred an' thirty-three cars bein' in th' procession.

Hubbard as an essayist had rather more organization than Billings; but, like Billings, he depended on good sayings to give his essays their zest. "Th' Use o' th' Nut" is a typical essay:

> Nine-tenths o' th' people go thro' this life without usin' ther nut. Lots o' folks die at seventy-five with bran' new, unscuffed brains, brains that have jest been cuddled up an' forgotten fer years, brains in ther original wrappers. In other words, most people tackle all th' great transactions o' life without stoppin' t' think, or if they do stop it's because o' cold feet, an' not thro' any exercise o' th' nut. Th' feller that drives a car should have his nut at his toes' tips at all times, an' th' feller that's importuned t' go int' somethin' where he kin double his $700 should consult his nut at once, retire t' a room, or water plug, an' think. Some folks talk fer hours without thinkin', or they'd never begin. "It never dawned on me," "I never once thought," "I never dreamed o' such a thing," are all familiar expressions that come from people with dormant thinkin' apparatuses. Results have showed that th' average voter don't use his nut any more than th' widows who invest ther money. "I wish I'd thought," says th' feller or widow, who's lost ever' thing. "It never occurred t' me," is another common stock expression very pop'lar with fellers who have missed rare opportunities, or lost out on th' chance of a lifetime. We all go too fast an' bust int' things too freely. The sober second thought allus comes mopin' along after th' car's ditched, or we've made a mess o' marriage, or th' savin's of a lifetime have gone glimmerin'. Then fer th' first time most of us discover that we've got a nut. This would be some country if ever' one used his nut instead o' lettin' a few glib, affable handshakers with brief cases do ther thinkin'. Pick up anybuddy an' try t' git his nut t' workin' an' see how you come out. He may say, "I never thought o' that before," but that's th' best you'll git. We don't believe eight fellers out o' ten even think they'll play golf. We believe they jest automatically neglect ther work an' play. Occasionally some feller really uses his nut an' still shows poor judgment, but that's due t' a faulty nut. Life is filled with tight places, an' at no time in all history wuz ther ever an age like t' day's, an age when we depend almost entirely on quick nut work lest we git skinned, or shot, or maimed—or poisoned.

It was in the short aphorisms, however, rather than in the longer essays on subjects like "Salesmanship,"

"Speedin'," "Th' Circus," "Popularity," and "Farmin'," that Abe was at his best. Kin Hubbard had tricks of his own that were worth something. His combination of two unrelated aphorisms into a single paragraph piled up disparities. He used some queer names of fellow-Hoosiers for allusions and quotations and tended to make them type characters—Miss Fawn Lippincott, a village belle; Young Lafe Bud, a dandy; Mr. and Mrs. Tilford Moots, who had domestic trouble; Miss Tawny Apple, who was rather brash in her dress and her sex life; Tell Binkley, the village failure who thought he knew about finance, and others who came into his talk every now and then down through the years. Finally, he had a way of putting together slowly unfolding sentences, the meaning of which was hidden to the last: "'I'll be glad when I'm found guilty, an' git a new trial, an' go free, an' have this mess over with,' said Mrs. Tilford Moots' niece, whose late husband wuz insured for eighteen thousand dollars." This rambling sentence came out in 1928, a year when a number of self-made widows were cleared of murder charges. Again: "'If she comes in t' night I'll try t' catch her in th' mornin' an tell her,' said Mrs. Tipton Bud, when somebuddy left a message for her daughter." This tragic story, with its poignant contrast between the old and the new generation, is developed in a similar way: "Uncle Mort Hickman, nearly ninety-eight, after cuttin' and splittin' four cords o' wood yisterday afternoon, wuz found frozen stiff in th' lane leadin' t' th' house by his four sons, who had been attendin' a billiard tournament."

These stories compressed into a sentence, with the climax falling neatly in the last word, were Hubbard's chief contribution to the art of expressing ideas humorously. Otherwise, this writer, who Will Rogers said "is writing the best humor in America today," did very well with little more than Billings had used many decades earlier.

II

"Ther's at least one instance," said Abe Martin, "where havin' enough rope didn' end disastrously, an' that's Will Rogers." It was natural that Hubbard and the cowboy humorist should admire each other, because the success of the humor of Rogers as well as that of Hubbard was largely the result of an ability to squeeze a great deal of good sense into a funny sentence.

Rogers was the more successful of the two. His life-story was a fantastic triumph of the sort that has made America an amazing country. Born in 1879 in a ranchhouse in Indian Territory, as he put it, "halfway between Claremore and Oologah, before there was a town in either place," he grew up in the cow country. He went to a country school and then to Kemper Military Academy, "a little while"—and his formal schooling was ended. His informal schooling included working in the Texas oil fields, punching cows for a number of years, service in the Boer War, travel with a circus in the Antipodes and the Orient, and vaudeville work in America.

He was in vaudeville, staging a lariat-whirling act, when he discovered that if he mixed talk with his roping tricks, the audience liked him better. Bit by bit he added anecdotes and sallies to his act, until he became famous as a wisecracking cowboy. In Ziegfeld's *Follies,* in 1914, he became a star, partly because he added comments on national and international affairs to his humorous monologues. From then on, the way was easy: by leaps and bounds he mounted to such prominence that when he died in an airplane accident in August, 1935, many felt his death to be a national calamity. Newspapers used column after column to rehearse his life-story, a coast-to-coast radio hookup carried a memorial program, and in the Senate, Majority Leader Robinson rose and said: "Probably the most widely known citizen in the United States and certainly the best beloved met his death some hours ago in a lonely and faraway place."

It is interesting to guess at the reasons for this great fame Rogers had. Undoubtedly, one thing that helped it a great deal was the novelty of a cowboy humorist. Perhaps even more important was the fact that he embodied for Americans a type which in some ways at that time seemed more representative of the life of the country than the farmer type did. And the way the screen plays of some decades had portrayed heroic western cowboys certainly had built up a friendly attitude—if not a worshipful one—toward the type.

Rogers' tremendous popularity doubtless was also partly the result of his getting to the people of America in more ways than any humorist had ever before used to reach the public. He became known first as a trouper with vaudeville companies swinging around the country. Then came Broadway engagements, with the metropolitan press giving him all the publicity usually given to a man who is an unusual kind of a stage celebrity. The silent moving pictures made his face and his gestures known to millions, and some of the lines he wrote to be flashed on the screen gave this huge audience samples of his wit. Then came the talkies, and the hesitant Rogers drawl charmed crowds who went to see him play Bill Jones in *Lightnin',* Hank in *A Connecticut Yankee,* Lem Morehouse in *Young as You Feel,* and other roles just as well suited to him. A fine contract lured him to the lecture circuit—and, like Artemus Ward, Mark Twain, and others, he traveled across the continent, appearing before many delighted audiences. The radio, too, carried his voice to hundreds of thousands of chuckling listeners. Meanwhile, he had begun to write—books at first, newspaper columns and magazine articles later. The take from these many activities was impressive—at its height about $20,000 a week. At the time he died 350 daily newspapers and 200 Sunday newspapers from coast to coast were using his pieces, and it was believed that he had about 40,000,000 readers. Never, even in the Gilded Age—the golden age for humorists—had any American jester reached such a huge audience.

Mr. Jack Lait, old-timer in the world of journalism, saw signs of the humorist's great popularity in the way the news of his death struck the world. He said:

Never in my lifetime have I seen a whole world so stunned and sorrow-stricken. . . . . In the years that went before, I have reported and handled for newspapers and press services the tidings of the passing of monarchs, ecclesiastical heads, dictators, saints. But never had or has anything approached the myriad human soul-reactions of the final "fade-out" of this. . . . man. . . . .

An editorial writer on one of the intellectual magazines noted with some wonder that on the day Rogers died everyone—waitress, garage man, white-collar office worker, professor, financier—was talking about his death, grieving about it.

III

Mr. H. S. Canby, an editor of the *Saturday Review of Literature* better acquainted than most people of the time with the history of American humor, was interested in the way Rogers followed old paths. Said he:

We Americans have had a long tradition of philosophers in homespun. . . . . Homespun in mind they have all been, which means, that whatever the source of their wisdom, its form and pressure was distinctively local to this continent, and many of them have been homely also in speech, self-made in knowledge, and blatantly provincial. . . . . The type has varied. . . . , although Will Rogers bred true, and was the perfect upcountry philosopher who would have been at home in Lincoln's law shop, or Red Gulch, or Down East on a Gloucester wharf. To the last dash and comma, his tricks were the same,—that combination of shrewd human philosophy as broad as human nature with a fundamental distrust of everything not made in America which has made us a trial to Europe and sometimes to ourselves.

The notion that Rogers wrote and thought like the great mass of philosophers in homespun before him had a solid basis. In several ways, of course, he was unique. His cowboy background, his experiences on the stage and in Hollywood, the fact that he lived in an age of airplanes and skyscrapers—all made him diverge somewhat from the exact pattern of earlier humor. But he had the old-fashioned horse-sense kind of a mind, and he won laughs in old ways.

Back of his humor, as almost everybody said who wrote about him, was a philosophy. When, in 1930, he was criticized because of the huge sum he was to be paid for a series of brief monologues on the radio, *World's Work* said, in his defense: "It seems to be his mission, under the guise of genial raillery, to tell us the hard, blunt truths about ourselves—truths about our politics, our civic standards, and our social habits. They are the sort of truths we do not always like to hear, but we will take them with a contagious chuckle. . . . ."

He himself thought that ideas made his humor what it was. When someone spoke to him about the poor grammar in his newspaper articles, he said, "Shucks, I didn't know they was buyin' grammar now. I'm just so dumb I had a notion it was thoughts and ideas." His feeling, he said, was that "A gag to be any good has to be fashioned about some truth. The rest you get by your slant on it and perhaps a wee bit of exaggeration, so's people won't miss the point." He started many of his pieces by saying, "Well, all I know is just what I read in the papers"; but he believed, as most of his readers did, that he had better thoughts concerning his reading than the average person did. He put it this way:

I'm just an ignorant feller, without any education, so to speak, but I try to know what I'm talking about. . . . . I do a lot of studying. . . . read editorials a lot. . . . when I go to a national convention I have to know what they're talking about to know what's funny. If I was just a clown, Borah and Read and Mellon and all those fellows wouldn't take the trouble to explain what they're drivin' at to me.

His mind worked in a way that appealed to his countrymen. He liked the ways of thinking he had learned in the cow country, feeling that they were good enough to carry him to success if he continued to stick to them. "I am just an old country boy in a big town trying to get along," he said. "I have been eating pretty regular, and the reason I have been is because I have stayed an old country boy." On the basis of his experience and what he saw had worked, he judged anything and everything—all the way from a little political squabble to international affairs. The Republican Convention of 1932, for him, was "kind 'er like a country picnic—you meet a lot of old friends from everywhere and see all the newspaper boys again." His remarks about the greatest Chinese philosopher showed his brain at work:

Confucius had some mighty pretty Sayings, but none of 'em have ever kept a Foreigner from coming in and gobbling up what he wanted. . . . Now, I am not taking anything away from Confucius. He must have been a wonderfuly smart man. From reading some of his sayings, I would judge him to have been a cross between our Abraham Lincoln, Elbert Hubbard and H. L. Mencken. But the things he said was for the Chinese; they wasn't meant for a half-baked Chinese that had a conglomeration Night Club and Tammany Hall political-method background. I bet if Confucius had known his people would adopt a lot of this modern-world foolishness, he would have written a different book, telling 'em to stay at home. He had life figured out for 'em better than any man in the world for any Nation, and to prove it, it worked for two thousand years; but he naturally thought they was going to stay Chinese.

It was typical of Rogers, the provincialist, to suggest the nature of the writings of an Oriental sage by comparing him with three American writers known to ordinary men, just as it was typical of him to call Paris "the Claremore, Oklahoma, of France." Like Franklin, he was able to test a moral system not by general principles but by the way it worked. Like Lincoln, he took for granted that even rules for living thought up by a sage had to be discarded after changes in conditions had made the old rules lose their usefulness.

IV

The results of such thinking on all sorts of subjects he made amusing by using many of the tried tricks of old-time American humorists. When he started out as a talker, he made use of a manner much like that of the old-time humorous lecturers. He did not wear the funereal expression so many of them had found valuable, but his loose-lipped, shy grin, his slow drawl, and his shambling walk on the platform gave him an appearance of diffidence, even of humorlessness, like that of many earlier lecturers. He had Artemus Ward's and Mark Twain's way of looking innocently surprised when the audience chortled at one of his bright remarks. On the whole, then, he posed as much simpler than he really was.

When he turned to writing, he often continued to use the old-fashioned device of acting like a fool. "The only pose in Will Rogers," said Mr. Lowell Thomas, "was the pretense that he was an ignorant and illiterate fellow." He was in the habit of saying, "I studied the fourth reader for ten years." He dotted his pages with poorly spelled words, thus getting back to a device which had not been used by most humorists since the time of the Civil War. Another way he had of showing his illiteracy—one not often used by American humorists before him—was the lavish misuse of capital letters. His grammar was bad, and he let on that he had little respect for it. "Grammar and I," he said, "get along like a Russian and a bathtub" and, again, "Maybe ain't ain't so correct, but I notice that lots of folks who ain't usin' ain't, ain't eatin'."

He used many of the kinds of expression that had long been useful to humorists. The old habit of linking together in one sentence a group of queerly assorted articles—a habit useful to Ward, Twain, Nye, and others—made possible such a remark as "Russia's a country that used to have four exports—dukes, grand dukes, princesses and whiskers." He had a liking for puns and malapropisms, as hosts of humorists had had before him: "Now the President says we're going to recognize the Czecho-Slovaks. We may recognize them but we will never pronounce them." The old device of the comic simile cropped up in sentences like "Americans are getting like a Ford car—they all have the same parts, the same upholstery and make exactly the same noises" and like "Eskimos are thicker here [in Alaska] than rich men at a save-the-Constitution convention."

Most of the pains he took with his writing went on polishing his lines until they did two things, both important: (1) they phrased a humorous idea in a way that *seemed* very casual and (2) they phrased the idea in just the way to make it most amusing.

> The guys that tell you they can be funny at any minute, without any effort, are guys that ain't funny

to anybody but themselves [he claimed]. I depend on the newspapers for most of my inspirations. Some days there is material for several good lines. Then there will be a week when there isn't a little thing worth mentioning. About once a month I turn out a gag that I get a big kick out of myself. That's a pretty good average.

He used the same sort of care Josh Billings did on phrasing. Often he wrote eight or ten versions of a sentence before he got one that suited him. But his expressions, for all their working-over, had to seem offhand, spontaneous, accidental.

Many of the things he did were in the character of a simpleton who behaved as foolishly in the presence of fame or greatness as only a very impudent person—or a fool—could be expected to do. On the stage in New York at the start of his career he found that if he made joking attacks on celebrities in the audience, both the celebrities and the audience enjoyed them, and he never forgot the formula. At a time when the Prince of Wales was getting much notoriety because he had tumbled off his horse in a number of steeplechases, the American met him in London.

"Hello, old-timer," Rogers greeted him. "How are you falling these days?"

The Prince won the humorist's approval by saying, "quick as a flash": "All over the place. I got my shoulder broke since I saw you last." "I hear you are a journalist now," the Prince went on. "This is no interview, remember; just renewing old acquaintanceship."

"Anything you say to me is just *ad lib,*" Rogers told him, "and nobody will ever know it but President Coolidge and America."

Or he was introduced to Coolidge, and the pucker-faced President said something through tight lips as they shook hands. Rogers leaned over as if he had missed some words and said:

"Pardon me. I didn't catch the name."

He thought it was a good joke, on a radio program, to announce that he would now introduce the President of the United States, and to mimic Coolidge's Yankee twang, saying: "It gives me great pleasure to report on the state of the nation. The nation is prosperous on the whole, but how much prosperity is there in a hole?"

Not long afterward he met Mrs. Coolidge, who told him that she could imitate her husband's voice better than the comedian did. "Well, Grace," he said to her, "you can imitate Cal's voice better'n me, but look what you had to go through to learn it." After an overnight stay at the President's mansion with the Coolidges, he reported, as if with the greatest innocence:

> I am the only Democrat who has slept in the White

House for a long time. . . . . Of course, the President's not understood. He's a nice fellow with a sense of humor. We spent last night swapping yarns. About eight o'clock the President began to yawn and at ten he fell asleep on me.

Like Jack Downing, therefore, Rogers told of his talk with great men in public affairs. Like him, he made fun of both sides, but like Jack's contemporary, Davy Crockett, he told stories which were not merely figments of the imagination but were based on actual experience. In the boom days of beautiful nonsense during which he thrived, a clown famous throughout the nation could actually turn into realities some of the fantasies which, in the 1830's, it had been mildly shocking even to imagine. In the 1830's, for example, no one would have thought of having Crockett stand up on the stage before a national convention and get off witticisms about the leading politicians, as Rogers did more than once. Like both the two earlier heroes, Will received many votes in various elections, and he was nominated for the presidency. Unlike the earlier men, Rogers was a candidate who really was given more than passing consideration by a number of people. Once, at least, his name was seriously suggested on the floor of the House of Representatives. Said Representative Everett B. Howard, "Rogers is a statesman, experienced, courageous, safe, and sound, and offers excellent material for the Presidency."

There were times, though, when the cowboy comedian took on, in his writings, a fictitious governmental job. Traveling abroad, he posed as "a self-made diplomat," writing reports to either the chairman of the Senate Committee on Foreign Affairs or to the President. In the assumption of this ignorant man that he, in his old blue serge suit, could and should do a better job than the diplomats, there was amusing evidence of almost sublime conceit. "Of course we have foreign Ambassadors over there," he said, "but they are more of a Social than a Diplomatic aid to us." Readers laughed at the frank and democratic way this traveler chatted with rulers. People were amused, too, by the way this diplomat, in contrast to those who were not self-made, kept his thoughts, findings, and conversations secret by publishing them first in the *Saturday Evening Post* and later in widely sold books. Finally, what he said about Europe had about as little diplomatic tactfulness as anyone could imagine.

"You know, of course," he said, for example, "or perhaps you have had it hinted to you, that we stand in Europe about like a Horse Thief. Now I want to report to you that this is not so. It is what you call at Amherst 'erroneous.' We don't stand like a Horse Thief abroad. Whoever told you we did is flattering us. We don't stand as good as a Horse Thief."

This cynicism about the relationship between America and other countries came out in many passages in the letters. The common sense of Rogers, as he believed, usually led him to favor our isolation from foreign affairs.

Let a nation do like an individual [he wrote]. Let 'em go through life and do and act like they want to, and if they can't gain friends on their own accounts, don't let's go out and try and buy it. . . . If we would stay at home and quit trying to prowl around to various conferences and conventions somewhere, we would be better off.

Undoubtedly he was a great force in behalf of isolationism, and probably such preaching, despite its sincerity, was his greatest disservice to his country.

Rogers' suspicion of Europeans and his democratic way of sizing up things with his humble mind and confidently making known what he had decided carry back one's memory to a time when another Westerner, Mark Twain, had looked at Europeans and European things and had made unflattering remarks with just as much confidence. Clemens, too, had been a sort of an unofficial ambassador, seeing the great men of many lands and chatting with them easily. Toward the end of his life, Twain had become almost as much of an oracle as Rogers, with reporters clamoring to hear his opinions about all sorts of subjects.

When Rogers died, not a few commentators thought of comparing him with Mark Twain. But there was one great difference between the two, a very significant one. The earlier humorist turned against whatever he disliked with a hate that was ferocious; Rogers had no hate. "When I die," he said, "my epitaph or whatever you call those signs on gravestones, is going to read, 'I joked about every prominent man of my time but I never met a man I didn't like.' I am proud of that. I can hardly wait to die so it can be carved." And again: "You folks know I never mean anything by the cracks I make on politics. I generally hit a fellow that's on top because it isn't fair to hit a fellow that's down." This meant that, though many people thought Rogers was a sort of unofficial preacher-at-large to the United States, the sermons he preached did not attack the popular sins of the day as ferociously as they might have done. Perhaps, though, more ferocity would have spoiled his humor—as it sometimes spoiled Mark Twain's; perhaps this funnyman, the latest of a long line of towering philosophers in homespun, went as far as anyone could who was as true to the traditions of his craft as Will Rogers was.

Norris W. Yates (essay date 1964)

SOURCE: "The Crackerbarrel Sage in the West and South: Will Rogers and Irvin S. Cobb," in *The American Humorist: Conscience of the Twentieth Century,* Iowa State University Press, 1964, pp. 113-33.

[*In the following essay, Yates explains the ways in which Rogers adapted and modified the tradition of nineteenth-century American humorists.*]

As a frontispiece to the revised edition (1960) of his book, *Native American Humor,* Walter Blair has drawn a circle of nineteenth-century humorists seated around a potbellied stove, evidently swapping yarns. If Professor Blair had added one of George Ade's self-made men, and portraits of Abe Martin, Will Rogers, Irvin S. Cobb, and possibly E. W. Howe, O. O. McIntyre, Walt Mason, and Ellis Parker Butler, he might have emphasized a point made in the text and in his *Horse Sense in American Humor,* the point, namely, that the nineteenth-century hot-stove tradition in American humor continued unbroken into the twentieth. This tradition—associated, as seen, with rugged individualism in business, caution in politics, and stability in the home—reached a new high in popularity in Will Rogers. Not without certain modifications, however.

ANOTHER SUCCESS STORY

For one thing, Rogers gave a western tinge to the tradition. Some earlier humorists had written humor while living in the West—George Horatio Derby (John Phoenix) in California; Edgar Wilson (Bill) Nye and M. C. Barrow in Wyoming, for example—but no humorist had achieved a national reputation while presenting himself as a western character. Rogers, on the other hand, began early to bill himself as "the cowboy philosopher," and although he got his start in humor on the eastern vaudeville circuits, he came honestly by his lariat and his western saddle. His father, Clem Rogers, was one of the first— and last—of the cattle barons during the brief period of the open range and the trail drive. Will once remarked, "My father was one eighth Cherokee and my mother one fourth Cherokee, which I figure makes me about one eighth cigar-store Injun." Many times Rogers stressed that his people were the first Americans and had met, not sailed on, the *Mayflower.* He came from both the economic and the ethnic heart of the Old West.

Kin Hubbard once said that, "No feller ever ort t' get too great t' register from th' little town where he lives." Rogers was born in a ranch house near Claremore, Oklahoma, and he always put down that town as his native place when he registered at hotels. His father was wealthy, but even in his teens Will preferred to make his way alone, and, after some country schooling and a two-year stay at Kemper Military Academy, he worked as a roughneck in the oil fields, punched cows in Texas and in Argentina, and traveled with a Wild West show in Africa, China, and Australia. As a result of the latter job, he began to appear on the stage as a trick roper. Probably by 1910 he was making wisecracks on current topics to pep up his act, and it was his homely verbal comedy as much as his rope tricks that got him a role with Ziegfeld's *Follies* in 1915.

Will's first two books, *The Cowboy Philosopher on the Peace Conference* (1919), and *The Cowboy Philosopher on Prohibition* (1919), were mostly collections of what he had said on the stage. In 1922, both the New York *Herald* and the McNaught Syndicate approached him with the notion that he should write a weekly humorous feature. He began for McNaught by imitating Mr. Dooley and presenting two quaint characters talking over the news, but he found he could not create characters—except for his own *persona*—nor write narrative. He tried putting his humor into epigrams and brief paragraphs, much as he had done orally, and his rise to popularity as a writer was shortly under way. Two years later he still had not quite learned that his natural media were the quip and the editorializing paragraph. When he added a daily feature he at first imitated the anecdotal style of Irvin S. Cobb, but he soon reverted to his natural methods.

Both features were soon running in dozens of newspapers; it is said he eventually reached one hundred million readers a year. In addition to the daily paper, Rogers' humor reached the public through the stage, the lecture circuit, the movies, and the radio. When he was killed in a plane crash in 1935, Senate majority leader Joseph E. Robinson announced that Rogers was "Probably the most widely known citizen in the United States."

Why did Rogers capture the public on a scale that probably surpassed even Mr. Dooley and Abe Martin? Blair has suggested that his cowboy origins helped. Through them he embodied a figure that people liked to feel was more representative of American life as a whole than was any farmer type; moreover (says Blair), he reached the public through more media than any other humorist had used. Other commentators have stressed that he was always just a little, but never too far, ahead of the main drifts of public opinion. Thus he was an early supporter of Wilson but quickly became cool to the League of Nations; he advocated "normalcy" before Harding—who might himself be called a crackerbox type—had unintentionally coined the word; he tried to sting the Hooverites into more action but became a traffic cop in blue jeans warning the Roosevelt cavalcade not to go too fast and too far.

It should be added that Rogers, at least in his role as a public man, was close kin to the mythical citizen on the make praised by William Graham Sumner, idealized by the Progressives, placed in a city tavern by Dunne, given wealth and a flighty family by Ade, and brought back to the village square by Hubbard. Behind the chaps and the lariat the public recognized the same familiar figure. Furthermore, Will knew how to impersonate—perhaps one should say, to *be*—several different varieties of this man. Thus, when he discussed prohibition, he appeared as a practical citizen who minded his own business and was skeptical of both the extreme wets and drys; in this role he appealed to millions who were sick of the whole issue. When he needled the public for its complacency during the nineteen-twenties and called for moderate reforms that would reduce political immorality and help the farmer, he appeared more like the enlightened citizen the Progressives had postulated, and masses of readers who were disgusted with the corruption in high places but apathetic when it came to doing something about it responded sheepishly and joyously.

George Ade had advised that to get on, one should keep on being a country boy. Rogers strove consciously to perpetuate the image of a rube from the wide-open spaces seeking his fortune. He reproved Percy Hammond, drama critic for the New York *Herald Tribune,* with, "Percy, I am just an old country boy in a big town trying to get along. I have been eating Pretty regular, and the reason I have been is because I have stayed an old Country boy." (Hammond was from Cadiz, Ohio.) In reply to criticisms from Ed Sullivan, columnist on the New York *Daily News,* Rogers referred to "us country columnists." Like Kin Hubbard and O. O. McIntyre, Will often used his rural background to suggest the wise fool, especially with regard to literacy and letters. "Grammar and I get along like a Russian and a Bathtub," he said, and he made a point of never having got beyond McGuffey's Fourth Reader (which was not true). However, he also stated that his public was not "buying" grammar but ideas—and left unspoken the thought that possibly he had a few worth expressing, "fool" though he might be where language was concerned.

About formal literature: "Vergil must have been quite a fellow, but he didn't know enough to put his stuff in English like Shakespeare did, so you don't hear much of him any more, only in high school and roasting-ear colleges, where he is studied more and remembered less than any single person." When it came to pictorial art, Rogers was far behind Mark Twain, who in *Innocents Abroad* had admired a few paintings. From overseas, Rogers wrote in 1926, " . . . I don't care anything about Oil Paintings. Ever since I struck a dry hole near the old home ranch in Rogers County, Oklahoma I have hated oil, in the raw, and all its subsiduaries. You can even color it up, and it don't mean anything to me. I don't want to see a lot of old Pictures. . . . So when I tell you about Rome I just want you to picture it as it is, not as it is in the guidebooks, but as an ordinary hard-boiled American like you and I would see it." Rogers here flattered the Babbitts—"hard-boiled" Americans all—in language much like theirs. In 1934, when Diego Rivera was dismissed by Nelson Rockefeller for putting Lenin and other radical figures into his murals at Rockefeller Center, Rogers sided with the millionaires and with the conservatives in art, in contrast to E. B. White (a graduate of Cornell), who spoofed both sides in a poem on the controversy. When the common man was threatened with culture, Rogers, like Dunne, was often there to defend him.

In Rogers, the professional humorist and the man were unusually close. "All I know is what I read in the papers," was almost a literal truth, according to Mrs. Rogers. Will really had been a cowhand, and whenever he visited his old haunts in Oolagah and Claremore, he was received by the local ranchers and townspeople with an affection that gives a true ring to such statements as "I am mighty happy I am going home to my people, who know me as 'Willie, Uncle Clem Rogers' boy.'" On the other hand, the public image and private man did not match perfectly. Will's visits to Oklahoma after he became famous were brief, though fairly frequent. In addition, Lowell Thomas claimed that "The only pose in Will Rogers was the pretense that he was an ignorant and illiterate fellow," and P. J. O'Brien writes that "Underneath Will Rogers' mask of 'ignorance' was a well-mannered and cultured man with a shrewd, trained mind." Both Irvin S. Cobb and Homer Croy qualify the epitaph chosen by Will, "He joked about every prominent man in his time, but he never met a man he didn't like." Cobb says that although Will certainly liked most people, he could express his dislike of a few in salty language and the epitaph probably referred to prominent politicians only. Croy asserts that Rogers had two fist fights.

Yet Rogers surely meant what he said when he told Max Eastman, "I don't like to make jokes that hurt anybody." Even in unguarded moments he rarely made such jokes. His kindliness, and the verifiable nucleus of truth in his claim to be "just folks" render his personality and his *persona* closer to each other than those of any other humorist examined in this book.

POLITICS AND DETACHMENT

Without an exhaustive and probably impossible study of public opinion during Rogers' career, it is not feasible to test the hypothesis that Rogers accurately voiced the immanent attitudes of the "big Honest Majority" in politics. If one goes ahead and assumes that he did so, Will's political opinions offer basic clues to what that majority were thinking and feeling. If one rejects the hypothesis, Will's public image and his views at least offer one more humorist's portrait, not only of the crackerbox oracle but of the solid citizen trying to think things through. This citizen shows traits of the man idealized by the conservative who distrusts reformers and asks only to be let alone, and traits also of his counterpart in the liberal mythology who participates in reform movements for the sake of getting the great corporations and militant unions to let him alone. Rogers tried to embody both images at once without sacrificing the approval of either faction. He declared once that, "I am just progressive enough to suit the dissatisfied. And lazy enough to be a standpatter." The pretense of laziness, a trait which is part of the stereotype of the wise oaf, helped to mask his inconsistency.

One of Rogers' favorite tactics was to enact the role of a presumptuous ass who has created for himself a fictitious government job or who assumes that he is the familiar of whatever President is in office. In this tactic he resembled Jack Downing, Davy Crockett, and Sut Lovingood. Like Crockett but unlike the other two, Rogers could, in part, support his pose of hobnobbing with leading political figures by pointing to the facts. Eminent politicians were eager to be interviewed by him. Whether wholly serious or exaggerated for humorous effect, much of his "advice" suggested the *naïf* who is unaware that he may give offense and who consequently speaks frankly in telling the President or some other prominent official what the "folks back home" are thinking. In fact, this *naïf* assumes that his boss in the White House will be glad to hear him, since they both are just two good men who need to talk things over. The offhand manner of Rogers with Presidents also reminds one of Mr. Dooley's "me frind Mac"

(McKinley) and "me frind Teddy." Rogers addressed the stately Wilson as "Pres." and wrote Coolidge that he was too busy to bother with seeing him, but he shrewdly warned Wilson against taxing the public to pay a veterans' bonus, and he voiced the isolationism of millions in the twenties by telling "Cal" that, "If we would stay at home and quit trying to prowl around to various [international] conferences and conventions somewhere, we would be better off."

On the whole, Will (because of his essential detachment from political strife) was closer to the conservative than to the liberal citizen, especially before the Great Slump. Aloofness toward factions was necessary if Will was indeed to speak for all the people, but it also stemmed from his real indifference to the outcome of party squabbles. His detachment was reflected in his view of politics as entertaining spectacle (an approach close to H. L. Mencken's). "Politics," he declared, "is the best show in America." From 1920 to 1932 he did not miss a national convention of either major party—but he went as an observer only. He received two votes in the balloting for the presidential nominee of the Democrats in 1928, but he himself never voted in an election. More than once he said, "This country runs IN SPITE OF parties . . ." (the emphasis is his). During the Smith-Hoover presidential contest he wrote a weekly column for *Life* as part of the burlesque compaign in that magazine for Will Rogers, candidate of the Anti-Bunk party. Earlier he affirmed that "No Element, no Party, not even Congress or the Senate can hurt this Country now; it's too big. . . . It's just the same as it was, and always will be, because it is founded on right and even if everybody in Public Life tried to ruin it they couldn't. This Country is not where it is today on account of any man. It is here on account of the real Common Sense of the big Normal Majority." The complacency of that majority during the Harding-Coolidge era is voiced in this statement of 1925; some of the moral apathy with which that majority received the disclosures of the Teapot Dome oil grab was criticized by Will in 1928:

> Its awful hard to get people interested in corruption unless they can get some of it.
>
> They [politicians] are great Guys personally, and they know in their own heart that its a lot of "Boloney," and if they are smart enough to make us feed em, why then we are the Yaps, not them.

In the hungry thirties Rogers affirmed his faith in the two-party system, but the final sentence in that affirmation reveals that he is still not deeply involved with the outcome of party battles. In June, 1934, he said, "So the whole thing is just a revolving wheel. One party gets in and through a full stomach and a swell head over-steps themselves and out they go. And the other gets in. And that's as it should be. For there would be no living with one of 'em if they knew the other one dident exist."

A STRONG, PATERNAL HAND

Outside the realm of party politics, Rogers' views were indeed neither conservative nor liberal, but composite.

He walked in the middle of the road, holding a view commonly labeled conservative: that government is essentially a business; and holding another, commonly held to be part of the Progressive-New Deal ideology, that a powerful, centralized federal government is a good thing. Neither view changed much with the times. "It's simply a mercantile business in town—that's all the Government is," Rogers said in the *Saturday Evening Post* of March 20, 1929, several months before the stock-market crash, and in 1935 he stated, "Business rises above politics in this country." Will's conservative and liberal views had in common a kind of executive paternalism: "If we were run by the Manager form of Government we would soon be paying so little taxes we would be lonesome," he said. He thought that the only way out of the Teapot Dome scandal was "to do as the Movies did, appoint a Will Hays to Wet Nurse the Oil Industry, and see if he can keep their Nose clean." By "Manager" government, Will meant the type of management that ran Standard Oil or General Motors, firms that the Senate and Congress would "bankrupt in two years" if they tried to run them.

According to Homer Croy, Henry Ford's "Peace Ship" in 1915 gave Rogers the chance for "his first big successful joke at the expense of a public figure." Will also made his share of cracks about the tin-lizzie. However, Ford soon became for Rogers a symbol of administrative know-how and power. Will was more than half serious in pushing the Ford-for-President movement in 1923. He said, "I expect if it was left to a vote right now by all the people, Mr. Ford would be voted for by more people than any other man." Concerning a report that every man working at the Ford plants had "to have his breath smelled every morning." Will, though admitting the strictness of the rule, declared that it was "absolutely necessary" and affirmed, "Now Mr. Ford is a very smart man and in passing these rigid rules I bet you he knows where to stop."

In 1929, Rogers spoke more cautiously of Ford: "It will take a hundred years to tell whether you have helped us or hurt us, but you certainly didn't leave us like you found us." However, in the following year he said, "I have always wanted to see Ford elected President," and in 1933, his verdict on the motor executive was, "More common sense than all of 'em." Evidently the cowboy philosopher thought that "Uncle Henry" was efficient but still simple of heart and tastes, like Ade's self-made tycoons and could therefore be trusted to run the Government in the interests of the common man without too much help from the commen men in Congress who lacked Ford's efficiency.

Rogers also admired the personality and policies of Benito Mussolini, who, he thought, was like Ford in being an efficient business manager. Will reflected the views of many Americans during the nineteen-twenties; Abe Martin said in 1927, "Nearly ever'buddy I've talked to would like t' borrow Mussolini fer a day or two. . . ." (Perhaps the emphasis should fall on the final phrase.) After interviewing the Duce in 1926, Will wrote:

Some over home say a Dictator is no good! Yet every successful line of business is run by a Dictator.

This Fellow has been to Italy just what Henry Ford has been to all those old Ash cans and empty bottles and old pig iron; he molded them into a working machine by his own mind and Dictatorship.

Rogers praised the Duce for ending unemployment and beggary, for his shipbuilding program, for his "No Strike in Italy" policy, and for his realistic rearmament of that country. He was facetious about the fascists' quelling some of their opponents by forcibly dosing them with castor oil—"Then you don't want to forget that that Castor oil will live on after he [Mussolini] has gone, and that, applied at various times with proper disscretion, is bound to do some good from every angle."

Rogers cared little for Hitler or for Huey Long, yet he was not opposed to modern authoritarianism as such. He did not favor the adoption of Soviet methods in the United States but he respected the Bolshevik aim of distributing wealth more equally. "Dictatorship is the best government in the world provided you have the right dictator," he wrote in 1933, having in mind the charges that Roosevelt had assumed dictatorial powers. The year before his death Will praised Dollfuss for his suppression of the attempted Nazi *Putsch* and said, "The Austrian chancellor has been visiting Mussolini and learning a lot. This fellow Benito is running a free school for dictators. They all come to him to learn how to put it over." (Before long Mussolini was visiting Hitler.) Will did not explicitly approve of the invasion of Ethiopia, but he criticized the British for their inconsistency in objecting to this action of a fellow imperialist.

Will's respect for executive power is surprising in a man who could hit hard, in his role as presumptuous clown, at both big-businessmen and politicians: "I tell you, the more I hear these big men talk, the more I realize I am the only one that is trying to uphold the rights of the common people." But Will was used to the one-man rule of the cattle empire; his point of view was that of the lone entrepreneur who distrusts both corporate wealth and organized labor, and looks to the executive branch of the Federal Government as the only force capable of keeping both off his back. Rogers' attitude toward labor is represented by his approval of the people who cooperated to keep the wheels turning during the general strike in Great Britain in 1926. His rural background undoubtedly contributed something to his distrust of labor unions, though he admired Samuel Gompers for his executive efficiency in building and running a huge organization.

Rogers' belief that the executive branch of a government is apt to work better than its legislative branch is also surprising in that he voiced it often during the nineteen-twenties, when the Chief Executives of the United States were relatively inactive and undistinguished and the Congress included such unusually able leaders as LaFollette, Borah, Johnson, Glass, McNary, Bankhead, and Norris.

Perhaps the fact that some of these leaders were specialists in preventing rather than in initiating action had something to do with Will's preference for the executive branch as a force for getting things done. However, one aspect of this preference was his qualified belief in what is now called the welfare state. When the boom in agriculture collapsed after World War I, he pleaded for federal relief for the farmers. In 1924 he made the then radical suggestion that the Government move to protect children from infantile paralysis. Later he praised Hoover's attempts to prod Congress into activity, and still later he applauded the "Happy moratorium!" declared by Roosevelt on bank debts (One Indiana banker's complaint to the Lynds revealed how some of Rogers' punches had hit home. He told the investigator that "Will Rogers didn't help any when he said it was a good idea for people to forgive their debts so that everybody could start clean again"). Rogers approved of the National Recovery Act, and also of the Administration proposals for the Tennessee Valley Authority and for the Bonneville power project—"He [President Roosevelt] told that the people could make their own electric energy cheaper than they were getting it. And say, by Monday morning he had the companies talking 'new rates.'" Although he was not given to summing up his New Dealism or any other views in neat principles, he clearly felt that the ordinary man should be protected from the powerful corporations by a benevolent state concentrated largely in a strong Chief Executive.

Because Rogers' executive paternalism has been generally neglected, it is here emphasized perhaps to the point of distortion. It existed alongside his somewhat contradictory view that whoever is in political office does not really matter much: "Nobody is making history. Everybody is just drifting along with the tide. If any office holder feels he is carrying a burden of responsibility, some Fly will light on his back and scratch it off for him some day." However, Will was most likely to make such statements during national conventions or at election time, in order to reduce tensions and preserve good feeling. He instinctively steered toward a middle ground.

AN OLD-FASHIONED MODERN MAN

Like most crackerbarrel philosophers, Rogers sometimes showed, under the mask of the wise fool, a mixture of shrewdness and of genuine naïveté. He saw all too well the inability of Congress to act when action was needed, and he appreciated the potentialities for good of a strong executive. Yet he wanted that executive to rule a vast and complex nation by the simple code of the individual rancher, a code surviving from pioneer days. He insisted that "the whole N.R.A. plan should be written on a post card. . . . The minute a thing is long and complicated it confuses. Whoever wrote the Ten Commandments made em short." This simple view recalls Davy Crockett, who had served briefly as a magistrate and who allegedly wrote, "I gave my decisions on the principles of common justice and honesty between man and man, and relied on natural born sense, and not on law learning to guide me;

for I had never read a page in a law book in all my life." Crockett finally fled civilization to the West from which Rogers came.

Other inconsistencies also stand out in Rogers' attitudes. Will was a crackerbox sage who had discarded the crackerbox for mass media rendered possible by modern technology—media that helped the ex-cowpuncher to earn, at one time, around $20,000 a week. Over one of these media, the radio, he delivered possibly his most often-quoted comment, a slam at another triumph of applied science: "We are the first nation in the history of the world to go to the poor house in an automobile." Yet he took a keen interest in aviation, another modern form of transportation which, like the automobile, was tying the far-flung prairies closer to the urban life that Will distrusted. Ironically, Rogers' interest in this new form of transport led to his death near Point Barrow, Alaska, when a plane piloted by Wiley Post, with Rogers as a passenger, crashed on August 15, 1935.

Not the least of Rogers' inconsistencies was the fact that under his approval of the welfare state ran a counter-current of skepticism about the liberal icon of progress. A letter of inquiry from Will Durant in 1931—when Rogers was anticipating the New Deal in his advocacy of farm relief and stricter regulation of banks—called forth one of Rogers' few statements of basic principle. He wrote to Durant, "Nothing don't mean anything. We are just here for a spell and pass on. Any man that thinks that Civilization has advanced is an egotist. Fords and bath-tubs have moved you and cleaned you, but you was just as ignorant when you got there. We know lots of things we used to didnt know but we dont know any way to prevent em happening." Such a distrust of the common man's "progress" must have met with the approval of Mencken, who also had a letter to Durant in the same volume. Rogers added, "Indians and primitive races were the highest civilized, because they were more satisfied, and they depended less on each other, and took less from each other. We couldent live a day without depending on everybody. So our civilization has given us no Liberty or Independence." His skepticism became almost nihilistic:

> Suppose the other Guy quits feeding us. The whole thing is a "Racket," so get a few laughs, do the best you can, take nothing serious, for nothing is certainly depending on this generation. Each one lives in spite of the previous one and not because of it. And dont start "seeking knowledge" for the more you seek the nearer the "Booby Hatch" you get. And dont have an ideal to work for. Thats like riding towards a Mirage of a lake. When you get there it aint there.

A man who believed in God but belonged to no church, Will closed his letter to Durant with an extremely vague comment on the supernatural basis of ethics: "Believe in something for another World, but dont be too set on what it is, and then you wont start out that life with a disappointment. Live your life so that whenever you lose, you are ahead." The philosophy indicated in this letter elimi-

nates the significance of society; it is frontier individualism carried to the point of anarchy. In its denial of progress, knowledge, and ideals, it also clashes with the assumptions of the Progressive-New Deal tradition. Here, despite his humanitarian leanings, Will suggests the conservative rather than the liberal citizen.

The fact that Rogers' popularity reached new heights during the depression suggests that the public was in the mood for a strong if unstable mixture of New Dealism, wry humor, and grassroots skepticism. If one adds to this mixture a respect for the Man on Horseback (like a cattle king) who Gets Things Done; nostalgia for one's rural origins; an inconsistent readiness to make use of modern technology; a pungent, proverbial style; and most important, the elusive essence that makes a man Will Rogers rather than just another ranch-hand; then one has the combination for becoming the best-liked humorist of his generation.

William R. Brown (essay date 1970)

SOURCE: "Will Rogers, American Adam," in *Image-maker: Will Rogers and the American Dream*, University of Missouri Press, 1970, pp. 70-87.

[*In the following essay, Brown examines Rogers's use of the "rugged individualist" philosophy in his work.*]

Will Rogers was dedicated to the vision of man as being intrinsically worthy. Growing up as he had in a new country in which there was no overcrowding to cheapen human life, living as himself the king of creatures in that new country, and being himself the unique product of the mixing of New and Old World cultures, he could reasonably be expected to value the unique individual. If such a dedication to the worth of the individual might be called American innocence, Rogers often combined with it a sidelong, wise glance that made him the wise innocent. Comments resulted such as that expressing belief in the generosity and goodness of the American people, whom he believed would forgive anything except stupidity. If he was innocent in not understanding the hullabaloo over a football player's running the wrong way, he was wise in seeing that what counted was the fact that the boy's mind wasn't standardized. The over-all effect, therefore, was that the saw of Rogers' words had teeth all the sharper because they were "cross-set" in their wise innocence.

At times, he stated head on a commitment to the powers and virtue of the common man. "No man wants to admit that he is average," Rogers once wrote, perhaps aware that Americans dreamed of their limitless potentiality. "Did you see the picture and specifications of the average man they located last year? That took all the joy out of wanting to be average," he added. It is clear in such a comment that being average meant being homogeneous; Rogers had little ever to say in praise of such a concept of the common man. "I never did go in much for this typical American stuff," he wrote in a daily squib. He preferred, rather, to talk about what he liked to call the "big Normal Majority"—the generality of "little" people who could not be categorized except by their powers of common sense, of balanced reason.

> This American Animal that I thought I had roped here is nothing but the big honest Majority, that you might find in any Country. He is not a Politician. He is not a 100 percent American. He is not any organization, either uplift or downfall. . . . He hasn't denounced anything. . . .
>
> He don't seem to be simple enough minded to believe that EVERYTHING is right and he don't appear Cuckoo enough to think that EVERYTHING is wrong. He don't seem to be a Prodigy, and he don't seem to be a Simp. In fact, all I can find out about him is that he is just NORMAL.

In these people, whether small town residents, farmers, ranchers, or, later, members of the nation's army of unemployed, Rogers apparently found great strength and powers. "We got some great people in this country," he wrote, "and they aint all on Wall Street, or at Luncheon Clubs, or in the Movies or in the Senate." Many of these great, little people were small city, small town, or rural folk. In the fall of 1925, Rogers began the first of a series of annual solo tours that took him from one end of America to the other. Later, he seemed impressed on two relevant levels by the little people's powers.

First, he expressed admiration for their acuity of judgment. "Read? Say, the audiences in the smaller towns make a monkey out of the big cities for knowing what is going on in the world. They know and read everything." Further, these Americans retained their powers of independent thought, Rogers said. "You can kid about the old rubes that sat around the cracker barrel, spit in the stove, and fixed the nation, but they were all doing their own thinking. They didn't have their minds made up by some propagandist speaker at the 'Get Nowhere' Luncheon Club." Such sentiment accorded well with the dream of the garden, with its sturdy yeoman as its hero, and therefore would harmonize with the agrarian dream of freedom.

Second, Rogers expressed a belief in the little people because of their powers of stamina. During the years of the locust, during the times of twenty-five cent wheat and nickel beef, of choking dust that drifted like snow along fence lines and on the lee side of barns and homes, during those times that in lusher farm areas would lead to futile farm holidays, he kept in touch with the little people. "When you ever have any doubt as to what might happen in these United States," he wrote, "go to the country and talk with the people and you will come back reassured." During the time of scourging in the cities, when those who were worst-off scavenged for garbaged vegetables and salvageable meat, Rogers stated his perception of their powers of stamina. "Many, many people out of work, some even in actual want, yet carrying on in

confidence, and in hope. When the little fellow, that is actually in want, can have faith in his government, by golly the big ones should certainly carry on, for they have never missed a meal so far." And again: "Fear has never come from the fellow with no job or no food. He has stood it wonderful. I doubt if a parallell [*sic*] will be found where millions hung on with such continued hope and patience as in this country." Rogers had seen these qualities of judgment and stamina in the big normal majority years before, in the time of abundance; he had seen that a time would come when crisis years would summon all the greatness of the common man:

> No element, no Party, not even Congress or the Senate can hurt this Country now; it's too big. There are too many men just like those Dog Team drivers and too many Women like that Nurse up in Nome [who by combined efforts prevented a diphtheria epidemic] for anything to ever stampede this old Continent of ours. . . .
>
> Even when our next War comes we will through our shortsightedness not be prepared, but that won't be anything fatal. The real energy and minds of the normal majority will step in and handle it and fight it through to a successful conclusion. A War didn't change it before. It's just the same as it was, and always will be, because it is founded on right and even if everybody in Public life tried to ruin it they couldn't. This Country is not where it is today on account of any man. It is here on account of the real Common Sense of the big Normal Majority.

Besides reflecting optimism for the future and thus being relevant to a dream of progress, such a statement is reminiscent of Whitman's belief that the powers of the common man enabled him to derive "good uses, somehow, out of any sort of servant in office." To be able to bring good out of evil is to be touched, at least, by deific power. Rogers spoke of the potential of the common man in America, appearing to be consubstantial with those who dreamed of the inherent greatness of the private citizen.

He did not speak of the infinite powers of man in the abstract. According to him, for instance, the big normal majority was keeping its sense of balance amid the partisan uproar over the effects of prohibition. He said he wanted the viewpoint of unemployed men on some of the government depression commissions, and he voiced approval of the levelheadedness of San Franciscans under the stress of the general strike of 1934. Rogers' words, in the context of events calling for affirmation of the dream of the dignity and worth of the individual, increased his authority, and he gained power by proving the potentialities of the common man. His words helped establish his emerging image as the dream-alive and made his imaged smile seem admiring and approving. They also helped identify him with the vision of the goodness of the common man in the dream of individual dignity.

Rogers gained the reputation of being one who attacked foibles, whether possessors of those frailities were congressmen, senators, big businessmen, preachers, celebrities, or the general public. Yet he never consistently vented Swiftian savagery toward the Yahoos; he was never so blackly pessimistic regarding the nobility and goodness of man as had been Mark Twain. Instead, without being a pollyanna, he concentrated on the better side of humanity. In his writings and talks, he expressed a belief in the goodness of the common man in two chief ways, through the concept of innate goodness and through his attention to instances of virtue.

First, in the tradition of Rousseau and his American followers, Rogers said that the man freed from the deteriorating influences of corrupt modern society is unspoiled, naturally good and happy. And if such a view would seem to contradict the dream of progress, it simply mirrors similar tensions within the constellation of ideas in the great dream itself.

> I doubt very much if Civilization (so called) helped generosity. I bet the old cave man would divide his raw meat with you as quick as one of us will ask a down and out to go in have a meal with us. Those old boys or girls would rip off a wolf skin breech clout and give you half of it quicker than a Ph.D. would slip you his umbrella. Civilization hasent done much but make you wash your teeth, and in those days eating and gnawing on bones and meat made tooth paste unnecessary.

The noble savage was also happy, not merely engaged in the pursuit of happiness. On the occasion of being asked by Will Durant for a statement of his "philosophy of living," Rogers typed his reply in open letter style to Durant. "There aint nothing to life but satisfaction," he began. "If you want to ship off fat beef cattle at the end of their existence, you got to have em satisfied on the range. Indians and primitive races were the highest civilized, because they were more satisfied, and they depended less on each other, and took less from each other." How did the present compare? "We couldn't live a day without depending on everybody. So our civilization has given us no liberty or independence."

Such statements on the goodness and happiness of the natural man could appeal to the ambivalence with which Americans regarded their spiraling technology. Perhaps every American who had longed to take a Huck Finn trip down the Mississippi in those depression days agreed with Rogers when he wrote in his daily wire in February, 1930, "The more you see of civilization, the more you feel that those old cavemen about had the right dope."

Rogers strongly implied the presence of decadence from the primitive ideal in "so-called civilized" members of society when compared to "primitive" individuals. On the other hand, he portrayed the goodness of his cultural contemporaries.

The second way in which Rogers identified materially with the dream of the virtue of the common man was his publication of instances of Americans' concern for their fellow men, a goodness of the highest sort. Many times in his career Rogers was to speak or write like the following, uttered in support of a Community Chest drive, as people all over the United States gathered to hear him and Herbert Hoover on an all-network radio broadcast. "I'll bet you that every town and city comes through," Americans heard Rogers say, and perhaps imagined him before the microphone—hat on and cud of chewing gum rolling in his jaws. "I have seen lots of audiences and heard lots of appeals, but I have yet to see one where the people knew the need, and the cause was there, that they didn't come through—even Europe who hates us and thinks we are arrogant, bad mannered and everything else, but they will tell you that we are liberal, dog-gone it, our folks are liberal."

Dispatches for his string of newspapers often attested to the virtue of the "big Normal Majority."

> Right here in Memphis today over twenty-five policemen went to a hospital and volunteered to give blood transfusions to a kid that was near death. I know that I am out of order in speaking of the good things that cops do, but I am one of the old-fashioned people who believes if somebody pounced on me I could holler for one and he would come and help me out without me having to pay him anything.

> The poor fellows can't catch many criminals as our towns have them too busy marking cars that have been parked too long.

On occasion, Rogers would blend other categories of the great dream with that of the worth of the individual. In a daily column showing the goodness of some of the former delinquents whom police had once managed to catch, he stirred in a strong flavor of the success dream:

> The most human thing I read in the papers today, or this month. The reform school in New Jersey gave a home coming and alumni meeting where over two hundred men who had been there as boys, lots of them now prominent, came back and told what they were doing. Some brought their wives and families with 'em. One told that he served five years there for larceny, and was now a big contractor installing burglar alarms in banks, and was bonded for $150,000.

> It didn't give their names, but it ought to, for I believe it would endear every one of their standing in their home communities. It would at least be a change from that old success formula, "I started as a newsboy."

Rogers was identifying with heroes of progress, as well as with those who trusted the basic virtue of the common man, when he told of the big-heartedness of the "boys" on the Western Air Express who bought toys and clothes and airdropped them for Christmas to an isolated western ranch family that had lost the father.

Will Rogers did not use the language of transcendentalism to state the dream of individual goodness; he wrote as though he had never heard of Rousseau or Whitman, and his own flights to the wildernesses of Mexico or to friendly ranches were probably only coincidences with, and not echoes of, Thoreau's sacramental idylls. Nevertheless, he wrote and said much in the general tenor of those dreamers of the dream; his words on the goodness of the common man had about them the breath of experience with nature. His faith, like that of Father Duffy's, seemed to be in humanity. If Rogers satirized foibles of humankind, he apparently did not do so in despair of the basic worth and virtue of people. If the common man had powers of judgment and stamina and possessed an innate goodness then, according to the dream, his self-fulfillment should follow if given the opportunity.

In performing the action corollaries of the dream, the ideal American should also reject whatever of the past stifled the individual, should seek and trust experience on all its levels, and then realize to a degree his highest development as a man as one who possessed the wisdom born of wise innocence, who kept a sense of irrepressible life for himself and who could also feel regard and devotion for others. Rogers used words that depicted a commitment to this program of action. In writing about his actions, he identified with the indirect level of the dream of the individual, and at the same time emerged as a hero of that vision.

"If every history or books on old things was thrown in the river. . . ." The word-twirling cowboy from Oklahoma seemed to his readers to turn away from the past in the best manner of the American Adam seeking his own fulfillment.

The past, for many Americans from Samuel Clemens to Henry James to Will Rogers, was bound up chiefly with Europe, with its layers and levels of custom, tradition, hierarchy, and achievement. On a trip to the Continent in 1926, Rogers visited France, Germany, Italy, and Switzerland, besides spending a good bit of time in England and Ireland. His reactions to the past as present in Europe were reminiscent of those of other "innocents abroad." Works of art, for instance, were too often thought to be great simply because they were old. "In the first place, I don't care anything about Oil Paintings. Ever since I struck a dry hole near the old home ranch in Rogers County, Oklahoma I have hated oil, in the raw, and all its subsidiaries [*sic*]," he wrote to the readers of *The Saturday Evening Post*. "This thinking that everything was good just because it was old is the Apple Sauce." Those venerable structures recalling past glories won little admiration from the touring cowboy philosopher, although other Americans avidly haunted them: "They get up early in the morning to start out to see more old Churches. Now a Church is all right, and they are the greatest things we have in our lives, but not for a steady diet." The only alternative to church-visiting was ruin-looking, but a "ruin don't just exactly spellbind me; I don't care how long it has been in the process of ruination. I kept trying to get 'em to show me something that hadent started to rue yet."

With the works of Michelangelo, the ruins of the Forum, and the birthplace of Columbus, it was the same reaction. Columbus' feat, after all, would have been more remarkable had North and South America been as small as Switzerland. With other figures from the European past, Rogers was equally irreverent. The Tudors, for instance, received cavalier treatment in a 1929 weekly newspaper article: "This old Henry was just an old fat big-footed . . . Baby," at the head of a country that "stood just about like the Red Sox in the American League." Henry as "a younger brother was just a Democrat, he had to take what was left," but as survivor of Crown Prince Arthur he "not only inherited the direct line to the King, but he took over all Prince Arthur's estate, including wife," Catherine of Spain, whose nation was "the General Motors in those days."

In view of such reactions, Rogers' general evaluation of Europe was inevitable. "I say there is nothing new there; we got everything over home, only bigger and better," he told his *Post* readers. As a matter of fact, Europe had almost nothing to offer the Eden-seeking American Adam liberated from the desert of the past, "You take the Guides and the Grapes out of Europe and she is just a Sahara. It's great for you to see, if somebody is paying for it, or paying you to do it. But just as a pure educational proposition or pastime, it ain't there."

To the American audience, such a rejection of the past as embodied in Europe was possibly more than simple chauvinism. Had the monarchy and the hierarchy welcomed the aspirations to self-fulfillment of the common man? Had not the great art works been patronized by a class of idle aristocrats? Was it not satisfying to be able to declare cultural independence by a casual dismissal of the European past? Whether justifiable or possible in any real sense, the act stood as a token of the worth of the man who could so dismiss the Old World.

Further, the rejected past need not be limited to European shores. "If a foreign Fiddler comes here, as soon as he is fumigated they throw him down and get a musician's dress suit on him, and put him in Carnegie Hall for a 'Recital,'" Rogers asserted in a 1926 weekly article. He was still at it in 1935. During a network broadcast revealing his own long-awaited "plan" for national recovery—a national lottery, based upon "sound" historical precedent at Yale and Harvard—he admitted that Harvard had been so disgusted with the football players paid for by lottery that "they never held any more lotteries and became so disgusted they took up the English language instead of the American language— and today . . . it's the only college that is carried on in a foreign tongue." Paul Revere's ride, the stories of houses where Revolutionary heroes reputedly slept, the history of Philadelphia, and other chapters in American history received a light touch that was free with details and accorded with the character of this new Adam who would be made uncomfortable, if not stifled, by the past-worshipping Daughters of the American Revolution.

Will Rogers as the American Adam seeking self-fulfillment projected an image of gay insouciance toward the past—his true identity was not to be found there. To the extent that books also represented that past and to the extent that a rejection of the past called for intuition in dealing with the present, Rogers expressed a trust in the broadest possible direct experience with the present. Life, itself—not books—was the textbook for the new man, the American, at the second stage of his search for self-fulfillment.

America's "natural" philosopher made the point strongest, perhaps, in a weekly article discussing letters he had recently received: "An educated man just teaches the things that he has been taught, and its the same that everyone else has been taught that has read and studied the same books that he has. But if these old fellows [like cattlemen] know anything, it come direct to them by experience, and not by way of somebody else." The knowledge gained from such direct experience provided "a lesson of every day life in every little animal or Bird we have"; it would create confidence in those to whom it came secondhand, for "they would know that it come from a prairie and not from under a lamp." Its possessor was the "old broad minded man of the world of experience," with whom the "Educated Guy" felt lost, "FOR THERE IS NOTHING AS STUPID AS AN EDUCATED MAN IF YOU GET HIM OFF THE THING HE WAS EDUCATED IN."

If the method of attaining knowledge and self-fulfillment was thus empiricism in its broad sense, the American Adam would be also an intuitive searcher. In the context of the hastily-devised measures for relief and recovery from the depression in the first Roosevelt years, Rogers spoke to his radio audience on the importance of intuition. "Now—my plan—my plan is: don't plan. Whatever you do, don't do it purposely—you know—live haphazardly—just kinda go through life haphazardly—well, even more than we are now." Even when Will Rogers wrote about his use of language to convey the results of his own experience and intuition, he added to his image as the American Adam, the natural man. Words, like men, animals, and events, required firsthand experience: "Course, the Greeks have a word for it, and the dictionary has a word for it, but I believe in using your very own for it," Rogers wrote, pointing out that unfamiliar words were detour signs to readers, who would cuss and take a different "route" next time. "I love words," he concluded, "but dont like strange ones. You dont understand them, and they dont understand you, old words is like old friends, you know em the minute you see em."

Thus, relying upon experience and his own intuitive ability to assimilate it meaningfully, Rogers went forth each day (in the eyes of his public) as had Whitman's eidolon—to meet men and creatures, and to know the earth and the sun in order to have the widest experience possible. The daily datelines told of places seen, people met, food eaten, and of sights, sounds, and affairs both ugly and beautiful. The dateline might read Pittsburgh, Wilkes-Barre, Utica, or New York City, in what Wolfe would later call the "good, green East." "New England," Rogers wrote, "the most beautiful place in the summer time, and for those that like their snow, its fine all the year round. Up state New York is great." Word came, too, from places like Chicago, Cleveland, and Kalamazoo: "All the Middle West, with its rolling prairies and big grain farms," he found to be great. From places like Denver, Butte, and Los Angeles, might come something like the following: "The Northwest, just anything in the way of scenery you want, any crops, any view. The whole Pacific Coast and its adjoining mountainous States. California, the Chamber of Commerce will take that up with you. . . . Nevada has a freedom and independent spirit that is slowly reaching out all over our land. Utah is a great state. . . . Colorado is our grand stand seat to see our world from." Or from the Southwest and places like Tulsa, Dallas, and San Antonio, might come observations like: "Texas? . . . Texas has got everything that any other State has and then 'Ma' and 'Jim' besides. Oklahoma? A lack of vocabulary is all that stops me. I should have stayed in Oxford another year to really have done justice to Oklahoma." With joyous hyperbole, he might add a note on disappointment of Republican hopes on election day there: "Why there is Republicans who live so high up in them skyscrapers in Tulsa and Oklahoma City that they aint been down to the ground since November eight [*sic*]." From the South, from Nashville, Birmingham, and Atlanta might come comments on sights seen earlier or yet to be seen. "Arkansas? Scenery, vacation land, fertility, beautiful women." Or he might mix in politics: "Was you ever down in Long Valley? There is a wonderful, beautiful poetical valley along the length of our great Mississippi River. Cities, beautiful, prosperous ones, hanging moss from century old trees. Charming and delightful people in this valley. Its not called Long Valley on any of your maps, its labelled Louisiana."

This is the kind of untethered experimenting that Whitman had dreamed of. From "Manahatta" to California, from the land of the live oak to "Kanada," the part-Cherokee son of the Mississippi Valley went in the company of all kinds of people, Whitman's "en masse," absorbing and reporting what he saw.

Along with all this, he typed out messages to his public that showed that in the course of such experiential grazing he was achieving a degree of self-fulfillment, his highest possible development as a man. In such a national role, he was the emblem of the dream of self-fulfillment. In at least three ways, Rogers showed that he was developing to their highest his powers and goodness. First, he was the wise innocent in his humor and his commentary. Second, he was the eternal boy in the sense that he seemingly retained a deep joy in life. Finally, he was the good friend of all, considerate of creatures and of his fellow man.

His posture as the wise innocent appeared to follow from a clear-eyed look at the past and from a breadth of experience. The result was a mixture of the sophisticated and the naïve, of the sly and the open, of the worldly and the visionary.

He may have understood the necessity of a consciously-practiced wise innocence. With his role as humorist, for instance, his strategy was to seem artfully unaware of the incongruity he was presenting. "You see," he told readers of a weekly newspaper article, "the subtle thing about a joke is to make it look like it was not a joke." His persona throughout his career was that of the country boy who only seemed to be taken in by the sights and wiles of the big town. Here is, for instance, the magazine article version of a joke that found its way into at least one movie and possibly into dozens of personal appearances. Rogers was trying to get a passport to Europe without being able to present legal evidence of his birth:

> "Well," I told her "Lady I have no birth certificate; and as for someone here in New York that was present at my birth and can swear to it, I am afraid that will be rather difficult." "Havent you somebody here that was there?" she asked. You know the old-time Lady's of which I am a direct descendant. They were of a rather modest and retiring nature, and being born was rather a private affair, and not a public function.
>
> I have no one here in New York that witnessed that historical event, and I doubt very much if even in Oklahoma I could produce any great amount of witnesses. My Parents are dead, Our old Family Doctor, bless his old heart, is no more. So what would you advise that I do? Will it be necessary for me to be born again, and just what proceedure [*sic*] would you advise for me doing so? . . . You see, in the early days of the Indian Territory where I was born there was no such things as birth certificates. You being there was enough. We generally took it for granted if you were there you must have at some time been born.

This is the same straight-faced pose of an innocence wiser than it seems as practiced by the sharp Yankee; it has the exuberance of the tall-story backwoodsman subdued but not repressed; it bespeaks a gay and poised spirit that is finding fulfillment.

Rogers practiced the art, too, when speaking on topical matters. In a time when Florida and California Chambers of Commerce jousted ceaselessly over comparative advantages of their topography and climates, Rogers—as a California mayor—seemingly innocently and good-naturedly strafed Floridian publicists in a daily telegram. He had, he said, rushed down to the pressroom of a Miami paper to get the details on an earthquake in California (for his family was there) but couldn't find any; he had found, though, details of a quake that was happening at the moment, "so I am not going to get excited till next Friday's earthquake. That's when they report a big one," he concluded, behind his mask of innocence. At times the mask would slip and loosen restraint on the exuberance; but in the fun Rogers had with blue-nosed prohibition, with puffy senators, with disarmament conferences, and all the rest, he consistently followed his dictum that the subtle thing about a joke was to make it look like it was not a joke. "There ain't nothing to life but satisfaction," he had said. He seemed in his humor to be getting satisfaction from what he experienced as he grazed all over the new Eden. In humor, his strategy was the wise *innocence.*

When he came to straightforward news commentary, his manner was that of the *wise* innocence. Rogers pretended to be more "dumb" than he was by prefacing many of his comments with expressions such as "All I know is what I read in the papers," "I'm just a dumb comedian," "Now, this is just a rough idea of mine," and variants of each. For Rogers' audience, perhaps, the effect of such disclaimers was at least twofold: They produced the effect of modesty of judgment appropriate to the wise practice of the golden mean and they magnified the words of wisdom that followed by decreasing audience expectations relative to that wisdom.

When Rogers combined with this posture of the American innocent the application of everyday principles to complex affairs, he did seem wise. To make the complicated National Recovery Administration work, "the whole NRA plan should be written on a postcard." For in these few words the NRA could be expressed: "Nobody can work a man over a certain number of hours (without extra pay) and nobody can pay anyone under a certain sum (no matter what line of business it was), nobody can hire children." How to stop war? The wise American innocent would apply the everyday principle of outlawed debts: If loot and reparations were limited, countries would be slow to start wars. Meantime, how to meet crises? With the everyday American principle of unsurprise: "Poor old 'Brink'. I dont know of anything we been on more of than we have it. We have tottered on the Brink so long and so much that I think the old Brink has got hand holts on it. I am beginning to believe we wouldent go over it on a bet," Rogers told his readers of a weekly article in 1934. Such words, tied closely to the experience of the intuitive American Adam, seemed wise to their readers who were themselves dedicated to the proposition that through "the school of hard knocks" comes wisdom and, therefore, the highest possible development of the individual's possibilities.

Speaking wisely-innocent words in his humor and commentary, Rogers gradually etched his own public portrait as the American Adam, a new man starting from new beginnings and developing his own powers to their fullest. Rogers showed himself to be the eternal boy in that he seemed always to have a dog or horse handy, and he wrote lovingly of them. One dog was "Sealingham," a gift of Lord Dewar in 1926. Five years later, the dog had met his death, and Rogers told readers, "We have petted him, complained at him, called him a nuisance, but when we buried him yesterday we couldn't think of a wrong thing he had ever done." On another occasion, a favorite family pony died, a pet of many years' standing. "I first saw him at a town in Connecticut, I think it was Westport," Rogers recalled, almost as if he were talking about a human acquaintance. "I liked him, and he come home with me, and I think he liked me." "Dopey," the safe pony on which all the children had learned trick riding, had been intimately connected with the Rogers family. "He never hurt one in his life. He did everything right. Thats a reputation that no human can die with."

In a final way, Rogers' messages pictured a man who was finding self-fulfillment. His words, revealing a continuing zest for life and the consideration for others that was part of the American dream's program for self-fulfillment of the individual, had the ability to say, "By Golly I am living now," in many ways. As already suggested, the joy of his humor, by itself, testified to his enjoyment of life. In addition, however, many times he wrote of the delights partaken of as the eternal boy. One delight was the navy beans cooked "Kinder soupy" with plenty of home-smoked ham and real corn pone at his sister Sallie's. With April came crocuses and the national pastime: "With the baseball season opened and Washington headed for another pennant, boy, Congress better be good from now on!" At the conclusion of the 1932 Olympics, he told those who had not attended, "You have missed the greatest show from every angle that was ever held in America." At Christmastime, readers might find that Rogers was busy replacing presents he had worn out by playing with them himself. A daily wire on what was to be his last birthday testified to Rogers' continuing joy in living and spirit of boyhood. "I am pretty sore today," he began. "Am looking for the ones that reminded me that 55 years ago today at Oolagah [sic], Indian Territory, on Nov. 4, 1879, a boy baby was born. Well, anyhow, I played a game of polo and roped calves all day, so there is life in the old nag yet." The same essence of boyishness clung to dispatches from trips around the world and to travels around this country. Any reader could conclude that he was getting satisfaction from living.

Though in his public portrait Rogers was the eternal boy, he was not an egocentric one, thoughtless of all but himself. In his dispatches, the cowboy philosopher expressed a love for comrades from both humble and high stations in life. Many times would appear a daily squib such as the following (which mixed in the dream of equality):

> "Mexico, Mo.—Tom Bass, well-known Negro horseman, aged 75, died here today."
>
> Don't mean much to you does it? You have all seen society folks perform on a beautiful three or five gaited saddle horse, and said, "My, what skill and patience they must have had to train that animal."
>
> Well, all they did was ride him in. All this Negro, Tom Bass, did was to train him. For over fifty years America's premier trainer, he trained thousands others were applauded on. . . .
>
> If old St. Peter is as wise as we give him credit for being, Tom, he will let you go in horseback and give those folks up there a great show, and you will get the blue ribbon yourself.

Whether the friend was mail plane pilot, governor of a state, or Speaker of the House, Rogers evidenced in his words the same degree of warm feelings. "If we haven't got any friends," he had written, "we will find that we are poorer than anybody." Rogers apparently was rich. "I am proud of the fact there is not a human being that I have got it in for. I never met a man I dident like," he professed—aware, of course, that liking (as does loving) admits of many degrees. For such a man, happiness seemed to be a possession rather than a pursuit.

In his public pronouncements, Rogers also showed consideration for the religions of others, perhaps the most personal of all matters. In a weekly article in 1933 he answered an inquiry from a Protestant minister and seemed almost to be Whitman's ideal American. "I was raised predominately [sic] a Methodist, but I have traveled so much, mixed with so many people in all parts of the world, I dont know now just what I am," he wrote. "I know I have never been a nonbeliever. But I can honestly tell you that I dont think that any one religion is the religion." If the Protestant minister were hoping for endorsement of his own sect, he was probably disappointed in the reply. Whitman, though, urging the ideal American not to argue about religion, would not have been disappointed, for Rogers consistently upheld an ecumenical attitude toward religion. As early as 1923, he told his newspaper audience, "Every man's religion is good. There is none of it bad."

In such messages, Rogers appeared to be considerate of others. Such an impression, paired with that of a man who is eagerly enjoying life itself, spoke relevantly of the dream of the common man's self-fulfillment.

In sum, Will Rogers identified himself materially with the dream of the dignity and worth of the individual by admiring the judgment and stamina of all the unique individuals who comprised "the big Normal Majority," and by expressing a belief in the natural goodness of man and the altruism of his cultural contemporaries. He also merged himself on a second level of the dream by projecting his own individual powers and goodness into the role of the new American Adam who first rejects the stifling past, then seeks broad firsthand experience, and, finally, finds a degree of self-fulfillment in wisdom, joy in life, and consideration for others.

Rogers also identified formally with the dream of individualism in his use of simple gesture and word. The vision of the dignity and worth of the individual held a sense of new beginnings—at its center was the new Adam, personification of the dream in his newness and wise innocence.

Rogers habitually used a gesture that gave him the appearance of the wise American innocent. As he would say words such as, "Course, that's just a rough idea of mine," or "Course, I'm just a dumb comedian," he would lower his head as though to look at the floor, but, instead, would raise his eyebrows and quickly and repeatedly alternate his glance between the audience and the floor. Used constantly in the context of uttered words, the gesture could well have taken on a conventionalized significance (renderable in word symbols) of "wiser-than-I-look." With such a symbolic function abstracted from the total stimulus, audiences could possibly associate meaning and gesture so strongly that the expression could be said to look like the wise innocent (instead of, for example, a groveling Uriah Heep). To the extent that the gesture suggested the wise innocence of the American Adam, it was an iconic symbol and a formal identification with the dream of the individual.

When Rogers used either written or spoken language, the form or appearance of the new Adam was only metaphorically such. But he did utilize the properties of written or spoken language to convey the sense of newness that was so much a part of the American Adam. That sense of newness came chiefly through bending words toward new significations—first, by artistically misapplying a word so that it was made to bear a new sense, and, second, by using slang.

The artful misapplication of a word is a figure of speech and, therefore, distinctly dependent upon the verbal language, itself. As Rogers applied the technique, the impression on his audiences may simply have been one of pleasing newness and of fresh use of language. In the guise of the past-rejecting Adam, he could remark that New England "is mangy with History"; in Genoa, he was going "church prowling," and the cardinal in Rogers' version of English history made possible Henry VIII's marriage to Catherine when he "thought of the bright idea of saying that Prince Arthur and Catherine were never married, that it was two other fellows." When he addressed himself to political matters as the *wise* innocent, he could report that Kansas had "sentenced" Charles Curtis to the Senate; he could hope, after the common man realized his own potential more fully, to see us "extinguish our office seekers every two years"; if the NRA were resubmitted to Congress after being declared unconstitutional, he would be sure that it went there under an "assumed name." Republicans, apparently, were not human beings counted in numbers: "You'd be surprised at the amount of 'em that's showin' up, you know"; on the other hand, senators who earlier had baited President Hoover had demanded unfairly that the President give them the whole "Menu" of a visit between the President and the English Prime Minister. Commenting upon other international events, Rogers took note of the knee breeches worn by diplomats received by the English King and took satisfaction from the fact that America's "Charley [Dawes] was the only one that didn't wear rompers." A few years before, he had professed astonishment over Mexican reaction to an earlier punitive expedition: "They dident appreciate the fact that they had been shot in the most cordial manner possible." By means of such word bending, Will Rogers achieved an effect of freshness in his language. Too, he suggested the new Adam in his use of slang.

One source of slang for him was the transfer of professional or occupational terms from their special vocabularies to a more general one, with an effect much like that of artful misapplication. From bookkeeping came the expression to describe the Ferguson couple in Texas, both of whom became chief executives of that state: "America's only Double Entry Governors." From Rogers' ranching experience came "round up" and "corralling beef" that he applied to corset making; a governor from Maryland had every "earmark" of a future President. From show business he drew many expressions and applied them outside the field: Nations had to "book" wars ahead; Moses' Biblical followers had been his "troupe"; our intervention in Nicaragua had been wrong because citizens of that nation had wanted to use only "home talent" in their civil war; present-day Nevada miners were "descendants of the original casts." This was slang at its best—fresh, vivid, and Adamic.

Another source for Rogers' slang lay in his naturalization of foreign words: From the Spanish *remuda,* he arrived at "remuther" as the name for a ready group of saddle horses; the front feet of cattle were "mongano"; the Spanish *frijole* kept its pronunciation but not its spelling when, as the eternal boy, he loved to eat "free holey" beans out on the range.

Besides using special terms in a more general sense and adapting foreign words, Rogers used shortened forms of words, onomatopoetic words, and coined words to achieve a fresh language.

A division into shares was a "divvy"; a reputation was a "rep"; diplomats wouldn't "dip," and the preferable ruins were those that hadn't yet started to "rue." His Ford car had gone "flooey"; talk about brinks was all "hooey"; talking was also "yowling" and "yapping"; a risqué foreign film was admittedly "snorty" in spots. A back belonging to a coward was a "Spine-a-Marino," and Oklahoma—with its frequent troubles with governors—was "IMPEACHerino." The Old Testament Adam "gave names to all cattle, and to the fowl of the air, and to every beast of the field." Will Rogers, as a new Adam, used new names for old ones.

By speaking directly of the principles of the dream of the dignity and worth of the individual, by using words to reveal his practice of the action corollaries of that dream, and by using the resources of language, itself, to suggest further the character of the new Adam, Will Rogers gained identification with one great category of the American dream. Of Americans who dreamed of the powers of the common man, Dixon Wecter observed in 1941, "Mother-wit and resourcefulness we love." Of Adam-worshipping Americans, he added this description of their affections:

> Manliness, forthright manners, and salty speech are approved. Love of the soil, of dogs and horses and manual hobbies and fishing, is better understood than absorption in art, literature, and music. . . . Also the touch of versatility and homely skill is applauded in a hero.

Thus, one face that Americans of the twenties and thirties may well have seen on Will Rogers was that of the new Adam. With that face alone he would have been attractive. With the addition of others—including that of the American democrat—he was a potential folk-hero.

Peter C. Rollins (essay date 1976)

SOURCE: "Will Rogers: Symbolic Man, Journalist, and Film Image," in *Journal of Popular Culture,* Vol. 9, No. 4, 1976, pp. 850-74.

[*In the following essay, Rollins argues that Rogers used his image to calm many of the social anxieties common to Americans at the time.*]

On August 15, 1935, Will Rogers and his pilot Wiley Post were killed in a plane crash at Point Barrow, Alaska. Exactly one week later, the offices of Twentieth Century Fox and Universal Studios closed at noon so that office workers could attend a special memorial service at the Hollywood Bowl "where over twenty thousand gathered to pay tribute to the memory of the beloved humorist." That evening, twelve thousand motion picture theaters across the country observed two minutes of respectful silence before beginning their evening programs.

Just before leaving for Alaska, Rogers had completed two films. At least previous to this dilemma, Hollywood had observed "an unwritten law forbidding the release of a picture after the death of a star." But in the case of Will Rogers, there were obviously other factors to be considered. In fact, the rationale behind the release of *In Old Kentucky* and *Steamboat Round the Bend* gives us a glimpse of the special relationship between Will Rogers and his American audience. After a long conference, Joseph Schenck (Chairman of the Board of Directors) and Sidney R. Kent (President) of Twentieth Century Fox determined that the release of these last two pictures would not have the same morbid overtones which might have accompanied a similar posthumous release of films by other actors: "Rogers was totally different from Valentino, Wallace Reid and Lon Chaney, where audiences appreciated their work. Rogers was loved as a man, as a national character, as the greatest of all home philosophers."

Joseph Schenck was right about the unique place of Will Rogers in the hearts of Americans. Although he never held political office, the popularity of his daily syndicated columns, his books, and finally his movies made him one of the most important molders of opinion in America from 1922 until his untimely death in 1935. In ways which this paper will attempt to articulate, Will Rogers as public person, as journalist, and as film star confronted and subdued many of the pressures and anxieties affecting his audience. A typical Will Rogers fan had very special ideas about Rogers' behavior as a private individual; he derived a special pleasure from the style of Rogers' journalism. With these elements in mind,

he attended and surrendered to the seductive nostalgia of Rogers' late films.

This paper will begin with a short discussion of the hopes and anxieties of post-World War I America, with the objective of establishing a context within which Rogers functioned both as ironic observer and symbolic person. The second section will attempt to specify which values were associated with Rogers as a "private" individual, and relate these imputed values to his penetrating and entertaining style of humor. The third and final section will sketch the evolution of the Rogers *persona* in film. In the last stage of his Hollywood career, Rogers became the best paid ($225,000 per film) and most popular male movie attraction. From 1933 until 1935, Will Rogers portrayed a film character who deeply moved his American audience. If correctly interpreted, these nostalgic rural dramas are as relevant as documents of the spirit of the 1930's as a book like *I'll Take My Stand* (1930). Like that famous protest against progress, the city, a declining estimate of man, the late films of Will Rogers portray an alternative society in which the best of traditional elements of the American national character could have free play. Franklin Delano Roosevelt was not alone in concluding that the sanity of Americans in the turbulent early decades of the twentieth century had been preserved because of the sympathy and humor of this complex companion of the American people.

I. THE TWENTIES: THE PRICE OF THE NEW

Americans in the 1920's were excited by the rapid changes going on around them, yet at the same time they were uneasy, for assuming the new identity as twentieth century urban Americans entailed a rejection of older modes of life and values. The tension induced by these changes led some Americans to strike out at the new. The infamous Red Scare inspired by A. Mitchell Palmer sought to stamp out the threat of bolshevism. Gathering new members among native-stock, rural Americans, the Ku Klux Klan expanded its crusade against change. Its new enemies included "the city, sexual freedom, modern life . . . [and] . . . liquor." While militant fundamentalists brought John Scopes to trial, the Daughters of the American Revolution and others who feared the rising political power of the immigrant launched their campaign for 100% Americanism. The majority of Americans attempted to find a place for themselves in this new world, but unquestionably all Americans in the period were curious about the much celebrated juggernaut of progress—was it steaming toward the good society or away from it?

Industrialism had posed increasing challenges since the end of the Civil War. Those native Americans who went to the city to profit from the new wealth and social mobility available there were rewarded handsomely. A ready supply of docile immigrant labor assured that quick-witted native Americans could rise to the top of the industrial heap. Yet for all their successes, these same newcomers to the good life of industrial America had their anxieties: "For millions of people torn from accustomed rural patterns of culture and thrust into a strange, urban environment, the meaning of industrialism lay in a feeling of uprootedness, in the disintegrations of old ways of life." Many of those who remained behind believed they were left out, creating the paradoxical situation in which the liberated were anxious, while the innocent were resentful.

The technique of mass production started what has been called a "second industrial revolution." The United States was transformed as this manufacturing technique was pressed into service to turn out large quantities of automobiles, radios, and other new inventions of the era. The advertising industry expanded its efforts to convince Americans that they required the massive number of goods which could now be produced. Americans were urged to consume, to buy on credit, to become part of this new economy of abundance. If they had money left when they finished shopping, Americans were advised to invest in the stock market. If they had no money left, they were assured that they could buy on the margin.

Parallel with these major changes in economic life, a "revolution in morals" was significantly altering the outlook of Americans. As the authority of religion declined, the gospel according to St. Freud gained true believers. The family had already lost its economic role; its power as an institution was further lessened by a host of pleas for individual liberation. As a result, many were bothered because new guides of conduct were not being offered to clothe the individual as he stripped off the corset of Puritanism. Perhaps the greatest consternation arose when the new woman appeared. Rather than a socially constructive idealist, like Jane Addams, she turned out to be the flapper and the flirt!

The liberation of writers in elite culture yielded the creative literary work of Hemingway, Faulkner, and Fitzgerald. But in popular culture liberation appeared to have unstopped the bottle of cheap-and-nasty: popular songs on the radio were titled "Hot Lips," "I Need Lovin'," "Burning Kisses," while popular magazines such as *Paris Nights* and *Flapper Experiences* covered the newsstands. Hollywood concentrated all of these pyrotechnic changes into one half-baked city, Los Angeles, California. Advertisements for the "smart" and "sophistocated" films produced there promised "brilliant men, beautiful jazz babies, champagne baths, midnight revels, petting parties in the purple dawn, all ending in one terrific smashing climax that makes you gasp."

According to Edward Sapir (a contemporary social scientist) industrialism, urbanism, advertising and the unreflective celebration of the individual all had worked to fragment the traditional culture of the West. Much like Will Rogers, Sapir was careful to explain that so-called "progress" in the early twentieth century was more a matter of material improvement than an advance in the quality of "genuine culture." Even the most well adjusted twentieth century American sensed a certain incompleteness in his life: "Even if he succeeds in making a fairly

satisfactory compromise with his new environment, he is apt to retain an uneasy sense of the loss of some vague and great good, some state of mind that he would be hard put to it to define but which gave him a courage and joy that latter-day prosperity never quite seems to have regained for him. What has happened is that he has slipped out of the warm embrace of a culture into a cold air of fragmentary existence." The price of material conquest of the environment had been paid for by an emotional tax on true happiness: "Here lies the grimmest joke of our present American civilization. The vast majority of us, deprived of any but an insignificant and cruelly abortive share in the satisfaction of the immediate wants of mankind, are further deprived of both opportunity and stimulation to share in the production of non-utilitarian values. Part of the time we are dray horses; the rest of the time we are listless consumers of goods which have received no least impress of our personality. In other words, our spiritual selves go hungry, for the most part, pretty much all the time."

From his elevated position as Professor of Anthropology at Yale, Edward Sapir could see the fragmentation of culture in a historical sweep that went back to the seventeenth century. On the level of popular culture, most Americans sensed the same inadequacies in their lives, but their frame of reference was smaller. Many sought solace in thinking of the 1890's as a lost Eden from which the America of their own post-war era had departed. At least as nostalgically recalled by these unsettled people, that earlier America had been a face-to-face society, a comprehensible world painted in primary colors:

> By 1932, the prewar years had taken on a luminescence that they did not wholly have at the time. In retrospect, the years before World War I seemed like a lost Arcadia. Men remembered county fairs and church socials, spelling bees and sleigh rides, the excitement of the circus train or the wild dash of firehorses from the station house, the cool smell of an ice cream parlor and the warm fragrance of roasted chestnuts. . . . They remembered people: the paper boy with his off-key whistle, the brawny iceman sauntering up the walk with his five-cent cake of ice, the Negro stable boys, the printers and devils in the newspaper offices. They recollected general stores: the bolts of calico and muslin, the jars of cinnamon and gunpowder tea, bins of dried peaches and cornmeal, kegs of mackerel, canisters of striped candy. From the vantage point of 1932, it seemed as though they had danced endlessly at tango teas and strummed mandolins every evening.

Not the realities of the 1890's, but the anxieties of the 1930's tempted Americans to reflect nostalgically on that earlier era, proving that people who burn their candles at both ends will frequently be burned by the hot wax.

II. WILL ROGERS: PUBLIC PERSON AND PUBLIC SPOKESMAN

Will Rogers was important to Americans in the 1920's and 1930's because he addressed his humor to their basic sense of rootlessness and loss. As a cowboy version of Rip Van Winkle, Rogers passed through this era of change, judging new developments by the standards of the 1890's. And despite the criticism he delivered, he somehow bridged the gap between the old and the new. Because he made the transition without losing his identity, his audience was intensely concerned with his highly publicized "private" life: in a world where divorces were increasing, Rogers remained happily monogamous; while his audience felt itself to be under constant pressure to perform, he seemed somehow to be unruffled. In an era of big government's delays, Will Rogers stood out as a symbol of ready sympathy and practical help for the distressed, for unlike his uprooted audience, he was still in contact with **"The Real Things of Life."**

A. ROGERS THE MAN: LIVING A LIFE IN PUBLIC VIEW

1. *Love and Marriage*

Will Rogers was admired from the beginning as a man who was somehow able to remain simple and pure, even in an age of puff and artificiality. He seemed miraculously unaffected by the erosion of values. His good qualities were highlighted further by his presence in Hollywood: "He became nonetheless dear to us because of the falsity of much that surrounded him: the spurious nature and illegitimacy of much of the screen threw him into relief as someone really genuine." Rogers' sexual purity was universally respected. Reviewers of the early Rogers films were surprised that he could succeed on the screen without pandering to the usual demands of romance and sex appeal. He was unique as a male film star in "outwitting the sexy fellows."

Many admired Will and Betty Rogers for holding their family together. One reporter, realizing how important this happily monogamous couple was to her audience, breathlessly told her readers the results of a telephone "interview over four thousand miles with a model married man." The readers necessarily understood that Hollywood was the leading edge of sexual liberation, and thus a city where the family was most endangered. In this context of dizzy freedom, "Will Rogers and his wife have been married longer than some stars, several times divorced, have been alive." Rogers himself encouraged the press to report this eccentricity. Proudly (and often) he proclaimed that he was "the only motion picture star who has the same wife he originally started with." The result of all this interest and self-promotion was that the Rogers household was celebrated as "an ideal home" where (in contrast with much of the rest of American homes) parents spent every free moment teaching the children or playing with them.

A review of Rogers' first talkie, *They Had To See Paris* (1929) clearly shows how intensely concerned his film audience was with this reputation for cleanliness and fidelity. When Pike Peters (Will Rogers) and his wife (Irene Rich) reach Paris, Mrs. Peters immediately begins to dress in the styles of the *beau monde*. In a bedroom scene, Pike, pleased by the way his wife looks in her new fashions, gives her a very innocent kiss. Rogers' audience was so involved with their public man off the screen, that there was a very intense response to this act on camera: When "he blushingly kissed her, the audience broke into happy applause. They knew it was Will's first screen kiss, and they realized that he never would have done it had it not been for the years of devoted friendship that had grown up between them in their pilgrimage to the top of the screen ladder. Also knowing Will's domestic happiness, the roof went off when he admitted that his kiss was almost like 'infidelity.'" The film audience admired the Rogers' for maintaining "a real house, even in Hollywood" because so many families in their own neighborhoods were disintegrating under the acid of change.

2. *Transcending the Pressures of Middle-Class Life*

Americans were fascinated by Will Rogers' ability to surmount the pressures of his busy life as entertainer, journalist, and film star. As an admiring newspaperman reported: "Will Rogers probably is the only person alive who can face the Associated Press totally unembarrassed. Big news is but the happenings of a small town to him. To him important personages are but fellers of his acquaintance." Rogers himself delivers a line in *Life Begins at Forty* (1934) in which summarizes the lesson which his viewers drew: "He solved the problem which all the world has been looking for—how to relax. Just to look at him makes me feel better."

Rogers' freedom from pressure was communicated in numerous ways. When radio was a new invention which stymied a number of professional performers, Will Rogers made his broadcasts extemporaneously. He conveyed the impression that he was too secure in himself to be worried. As one commentator noted, Rogers was "the only guy in radio who dares to hem and haw away air time." Rogers' movie fans were aware that he was equally blase on the movie set. Part of the delight in viewing a Rogers movie was watching Rogers deviate from the script, and seeing the problems which his improvisation caused for his fellow actors. While this horseplay might have been a pleasure for an audience accustomed to being programmed during working hours, it caused some consternation and confusion on the movie set at Twentieth Century Fox. Rochelle Hudson (who played the young female in *Dr. Bull, Mr. Skitch, Judge Priest, Life Begins at Forty*) admitted that Rogers' liberties with the script caused her great distress, for she never recognized her cues. As she recalled, Rogers' proclivity for improvisation left her "listening for cues that never came . . . had me ad libbing to myself in my sleep long before my first picture with Bill was finished." A young and ambitious John Ford (forewarned about the insouciance of Will Rogers and Irvin Cobb on the set) began the filming of *Steamboat 'Round the Bend* (1935) with the simple but knowing question: "Does either of you two gentlemen have the faintest idea of what this story is about?"

Will Rogers' screen audiences were delighted by his improvisations, for his liberty even from the verbal restrictions of a script conveyed the impression that he was a man at ease with himself who (unlike his middle-class audience) was capable of transcending the petty demands of a busy life. One reviewer accurately spoke for millions when he said that "You feel, somehow, that he has captured the secret of being happy, and that if you watch the screen carefully, this secret may be yours." As with the other virtues described in this section, the audience believed that this secret applied to Rogers the man as well as the Rogers *persona* on the screen.

3. *The Sympathetic Spirit*

Rogers' humanitarian activities were widely followed and admired. When an earthquake destroyed Managua, Nicaragua in 1931, Will Rogers flew south to lend his name to fund raising efforts; after floods ripped through the lower Mississippi Valley in 1927, Will Rogers was on the spot to entertain and to ease the pain of the dispossessed; when Oklahoma and surrounding states became a "dust bowl" during the famous drought of the 1930s, Rogers stumped Oklahoma and Arkansas for the Red Cross. The itineraries of what were called his "tours of mercy" boggle the mind of the ordinary mortal. His contemporaries found it difficult to believe that a man could do so much for so many without some kind of mission of love inspiring him. One contemporary went so far as to call these tours as representative of Will Rogers' "Christ-like spirit of giving." When they reported these tours, newsmen did not hesitate to contrast the personal concern demonstrated by Rogers with the foot-dragging and bureaucratic bungling of a big and indifferent government. There is little doubt that by circumventing the red tape and empty debates, Will Rogers gave many forgotten men in the age of Coolidge and Hoover the sense that someone of national stature was personally concerned about their suffering.

A newspaper cartoon entitled "Relief Map of Oklahoma" conveys this message. Rogers managed to visit almost every major city and county seat of Oklahoma during the disastrous drought of the thirties. The people of his home state were obviously pleased with the $225,000 in financial relief which these tours yielded, but this cartoon-map has nothing to say about physical or fiscal relief. In fact, it is really not a map at all, but a close-up of Will Rogers: in the foreground, blocking out all but the eastern and western extremities of the outline of the state, is the smiling face of Will Rogers, his hat on the back of his head, and his boyish grin warming our hearts. The cartoon really celebrates the spiritual and psychological relief which Will Rogers' humor brought to suffering people. Other stories and cartoons of this kind make it certain that victims of flood and other natural disasters were relieved when they heard the announcement (this from a New Orleans newspaper) "Will Rogers is Coming!"

A writer for the *Jacksonville Journal*, Jacksonville, Florida, summed up the profound effect of Rogers' per-

sonal charity. Note the emphasis in this response upon Rogers' spiritual use of one of the principal symbols of the age of technology:

> Giving wings to most people does not add to their ability to be of benefit to the world . . . though it may increase their economic efficiency. . . . But when a genius such as Will Rogers got wings, he becomes a sort of superman, not by reason of a superiority of attitude, but by the multiplication of his contacts with human creatures who need a bit of cheer in their helplessness or weariness or misery. Like St. Francis, he is a lover not of mankind, at large, but men as individuals. St. Francis used the 'shabby expedient' of a rope to tie around his waist in his spiritual vocation; Will Rogers used it to humanize his philosophy. And the good he does in this world is increased by his mobility.

As a representative person, Will Rogers embodied a ready sympathy, a freedom from the selfishness which seemed to be the guiding spirit of the materialistic American twenties. In a society where members of the same apartment building did not know each other, Will Rogers seemed to convey the idea that cities and nations (through his example) could be linked by neighborly bonds of affection: "He comes nearer being a *Jongleur de Dieu* than any modern world personage—a jongleur and a troubador in one—not for a single community, but for thousands of cities and for the remotest cabins. To have wings for such a service is not merely to minister to more people directly; but is to carry them the human kindness of others and to bring these people into wider human relationships."

4. *"The Real Things of Life"*

The news surrounding Will Rogers' response to his sister's death binds together many of the values and qualities which his audience identified with Will Rogers the "private" man. One report may stand as a representative of the whole. **"The Real Things of Life"** begins with an explanation of Rogers' wealth and popularity as an entertainer and journalist. The major point of the article (and a very important one for Rogers' followers) is that no matter how successful, how far on top of the heap, Will Rogers proudly kept his spiritual roots in the soil of Oklahoma.

The articles about the death of Rogers' sister and his response to it emphasize two incidents. The first occurs while Rogers is entertaining a convention hall filled with ministers. As he delivers his planned comic lines, Rogers is overwhelmed by the thought of his sister's suffering, and breaks into tears. With an immediate change of mood, Rogers asks the assembled clergy to pray for his sister, Mrs. C. L. Lane. Far from ridiculing Rogers' display of emotion, an admiring reporter wrote: "He could not hide his sorrow, nor would it have been more manly in him to suppress his tears."

The second incident involves Rogers' response to a newspaper story which he saw while returning to

Claremore, Oklahoma to attend his sister's funeral. Perusing a state newspaper, he noticed a headline calling his sister "Mrs. C. L. Lane, sister of famous comedian, Will Rogers." Rogers' response was noted well because it reaffirmed his respect for rural America, even though he was himself a success in the new world of the city. After seeing the headline, he attempted to correct what he saw as a very false impression. Reflecting about the reverent, mourning crowds of country people, he demonstrated his respect for **"The Real Things of Life"**: "It's the other way around. I am the brother of Mrs. C. L. Lane, 'The Friend of Humanity.' And I want to tell you that as I saw all these people who were there to pay tribute to her memory, it was the proudest moment of my life that I was her brother. And all the honors that I could ever in my wildest dreams hope to reach, would never equal the honor paid on a little western hilltop among her people to Maude Lane. If they love me like that at the finish, my life will not have been in vain."

Such a statement of respect for the values and judgment of small town America had broad resonances in 1925. The revolt from the village had long before become a trendy cause in popular and serious literature: Sinclair Lewis added the word "Babbitt" to the American language in 1922 when his searing portrait of the Middle Western businessman was published; *soi-disant* sophisticated readers of H. L. Mencken's *American Mercury* (1924-33) were learning to chortle over the strange and antiquated manners and morals of the "booboisie" of the American hinterland. This was indeed a period when "The midwest stood for all that was tedious, humdrum, and false about human existence." Within this context of contempt for rural America, Rogers' newspaper audience was impressed by his emotional reaction to his sister's death. Unquestionably, Rogers' followers were probably reading at least some of the writings of Lewis and Mencken, but they were impressed (and perhaps reassured) by this incident. Clearly, Rogers had his feet in basic old American values even though he was living in the urban world and earning one of the highest salaries in show business.

His audience may have made the same rise, but they feared that they had lost touch with a society which could value people for non-economic virtues. In contrast, Will Rogers had made the same passage to the new without losing touch with the old. His ability to bridge the gap (and their capacity to admire him for doing it) salved their consciences. As one Hollywood acquaintance summed up Will Rogers' unusual capacity to keep his feet planted in both realms, "Bill is perhaps the world's most widely travelled citizen with the hometown feeling completely untouched." Thus, to a disturbed and mobile people, Will Rogers "represented something fundamentally honest in human nature, something which, in the hectic movement of the passing time, we seem to be in danger of forgetting and eventually losing."

B. ROGERS THE JOURNALIST

Because Americans imputed so many anachronistic (yet estimable) characteristics to Will Rogers, they willingly turned in their confusion to his newspaper column every morning for a dose of common sense. Will Rogers seemed to be uncorrupted by the fads of the period, and this exemption convinced people that he (unlike them) could look straight at the new and see whether or not the Emperor had on a new set of clothes. Frequently (to the relief of his audience) Rogers saw that the Emperor was naked.

1. *The Old (the Essential), the New (the Inessential), and the Crash (a Judgment)*

While Will Rogers is remembered today as simply a "humorist," his contemporaries were very much interested in Rogers as a moralist. The moralism of his social commentary was rendered in his humor as much by a dramatic technique which runs through it as by the actual words he used. The basic inner technique of Rogers' humor is implicit in the relationship which he articulates between himself as an observer and the modern world which he reports for us. The observer in Will Rogers' humorous journalism is always an "old boy" from Claremore, Oklahoma who has been by-passed by the germs of fashion. We are always forced to assume that this speaker has some kind of contact with a core of uncorrupted, "natural" rural values. Because our speaker is pre-modern, pre-urban, he can see through many of the artificial problems which perplex urban man.

The society and leaders observed in Will Rogers' humorous journalism are usually associated with ideas, institutions, inventions, or problems which are new to the twentieth century. As Rogers' innocent eye scans the contemporary horizon, it focuses quickly on the exaggerated sense of self-importance which urban man is always guilty of claiming for himself. The lesson which Rogers tries to communicate is that men in cities, in corporations, at the head of big governments and major political parties may have convinced themselves that they are important to the world, but our rural commentator who is closer to nature knows better. Since men's pride is the subject of so much of Rogers' commentaries, it should be underscored that the insights which he presents are penetrating not because of his special intelligence, but by virtue of the perspective of the human comedy which his rural (and pleasantly backward) location gives him. Only in exceptional cases (the pilot Lindberg is one) does a product of the twentieth century prove itself to be a match for a counterpart in the nineties. We are told both explicitly (by argument) and implicitly (by metaphor) that people at the turn of the century knew who they were and what they wanted, but that twentieth century American man (because he has lost his roots) is pursuing a set of hollow and trivial goals.

Rogers' device of speaking for an older value system is especially obvious in the following criticism of Reno's infamous (and then shockingly new) divorce mill: "Lawyers meet the trains and line up and holler out the same as porters do down South at depots for Hotels. They got lawyers there that can get you loose from an Octopus.

Lots of the women buy . . . cottages . . . till their proba-tion is over. Lots of them keep their houses there, and then use them when they come back on the next case. Some women have as many as four or five 'notches' on the same house, showing that they had got their man." The humor in this passage is created by the speaker's attitude: he is a curious innocent looking on in bewilder-ment. The moralistic judgment of this passage is implicit in the verbal pictures which are presented, especially the metaphor of the female as gunslinger. A society in which such chaos reigns is obviously decadent and corrupt.

Surveying a modern civilization which produces so much that the institution of advertising has been needed to force people to consume, Rogers tartly observes that "One-third of the people in the United States promote, while the other two-thirds provide." The judgment in this remark stems from Rogers' adherence to the older ethic of work and productivity rather than the goals of leisure and consumption so praised by twentieth century men, especially by the ubiquitous voice of advertising. To Rogers' mind, advertising was especially dangerous be-cause it frequently convinced people to relinquish valid old truths that had been tested over years. Such a nega-tive judgment is the buried irony of the famous phrase which became a sort of verbal signature for Rogers the journalist. While the phrase "All I know is what I read in the papers" led most of Rogers daily articles, it did *not* mean what it literally said, but precisely the opposite. Rogers despaired that the average middle-class American in his audience swallowed the reports of the press and the claims of advertisers whole each morning along with their new vitamin pills. To his peril, it was the average American who knew only what he read in the papers. As a man who represented a fading value system, which had been forgotten by mass media, it was Rogers' purpose to hold the perspectives and information of these opinion *creating* newspapers up to the light of his older, tested truths.

While Will Rogers the humanitarian certainly did not gloat over the stock market's resounding crash and the subsequent economic depression, he did believe that the depression confirmed the criticism which he had been delivering all through the twenties. Although Rogers ex-pressed himself in homier language, his critique was not unlike that which we saw voiced by the anthropologist, Edward Sapir. While Sapir, the academic, explained that Americans were living in a "spurious culture," Rogers summed up his criticism in the famous insight that "there ain't no civilization where there ain't no satisfaction, and that's what's the trouble now, nobody is satisfied." One quip by Rogers is particularly devastating: "Two hundred years from now, history will record: 'America, a nation that flourished from 1900 to 1942, conceived many odd inventions for getting somewhere, but could think of nothing to do when they got there.'" His very famous observation that "America is the only nation to go to the poorhouse in an automobile" is a compression of this ironic criticism of the mindless worship of technology. As the depression deepened, so did Rogers' vision grow darker, bordering on a very uncharacteristic despair. Shortly before his death, he wrote that "Civilization is nothing but acquiring comforts for ourselves, when be-fore civilization they were so hard they didn't need em. We will strive to put in another bath, when may-our neighbors cant even put in an extra loaf of bread."

2. *Let Me Play With Your Problems*

Because Will Rogers had faith that men could survive both their problems and their leaders, he was fortunately spared the kind of despair which the last quotation seems to reflect. For although he was a political commentator for most of his adult life he believed that "history makes itself, and statesmen just drag along." For some men, such a conclusion could be fatalistic, but in Rogers the message which is hammered home repeatedly is that we should not take our politicians, intellectual systems or ourselves as seriously as we do—life is more fun and less taxing when we learn to see that man is not at the center of the universe. Rogers could remain aloof even during the crucial presidential election of 1932. In response to the exaggerated predictions of gloom by both candidates, Rogers retorted that "This country is a thousand times bigger than any two men in it or any two parties in it. This country has gotten where it is in spite of politics, not by aid of it. That we have carried as much political bunk as we have and still survived shows we are a supernation." Given this perspective, Rogers advised the candidates to take a rest and let the people make up their minds: "Get the world off your shoulders and go fishing. Then come back next Wednesday and we will let you know which one is the lesser of two evils of you."

In the "playful" (*vs.* the "moralistic") vein of his journal-istic humor, Rogers seems to have appointed himself to be a translator of the new to the American people. In this role, he strives not so much to judge the new as to play with it as his audience looks on with admiration. On first inspection, many of these verbally playful articles seem superficial. After all, they formulate no solutions for the problems which they discuss. Such an analysis misses the real point of these articles—in them, Rogers is not at-tempting to formulate answers so much as to give his audience a sense that the novelty discussed is not so awesomely complex and threatening as it might appear at first. Rogers' major goal in these articles is not to turn out stock answers to the daily headlines. He modestly wished to slow down their impact on the mind of his audience. If he could only juggle them long enough, the result would be that his audience could deal with them more sensibly. Some small sampling of these playful ar-ticles is necessary to counterbalance the impression that Rogers was strictly a moralist. In the following daily tele-gram, Rogers sends President Coolidge a mock warning about the popular tune, "Valencia." It is on its way to poison the public mind of America: "My dear Mr. Presi-dent: There will be a song hitting you now if it hassent already hit you. Do what you can to keep people from going entirely cuckoo over it. It is in exchange for 'Yes, We Have No Bananas,' and is called 'Valencia.' It ain't the Piece—it's all right—its the amount of times they will play it. Have Ear Muffs ready." This is the voice of a man who delights in the absurdities of popular culture!

Rogers' capacity to make his readers laugh at their own frenetic involvement in change must have released psychological tensions. In one telegram that became famous Rogers observed: "Give an American a one-piece bathing suit, a hamburger, and five gallons of gas and they are just as tickled as a movie star with a new divorce." Here Rogers addresses himself directly to manifestations of the rapid changes in the moral, social, and physical environments: the one-piece bathing suit was considered to be a daring symbol of rebellion from Victorian prudery; the hamburger is the snack of a society which is in a hurry (and probably not exactly sure where it is going); the automobile is obviously a symbol of the new industrial civilization. The final, synthesizing line about the movie star with a divorce gives the description a special twist. The reader *does* feel guilty and confused about the rapidity with which his life is changing in all sectors, but he knows that he is not as fallen as the movie star. The inappropriate conjunction in this humorous comparison helps the reader to feel reassured that he has not yet gone off the deep end, for all his movement away from the certainties of the nineties.

To the obvious delight of his audience, Rogers would "play" with the most unplayful of problems. The growing combativeness in Europe and Asia was no laughing matter to Americans in the twenties and thirties. Rogers could not hold back, however, because he was driven to be the representative tester of the new: "Japan wants a 'Monroe Doctrine' with them playing the part of Monroe, 'doctoring' on China. Not only 'doctoring,' but operating." Here is a line directed at events which were in the papers of the previous day. What Rogers succeeds in doing here is subtle, but essential to understanding the appeal of his daily articles. In a short space, he has summarized the nature of the threat. He then exaggerates the justifications of the belligerent so that they appear ridiculous and self-criticizing. Finally, he provides a summary judgment of the problem. When a typical reader of Will Rogers' daily article put down the newspaper, the problem was no less real to him, but it was certainly psychologically more manageable. With numerous messages of violence, war, and depression pouring into the press from all points in the world, people needed to laugh so that they could function. Rogers' humorous treatment helped insulate the shocks. As one of the townspeople says in *The Will Rogers Story,* (starring Will Rogers, Jr.), "You don't tell us much, Will, but you sure do keep us laughing."

Speaking in his moralistic voice, Rogers could conclude about the depression that it wasn't "Hoover, the Republicans, or even Russia that . . . [was] . . . responsible. I think the Lord just looked us over and decided to set us back where we belonged." But for all his criticism, Rogers had a deep faith in the ability of the American people to adapt. To help them with their adaptation,

Rogers undertook for himself the role of reducing massive, abstract threats in politics and society to manageable proportions. By making Americans laugh at Japan's Monroe Doctoring, he skillfully provided a catharsis for real and profound tensions. The common denominator which links Will Rogers' moralistic journalism to his playful journalism is his explicit and articulate discussion of the new and challenging in the contemporary setting.

Unlike his journalism, Will Rogers' films appear to have no relation at all to contemporary events and themes. We search these films in vain for the excoriator of advertising, or the debunker of disarmament conferences. We cannot even find the intransigent foe of the one-piece bathing suits. For this reason, the question immediately poses itself: Why is the *persona* which Rogers portrays in his films so out of touch with twentieth century America? Are these merely flimsy "entertainment films" which are intentionally irrelevant? Or is it possible that below the surface of Will Rogers' films there is a symbolism and a mood which spoke clearly to the millions who flocked to see them? Is it possible that the problems of the 1920's and 1930's which Rogers dealt with in his journalism are latent within the films in a coded form, waiting to be decoded by the historian who is both sensitive to the historical issues and the effects of film?

III. WILL ROGERS IN FILM: FROM COWBOY TO UNCLE WILL

A scene from the (now lost) film, *One Day in 365,* is a convenient place for us to begin a discussion of the film career of Will Rogers. Will is sitting in the sunroom of his beautiful house in Santa Monica Canyon, reading the newspaper. The headline reads: "REGARDLESS OF DISARMAMENT PLANS, THERE ARE RUMBLINGS OF WAR." Will looks up from his paper and says to Betty Rogers, "I guess the Republicans want another war, to show how much better they can run it than the Democrats." When he finally finishes reading the paper, he throws it down in disgust saying, "Same old junk—murder and divorce—the people who were divorced last year are being murdered this year."

In this scene we are watching Rogers humorously combine both the moralism and the capacity to "play" with elements of the contemporary world. It is of interest in our discussion of Rogers on the screen because its relevance to current events is atypical. Rogers played many parts on film, but the common characteristic of all of them was their removal from pressing contemporary issues. And the longer Rogers remained in Hollywood, the farther back into an Arcadian pre-industrial past his characters moved.

Will Rogers made his first film, *Laughing Bill Hyde* (1918) while twirling his rope on the stage of Zeigfield's *Follies.* Not surprisingly, he was cast as a cowboy in various melodramatic and comic roles. Rogers had real problems with his audience in these first films. New York critics who knew Rogers from the *Follies* brought an understanding of his humor to the films and this preparation helped them to understand the silent film character. On the other hand, the general public was indifferent because it had not yet been properly exposed to this fresh breeze of air from the West. Records show that Samuel Goldwyn lost at least $40,000 on these early films.

After a short time as a cowboy, Rogers developed a second film *persona.* Called "Jubilo," this figure is a rural clown, a perpetual loafer who floats through society getting himself into trouble and avoiding work whenever possible. Jubilo is an eccentric figure whom we love despite his numerous flaws. He is distinctly unlike the late, philosophical Rogers *persona:* Jubilo can fall in love, and even has a few (rather athletic) fist fights.

Rogers experimented with satire in two uproarious silent films. In *Doubling For Romeo* (1921) Rogers humorously spoofed the swashbuckling film romances of Douglas Fairbanks, Sr.: Rogers swings from chandeliers, holds off hundreds of opponents with his single sword, and captures the girl of his dreams. In the process, he takes advantage of the opportunity to expose the absurdities of the conventions of Hollywood's popular love pictures. In a second film, *Two Wagons, Both Covered* (1923) Rogers satirized the sententious epic of the silent era, *The Covered Wagon*—a kind of frontier *Ben Hur* of its day. As an authentic westerner who had grown-up with pioneers, Rogers relished this opportunity to mock those who spun romances about the settlement of the American West.

During Rogers' middle film period (1929-1932) he developed a fourth screen *persona,* one which would have been readily recognized by his daily readers. In these portraits of an Innocent Abroad, Rogers plays a simple down to earth figure (usually from Claremore, Oklahoma) who is forced to travel outside his provincial world to Washington *(Going to Congress),* New Orleans *(Handy Andy)* or Europe *(They Had To See Paris).* The Innocent is usually forced out of his normal environment by his wife, who usually aspires to be a sophisticated and "broad minded" citizen of the twentieth-century city. In a few instances, some local political faction accidently elects the Innocent to Congress. The humor in all of these films about the Innocent Abroad derives from the interplay between the central character and the corrupt people of the urban centers which he is forced to visit. In most cases, Will Rogers overwhelms the corrupted urban men by the sheer force of his ebullient personality.

In playing these roles as the Innocent, Rogers began to show that he was more than merely a good actor. One reviewer discerned that Rogers tapped deeper, national themes: In speaking of Pike Peters (a character protrayed by Rogers in *They Had To See Paris,* 1929) the reviewer noted that "Will Rogers has become a national character, infinitely more characteristic of America than the grotesque figure of Uncle Sam. It would be an artistic and patriotic crime to let such a film character [i.e., the Innocent Abroad] die." The reviewer and his public were not disappointed, for *So This is London* (1930) provided

Rogers with the same kind of ironic contrast between solid provincial and an effete society.

America's new place in the international world determined the strong response to Rogers in this role. While America had refused to enter the League of Nations, the facts of international life could not be denied—the United States was the most powerful nation in the world, but was still unsure of its place and its role. Rogers' Innocent Abroad films gave Americans a confident sense of poise in the international setting. The message of these films is always that older civilizations may have posted their claims to pre-eminence before the United States, but post-war realities obviously showed that the United States was the only country in the world whose spirit had not been broken by the experience of the Great War. As one discerning reviewer reported, Rogers not only gave Americans confidence inspiring self-image, he also conveyed a better picture of American character and values to the outside world:

> There was always the quiet homely voice and the loveable smile to keep us in touch with the things we knew and understood. He was a Westerner talking to Westerners in a language and with an awkward grace readily comprehended. He was the epitome of the spirit of the West: open-handed, free and easy, loquacious, oddly philosophical, genuinely sentimental with a smile ever within reach—one of the boys. And we liked to think that this was the picture of us that he carried to other and far corners of the world, where people, not knowing us too well, were apt to think of us as uncouth and six-shooting.

The advent of sound films effected a transformation in what Rogers could convey to his audience. Prior to sound, viewers missed much of Rogers' special humor if they were not prepared by a night at the *Follies,* or exposure to Rogers' daily column. With sound, it was impossible to miss his mysterious, radiating humanity. Speaking of this power to project a lovable personality, a reviewer of Rogers' first talkie, *They Had To See Paris,* noted that: "This picture changes all [the difficulties of communication in the silent films]. Rogers' shadow is almost a living thing. The wit is spontaneous and droll . . . the disarming humanness of the man envelopes the screen, the orchestra and the auditorium with one surging feeling of brotherhood."

What was now needed in the era of sound was the proper screen "vehicle" for the Rogers personality. Of importance in selecting that role was the awareness that the camera could supply much of the atmosphere for the Rogers *persona,* that Will Rogers in a film could say less and actually personify the values which had guided his "private" life and his journalistic commentary. The final Rogers films portray him as a small town figure. He is no longer the cowboy, the clown, the satirist, nor even the innocent abroad, but a very different symbol of a harmonious America before the turn of the century. He lives in the mythical world which we have seen Americans nostalgically projecting back into the 1890's because of the pressures they feel themselves to be under in the 1930's.

Actually, Rogers had experimented with the small town role during the 1920's. One critic was extremely impressed by its possibilities, given Rogers personality and style. In a review of *Jes Call Me Jim* (1920) he noted the kind of effects which would later be attributed to the Rogers of the later sound films—that he was not merely amusing his audience, but conveying a much needed message of brotherhood and a refreshingly positive perspective on human possibilities. In this way, Rogers was showing that his films performed a social function: "Will Rogers' . . . good natured personality seems to spread throughout the world a sense of happiness and kindness. I suppose a man like this, acting as he does before almost countless millions, does more good to this old earth than scores of preachers and philanthropists; able to reach more hearts than can be reached through any other medium.

In *State Fair* (1933) Rogers came back to this role. Audiences, executives at Twentieth Century Fox, and critics all recognized immediately that this was the ideal role for Rogers because it placed him "in a day when American village life was far more isolated than it is today." Celebrating that "Will Rogers Restored Picture Themes to Provincial Subjects," a reviewer captured the essence of this universally positive response: "*State Fair* taught Rogers his correct *metiér* and it taught the industry that pictures concerning inland, provincial characters were more appealing than penthouses and gunspattered pavements." The reviewer concluded that Rogers' nostalgic pictures had tapped a "forgotten public" which "had lost interest in crime and so-called 'smart' films [and had] stayed away entirely from cinema."

At least in the beginning, both the film critics and this "forgotten public" shared a common enthusiasm for these rural films. Some critics thought that they saw a "complete metamorphosis [in Rogers] from amusing philosopher into character actor." Other critics saw that Rogers after being a cowboy, clown, innocent abroad, had finally stumbled upon the right character for the screen. But after the formula was repeated a few times, critics tired of the rural Rogers "vehicle." Ironically, while the film critics stopped applauding Rogers' films, the American public swarmed to them in ever-increasing numbers, and film retails for Fox averaged about $2.5 million per film. The irony of this disaffection of the critics was that Rogers had begun his film career as a darling of the critics but a box-office failure; in these late films, Rogers was obviously appealing to real and profound popular emotions, emotions that could easily be overlooked by a critic interested in film as an art form. For the average viewer of these films did not buy his ticket to see art, but for the psychological relief and fatherly support which Rogers seemed to offer.

If we ignore the artistic merits of the late films and keep a clear focus on the response of the viewer, we begin to see why Rogers refrains from commenting directly on current events. The world of the late Will Rogers films is purposefully insulated from contemporary strains and pressures. For this reason the viewer's psychological "pay-off" from these rural dramas was the opportunity to temporarily escape from the world of ethical confusion, depression, and impending war. In *David Harum* (1934) this place is called "Homeville," a term which we will use hereafter to describe the nostalgic, pre-industrial world which we find in all of the late films of Will Rogers. Economic breakdown, the separation of a democratic society into rigid classes, the professionalization of knowledge may exist in this world of the later films, but in a special form. In Homeville, all of these threats are reduced to human proportions. They may challenge the wits of Homeville's citizens, but they never seem to be overwhelming.

Because the challenges to happiness and fulfillment have been reduced, the Will Rogers *persona* in Homeville can deal with them. (Rogers in these last films will hereafter be called "Uncle Will" because of his avuncular role.) In a few instances, Uncle Will enlists the aid of the threatened, but most often he is capable of solving the problems by himself. He is really more than just an inhabitant of Homeville: he is its superintending consciousness. Uncle Will has a special insight into the human heart. Because of this special power, and because every problem in Homeville has a human face, Uncle Will is a master of this world.

The best metaphor for the perspective given the viewer of the late Rogers films is probably that of a telescope which we look through backwards. The result of looking at the world in this perspective is that everything appears smaller and therefore less challenging to the viewer. The remainder of this essay will look closely at two films, *David Harum* (1934) and *In Old Kentucky* (1935) in an attempt to show how this miniaturizing process takes place in two specific cases.

A. *DAVID HARUM* (1934)

The first scene of *David Harum* (1934) could not be more explicit about the function of the late Rogers' films to transport the viewer back into a simpler past. Will Rogers plays a rural banker who has come to the big city of New York to visit General Woolsey, a banker on Wall Street. The panic of 1893 has forced the General to close his doors recently. Consequently, the General is very curious to know how Uncle Will can remain open for business during times of "depression, unemployment and starvation."

David Harum's answer is hardly an answer at all. Its dramatic purpose is to accentuate the differences between the two worlds which these men inhabit: the General lives in the city which has proven itself to be out of balance; Uncle Will lives in the country where people may not be good, but the proximity of men to each other assures that they are always under control. Harum explains to the General: "Well, General, I go a long way on character, and after I've gone a long way on character, I check on collateral. Then I give 'em half of what they ask for."

This statement says something about the volume of business which Uncle Will does up in Homeville. He knows everybody in Homeville, and he also realizes that it is "human nature" for borrowers to pad both their loan requests as well as to overestimate their ability to provide collateral. Fully aware that even his best clients will cheat, Uncle Will gives them half of what they request—which, ironically, is probably what they really need! The point of all this is that the urban banker is a victim of impersonal economic forces which he cannot control. David Harum's Homeville, on the other hand, is never affected by anything as abstract as twenty-one year periodic economic cycles. As David explains, the people of Homeville are not dependent on a fickle outside market for their prosperity. Because they are closer to nature they are self-sufficient and can therefore "roll their own" in hard times.

The young male figure enters *David Harum* with troubles not entirely foreign to a 1930 audience. John Lennox's father recently committed suicide because of his heavy losses on the stock market. To compound John's problems, his calculating, urban fianceé has closed out their engagement as she would a savings account—there is no more money in it. John has been searching for a job in a city that has none to offer. But because this is the panic of 1893 (and not the depression of the 1930's) John has recourse to the country to renew his chances for a good life. General Woolsey cannot help John personally, but he makes arrangements for David Harum to take John into the bank up in Homeville. When John leaves the befuddled city for the stable, self-sufficient countryside, he remarks pointedly: "Thanks, General—I want to get away from the city and get to work."

Homeville is unlike the impersonal city because it has a superintendent of hearts. Uncle Will is there to assure that a money problem never becomes an obstacle to individual fulfillment. Because of Uncle Will's ever present concern, the inhabitants of Homeville are rewarded on the basis of personal virtue rather than because of the intelligence, class, or sophistication which the world may have given them.

John Lennox (as an urban man who must learn to get some roots back into "the real things in life") has severe initial difficulties with the primitive conditions of Homeville. On the stormy night of his arrival, he finds the kitchen of the local hotel closed, and learns that if he wants to use the tub, he must pay extra for such a luxury. Upstairs, he finds that the ceiling of his room leaks, and that the broken pane in his window is not interfering with the play of the rain. The night clerk of the hotel informs John that the town's only carpenter will fix the window when his rheumatism improves—which will probably be never. The purpose of building up these details of back-

wardness and inefficiency is to communicate clearly that we are living in a world where work is not the most important part of life, where people take their time because they are ignorant of the city's tread-mill of ambition and selfishness. As a result of not being obsessed by the Protestant ethic, the people of Homeville are happy, even if they are unwashed and a little behind on conveniences.

Uncle Will (as David Harum) personifies Homeville's indifference toward work and money. The more we watch Uncle Will in this film, the more we conclude that he is liberated from all material concerns. In order of their priority, his worldly interests seem to be: horse trading; ring toss (played in his office with his pocket knife stabbed into the middle of his papers as a pole); and fishing. Uncle Will even has difficulty making it to his office at all on many days because of the chances for horse trades and conversation along the way.

If considered closely, the six horse trades in *David Harum* fit into the overall pattern of reduced threats that we find in Homeville. As explained by Uncle Will to his skeptical sister, the golden rule of the horse trade is "Do Unto Others What They Want to Do Unto You." Translated into the world of the 1920's and 1930's as a business ethic, this is precisely the doctrine of the survival of the most aggressive and dishonest which led to disaster. Yet in the setting of Homeville, the false representation and sharping of the horse trades seem quaint and entertaining, for what is destructive in Hooverville can be transformed into humor in Homeville.

David Harum's business practices as a banker reflect his easy-going attitude, his charity, but also his power to see into the human heart. David Harum's opening lines taught us that human beings are neither good nor bad, but a little of each. Because they can easily go astray, they cannot be completely trusted; but because they are not completely evil, we should not be completely cynical.

The film also indicates that a small town is an ideal social unit, because in a small town people have an opportunity to study one another over a long period of time. In sum, Rogers communicates to his audience that the small town is an ideal society, not because people act better there, but because in a small town a better watch can be kept over a wayward human nature.

Uncle Will's behavior as a small town banker reflects this basic philosophy. When an impoverished widow cannot keep up with the payments on her mortgage, Uncle Will discovers a "forgotten" bank account which clears her of debt. This tender act of charity is followed by an entirely different scene which demonstrates that for all his charity, Uncle Will is no sentimentalist who can be outwitted by the worldly. Immediately after his scene with the widow, Uncle Will is confronted by a burly customer who arrogantly refuses to pay his loan on time, claiming that an improper signature of his co-signer makes him exempt from prosecution. Uncle Will looks out of the corner of his eye—he knew that this confrontation would come eventually—and slyly explains to the defaulter that he had obtained the proper signature months earlier in anticipation of this ploy. The note must be paid. This revelation leads to a fist fight, and although no one is hurt in the uproar, a significant message comes through: If you are angry in Homeville, you can actually identify and take a swing at your oppressor. This personalized environment which allows the individual to let off steam contrasts with the frustratingly complex world of Muley Graves in Steinbeck's *Grapes of Wrath,* Unlike that impersonal setting of land companies, banks, and distant corporations, the forces that operate in Homeville always have a human face and heart. As noted, the charitable spirit of Uncle Will controls Homeville because he has special powers to see into the human hearts of his small town.

Uncle Will's inveterate matchmaking in these last films tells much about his concern for particular human hearts. Reviewers tired rather quickly of the Kent-Venable mating that is repeated over and over again in the late films, but the mass audience kept coming back for more. To understand the full effect of these love-matches, we must realize that everyone in the audience understood that Rogers was in no way interested in the young girls he helps to find their man. One reviewer summarized the audience's sense that Rogers was a "sympathetic and comforting 'old man': If ever a man was a father, it's Will. When Ann comes up to Will's bedroom [at the opening of David Harum] while he is dressing, there is no embarrassment. With any other actor, the audience might smirk and think naughty thoughts. But with Will, he is so much the father type, naughtiness occurs to nobody." These romances are really of no interest in themselves, but they have a function in the late films. Just as marriages in nineteenth century novels frequently have social and other signifiances, so the presence of separated young people in the late Rogers films is used to convey a deeper meaning. Simply, the young lovers exist in these films so that Uncle Will can have something loving to do.

It is not difficult to decode the appeal of this element of the late films. Rogers' audience was living in a world which was growing increasingly *im*personal. Not only community feeling, but the small loyalty demanded by the nuclear family was becoming exhausted as the result of the intellectual and economic strains. The appeal may have been sentimental, but an image of such a man as Rogers was very much needed by his audience to counterbalance this drift toward depersonalization. In a treacherous world which seemed to be out of control, here stood a sympathetic personality, completely unselfish, concerned with warding off harm rather than amassing power. Viewers of the late films were shown lovers who were separated because of financial differences (*David Harum*); the law's delays (*Steamboat Round the Bend*); the dishonesty of a spoiled rich boy (*Life Begins at Forty*); the covetousness of city folk (*In Old Kentucky*). Fortunately for the young lovers, in all these cases

democratic Uncle Will is present to help. He manipulates the people of Homeville (and even the weather) so that these barriers can be surmounted. The result is that the young people finally recognize that they are just human beings, and that the differences which seemed so insuperable are really artificial and flimsy when weighed against the inner promptings of the heart. As a result of all this matchmaking, Rogers comes to represent a disinterested spirit of brotherhood. And while this message is transmitted in the later films through a flimsy set of conventions, the ultimate effect upon the audience is to demonstrate that we Americans still have the capacity to transcend our materialism and our growing class barriers.

Our superintendent of hearts frequently calls into play some forms of *deus ex machina* to extricate him and his friends from the predicaments in which they find themselves. The most absurd of them all (from *In Old Kentucky*) is worth relating for its unreality and its appeal. Grandfather hires a rainmaker to salt the clouds so that the track will be wet during the climactic race. When the rainmaker's standard concoctions fail, he ties a bundle of dynamite to a cluster of balloons and hopes for the best. When the balloons fail to lift the dynamite, the bundle slams into a water tower near the finishing stretch, with the result of completely flooding the track. Because the track is flooded, the Martingale horse, Blueboy, comes from behind at the last moment to win the race. His victory ends all of the personal difficulties and family feuds which the viewer has become familiar with during the film. Only in Homeville, the land of wish-fulfillment, can such *dei ex machinii* grind out their answers without complaints from the audience!

Here the theme of the use and abuse of power enters in a coded form. We have already indicated that Uncle Will is the benevolent dictator of Homeville. Always a critic of men who aspired to hold power, how does Rogers on the screen avoid the abuses which he found in others? Here the contrived conclusions of the films find their meaningful (and comforting) place. Certainly most of the films achieve their happy endings in this way: In *Judge Priest,* Uncle Will persuades his Southern jury to acquit his client by playing "Dixie" outside the courtroom window at the right moment; in *Steamboat Round the Bend* a race, which eventually joins the lovers and saves an innocent man's life, is won because an unexpected supply of patent medicine (with a high alcoholic content) is discovered at the last minute to be useful as a high energy fuel; *In Old Kentucky* ends with a horse race in which the track becomes providentially muddy. In every case cited, Uncle Will sees to it that all the love knots are tied, and that society's conflicts are resolved—but always without an overt display of power. Uncle Will always gives us the impression that he has somehow transformed power into love. Unlike political and business leaders outside the theatre, he has the gods on his side. In all of the late films, the viewer is encouraged to identify with the young lovers, to experience their (temporary) sense of tension and unfulfillment, but then gradually to be rewarded by the tutelary deity of Homeville, Uncle Will. The viewers who succumbed to these love stories may have been guilty of taking an emotional holiday, but we can understand their deep need for such an escape when we consider the world that awaited them outside the theater. In these hours of escape, the viewers could smile at the pleasing notion that John Lennox and Ann Madison are married at the conclusion of *David Harum*. The viewers could applaud John and Ann's decision to remain in Homeville rather than return to the city. Unfortunately, the viewers of *David Harum* could not lean on the comforting spirit of Uncle Will, nor could they stay in the protected landscape of Homeville; they had to go home when the lights went on.

B. *In Old Kentucky*

Much of what has been said about Homeville and Uncle Will applies to the Rogers figure and the community portrayed in one of his last two films, *In Old Kentucky* (1935). The story brings two very different families into conflict: The Martingales are an out-at-elbows rural family whose very special horse, Blueboy, is coveted by a neighboring gentleman farmer and his daughter (the Shattocks). Somewhere in the past, a piece of property was added illegally to the Shattock farm, initiating a feud between the two families. Uncle Will in this setting plays a horse trainer, Steve Tapley, who is especially concerned about the boy and girl who are separated by the feud.

The style and behavior of the Shattocks symbolizes that the city is encroaching upon the countryside. Grandpa Martingale becomes the center of controversy, because he is still angry about the stolen piece of land. He aims his shotgun at the Shattock automobile whenever it passes the Martingale house. But Grandpa never fires. Viewers quickly learn that Grandpa is an eccentric old man who is really quite harmless. Nevertheless, because they are city people, the Shattocks know how to call the impersonal force of the law into play. They file a complaint against Grandpa, with the hope that legal pressure will force the Martingales to sell their horse, Blueboy.

As Steve Tapley, Uncle Will is hard pressed to avert a tragedy. After all, he is a mere horse trainer in this film, and therefore lacks the social leverage which was his when he was David Harum, Homeville's only banker. Nevertheless, Uncle Will lives up to the occasion because in Homeville (unlike Hooverville) character is the source of power, not money or social position. For this reason, a social inferior like Uncle Will who can see into the human heart can gain complete control: With his insight into the darker regions of the human heart, Uncle Will can anticipate the ploys of the Shattocks as they attempt to buy (or steal) Blueboy; with his more tender concern for individuals, Uncle Will can assure that Nancy Martingale and Lee Andrews are eventually matched.

As in *David Harum,* so here, Homeville brings threats to manageable proportions. For example, we note almost immediately that class divisions exist. The Shattocks exhibit the worst characteristics of the American rich: they dress according to the latest fashion; they have an affected accent which has obviously been learned rather than acquired; they have themselves chauffeured around Homeville in an enormous Packard touring car. In distinct contrast, the Martingales are unaffected citizens of Homeville: Grandpa still dresses like a farmer; young Nancy is always in a loose sweater and riding clothes; and when the Martingales travel, they either bounce along on a buckboard or ride one of their fine horses. At their farm, the Shattocks have hordes of retainers, while the Martingales do their own work.

In *In Old Kentucky* Rogers takes the opportunity to comment on the new woman. Her superficiality and artificiality is contrasted with the virtues of Nancy Martingale, a woman of older America. While Ms. Shattock is identified quickly by her dress, her accent, her snobbery as the bitch that the new woman has become, Nancy Martingale shows herself to have feeling for animals (always a cardinal virtue in Homeville). Nancy also knows enough to rely on Steve because she seems to recognize in him both a confidant and guardian angel.

A scene in which Uncle Will visits a dress shop in the city most effectively contrasts the life styles of the urban Shattocks and the rural Martingales. A kick-off dance at the local country club has been planned for the night preceding the big race. Knowing that Nancy cannot afford a dress for herself, and aware that she must be at the dance to meet her young man, Uncle Will decides to take direct action. In this scene, Rogers tries to develop at some length the distance between the sensibility of an older, rural America and the worldliness of the contemporary American mentality that is reflected in women's fashions. The store owner who greets Uncle Will speaks and acts more like a madame of a bordello than a saleswoman. From the beginning, she and Uncle Will operate under a misconception: he wants a modest dress for his young employer; the manager of the dress shop thinks that he wants something spicy for a mistress. While Uncle Will is muttering to himself in a corner, the madame parades out six or seven models who line up behind him half dressed (or half undressed) in diaphanous nightgowns and peignoirs. When Uncle Will turns around to see what has been brought out, he is shocked. Averting his eyes, he apologizes profusely for stumbling into the ladies dressing room! When the confusion is finally cleared up, Uncle Will buys a white, high necked, long-sleeved dress which is more consonant with his old-fashioned ideas about women. Predictably, on the night of the dance, Arlene Shattock is wearing one of the low-backed, clinging gowns which made Uncle Will blush. The lesson is obvious—in her covetousness and in her dress, Arlene has shown herself to be all that is bad about the new woman. On the other hand, Nancy Martingale shows herself to be an old-fashioned girl who knows that she must rely upon the guidance and strength of the men around her.

In Old Kentucky miniaturizes the problem of the professionalization of knowledge, a twentieth-century development which Rogers spoke about frequently in his columns. Rogers was extremely suspicious of professional or school-trained experts, for he suspected that they frequently ascribed expertise to their work when none really existed. Whether bogus or not, the idea of the world becoming too complicated for the average man to understand was very much on the minds of Rogers' audience.

Dr. Lee Andrews enters Homeville as a representative of professional learning. Whereas Uncle Will became a trainer by working with horses, Dr. Andrews has taken copious notes in the classrooms of Kentucky's new agricultural and mechanical college. Within the setting of Homeville, this symbol of complexity is quickly subdued by Uncle Will. Not only does Lee show complete respect for the old-fashioned trainer, the young doctor is entirely dependent upon Uncle Will in his love match with Nancy Martingale.

In Old Kentucky thus presents (and reduces) the problems of a society breaking down into rigidly isolated classes, of a new morality and a new woman, of the professionalization of knowledge. All of these unsettling developments are presented in such a way that we do not see them as a clear demonstration that our world is becoming increasingly perplexing and violent. Instead, our response (like our response to Will Rogers' "playful" journalism) is one of reassurance—Uncle Will's presence on the screen has lessened their impact upon us. Throughout, the most important factor is that the environment and the people in Homeville are entirely malleable under the workings of the spirit of Uncle Will. Millions of Rogers' fans must have watched such resolutions of conflict with satisfaction. They must have been impressed by what one contemporary reviewer noted was Rogers' power "to set right all the troubles of the impulsive people around him." Given a sympathetic understanding of the forces affecting Americans in the 1920's and 1930's, it is difficult to vouchsafe them their inner need to love such a symbolic man. He meant so much to his people in a time of change and deprivation because he presented them with an image of what Americans had been told to believe was the best in their national character. In preserving this image of humanity and love, Rogers was making no small contribution to the sanity of Americans in a world rushing toward international violence. A reviewer of *In Old Kentucky* hit upon some of the essential positive factors of Rogers' contribution as man and as a film image. These late Homeville movies reassured Americans (especially frenzied New Yorkers) "about the solidity and innate common sense of this country." While the reviewer granted that Rogers was probably playing "himself," he felt compelled to add that as a representative figure, Rogers supplied welcome reassurance in an era of bad news: "Will Rogers has a curious national quality. He gives the impression somehow that this country is filled with such sages, wise with years, young in humor and life, shrewd, yet gentle." Most importantly for the reviewer, "He is what Americans think other Americans are like." After the erosion of values in the twenties, after the economic disaster of the thirties,

Americans were indeed fortunate to have such a public person to keep a hopeful image of American values and optimism bright.

Peter C. Rollins (essay date 1991)

SOURCE: "Writing a Contemporary Column in `The Spirit of Will Rogers': An Exercise in Practical Criticism," in *Journal of American Culture,* Vol. 14, No. 2, 1991, pp. 59-68.

[*In the following essay, Rollins explains his attempt to revive the Will Rogers tradition in his own writing.*]

Will Rogers had an enormous impact on the people of his time, but sometimes I wonder if he realized the tyranny he would have over the lives of a small group of scholars long after his death. The Will Rogers writing habit can become a sickness leading to otherwise unaccountable behavior! For example, in 1935, Tulsa lawyer David Milsten published a book entitled *An Appreciation of Will Rogers,* a volume which took a regional slant on the national humorist. Lacking anything new to say, but still infected by Will Rogers enthusiasm, Milsten brought out the same book under the title *The Cherokee Kid: Life of Will Rogers* in the 1970s, a volume timed to reach the bookstores at the moment Mr. Milsten was being considered for the Will Rogers State Commission. Scholars like Fred Roach—a fellow speaker—and I have been guilty of glutting the Will Rogers market. Professor Roach's dissertation is entitled *Lariat in the Sun: The Story of Will Rogers;* it is an analytical biography of the great Oklahoman. Since completing his dissertation in 1972, Roach has gone on to write a number of excellent interpretive articles. He has contacted the illness, carrying it as far East as Marrietta, Georgia.

I, too, suffer from Rogers fever. When I first appeared on the campus of Oklahoma State University, I was assigned for a quarter of my allotted "time" as a teacher to the Will Rogers Publication Project. From 1972 until a few months ago, the project edited and published *The Writings of Will Rogers* (22 volumes), a massive collection of previously published and unpublished works spanning Rogers career in print, radio, and film. Just last week, the bound copies of a comprehensive index to the series went on sale, officially bringing the project to a close. While with the project, I wrote a number of interpretive introductions to the volumes we printed: little did I know that I was contracting a lasting ailment. My first signs of Will Rogers fever occurred at national Popular Cultural Association meetings during the 1970s where I assembled films for evening screenings and chaired panels about Will Rogers. From 1972 to 1981, I plead guilty to publishing seven journal articles on the Oklahoman; in addition, I was the producer/director of a motion picture about Rogers which was entitled *Will Rogers' 1920s: A Cowboy's Guide to the Times* (1976). For a week or two, I thought about radio programs, but the fever subsided.

Strangers can only catch a glimpse of the etiology of the sickness. After watching my film one evening at a professional meeting in Boston, a scholar came up to me and very nearly identified the problem when she asked: "You call that work?" Professor Roach and I know what she was talking about: working with the Will Rogers materials is simply too much fun, an activity as difficult to avoid as the Braum's ice cream shops in Texas and Oklahoma towns. Not only are the materials a delight in themselves for the interdisciplinary scholar, the plenitude and organization of papers at the Will Rogers memorial invite the lazy researcher who likes to have all his documents in place—dated, labeled, filed, and indexed. This fever can be enervating.

In 1982, I devised what I thought would be an antidote for the sickness: I was invited by editor and scholar Thomas Inge to write one of the Greenwood Press books in popular culture and I became determined to pack everything I knew into the study. It would be my way of purging the system of the Will Rogers bug—or so I thought. Unfortunately, as interlibrary loans began pouring in, I could feel my fever rise. As I went back into the Will Rogers materials themselves, the thermometer continued to climb. Like all Will Rogers scholars when they are overtaken by the malady, I began to bring home the best of the *bonmots* encountered during the day: I was sure my wife could not resist hearing lesser known Rogersisms. Although my motives were healthy, I was passing on the sickness.

A FIRST ATTEMPT: "THE WILL ROGERS TIME MACHINE"

At some point, my wife suggested that the public might like to hear Will Rogers comment on issues of the 1980s. We talked about a series called "Will Roger Says," articles which were syndicated for three or four years during the 1970s. "Will Rogers Says" consisted of short paragraphs edited by Bryan Sterling, a New Yorker who has managed to live with Will Rogers fever by commercially exploiting the Rogers heritage in every conceivable way. The Bryan Sterling articles were very brief, direct quotes from Rogers. Local Newspapers subscribing to the series received a week's supply at a time and were asked to insert the short statements in coordination with daily headlines. In that way, the dated Rogers pieces would appear to address recent events.

We felt that the Sterling attempts were too short; they did not allow Rogers to do much more than mention a topic. Our alternative was based on a past *vs* present approach in a series called *The Will Rogers Time Machine*. Articles featured two vertical columns: on the left was historical and narrative material supplied by us to provide background for current issues; this column also described historical parallels. The right column contained an extended quotation form Will Rogers taken from his writings; obviously, the observations by Rogers were selected to bridge the gap between the "Then and Now" of the left column. Here are a few examples of the series we initially envisioned. The first installment addresses the issue of fast foods, a topic which seems to be of constant concern to Americans.

*The Will Rogers Time Machine
Turns to Fast Foods*

Now:

In 1982, there is an increasing awareness of the deficiencies of fast foods. Not only are they poor sources of nutrition, their connection with the automobile links them to a pervasive rootlessness in our society.

Then:

During the 1920s, an era of infatuation with technological progress, Will Rogers observed that the fast food craze—then focused on the hamburger—and dependence on the automobile were developments which would not be entirely good for American culture.

Rogers:

Give an American a one piece bathing suit, a hamburger, and five gallons of gas, and they are just as tickled as a movie star with a new divorce.

As with all other articles in the series, there are three components: "Now," "Then," and "Rogers." Our thought was that the reader—once adapted to the layout of the series—could let his eye travel to any of these items in a sequence of his choice. Some might plod through the offering from "now" to "then" to "Rogers" in the obvious sequence; on the other hand, the Rogers fan might reverse the order and go immediately to Rogers and then trail back to either or both of the historical framing elements. He could glean as much entertainment and information as wanted on any particular day. Serious readers could muse over the full triad. We felt that the plan was clearly a substantive improvement over the Brian Sterling snippets.

The recent resignation of Secretary of the Interior James Watt made a second example especially pertinent:

*The Will Rogers Time Machine
Turns to Conservation*

Now:

The fate of wilderness areas has been endangered by a combination of forces to include our dependence on foreign oil, and some observers would add, our dependence upon Secretary Watt for Conservation administration.

Then:

Will Rogers regretted the onrush of a civilization which quickly boxed up the open plains of Oklahoma during his youth. For him, the passing of frontier life and values was a fact, not a metaphor.

Rogers:

We are going at top speed, because we are using all our natural resources as fast as we can. If we want to build something out of wood, all we got to do is go cut down a tree and build it. We didn't have to plant the tree. Nature did that before we come. Suppose we couldn't build something out of wood till we found a tree that we had purposely planted for the use. Say, we never would get it built . . . We are certainly setting pretty right now. But when our resources run out, if we can still be ahead of other nations then will be the time to brag; then we can show whether we are really superior.

Like other clusters in our series, this evocation of national concern for the environment does justice to the need for historical perspective on Rogers' work while allowing him to speak at length. Not everything Will Rogers said rang with profundity, but the combined poetry and prophesy of this quotation gives focus to both the contemporary and the historical dimensions of a headline issue.

You are wondering: "What happened to their first experiment in Will Rogers journalism?" We prepared and submitted a series of articles for consideration by local editors and their syndicate. Unfortunately we chose the wrong editor at the *Stillwater News Press* to be our contact: We later learned that he was a family member who was brought on staff because he could perform no useful work elsewhere! After fifteen months, we are still waiting for a response to our experiment with the *Will Rogers Time Machine.* When our slow-moving Stillwater newspaperman finally replies, I suspect we will be told that the *The Will Rogers Time Machine* takes up too much space and is didactic. He and the syndicate will find the quick-and-dirty approach of Bryan Sterling sufficient. Naturally, we feel that such low standards will be an insult to the readers of his paper and to the Will Rogers tradition.

A SECOND ATTEMPT: "THE SPIRIT OF WILL ROGERS"

From our point of view, the *Time Machine* project had a very specific deficiency: producing the article was too much like work; the creative process lacked spontaneity and verve, the spirit of Will Rogers. As we talked about alternative strategies, we discovered that we were not so much interested in celebrating the great Oklahoman as tapping the sense of play and transcendence radiated by a typical Rogers article or radio program or film. Driven by the Will Rogers fever, we devised a more cheerful approach: we would ignore the actual words of Will Rogers; we would not attempt to put current issues into historical perspective. Instead, we would isolate some of the devices of American humor which Rogers employed and then apply them ourselves to recent events, issues, and people in the news. The notion combined the fever's delirium and delight: we would satirize our own times through the *persona* of Will Rogers! We would vicari-

ously participate in *The Spirit of Will Rogers* rather than attempt to exhume it from a dead past.

Our first step toward entering *The Spirit of Will Rogers* was to agree upon appropriate rhetorical devices. There is an entire library of books on American humor to which interested readers can turn for a detailed itemization of comic devices characteristically employed by American humorists from Benjamin Franklin to Art Buchwald. As practitioners, we singled out a limited number of devices for our use. (The fact that our articles were written during the cocktail hour further encouraged a certain lack of academic rigor.) First, we planned to use the staple Will Rogers device of the naive innocent who claims to "know" only what he reads in the papers. What Rogers meant by the famous introductory line was that he had difficulty—as an innocent—deciphering the goodness and purpose of much in the news. So many of Will Rogers' articles explore the stupidity of public actions in the light of common sense. The humor of his observations was the result of pondering the distance between his unaffected outlook and the arcane values of men and women in the public view. For the Rogers *persona,* making sense out of the news was no easy feat. Supporting the naive innocent perspective would be a reference in every article to an actual event in Will Rogers' life: not only would such an allusion add authenticity to our fabricated observations, it would also underscore the "then and now" theme we had attempted in our previous venture, *The Will Rogers Time Machine.* Within this new context, the old would be identified as being healthy, useful, appropriate while the new was misled, distorted, deviating from the norm. Just as Will Rogers accentuated his Oklahoma heritage to call developments of an urbanizing and industrializing America into question, we would constantly use a nostalgic view of the past to satirize the present.

Whenever possible, we would attempt to discuss abstract issues through particular images. Looking back at the representative *Will Rogers Time Machine* article . . . , notice how Rogers, in discussing American rootlessness, does not invoke high level abstractions. Instead, he concentrates on particular images: the one piece bathing suit, the hamburger, the gasoline, the movie star with a divorce. These particular images collide to evoke abstractions in the mind of the reader. Through them Will Rogers turns a serious comment about American society into a fast-paced comic montage. Whenever possible, we vowed to follow the same poetic technique. Like Rogers, we would not always go for the obvious particular image: note in the example already cited that Rogers does not mention the automobile or a nation on wheels—two obvious connections; instead, he selects images which are on the periphery of the subject and then moves them toward the center. The effect is to confuse and to tickle the reader with just a bit of irrelevance. We, too, would seek particulars off the beaten track. (For examples of this technique, see the discussions of "Washington hairsplitting". . . and the article on "vipertuperation" . . . [that follow].)

Word play would be as important for us as for the Oklahoman. Although Rogers could write perfectly grammatical letters to family and friends, he was prone to illiterate usage whenever such ignorance had rhetorical value; it seemed silly for us to not exploit the device. Whenever useful, the Rogers *persona* speaks ungrammatically. In addition, puns were a constant part of the Will Rogers' written and oral humor—not to mention their revered place in the stock-and-trade of all American folk humorists. The pun could help us in a number of ways: the innocent *persona* could emphasize his confusion with modern ways through his inability to comprehend modern usage; and from our point of view, the pun could serve as a valuable tool for quick transitions from one subject to another. Finally, for those of us who get into the spirit of Will Rogers, there is a special use for the pun: it gives a sense of power in which words become more important than the things they signify. To manipulate the words gives a brief sense of superiority over the terrors of modern life which they describe. It seems clear that one of the rewards for the Jazz Age and Depression era reader of Will Rogers was the way in which Rogers could rope and tackle even the biggest issue with his verbal lasso. If insight was not always the reward of a Will Rogers article, relaxation of tension was an inevitable by-product. People could go back to the news with some sense that the national spirit—as articulated by Will Rogers—was sturdy enough to laugh off difficulties. Writing *The Spirit of Will Rogers* columns gave us, the writers, a sense of relief; we hoped that in using the mask of the wise innocent and by word manipulations we could pass that sense of delight and laughter along to readers.

Our final goal was to be challenging with allusions. We hoped to make readers think; if possible, we wanted them to leave the articles with a question or two about historical references. This goal ran directly counter to the strategy of the previous didactic series *The Will Rogers Time Machine.* Somehow, the notion of focusing on particulars, shifting from one topic to another quickly by means of puns encouraged a dimension of mystery. The voice of our *persona* would be the voice of a rural clown set loose in an urban world, but the clown would be a *wise* innocent. There would be knowledge hidden in the hayseed, and this sense of wisdom is as important as play for those who know the true "Spirit of Will Rogers."

The format of the articles reinforced the themes we wanted to stress. At the upper-left, a small graphic depicts Will Rogers dressed in chaps, wearing a cowboy hat, and seated at a portable typewriter—presumably churning out a daily article (like the one below) between scenes on a Hollywood set or between shows at Ziegfeld's *Follies.* Each article was surrounded with a border which resembled rope, emphasizing the cowboy tradition and adding to the frontier flavor. Finally, each article would be given a closing which would emphasize the point of view of the particular piece: in speaking of taxes, the Rogers *persona* closes for the consumer; when the subject is campaign slogans, he calls himself a "Country Chairman," alluding to a very funny film made by Rogers

in 1935. Each detail added to the message of the body of the article.

Some specific examples from *The Spirit of Will Rogers* series will clarify the generalizations. Here is an article which we wrote during the White House battle of the barbers in 1982:

ON WASHINGTON HAIR-SPLITTING

All I know is what I read in the papers and this White House barber business beats academics at splitting hairs. Now I don't mind getting myself shorn 'til my ears start itchin', and the ole boy they had there did my kind of cut.

Of course, nowadays, there's this unisects stuff, which confuses me. Is it a new religion or somethin'? Is it a tire company? Does it mean that everyone will do his own part?

If Mr. Stockman spent more time with his calculator and less time with the blow dryer, he probably wouldn't have ended up in The Atlantic. The President never comes in for personal business— he always asks for budget cuts. The armed services look mighty ragged lately: they seem to have gone to the shag.

Yours from the heir apparent,
The Spirit of Will Rogers

Following a device of Will Rogers, the article focuses upon a trend in style, but trips over a number of significant political and economic matters—seemingly by accident. The imagery unifying the article relates to a controversy which had recently come to a "head" in the White House: the proprietor of the barber shop had fired a husband/wife styling team. Newspapers carried the story and more than one network aired indepth, investigative reports, to include comments from White House advisors and—of course—from the disgruntled couple as they carried their blow dryers off the White House grounds. It was the kind of squabble which Will Rogers loved to exploit.

Paragraph one of our article begins with the standard opening, a statement which propels the *persona* into events which he cannot quite understand. Since the immediate audience for the articles consisted of academics, we introduced a pun about "splitting hairs" and let the jibe fall on intellectuals. Rogers then talks of being "shorn" the way animals would be cropped and speaks in the diction of country bumpkin. He sides—humorously—with the proprietor of the shop and makes it clear that he has no sympathy for new trends in not-so-masculine coiffeur.

In paragraph two, confusion continues. Poor Rogers does not know how to spell "unisex." In a desperate attempt at phonetics, he writes "unisects" and then stumbles over possible meanings. As he struggles for clarity, he indirectly plays with such notions as the Unification Church, and the Uniroyal Tire Company. He then injects the idea of social responsibility, wondering if everybody is doing "his part."

David Stockman was one of the White House advisors interviewed for a network story on the hair affair. Rogers pounces on this controversial figure to ridicule a near-fatal attraction to media. Focusing on the particular image of a blow dryer, rather than uttering an abstraction such as "conceit" or "vanity," Rogers asserts that internal weakness invited the infamous exposé of Stockman in *The Atlantic Monthly*. The negative aspect of the scandal is emphasized by wording the description so that "the Atlantic" is a pun: we mean both that he almost got thrown in the ocean and that the story appeared in a Boston-based magazine. Naturally, the idea of the Reagan Administration's budget director led to a consideration of the budget cuts that are at the heart of Reaganomics.

Ronald Reagan's budgetary policies are introduced by particular images. The president is described as so busy that he only has time for the barber to work on "budget cuts." Many people feel that President Reagan's emphasis on military spending is in hypocritical contradiction with his promise to heal the economy. The military—who should be interested in close-cropped hair—are at first shown in a negative light: they are ragged; their hair is too long. Rogers then explains this anomaly in a particular image—the shag—to stress that it is unnatural for the military not to exercise the same fiscal responsibility while others get their "cuts." The hair images serve as a braid threading together a number of topics, all of which focus on the absurdities of life inside the Washington beltway.

By signing the article from the "heir apparent," Rogers indicates that he is the American spirit of common sense ready to take over if things get too unbalanced next to the Potomac. However silly our elected officials become, Rogers assures us that there is always a reservoir of good sense and decency in the nation to counterbalance mistakes made in Washington. In the days of Will Rogers, such a message inspired confidence as well as laughter; in our own time of centralized government and instant communications, we hoped to convey a similar sense of transcendent play.

Perhaps because we wrote the articles in the evening just before dinner, one of our favorite efforts deals with the novelty of microwave ovens. In this case, the Oklahoma cowboy shows his perplexity and confusion in connection with a technological revolution.

The first paragraph follows Rogers' practice of twisting the lead "all I know is what I read in the papers" to suit each novel situation—in this case, the appearance of microwave ovens as a standard offering of appliance stores.

In paragraph two, the old days are pictured in a poetic way. The home kitchen and smokehouse are depicted as being in Oologah—Rogers' actual birth place—rather than in Claremore—which he usually cited as his home-

town. The Indian name gives a frontier flavor, as do references to ribs and spices—the Westerner's favorite fare. The reference to the fire at Will Rogers' sister's home is a factual one, lending authority to the *persona;* however, the remark about aroma is more geared to nostalgia than factual accuracy. Obviously, sister Maud never considered such compensations at the time of the accident!

The third paragraph brings the innocent into conflict with change. He mourns the passing of real cooking, the slow way: food colors and textures are often lost in the electronic era; the name "TV dinner" frustrates him, but there is wisdom in describing them as products of a machine-oriented society; finally, he is right in guessing that the ritual of family meals has been further disrupted by the ease with which leftovers can be recycled for individual consumption. Our *persona's* confusion about clock mechanisms on microwaves further underscores novelty. Is the machine a clock or is it an oven? The closing for the article comes back to primary ingredients of cooking which a cowboy could recognize: fire and smoke. There may be discomfort in such an arrangement, but an open fire is closer to the real things in life.

This article resembles a great number of pieces which Rogers produced—especially during the 1920s. As a social observer interested in values as well as politics and economics, Rogers felt compelled to count the potential loss associated with every new gadget. When the Depression increased in severity during the 1930s, Rogers reminded Americans that they had too blithely accepted technological innovations without exploring their human impact.

ON MICROWAVE OVENS

All I know is what I see in appliance stores and these microwave ovens have me stumped.

In our kitchen back in Oolagah, nothing was more memorable than the aroma of dinner cooking through the day—beans, ribs and sauces. My sister's smokehouse once set fire to her home, but the aroma almost made up for the damages.

Nowadays, people have these microwaves, but what have they lost? It will cook your roast, but no one will eat it because it's not brown. The only square meal will be a TV dinner, and who eats TVs for dinner? It makes leftovers so good, people have gone for years without a second meal! In the old days, people said: "Where there's smoke, there's fire." Nowadays, they say: "Where there's a skittish pacemaker, there's a microwave."

Golly, I don't know if I'm resetting my clock or cooking leftover chili.

Yours by the campfire, smoke and all,
In the Spirit of Will Rogers

Some of the articles, like the one dealing with campaign slogans, are examples of pure word play:

ON CAMPAIGN SLOGANS

All I know is that there is an election coming up next year and everybody is working on slogans.

Back in the 1920s, President Coolidge said he did not choose to run. He knew the flavor would run out after 1928. So "Life Magazine" put me up as the "bunkless candidate"—by which they meant I told the truth, not that I didn't have a place to sleep.

Politicians today have a tough job. Those who got caught in the Abscam scandle better ask for a fair sheik.

Gay congressmen will have to take a lesson from the old organist, don't turn to the wrong page.

If a congressman orders a coke, it better be from a vending machine.

Now that we've all had a long class on supply-side economics, we can go on to other matters; it won't be necessary to "stay the course."

I am for slogans with a down-home flavor. My kind of politician would say, "If I do any dipping while in office, it will be skinny dipping."

> Your County Chairman,
> The Spirit of Will Rogers

After a standard twist of the "all I know . . . lead, the article refers to a 1928 campaign in which *Life Magazine*—then a publication specializing in satire—supported Will Rogers for president. "Bunk" was a popular word in the 1920s—perhaps because it was in such abundance—and Rogers was proclaimed as a "bunkless" candidate who would speak his mind on major issues. The whole effort resulted in some of the most delightful writing in the Will Rogers canon. The remainder of our article is a survey of the early 1983 political scene, stressing embarrassing revelations which politicians will have to cover over with flowery rhetoric. Surveyed are "abscam" defendants; congressmen with kinky sexual histories—alas, we did not know at the time that one was Congressman Studs—or drug records; finally, there is word play in connection with the then pro-Reagan motto about "staying the course."

As it opens, so the article closes with references to earlier, simpler behavior patterns. Cowboys live in bunkhouses where there is no need to be concerned with duplicity. Even country politicians—as Will Rogers and Steppin' Fetchit demonstrate in their film *County Chairman* (1935)—cannot go too far from the straight and narrow. Their efforts at political manipulation are harmless because power is not centralized and there is no treasury to rob. For such office holders, skinny dipping is the only kind of dipping. Framed by rural values, the article tries to take some of the sting out of recent examples of public corruption, offering the consolation that these ex-amples of malfeasance are exceptions to, not the norm of, congressional behavior.

CONCLUSION

The articles in our 1982-1983 series addressed a number of national issues, always with the Will Rogers touch. The president's unsuccessful attempt to boycott the Siberian pipeline was explored, stressing the shameful haste with which our NATO allies rushed to aid the Soviets. The impact of a new gas tax on truckers was considered against the background of concurrent Congressional pay raises. Will Rogers proposed his own "Cowboy Diet" to compete with the veritable feast of offerings to overweight Americans, satirizing along the way the Beverly Hills Plan, the Richard Simmons Diet, and the near-fatal Scarsdale approach. The crisis of Social Security was discussed, with Rogers suggesting a quick measure to help the old: he proposed that the federal government nationalize McDonald's and launch a "mac attack" on hunger among the elderly. The influence of motion pictures—always a concern of Will Rogers—was assayed in connection with the impact of *Ghandi* on an impressionable sailor who refused to wear her uniform after seeing the cinematic epic. Local and regional matters recognizable to national readers were also exploited for humor and insight.

Our series *The Spirit of Will Rogers* came to a close when *The Daily O'Collegian* (our student newspaper) ceased publication for the spring of 1983. We mailed out bound copies of our articles to at least twelve syndicates in the Middle West, the East, and the West. Over the summer, rejections trickled back, flooding the plains with disappointment. No one seemed to share our interest in communing with *The Spirit of Will Rogers*. The rejections forced us to reconsider the project, why we enjoyed it while others found so little savor.

Personal factors account for our special attraction to the Will Rogers project. Both of us are from Republican families once dominant in our home towns, but now politically inactive. As Richard Hofstadter has pointed out in *The Age of Reform* (1955), victims of status revolutions often exaggerate past virtues as a result of unhappiness with present realities. During his own time, Will Rogers' social commentary may have had such an appeal for white, middle-class Americans who typically subscribed to the *Saturday Evening Post*, and who typically suspected that unfriendly changes were in motion. In any case, it was certainly one of our delights in *The Spirit of Will Rogers* to reject the present in preference for an idealized past. Even if that past was a product of our creation, we needed it as a standard to measure a fallen present. In the era of *The Preppy Handbook*, the ploy did not help us with distribution and syndication. I suspect that there are very few editors nowadays who long for the decades when WASPS were in flower!

Certainly one of the pleasures of a typical Will Rogers article—and we hoped of our *Spirit of Will Rogers* series—was the delight in word play, but audiences seemed unwilling to be entertained by our verbal wit. We consciously imitated the Rogers technique of addressing problems through verbal manipulation—either through puns or some other form of linguistic misunderstanding which might require a series of verbal manipulations to attain clarification. Our article on the Washington snake incident of April, 1983 highlights both the joys of word play for us and the difficulties in reaching a contemporary audience:

ON RECENT HISTORY

All I know is what I read in The Washington Post and I hear two snakes got out of the zoo the other night.

Slithered into a trash bag and went for a bus ride. When the kid who took them was bit, they had to send back to my home state, Oklahoma, for anti-venum syrum.

Back in the 1920s that was my job, to take the poison out of the political system, to turn congressional vipers into wet noodles. You know a laugh can neutralize lots of hissing.

This kid in Washington had the right idea. Maybe congressmen would understand the current recession better if they got out of their cages and rode in buses like ordinary folk. Maybe they'd stop snapping at the president so much. Let him send through programs without sharpening their fangs on 'em. In these tough times, we need cooperation in our system, not all this snake oil business.

Yours for common sense instead of vipertuperation
The Spirit of Will Rogers

The stolen snake story was given special attention in Oklahoma because our state supplied the anti-venom vaccine used to save the young Washington boy. From our point of view, the occasion served as a basis for an extended metaphor, with hints of the Garden of Eden, the devil, and opportunities for puns.

In the third paragraph, Rogers compares himself to the vaccine in that he took upon himself the job of neutralizing venomous national debates. There are a host of testimonials by contemporaries of Will Rogers to substantiate such a claim: his humor did ridicule excesses without provoking anger; his daily and weekly articles on current events boosted national morale, encouraging Americans to work together in spite of differences.

The fourth paragraph continues the snake metaphor, but twists and turns to subjects such as the recession, the distance between our representatives and real Americans who use mass transit, and the unnecessary fractiousness which inhibits important government action in hard times. The overall effect of the final paragraph is to ridicule myopic officials who use their natural reflex to substitute debate for action.

The article closes with a meaningful pun. Throughout, we condemn the vituperation of Washington, but Rogers confuses the word with the word for snakes. We were especially pleased with the overall scheme of the article because it took peripheral news and made it a basis for general statements. Summing up the issues in the pun "vipertuperation" seemed to us to be a masterstroke. We had given the article all of the Rogers touches: a depth of historical awareness, contemporary insight, and a sense of play.

We were disappointed that sample audiences could not concur with our judgment. Our undergraduates claimed that they could not understand the references, even when they had seen and heard the snake story previously on the nightly news. Always wary of the printed word, colleagues in the English Department studiously ignored the articles; for them, they did not exist. The only genuine response came from the English building's janitor and his wife who came by our offices after working hours. And then there was the fourth grade child of our medievalist: he enjoyed the articles. As a result of indifference by our readers, we have *temporarily* ceased our efforts.

We are now trying to cure ourselves of Will Rogers fever. We make an effort not to mention his name or to invoke his gift of laughter during the evening news, no matter how depressing or absurd the reports. We have also vowed not to attempt any new Will Rogers projects—that is, *after* we finish our long-planned radio series and *after* we complete the film project which came to mind just the other day.

Ben Yagoda (essay date 1993)

SOURCE: "Reversible Figure: Will Rogers and Politics," in *Will Rogers: A Biography,* Alfred A. Knopf, 1993, pp. 285-303.

[*In the following essay, Yagoda provides an explication of Rogers's political beliefs.*]

Politically, Will was a little hard to pin down. What was one to make of a columnist who, as occasion demanded, would praise Calvin Coolidge and Al Smith, Dwight Morrow and Robert La Follette Jr., William Borah and Franklin D. Roosevelt? The inconsistency, however, was more apparent than real; certainly Will was not unaware of the sizable differences among these men of affairs. It was just that as he developed as a commentator through the 1920s and into the 1930s, he was able to pick and choose his issues, never blindly casting his lot with any camp. One explanation for this catholic perspective is his childhood and youth in the Indian Territory, whose political parameters corresponded in no way with those of the twentieth-century United States, and which therefore spared him partisan baggage. Another is his own resistance to doctrinaire ideology in any form.

His main impulse was a broad neo-Jeffersonian populism tempered by an across-the-board skepticism. He had a general and instinctive distrust of bankers, big business, and Wall Street. (Talking to a banquet a few months after Herbert Hoover took office, he offered a scathing, difficult-to-dispute two-sentence assessment of Hoover's laissez-faire predecessor: "Coolidge went in and just turned his head. And say, brother, if you didn't get yours then you was just dumb.") Pro-income tax and antitariff, he doggedly stuck up for the farmers, whom he (correctly) saw as getting the blunt end of Republican economic policies of the 1920s. He felt that consumer buying on credit and stock-market speculation, both of which reached unprecedented proportions by the end of the decade, were something close to an evil and he (correctly) felt they would end in disaster. But unlike many populists, Will was no proselytizer. He saw Prohibition— a divisive litmus test in the Democratic party for more than a decade—strictly as a political issue, with negligible relevance to morality or the public good; the position got him into trouble with many of his rural admirers, including his pious sister Sallie. "Talking about Prohibition is like whittling used to be," he said in a radio broadcast in 1930. "It passes away the time but don't settle anything." And he found stridently racist Bible-thumpers like Alabama Senator Tom Heflin distasteful. He simply didn't trust crusaders, which was why he never warmed to William Jennings Bryan, Huey Long, or, for that matter, Woodrow Wilson.

Another area of contention with Wilson and Wilsonians was in the realm of foreign policy. His skepticism about the efficacy of the League of Nations, the World Court, and the succession of international conferences held in the twenties and thirties qualified him as an isolationist, although unlike many people traditionally designated as such he was consistent, opposing U.S. military intervention in such places as Nicaragua, Mexico, and the Philippines, as well as Europe. At the same time, he favored a strong military—especially, of course, in the air—and had little doubt that there would eventually be another world war. In the matter of World War I debts owed to the United States by its European Allies, he was a strict collectionist, a stance that left him open to the wrath of internationalist voices such as Walter Lippmann and *The New York Times*. But Will's position had less to do with ideology than with the commonsense feeling that money borrowed ought to be paid back. He approvingly quoted Coolidge's five-word assessment: "They hired it, didn't they?" ("They" being the Allies, "it" being the money.)

Will was famous for making fun of Congress—a good half of his most famous quips were directed at that body's collective denseness, crookedness, and/or inefficiency. There was a venerable tradition for this sort of thing, participated in among others by Twain, who once observed, "It could probably be shown by facts and figures that there is no distinctly native criminal class except Congress." Like Polish jokes or mother-in-law jokes, swipes at Congress had entered a rhetorical realm in which the message imparted was subordinate to the convention itself, and its relative truth was of little consequence. But the way Will returned to the theme, again

and again and again, bespoke a genuine disdain on his part for legislators (in general—typically, he had nothing but praise for most of them as individuals); he saw their posturing, blatant pork-barreling, and sheer windiness as a permanent, only slightly less egregious version of the endless 1924 Democratic convention that had so infuriated him. Drawing any conclusions from the fact that the country's most celebrated Congress-basher was the son of a three-term Cherokee senator and master legislative politician would require aggressive speculation. But the irony is no less striking for that.

Will genuinely admired Mussolini for taking the reins of power as completely as he did, thus bypassing the messy legislative process, and as late as 1933 remarked, "Say, Mussolini could run this country with his eyes shut, in fact that is the way our Congress has been running it." When a San Diego newspaper criticized this comment and pointed out some of the drawbacks to life in Italy, Will responded to the "long winded editorial" with a personal letter that averred, "Dictatorship is the best government in the world provided you have the right dictator."

Statements like that lent credence to the proposition that Will was a mere comedian and not to be taken seriously as a political commentator. As such, they were welcomed by more conventional pundits, who were habitually bemused by the political and popular influence he wielded. Arthur Brisbane, the dully oracular author of the "Today" column in the Hearst papers, frequently made patronizing remarks about the very "useful" (faint praise indeed) Will Rogers. (In 1931, Brisbane wrote that Will's "early training at Eton and Oxford" made it hard for him to maintain the "cowboy style"—a weak joke that revealed more about Brisbane than Will.) In the pressroom of the 1928 Republican convention, with Will (and a reporter from the St. Louis *Post-Dispatch*) present, H. L. Mencken, the sage of Baltimore, fumed at Will's influence in the body politic.

> "Look at the man," he shouted. "He alters foreign policies. He makes and unmakes candidates. He destroys public figures. By deriding Congress and undermining its prestige he has virtually reduced us to a monarchy. Millions of Americans read his words daily, and those who are unable to read listen to him over the radio. . . . I consider him the most dangerous writer alive today."

> "Come on, now, Henry, you know that nobody with any sense ever took any of my gags seriously," remonstrated Rogers.

> "Certainly not," was the retort. "They are taken seriously by nobody except half-wits, in other words by approximately 85 percent of the voting population."

Mencken's outrage was in some measure mock (the *Post-Dispatch* reporter is no help in trying to determine the exact proportion). But there was an undercurrent of seriousness in his tirade as well.

The good gray *New York Times,* which by the time Will started writing for it had assumed its identity as the voice of what would later be called the Eastern Establishment, never knew quite what to make of its cowboy columnist. From the beginning of his association with the *Times,* in 1922, it was an odd fit, a fact the paper recognized two years later when it dropped his weekly column. (The McNaught syndicate had also been angling for a hefty rate hike at the time.) In January 1927, just months after his daily telegram had begun, Arthur Hays Sulzberger, who had married Adolph Ochs's daughter and would become publisher of the *Times* on Ochs's death in 1935, sent his father-in-law a memo asking, "Don't you think Will Rogers is getting pretty bad—and if so that we have been paying him long enough to feel that we have wiped out any obligation that we may have incurred last summer [when Will filed from Europe for free]?

My suggestion would be that we give him due notice of desiring to stop at the earliest possible time."

Ochs didn't follow the advice. But he—and the editors who worked for him—consistently treated Will with condescension. A reader once wrote in to complain that Will was "going into fields that are outside of his jurisdiction" and wanted the *Times* to "swap" him for Walter Lippmann, then with the New York *World.* "It has been our idea," replied managing editor Edwin "Jimmie" James (who doubtless wished he could make the trade), "that our readers understood that he wasn't presented as a serious oracle, but as a jokesmith." This was not Will's self-assessment. Since his 1926 European trip, he had considered himself a bona fide reporter. The *Times* did not. In 1930, in London to cover the disarmament conference, Will received this cable from Ochs:

AM SURE YOU SHARE OUR HOPE FOR SUCCESS OF DISARMAMENT CONFERENCE. IN THAT BELIEF SUGGEST YOU DO NOT UNWITTINGLY EMBARRASS THIS COUNTRY'S NOBLE PURPOSE IN ENDEAVORING TO PRODUCE GOOD LASTING RESULTS. LETS TRY TO BE HELPFUL

He got the same treatment the following year. Before his trip to Manchuria, he asked Ochs for credentials indicating that he was a *Times* correspondent. The publisher's return telegram answered in the negative and included, by way of explanation, a memo written to Ochs by F. T. Birchall, James's predecessor as managing editor:

It should be remembered that neither the Japanese nor the Chinese know Mr. Rogers, nor will they be able to understand his keen wit. These two are perhaps the most sensitive nations on earth. They have no sense of humor, and if he is going to be humorous, he will be misinterpreted and misunder-stood. . . . On the other hand, if Mr. Rogers proposes to be a serious correspondent, it should be borne in mind that it would take a long time to convince the public that he had become one. . . . Also a good Far Eastern correspondent requires years of training and absorption of history and customs. . . .

Whether the situation be drawn out or short lived, Mr. Rogers will be better able to comment from Beverly Hills, basing his material on what he reads in the Times.

On at least two occasions, the *Times* killed Will's column, the first time explaining the censorship by sending him this supercilious anonymous wire: "WE DID NOT USE YOUR PIECE TONIGHT. WE DO NOT CARRY ATTACKS ON CHARACTER OR CREDIT. [The author adds in a footnote: "The 'attack' in question came in a 1933 column criticizing what would later be known as the 'trickle-down' theory. 'The Reconstruction Finance Corporation is made up of fine men, honest, and mean well and if it was water they were distributing it would help the people the plan was meant to help,' Will had written. 'For water goes down hill and moistens everything on its way, but gold or money goes uphill. The Reconstruction loaned the railroads money, medium and small banks money, and all they did with it was pay off what they owed to New York banks. So the money went uphill instead of down. You can drop a bag of gold in Death Valley, which is below sea level, and before Saturday it will be home to papa J. P. [Morgan].'

In the second column, Will wrote, 'Frank Phillips, of oil fame was out the other day, said he was going to Washington. The oil men were going to draw up a code of ethics. Everybody present had to laugh. If he had said the gangsters of America were drawing up a code of ethics, it wouldn't have sounded near as impossible.'"]

Usually, Will grinned and bore this sort of thing. Once, he didn't. Late in 1932, England and France asked for postponement of their next war-debts payment. Will would have none of it. "One message of three words," he wrote, "will make every nation in Europe dig it up and send it over by plane, they would be in such a hurry to get it here—'Pay or default.'" He hammered home the theme in several other columns. The stance went counter to the prevailing view (editorially endorsed by the *Times* and Lippmann) that debts should be canceled, or at least their terms adjusted, and the newspaper received a spate of irate letters, including one from a recent Harvard graduate named Charlton Ogburn, who accused Will of "destructive obscurantism," called him "the most vociferous expositor of the 'hick' or 'dirty foreigner' viewpoint in the country," and accused the *Times* of "augmenting his already appalling influence." An editor wired Ogburn's letter to Will for reply and noted in a memo to James, the managing editor, "No answer to this tonight. Will probably is looking up the big words, or having someone interpret it for him." But Will did puncture Ogburn's pretensions masterfully in a wire that was addressed to James and published in the Letters to the Editor section. (" . . . HE MADE ME MAD JIMMIE, HE CALLED ME A 'BUCOLIC WIT,'" wrote Will. "JIMMIE I AIN'T HAD THAT SINCE I WAS A CHILD. . . . ") It was followed by eleven letters from readers: five pro-Will, six con.

The next day, the newspaper itself half-apologized for Will's views, in an editorial that swelled with condescension. "Let the raw, untutored voices be heard," it stated, and concluded: "Mr. Rogers will doubtless recall the advice of Matthew Arnold not to be disturbed by 'the fever of a differing soul.' The Times tries not to be." But Will got the last word in his daily telegram the following week:

> I would like to state to the readers of THE NEW YORK TIMES that I am in no way responsible for the editorial or political policy of this paper.
>
> I allow them free reign as to their opinion, so long as it is within the bounds of good subscription gathering.
>
> But I want it distinctly understood that their policy may be in direct contrast to mine.
>
> Their editorials may be put in purely for humor, or just to fill space.
>
> Every paper must have its various entertaining features, and their editorials are not always to be taken seriously, and never to be construed as my policy.

It's worth noting that, except for the (not uncommon) use of *reign* for *rein* in the second sentence, the entire column contains not a single error of punctuation, grammar, or spelling.

In his next weekly article, Will put forth a lengthy defense of his political seriousness. He remarked that he'd noticed a lot of people writing to the papers, saying, "I read Will Rogers, but why does he have to dabble in politics. Let him stay on funny stuff where he belongs."

> Well if they would just stop to think I have written on nothing but politics for years, you never heard me on a mother in law joke. It was always about national or international affairs. . . .
>
> Where do these other fellows get all of their vast stores of knowledge. I never hear of 'em going any place. If I write about Mexico, I have been down there a half a dozen times. Nicaragua, I been there twice and found out things that I couldent ever have by reading about it. Crossed India at the height of their troubles, been in Europe and talked debts till I had everybody's angle over there. There is not a state in this country that I am not in ever once in awhile. Talk to everyone, get the ranchers' and farmers' angle.
>
> Those New York writers should be compelled to get out once in their lifetime and get the "folks" angle. I know and have known all the time that the real backbone people of America wasent going to cancel any debts. They would never have given the moratorium if it had come to a vote of them. All your Lippmans and all your cancellationists in New York can write their economic theories that want to, but they dident know a thing about our people.

Will's point was well taken. But he was also protesting too much. He wanted to be taken seriously, yes, but at the

same time he wanted to retain the comedian's privileges of hyperbole, selectivity, and deflection. He would still frequently back away from the logical conclusion of his comments, still undercut his criticisms of politicians and big business with a public courting of Calvin Coolidge and John D. Rockefeller, still avoid topics or positions that couldn't be explored without running the risk of dullness, still never allow himself to go for more than a few sentences at a time without saying something funny. He still refused to recognize evil. As a result, he became the political equivalent of a reversible figure—the psychological test in which a wavy line on a blank page can be seen to be either a table lamp or a human profile, depending on which side of the line one concentrates on. If you looked one way at Will, he was a jokesmith; if you slightly modified your angle of perception, he was a sage. Far from bothering Will, the ambiguity suited his purposes perfectly.

And, of course, it helped bolster his remarkable popularity. If he had rigorously followed his positions to their logical conclusions, he would have lost the allegiance of millions. As it was, he was adored by Prohibitionists, Wall Street bankers, senators, tariff supporters, internationalists, even Cancellationists with more of a sense of humor than Charlton Ogburn had. Whenever a Rogers opinion was unpalatable, they could with minimal effort shrug it off and turn it into a mere joke.

By the late 1920s, in any case, Will had become a figure of real influence in American politics. He was read every day by millions, many of whom uncritically adopted his views as their own; most of the others at least looked on them sympathetically. This was not lost on politicians, who, over and above the honest affection they generally felt for Will, knew better than to overlook what he had to say on the issues. In 1930, a "Washington statesman" was quoted in *American Magazine* as saying, "You can never have another war in this country unless Will Rogers is for it." Also significant was a subtle but unmistakable sea change in the public climate (a change Will had much to do with bringing about): Suddenly, appearing to be a good sport, a regular guy, had become an important political consideration. In 1933, when Will announced over the radio that he planned to step down as congressman-at-large, Vice President Garner and no fewer than fifty-eight senators (nearly a two-thirds majority!) beseeched him to reconsider. Indeed, in the years since Will's gibes had ruffled Warren G. Harding's feathers, only one politician, Chicago's Mayor William "Big Bill" Thompson, had been foolhardy enough to take him on publicly. [The author adds in a footnote: "In 1930, in the depths of the Depression, Thompson had put forth a plan to solve the city's economic woes with a lottery, and Will had taken a shot at it in his column.

'All I have to say,' stated Thompson, 'is that if Will Rogers has made so much money that his head is so swelled that he thinks it is funny to crack jokes about people who are starving, I hope to God he goes broke and gets hungry himself and he won't crack any more jokes about those who have to accept charity.

'He has pulled some pretty brutal and unfair stuff about me in years gone by, which means nothing to me, because I consider the source from which it comes. When this nation is suffering and people are hungry, a wisecracker that belittles the condition and efforts of anyone to correct it is to me the cheapest skate on earth.'

The next year Thompson was out of office."]

No doubt many seethed at him in private. One such was Harold Ickes, secretary of the interior under Franklin Roosevelt. Will had criticized him for wanting to change the name of Hoover Dam and had commented, during a radio broadcast, that at least there were no plans to call it "Ikey's Dam." Few things made Ickes angrier than to hear his name subjected to that particular mispronunciation, and the morning after the broadcast he was livid with rage. "He never again had anything to do with Will Rogers," said an Ickes aide.

Will testified before Congress on the question of flood relief in 1928. Beyond that, he was a frequent, savvy, and welcome presence in the hallways of the Capitol and in informal summits of the powerful. Senators came to his ranch, hat in hand, to talk politics. At the 1928 Democratic convention, he drew Al Smith aside and pleaded with him to withdraw his candidacy. "Wait four years," a Smith associate remembered Will saying. "Nobody ever killed Santa Claus. Times are too good, you can't win in so prosperous a year." If Smith had followed the advice, he would have had a much better chance in 1932, and American history could have been very different. Will was also an unofficial adviser to Frederick Davison, Clarence Young, and David Ingalls, who as (respectively) assistant secretary of war, assistant secretary of aeronautics, and assistant secretary of the navy in the Hoover years were collectively responsible for the nation's aviation policy. [The author adds in a footnote: "Years later, Davison recalled a day when he, Young, Ingalls, Amon Carter, and Will met at his house for cocktails. Knute Rockne had recently died in a plane crash, and the topic under discussion was whether the airlines should provide parachutes. Ingalls, Davison, and Will said yes; Young thought it would be too impractical.

I remember Young saying, 'Take that accident. You probably wouldn't have saved more than one out of the whole bunch.'

Will Rogers with that funny little smile of his looked at the ceiling and said, 'Well, wouldn't he have been tickled.'"]

The friendships Will had cultivated over the years were bearing fruit as his cronies advanced up the ladder of power. His friend Joe Robinson of Arkansas, the Democratic leader in the Senate since 1923, was picked by Smith to run for Vice President in 1928. Nick Longworth died in 1931, but he was succeeded as Speaker of the House by John Nance "Cactus Jack" Garner, a hard-drinking, plain-talking, white-haired Texan Will had known and liked for years (and who will always be remembered for the immortal remark, "The vice-presidency isn't worth a bucket of warm piss"). On the two or three trips he made to the capital each year, Will would use Garner's office as home base, dumping his gear there before prowling the corridors. He also had long been friendly with Franklin Roosevelt, a fifth cousin of Theodore who had been the Democrats' vice-presidential nominee in 1920 and who was elected governor of New York in 1928. Their admiration was sincere and mutual. In 1930, Roosevelt was reelected by a plurality of more than 700,000 votes, and Will wrote in his daily telegram, "The Democrats nominated their President yesterday, Franklin D. Roosevelt." The following year, in a letter to Will, Roosevelt implored him to come to Albany sometime "and talk to me of cabbages and kings! I want to see you, Oh, most excellent of philosophers."

By the time Roosevelt wrote these words, the country was two years into the worst depression in its history. It was a moral and political crisis as well as an economic one, and it provoked Will, as nothing had before, to transcend reversibility, to take a firm, serious, and provocative stand.

Like virtually everyone else in the country, he had no idea that the stock market crash of October 1929 would be followed by a severe slump. Given his frequently expressed distaste for financial speculation, his initial reaction was not surprising. "Oh it was a great game while it lasted," he wrote in November. "All you had to do was buy and wait till the next morning and just pick up the paper and see how much you made, in print. But all that has changed, and I think it will be good for everything else. For after all everybody just can't live on gambling. Somebody has to do some work."

In the following months, as the economy continued to turn downward, Will continued to be attracted to the view that hard times might be a good thing in the long run. Americans had been living beyond their means, and financing it all on credit; the slump had brought us down to earth. "It's really not depression, it's just a return to normalcy," he wrote. "It's just getting back to two bit meals and cotton underwear, and off those $1.50 steaks and silk Rompers. America has been just muscle bound from holding a steering wheel. The only callus place we got on our body is the bottom of the driving toe." The temptation, for Will, was to see the Depression as a kind of all-purpose moral cleanser, wiping away the excesses of the 1920s and allowing old-time values to shine once more. "You know this darn thing has made the whole country better off in a lot of ways," he wrote on another occasion. "It's done away with four-flushing. If a man hasent got it, he don't mind telling you right out that he hasent. . . . It's brought out some mighty good qualities in lots of people. There is a spirit of better fellowship among everyone I think."

But as it became clear that there would be no quick upturn, he was forced to come to terms with the fact that any bracing effects the Depression might have had were as nothing compared to the suffering it had wrought. Seven million people had neither a job nor the hope of finding one; untold thousands were without sufficient food or shelter. Will's Red Cross relief tour in the winter of 1931 showed him how bad things really were among farmers, who had to face the consequences not only of drought but of price drops of up to 90 percent over the previous twelve years. Something was not right. Hoover's State of the Union address in December 1930 was a rather pedantic attempt to explain the causes of the Depression, which to Will was beside the point: "Our rich is getting richer, and our poor is getting poorer. That's the thing that these great minds ought to work on."

A month later, he returned to the theme. In England, Arkansas, an armed force of some five hundred people had demanded food from Red Cross officials, graphically illustrating how desperate things were. Yet Congress and the Hoover administration refused to provide any direct relief. Will didn't blame Hoover for the slump ("Mr. Coolidge and Wall Street and big business all had their big party, and it was just running out of liquor when they turned it over to Hoover," he would write), but the government's inaction left him incredulous. "If you live under a Government and it don't provide some means of getting work when you want it and will do it, why then there is something wrong," he wrote. "You can't just let the people starve, so if you don't give 'em work, and you don't give 'em food, or money to buy it, why what are they to do? What is the matter with our Country anyhow?" He proposed that the government hire the unemployed for massive public-works projects, to be paid for by "a higher surtax on large incomes." "It may not be a great plan," Will concluded, "but it will DAM sure beat the one we got now."

Franklin D. Roosevelt would adopt Will's plan almost to the letter, but his inauguration was still more than two years away. In the meantime, the masses were becoming less willing to accept their lot. A general conviction was emerging that some kind of revolution was a distinct possibility. In the fall of 1931, editor William Allen White warned that unless the government provided effective relief, the winter would see "barricades in the street." His prediction appeared to be borne out the following March, when the police opened fire on a group of three thousand protestors at a Ford plant in Dearborn, Michigan, killing four of them. In the spring, World War I veterans from around the country, demanding immediate payment of a bonus they were scheduled to receive thirteen years later, marched on Washington. Twenty thousand strong, they peacefully camped out in shanytowns on the Anacostia Flats until July, when soldiers under the command of General Douglas MacArthur, bayonets flashing, drove them from the city.

It would take a very long stretch to call Will Rogers a radical. His resistance to doctrinaire ideology of all kinds ruled out any attraction to communism or its variants; indeed, all his views were informed by a visceral (not

political) conservatism, and he was in fact a frequent target of leftist voices. "Will Rogers likes to pose as 'home folks,'" complained a socialist newspaper, "but the truth is he's a millionaire. He has never written a word in support of a worker on strike. He has never spoken a sentence that doubted the divine justice of the capitalist system. Many of his wisecracks reveal a hidden sympathy for the Fascist type of Demagogue." (The second and fourth sentences were accurate, and, if we set aside the question of whether Will was posing, the first was as well. The third was not.) But, reversible as always, Will was subject to divergent interpretations. Woody Guthrie, a Dust Bowl Oklahoman whose left-wing credentials are beyond dispute, was once asked who his heroes were. He gave two names: Jesus Christ and Will Rogers.

One observer bemused by the paradox was his son Bill. A self-described "intellectual snob" who was cultivating a fashionable radicalism in the early 1930s, Bill once collared his father and said, "Dad, you've been jumping on the bankers day after day. Don't you see the implications of what you've been saying?" Will brushed him off: "He didn't feel he had to be consistent," Bill Rogers says now.

But in 1931 and 1932, the spectacle of a government seemingly uninterested in addressing its people's suffering elicited a palpable anger in Will. On Washington's Birthday 1931, he wrote bitterly that Washington "would have seen our great political system of 'equal rights to all and privileges to none' working so smoothly that 7,000,000 are without a chance to earn their living." He was unimpressed when Congress convened early to discuss the unemployment question: "Well, I believe if I was unemployed and hungry I would want a little more substantial help than just the thought of 'our boys' being gathered in Washington."

Hoover recognized Will's unique position in the country and tried to use him to help build support for his program to fight the Depression, such as it was. But the President understood neither the Depression nor public relations. Once, he met with Will and merely requested a few antihoarding jokes. Another time, he tried to explain his opposition to direct relief. "Had a long talk with the president this morning," Will reported to his readers. "He sincerely feels (with almost emotion) that it would set a bad precedent for the government to appropriate money to the Red Cross." The parenthesis was damning.

On October 18, 1931, Hoover was scheduled to make a radio speech on the issue of unemployment, for which he had devised a two-pronged strategy—convincing the country that the problem was not as bad as it seemed and convincing local groups to raise money for relief. [The author adds in a footnote: "The chairman of the President's Organization for Unemployment Relief (POUR), formed in August 1931, was Walter S. Gifford, the president of AT&T. In January 1932, he told a Senate Subcommittee, 'My sober and considered judgment is that at this stage

. . . Federal aid would be a disservice to the unemployed.' An exasperated senator complained, 'You are always hopeful!' 'I find it pleasant, Senator, to be hopeful,' was Gifford's reply.'] He asked Will to speak on the broadcast, and he did. This was another miscalculation on the President's part. Will said all the right things, asking towns and cities to do their part and even venturing the opinion that Hoover "would rather see the problem of unemployment solved than he would all the other problems he has before him combined." But he also confronted the issue with a solemn and eloquent fervor that put the administration's inaction to shame:

> Now we read the papers every day, and they get us all excited over one or a dozen different problems that's supposed to be before the country. There's not really but one problem before the whole country at this time. It's not the balancing of Mr. Mellon's budget. That's his worry. That ain't ours. And it's not the League of Nations that we read so much about. It's not the silver question. The only problem that confronts this country today is at least 7,000,000 people are out of work. That's our only problem. There is no other one before us at all. It's to see that every man that wants to is able to work, is allowed to find a place to go to work, and also to arrange some way of getting more equal distribution of wealth in the country.

If the notion of Will Rogers as a presidential candidate had caught Americans' imagination in booming 1928, how much more attractive must it have been in 1932, when the country seemed on the verge of collapse. In the intervening four years, moreover, Will's stock had risen even higher. His credentials as a political sage were now established beyond question, and as a result of his humanitarian efforts he had become a nearly universally admired, and in some circles venerated, figure. In an extraordinary editorial written after Will's drought-relief tour and his goodwill mission to Latin America in 1931, *The New York Times* itself compared him to St. Francis of Assisi and praised him for "flying over great stretches of GOD's earth to make it as much of heaven as possible while still a very human mortal." His efforts on behalf of the suffering, in the *Times'* opinion, were "suggestions of a kind of angelic service, though the angel be of a very masculine type and very different from the conventional one."

Newspapers started promoting a Rogers candidacy in 1931, jokingly at first but more seriously by the month. In July, a Kentucky paper reported that "it is beginning to look as if the possibility exists of Rogers being taken seriously as a possible candidate." He was endorsed by the Oklahoma League of Young Democrats; Governor James Ferguson of Texas said he would be no more out of place in the White House than was Lincoln or Andrew Jackson. The *Home Friend* magazine got on the bandwagon early in 1932. "Little did we realize when we published the article about Will Rogers being the man we need in the White House," it reported in a subsequent issue, "that it would arouse so much favorable comment, and strike such a sympathetic chord in the hearts of our readers." *The Home Friend*'s editor copied out some of the responses and sent them on to Will. Mrs. C. W. Webb of Oklahoma wrote in to say, "If he could be prevailed upon to accept, I believe he would simply be the saviour or redeemer of our beloved U.S.A." A. C. King of Pennsylvania said, "In my intimate group of friends with whom I chat and play I find manufacturers, clerks, professional men, farmers and laborers, and I have heard your suggestion spoken of hundreds of times within the last few months, and the unanimous opinion that he could handle the job, and give us the faith and confidence we need at this time."

As a publicity stunt, a movie magazine sent a young man around the country in a car bearing a WILL ROGERS FOR PRESIDENT banner. He was surprised to find genuine interest in the idea, and repeatedly had to hurry out of town to escape people's demands to know the particulars of Will's platform.

Even Roosevelt, favored to bear out Will's prediction and win the Democratic nomination, appeared concerned about the possibility of a Rogers candidacy. "Don't forget you are a Democrat by birth, training and tough experience," he wrote Will in June, four weeks before the convention, "and I know you won't get mixed up in any fool movement to make the good old Donkey chase his own tail and give the Elephant a chance to win the race."

As Roosevelt knew very well, conditions in the country were such that, more than at any other time in its history, a candidate outside the political mainstream had an opportunity to attract a sizable following. Sinclair Lewis recognized this in his 1935 novel *It Can't Happen Here,* in which a plainspoken Vermonter is elected to the White House (and proceeds to install a fascist regime). That same year, Louisiana's Huey Long—blasting big business and promoting a redistribution of wealth—attracted enough support that he was considered a serious presidential contender until his assassination in September. Probably even more than Long, Will would have been able to tap the longings and resentments of the large portion of the country that had been abandoned by conventional politics. But unlike Long, Will had no interest in power. Furthermore, becoming President would have meant a cut in pay of more than 75 percent. There is, in any case, no evidence that he gave any serious consideration to running. When a *Collier's* magazine writer boosted his candidacy, he responded in his daily telegram: "Will you do me one favor? If you see or hear of anybody proposing my name either humorously or semiseriously for any political office, will you maim said party and send me the bill?"

To a friend he wrote, "I couldn't be a politician in a million years. I like to go my own way, and I don't believe I could take dictation. It sure would be an honor, and worth all the monetary sacrifice, but I am going through my life making up my own mind. . . ."

The 1932 Democratic convention began in Chicago on June 27 (the Republicans having already renominated

Hoover). On the opening day, during a recess, Will made an impromptu speech that was greeted with gales of laughter. "If some fellow got up and nominated Rogers right then," wrote a Chicago newspaper, "he'd have got two-thirds of the vote as quick as a secretary could have called the roll." Heywood Broun, an admirer since the *Follies* days, wrote, "I think it is a little ironical that the same convention which thinks Will Rogers is a clown accepts Huey Long as a statesman."

But Roosevelt was the man of the hour. Two years younger than Will, he had risen rapidly in the Democratic party, serving in the New York State legislature and as assistant secretary of the navy before receiving the vice-presidential nomination at the age of thirty-eight. The loss in the 1920 campaign was followed by personal calamity the next year, as he was stricken with polio and paralyzed from the waist down. Through sheer perseverance, he recovered the partial use of his legs, and, where previously he had struck many as a callow child of privilege, he emerged from the ordeal with a new and unmistakable authority and presence. While he held no office until 1928, he maintained and solidified his standing in the party, chiefly through his rousing nominating speeches for Al Smith at the 1924 and 1928 conventions. As Will had recognized, his overwhelming re-election as New York governor in 1930 had pegged him as the Democrats' strongest candidate in an election that, because of the Depression, appeared unlosable.

But when the first ballot was taken in Chicago on June 30, 1932, Roosevelt was still short of the necessary two-thirds of the vote; both Smith (now his bitter rival) and Garner (running with the support of William Randolph Hearst) received significant support. Oklahoma's twenty-two votes had been pledged to its eccentric governor, William "Alfalfa Bill" Murray, who had served with Clem Rogers at the constitutional convention of 1907. During the second ballot, Murray stood up and announced he was throwing the votes to "that sterling citizen, that wise philosopher, that great heart, that favorite son of Oklahoma, Will Rogers." At that very moment, Will was in the press box, fast asleep. "He came out of the trance dazed but smiling," reported *Editor and Publisher,* "and let out a long, loud laugh when he learned what had happened." Oklahoma switched its votes from Rogers to Roosevelt on the third ballot, and the New York governor won on the fourth. On hearing the news, Roosevelt took an airplane from New York to Chicago—the first presidential candidate to fly. He chose Garner for his running mate.

Will made no official endorsement, but there wasn't a soul in the country who thought he preferred Hoover. When Roosevelt went to Los Angeles in September, it was Will who introduced him to the cheering crowd of more than eighty-thousand at Olympic Stadium. "This is the biggest audience in the world that ever paid to see a politician," Will said as Roosevelt lifted back his head and roared with laughter. "Franklin—I can call you Franklin, for I knew you before you were Governor or even Assistant Secretary of the Navy. I knew you when you first started in your career of nominating Al Smith for office. As a young man, you used to come to the Follies, and I would call on you from the stage to say a few words, and you would get up and nominate Al Smith for something."

After the expected landslide, Will typed out the draft of a night letter to the President-elect in Warm Springs, Georgia, where he regularly repaired for the healing waters. It is an extraordinary document, displaying not only Will's affection and concern for Roosevelt but also his own unique position in the country. If anyone could presume to sit a President-elect down and give him some fatherly advice, it was Will Rogers. "I dident wire you on your election because I knew you wasent reading any of em anyhow," he began.

> Now that all the folks that want something are about through congratulating you I thought maby a wire just wishing you could do something for the country when you get in, and not wishing anything for me, well I thought the novelty of a wire like that, when it was backed up by the facts, might not be unwelcome.
>
> Your health is the main thing. Dont worry too much. A smile in the White House again (by the way when was the last one?) why it will look like a meal too us. Its the biggest job in the world, but you got the most help in the world to assist you. Pick you some good men, and make em responsible for their end. If Europe dont pay up, fire your sectry of the treasurer and get one that will make em pay. If people are starving and your granaries are full, thats your secretary of agricultures business is too feed em. If Nicaragua wants to hold an election, send em your best wishes but no Marines. Dissarm with the rest of the world, but not without it. And kid Congress and the Senate, dont scold em. They are just children thats never grown up, they dont like to be corrected in company. Dont send messages to em, send candy. Let your secretary of state burn up the notes that come from Europe, dont you have to attend to a little thing like that. Europes not going to do what they "threaten to do," all those things are just something to give diplomats an excuse for existing. Dont let these state governors like Pinchot, and all those get in your hair. A state is too the federal government, what an "honery" relation is too any of us. The more you do for em the more they expect. Keep off the radio till you got something to say, if its a year. Be good to the press boys in Washington, for they are getting those "Merry Go Rounds" out every few weeks now. Stay off of that back lawn with those photographers unless you got a Helen Wills. Or your fifth couzin, Alice Longworth. Nothing will kill off interest in a president quicker than "weeklys" with chamber of commerces, and womens political organizations. Now if some guy comes running into your office telling you "what Wall Street was doing" that day, tell him "Wall Street? Why there is 115 million of my subjects that dont know if Wall Street is a thoroghfare, or

a new mouth wash, its happenings dont interest me." Why Govenor you can go in there and have a good time. We want our president to have some fun, too many of our presidents mistake the appointment as being to the Vatican and not to just another American home.

And about people wanting jobs, just pass them on down to the next in line, and there is so many working for the government, that by the time they reach the lowest government employee, why the applicant will be beyond the government age limit. Why you handled more different kinds of people as govenor of New York than you will have in the U.S. and if Tammany comes around telling you "what they did," you just tell em, "Yeah?, I know what you did, and thats why you better keep quiet." So go in there and handle this thing just like it was another job. Work it so when we see you in person or pictures, we will smile with you, and be glad with you. We dont want to kill our presidents, but it just seems our presidents want to die for us. If we are going to blow up as a country lets be good sports and blow up with a smile.

Now if you dont like these rules I can send you some more, but you will get the next bunch collect. Just dont get panicky. All you have to do is manage 120 million "hoodlums," and the higher educated they are the bigger hoodlums they are, and the harder to manage. The illiterate ones will all work, and you will have no trouble with them, but watch the ones that are smart, for they have been taught in school they are too live off these others. In fact this last paragraph is about all that is the matter with our country.

Yours with all good wishes,
Will Rogers.

Roosevelt was inaugurated on March 4. The following day, invoking emergency powers, he declared a national bank holiday. Will was impressed. "America hasn't been as happy in three years as they are today," he wrote in his daily telegram.

No money, no banks, no work, no nothing, but they know they got a man in there who is wise to Congress, wise to our big bankers and wise to our so-called big men.

The whole country is with him. Even if what he does is wrong they are with him. Just so he does something. If he burned down the Capitol we would cheer and say, "Well, we at least got a fire started anyhow." We have had years of "Don't rock the boat," go on and sink it if you want to, we just as well be swimming as what we are.

Not surprisingly, FDR's usurpation of legislative author-ity struck a responsive chord with Will. In the middle of March, Roosevelt more or less unilaterally effected a modification of the Volstead Act, permitting the sale of beer, and Will could only shake his editorial head: "It just shows you what a country can do when you take their affairs out of the hands of Congress." Will liked every-

thing about Roosevelt. On April 30, he began a Sunday-evening network radio program and devoted his talk to the President, concluding, "That bird has done more for us in seven weeks than we've done for ourselves in seven years." A few weeks later, he compared the President to Moses and said, "He swallowed our depression. He has inhaled fear and exhaled confidence."

One of the things Roosevelt's Hundred Days made clear was that he was a new kind of President, a President who was not formal or distant or unapproachable in any way, yet who retained an unmistakable dignity, compassion, and sense of purpose. He conducted himself, as Will had advised, in a manner that made people happy when they saw him. Roosevelt's greatest innovation in the area of communications actually went against Will's counsel to stay off the radio for a year. He had his first Fireside Chat on March 12, and the way his voice came into the nation's living rooms bolstered the sense people had that he was trying to reach out to them personally. In truth, he had not a little in common with Will Rogers, his fellow radio communicator. FDR's second Fireside Chat was scheduled to air Sunday, May 7, after Will's own pro-gram. When the Rogers show was over, the White House phoned NBC and said the President wanted to know what Will had said; could a transcript of his remarks be read over the phone? The parallels between President and humorist were so striking that a guest on his show once remarked to Will, "Some people are wondering if the President is writing your speeches or you're writing the President's speeches."

Roosevelt boosted the nation's morale. His decisive moves did give it a much-needed display of direction and action in the White House. But the fact remained that they did not immediately (or even gradually) end the Depression. Nineteen thirty-three, 1934, and 1935 were hard years, better only marginally, if it all, than their predecessors. A reader of Will's columns of that period would have no way of knowing this. Over the previous two and a half years, he had repeatedly decried the plight of the poor, the hungry, and the unemployed; now, it was as if they suddenly had money, food, and jobs.

Will had made such a turnabout once before—in 1908, when an acceptance of his marriage proposal by Betty Blake was followed by the permanent disappearance of the despair and emotional frenzy of the preceding months. His foray into advocacy had been provoked by extraordinary circumstance, and was as anomalous and uncomfortable as his soul-baring had been. He gratefully seized on Roosevelt as a savior, and he turned his atten-tion to other things.

Joel Schechter (essay date 1994)

SOURCE: "David Crockett Goes to Washington, Will Rogers Stays Home," in *Satiric Impersonations: From Aristophanes to the Guerrilla Girls,* Southern Illinois University Press, 1994, pp. 34-45.

[*In the following excerpt, Schechter examines Rogers's use of satire in his writings and performance.*]

Long before a former Hollywood actor entered the White House, theater was inextricably linked to American politics by Congressman David Crockett. Crockett's collusion with his impersonators in the 1830s initially advanced his career and then harmed it. At the same time professional actor James Hackett popularized Crockett's persona in a stage play promoted by the Whig Party, the Congressman performed a lesser role assigned by the Whigs, as party celebrity. He was miscast in a road show that took him to New England dinners and to a Fourth of July celebration in Philadelphia, far from the electorate in Tennessee. The role cost Crockett his seat in Congress, which he lost in 1835. His impersonator, Hackett, fared better; he continued to portray the colorful politician onstage for two decades.

Almost a hundred years later, Will Rogers reacted against traditional party politics (and roles like Crockett's that support the politics of spectacle) with a satiric Presidential campaign. Rogers ran for president as the Anti-Bunk candidate in 1928. He argued that the Democratic and Republican parties offered voters bunk and said the candidates on tour were no better—in fact less entertaining—than a circus. The comedian negated boasts by Hoover, Smith, and their parties with his own promises to deliver nothing. "I have made a lot of promises, but they were only political promises, and I have no idea of keeping them," Rogers pledged before the election.

Will Rogers was a far more popular entertainer than his opponents in 1928, but he refused to turn his campaign into a spectacle like theirs or Crockett's. He would not play the role expected of national candidates in his satiric impersonation of one. "The less a voter knows about you the longer he is liable to vote for you," he joked as he declined to travel across the country for public appearances during his campaign. As will be seen, in his mockery of Smith and Hoover, Rogers became the antithesis of Crockett. Where Crockett promoted Whig policy through public tours and semicomic literature published in his name, Rogers did not campaign in person. His 1928 race for office was conducted in the pages of *Life,* a weekly humor magazine (not to be confused with the Henry Luce journal).

The cowboy-philosopher regarded the other candidates as comedians and found their roles humorous, but he said he was the only intentionally funny candidate. After Hoover won the election, Rogers told the public, "You made your choice, now go ahead and regret it. You will have no fun during the next four years. I would have given you a million laughs just by repeating the things I heard congressmen say."

Like Congressman Crockett in 1833, Will Rogers occasionally repeated humor written for him by a ghostwriter. Some of the speeches for his 1928 campaign in *Life* were written by the magazine's editor, Robert Sherwood.

(Rogers once praised Sherwood's work by saying, "That was a good piece I wrote for you last week.") Most of the time, however, he was paid five hundred dollars for each article he gave *Life,* and that was ample motive to write his own material. Crockett, by contrast, let someone else write his material too often for his own good.

CROCKETT'S ECCENTRICITIES

According to Mody Boatright, Whig Party ghostwriters initially published a spurious autobiography of Crockett to discredit him and Andrew Jackson, who was president from 1829 to 1837. Jackson's reputation as a Tennessee frontiersman was a political asset. Instead of being linked to urban corruption and big money backers, he was associated with the spirit of the common man and a new democracy.

The Whigs countered this imagery by portraying Crockett, another Tennessean, as an ignorant backwoodsman and a comic boaster. Boatright quotes the autobiography, *Sketches and Eccentricities,* to support his thesis that the book was an anti-Jackson literary hoax. At one point, the alleged author of the book announces, "I'm that same David Crockett, fresh from the backwoods, half-horse, half-alligator, a little touched with the snapping-turtle . . . can whip my weight in wild cats . . . hug a bear too close for comfort, and eat any man opposed to Jackson." The implication is that only associates of wild animals would befriend Andrew Jackson.

The book backfired according to Boatright; it flattered Crockett and made him popular. He joined Whig opposition to Jackson, and the Whigs wrote more for him.

Vernon Parrington has noted that Whig Party literature increased Crockett's reputation and the party's own standing as the choice of Tennesseans. While Jackson's populism had the support of farmers, industrial laborers, and backwoodsmen who helped elect him, the president's greatest supporters were largely ignored by the aristocratic Whigs prior to Crockett's tenure of office (1827-31, 1833-35). Crockett's entry into Whig ranks brought them the trappings of populism, but they were a party far friendlier to bankers than farmers.

Andrew Jackson frequently spoke out against "monied capitalists" and opposed the concept that government exists largely to serve private enterprise. When the Whigs adopted Crockett as their representative of new frontiersmen and rugged individualism by appealing to the Congressman's ego and inflating his self-importance, his individualism became synonymous with laissez-faire capitalism. At a time when Jackson objected to the Second Bank of the United States, and said it was serving special interests rather than the American people as a whole, Crockett joined the Whig defense of the bank. He had reason to approve of that institution; at least once the bank had generously forgiven a debt Crockett owed.

Crockett also came to support the Whig program for tariffs protecting Northern industry, although the tariffs did no particular good for his home state. His alliance with the Whigs may have cost the congressman his seat, even his life. Parrington notes that Crockett lost the backing of his electorate when he broke with Jacksonian populism, and when he lost the congressional election in 1835, "in a fit of anger he quitted his family and the state of Tennessee, went off on a mad chase to Texas, and in March of the next year fell at the Alamo. Vain, ignorant Davy Crockett . . . went down to Jericho and fell among thieves."

Before the voters in Tennessee turned against Crockett, he left them for a Whig-sponsored tour of the East Coast. Parrington reports that the colonel was "paraded at meetings by Daniel Webster, given great dinners, applauded for his rustic wit and homespun honesty. . . . Wherever he went he was taken in charge by young Whigs. Everything was carefully arranged beforehand." Crockett's autobiography also intimates that others led him to play politics as actors play roles. He wrote that in 1834 when crowds at Barnum's in Baltimore "called on me for a speech . . . I was compelled once more to play the orator." He sounds like a reluctant speaker.

Crockett did not always have to play the role of orator. During Crockett's years in Congress, the actor James Hackett performed as Nimrod Wildfire, a popular stage hero modeled after the Tennessean, in *The Lion of the West*. Hackett was, so to speak, Crockett's understudy, and the Whigs may have promoted the actor's tours in *The Lion of the West* much as they arranged Crockett's own public appearances.

COLONEL CROCKETT AND HIS UNDERSTUDY

> What a pity it is that these theatres are not contrived that everybody could go; but the fact is, backwoodsman as I am, I have heard some things in them that was a leetle too tough for good women and modest men; and that's a great pity, because there are thousands of scenes of real life that might be exhibited, both for amusement and edification, without offending.
>
> —Colonel David Crockett,
> *Life of David Crockett*

Crockett watched *The Lion of the West* himself in Washington, D.C. In 1833 his understudy, James Hackett, appeared as Nimrod Wildfire at the Washington Theater. Before the performance began, the audience cheered Crockett's arrival. Before the first word was spoken, the audience cheered Hackett as he bowed toward the congressman. Crockett in turn bowed toward the actor portraying him, and the audience burst into applause. It must be said that Crockett was a greater showman than Hackett, since the congressman had invited the actor to impersonate him on the Washington stage in the first place. He was bowing toward his own stage production and offering his own "scene of real life" to the audience.

Crockett attended theaters in New York, Baltimore, and Philadelphia as well as Washington, and his autobiogra-

phy suggests that the congressman was the featured attraction at least once. He, and not a play based on him, became the "scene of real life" at New York's Bowery Theatre in 1834. Again he sounds a note of regret as he recounts an episode of forced public appearance:

> When I got back to the hotel [in New York], I found the bill for the Bowery Theatre; and it stated I was to be there. Now I knew I had never given the manager any authority to use my name, and I determined not to go. After some time, I was sent for, and refused; and then the head manager came himself. I told him I did not come for a show; I did not come for the citizens of New York to look at, I come to look at them. However, my friends said it would be a great disappointment, and might harm the managers; so I went, and was friendly received. I remained a short time, and returned. So ended the first day of May, 1834.

Crockett's name could have been placed on the bill by the theater managers or by the Whig politicians who promoted his East Coast tour during April and May of 1834. That the Bowery Theatre featured a play about Major Jack Downing, "a sort of Yankee Davy Crockett," a week before Crockett's billing, no doubt increased public interest in his visit. And James Hackett performed another play about Jack Downing two weeks later on 10 May at the Park Street Theater across town. Crockett may not have asked for billing at the Bowery, but the Whigs and theater managers knew his "real life" appearance would be as welcome as any actor portraying a rough-hewn folk hero.

In retrospect, it is difficult to say which version of David Crockett was more popular during his lifetime: the legendary one of stage and almanacs or the one who acknowledged the legend with a bow at various theaters. Perhaps it does not matter, since Congressman Crockett advanced both versions during his lifetime, and they became inseparable. Francis Hodge noted of Crockett and Hackett that "the line between the man in public life and the nineteenth-century actor was not clearly discernible, and as far as the public was concerned the actor frequently took second place in the continuing competition between the platform and the stage." Crockett was fortunate to have places on both the politician's dais and the stage, although sometimes an actor stood in for him at the theater.

The man who has been portrayed pictorially for a century as a hunter in a coonskin cap first acquired that hat on stage when James Hackett wore it in *The Lion of the West*. Crockett himself never wore such a hat as far as we know. Crockett scholar James Atkins Shackford notes a comparable transfer of art into life when he found Hackett's stage dialogue reappearing in St. Clair Clarke's Crockett biography, *The Life and Adventures of Colonel Crockett of West Tennessee*, published in 1833.

In one scene, Wildfire recalls that after he fought a riverboat man and the stranger bellowed "enough," he was told by his conquest, "You're a beauty anyhow, and if you'd stand for Congress I'd vote for you next election." Wildfire answered, "Would you? My name's Nimrod Wildfire. Why, I'm the yaller flower of the forest. I'm all brimstone but the head, and that's aky fortis [strong waters]." In the 1833 *Life,* Crockett tells the same story, with one significant change. After the stranger says, "If I know'd your name I'd vote for you next election," the backwoodsman replies, "I'm that same David Crockett." The call for votes occurs in both versions, only the biography names Crockett, not Wildfire as the favored candidate. Crockett needed all the votes he could get that year, and in fact he was reelected for his last two-year term in 1833.

Shackford proposes that *The Lion of the West* benefited from Whig support as much as the books, *Colonel Crockett's Tour to the North and Down East* and *Life of Martin Van Buren,* both published in 1835 under Crockett's name, although Whigs wrote them.

"NO REFERENCE TO MY PECULIARITIES"

The author of *The Lion of the West,* James Kirke Paulding, denied that he based Nimrod Wildfire's character on Crockett. Paulding's son published a letter attributed to Crockett, in which Crockett thanked the playwright for his "civility in assuring me that you had no reference to my peculiarities." The letter, according to Shackford, could have been a Whig stunt, "a literary hoax which may have been an essential part of the whole Whig campaign to make David a more powerful anti-Jackson weapon in the hands of the friends of the U.S. Bank." Paulding wrote *The Lion of the West* to win a contest in 1830 after actor James Hackett offered a three-hundred-dollar prize for "an original comedy whereof an American should be the leading character." It is doubtful that Whigs were behind the contest or its outcome. (Paulding was appointed to the cabinet position of navy secretary by President Martin Van Buren in 1838. His political connections to Van Buren were probably not improved by his play about Whig favorite Crockett, whose 1835 book strongly criticized Van Buren.)

According to Shackford, *The Lion of the West*

> tremendously nationalized and pictorialized the name reputation of David Crockett, and precipitated about his name much of the current tall-tale legend of the West. . . . Noting how similar were the materials which entered into both [the play and the 1833 *Life*], we become increasingly convinced that the tie-up of *The Lion of the West* with David Crockett could not have been merely accidental.

By publishing other books about Crockett and arranging his tour, the Whigs capitalized on Hackett's play, if they did not actually promote it. Consider Crockett's 1834 visit to the Chestnut Street Theater in Philadelphia. Three years before, *The Lion of the West* was performed there for five nights; it returned a year later in 1832, further laying the ground for Crockett's visit to Chestnut Street

on 4 July 1834. He reports in his autobiography that "immediately upon its being announced that I had arrived, I was called on from all quarters for a speech. [I] . . . made a short address. They gave me two or three thunders like you hear on the stage, and then went on with the show." He was only the curtain raiser but the theatergoers must have loved his oration. It is too bad the Philadelphians could not vote for Crockett in Tennessee; he lost his office a year later.

His stand-in, Nimrod Wildfire, remained popular much longer, as James Hackett toured the play for two decades in England, Ireland, and America. He sometimes portrayed Wildfire in a solo show through monologues selected from the text; that was the form in which Crockett's stage image reached Washington in 1833.

If promotion of the play was part of a Whig hoax, Crockett himself participated. Perhaps he did not write the letter to Paulding denying that Wildfire resembled him, but he most certainly bowed to his impersonator in 1833 and accorded the work recognition as an acceptable representation (or misrepresentation) of him. Also, whatever hesitations he may have had, he visited the same theaters in which the play was performed (Park Street Theater, New York; Chestnut Street Theater, Philadelphia; Washington Theater, Washington, D.C.) and spoke to the audience when asked. He played as cast in a road show that continued until his electoral defeat in 1835.

KEFAUVER'S COONSKIN CAP

Walt Disney renewed the popularity of the Crockett legend in 1955 by releasing several television films—and one full-length movie—based on the pioneer-politician's life. Businessmen seeking to profit from the revival manufactured replicas of the coonskin cap Crockett never actually wore. Millions of children imitated Crockett by wearing these caps as Fess Parker had on television, while portraying the legendary man. I confess I wore one, too. In 1956, Senator Estes Kefauver, from Crockett's own state of Tennessee, donned a coonskin cap during his campaign to become the vice-president of the United States. The cap the Whigs made famous became a famous political wig. But Kefauver lost the electoral race. Margaret J. King notes that while Kefauver "appropriated the Crockett symbol popularized by television . . . five years earlier, the 1951 Kefauver Hearings on Interstate Crime had ascribed to television the role of an agent of corruption." Kefauver came to regard television and its imagery as a necessary part of political campaigning—much as the Whigs had turned to literary and stage fiction to advance their program a century earlier. Incidentally, Fess Parker considered running for Congress after his Disney series, but he remained in Hollywood, an actor to the last.

WILL ROGERS AS THE ANTI-CROCKETT

> Personally I think the Camera has done more harm for Politics than any other one faction. Everybody would rather get their picture than their ideas in

the paper. What does the platform of a Political party amount to compared to the photography! There is 10 cameras to every plank in the platform. Speakers get up early in the morning not to find out how their speech was received by the Press, but how the Pictures turned out.

—Will Rogers, *How We Elect Our Presidents*

Will Rogers was a comedian whose career differed considerably from David Crockett's. Although both have been regarded as colorful public speakers from rural America, Rogers was always a stage and screen performer, not a politician. Onstage he was the opposite of James Hackett's Wildfire: instead of promoting a political party's candidate or recounting how a riverboat man came to vote for a Whig, Rogers would debunk the existing parties and touring candidates from his perspective as a newspaper-reading, lasso-twirling cowboy. "I am not going around the country making a monkey out of myself just to see what kind of a man they would have in the White House if elected," he wrote in 1928, adding, "I did all that before I was nominated."

Once Rogers briefly abandoned his cowboy persona and became the president of the United States by impersonating Calvin Coolidge on the radio. According to Donald Day, Rogers copied Coolidge's voice in January 1928 so well that millions of radio listeners thought they heard the president say:

> I am proud to report that the condition of the country as a whole is prosperous. . . . That is, it's prosperous for a Hole. . . . There is not a "hole" lot of doubt about that. . . . Everybody that I come into contact with is doing well—Hoover, Dawes, Lowden, Curtis and Al Smith are all doing well. . . . Mellon [Secretary of the Treasury] has saved some money, for the country, and done very well for himself.

The speech continued in this comic vein, suggesting that an elect few were prospering, undercutting Coolidge with his own voice and catch phrases. Many listeners whom Rogers felt Coolidge had misled were now misled by the comedian or entertained by him at the president's expense. Coolidge wrote Rogers a letter saying he knew the parody was done "in good-natured amusement, and not to give it a moment's worry," according to Rogers but Donald Day thought that the impersonation deeply offended the President.

Having demonstrated that he could speak as well as an incumbent president, Rogers next campaigned for the office himself in one of his longest-running acts of political satire. As noted earlier, he became a third party candidate for president, running against Hoover and Smith on a platform opposing bunk. His supporters in the 1928 campaign were known as the Anti-Bunk party. Through comic speeches and statements Robert Sherwood printed for him in *Life* magazine, Rogers campaigned against the hyperbole and lack of distinction evident in the platforms of other parties' candidates. (Henry Ford, author of the

statement that "history is bunk," endorsed Rogers' antibunk campaign, as did Robert Benchley, Eddie Cantor, and Amelia Earhart.)

The Whigs promoted Crockett's candidacy and their party's anti-Jackson programs through inflation of the pioneer's reputation and publication of legends about him. Rogers chose to deflate his opponents by suggesting they had nothing special to offer voters, and neither did he. His campaign platform, published in an August 1928 issue of *Life,* constituted a sort of minimalist politics, eliminating from his own pronouncements all the false promises and patronage built into the other campaigns:

> Our support will have to come from those who want nothing and have the assurance of getting it. This means that we won't pay a cent for votes. We want the voters but they must be amateurs.
>
> Whatever Hoover and Smith promise you we'll rise 'em by at least 20%.
>
> We're going to eliminate party leaders, slogans, boll-weevil, luncheon clubs, vice-presidents, sand, fleas, conventions, golf pants and lots of other things.
>
> If elected I positively and absolutely agree to resign.

Will Rogers spoke not with the authority of an elected official or an actor impersonating a congressman (as Hackett did), but rather as a man who knew rural America and favored ordinary people over big business. Responding to Hoover's proposals to improve farm efficiency, Rogers asked: "Will the cows and chickens cooperate with this scheme? Well, I've met up with a few cows and chickens myself, and never saw one yet that understood the Ethics of Big Business." His friendship with cows and chickens is a far cry from Crockett's wrestling with bears and alligators.

The role of plainspoken, innocent farmhand was played somewhat disingenuously by Rogers; he was, after all, a highly successful national entertainer and honorary mayor of Hollywood. As a veteran of the vaudeville stage and the screen world, he knew how legends and artful fiction could mislead the public. And that knowledge enabled him to offer the public another, more knowing series of statements in 1928. He compared politicians at conventions and on campaign tours to film stars and entertainers. The candidates were not as entertaining as professional actors and directors, but they still sought the limelight, particularly when a film camera focused on it: "There is no other line of business that any of them could get in where they would get one tenth part of the publicity they get in public office, and how they love it! Talk about Actors basking in the limelight! Say, an old Senator can make an Actor look like he is hid under a barrel." Rogers anticipated our own times when, as a presidential candidate, he defended the profession of show business against competition from politicians. He lost the race in 1928, and it could be argued that Hollywood lost its competition with Washington around the same time, as the radio, stage, and screen became increasingly popular campaign grounds for American politicians. Rogers criticized the self-promotional, circuslike tours Hoover and Smith conducted in 1928 while he stayed at home:

> I hope there is some sane people in this country who will appreciate dignity and not showmanship in their choice for the Presidency.
>
> I have no free shows to give around the country, and no one to pay my way to them, in return for cabinet positions afterwards.
>
> So if your town wants to have a holiday wait til Ringling Circus comes along and see a GOOD show.

He declined to travel around the country campaigning, but he knew staying home was not the way to win an election in the age of political spectacle: "Our party has placed Dignity above showmanship, so the majority of people don't even know I'm running." To this day, most historians asked about the presidential campaign of 1928 will tell you Hoover defeated Smith; they forget Rogers ran. That is their misfortune, and ours, because his campaign speeches collected in a volume titled *He Chews to Run* remain enormously entertaining as a commentary on political modesty, the anti-Crockett philosophy in the age of political showmanship. . . .

FURTHER READING

Bibliography

Rollins, Peter C. *Will Rogers: A Bio-Bibliography.* Westport, CT: Greenwood Press, 1984, 282 p.
  Includes biographical, bibliographical, and critical essays on Rogers, in addition to numerous lists of works by and about him.

Biography

Cooke, Alistair. "Will Rogers." *One Man's America,* pp. 173-80. New York: Alfred A. Knopf, 1952.
  Fond reminiscence.

Croy, Homer. *Our Will Rogers.* New York: Duell, Sloan and Pearce, 1953, 377 p.
  Account by a personal friend of Rogers's that attempts to present his life truthfully, "mole and all."

Day, Donald. *Will Rogers: A Biography.* New York: David McKay, 1962, 370 p.
  Biographical examination of Rogers's "Americanness," attempts to place his life and career within their historical contexts.

Love, Paula McSpadden, ed. *The Will Rogers Book.* New York: Bobbs-Merrill, 1961, 218 p.
  Compilation of Rogers's statements on various topics.

Payne, William Howard, and Lyons, Jake G., eds. *Folks Say of Will Rogers: A Memorial Anecdote.* New York: G. P. Putnam's Sons, 1936, 224 p.
  Compilation of reminiscences about Rogers.

Yagoda, Ben. *Will Rogers: A Biography.* New York: Alfred A. Knopf, 1993, 409 p.
  Extensive biographical account with copious notes and documentation.

Criticism

Lucas, E. V. "Three American Humorists." *Only the Other Day: A Volume of Essays,* pp. 95-105. London: Methuen, 1936.
  British perspective on Rogers's personality. Lucas also discusses Artemus Ward and Josh Billings.

Smallwood, James M. "Will Rogers of Oklahoma: Spokesman for the 'Common Man.'" *Journal of the West* 27, No. 2 (April 1988): 45-9.
  Overview of Rogers's life and career.

Wertheim, Arthur Frank, ed. *Will Rogers at the Ziegfeld Follies.* Norman, OK: University of Oklahoma Press, 1992, 268 p.
  Compilation of Rogers's writings during the time he was performing on Broadway.

Additional coverage of Rogers's life and career is contained in the following sources published by Gale Research: *Contemporary Authors,* Vols. 105, 144; *Dictionary of Literary Biography,* Vol. 11; *DISCovering Authors* (Multicultural); and *Native North American Literature.*

Erich von Stroheim

1885–1957

(Erich Oswald Stroheim) Austrian-born American film-maker, actor, and novelist.

INTRODUCTION

A prominent figure in the early years of the motion picture industry, Erich von Stroheim is regarded as an innovative director of silent films and as a gifted actor whose famous portrayal of a cruel Prussian army officer earned him the popular appellation "The Man You Love to Hate." Witty, sophisticated, and satirical, his epic-length films, most of which were dramatically reduced in size and heavily edited before being released to the public, depict a world of cynicism, greed, decadence, and corruption often set in post-World War I Europe or the closing days of the Austro-Hungarian Empire. Stroheim's cinemagraphic style is typified by his meticulous attention to detail, construction of lavish sets, and dark evocations of mood using innovative lighting effects and filmic composition. He wrote and directed nine films, including his directorial masterpiece, *Greed* (1923), which was originally some 40 reels (more than seven hours) long. An obsessively perfectionistic director, Stroheim clashed with studio executives on many occasions when the demands of his extravagant, even self-indulgent productions ran over-budget. By the late 1920s Stroheim's films ceased to provide mass audience appeal or profits for the major film studios. Unwilling to sacrifice his artistic vision to monetary imperatives, Stroheim ceased to direct, and instead focused on acting, winning international acclaim for roles in such films as *La Grande Illusion* (1937) and *Sunset Boulevard* (1950).

Biographical Information

Stroheim was born in Vienna, Austria, on 22 September 1885. His father was a middle-class Jewish hat manufacturer, and not a member of continental aristocracy, though Stroheim continued to perpetuate this fiction throughout his lifetime, adding the title "von" to his name in order to create the illusion of nobility. Sometime between 1906 and 1909 Stroheim emigrated to the United States and was eventually granted citizenship in 1926. He undertook a variety of jobs until 1914 when be began acting in bit parts in the films of John Emerson and D. W. Griffith. Small roles in Griffith's *The Birth of a Nation* (1915) and *Intolerance* (1916) also afforded Stroheim a measure of fame and the opportunity to assist in directing these and other films. By 1917 he had performed his famous role as a Prussian officer in the motion picture *For France*, for which he was billed "The Man Who You Love to Hate." In 1918 he sold the screenplay for *Blind Husbands* to Universal Studios and

directed the film. Three years later he directed his first international success, *Foolish Wives* (1921). Conflicts with producers over stories, budgets, and methods throughout the 1920s— including his legendary clashes with Universal's Irving Thalberg—led to a decline in esteem for his work in Hollywood. By January 1929, filming of his *Queen Kelly* was halted, and the picture was not completed in his lifetime. Destitute by the mid-1930s, Stroheim concentrated on his acting career and left the United States for France. Between 1929 and 1955 he acted in numerous films, reprising his Prussian role for Jean Renoir's *La Grande Illusion*. Stroheim died in Maurepas, France on May 12th, 1957.

Major Works

Stroheim's first three films, *Blind Husbands*, *The Devil's Passkey* (1919) and *Foolish Wives* represent his exploration of a common theme, the corrupting power of European decadence over American innocence and simplicity. In each picture Stroheim portrayed a love triangle of sorts, featuring an undiscerning husband whose unhappy wife is seduced by a cynical and sardonic aristocrat—played by Stroheim in *Blind Husbands* and *Foolish Wives*. The latter film complicates the formula by highlighting the wantonness of its female lead, and features elaborate social settings, lavish banquets, and provocative boudoir scenes. Set in Vienna just prior to and during the First World War, *Merry-Go-Round* (1922) is a dark story of love between an Austrian count and a circus girl. Stroheim's career reached a significant turning point with the production of his fifth film, *Greed*. Based on Frank Norris's novel *McTeague*, the picture represents Stroheim's psychological study of avarice and its consequent moral degradation. Largely realistic, but with expressionistic touches, *Greed* details McTeague's murder of his wife, Trina, after she has won $5,000 in a lottery and contains disturbing images of the sewers of San Francisco and an unsettling murder scene in California's Death Valley. *The Merry Widow* (1925) is an adaptation of the ironic operetta of the same name, while *The Wedding March* (1927) and its sequel *The Honeymoon* (1928) bear similarities to *Merry-Go-Round*, sharing the theme of love between social classes. Stroheim asked to have his name removed from the credits of *Walking Down Broadway* (1933), his last film and only one in sound, because the work in its publicly released form had been rewritten and largely reshot.

Critical Reception

Reaction to Stroheim's work underwent considerable reassessment during his own lifetime, ranging from the critical success of his silent films *Foolish Wives* and *Greed*—which led to his being named one of the world's six best directors in 1925—to the virtual destruction of his reputation only five years later. In addition, while the advent of talkies contributed to the end of his career as a filmmaker, Stroheim rebuilt his popular reputation through acting over the next three decades. In the years since his death, Stroheim's directorial work has likewise been vindicated by critics who acknowledge that his films were distorted by the studios that so extensively edited them, sometimes removing three quarters or more of the footage that Stroheim intended to include. Likewise late twentieth-century scholars consider *Greed* to be not only his personal masterpiece, but also a classic example of realistic American filmmaking, and place Stroheim among the greatest directors of silent film.

PRINCIPAL WORKS

Blind Husbands (film) 1918
The Devil's Passkey (film) 1919
Foolish Wives (film) 1921
Merry-Go-Round (film) 1922
Greed (film) 1924
The Merry Widow (film) 1925
The Wedding March (film) 1927

The Honeymoon (film) 1928
Walking Down Broadway (film) 1933
Paprika (novel) 1935
Queen Kelly (film) 1985

CRITICISM

Peter Noble (essay date 1950)

SOURCE: "Stroheim, Sex and Symbolism," in *Hollywood Scapegoat: The Biography of Erich von Stroheim*, The Fortune Press, 1950, pp. 82-92.

[*In the following essay, Noble examines Stroheim's portrayal of sexuality.*]

> Thanks to Stroheim the women and young girls of America learned to prefer the slick, insolent archdukes, whose kisses burned like the lash of a whip, to the bucolic American heroes. He was the true creator of a sophisticated cinema.
>
> [*Herman Weinberg* in *Film Art (Spring 1937)*]

> *Foolish Wives* is an insult to every American . . . Stroheim has made a film that is unfit for the family to see; that is an insult to American ideals and womanhood. It gives an insight into Continental morals and manners such as only, so far, we have been able to get from certain books and paintings.
>
> [*Photoplay (March 1922)*]

> Stroheim taught the Americans how to make love.
>
> [*Oswell Blakeston* in *Film Quarterly (Spring 1947)*]

Hollywood without sex would hardly be Hollywood at all. Since the very beginnings of movies the primary objective of most film producers has been to turn out motion pictures which act as a visual process of sexual stimulation or sublimation, believing that every young person in the audience imagines himself—or herself—to be the central character in the love scenes being enacted on the screen. There is nothing new in this; the one aspect of the cinema which has remained constant for more than thirty years is the unlimited variation of the sex or love theme. Stroheim played a most important role in developing this theme beyond the vulgarities and crudities of the early silent cinema. He was a pioneer, and can be said to have exerted a stronger influence on this aspect of films than any other Hollywood director, even including Lubitsch.

Curiously enough, little is known of Stroheim's legitimate—and illegitimate—sex life. There have been murmurings of an unhappy love affair back in Vienna; in California he was married three times. His first wife was Dr. Margaret Knox of Oakland, California, who died in

1915. His second wife, May Jones, a designer for D. W. Griffith, was the mother of his eldest son, Erich, now an assistant director at Twentieth Century-Fox Studios in Hollywood. Stroheim's third wife, following his divorce in 1918, was actress Valerie Germonprez, whose brother Louis was Von's devoted assistant director for ten years. She was the mother of Stroheim's second son, Josef Erich.

Whether Stroheim's deep interest—some have termed it an obsession—with sexual themes in his films was an expression of his own sublimated desires is doubtful, but it is certainly curious that the man who did more to bring a sophisticated approach to sex into the silent cinema was himself a loving and faithful husband for more than thirty years. This is yet another paradox in Stroheim's paradoxical life.

Stroheim's celluloid world is a world of swaggering seducers, of light-hearted love affairs, of kings, dukes and counts making love to servant girls and tavern maids, of princes abandoning their thrones for love of pretty little working-class girls, of intrigue and sacrifice—in short, of Romance. Yet it is also a world of sordid affairs, of adultery, plots, deception and broken faith. Stroheim's philosophy is simple. In the credit titles of *The Devil's Passkey* the director reproduced a quotation from the American philosopher Elbert Hubbard: "To be deceived is less shameful than to be suspicious", and his delineation of suspicious husbands was always considerably more unsympathetic than that of his erring wives. His moral outlook was a protest derived from what he had experienced in his adolescence. He had lived in a world of intrigue and lasciviousness. At court he had seen drunken officers at midnight dragging protesting maidservants into their quarters until he was sickened by the lechery with which he was surrounded. Himself a studious and aesthetic person, he was repelled by the indications of sexual licence which he encountered everywhere in the environment of the Hapsburgs' Palaces. This resentment expressed itself many years later in his films, for although he seemed to have little or no sympathy for the weak wives and the suspicious husbands, reserving this for such seducers as Lieutenant von Steuben (*Blind Husbands*), Rex Strong (*The Devil's Passkey*) and Count Karamzin (*Foolish Wives*), punishment was always meted out to the villains in the final reel. He had a strong moral code, and villainy was always justly punished. In *Blind Husbands* the officer was dashed to death on the Alps, while in *Foolish Wives* Karamzin's body was stuffed into a sewer, thus satisfying the moral dictates of the American censor—and perhaps even Stroheim's own sense of fitness. One will never know whether he took sides on the question of justification for unlimited sexual licence on the part of his officers and aristocrats. There is much in his work to indicate that although he seemed to revel in detailing their glamorous exploits, yet his sense of justice, perhaps even his own moral character, saw to it that they were eventually punished in the Victorian manner. Or maybe he was merely bowing to the dictates of the public?

There were other aspects of Stroheim's approach to sex, aspects which were far in advance of his times. Not all his villains were straightforward seducers. I have referred elsewhere to his handling of that remarkable character Baron Sadoja in *The Merry Widow*. Sadoja, on the surface, was yet another in the list of Stroheim's sexy villains. He was, however, lecherous to a degree only hinted at by such as von Steuben and Karamzin, and what made him more unpleasant was the fact that he was a hideous, raddled old man whose main pleasure was obtained from the defloration of young girls. The Baron's particular form of sexual delight appeared on the surface to be the bending of a young girl's will to his. It seemed that he was convincing himself that his rheumatic old body was still able to make its conquests and that his disappearing virility could summon new strength from the conquests of young flesh. The scene in *The Merry Widow* in which Sadoja prepares himself for the wedding night with his new bride, is almost sickening in its sensuality. Carefully he gets his person, ready for the nuptials, the while peering through a crack in the door at his young wife, now undressing, now in her negligée. Finally, with the aid of his sticks, the crippled baron hobbles into the bedroom, eager and ready for the conquest for which this time he had paid the price of marriage. Here was one who had not been an easy pigeon. She had demanded that marriage accompany his propositions, and Sadoja, eager for a culminating victory to his series of sordid affairs, had finally acquiesced.

As he throws away his sticks and surveys with glistening eyes and slavering mouth the lovely body of his bride (clad in diaphinous black negligée) Sadoja's heart begins to beat wildly. Slowly he approaches the girl, more a victim than a wife, and as she shrinks back trying to conceal the repulsion she feels, Stroheim's camera dwells lovingly on close-ups of their expressions. Here was stark sexual realism in a scene which was so startling that even to see it today makes one wonder how it passed the censor in 1925. As Sadoja grasps the shrinking body of the girl his heart, which has been pounding at breakneck speed, suddenly stops. The sexual excitement has been too much for him; his withered body cannot stand the strain of yet another orgasm, and he collapses in a death struggle.

This is, perhaps, straightforward enough, but the director dwells, with engaging detail, on other aspects of Sadoja's sex life. The baron is a fetishist, his particular interest being a collection of ladies' high-heeled shoes and slippers which he keeps in a cupboard in his bedroom. Each pair represents a conquest, each pair carries the scent of yet another girl who has fallen victim to his salacity. In a classic scene, Stroheim's camera points to the Baron's trembling fingers as he fondles pair after pair of the shoes. One can only conjecture at what the censor was thinking when he allowed this one through! And again it is interesting to ask how such scenes were viewed by the great American public. Did they object? It is too much to expect that more than a handful of cinemagoers understood the true significance of this aspect of Sadoja's character. Even today such a sequence would be considered "daring".

To have made that old operetta success **The Merry Widow** into a sophisticated and subtle film, fraught with sexual significance, must be counted a distinct triumph for the young director. Seeing it today, one is still impressed, one continues to be amazed at its audacity and adult approach.

Merry-Go-Round, The Merry Widow, The Wedding March and **Queen Kelly**—all these were concerned with a society which Stroheim knew, loved and hated, for although some of his screen courts were given some fictitious names, it always remained Vienna. Why do Stroheim's thoughts always turn to the dazzling court of Old Vienna? Because he belongs by right to palaces, because he is a natural king. That is why he wrote the story, which was never—unfortunately—filmed, of the Emperor who had to wash the feet of the poor while they were offered, by an endless line of powdered flunkeys, delicacies on silver salvers which they were forbidden to eat—the ritual feast of the king by right who can protect his subjects, provided they acknowledge his absolute supremacy.

Of course Stroheim is at home with ritual, for he is himself the incarnation of the most secret of all rituals—the fertility of the universe. Note his obsession with candles in **Merry-Go-Round, Wedding March** and **Queen Kelly**—candles, the age-old symbol of fertility. Remember that it was Von who ordered twelve apple trees to be covered with one million blossoms of wax for a scene in **The Wedding March**. It was Von who always triumphed over human frailty, who made a mockery of the insignificant amours of his puppet characters. Stroheim put his secret thoughts on to the screen, and with them his secret desires. Glamour is a glamorous word—for sex. With Stroheim the glamour is intensified to kingship. It is the primitive, undeniable potency which gave some dark monster dominion over a herd of enemies in the early days of the world. It is the ultimate of male dominance. It is sex in sledge-hammer blows. It transcends the pretty world of the publicity agent, the drawing room flirtation. It conquers and commands. Stroheim's heroes had potency. They had sex and personality. Potency may not be a pretty idea for puritans, but it will bring them to their knees, as it brought Stroheim's detractors to their knees, amazed at the man's authority.

Lotte Reiniger, the creator of delightful black-lace silhouette films, once told Oswell Blakeston: "I am no schoolgirl, yet when I talk to Stroheim I find myself blushing." This is a ridiculous confession for such a sophisticated person as Mrs. Reiniger, but there is nothing ridiculous about the force which emanates from Von as a person, and from Von as a creative genius of the cinema.

His first picture, **Blind Husbands,** was a straightforward story of a seducer and his fate, a fate which was almost preordained in the Victorian style. Lechery was punished, and Stroheim was content. In **The Devil's Passkey** the illicit lovers were allowed to go unpunished; the director was more concerned with condemning the husband's suspicions than the wife's infidelity. In his next, **Foolish Wives,** Stroheim went further. The last reel saw Count Karamzin dead, murdered by an avenging father, but the sympathy of the director was obviously with the count. Living on his wits in Monte Carlo, Karamzin kept an intriguing *menage à quatre,* consisting of himself, his two pretty "cousins" and a maidservant who is infatuated with him. The Russian count has made seduction and blackmail his business, and his "cousins" act as partners in his misdeeds. In addition the count is obviously having love-affairs with both of them; there are several sly interpolations revealing the occasional jealousies which disturb the peace of the villa. Charming and "Continental" as this might appear—or shocking, whichever way you look at it—the situation was further complicated by Karamzin's rather sordid affair with his middle-aged maidservant.

He is apparently a man of astonishing sexual virility. After dallying amorously with a potential victim in her flat while her husband is engaged on business, he returns home to the arms of whoever of his "cousins" happens to be available. Late at night the eager maidservant slips surreptitiously into his bedroom, where she spends an hour alternately crying with shame and making unashamed and violent love to her master. Certainly Stroheim's creation, Karamzin, fulfilled the desire of every male member of the audience to be the sexual ruler. Here was a man who took what he wanted, who was sexually free. Here was a libertine with charm, here was a man who knew how to live, who knew a woman's place in a man's world. The "harem approach" of Karamzin in **Foolish Wives** found a ready response in the complacent American male, and, not unnaturally in the sexually frustrated American woman.

Stroheim taught Americans more about love than any other director had done previously. He set up a ritual of fertility, surrounding unfaithfulness with glamour, symbolising sexual power as the central plank of living. Stroheim's male characters all had this power and one knows that power cannot deceive its own promise. In a Stroheim film things will really happen. Here is no deception such as one finds in the quasi-Freudian textbooks which raise our hopes too high. One reads in Jung, Freud and Krafft-Ebing of men who want to drink their mothers' blood. Something epic, something colossal—but it never happens. Instead the wishes sublimate—they drink a cup of tea. They perish in a sink of their own frustration. But Stroheim—one can easily imagine him drinking blood—not in reality, but involved as it were in that world of clash and clangour which he made peculiarly his own—the world of glittering Viennese Courts, of gallant men and willing maidens, of pomp and splendour, of the jewelled princesses in their lovers' beds and the dead cats in the dustbin. In Stroheim's world there is potency, not sublimation, reality not fantasy.

Stroheim's strength and imagination led him to conceive films which would terrify lesser men. He is a man with a blinding power of fantasy. It was he who wrote a powerful and moving story of a man who fell in love with a woman with no legs. Yet where was the producer who had Stroheim's courage to produce this epic? The opening shot was a side-show in a circus: "See the woman with no legs! See the woman with no legs!" screamed the neon signs outside. The next shot showed the freak herself, a beautiful girl with a sad, strange face, squatting on a velvet cushion. The camera moves into a huge close-up of her face, then moves back to take in first her deformed body, and then the half-horrified, half-giggling faces of the spectators. "She must be a fake." "Her legs must be hidden away under the cushion." "It is all done by mirrors." So runs the tenor of the comments. Then to a vivid close-up of a sensitive-faced young man standing at the back of the crowd and looking at the girl with love and longing. She sees his look, but ignores the silent pleading of his eyes. And so on—and on—into the vivid, exciting and unusual story of a great love which transcends all normal sexual relationships. But could Stroheim get a producer to look at his script? Certainly not.

But producers fell over themselves to take Stroheim's scripts about love and pretty romance. Yet they themselves were the last to realise the hidden implications in the finished films. Did they think twice when they saw the Sadoja episodes in *The Merry Widow*? And what did they make of Stroheim's preoccupation with cripples? (e.g., *Foolish Wives* and *The Wedding March*). And there is that strange incident in *Foolish Wives* where Karamzin, still maintaining his love affairs with four women at the same time, yet gives up an evening at a great ball in Monte Carlo to climb into the bedroom window of a mentally deficient child. Did the producers see nothing strange in this incident in *Foolish Wives*? Did they not ask themselves "Why should this successful rake be obsessed with a poor, ugly idiot?" Why, indeed, was the handsome Karamzin so anxious to possess the girl? And did he rape her with the knowledge that this would lead to his death at the hands of her father? Did Karamzin possess a death complex? Did he realise that this was to be his last affair? Did he enter the girl's bedroom knowing that this pitiful character had lived for fourteen years without any kind of sexual love, and would welcome his advances? Was this his last sacrifice? Was it merely lasciviousness—or was something deeper implied? These are questions raised in our minds after seeing *Foolish Wives*. The incident of the counterfeiter's daughter must remain one of the most intriguing of all the Stroheim mysteries.

Powerful as this rape scene was, the classic rape sequence of the silent screen occurred between George Siegmann and Mary Philbin in Stroheim's fourth film, *Merry-Go-Round*. As Clifford Howard remarked (in *Close Up*): "The whole film, powerful and impressive, was notable for its wholly gratuitous violence and intensification of the anti-pathetic aspects which any such scene must hold." This film also featured a sub-plot concerning the affair between the countess (Dorothy Wallace) and the groom (Sydney Bracey). Their love scenes in the stable were daring to a degree never before witnessed on the Hollywood screen. One reviewer condemned the film as a "glorification of animal passion", which indeed it was. Stroheim never denied that his films were "real", and his love affairs far from merely "pretty-pretty". In *Merry-Go-Round* he anticipated D. H. Lawrence's *Lady Chatterley's Lover*.

Encouraged by the success of his sophisticated and daring treatment of sex themes in his first four films, Stroheim introduced what amounted to a rape sequence into his masterpiece *Greed*. The film was full of striking realism (e.g., the love scenes between McTeague and Trina on the sewer pipes, and the almost-sickening sequence when dentist McTeague pulls out one of her teeth.) On their wedding night, McTeague, a clumsy but gentle giant in everyday life, becomes a fearsome would-be rapist to the sexually innocent bride. Knowing nothing of the gentler and more spiritual sides of love-making, and having had no experience of sexual love-play, the newly married couple awkwardly enter their bedroom. The girl is obviously frightened, and will not respond to her husband's clumsy attempts at love-making. Finally, McTeague grabs her in a kind of desparation, and in much the same way as John Steinbeck's tragic creation Lennie unwittingly kills the mice and kittens he loves to pet, in *Of Mice and Men,* so McTeague destroys the love of Trina. She never recovers from the pain and fear of that night, and her sex phobia continues throughout her married life. Haunting her is the memory of that dreadful conquest. Whether legal or otherwise, rape is not a pretty thing, and this aspect of *Greed* was sickening and powerful and in true Stroheim tradition. Trina's subsequent mental development was a revelation of Stroheim's grasp of fundamental psychological phenomena which marked his pictures out as years ahead of their time. To modern cinemagoers, steeped in Freud—or rather Hollywood's idea of Freudian teachings, which is not perhaps the same thing—the process of Trina's sexual sublimation in *Greed* would seem to be eminently simple. Her obsession with gold, and her sexual coldness towards her husband would appear to go hand in hand. Trina begins to love gold with an almost sexual passion. She realises that money can give her power over her husband—power to repel him, to keep him at arm's length. The coins become a fetish. As she lies in bed at night she allows the gold she has saved through years of parsimony to trickle down her wasted body. She lies flat on the mattress of her ugly brass bedstead and pours the coins over her pathetic bosom. Gold is her lover. Gold is her god. Gold replaces the sexual love which she is psychologically incapable of accepting from the man she can only view as her rapist-husband. And he, bewildered by something which is beyond his powers of comprehension, and angered at her coldness and refusal to be a real wife to him, becomes a drunkard and a murderer.

The critics who hailed *Greed* as one of the greatest silent films of all time, unanimously declared that the theme—

that lust for gold destroyed lives—was almost Victorian in its moral appeal. Even they failed to discern the emotional and sexual undertones which marked the film out as unusual, as a classic piece for the collector. *Greed* was a powerful novel, but it became in Stroheim's hands an even more powerful and memorable film. In it McTeague, the strong dominant male, was defeated, however. He had fashioned the means of his own destruction. For Stroheim, obsessed with male fertility as he was, and forever conscious of male dominance, realised that the strength of woman was as strong in its negative fashion, in its non-acquiescence, in its sexual coldness, as man's, the male ego, both sexual and psychological. In his novel *Paprika* some years later he developed the theme of feminine sexual sadism.

Greed was an extraordinary film, which nevertheless fits unevenly into the Stroheim cycle. It was entirely different from the themes of *Blind Husbands* or *Foolish Wives,* and far removed from the Court intrigues of *Merry-Go-Round* and *The Merry Widow.* Stroheim revealed himself to be a veritable master of the delineation of tragedy and realism as well of sophisticated romance.

Merry-Go-Round and his seventh film, *The Wedding March,* were similar in many respects. Each dealt with the dying aristocracy of Stroheim's own birthplace, Vienna, and each examined the situation of an aristocrat falling in love with a commoner. In the former it is an Austrian nobleman (Norman Kerry) and a working-class girl (Mary Philbin), whose romance is destroyed by the declaration of war, and his subsequent campaign. In the latter the "hero" is a prince who falls in love with the daughter of a Viennese violinist only to leave her when he is forced by his father to marry the crippled daughter of a corn-plaster magnate, because his family needs money to prop up its disappearing prestige and position. (The marriage, incidentally, is "arranged" in a brothel by Nikki's drunken father and the magnate—a typical Stroheim touch, expressing his intense disgust in the most dramatic way possible.) Stroheim himself played Prince Nikki in *The Wedding March,* with Fay Wray as the girl he loves, and Zasu Pitts as Cecilia, the rich cripple who becomes his bride. The limping princess is a pitiable figure, and the director appears to revel in her affliction. In scene after scene she is made to limp the length of a long room in full view of the camera, and even in the wedding sequence Stroheim's camera follows her relentlessly as she limps all the way up the long aisle to her husband-to-be, waiting, a trifle impatiently, at the other end. With a flicker of his eyes Stroheim reveals the faint distaste, intermingled with pity, which he feels for the girl he is being forced to marry. The wedding scene was extraordinarily well acted, by both Stroheim and Zasu Pitts, and remains a highlight of the director's career, for its sensitivity, pity and undertones of poetry. *The Wedding March* is a film of rare atmosphere.

Like *Merry-Go-Round,* it featured a remarkable rape scene, however. Stroheim still revelled in his favourite character, that of the dominant male. (He was to develop this character along his own individual lines in the talk-

ing films in which he starred—*Three Faces East, Friends and Lovers, As You Desire Me* and *Fugitive Road* in Hollywood, and *Marthe Richard, Alibi* and *Gibraltar* in France—the strong, brutal male, not handsome but almost terrifying in his sexual power and implicit male mastery.) In the earlier film it was George Siegmann, the owner of the Merry-Go-Round, who portrayed the burly rapist, while in *The Wedding March* Mathew Betz played the loutish Schani, the butcher, who wants Mitzi passionately and almost manages to satisfy his lust when she is heartbroken over her lover's marriage to Cecilia. The rape sequence in the slaughterhouse (and who but Stroheim would envisage this?) when Schani struggles with her on the sawdust floor, is sickening in its intensity. The pathetic struggles of the girl, fluttering like a bruised butterfly caught in a net, the bestiality on the face of the man relentless in his lust, the blood dripping into the sawdust from a huge ox carcass hanging from the ceiling—here was a terrifying instance of Stroheim's power to create life from celluloid. The threshing bodies in the sawdust—the coagulating blood on the floor—this was Stroheim the realist. Yet the love scenes between Nikki and Mitzi were gentle, tender, almost lyrical. Their sad love story was told with a kind of detached poetry, and all their scenes were moving in the extreme. It revealed another facet of the director's artistry—the gentle lyricism totally opposed to his sardonic approach in *Blind Husbands* and *Foolish Wives.* His attitude to love in his previous films could hardly be said to be lyrical or poetic. On the contrary it was savage, sardonic, lusty and brutal. Love was not the word which could possibly apply to the relationships between the officer and the doctor's wife in *Blind Husbands,* between Strong and the playwright's wife in *The Devil's Passkey,* between Karamzin and the American ambassador's wife in *Foolish Wives.* Note by the way, how Stroheim attacked the conventions of marriage and the American male at one and the same time. His "blind husbands" were invariably Americans, while his charming seducers, although justly punished—for the Censor's benefit one feels—were all Continentals. In *Merry-Go-Round* Stroheim allowed himself one or two less sardonic moments in the scenes between the Prince and his little girl from the suburbs. *Greed* was distinguished by a crushing brutality, and *The Merry Widow* by polished cynicism.

With *The Merry Widow,* Stroheim excelled himself in his efforts to point the decadence of the aristocrats and officers in the prewar Viennese Court. Many of his sequences were censored. It has been rumoured that they included some too-passionate love scenes between Prince Danilo and Sally O'Hara, and orgy sequences in the private rooms of the officers. The censors deleted, it is said, a sequence which took place in a locked ballroom where an orchestra of naked women played music while the drunken officers caroused and made violent love on the splendiferous velvet settees and divans which surrounded the dance floor. All that remains of these sensational scenes are a few stills, some of which are in the possession of the American critic, Herman Weinberg. But think of it—an orchestra of naked women sedately playing violins and cellos while orgies were taking place before them! Only Stroheim could create such a scene. Even if it didn't happen, one would like to think it did!

In *Queen Kelly,* made in 1928, Stroheim, managed to get a naked queen into the script, in spite of the censors. Played by Seena Owen, this character is the mad queen of a Ruritanian kingdom who always walks around her palace completely unclad except for a large white cat which she clutches in her arms. She even continues to fondle the cat when she takes her bath. It is the only thing she loves. For her fiancée she has nothing but a feeling of possessiveness, expressing this—and who knows what else?—when she whips pretty Patricia Kelly the schoolgirl whom her Prince loves. In this one scene the queen permits herself to wear a long black robe, almost as if she feels too shy to let herself be seen unclad by the victim of her flagellation. Curious? Yes, indeed; *Queen Kelly* abounded in such "curiosities".

Queen Kelly was never released owing to the coming of talking films, but those who have seen it declare that, it is a truly remarkable piece of work. Three years afterwards Stroheim directed his first sound picture, *Walking Down Broadway,* in which he dealt with the relationship between two girls, one of whom was jealous of the other's success with men. A curious and highly individual picture, quivering with sexual undertones, and reminiscent of the pages of Krafft-Ebing, it thoroughly frightened the Fox officials who commanded a private viewing. It was too powerful, too sordid, too shocking to be shown, they declared. And it was shelved, leaving imaginations to run riot. Thus ended an era unequalled in the history of the cinema, the period when Stroheim's theory of male dominance prevailed, the era of a group of American films which have since been unequalled for their daring and courage. Stroheim's career for twenty years has been restricted to acting and writing, but even so he had brought his strong, powerful—and highly sexual—presence to bear on a score of films of varying quality. Today he still reminds us of the time when his work represented the most sophisticated approach to sex ever seen on the screen. Who, today, would dare to make a picture like his *Walking Down Broadway,* where the feelings of the character played by Zasu Pitts for the girl played by Boots Mallory were "not quite motherly, not quite sisterly, but a great deal more than either?" Even *implied* Lesbianism is taboo in the cinema. But nothing was taboo to the fabulous Stroheim. Only his daring and lusty novel, *Paprika,* which "uncovers the sadism inherent in the sexual plexus of a woman", issued in England in a cut version, gives some indication in literature of the approach which labelled him twenty years ago as one of the great masters of the literature of the cinema, the De Maupassant of the screen, the Austrian who taught the Americans how to love.

André Bazin (essay date 1949)

SOURCE: "Erich von Stroheim: Form, Uniform, and Cruelty," in *The Cinema of Cruelty: From Buñuel to Hitchcock,* edited by Francois Truffaut, translated by Sabine d'Estree with Tiffany Fliss, Seaver Books, 1982, pp. 3-16.

[*In the following essay, which was originally published in 1949, Bazin considers themes of violence and cruelty in Stroheim's films.*]

ERICH VON STROHEIM: FORM, UNIFORM, AND CRUELTY

The films of Erich von Stroheim rightfully belong to the critics and filmmakers of the post-World War I period. And his work cannot be well known by anyone who is unfamiliar with the last five years of silent films. Perhaps because it is more recent than that of Chaplin and Griffith, his work needs some time to acquire the objectivity bestowed upon it by retrospectives and historical criticism. Whether by coincidence, accident, or predestination, his films are among the most difficult to view today. His relatively short but brilliant oeuvre exists only in the memories of those who were dazzled by it at the time it was released, and in the respectful admiration they felt for him—and admiration shared by the present generation.

I am not old enough to have seen Stroheim's films when they were first shown, and this means that, when I write about him, I can never compensate for not having been on this cinematic road to Damascus.

We not only lack enough historical perspective and critical documentation to appreciate Stroheim but we are also dealing with a psychological complex unique in the annals of films. A kind of fear, a sacred horror, tacitly relegates him to the Hades of film history. Perhaps that is why it is so difficult to find—among the comments and testimonials of those he most influenced (such as Renoir) or those who most admired him—anything except wild superlatives and value judgments that one would be hard pressed to justify.

We all know how original his subjects and his own character were, as we know that he turned upside down the erotic themes on the screen at a time when Valentino was at the peak of his glory in America while a new art film was emerging in France. We can still glimpse something of these themes in Stroheim-the-actor that we admire today. But nonetheless we must ask ourselves if his importance does not lie in the audacity of his subject matter and the tyrannical violence that is always present in his films. It is therefore fairly difficult to understand the widespread influence he had—an influence which continues today. Because, ultimately, what is admirable about him is precisely the most inimitable portion of his work. If Chaplin has been influential, although less so than Stroheim, his influence comes almost exclusively from word of mouth. In his films when he does not appear as an actor one perceives ultimately the secrets of his style, his stage setting, and direction. Just as Chaplin is at the core of his work, which cannot be discussed without somehow explaining the character himself, Stroheim cannot remove himself from *Foolish Wives* and *Greed,* in which he has no acting part. If any work in film history, with the exception of Chaplin's, has attained the strictly exclusive expression of its creator, it is that of Erich von Stroheim. That is why studying his work will perhaps allow us to unmask a false aesthetic problem and resolve a critical paradox.

The paradox is this: an aesthetic revolution involving radical renovation in the formal design of the direction is often only the direct result of an actor's performance, of his basic need to express his inner feelings. The perfect example is still Chaplin. But if we are wrong in thinking that Chaplin invented nothing so far as directing is concerned, and that his film cutting did not involve any particular narrative aesthetic, it is nonetheless true that his importance can be considered to be secondary in this respect. With Chaplin, the actor has almost totally taken over the film. This does not mean, however, that the same holds true for all actors' films. It is simply that Chaplin's style, deriving from music halls and Mack Sennett, had *already* found its full expression in films made *before* Griffith. Editing supplied almost nothing. Another actor might need other resources, and Stroheim, working after *Broken Blossoms* (1919) and *Intolerance* (1916), found it difficult to express himself when faced with the rather strict laws of film editing. It was because of these laws and other formal film practices that Stroheim had to assert himself, just as he did with the scripts of the time.

To explain Stroheim's directing and staging we almost have to resort to an introductory psychoanalysis of his persona. Let's start by admitting that his work is dominated by sexual obsession and sadism, and that it develops under the aegis of violence and cruelty. The message we must look for in *Greed* or *Foolish Wives,* as in *Intolerance,* is simply of a social or moral thesis. It is a kind of one-track testimonial, a unique and selfsame affirmation of personality, a startling vision of the world seen through a prism colored by consciousness—or rather by the unconscious. For Stroheim, a film was merely the most efficient means of affirming his character and his relationships with others, particularly women. It is worth emphasizing here that Stroheim's message did not have much impact on the literature of his time, nor would it on today's. And it is obvious that Stroheim can be considered tame when compared to the many daring, psychological novels that have been published in the last fifty years. Yet we must refrain from believing that what is conventionally called "subject matter" enjoys, albeit potentially, an existence that is independent of the means of expression that render it perceptible to us. Stroheim would doubtless have been a mediocre writer, but his advent at a certain moment in film history and the actual choice of this particular art form make him equal to the greatest writers. The significance of a theme and the power of a subject are concomitant with the time of their appearance in relation to the history of the art form that sustains them, as well as with the evolution of genres, or styles. If we consider Stroheim as the Marquis de Sade of film, although his novel *Paprika* is not really innovative,

the fact remains that the magnitude and originality of a work can, in the final analysis, be measured only by the art form to which it belongs.

Let me stop this aside and return to Stroheim's position in the cinema of his time. Griffith had reinvented films and taught the whole world the laws of editing. De Mille's *The Cheat* (1915) brought about a roughly comparable revolution to film acting. By using either theatrical or simplistic acting, he invented a kind of cinematic syntax to express emotion. After all, Chaplin—as much through his acting as through his narrative style—had taught us the cinematic value of ellipse and allusion. With him, screen artistry attained the sublime by what it did *not* show us. This was also the period when Valentino's erotic bel canto were the rage and when the feminine ideal of the vamp was soon to be imported from Germany. If an attempt is made to synthesize this aesthetic juncture it could be defined, with respect to its basis, by the triumph of the mythological star, crystallizing, as Malraux said, some powerful collective, unconscious instinct. With respect to style, it could be defined by the ultimate implantation of a specific screen language that was basically elliptical and symbolic. Griffith's great discovery was, in effect, having taught the cinema that it was not just capable of *showing* but of *telling;* not just *reproducing,* but *describing.* By analyzing reality through the isolation of a certain fragment outside of its context and by arranging such shots in a certain way in time, the camera was no longer restricted simply to recording a story. It created the story to its own advantage, which could not be simply grasped by photography.

The importance of Griffith and the discovery of editing is immeasurable. And Stroheim's films could not have the same meaning *before* or *after* Griffith. This language had to exist before its destruction could be called an improvement. But what is certain is that Stroheim's work appeared to be the negation of all the cinematic values of his time. He will return the cinema to its main function; he will have it relearn how to *show.* He assassinated rhetoric and language so that evidence might triumph; on the ashes of the ellipse and symbol, he will create a cinema of hyperbole and reality. Against the sociological myth of the star—an abstract hero, the ectoplasm of collective dreams—he will reaffirm the most peculiar embodiment of the actor, the monstrosity of the individual. If I had to characterize Stroheim's contribution in one phrase, however approximate, I would call it "a revolution of the concrete."

Thus we see that what Stroheim wanted to say on film was the very opposite of what the screen was able to express at that time. An actor to the point of exhibitionism, Stroheim wished first and foremost to show himself. His legendary taste for uniforms is the least important sign of this, yet the most expressive. Around this personality, whose particular originality contained a prodigious will to power, was organized the Stroheimian directing and staging—like concentric circles when a stone is thrown. It goes without saying that Stroheim's genius lies in the fact that his tyrannical pride did not lead him to seek the lion's share of closeups, as was the foolish conceit of most film stars. If he reigns on screen it was not by the square foot but through the constraint whereby people or things resemble him or submit to his will. One cannot resemble ideas, and one can only reign over people; myths do not suffer when whipped; sadism needs human flesh and nerves; only thus can it triumph over our hearts. This explains the realism of Stroheim's direction and his use, which was revolutionary at the time, of natural sets, or at least faithfully reconstructed sets that had true dimensions. Orson Welles would later make use of the famous Stroheim ceilings. Stroheim did not ask his actors to convey feelings through acting, according to a vocabulary and syntax of gesture transposed to expressive ends. On the contrary, he asked them to reveal themselves as much as possible, to bare their features without shame. Nothing but the disorder of the human appearance should acquaint the audience with this interior world. Unfortunately, I have seen *Greed* only once. Despite the famous final sequence in the desert, the image that remains engraved in my memory is the unbearably erotic scene at the dentist. Let's not dwell on the Freudian symbol of the tooth that haunts the whole first part of the film, as does all the paraphernalia of the dentist's office that is used as a prelude to love. Since the young woman can no longer bear the pain of the drill, the surgeon puts her to sleep. Only her face emerges from the white cloth that protects her. It is at this point that the man is overwhelmed by uncontrollable desire. There is a kind of sexual fury that Stroheim does not justify by the logic of the situation (a defenseless woman), but by what he shows us of the heroine's face. He literally succeeds in photographing her sleep: we see the slight twitching of her skin, minute muscular movements; the nervous trembling of her lip or eyelid imperceptibly disturb a face on which we read drug-induced troubled dreams. The man's mounting desire (the camera shows us his face with the same indiscretion) is not intimated by the editing or even by his acting. If we participate, ad nauseam, in this scene it is due to a sort of carnal incantation that emanates from so much physical evidence. Stroheim's actors do not cry glycerine tears. Their eyes are not more of a mirror of the soul than are the pores of a perspiring skin.

Nothing of what I have said up to now would be totally incompatible with a classical conception of staging or directing. Stroheim would be merely an amazing scriptwriter and a director of first-rank actors if the cutting and the forms themselves of the narrative did not corroborate and complete the sense of these working methods. The professional vocabulary of film is unfortunately too poor and ambiguous. The terms "editing" and "cutting" indiscriminately conceal technical or aesthetic realities that are absolutely different. Therefore I must paraphrase, because of my inability to justify personal definitions. Before Stroheim, and even today, in ninety out of one hundred films, the unity of cinematic narrative was, and still remains, the "shot" in Griffith's style—a discontinuous analysis of reality. Stroheim also used close-ups and broke up a scene during the shooting. But the division

that he made the event undergo, by force of circumstances, did not stem from the analytical laws of editing. If Stroheim's narrative could not, for obvious technical reasons, escape the discontinuity of shots, at least it was not based upon this discontinuity. But, on the contrary, what he was obviously looking for was the presence in space of simultaneous events and their interdependence on one another—not a logical subordination as with montage, but a physical, sensual, or material event. Stroheim is the creator of a virtually *continuous* cinematic narrative, tending toward permanent integration with all of space. Unfortunately the technical and aesthetic state of filmmaking at the time prevented him from perfecting this new cutting, for without knowing it, he was inventing what would later become the language of sound films. A "continuous" cutting is in fact inconceivable with a reality in which only visual images can be reproduced, excluding the reality of sound. The absence of sound leaves fatal lacunae in the narrative, lacunae that can only be filled by an appeal to the added symbolism of the acting or the editing. It was necessary to wait for sound and, among other discoveries (or rediscoveries), depth of field before directors could really refine the cutting as Stroheim envisioned it. This is what Renoir did, especially in *The Rules of the Game* (1939), where he managed to dissolve the idea of shots in a reality of liberated space. However, the appearance of sound was necessary to grant Stroheim the place which was rightfully his and which he deserved. He would have been the Griffith of sound films, but his message was only temporarily and partially understood. From time to time in a modern film we find a shot from *Foolish Wives* or *Greed* (for example, the ending of *Manon* by Clouzot, 1949). If there is a cinema of cruelty today, Stroheim invented it. But those who borrow an idea or a situation from him do not always know how to draw their inspiration from his technique. This is because this technique is perhaps more terrifying than his subjects. More professional courage and above all more imagination are needed to be faithful to Stroheim's narrative technique than are needed to draw inspiration from his themes. I can't really think of anyone beside Renoir who knew how to do it; but I also see Orson Welles's sequence shots as a continuation of Stroheim's narrative style. Almost everything that is really new in film in the last twenty years has some affinity with Stroheim's work. Even today he is largely misunderstood, but his message runs deep, and we keep seeing it resurface here and there. The time has not yet come when sound films cease to be under Griffith's domination and move on to Stroheim and Murnau.

STROHEIM LOST AND FOUND (*DANCE OF DEATH*)

Those who remember **Greed, Foolish Wives,** and **The Wedding March** know that if films possess a remarkable actor in Stroheim, it is an understatement to say that films lost one of the world's greatest directors—perhaps the greatest after Chaplin. For Stroheim, the roles of actor and director were inseparable. Under the guidance of other directors, Stroheim lost his greatest originality, even as an actor. The character he is usually made to play nowadays is only the shadow of the one that rocked the film world in 1925. It is true that Stroheim had enough character to continue to be an astonishing actor—in spite of this loss of substance. But the fact is that since *The Grand Illusion* he has continued to bury himself in a more and more physically and morally stereotyped character, one who is opposite of the hero in **Foolish Wives** and **The Wedding March**. Whether playing the part of the international adventurer in *Storm Over Lisbon* (1944) or the Prussian officer in *The Grand Illusion,* Stroheim has obviously become softhearted. Beneath his terrible mask seamed with scars, the shaved head, behind the unsettling silence, behind the brutality with which he drinks a glass of liquor, a repressed and sometimes delicate sensitivity is hidden. And even when entrusted with a "bad guy" role, it never goes very far. The scriptwriter easily gets rid of him through a disgraceful suicide which reveals, in the final analysis, that the villain was not really very dangerous. Frozen in a certain attitude, and displaying the tics of his early roles, Stroheim in reality saw himself dispossessed, by those who used him, of what was the essence of his genius. The former Marquis de Sade of film is today most often only a bogeyman of detective films or a misunderstood softie.

Stroheim's revelation and revolution were the results of unbridled and limitless psychological violence. We undoubtedly owe him the only "imaginative" films in which movies dared to be wholly realistic, where no insidious censorship, however subjective, limited his inventiveness and expression. These films were true to life and as free as dreams. But it would take too long to explain how, motivated only by the desire to dig deeper into his character, Stroheim was also led to invent—like Chaplin—a new aesthetic of direction, whose lessons would be prophetic. But here I only wish to speak of Stroheim the actor.

Unfortunately, several months after the announcement that he would participate in adapting **Dance of Death,** very disturbing rumors began to circulate. It was said that Stroheim "added" many things to Strindberg. The film took place twenty years before the time in the play and tongues began to wag that Stroheim was less concerned with being faithful to the play than to giving himself the opportunity to make himself look younger as well as don as many uniforms as possible. Under these conditions, one had every right to fear that the film was, on one hand, a betrayal of Strindberg's work, which was already difficult to adapt and, on the other hand, sanction of the decadence of a man who was naïvely prisoner of his most unbearable bad habits.

Not only is Marcel Cravenne's **Dance of Death** a tour de force of adaptation (in collaboration with Michel Arnaud, dialogue by Jacques-Laurent Bost) but we also are indebted to him for an almost unrecognizable Erich von Stroheim, in that he no longer resembled the artificial image of the last ten years, but looked like himself.

It is certain that without Stroheim as an actor, there would have been no special reason for bringing **Dance of Death** to the screen. His astonishing personality is the focal point of the film. For the first time since *The Grand Illusion,* Stroheim found a role worthy of him and a director who knew how to elicit the best from him. It seems as if Marcel Cravenne, through an intelligent and critical respect for his actor, was able to make his innermost personality reappear. This was not always easy, as Stroheim had his own set ideas. It is unfortunately true that his scenario was indeed set "twenty years earlier." Haunted by the idea of his former persona, Stroheim wanted to recapture it by returning to the age he was then. Without Stroheim's knowledge, and sometimes by resorting to guile—for example, taking advantage of his actor's fits of temper—Marcel Cravenne was able to egg him on to interpret a role that the latter saw differently. That is why many scenes, which are not in the finished film, had to be shot—to please Stroheim, so that he would agree at another point to act as the director wished. If in art the result only counts, Marcel Cravenne was right, since, because of him or in spite of him, it is really Stroheim whom he gave back to us. Of course, he no longer has the almost unbearable violence shown in **Greed,** but certain scenes, at least fleetingly, contain a flash of blinding cruelty. The famous sword dance in which the old alcoholic officer, who suffers from a heart condition, dances until he drops, is particularly haunting. You must also see him chasing his wife with the tip of his sword in a kind of terrifying and ambiguous banter, or striking her with a whip on the stairway of the castle, to recognize the strange and fascinating uneasiness. He is like a flame in the cinematic hell which he himself created and which twenty years of cinema contrived to forget.

Erich von Stroheim (essay date 1955)

SOURCE: "Introducing *The Merry Widow,*" in *Film Makers on Film Making: Statements on Their Art by Thirty Directors,* edited by Harry M. Geduld, Indiana University Press, 1967, pp. 74-8.

[*The following essay is a transcript of Stroheim's introductory remarks to a 1955 showing of* The Merry Widow.]

. . . I would like to introduce to you my friend, my collaborator, Denise Vernac . . . [applause]. . . . It is always a very bad sign when a director has to speak before one of his own films . . . [laughter] . . . because he will be making excuses . . . and that is exactly what I want to do. I have many reasons for it and for asking your patience. In the first place, because I speak very poor French. Secondly, because this film, **The Merry Widow,** was made thirty years ago. It is a very long time. In those days we did not have the techniques and equipment we have today, for instance, lighting, color, sound . . . And then, this film that you are going to see, this copy is a . . . [Denise Vernac: "contretype" . . .] a contretype from a completely different version. This is a 16mm. copy and it will be projected on a regular-size screen and for that reason the images will not have the sharpness of focus. . . . Also, we don't have music. It was necessary, this very afternoon, to arrange something during the last two hours. In the old days, the M.G.M. company had experienced composers who prepared scores for the theatres which had orchestras. The smaller theatres, naturally, had only pianos—that's all. Tonight we have a very intelligent, extremely . . . [Denise Vernac: "able" . . .] able musician who will do his best.

Naturally, I like drama . . . tragedy. . . . But the producers do not like it. . . . They like only what brings money, and in my youth I hated money, although today . . . [laughter and applause]. Therefore I never wanted to direct stories for infantiles like that . . . [laughter] . . . but because, before I embarked on *The Merry Widow,* I had made a great tragedy . . . when I say "great," I mean in length . . . [laughter] . . . and a great story. . . . It was not my story this time—it was one of the greatest stories written by an American, Frank Norris, a student of Zola. And this film was, as the company said, a complete, a complete . . . [Denise Vernac: "fiasco" . . .] fiasco . . . [laughter] . . . because it was not this company that gave me money to make the film but another one, which had supervised me during the shooting but which did not have a money interest in the film! It is very simple—the company did not give the film enough publicity and made it also into a financial fiasco, probably. However, for me, it was a great success artistically. I had always wanted to make a great film, a good film and a long one, too, with an intermission—at a psychologically suitable moment—to give the audience time for dinner as the great Eugene O'Neill did in . . . [Denise Vernac: *"Strange Interlude"* . . .] *Strange Interlude.* He did it several years after me. I wanted to do it in *Greed.* . . . And I made the film. But it was too long for the producer, because he did not think about screening it in two sittings, as I did. So, the company hired a man who had never read Norris's book, did not know anything about my editing ideas, and was ordered to edit it . . . so he edited it . . . [laughter] . . . he edited it. . . . When, ten years later, I saw the film myself, for the first time, it was like seeing a corpse in a graveyard. I found it in its narrow casket among plenty of dust and a terrible stink . . . [laughter]. . . . I found a thin part of the backbone and a little bone of the shoulder. And, naturally, I became sick, it made me very sick, because I had worked on this film for two years of my life without any salary. Try to play this on your piano . . . [laughter] . . . two years with a sick woman, with a sick child, very sick, with polio—and me, working without a salary on this film, for two years! At the end of the two years, I thought: if this film comes out the way I made it, I will be the greatest film director living. . . . But, when it was edited like this. . . . And, after all this fiasco, imagine, a producer coming to me and asking me to direct for him a film called *The Merry Widow*! He bought the rights to it for a great sum of money, dollars, not Belgian francs . . . and he had nothing for his money but the title, since the success of *The Merry Widow* was in its music. The story itself was ridiculous, or almost ridiculous. Naturally, I did not want to make it. And, besides, I had never had stars, because I don't like stars—

both men and women stars. Particularly women . . . [laughter] . . . because they have ideas. . . . When I direct, it is me who has the ideas. It is me who directs. So, to please me, the Company forced me to accept two stars, not one. Two! . . . [laughter]. . . . Mae Murray, who always played under the direction of her husband, a very great man, very great, six-feet-three, and a very gentle man. I could make a comparison between a Saint Bernard dog . . . [laughter]. . . . She, herself, if I may say so . . . was very active, very agile, too active . . . [laughter]. . . . So this grand man and this little woman . . . you know very well who won the battle . . . [laughter]. . . . It was always Mae Murray, it was always she who won and the big Saint Bernard did exactly what his wife told him to do. But it was very different with me, since I was not married to this woman . . . [laughter]. . . . No. She was very gentle, but she had ideas . . . [laughter] . . . and, as I said before, I have ideas myself. So these two ideas . . . [laughter] . . . clashed. One time we had a terrible battle, during the embassy ball scene, and it was terrible because I had 350 extras in it who loved me very much . . . it was always the workers who liked me, not the producers—the workers . . . do you see the difference? . . . [laughter and applause]. So this woman thought . . . it was after the First World War . . . and she called me "dirty Hun." . . . Naturally, I did not like it, since I was born in Austria, in Vienna, and since she was born in Vienna, too . . . [laughter]. . . . As a matter of fact, she was born in Czechoslovakia, but then I did not see much difference . . . [laughter] . . . and since my workers, my extras understood that this meant the end, they took off their uniforms and threw them on the floor. . . .

I want to tell you a very, very strange story. You will permit me to sit down [he sits down on the podium]. Thank you. Because this is a very strange story . . . [laughter]. . . . I am very superstitious, also religious, and in many cases that goes together, as you know. I had troubles with Mae Murray, as I said already, and also troubles with electricity, lamps, with the helpers, with everybody. And it was strange, because it had never happened that way before. So, after the duel with Mae Murray, I was discharged by the company, but really . . . [laughter]. . . . But I almost forget to tell you my story. . . . Since I am very superstitious and a mystic, I used to visit a certain voyeuse [Denise Vernac: "voyante" . . .] voyante . . . [laughter] . . . so, before I started workng on *The Merry Widow,* at the time when the company approached me, I naturally went first to my friend Madame Ora . . . [laughter]. . . . She was an old woman, only an EAR, so I asked her what would be the outcome, should I make the film or not? She waited a little while, just enough to give the necessary weight, and said that I should "absolutely do it" because it will be a great feather in my hat . . . [laughter]. . . . In California nobody wears a hat, and I did not have a hat—but she assured me of great success, a large feather, a beautiful plume in my hat, *bon! So* I started the film, I was discharged, and I came immediately, the first thing I did, to my adviser, Madame Ora. I told her that I was discharged and that the president of the company had shown me the doors himself and that, in my turn, I'd given him a few words which he will never forget, and that I am in the street now. What should I do? And you have assured me that this will be a large feather in my hat! The Madame said to me: "Monsieur von Stroheim, I can't change my idea. You will continue tomorrow on *The Merry Widow,* you will direct it tomorrow, and it will be a great success and it will be a feather in your hat." I said, "Madame, you have not understood me correctly. I am in the street. . . . [laughter]. . . . No, Monsieur, it is you who does not understand. You will be continuing tomorrow morning." And this was six o'clock in the afternoon. And she says to me, further, that now, this very moment, there are four or five men in my Los Angeles home waiting to see me . . . regarding tomorrow's work. I said, "But this is ridiculous, isn't it?" And she says, "They are in uniforms . . ." [laughter]. . . . And it was the time of prohibition in California, and I, like a good citizen, had plenty of whiskey in my house . . . [laughter] . . . and a few whiskeys in my car, just like that . . . [laughter]. . . . That meant this . . . [laughter] . . . years not in a private prison but on the island of Alcatraz. . . . So I hurried home, and, believe it or not, there were four men waiting and they were in uniforms. But they were not policemen but from the staff of the company, sent by the president himself to speak with me, to ask me to continue work on the film the next morning! That was too much . . . too strange. During the night the president sent his men twice more, just to be sure that I would definitely be at work the next morning, at 8:30 . . . counting thirty minutes for peace talks. . . . *Oui!* Madame Ora was right. I continued directing, it was one of the great successes of its time, and it was chosen by the critics of America as the best film of 1926. That, perhaps, is not such a great credit in itself, since, probably, the other films were very bad . . . [laughter]. . . . At any rate, this film has made for its company four and a half million . . . though not for me. I had twenty-five per cent of it. How much do you think I received? . . .

I thank you once more and ask you to have patience because the film is thirty years old; this print is only a 16mm. version projected on too large a screen, and I don't have the sound or the color or the cinerama. . . . I have nothing. And so I have made all the possible excuses that I could think of. All the good things in this film were made by me. The things that are no good in it were made by others.

William K. Everson (essay date 1957)

SOURCE: "Erich von Stroheim," in *Films in Review,* Vol. VIII, No. 7, 1957, pp. 305-14.

[*In the following essay, Everson surveys Stroheim's films.*]

Erich von Stroheim's death in Paris on May 12, 1957, has further reduced the rapidly diminishing number of directorial "giants" of the silent screen. First Murnau,

then Griffith, Eisenstein and Pudovkin. With Stroheim's death, only two are left—Carl Th. Dreyer, the greatest living silent director, and probably the greatest director making films today, and Charles Chaplin, whose latest film appears to be a disappointment and an unhappy swan song.

Though not the most important of the seven "giants" just named—any such selection is necessarily arbitrary—Stroheim was certainly the most colorful, the most publicized, and the most maligned. He was attacked out of all proportion to his "crimes" by his enemies, and defended out of all proportion to his achievements by his friends.

From the beginning, Stroheim was an egotist and his talent an *individual* one. Even when playing a bit role in an early film he *had* to make an impression on the audience, he *had to be noticed.* In *Ghosts,* an early Fine Arts feature under Griffith's supervision, Stroheim had an unimportant bit as an office clerk. Though the key action was taking place elsewhere on the screen, Stroheim cunningly diverted attention to himself by squirmings and other movements as he pored over a ledger, figured, calculated, angrily erased as he found an error. Then, when one of the principal players tapped him on the back to ask a question, Stroheim whirled around with a look of outrage at having been disturbed in his work! The immediate insertion of a title prevented Stroheim from milking the scene any further.

In 1916's *Old Heidelberg,* well and charmingly played by Wallace Reid and Dorothy Gish, Stroheim built an already large role into something much more. He played the valet of the student prince, the one who constantly recalled his master from the paths of pleasure and love to duty, Stroheim played the valet with such venom that he practically made an arch-villain of an unimportant flunky.

Stroheim's "influence" was in evidence elsewhere in *Old Heidelberg* too, for he also worked on it as military advisor and assistant director. The militaristic precision of the students' singing rituals, and of a duelling sequence, showed more of Stroheim than of either the official director (John Emerson) or supervisor Griffith.

In another Fine Arts film of the same period—*His Picture in the Papers,* one of the best and cleverest of the early Douglas Fairbanks movies—Stroheim embellished his villainous acting routines by the vivid but hackneyed device of a black eye-patch.

At Fine Arts, from 1914 to 1917, Stroheim worked with D. W. Griffith in a number of capacities—as actor, assistant director, military advisor, art director, and above all, as an embodiment of what World War I propaganda meant by "Hun."

Stroheim idolized Griffith and considered him the one real genius of the motion picture. He also considered him his friend. When Griffith died Stroheim delivered a memorable tribute via London's BBC (on December 30, 1948). He began by saying that he had been asked to speak for approximately 15 minutes but that "fifteen hours wouldn't be nearly enough."

Despite Stroheim's devotion to Griffith, and his oft-repeated declaration that he had learned filmaking from working with him, the films he directed show no "Griffith influence" of any kind—unlike the films of such of Stroheim's contemporaries at Fine Arts as Chester and Sidney Franklin, Raoul Walsh, and others.

While Stroheim learned the *mechanics* of the movies from Griffith, he learned nothing from him philosophically. The *types* of stories they told were antipathetic, and so was the *way* they told them. Griffith liked to find beauty amid squalor and despair (*Broken Blossoms, Isn't Life Wonderful?*), Stroheim preferred to find ugliness and depravity amid luxury and elegance (*Foolish Wives, The Merry Widow*). For Griffith the *means* were often as important as the story itself—his films had elaborate friezes of cross-cutting, panel shots, vignettes, cut-backs and other technical and dramatic devices to heighten a theme's excitement and power. To Stroheim only story mattered. He rarely moved his camera, the editing was plodding and straightforward (in this Stroheim resembled Chaplin).

Blind Husbands (Universal 1919) was Stroheim's first directorial venture. The script was an adaptation by him from his own novel, and, since he starred in it too, it was very much a one-man undertaking. The story elaborated Stroheim's strange dichotomy: preoccupation with sex counter-pointed with an excessive morality requiring the transgressor to be *more* than punished for his sins.

Blind Husbands was a disciplined film. The discipline came from Stroheim himself—a fact that makes it hard to excuse his subsequent outrageous extravagances of plot and direction.

Following *The Devil's Passkey,* a triangle romance which some think better than *Blind Husbands,* Stroheim directed the famous, and notorious, *Foolish Wives* ('21). This was the film that first caused the critics to call his pictures "epics of the sewer" with "the atmosphere of a pig-stye." *Foolish Wives* ought not to be attacked merely for being tasteless and revolting, for such was Stroheim's intention, and this film was a success in that regard at least.

A great deal of the footage that Stroheim shot for *Foolish Wives* was never used. The cries that went up, and can still be heard, of "butchering" and "mutilation," are rather disingenuous. No doubt some of the unused footage may have been good, and even spectacular. It would be fine to see it. But I doubt if any of it could have helped make *Foolish Wives* a whole. The nine reels that were released, ineptly edited to be sure, contain no indication of greatness, cinematic or otherwise, and are often just plain dull.

Merry-Go-Round, which followed, convinced almost everyone that Stroheim was doomed, in his exploitation of "daring" content, to self-defeating extravagances. Nevertheless, when he was removed from this picture, and replaced by Rupert Julian, there was no lack of people who called him a "martyr."

Merry-Go-Round is very curious, and more than a little reminiscent of parts of Stroheim's novel *Paprika,* with a romanticized novelettish story only *half* taken seriously by Stroheim himself. Yet it has some truly great sequences—the pursuit of the helpless heroine (Mary Philbin) by the evil operator of the merry-go-round (George Siegmann) around the deserted carousel at night; the wild party in the bordello; some of the war scenes; the commentary on the depravity of palace life.

These were great moments in a rather ponderous film. Other scenes, incredibly flat, were obviously shot by another director. Stroheim made many *had* scenes, but he never made "flat" and uninteresting ones. Nevertheless, on the whole *Merry-Go-Round* is quite good.

The Stroheim clacque still echoes Stroheim's claim that only a few feet shot by him remain in the picture. From this it is possible to draw one of only two conclusions: a) Rupert Julian was as good a director as Stroheim to have achieved the great scenes; b) Stroheim was the worst possible authority on his own pictures.

The latter conclusion is the more likely. Rupert Julian's best pictures (*Merry-Go-Round* and *Walking Back*) were done *with* another director. The films he directed alone (e.g., *The Yankee Clipper*) were routine. Stroheim, in later years understandably bitter, preferred to repudiate work that may have been *spoiled,* but was certainly not *ruined* by others. Indeed, Stroheim's comments in later years were unreliable, as was proven by his repeated statements that he had never seen *Greed*. It is a matter of record that he saw it at least once at the Museum of Modern Art in New York.

Greed was begun, under the title *McTeague,* for Sam Goldwyn, but by the time it was finished Goldwyn had sold out to Metro. Stroheim, who had made the film unhampered, then found himself up against an old enemy, Irving Thalberg, with whom he had had "trouble" at Universal over *Merry-Go-Round*. Both Thalberg and Louis B. Mayer opposed Stroheim's plan to release *Greed* as he had shot it—or even in a very much condensed version of 18 reels. Ten reels was the maximum they would allow. Whereupon Stroheim washed his hands of the whole matter and alleged that the film was handed to " . . . a cutter, a man earning $30 a week, a man who had never read the book nor the script, and on whose mind was nothing but a hat. He ruined the whole of my two years' work."

Such comments are unfair, and sympathy for Stroheim, and understanding of what *Greed* had meant to him, should not condone such charges. *Greed* was cut with respect and care and its editing is masterly. It *looks* as though it had been shot that way, and anyone ignorant of the film's history is not aware of gaps in story or continuity. The editing of *Greed* was not a job of slick condensation, or of covering-up for missing sequences. It was a creative work in itself. Critics are unanimous that *Greed* is a motion picture masterpiece, and this judgment is based on the "butchery" of this cutter, not on Stroheim's original conception or on all the footage he shot.

Here, again, the unused material may have had wondrous quality—some stills of it so indicate. But whether *Greed,* two or three times longer than the released version, would have been great, is something else again. Certainly some of the simplicity and directness of theme, so striking in the ten-reel version, would have been lost in a longer treatment complicated by sub-plots and macabre dream sequences. It is too bad the original footage is not available in its entirety, to be seen by all who so wish. It is also too bad that many who have not seen this footage nevertheless assume it is the substance of which the ten-reel *Greed* is a pale shadow.

It's really quite bizarre that *Greed* continues to be disparaged by the very people who admire Stroheim the most.

Metro's experience with Stroheim over *Greed* did not finish him as a director. While extravagance has never been a Hollywood crime, and never will be, unnecessary extravagance *is*. One can easily sympathize with producers when they see large sums of money going into footage that could not possibly get on the screen—either because it is sure to be censored, or because there is just too much of it.

Stroheim Versus The Producers became a minor cause celebre in the Hollywood of the '20s. It was well-promoted by Stroheim and was worked up by his adherents into Art vs Industry fustian. Which was all pointless and did Stroheim no good. Stroheim was indubitably an artist, but it is not artistry to refuse to recognize the requirements of a medium. Nor was it a crime against art for producers to refuse to allow Stroheim to go on doing things HIS way. The yaps and yawks of Stroheim's clacque about "money men," "button hole men" and "money grubbers" were the unthinking reactions of those who do not know, or understand, the economics of filmmaking.

The producers were *not* unaware of Stroheim's talent nor disdainful of it. Within two years of *Greed,* Metro gave Stroheim a relatively free hand with *The Merry Widow*.

Although there was considerable cutting on *The Merry Widow,* chiefly of scenes of blatant sex, Stroheim seemed at the time satisfied, and since *The Merry Widow* was also a financial success, Metro was happy too.

The story, with a passing nod to the operetta by Leon & Stein, was Stroheim's. So was *all* of the direction. Hence

The Merry Widow is a rather complete example of Stroheim's cinematic ability and range. I find nothing in it to support the claims of those who say that an unexpurgated *Foolish Wives* would be a masterpiece. The decor, backgrounds, atmosphere—are wonderful. Individual incidents, particularly those involving Baron Sadoja, have an outré sort of power. But the silliness of the plot cannot, and should not, be excused on the ground that Stroheim himself was not taking it seriously. Superb backgrounds and good moments do not of themselves make a good picture. The principal fault of *The Merry Widow* is the unforgivable fault. It's a bore.

From the commercial success of *The Merry Widow* Stroheim coasted to Paramount, a company not prone to experimentation, and certainly not given to art for art's sake. Actually, Stroheim went to work for his friend Pat Powers, who, as an independent, was producing *The Wedding March* for Paramount release.

The result was another imbroglio, with Stroheim being accused of pointless extravagance, and he refusing to allow. Paramount to cut the second half of *The Wedding March*. Only the first half of it was released in the US.

Stroheim's final contributions to the silent screen were *Tempest* and *Queen Kelly*.

The former, a John Barrymore vehicle, was merely written by Stroheim. It has a colorful script with a Russian revolution background, and many touches typical of Stroheim, who, in writing it, transferred the depravities and intrigues of the Hapsburgs, about which he was so ambivalent, to the Romanoffs.

Queen Kelly was the last of Stroheim's extravaganzas about Cinderellas in the midst of court intrigue. It was never completed, and the six reels that were put together—but never released—seem absurdly tame when compared with the material Stroheim wanted to put into the concluding reels.

Stroheim was a good story-teller, with a genuine flair for combining the un- and the over-ripe. *Queen Kelly*'s rambling, crazy and spectacular plotline *could* have made an exhilarating film. It *might* have been grand fun, but it almost certainly wouldn't have been art. When it was abandoned, Stroheim-ites at once took the line of "another suppressed masterpiece." It cost Gloria Swanson, who had formed her own company to produce it, her fortune.

The courage of one's convictions is an important virtue for a filmaker, but so—and this is something Stroheim never learned—is the realization that wilfullness is not wisdom. True, there was no valid reason why Stroheim's films shouldn't run longer than 10 reels. Long before he started directing, audiences had sat still, and totally engrossed, for the 12 reels of *The Birth of a Nation.* They had also grown restless during the 13 reels of *Intolerance.* Since a long *Greed* could have been expected to duplicate the fate of *Intolerance* rather than the success of *The Birth of a Nation,* the agitation of Thalberg and Mayer is at least understandable.

When *Intolerance* failed, Griffith recognized the need for compromise, and, instead of launching into another costly prestige feature, and risking the money of investors and studio, he played it safe with a number of programmes that were not great, but were decidedly good. When the time was ripe, he made *Broken Blossoms.* He then did more "commercial" features ("commercial" is by no means inevitably a synonym for "inartistic") until he could afford an almost certain boxoffice failure, but artistic triumph, *Isn't Life Wonderful?* Griffith was thus able to keep active, and his films that survive today more than justify that policy.

How much better it would have been for Stroheim had he been content to direct comparatively routine films like **The Devil's Passkey** in between each major effort. Not only would he be better represented in screen history, but in all probability his important films would have reached the screen intact. For he would have mastered his craft, and need not have feared each film would be his last, and need not have rushed pell-mell into each film, repeating the excesses he knew would end in a debacle. Stroheim had a kind of integrity, but it was certainly not accompanied by wisdom.

Stroheim's last directorial assignment was **Walking Down Broadway** for Fox in '33. A recent perusal of its original script—by Stroheim—reveals power as well as many echoes of **Greed**.

Once again, Stroheim's footage was not released. It was revamped, and re-shot by Alfred Werker, and released as **Hello Sister.** The reason for this has never been clearly established. Stroheim's footage was certainly *intended* for release at one time, as the fan magazines carried page advertisements of it with full credit to Stroheim, and even reviewed it. It had been economically made, and wasn't even of major importance on the current schedule.

Its withdrawal is a mystery Stroheim never dispelled. Perhaps the big "moral cleanup" of movies then impending, made Fox unwilling to incur disfavor with a comparatively unimportant film. Also, Fox was having very serious corporate troubles at that time.

After sound came in, except for **Walking Down Broadway,** Stroheim reverted to writing and acting. He had not forgotten the scene-stealing tricks he had practised as far back as *Ghosts.* In *As You Desire Me* (MGM, '32) he stole all of Garbo's thunder in one scene—even though she was in the foreground, and talking. Standing silently in the background, he listened politely to her—at the same time bending his knees and flicking ash from his cigarette by an elegant flourish of his cane.

Stroheim gave some of his best performances in the '30s, even in cheap quickies. He was wont to sneer at these performances and to say he did them for money. In *Crimson Romance,* e.g., he said he acted "like an automaton." *Crimson Romance* was a cheap little film, built mainly around stock footage from *Hell's Angels,* but it was a well-made film (for a small company like Mascot), and Stroheim's performance contained many little tricks and nuances which could not have been present in the script, and would *not* have been present in the film, had he been performing "like an automaton".

Stroheim was never a great actor, but he was a good one, and, in between villain and Hun roles, he delivered some surprisingly effective "gentle" performances—particularly in the French films *La Grande Illusion* and *Les Disparus de Saint Agil.* And he was responsible for some good scripts at MGM in the early '30s and for some good ones in France.

It is unfortunate that the very fine **La Danse de la Mort** of the mid-'40s has never been released in this country. Written by Stroheim—from Strindberg's play—and starring him, it is one of the most interesting of all his pictures.

In some of the films in which he acted there are traces of Stroheim in the direction. The cheaper companies, utilizing directors who at best were no more than competent, often welcomed his suggestions, and more than one such director gladly used Stroheim's directorial ideas. But most of the larger companies did *not* welcome his directorial cooperation, and more than one deal for his acting services fell through when it became apparent he wanted to have a say in other than acting matters. If the role was of no interest to him, Stroheim would *insist* he be hired to direct as well. At worst, he would lose a role he didn't want. At best, there was a chance someone might agree, and he would be directing again. No such chance ever came.

It is reported that Stroheim would arrive on the set of *Alraune,* a German film of a few years ago that was directed by Rabenalt, every morning with a fresh script and the explanation that he'd re-written everything, and then demand that they shoot it *his* way that day. At first Rabenalt fought him, but then decided to humor him. It was shot *both* ways—Stroheim's way, and the way Rabenalt originally intended. Presumably none of the Stroheim-inspired footage was used. At least I hope it wasn't, for *Alraune* is wholly mediocre, and is distinguished only by Stroheim's performance.

Ironically, one of Stroheim's quirks was responsible for the long delay in the release of *Alraune* in the US. His contract stipulated that if *Alraune* were dubbed into English only *he* could dub his voice. Unfortunately, no price was mentioned, and when American release seemed imminent, Stroheim's price was far too high. To have released it here without dubbing would have been fruitless, since *Alraune* has not sufficient merit for art-houses and can only be sold on its stars—Stroheim and Hildegarde Neff—and its lurid and sexy plot. It is now said the problem was solved before Stroheim's death and that *Alraune* will be released here shortly.

Stroheim once wrote: "If you live in France and you have written one good book, or painted one good picture, or directed one outstanding film, fifty years ago, and nothing ever since, you are still recognized as an artist, and honored accordingly. People take their hats off and call you maitre. They do not forget. In Hollywood—in Hollywood, you're as good as your last picture. If you didn't have one in production within the last three months, you're forgotten, no matter what you have achieved ere this. It is that terrific, unfortunately necessary, egotism in the make-up of the people who make the cinema, it is the continuous endeavor for recognition, that continuous struggle for survival and supremacy, among the newcomers, that relegates the old-timers to the ashcan."

Unlike most of Stroheim's strictures against Hollywood, *that* one is true. Hollywood *does* neglect its own.

If it takes only one great film to merit the accolade of "maitre," Stroheim has it in **Greed**. Whether he disapproved of the ten-reel version the world knows, or not, it is one of the great motion pictures of all time.

His friends would do better by his memory if they exalted **Greed** as proof of his greatness, and *forgot* the so-called "mutilated masterpieces" and the discarded reels of bordello and orgy sequences.

Joel W. Finler (essay date 1968)

SOURCE: "Norris & McTeague," in *Stroheim,* University of California Press, 1968, pp. 23-97.

[*In the following essay, Finler provides a scene-by-scene analysis of* Greed.]

Stroheim's . . . film [**Greed**] was shot for the Goldwyn Co. It was to be a vast adaptation of Frank Norris's novel *McTeague.* The fidelity of the screenplay to the novel is such that any consideration of the film should involve Norris as well as Stroheim.

Frank Norris was born in Chicago in 1870. He lived and studied for a while in San Francisco, but much of his life was spent travelling as a foreign newspaper correspondent. When he died at the age of thirty-two he had completed a number of stories and novels. With a very different background and career, Stroheim shared some of Norris's creative vision.

Norris was a dedicated writer who detested the kind of novel which was popular during the 1890's and which he called 'the literature of chambermaids'. He also regarded Realism as merely the attempt to describe life in a truthful and accurate way. He wished, rather, to probe further beneath the surface, to explore the basic and primitive drives which he thought determined man's actions, in conjunction with other influences like environment and heredity. Norris was the leading American exponent of Naturalism and follower of Emile Zola.

The basis for the Naturalist literary approach had grown directly out of the general intellectual climate of the nineteenth century, influenced by the latest scientific findings. The new reliance upon scientific data gained through objective experiment and observation was a prime influence. It was an aim in the efforts of the Naturalist writers to remain as objective as possible in describing in detail real places in which some of the actual events of their books had taken place. More important still was the influence of Darwinism: evolutionary doctrine had supplied them with the basis for relating man closely to nature through a determinism which viewed him as a primitive brute governed by his instincts and limited by heredity and environment.

All of these elements can be found in *McTeague,* an archetypal Naturalist novel. Norris's familiarity with the Polk Street area of San Francisco comes through in the novel's accuracy of detail. Almost every aspect of setting and characterization which would be necessary in translating the book to the screen is dealt with in meticulous detail. In McTeague himself Norris brought the Naturalist concept of man to life.

The strictly objective style of the novel requires that all the characters appear as relatively simple people who can be depicted adequately through description of their external behaviour. This is especially true of McTeague, the principal character. In fact, Norris frequently emphasizes his impulsive stupidity and the primitive nature of his motivations. The Naturalist approach was most effective in dealing with uncomplicated, uneducated characters, who were particularly vulnerable to the vicissitudes of fortune.

The novel centres around the marriage of McTeague to Trina. Here Norris was able to make a detailed study of the interaction between two very different characters. In this he shows a remarkable grasp of psychology, particularly in his portrayal of Trina.

Norris's debt to Zola is considerable. When McTeague loses his dental practice, the decline of the couple recalls *L'Assommoir,* while the character of McTeague is closely related to *La Bête Humaine.* Both of these books are included in the vast series of novels set in France during the Second Empire, *The Rougon Macquart.* Both have been filmed: *L'Assommoir* as *Gervaise* by René Clément and *La Bête Humaine* by Jean Renoir and Fritz Lang as *Human Desire.* The visual and dramatic qualities of Naturalist novels make them particularly suitable for filming.

As in *La Bête Humaine,* Norris suggests McTeague's latent hereditary weakness by reference to his alcoholic father. Nowhere can the extent of Stroheim's commitment to the Naturalist credo be more fully understood than in his portrayal of the death of McTeague's father from alcohol. This is included in the original prologue and introductory section which Stroheim added to the Norris novel. Otherwise the film is a remarkably close translation to the screen, and indicates the similarity in the attitudes of the two men. Norris was rebelling against the popular American fiction of the 1890's just as *Greed* was a reaction against the typical Hollywood product of the 1920's. Predictably enough, the reactions to both film and novel were similar. They were attacked for the vulgarity and sordidness of their 'realism'.

However, in Stroheim's film, as in the original novel, the goal was not 'realism' but 'Naturalism'. In other words, the aspiration towards a certain objectivity and realism was balanced by the frequently exceptional even pathological nature of many of the characterizations. These are the extraordinary creations of a vivid literary imagination and have only a slight connection with the objective observation of the life of the time.

Too often Stroheim's film is quoted as an example of Realism in the cinema. This error is encouraged by the fact that the film was shot on location and by the subsequent mutilation of the released version, which eliminated many of the 'non-realistic' elements. The powerful characterization and fantastic plot of Norris's novel probably intrigued Stroheim just as much as its vivid visual qualities and contemporary American settings. Stroheim was committed without qualification to both style and content of the original.

Stroheim's cinematic Naturalism was an attempt, following Norris's lead, to probe beneath the surface of life and human behaviour. He too saw the use of actual locations as a way of lending added force and meaning to the weird and fantastic elements of the story, and in this he discovered a principle which is of fundamental importance to the cinema.

The cinematic medium gave new life to the principles which had motivated Norris and other Naturalist writers. Their scrupulous attention to the smallest details of the characters' dress, behaviour and gestures, as well as to their surroundings, frequently required extended and laborious description. The cinema could convey all this with more ease and greater effect. Norris could incorporate into his novel the circumstances of a particularly gruesome murder about which he had read in a newspaper. But Stroheim was able to shoot his film on location in the very house where the actual murder had taken place.

Most of the novel is set in the Polk Street district of San Francisco among the lower middle class milieu of small traders and Norris's original title was *The People of Polk Street*. To recreate the atmosphere of the novel, Stroheim naturally shot the film in this very section of San Francisco. As he himself recalled:

I had rented a house on Laguna Street in San Francisco, furnished the rooms in the exact way in which the author had described them, and photographed the scenes with only very few lamps, making full use of the daylight which penetrated through the windows. Of course, this was not always to the camera-man's liking, but I insisted . . . and we got some very good photographic results. In order to make the actors really feel 'inside' the characters they were to portray I made them live in these rooms (a move which was favourably received at the studio since it saved the company some hotel expenses!)

This setting was of paramount importance as the rise and fall of the McTeagues takes place in this one boarding house. Thus, a unity of place throughout much of the film (and novel) allows familiarity with the location and neighbours to develop. Marcus, old Mr Grannis and Miss Baker all occupy single rooms in the house along with other minor characters. Zerkow, the junkman, lives in the shack adjoining the rear.

When McTeague loses his dental practice, he and Trina move from their three-room flat into a back room in the same house. Some time later the one-room shack in the back yard becomes vacant. To this the McTeagues finally move after Mac has lost his job at the factory. At this point in both novel and film it is clear that the couple have sunk as low as is humanly possible. The scene is described by Norris:

The one room grew abominably dirty, reeking with the odours of cooking and of 'non-poisonous' paint. The bed was not made until late in the afternoon, sometimes not at all. Dirty, unwashed crockery, greasy knives, sodden fragments of yesterday's meals cluttered the table, while in one corner was the heap of evil-smelling dirty linen. Cockroaches appeared in the crevices of the woodwork, the wallpaper bulged from the damp walls and began to peel. Trina had long ago ceased to dust or to wipe the furniture with a bit of rag. The grime grew thick upon the window panes and in the corners of the room. All the filth of the alley invaded their quarters like a rising muddy tide.

Between the windows, however, the faded photograph of the couple in their wedding finery looked down upon the wretchedness, Trina still holding her set bouquet straight before her, McTeague standing at her side, his left foot forward, in the attitude of a Secretary of State; while near by hung the canary, the one thing the dentist clung to obstinately, piping and chattering all day in its little gilt prison.

And the tooth, the gigantic golden molar of French gilt, enormous and ungainly, sprawled its branching prongs in one corner of the room, by the footboard of the bed. The McTeague's had come to use it as a sort of substitute for a table . . .

Such a passage is typical of the detailed description in which the novel abounds. Stroheim was able to draw upon it throughout the designing and shooting of the film. However, the closeness of novel and film means that much of the literary criticism of Norris's novel is equally applicable to the film, although few literary critics appear to be aware of the film's existence. For example, Maxwell Geismar's book on the American novel from 1890 to 1915 (entitled *Rebels & Ancestors*) includes the following passage:

> McTeague *was in this respect a study of greed; of a 'passion' in the manner of the 19th century French and English authors, that feeds upon and consumes the normal range of human emotions . . . The novel was in fact structured upon images of gold, and one notices again, in Norris's case, that these early realists and naturalists were consciously using the techniques of a literary symbolism. In a story of mutual disintegration, too, the McTeague's move from cheaper to cheaper rooms, while both husband and wife, gnawing and preying upon each other in their economic desperation, are driven to the extremes of their idiosyncracies.*

How appropriate that Geismar should have been struck by the novel's symbolism, for this aspect of the novel had undoubtedly appealed to Stroheim as well. One of the novel's working titles was *The Golden Tooth*, an image which dominates both novel and film. Stroheim had originally planned to have the various gilt objects in the film, such as the giant tooth and the bird cage, hand-coloured to suggest their relation to the symbolic insert shots which were to be included at various points. These shots were among the few additions by Stroheim to the material provided by the novel. Others were the addition of a second pet bird and the funeral procession which passes by the window during the wedding.

If similar passages from novel and screenplay are placed side by side, the close relationship of the two is frequently remarkable.

> 'But tell me, Mac, did you get a place?' McTeague turned his back on her. 'Tell me, Mac, please, did you?' The dentist jumped up and thrust his face close to hers, his heavy jaw protruding, his little eyes twinkling meanly.
>
> 'No', he shouted. 'No, no. Do you hear? No.'
>
> Trina cowered before him. Then suddenly she began to sob aloud, weeping partly at his strange brutality, partly at the disappointment of his failure to find employment.
>
> McTeague cast a contemptuous glance about him, a glance that embraced the dingy, cheerless room, the rain streaming down the panes of the one window, and the figure of his weeping wife.
>
> 'Oh, ain't this all fine?' he exclaimed. 'Ain't it lovely?'
>
> 'It's not my fault,' sobbed Trina.
>
> 'It is too,' vociferated McTeague. 'It is too. We could live like Christians and decent people if you

> wanted to. You got more'n five thousand dollars, and you're so damned stingy that you'd rather live in a rat hole—and make me live there too—before you'd part with a nickel of it. I tell you I'm sick and tired of the whole business.'
>
> An allusion to her lottery money never failed to rouse Trina.
>
> 'And I'll tell you this much too,' she cried, winking back the tears. 'Now that you're out of a job, we can't afford even to live in your rat hole, as you call it. We've got to find a cheaper place than this even.'
>
> 'What!' exclaimed the dentist, purple with rage. 'What, get into a worse hole in the wall than this! Well, we'll see if we will. We'll just see about that. You're going to do just as I tell you after this, Trina McTeague,' and once more he thrust his face close to hers.
>
> 'I know what's the matter,' cried Trina, with a half sob: 'I know, I can smell it on your breath. You've been drinking whiskey.'
>
> 'Yes, I've been drinking whiskey,' retorted her husband. 'I've been drinking whiskey. Have you got anything to say about it? Ah, yes, you're right, I've been drinking whiskey. What have you got to say about my drinking whiskey? Let's hear it.'
>
> 'Oh! Oh! Oh!' sobbed Trina, covering her face with her hands. McTeague caught her wrists in one palm and pulled them down. Trina's pale face was streaming with tears; her long, narrow blue eyes were swimming; her adorable little chin upraised and quivering.
>
> 'Let's hear what you got to say,' exclaimed McTeague.
>
> 'Nothing, nothing,' said Trina, between her sobs.
>
> 'Then stop that noise. Stop it, do you hear me? Stop it.' He threw up his open hand threateningly. 'Stop!' he exclaimed.
>
> Trina looked at him fearfully, half blinded with weeping. Her husband's thick mane of yellow hair was disordered and rumpled upon his great square-cut head; his big red ears were redder than ever; his face was purple; the thick eyebrows were knotted over the small, twinkling eyes; the heavy yellow mustache, that smelt of alcohol, drooped over the massive, protruding chin, salient, like that of the carnivora; the veins were swollen and throbbing on his thick red neck; while over her head Trina saw his upraised palm, callused, enormous.
>
> 'Stop!' he exclaimed. And Trina, watching fearfully, saw the palm suddenly contract into a fist, a fist that was hard as a wooden mallet, the fist of the old-time car-boy. And then her ancient terror of him, the intuitive fear of the male, leaped to life again. She was afraid of him. Every nerve of her

quailed and shrank from him. She choked back her sobs, catching her breath.

'There,' growled the dentist, releasing her, 'that's more like. Now,' he went on, fixing her with his little eyes, 'now listen to me. I'm beat out. I've walked the city over—ten miles, I guess—an' I'm going to bed, an' I don't want to be bothered. You understand? I want to be let alone.' Trina was silent.

'Do you hear?' he snarled.

'Yes, Mac.'

The dentist took off his coat, his collar and necktie, unbuttoned his vest, and slipped his heavy-soled boots from his big feet. Then he stretched himself upon the bed and rolled over toward the wall. In a few minutes the sound of his snoring filled the room.

Trina craned her neck and looked at her husband over the footboard of the bed. She saw his red, congested face; the huge mouth wide open; his unclean shirt, with its frayed wristbands; and his huge feet encased in thick woollen socks. Then her grief and the sense of her unhappiness returned more poignant than ever. She stretched her arms out in front of her on her work-table, and, burying her face in them, cried and sobbed as though her heart would break.

The rain continued. The panes of the single window ran with sheets of water; the eaves dripped incessantly. It grew darker. The tiny, grimy room, full of the smells of cooking and of 'non-poisonous' paint, took on an aspect of desolation and cheerlessness lamentable beyond words. The canary in its little gilt prison chittered feebly from time to time. Sprawled at full length upon the bed, the dentist snored and snored, stupefied, inert, his legs wide apart, his hands lying palm upward at his sides.

At last Trina raised her head, with a long trembling breath. She rose, and going over to the washstand, poured some water from the pitcher into the basin, and washed her face and swollen eyelids, and rearranged her hair. Suddenly, as she was about to return to her work, she was struck with an idea.

'I wonder,' she said to herself, 'I wonder where he got the money to buy his whiskey.' She searched the pockets of his coat, which he had flung into a corner of the room, and even came up to him as he lay upon the bed and went through the pockets of his vest and trousers. She found nothing.

'I wonder,' she murmured, 'I wonder if he's got any money he don't tell me about. I'll have to look out for that.'

The film version corresponds very closely:

Medium shot of Trina and McTeague in their dingy room. Trina touches him on the arm, says:

Title: 'Did you get a place?'

Back to scene, McTeague turns his back on her. Trina holds him by the sleeve, says: 'Tell me, Mac, please. Did you?' Mac turns around and thrusts his face close to hers.

Medium close up, both in, Mac's heavy jaw protruding, his little eyes twinkling meanly, says, 'No! No! do ya hear? NO!' Trina cowers before him, then suddenly she begins to sob, sits down in chair, puts her head in her hands and cries.

Medium shot of McTeague gazing around the room.

Close up of unmade bed.

Medium shot of McTeague.

Close up of dirty dishes in basin.

Medium shot of McTeague.

Close up of two birds in cage fighting.

Medium shot of McTeague with cynical smile, says:

Title: 'Ain't that fine?'

[Close up McTeague.

Title: 'Ain't it lovely?'

Back to scene, Trina looks up sobbingly, says, 'It isn't my fault.'

Close up, McTeague says: 'It is too', and continues:

Title: ' . . . we could live like Christians—you got more than five thousand dollars and you're so damn stingy that you'd rather live in a stinking rat hole . . . '

Back to scene. He points at room, continues speaking:

Title: ' . . . before you'd part with a nickel of it. I'm sick and tired of the whole business.']

Back to scene, Trina rises.

Close up Trina from his angle. She turns toward him, tears running down her cheek. But she gets sore, speaks:

Title: 'I won't have you yell at me like that.'

[' . . . and now that you're out of a job, we can't afford to live even in this rat hole.']

Back to close up of McTeague, purple with rage, [says: 'What, get into a worse hole than this? We'll just see about that!] never taking his eyes off her, slowly comes toward her with lowered head. She doesn't give an inch.

Medium close up of Trina and McTeague.

Close up of McTeague's face looming close.

Medium close up of Trina and McTeague.

Giant close up of McTeague's face.

Medium close up of McTeague's face close to Trina's: he spits every word like a snake into her face, speaks:

Title: 'You're going to do just as I tell you after this—Trina McTeague!'

Back to scene. Trina gets a whiff of his breath, 'You're drunk, I know.' McTeague smiles cynically, says:

Title: 'Yes, I been drinkin' whiskey . . . ' ['What ya got to say about it?']

Back to scene. Trina sobs, covering her face with her hands. McTeague catches her wrist in one palm and pulls it away. Her face is streaming with tears, her adorable little chin upraised and quivering. McTeague speaks: 'Let's hear what you got to say.' [Trina shakes her head, sobbing, says 'Nothing'.]

Medium shot of McTeague's head and shoulders and Trina's face, crying. [McTeague speaks: 'Then stop that noise'.

Title: 'Stop it! Ya hear me?']

Close up of McTeague's face.

Close up of Trina's face.

Back to scene. Mac yells again 'Stop it'. He raises his open hand, yells, 'Stop!' Trina looks at him fearfully.

Close up. Trina watching, frightened, looks from his face to his hand.

Shot from her angle of McTeague's terribly large open hand that suddenly contracts into a fist.

[Back to close up of Trina. She is terrified. She chokes back her sobs.]

Back to scene. Both in. McTeague says: 'That's more like it.' He shoves her onto the bed. She rises as McTeague speaks:

Title: 'I'm beat out and I don't want to be bothered!'

Back to scene. Trina nods, answers, 'Yes'. McTeague turns and snarls; he hits her, and shoves her out of the way, then takes off his coat and falls onto the bed with his boots still on.

[Close up of Trina. She cranes her neck and looks at Mac. She goes to table, sits down, stretches her arms in front of her, buries her head in them, and cries and sobs as though her heart would break.

Close up of window pane, sheets of water pouring down outside.]

Close up of canary cage: the two birds are fighting.

Close up of McTeague's face, mouth wide open, snoring to beat the band.

Close up from baby tripod of Trina at the table. She raises her head (coming even closer to camera), thinks, looks over at Mac, then looks back into space, says:

Title: 'I wonder where he got the money . . . to buy the whiskey?'

Back to close up of Trina, thoughtful, with finger characteristically held to her lip.

[Medium shot. She rises, goes over to bed, picks up coat which had fallen to floor, goes through pockets, doesn't find anything, sneaks over to bed, watches him very carefully, goes through the pockets of his pants. She finds nothing.

Close up of Trina with finger on her lip, says:

Title: 'I wonder if he's got any money he don't tell me about. I'll look out for that.' Back to close up.]

Iris out on Trina's face.

The final close-up of Trina's finger held thoughtfully to her lips again reminds us of the Naturalists, who were fond of singling out a particular gesture or phrase to typify the character and using it throughout the novel as a kind of leitmotif. Stroheim uses this habit of Trina's in the same way.

No comparison of the film and novel should ignore the suggestion that in some ways Stroheim may have been mistaken in remaining so faithful to Norris. The dramatic and visual elements of the novel positively benefited from the translation to the screen, like the climax in Death Valley which appears weak in the novel. But some aspects of the film predictably suffered from the very same flaws as the book. The comments of Van Wyck Brooks on the novel are equally applicable to the film:

> There were defects in McTeague, however . . . The characters were too often types, personifications of ruling passions who repeated the same phrases and actions as if they were machines. Trina's avarice was overdone, Zerkow's greed was monstrous, Maria retold too often her tale of gold, and the old bookbinder and the spinster in the flat might almost have been figures in a puppet-show. And could one have lacked the power of will as completely as McTeague, who had certainly not been presented as entirely spineless? Was it plausible that he should have sunk without a struggle from the moment when the authorities discovered that he had no licence? Accepting the naturalistic formula in which nothing exists but natural forces, was it natural, was it in character, for McTeague to behave so—to go down like a felled ox and end by murdering Trina, when he had been described as

good-natured, obliging, and forgiving?

This criticism of the novel is excessively harsh, but there is no doubt that the weakness of the subplots undermined the work as a whole. This was probably also true of the film, and made the subplots seen ripe for cutting. Their elimination from the final version of the film might suggest that the reduction in length was not entirely a matter of mutilation. This idea needs to be dealt with in the context of the various stages of the film's production and re-editing.

Stroheim had often expressed his desire to put a novel on the screen virtually complete without the abridgement which was thought to be part and parcel of screen adaptation. He had wanted to make a film from Norris's novel for many years, but such a powerful and uncompromising story was generally considered to have little commercial appeal. However, in 1923 Stroheim managed to interest Sam Goldwyn in the project.

Although the Goldwyn Company financed the film, Stroheim was his own producer in the sense that he arranged and managed all the details of the production himself. He employed his usual camera crew and assistants together with many of the actors who had appeared in his other films. Apart from writing the screenplay and directing, Stroheim also collaborated with Richard Day in designing the film.

The city scenes in *Greed* were shot entirely on location in and around San Francisco. Since the novel's climax had taken place in Death Valley, Stroheim naturally decided to film it there, although the conditions were the most difficult imaginable. He had been struck by Norris's descriptions of the Valley, and it could not be matched in appearance by any other location in the world.

The best guide towards visualizing the film as it appeared in its original form is obviously Stroheim's own screenplay, which has been published by the Belgian Cinémathèque. Fortunately a large number of stills exist from cut sections of the film; one of these shows Stroheim himself as a balloon-seller and suggests that he made a pre-Hitchcock cameo appearance in the film. The most easily accessible source of all is the Norris novel.

A careful comparison of the ten-reel final version of the film with the original screenplay suggests that three-quarters of the film has been cut, and this tallies exactly with those references which mention an original length of forty-two reels, or ten hours. However only about seven and a half hours resulted from the faithful translation of the novel to the screen. The additional amount is represented by Stroheim's extended prologue, which he added to the content of the novel.

During the very period that Stroheim was filming and editing *Greed,* the Goldwyn Company was merged into a new and larger studio, Metro-Goldwyn-Mayer, headed by Louis B. Mayer. Irving Thalberg, the producer with whom Stroheim had often tangled at Universal, was hired by Mayer to serve as his executive producer. Both men were less than sympathetic to Stroheim's *Greed* project, which was very far from their ideal of screen entertainment.

Stroheim himself had reduced the film to twenty-four reels, for exhibition in two parts separated by an interval. When the studio still objected, he gave the film to his friend Rex Ingram, who managed to edit it down to eighteen reels which he considered the bare minimum. In either of these versions, running for four or five hours, the film was probably the ideal compromise between Stroheim's original conception and the demands of the releasing studio.

In order to produce this length, both subplots had probably been eliminated and the opening section reduced, along with some marginal aspects of the central plot. The subplots had obvious weaknesses: the Maria-Zerkow story was excessively melodramatic, while that of Grannis and Miss Baker was incredibly naive and sentimental. The opening scenes had not been part of Norris's novel and could justifiably be eliminated for that reason. Nevertheless, the stills and screenplay suggest that the opening (like the subplots) had included some original and effective cinema, and this is confirmed by the fragment which remains of the prologue at the mine. These cut sections included much material which was typically Stroheimian, and essential for relating *Greed* to his other films. There is no contradiction involved here, but rather a paradox: some of Stroheim's best work may have involved characters like Zerkow and McTeague Sr, who were the most expendable in relation to the central plot.

The eighteen-reel version of the film was still not considered short enough by MGM and it was given to an anonymous studio cutter unfamiliar with the novel and Stroheim's conception of it. He reduced *Greed* to ten reels, the version in which it was finally released. All that now remained of the film were the bare bones of the central plot concerning McTeague and Trina, and even this was often less than clear.

The reduction had been divided between the elimination of subplots and of most of the opening section, and some reduction in the main plot. Since Stroheim's technique generally included important details within the individual shots, the shortening of the film was largely a matter of eliminating complete scenes rather than cutting or rearranging shots within a scene. The scenes which remain tend to be fairly complete, with occasional shortening of beginnings and ends. Most fortunate of all, the order of the scenes has not been altered, with the single exception of the fight between McTeague and Marcus in the pub.

The cutting has necessitated the alteration of many of the titles which had been carefully composed by Stroheim or quoted from the original novel. Many of the new titles appear as facile and poorly-worded attempts to bridge gaps in the story. Some are just inept. For example, the opening sequence of violence at the mine is abruptly concluded with the title, 'Such was McTeague', which invariably causes amusement in the audience.

One final corollary of the film's reduction which has been entirely neglected by the critics is the inevitable distortion in meaning of the scenes that remain. They are all given a weight which Stroheim himself could never have foreseen. Instead of Trina's miserliness developing over a long period of time through many little incidents and only occasionally resulting in open clashes with her husband, all that remain are the few climactic scenes. The film suffers from a concentration, in which one intensely dramatic scene follows another without any respite.

Some writers have suggested that the present version of *Greed* is so powerful and intense that they could not have taken any more, implying that it is just as well that the film has been severely cut. In fact the four or five hour version would have proved both closer to Stroheim's original intentions and easier to appreciate, with the climactic scenes more naturally spaced within the film's proper development.

Stroheim's technique of filling each shot with interesting details and keeping backgrounds always in focus means that many details which are not explicitly mentioned remain accessible to the perceptive viewer. Although the altered titles make no reference to the decline in living quarters which parallels the deterioration in the McTeague's marriage, the changes are quite apparent. In fact, various shots in the hallway of the boarding house help to locate McTeague's dental parlours and apartment toward the front of the house, while later in the film they occupy a little room at the back, on the same floor. And although the important motif of the giant gilt tooth has been eliminated, it can still be glimpsed in their little room, serving as a makeshift table.

A brief summary of the film's plot:

PROLOGUE: 1908. A gold mine in the mountains of California. Young McTeague works in the mine. When his alcoholic father dies, his mother takes advantage of the opportunity to send him away as an apprentice to a travelling dentist. When she dies, five years later, McTeague uses his small inheritance to set up a dental practice in San Francisco. End of prologue.

1918. The film itself opens with an introduction to Mac's friend and neighbours on a typical Saturday. The action of the novel begins one Sunday when Mac is relaxing in the dental parlours which also serve as his lodgings. His friend, Marcus, arrives to tell of an accident which has injured the teeth of his cousin, Trina Sieppe. On the Monday, Trina becomes Mac's patient—the opening of the cut film. After treating her for a few weeks, Mac has fallen in love. He confesses this to Marcus, who chivalrously renounces her to Mac and even takes him on a picnic with Trina's family. Mac courts Trina. She wins $5,000 in a lottery. But Marcus has become jealous, and the two men have a fight. McTeague and Trina are married. End of Part One.

1923. Mac and Trina have been happily married for three years when Mac and Marcus have a second fight. Out of spite, Marcus reports Mac to the dental authorities before leaving San Francisco. After Mac loses his practice, the marriage deteriorates quite rapidly as they become increasingly isolated from their friends and relatives. Trina grows more miserly, while Mac has taken to drink and tormenting his wife physically. Finally, he robs and abandons her. But he returns some months later to murder her and rob her of the $5,000 lottery prize. He flees back to his old home at the mine. Sensing that he is pursued, he heads across Death Valley. Here he is caught by his former friend Marcus, who has joined the posse. Both men die in the desert.

The opening shots of *Greed* are like a documentary film on the workings of a gold mine in the Western United States at the turn of the century. They appear much as Stroheim had planned them. But this small fragment of the mine sequence is all that remains of the entire first quarter of the film. In addition to the prologue at the mine, this section should include the arrival of McTeague in San Francisco and an introduction to the characters and milieu of Polk Street, where he lives and practises dentistry. Most of this section was original Stroheim material, based on a few brief suggestions from Norris regarding McTeague's origins. It is the one section of the film not closely adapted from Norris's novel and thus was vulnerable to cutting. The original two and a half hours have been reduced to seven minutes of prologue.

The young McTeague, simple but powerful, is first seen working at the mine where his father is shift boss and his mother is cook. In the opening sequence he rescues a wounded bird. A giant close-up stresses the incongruity between the large man and the tiny bird: here the influence of Griffith is evident. McTeague's sudden transformation from gentleness to violence, when the bird is knocked from his hand, anticipates his later fight with Marcus in the pub.

When McTeague leaves the mine, apprenticed to the travelling dentist, he takes only a few treasured possessions with him—his concertina, a twenty-dollar goldpiece, a watch on a chain with a tooth-locket, and a bird cage containing the wounded bird which he has adopted as a pet. Each of these objects has symbolic associations which are developed throughout the film: leitmotifs reflecting on the character of McTeague.

The pet bird, in particular, serves as a reminder of his original home at the mine, throughout his travels and his life in San Francisco. Like Orson Welles's Charles Foster Kane, McTeague is the unwitting victim of an ambitious mother who wants to see her son 'rise in life', away from the rough environment and unhealthy influence of his drunken father. McTeague's pet bird, like Citizen Kane's sled, comes to symbolize his 'lost innocence' and his nostalgia for his old home. The caged bird is also an image of McTeague's own alienation in the city.

McTeague and his pet are inseparable. Pursued into Death Valley at the film's conclusion, McTeague still carries the bird-cage, thus making it particularly easy for the law to follow him whereever he goes. His dying act is an effort to free the bird. Kane died with the word 'Rosebud', the name of his sled, on his lips. Both films have come full circle. Kane's childhood sled goes up in flames after his death, and McTeague's pet bird dies with him in the midst of Death Valley.

By opening **Greed** at the mine, Stroheim has given the film a form that the novel lacked. Opening and closing sections among the mountains and deserts of the Far West frame the main part of the film set in and around San Francisco.

Before McTeague's arrival in San Francisco, we see one revealing episode in his experience as assistant to the travelling dentist. He is helping to treat a young couple. At first McTeague is so embarrassed by the young woman that he has to exchange patients with the dentist. Then he finds it difficult to operate the forceps in the young man's mouth, puts them aside, and finally pulls the tooth with his bare hands.

McTeague's apprenticeship ends about five years later, when the death of his mother provides him with the money for setting up his own dental practice in San Francisco. From here onwards the film centres on the house in Polk Street, where he and many of his friends live. We are introduced to the milieu of boarding houses and shop-keepers living above their little shops on a typical Saturday. The movements of the various characters are inter-related in a sequence which comes to life in a remarkable way, even on paper (i.e., as it appears in the original screenplay).

This sequence revolves round the volatile Marcus, who is as lively and excitable as McTeague is dull and plodding. As the foil to McTeague, friend at the beginning of the film, bitter enemy by the end, Marcus comes close to stealing the first half of the film with his wild antics and gestures.

He works at the dog hospital owned by Mr Grannis, where he is first seen asphyxiating some puppies. On his return from work, Marcus shows his flashy new neck-tie to McTeague who lives in the same house. The other lodgers are forced to wait for Marcus to finish his bath, as he has a date with Trina, his cousin and girl-friend.

Stroheim intercuts the movements of the various characters in this sequence, which introduces the two main sub-plots: the romantic story of Mr Grannis and Miss Baker and the sordid tale of Maria, the charlady, and old Zerkow, the junkman. From McTeague eating his meal Stroheim cuts to Trina shopping and then to Marcus, who is on his way to meet Trina and bumps into his friend McTeague at the door. Mac is just returning with a new bird and cage which he had purchased at the nearby pet shop owned by a nice little old lady, just like his mother.

Lasting for about an hour in the original film, this section suggests the relationship of plot, subplot and symbolic motifs, and the mixture of objective and subjective, that was characteristic of Stroheim's original conception. Shooting the entire film on location, Stroheim showed a remarkable feeling for contemporary San Francisco, but the realistic backgrounds were always used dramatically and blended with the fantastic or grotesque.

A realistic shot shows McTeague returning home along the street late on Saturday evening and gazing up at his window, imagining how a large gilt tooth sign would look there: *Shot from his angle of bay window into which dissolves the large gilded tooth, suspended from iron rod.*

The only subjective shot remaining in the film is Mother McTeague's vision of her son substituted for the travelling dentist, as she watches him getting paid for extracting a tooth. This shot is accomplished by Stroheim so smoothly and naturally that it fits unobtrusively into the otherwise realistic prologue at the mine.

Many of the subjective sequences in the original version concern the Maria and Zerkow subplot which is so bizarre as to border on the surrealistic. Most of the scenes between them take place in Zerkow's squalid shack in the alley behind McTeague's boarding house, reflecting a Zolaesque blend of heightened realism with the grotesque. The first of the symbolic insert shots which recur throughout the film occurs when Maria tells Zerkow a fantastic story of the solid gold dinner service which once belonged to her parents. But the one surviving shot of the dinner service has been placed at the end of a scene concerning Trina. Other insert shots should have been included at appropriate points throughout the film. These inserts were conceived by Stroheim and have no stylistic counterpart in the novel. They were to be tinted a golden colour like various objects in the film itself, including McTeague's bird cage and his large gilt tooth sign, to stress their symbolic associations. Only three of these symbolic shots remain in the mutilated film and these have been included at the wrong points.

Completely eliminated from the film are the characters of Zerkow and McTeague's degenerate father, both true Stroheimian creations. In one extraordinary scene, McTeague Sr was seen in a drunken stupor leading to hallucinations and raving, which only ended when he dropped dead, poisoned by alcohol. The squalor of the saloon-brothel, where McTeague Sr is fond of drinking, foreshadows the subplot between Maria and Zerkow; this, in turn, serves as a grotesque parody of the marriage of McTeague and Trina and suggests the decline which McTeague himself is to undergo by the film's end. The final subplot concerning the romance of an incredibly shy and innocent old couple, Mr Grannis and Miss Baker, contrasts so strongly with the other characters and events in the film that it adds yet another touch of incongruity to the film's already weird mixture.

The virtual elimination of all subplots has reduced most of the minor characters to an occasional passing appearance, if their roles have not been cut out entirely. The subplots should have provided a counterpoint to the development of the relationship between McTeague and Trina throughout the film: a great strength of Stroheim's direction is the interaction between major and minor characters. This gives an importance to the minor parts and exemplifies Stroheim's antagonism to the star system, an attitude that led him to work wherever possible with his own stock company of actors.

Most important of all, the mutilation of *Greed* is not confined to a reduction in length, but has resulted in the complete destruction of the original balance between the realistic and naturalistic, and the weird, bizarre or subjective elements, with the cuts concentrated on the latter. Though *Greed* continues to be regarded as Stroheim's one uncompromisingly realistic film, it had originally much more in common with his other films than is generally realized. All that remains is the realistic core of a film which was meant to combine many different elements, the underlying realism being used by Stroheim to give an added force to the strange and unrealistic aspects of the story, in accordance with the Naturalistic philosophy of Norris and Zola.

At the end of our introduction to San Francisco on this particular Saturday, Stroheim had shown Marcus meeting Trina Sieppe and going to dinner with her family. This German-Swiss family of caricatures provided Stroheim, once an immigrant himself, with the opportunity for a bit of harsh satire. Marcus stays overnight, and the following day is vigorously pushing Trina on a swing, when the rope snaps. Her injury brings the first note of discord into their relationship. ('It's your fault Marc, now I'm disfigured for life.')

Later the same day Marcus arrives back at Polk Street. He drops in to see McTeague, and asks him to fix Trina's damaged teeth. In this, the opening scene of Norris's novel, Marcus finds Mac relaxing, stretched out in his dental chair by the bay window with his concertina nearby, 'reading the paper, drinking his beer, and smoking his huge porcelain pipe while his food digests; cropfull, stupid, and warm'.

The truncated version of the film proper begins on the following day, Monday, when Marcus brings Trina to Mac's dental surgery. The missing ten reels have been replaced by a single title:

> Mac learned dentistry after a fashion, through assisting the charlatan . . . and, years later on Polk Street in San Francisco, 'Doc' McTeague was established.

Mac is just finishing work on old Miss Baker when Marcus and Trina arrive. While they are waiting, Maria, the charwoman, approaches and persuades Trina to buy a lottery ticket.

Mac decides that one of Trina's teeth will have to come out. However, her natural distress at this news has been distorted in the released version by a new title which reads: 'That will cost too much, won't it?' At the very first opportunity, a crude attempt has been made to introduce Trina's stinginess into the film.

This scene has been drastically shortened and the ending has been eliminated. It was meant to show the great impact on McTeague of his first encounter with Trina. He is not used to being close to young women. After she has gone, Mac is standing helplessly by the dental chair when he suddenly notices Trina's extracted tooth. He carefully wraps the tooth in a scrap of newspaper and puts it into his waistcoat pocket to keep.

The reduction and alteration of this opening scene is on the same pattern as the cutting throughout the rest of the film. Apart from the removal of subplots and of many scenes in the main plot, the beginnings and endings of many of the remaining scenes have been cut. The reactions of McTeague and Trina to each other, when they are alone, have often been edited out, wrecking Stroheim's intended development of their relationship.

The quality of the acting is sometimes brought into question by abrupt changes in mood and gaps in the characters' development. Poorly-worded titles are meant to fill in large gaps in the story caused by the ruthless cutting, but various aspects still remain unclear. Since Trina's obsession with money is at the heart of the story, a crude attempt is made to suggest it in some new titles. But Stroheim's careful development of her character in detail can not be so easily replaced. Her excesses were originally counter-balanced by aberrations in other characters (largely omitted from the cut film), like McTeague's own obsession with the bird and the giant gilt tooth and Zerkow's obsession with the solid gold dinner service.

Finally, after two weeks of treatment, comes Trina's last visit. McTeague cannot resist kissing her while she is under the influence of ether, but her first words when she revives are: 'I never felt a thing'. This title has been cut, and so has Mac's immediate proposal of marriage, which she refuses. Without the missing footage, it is impossible to understand why the couple are so ill at ease when Marc returns. They both look so glum that he begins clowning to make them laugh.

The scene ends with Mac looking through the bay window as Trina and Marcus leave. Shooting from a specially raised platform, Stroheim is able to show us McTeague in the foreground watching his two friends boarding the tram in the street below, thus underlining Mac's feeling of loss at Trina's final departure. This is the first point at which Stroheim has consciously made use of depth of focus, although cars and people passing in the street below had been clearly visible through the large bay window during the scenes in the dental parlour.

The next section (cut in the released version) shows how McTeague's normal pattern of life has been disrupted by his encounter with Trina. He is off his food, and generally out of sorts, but he goes on cherishing Trina's extracted tooth. Marcus's first remark as they sit in the corner of a pub on the boardwalk by the sea is: 'What's the matter with you these days, Mac? Huh?' While the conversation goes on indoors, continuous background interest is provided by a steady stream of passers-by who can be seen through the windows. Again the end of the scene is cut, including Marcus's offer to take McTeague on a picnic with Trina and her family, who have not yet appeared in the shortened film.

Mac meets the Sieppes on the picnic excursion, and is noticeably ill at ease at seeing Trina once again. The scene at the railroad station is one of the few group scenes remaining in the film. It shows Stroheim's gift for organizing a sequence in depth: Popper Sieppe arranges the family in the foreground, while the others continue their conversation in mid-ground; little Owgooste runs off to watch the train which passes in the background and is hastily fetched back by Mommer; Popper marches to the head of the column. (All this is shot in a single, one-minute take.) Finally, the group marches off, led by Popper doing the goose step. This shot is said to have caused riots in German cinemas. The scene at the entrance to the fair is similarly organized in depth with Marcus buying the tickets at the left of the screen while conversations are going on in the foreground and the back ground.

Little of this picnic scene remains, apart from a superb merry-go-round shot in which the wooden horses come riding out of the fade-in with McTeague in the lead with the camera in front of him on the platform itself. In the evening the group return to the Sieppes' house where Mac and Marcus are to spend the night. The concluding sequence of this section shows McTeague's ecstasy at finding himself alone in Trina's room among all her clothes and personal possessions.

Weeks passed, and March rains put a stop to their picnics . . . but McTeague saw Trina every Wednesday and Sunday.

For once, the title is not merely filling a gap in the original film. We notice the growth of their relationship in the natural way that Trina holds McTeague's arm and leans on him as they walk, or holds him for support as she hops on to the sewer. (The crude title: 'Let's go over and sit on the sewer', doesn't appear in Stroheim's own screenplay.) We can sense Trina's growing dependence on him. A brief cut in this scene eliminates a further reference to the tooth motif: 'Some day I am going to have a big gilded tooth outside my window for a sign', says McTeague, revealing his one great dream to Trina. 'Those big gold teeth are beautiful, beautiful, only they cost so much I can't afford one just now'.

After this scene by the railroad tracks a major piece of mutilation has eliminated the following short sequences:

Trina's reaction at home to Mac's kiss; another meeting between them when a kiss from Mac again stifles her objections; various conversations between Mac and Marcus in the course of which Marcus suggests a theatre party to celebrate the engagement—the slow-thinking McTeague is still dependent on his friend's suggestions. We should also be shown McTeague's difficulties in coping with the theatre box office, and finally the evening at the theatre intercut with the arrival of the man from the lottery company at the house on Polk Street.

The truncated film resumes as Mac, Trina, Mommer Sieppe and Owgooste are leaving the theatre. As they arrive back at Mac's house and are just entering the door, we see them react to the commotion upstairs. Although, evidently, the audience cannot hear the sounds that are part of the action in a silent movie, this is an example of Stroheim's natural treatment of sound.

A sinister-looking stranger, like the symbol of Fate found in many German films of the period, steps forward, bows to Trina, and, speaking 'with the mien of an undertaker', informs her that she has won the $5,000 lottery prize. Marcus tries to hide his disappointment behind his usual cynical pose. Much of the celebration in the dental parlours has been cut, but for some reason, a shot of Maria, the charwoman, stealing some of Mac's dental gold, remains. This is the only remaining suggestion of the sub-plot between her and old Zerkow, to whom she sells the gold.

Maria is the last guest to leave, allowing Mac and Trina to be alone for the first time all evening. We are shown the natural way in which the couple behave together, Trina adjusting McTeague's tie before the two embrace. There is more than a hint of malice in Marcus's interruption at this moment.

The scene ends at the dog hospital where Marcus works. There is a brief glimpse of a passing streetwalker. The shots of Marcus in the doorway 'cursing his luck' was clearly meant to lead directly into the pub scene when he fights with Mac for the first time. This is the one occasion when the position of a scene has been altered from the original. This destroys the logic of the original plot, leaving us no explanation for Marcus's behaviour at the wedding or for the substitution of old Mr Grannis as best man. Crudely intercut shots of Trina shining her gold pieces have been edited in from a later portion of the film.

Stroheim builds up the tension in the pub in a single longish take: Mac in the background of the shot packs and lights his pipe, and as he starts puffing, the scowl on the face of Marcus who is near the camera, starts to deepen. Marcus squirms in his seat and begins turning a coin on the table with increasing rapidity until he can bear it no longer. He turns to Mac and says:

Say, for God's sake, choke off on that pipe! If you've got to smoke rope, smoke it in a crowd of muckers. Not among gentlemen.

The scene probably appears much as Stroheim shot it, with the various alterations from the original screenplay merely carrying through Stroheim's own decision to condense the two original pub scenes into one.

In the climax to the scene, Marcus breaks McTeague's pipe and throws a knife at him before disappearing through the door. At this point in the filming, Gibson Gowland refused to allow a real knife to be used, even if thrown by a professional knife-thrower. The incident, which shows Stroheim's continual striving for authenticity in front of the camera, has most recently been told by Joseph von Sternberg in *Fun in a Chinese Laundry*. Completely oblivious to the fact that a knife has been thrown at him, McTeague goes storming out of the pub in pursuit because Marcus has broken his favourite pipe.

He arrives home, still in a rage, to find a large packing case awaiting him. He opens it and his anger evaporates immediately. It's the giant gilt tooth sign which he had always dreamed of hanging from the window of his dental parlours, a birthday present from Trina.

> *McTeague tears away the excelsior; suddenly he utters an exclamation. Close up, from his angle; it is the golden molar, his greatest ambition in life. Back to scene, he very carefully removes the rest of the excelsior and lifts the ponderous tooth from its box, sets it upon the marble-top centre table; he circles about the golden wonder, touching it gingerly with his hands; he sits down, gazes at tooth in ecstasy. Fade out.*

Stroheim's description in his screenplay is virtually identical to that of Norris who treats the scene with equal relish:

> *How immense it looked in that little room! The thing was tremendous, overpowering—the tooth of a gigantic fossil, golden and dazzling. Beside it everything seemed dwarfed. Even McTeague himself, big boned and enormous as he was, shrank and dwindled in the presence of the monster. As for an instant he bore it in his hands, it was like a puny Gulliver struggling with the molar of some vast Brobdingnagian.*

Having begun with an extracted tooth, the romance between Trina and McTeague has reached its symbolic climax in McTeague's dental parlours. Trina's little tooth, which Mac had so carefully kept, has now grown to giant proportions. The tooth symbolizes both the development of the love between Trina and Mac, and the gradual alienation of their friend Marcus, which is now complete. The very first discord between Marcus and Trina had arisen through the accident when Trina's teeth were broken. It was further aggravated by her lottery winning, which has now provided the money for the gift. The fight between Mac and Marcus and the arrival of Trina's gift appropriately coincide. In appeasing McTeague's anger, the giant tooth underlines Trina's replacement of Marcus as the most important character in the story next to McTeague. From this point on, Marcus fades into the background until his dramatic and unexpected reappearance after Trina's murder. The tooth motif can be traced back to the prologue at the mine, where the travelling dentist makes his first appearance in a buggy which has a large tooth symbol hanging from the roof. When McTeague leaves the mine, he takes a tiny tooth locket with him. But the final comment on this theme is only supplied by Norris near the conclusion of the novel when Mac returns to his old home at the mine.

> *In the Burly drill he saw a queer counterpart of his old-time dental engine; and what were the drills and chucks but enormous hoe excavators, hard bits, and burrs? It was the same work he had so often performed in his 'Parlours', only magnified, made monstrous, distorted, and grotesqued, the caricature of dentistry.*

Here is a mechanical counterpart to the inflation of the tooth to giant size.

Mac and Trina are now on bad terms with Marcus, and Trina's family is planning a move to Los Angeles straight after the wedding. Our interest centres exclusively on the married couple. A short scene at the Sieppes' shows the family in the final stages of packing for the move south. Mommer Sieppe manages to get Marcus to shake hands with McTeague, but he still refuses to be best man at the wedding.

The wedding takes place in the photographer's rooms adjoining Mac's dental parlours. Consisting of bedrooms, sitting-room and a small kitchen, they have been furnished by Trina and taken over as their new flat. In this scene, virtually the entire collection of major and minor characters, cripples and grotesques are brought together, dressed in their Sunday best and demonstrating all their middle-class pretensions.

As the wedding ceremony is concluding by the window, a funeral can be seen passing on the street outside, including a crippled boy walking with a crutch. This is the most famous example of Stroheim's use of deep focus and has no direct antecedent in the novel. Norris had suggested the dismal wedding atmosphere by referring to a 'persistent sound of sawing', coming from somewhere in the building, which could be heard throughout the wedding ceremony. It has been concluded that Stroheim included the funeral as a visual equivalent to the sawing sound. In fact, both the funeral and various shots of a hand sawing wood are *both* included in Stroheim's screenplay.

Another Stroheim invention is the sequence in which McTeague presents Trina with a wedding gift of two love-birds in a cage. She can hardly conceal her disappointment and Marcus is downright contemptuous. Only little old Miss Baker, who is like McTeague's own mother and the old lady in the pet shop, appreciates the sincerity of the gift.

Since the Sieppes are just departing for their new home in southern California, one can understand the drama of the leavetaking scene, particularly between Trina and her mother. This is the last time that Trina will ever see her family. When at last Mommer is gone, Stroheim emphasises Trina's loneliness with the instruction: 'grind on closed door for six feet.'

Trina returns to the flat frightened and with tears in her eyes. Norris's description makes it clear that Stroheim has even been faithful to the novel in the lay-out of the McTeague's flat:

> The hall was empty and deserted. The great flat around her seemed new and huge and strange; she felt horribly alone . . .
>
> She went down the hall, by the open door of the sitting-room, going on toward the hall door of the bedroom.
>
> As she softly passed the sitting-room she glanced hastily in . . . The table itself, abandoned, deserted, presented to view the vague confusion of its dishes, its knives and forks, its empty platters and crumpled napkins. The dentist sat there leaning on his elbows, his back toward her; against the white blur of the table he looked colossal . . .
>
> Trina entered the bedroom, closing the door after her. At the sound, she heard McTeague start and rise.
>
> 'Is that you, Trina?'
>
> She did not answer, but paused in the middle of the room, holding her breath, trembling.
>
> The dentist crossed the outside room, parted the chenille portieres and came in. He came toward her quickly, making as if to take her in his arms. His eyes were alight.

As Mac and Trina kiss, Stroheim shows a close-up of Trina's white satin slippers standing on tiptoe on McTeague's large black shoes. Their embrace is intercut with a shot of the two love birds in their cage. The camera, which had begun to back away at the beginning of their kiss, continues to withdraw discreetly as Mac approaches and draws the portières.

As originally planned, the wedding concluded the first half of the film. The second part began with following title:

> The first three years of their married life wrought little change in the fortunes of the McTeagues. Instead of sinking to McTeague's level, as she had feared, Trina made McTeague rise to hers.

This was altered in the cut version to read:

> The early months of married life wrought changes. Since her lottery winning Trina feared their good luck might lead to extravagance and her normal instinct for saving became a passion.

The new title is a weak attempt to explain Trina's obsession, which has not yet appeared in the film. It has probably misled many critics into connecting her obsession with the wedding night. A typical reaction is that of Gavin Lambert:

> . . . the shy, virginal Trina marries the genial but brutish dentist McTeague, and a clumsy wedding night leaves her impregnably frigid and terrified. Her desires are twisted into one direction only, the acquisition of gold.

Peter Noble's biography of Stroheim makes a commendable effort to relate this scene to Stroheim's other films. But instead of relating it to other love scenes or wedding nights, he compares it to the *rape* scenes:

> Encouraged by the success of his sophisticated and daring treatment of sex themes in his first 4 films, Stroheim introduced what amounted to a rape sequence into his masterpiece **Greed** . . . On their wedding night, McTeague, a clumsy but gentle giant in everyday life, becomes a fearsome would-be rapist to the sexually innocent bride . . . She never recovers from the pain and fright of that night, and her sex phobia continues throughout her married life. . . . To modern cinemagoers, steeped in Freud, the process of Trina's sexual sublimation in **Greed** would seem to be eminently simple. Her obsession with gold, and her sexual coldness towards her husband would appear to go hand in hand. Trina begins to love gold with an almost sexual passion . . .

All this is pure speculation, supported by the badly altered titles. There is not the slightest suggestion of sexual incompatibility between Mac and Trina, and Norris's novel is quite explicit on this point:

> Suddenly he caught her in both his huge arms, crushing down her struggle with his immense strength, kissing her full upon the mouth. Then her great love for McTeague suddenly flashed up in Trina's breast; she gave up to him as she had done before, yielding all at once to that strange desire of being conquered and subdued. She clung to him, her hands clasped behind his neck, whispering in his ear; 'Oh, you must be good to me—very, very good to me, dear—for you're all that I have in the world now.'

Altered titles and severe cutting have done their damage. This central section of the film is the most seriously mutilated of all, with every other aspect of the story neglected in favour of Trina's developing obsession. The effort is self-defeating as her neurosis can only be understood properly within the context of her relationship with McTeague and her own family background, both of which have been badly cut. In the original film her miserly qualities had only revealed themselves briefly and at intervals in the development of her relations with Mac, originating in her addiction to saving even before her marriage, but remaining both tolerable and understandable, balanced against the other unusual characters and situations.

Unfortunately, we see very little of the McTeagues' happily married life together and the beneficial influence which Trina has upon Mac's slovenly 'bachelor habits'. Without this we cannot fully appreciate the extent of their later degradation. Not only do we have little understanding of their normal life together, but the cutting puts a disproportionate emphasis upon those scenes which do remain, such as that of Trina emptying Mac's pockets while he sleeps, an emphasis which obviously could not have been foreseen by Stroheim. Their visit to a house which is to let, is terminated by an inept title stressing her meanness.

It is important to remember that Trina's obsession emerges only after McTeague has lost his dental practice, and its development parallels their general decline. Her tendency to excessive stinginess had earlier been carefully kept under control, outweighed by her love for Mac. Of course, the temptation is always there, as it is so easy to take advantage of the slow-thinking McTeague: Maria, for example, steals bits of his dental gold.

In an attempt to disguise the severe cutting here, the pub fight between Marcus and McTeague has been transposed to this point, replacing their second fight at a picnic. Whereas the earlier fight brought their friendship to an end, this one has even more serious consequences.

A brief glimpse of the McTeagues embracing is interrupted by Marcus knocking at the door as he had done on the night of their engagement. As the three sit at the table, Trina tries to gesture to Mac behind Marcus's back, but Marcus smiles, knowing that he now has the upper hand. The situation is symbolized by the intercut shots of Marcus's cat in pursuit of the two birds. And a few days after Marcus's departure, the cat is again seen pursuing the birds in McTeague's bay window as he reads the fateful letter telling him that he is no longer allowed to practice dentistry without a recognized diploma.

The loss of McTeague's dental practice and Trina's refusal to give up any of her savings make it necessary for them to give up their flat. They move into a single room at the back of the same boarding house. The auction sale at which they sell most of their things has been cut, including a superb ending in which the couple, left alone in the now bare flat, recall their wedding day (which appears in flashback).

Because of numerous cuts, we next see the McTeagues when they have already adapted to an entirely new way of life. Their decline has begun. In accordance with Naturalist principles, their economic decline parallels a further deterioration in their marriage. Trina's avarice and Mac's stubborn intractability continue to feed on each other. Her obsession has been further stimulated by the proceeds of the auction sale, while Mac has only grudgingly come to accept the change in living quarters.

Their ugly room remains in a constant state of disorder, which is first presented to us through the montage sequence which opens the scene. Trina now works all day at her woodcarving, and Mac is employed at a surgical equipment factory. His glorious gilt tooth has to serve as a makeshift table and can be glimpsed for a moment in the background.

Their deterioration is shown in the one key sequence of scenes which survives from this part of the film. Having lost his job, Mac arrives home early. Trina takes all his money and immediately sends him off to look for another. In a brief scene outside the boarding house, Maria points out McTeague to a group of gossiping neighbours. Mac, who has been caught in the rain, is passing Frenna's saloon when his friend Heise insists on buying him a whiskey. By the time he returns home, he is drunk and angry. For the first time Mac stands up to Trina: a direct result of her own stinginess. Their fight is intercut with the two birds fighting in their cage. Mac's success as a dentist had represented a triumph over both heredity and environment, represented by his drunken father and the rough life at the mine. In this scene he appears for the first time as the archetype of the Naturalist man.

Mac's brute strength, developed by work in the mine, had a primitive, animal quality which went with the giant trees and mountains and the powerful machinery of the mine itself. Near the end of the film he will instinctively be drawn back to his old home and life at the mine:

> The still, colossal mountains took him back again like a returning prodigal, and vaguely, without knowing why, he yielded to their influence—their immensity, their enormous power, crude and blind, reflecting themselves in his own nature, huge, strong, brutal in its simplicity.

Before meeting Trina, McTeague had lived contentedly with a few simple pleasures represented by his pipe, concertina, pet bird and steam beer. Then he is caught up in a progression of events over which he has no control. Slow-thinking and good-natured, he had allowed Trina to take advantage of him and had even accepted the loss of his dental practice. Now without any job he is at the mercy of his environment, a prime example of the Darwinian concepts which had so appealed to the Naturalist writers. The convincing way in which McTeague's transformation is portrayed testifies to the achievement of Norris whose understanding of human psychology goes beyond the occasional naiveties of the Naturalist point of view.

McTeague has become a primitive 'bruteman' governed by his instincts alone and stimulated by his new taste for whiskey. In order to extract money form Trina, he tortures her, twisting and biting her fingers, which have been made sensitive by long hours of woodcarving. As they fight, the walls behind them are still decorated with various souvenirs of their wedding.

After Zerkow has murdered Maria and himself committed suicide, Trina immediately sees an opportunity to move into even cheaper quarters, although she was the first one to find Maria's dead body and Maria still haunts her dreams. Trina forces McTeague to move once again, into the old junkman's shack in the back yard.

Their room had been dirty and untidy for much of the time, but the shack stays in a permanent state of filth. Trina and Mac negglect their own appearance more than ever. Trina no longer takes care of her long hair and often goes about all day in her dressing gown. Mac is unshaven and never wears a suit or tie. By this point in the film she and Mac have sunk to the level of McTeague Sr or of Maria and Zerkow. Earlier in the film these subplots had provided a contrast with the McTeagues. The character of Maria, in particular, anticipates the development of Trina in her ability to take advantage of Mac. By the end of the film, Trina too has become a charlady and is murdered by her husband.

However, the conclusion of the alternate subplot, between old Mr Grannis and Miss Baker, does provide a contrast with the degradation of the McTeagues. Intercut with the final scene showing the dismal life of Trina and Mac in the shack, are the last idyllic glimpses of the old couple who are now married. We see them holding hands and kissing in the park, like young lovers, among apple and peach blossoms. Back at the boarding house the partition dividing their single rooms is taken down.

Torn and frameless, the McTeagues' wedding portrait still hangs on the wall of the shack. Its only meaning for Mac is to remind him of the magnificent wedding dinner. He decides to sell his gilt tooth and with the money sends Trina to buy some meat for a proper meal. Trina has now become so obsessed with her money that she is completely oblivious to the workings of McTeague's slow mind. Whereas she was once shrewd enough to outsmart him, she's now blinded by her obsession. While she schemes to cheat him out of part of his change, Mac is making plans to outsmart *her* for once.

After the meal is finished Mac sets off to go fishing, as usual, in spite of the rain. And he decides to take the birds with him. Ignoring this obvious clue to his intentions, Trina goes so far as to suggest that he should sell them.

A single shot outside the shack shows the rain pouring down as it did on the fateful day when Mac lost his job and started drinking. Eliminated from the film is his return later that same day, while Trina is out, to take all the money from her trunk. (The original $5,000 is still safely invested in her uncle's business.)

When Trina returns to find the money gone, she becomes quite ill. The doctor who is called notices her damaged fingers and is forced to amputate. No longer able to carve wood, she becomes a charlady, living alone. A letter informs her that her family have emigrated to New Zealand, and, with Mac gone too, she has nothing in the world but her $5,000.

And with all her gold she was alone . . a solitary,

abandoned woman. Interior of Trina's room, bed is open, she is standing in petticoat and shirt in front of bed, pouring gold pieces on to the sheets from chamois bag, match box, as well as from canvas bag; with mad delight she spreads it, takes cushion away, looks around, then drops her petticoat. She stands in long shirt, she looks toward light, runs over to door, tries it, runs back. Close up—shoulders in, her hands gather the shirt, she pulls it over her head, drops it, her hands turn out the light.

Long shot—with one thin streak of light, lighting her nude body stepping into bed.

Close up—Trina in bed, shoulders in, her hands pour gold pieces over her nude shoulders; she has actual physical delight; she smiles a bit.

When McTeague returns, having exhausted her money (but still carrying the bird cage), Trina's reaction is understandable. Since the truncated version of the film never refers to the robbery, it is easy to miss the broader meaning of her reply to him:

McTeague: 'I wouldn't let a dog go hungry.'

Trina: 'Not if he'd bitten you?'

Trina is also made to appear less sympathetic by the disappearance of the end of this scene, when she relents at the last minute, and tries to call McTeague back. She breaks down and cries when she realizes that Mac has already gone.

A few days later Trina is just concluding her work, surrounded by Christmas decorations, when McTeague appears at the door in silhouette. The dim lighting recalls their first kiss in the station shed during the storm. Mac's face looms up menacingly in close-up, heralding a dramatic climax. But the murder itself is portrayed with great restraint and in this Stroheim is again following the lead of Norris. If anything, the physical violence appears all the more terrible for being indistinctly visible in the shadows or hidden by dividing doors. Afterwards, McTeague emerges from the darkness and wipes the blood from his hands.

Mac has ostensibly murdered Trina for her money, but he never seems much interested in it, nor does he spend any of it. Instead, he heads straight back to his old home at the mine.

Straight as a homing pigeon and following a blind and unreasoned instinct Mac returned to the Big Dipper Mine.

Here as elsewhere in the film, Stroheim's original title quotes exactly from Norris.

McTeague goes back to work in the mine before some inner sense warns him that he is being pursued. Heading further away from San Francisco, he crosses the mountains on foot, still carrying his concertina and bird-cage along with the sack of gold coins.

He teams up with an old prospector, but feels that he is still being followed. Only then does he decide to shake off his pursuers by heading across Death Valley. Here the truncated film resumes, moving toward a final chase climax which matches any by D. W. Griffith.

The film's greatest improvement over the novel is this chase sequence: it comes across with effect on the screen as we cut from pursuer to pursued, but is particularly awkward to handle on paper. Norris had been uncertain how to end the book and had put it away unfinished, only adding the present ending a few years after writing the rest of the book.

The novel follows the progress of McTeague until his unexpected encounter with Marcus in the midst of Death Valley.

> *Suddenly there was a shout.*
>
> *'Hands up. By damn, I got the drop on you!'*
>
> *McTeague looked up.*
>
> *It was Marcus.*

Then the action is left suspended while the author launches into an awkward three-page explanation of Marcus's life since leaving San Francisco and how he happens to have arrived in Death Valley. Marcus has not been mentioned since he reported Mac to the dental authorities. The novel is concluded in the five remaining pages.

McTeague's last act is to release the pet bird from its cage, but it is now too weak to fly. Mac dazedly sits awaiting death with the bag of spilled coins nearby, as the sun beats mercilessly down on the desert. The final, extremely long shot includes the lone figure of McTeague as a tiny spot in the distance, surrounded by an endless expanse of desert.

SCREENPLAY

> *Close up of a canvas sack with spilled money.*
>
> *Medium close up, McTeague and Marcus both in. The two look at each other. They (both) get the same idea. McTeague makes a step forward, says: 'I guess,'*
>
> *Title '. . . even if we're done for, I'll take some of my truck along.'*
>
> *Back to scene, Marcus very aggressive, puts his hand against Mac's chest and says: 'Hold on'.*
>
> *Title: 'I ain't so sure 'bout who that money belongs to'.*
>
> *Back to scene, Mac says: 'Well, I am'. They look at each other with ancient hate. Mac speaks:*

> *Title: '. . . . . don't try and load that gun either'.*
>
> *Closeup of McTeague. He fixes Marcus with his eyes.*
>
> *Closeup of Marcus dragging handcuffs from his pocket as he holds revolver in other hand like a club.*
>
> *He speaks:*
>
> *Title: ['You soldiered me out of that money once, and played me for a sucker. It's my turn now.]*
>
> *Don't lay your fingers on that sack.'*
>
> *Medium shot, both in. Marcus bars McTeague's way.*
>
> *Big head close up of McTeague; his eyes draw to fine twinkling points.*
>
> *Close up of his fists knotting themselves like wooden mallets.*
>
> *Back to scene, medium close up. Mac moves a step nearer to Marcus, then another.*
>
> *Medium long shot. Suddenly the men grapple. In another instant they are rolling and struggling on the white ground.*

NOVEL

> *. . . In an instant the eyes of the two doomed men had met as the same thought simultaneously rose in their minds. The canvas sack with its five thousand dollars was still tied to the horn of the saddle.*
>
> *Marcus had emptied his revolver at the mule, and though he still wore his cartridge belt, he was for the moment as unarmed as McTeague.*
>
> *'I guess,' began McTeague coming forward a step, 'I guess, even if we are done for, I'll take—some of my truck along.'*
>
> *'Hold on,' exclaimed Marcus, with rising aggressiveness. 'Let's talk about that. I ain't so sure about who that—who that money belongs to.'*
>
> *'Well, I am, you see,' growled the dentist.*
>
> *The old enmity between the two men, their ancient hate was flaming up again.*
>
> *'Don't try an' load that gun either,' cried McTeague, fixing Marcus with his little eyes.*
>
> *'Then don't lay your finger on that sack,' shouted the other. 'You're my prisoner, do you understand? You'll do as I say.' Marcus had drawn the handcuffs from his pocket, and stood ready with his revolver held as a club. 'You soldiered me out of that money once, and played me for a sucker, an' it's my turn now. Don't you lay your finger on that sack.'*

Marcus barred McTeague's way, white with passion. McTeague did not answer. His eyes drew to two fine, twinkling points, and his enormous hands knotted themselves into fists, hard as wooden mallets. He moved a step nearer to Marcus, then another.

Suddenly the men grappled, and in another instant were rolling and struggling upon the hot white ground.

Jonathan Rosenbaum (essay date 1974)

SOURCE: "Second Thoughts on Stroheim," in *Film Comment,* Vol. 10, No. 3, 1974, pp. 6-13.

[*In the following essay, Rosenbaum re-examines Stroheim's canon, noting especially the discrepancy between the "legend" of the director and his actual work.*]

PREFACE

> *Total object, complete with missing parts, instead of partial object. Question of degree.*
>
> —Samuel Beckett, "Three Dialogues"

Two temptations present themselves to any modern reappraisal of Erich von Stroheim's work; one of them is fatal, the other all but impossible to act upon. The fatal temptation would be to concentrate on the offscreen image and legend of Stroheim to the point of ignoring central facts about the films themselves: an approach that has unhappily characterized most critical work on Stroheim to date. On the other hand, one is tempted to look at nothing *but* the films—to suppress biography, anecdotes, newspaper reviews, reminiscences, and everything else that isn't plainly visible on the screen.

Submitting Stroheim's work to a purely formal analysis and strict textural reading of what is there—as opposed to what isn't, or might, or would or could or should have been there—may sound like an obvious and sensible project; but apparently no one has ever tried it, and there is some reason to doubt whether anyone ever will. Over the past fifty-odd years, the legend of Stroheim has cast so distinctive a shadow over the commercial cinema in general and his own work in particular that the removal of that shadow would amount to nothing less than a total skin graft; above all, it would mean eliminating the grid through which his films were seen in their own time—a time that, in many crucial respects, remains our own.

From one point of view, Stroheim's films only dramatize problems of directorial control and intention that are relevant to most Hollywood films. They dramatize these problems, however, in a particularly revealing way: we remember his best works (**Foolish Wives, Greed, The Wedding March, Queen Kelly**) not merely because of their power—which is considerable—but also because of their *will to power,* which is always even more considerable. We are constantly brought up against the problem

of considering his films as indications and abbreviations of projected meta-films that were either reduced and re-edited by the studios or, in the case of **Queen Kelly,** never completed in any form.

It is central to Stroheim's reputation that he is valued today more for the unseen forty-two-reel version of **Greed** than the ten-reel version that we do have. And if history and legend have conspired to install Stroheim as an exemplary figure in cinema—virtually the patron saint of all directors who have suffered at the hands of producers—it is precisely because of this discrepancy, the gap between the power and control that was sought and the amount that was visibly achieved.

How are we made aware of this discrepancy? Certainly we sense it almost as much in Stroheim's acting in the films of others as in his own projects—not simply because of all the dictatorial parts, from Prussian officers to assorted lunatics, but in the very style of his delivery, the very manner of his presence. Consider the sublime and all-but-hallucinatory tedium of his first role in a sound film, James Cruze's *The Great Gabbo,* when he seems to speak each line at roughly half the speed of everyone else in the cast; here one can witness the will to power in a strictly temporal arena—the apparent desire to remain on the screen as long as possible—lending to the part of the mad ventriloquist an intolerable tension and demonic mulishness that go well beyond the melodramatic demands of the plot, as though he were pulling at his character like taffy to see how far it could stretch before breaking. Insofar as a single performance can be compared to an entire film, it is likely that the duration of the original version of **Greed** was motivated along similar lines.

The opening credits of **Greed, The Merry Widow,** and **The Wedding March** alert us to Stroheim's aspirations before anything else appears on the screen: the first two are said to be "personally directed by Erich von Stroheim," the third is labeled "in its entirety an Erich von Stroheim creation." But if accepting Stroheim's legend means submitting to a fiction—a supplement, in many cases, to the fictions that he filmed—denying it is tantamount to imposing another, alternate fiction. (However much we may ever learn about Stroheim, it's highly unlikely that we'll know enough to do away with fictions entirely.) Bearing this in mind, an attempt will be made here to *isolate* his legend whenever possible, but not to dismantle it.

I

> *It is bad for man to believe he is more almighty than mountains.*
>
> —Sepp (Gibson Gowland) in **Blind Husbands**

Some favorite devices, recurring frequently throughout Stroheim's work: a long shot dissolving into a medium shot of the same character, a camera movement that turns a medium shot into a close-up, and an upward or downward pan taking in the whole body of a character. Each represents a different way of taking a closer look at someone—the first usually introduces characters, the second permits an increasing concentration of dramatic focus and detail (like the extraordinary track up to the face of Dale Fuller, the exploited maid in *Foolish Wives,* where we're enabled to see revenge being hatched in her eyes), and the third is more in the nature of an inventory.

Eyes have an unusual authority in Stroheim's films, and what is frequently meant by his "control of detail" is his uncanny gift for conveying information through an actor's eye movements. How someone looks and sees is always a central character trait, and the story of each film is partially told in glances.

A memorable example occurs as one of the privileged camera movements in *The Wedding March,* when Mitzi (Fay Wray), standing in a crowd, looks up at Prince Niki (Stroheim) sitting on a horse, and an upward pan gives us her exalted estimation of him. We can trace this shot all the way back to *Blind Husbands,* Stroheim's first film (1918), when Erich von Steuban (Stroheim) first encounters "Silent Sepp," the local Tyrolean mountain guide. Each sizes up the other in a separate pan: Steuban looks at Sepp, a slow pan from feet to head; Sepp looks at Steuban, a slow pan from head to feet. The central metaphysical conceit of the plot is hung on these two camera movements. Significantly, they are repeated in different but related contexts near the end: a slow pan all the way up the mountain on which the climactic struggle will take place, introduced as "The Pinnacle" (Stroheim's own original title for *Blind Husbands*) and which Dr. Armstrong (Sam de Grasse) and Steuban are about to ascend; and in the midst of this struggle, while Armstrong stands over Steuban, clenching him by the throat—a slow pan from Steuban down the mountain to the rescue party of soldiers and others, including Sepp, making their way up.

From top to bottom, from bottom to top: thematically and dramatically, all of Stroheim's films refer to this basic pattern. *Blind Husbands* provides at best only a rough sketch of what is to follow, but the essential lines are already there. Sepp is the pinnacle, the higher aspiration, and also something of a dumb-ox innocent, earthy and inert, who prevents Steuban from seducing Mrs. Armstrong (Francelina Billington) by appearing in the hotel corridor at just the right moment. (A cryptic monk appearing out of a rain storm in *Foolish Wives* functions identically.) Steuban is the depths, the lower aspiration, the grim, deadly, and well-dressed seducer, full of bluff and pretension. In between stand the Armstrongs, an American couple, naïve without being simple or wise (like Sepp), adventurous without being irresponsible or pretentious (like Steuban)—two free-floating characters who are, by extension, ourselves: likable zeros susceptible to the influences of a Sepp *or* a Steuban.

These and several other characters in *Blind Husbands* represent archetypes traceable back to the nineteenth-

century novel. The credits indirectly acknowledge this heritage by claiming that the film is derived "from the book *The Pinnacle* by Erich von Stroheim," an apparently imaginary work that no visible research has ever uncovered—much like the book *Foolish Wives* that the heroine of *that* film is shown reading. If the "realist" tag assigned to Stroheim often seems today like an outdated literary category—and one that might make Stroheim seem more outdated than he actually is—this is equally the case with his first literary models, Zola and Norris. The fictional worlds of all three are so charged with metaphysical forces and intimations of fatality that the "realism" they project is not one in which free will predominates; characters are usually doomed to be what they are by class and social position, heredity, mysterious turns of fate, or some malign combination of all three.

Steuban and the Armstrong couple can easily be seen as first drafts of Karamzin and the Hughes couple in *Foolish Wives*—an elaborated remake in many respects. (*The Devil's Passkey,* made during the interval between the two, is a lost film today, but existing synopses indicate it to be another version of the same plot, which remained with Stroheim for years: Stroheim completed a new script based on *Blind Husbands* in 1930, which he planned to film in sound and color.) But the distance traversed between Stroheim's first and third film is cosmic, even though only three years separate them. Vaguely sketched essences of character and locale became "three-dimensional" embodiments—not merely ideas expressed, but ideas incarnated—and we leap from an apprentice work to something closely approximating a mature style.

II

They are showing only the skeleton of my dead child.

—Stroheim after the release of *Foolish Wives*

Comparing the Italian and American prints of *Foolish Wives* in *Cahiers du cinéma* No. 79, Jacques Rivette observed that they differ not only by length, order of sequences, and editing within scenes, but also by the fact that they don't always have identical "takes" of the same shots. He offers the very plausible hypothesis that the longer Italian version corresponds much more closely to Stroheim's, while the American print is the version recut by Universal after the film's New York premiere. It seems quite possible—I haven't seen the American print in a few years—that the remarkable close-up of Dale Fuller's storytelling eyes and the fire-fire-truck montage, as described here, exist only in the Italian version.

A particularly troubling problem with both versions is the absence of what must be considered the film's climactic sequences: the rape of Ventucci's half-witted daughter (Malvine Polo) by Karamzin—or "Karamazin," according to Thomas Quinn Curtiss—resulting in the murder of Karamzin by Ventucci~ (Cesare Gravina); and after Ventucci's depositing of Karamzin's body in a sewer (visible in both versions), the corpse shown at dawn in the midst of garbage floating out to sea; and Mrs. Hughes giving premature birth to a child, which brings about a reconciliation with her husband. (These scenes are all indicated in Stroheim's synopsis.)

Lacking these scenes, our understanding of Karamzin's function in the film remains incomplete. Unless we can see the contrast between his magisterial first appearance by the Mediterranean and his exit as "rubbish" in the same setting, the trajectory of his scurrilous career is not fully articulated. And without the birth of the Hughes's child—apparently suggesting a quasi-mystical resurgence of life out of the ashes of corruption—his death fails to achieve the proper resonance. But despite these and other regrettable lacunae, Karamzin remains Stroheim's most complex and fascinating character outside of **Greed** and provides the occasion for his definitive performance.

The differences between Karamzin and Erich von Steuban are so closely related to the differences between Stroheim's authority as a director in each film that it is difficult not to see both characters as partial autobiographical counterparts. Karamzin displays all the low traits of Steuban, from vanity to cowardice, but two crucial characteristics are added: he is an impostor; and he is mainly out for money. Moreover, he is something of a professional con man while Steuban is at best a promising novice in the arts of deception, too often a fumbler to convince us that he is truly malignant. Both characters are identified with an "artistic" sensibility: one of Steuban's ploys with Mrs. Armstrong is to play soulfully on the violin along with her piano, while **Foolish Wives** invites us to relish Karamzin's more subtle methods of enticement, delight in his grander fabrications.

A classic instance of Stroheim as trickster: the episode of the armless veteran. Already, in contrast to **Blind Husbands,** he is firmly establishing a very specific milieu and period in which to locate his story—Monte Carlo just after the War, where veterans on crutches and kids playing soldiers (some of whom seem to mock and "see through" Karamzin's postures) form an essential part of the background. Because we don't realize that the stolid man who, early in the film, neglects to pick up Mrs. Hughes's gloves is armless, we assume that he's around merely to indicate the kind of courtesy that she's accustomed to receiving, and to provide Karamzin with an opportunity to display his own gallantry. The second time the man appears, exhibiting similar behavior in an elevator, we might imagine him to represent some sort of running gag. Then, when we discover he is armless, we are brought up short, and moved to pity: a strong ironic point has been scored. But Stroheim refuses to stop there. As Mrs. Hughes proceeds to fondle and caress one of the veteran's armless sleeves, pity quickly turns into disquieting morbidity, and what we've previously been led to ignore we're now obliged to dwell upon. In a brief instant that illuminates the rest of the film, comedy turns into tragedy and the tragedy becomes a fetish. It is a remarkable transformation of tone, created throughout by a series of false narrative expectations . . . If **Blind Hus-**

bands squats somewhere uncomfortably between a "symbolic" play and a cheap novella, **Foolish Wives** all but invents the novelistic cinema.

How does **Foolish Wives** resemble a nineteenth-century novel? By turning the spectacle of Griffith into an analysis of social and psychological textures—Monte Carlo was his *Intolerance* set—Stroheim asks us to move around in his frames and episodes in a way that grants us some of the freedom and leisure of a reader's experience. Griffith's suspense montage has enough Kuleshovian (and Pavlovian) effects to deny the spectator the opportunity to use much of his intelligence. This creates momentum, to be sure, but Stroheim usually sweeps the spectator along with a different kind of persuasion. Griffith either lulls or harasses you into the role of just plain folks; Stroheim starts with the assumption that you're witty, discerning, and twice as sophisticated as the fellow sitting next to you. Karamzin may be a sneak fooling that American ambassador and his wife with his phony credentials, but he doesn't fool us.

We hate him because he is evil; we love him because we know him: that's probably why we love to hate him. Stroheim loves to hate him too; it is something he is sharing with us as much as showing us. It is a very strange process: what the actor creates, the filmmaker annihilates and the portrait is as merciless as the character. He is confidential about what he shows us, like a novelist; he tells us the kind of things that are going on behind closed doors, when certain people are out of earshot. He wins our confidence by telling us secrets.

III

I had graduated from the D. W. Griffith school of filmmaking and intended to go the Master one better as regards film realism. In real cities, not corners of them designed by Cedric Gibbons or Richard Days, but in real tree-bordered boulevards, with real streetcars, buses and automobiles, through real winding alleys, with real dirt and foulness, in the gutters as well as in real castles and palaces. . . . I believed audiences were ready to witness real drama and real tragedy; as it happens every day in every land; real love and real hatred of real men and women who were proud of their passions.

—Stroheim, date unknown

It is witty for Godard to suggest that Méliès made documentaries, and rewarding to look at Feuillade's films under that aspect; but Stroheim turned the fiction film into the documentary in a much more central and decisive way. He did this above all in **Greed,** and not so much through "stripping away artifice" as by reformulating the nature that his artifice was to take.

This was not simply a matter of shooting **Greed** on locations. More crucially, it was a direct confrontation with the challenge of adapting a literary work. *McTeague* is a work of fiction that impressed Stroheim and his contemporaries for its "realism"; by attempting to arrive at an equivalent to this literary mode, Stroheim wound up having to deal exhaustively with all of the essential problems inherent in adapting *any* fictional prose work. There was certainly no filmmaker prior to Stroheim who attacked these problems in quite so comprehensive a manner, and it is arguable whether there has been anyone else since. For this reason alone, *Greed* remains a laboratory experiment of the first importance—valuable for its failures as well as its successes, and comprising a virtual textbook on some of the formal issues that it raises.

When Stroheim filmed *Greed* Kenneth Rexroth tells us in the Signet edition of Norris's novel, "he is said to have followed *McTeague* page by page, never missing a paragraph. We'll never know because the uncut *Greed*, greatest of all movies, is lost forever." To understand the important aspects of Stroheim's adaptation, the first step is to dismiss hyperbole of this sort and work with the materials available: the novel, Stroheim's screenplay, the version of *Greed* that we *do* have, and the existing stills of scenes that were cut from the film.

The first thing that the published script tells us is that an enormous amount of material has been added to the novel, particularly in the opening scenes. About sixty pages—nearly one-fifth of the screenplay—pass before we reach McTeague eating his Sunday dinner at the car conductors' coffee joint, the subject of Norris's first sentence. Mac's life prior to his arrival in San Francisco is conveyed by Norris in a brief résumé of two paragraphs; in the script it consumes twenty-five pages. A brilliantly designed sequence that runs even longer, and is completely missing from the final version of the film, introduces us to all of the major characters on a "typical" Saturday afternoon that precedes the novel's opening.

Interestingly, this sequence is largely constructed around cross-cutting between characters whose interrelations in the plot have not yet become clarified—and in the case of Mac and Trina, between characters who have not yet even met—so that the juxtapositions are unusually abstract, even from a thematic point of view. As an approach to narrative that was already common to prose fiction but far from being a convention in cinema, this is probably the most "advanced" and experimental departure in the script: nearly everything that takes place is descriptive and inconsequential as plot, and each character is linked into an overall pattern of significance that nothing in the story has yet justified. Harry Carr, one of the only people who saw *Greed* in its complete form, may have had this sequence partially in mind when he compared the film to *Les Misérables* and remarked that "Episodes come along that you think have no bearing on the story, then twelve or fourteen reels later, it hits you with a crash." (*Motion Picture Magazine,* April 1924.)

Undoubtedly the most problematical element in Stroheim's adaptation is its use of repeated symbolic motifs—shots of gold, greedy hands, animals and other emblems—which seem to be a direct misapplication of literary principles to cinematic structures. The recurrent image in *McTeague* of Mac's canary "chittering in its little gilt prison"—a phrase repeated with slight variations in many contexts, before it appears as the final words in the novel—works symbolically and "musically" because it is laced smoothly into the thread of the narrative, with no breaks in discourse or syntax. But in *Greed* the repeated images have the disadvantage of interrupting the narrative, usually without adding any useful perspectives to it: they are like footnotes that mainly say "Ibid." In their limited use in the film that we have and their *implied* use in the script, they tend to seem like dead wood clinging to the rest of the film.

The script further leads us to suspect that many of the motifs are repeated without variation—like the mother rocking the cradle in *Intolerance*—and occasionally without any naturalistic explanation, like the shot of wood being sawed, which recurs no less than eight times during the wedding sequence. Such a shot is a purely abstract intrusion, but not one that serves to expand the narrative; like Tolstoy's historical arguments in *War and Peace,* it seeks to contract the total picture into a graspable, didactic design. And it fails, one can argue, for roughly the same reason that Tolstoy fails—because Stroheim has more to show than he has to say. The world he creates in the wedding sequence alone overwhelms anything he has to say about it: it is too rich to accommodate supplementary lessons.

Which brings us back to the "realism," the documentary aspect of *Greed*. Clearly one of its most extraordinary aspects remains the unusual conviction of the performances, which is apparent even in the random instants offered by stills. Look at any frame enlargement from *Greed* showing ZaSu Pitts, Gibson Gowland or Jean Hersholt and you'll see not a familiar actor "playing a part," but a fully rounded character *existing*—existing, as it were, between shots and sequences as well as within them (or such is the illusion). How many films in the history of acted cinema would pass this elementary litmus test? Certainly not *Citizen Kane;* perhaps *The Magnificent Ambersons,* a film whose achievement (and mutilation) parallels that of *Greed* in many important respects.

One recalls André Bazin's famous remark about Stroheim: "In his films reality lays itself bare like a suspect confessing under the relentless examination of the commissioner of police. He has one simple rule for direction. Take a close look at the world, keep on doing so, and in the end it will lay bare for you all its cruelty and its ugliness. One could easily imagine as a matter of fact a film by Stroheim composed of a single shot as longlasting and as closeup as you like."

This is the spirit of documentary—a tendency that is equally present in Stroheim's introduction of outside chance elements into his fictions. It's not so much a matter of letting random accidents creep into the staged actions (as in Léonce Perret's 1913 melodrama *L'Enfant de Paris,* when a friendly dog wanders into a shot at the heels of an actor) as a sort of semi-organized psycho-drama, exemplified in a scene missing from current prints of **Greed:** When Trina discovers Maria Macapa with her throat slit, she runs out of Zerkow's junk house and hysterically reports the murder to the first people she sees. Stroheim shot this sequence with hidden cameras, and the responses came from passersby who were not aware that a film was being made. When Samuel Fuller used a similar technique at the beginning of *The Crimson Kimono* (1959) and Godard followed the hero of *Le petit soldat* (1960) down the streets of Geneva holding a gun, they were drawing on a common principle that Stroheim had already made extensive use of thirty-five years ago.

IV

O Love—without thee marriage is a savage mockery.

—opening title of **The Wedding March**

Greed stands at roughly the halfway point in Stroheim's fifteen-year career as a director, constituting both a caesura and a change of direction in his *oeuvre.* Four features precede it and four follow it, and beneath the continuity of certain undeniable stylistic and thematic traits, Stroheim's preoccupation with realism, his concern with narrative, and the nature of his ambition all undergo important transformations.

The first thing to be said about **The Merry Widow,** the film immediately following **Greed,** is that it represents a nearly total inversion of the former's approach: after filming his least compromised, most "realistic" work, he promptly made a film that was his most compromised and least "realistic." At its best, **The Merry Widow** has a lightness of touch and a grace of movement suggesting a pre-sound musical, with an idealized fairy-tale landscape (clearly established in the opening shots) that necessitates a very different kind of discourse. The most striking offbeat elements in this Hollywood dream bubble—Prince Mirko (Roy D'Arcy) and Baron Sadoja (Tully Marshall)—figure in the overall scheme in a way that is analogous to the "marginal notations" of irreverence that characterize most of Buñuel's films in the Fifties: they offer ironic swipes at the conventional aspects of the material without ever seriously threatening the root assumptions of these conventions.

Prince Mirko is an obvious derivation of Erich von Steuban and Count Karamzin, but his role here is not as central: as a foil to the romantic figure of Prince Danilo (John Gilbert), he can not wield the same kind of lethal authority. Similarly, the more grotesque part of Baron Sadoja—a "first draft," as it were, of the even more monstrous Jan Vooyheid, incarnated by Tully Marshall in **Queen Kelly**—is allowed to function as a grim commentary on the action and an intrusion on the central love story, but at no point is he really permitted to dominate the film.

Regarding **The Merry Widow** as a transitional work, one can perhaps best understand Mirko and Sadoja not as

"realistic" intrusions—they are anything but that!—but as rebellious counter fantasies provoked by the more conventional fantasies embodied by Danilo and Sally O'Hara (Mae Murray). If the earlier films were an attempt to subvert Hollywood from an outsider's position—eliminating the characteristically romantic leads, and in the case of **Greed,** literally moving out of the studios to locations—**The Merry Widow** announces the counterstrategy of boring from within. There is more than one prefiguration of this procedure in **The Merry Widow.** The most celebrated instance occurs in the theater, when Sadoja, Mirko and Danilo each look at the dancing heroine through opera glasses: the first concentrates on her feet, the second on her body, the third on her face.

Another noticeable shift in Stroheim's style is a somewhat different use of durations in relation to narrative. In the silent films after **Greed,** despite Stroheim's continued interest in making long films, the novelistic aspect becomes less important, and the ritualistic, ceremonial aspects of duration gradually come to the fore—the obsessive desire to keep looking at something not in order to "understand" or "decode" it, but in order to become totally absorbed in it, transfixed by it; not to penetrate the surfaces of things, but to revel in these surfaces. As suggested earlier, the aggressivess of Stroheim's camera eye ultimately leads to a kind of passivity. In the films after **Greed,** this change becomes much more explicit. The belligerent eye of the skeptic gradually turns into the passive eye of the voyeur.

This generalization tends to oversimplify a great deal of Stroheim's work, and probably shouldn't be taken as literally as it is stated above; but it does help to account for the peculiarly dreamlike elongations of actions and scenes in **The Merry Widow, The Wedding March,** and **Queen Kelly.** A simple comparison might help to clarify the difference: when the camera slowly approaches Dale Fuller's face in **Foolish Wives** to reveal the revenge plans being formed in her eyes, the lingering effect has a purely narrative function, permitting us to watch a *process* more clearly than we could otherwise. But when the camera slowly tracks up to the face of Mae Murray in her wedding dress, and then recedes a bit to frame her entire figure as she proceeds to tear up the dress, we are being asked to concentrate on her primarily as an *object;* the "process" at work is chiefly the camera movement itself. We can intuit that the character's visible distress leads to her act of violence, but the steps leading from A to B are implied more than chronicled. They are the scene's justification, but not its major focus.

Nor is it just a question of the relative lack of virtuosity in Murray's performance. Gloria Swanson's performance in **Queen Kelly** is quite adept in its development and exposition of motives. But this is no longer the camera's primary subject: virtually all of the characters in Stroheim's last silent films exist as essences, fixed points of reference—"static essentials," to borrow Pavese's phrase. That Stroheim intended to show Kelly undergoing a complete transformation—from innocent to brothel madam to queen—must be acknowledged, but the evidence of this change was not recorded on film; it isn't until *Walking Down Broadway* that we find a visible (if partial) throwback to a "narrative performance" in the part of ZaSu Pitts as Millie.

The Merry Widow announces a more static view of action and character; *The Wedding March* and *Queen Kelly* both epics of slow motion, expand and sustain it. It is hardly accidental that religious and military ceremonies figure so importantly in these films—they, too, are "static essentials." The "realistic" impulse goes through no less pronounced a change: the European countries of *The Merry Widow* and *Queen Kelly* are fantasy kingdoms, and even the celebrated accuracy of detail in the Vienna of *The Wedding March* is subject to fanciful additions (e.g., the use of the wedding march in a Catholic ceremony) and idealizations. "I am through with black cats and sewers," Stroheim is reported to have said while making the film. "I am going to throw perfumed apple blossoms at the public until it chokes on them. If people won't look upon life as it is, we must give them a gilded version."

And a gilded version is what *The Wedding March* supplies. Even though the villain Schani (Matthew Betz), a pigsty and a slaughterhouse are all clearly intended to offset the apple blossoms, these supposedly "realistic" elements are just as idealized as the romantic ones. Next to Stroheim's other villains, Schani is a crude cardboard cutout who is never allowed to expand beyond a few basic mannerisms (mainly spitting); and the other major characters—Prince Nicki (Stroheim), Mitzi (Fay Wray) and Cecelia (ZaSu Pitts)—are unusually simplistic creations for Stroheim.

One could be charitable (and many critics have been) by regarding the figures and themes of *The Wedding March* as mythic distillations of their counterparts in previous Stroheim films; or one can be less charitable and regard them as inert calcifications—rigid prototypes whose original *raison d'être* is lacking. *The Wedding March* is generally accorded a high place in the Stroheim canon, and it must be admitted that it has a magisterial, "definitive" quality that is missing from most of his other work. But speaking from a minority viewpoint, I might argue that a certain price has to be paid for this rather self-conscious classicism. Apart from rare scenes—like the remarkably subtle exchange of looks and gestures between Nicki and Mitzi during the Corpus Christi procession—the action, characters, and symbolic motifs (e.g., the Iron Man) are so schematically laid out that they assume a certain thinness; investigation is consistently bypassed for the sake of a polished presentation, and the eighth time that we see Schani spit could just as functionally be the second time or the ninth.

Seen purely on its own terms, *The Wedding March* is undeniably an impressive work. Offering us spectacle more than drama, it is a stunning display of lavishness and an ironic commentary on a particular kind of royal decay lurking underneath. It is only when we place it alongside *Foolish Wives, Greed,* and *Queen Kelly* that we can understand its limitations. What these films (and even the others, to lesser degrees) possess that *The Wedding March* lacks is an acute sense of *transgression*. And it is precisely this sense that makes *Queen Kelly,* for all its own limitations, a more pungent and exciting work. If *The Wedding March* converts many of the familiar Stroheim themes into a series of dry homilies and mottoes, all suitable for immediate framing, *Queen Kelly* converts many of these same themes into a species of delirium—a possessed work of hypnotic, almost hallucinatory intensity. In contrast to the icy elegance of *The Wedding March, Queen Kelly* breathes fire.

It is trashy, yes; but in the best sense, like Matthew G. Lewis's *The Monk* and Faulkner's *Sanctuary*. And at certain moments it achieves an elegance of its own, an elegance recalling that of a Nathanael West or a Georges Bataille, at least in stylistic control and continuity.

Which is not to praise *Queen Kelly* for its literary qualities: it has none, or at least no more than Stroheim's novels like *Paprika* do. On the contrary, *Greed* and location work aside, it is the most "cinematic" of his films, the one most alive to the medium's formal possibilities. The lighting is his most richly orchestrated, the camera moves about with an unprecedented freedom (assuming the hero's angle of vision, for instance, as it scans the doors in the convent for Kelly's room), and the use of duration has never been quite as operative as it becomes here. *Queen Kelly* is Stroheim uncensored—which is to say, more kinky, due to the effect and implications of the durations, than he probably ever intended it to be.

The unnatural protraction of the fire-side seduction scene and (most particularly) the marriage of Kelly to Jan Vooyheid over the figurative and literal corpse of her aunt, would probably seem more sentimental and less carnal if they were trimmed down to conventional lengths. As they stand, they tend to create an emotional detachment in the spectator by making the actors and settings into purely aesthetic objects, delectable or abhorrent surfaces arranged in such a way that the possibilities of identifying with them or sentimentalizing them are decreased. Considering the *increase* in sentimentality in all of Stroheim's films after *Greed,* this is rather a throwback to the dryer, more "scientific" style of his earlier period, but here it is exercised on a fictional world that is substantially more metaphysical and dreamlike, and less concerned with sociological and psychological matters. *Queen Kelly* is probably the closest thing in the Stroheim canon to an abstract work, a self-enclosed film that secretes its own laws. The sense of transgression that we experience in the previous films is always grounded in morality; here it seems to come to life as a direct expression of the id—as when Queen Regina (Seena Owen) beats Kelly with a whip across an enormous hall, down a grand flight of steps, and out the door of the palace—and morality mainly seems to figure in the action like the memory of a bad dream.

Unconsummated lust, a sustaining leitmotif throughout Stroheim's work—a stale-mated struggle reflected in the pull between the nineteenth and twentieth-century aspects of his art—is finally stretched out into a slow-motion revery that is studied as if it were taking place under a microscope. Vooyheid is even literally seen as an insect, when he appears in the final marriage-and-death sequence comprising the recently discovered "African footage: a scarred preying mantis on crutches, with a cigar in his teeth (or fist) and various objects sticking out of his pockets like additional legs, and a tongue that moves over his lips like a feeler.

He and Kelly stand on opposite sides of the aunt's deadbed; a wedding veil is fashioned out of a bed awning by some local prostitutes. Intercut with close-ups of Kelly in tears are shots of the black priest—who, like her, is dressed in white—from her viewpoint, blurring (to suggest tears) and then turning into an image of Prince Wolfram in white robes; another blur, and the Prince is in a black uniform; still another blur, and we return to the black priest in white. When her aunt expires, Kelly throws herself down on the body; the priest kneels; and then Vooyheid, who is kneeling, slowly raises himself on his crutches until he is the only figure standing.

As far as the silent cinema is concerned, this Manichaean spectacle constitutes Stroheim's last rites: an arbitrary ending, perhaps—it was certainly not the one he had in mind for **Queen Kelly**—but an appropriately emblematic conclusion nevertheless. With the death of the aunt, we arrive at the imminent loss of innocence and the ascension to power of pure evil—a lurid ellipsis and a suspension of possibilities that were already rather explicit in **Blind Husbands**. But the "message" is no longer, "Watch out for him!" It has become, simply, "Look at him!" And were it not for the somewhat problematical footnote provided by **Hello, Sister!,** one might say that Stroheim's career as a director ends at roughly the same time that virtually all remaining pretense of free will vanishes from his imaginary kingdom.

EPILOGUE

Do you like funerals? I saw the cutest one last Saturday. . . . I'm just a fool *about funerals!*

—Millie (ZaSu Pitts) in *Hello, Sister!*

Even in its mutilated, garbled, and partially reshot form, **Hello, Sister!,** the release version of **Walking Down Broadway,** is recognizably Stroheim for a substantial part of its running time. The "final shooting script" of **Walking Down Broadway**—dated 8/9/32, assigning story and continuity to Stroheim, and dialogue to Stroheim, Leonard Spigelgass, and Geraldine Nomis—helps us to understand some of the original intentions, but also suggests that even in its original state it would have been a minor Stroheim work. The absence of certain audacities and eccentricities in the release version—which include Mac (Terrance Ray) on a dance floor "[holding] up his

middle finger at Jimmy," jokes about Prohibition, and various things relating to Millie (such as her pet turtle Lady Godiva and her dialogue with Miss Platt, a middle-aged hunchback)—are somewhat offset by various banalities that are also missing. The ending of the film that we have is a standard Hollywood clincher; but it is hardly much worse than the one prefigured in the script, in which "Peggy and Jimmy walk close to show-window and look. Wax baby in Nurses' arms—as before—except window is dressed for Easter." Peggy says "(Motherly): isn't it *cute?*" Jimmy says "(Fatherly): *Sure* is!" And "They draw close together and look at each other admiringly."

Much of the interest in **Hello, Sister!** today derives from the opportunity to see Stroheim recasting many of his most familiar procedures in the context of sound. The repetitive character trait that would have been expressed visually in **The Wedding March**—e.g., Schani spitting—is conveyed here in the dialogue: Mac uses the phrase "Catch on?" nearly two dozen times in the script, much as Veronica (Françoise Lebrun) continually makes use of "un maximum" in Jean Eustache's recent *The Mother and the Whore*. Elsewhere the dialogue often becomes less functional and tends to distract from the visuals. The Southern and New York accents of Peggy (Boots Mallory) and Jimmy (James Dunn) are important aspects of the characters, but their narrative function is not controlled in the way that the actors' visual presences are. When Jimmy provokes Millie's sexual jealousy in a scene near the end by refusing her help ("You're all right, Millie—but you wouldn't understand"), the extraordinary expressiveness of ZaSu Pitts's reaction—the way her eyes flare up at his casual dismissal—is as striking as the close-up of Dale Fuller already alluded to in **Foolish Wives**. (The relationship doesn't stop there: both characters suffer from sexual rejection, and take revenge by starting fires which provoke the grand finales of both films.) But Pitts's acting in this case becomes the *subtext* of the dialogue rather than vice versa, a classic instance of the way that sound films often teach spectators not to see; the mystery inherent in her character tends to be minimized by the "explicating" power of the dialogue, and what might have been twice as powerful in a silent context can easily escape attention here.

To some degree, the dialogue in **Hello, Sister!** only makes more explicit some of the schematic simplifications of character and situation that are constants in Stroheim's work, negating some of the openness and the demands on the spectator's imagination imposed by silence. In every silent Stroheim film but **Greed**, the sound of English or American voices invading the continental kingdoms would surely have worked as an alienating factor. **Hello, Sister!,** which relates back to **Greed** in many respects (Mac and Jimmy are derived from Mac and Marcus, and even a lottery figures comparably in the **Walking Down Broadway** script), is set in New York, and doesn't have to deal with this problem—indeed, the accents and inflections here are aids to verisimilitude—but at the same time, the screen is no longer quite the tabula rasa that it was, and the characteristic Stroheim Stare (the trained concentration of the camera on his fictional world) recedes somewhat under the verbiage, which frees us partially from the responsibility of looking.

The major stylistic developments in Stroheim's career took place between *Blind Husbands* and *Foolish Wives.* One can speak of additional developments up through *Greed,* but after that one can principally refer only to certain simplifications and refinements. This is surely characteristic of Hollywood cinema in general, where Howard Hawks can devote a lifetime to refining *Fig Leaves* and *A Girl in Every Port,* and even a director as "experimental" as Hitchcock is periodically forced to retreat to the formulas of earlier successes. In the case of a maverick like Stroheim, the miracle—apart from his remarkable early development—is not that he wasn't able to develop his style after *Greed,* but that he was able to make further films at all.

And in order to do so, he clearly had to pay a price. Whether or not future work in sound films would have led to other stylistic developments is impossible to determine; at best, all that *Hello, Sister!* suggests is the desire to accommodate his style to sound rather than to expand its basic options. Considering its relatively small budget, *Blind Husbands* can be seen as another sort of accommodation; and in a sense the evidence of the best in *Hello, Sister!* is comparable. It marks Stroheim as a promising director.

Tom Milne (essay date 1985)

SOURCE: "Sparing No Hint of Verismo," in *Sight & Sound,* Vol. 54, No. 4, 1985, pp. 301-2.

[*In the following essay, Milne examines a restored version of Stroheim's* Queen Kelly.]

Hitherto, prints of *Queen Kelly* have ended, satisfactorily if unsatisfyingly, with Gloria Swanson's despairing leap from the bridge (followed, in the version issued by Swanson in 1931, by a coda not directed by Stroheim in which Prince Wolfram made it a double suicide). Although the watchman is seen jumping to the rescue, making it obvious that the convent-bred innocent deflowered by her princely admirer would in fact be saved and go on to justify the title through her subsequent metamorphosis into Queen Kelly, it worked well enough as a typical Hollywood tale of the bitter-sweet wages of sin, rendered untypical by the magnificence, the daring and the detail of Stroheim's imagery. The sense of dissatisfaction lay in the lack of any clue, even if one knew in broad outline how the story was to continue, as to how Stroheim would contrive to escalate this somewhat linear bitter-sweet ambience into his own uniquely characteristic blend (cf *The Wedding March*) composed of equal parts of pure cynicism and pure romanticism.

The present version of *Queen Kelly* (Contemporary), 're-stored' by Kino International with the aid of titles, stills

and some fifteen minutes of footage from the African sequences shot by Stroheim before Swanson called a halt to the production, offers at least some of the answers. Easy to recognise the Stroheim touch in the arbitrarily cruel hand of fate which, not content with toppling Patricia Kelly from the ecstasy of her tryst with Prince Wolfram into the agony of being whipped from the palace by the mad queen, imagines the ultimate degradation of forced marriage to a filthy, gin-sodden, slaveringly lecherous and ageing cripple.

Stroheim spares no hint of verismo in the accumulation of squalor, which makes it unequivocally clear that the establishment Patricia Kelly is to inherit from her dying aunt in Dar-Es-Salaam is more bordello than dance-hall or gin-mill. He adds the final turn of the screw by having Tully Marshall, as the obscenely lascivious cripple, scuttle around Swanson on his crutches like some repellent arachnoid ensuring that the fly caught in his web is too securely enmeshed to escape. Directed with extraordinary intensity, almost gloatingly revelling in details of sweaty venality and squalid sexuality, these scenes arouse a sense of physical revulsion which is almost tangible, as events proceed inexorably towards what is in effect a wedding funeral. As the last rites are administered to the dying aunt, Patricia and the cripple, assembled at her beside as chief mourners, are first pledged to each other by the dying woman and then married as she literally croaks on the sidelines. Yet unexpectedly and almost inexplicably, the glittering splendours of the royal palace from the first half of the film are echoed, dimly but unmistakably, as the dingy African shack is transformed not only by the pristine whiteness of the black priest's robes, the pyx, orb and censer wielded by his acolytes, the candles that soften the harsh light, the flowers that bring memories of romance, but by the gracefully flowing lines of the mosquito net pressed into service as a wedding veil for the bride.

Although Stroheim's extravagance is generally cited as the main reason why production was halted on *Queen Kelly* with more than half the film still to be shot, Gloria Swanson's autobiography innocently reveals that moral outrage was an equally important factor. Already shocked to realise, in viewing the rushes, that Stroheim had slipped in a reaction shot of Walter Byron (as Prince Wolfram) amusedly sniffing the drawers that Patricia Kelly hurls at him in embarrassment after inadvertently losing them on their first encounter, Swanson revealingly commented, 'Since everything else was so beautiful, I decided not to exercise my veto on the matter until the proper time came.' But the African scenes evidently brought that proper time forward, since they seemed to her not only 'rank and sordid and ugly'—which they were—but 'utterly unrelated to the European scenes and the characters in them'—which is nonsense unless one is thinking in terms of pure Hollywood convention.

On the contrary, in fact, the African scenes are clearly designed as a mirror image reflecting the European ones, and demonstrating the extent to which a little cosmetic decoration—like the perfume once used by aristocrats to mask the odour of unwashed bodies—can transform ugliness into beauty. Throughout the first half of the film, in the context furnished by Seena Owen's marvellous mad queen—the very epitome of Stroheimian-Ruritanian degeneracy—Prince Wolfram seems more sinned against than sinning. Although he is first seen falling off his horse in a drunken stupor after a night of debauchery with his military cronies and some complaisant courtesans, and although he engineers the seduction of innocent Patricia Kelly with the cunning of a master, he can still play the romantic hero since he is presented as another helpless fly struggling against the spider of Queen Regina's cruelly selfish whims and jealousies. Yet his cigar butts *do* litter the ashtray in her bedroom with their betraying presence; and when his mirror image is presented in the person of the crippled trader, one is invited to wonder just how far the queen's madness is a reaction to the cooling of what may once have been his ardent passion, and how far his initial pursuit of Patricia Kelly—though later transformed into genuine love, perhaps simply by the overwhelming ambience of moonlight, roses and innocence—was motivated by the same pure lust that activates the cripple.

With this intimation that the idyllic tryst between Patricia and Wolfram in the palace heralded not only her downfall but also his first step on the road to redemption, a characteristically romantic Stroheim schema is adumbrated whereby the ex-roué and the new brothel madam could meet again—and love—on equal terms. Unlike the original prints, this reconstituted version makes for a satisfying conception but unsatisfactory viewing, in that the 'reconstitution' brings the truncation of the film even more forcefully to mind than before. With explanatory titles swept aside by the overwhelming intensity of the images, *Queen Kelly* now leaves one nursing, willy-nilly, a sense of disgust at the gleeful miserabilism which abandons poor Patricia Kelly to rot in the clutches of a monster. One would not willingly dispense with the pleasure afforded by the African footage; but one is, in a sense, further from Stroheim's intention than ever.

Thomas K. Dean (essay date 1990)

SOURCE: "Thematic Differences between Norris's *McTeague* and von Stroheim's *Greed,*" in *Literature Film Quarterly*, Vol. 18, No. 2, 1990, pp. 96-102.

[*In the following essay, Dean discusses the differences between Stroheim's* Greed *and the original novel on which it was based.*]

The surprisingly few critics who have compared Frank Norris's novel *McTeague* and Erich von Stroheim's film adaptation *Greed* invariably assume that Norris is an imitator of Emile Zola rather than an author with his own thematic program, and they fail to take into account von Stroheim's consistent Judeo-Christian sin/punishment ethic that informs all his other films. The common belief

is that von Stroheim's adaptation is a sentence-by-sentence reconstruction of an ersatz Zola novel. I wish to compare *McTeague* and *Greed* once again with a greater awareness of both artists' thematic agendas. To illustrate the differences between the novel and film, I will focus on a specific image in the film, that of McTeague kissing his bird as he releases it while dying in the desert at the end of the film, which subtly but fundamentally alters the philosophical framework of Norris's tale of avarice and atavism.

McTeague's delicate act of compassion at the end of von Stroheim's film seems out of character for Norris's McTeague, who has experienced an atavistic decline into a brute state. This degeneration is not necessarily a replication of Zolaesque naturalistic thematics and "scientific method," however. Of course, it would be foolish to claim that Norris was not influenced by Zola, as Lars Åhnebrink has definitively demonstrated. Norris shares with all the French naturalists an interest in documentary detail and at least some philosophical interest in questions of evolution and degeneration. But Norris's interest in Zola lies primarily in what he calls Zola's "Romanticism," his sensational subject matter and grandiose effects, not his deterministic philosophies. While Norris recognizes the existence of a fundamental human beast in *McTeague* (and other novels), he does not believe in an inevitable decline to that state. Actually, neither does Zola, if one reads *The Experimental Novel* carefully, but Zola's goal in most of his novels is to pointedly engender, depict, and study that decline. Norris does so in only two of his novels, *Vandover and the Brute* and *McTeague*. If one were to take his complete corpus into account, one would see that Norris's concerns are more far-reaching.

Norris's major concern in his novels is the problem of disconnection from vital experience in favor of aestheticization and intellectualization. He explores this problem in his criticism through a dialectic of "Life" and "Literature." "Life," which Norris finds a positive force, means firsthand, natural experience, and "Literature," a negative force, means secondhand, artificial experience. The concept of "Life" encompasses emotion, instinct, passion, violence, strength, and a vital connection to nature in living one's life and depicting it in art. Norris's concept of "Literature" focuses on cultivation away from what he sees as basic to human nature, and encompasses overeducation, aestheticization, refinement, artificiality, weakness, and devotion to mannered social intercourse over natural emotion. Norris's criticism is rife with exhortations to authors to experience the world, since vital literature, to be true, is "dependent solely upon fidelity to life for existence," and "it must be practiced in the very heart's heart of life, on the street corner, in the market place, not in the studios." The spectrum of Norris's novels, then, explores varying degrees of success and failure at his characters' aligning themselves to the proper life forces. *Blix,* for example, depicts characters flourishing when they practice honest and sincere love for each other rather than high society social conventions. Although *The Octopus* ends in tragedy for most of the characters,

Norris ends the novel with an affirmation that the forces of the Wheat and of the world are working themselves out to a positive end. *McTeague,* thus, does not suggest a universal application of the character's experience but presents an illustration of the consequences of mistaken living.

McTeague has chosen to find meaning in life through middle-class materialism as an end to itself. Aside from his lust for Trina, McTeague see the fulfillment of his human destiny in middle-class order and material comforts, in evenings in the parlor with his concertina, his pipe, and his bucket of steam beer. McTeague has failed to see that such pursuits are not ends unto themselves, but means to spiritual fulfillment, the same mistake that Walt Whitman saw most Americans making. McTeague is a case of arrested development, failing to move beyond the stage of materialistic acquisition to what Whitman would see as the latent spirit of the common man, the "ensemble-Individuality," and what Norris would see as "Life." For Norris, materialism for its own sake is a false intellectual construct and thus a false force with which to align oneself in the conduct of life. This tenuous framework is easily destroyed in the novel by the machinations of Marcus Schouler. Without this construct, McTeague has nothing left but his animal essentialism, an admittedly necessary component of "Life" for Norris, but not one to exist alone in its purest form. McTeague's hereditary alcoholism, his constitutional criminality, and his greed take over to propel him to this bestial state. In such a pure animal state, then, Norris's McTeague would never have kissed the bird at the end of the tale as von Stroheim's McTeague does.

It comes as no surprise that Erich von Stroheim would find *McTeague* striking sympathetic chords with himself, and thus it is understandable that one could easily conclude that Norris and von Stroheim are philosophical blood-brothers. Von Stroheim, too, railed against mannered sentimental fare, which Norris saw as over-aestheticized "literary" claptrap. The director insisted that his film would provide his viewers with 'knowledge of life as it is. . . . not . . . the shallow trash of mother love, father love, sister love'." As with Norris essential components of depicting "real life" are the shocking, the grotesque, even the lascivious, and the director announced with pride in an interview with Edwin Schallert that he intended to adapt Norris's novel as "a sinister and lasting triumph of sordid, though intense and magnificent, naturalism." And, as with Norris, von Stroheim emphasized the necessity for convincing realism through documentary detail. Von Stroheim was perhaps the most exacting Hollywood director of all time, and his legendary insistence on realistic detail reached its apex in *Greed,* especially in his refusal to use any studio sets, which led him to film in such locations as the actual closed Big Dipper Mine and Death Valley itself.

Thematically, Norris and von Stroheim do seem to intersect at first, for McTeague's attempt to rise above his bestial nature is rooted in establishing middle-class material comfort in both novel and film, and thus a "documentary method" of realistic detail emphasizing the material reflects characterization and theme. When atavism takes over, McTeague's physical and spiritual decline is constantly equated with the concurrent corruption of and loss of his material world. The $5000 has become meaningless in its inability to produce a material existence, so McTeague's life has become meaningless, and annihilation seems his inevitable end. It is only fitting that Mac's death occurs in perhaps the most material-less place on the earth, the desert, reflecting the loss of his goals, the wasteland of his spirit, as well as the death of his body. Since the novel emphasizes the material milieu as both reflection of and contributor to the character's decline, a visual representation of the story, a film adaptation, has a great chance for success. And it really comes as no surprise that von Stroheim would be the director to take up the challenge, for his strength as a director lies not in his editing, but in his *mise-en-scène.* Meaning is created through his accumulation of detail and the composition of his shot, not through the relationships between shots, the editing.

With such close affinities between Norris and von Stroheim, one could easily conclude that reports of von Stroheim's reputed sentence-by-sentence reconstruction of the novel must be accurate. But this is a blithe assumption, and an important detail like McTeague's kissing the bird at the end of the film casts doubt on the idea of direct thematic correspondence between novel and film. We have seen that a more comprehensive understanding of Norris's work can lead to a more accurate understanding of his novel. Likewise, a more comprehensive understanding of von Stroheim's work can lead to a more accurate understanding of his film and ultimately an explanation of the differences in McTeague's behavior at the end of the novel and the film.

Taken as a whole, von Stroheim's films work within a surprisingly consistent and rudimentary moral system despite their fascination with the grotesque and the licentious. As Joel Finler says, "the heroes may not always emerge victorious, but the villains invariably die horrible deaths." Evil never goes unpunished in von Stroheim: the seducer von Steuben of *Blind Husbands* falls to his death off the top of a mountain; the impostor/seducer Count Karamzin of *Foolish Wives* is murdered and stuffed down a sewer; in the epic tales of decadent turn-of-the-century Vienna, the prince who would be commoner inevitably loses the girl.

Concomitantly, Christian symbols loom over practically all the characters, sets, and action: the crucifixes, mountain-path shrines, and the sign in von Steuben's bedroom that ironically reads "In the Alps, there is no sin," all in *Blind Husbands;* the crucifix looming over Karamzin as his tower of seduction burns, and the powerful, haunting, almost iconic hollow-eyed monk who stares judgmentally through the Count in *Foolish Wives;* the ever-present crucifixes that appear throughout *The Merry Widow* and *The Wedding March,* and on and on. If there is any "force" determining lives in von Stroheim's films, it is the inevitable fundamentalist Christian judgment of sinners. As virtually all his characters are examples of one form of degradation or another, von Stroheim seems to view humanity as corrupt, decadent, and fallen, from the highest levels of Austrian aristocracy to the lowest levels of poverty-stricken junkmen. There is no evolution, no attempt at human progress and development through alignment with proper forces; there is only sin, a fully-developed humanity that has chosen to disobey God's morality and that has tumbled into iniquity. Despite the grandeur and breadth of von Stroheim's celluloid canvasses, their thematic dimensions are narrow and conventional.

Given von Stroheim's thematic consistency in all his other films, it seems prudent to place *Greed* in this context. The overt Christian symbolism is missing in *Greed,* but a series of subtle images does accumulate. Most immediately, Trina's headdress as McTeague performs dental work on her comes to mind. The resemblance to a nun's garb is unmistakable, and it is here that McTeague's "sinful" lust for the unconscious patient asserts itself (the rhetoric in both novel and film about McTeague being unable to subdue his animal passions suggests his desire is sinful.) A religious prohibition, however, surrounds Trina in the form of distinct Christian symbolism. Another important scene in the development of McTeague's lust for Trina occurs at the train stop during the rainstorm. Here McTeague proposes to Trina, kisses her violently, and declares that "I've got her!" Overlooking the two on the wall of the depot is an advertisement for "Pluto" drinking water, suggesting that what has transpired may be the work of the devil. The other great sin in the film is, of course, greed, and the Pluto drinking water appears again at Trina's bedside when she decides not to send money to her needy mother. Even more blatantly, one of the earliest scenes depicting Trina's growing miserliness occurs when she tricks Mac into buying her some lilies, saying she hasn't enough money when her purse is brimming. This scene takes place in front of a church, recalling von Stroheim's more obvious technique of overt Christian symbolism looming in judgment. Finally, the most heinous sin of all, Mac murdering Trina for her $5000, takes place in the kindergarten with a "Merry Christmas" banner and other Christmas decorations framing the act.

McTeague in *Greed* is fated to punishment for his sins and destruction by inherited tendencies, whereas in Norris, inherited tendencies destroy him only after his alignment with the wrong forces. But, given von Stroheim's implicit Judeo-Christian proclivities, these traits are inherited as a result of the Fall, and Original Sin is to be perpetually punished by God. In Norris's universe, there is potential for human development, though humanity's downfall is in fact determined if that potential is not reached, due to its bestial base nature. In von Stroheim's morally corrupt universe, there seems to be no human potential, as humans are from the beginning naturally depraved, almost in a Calvinistic sense.

Taken with this understanding of Norris's and von Stroheim's thematic concerns, McTeague's simple gesture at the end of the film produces important ramifications for his character. Von Stroheim emphasizes a compassionate part of McTeague's nature more than Norris by placing a shot of McTeague kissing a bird at the mine at the beginning of the film, an image that is powerfully imbedded in our visual memory due to its early placement, coloring our perception of McTeague throughout the narrative. The bird imagery is developed further with McTeague's canary. In both novel and film, the actions of the bird parallel the actions of its owner. As Charles Wolfe notes, in the film it "hops in its cage when he kisses the etherised Trina, happily accepts a mate when Mac marries, nestles with its companion when Mac and Trina embrace, and fights when Mac and Trina quarrel." In the film, the second bird which is introduced dies when Trina is murdered, and in both novel and film, the original bird becomes progressively weaker as McTeague regresses toward the brute throughout the Death Valley trek. But more importantly, the canary suggests that there are gentleness and civilization within the brute McTeague, and the film emphasizes it to a greater degree than the novel. In the novel, the cage is a gilt prison for this less brutish side, and, as Don Graham notes, "represents the civilization available to McTeague." McTeague then does not properly utilize the forces of that civilization available to him, the forces of Norris's "Life," and he swiftly regresses to the primitive that is so near to the surface.

In the film, however, McTeague does not lose that civilized aspect, even at the bitter end. Despite humanity's natural depravity, which does not equal primitiveness, it still struggles to attain closeness to God through ultimately futile attempts at obeying God's moral imperatives. Such attempts are vestiges of a pre-lapsarian goodness. At the wedding in the film, for example, McTeague presents Trina with a second canary, an event that does not occur in the novel. The caged, more "civilized" side is doubled, indicating the characters' strong belief and trust in the integrity and civilizing influence of Christian matrimony. In addition, McTeague's "theme song" is changed for the film. For the most part, Norris has him playing his "six mournful concertina airs" and singing the portentous "No one to love, none to caress,/Left all alone in this world's wilderness," suggesting the hollowness of his middle-class existence and the imminent degeneracy in the wilderness of Death Valley. In the film, however, he is "Nearer My God to Thee" from the start. Of course, in a depraved world, these attempts at spiritual fulfillment are futile. Punishment for sins inherited and committed (for McTeague, greed, lust, alcoholism, and murder) is humanity's only fate.

In both film and novel, then, McTeague carries the bird cage with him through the burning desert, and just as he is devastated, the bird, his hope for something better, is "chittering feebly." McTeague has sunk to the lowest level, doomed to death, chained to the bludgeoned Marcus, in the inferno of the sandy wastes. The film alters the end, however, by having the gentler side of McTeague return. He gently takes the bird, caresses it, and in a repetition of the gesture that opened the film, kisses it. His final act is to release the bird, the human spirit that makes one final dramatic attempt at triumphing over its punishment, before it falls dead to the ground. In von Stroheim's Judeo-Christian context, then, this compassionate humanity, as represented by the bird, is merely an icon of the already-lost spiritual potential of fallen humanity. It is a pre-lapsarian vestige with no potential, but it remains extant, as McTeague's fate is more a punishment for basic human evil than a degeneration. For Norris, on the other other hand, McTeague has lost his real and exploitable human potential once he aligns himself with materialism and has that incomplete and thus false framework knocked out from under him. McTeague cannot even feebly attempt to free the potential human spirit at the end of Norris's novel since it no longer exists. He has forsaken the potential for a false ethic, and is left with only a prehistoric brutality.

With a fuller understanding of Norris's and von Stroheim's philosophical contexts, it is easy to see that *McTeague* and *Greed* are about very different views of the universe and are not doppelgangers. Whereas Norris is working with an artistic/philosophical system of "Life" through a vital connection to the natural world and experience, and which posits humankind's potential for development through alignment with proper natural forces, von Stroheim is working in a traditional Judeo-Christian tradition in which humanity is from the start essentially corrupt and naturally depraved, and in which its determined fate is punishment of sin. Ultimately, we must remember that the adaptation process filters materials through a different medium and a different artistic/philosophical consciousness, which will inevitably transform the work in question. With this reminder, perhaps critics can avoid the quick assumptions that have marred the understanding of such works as *McTeague* and *Greed* in the past.

Jared Gardner (essay date 1994)

SOURCE: "What Blood Will Tell: Hereditary Determinism in *McTeague & Greed*," in *Texas Studies in Literature & Language,* Vol. 36, No. 1, Spring, 1994, pp. 51-74.

[*In the following essay, Gardner examines the realism of Stroheim's films and Frank Norris's novels.*]

> We Anglo-Saxons are a fighting race. . . . Civilization is far from that time when the fighting man can be dispensed with.
>
> —Frank Norris (*Literary Criticism*)

> Against these assaults of inferiority . . . where can civilization look for its champions? Where but in the slender rank of the racially superior . . . this "thin red line" of rich, untainted blood which stands between us and barbarism or chaos.
>
> —Lothrop Stoddard

In the short history of film's silent era there were five adaptations of stories by Frank Norris. Two of these, the first and last, were significant moments in the development of American cinema. D. W. Griffith's *A Corner in Wheat* (1909), a one-reel condensation of Norris's "A Deal in Wheat," has been explicated elsewhere in terms of Norris's influence both on the film and on the technical innovations it introduced. However, Erich von Stroheim's *Greed* (1924), while regularly cited as one of the most ambitious films of the period and as the most faithful adaptation of a novel ever attempted, has not been accorded significant study of its relationship to its literary source. The criticism abounds in apocryphal accounts of the production of Stroheim's forty-five-reel transcription of Norris's novel and of its dismemberment at the hands of the studio system. It is Hollywood's Frankenstein, and though film historians relish in the creation and destruction of the monster, it remains to be explained why Stroheim created it in the first place.

Relying on troubling equations of the aims of literary naturalism in the 1890s with cinematic realism of the 1920s, Stroheim's manifestos on cinematic "realism" are cited as evidence of the ideological bond he shares with Norris, and his use of the static camera and the long take are summarily equated with Norris's stark focus on the characters and conditions of Polk Street. Yet such explanations seem unsatisfactory when considering what could have made this story of an immigrant community written by an aristocratic Harvard boy so central to the vision of an immigrant son of a Jewish hatter, a son who had in a few short years rewritten himself to become Erich von Stroheim, born of Austrian nobility to be the greatest director since D. W. Griffith. And they fail to answer the larger questions surrounding the preoccupation of early film with literary realism and naturalism as it attempted to define itself. What did Stroheim learn from Norris? What "realism" could they have shared?

To begin answering these questions, we must examine Norris's early writings from a standpoint that has been largely neglected. Though much has been said about the relation of Norris to Social Darwinism, the nativist theories articulated in Norris's own work have been largely ignored. To reconstruct this complex ground, I shall begin by outlining the intersections of naturalism and nativism at the end of the nineteenth century. After locating Norris's early work within this emerging logic, I shall discuss the nativism of the 1920s, its anxieties regarding heredity, and its authorization of the response to the new immigration. Finally, turning to *Greed,* I shall examine the film as an attempt to negotiate Norris's fledgling nativism (and, implicitly, the fully developed nativism of the 1920s), a response acted out within the last stronghold of the assimilationist dream: 1920s Hollywood.

In October 1893, an Irish laborer named Pat Collins brutally murdered his wife in the kindergarten where she taught. The story caught the eye of Frank Norris, then a senior at Berkeley. He had just finished a year of studying under the acclaimed American Social Darwinist, Joseph Le Conte, and he had recently discovered Zola. The account of the murder reached Norris as he had begun to move from the evolutionary optimism of Le Conte toward the darker determinism of Zola, and the story remained with him over the next few years as he began making plans for his first novel.

Le Conte, Norris's favorite teacher and one of the most widely read evolutionary theorists in this decade of popular science, preached a millenarian vision of the ultimate destiny of man. Social Darwinism, in its migration to America in the 1870s and 1880s, brought about a marriage of religion and science where Europeans had found only opposition, and Le Conte devoted his career to proving that evolutionary science and faith in the spiritual advancement of man were not mutually exclusive. For the American Darwinists of the time, man was moving toward a final stage of evolution, and the struggle now being waged was the fight for final supremacy between the spirit and the body: "Man is born of Nature into a higher nature. He therefore alone is possessed of two natures—a lower, in common with animals, and a higher, peculiar to himself. The whole mission and life-work of man is the progressive and finally the complete dominance . . . of the higher over the lower" (Le Conte). It was a struggle certain to be won by the forces of progress. As John Fiske, another influential U.S. evolutionary optimist, promised in 1884: "The most essential feature of Man is his improvableness. . . . The changes have been so great that in many respects the interval between the highest and the lowest men far surpasses the interval between the lowest men and the highest apes."

What gets left behind in this great march forward is "lowest man," crucial in his double function as both the proof of man's progress and the site of man's continuing struggle. American Darwinism saw the criminal deviant as a throwback, a laggard in the race toward man's perfection, and its scapegoated victim. Entering the twentieth century, man existed in a state of uneven development with the interval daily growing between the evolutionary vanguard and their atavistic brethren; the criminal served as the motivation for the final act of "throwing off the Brute-Inheritance" (Fiske). Crime was thus a catalyst in natural selection; as the sociologist Arthur Cleveland Hall promised: "Crime is an inevitable social evil, the dark side of the shield of human progress. . . . The production of crime and criminals is one of the saving processes of nature, substituting a lesser for a greater evil, promoting upward progress at a smaller cost."

For Norris, after a year with Le Conte, Zola's darker naturalism must have constituted a rebellion of sorts, a rejection of the blithe optimism of the popular scientists in his own country. But why Norris would have been drawn away from this optimism, and why the account of Collins's murder became so central for him at this moment, is not fully explained by the influence of Zola. Attempts to line Norris up with the dark side of evolutionary theory as he encountered it in Zola or in Max Nordau's *Degeneracy* fail to read through the local

framework within which Norris's anxious vision of America's destiny was generated. It is in what is often bracketed and dismissed as Norris's "Anglo-Saxonism" that we locate the nativist anxieties that captured Norris's imagination at the time he was writing *McTeague*.

The 1890s saw the reawakening of a xenophobia that had lain dormant since the Civil War. Increasing immigration, coupled with labor unrest and economic depression, resulted in the first wave of modern nativist legislation. However, as John Higham tells it, the scientific optimism of men such as Le Conte and Fiske worked to hold this emergent nativism temporarily in check: "To a generation of intellectuals steeped in confidence, the laws of evolution seemed to guarantee that the 'fittest' races would most certainly triumph over inferior competitors. . . . Darwinism, therefore, easily ministered to Anglo-Saxon pride, but in the age of confidence it could hardly arouse Anglo-Saxon anxiety." For the majority of the theorists of race and immigration in the 1890s, faith was maintained in the defensive powers of American soil and Anglo-Saxon blood. But the emerging social sciences—especially criminology as it came to America through the writings of Cesare Lombroso—found reason to look to the growing number of immigrants with increasing foreboding.

As the passages from Le Conte and Fiske illustrated, one of the questions haunting social science of the time was how, if man is the summit of evolution, can so many criminals exist? Criminology, with its attempts to identify, classify, and ultimately regulate the lower rungs in man's evolutionary ladder, was founded to answer the question. Autopsying and measuring hundreds of criminals, Lombroso identified the criminal man's physical characteristics: he was a primitive man, an "atavistic being who reproduces in his person the ferocious instincts of primitive humanity and the inferior animals." In the United States, this throwback was identified increasingly with the immigrant populations; and with the rising tide of immigration, confidence in natural selection's ability to deal with the atavistic elements of the population was shaken. By the 1890s, criminologists were examining the effects of immigration on the genetic makeup of the United States, mapping the inroads of Lombroso's Criminal Man into society, reading crime as an invading germ in an otherwise natural field of evolution. Thus, criminology, founded upon a disease model of criminality coincident with an unprecedented wave of immigration, led to speculations that would not be voiced explicitly until eugenics offered new authority in the following decade: immigrants are breeding a nation of criminals in the United States.

Stephen Jay Gould writes, "Lombrosian criminal anthropology had its primary influence in bolstering the basic argument of biological determinism about the roles of actors and their surroundings: actors follow their inborn nature. To understand crime, study the criminal, not his rearing, not his education, not the current predicament that might have inspired his theft or pillage." All that was necessary was a few lines of racial background, a brief history of family violence, and the outline of the square jaw and sloping forehead—this was the recognizable criminal. So Norris could sum up McTeague's background in a paragraph describing the father's alcoholism and the son's inherited feeble-mindedness and square jaw. These few strokes, coupled with a heavily inflected ethnic tag imbedded in the title character's name ("Teague" as an epithet for Irishman), and Norris was ready to proceed with his examination of the criminal immigrant "type."

In the articles describing the murderer, Norris found examples of how to quickly sketch the "Type." In the *Examiner,* he read of "Patrick Collins, the savage of civilization," saw "What the Murderous, Human Beast Looks Like," and probably shared the author's educated guess that "if a good many of Patrick Collins' ancestors did not die on the scaffold then either they escaped their desert or there is nothing in heredity." The fact that the man was "Born for the Rope" is proven by his face, "not degraded, but brutish. That is to say, he is not a man who has sunk, but one who was a beast to start with. The face is broad, the brown eyes are set wide apart, the nose is flattened at the bridge and is broad as a negro's. The jaw is heavy and crue." Norris too believed that what a man will come to can be described with equal facility by an Irish name, an alcoholic father, and a "square-cut" head, "the jaw salient, like that of the carnivora" (Norris, *McTeague*).

At the time he was working on *McTeague,* Norris wrote a series of stories that illustrated his increasing preoccupation with the "type" of the immigrant criminal and the threat he posed to the "thoroughbred" American. The hero of two of the earliest of these stories is a man named Shotover, "American-bred and American-born, and his father and mother before him and their father and mother before them, and so on and back till one brought up in the hold of a ship called the *Mayflower,* further back than which it is not necessary to go" (Norris, *Works*). In "A Defense of the Flag" (1895), Shotover discovers the Irish flag flying over City Hall on St. Patrick's Day and proceeds to replace it with the U.S. colors. It is a stand he must take for the progress of his nation: "The great American city, with its riches and resources, bulging with the life and energy of a new people, young, enthusiastic, ambitious, and so full of hope and promise for the future, all striving and struggling in the fore part of the march of empire, building a new nation, a new civilization, a new world, while over it all floated the Irish flag." While his compatriots rest confident in their supremacy, Shotover alone recognizes the dark possibility that over this "new civilization" might one day fly the flag of a degraded immigrant race. And in Shotover's lone stand against the mob that comes for him, Norris attempts to prove that Shotover's fears are not groundless: "In the books, the young aristocrat invariably thrashes the clowns who set upon him. But somehow Shotover had no chance with his clowns at all. . . . their way of fighting was not that which he had learned at his athletic club."

In "Thoroughbred" (1895), Shotover again confronts an immigrant mob, this time marauding Chinese invading the ancestral grounds of his fiancée. Here Norris sets up the "thoroughbred" as the nation's saving grace when the Chinese mob "recoil[s] before the figure of a slightly built young man in tennis flannels who stood upon the topmost step with a cigarette in his mouth and a heavy dog whip in his hand. . . . [R]ecognizing, with a crowd's intuition, a born leader and master of men [they] felt themselves slipping back into the cowed workmen and opium-drugged half-castes of the previous week, and backed off out of reach." Shotover and the family dog "kept the crowd in check, thoroughbreds both."

As he worked on *McTeague* in 1897, his stories and sketches increasingly moved away from the promise of the triumph of the thoroughbred, seeming instead to prophesy his contamination. "A Case for Lombroso" tells of the destruction of a "torrowbred [*sic*]" Harvard boy named Stayne, who is corrupted by the unnatural lust of a girl whose "race was almost exhausted, its vitality low. . . . To-day Cresencia might have been called a degenerate." Stayne is stainless in every way until he mixes with her "red-hot, degenerate blood," after which he is transformed into a sadistic brute. The story ends with the significant moral: "Stayne's name has long since been erased from the rolls of his club." We learn that even the thoroughbred, if he does not protect himself, can degenerate through sexual contact with a degraded race. It is the duty of the "club" to prevent such contamination.

Throughout 1897 Norris's articles bear witness to a growing obsession with the degenerate, in sketches on the "type" in "Brute," "Fiction Is Selection," "New Year's at San Quentin," "A Lag's Release." In his sketch on the immigrant poor in "Among Cliff Dwellers," he seems to be describing a paranoid vision for the future of his nation: "The hill is swarming and boiling with the life of them. Here on this wartlike protuberance bulging above the city's roof a great milling is going on, and a fusing of peoples, and in a few more generations the Celt and the Italian, the Mexican and the Chinaman, the Negro and the Portuguese . . . will be merged into one type. And a curious type it will be." What this "type" will be is a central preoccupation for Norris during these years. These sketches, all written within months of each other, help us understand how Norris was approaching his immigrant subjects in *McTeague.* The novel's working subtitle was "The People of Polk Street," and the "mixed character" of the community was as much Norris's subject as the tragedy itself. While one early reviewer questioned the racial superiority implied by the novel, "standing off and explaining the characters in a way that suggests superiority," the failure of modern critics to address and account for Norris's theories of race and heredity has allowed a powerful, albeit disturbing, undercurrent of *McTeague* to go unexplored. And for Stroheim, as an immigrant aggressively attempting to subvert racial determination through his career in film, this aspect of the novel was precisely what he had to confront in his attempt to tell his "American story."

"The People of Polk Street" are each determined by the racial and bestial characteristics that make them who they are for Norris. McTeague is "bull-like," "an elephant" who "seemed to have no nerves at all." Trina is "almost infantile," with "a certain feline eagerness of expression." Zerkow, the Polish Jew, has "clawlike, prehensile fingers" and "gets so mad [he] rolls on the floor and scratches himself." Maria is "a greaser," "a strange woman of a mixed race." Marcus throws his knife "greaser style" and bites McTeague's ear like an animal. And as these characters intermarry and procreate, they produce only mutants and animals. All the children in the novel are further degenerations from their adult prototypes. August Sieppe is portrayed as a simpleton: "His eyes were starting from their sockets, his chin had dropped upon his lace collar, and his head turned vaguely from side to side with a confused and maniacal motion." The marriage of Maria Macapa and Zerkow results in the birth of "a wretched sickly child with not even strength enough nor wits enough to cry. . . . It had not even a name, a strange, hybrid little boy . . . combining in its puny little body the blood of the Hebrew, the Pole, and the Spaniard."

But it is the marriage of Trina and McTeague that is most grotesquely unfruitful. Trina, unable to produce a child, turns instead to her inherited skill: toy making, carving Noah's animals with machinelike regularity. These animals are the only beings she produces in the story, but it is only the animals, not the human family of Noah (the bearers of the covenant with God), that she is able to create. Mark Seltzer identifies an anxiety in naturalism over production and generation that reveals itself in "the desire to project an alternative to biological reproduction, to displace the threat posed by the 'woman people'." Here the threat posed by biological reproduction is implicitly the threat of the mixed marriage, and by forbidding Trina to make the human figures (manufactured instead by a machine), Norris exposes the link between this naturalist anxiety and nativist fears.

At the height of his ambition, McTeague imagines himself "as a venerable patriarch surrounded by children and grandchildren," yet he ends up surrounded by nothing but Trina's menagerie. But Trina works to turn this bestiary production into a reproductive model, filling out "a nest egg" from "the pittance she derived from the manufacture of the Noah's ark animals." Fanatically saving her money in a chamois bag that grows full and round beneath her bridal dress in her trunk, she feeds her nest egg from the income derived from other people's children, the "thousands and thousands" that purchase her animals and, later, the charity children that populate the kindergarten where she is charwoman. When Mac robs her, stealing her unborn child from her, she weeps over her empty bag "as other women weep over a dead baby's shoe." In a barren and degraded mixed marriage, Trina can produce nothing but animals and a full sack under her dress. Her "good fault," for Norris, is that she does not put her "nest egg" into circulation. She hoards, responding to her "peasant blood" of a "hardy and penurious race" but also

to an innate fear of reproduction that characterizes her throughout the novel. Her "good fault" allows McTeague's stock to die finally in the barren, primeval desert of the novel's conclusion. As Marcus preaches, "The masses must learn self-control. . . . Decrease the number of wage earners and you increase wages." Trina's "good fault" is that she "had always been an economical little body" conditioned to save and not to spend the egg beneath her bridal dress.

This is a novel in which blood tells all, despite the characters' attempts to silence its pronouncements. We witness the attempts of the residents of Polk Street to forge alternate heredities, to evade the determination of race. McTeague imagines himself as "patriarch," father of "Daniel": "Daniel would have little children. McTeague would grow old among them all . . . surrounded by children and grandchildren." Maria fantasizes that she is the daughter of a wealthy coffee merchant. Even Zerkow, the Polish Jew, the most mixed (and, therefore, degraded) character in the novel, seeks to replace his tainted blood with a pure bloodline, imagining "money as if it had been the blood of his veins." And they all dress up in costume: Marcus playing the cowboy hero; Mr. Sieppe marching around as a Bismarckian commander; on the night of the theater party, McTeague arrives in a Prince Albert coat, dressing as the Germanic prince who becomes prince-consort to Victoria; and Little August, in his Fauntleroy costume, is dressed as the naive American boy who becomes heir to a British estate. Norris points to these costumes to expose the assimilationist ambitions of these immigrants, ambitions that Norris brutally denies at every turn.

While the novel focuses on two doomed parallel mixed marriages, it does present one romance that rises above the squalor and the poverty of the surroundings. In the relationship between the Old People, the novel's two Anglo-Saxons, Norris offers proof that environment is not responsible for the fate of the immigrants. Suffering under the same conditions as these newer immigrants, Old Grannis is able to contribute toward the progress of society with a patented invention: a book-binding machine on which he sews issues of *The Breeder and Sportsman*. As his fortunes prove, blood makes all the difference. As for the rest, like McTeague, they are all fated by the tainted blood running through them: "The foul stream of hereditary evil, like a sewer. The vices and sins of his father and of his father's father, to the third and fourth and five hundredth generation, tainted him. The evil of an entire race flowed in his veins." Ultimately, in the immigrants' failure to reproduce and in their violent self-destruction, an innate confidence in natural selection is at work in Norris's conclusion. He falls back upon his teacher's confidence, believing finally in the tendency of evolution to kill off the degraded races populating San Francisco. The fantasy he projects in the novel's conclusion has McTeague withdraw from the city, back to his personal origins at the mine, and finally to find his "natural"—that is, inevitable—end at a mythical point of evolutionary origins in Death Valley, the lowest point in the United States, three hundred feet below sea level.

Survival of the fittest requires a natural field upon which selection will take place. The artificial imbalance that immigration was engendering threatened the otherwise immutable plan of Anglo-Saxon triumph. By the early twentieth century, the link Norris had articulated in 1897 between naturalism and nativism, between fate and race, was "proved" by the work of American eugenics. Appropriating Binet's speculations into the connection between intelligence and heredity, hereditarians in the early part of the century reified blood to the level of inevitability and, in so doing, lost confidence that the United States was winning the war with its foreign invaders.

Eugenicists in the United States identified two sites of infection that science would be called upon to regulate: uncontrolled reproduction from within and massive immigration from without. Following H. H. Goddard's study of inherited feeble-mindedness in *The Kallikaks,* eugenicists worked to classify and regulate the forces that endangered U.S. stock. Goddard was invited to Ellis Island in 1912-13 to judge the mental condition of the immigrants flooding into the country, and employing visual observation and a modified Binet test, he pronounced "that the immigration of recent years is of a decidedly different character from the early immigration. . . . We are now getting the poorest of each race." Goddard's followers spent World War I testing soldiers, revealing an average intelligence far below what was expected and justifying their own worst fears. No longer secure that man was naturally progressing, the eugenicists insisted that man's genetic pool had to be regulated. By 1923 eugenicists were able to argue that "the curve indicates a gradual deteriorioration in the class of immigrants examined in the army. . . . The average intelligence of succeeding waves of immigration has become progressively lower." And racist thinkers could now speak with scientific authority: "America's immigration problem is mainly a problem of blood. For over a generation America has been changing her blood. . . . Three or four shiploads have been landing at Ellis Island every week. If they are allowed to breed the future 'typical American,' then the future typical American is going to be as devoid of personal beauty as this vast mass of humanity."

These anxieties were in no way limited to the scientific community. Eugenicists fed off of a popular hysteria, providing documentation and statistics to back up the growing anxiety that unregulated immigration was bringing about racial suicide. Blood now told all there was to tell: "The racial effects of immigration are more far-reaching and potent than all others. Recent discoveries in biology show that in the long-run heredity is far more important than environment or education. . . . They also show what can be done in a few years in altering species, and in producing new ones with qualities hitherto unknown; or unknown in combination." In 1924, responding to these discoveries, Virginia permitted sterilization

of patients confined for feeble-mindedness. The statute was defended by Justice Oliver Wendell Holmes: "It is better for all the world, if instead of waiting to execute degenerate offspring for crime . . . society can prevent those persons who are manifestly unfit from continuing their kind." As Goddard defended sterilization, "The operation itself is almost as simple in males as having a tooth pulled." At the same time, eugenicists successfully lobbied the House Immigration Committee for stricter controls of the external threat of new immigration. Eugenics, the revival of the Ku Klux Klan, and the prophecies of such best-sellers as Madison Grant's *The Passing of the Great Race* and Stoddard's *The Revolt against Civilization,* worked to make possible the first significant restrictions on immigration. Higham writes, "Public opinion echoed the perturbations of the nativist intelligentsia as never before. The general magazines teemed with race-thinking, phrased nearly always in terms of an attack on the new immigration." Goddard's call for genetic sterilization—as easy as "having a tooth pulled"—and the anti-immigration violence fueled by the Klan under the leadership of another tooth-puller, the dentist Hiram Evans, rose to its climax with the passing of the Immigration Act of 1924.

The Jews most bore the force of this hostility in the early 1920s (Higham). Their increasing numbers and their phenomenal success in the very entertainment industries that were being held responsible for the collapse of old American values led to increasing anti-Semitism by this union of racial science, politics, and popular hysteria. The film industry, where Jews held highly visible positions of power, became a focus of vicious attacks.

During these two years, 1923-24, in which the nativist movement was rising to its climax, Erich von Stroheim was in San Francisco working on the film of his dreams: the complete and faithful adaptation of Frank Norris's *McTeague.* It was to be the greatest film ever made, his claim to the throne of D. W. Griffith. It was to be the proof that Stroheim could tell an "American story": "It has always been my determination to produce the story exactly as it was written. They have said I could not make an American story and I want to prove that I can." And in choosing *McTeague* as his "American story," Stroheim went to the heart of the culture's challenge to his assimilationist ambitions.

Erich Stroheim, son of a Jewish hatter and a deserter from the Austrian army, arrived on Ellis Island in November 1909, the same year that Griffith filmed the first adaptation of Norris for the screen. As part of the largest wave in immigration history, Stroheim, as just another Jew, had little hope of meeting with success. Instead, he reinvented himself for the immigration authorities as a man from whom much could be expected: Erich Oswald Hans Carl Maria von Stroheim, son of a German baroness and an Austrian count, practicing Catholic, second lieutenant, and noble emigré. As his biographer, Richard Koszarski, writes, "From the day Erich von Stroheim landed in America he treated his early life as a fiction, and to the day he died he stuck to the outline of his story with only minor embellishments. As an artist von Stroheim chose to make his own life his prime artwork."

How this man, who successfully claimed a false title, religion, and genealogy, came to be so obsessed with Norris's story is a subject rich with coincidence. Among his early acts of self-fictionalizing was the claim that he had early on authored a play called *The Black Mask* that was running in San Francisco when he had lived there in poverty with his first wife in 1913. The play, which he did not write, tells of a disfigured maniac who hides behind a black mask and wins his bride by holding her over an open mine shaft. Unraveling the significance of this claim leads us in several directions and provides some insight into the anxieties plaguing the young Stroheim's own "American story."

Stroheim himself would one year later play a madman in a black mask, in his first acting role as a blackface soldier in *The Birth of a Nation*. And it was while working for Griffith in semistarvation as an extra that he first read *McTeague*. Further, in the same year that *The Black Mask* was running, Stroheim himself acted out its central role by assaulting his wife, precisely the violence Norris would have scripted for him. Margaret Stroheim was granted a divorce on the grounds of extreme cruelty, and in the hearings it was revealed that Stroheim had turned to drinking and running through the streets screaming, "You God damn dirty beast, I have you and your mother in my fist and I am going to squeeze you." Stroheim must have seen himself behind the black mask, a man disfigured by heredity, disguising his racial identity but still unable to escape the role to which Norris had fated him. Thus, in one minor (and easily disproved) element of the fiction Stroheim created for his life lie the disparate strands that bind his story to Norris's novel. *McTeague* had told him what he was born for by being born a Jew; that try as he might to claim an alternate identity, he was doomed to violence and degeneration. Stroheim, having left his Judaism with his old country, now stood in Griffith's lot behind the twin masks of Austrian nobility and blackface, reading the novel that spelled out his fate in his new country. Stroheim had already been found guilty by the courts of extreme cruelty, failed to support his wife, and turned to drink, so Norris's novel must have seemed to prophesy his destiny as he put on his blackface for three dollars a day. Seeing himself in *The Black Mask,* he worked to wrest himself free from the starring role, to align himself instead with the authorial voice—a claim made especially interesting by the fact that the star of *The Black Mask* in its San Francisco run was Holbrook Blinn, the man who would star in the first film adaptation of *McTeague* in 1915. He wanted to be Norris, not McTeague; to be the playwright, not the man in the black mask; and most important, he wanted to be Griffith, not the man in blackface. His ambition to direct, like his desire to author the fiction of his life, was an attempt to escape the life that nativist America was attempting to script for him. In claiming authorship of *The Black Mask,* Stroheim was claiming power to author his own life. It is

telling that he would be one of the only early directors to star in most of his own films, and in directing *McTeague,* he redirected the story of the immigrant away from the predetermination from which he had to escape if he were to survive in America.

In 1915, the year the novel's first adaptation was being filmed, Stroheim was hard at work for Griffith in his second major spectacle, *Intolerance.* Stroheim received billing in the film as "Count von Stroheim" in the role of a Pharisee. His increasingly aggrandized title, placing still more honorifics between his given and his inherited name, arose from the fact that the roles he was now playing were pushing him closer to home. Griffith was forcing him back toward his true racial identity, sending Stroheim to Los Angeles's Jewish quarter to round up "old men with patriarchal beards" and filming him chanting the Pharisee prayer: "Oh Lord, I thank thee that I am better than other men." "In other words," as Werner Sollors reads the legacy of this prayer, "Thank God I am not ethnic!". Griffith had Stroheim playing the most orthodox of Jews as an example of the "intolerance" that crucified Christ, but in chanting the Pharisee prayer, Stroheim is again putting on a double mask, this time playing the Jew he had disowned while at the same time speaking the nativist rhetoric that threatened to call him out. Stroheim's other role in the film is in the crucifixion scene itself; as he remembers it, "I'm one of those guys yelling 'Crucify Him'." Although he clearly enjoyed the irony of this role, Stroheim once again found himself directed in a role that put him on the wrong side of the fence. In his own career as a director, which began three years later, Stroheim was to rewrite the story with himself as the greatest martyr that film has ever known and with the Hollywood Jews as the ones shouting "Crucify Him!"

Stroheim began his career with Griffith, the man who made film respectable to middle-class audiences. As Michael Rogin has shown, it was in the first and greatest of his spectacles, *The Birth of a Nation,* that Griffith created an entertainment that capitalized on middle-class anxiety of racial stain. Until Griffith, movies were primarily the entertainment of the poor immigrant communities, often as part of a vaudeville review, and *McTeague* contains one of the first appearances of the motion picture in fiction. Capping an evening of slapstick and song, McTeague and his guests are treated to "The feature of the evening, the crowning scientific achievement of the nineteenth century, the kinetoscope." The film presentation, a street scene in San Francisco, is indeed exciting: "The kinetoscope fairly took their breaths away," and McTeague was so "excited . . . [h]e began to feel that he was a man of the world."

Initially, it was simply the technical wonder of the medium that attracted viewers, but soon new selling points had to be discovered to maintain repeat consumption and to expand the market to more respectable audiences. The industry turned to the novel. Griffith, who began his career embarrassed to be participating in so lowly a form of entertainment, devoted himself to turning film into a high art, relying increasingly on literary sources. His determination to tell the story of the racial threat posed by miscegenation required a longer format than the standard two reels to carry the full impact of his source material, Thomas Dixon's *The Clansman*. Griffith sold investors on the unprecedented length of *Birth* by proving that this novel would lose its force in condensation. Investors, eager for the spending money of the novel-reading audience, took the bait. Thus, the novel, in the form of Dixon's racist epic, was used to transform film from an immigrant entertainment into a middle-class art form.

Stroheim took Griffith's reliance on novelistic authority to its ultimate end in his determination to expand narrative cinema into a form fully commensurate with the nineteenth-century realistic novel. At the same time, he also tried to take something back. By the time he became a director, there was no longer a need on the part of the industry to justify itself to the middle class. Having captured the middle-class viewers, the industry was busily engaged keeping them watching, protecting their sensibilities, and justifying their world view. Responding to Harding's call for "normalcy," the immigrants who founded the studio system devoted themselves to maintaining their respectable pastime by keeping immigrants off the screen. With anti-Semitism on the rise and Jewish prominence in Hollywood increasingly under attack by such nativist institutions as Henry Ford's *Dearborn Independent* and the Klan, the Hollywood Jews worked hard to defuse themselves as a source of the hostility. As Neal Gabler writes, "While the Hollywood Jews were being assailed by know-nothings for conspiring against traditional American values and the power-structure that maintained them, they were desperately embracing the values and working to enter the power structure. Above all things, they wanted to be regarded as American, not Jews; they wanted to reinvent themselves here as new men."

As part of this effort, the industry appointed an internal censorship office under the command of Harding's postmaster general, Will Hays, to devise the "purity code" under which the industry would operate for the next forty years. The stakes were now enormous. By capturing the middle-class audience, film had realized substantial profits and the growing interest of Wall Street investors. Gone were the days of the nickelodeon; now one could pay up to five dollars for a Griffith premier. As investors began capitalizing on the potential of Hollywood, controlling the industry's efficiency and product became increasingly crucial, and the early 1920s saw the rise of the supervisor-producer whose primary loyalty lay with the investors.

Almost immediately as a director, Stroheim ran afoul of both the "purity code" and the new studio system in the form of the archetypal central producer, Irving Thalberg. Thalberg was the model of the new breed of producers, controlling all film activities and finances. Stroheim, who wanted to be the next Griffith, had to operate in a system Griffith had never known, with an accountant between him and his vision. Thus Stroheim famously became the first martyr to the producer system of production. None of his films appeared in the form he intended, and in 1922 his film *Merry-Go-Round* was taken entirely out of his hands by Thalberg and given to another director to complete. Unwilling to continue at Universal under Thalberg's thumb, Stroheim went to Goldwyn to film the story he had been planning ever since he entered the business: *Greed*.

Greed went against the tide of early 1920s movie making in almost every way. It was bleak and tragic when Hollywood was filming Cinderella stories; it featured unglamorous and unknown actors when studios were capitalizing on the star system; and if focused on the working poor at a time when DeMille and others were fueling America's obsession with the rich and extravagant. *Greed* was an exception to Stroheim's own history as a director as well. It was his first film that he neither authored or starred in, and it was the first that was not centered around his standard plot vehicle of seduction and decadence in Old Vienna. It was also the first film ever made with a personal dedication: "To My Mother." To understand why Stroheim made this picture and why he felt the need to dedicate it to a mother whom he had fictionalized out of existence, we must compare the film's shooting script to the novel, not to note, as is often done, how closely Stroheim followed the novel, but to read the moments when he purposefully changes Norris's story to his own.

It is quite apparent from the script of *Greed* that Stroheim worked with the novel open beside him. The bulk of the scenes are transcribed literally, right down to Stroheim's somewhat awkward use of Norris's Americanisms in his stage directions. So completely did Stroheim sell his legendary fidelity to the novel that all of the reviews focused around his determination to translate the realism of Norris to the screen, and even today no one questions the legend of Stroheim's complete subservience to the novel. As Stroheim declared during production:

> It is possible to tell a great story in motion pictures in such a way that the spectator . . . will come to believe that what he is looking at is real. . . . Dickens, De Maupassant, Zola, Frank Norris and other brilliant writers have caught and reflected life in their novels. . . . There must be more realism on the screen, and it is my humble ambition to furnish some of it. It is with that idea that I am working hard on Norris's "McTeague," which will be introduced on the screen under the title of "Greed."

Throughout, Stroheim repeatedly asserted the novel as the source of the film's "realism."

The movie opens with the title, "From the American Classic," and then cuts to a shot of the novel opening slowly to reveal an epigraph, ostensibly from the novel but actually borrowed from a Norris essay, "The True Reward of the Novelist" (1901):

I never truckled; I never took off the hat to Fashion and held it out for pennies. By God, I told them the truth. They liked it or they didn't like it. What had that to do with me? I told them the truth, I knew it for the truth then and I know it for the truth now.

—Frank Norris (*Greed*)

Stroheim is using the bravado of this essay to get Norris to speak for him as he embarks on a project that he is aware might well ruin him. But Norris's is a difficult voice to claim as his own, even as it is precisely the voice he most desires; for this same essay strictly proscribes Stroheim by its very terms of address, as Norris assures himself, "We are all Anglo-Saxons enough to enjoy the sight of a fight." And while Stroheim attempts to appropriate Norris's declaration of independence for his own, Stroheim would be forced to remove over eight hours of his film to financial and moral censors and would be ultimately drummed out of Hollywood as a financial and moral failure. Norris, on the other hand, willingly performed his own censorship when the slightest breath of scandal appeared around the publication of *McTeague*. Eager for a British edition of his first novel, but facing the nervousness of his publisher over one scene, Norris removed the offending bit of "realism" without protest. As Robert Morace points out,

> Late in his career, Norris defiantly claimed that he had "never truckled," he didn't mention that he had, however, rewritten passages in two novels . . . that reviewers of the earliest printings had found objectionable. This is not to say that Norris did indeed truckle, merely that he didn't really have to. His relationship with his readers was not antagonistic . . . rather, it was one of accommodation.

This is precisely the point: Norris was writing a novel to an imagined audience of fellow Anglo-Saxons who shared his position of superior fascination with the world of the immigrant poor and his anxieties about the effects they might have on the future of the nation. Stroheim, in adapting Norris's novel and holding it up as the preeminent example of literary realism, is claiming an alliance with Norris; but at the same time his effort at assimilation leads him subtly to rewrite the focus of the story in such a way as to claim assimilation as a possibility and environment as an explanation for degeneration that is at least commensurate with that provided by blood.

Stroheim appears to have run into problems almost immediately. He worried over the fact that Norris presents the reader with McTeague already set up at Polk Street with only a few short lines describing his background. In his most obvious structural change to the novel, Stroheim added over an hour of material describing in detail how McTeague came to be where and what he is. Beginning his film at the Big Dipper Mine in 1908 (the year before Stroheim himself set out for America), Stroheim constructs an allegory for his own immigration to San Francisco. But where Norris's novel rested on the assumption

that a few lines of hereditary background doomed McTeague to his fate, Stroheim struggled to expose the details, the extenuating circumstances, that transformed McTeague into a brute. He went directly against the hereditarian belief that blood told all, and attempted to show in detail how the environment conspired to make the criminal, portraying the drudgery of work at the mine, the debauchery of camp life, and the violence of Father McTeague's alcoholism in gruesome detail (where Norris portrayed a father who drank every fourteenth day, Stroheim had him drinking the other thirteen as well).

And against it all, Stroheim invents a Mother McTeague who was good, hardworking, and full of ambition for her son's escape. We see her imagining her son alternatively at "an elegantly furnished office with one solitary desk at the centre" (*Greed*) and accepting money as a dentist. When an itinerant dentist offers to take Mac into the big city to teach him a profession, Mother McTeague gives up her son and sends him off with her hard-earned savings. The figure of the mother, Stroheim's own invention, is linked to his own by the dedication. The mother in Stroheim's film provides an alternate heredity of goodness, an image of the immigrant who has maintained dignity despite the misery of her conditions. The father becomes the repository of the "bad seed." We can see how important this distinction is to Stroheim in one title that he first adapted from the novel as "But below the fine fabric of all that was good in him ran the foul stream of hereditary evil, like a sewer," but which he later changed to, "But below the fine fabric, bred of his mother, ran the foul stream of hereditary evil . . . the taint of generations given through his father." Blood still tells, but it no longer tells the whole story.

We see a similar transposition of determining forces in another scene; where Norris emphasized the degeneration of the progeny of the mixed marriage of Maria and Zerkow, Stroheim carefully works to lay the blame on environment, on one hand, and on the sins of the father, on the other. As he filmed the scene, Stroheim invented an incident to account for a death without laying blame on race or mother. The baby is killed, not by heredity but by Zerkow, who dilutes the baby's milk with wash water. Where *McTeague* told of a baby who died because Norris could not imagine the monster he would be if he had lived, Stroheim's version has the baby fall victim to the violence and greed of the father.

Stroheim hired comic actors for the central characters and encouraged them to perform their roles as such. The same characters who were animals for Norris became vaudeville comedians for Stroheim. Establishing a sympathetic reaction to the homely, overacted characters, Stroheim lets his camera linger hard and long on the environment that surrounds them. His camera inverts the emphasis of Norris's pen: where Norris held the Lombrosian belief that it was the character of the criminal that must be studied while the environment need only be sketched in broad strokes, Stroheim maintained the immigrant's belief that the environment was the source of the immigrants' failures. Focusing on the rats in the sewer, the closeness of the living conditions, and the dimness of their prospects for acculturation, employment, or advancement, Stroheim tells a very different story. The bleakness of Norris's novel is centered around the characters; the brutality of Stroheim's movie is focused on the surroundings they are forced to live in. It is this focus on the underbelly of the U.S. city that led the middle-class audience to reject his film as unpalatable precisely where Norris's story had been judged a fascinating "study of the people who were on the verge of the criminal class."

Stroheim's notorious fight with the studio for his "realism" was entirely waged over authenticity of environmental detail. To get his actors ready for their parts, he forced them to live for months under the same conditions that the characters would have lived. He sought out the exact locations that Norris described, from Polk Street, to the Big Dipper Mine three thousand feet underground, to Death Valley itself. He made his actors respond to the poverty of their conditions, as opposed to the heredity that Norris had scripted for them. When the studio asked him to film the final sequence in the dunes outside Los Angeles, Stroheim insisted on Death Valley at the hottest time of the year. The environment was what he had to capture in this film. It was as if he wished the audience to experience the environments in which Norris placed his characters in order to prove that Norris had it all wrong. Who would not become McTeague living in these conditions? As Jean Hersholt, the actor who played Marcus, remembers the Death Valley sequence: "I swear that murder must have been in both our hearts as we crawled and gasped, bare to the waist, unshaven, blackened and blistering and bleeding, while Stroheim dragged every bit of realism out of us." At the very least, his *actors* experienced "realism" as Stroheim meant to show it.

We can only speculate as to the relation Stroheim articulated for himself between the film and his own immigrant story. But beyond the dedication, there are other clues that point toward his identification with the characters and, at the same time, his need to distance himself from them. He posed for publicity shots in which he dressed as a railroad worker, emphasizing for the press that he once held a job as a laborer in northern California. In one photo, he is swinging a pick and shovel; in another he is shooting craps with black and Mexican workers. Yet even while underscoring these biographical connections, he was also busily reasserting the "nobility" that had been his selling fiction since his arrival in the United States: as the *New York Times* reported, "the 'von' now reappears after a complete, if temporary, eclipse."

In the fantastical accounts that grew up around the production in the contemporary press, Stroheim's commitment to "realism" became synonymous with the director's incredible extravagance on behalf of authentic detail. The *Chronicle* revealed Stroheim's "effort to have everything in his picture just as it would be in real life," and

Stroheim himself proclaimed in one production interview:

> The audience must know that what von Stroheim produces is done with the utmost honesty and is just as reliable as the National Geographic Magazine or the Encyclopedia Britannica. Audiences know this, I believe. They think von Stroheim will stand up and fight for correctness of detail; that he is willing to suffer the consequences; that he is willing to go to damnation for his convictions. And he is. Because everything he puts before the eyes of an audience must be that thing itself—the real thing.

Stroheim recognized that it was Norris's scientific discourse that he must claim for his own project—the reliability of *National Geographic* as the source of popular conceptions of foreign races and of the *Encyclopedia* as the repository of fact. He needed to claim their authority as his own, to rewrite *McTeague* from a story in which blood tells all to one in which environment speaks its part—into which assimilation is reinscribed as a possibility in a decade that increasingly perceived the Melting Pot as a failed model.

Andre Bazin identifies Stroheim's cinematic contribution in his camera's gradual overlaying and accretion of detail, the point of view that moves little while staring long and hard at its subject: "In his films reality lays itself bare like a suspect confessing under the relentless examination of the commissioner of police. He has one simple rule for direction. Take a close look at the world, keep on doing so, and in the end it will lay bare for you all its cruelty and its ugliness." Just as Griffith's development of the cross-cut has been located, at least in part, in the work of Frank Norris, so too might Stroheim's own stylistic innovations be found in his interaction with this same author. Maintaining a static camera and relying on the long take with very few intertitles, Stroheim shows the environment as it lays itself bare in "its cruelty and its ugliness"; the poverty of the immigrant's life "confesses" its part in the crime.

While Stroheim was frantically trying to edit the forty-two reels he ended up with down into a presentable format, Goldwyn merged with Metro to become Metro-Goldwyn-Mayer, and in what must have been his worst nightmare, Stroheim found his film once again under the thumb of Irving Thalberg. After several attempts to cut the film with the help of sympathetic friends, Stroheim presented a ten-hour version to the studio and pleaded his case. Thalberg immediately farmed the film out to a cutter who had read neither the script nor the novel. It was returned at the acceptable length of two hours.

Interestingly, in cutting the background sequence of McTeague's life in the mine, Thalberg reduced it to a few short scenes that mirrored quite closely the original novel. And in place of all the detail that Stroheim had found so vital to explain McTeague's actions, the editors, like Norris, found it sufficient to have brief examples of McTeague's work in the mine and his irrational violence.

Titles inserted into the picture at this point ("Such was McTeague") replaced the many scenes in which Stroheim had labored to prove that such need not have been McTeague at all. In the studio's attempts to remain under budgetary, time, and censorship constraints, McTeague's story was reduced to blood once more.

Despite MGM's attempts to salvage the picture, it had the effect they feared. They spent enough for four pictures and ended up with one financial flop. The reviewers responded to the film as an assault on their middle-class values:

> I do not remember ever having seen a picture in which an attempt was made to pass as entertainment dead rats, sewers, filth, rotten meat. . . . all these things and more are found in *Greed;* they will turn inside-out the stomach of even a street-cleaner.

> Imagine any girl keeping company with a young fellow urging him to take her to see *Greed* when she knows the night that she sits through it he is going to sour on every thought that has to do with marriage. (*Variety*)

Thalberg edited the movie to a presentable length, but could not re-edit the camera's gaze away from the "dead rats" and "rotten meat" and back toward Norris's more genteel entertainment of racial types and criminal natures.

Stroheim referred to all of his movies as his "children," using the metaphor to justify his fierce devotion to their development. To none of his "children" was he more devoted than to *Greed*. Yet each film he made was taken from him, cut up, and sent into the world in a format suitable for the 1920s United States. "They are showing only the skeleton of my dead child," he had moaned after the editing of *Foolish Wives*. And each of his children he disowned, refusing even to look at the final version of *Greed* and failing to keep a copy of the film in its original state. Although it is that mythical *Greed,* the "nitrate Holy Grail," that has proved a virtual obsession to the Hollywood critics who followed, it was not the film on the cutting room floor that interested Stroheim (Everson). It was the child that the public would see that he cared for, and this child was no longer his own. It was taken from him to be Americanized, and to be Americanized in the 1920s meant the validation of the nativist perspective early articulated by Norris in the 1890s. Stroheim mourned *Greed*'s fate: "My picture was arbitrarily cut. . . . The rest of the negative was burned to get the 43¢ worth of silver out." The sterilization performed on his films, "simple . . . as having a tooth pulled," led to his ruin as a director and his exile from the United States.

Writing on *The Birth of a Nation,* narrative film's founding spectacle that climaxes in the Klan's castration of a black rapist, Rogin showed how "American movies were born . . . in a racist epic." Looking at *Greed,* we can see how American cinematic realism met its end in Stroheim's attempt to rewrite the script of hereditary determinism and racist fears that Norris and Griffith had monumentalized as middle-class entertainment.

FURTHER READING

Criticism

Film Culture: The Motion Picture and TV Monthly IV, No. 3 (April 1958): 1-22.
>   Contains articles on Stroheim's life and film career by various contributors, including Stroheim's own introduction to *The Merry Widow* and an essay on his cinemagraphic style.

Koszarski, Richard. *The Man You Loved To Hate: Erich von Stroheim and Hollywood*. Oxford: Oxford University Press, 1983, 343 p.
>   Detailed examination of each of the films that Stroheim directed in light of "his great contribution to cinema: his ability to marshal the resources of mass production in the service of a single artistic vision."

————. "A Film That Almost Got Away." *American Film* X, No. 5 (March 1985): 15-16, 18.
>   Chronicles the shooting of *Queen Kelly*, abandoned in 1928 but completed and restored from rare footage in 1985.

————, and William K. Everson. "Stroheim's Last 'Lost' Film: The Making and Remaking of *Walking Down Broadway.*" *Film Comment* 11, No. 3 (May-June 1975): 6-19.
>   Recounts the filming history of *Walking Down Broadway*.

Noble, Peter. "The Man You Love to Hate." *Theatre Arts* XXXIV, No. 1 (January 1950): 22-27, 92-95.
>   Overview of Stroheim's career as a film director.

Sarris, Andrew, ed. "Erich von Stroheim." In *Interviews with Film Directors*, pp. 429-36. Indianapolis: The Dobbs-Merrill Company, Inc., 1967.
>   Includes a selection of quotes and stories told by Stroheim and a transcript of his introductory remarks to *The Merry Widow*.

Schwerin, Jules V. "The Resurgence of von Stroheim: Hollywood's Earliest Writer-Actor-Director." *Films in Review* 1, No. 3 (April 1950): 3-6, 43-44.
>   Anecdotal survey of Stroheim's film career to his role in *Sunset Boulevard*.

Weinberg, Herman G. *Stroheim: A Pictorial Record of His Nine Films*. New York: Dover Publications, Inc., 1975, 259 p.
>   Contains a synopsis, cast list, and credits for each of the films that Stroheim directed.

Wolfe, Charles. "Resurrecting *Greed*." *Sight and Sound* 44, No. 3 (Summer 1975): 170-74.
    Analysis of expressionistic imagery in Stroheim's great realistic film, *Greed*.

H. M. Tomlinson

1873-1958

(Full name Henry Major Tomlinson) English journalist, essayist, travel writer, novelist, and critic.

INTRODUCTION

Esteemed as a perceptive journalist and impassioned correspondent during World War I, Tomlinson wrote numerous books of essays and critically acclaimed novels. All of his works, including his reminiscences and autobiographical sketches, reflect his three overarching passions: England, the love of travel, and his hatred of war.

Biographical Information

Tomlinson was born in Wanstead, Essex, near the docks where his father worked. Raised with an abiding love of the sea, he was obligated after his father's death to help support his family by working in a local office. Encouraged by his mother to read extensively, Tomlinson developed a keen interest in literature. While working as a clerk in a shipping company, he published several articles in local newspapers. His career as a journalist began in 1904 when he was hired by the *Morning Leader* to cover stories having to do with shipping and seafaring. One assignment, in which he sailed on the first English vessel to travel 2,000 miles up the Amazon river, resulted in his first book, *The Sea and the Jungle* (1912). With the outbreak of war in 1914, Tomlinson covered the hostilities for the *Morning Leader* and the *Daily News* from Belgium and France, sending back sobering reports of brutality and carnage; he was eventually relieved of his correspondent's duties because his writings were determined to be too "humanitarian," that is, not supportive enough of the war effort. After the war, he served as literary editor for the journal the *Nation,* traveled widely, and wrote essays and novels. He died in London and is buried in a church cemetery near his summer home in Dorset.

Major Works

Tomlinson's best-known work was his first, *The Sea and the Jungle.* This nonfiction book is a chronicle and vivid description of what he saw during his voyage on the *Capella,* a tramp steamer that sailed from the mouth of the Amazon river in northeastern Brazil to San Antonio Falls near the Brazil-Bolivia border. The work has been praised for its portrait of the tropical jungle landscape. *Old Junk* (1918) is a collection of essays on a wide variety of topics, including ships and sailing, life in small fishing villages, and aspects of soldiers' experiences during the First World War. John Lingard described the volume as possessing a "unifying fascination with the

revelation of unexpected beauty, value, or even horror, in the apparently banal or everyday." The first book Tomlinson wrote after the war, *London River* (1921), contains eleven elegiacal essays on life along the Thames and the importance of the river to the people of London. Tomlinson returned to the theme of war in *Waiting for Daylight* (1922), a collection of essays about his reactions to modern warfare. While many of the pieces do not directly address the war—his topics include the writings of Thomas Carlyle, the figureheads of sailing ships, and travel books—the book's central premise is that the war robbed the world of its innocence, permanently changing the nature of serious discussion on any topic. In *Gifts of Fortune and Hints for Those about to Travel* (1926) Tomlinson sought to write about those things that can provide solace and wonder in the postwar world. Reviewing this essay collection, D. H. Lawrence wrote that Tomlinson was "a man who sets new visions, new feelings sensitively quivering in us." Tomlinson's first novel, *Gallion's Reach: A Romance* (1927), is a somewhat autobiographical tale about a young Englishman who works as a clerk for an importing company and yearns for adventure on the high seas. During a business-related quarrel over labor relations, the protagonist, Jim Colet, accidentally kills his boss. The body of the novel concerns Jim's escape aboard the ship *Altair,* describing its adventurous journey from Rangoon, to Malaya, and back to England. The book was a moderate popular success, and critics generally regarded the descriptive passages as more accomplished than the plot and character development. *All Our Yesterdays* (1930), Tomlinson's second novel, is a kind of cultural history of England, encompassing the years from the end of the Boer War through 1919. As with *Gallion's Reach,* critics found the book's strengths to be its extensive expository passages, sections in which Tomlinson discussed the state of English society at the time; the abundance of these pieces, however, is generally believed to weaken the work as a novel. *Out of Soundings* (1931) is a collection of essays, many of which examine in a critical light various aspects of modernity, or "progress." For example, several essays discuss the deleterious effects on the natural world and on humanity of the movies, cars, and airplanes. Lingard noted that Tomlinson's critiques are "never reactionary, however, and his arguments are often quietly reasonable." While Tomlinson's hatred of war is a recurring motif in almost all of his works—even in those not obviously about the subject, he addresses the theme from a variety of oblique angles—*Mars His Idiot* (1935) directly presents his views on the matter. However, critics regard this as his weakest book, noting in particular an "uncharacteristic shrillness" in the tone and temper of the prose. Despite his attitudes toward war, Tomlinson supported England's role in the Allied effort during World War II. Referring to Nazi Germany, he wrote in *The Wind Is Rising* (1941), a book of essays on British life during the war, that an "abominable dominion has to be overcome." *A Mingled Yarn: Autobiographical Sketches* (1953) is primarily a compilation of previously published essays; it includes four short works of autobiography, one of which is a tribute to his wife, Florence. Tomlinson's last work, published shortly before his death, was *The Trumpet Shall Sound* (1957), a novel that depicts the effects of World War II on the upper-class Gale family, who are presented as emblems of the larger British society.

PRINCIPAL WORKS

The Sea and the Jungle (nonfiction) 1912
Old Junk (essays) 1918
London River (essays) 1921
Waiting for Daylight (essays) 1922
Tidemarks: Some Records of a Journey to the Beaches of the Moluccas and the Forest of Malaya, in 1923 (travel) 1924; also published as *Tidemarks, Being Some Records of a Journey to the Beaches of the Moluccas and the Forest of Malaya in 1923*
Gifts of Fortune and Hints for Those about to Travel (travel) 1926

Under the Red Ensign (travel) 1926; also published as *The Foreshore of England: Or, Under the Red Ensign*
Gallion's Reach: A Romance (novel) 1927
Illusion, 1915 (short stories) 1928
Thomas Hardy (criticism) 1929
All Our Yesterdays (novel) 1930
Between the Lines (lectures) 1930
Norman Douglas (criticism) 1931
Out of Soundings (essays and short stories) 1931
The Snows of Helicon (novel) 1933
Mars His Idiot (nonfiction) 1935
Pipe All Hands (novel) 1937; also published as *All Hands!*
The Day Before: A Romantic Chronicle (novel) 1939
The Wind Is Rising (journal) 1941
The Turn of the Tide (journal) 1945
Morning Light: The Islands in the Days of Oak and Hemp (novel) 1946
The Face of the Earth: With Some Hints for Those about to Travel (essays) 1950
Malay Waters: The Story of Little Ships Coasting Out of Singapore and Penang in Peace and War (nonfiction) 1950
A Mingled Yarn: Autobiographical Sketches (essays) 1953
The Trumpet Shall Sound (novel) 1957

CRITICISM

Robert Lynd (essay date 1923)

SOURCE: "Mr. H. M. Tomlinson," in *Books and Authors,* G. P. Putnam's Sons, 1923, pp. 252-59.

[*In the following essay, Lynd offers an appreciation of Tomlinson and his works.*]

Mr. Tomlinson is a born traveller. There are two sorts of travellers—those who do what they are told and those who do what they please. Mr. Tomlinson has never moved about the world in obedience to a guide-book. He would find it almost as difficult to read a guide-book as to write one. He never echoes other men's curiosity. He travels for the purpose neither of information nor conversation. He has no motive but whim. His imagination goes roaming; and, his imagination and his temper being such as they are, he is out on his travels even if he gets no farther than Limehouse or the Devonshire coast. He has, indeed, wandered a good deal between Limehouse and Devonshire, as readers of *The Sea and the Jungle* know. Even in his more English volumes of sketches, essays, confessions, short stories—how is one to describe them?—he takes us with him to the north coast of Africa, to New York, and to France in war time. But the English sketches—the description of the crowd at a pitmouth after an explosion in a coal mine, the account of a derelict railway station and a grocer's boy in spectacles—almost equally give us the feeling that we are reading the narrative of one who has seen nothing except with the fortunate eyes of a stranger. It is all a matter of eyes. To see is to discover, and all Mr. Tomlinson's books are, in this sense, books of discoveries.

As a recorder of the things he has seen he has the three great gifts of imagery, style and humour. He sees the jelly-fish hanging in the transparent deeps "like sunken moons." A boat sailing on a windy day goes skimming over the inflowing ridges of the waves "with exhilarating undulations, light as a sandpiper." A queer Lascar on a creeping errand in an East-end street "looked as uncertain as a candle-flame in a draught." How well again Mr. Tomlinson conveys to us in a sentence or two the vision of Northern Africa on a wet day:

> As for Bougie, these African villages are built but for sunlight. They change to miserable and filthy ruins in the rain, their white walls blotched and scabrous, and their paths mud tracks between the styes. Their lissome and statuesque inhabitants become softened and bent, and pad dejectedly through the muck as though they were ashamed to live, but had to go on with it. The palms which look so well in sunny pictures are besoms up-ended in a drizzle.

Mr. Tomlinson has in that last sentence captured the ultimate secret of a wet day in an African village. Even those of us who have never seen Africa save on the map, know that often there is nothing more to be said. Mr. Tomlinson, however, is something of a specialist in bad weather, as, perhaps, any man who loves the sea as he does must be. The weather fills the world for the seaman with gods and demons. The weather is at once the day's adventure and the day's pageant. Mr. Conrad has written one of the greatest stories in the world simply about the weather and the soul of man. He may be said to be the first novelist writing in English to have kept his weather-eye open. Mr. Tomlinson shares Mr. Conrad's sensitive care for these things. His description of a storm of rain bursting on the African hills makes you see the things as you read. In its setting, even an unadorned and simple sentence like—

> As Yeo luffed, the squall fell on us bodily with a great weight of wind and white rain, pressing us into the sea,

compels our presence among blowing winds and dangerous waters.

But, weather-beaten as Mr. Tomlinson's pages are, there is more in them than the weather. There is an essayish quality in his books, personal, confessional, go-as-you-please. The majority of essays have egotism without personality. Mr. Tomlinson's sketches have personality without egotism. He is economical of discussion of his own tastes. When he does discuss them you know that here is no make-believe of confession. Take, for instance, the comment on place-names with which he prefaces his account of his disappointment with Tripoli:

> You probably know there are place-names, which, when whispered privately, have the unreasonable power of translating the spirit east of the sun and west of the moon. They cannot be seen in print without a thrill. The names in the atlas which do that for me are a motley lot, and you, who see no magic in them, but have your own lunacy in another phase, would laugh at mine. Celebes, Acapulco, Para, Port Royal, Cartagena, the Marquesas, Panama, the Mackenzie River, Tripoli of Barbary—they are some of mine. Rome should be there, I know, and Athens, and Byzantium. But they are not, and that is all I can say about it.

That is the farthest Mr. Tomlinson ever gets on the way towards arrogance. He ignores Rome and Athens. They are not among the ports of call of his imagination. He prefers the world that sailors tell about to the world that scholars talk about. He will not write about—he will scarcely even interest himself in—any world but that which he has known in the intimacy of his imaginative or physical experience. Places that he has seen and thought of, ships, children, stars, books, animals, soldiers, workers—of all these things he will tell you with a tender realism, lucid and human because they are part of his life. But the tradition that is not his own he throws aside as a burden. He will carry no pack save of the things that have touched his heart and his imagination.

I wish all his sketches had been as long as **"The African Coast."** It is so good that it makes one want to send him travelling from star to star of all those names that mean more to him than Byzantium. One desires even to keep him a prisoner for a longer period among the lights of New York. He should have written about the blazing city at length, as he has written about the ferries. His description of the lighted ferries and the woman passenger who had forgotten Jimmy's boots, remains in the memory. Always in his sketches we find some such significant "thing seen." On the voyage home from New York on a floating hotel it is the passing of a derelict sailing ship, "mastless and awash," that suddenly re-creates for him the reality of the ocean. After describing the assaults of the seas on the doomed hulk, he goes on:

> There was something ironic in the indifference of her defenceless body to these unending attacks. It mocked this white and raging post-mortem brutality, and gave her a dignity that was cold and superior to all the eternal powers could now do. She pitched helplessly head first into a hollow, and a door flew open under the break of her poop; it surprised and shocked us, for the dead might have signed to us then. She went astern of us fast, and a great comber ran at her, as if it had just spied her, and thought she was escaping. There was a high white flash, and a concussion we heard. She had gone. But she appeared again far away, forlorn on a summit in desolation, black against the sunset. The stump of her bowsprit, the accusatory finger of the dead, pointed at the sky.

We find in **"The Ruins"** (which is a sketch of a town in France just evacuated by the Germans) an equally imaginative use made of a key incident. First, we have the description of the ruined town itself:

> House-fronts had collapsed in rubble across the road. There is a smell of opened vaults. All the homes are blind. Their eyes have been put out. Many of the buildings are without roofs, and their walls have come down to raw serrations. Slates and tiles have avalanched into the street, or the roof itself is entire, but has dropped sideways over the ruin below as a drunken cap over the dissolute.

And so on till we come to the discovery of a corn-chandler's ledger lying in the mud of the roadway. Only an artist could have made a tradesman's ledger a symbol of hope and resurrection on a shattered planet as Mr. Tomlinson has done. He picks out from the disordered procession of things treasures that most of us would pass with hardly a glance. His clues to the meaning of the world are all of his own finding. It is this that gives his work the savour and freshness of literature.

As for clues to Mr. Tomlinson's own mind and temper, do we not discover plenty of them in his confessions about books? He is a man who likes to read *The Voyage to the Houyhnhnms* in bed. Heine and Samuel Butler and Anatole France are among his favourite authors. There is nothing in his work to suggest that he has taken any of them for his models. But there is a vein of rebellious irony in his writing that enables one to realise why his imagination finds in Swift good company. He, too, has felt his heart lacerated, especially in these late days of the world's corruption. His writing would be bitter, one feels, were it not for the strength of his affections. Humanity and irony contend in his work, and humanity is fortunately the winner. In the result, the world in his books is not permanently a mud-ball, but a star shining in space. Perhaps it is in gratitude for this that we find it possible at last even to forgive him his contemptuous references to Coleridge's *Table-talk*—that cache of jewels buried in metaphysical cotton-wool.

Edmund Blunden (essay date 1925)

SOURCE: "H. M. Tomlinson," in *Edmund Blunden: A Selection of His Poetry and Prose*, edited by Kenneth Hopkins, Rupert Hart-Davis, 1925, pp. 303-08.

[*In the following essay, originally published in 1925, Blunden praises Tomlinson's writing style and ability to evoke landscapes and scenes.*]

The author of *The Sea and the Jungle* has not had his share of the talk about the moderns. Neither personal nor critical studies of H. M. Tomlinson have multiplied, though such things are by no means out of fashion. He himself probably never thinks of this comparative neglect, and would, I believe, respond to an interview with something like Hamlet's "I am too much i' the sun". He has a not inconsiderable company of admirers, but their number should be ten times as many. I maintain it; for I would maintain this also, that at his best (and he is as consistent as anybody) Mr. Tomlinson writes the best prose in England now.

In his early days he was in a shipping office in Poplar. Call it dreary. Then read his version, "**A Shipping Parish**". He remembers the last of the China clippers in the Thames, and sees in an old Lloyd's Register forms of ancient beauty not yielding anything to the Grecian Urn which apotheosized Keats. Not all the writing of his youth was done in the mysterious ceremonies of ship's business. Somewhere or other there may yet survive a copy of the proceedings of a Dockland literary society, and I am looking for that copy; it contains H. M. Tomlinson's first contribution to print. He told me himself, without a blush, without one longing look behind, that at the time of his marriage there was a bonfire in his garden, and in the bonfire a stack of his manuscripts ended their short existence. There were famous precedents, of course, but Mr. Tomlinson ought to plead guilty without any appeal.

Of Fleet Street he has seen plenty—enough, one gathers; thither his pencraft took him, thence editors dispatched him to football cup finals and murder scenes ("a cross indicates the spot where the body was found"). I should say, from his still glorious agility in jumping on and off motor-buses in their middle course, that he was an invaluable reporter. He tells me that the famous football players of years ago were really great at the game; he lingers over their names somehow as he reconsiders the *Cutty Sark,* and the *Samuel Plimsoll.* To-day, he hints—but let them go; he writes nothing about the new football. It was in his Fleet Street days that he had the chance to join a voyage to the Amazon, the fruit of which is *The Sea and the Jungle.* What did the editor of the *Morning Leader,* that vanished glory, foresee of this when he let his subaltern depart southwards?

The war reverberates less through the "best sellers" and "intellectuals" than it does through Mr. Tomlinson's recent essays, and the reason is that he was in it. From the first legendary, crusade-like days, through the seemingly endless monotonies of destruction and dirt which so marvellously came to an end, he was a witness. There can be only a few who understand the experience of the soldier so well; few who will talk over so profoundly, so freshly the extraordinary contrasts of Flanders in the days of decision. It is hard to communicate the strange confusion of acceptance and despair which filled those far-off times, but when two survivors are much in one another's company, they are apt to speak of what was with an intensity of mutual comprehension. "Any book which refers," wrote Mr. Tomlinson lately, "especially in an offhand way, to Merville, Estaires, Bailleul, Laventie, Armentières, Strazeele, Locre and so on, abolishes my other immediate circumstances and has me in bond." And I may comment that, on many a morning when the printers had sent their boy to the office for some urgent proof corrections or fill-ups, Mr. Tomlinson has begun to refer in an offhand way to those and many other places once known desperately well, and has abolished my sense of time and duty, and held me in bond. The Ancient Mariner is "nothing to it".

Towards the end of the strange events in Flanders, Mr. Tomlinson's kind of reporting was attacked by one of the countless committees of those times on the ground of its being too human, and he returned to England, becoming Literary Editor of the *Nation.* The office of that great journal overlooked the Thames and the Embankment, and a familiar picture of Mr. Tomlinson to many of us will be framed by his tall window there, while the hazy waterside buildings seen beyond, especially one with two stone lions on it which he used to consider as spiritual targets, will be his background. Forget not yet, sweet memory, the heaps of new novels and economic manuals which might be perhaps a too gaudy foreground; and, if we pursue the old style of portraiture throughout, let his elbow rest on Melville's *Moby Dick* and his eye on a stack of manuscript.

On the transference of the *Nation* to new proprietors, the former set of contributors (and a more remarkable array of intellectual power and journalistic skill it would be tantalizing to seek) almost all departed. I may have been the junior among those writers, and, as the law-court column says, I felt my position keenly. The breaking up of such a gallant company of fighters for truth and beauty was an event like the death of an intimate; and it was far from surprising that the Literary Editor soon afterwards went off very quietly to Malay. I think he would have gone to Flanders, but circumstance determined his travels, and the sea and the jungle were his old love. He took chances in the East Indies. There are places which previously no white man had reached, and to some of these he went out of sheer polarity-sense from what I am able to visualize.

And now again Mr. Tomlinson is engaged in periodical literature in London, editing his part of the *Weekly Westminster,* and contributing to other torch-bearing magazines. The reader must not suppose him to be solemnly and utterly attached to an editorial desk, for among other activities he has a habit of getting about. He is a naturalist of fresh and accurate disposition. You may find him in picture-galleries, or in tithe-barns, or hovering over a barrow of unpromising old books.

He himself has added to literature at least five books, and if he does not increase that total very considerably, it will be counted a black mark against him, for he writes with perennial personality; his works are his own. They have an emanation, a radiance and a smiling integrity which he could not omit from his writing even if for some reason or other he wished to try. The list of his books, so far as I know, is made up thus: *The Sea and the Jungle,* published in 1912, and reprinted in 1913 and 1920: *Old Junk,* 1918: *London River,* 1921: *Waiting for Day-light,* 1922: and *Tidemarks,* 1924. Each of these volumes has its distinctive reference, and shall be here indicated in brief sort in a separate paragraph.

In *The Sea and the Jungle,* Mr. Tomlinson takes us in a tramp steamer out of Swansea in coal dust and snow, and Christmas finds us off Madeira. A little later we pass through the curious gateway of Para into the country of the Amazon; as an old-fashioned poet says,

> The mighty Orellana. Scarce the Muse
> Dares stretch her wing o'er this enormous mass
> Of rushing water.

That way the *Capella* goes for two thousand miles, but the old poet was right. Mr. Tomlinson's record is a majestic confession that the Amazon region is "an impenetrable density of green and secret leaves", but against that solemn invincible umbrage he reveals the brilliant importunities of insect, of animal, of man, so that the mind is filled with intense wonder.

The peripatetic of modern short story must have his copy of *Old Junk,* a set of sketches chiefly nautical. He should read it all, and perhaps it will be **"The Lascar's Walking-Stick"** which will indispose him for some of the amorous episodes which often seem to concentrate the spirit of the age. The story concerns a man named Hammond, of whom more could be said—and Mr. Tomlinson will perhaps say it in his book on the European war. It is brief. It also concerns a walking-stick with a handle like the head of a snake, and an old Lascar who owned it. The walking-stick began to wriggle, and the Lascar was rescued by the police from the Limehouse crowd. But consult Hammond in Mr. Tomlinson's report.

A drawing of the foreshore at Limehouse, the idly lapping river, the unhandsome craft tied up to the wharves, the erratic piles of houses in the grey sky, the gulls and the streaks of smoke, is the frontispiece to *London River.* It is a poet's book, in a manner; for herein Mr. Tomlinson gives us more of the dream quality than elsewhere. I should say also that it is a book for the lovers of Lamb, for in it one hears a century later that most strong, sweet, most immutable undersong which inspired Elia. And Mr. Tomlinson's rich and strange region, like Elia's, is no distant ground; no fabulous flight nor necromancy is wanted to find Wapping High Street.

The troubles and the after-troubles of war are complications which few of our great literary artists have attempted to portray. When will Mr. Tomlinson give us his war-book? Yet, if he does not—if something seals his lips on his ultimate psycho-history—he has given many an acute and profound rendering of war experience here and there. *Waiting For Day-light* opens in Ypres, the 1915 Ypres—before my time. It closes by the Serpentine in 1921. It is a document of searching particularity upon those incredible years between, and matters relative to them. Mr. Tomlinson is a man who has a habit of noticing awkward details, and when he catches Ruskin in the act of calling war "noble play", or observes a working man reading Swedenborg, he is apt to set forth difficult nuts for the teeth of the Philistines.

His latest work, *Tidemarks,* is akin to his earliest. It is an archipelago itself, of large and opulent, of fierce and bitter, of laughing and crying scenery. It is a treasury of his spiritual and technical gifts, which blend in a prose not to be bedimmed by a close collocation with the resplendence of Herman Melville, nor seeming in the least insensitive if heard in alternation with Charles Lamb. Since the reviewer of *Tidemarks* cannot fail to quote from it, I return to the previous volumes for a glimpse or two of this modern master.

Picture the upper Amazon; let a certain Jim, who takes little water with it, navigate a canoe with the author and a box of dynamite in it to a creek, to catch fish. Jim is a trifle dreamy, at the beginning, and his way of fixing his fuse, lighting it and dropping the explosive into the sullen forest water is sufficiently menacing. And then—

> "It sank. There were a few bubbles, and we sat regarding each other in the quiet of a time which had been long dead, waiting for something to happen in a time to come. At the end of two weeks the bottom of the river fell out, with the noise of the collapse of an iron foundry on a Sunday. Our boat tried to leap upward, but failed. The water did not burst asunder. It vibrated, and was then convulsed.

> Dead fish appeared everywhere, patches of white all round; but we hardly saw them. There was a great head which emerged from the floor, looking upwards sleepily, and two hands moved slowly. These quietly sank again. The tail of the saurian appeared, slowly described a half circle, and went. The big alligator then lifted itself, and performed some grotesque antics with deliberation and gravity. Then it gathered speed. It rotated, thrashed and drummed. It did all that a ten-horse-power maniac might. I think the natives shrieked. I think Jim kept saying "hell"; for I was conscious only with my eyes. When the dizzy reptile recovered, it shot away among the trees like a torpedo.

> We went home. That night I understand the second mate was kept awake listening to me, as I slept, bursting into spasms of dreadful merriment.

After this alligator, it is difficult to return to the proper subject of my article; but one point remains to be touched upon. For years past Mr. Tomlinson has been writing the liveliest and soundest literary criticism; his modesty has probably caused him to recoil from suggestions that he should collect his many papers in that way; but when he at last does so, the weather will be fine, and the birds will sing in the branches.

J. B. Priestley (essay date 1927)

SOURCE: "H. M. Tomlinson," in *Saturday Review of Literature,* Vol. 3, No. 23, January, 1927, pp. 477-78.

[In the following essay, Priestley praises Tomlinson's realistic portrayal of his travels.]

Most of his readers, perhaps all but the most astute, would be surprised if they met him. There is nothing of the traveler about H. M. Tomlinson. He is not bronzed, hearty, hail-fellow-well-met, nor does he carry with him any suggestion of great distances and strange suns. Yet his appearance, I think, is significant, revealing not a little of his secret. At a first superficial glance, he looks like a rather hard-bitten city clerk. At a second glance, he looks like a gnome, who has come up from some elfin solitude to observe the stir of things on the bright surface of the world, to see men hurry down long streets, swing up to their navigating bridges, or dive below to their engine rooms, and harry their little ships across the globe to some fantastic heart of darkness. These two contradictory appearances bring us close to the secret of his unique power as an essayist of travel. His work would not have the force it has unless he were at once the city clerk, that is, the man who knows the life of the dark streets, and knows what it is to escape, and the elfin recorder, with such a wealth of exact yet luminous imagery, who travels here, there, and everywhere in search of strangely significant facts. He is not to be confused with those writers—and there are not a few of them—who deal largely in the same wares, the docks and the old clippers, and little ports on the edge of the jungle, for the purpose of achieving cheap romantic effects. Theirs is the way of easy escape. Although, to the casual observer, he may seem to travel the same path, actually his way is very different, for it is that of hard escape.

. . . . .

He does not turn his back on hard facts, and lose himself and his reader in romantic glamour. He has a lightning eye for a fact, and a grim, ironical appreciation of the hardest of them. This does not mean that poetical glamour does not exist for him. On the contrary, he continually recognizes its presence with all the gusto of the true romantic, and it is for him the beginning of things. Time and again, he admits it:

> You probably know there are place-names, which, when whispered privately, have the unreasonable power of translating the spirit east of the sun and west of the moon. They cannot be seen in print without a thrill. The names in the atlas which do that for me are a motley lot, and you, who see no magic in them, but have your lunacy in another phase, would laugh at mine. Celebes, Acapulco, Para, Port Royal, Cartagena, the Marquesas, Panama, the Mackenzie River, Tripoli, or Barbary—they are some of mine.

That essay—perhaps the finest of all his shorter papers—called **"A Shipping Parish"** from *London River,* in which he laments the vanished glories of Poplar, is made up of exact detail observed against a vague, glamorous background of dim horizons and lovely lost ships. He hugs with delight his knowledge that the sea creeps almost into the heart of London, that you have only to go a little way past the offices of Fenchurch Street to arrive at the foreshore, where there are saloons full of men whose talk may be pieced together to form an epic. He tells us how, when a boy, he had to take some documents to a vessel loading in the London dock:

> She was sailing that tide. It was a hot July noon. It is unlucky to send a boy, who is marked by all the omens for a city prisoner, to that dock, for it is one of the best of its kind. He had not been there before. There was an astonishing vista, once inside the gates, of sherry butts and port casks. On the flagstones were pools of wine lees. There was an unforgettable smell. It was of wine, spices, oakum, wool, and hides. The sun made it worse, but the boy, I think, preferred it strong. After wandering along many old quays, and through the openings of dark sheds that, on so sunny a day, were stored with cool night and cubes and planks of gold, he found his ship, the *Mulatto Girl*. She was for the Brazils.

The Master, the very figure for a boy's eye, told him that there was a berth for him if he would go along. But the boy did not go, and "never heard again of the Mulatto Girl." You might say that he has spent the rest of his life looking for her.

Here then, obviously, is the desire to escape. We could not deny it even if we would. Escape is the secret of the magnificent gusto that we discover in his first book, **The Sea and the Jungle,** a book that has no single passages equal to some of the finest things in his later volumes but is, nevertheless, his most sustained and perhaps his best performance. At the beginning of that book, we meet again that "City prisoner," now grown up. On a certain grimy morning, he catches the inevitable 8:35 for the City and finds himself once more caught in the dreary routine, a squirrel turning in a cage. A few bitter paragraphs dismiss the whole foolish business. But then the Skipper arrives; the Skipper, bound for the very heart of the Amazonian forest. "I saw an open door," he tells us. "I go out. It was as though the world had been suddenly lighted, and I could see a great distance." Once more he is asked to go, and this time he goes. The adventure begins with Swansea in the black rain, but he can chant: "Now do I come at last, O Liberty, my loved and secret divinity! Your passionate pilgrim is here, late, though still young and eager-eyed." The rest, that long journey through the grey tumult of the Atlantic to the steaming reaches of the Amazon, we know or should know if we have any love of travel and good writing. It is related in some of the best descriptive prose of our time.

. . . . .

But to honest minds (and here is a burningly honest mind), there is no such thing as absolute escape. We only move from one set of responsibilities to another. Liberty only confers upon us the power of making our own and possibly sterner choice. The sea demands a routine more exacting and inflexible than that imposed by bank managers or editors, and a man without a romantic imagination, a Dr. Johnson, has good warrant for preferring a

gaol to a ship. Given that glamour we have already noted, the case is altered, but an honest mind cannot escape into the very blue of idle hours and pretty adjectives. What Tomlinson did was to escape from a dreary routine to an heroic routine, and it is this that binds him, as it did Conrad, to the men of the sea, who, in an age when so many of our activities are petty and muddled and cynical, are still able to do their duty, simply and stoutly. Theirs is one of the eternal and symbolical callings. Conrad saw this, and thus was able to turn a quarter-deck into an arena of tragic circumstance, to express through an account of some schooner in heavy seas an heroic vision of this life. There is a similar attitude of mind to be found in many of Tomlinson's grim and vivid records, and it has brought him some of his finest passages. Consider the moving significance, for example, of his description of the derelict. He watches the seas pouring over it, watches it all from the deck of an enormous New York liner, and then concludes with this:

> There was something ironic in the indifference of her defenceless body to these unending attacks. It mocked this white and raging post-mortem brutality, and gave her a dignity that was cold and superior to all the eternal powers could now do. She pitched helplessly head first into a hollow, and a door flew open under the break of her poop; it surprised and shocked us, for the dead might have signed to us then. She went astern of us fast, and a great comber ran at her, as if it had just spied her, and thought she was escaping. There was a high white flash, and a concussion we heard. She had gone. But she appeared again far away, forlorn on a summit of desolation, black against the sunset. The stump of her bowsprit, the accusatory finger of the dead, pointed at the sky.

There is the ring of genuine tragic feeling in this clean and strong prose, all the more moving because of its reticence.

There is a difference, however, between our author and Conrad, and it is a difference as important as their likeness. Conrad was himself a seaman, and shadowed forth his views of things indirectly, by way of romantic narrative. Tomlinson, on the other hand, is, as we have seen, an escaped "City prisoner," now a traveler, a recorder of his impressions; indeed, perhaps the shortest description of him is that he is a reporter of genius. He has been endowed with an amazingly sharp eye and a prose style that is at once unusually vivid and exact. If newspapers were still produced for intelligent people, and were not afraid of detached yet eager minds, their editors would want to send him out every hour of the day and night and would not stop short of kidnapping to secure his services. There is nothing he cannot make as memorable to a reader as one of that reader's own unusual experiences. He can drain a scene, a figure, an event, of all its color and bloom and salt and tang. It is only just to Fleet Street to add that this fact was realized and that for some years he was one of its special descriptive writers. He was sent to the scenes of various catastrophes, and finally arrived on the scene of the greatest catastrophe of all, being for some time a war correspondent. In this capacity he was not a success: he saw too much and felt too much. The ideal reporter sees this life as something of a show; the less he feels the more able he will be to reproduce the official emotions expected of him; at heart he should regard a European war merely as a glorified circus, content to sharpen a few more pencils when faced with the enlarging vistas of death and international ruin. At the front, Tomlinson found again that heroic routine, but now it was robbed of all the glamour of great distances, the poetry of fantastic names, and his experiences there left him a legacy of not ignoble bitterness. Hence the difference between the author of *The Sea and the Jungle,* written before the war, and *Waiting for Daylight,* whose grim title tells its own story.

A glance at his situation reveals its irony and probably explains the ironical twist that has been given to his thought. He is a reporter of genius because he brings so much mind and heart to the task, but, as we have just seen, it is perhaps better that a reporter should not have too much mind and heart. His task is to be an onlooker, an eager spectator, an epicure of curious scenes, a creator of vivid pages, and nothing more. There are numbers of men with great talent who do not ask to be anything more, and some of them made reputations during the war. But such a one as H. M. Tomlinson naturally revolts against being a mere spectator, against his task of finding new adjectives with which to conjure up the vision of death and disaster. Continually he finds himself where terrible things are happening, but neither one of the victims nor one of the rescue party, simply a man with a notebook and pencil. Send such a man, with his needle-sharp eyes and ears, his taut nerves, his blazing, honest, sensitive mind, to the front, not to take part in the ghastly business, to march and dig and shoot until he has blunted his tragic sense of what is happening, but to go here, there, and everywhere, describing what he sees and hears, missing nothing—and you have condemned him to Hell. Small wonder that he should emerge far more embittered by his experience than those of us who were actual soldiers, for we were in it, and, therefore, could afford to forget about it, whereas he was looking on, watching, watching, while a hundred thousand lads went tramping past to die. And even where the War was not in question, the position of such a writer as Tomlinson would still not be easy. If he goes to sea, it is not as a seaman, who can lie back and think no more about things once his watch is done, nor yet as a mere passenger, who knows nothing, who is all innocence, merely so much superior freight. Thus he is condemned never to take things easily, and has more responsibility, in the honest depths of his mind, than the skipper himself, for the skipper has only the ship and the crew and the freight on his back, but this brooding spectator of heroic routine has skipper, ship, crew, freight, the wide sea itself, on his back. Naturally despising the rôle of mere idle spectator, delicate and heartless collector of sensations, he has no alternative but to feel passionately about the life he has escaped into, to share—as it were—every watch, climb to every mast-head, to go down with every doomed ship.

This is what I meant by "hard escape." It is this (and a greater mastery of prose style) that distinguishes H. M. Tomlinson from those other writers who talk of clippers and jungles. Romance is there—the strange distant light has never gone out—but it is something seen between bouts of wrestling with hard facts. Remove him from these scenes of heroic routine, touched with fantastic beauty, and you have an ironist of a sardonic and uncompromising temper. His reading is significant, for when he has reluctantly set aside the great simple voyagers, his men are Swift and Heine and Butler and Anatole France. Criticism is not really his business at all, though for some years he was engaged in it. He could probably write about a few books and authors better than any man living, but for the rest, he is no critic. His demands are too narrow and personal, and he would rather explore the world than other men's minds. He would seem to pass by the light graces of life and literature with a shrug. Sentimentalism makes him angry. Hearing the seas forever roar behind him, seeing once more the image of young men going to die, he is inclined to make the mistake, common to such masculine tempers, of thinking that the things spiced with terror and danger have a superior reality and significance. But though he may be unduly embittered at times, he is anything but soured, and is far removed from certain contemporary authors who assail the universe and their fellow creatures because vanity is eating out their hearts. He might be excused if he were sometimes bitter about his own affairs and not about all the noble doomed things in this world. I for one would forgive him (though I doubt if the occasion will ever arise) because I think he has been badly treated. It would not be easy to give the author of *The Sea and the Jungle, Waiting for Daylight, Old Junk, London River, Tidemarks,* and this last and characteristic book on travel, *Gifts of Fortune,* his full due, for the hour is not ripe, but at the present time, their author, who is undoubtedly the master in his own kind of work and one of the best prose writers we have, is still suffering from what seems to me shameful neglect, both on the part of the critics and the English public. Fortunately, there is still time for this to be remedied, but meanwhile—and I am reluctant to make the admission—it looks as though yet another name will have to be added to the list of notable English authors who have been given an earlier and more generous welcome in America.

John Freeman (essay date 1927)

SOURCE: "Mr. H. M. Tomlinson," in *London Mercury,* Vol. 16, No. 94, August, 1927, pp. 400-08.

[*In the following essay, Freeman describes Tomlinson's journeys as portrayed in his writings, particularly* The Sea and the Jungle.]

I

Nothing now is left remarkable, except the flatness of the world; curiosity has destroyed whatever is curious, and invention has overtaken invention until we are fatigued by wonders and retreat into the unfathomably familiar.

It is not Mr. Tomlinson that leads me to talk thus, but the announcement, recently made, that liners are ready to take you a thousand miles up the Amazon into the heart of America. Years ago Mr. Tomlinson made this journey in a steamer full of Welsh coal, the first ocean steamer to penetrate so far among so many dangers; and now a liner will carry you with a tourist's ticket into the very heart of the obscure, and the hosts of wingless guardians of the mystery will flee from the wrath of the bacteriologist. Next year, I suppose, a convoy of palaces will steam a thousand miles further, into the never yet shaken darkness of the watery jungle, and listless throngs will finger their diaries and think, as they stare far down at the water, of last year at Dieppe, last month at Wimbledon, or last week at the London Pavilion.

It was not thus that Mr. Tomlinson made his journey, nor in this spirit that he recorded it in *The Sea and the Jungle,* his best book. He reveals himself in this narrative without being aware (I am sure) how much of himself he is revealing, and indeed without greatly caring. Nothing very wonderful happens to him or his ship, but everything that happens serves to reflect his image in motion; and of all, the chief events and the chief revelations refer to his contacts with ordinary human beings. Few writers have less invention but few have a better imagination. He sees things as poets do, in an imaginative light, not in their parts but as wholes, not rationally but by intuition; and even as he looks he is thinking of something else through which, in a moment, he is gazing more steadily, fondly and faithfully until the visible is charged with the reality of the invisible.

II

But to write thus of Mr. Tomlinson is to begin at the end. I ought to have said first of all that *The Sea and the Jungle* tells of a voyage in a tramp steamer from Swansea to Para in the Brazils, and then two thousand miles between the forests of the Amazon and the Madeira, in 1909-10. Parts of the story were published here, there and anywhere, for Mr. Tomlinson is a journalist, but the upgathering of the parts, or waves, is perfect and the whole moves like a tide. He presents his story as the story of an escape from London, a casual felicitous escape from home, streets, winter, care; a long slow voyage into the homeless tropic world; and then a hurried return to all he had fled from. He has not that "lust" of travel which the cultured are supposed to share and which means no more than an appetite for something to keep them from thinking closely and feeling sharply. He travels because he is by nature a dreamer, and he writes because he is by circumstance a rebel. His mind falls into the order of dreams, the dreams recur and stimulate him again and again to fresh journeys; in the breath of dreams he sees the same images, like figures in smoke, and he returns to the same early country of childhood's memory, the same admired characters and scenes of manhood's

memory, repeating what he loves because he loves it and because it revolves and in its turn possesses him again. Yet there is nothing dreamlike in what he tells, and perhaps his best prose is given to the sharp, clear, and simple telling of simple matters—of the rust of an anchor, the coldness of seas, the unexpectedness of stairs and passages in rough weather. Of these and a hundred other items he writes as the most businesslike, dreamless alderman would write if he could. For a long while, he says, the steamer was a harsh and foreign thing, unfriendly to the eye, hard to understand; but he learned to know her faults and now would resent any change:

> The two little streets of three doors each, to port and starboard of her amidships, the doors that open out under the shade of the boat deck to sea. There, amidships also, are the Chief's room and the galley, the engineers' messroom, and the engine-room entrance; but these last do not open overside, but look aft, from a connecting alley which runs across the ship to join the side alleyways. Forward of these cabins is the engine-room casing, where the 'midship deck broadens, but is cumbered with bunker hatches (mind your feet, at night, there); and beyond, again, is the chart-room, and over the chart-room the bridge and the wheel-house, from which is a sheer long drop to the main deck forward. At the finish of that deck is an iron wall, with the entrance to the mysterious forecastle in its centre; and over that is the uplifted head of our world watching our course, a bleak windswept place of rails, cable chains, and windlass. The poop has a timber deck, and there in fine weather the deck chairs are. The poop is a place needing exact navigation at night. Long boxes enclosing the rudder chains are on either side of it. In the centre is the saloon sky-light, the companion, the steward's ice-chest, and the hand-steering gear. Also there are two boats. I gained my night knowledge of the poop deck by assault, and retained my gains with sticking plaster. I am really proud of the privilege which has been given me to roam now this rolling shadow at night.

He shows something childlike and candid in his stare at strange things, counting and looking at them—familiar enough to others—as though no one had ever seen them before. It is as if Robinson Crusoe or John Bunyan had gone to sea in a tramp steamer and confronted that anchor, that heavy swell, those stairs and passages, and gazed half in doubt, half in delight. Thus it is that *The Sea and the Jungle* gives you immediately a double view—of what the writer sees with his unaccustomed stare, and of the fresh receptive mind touched by the succession of images and wonders. And all is so simple that there is an effect of cunning in the simplicity, the plain thing being enriched, yet no more complicated than is the tree by its shadow, which as you look becomes indeed a part of the tree.

In this he is at a great distance from Joseph Conrad. Like Mr. Tomlinson, Conrad was poor in invention, although he was uniquely rich in imagination; but it was Conrad's habit to complicate things endlessly, often without enriching them, while Mr. Tomlinson, as I have said, enriches without complicating them. All such comparisons are as stupid as comparisons of beast with beast and flower with flower, but like many stupidities they are for a time inevitable, and it will be long before a writer on the sea can escape being damned because he is not Conrad, but himself. Perhaps the main point of difference between the two is in style, and of this I shall be speaking in a moment; and the main point of likeness—since comparisons which are inevitable as well as stupid must be faced—is the moral one. Conrad was essentially and utterly simple-minded, with the simplest and most unfailing morality; and this at any rate Mr. Tomlinson shares. Integrity, faith, religiousness of heart—these pervade, stimulate and stiffen the work of both; but in Mr. Tomlinson they fortify the English puritan who has never been sophisticated by the sight of evil or embittered by renouncing it, but hates it, rather, instinctively, as one man hates oil with his food, and another theatres. Hence you feel at ease with him, for you know where he is and where he will be: he is as firm as a hawthorn, as sound as an apple, and in his looks is a good deal like both.

III

This impression of a personal character is one of the clearest and happiest impressions you receive from his books. In *The Sea and the Jungle,* especially, the personality is pure of theory, for being away from the life of cities and hasty civilisation there is little for the traveller to demur to and denounce. The rebel is quiet, and I think the work gains therefore in quality, for although rebellion may be native and hate may be as strong as admiration, a rebel in great things may become querulous in small. Mr. Tomlinson is naturally of those who now and again produce the doctrinaire, the liberals who can so readily, and so sincerely, proclaim ideas which other parties adopt. They pick the pocket of the future, but the profits pass to the tory fence or the labour fence; and so the liberals remain of all men the most miserable. It is not wonderful, therefore, that they become exacting and over-righteous, though still hardy, intrepid, bearded animals, less crude than the wolves on their left and less amiable than the oxen on their right. Mr. Tomlinson is a born liberal, but he has escaped the pressure of their circumstances and all but wholly escaped their dolorous readiness to complain. Some men are saved by humour, some by triviality, being unable to take a wrong seriously, some by honesty, being unwilling to exaggerate a wrong. Mr. Tomlinson shows little humour and is incapable of triviality, and is saved by the honesty of his heart and the sanity of his mind. Men err, they are foolish and selfish and often incapable of acting for the common good, they have built abominable cities and there is no fire to descend on the plain and purge them or destroy them; but he sees nevertheless that the world has infinite capacities, and that present evil is not a sudden corruption but an item in a sequence, a link in a chain. He is, in short, at once free from the loathsome optimism of the materialist, and the feeble pessimism of the idealist; and

whenever he tries to philosophise, cheerfulness breaks in as it did on Johnson's friend.

The Sea and the Jungle, then, is his best book not only in its literary quality but also in its outline of his character, and this is drawn firmly in his admirations. Here is a passage which is in no way emphasised, a mere page in a chronicle of common events:

> The construction camp was not more than a month old. Perched on an escarpment by the line was a row of tents, and at the back of the tents some flimsy huts built of forest stuff. They stood about a ruin of felled trees, with a midden and its butterflies in the midst. Probably thirty white men were stationed there. They were then throwing a wooden bridge across the Caracoles. Most of them were young American civil engineers, though some were English; and when I found one of them—and he happened to be a countryman of mine—balancing himself on a narrow beam high over a swift current, and, regardless of the air heavy with vapour and the torrid sun, directing the disposal of awkward weights with a concentration and keenness which made me recall with regret the way I do things at times, I saw his profession with a new regard. I noticed the men of that transient little settlement in the wilds were in constant high spirits. They betrayed nothing of the gravity of their undertaking. They might have been boys employed at some elaborate jest. But it seemed to me to be a pose of heartiness. They repelled reality with a laugh and a hand clapped to your shoulder. At our mess table, over the dishes of toucan and parrot supplied by the camp hunters, they rallied each other boisterously. There was a touch of defiance in the way they referred to the sickness and the shadow; for it was notorious that changes were frequent in their little garrison. They were forced to talk of these changes, and this was the way they chose to do it. As if laughter was their only prophylactic! But such laughter, to a visitor who did not have to wait till fever took him, but could go when he liked, could be answered only with a friendly smile. Some of my cheery friends of the Caracoles were but the ghosts of men.

Fever was not the only foe, for the plague of poisonous flies provoked a courage less conspicuous, perhaps, but not less real, even when the peril was ignored as the Chief Engineer ignored it. Mr. Tomlinson cannot dissemble his admiration of men moving so confidently in a haunted region, and certainly, by his expression of it, gives a sharper sense than Bates shows (in his *Naturalist on the Amazon*) of a land of flies that would satisfy even Mr. Abercrombie's imagination of their horror.

IV

It may be freely admitted that Mr. Tomlinson's other books are not all equal to *The Sea and the Jungle.* Some are precisely journalism, and the wisdom of collecting the items may be doubted, for when he reviews books, the poems, for instance, of Mr. Conrad Aiken, he shows that he is less interested in what men say than in what they do and the world they inhabit. Ideas attract little interest and no warmth in his regard, and so his reprinted reviews are not the things to compel a new reader's attention, and perhaps the best to be said for them is that there is nothing to repel it, certainly not that cleverness which, he sees, is craved only by the brain-sick, as drink is craved by a morbid body. There is, moreover, another difficulty in the way of esteeming some of his writings, namely, that they present him as a man exasperated by the wantonness of the war. Exasperation enters into chapter after chapter on one thing after another—an exasperation as honest as the day, as right as rain, but also, it must be owned, as unexhilarating as rain. Looking at such chapters as literature and not as evidence of propaganda, the inflammation which frets them is seen as a real weakness, and if it is indifference which makes us turn the pages rather hastily now, it is an indifference which even Mr. Tomlinson, in his innumerable spurs and flicks, does not dissipate.

But the war is left behind in his more recent books, and in *London River* (1921) is already put by. A particular interest now creeps in:

> Nothing conjures back that room so well as the recollection of a strange odour which fell from it when its door opened, as though something bodiless passed as we entered. There was never anything in the room which alone could account for the smell, for it had in it something of the sofa, which was old and black, and of the lacquered tea-caddy, within the lid of which was the faint ghost of a principle indefinably ancient and rare; and there was in it, too, something of the shells. But you could never find where the smell really came from. I have tried, and know. A recollection of that strange dusky fragrance brings the old room on a summer afternoon, so sombre that the mahogany sideboard had its own reddish light, so quiet that the clock could be heard ticking in the next room; time, you could hear, going leisurely. There would be a long lath of sunlight, numberless atoms swimming in it, slanting from a corner of the window to brighten a patch of carpet. Two flies would be hovering under the ceiling. Sometimes they would dart at a tangent to hover in another place. I used to wonder what they lived on. You felt secure there, knowing it was old, but seeing things did not alter, as though the world were established and content, desiring no new thing. I did not know that the old house, even then, quiet and still as it seemed, was actually rocking on the flood of mutable affairs; that its navigator, sick with anxiety and bewilderment in guiding his home in the years he did not understand, which his experience had never chart-ed, was sinking nerveless at his helm. For he heard, when his children did not, the premonition of breakers in seas having no landmark that he knew; felt the trend and push of new and inimical forces, and currents that carried him helpless, whither he would not go, but must, heartbroken, into the uproar and welter of the modern.

It is the touch of himself, himself among the long-acquainted docks and quays of *London River,* that gives a peculiar value to the book bearing this for title, and incites him to descriptions that are vital and moving because they preserve for him what he most loves in the world—the lines of a sailing ship, the heavy strength of sailors buffeted by misfortune, the violence and the beauty of the sea. I think a barquentine, he says, the most beautiful of ships, the most aerial and graceful of rigs, memorable as a Greek statue; and added "to her beauty of line there went a richness of colour which made our dull parish a notable place. . . . You could believe there was a soft radiation from that ship's sides which fired the water about her, but faded when far from her sides, a delicate and faery light which soon expired." And throughout his remembrance of Dockland—"once we were a famous shipping parish"—there is an entangling of memories and regrets, that familiar sense of passed and passing, which may so easily be overcharged but which none the less, by a truthful man, may be uttered in words that we cannot and would not forget. He was born where he could hear even in his cradle the ships of London River, and before he became a writer was familiar enough with sailors and freights; and so there is something solid at the base of his reminiscence, and whatever romantic hue is apparent now when he speaks of ships and water is reflected from a lamp lit in childhood and still undarkened. Too sparingly are the reverting glances allowed, and I wish he might be persuaded to indulge his fondness and add to that literature of remembrance which is surely of all prose writing the most endearing and durable.

v

But while he keeps us waiting for this Mr. Tomlinson asks us to be content with a volume akin to *London River,* one of a series intended to show the state of English commerce—shipping, agricultural and industrial—in 1926, his own contribution being the most vivid of studies and also, I fancy, the most personal and odd book to crush into uniformity. I wish that other treatises on political disease were half so stimulating and persuasive; it is impossible to disagree with a man who writes so well, plucks you by the sleeve and has your sympathy before you begin to think. This is how he speaks of English shipping in *Under the Red Ensign* (1927):

> I can be as doting in an old shipyard as are others in the cloisters of their old schoolhouse. The junk and lumber and the tradition affect me. There are ghosts about. I cannot believe there is much that London reveals by chance to the curious, or even to the cunning, which hints her story with deeper implications than that show of the Thames from Duke Shore, of Limehouse. On one hand is the reach of the Lower Pool and on the other is Blackwall Reach beginning the loop about the Isle of Dogs. The day is grey, the tide full, the ships pass, and there smoulders modern London, obscure and grim, where the labour of the Nobodies keeps our chimneys smoking and feeds with oil the light for our rare midnight studies. How could even a stranger come in with the flood tide, and approach that immense and central gloom which seems not a city but an ominous darkening of the heavens, a

warning of the dubious enterprise of beings who have rebelled against the light and have dowsed even the sunset into smoking anger, and not be awed by the greatness of it, by the shadow of a tradition he does not know? But the tradition of that city, though darkness is its sign, is not ignoble, for the artless souls who made it and who still keep its fires, cannot be said to have laboured only for pay. They must have felt, though from what instinct we shall never know, that man must live by more than what goes into his mouth. They will endure for a ghostly idea, and perish for it, just as though they were Christian souls. We have witnessed that in recent years.

The whole chapter is sustained at this note, to the prejudice, no doubt, of social economics but to the great advantage of Mr. Tomlinson's personal account of his search for the truth about shipping. He collects statistics but avows that he does not know how to use them; and he collects impressions and characters, sounds and colours, and makes a picture of a precarious industry which no one else could paint so well. Some of his chapters remind me of a writer who has been so lightly neglected—for it is easy to neglect what is truthful but unassertive, and follow after foreign idols—and whom Mr. Tomlinson himself might admire, the late Frank Bullen. For Bullen possessed an earnest, instinctive admiration of the same men as Mr. Tomlinson writes of, and he has only been forgotten because of the buzz of worse writers. Mr. Tomlinson has, however, the advantage of a knowledge gained from his journalism, a knowledge of the way things are going under the monstrous engine of progress. All good workers are artists, he says, lamenting that their pride should be wasted on something vast and sightless; and they have found reason to watch in horror the movements of the imperial State. We have been overtaken by industrial science, and calamity has fallen because we do not yet comprehend the energies we have unloosed; the clutch is slipping and the power is wasting noisily, while nobody knows what to do—"it is becoming clear to us that a long-continued concentration upon mechanics may put out the light of the mind." But the poet with his dream of beauty, and the savant with his dream of truth, these may yet be saviours, and it is not prosperity we need so much as another attitude of mind—the poet's. And thinking thus, recalling the false confidence of the past, and seeing the present failure of all confidence, he is able to look for a better comprehension of "those awful and nonsensical words," the Beatitudes; the state of British shipping in 1926 having been forgotten long before the last page is reached.

Even Mr. Tomlinson's travel books are not more romantic in essence than this study in economic conditions, and when he writes *Tidemarks,* a record of an Eastern journey in 1923, he does not make Malaya and Singapore more alluring than London's river and "our shipping parish." A man cannot be born and bred in several places at once, and it is because that gorgeous East was not his cradle that Mr. Tomlinson has not succeeded in lifting its heavy oppression from our minds. His record is as good as he can make it, but the disenchantment which he feels in looking back is shared by the reader. Inevitably one reads his story with an eye on *The Sea and the Jungle,* and finds that he is repeating an experience; his observation no doubt is more skilled but not so fresh, there is less of the adventurer and more of the tourist, less to tell of what few of us can attempt and more of what all of us can so easily enjoy. We are aware, he remarks, that even our own street may sometimes give us the sensational idea that we really do not know it. He refuses to distort his brief span by trying to crowd every experience into it and does not answer his own question: *What are the significant things in travel?* for an answer is needless. He carries the unfamiliar about with him—can Ternate and Tidore be stranger? Certainly the East is scarcely strange now, since Java uses holiday posters as vivid as Bournemouth's, and the cinema theatres in the dark groves present the same films of faithless wives and bold burglars as we enjoy in London. When someone tells him there is nothing in the world like Borobudor, he answers, "This poor world is overloaded with Borobudors. We struggle beneath them, yet nothing will satisfy you but you must dig out another from the forest which had fortunately hidden it." And once again the supreme discovery is the exaltation of homecoming and the renewal of a million ancient contacts:

> England! That shadow was the indenture on the very stars of an old grandeur, the memory impressed on night itself, blurred but indelible, of an ancient renown. It was the emanation of an idea too great for us to know; the unsubstantial reminder in my isolation and misgiving of wonderful things almost forgotten, of the dreams and exaltations of splendid youth, of the fidelity of comrades, of noble achievements, of our long-passed intimate sorrows, of precious things unspoken but understood, of our dead.

His attitude towards mere signs and wonders is developed in *Gifts of Fortune* "with some hints for those about to travel." We are often told that travel gives light to the mind, but he wonders whether it does. "Light comes to us unexpectedly and obliquely"—what can reach us in a floating cabaret, in the midst of organised amusements? To Mr. Tomlinson this oblique light suggests a life and a tendency outside our own, indifferent to our crises:

> At sunrise to-day, on the high ridge of the shingle which rose between me and the sea, six herons stood motionless in a row, like immense figures of bronze. They were gigantic and ominous in that light. They stood in another world. They were like a warning of what once was, and could be again, huge and threatening, magnified, out of all resemblance to birds, legendary figures which closed vast gulfs of time at a glance and put the familiar shingle in another geological epoch. When they rose and slowly beat the air with concave pinions I thought very Heaven was undulating. With those grotesque black monsters shaking the sky, it looked as though man had not yet arrived.

These phrases are taken from the conclusion of a chapter entitled "On the Chesil Bank," and remind me once more that this "light" falls on him almost peculiarly amid English scenes, within sight and sound of the sea; for they travel farthest who travel least and do not encumber their vision with objects half seen in the delirium of speed. It is the reflective mind that is the seeing mind, and as I have already suggested it is in his power of presenting things in a double vision that Mr. Tomlinson shows his true value as a writer.

His prose style needs little comment, for its virtues are clear and make their own way, and the passages already cited may be looked at again for illustration. Sometimes he indulges himself with the short, sharp staccato sentence, one following another like barks, loud and arresting it is true, but seldom pleasant and seldom as effective as here:

> And what were those ivory figures leaping and shouting in the shallows? As I watched them in that light a doubt shook me. I began to wonder whether I knew that little ship, and those laughing figures, and that sea. Who were they? Where was it? When was it?

Usually, the serenity of his mind is shown in the easy breathing of his sentences, their rhythm being palpable yet not formal. His prose is full of light and movement; if he writes of the sea it is untragically and without seeking ponderous phrases, and if he writes of men they are unsophisticated figures in his narrative. His tendency is lyrical, and the serene, ripe ardour which might have gone into poetry has liberated his prose and made it, without extravagance, personal, and without artifice, bright.

Frederick P. Mayer (essay date 1928)

SOURCE: "H. M. Tomlinson: The Eternal Youth," in *Virginia Quarterly Review,* Vol. 4, No. 1, 1928, pp. 72-82.

[*In the following essay, Mayer disputes the comparison of Tomlinson with Joseph Conrad, noting Tomlinson's unique abilities as a writer.*]

I

Because his book is labeled fiction, H. M. Tomlinson, with the publication of his first novel, *Gallions Reach,* is gaining fame. Before, Tomlinson, essayist and traveler, enjoyed but a limited distinction. Recently, however, and mainly through *Gallions Reach,* there has grown a Tomlinson vogue. He has been praised as "a second Conrad."

The truth is, Tomlinson does not derive from nor resemble Conrad. *Gallions Reach*—the book by which Tomlinson's name is linked with Conrad's and by which Tomlinson is becoming popularly known—has added no inches to Tomlinson's literary stature. As a novel, it is a doubtful success and then succeeds only

where Tomlinson reached distinction many years ago in his seven travel books of essays, some of them now quite old. These books are: *The Sea and the Jungle, Old Junk, London River, Waiting for Daylight, Tide Marks, Gifts of Fortune,* and *The Foreshore of England.* Both Tomlinson and Conrad write about the sea; that is their chief agreement. If that makes them alike, then Jane Austen and Sinclair Lewis are similar, because they both write of small towns; and Felix Riesenberg and Edith Wharton resemble each other because they both write of New York. Tomlinson can stand on his own feet.

Who is H. M. Tomlinson? His name heads frequent articles in *Harper's* and *Century,* and he has published books and essays for twenty years. But his fame is recent. In an unpublished biographical essay, he says,

> It seems to me an impossible task to interest strangers in such an early history as mine. That is all private litter, except for what has appeared in my books. My existence has been uneventful and unmarked; except, I fear, by the Recording Angel. And when he publishes it, some day, I do not expect a ripple of excitement to pass round the Judgment hall. It will be heard only in dreary resignation by the few who are still waiting their turn while the T's are being worked through.

But this humility is not warranted. Tomlinson's life has been eventful beyond most. He has gone to the Malays and to the Amazon; he has reported wars and explored London; he has worked for ships and on ships. He is now past fifty—a veteran journalist; his first book was published when he was thirty-eight. That was *The Sea and the Jungle* and laid the foundation for what is rapidly becoming fame.

II

The present vogue for Tomlinson is not hard to understand. But it is surprising that it did not happen long ago. What he writes about has been popular since Homer and *Beowulf.* The old sea has always been a wonder. Boys whittle boats and watch twigs swirl downstream in a creek. Men squander afternoons in summer seeing ships unload in harbor, and poor fellows from offices dream of cruisers outward bound. There is a charm about it, just as Herman Melville said there was. And all his life Tomlinson has lived around ships. He has written much about them and the strange lands to which they sometimes go. His tale has always been strange and full of things most of us cannot see. The magic of the ocean is in it.

Yet, this vogue comes from more than Tomlinson's use of the sea and ships for subjects. Tomlinson, better still, gives his readers enthusiasm. For him the world is born new every morning. He has never lost a boy's pleasure in a new sight or sound or smell. That, in an old world, ought to assure him of fame. Tomlinson has never sought eternal youth—he is the eternal youth. Men who grow old lose the capacity for enjoying things. They think less and less of their birthdays—except to count them morosely—

and they care nothing for candles and a cake. To use a figure, Tomlinson can still enjoy a birthday party. For him, at each affair, there never was another party like it and never such a fine company gathered together.

To read *Tide Marks* and see how surprising it is to Tomlinson to set sail on a ship; to see how splendid all the sailors are and how glorious every prospect (nor is man vile), is to be convinced that Tomlinson never rode a ship before. You believe he is young, inexperienced. You become startled to learn that although he may be easy to surprise, he is not young in years or in experience. You wonder at his fifty or more years.

This youth, or freshness, is a quality of good literature. We must grant Tomlinson much for it. Many wise men regret its passing. Wordsworth always did: "Our birth is but a sleep and a forgetting. . . ." Longfellow bewails his lost youth, and when we look for what distinguishes an artist from other men, we usually come back to this freshness which enables him to enjoy what is to other men dull or stale.

There is a subtle suggestion in this which hints, however, that Tomlinson is mature despite his youthful zest. Where young writers wage combat, Tomlinson never grows angry. He has lived too long to think that eccentric battles against restrictive convention avail. He brings heightened delight instead of growing pains. Such peace is not often found in young men.

III

But criticism, as usual cold and somewhat clammy, cannot accept this enthusiasm without what may be some derogatory qualifications. It must be remembered, however, that whatever adverse judgement may, within this article, be passed, it is, nevertheless, the opinion of a reader who has found in the prose of H. M. Tomlinson a steadfast pleasure.

Enthusiasm, or freshness, is never good because of itself. Freshness is either arrested development—immaturity—or genius—hypermaturity, to use a parallel phrase. Sherwood Anderson, in some of his moments of infantile admiration, may stand as an example of the freshness of immaturity. John Keats, who delights justly in a nightingale, represents the freshness of genius.

Is the delight of Tomlinson's the one or the other? Let us take up the case of arrested development first.

One way to keep enjoying experience and to get what the motion pictures term, so justly, a thrill, is to hypnotize yourself into thinking every strange view perfect and every visible man splendid. It is the way of the professional optimist, and it implies shutting your eyes to all evil and surrendering your common sense. It means neglecting what your senses tell you smells bad or tastes bad and it means neglecting what your mind tells you is ugly or miserable or unhappy. Such delight in a young world is a symptom of arrested development.

That way of enjoying life lacks common sense. It wants perspective and wisdom. It is the way of the traveler who comes back from his journey full of the glory of himself . . . he has seen so much; he has discovered this, and this, and this. He has no sense of the other man's experience, no realization that other men may have seen all this years ago without shouting so loudly about it. He forgets that the enthusiasms he has may not be those of other people, and he may bore instead of please his listeners. Such freshness is the result of a young mind rudely shocked and unable to grasp what has hit it. This is not Tomlinson. He is not a professional optimist. He is not a babbling mouth.

A second example of arrested development is exhibited in getting enthusiastic over things not worth your enthusiasm. There are trivial minded men—and they write books—who are pleased inordinately by the lavender pastel shades of smoke and fire from a blast furnace at night. They do not understand what labor and pain go into the making of those pretty colors they adore. The lover of the lights must not forget their meaning. Women lavish affection on dogs and cats. Similarly, artistic delight can be lavished on trivialities, and since there are more trivial things in the world than there are valuable, petty-minded enthusiasts can be perpetually amused.

In English literature there are many things which seem through centuries to have given lasting pleasure. They are, some of them, the stars, flowers, stretches of country and forest in mid-summer, the smile of a beautiful girl, the sound of a brook at night, the gentle animals on a farm. To find that your heart can lift up when you see daffodils is to be young in the right way. It is no sign of arrested development. It is an indication that you have not been dulled by living. The clouds of glory have not all passed away. The prison house has not yet built its walls. To hypnotize your mind into unvarying enthusiasm or to be pleased by ignoble things is a sign of arrested development. To have the capacity to enjoy what is worth your devotion is one of the marks of genius.

IV

H. M. Tomlinson, then, does seem to get excited over the proper things. His is a genius for discovery, and a genius for appreciation. He has an unusual ability to find pleasure. But there is this detraction. Although he gets his pleasure from things honestly worth the effort, I sometimes wonder whether they are worth the amount of enthusiasm which he expends.

In *Tide Marks,* Mr. Tomlinson describes a splash bath, one of those tropical inconveniences by which many Europeans on tour have kept themselves clean. Now, a splash bath, I am told, is a novelty, rudimentary, honest, but nevertheless a very ordinary and sometimes messy substitute for the delights of sanitary plumbing. To the traveler weary of civilization, it may seem refreshing in its Biblical simplicity, but it is, after all, a splash bath.

But to Mr. Tomlinson there never was such a thing as a splash bath! There never will be again so splendid, so delightful, so humorous, so insinuating a diversion as a splash bath! It pleases him in the same unmeasured way as a tin toy gratifies a youngster. He will not eat, he will not sleep, he will not work while he has a splash bath. True, sometimes Mr. Tomlinson plays with his delight in a thoroughly knowing and sophisticated way. He tells us, by his style, "This is just fooling; it isn't worth much; but it amuses us both." He realizes his own extravagance and sometimes plays on it. That takes some of the sting away. It makes him less of an enthusiast.

It shows us our answer. Tomlinson does possess a certain genius, even though he steadily grows rapturous where passing interest would be sufficient. But he does find joy in the honest and simple things of experience. He is able to keep his ability to be surprised, and he can laugh at objects even while he relishes them.

V

This brings us to the dangers of Tomlinson's style and structure.

In general, all this can be put down by saying that Tomlinson's writing is a highly personal method of explaining the world. It is only the world impinging upon his own consciousness that counts, not the great sweep of life which may be more important but which has not touched his senses. He has little objectivity. His attitude colors reality. This is usually a delightful color, but that is beside the point.

No author ever achieves perfect objectivity. What I mean, though, is the desire on the part of many men to discover the great meaning of the world even when that world's action has not become a personal experience. It is what might be termed an abstract philosophy. Tomlinson has little of this; he lives in a world of vivid sights and sounds and smells, and he communicates these with rare skill. He "philosophizes" much, but he never drops his enthusiasms sufficiently to order them and to give them intellectual plan and relative importance. It is not that he neglects the cosmic, but he invokes it on almost every subject and with equal fervor.

If Tomlinson had no more than an attitude to communicate, he would be bad. He has more, despite what has just been said. But he is not able ever to create more than himself. In his own mind, I dare say, there lies a scheme of faith and a way of life as beautiful as his prose, but what I get from his books is always the intimate sense of a new concrete experience. There is seldom any valuable intellectual residue. I am not trying to lecture an author for failing to write as I want. This is merely an evaluation of Tomlinson, the eternal youth.

John Keats used to write about "negative capability." By that he meant the ability of a poet to forget himself in the intensity of things greater than himself. Keats did it. Tomlinson cannot forget himself. It is too wonderful that all this should have happened to him. He is a traveler and he writes travel essays because such writings are the reactions of objects and persons and places on one observer. They require almost no objectivity and take energy from their surcharge of personality. They are not the highest type of literature, certainly. That objectivity which let Thomas Hardy picture men and places and let him forget himself—and lets us now forget the author— is the path to genius of the first rank.

VI

Tomlinson's enthusiasm for new experiences finds permanent expression in his style, which partakes of the good and bad qualities of enthusiasm in general.

A repetition of exclamatory delight always loses conviction. That is one trouble with the Tomlinson books. The enthusiasm of the author tends to persist after the reader has stopped being enthusiastic. The sensations of wonder and surprise are worked upon until the effect resembles boredom. In more than one of his books, we begin by being told that the author felt securely bound to the ordinary routine of office work, and suddenly a voyage to unknown seas projects itself upon him and becomes an amazing reality. Now, that is a fine thing and it is worth writing about. It is the supreme satisfaction of any vacation, and it is the great delight of travel—finding yourself where by rights you ought not to be. But after more than one book starts out with the general unbelief of the author in what Heaven sends him, you begin to wonder why he cannot get used to it, and, however slightly, expect it. The beginnings of *Tide Marks* and *The Sea and the Jungle* are evidences of this trait, and the same note is struck in the other books.

The style of the Tomlinson prose, smooth as it is, lacks economy. It is true that Tomlinson strikes a high level in descriptive travel sketches, and often, in his books, he reaches what he set out to capture, the magic of a tree or jungle village or stretch of sluggish water. He writes steadily better prose than many other living Englishmen of the most applauded names. He is always interested, usually interesting, and he knows what prose rhythms mean—sometimes to his own detriment.

That is the trouble. His exuberance of observation makes his style exuberant. He fills a page with words, when two lines would be more effective. He forgets that dwelling on an emotion sometimes takes the fire out of it. He uses rare words and too many words; he indulges in circumlocution. He gives personality and purpose to inanimate things and plays with ideas while he is on the road to a more important thought. All this is evident in the beginnings of *Gallions Reach*. Such circumlocutions are not so easily noticed in essays, because the essay is the great store house of casualism. But in what is called a novel, overwriting may be worse than no writing. Fluency may harm as much as effort.

Here is a description of scrub women in a London office building. The picture is absurdly ornate for so ordinary a theme; it may be amusing to write in this way, but it is circumlocution and "fine" writing. It lacks simplicity and calls attention to the words instead of to the idea. There is much like this in the Tomlinson prose.

> Between those hours the arid and hollow limestone, where nothing grows but ciphers, is thronged with a legion as intent and single minded as a vast formicarium. Before those hours, and at night, it is as silent as the ruins of Memphis, and as empty, except for a few vestals with brooms and pails who haunt the temporary solitude on their ministration to whatever joss presides over numerals.

It is true that only an unspoiled mind can look at scrub women with such interest and playfulness; it is equally true that such prose is florid and wordy and inexpertly phrased for such essentially simple realities as the women who scrub floors.

Gallions Reach shows Tomlinson's structural limitations. He has not written a novel, despite its name. It is, at its best, a good travel narrative; at its worst, it is a novel with poor motivation and a creaking and disjointed plot. To see its weakness one need only compare it with the work of an able craftsman of novels, Willa Cather, a woman whose gifts are consistent with the demands of the type. *Death Comes for the Archbishop* is not a travel essay of New Mexico. It is an objective character study of a real man's life in New Mexico, with a clear pattern, strong motivation, unity, and shape, even though the mood of the place bulks large. *Gallions Reach* is merely another interpretation of Tomlinson. *Death Comes for the Archbishop* is much more than another interpretation of Willa Cather. It is an interpretation of the Archbishop, and we forget the author while we read. We can never forget Tomlinson in *Gallions Reach*. His personality as an essayist takes possession of what should have been pictures of other people.

Moreover, novels need characterization of real people. The only real character Tomlinson sketches in fully in his book is that of himself. It is a picture of a gentleman. I do not see how anyone can read a book of Tomlinson's without wanting to know and talk to the author. But create other people he has not yet done. Those ecstatic critics who compare Tomlinson's novel to any of Conrad's must have forgotten the variety and reality of the men and women in Conrad's tales. They are seldom too bad or too good; they are both, like people on the street.

VII

All talent is not of one sort. Though a man may want to write one thing, he often does another better. So it is with Tomlinson; he can cultivate with distinction his own garden. As yet, he has not revealed his probable talent as a novelist. His readers will, of course, welcome that day, if it ever comes, when he does amplify what he has already done into a well-rounded piece of prose fiction.

Literary history is full of examples of able writers whose ability was of one sort only. I recall Henry James and his unfortunate excursions into the drama; Stevenson and his poor plays; George Eliot and her regrettable poetry.

To say things that limit your admiration of a man you admire is especially hard in these days of slipshod superlatives. Every new book steams with the effusions of the publishers. Great names recommend a new book as "cruel and devastating beauty" (whatever that may be!) . . . "a unique contribution to English letters" . . . "the start of a new type of English prose" . . ."the finest poetry since Keats" . . . "rich and magnificent." In the light of such glowing praise any more exact comment seems grudging. To say that you read Tomlinson with pleasure and to say that you like his enthusiasm and vivid pictures and humor and decency seem a paradox these days unless you go the whole way and—ignoring all else—say that the book is perfect.

H. M. Tomlinson is an able essayist, one of the few noble practitioners of a noble but vanishing art. I know of no other man who can give me so intimate a picture of what he has seen. The reality and immediacy are, often, magical. I look on lands I never saw, and I see them with my own eyes. I forget that my life has routine and that it sometimes grows dull. I catch the moment when the ship first trembles as she leaves the dock, and I go out to sea, where I cannot often go. H. M. Tomlinson's youth carries me on to voyages I would never take without his energy and excitement. He is young enough, at fifty, to relish living in this world. The light of the sun on London River and the sweep of rain across a ship's prow at night are still unbelievably new. The sight of an office building still makes him think strange and unbound thoughts. He has not yet, in those terrible words of a cynical world, "settled down."

H. M. Tomlinson has delight enough to live his life out. He has promise of more than that richness which he has already given. It is only of a man with youth that one can apply the word, promise. Yet that seems a just word. Whether he writes another book or not, Mr. Tomlinson gives promise of more in him than has yet come out, of more to life than we who live it ever see.

Odell Shepard (essay date 1931)

SOURCE: "In the Great Tradition," in *Yale Review*, Vol. 20, No. 4, June, 1931, pp. 843-44.

[*In the following review of* Out of Sounding, *Shepard praises Tomlinson's ability to evoke a mood of nostalgia.*]

Until one has read halfway through this book [*Out of Soundings*] one regards it as merely another collection of random essays such as Mr. Tomlinson has given us before and may, if we are lucky, give us again. Gradually there emerges, however, not so much a plan and purpose as a tendency of thought or tone of feeling, perhaps not entirely conscious in the author's mind, which produces at least the unity of mood. By the time the reader lays down the book he is likely to feel that it is one of the more poignant expressions of nostalgia for the more secure and orderly and human world which most of us can still remember. Without anger or any outcry Mr. Tomlinson mourns the passing, in our time, of many things fair and frail that have delighted human hearts for hundreds of years and that nothing can now save; he deplores the devastation of sanctuaries recently ours which we cannot preserve for our children. Less concerned with causes than with effects, he gives us no more novel explanation of these inevitable losses than those provided by the Great War and the Machine. For he is little of a philosopher but much of an artist; and so he is most effective when speaking, with a sort of quiet ecstasy that borders pain, about the delicate beauty of his England, so easily soiled past recall, or about the barque in full sail which he once overtook and saw at dawn from the bridge of a steamship. The most memorable essay in the volume is that concerning Thomas Hardy, which is a requiem less for a man than for an epoch. Yet the reader is likely to recall with greatest pleasure the extremely deft symbolism of **"The Wreck,"** with its reverberations of tragedy that roll like thunder up and down the mind, and, at the other extreme of the literary gamut, the charming humor of the tribute to **"Joey,"** a pet owl.

It would be almost an impertinence to point out once more that Mr. Tomlinson is a writer of prose in the great tradition, one of the very small and dwindling band of writers who manage style not as a decoration but as a means of heightened expression. He has no exceptional funds of knowledge or experience, and his thought is neither novel nor deep; but humor he has, good sense, the gift of the flashing phrase, and wide acquaintance with beauty. This is enough to make any book of his worthy of attention.

Although it is handsomely printed and bound, the volume is too heavy, too large, and it costs too much.

D. H. Lawrence (essay date 1936)

SOURCE: "Review of Books: *Gifts of Fortune,* by H. M. Tomlinson," in *Phoenix: The Posthumous Papers of D. H. Lawrence,* edited by Edward D. McDonald, The Viking Press, 1936, pp. 342-45.

[*In the following essay, Lawrence declares Tomlinson to be not a travel writer, but a writer exploring what Lawrence calls "coasts of illusion," meaning travel by mind and soul to a world uncorrupted by disillusionment.*]

Gifts of Fortune is not a travel-book. It is not even, as the jacket describes it, a book of travel memories. Travel in this case is a stream of reflections, where images inter-

twine with dark thoughts and obscure emotion, and the whole flows on turbulent and deep and transitory. It is reflection, thinking back on travel and on life, and in the mirror sense, throwing back snatches of image.

Mr. Tomlinson's own title: *Gifts of Fortune: With Some Hints to Those About to Travel* is a little grimly misleading. Those about to travel, in the quite commonplace sense of the word, will find very few encouraging hints in the long essay which occupies a third of this book, and is entitled, **"Hints to Those About to Travel."** The chief hint they would hear would be, perhaps, the sinister suggestion that they had better stay at home.

There are travellers and travellers, as Mr. Tomlinson himself makes plain. There are scientific ones, game-shooting ones, Thomas Cook ones, thrilled ones, and bored ones. And none of these, as such, will find a single "hint" in all the sixty-six hinting pages, which will be of any use to them.

Mr. Tomlinson is travelling in retrospect, in soul rather than in the flesh, and his hints are to other souls. To travelling bodies he says little.

The sea tempts one to travel. But what is the nature of the temptation? To what are we tempted? Mr. Tomlinson gives us the hint, for his own case. "What draws us to the sea is the light over it," etc.

There you have the key to this book. Coasts of illusion! "There are other worlds." A man who has travelled this world in the flesh travels again, sails once more wilfully along coasts of illusion, and wilfully steers into other worlds. Take then the illusion, accept the gifts of fortune, "that passes as a shadow on the wall."

"My journeys have all been the fault of books, though Lamb would never have called them that." Mr. Tomlinson is a little weary of books, though he has here written another. A talk with seamen in the forecastle of a ship has meant more to him than any book. So he says. But that is how a man feels, at times. As a matter of fact, from these essays it is obvious that books like Bates's *Amazon,* Conrad's *Nigger of the Narcissus,* and Melville's *Moby Dick* have gone deeper into him than any talk with seamen in forecastles of steamers.

How could it be otherwise? Seamen see few coasts of illusion. They see very little of anything. And what is Mr. Tomlinson after? What are we all after, if it comes to that? It is our yearning to land on the coasts of illusion, it is our passion for other worlds that carries us on. And with Bates or Conrad or Melville we are already away over the intangible seas. As Mr. Tomlinson makes very plain, a P. & O. liner will only take us from one hotel to another. Which isn't what we set out for, at all. *That* is not crossing seas.

And this is the theme of the Hints to Those. We travel in order to cross seas and land on other coasts. We do not travel in order to go from one hotel to another, and see a few side-shows. We travel, perhaps, with a secret and absurd hope of setting foot on the Hesperides, of running our boat up a little creek and landing in the Garden of Eden.

This hope is always defeated. There is no Garden of Eden, and the Hesperides never were. Yet, in our very search for them, we touch the coasts of illusion, and come into contact with other worlds.

This world remains the same, wherever we go. Every ship is a money-investment, and must be made to pay. The earth exists to be exploited, and is exploited. Malay head-hunters are now playing football instead of hunting heads. The voice of the gramophone is heard in the deepest jungle.

That is the world of disillusion. Travel, and you'll know it. It is just as well to know it. Our world is a world of disillusion, whether it's Siam or Kamchatka or Athabaska: the same exploitation, the same mechanical lifelessness.

But travelling through our world of disillusion until we are finally and bitterly disillusioned, we come home at last, after the long voyage, home to the rain and the dismalness of England. And how marvellously well Mr. Tomlinson gives the feeling of a ship at the end of the voyage, coming in at night, in the rain, the engines showed down, then stopped: and in the unspeakable emptiness and blankness of silent engines and rain and nothingness, the passengers wait for the tug, staring out upon utter emptiness, from a ship that has gone suddenly quite dead! It is the end of the voyage of disillusion.

But behold, in the morning, England, England, in her own wan sun, her strange, quiet Englishmen, so silent and intent and self-resourceful! It is the coast of illusion, the other world itself.

This is the gist of the Hints to Those About to Travel. You'll never find what you look for. There are no happy lands. But you'll come upon coasts of illusion when you're not expecting them.

Following the Hints come three sketches which are true travel memories, one on the Amazon, one in the Malay States, one in Borneo. They are old memories, and they gleam with illusion, with the iridescence of illusion and disillusion at once. Far off, we are in the midst of exploitation and mechanical civilization, just the same. Far off, in the elysium of a beautiful spot in Borneo, the missionary's wife sits and weeps for home, when she sees an outgoing ship. Far off, there is the mad Rajah, whom we turned out, with all kinds of medals and number-plates on his breast, thinking himself grander than ever, though he is a beggar.

And all the same, far off, there is that other world, or one of those other worlds, that give the lie to those realities we are supposed to accept.

The rest of the book is all England. There is a sketch: **"Conrad Is Dead."** And another, an appreciation of *Moby Dick*. But for the rest, it is the cruel disillusion, and then the infinitely soothing illusion of this world of ours.

Mr. Tomlinson has at the back of his mind, for ever, the grisly vision of his war experience. In itself, this is a horror of disillusion in the world of man. We cannot get away from it, and we have no business to. Man has turned the world into a thing of horror. What we have to do is to face the fact.

And facing it, accept other values and make another world. "We now open a new volume on sport," says Mr. Tomlinson, "with an antipathy we never felt for Pawnees, through the reading of a recent narrative by an American who had been collecting in Africa for an American museum. He confessed he would have felt some remorse when he saw the infant still clinging to the breast of its mother, a gorilla, whom he had just murdered; so he shot the infant without remorse, because he was acting scientifically. As a corpse, the child added to the value of its dead mother."

We share Mr. Tomlinson's antipathy to such sportsmen and such scientists absolutely. And it is not mere pity on our part for the gorilla. It is an absolute detestation of the *insentience* of armed, bullying men, in face of living, sentient things. Surely the most beastly offence against life is this degenerate insentience. It is not cruelty, exactly, which makes such a sportsman. It is crass insentience, a crass stupidity and deadness of fibre. Such overweening fellows, called men, are barren of the feeling for life. A gorilla is a live thing, with a strange unknown life of its own. Even to get a glimpse of its weird life, one little gleam of insight, makes our own life so much the wider, more vital. As a dead thing it can only depress us. We *must* have a feeling for life itself.

And this Mr. Tomlinson conveys: the strangeness and the beauty of life. Once be disillusioned with the man-made world, and you still see the magic, the beauty, the delicate realness of all the other life. Mr. Tomlinson sees it in flashes of great beauty. It comes home to him even in the black moth he caught. "It was quiet making a haze," etc. He sees the strange terror of the world of insects. "A statue to St. George killing a mosquito instead of a dragon would look ridiculous. But it was lucky for the Saint he had only a dragon to overcome."

Life! Life exists: and perhaps men do not truly exist. "And for a wolf who runs up and down his cage, sullenly ignoring our overtures, and behaving as though we did not exist, we begin to feel there is something to be said."

"And consider the fascination of the octopus!"

"I heard a farmer," etc.

"At sunrise today," etc.

"Perhaps the common notion," etc.

One gradually gets a new vision of the world, if one goes through the disillusion absolutely. It is a world where all things are alive, and where the life of strange creatures and beings flickers on us and makes it take strange new developments. "But in this estuary," etc. And it is exactly so. The earth is a planet, and we are inhabitants of the planet, along with many other strange creatures. Life is a strange planetary phenomenon, all interwoven.

Mr. Tomlinson gives us glimpses of a new vision, what we might call the planetary instead of the mundane vision. The glimpses are of extreme beauty, so sensitive to the other life in things. And how grateful we ought to be to a man who sets new visions, new feelings sensitively quivering in us.

Helen and Richard Altick (essay date 1943)

SOURCE: "Square-Rigger on a Modern Mission," in *College English,* Vol. 5, No. 2, November, 1943, pp. 75-80.

[In the following essay, the Alticks discuss Tomlinson as an anti-war writer.]

Henry Major Tomlinson in the era-between-wars was one of those writers against war whom Mr. MacLeish has categorically accused of having contributed much to the so-called "psychological disarmament" of the democracies. History will decide whether eventually he will be sanctified as a passionate but unheeded prophet or assigned a particularly bleak station in the outer darkness as an unwitting but effective saboteur of democratic morale. The results of the present war must first be in, and the crusade against war given a chance to revive, before we can be sure what the writers of anti-war tracts in the 1920's and 1930's really did to us. Meanwhile, Tomlinson's books remain—a long list of them—full of bitterness eloquently expressed; and Tomlinson himself, approaching the age of seventy, observes the battle for the *Atlantic Monthly.* And while a definitive critique of his work would still be premature, the most important chapters of his career were ended irrevocably in the first days of September, 1939. Hence a retrospective glance at Tomlinson against the background of the present war is certainly in order.

He has a place all his own among the writers who are supposed to have "softened" us for the ordeal of the present day; he might even be called the dean of the group. The most typical and most famous literary expositors of disillusionment, men like Hemingway and Remarque and Dos Passos, whose names occur in Mr. MacLeish's famous speech, were young men in 1914. They were to be disillusioned first of all by the first World War. Tomlinson, however, had drunk his bitter draft long before Sarajevo, and the war merely added desperate emphasis and urgency to convictions he had long entertained. While he was, in some respects, a most effective ally of the younger writers in their in-

dictment of war, he was not one of them. He was the man the older generation of British writers sent to redeem the idiot of Mars; and he brought to his task something of the temperament of a Cunninghame Graham or a W. H. Hudson.

"Down Poplar way," in the 1870's, was no place for a congenital romanticist to be born. It was the twilight of the gods—twilight of the era that had seen tall-masted ships by the score thrusting their bowsprits far across the wharves and waterside streets of the East End. But the funereal pall of smoke had not yet settled so thickly over London River that Tomlinson as a youth could not know the glory that had been the sea in the days when his own father had found satisfaction and prosperity in sailing his bark to the corners of the earth. Darkness, however, fell: his father came home for good, and ugly slab-sided steamers elbowed the graceful clippers from East India docks. Tomlinson early sensed the meaning of "progress," and he did not like it.

There is one particular misconception embraced by all youths whose romantic instincts are most keenly aroused by the smell of salt air and the sight of a brig standing out to sea. That misconception is: commerce is for adventure, not for money-making. Boys who stand gazing (as Tomlinson did) into ship-outfitters' windows filled with compasses, sextants, sounding-machines, and signaling gear, and who when they are men must give their books such titles as *Gallions Reach, Pipe All Hands, Tide Marks, Under the Red Ensign, Waiting for Daylight,* and *Between the Lines*—such boys never get over the crushing discovery that grown men go down to the sea in ships not for the mere thrill of it but rather for the sake of certain rewards calculable in pounds and shillings. Tomlinson was no exception. To discover the sordid truth about the uses of the sea roads was his first and greatest disillusionment—and it occurred long before the turn of the century.

From the first, both by instinct and by circumstance, he was the enemy of mechanization and amalgamation—two words ugly in themselves and with overtones infinitely uglier to a young man of Tomlinson's disposition. "Commerce" in all its significances was anathema to him. Even in his first book, *The Sea and the Jungle,* in which his romantic gusto found its freest and most memorable expression, occur many intimations that he was aware of the crass motives behind all high adventure, even the journey of the rusty tramp "Capella" across the Atlantic and far up the Amazon. Somebody in Park Lane or Wall Street has an idea; men die by the hundreds in the Brazilian jungle, but the railroad they were sent to build is somehow completed; freights of precious rubber move down the tracks and eventually cushion the motorcars as they purr down Park Lane or Wall Street. "The chap who had the bright idea, but never saw this place, and couldn't live here a week, or shovel dirt, or lay a track, and wouldn't know raw rubber if he saw it, he'll score again. Progress, progress! The wilderness blossoms as the rose. It's wonderful, isn't it?"

Equally wonderful, to him, was the launching of a warship at Liverpool. It had cost the price of seven cathedrals or fifteen thousand homes, "and a disciple of Jesus was blessing her huge guns, while choristers chanted praise to whatever deity may approve of that honor." He knew why the warship had to be built; he saw, as clearly as a ship's captain can read the shifting of the wind and the darkening of the sky, that commerce—the hated commerce that had sent old barks to rot at their moorings—bred imperialism; and imperialism brought international rivalries, and soon the warship would be needed. . . . . And so, with the realistic eye sharpened by years in the newspaper trade, he foresaw the coming of the first World War. But he was not quite prepared for it. Hating the idea of war, the misbegotten idiot son of trade, he still did not know what war was.

His calling as journalist took him to France. There, seeing the fine British uniforms he had lately watched on parade now caked and sodden with mud, and encountering first a child's doll in a roofless French cottage and then a whole graveyard full of bodies disinterred by a bomb, his rankling hatred of industrial civilization and all its unholy works—not failing to include the politicians and the enfranchised though still ignorant masses—was transformed into horror. No inspiration did he find in the mud of the Somme, says Tomlinson, no visions at Vimy Ridge; but only horror and an overwhelming sense of the obscenity, the irredeemable degradation of war.

In book after book, in the manner of a stricken man who can find relief from the grim phantasms that infest his mind only by constantly objectifying them on paper, Tomlinson wrote of the war as he had seen and felt it. It may be true, as some of his less patient readers urged, that he wrote so persistently about the war (it could not be kept out of even his most Conradian sea-pieces) that it became less of a horror than an unmitigated nuisance. And yet the heavy note of irony that pervaded all his writing gave it a certain undeniable power. Readers who tired of the officers' huts in France and the look of the mangled bodies of British youths could still be fascinated by Tomlinson's fierce sincerity. The passage in *Mars His Idiot* which describes the advent of a bomb in a great London printing establishment, where hundreds of neighbors, among them women heavy with child, had taken shelter from the raid, is unforgettable, however much the tenderhearted might wish to erase it from memory. "It looks like the final abomination, beneath which man cannot sink. If man can insult his Maker, there he did it. To procure abortion with a bomb!"

He saw war as the final negation of all that is jocund and fair in Christianity, in Western civilization, in life itself. Highly characteristic of him is this wryly antiphonal paragraph describing no man's land on Christmas, 1916:

It rained next morning. This was Christmas Day. We were going to the trenches. Christians awake, salute the happy morn. There was a prospect of straight road with an avenue of diminishing poplars going east, in an inky smear, to the Germans and infinity. The rain lashed into my northerly ear, and the A.S.C. motor-car driver, who was mad, kept missing three-ton lorries and gun limbers by the width of the paint. One transport mule, who pretended to be frightened of us, but whose father was the devil and his mother an ass, plunged into a pond of Flanders mud as we passed, and raked us with solvent filth. We wiped it off our mouth. God rest you, merry gentlemen. A land so inundated that it inverted the raw and alien sky was on either hand. The mud clung to the horses and mules like dangling walnuts and bunches of earthy and glistening grapes. The men humped themselves in soddened khaki. The noise of the wheels bearing guns was like the sound of doom. The rain it rained. O come, all ye faithful!

It was this note of irony, never tender, never subtle, which gave his writing its distinction.

The ink was scarcely dry on the document of Versailles before Tomlinson was aware of the renewed fall of the barometer that heralded a greatest catastrophe to come. His dour realism where international affairs were concerned informed him of the true nature and probable consequences of the things that had been done in the name of peace. The blessings of the machine age were multiplied; children starved, whole cities went on the dole, and fat shipowners, like Perriam in *Gallions Reach,* grew rich. Home from a trip to the Far East in 1923, he denounced the building of the Singapore naval base as a blunt provocation of war. Year by year through the twenties and thirties he watched the storm clouds gather, positive that the cataclysm, when it came, would be the worst yet. With it would come the end of the capitalistic system—and good riddance, Tomlinson said, although he was not happy when he thought of what might come in its place.

The present war has seen Tomlinson for the most part drifting out of control. Superficially what he has written since the rape of Poland reads like a negation of his old principles; for he has proclaimed that this war is different. It is a necessary war—a war against barbarism and the threat of world enslavement. Forgetting his old indictments of wanton British selfishness and stupidity, he has somehow had a renewal of faith. He concentrates his gaze upon the cliffs of England and the hovering ghosts of Wat Tyler, John Ball, Sam Weller, Nelson of Trafalgar, and numerous unidentified bombed-out Cockneys from the shipping parishes; and in that mystical sight he seems to find promise of a new and brighter world to come.

Tomlinson thus has joined the ranks of the propagandists in the second World War. This is, after all, not as surprising as it might seem at first glance. He has said recently that he would not amend a single line in *Mars His Idiot;*

nor is it necessary for him to do so. He still hates war to the very depths of his nature. But when the typhoon strikes, one battens down the hatches and does his best to ride out the storm.

His position, however, is anomalous; and he has been so obviously embarrassed by it that whatever influence he wielded up to the last few years must now be largely lost. His show of optimism can no more keep him on a straight course than an oar can guide a four-masted schooner. He is, to all intents and purposes, rudderless. But actually he never was very sure of where he was going. Even in his best days, his charts and steering gear never were of the best quality obtainable.

The Tomlinson of the great anti-war crusade never did steer by reason. His was not primarily a revulsion from war as an insult to the human intellect (although, of course, he recognized that war was this as well); he hated war because it is the final indignity committed against the spirit of man by the forces man himself has unleashed. It is the most horrible manifestation of a civilization that has no place for square-riggers. Tomlinson's protest against war was, above all, the protest of an outraged dreamer who found himself in a world that was distinctly not to his liking.

The shadowy quality of his present optimism is proof enough of the essentially negative character of his thought. We have been left in no doubt as to the things that repel him—trade's transformation of Poplar from a cheerful, prosperous port to a grimy slum; the greedy agents of British imperialism as they seduced Nature's brown children with bribes of tinned meat and oil; the brass-hats of the war office happily applying in 1915 the lessons they learned in the Boer War. We have had much more difficulty in discovering his positive values. It is true that as a man with the essayist's contemplative turn of mind he has a capacity for the hearty enjoyment of life; indeed, he is able to enjoy anything in the world that is not tainted by the curse of technological civilization. But that in itself never went far toward solving the most poignant question he proposed, directly or implicitly, in book after book: How can we save ourselves?

If he had had a positive, well-developed credo with which to answer that question, Tomlinson would have won for himself a position in contemporary literature far higher than that which he now holds. He would be remembered as a crusader *for* something, rather than as an indefatigable rebel *against* something. As it is, literary historians are inclined to dismiss him as an exponent of "a somewhat tiresome middle-aged liberalism."

For, as his latest essays have shown once again, the only refuge he has ever found from the cataclysmic implications of machine civilization has been in a cloudy, mystical faith in the potentialities of the individual man. Sometimes he reminds one more than a little of Rousseau. He would move the stunted nobodies of Bethnal Green to the jungles of the Amazon. Seeing the prodigality of Nature, they would realize the tyranny of what they had been taught to believe was civilization, and forthwith they would break their bonds; "they would begin with dignity and assurance to compass their own affairs, and in an enormous way; and they would make hardly a sound as they moved forward, and they would have uplifted and shining eyes." His heroes are all individualists, men who have refused to be stifled by society's insistence on conformity. They are humble men, most of them, but courageous and confident. A talented architect renounces his professional future for the sake of defending an ancient temple against commercial exploitation. The captain of a stricken ship proudly declines the offer of a tow by a mail steamer. A British soldier goes out under fire to hold up a wounded German and give him water, and his platoon officer reports that fact as characteristic and admirable. These are the nobodies who step in when

> the well-born, the clever, the haughty, and the greedy, in their fear, pride, and wilfulness, and the perplexity of their scheming, make a general mess of the earth. Forthwith in a panic they cry, "Calamity cometh!"
>
> Then out from their obscurity, where they dwelt because of their low worth, arise the Nobodies, because theirs is the historic job of restoring again the upset balance of affairs. They make no fuss about it. Theirs is always the hard and dirty work. They have always done it.

Unfortunately, Tomlinson, like everyone else who has found solace in the belief that men of good will can return the earth to its pristine purity, has failed to reconcile this glowing faith with the distrust of democracy *en masse* which usually accompanies it. Neither he nor anyone else can quite explain why it is that men who separately are supposedly sweet-natured, generous, and intelligent can be transformed, by merely being brought close to one another, into "the multitude, that limitless repository of instincts and emotions that can be enlisted for service by skillful men seeking wealth and power." Tomlinson's frail ship of hope inevitably founders on this rock.

And so, as the whistling-in-the-dark tone of his essays written during the Battle of Britain reminds us, Tomlinson contributed little more to the anti-war literature of our era than a sense of comprehensive horror. All he could do, after writing one terrible indictment after another of commercialism and militarism, was to indulge in a pleasantly nebulous and thoroughly unconvincing confession of faith in the ultimate victory of man's goodness. His writings against war were heavy with a conviction which he never squarely faced: a conviction of futility. He could offer no positive program for the redemption of modern civilization, because he could not believe in any. His disillusionment, begun in Poplar's tangle of spars and rigging, was too complete. His magnificent mission was doomed to failure.

Alva A. Gay (essay date 1958)

SOURCE: "H. M. Tomlinson, Essayist and Traveller," in *Studies in Honor of John Wilcox,* edited by A. Dayle Wallace with Woodburn O. Ross, Books for Libraries Press, 1958, pp. 209-17.

[*In the following essay, Gay discusses Tomlinson's pre-1940 works.*]

In 1950 the Londoner, H. M. Tomlinson, journalist, novelist, essayist, traveller, published a collection of essays under the title *The Face of the Earth.* One wonders to how many of those who chanced upon it the name of its author evoked nostalgic memories of other of his books not reread in years. To most readers born between the 1914 and 1939 wars the name would probably be no more than just that—a name. But to older readers was there recollection of *The Sea and the Jungle, Old Junk, London River, Tide Marks*? The essays collected in *The Face of the Earth* themselves constitute a backward glance. They are, the author remarks, "remembrances . . . salvaged from books lost in the last war." "It was thought proper," he goes on to say, "to save them; oblivion is inevitable, but it need not come too soon." And he was right; oblivion need not and should not come too soon to his work. There is place for the minor as well as the major, for the quietly persistent tone as well as the shout. One can be delighted and bemused and moved, if in a different way, by Charles Lamb and Thoreau as well as by Herman Melville and Dostoyevsky. Henry Major Tomlinson has been persistent. Although the bulk of his best work was written prior to the outbreak of the second war, at no time since then has he dropped from sight completely. During the war appeared *The Wind Is Rising* (1941), reactions to life in wartime Britain; in 1950, *Malay Waters,* a tribute to the officers, the men, and the little ships of the Straits Steamship Company, "coasting out of Singapore and Penang in peace and war," as the subtitle reads; in 1953, in his eightieth year, *A Mingled Yarn,* a collection much like *The Face of the Earth,* consisting for the most part of earlier essays and sketches; in addition to these, scattered essays that have appeared in a popular travel magazine and elsewhere, and early in 1957 *The Trumpet Shall Sound,* a novel. It is, however, with the Tomlinson of the years prior to the 1940's that I wish to concern myself—not the writer of such novels as *Gallions Reach* (1927) and *All Our Yesterdays* (1930), but the meditative observer, the traveller, the social critic, the author of *The Sea and the Jungle* (1912), *Old Junk* (1918), *London River* (1921), *Tide Marks* (1924), *Gifts of Fortune* (1926), and "**Log of a Voyage, 1935,**" published in *The Turn of the Tide* in 1947.

A frequenter of dockside Thames, as he is seen in *London River,* almost, one hazards, its familiar spirit—he was born in 1873 in one of the shipping parishes—a keenly observant lands-man with a love of the sea in its every mood, a love, albeit, somewhat tempered with a knowledgeable fear, and a voyager on most of the oceans of the world, he has an understanding of ships and those who make their living from them and of the sea in its many aspects. The majority of his best books and essays are about the sea and those who live on it. So much has the sea meant to him that often in writing of land matters he uses imagery drawn from it. In "**Drought**" (*Gifts of Fortune*), describing the encroachment of a city's residential suburb into what had been a peaceful rural village, he notes that the slopes of the adjacent down hang over mason and carpenter like the solidified roller of the sea, a grove of trees riding its back like a raft. And in "**A Devon Estuary**," in the same volume, the seaside village of Burra becomes a part of a great ship:

> This village, which stands round the base of the hill where the moors decline to the sea and two rivers merge to form a gulf of light, is one I used to think was easily charted. But what do I know of it? The only certainty about it to-day is that it has a window which saves the trouble of searching for a better. Beyond that window the clouds are over the sea. The clouds are on their way. The waters are passing us. So, when I look out from my port-light to learn where we are, I can see for myself there may be something in that legend of a great stone ship on an endless voyage. I think I may be one of its passengers. For where is Burra? I never know. The world I see beyond the window is always different. We reach every hour a region of the sky where man has never been before, so the astronomers tell us, and my window confirms it. Ours is a celestial voyage, and God knows where.

But what of the voyages across the seas of the world? I cannot here do justice to them. I can hope only that what I give will sharpen curiosity so that the reader will seek to discover for himself Tomlinson's landfalls and horizons. An early voyage, his first he states, is described in "**Off-Shore**" (*London River*), the account of a voyage by steam trawler, the *Windhover,* to the cod fleet on the Dogger Bank in the days of the Russo-Japanese War. He tells of the almost futile search through several days of stormy, North Sea weather for the trawler fleet, which should have been found directly. Tomlinson was considered a Jonah, but this distinction did nothing to diminish his delight in the prospect of endless ocean upheaved and of leaden sky. The ship herself was for him as sentient a creature as any aboard her, when she pointed her stem to the clouds as she climbed a wave, or lifted her stern to let a mass of hissing gray water pass beneath her keel. Characteristic of the exactness of detail with which he can report what he has seen is the view of the *Susie,* a trawler his skipper hailed in his zig-zag search for the lost fleet: "I shall always see her at the moment when our skipper began to shout through his hands at her. She was poised askew, in that arrested instant, on a glassy slope of water, with its crest foaming above her. Surge blotted her out amidships, and her streaming forefoot jutted clear. She plunged then into the hollow between us, showing us the plan of her deck, for her funnel was pointing at us."

Another voyage, the subject of "**The African Coast**" (*Old Junk*), took him from Algiers to Tripoli in Barbary on the cargo steamer *Celestine,* with an ebullient French-man as master. Again there was a storm—"the barometer, wherever I am, seems to know when I embark. It falls." There had been earlier on his trip from England to Algiers, sun bright glimpses of the land, but off Bougie, "That shining coast which occasionally I had surprised from Oran, which seemed afloat on the sea, was no longer a vision of magic, the unsubstantial work of Iris, an illusionary cloud of coral, amber, and amethyst. It was the bare bones of this old earth, as sombre and foreboding as any ruin of granite under the wrack of the bleak north."

Years later he embarked by cargo ship for the Mediterranean again, this time with a grown son, whose first voyage, when he was a boy, Tomlinson described in **"Initiation"** (*Old Junk*). The voyage was a leisurely one, with halts at Casablanca, Gibraltar, Malta, Patras, Piraeus (where the ship sailed unexpectedly without them to its next port, while they were on the Acropolis), Istanbul, Ismir, and Alexandria. In his account are the description and reflection that we come to recognize as the hall marks of the man's work: "A mile to port a schooner was dim within the curtain of a cloud, but . . . a beam of [sunlight] found her, and she was radiant in an instant. She became more glorious than a ship ever is. As she heeled she flashed, as if giving out fire. She was signalling eternal renown to us."

The Sea and the Jungle and *Tide Marks* are his two major travel narratives. Concerned with his experiences on his first crossing of the Atlantic, the first covers a voyage from Wales to Brazil and two thousand miles up the Amazon and its tributary, the Madeira, to Port Velho at the San Antonio Falls. The trip was made in the *Capella,* a collier drawing twenty-three feet laden, carrying primarily a cargo of "patent" fuel for a railway construction project. The first part of the book is of the westward crossing—the sea. The ship, almost as soon as the pilot was dropped, was struck by a gale of steadily increasing velocity that, by the time she was out of the Bristol Channel, reached near hurricane force. Few writers that I know of have written so convincingly of the unrelenting fury of the sea as Tomlinson has written here, and I have not forgotten Conrad's power *Typhoon.* He concentrates his attention not so much on the damage inflicted by wind and weight of water as upon the *Capella's* dogged persistence fighting her way over each monstrous wave hurled against her. She was hurt once and almost overwhelmed when the cover of number three hatch came free. But there was finally relief, and the remainder of the crossing was under a hot sun and warm showers, through slowly surging tropic waters. There follows the second part, the arrival at Para and the long voyage up the rivers, with the *Capella* like a captive creature. Foliage brushed her rigging on occasion, and the fraying of her cable, when she anchored, through the friction of current-borne debris was a constant worry to the first mate. At Port Velho, Tomlinson took a trip further inland to the end of the railway construction and beyond. His breakneck return by mule and handcar to avoid missing the sailing of

the ship is a nightmare of speed. To present the book thus summarily is, of course, to miss completely the subtle portraiture, descriptive power, and thoughtfulness that are its marrow.

Tide Marks carries the reader to Singapore and beyond to the island of Ternate in the Dutch East Indies, with stops at Borneo, Java, and Celebes. Returning to Singapore, Tomlinson then made an excursion into the Malayan jungle. This book, satisfying in its own way, lacks the lyric and meditative tone of its predecessor but it has brilliantly realized vignettes of the tropics, both marine and insular. Its high points are the scramble up Ternate's volcanic peak and the sojourn in the jungle with the affliction of ubiquitous and determined leeches.

In the foreword to the first illustrated edition (1930) of *The Sea and the Jungle* Tomlinson chides the original reviewers of the book for their failure to hear the accents of the author who stood in his immediate background, Thoreau. There and elsewhere his indebtedness is evident. Consider the following from **"Some Hints for Those about to Travel"** (*Gifts of Fortune*):

> It is the chance things in travel that appear to be significant. The light comes unexpectedly and obliquely. Perhaps it amuses the gods to try us. They want to see whether we are asleep. If we are watchful we may get a bewildering hint, but placed where nobody would have expected to find it. We may spend the rest of the voyage wondering what that meant. A casual coast suddenly fixed by so strange a glow that one looks to the opposite sky fearfully; the careless word which makes you glance at a stranger, and doubt your fixed opinion; an ugly city, which you are glad to leave, transfigured and jubilant as you pass out of its harbour; these are the incidents that give a sense of discovery to a voyage. We are on more than one voyage at a time. We never know where Manoa may be. There are no fixed bearings for the City of Gold.

The attitude toward experience is the same in both men and both are keen observers of the world of nature. Tomlinson, however, takes the waters of the oceans of the world for his province and the great jungles of the New World and of the Malay Archipelago. Thoreau had only the narrowly circumscribed shores of Walden Pond and the New England wood lot and meadow. The movements of one for most of his life were within a ten-mile circle; the other has sailed the seven seas. Tomlinson, in **"Log of a Voyage, 1935,"** writes of his son and himself: "Though we were in the same ship, the two of us must make separate voyages with varying experiences. We should share the same daylight, see the same landfalls at the same time, yet reality for each of us would be anything you like to name. The sea, ancient and changeless, could not reconcile us with its hint of continuity, the same yesterday, today, and for ever." The cabin of a ship at sea serves the same purpose as another man's hut beside Walden Pond.

Like Thoreau, Tomlinson decries the drift of the times. The former deplores the frenetic, and to him inconsequential, quality of the daily press; the latter is distressed that the umbilical cord of radio binds a ship at sea to the news of the world and to the land, so that even the master of a ship "is on a length of string, and an office boy in the owner's office often pulls it, to let him feel the brevity of his liberty." There is virtue in isolation. In *The Sea and the Jungle* he writes of his feeling in mid-Atlantic on the fortunately radioless *Capella:* "we confessed, with ease at the heart, and with minds in which nervous vibrations had ceased, that we must have reached the place that was nowhere, and that now time was not for us. We had escaped you all. We were free. There was not anything to engage us. There was nothing to do, and nobody who wanted us. Never before had I felt so still and conscious of myself." To him a ship's radio is but another example of a mechanization of life that can lead only to the merging of the individual difference in the dull gray mass of uniform humanity. This theme he develops in **"Log of a Voyage, 1935"**:

> From Shanghai to Istanbul, people are merging into a uniformity as featureless as the wooly flocks; as if we, too, were mass-produced, like our opinions, our habits, and our flats. . . . There is no excuse for sameness and flatness. It is a crime against the intelligence. Uniformity is the abortion of creation. It is not harmony, but monotony, like the drone of our engines, and numbs thought. It means the death of freedom of the mind, and so the end of the soul's adventure; the hopeful old story of our beginning in a garden will be empty of its purport, for the spirit will be frustrate, good and evil the same, and our eyes blind to the glory of the Lord, should it be revealed.

And again:

> . . . it appears today as if there were but one good we all should respect, whether we want to or not: we must bow to the political use of power directed to full control of the lives of our fellows. The last aim of reason, therefore, is to refuse to human life the use of reason; so down we go to the uniformity of sheep. But will we go down? There is sure to be trouble about that. The individual soul forever, in London, and Pekin, and every Kaffir kraal, against all the assumptions of outside authority!

But I would not imply that his is only a derivative importance. There are echoes of Thoreau in his work, yet what he has felt is a reflection of his own individuality, and what he has seen has been viewed from his own angle of vision. And all of it has been set down in a style superbly and exactly molded to his purpose. He is a skilled craftsman of word and phrase.

Tomlinson has not received the serious and extended consideration that his work deserves. Collections of his earlier essays, as has been remarked, have been reprinted in recent years, and one of his pieces—**"The Derelict"** (*Old Junk*)—has strangely been included in Bennett Cerf and Henry C. Moriarity's *An Anthology of Famous Brit-*

ish Stories, although it is a narrative sketch rather than fiction. Little attention, however, has been paid either to his ideas or to his richly metaphoric prose. In part this neglect is undoubtedly due to the fact that much of what he has said so well as a critic of society has been included in his meticulous rendering of persons and places, of landscapes, seascapes, and personalities—in his travel essays, that is. Creative in quite a different sense from fiction, first rate travel literature nevertheless challenges critical insight.

Without question, it seems to me, he belongs to that noble fraternity of travellers among whom are found the James Boswell of *A Journal of a Tour to the Hebrides,* the Thoreau of *A Week on the Concord and the Merrimack Rivers,* the George Borrow of *The Bible in Spain,* the Charles Doughty of *Arabia Deserta,* the George Gissing of *By the Ionian Sea,* the Henry James of *The American Scene,* the Norman Douglas of *Old Calabria,* the D. H. Lawrence of *Sea and Sardinia,* the E. E. Cummings of *Eimi.* Of such as these Tomlinson may be said to write, and it can be written of him as well: "We borrow the light of an observant and imaginative traveller, and see the foreign land bright with his aura; and we think it is the country which shines."

Derek Severn (essay date 1979)

SOURCE: "A Minor Master," in *London Magazine,* Vol. 18, No. 11, February, 1979, pp. 47-58.

[In the following essay, Severn offers a post-centenary appreciation of Tomlinson's work.]

The changes of taste and fashion since the war have suppressed, at least for the time being, a number of distinguished reputations. One thinks, for example, of R. C. Hutchinson, William Gerhardie, Hugh Kingsmill, Forrest Reid and R. B. Cunninghame Graham. H. M. Tomlinson is another of the casualties. His centenary in 1973 passed without notice, and not one of his thirty books is now in print in this country. But he was a writer of singular integrity and individuality who published nothing that was not distinguished, whether in essays and criticism, or works of travel, or novels—though these were, in strict terms, the least satisfactory of his books, the whole being usually less than the sum of the parts. Even the most ephemeral of his books, the commentaries and reflections on public affairs that belong now to the historian's province, are worth rereading as records of the responses of a sensitive, wise and humane observer at a time when the world was being torn apart.

Tomlinson was his own man; his mind was reflective; and his style, though it can move in the space of a sentence from the colloquial to the eloquent without a perceptible change of gear, is essentially a tone of voice, for his personality pervades everything he wrote. Yet that personality is elusive and not easily defined. The voice is quiet, too quiet to impose itself in an age when not a few literary reputations from Proust onwards have owed as much to carefully organized publicity as to intrinsic merit. Tomlinson went his own way, writing, as far as his finances allowed, the things he wanted to write, and said the things he wanted to say to those who cared to hear them. However, no more than Conrad, about whom he wrote with fine discrimination and to whom he was unperceptively compared, did he admit one to the private areas of his life. Even his entry in *Who's Who* gave only his initials, not his Christian names; and to a suggestion that he should write his autobiography he replied, 'It's all in the books.' So it is; but although at the end of his life he published an essay entitled **'A Mingled Yarn'** about his early years one must look within the work to find the man.

Yet the facts are sufficiently interesting, for he was self-made both as a man and as a writer. He was born in the East End of London, the son of a foreman in the East India Dock. Three things stayed with him from his childhood: his sympathy for the poor, for the shadow of poverty, which merged imperceptibly into the shadow of the workhouse, lay darkly over Poplar in the 'seventies and' eighties of the last century; his passion for the sea (the masts of clippers in Blackwall Reach were among his earliest impressions); and his love of books and music, which he inherited from his father. The writer in him emerged early: he was a scribbler, he said, from childhood, but 'judiciously burned it all'. His father's death when he was thirteen put an end to his education, and he took a job at six shillings a week in a shipping office in Leadenhall Street, not far from the place where Lamb had worked for the East India Company. 'My youth,' he wrote, 'was spent among the bills of lading and the cargo manifests of the clippers.' Sailor-fashion, he knew the ships as living things: *Thyatira, Blackadder, Euterpe, Charlotte Padbury, Briarholme, Loch Garry, Duchalburn, Dharwar* and many others. He knew the *Cutty Sark,* and the *Torrens* when Conrad was one of her officers, though it was not until many years later, when both were established writers, that he came to know Conrad himself. He discovered Dickens, Stevenson and Carlyle, Hakluyt and Cook's *Voyages;* he read entomology, and made himself a sufficiently competent geologist to be invited to join an expedition to the Arctic; but his health was too frail to allow him to accept.

The job in the shipping office grew irksome, but he found no way of escape until, at the age of thirty-one, when he was already married and his first child was about to be born, he quarrelled with his employer and walked out— an incident which he used and embellished many years later in his first novel, **Gallions Reach**. With no more published work behind him than a handful of articles in halfpenny journals he presented himself on the spur of the moment to the editor of the *Morning Leader,* a Radical paper which later became the *Daily News,* and was given a job. Almost at once he went to sea, to cover naval manoeuvres and the winter labours of the fishing fleet on the Dogger Bank.

Tomlinson stayed with the paper for thirteen years, and then became the Literary Editor of *The Nation* under its great editor, H. W. Massingham, whose austere integrity prompted, long afterwards, one of the finest of Tomlinson's portrait-essays. Massingham demanded of men in public affairs a straightforwardness equal to his own, and it was he, more than anyone else, who destroyed Lloyd George's reputation. When Liberal ministers who failed on issue after issue to live up to his exacting ethical standards could no longer tolerate the trenchancy of his criticisms, and *The Nation* drifted into financial difficulties, J. M. Keynes rescued it on condition that its policy would be changed. Massingham was abruptly dismissed, and Tomlinson elected to go with him. 'There was,' he said, 'nothing else to do.' Soon afterwards the success of **Gallions Reach** gave him a measure of independence, and in the last thirty years of his life he produced more than twenty books.

Reading them after the lapse of a generation or more one sees that Tomlinson's place is with the lesser masters who make up the secondary but essential literature of their time. Too disparate to form a *corpus,* and too modest in intention to claim the status of major work, his books impress by the singular consistency of their quality and by the strength and individuality of the mind which informs them all. Without puritanism, and with a puckish humour to which puritanism is wholly foreign, he concealed behind the quietness of his manner great toughness and austerity. 'I see no essential difference,' he said in a lecture at Harvard, 'between Isaiah and Swift as men with something to say to us. I am unable, I mean, to separate religion and literature. For me they are the same. The writer who would give his public what it wants, with his tongue in his cheek, is in the same class exactly as the other fellow who once took pieces of silver in payment for treachery.' Faithful to this credo, he wrote slowly, and gave the same care to an article for a magazine as to a chapter of a book which might, perhaps, survive. He was a journalist at a time when journalism approached, and often achieved, the condition of literature more frequently than it does now, and when the essay, a form which was particularly congenial to his reflective mind, was still practised with elegance, trenchancy and wit. An enterprising publisher might find material for a couple of notable volumes among his occasional pieces, for there were none in his generation who wrote better than he, and few who wrote as well. He had the journalist's facility for finding something worthwhile to say about even the least promising of subjects: even so slight a matter as a visit to an offshore sand dune or an almost uninhabited island could draw from him an essay worthy of a place in any anthology of English prose:

> O'Keefe himself was a man who would have raised no comment as an under-steward in a Portuguese ship. He did not speak English, and could not make out why we were there.

> I ignored him that morning on the jetty, after my first greeting, and stared overside. A rose-coloured lory, perched near me on the rail, made a friendly

noise and sidled towards me. This parrot was less foreign than O'Keefe. I tried lazily to detect the surface of the water beneath. If you looked straight at the glass it had no surface. Your gaze, as though too heavy for this equatorial sort of water, fell to the bottom, to coral shrubs the colour of the parrot, to hummocks that were olive-green, to a garden five fathoms down. I could see suspensory groups of stalkless blossoms, or else they were fishes, beneath me. Those coloured particles were free, and they drifted about invariably true to their own colour and kind. They were never confused. The numerous vivid atoms of each group, in the denser air below, sparkled ruby or gold, and the company of each sort moved as one body, invisibly attached. One swarm of them, glittering like a constellation before the dark opening of a cave, suddenly dispersed in minute flashes of blue lightning. Another cluster were of saffron with black stripes, and they were swaying in a draught I could not feel up above; they slowly dissolved, and then reappeared to sway elsewhere. I was only looking on; in the heat of the day the sight was the only sense which kept awake. An array of shining torpedoes swept into the transparency, and the little flowers vanished. The glass below me trembled, the bottom of the sea wavered, reticulated, and faded. Now I could see its surface.

There are scores of passages of this quality to be found in Tomlinson's work. What Conrad said of W. H. Hudson is equally to be said of him: 'One cannot tell how this fellow gets his effects. He writes as the grass grows.' Without literary self-consciousness, without reaching after effect, he evokes a mood as easily as an image, a mystery as surely as a fact. His style defeats analysis, for the simple reason that (as Frank Swinnerton, who knew him well, has testified) he wrote as he spoke; yet a moment's examination of any paragraph is sufficient to show that this talk has the grace of music and a precision of diction almost too delicate for conversation. Like the greatest passages in *The Prelude,* his descriptive prose mirrors his material without appearing to impose upon it either tone or form, yet in doing so distils from it the purest poetry.

Although he is remembered, if at all, as a travel writer, he wrote only two travel books, if one discounts **South to Cadiz,** which is really a volume of essays prompted by his journey through Spain. He was nearly forty, with his literary personality already formed, when he published in 1912 **The Sea and the Jungle,** the first, and for many years one of the best-known, of his books, though it came only slowly to public attention. His brother-in-law, who was to command the steamer *Capella* on a voyage from Swansea to Porto Velho, two thousand miles up the Amazon and Madeira Rivers, offered him a berth as purser, and Tomlinson's editor gave him leave to go, on the understanding that he would send back a series of articles on the journey. These articles, which were based on Tomlinson's diary, formed in turn the basis of one of the outstanding records of travel of this century—a book worthy of a place on the same shelf as Wilfred Thesiger's *Arabian Sands,* Patrick Leigh Fermor's *The Traveller's*

Tree and the best of Freya Stark. When a man can write like this it is his mind as well as his subject that fascinates, since the poet in him has a relish for experience that his imagination intensifies:

> There was one sunset when the overspreading of violet clouds would have shut out the day a little too soon, but that the canopy was not closely adjusted to the low barrier of forest to the west. Through that narrow chink a yellow light streamed, and traced shapes on the lurid walls and roof which narrowly enclosed us. This was the beginning of the most alarming of our daily electrical storms. There was no wind. Serpa, and all the coast facing that rift where the light entered our prison, stood prominent and strange and surprised us as much as if we had not looked in that direction till then. The curtain dropped behind the forest, and then all light was shut out. We could not see across the ship. As we knew how strong and bright could be the electrical discharges (though they were rarely accompanied by thunder) when not heralded in so portentous a way, we waited in some anxiety for this display to begin. It began over the trees behind Serpa. Blue fire flickered low down, and was quickly doused. Then a crack of light sprang across the inverted black bowl from east to west in three quick movements. Its instant ramifications fractured all the roof in a network of dazzling blue lines. The reticulations of light were fleeting, but never gone. Night contracted and expanded, and the sharp sounds, which were not like thunder, might have been the tumbling flinders of night's roof. We saw not only the river, and the shapes of the trees and the village, as in wavering daylight, but their colours. One flash sheeted the heavens, and its over-bright glare extinguished everything. It came with an explosion, like the firing of a great gun close to our ears, and for a time we thought the ship was struck. In this effort the storm exhausted itself.

There is in Tomlinson's observation of the world a quality of innocence which is entirely deceptive. Encountering the Amazonian jungle for the first time, and determined that nothing should escape his attention, he says, 'It was like being born into the world as an understanding adult.' Exactly so: for the morning-of-creation freshness of his perception is qualified by a drily humorous, ironic reflection (or it may be only an epithet) that implies a judgment more often than it states one; and where the comment is explicit it is likely to be trenchant, as in his discovery that the aboriginal natives of this region, unlike those of his native Poplar, who are two thousand years more advanced, have no need of a Poor Law, and that if he encounters a hungry child the men of that village are hungry too. Whatever he notices is set in a swiftly-sketched context, and gains depth by being referred to some other aspect of experience—a mantid in the corner of a hut, 'chewing a fly exactly as one would an apple' (Tomlinson remembered this extraordinary green insect fifteen years later when he wrote **Gallions Reach**); palm-leaf huts 'forced down' by the overhanging forest 'to wade on frail stilts'; the odour of a warehouse, 'evasive, sweet and pungent, as barbaric a note as I found in Pará'. And behind it all is the sense that the few tiny fragments of civilisation that have attempted to establish themselves in the jungle, which is teeming with unsuspected life and may erupt at any moment into an act of violence, are fragile to the last degree, civilised in name more than in fact, and exist only on sufferance. For Tomlinson's sensibility, though never cultivated for its own sake, was finely tuned, and as responsive to mood as to the appearance of everything he encountered. The sense of the numinous was with him always. 'Life is a mystery,' he wrote, 'and always will be.' And so there are presences in his world, whether he is thrusting into a jungle, or strolling along Chesil Beach, or walking down Ludgate Hill after a night's bombing. What they are he does not attempt to say: it is sufficient to be aware of them. His descriptive passages suggest again and again an unfathomable depth beneath appearances, a dimension of reality that is sealed off from the literal, prosaic mind.

Tomlinson's second travel book was *Tidemarks* (1924), a record of a journey to the Moluccas and Malaya, and like *The Sea and the Jungle* a work of great distinction. The experiences that it records provided him with much of the material for the first of his six novels, *Gallions Reach* (1927), which won him the Femina-Vie Heureuse Prize. There are fine things in this novel—a memorable description of a shipwreck, and a sustained and even more impressive passage concerning an expedition into the interior of Malaya, together with a hundred incidental felicities. Yet it fails of its effect: the moral problem inherent in its plot is evaded in favour of pure narrative, so that the ending, which circles back upon the beginning, seems arbitrary and ill-prepared.

In this it is typical of Tomlinson's novels. Although they all contain admirable things, they are nevertheless the least of his work, since a dimension is lacking. His imagination was not of the creative order. It could embroider and embellish his own experience, but could not range far beyond it, so that he was quickly out of his depth on those occasions when he tried to describe a *milieu* or a situation that he did not know. And although he could create a dramatic situation he was unable to develop it, or to fuse situation and character in such a way that each advanced the other. His narrative tended to develop serially, and was not closely woven. Above all, he lacked the gift of empathy: his curiosity, though widely and sympathetically diffused in whatever surroundings he found himself, was not especially kindled, as a novelist's must be, by the variousness of human psychology. His characters are drawn from the outside, and when he enters into their minds it is largely his own mind that he reveals. Moreover, the quickness of his eye is not matched by sharpness of ear, so that the ring of his dialogue is not quite true. Yet he could tell a story, if it were not a long one, magnificently, and the five chapters of *Gallions Reach* describing the shipwreck are of classic quality. He was compared to Conrad for them, but that was unnecessary. He did not write like Conrad: he wrote as well as Conrad. Indeed, in one respect he wrote better, for his prose had gained from his experience as a journalist a

flexibility which Conrad did not achieve until late in life, when his sea stories were far behind him.

One other of Tomlinson's novels, *All Our Yesterdays* (1930) achieved a substantial *succès d'estime,* but again its elements fail to cohere. It is memorable as the nearest thing that Tomlinson wrote to a volume of war memoirs, but philosophizing intrudes fatally upon its narrative: he could not keep it out. The philosopher in him was compounded of elements seemingly disparate, yet curiously fused. He had the social conscience of a Radical who has known poverty in his formative years, the longing for harmony of a contemplative whose sensibilities are delighted by beauty and rasped by uncouthness in private or public affairs, the integrity of a man who instinctively measures all experience against a scale of values, and the wry humour of an observer who can extract richness from every situation yet has learned not to expect a great deal from humankind. Although he cherished goodness, he had seen too much of the grubbier aspects of experience to be other than quietly sceptical about human activity. Without being didactic he was always a moralist and an ironist, alert to the discrepancies between public faces and private meanings.

His irony is delicate and deadly, and lurks always near the tip of his pen: you never know when a casual comment will dissolve a layer of pretentiousness or humbug that you had not noticed was there, and reveal beneath it a value too long tarnished by custom or neglect. There is no malice in this irony: it is a cleansing agent; and it calls for some alertness in the reader, for it may well not be noticed unless you are on the lookout for it—until, that is, your ear is attuned to this grave, slightly mocking prose and can catch its vibrations. Tomlinson was profoundly aware of what L. H. Myers called 'the deep-seated spiritual vulgarity that lies at the heart of our civilisation', and the best of his irony was directed towards the exposure of its shallow assumptions and easy optimism. He stood at a slight angle to our common experience, so that he saw things a little differently, and saw through them because he did not commit the vulgar error of approaching them through the intellect alone. He shared intuitively the oriental and Celtic awareness that truth is to be found in the quietness of a man's own heart, if the clamour of the world can be sufficiently stilled to let him hear it. But it was not oriental philosophy that formulated his quietism: the authors who influenced him most were Emerson, Thoreau and Whitman—and one other. 'Plato', he said with his tongue in his cheek, 'has been the ruin of me.' He seems never to have made an open avowal of religious belief, but here and there in his work a hint is given that the dignity and restraint of his civilised mind rested upon the gift of faith.

His criticism, which is incidental to his other work, reflects his acceptance of mystery. He distrusted those intellectual formulations which tell us too little because they are too narrow, too precisely defined, and so cannot suggest the inexpressible, and because the critic who professes to take the measure of a mind greater than his own is guilty of unpardonable presumption. Writing of El Greco he says:

> It might be as well simply to admit that when an artist evidently knows what we know, yet makes that knowledge appear to be extraordinary, his oddity is but the experience of a value which cannot be seen from where we stand. We are not wrong; we are right, within our own confine; but he is aware of an extension invisible to us.

On occasion his criticism could be devastating, as in his discussion of Sir Winston Churchill's *The World Crisis* in the essay **'A Footnote to the War Books'**. Churchill's history of the First World War had been acclaimed as great prose. Tomlinson commented:

> We should know something of prose, for we are not unaware of Browne, Bunyan, Swift, Sterne and Lamb. There are also Melville, Hardy and Doughty. So there is not much excuse for us when deliberately, after a critical scrutiny, which suggests we have a right to judge, we give to limelight the honour which should go to the broadening of dawn.

And then, by quotation and analysis, he quietly demolishes these extravagant claims. What offended him was the theatrical falsity of Churchill's diction, the striving after melodramatic effect, which insulted with its twopence-coloured imagery the unpretentious courage and endurance of those who fought. 'It is, I should say, eloquence in an Eton collar on Speech Day. It is intended to impress us; and we may doubt that genuine eloquence ever so intends . . . If we think we ought to be eloquent because the subject deserves it and try to be, then we are not. The test for a war book is the same as that for any other sort of book.' Yet, as he made clear in *The Wind is Rising* (1941), his admiration for Churchill the war leader fell only a little short of reverence.

Behind such criticism lay Tomlinson's experience as a war correspondent on the western front. He was sent to France as soon as war was declared in 1914 and was attached to British G.H.Q. For three years he endured the worst of it, and his hearing was permanently damaged by gunfire; but he was not permitted to see the war out. In 1917 Lord Northcliffe's representative on the Newspaper Publishers' Association objected that he was too 'humanitarian', and he was recalled. It was then that he joined Massingham on *The Nation*.

He was once asked why he did not write a book about the war; but, he said, 'it occurred to me that a cynical enemy could accuse me of having written about nothing else since 1914'. In consequence he has never been considered as one of that group of writers who gave the First World War a literature of its own; yet the many passages in his books which deal with what he saw are in no way inferior to the work of Graves, Blunden or Sassoon. Like every writer who went through that experience Tomlinson was profoundly and permanently affected by it, and he put more of his deepest self into his war writing than into any of his other work. *Waiting for Daylight* (1921), *Mars His Idiot* (1935), *The Wind is Rising* and *The Turn of the Tide* (1945) are essential reading for those who would know what kind of man this was who wrote with such distinction of mind and showed such quiet scorn for the babble and stridency of publicists. These commentaries impress us now not for their measured gravity alone, the equilibrium which they maintain between involvement and detachment, but for their clear-sightedness. Thirty years on we forget how difficult it was to stand back, to retain one's sense of perspective; but Tomlinson was a difficult man to fool. He had been through war and seen through the misrepresentations of official spokesmen and apologists; but he had also achieved his own perspective, and it could not be shaken by either propaganda or disaster. Knowing clearly the values by which he lived, and for which wars might justifiably be fought, he was unlikely to suppose that salvation could be found through political programmes. When war came again in 1939 Tomlinson had his own word for it: 'the Nazi outrage against civility'. That word, exactly chosen, recurs again and again throughout *The Wind is Rising*, which is a notebook kept during the year from August 1939 until just after Dunkirk. It has overtones of courtesy, dignity, respect and order, fragile things which are the first to go when there are bombs about; and it has little to do with the pronouncements of politicians. One is reminded of a book by another writer whose mind was cast in a similar mould, and who wrote as well as Tomlinson: C. E. Montague's *Disenchantment*. Tomlinson took the long view, and noted, in prose more elaborate than usual, an irony that others did not perceive:

> Once a man dreamed of a little engine to move more powerfully than others through internal combustion; and lo, our ghastly night sky, and the dead in the cellars! To a mind receptive of novelty came that revelation, and we welcomed it as a device to bring men nearer to each other; in truth, it happened that men could in reality mount up with wings as eagles, though borne aloft not by the power of the spirit which moved the prophet to chant of a joy to be. And the extraordinary outcome of this gift of wings? We are troglodytes again. We have gone to earth. We dread the light while fearing the dark. Human infants are born in subterranean passages, and stay there.

So too with the end of the war: 'How if, when we have victory, we have our worst selves to fight?' he wrote in 1945, when this was not a popular sentiment with an exhausted nation. 'Never yet has there appeared on this earth a fair democracy; it has not yet been called up. Such a community could only appear at the call of wisdom, which has been named the fear of God; so men till now have not enjoyed its liberty. That liberty can be had but at a price; a price men may be reluctant to pay, I suppose, even for residence within the jurisdiction of Zion. They are slow to give up anything, even the causes of their tribulations . . . It is not so easy as it seems to give our best to society instead of our worst, for our existence is suffered by our neighbours not on the highest terms but on the lowest.'

Tomlinson lived long enough to see his forebodings become reality: he died in 1958, and faded out of public memory. Which is a pity, because his work is literature, and even the most ephemeral of his books, the war commentaries, are grounded in values that need to be perpetually reasserted. Reading him again it is not difficult to believe the inscription on his gravestone at Abbotsbury in Dorset—an epitaph adapted from Hardy, whose work he loved: 'He was a good man, and did good things.'

FURTHER READING

Criticism

Alcorn, John. *The Nature Novel from Hardy to Lawrence,* pp. 53-55. New York: Columbia University Press, 1977.
Brief discussion of *The Sea and the Jungle* in which Alcorn compares it to Joseph Conrad's *Heart of Darkness* (1902).

Bergonzi, Bernard. *Heroes' Twilight: A Study of the Literature of the Great War,* pp. 186-89. London: The Macmillan Press, 1980.
Examines Tomlinson's depiction of war in *All Our Yesterdays.*

Crawford, Fred D. *H. M. Tomlinson.* Boston: Twayne Publishers, 1981, 260 p.
Biographical and critical examination of Tomlinson's life and works.

Review of *The Sea and the Jungle,* by H. M. Tomlinson. *The Dial* 54, No. 644 (16 April 1913): 348.
Brief, favorable assessment.

Hopkins, Kenneth. "Introduction." In his *H. M. Tomlinson: A Selection from His Writings,* pp. 11-19. London:

Hutchinson, 1953.
Laudatory overview of Tomlinson's career and body of work.

Krasner, James. *The Entangled Eye: Visual Perception and the Representation of Nature in Post-Darwinian Narrative,* pp. 116-22. New York: Oxford University Press, 1992.
Discusses *The Sea and the Jungle* and the implications of Tomlinson's use of urban architectural metaphors when describing the natural world.

Ratcliffe, S. K. "Foreword." In *Old Junk,* by H. M. Tomlinson, pp. 11-16. New York: Alfred A. Knopf, 1923.
Overview of Tomlinson's life and laudatory introduction to the works collected in *Old Junk.*

————. "The Ultimate Ordeal." *Saturday Review of Literature* 25, No. 12 (21 March 1942): 7.
Favorable review of *The Wind Is Rising.*

Swinnerton, Frank. "Four Journalists." In his *Figures in the Foreground: Literary Reminiscences 1917-1940,* pp. 116-35. Garden City, N. Y.: Doubleday and Company, 1964.
Anecdotal discussion of Tomlinson's life and career.

Taylor, Mary A. "More Evidence of H. M. Tomlinson's Role in the Melville Revival." *Studies in American Fiction* 20, No. 1 (Spring 1992): 111-13.
Brief presentation asserting Tomlinson's enthusiasm for Herman Melville's novel *Moby-Dick* (1851). The essay includes an extended excerpt from a letter in which Tomlinson states: "But *Moby Dick . . .* ah, the secret is out! That's the Immense book of the sea."

West, Rebecca. "A London Letter." *The Bookman* (New York) 69, No. 5 (July 1929): 518-23.
General discussion of Tomlinson's writing occasioned by his winning a literary prize.

Hans Vaihinger

1852-1933

German philosopher.

INTRODUCTION

One of the foremost early twentieth-century scholars of the German philosopher Immanuel Kant, Vaihinger also conducted extensive philosophical investigations into the role that "fictions" play in various aspects of human life. His major work, *Die Philosophie des Als-Ob (The Philosophy of "As If")* (1911), stresses the usefulness and value of false ideas for both individuals and social groups. Influenced by the German philosopher Arthur Schopenhauer, Vaihinger espoused a thoroughly pessimistic view of the world and famously defined mankind as "a species of monkey suffering from megalomania."

Biographical Information

Vaihinger was born in Nehren, now known as Baden, just outside Wuerttemberg in Germany. He was educated in theology in nearby Tübingen and later received his Ph.D. in philosophy from the University of Leipzig. In 1877 he began his long career as a teacher at Strasbourg, where he would remain for seven years, and then moved on to the University at Halle in 1884. During his tenure there, he founded the periodical *Kant Studien,* and the Kant Gesellschaft (an academic society) in 1904. Poor health, notably extreme nearsightedness, eventually drove Vaihinger into retirement in 1906 at the age of fifty-four. It was in the period immediately following that he completed the work for which he is most famous, *The Philosophy of "As If,"* published in Germany in 1911. He continued to involve himself in academic matters later in life, preparing a yearbook of philosophy and philosophical criticism in 1919. Vaihinger died in December 1933.

Major Works

Vaihinger distinguished himself with a number of works on Kant, including a two-volume critique entitled *Commentar zu Kants Kritik der reinen Vernunft* (1881-1892), as well as a study of Friedrich Nietzsche, *Nietzsche als Philosoph.* Vaihinger's own philosophical work revolved around his notion of "fictionalism" or the "As-If": based on the Kantian assertion that the human mind tortures itself with insoluble problems, searching for truth where no possibility of achieving the truth exists. The "As-If," for Vaihinger, is the necessary fiction of human thought, the assumption of truth even in the face of clearly false ideas, which, he postulated, made thought and indeed life itself possible. He went on to argue that ideas like "immortality" or "freedom" were meaningless, but that humanity still manages to make use of them in

beneficial ways. Vaihinger developed his "fictionalism" in two substantial works, *The Philosophy of "As-If"* and *Der Atheismusstreit gegen die Philosophie des Als Obs und das Kantische System* (1916). In both, he stressed the value and usefulness of clearly false statements, and worked to unseat "the truth" from its discursive prominence, claiming that certain aspects of the world are inherently irrational and incomprehensible, that the "truth" of these aspects, if it exists at all, cannot be grasped by the human mind.

Critical Reception

Vaihinger set himself against the skeptics, positivists, and materialists of his time by asserting that doctrines should not be evaluated by their truth, but by their utility and ethical affect. As such, many prominent figures in opposing schools of thought, including materialist H. L. Mencken, took a dim view of Vaihinger's work and criticized his books publicly. Nevertheless, Vaihinger was generally well received both in Germany and abroad, especially in America. While he never managed to draw as much attention to himself as some of his contemporaries, the ideas associated with the "As-If," as well as Vaihinger's accomplished Kantian criticism, found and maintained a broad base of sustained interest in academic circles.

PRINCIPAL WORKS

Gothe als ideal universeller Bildung (lecture) 1875

Hartmann, Duhring, und Lange: Zur Geschichte der deutschen Philosophie im XIX Jahrhunderts (philosophy) 1876

Commentar zu Kants Kritik der reinen Vernunft (philosophy) 1881-1892

Nietzsche als Philosoph (philosophy) 1902

Die transcendentale Deduktion der Kategorien (philosophy) 1902

Die Philosophie in der Staatsprufung (philosophy) 1906

Die Philosophie des Als-Ob: System der theoretischen, praktischen, und religiosen Fiktionen der Menschheit auf Grund eines idealistischen Positivismus, [The Philosophy of "As-If": A System of the Theoretical, Practical, and Religious Fictions of Mankind, translated by C.K. Ogden] (philosophy) 1911

Der Atheismusstreit gegen die Philosophie des Als Obs und das Kantische System (philosophy) 1916

Zu Kants Gedachtnis [editor, with B. Bauch] (philosophy) 1904

CRITICISM

Havelock Ellis (essay date 1920)

SOURCE: "The World as Fiction," in *The Nation,* Vol. XXVIII, No. 4, 1920, pp. 134-36.

[In the following essay, Ellis reviews The Philosophy of "As If."*]*

It is noted of the young men of to-day—the after-war generation as they already regard themselves—that they suffer from disillusion. The world has not turned out as they had expected it would turn out, or, the weaker ones might say, as they had been taught to expect it to turn out. They feel home-sick wanderers in the Universe, new Werthers or new Obermanns, as the case may be, searching the horizon for the apparition of some new Romanticism to solace their sick souls.

The world is, as it has ever been, infinitely rich. We hang on to it by a thread here and there, among innumerable threads, and the thread snaps, and we cry out that it is a rotten world. But the thread was of our own choosing; it was our business to test it and to prove it. If we were deceived we were only deceived in ourselves. The world remains infinitely rich.

It is possible that some to-day may turn with interest to a book—it happens to be a German book—which they never turned to before or probably never heard of although its significance was recognized even when it appeared three years before the war. It was written many years earlier than that. Dr. Hans Vaihinger the author of *The Philosophy of the As If* (*Die Philosophie des Als Ob*) had been known as one of the profoundest students of Kant. It was in Kant that he discerned the core of his own philosophy concerning the practical significance of fiction in human life. It is by no means the idea that has traditionally been found in Kant—for Kant was himself not clear about it and his insight was further darkened by his reactionary tendencies—but it is that which under various disguises has inspired some of the most influential philosophers of recent times, and it was Vaihinger first of all who, secretly and unknown, elaborated it. He was not only the first but the most thorough-going exponent of this vision of the world. Nietzsche, the Pragmatists, Bergson, Croce, Bertrand Russell, have all expounded some aspect of a conception which finds its unadulterated essence in a book they had never seen until their own systems had been formulated.

Vaihinger certainly had his first stimulus from Kant, in whose philosophy (he is perhaps the chief living exponent of it) he found that the "as if" view of belief and conduct played an extraordinarily large though overlooked part, and was even his special and personal way of regarding things; he was not as much a metaphysician, Vaihinger argues, as a metaphorician. But Vaihinger soon found almost the same attitude more or less ex-

pressed or implicit in various other thinkers, notably in F. A. Lange, of the famous "History of Materialism," whose view of the value of poetic conceptions for science and for life made him the immediate precursor of Vaihinger.

It was in 1876-7 that Vaihinger wrote his book, a marvellous achievement for so youthful a thinker, for it would appear that he was then only about twenty-five years of age. A final revision it never underwent, and there remain various peculiarities about the form into which it is cast. A serious failure in eyesight seems to have been the main reason for delaying the publication of a work which the author felt to be too revolutionary to put forth in an imperfect form. He preferred to leave it for posthumous publication.

But the world was not standing still, and during the next thirty years many things happened. Vaihinger found the new sect of Pragmatists coming into fashion, with ideas resembling his own, though in a cruder shape, which seemed to render philosophy the *meretrix theologorum.* Many distinguished thinkers were working towards an attitude more or less like his own, especially Nietzsche, whom (like many others even to-day) he had long regarded with prejudice and avoided, but now discovered to be "a great liberator," with congenial veins of thought. Vaihinger realized that his conception was being independently put forward from various sides, often in forms that to him seemed imperfect or vicious. It was no longer advisable to hold back his book. In 1911, therefore, *Die Philosophie des Als Ob* appeared. Therewith the author's life-work was done; he still lives, in blindness and retirement, at Halle, and is still able to preside over the meetings of the Kant Society.

The problem which Vaihinger set out to solve was this: How comes it about that with consciously false ideas we yet reach conclusions that are in harmony with Nature and appeal to us as Truth? That we do so is obvious, especially in the "exact" branches of science. In mathematics it is notorious that we start from absurdities to reach a realm of law, and our whole conception of the nature of the world is based on a foundation which we believe to have no existence. For even the most sober scientific investigator in science, the most thorough-going positivist, cannot dispense with fiction; he must at least make use of categories, and they are already fictions, analogical fictions, or labels, which give us the same pleasure as children receive when they are told the "name" of a thing. Fiction is indeed an indispensable supplement to logic, or even a part of it of equal rank; whether we are working inductively or deductively, both ways hang closely together with fiction, and axioms, though they seek to be primary verities, are more akin to fiction. If we had realized the nature of axioms, the doctrine of Einstein, which sweeps away axioms so familiar to us that they seem obvious truths, and substitutes others which seem absurd because they are unfamiliar, might not have been so bewildering.

Physics, especially mathematical physics, Vaihinger explains in detail, has been based, and fruitfully based, on fictions. The infinite, infinitely little or infinitely great, while helpful in lightening our mental operations, is a fiction. The Greeks disliked and avoided it, and "the gradual formation of this conception is one of the most charming and instructive themes in the history of science"—indeed one of the most noteworthy spectacles in the history of the human spirit; we see the working of a logical impulse first feeling in the dark, gradually constructing ideas fitted to yield precious service, yet full of hopeless contradictions, without any relation to the real world. That absolute space is a fiction is no new idea. Hobbes had declared it was only a *phantasma;* Leibnitz, who agreed, added that it was merely "the *idolum* of a few modern Englishmen," and called time extension, and movement *choses idéales.* Berkeley, in attacking the defective conceptions of the mathematicians, failed to see that it was by means of, and not in spite of, these logically defective conceptions that they attained logically valuable results. All the marks of fiction are set on the mathematician's pure space; it is impossible and unthinkable; yet it has been proved useful and fruitful.

The tautological fiction of "Force"—an empty reduplication of the fact of a succession of relationships—is one that we constantly fall back on with immense satisfaction and with the feeling of having achieved something; it has been a highly convenient fiction which has aided representation and experience. It is one of the most famous, and also, it must be added, one of the most fatal of fantasies. For when we talk of, for instance, a "life-force" and its *élan,* or whatever other dainty term we like to apply to it, we are not only summarily mingling together many separate phenomena, but we are running the risk that our conception may be taken for something that really exists. There is always temptation, when two processes tend to follow each other, to call the property of the first to be followed by the other its "force," and to measure that force by the magnitude of the result. In reality we only have succession and co-existence, and the "force" is something that we imagine.

We must not, therefore, treat our imagination with contempt, as was formerly the fashion, but rather the reverse. The two great periods of English philosophy, Vaihinger remarks, ended with Ockham and with Hume, who each took up, in effect, the fictional point of view, but both too much on the merely negative side, without realizing the positive and constructive value of fictions. English law has above all realised it, even, he adds, to the point of absurdity. Nothing is so precious as fiction, provided only one chooses the right fiction. "Matter" is such a fiction. There are still people who speak with lofty contempt of "Materialism"; they mean well, but they are unhappy in their terms of abuse. When Berkeley demonstrated the impossibility of "matter" he thought he could afford to throw away the conception as useless. He was quite wrong; it is logically contradictory ideas that are the most valuable. Matter is a fiction, just as the fundamental ideas with which the sciences generally operate

are mostly fictions, and the scientific materialization of the world has proved a necessary and useful fiction, only harmful when we regard it as hypothesis, and thus possibly true. The representative world is a system of fictions. It is a symbol by the help of which we orient ourselves. The business of science is to make the symbol ever more adequate, but it remains a symbol, a means of action, for action is the last end of thinking.

The atom, to which matter is ultimately reduced, is regarded by Vaihinger as equally a fiction, though it was at first viewed as a hypothesis, and it may be added that since he wrote it seems to have returned to the stage of hypothesis. But when with Boscovich the "atom" was regarded as simply the bearer of energy, it became literally "a hypostatized nothing." We have to realize at the same time that every "thing" is a "summatory fiction," for to say, as is often said, that a "thing" has properties, and yet has a real existence apart from its properties, is obviously only a convenient manner of speech, a "verbal fiction." The "force of attraction," as Newton himself pointed out, belongs to the same class of summatory fictions.

Vaihinger is throughout careful to distinguish fiction alike from hypothesis and dogma. He regards the distinction as, methodologically, highly important though not always easy to make. The dogma is put forward as an absolute and unquestionable truth; the hypothesis is a possible truth, such as Darwin's doctrine of descent; the fiction is impossible, but it enables us to reach what for us is relatively truth, and, above all, while hypothesis simply contributes to knowledge, fiction thus used becomes a guide to practical action and indispensable to what we feel to be progress. Thus the mighty and civilizing structure of Roman law was built up by the aid of what the Romans themselves recognized as fictions, while in the different and more flexible system of English law a constant inspiration to action has been furnished by the supposed privileges gained by Magna Carta, though we now recognize them as fictitious. Many of our ideas tend to go through the three stages of Dogma, Hypothesis, and Fiction, sometimes in that order and sometimes in the reverse order. Hypothesis especially presents a state of instability which is unpleasant to the mind, so it tends to become either dogma or fiction. The ideas of Christianity, beginning as dogmas, have passed through all three stages in the minds of thinkers during recent centuries; the myths of Plato, beginning as fiction, not only passed through the three stages, but then passed back again, being now again regarded as fiction. The scientifically valuable fiction is a child of modern times, but we have already emerged from the period when the use of fiction was confined to the exact sciences.

Thus we find fiction fruitfully flourishing in the biological and social sciences, and even in the highest spheres of human spiritual activity. The Linnæan and similar classificatory systems are fictions, even though put forward as hypotheses, having their value simply as pictures, as forms of representation, but leading to contradictions and liable to be replaced by other systems which present more helpful pictures. There are still people who disdain Adam Smith's "economic man," as though proceeding from a purely selfish view of life, although Buckle, forestalling Vaihinger, long ago explained that Smith was deliberately making use of a "valid artifice," separating facts that he knew to be in Nature inseparable—he based his moral theory on a totally different kind of man—because so he could reach results approximately true to the observed phenomena. Bentham also adopted a fiction for his own system, though believing it to be a hypothesis, and Mill criticized it as being "geometrical"; the criticism is correct, comments Vaihinger, but the method was not thereby invalidated, for in complicated fields no other method can be fruitfully used.

The same law holds when we approach our highest and most sacred conceptions. It was recognized by enlightened philosophers and theologians before Vaihinger that the distinction between body and soul is not different from that between matter and force, a provisional and useful distinction, that light and darkness, life and death, are abstractions, necessary indeed, but in their application to reality always to be used with precaution. On the threshold of the moral world we meet the idea of Freedom, "one of the weightiest conceptions man has ever formed," once a dogma, in course of time a hypothesis, now in the eyes of many a fiction, yet we cannot do without it, even although we may be firmly convinced that our acts are determined by laws that cannot be broken. Many other great conceptions have tended to follow the same course: God, the Soul, Immortality, the Moral World-Order. The critical hearer understands what is meant when these great words are used, and if the uncritical misunderstand, that, adds Vaihinger, may sometimes also be useful. For these things are Ideals, and all Ideals are, logically speaking, fictions. As Science leads to the Imaginary, so Life leads to the Impossible; without them we cannot reach the heights we are born to scale. "Taken literally, however, our most valuable conceptions are worthless."

When we review the vast field which Vaihinger summarizes, we find that thinking and existing must ever be on two different planes. The attempt of Hegel and his followers to transform subjective processes into objective world-processes will not work out. The Thing-in-itself, the Absolute, remains a fiction, though the ultimate and most necessary fiction, for without it representation would be unintelligible. We can only regard reality as a Heraclitean flux of happening—though Vaihinger fails to point out that this "reality" also can only be an image or symbol—and our thinking would itself be fluid if it were not that by fiction we obtain imaginary standpoints and boundaries by which to gain control of the flow of reality. It is the special art and object of thinking to attain existence by quite other methods than that of existence itself. But the wish by so doing to understand the world is both unrealizable and foolish, for we are only trying to comprehend our own fictions. We can never solve the so-

called world-riddle because what seem riddles to us are merely the contradictions we have ourselves created. Yet though the way of thinking cannot be the way of being, since they stand on such different foundations, thinking always has a kind of parallelism with being, and though we make our reckonings with a reality that we falsify, yet the practical results tend to come out right. Just because thinking is different from reality, its forms must also be different. Our conceptions, our conventional signs, have a fictive function to perform, and thinking is, in its lower grades, comparable to paper money, and in its higher forms it is a kind of poetry.

Imagination is thus a constitutive part of all thinking. We may make distinctions between practical scientific thinking and disinterested æsthetic thinking. Yet all thinking is finally a comparison. Scientific fictions are parallel with æsthetic fictions. The poet is the type of all thinkers; there is no sharp boundary between the region of poetry and the region of science. Both alike are not ends in themselves, but means to higher ends.

Vaihinger's doctrine of the "as if" is not immune from criticism on more than one side, and it is not indeed always quite congruous with itself. Nor can it be said that he ever really answered the question with which he set out. In philosophy, however, it is not the attainment of the goal that matters, it is the things that are met with by the way. And Vaihinger's philosophy is not only of interest because it presents so clearly and vigorously a prevailing tendency in modern thought. Rightly understood, it is a fortifying influence to those who see their cherished spiritual edifice, whatever it may be, fall around them and are tempted to a mood of disillusionment. We make our own world; when we have made it awry we can remake it, truer to the facts. It will never be finally made; we are always stretching forth to larger and better fictions which answer more truly to our growing knowledge and experience. Even when we walk it is only by a series of regulated errors, Vaihinger well points out, a perpetual succession of falls to one side and the other side, and our whole progress through life is of the same nature; all thinking is a regulated error. For we cannot, as Vaihinger insists, choose our errors at random or in accordance with what happens to please us; such fictions are only too likely to turn into deadening dogmas; the old *visdormitiva* is the type of them, mere husks that are of no vital use and help us not at all. There are good fictions and bad fictions (we had too many opportunities to study the latter class during the war), just as there are good poets and bad poets. It is in the choice and regulation of our errors, in our readiness to accept ever closer approximations to the unattainable reality, that we think rightly and live rightly. We triumph in so far as we succeed in that regulation. "A lost battle," Foch, quoting De Maistre, lays down in his *Principes de Guerre,* "is a battle one thinks one has lost"; the battle is won by the fiction that it is won; and it is so also in the battle of life, in the whole art of living. Freud regards dreaming as fiction that helps us to sleep; thinking we may regard as fiction that helps us to live. Man lives by imagination.

The New Statesman (essay date 1924)

SOURCE: Review of *The Philosophy of 'As If,'* in *The New Statesman*, Vol. XXIII, No. 588, July, 1924, p. 472.

[*In the following essay, the reviewer finds Vaihinger's theory in* The Philosophy of "As If" *to be "indistinguishable from Pragmatism."*]

In the slow crystallisation of the amorphous mass of thought which we label "Modern Realism," one of the most significant developments has been the reinterpretation of Kant. Hans Vaihinger has been the genius of this movement. To him more than to any other is due the credit of rescuing the philosophy of his great fellow-countryman from the gentle tyranny of his Hegelian paraphrasers. His keen and sympathetic understanding of English philosophy aided him in this work to no slight extent; as it helped to make him, in the years before the War, a far-sighted critic of his country's policy and a prophet of the disaster which has overtaken her. The translation into English of his greatest contribution to constructive thought—*The Philosophy of "As If"*—will find a warm welcome from all who have followed the tendencies of modern metaphysics.

The centre of gravity in Vaihinger's philosophy lies in an exuberant emphasis upon the constructive activity of the mind in all scientific procedure. His thesis has its source in those passages of the *Critique of Pure Reason* which stress the logical function of the imagination, the regulative Ideas of Reason, and the Antinomies. Kant had shown that our science can proceed only through the assumption of ideas which cannot be shown to be valid, because in the nature of the case they cannot be realised in experience. Vaihinger holds that these ideas can be shown to be false as well as necessary. With this in mind he proceeds to exemplify throughout the entire range of scientific, philosophic and religious thought the use of ideas which are not only false and necessary, but consciously so. The mathematician treats the circle *as if* it were a polygon with an indefinitely large number of sides, the physicist treats the heavenly bodies *as if* their mass were concentrated at a point; the biologist treats evolution *as if* it were purposive; the lawyer treats the adopted child *as if* it were a natural child. In these instances the scientific mind advances to the solution of its problems by a method of conscious fiction. It treats the unfamiliar as if it were an instance of the familiar, knowing all the while that it is not. Science is right in so doing, as is shown by the fact that most of its great modern triumphs have waited for their achievement upon the invention of just such fictional methods. To deny the mind's right to proceed in this way would be to wipe modern science entirely off the slate.

This is a summary statement of what we might call the "Special Theory" of the "As If." Logically, it succeeds in distinguishing a new type of judgment—the fictional—from the hypothetical with which it has hitherto been confused. A scientific hypothesis hopes to be true, and is scrapped whenever it is proved false: but a scientific fiction never claims to be true; it is used as an artifice, and the error which it involves is compensated in the final result by an antithetic error which cancels it out. Metaphysically, by means of the wide range from which the examples are chosen, and the lucidity with which they are classified and discussed, it vindicates brilliantly against many forms of realist theory, the presence of a constructive mental activity in the logical processes by which we attain knowledge.

But Vaihinger is not content with this important result. It is only the foundation of a General Theory which envelops the whole field of philosophy. The theory of fiction invades the whole domain of legitimate hypothesis and then proceeds to the conquest of the realm of ascertained truth. Not only does thought make use upon occasion of fictional artifices, it can make use of nothing else. Not only is the Atom a fiction, together with Matter and Personality, Free-will and the Differential Calculus, Force and the Deity; but the categories of thought are fictions, and also all our general ideas. Nothing remains standing before the ruthlessness of the attack, except only the observable regularity of the sequences of our sensations. The world of ideas as a whole is a tissue of fictions, an elaborate and essential falsehood.

> The whole conceptual world is inserted between sensations; these alone are ultimately given.

> The goal of all science, the reduction of all happenings to atomic movements in space, is in fact an attempt to reduce all existence to ideational constructs of a purely fictional nature.

Vaihinger is not blind to the general implications of such a philosophy. "Mankind," he tells us, "is beginning to realise to an increasing extent that understanding is only an illusion, that life and action are based upon illusions, and lead to illusions." Yet in spite of this he refuses to be called a sceptic. The theory sounds sceptical only because we are such incurable optimists and expect more than we can have.

> The wish to understand the world is not only unrealisable, but also a very stupid wish.

We ought to be content with our illusions, because:

> The Ideal, the Unreal, is the most valuable; men must demand the impossible even if it leads to contradictions.

After all, thought is not an end in itself, but an instrument for the service of life.

> The actual purpose of thought is not thought itself, but behaviour and ultimately ethical behaviour. . . . We do not understand the world when we are pondering over its problems, but when we are doing the world's work.

The final result seems to be indistinguishable from Pragmatism. Vaihinger denies the identification, apparently because he refuses to say that a fruitful fiction is *true* because it works. Yet he maintains that we can no longer talk about truth at all, in the ordinary sense. "Truth is really merely the most expedient type of error." In other words, Truth itself is not truth but fiction, and the dispute with the Pragmatist is but a question of terminology. This is hidden behind the screen of "experience and intuition, which are higher than all human reason." In sensation and the regularities of sense-experience, we are at least face to face with reality and fact. Surely in this the great Kantian has forgotten his Kant. A "sensation" is as much a fiction as an "atom." And the perception of the regularities of sequence involves recognition and the categories. For how can I remember except by treating what is a present experience *as if* it were a past one? Thus if Vaihinger's General Theory is right, the whole field of experience, sensory and conceptual alike, is an *as if* that refers to nothing, a fiction created out of nothing, so far at least as it has any form. And, indeed, the General Theory makes the Special Theory meaningless, because it leaves no room for the essential distinction between "fiction," "hypothesis" and "fact."

The American Mercury (essay date 1924)

SOURCE: "Philosophers as Liars," in *The American Mercury,* Vol. 111, No. 10, October, 1924, pp. 253-55.

[The following review offers a negative opinion of The Philosophy of "As If," *finding Vaihinger to be a "dull" writer and his ideas "obvious."]*

This is a work that has had a great popular success in Germany, and is now gradually penetrating to foreign parts. It was first published in 1911 and is at present in its sixth edition; there is also a somewhat shorter *Volksausgabe.* Havelock Ellis, always alert for intellectual novelties, wrote an article about it four or five years ago, and there is already a small but active body of Vaihingeristas in England.

Like his master, Kant, and most other German philosophical writers (let us not forget the brilliant exceptions, Schopenhauer and Nietzsche!), Vaihinger is an extremely dull author, much given to long and complex phrases and to laborious repetitions. Nor has his translator, Mr. Ogden, done anything to rescue him from the labyrinth in which he wanders. On the contrary, the English version of the book is often even more vexatious than the original German. I point to one dreadful example: the translation of *Vorstellungsgebilde* as *mental constructs.* Is *construct,* then, an English noun? I doubt it. The noun, I believe, is *structure.* But even *structure,* in this place, would be clumsy, for what Vaihinger oviously means is *image.* I cite a typical sentence: "Er wäre es auch, wenn die Vorstellungsgebilde unmittelbare Abbilder des Seins wären." Ogden turns this into: "This would hold true even if our mental constructs were direct reflections of

reality." Why not make it: "It would be so even if our mental images were direct images of reality?"

But despite all this pedantic fustian there is a clear idea in the book, and it is this: that man is so constituted that he cannot carry on the business of thinking without making frequent use of assumptions that are untrue, and known to him to be so—that he needs fictions as well as facts. Vaihinger makes a clear distinction between fictions and hypotheses—a distinction too often neglected by other philosophers. A hypothesis may not be true, but it is at least something that someone believes may *become* true: it is an attempt to approach the truth by a plausible guess. But a fiction is admittedly *un*true, and its use is simply to get over an impassable place by throwing in logs and calling them solid rocks. In the jargon of the lawyers the former is a *praesumptio juris* and the latter a *fictio juris.* It is a *praesumptio juris* that when a man and his wife lose their lives together, as in a shipwreck, the wife dies first, as the weaker of the two. It may not be true in any given case, but it is at least probable in all cases, and so it is presumed to be true whenever the actual facts cannot be established. A legal fiction is quite different. It is an assumption that is admittedly not true: for example, that a glass of beer containing one half of one per cent plus one hundredth of one per cent of ethyl alcohol by volume is intoxicating.

In all fields of thought both hypotheses and fictions are constantly made use of. The former, as knowledge increases, often harden into laws, *i.e.,* statements of actual fact. The atomic theory has shown some signs of doing that of late, though Vaihinger, writing of it so recently as 1911, treated it as if it were almost a fiction. Darwin's theory of natural selection began as a hypothesis, changed into a law, and is now a hypothesis again, with some chance of ending as a fiction. Adam Smith's notion that man in society is moved only by self-interest began as a working hypothesis, was turned into a law by uncritical enthusiasts, and is now generally held to be a pure fiction. But a fiction never becomes a hypothesis, though it may be transiently mistaken for one. Its essence is that it is known to be untrue. Its use is that it bridges the gap between two truths. Man can think only in logical patterns, and when there is a vacant space he must fill it as best he may, or stop thinking altogether.

It is difficult to understand why all this should have kicked up so much pother. What Vaihinger says, in the main, is quite obvious. True enough, he supports it with a great many concrete examples, taking from all the known sciences and pseudosciences, from mathematics to metaphysics. His erudition is genuinely colossal. But, as he himself frankly shows, his chief notion, that the use of fictions is necessary to thinking, was known to other men years and years ago; a large part of his volume, indeed, is given over to demonstrating the fact. Once he has demonstrated it, what follows? Nothing follows. The human mind, at its present stage of development, cannot function without the aid of fictions, but neither can it function without the aid of facts—save, perhaps, when it is housed in the skull of a university professor of philosophy. Of the two, the facts are enormously the more important. In certain metaphysical fields, *e.g.,* those of mathematics, law, theology, osteopathy and ethics—the fiction will probably hold out for many years, but elsewhere the fact slowly ousts it, and that ousting is what is called intellectual progress. Very few fictions remain in use in anatomy, or in plumbing and gas-fitting; they have even begun to disappear from economics. Vaihinger's work is thus not a system of philosophy, in any true sense; it is simply a foot-note to all existing systems. Moreover, it is not a foot-note of much solid value. It is curious, but it is unimportant.

C. E. Ayres (essay date 1924)

SOURCE: "With Benefit of Fiction," in *The New Republic,* Vol. XL, No. 518, November, 1924, p. 254.

[*In the following essay, Ayres finds Vaihinger's views to be a valuable supplement to the body of Pragmatist works.*]

Truth, we have been told again and again by the philosophers, is the object of all thinking. But is it? Thinking is part of living. It would be strange indeed if the object and the reward of thinking were at odds with the necessities of life. A broader definition must take account of the contribution of thinking to living: the object of thinking is to facilitate living. This does not mean that whatever does so is true; but it may mean that any thinking which safeguards or enhances life is successful thinking, to which questions of truth are quite subordinate.

Indeed, that is precisely the contention of this book. Vaihinger's idea, at bottom as simple as it is startling, is that many of the most prominent and fundamental conceptions of human thought are consciously false. As conceptions they have a meaning and a value; but the things they represent do not exist. Nobody supposes that they exist. They are deliberate fabrications which men employ to facilitate their other dealings with actual reality. Vaihinger does not mean hypotheses. Neither does he mean myths. He means acknowledged falsehood. When he insists that far off, divine events are fictions in the minds of thinking people he intends to say not that they are guesses at what may be true, nor that they are legends of dubious though perhaps convincing authenticity, but that they are not true at all even in the minds that hold them. They are consciously imaginative constructs in a region of speculation that is known to be beyond the power of the intellect to establish any sort of truth. The hypothesis is a picture, formulated upon scanty data, perhaps, by constructive imagination, yet intended as the closest approximation of actuality that is possible under the circumstances. If it proves out, it will take its place among the "facts" as a true picture of genuine reality. A myth is a traditional account of certain events no longer subject to verification. But here again its character is determined by the fact that some people take it to be factually true. Fiction, the "als ob," is quite different. It is not a guess at the unknown. The thinker who employs it has no expectation of bringing it to verification. On the contrary, he intends it as an artifice, an intellectual scaffolding that will never solidify into masonry however invaluable it may be in all the building operations that go on in its vicinity.

The fictions which Vaihinger is aiming at are, of course, the sublime make-believes of religion and philosophy. Those matters of faith, about which human thinking has always turned as upon an axis, are myths in the minds of many people. For some they may even seem to be hypotheses. But their most persistent definition has been in terms of faith. Now faith, the belief in things "which you know ain't so," is precisely the artifice of "als ob." It is not a picture of the actual; it is a representation of the necessary. Logically, this discrimination is very simple. Any irrational number illustrates it perfectly. Thus a moment's reflection will reveal to anyone that the number zero (let alone infinity, or the square root of minus one) is a different sort of figure from three or quintillian. Those numbers can be reached by counting physical objects. Not so zero; it appears only through calculation, and there as an artificial entity, like the body of a corporation. For that purpose its meaning is clear; yet as a designation applying to actual objects it must always remain hopelessly absurd. "The milkmaid whistled as she milked her zero cows!" The very absence from the language of the ordinal corresponding to zero (as, third, second, first, "zeroth") shows that our habits, more discriminating than intelligence, have recognized it as a mathematical "as if."

This may seem, for an instant, an undignified interpretation of the highest attainments of the human spirit. But the theory of fiction is as serious as the conceptions with which it deals, and those are, primarily, the "ultimate realities" which mark the furthest excursions of the mind into the region beyond the finite world of material events. The dogmas of the faithful are many and various. Throughout all the flux of human civilization a constant succession of Ultimates has moved unbroken, each claiming to be the final truth and none substantiating the claim except by the internal evidence each, presumably, contains of its own superior reasonableness or authenticity. To this panorama of ultimate realities Vaihinger would apply the philosophy of "als ob" like a chemical resolvent. The reaction is immediate. Any theory of metaphysical (or theological) ultimates proves out at once as a "fictional construct." Among the unenlightened matters of faith may become confused with matters of fact. Vaihinger calls particular attention to the historical metamorphosis that overtakes any philosophy when it becomes widely diffused. Beginning as an intellectual artifice of the enlightened it gradually becomes a legend among illiterates. To the poet the gods are an aid to poesy; to the vulgar they are matters of fact just beyond the reach of immediate verification but no different in essence from any clod.

The theory of the "as if" is exciting enough in itself. But its close resemblance to certain other notions that have been reshaping contemporary thought makes it doubly interesting. This connection between fiction and mythology suggests one affinity. Another one is the unconscious make-believe that psycho-analysis has revealed. The conscious fiction which Vaihinger proposes looks like a new member of a familiar family.

Indeed, we are not wholly unacquainted with it in its own proper garb. The "als ob" is a special case of a general logical theory better known in the United States than in Germany, the "instrumental logic" of the pragmatists. Vaihinger has worked out a special interpretation of the more than rational constructions in which philosophy and theology abound; pragmatism has developed a complete account of the thinking process and a general conception of truth in which the "als ob" takes its place. Says Vaihinger, conscious fiction is not factually true, though it is valuable and significant in human life. Says pragmatism, no truth is true except in relation to the part it plays in human life. Vaihinger has made a most penetrating discrimination between factual truth and, to supply a term, inspirational truth. James and Dewey have exhibited truth not in two colors but in all the shades of the spectrum. The value of Vaihinger's work lies in its significance as supplementary to these other studies in the fictions by which men live. Its chief deficiency is that it has not recognized relationship.

Hans Vaihinger (essay date 1924)

SOURCE: "Autobiographical" in *The Philosophy of 'As If': A System of the Theoretical, Practical and Religious Fictions of Mankind,* translated by C. K. Ogden, Harcourt, Brace & Company, Inc. 1924, pp. 23-48.

[*In the following essay, Vaihinger explains his reasons for and method of writing* The Philosophy of "As If."]

I was born in a Swabian parsonage near Tübingen in 1852 and so I grew up in a very religious atmosphere. It was not exactly bigoted, but it had a limited horizon, for instance, the names of the Liberal Hegelian theologian Baur of Tübingen, the so-called "Heathen Baur" and his disciple, David F. Strauss, were spoken of with horror in our home. My father, who was the author of a good many theological works, had written a pamphlet against Strauss. When I was twelve years old I was given into the charge of an excellent master and teacher in Leonberg, Sauer, who was at that time a tutor and who became many years later one of the prominent figures at the Stuttgart Grammar School. Sauer awakened the ambition of his pupils by telling them how Kepler in the 17th century and Schelling in the 18th century had sat on the benches of that ancient school of Latin. I was his favourite pupil and he used to tell me too about his Sanskrit studies, which he carried on under the influence of Professor Roth of Tübingen University. He was especially interested in the great Mahabharata epic and occasionally at the end of the les-

son in religion he would tell us how this Indian epic contained the same sort of legends as the New Testament. The stories of the Old and New Testament had already awakened doubts in my mind, so I was gradually led to the conception of the ethical value of the myth. Generally speaking, Sauer's attitude was one of rationalistic theism with a solid moral basis. I had already reached this way of thinking at the time of my confirmation (1866). This ethical theism was a great help to me in those years, but from the time that I entered the Stuttgart Grammar School it gradually and imperceptibly evolved into pantheism, based on a deep love of Nature. During this period of transition, in 1868 I came across Herder's book on the History of Mankind, which appealed to my state of mind by its mixture of theism and pantheism, and to which I owe a great deal. It gives such a wide and lofty view of the whole development of the history of mankind, extending from the earliest origins onwards through all kinds and varieties of civilization. The idea of evolution became one of the fundamental elements of my mental outlook. Herder draws special attention to the evolution of spiritual life out of its first animal origins, and he regards man always as linked up with that Nature from which he has gradually evolved. Thus in 1869, when I first heard Darwin's name and when my schoolfriends told me about the new theory of man's animal ancestry, it was no surprise to me, because through my reading of Herder I was already familiar with the idea. In later years there has been much discussion as to whether Herder can be called a forerunner of Darwin. At any rate in my case Darwin's theory of descent added nothing new to what I had learnt from Herder.

Naturally I carried these studies further in later years, but from that time onwards one of the fundamentals in my philosophy has been this fact of man's animal ancestry. About this time I came under Plato's influence, which acted as a counter-balancing factor. I read the usual *Dialogues* and the *Apology,* but our Professor was old and though very thorough he was dull and kept us to the grammatical side. His routine teaching made nothing like the same impression on me as three lessons from a young teacher called Breitmaier, who came to replace him during an illness. He read to us in Greek the myth in the *Phaedrus* on the nature of the soul, and the description of the cave from the *Republic*. This opened up a new world to me, the world of "Ideas," and as he also spoke of Plato's myths, the seed was sown then of that conception which later I myself named the "World of 'As if'".

The Introduction to Philosophy which was customary at that time in South Germany, with its bare outlines of logic, psychology and ethics, played quite an insignificant part compared with the revolutionary ideas which I was discovering for myself. This was all the more marked because our professor was Gustav Pfitzer, the poet made notorious by Heinrich Heine. But I should like to pay him a tribute of admiration here, because he was a man of noble character and my feeling for him as a personality was one of absolute reverence. The opposition which I expressed in 1905 to the Introduction to Philosophy as a separate branch of instruction derives from my own earlier experience. In the same dissertation *Philosophy in State Examinations* (1905) I urged on the other hand that philosophy should be the general principle of instruction in all subjects and I drew attention particularly to the "opportunist method" of philosophy, which emphasizes points of philosophical significance when the occasion arises in other branches of study. I found an example of this in 1870 in the excellent teaching of our Headmaster, K. A. Schmid, who has made a name for himself as the editor of a large Encyclopædia of Education in many volumes. In an extra class of advanced pupils he used to hold grammatical discussions on complicated problems of Latin syntax and he taught us to overcome, difficulties by a strict logical analysis of conjunctions and their various uses. The double conjunction 'As if' was not mentioned, but it was this accurate logical training which later enabled me to recognize in the grammatical formation 'As if' the Fiction which has such logical significance.

Last but not least I must mention Schiller's poems and treatises, for they too had an important influence on me at that period. Every earnest young student is inspired and fired by Schiller, but this Swabian poet had a special appeal for me, because he had played a great part in the history of my mother's family. My great-grandfather, Professor Balthasar Haug, was Schiller's teacher and his son, the epigrammatic poet Friedrich Haug, was Schiller's friend. Schiller's philosophic poems, in which he contrasts the ideal world of pure form with the empirical world, were easily linked up with the Platonic influences mentioned above. Many of Schiller's verses made an indelible impression on me, for instance the words "In error only is there life, and knowledge must be death", words which in certain respects have become the foundation of my theory of Fiction. Schiller's philosophical treatises were of course still too difficult for me to attempt, but I understood his theory of play as the primary element of artistic creation and enjoyment; and it had great influence on the development of my thought, for later on I recognized in play the 'As if', as the driving force of æsthetic activity and intuition.

Thus equipped, I entered the University of Tübingen in the autumn of 1870, as a student at the residential Theological College there. At Tübingen memories still linger of the many great figures who have passed through its University: Schelling, Hegel, Hölderlin, Waiblinger, Baur, Strauss, Vischer, Zeller and many others. In my time the University was run on very liberal lines and great freedom was, and still is, given to the students to allow them to develop in their own way. In the first four terms especially, they are given a very thorough grounding in philosophy. My first term was devoted to ancient philosophy, the second to later philosophy up to Kant, the third to the period from Kant to Hegel, and the fourth from Schleiermacher onwards to the philosophic foundations of dogmatism. First-rate coaches gave us careful instruction on an independent scientific basis and they also supervised the working out of philosophic treatises by the students, who were encouraged to think freely for themselves. No obstacles were placed in the path of my philosophical development. On the contrary, I was encouraged on all sides, especially when I started a prize essay for the faculty of philosophy on **"Recent Theories of Consciousness."** For this work, which took me a year, I received first prize in the autumn of 1873, and this enabled me to travel in Switzerland and North Italy. This prize essay was also the decisive factor in making me abandon my theological studies which I had started with much hesitation. My transition to pure philosophy was made easy for me in every way. Thus I have good reason to remember the Theological College of Tübingen with gratitude, particularly Professor Buder, the open-minded and kind-hearted Director at that time.

Sigwart was of course the most prominent of all the lecturers on philosophy. His lectures on the History of Philosophy, on Psychology, and above all naturally on Logic were splendid and I owe much to them. In exercises also, particularly on Schleiermacher, I learnt to admire his penetrating mind and his broad outlook. Yet I cannot say that I was a disciple of Sigwart, in the sense that I accepted the fundamentals of his philosophy. What did not appeal to me was his absolutely teleological conception of the universe, which was bound up with the theological, or rather theologising metaphysic that he had derived from Schleiermacher. Therefore, unlike me, who was spending more and more time in scientific study, he had little sympathy with the new scientific theory of evolution. Sigwart certainly revolutionized logic, but in the real problems of philosophy, particularly in the question of the mechanical conception of Nature, he was too timid for my taste.

With regard to this latter problem, Liebmann who was then a lecturer, helped me much, but unfortunately for me he was shortly called away. The other regular professor, Reeff, had built up a system of his own on the foundations of Schelling's teaching, but this had only a passing effect on my philosophical development. What I did retain, however, was the view which he frequently expressed, namely, that a philosophic system need not be regarded as true simply because it satisfies the emotions; whoever seeks this satisfaction must not go to the philosopher to find it; philosophy must give light, but it need not give warmth. Köstlin, an enthusiastic Hegelian, gave us brilliant and inspiring lectures on æsthetic questions, but when he tried to win me over to Planck, I refused to follow him.

So really I had only myself to fall back upon. In my first term the teaching of the Greek nature-philosophers made a great impression on me, because of their close similarity with the modern theory of evolution. Anaximander appealed to me especially also because of his profound words on the vengeance which all separate existences must suffer. An incomplete treatise *Anaximander and the Indeterminate* resulted, and in it I anticipated much of what Teichmüller afterwards said about him. I also worked at Aristotle very thoroughly. In my second term

Spinoza absorbed me by his consistency and his dispassionate conception of the universe.

But the impression made upon me by Kant was very different from the rest. In every respect he freed my mind, without fettering it. The bold theory of the ideality of space and time always liberates the mind from immediacy, from the pressure of the material world, even although one soon recognizes that in the long run it is not tenable in that form. But what impressed me most was Kant's discovery of the contradictions with which human thought is faced when it ventures into the realm of metaphysics. Kant's theory of antinomies had a profound influence on me. I derived permanent value not only from his theory of the limitation of knowledge to experience, but also from his doctrine that action, the practical, must take the first place, in other words the so-called supremacy of practical reason. This seemed to appeal to my innermost being.

Thus it was natural that the systems of Fichte, Schelling, and Hegel, in spite of their wonderful architecture and their wide range, could not hold me for long, although in accordance with the plan of studies of the College I had concentrated on these three systems. It was Fichte's preference for the practical and Hegel's theory of contradiction and its significance for human thought and reality that appealed to me most.

The official plan of studies passed from the "German Idealism" of Fichte, Schelling and Hegel direct to Schleiermacher. But I followed my own course and turned to Schopenhauer, who until then had been ignored, even despised by the Faculty. But I had got hold of E. von Hartmann's *Philosophy of the Unconscious,* which was making a great stir at the time, but which of course was officially non-existent for the College, and it led back to Schopenhauer, whose name was constantly being mentioned in all current literature. So I went straight to the source and studied Schopenhauer very thoroughly.

Schopenhauer's teaching gave me much that was new and great and lasting, pessimism, irrationalism and voluntarism. The impression which he made upon me was, although not extensively, yet certainly intensively greater than that of Kant. In order to explain this, I must go further afield. In all the systems of philosophy which I had hitherto met, the irrational aspect of the world and of life had not received attention, or at least adequate attention. The ideal of philosophy was to explain everything rationally, that is to say, by logical conclusions to prove it rational, in other words logical, significant, fitting. The Hegelian philosophy came nearest to this ideal, and it was considered the supreme achievement of philosophy. This ideal of knowledge, however, had failed to satisfy me, for my mind was far too keen and critical not to see the irrational element in Nature as well in history. From my earliest days I had come across countless manifestations of the irrational in my immediate surroundings. It may sound strange, but it is a fact that my physical constitution had much to do with this also. From the very

beginning, extreme short-sightedness has hindered me in all my activities. Whereas my nature impelled me to action, to energetic movement, to activity in every form and aspect, this physical defect forced me into reserve, passivity, loneliness. This glaring contrast between my physical constitution and temperament has always struck me as absolutely irrational, and it has sharpened my senses to notice all the other irrational aspects of existence. I therefore considered it to be a lack of sincerity in most systems of philosophy, that they tried more or less to hide the irrational side. Now for the first time I came across a man who recognized irrationality openly and honourably, and who attempted to explain it in his system of philosophy. Schopenhauer's love of truth was a revelation to me. I did not follow his metaphysical constructions, because since I had studied Kant the impossibility of all metaphysics had seemed to me to be obvious. But that part of Schopenhauer's teaching which can be established empirically became my lasting possession and a source of fruitful inspiration, particularly in so far as it could be linked up with the theory of evolution, which was then much to the fore, and with the theory of the struggle for existence.

I have already mentioned that what appealed to me most in Kant and in Fichte was their emphasis on the practical aspect. In Schopenhauer I found this same tendency, but much clearer, much stronger, much more comprehensive. With him it was not the rather nebulous "practical reason", but the empirical psychological element of "the will" which was placed in the forefront. To me much that had hitherto been inexplicable seemed suddenly to be explained or at least explicable.

What struck me most was his proof of the fact that originally thought is only used by the will as a means to its own ends, and that only in the course of evolution does thought free itself from the bonds of the will and become an end in itself. Schopenhauer has already shown how the brain of animals is quite small, yet is large enough to act as an organ for the execution of the will's purposes, whereas in the higher animals, and particularly in man, it has grown out of all proportion. Darwin's theory of evolution, which was being worked out at this time, corroborated Schopenhauer's contention, which gave me a fundamental insight into reality.

This theory of Schopenhauer's seemed to me to be so fruitful that it called for expansion and general application. In my notes of the years from 1872 onwards this universal "Law of the Preponderance of the Means over the End" is constantly recurring. Everywhere I found evidence that an original means working towards a definite end has the tendency to acquire independence and to become an end in itself. Thought, which originally serves the purposes of the will and only gradually becomes an end in itself was the most obvious special case of a universal law of Nature that manifests itself in new forms always and everywhere, in all organic life, in the processes of the mind, in economic life, and in history. Unfortunately at that period I never managed to publish this "Law" and said nothing more about it when many years later Wundt produced his theory of the "Heterogeny of Purpose," which expresses the same idea. I maintain, however, that the expression "Law of the Preponderance of the Means over the End" gives the idea of the theory much more clearly and distinctly.

This theory of Schopenhauer's, that fundamentally thought is dependent on the purposes of the Life-will and has developed into an end in itself only as it were against all laws, became linked up in my mind with Kant's theory that human thought is bound by certain limits and that metaphysical knowledge is impossible. This limitation of human knowledge to experience, which Kant emphasizes over and over again, no longer struck me as a deplorable deficiency in the human mind, compared with a potential higher form of mind, not bound by these limits. This limitation of human knowledge seemed to me now to be a necessary and natural result of the fact that thought and knowledge are originally only a means to attain the Life-purpose, so that their actual independence signifies a breaking-away from their original purpose; indeed, by the fact of this breaking-loose, thought is confronted by impossible problems, which are not merely insoluble to human thought while possibly soluble to a higher form of thought, but problems which are utterly impossible to all forms of thought as such. This conviction has become one of the most solid foundations of my conception of the universe, and since that time it has grown within me and has crystallized with the years into an ever clearer form.

Another powerful influence on these same lines made itself felt about this time (1872-73), when Adolf Horwicz' book *Psychologische Analysen auf physiologischer Grundlage* came into my hands. In this work Horwicz showed that all psychology is based on the so-called scheme of reflexes: sense-impressions following upon stimulation, ideas leading up to thought, expressive movement and volitional action. The simplest reflexes are motor phenomena following upon stimulation. These stimuli must result in elementary feelings, which release corresponding movements, representing the most elementary beginning of volitional actions. In the interval between these impressions on the one hand and the motor expression on the other hand ideas come to the surface, first in an elementary form, but growing more and more complicated, so that in their highest form they may be described as Thought-processes. Thus the idea and later on the thought appear as merely a bridge, an intermediary between impression on the one hand and expression on the other hand. This theory, which Horwicz worked out most carefully and comprehensively, fitted in very well with the idea that I had derived from Schopenhauer, namely that thought originally is only a means for the purposes of the will, and both ideas coincided with the conviction that I had gained from Kant as to the supremacy of the practical.

As I have already mentioned, I was at this time not only working at the study of philosophy and its history, but was chiefly occupied with the great ideas which were revolutionizing science at this time. Firstly, I was interesting myself in the application, in every sphere of Nature, of the mechanical theory, with special reference to the "Law of the Conservation of Energy," secondly I was studying the new aspect taken on by the organic sciences as a result of Darwin's theory of evolution and the theory of selection involved in this, namely the mechanical, automatic selection of the fittest through the so-called "Struggle for Existence". In all branches of inorganic and organic science I endeavoured to get not only a general survey, but so far as conditions allowed, a special knowledge of the most important aspects. I seized every opportunity of keeping abreast of the movement, not only by reading the special books, but also by getting into personal touch with scientists. Thus I came into contact with Hüfner, the Professor of Physiology, and one day I had an interesting discussion with him, on the Life-force. With youthful prejudice I spoke very strongly against it, as an antiquated and useless theory. He granted that my objections were in part justified, but he pointed out that the application of this idea was expedient on practical grounds and might be not only permissible, but even necessary, although it might be regarded as false or at least not quite theoretically justified. He gave me his book on the Life-force which had just appeared.

A new seed was sown in my mind by all this and it has proved to be of the most lasting and decisive importance. It made me look carefully for arguments on the same lines and I collected examples from all the sciences. I had all the more opportunity for this, because I was not only studying many branches of science, but with real universality I was seizing every occasion of exploring new scientific fields, in which personal acquaintances had to help me as much as books.

In my last year at Tübingen, from the autumn of 1873 till the summer of 1874, I studied principally the classical languages, Greek archæology and Germanic philology. As I was able in the autumn of 1873 formally to give up the study of theology, which I had nominally carried on *ex professo* until then, according to the wishes of my parents, I had to become reconciled to the plan of lecturing in a university. So in this last year I attended classes in classical and Germanic philology. What attracted me most in classical philology was Greek art and in Germanic philology the evolution of language, which at that time, thanks to Schleicher's Indo-Germanic Grammar was being treated in accordance with the theory of evolution. I also began the study of Sanskrit under Roth.

What interested me most in these classes and in the history class which I also attended, was the practical contact with the exact methods of science. Ever since I had come under Sigwart's influence, I had been interested in Logic, not only for its formal aspect but especially for methodology, and now I had a welcome opportunity of collaborating in the practice of scientific methods and the formulation of theoretical conclusions from them.

In the summer of 1874 I graduated from Tübingen with a prize dissertation on **"Recent Theories of Consciousness"**, in which classical and Germanic philology appeared as subordinate sections.

But now the ground was burning under my feet. I had spent four years in Tübingen. According to the regulations of the College I had to spend eight sessions there. All that I could get out of Tübingen I had richly gained with hard, honest work. Now it seemed advisable to complete my one year of voluntary military service, and for this, according to the custom of many of my South German countrymen, I chose Leipzig, in whose celebrated University I could learn so much that was new and important.

Before leaving my home, however, I was anxious to consult some men of learning about a question that was troubling my mind. At the grammar school in Stuttgart I had turned from theism to pantheism, and at the University of Tübingen I had evolved from pantheism by way of Kantian agnosticism to a position closely approaching Schopenhauer's atheism. Now the question arose, as to what attitude one should take on this basis of theoretical atheism towards the historical forms of the Church, and to religious dogma with its historical origins, and whether one was obliged to adopt an absolutely negative attitude towards the positive Church. To my mind this did not seem to be necessary. My studies in Greek mythology, particularly its expression in ancient works of art (at that time called "Art Mythology") had taught me that, according to the custom of the cultured Greeks and Romans, and as I had noticed earlier in Plato, one may regard and treat these myths as "myths" and yet (or rather just because of this) continue to esteem such fictions for their ethical and æsthetic value. On this matter I wanted to hear the opinion of the three wise men of Swabia, at that time her most famous sons:—David F. Strauss, who had analysed the stories of the Bible, particularly of the New Testament, and the formulæ of dogma as "myths"; Friedrich T. Vischer, who earlier had made a strong attack on the Church but who, as an historian of art, could not get on without the myths of the Church; and lastly Robert Mayer, who discovered the law of the Conservation of Energy and who combined a strictly mechanical conception of Nature with a strong religious sense. I already had relations with Strauss, whose *Old Faith and the New* was making a great stir at the time. It was easy for me to see him, but I found him on a bed of sickness which a few months later was his death-bed. So our talk could not go very deep, but he gave me an introduction to his old friend Vischer. This latter, however, would only talk on his one favourite subject of those days, "the decline of the German people since 1871", on which he had publicly spoken on various occasions. He wanted to hear my opinion as a representative of the younger generation. I would not at that time quite agree that it was a "decline", but I had to admit that even I had noticed signs in the younger generation of boasting and arrogance and also an underestimation of the neighbouring civilizations. The French, who had been so gloriously defeated, were un-derestimated both on the ethical and cultural side. But what seemed to me much more dangerous was the universal misunderstanding and even contempt felt for the English. From my earliest years I had known many English people, and I had learnt to recognize, together with their peculiarities, their ability and reliability. Moreover, I had the greatest admiration for their literature, and the names of Hume and Darwin had made the English doubly dear to me. But here in Vischer there seemed to me to be something lacking, because he only knew the English from a distance and had no admiration for Hume and Darwin. My visit to R. Mayer was accidentally prevented.

When I arrived in Leipzig, in September 1874, I presented myself at once for military service. But because of my eyes, which even then were abnormal, I was not accepted. From one point of view this was a great blow to me, because I was fond of all sports and particularly of the military gymnastics which the Swabian Professor Jäger had introduced, and I should have liked to develop this side of my active nature. On the other hand, I naturally welcomed with enthusiasm the free time which I saw ahead of me, and at once employed my leisure in carrying out a long-standing desire. In Tübingen I had become acquainted with nearly all the sciences, but of one I still knew no more than what I had learnt at school, namely mathematics; and this was a source of growing distress. Our teacher of mathematics in Stuttgart was Professor Reuschle (also a friend of David F. Strauss) who had made a name for himself by his theory of the prime numbers, but who had no gift for teaching. I had tried to get on by studying alone (I got the suitable textbooks out of the public library), and I had achieved considerable success, but in Tübingen I had no time to follow up these studies. Now with real avidity I threw myself into analytic geometry and the infinitesimal calculus. Both these lines of study revealed wonderful new truths to me that had originated in the minds of Descartes and Leibniz. Besides this, they gave me striking examples of methodic fictions, which were of great importance for the continuation of the methodological investigations which I had started in Tübingen. So altogether these studies were very fruitful.

In another direction, these winter days of 1874-75 were of decisive importance. It was about this time that the second edition of Friedrich Albert Lange's *History of Materialism* appeared in its enlarged form and with the addition of much scientific material. I had come across the first edition of this work in Tübingen, and it had filled me with admiration, but it made no deeper impression on me because the scientific apparatus of the book in its original form was inadequate. Now, with that defect remedied, the material fell into my hands at the right moment. Now at last I had found the man for whom I had sought in vain during those four years in Tübingen. I found a master, a guide, an ideal teacher. The spirit which urged me onwards more or less vaguely, dominated him with complete clearness and perfection of form. On the one hand he had the highest respect for facts, and an exact knowledge of the natural sciences, together with mastery over the whole history of civilization; on the other hand he was an expert in Kantian criticism, with views modified and extended by Schopenhauer. Above all, he was a man of high ethical ideals, and with regard to religious dogma he combined the strongest radicalism in theory with the most broad-minded tolerance in practice. I had striven for this myself, but never before had I found all these qualities in one person. All that I had striven for and aimed at stood before my eyes as a finished masterpiece. From this time onwards I called myself a disciple of F. A. Lange. Naturally I read his other publications, particularly his book on the "Labour question", and his activity in this sphere also showed me that he was a man of wide vision and warm heart.

What gave the *History of Materialism* its particular value for my special studies of this period was that from my point of view F. A. Lange was on right lines even in regard to the methodic problem of fictions. On the other hand he showed a certain hesitation and vagueness on this point, so that I hoped, on the basis of my further thorough research, to be able to go further than he in this special question.

About this time I found another source of help in the same direction. The two old disciples of Herbart, Drobisch and Struempell were then teaching in Leipzig. Herbart's name had hardly ever been mentioned in Tübingen, but now my studies led me to him and I found in him very valuable examples of a theory of fiction, which he tried to apply in a practical form to his own philosophy. At the same time I was naturally drawn to a much deeper study of Herbart's psychology, and psychology in general; and through the influence of that ardent disciple of Herbart, Dr Susanna Rubinstein, who was then living in Leipzig, I got to know Volkmann and Lazarus. All this strengthened me in the conviction that, without psychology, philosophy and also epistemology are and can only be a methodic abstraction, which can be brought to no systematic conclusion.

Avenarius, whom I got to know at "The Academic Philosophical Society" which he had founded, influenced me in the same direction. He advised me to read Steinthal, whose *Introduction to Psychology* became one of the bases of my philosophy. His theory of the transformation by apperception of the material given to the senses has remained with me ever since.

I derived great profit from Avenarius in so far as he was a pungent critic of Kant's theories. This prevented me from regarding Kant's philosophy as dogma, but anyway I was not inclined to do this. I could not follow Avenarius, however, in his radical empiricism, or rather positivism. He realized quite rightly that the ideas of substance, causality etc. are imposed subjectively by the psyche on the given, yet for this very reason, according to "the principle of the least energy", he wanted to eliminate them completely from human thought. But I held

that they are suitable fictions, which must be retained because of their utility.

In the autumn of 1875 Wundt came to Leipzig. His first lecture was on logic and I listened to it with great interest and profit. He appealed to me in every way. For his sake I should have liked to remain on in Leipzig, and I had already planned a *Journal of Pure and Applied Logic,* in which I hoped to interest him. But family matters called me back to South Germany. I was only able to have one more term in the North, and that was to be in Berlin, where the Swabian, Eduard Zeller, was actively at work. The help which I got from him and from his friend Helmholtz, and also from Steinthal, Lazarus, Lasson and Paulsen was more or less valuable to me, but what was really important was that I came across the writings of Gruppe, who had died shortly before this, and they were most useful for my theory of fiction. My private studies were devoted mostly to David Hume and John Stuart Mill, whose exact knowledge was decisive for my philosophic attitude.

At the same time, during my Berlin days in the summer of 1876, my first book on philosophy was published, *Hartmann, Dühring and Lange*—a critical Essay on the History of Philosophy in the Nineteenth Century. It consisted of lectures which I had given in the Academic Philosophical Society at Leipzig. The author of the *History of Materialism,* with his Kantian tendencies, seemed to me to strike the happy medium between the spiritualistic metaphysics of E. von Hartmann on the one hand and the materialistic positivism of E. Dühring on the other hand. In Berlin I had got to know these two men personally. In my book I also announced the early publication of my investigation of Fictions.

For family reasons I had to choose a University near my South German home in which to take up my residence as a lecturer; so in the autumn of 1876 I moved to Strassburg, where I received a welcome from Laas. In his recent work on Kant's Analogies of Experience he had drawn a sharp line between himself and the Kantian, or rather Neo-Kantian, A-priorism or "Transcendentalism," and he was gradually approaching that radical attitude which he took up some years later in his three-volume treatise on Idealism and Positivism. He was the unprejudiced man of whom I stood in need. He was able to do justice to my own attitude. He was busy just then with the study of John Stuart Mill's *Examination of Sir William Hamilton's Philosophy,* in which I joined him, all the more readily because this was really a continuation of my Berlin studies of Hume and Mill. The resolution of so-called reality, from an epistemological or psychological point of view, into "Sensations and possibilities of sensation" seemed both to him and to me to be the correct analytical way. On the other hand Laas resembled Avenarius, who was related to him, in his positivist tendency to eliminate all further subjective additions as unjustified and useless, whereas I was always anxious to emphasize and keep hold of the practical value and use of these theoretically unjustifiable conceptions of the older idealism.

During the latter part of the year 1876, for my inaugural dissertation, I wrote down my thoughts in a large manuscript, to which I gave the title "Logical Studies. Part I: The Theory of Scientific Fictions." As I had been carefully collecting the material for several years and had gone into it most thoroughly many times, the writing of it did not take me long. I handed in my MS. in the New Year and at the end of February 1877 I received my *venia legendi*. The work which received this recognition from the Faculty is exactly the same as what was published in 1911 as the "Part I: Basic Principles" of *The Philosophy of 'As If'*. In it I developed the whole system of scientific fictions, that is to say the 'As if' treatment, applied practically to the most varied aspects of science, and I tried to give an exhaustive theory of this manifold 'As if' process.

But like Laas I regarded this dissertation only as a rough outline, in need of much supplementing and correction, so I made use of the next two years, so far as my lectures allowed me, to work at my MS. My father's death compelled me to look out for some more remunerative occupation, and so I made a very advantageous agreement with the generous and far-sighted Stuttgart publisher, W. Spemann, to produce a *Commentary on Kant* for the centenary in 1881 of his *Critique of Pure Reason*. I had then just started a far more thorough study of Kant, particularly his 'As if' theory, and in the course of this I had found in his *Prolegomena* that "misplacement of pages" which had passed unnoticed by many thousands of Kant readers for nearly a hundred years, but which is generally recognized by science nowadays. So I hoped, by application of the philological method, and by penetrating logical analysis, to further the study of Kant. But, as I have said, this new work was only a means to an end, and I hoped in a few years to be able to return to my researches on Fiction.

The above-mentioned "Law of the Preponderance of the Means over the End", which unfortunately I neglected to formulate theoretically and publish at the right moment, has proved in a practical sense very momentous in my own life. When, in 1884, the first volume of my *Commentary on Kant* brought me an appointment as special Professor at Halle, I hoped soon to be able to finish the other volumes there. But my lectures on the one hand and bad health on the other held up the publication of the second volume until 1892. In 1894 I was appointed regular Professor in Halle, and in 1896 I founded the *Kantstudien* as a means of helping on my work. But even this means preponderated over its own end. My work on the *Commentary* became secondary to the new periodical. When in 1904 the centenary of Kant's death was celebrated, circumstances seemed to make it my duty, in order to promote the *Kantstudien,* to start a Fund to defray the costs. This Fund was a success, but its organization necessitated the foundation of a Kant Society and this gradually became more and more an end in itself and

took up too much of my time and strength, although I was fortunate in having most efficient help in all these undertakings. Thus the means always triumphed over the end for whose sake it had been called into being, and robbed the original end of its life-force.

In 1906, in the midst of all these curious complications and crossings of my original intentions, a misfortune unexpectedly brought a happy solution, and enabled me after twenty-seven years to return to my original plan, which I had given up in 1879. The misfortune was the weakening of my eyesight, so that it became impossible for me to continue my lectures, or the special classes which I particularly enjoyed. So I had to give up my official duties. The eyesight still remaining to me was just sufficient to allow me to publish my MS. I got my Dissertation of 1876 copied, and introduced a number of small editorial alterations. This comprehensive MS. now forms "Part I: Basic Principles" of *The Philosophy of 'As If'* I also completed the revision which I had made between 1877 and the beginning of 1879 on the basis of the reviews of that time, and this forms the Part II (Special) of the complete work. This part took me two and a half years because of my bad eyesight, and Part III (Historical) took me another two and a half years. Between 1877 and 1879 I had made a note of the most important 'As if' passages in Kant's works, and I now completed this in an exhaustive manner, so that I was able to produce a monograph on Kant's 'As if' theory of nearly one hundred pages. The exposition of Forberg's religion of 'As if' also took me a long time, and so did the development of F. A. Lange's "Standpoint of the Ideal," with which I had much in common. But what took longer still was the final section on Nietzsche's theory of Fictions, which he had condensed into a few pages. It was the Spring of 1911 before the work appeared.

I called this work, *The Philosophy of 'As If'*. because it seemed to me to express more convincingly than any other possible title what I wanted to say, namely that 'As if', i.e. appearance, the consciously-false, plays an enormous part in science, in world-philosophies and in life. I wanted to give a complete enumeration of all the methods in which we operate intentionally with consciously false ideas, or rather judgments. I wanted to reveal the secret life of these extraordinary methods. I wanted to give a complete theory, an anatomy and physiology so to speak, or rather a biology of 'As if'. For the method of fiction which is found in a greater or lesser degree in all the sciences can best be expressed by this complex conjunction 'As if'. Thus I had to give a survey of all the branches of science from this point of view.

But it was not only a methodological investigation that I was attempting. The study of fictional thought in all branches of science had led me gradually to extend these investigations to philosophy itself, particularly to epistemology, ethics and the philosophy of religion. Just as my investigations into the function of 'As if' had arisen out of a definite view of the world so again this developed independently into a universal system of philosophy—I gave it the name of "Positivist Idealism" or "Idealistic Positivism". As I have already mentioned, Ernst Laas had published between 1884 and 1886 a three-volume work on Idealism and Positivism, in which he attacked Idealism and championed Positivism. The positivist attitude was also represented in Germany by Mach, Avenarius and to a certain extent by Schuppe, and it found particular favour with the scientifically inclined (but the name Positivism was never placed in the forefront of any programme). The chief currents of German philosophy, however, were certainly idealistic, though in different ways. Between these one-sided views it seemed to me that a compromise was necessary, all the more so because attempts of this kind had met with success in other countries. I considered that the time had come to announce the union of Idealism and Positivism. The result has proved that the right word was spoken at the right moment.

The term "Scepticism" has occasionally been applied to the Philosophy of 'As if' and its systematic doctrines; but this is not correct, for scepticism implies a theory which raises doubt or questioning to the dignity of a principle. The Philosophy of 'As if', however, has never had a trace of this attitude. In a simple and straightforward investigation it proves that consciously false conceptions and judgments are applied in all sciences; and it shows that these scientific Fictions are to be distinguished from Hypotheses. The latter are assumptions which are probable, assumptions the truth of which can be proved by further experience. They are therefore verifiable. Fictions are never verifiable, for they are hypotheses which are known to be false, but which are employed because of their utility. When a series of hypotheses in mathematics, mechanics, physics, chemistry, ethics or the philosophy of religion are shown in this way to be useful fictions and so justify themselves, surely this does not imply scepticism. The reality of these hypotheses is not doubted; it is denied on the basis of the positive facts of experience. The expression "Relativism" would be more applicable to the Philosophy of "As if", in so far as it denies all absolute points (in mathematics just as in metaphysics) and shows a natural affinity with the theory of relativity both of the past and the present.

The use of the term "Scepticism" as applied to the Philosophy of 'As if', has no doubt been partly due to the doubt with which this philosophy regards metaphysical realities, particularly God and immortality. But the above consideration applies in this case also. In the Philosophy of 'As if' I have never attempted to hide the fact that I regard these conceptions as Fictions of ethical value. My conviction in this respect is clear, simple and decided.

Many people of course confuse the technical expression involved here and think that they can discover in the Philosophy of 'As if' not exactly "Scepticism", but "Agnosticism". This latter system teaches that human knowledge is confined within more or less narrow limits and speaks of the Unintelligible, the Unknowable, according to Spencer's definition. Naturally the Philosophy of 'As if' also holds that knowledge has certain limits, but not in the sense that these limits bound only human knowledge, while they are non-existent for a superhuman knowledge. This is the theory of Kant and Spencer. It is the old complaint that the human mind is confined by narrow boundaries, which do not limit the higher forms of mind. My opinion is that these boundaries of knowledge are not implicit in the specific nature of man as compared with other possible minds of a higher order, but that such limitations are part of the nature of thought itself; that is to say, if there are higher forms of mind, these limitations will affect them and even the highest Mind of all. For thought originally only serves the Will to Life as a means to an end, and in this direction also it fulfils its function. But when thought has broken loose from its original aim, according to the Law of the Preponderance of the Means over the End, and has become an end in itself, it sets itself problems to which it is not equal because it has not developed for this purpose; and finally the emancipated thought sets itself problems which in themselves are senseless, for instance, questions as to the origin of the world, the formation of what we call matter, the beginning of motion, the meaning of the world and the purpose of life. If thought is regarded as a biological function, it is obvious that these are impossible problems for thought to solve, and quite beyond the natural boundaries which limit thought as such. From this point of view, we have no inclination to fall back on the favourite old grievance about the limitations of human knowledge. At most we may complain that the Law of the Preponderance of the Means over the End has led us to ask questions which are as unanswerable as the problem of $\sqrt{-1}$. A moment of reflection will show that all knowledge is a reduction of the unknown to the known, that is to say a comparison. This proves therefore that this comparison or reduction will somewhere stop automatically. In no sense, therefore, can the Philosophy of 'As if' be called scepticism or agnosticism.

In the same way we can dispose of another objection which is raised against the Philosophy of 'As if', namely that the concept of reality implied in it is not uniform: on the one hand all reality is reduced to sensations, or sensational contents (in the sense of Mill's theory of "Sensations and possibilities of sensation"); on the other hand the concept of reality in the natural sciences, which reduce everything to the movement of matter and the smallest constituents of matter, is constantly being employed, sometimes tacitly, sometimes expressly. And with this is bound up the question, how to unify these two concepts of reality represented by the Philosophy of 'As if'.

One might admire the perspicacity of this discovery of a twofold concept of reality in the Philosophy of 'As if', if one were not surprised at the short-sightedness of the subsequent question. I am going to ask a question in return. Has any philosophical system of ancient, modern or present times ever succeeded in bringing these two spheres into a logical, rational relation? These two hemispheres of reality, expressed briefly on the one hand as the world of motion and on the other hand the world of consciousness, have never been brought into a logically satisfactory relation by any philosopher. They will never be brought into a definitely unified association by any rational formula. We stand here at a point where an impossible problem confronts our reason. This question is just as impossible of solution by rational methods as the question of the purpose of existence. Although we, who ask this question, permanently unite in our nature these two halves of reality, or rather just because the divergence, or the obvious contradiction, between motion and consciousness runs all through our own being, our mind is not in a position to answer satisfactorily this fundamental question or this so-called world-riddle.

Therefore he who would criticize any system of philosophy, or the philosophy of "As if" in particular, for not answering this question, is in the same intellectual position as a man who would reproach a mathematician for not solving the problem of the squaring of the circle in his text-book of geometry, or a technical engineer for not dealing with the construction of the *perpetuum mobile* in his text-book of engineering.

In discussing ultimate world-problems, one is always coming up against this rationally insoluble antithesis between motions of matter and particles of matter on the one hand and on the other hand sensations, or rather contents of consciousness. For the philosopher who deals with the analysis of our contents of consciousness, this analysis ends everywhere with our sensations on the psychological plane and with our sensational contents on the epistemological plane. The world is to him an endless accumulation of sensational contents which, however, are not given to us and to him without plan, but in which certain regularities of co-existence and succession can be found. These sensational data—what Windelband calls "Gegebenheiten" and Ziehen "Gignomene"—these events crowd upon us more or less irresistibly; indeed they even cast a lasting fear over us, for we have to rule our lives according to them, in constant expectation of their appearance. This world of sensational contents is the material with which alone the philosopher as such can deal. But on the other hand, the philosopher must recognize for good or ill that the scientist constructs quite a different sphere of reality, the world of motion, the mobile world. To construct a rational relation between these two worlds is an impossible desire of our understanding, which fundamentally is not fitted for the theoretical solution of world problems, but only for the practical service of the will to live.

Naturally the human mind is tormented by this insoluble contradiction between the world of motion and the world of consciousness, and this torment can eventually become very oppressive. One would be well advised to remember how Kant had already pointed out that there are problems which mock us perpetually, but which we cannot get rid of. But there is one solution of this and similar torturing questions; for in intuition and in experience all this contradiction and distress fades into nothingness. Experience and intuition are higher than all human reason. When I see a deer feeding in the forest, when I see a child at play, when I see a man at work or sport, but above all when I myself am working or playing, where are the problems with which my mind has been torturing itself unnecessarily? We do not understand the world when we are pondering over its problems, but when we are doing the world's work. Here too the practical reigns supreme.

I will end by summarizing all the conclusions which are expressed in the Philosophy of 'As if', or which form its basis or arise out of it, as follows:—

(1) Philosophical analysis leads eventually, from an epistemological standpoint, to sensational contents, and from a psychological to sensations, feelings and strivings or actions. Scientific analysis leads to another concept of reality, to matter and the smallest constituents and motions of matter. Naturally it is impossible for the mind as such to bring these two spheres of reality into a rational relation, although in intuition and experience they form a harmonious unity.

(2) The strivings which probably exist in the most elementary physical processes develop in organic beings into impulses. In man, who has sprung from the animal (and to a certain extent in all the higher animals) these impulses have evolved into will and action, which is expressed in movements and caused by stimuli or by the sensations arising from stimuli.

(3) Ideas, judgments and conclusions, that is to say thought, act as a means in the service of the Will to Live and dominate. Thought is originally only a means in the struggle for existence and to this extent only a biological function.

(4) It is a universal phenomenon of nature that means which serve a purpose often undergo a more complete development than is necessary for the attainment of their purpose. In this case, the means, according to the completeness of its self-development, can emancipate itself partly or wholly and become established as an end in itself (Law of the Preponderance of the Means over the End).

(5) This Preponderance of the Means over the End has also taken place in thought, which in the course of time has gradually lost sight of its original practical purpose and is finally practised for its own sake as theoretical thought.

(6) As a result, this thought which appears to be independent and theoretical in its origins, sets itself problems which are impossible, not only to human thought, but to every form of thought; for instance, the problems of the origin and meaning of the universe. To this category belongs also the question of the relation between sensation and motion, popularly known as mind and matter.

(7) These endless, and, strictly speaking, senseless questions cannot be answered by looking forwards but only by looking backwards, by showing how they arose psy-

chologically within us. Many of these questions are just as meaningless, as for instance the problem of -1.

(8) If intellectualism or rationalism be identified with the assumption of an original theoretical reason as an inherent human faculty with certain problems to be determined by it, then my exposition must be termed anti-rationalism or even irrationalism, in the same sense in which histories of modern philosophy, for instance that of Windelband, speak of "idealistic irrationalism".

(9) From this standpoint all thought-processes and thought constructs appear a priori to be not essentially rationalistic, but biological phenomena.

(10) In this light many thought-processes and thought-constructs appear to be consciously false assumptions, which either contradict reality or are even contradictory in themselves, but which are intentionally thus formed in order to overcome difficulties of thought by this artificial deviation and reach the goal of thought by roundabout ways and by-paths. These artificial thought-constructs are called Scientific Fictions, and distinguished as conscious creations by their 'As if' character.

(11) The 'As if' world, which is formed in this manner, the world of the "unreal" is just as important as the world of the so-called real or actual (in the ordinary sense of the word); indeed it is far more important for ethics and æsthetics. This æsthetic and ethical world of 'As if', the world of the unreal, becomes finally for us a world of values which, particularly in the form of religion, must be sharply distinguished in our mind from the world of becoming.

(12) What we usually term reality consists of our sensational contents which press forcibly upon us with greater or lesser irresistibility and as "given" can generally not be avoided.

(13) In these given sensational contents (which include what we call our body) there is an abundance of regularity in co-existence and succession, investigation of which forms the content of science. By means of the sensational contents which we call our body, we can exercise greater or lesser influence on the rich world of the other sensational contents.

(14) In this world we find on the one hand a very great number of relations of fitness, on the other hand much that is not fitting. We have to take this as we find it, for there is little that we can alter. It is a satisfying Fiction for many to regard the world as if a more perfect Higher Spirit had created or at least regulated it. But this implies the supplementary Fiction of regarding a world of this sort as if the order created by the Higher Divine Spirit had been destroyed by some hostile force.

(15) It is senseless to question the meaning of the universe, and this is the idea expressed in Schiller's words: "Know this, a mind sublime puts greatness into life, yet seeks it not therein" (*Huldigung der Künste*, 1805). This is positivist idealism.

The journal which I founded in 1919 with Dr Raymund Schmidt, *Annalen der Philosophie* ("with particular reference to the problems of the 'As if' approach"), has been very useful in spreading and intensifying this positivist idealism or idealistic positivism. It represents quite a new type of journal, for its contributors include not only professional philosophers (Cornelius, Groos, Becher, Bergmann, Koffka, Kowalewski) but also eminent representatives of the most important branches of science, the theologian Heim, the lawyer Krückmann, the doctor Abderhalden, the mathematician Pasch, the physicist Volkmann, the biological botanist Hansen the economist Pohle, and the art-historian Lange. It thus demonstrates in a practical way that philosophy can only advance in the closest co-operation with the individual sciences and that philosophy, although it has much to give to the individual sciences, yet has much more to learn from them. It is from this interactivity alone that a fruitful and lasting compromise and reconciliation between positivism and idealism can take place—at least in the manner in which this is the deliberate and fundamental aim of the Philosophy of 'As if'. The critical examination of the use of the different methods of the 'As if' system in the most varied branches of science must on the one hand promote the scientific theory of method; and on the other hand the right method must also be found of finally reconciling the positivism of facts with the "Standpoint of the Ideal" (F. A. Lange). This analysis and this synthesis must be mutually complementary.

E. Jordan (essay date 1926)

SOURCE: "Reviews of Books," in *The Philosophical Review*, Vol. 35, No. 4, 1926, pp. 370-75.

[*In the following essay, Jordan reviews* The Philosophy of "As If," *noting the work's significance to philosophical methodology.*]

This translation of the **Philosophy of 'As If'** is "based upon the definitive Sixth Edition of the original, revised for the purpose by the author, who himself undertook the task of abbreviating various passages of purely historical interest or otherwise superfluous in an English version. In response to many suggestions, Professor Vaihinger's own account of his Life-work and of the spirit in which **The Philosophy of 'As If'** was written has been added by way of General Introduction, and this, together with an Analytical Table of Contents and a double Index, should add considerably to the interest and utility of the volume" (Translator's Note). In the Autobiography the author explains that the ideas incorporated in the volume were in process of development through the long period between 1876 and 1911.

The result is a solid and exhaustive, even if not perhaps finally conclusive, contribution to the discussion of the basic problems of philosophical methodology. As the work was originally published as early as 1911, it may be taken for granted that the author's point of view and the fundamentals of his philosophy are generally known. The book represents the extreme analytical tendency which has reached its fullest development in British empiricism—the author acknowledges his primary indebtedness to Hume and Mill—and, while the author regards himself as a follower of Kant, it is primarily the analytic and positivist aspect of Kant which gives both form and content to the work. Accepting the more rigoristic limits which Kant imposed upon concepts of scientific method in the distinction between constitutive and regulative principles, the author adopts the element of sense-content as the criterion of truth, and relegates to the realm of 'fiction' all the formal aspects of experience through which the relations of sense-fact are mediated. But the contradiction involved in accepting as a criterion of truth something the nature of which is incommensurable with every known character of truth leads the author to adopt a fiction which is fatal to all 'practical' philosophies—the fiction that truth, in so far, at least, as it affects the significance of thought-constructs, is a matter of utility.

Under this conception, a logical device that is found useful is a fiction; and this is defined as a concept known to be false but yet is found capable of yielding practically useful results. How anything could be known to be false while all the methods of knowledge are vitiated by the fictive uncertainty appears here as a somewhat baffling question. However, it is not difficult to show that the fundamental concepts of mathematics and science and of ethics, law, etc., as well, also the multitudinous forms of 'let's play' found necessary or convenient in simple practical relations have no several or one-to-one correspondence to sensibly determined objects; but just that seems to be the purpose of the book, and the result is an extraordinary amount of repetition as well as an unnecessary attempt to apply the doctrine of fictions in every conceivable circumstance. If such were all that the forms of thought mean in their logical implications, and the author goes beyond the practicality of his weaker brother the American pragmatist in recognizing that questions of truth are logical and not psychological or biological, the proof of the fact in one instance would be not only sufficient ground for the author's voluntarism and pessimism, but also would furnish a justification for the scepticism and intellectual nihilism which are inherent in all narrowly 'practical' philosophies. Thus the author is justified, on his sensationalistic presuppositions, in arguing that any logic which presupposes agreement between thought and reality is a false logic, since the agreement cannot be shown in any instance while the real is assumed to be identical with sensuous content. He is also justified in arguing that the dogma that the reason is altogether incapable of making any contact with the real is a self-destroying scepticism, a scepticism which would deny justification to the attempt to write a thick book on the 'as if.' So the only way out is Hume's "I dine, I play a game of backgammon," etc., which the author states

thus: "When I see a deer feeding in the forest, when I see a child at play, when I see a man at work or sport, above all when I myself am working or playing, where are the problems with which my mind has been torturing itself unnecessarily?" The doctrine that truth is utility is more useful than the doctrine that it involves a courageous facing of the possibility that there are reals other than those determined in sensation alone, in that it enables its advocate to stick his head in the sand.

But the author attempts to face the logical issue squarely in the question of the relation of the fictive construct to the principles of analogy and hypothesis. The fiction furnishes a useful standard with which to compare the real of sense experience. It is thus merely an expedient which aids in description, and presumably leads to the abstract generalizations which science tends to create. But why not face the fact that the ideal or fictive construct is itself derived from a synthesis of the characters of particulars, and thus transcends the generalization in a real universal? Analogy and hypothesis are and remain meaningless until they find their equilibrium in a principle, and until the fictive construct attains the status of a guiding criterion there is no point to assimilating its imaginary characters with sensory characters given in fact. Again, in the relation of the fiction to the hypothesis, the same weakness of the sense criterion appears. The fiction, says the author, is known to be false, and yet it points to the reality through its utility. The hypothesis, on the contrary, is a proposition on the way to being either validated by proof, or eliminated as useless. But it is difficult to see how it becomes anything other than a thought construct, even though it should become one of the ultimates of mathematics, and as a thought construct, it remains, for the author, still short of identification with the sensory given which he insists it must do if it is to be real. That is, on his own presuppositions, logical validity, though complete and demonstrable, is no nearer the reality than the mind's first and faintest interpretative hint; and the hypothesis which has become even an axiom remains a fiction still. So the author's acceptance of irrationalism is understandable. He has at the outset accepted as the only type of the real an element which is, because of its own nature, unrealizable, consequently all thought effort expended upon it is foredoomed to failure, and all thought instruments and media to it are *a priori* false. It is also at this point an interesting question, while truth and reality are matters of actual or possible sensations, how *anything* could be *known* to be false. *How* I can *now* know, on a sensationalistic theory of truth, that I never can experience a given sensation, is an interesting situation for the sensationalist.

But somewhere between the pure fiction and the pure hypothesis there is plenty of room for that instance of the type which, as constructed by thought on a basis of the order or orderliness of the given, is the real or concrete universal, or the species through which the real, including the useful, gets what significance is due to it. The treatment of the thought construct as a useful fiction is itself thus the prime instance of the pure fiction, the fiction which is by no methods realizable; so the fiction theory is itself the typical pure fiction. There are of course no grounds for denying that in the thought process there are many abstract symbols used primarily in the function of giving stability to thought elements while memory is engaged in endowing bodies of them with effective order; that is, meanings are symbolized in sensuous forms while their organization into higher unities is being effected by the synthetic functions of memory and imagination; it is equally true that these symbols are dropped the moment they become 'useless' to the unity effected and thus cease to be instrumental to the continuity of the thought process: there *are* fictions or methodological devices used in thinking, devices that are even used up in thinking, but that does not justify the monstrous conclusion that there are no substantive elements in the thought process besides the sense data.

Thus it is questionable whether a philosophy in its logical aspects can be constructed incidentally and as a by-product of the process of epistemological research. If a philosophy is to be a system of consistent convictions about reality, then a methodology will miss being that just by the difference between incontrovertible fact and the mere subjectivity of a mental state. And if sensation is taken as the characteristic mental state, the element of reality in fact will disappear in the instant that sensation is shown to have no independent status in the real, and that sensation has no real status is about the only indubitable result of the science of psychology. The hypothesis which makes a mental state the veritable real or the criterion of truth is disproved upon the discovery that the mental state has no contacts through references to the fact system whose rationality necessitated the hypothesis, and there is nothing left for the hypothetical real but to symbolize a useful but bootless abstract process. It is thus that utility issues in futility when made an instrument of logic, and the pursuit of the real is abandoned in the interest of a mental state, a mere groundless attitude. As a necessary result of the insufficiency of his method, therefore, the author abandons philosophy, and accepts what comfort he can get from the negative attitudes of pessimism and irrationalism. The attempt to justify the substitution of an emotional attitude for a consistent philosophical point of view, and to mediate the substitution with a logical process which justly claims the respect of instructed minds, in fact, compels that respect, should serve in its sorry issue as a significant hint to other pragmatists. It represents a degree of utility and practicality so proficient as to deceive itself, in spite of the fact that its candor is throughout unquestionable. For those who see the weight of such a contradiction in logic, which at the same time carries with it so compelling an ethical and religious significance, the question of the ontological status of 'mere' attitudes becomes itself the ground of a system of hypotheses for a real practical philosophy. But no such practical philosophy is yet written, and the author's pragmatics gives him no hint of its possibility.

But the book is of extraordinary value, just because it treats the fiction theory with the thoroughness which it merits, and because in doing so it furnishes in its sceptical and negativist issues an interesting but overwhelming *reductio* of the various prevailing types of 'practical' philosophy. Its appearance in English at this time when the theory of legal fictions is being turned to a criticism of social theory will contribute greatly to philosophical utility even if it adds little or nothing to a sound appreciation of philosophical methodology.

George Santayana (essay date 1952?)

SOURCE: "Vaihinger," in *Physical Order and Moral Liberty: Previously Unpublished Essays of George Santayana*, edited by John and Shirley Lachs, Vanderbilt University Press, 1969, pp. 305-14.

[*In the following essay, which remained unpublished during the author's lifetime, Santayana discusses Immanual Kant's influence on Vaihinger.*]

In the year 1888 at the University of Berlin, I remember hearing Georg Simmel delicately describe ten different philosophies, each of which professed to distil the central and only valid meaning of the Kantian revolution. Of these systems perhaps the most incisive was that of Vaihinger, which has now been re-edited and sensationally set before the public as the "Philosophy of the As If," or as we might say in modern English, or rather American, the Philosophy of Bluff.

Vaihinger admits that in the wisdom of the Sage of Koenigsberg bluff was not the only ingredient; but he collects a hundred pages—by far the most interesting in his book—of quotations from Kant's writings; and if these passages could be allowed to stand alone they would seem to establish a curious paradox: that in that famous philosopher's meagre little body there had lived a desperately romantic soul, and that those labyrinthine paragraphs hid the most pessimistic of doctrines. Probably the truth is that Kant, the man, began by possessing the humane virtues and sanity of the Eighteenth Century, and that in his person he never lost them; but like many of his contemporaries he tended to admit principles which, if carried out ruthlessly, would undermine all sanity and virtue. For instance, Kant proved to his satisfaction that the human mind creates its idea of the world; an assertion which might pass for a truism, at least with anyone who has considered the history of science or the biological basis of thought. But in proving this harmless assertion, he seemed to himself to be proving another also: namely, that the human mind creates the world itself, which is nothing but the human idea of it: and this second position, when generalised, implies that no idea can have any object but itself, that knowledge is impossible, and that no truth exists, to be the standard of ideas. We are thus brought to the edge of a veritable abyss, yet we are not frankly pushed over; for it is a rule of this game to maintain a perpetual equivocation and never to ask whether we are speaking only of our idea of a thing or of that thing itself.

Let us, however, in order to play the game, leave this equivocation for a moment unchallenged. Kant's next move will be to set up, on moral grounds, certain tenets which he called postulates of practical reason. Leibniz and the psychological idealists had accustomed the learned to the sentiment that each mind is shut up in its own shell and each man confined to his personal experience; yet practical reason leads us to postulate objects on which our action may be directed and whose presence and character may be signalled to us by our senses and thoughts; every sense and every language making this report in its own terms. By animal faith or by religious faith (which are two forms of practical reason) we may accordingly reach a sufficient knowledge of the powers, divine or natural, by which our experience is controlled: and this without denying our psychological isolation, which is only another name for our personal existence and spiritual integrity.

According to such a view, the first, perhaps the only, postulate of practical reason would be the existence and order of the material world; and we might go on living confidently in it, like the other animals, our critical philosophy having rendered us soberer, but not less natural men. I say soberer, because we should now recognise that our assurance in regard to matters of fact is presumptive only, however safe and true the presumption may be; and also that, in its substance, our knowledge is a phase of imagination, a creature of the thinking soul; so that while our bodies are busy in the world of matter, the report of it which reaches our minds is an echo only, and a poetic image.

Such, however, is not Vaihinger's view, nor on the whole was it Kant's; for Kant's practical reason did not postulate the existence of the material world. This world for him was only an idea of pure reason, or of science: and we may be surprised to learn that what practical reason postulates is rather the existence of free-will, of God, and of immortality. Here we might well exclaim with Cicero: *Ubinam gentium sumus?* Where on earth are we? For we do not seem to be on earth at all. Yet we are: we are at Koenigsberg in East Prussia; we are listening to the public deliverances of a professor, an official of a Lutheran State; and we are witnessing the difficult fusion in his mind of religious tradition and the system of Leibniz on the one hand with the scepticism of Hume and the sentimentality of Shaftesbury and Rousseau on the other. The word "practical" must not mislead us, as if it referred to action in the world, and to its implications: "practical" here means ethical, and the implications concerned are those involved in puritan moral sentiment. God, free-will, and immortality are indeed the postulates, not of the arts of daily life, but of an attenuated Protestant theology and of a puritan moralism seeking to justify itself metaphysically. Kant was not thinking of practice at all, but of conscience; and he was expounding the possible postulates of conscience when conscience has become superstition.

Very well; let this be the second move in the game, and let us consider the resulting position; which is not a little puzzling. For here again there is a crucial question which we are forbidden to ask. We must not inquire whether these, or any, postulates of practical reason are articles of faith, suppositions which are believed to be true in fact, like the postulate that the sun will rise as usual tomorrow morning, although pure reason may not be able to establish them; or whether on the contrary they are *mere* postulates, like the postulate that if I take a ticket for the lottery, I shall draw the big prize, not believed to be true, yet needed as a false lure or mock goal in the game of life. If God, free-will, and immortality existed in fact, we should still need to posit them as objects of faith; for since they would exist on their own account they could not possibly be parcels of our personal experience or imagination, as are our ideas of them. Such faith would be clear, it would be modest, it might even be true; but if Kant had stopped there, without insensibly slipping into the opposite view, how would he have differed from a poor scholastic, and where would have been his new, colossal, and earth-shaking philosophy? Yet the alternative position, to which logic might seem to drive him, and which Vaihinger tries to assume, is plainly untenable. For if the postulates of practical reason were unequivocally false, it would surely not be virtue to live as if they were true, but folly and crime. Can practical reason compel us to be foolish, and can the essence of duty be never to cease from crime?

I might postulate that an aged uncle was about to make me his heir, and I might hope, without believing, that some day when I opened the morning paper, behold, my postulate would turn out to have been true; so that the debts contracted by me in the days of my postulate might then be actually paid, and I might pose henceforth as an honest man, or at least as a lucky scoundrel. Or without waiting for a fabulous uncle, my practical reason might postulate that I was already in possession of boundless wealth, though pure reason might show me to be a pauper; and I might proceed to sign cheques lavishly in consequence, until arrested for obtaining food, lodging, raiment, and love under false pretenses. Which of these kinds of postulates does the As If philosophy recommend?

Perhaps the benign Kant inclined to the former, and *hoped* that an unknowable uncle might turn out to have existed: but Vaihinger has no such evanescent weaknesses. The heroism and pessimism of his position, which he attributes to Kant in spite of the latter's benignity, requires that the postulates imposed upon us should be avowedly false. Indeed radical transcendentalism, pure subjectivity, and profound paradox require this interpretation; without it, why should Vaihinger, or why should Kant, be a revolutionary genius? The same, in all its romantic violence, was the attitude of Fichte, and also of Nietzsche. It forms the core of the philosophy of *Bluff as the Principle of the Universe*.

Goethe noted with approval that the new German philosophy came to turn dogmas into postulates; and as a matter of method, something of the sort has happened in the sciences, of which Goethe perhaps was thinking. His own philosophy, however, was not of this kind. Where he did not lean on Spinoza, who was an honest dogmatist, he set observation above hypothesis, and disliked to think of any mechanism behind the fair face of nature: her secret was rather to be learned by intuition of her luminous aspects. For this sentiment Spengler, a botanist in history, esteems Goethe to be a great philosopher: and I should agree, in so far as intuition of sensuous or poetic essences seems to me a happier exercise of the mind than the investigation of causes; yet the latter, as Virgil says, is the concern of practical reason, and makes the happy farmer. In any case, the expedient of postulates is something intermediate; bluff, like doubt and like lying, is a marginal phenomenon. If no one ever really held a good hand, the wiliest and most taciturn gambler could never bluff. It is assured knowledge of fact, filling in the background, that lends plausibility to hypotheses and to postulates; and, if they are true, supplies their ulterior verification. Even when, on intellectual grounds, our expectation is of the slenderest, we entertain the possibility that our suppositions may be true in fact: otherwise the assumption would be meaningless. And not only are postulates marginal in origin, but in their moral force they are unstable; for it is psychologically impossible to accept a postulate and to live by it without presently believing it to be true; in other words, without turning it back into a dogma. Megalomania, indulged, becomes insanity, and sensation, acted upon, becomes perception and belief.

There was a subtle irony, doubtless unconscious, in Kant's choice of his postulates. Had he postulated that which practical reason actually needs to assume, namely, the existence and order of the material world, it would have been only what every sane man assumed already, what in practice everybody believes, and what every turn in life confirms. But he chose rather to postulate the existence of free-will, of God, and of immortality, for fear that they might be forgotten and that people might live happy without them. Absolute conscience itself, which seemed to him to dictate those postulates, might then be eclipsed. Faith in things true or probable or at least possible would have been but base earthly wisdom in his eyes, and disgraceful heteronomy: the autonomy of absolute conscience positively demanded that we should live by the light of postulates which we were willing should be false. Otherwise the purity of the moral will would have been contaminated with considerations about matters of fact.

Was this a merely personal extravagance? Far from it: it was romanticism revealing its principle; it was subjectivism attempting to be logical. A critic looking for proofs or refutations might prize it as a *reductio ad absurdum* of all modern philosophy: but a critic himself somewhat romantic, and interested in the life and passion animating no matter what folly, will prefer to think of it as a symptom. The romantic hero need not be a philosopher: he need not trouble himself to assert or deny the existence of God or matter, hell or heaven. He is necessarily an egotist, and can be concerned with these things only as with the giants and dwarfs, the weeping maids and rollicking taverns of his adventures: they will be foils for his courage and food for his dreams. Nothing is altogether real to

him except his capacity to feign: his pose is the centre of his universe. And eventually this pose will be more exciting, and more sincere, if it is somewhat paradoxical. Heaven, he will say to himself, if it existed, would be a bore; hell might be better worth trying; God and matter may be real, but the one is a tyrant and the other a nuisance. He will defy God by his heroism and exorcise matter by his subjectivity. After he has denaturalised these objects in this way and made their supposed reality relative to himself, it will not take much critical acumen on his part to perceive that he need not believe in them at all. Yet in that case, with what counters shall he play, and on what shall he exercise his virtue? Evidently on the *idea* of these, or of other such things; on the *illusion* of their existence. Thus, by the sheer force of his romanticism, he will be brought to the philosophy of false postulates, and to the vital duty of bluffing.

The revival of this doctrine (which might seem rather out of date) is perhaps a symptom of our times: while the philosophers are returning to scientific cosmologies, the uncertainty of these systems, and the uncertainty of everything, brings the notion of living by assumptions, yet without faith, near the public mind. Our contemporaries are deeply engaged in bluffing; not lavishly, for some ulterior clear purpose, but helplessly, by virtue of the commitments under which they groan. You or I may feel that these commitments were unnecessary, but we may lack the courage and the time to criticise them. Therefore we go on bluffing in religion, in art, in politics, in sport, even in science and in our airs of happiness. No doubt bluff has always prevailed in some measure in human society, because society is necessarily artificial; suppression and hypocrisy are inevitable, if we set about to establish order in public or integrity in private. Men must live up to their assumed characters, as they must live up to their clothes. But the peculiarity of our age is that the safety valve is closed: we see no issue out of our vanities. Bluffers in other ages, when they felt ruined and sick of the game, knew how to repent; they could turn with a clear mind to religion, to patriotism, or to superb understanding. Today if we turned to such things, most of us would be conscious of bluffing more than ever. We therefore often accept this necessity with bowed heads, somewhat in Vaihinger's spirit. We nerve ourselves sadly to play the game out, whatever it may be, in which we find ourselves engaged. We have habits, affections, responsibilities, which it would be too great a wrench to disown, ignorant as we are of any better allegiance. We therefore suffer our discredited postulates to carry us, if they can, a little father on the road to nothingness.

FURTHER READING

Flewelling, Ralph Tyler. "Our 'As If' World." *The Personalist* VI, No. 2 (April 1925): 133-135.
  Notes the materialist reaction to *The Philosophy of "As If,"* stating: "We recently ran across such a screed

of misunderstanding from Mr. Mencken." Flewelling nonetheless concludes that Vaihinger's book "seems one of the very few real contributions to the literature of philosophy in recent years."

House, Floyd N. Review of *The Philosophy of "As If,"* by Hans Vaihinger. *The American Journal of Sociology* XXXI, No. 5 (March 1926): 684-685.
    Concludes that *The Philosophy of "As If"* "is a book of one idea, but that one idea is a very important one for the social scientist."

Porter, Alan. "As If." *The Spectator* 133, No. 5011 (12 July 1924): 61-62.
    Hostile review asserting that *The Philosophy of "As If"* is "Right in detail, wrong in emphasis—the worst one could say of a philosopher." The reviewer makes extensive reference to Buddhist scriptures.

Additional coverage of Vaihinger's life and career may be found in the following source published by Gale Research: *Contemporary Authors,* Vol. 116.

Twentieth-Century
Literary Criticism

Cumulative Indexes
Volumes 1-71

How to Use This Index

The main references

> Calvino, Italo
> 1923-1985.....CLC 5, 8, 11, 22, 33, 39,
> 73; SSC 3

list all author entries in the following Gale Literary Criticism series:

BLC = Black Literature Criticism
CLC = Contemporary Literary Criticism
CLR = Children's Literature Review
CMLC = Classical and Medieval Literature Criticism
DA = DISCovering Authors
DC = Drama Criticism
HLC = Hispanic Literature Criticism
LC = Literature Criticism from 1400 to 1800
NCLC = Nineteenth-Century Literature Criticism
PC = Poetry Criticism
SSC = Short Story Criticism
TCLC = Twentieth-Century Literary Criticism
WLC = World Literature Criticism, 1500 to the Present

The cross-references

> See also CANR 23; CA 85-88;
> obituary CA 116

list all author entries in the following Gale biographical and literary sources:

AAYA = Authors & Artists for Young Adults
AITN = Authors in the News
BEST = Bestsellers
BW = Black Writers
CA = Contemporary Authors
CAAS = Contemporary Authors Autobiography Series
CABS = Contemporary Authors Bibliographical Series
CANR = Contemporary Authors New Revision Series
CAP = Contemporary Authors Permanent Series
CDALB = Concise Dictionary of American Literary Biography
CDBLB = Concise Dictionary of British Literary Biography
DLB = Dictionary of Literary Biography
DLBD = Dictionary of Literary Biography Documentary Series
DLBY = Dictionary of Literary Biography Yearbook
HW = Hispanic Writers
JRDA = Junior DISCovering Authors
MAICYA = Major Authors and Illustrators for Children and Young Adults
MTCW = Major 20th-Century Writers
NNAL = Native North American Literature
SAAS = Something about the Author Autobiography Series
SATA = Something about the Author
YABC = Yesterday's Authors of Books for Children

Literary Criticism Series
Cumulative Author Index

Anderson, Robert (Woodruff)
1917- . . . . **CLC 23; DAM DRAM**
See also AITN 1; CA 21-24R; CANR 32;
DLB 7

Anderson, Sherwood
1876-1941 . . . . **TCLC 1, 10, 24; DA;**
DAB; DAC; DAM MST, NOV; SSC 1;
WLC
See also CA 104; 121; CDALB 1917-1929;
DLB 4, 9, 86; DLBD 1; MTCW

Andier, Pierre
See Desnos, Robert

Andouard
See Giraudoux, (Hippolyte) Jean

Andrade, Carlos Drummond de . . . . . . **CLC 18**
See also Drummond de Andrade, Carlos

Andrade, Mario de 1893-1945 . . . . . **TCLC 43**

Andreae, Johann V(alentin)
1586-1654 . . . . **LC 32**
See also DLB 164

Andreas-Salome, Lou 1861-1937 . . . **TCLC 56**
See also DLB 66

Andrewes, Lancelot 1555-1626 . . . . **LC 5**
See also DLB 151, 172

Andrews, Cicily Fairfield
See West, Rebecca

Andrews, Elton V.
See Pohl, Frederik

Andreyev, Leonid (Nikolaevich)
1871-1919 . . . . **TCLC 3**
See also CA 104

Andric, Ivo 1892-1975 . . . . **CLC 8**
See also CA 81-84; 57-60; CANR 43;
DLB 147; MTCW

Angelique, Pierre
See Bataille, Georges

Angell, Roger 1920- . . . . **CLC 26**
See also CA 57-60; CANR 13, 44; DLB 171

Angelou, Maya
1928- . . . . **CLC 12, 35, 64, 77; BLC; DA;**
DAB; DAC; DAM MST, MULT, POET,
POP
See also AAYA 7, 20; BW 2; CA 65-68;
CANR 19, 42; DLB 38; MTCW;
SATA 49; YABC

Annensky, Innokenty (Fyodorovich)
1856-1909 . . . . **TCLC 14**
See also CA 110; 155

Annunzio, Gabriele d'
See D'Annunzio, Gabriele

Anon, Charles Robert
See Pessoa, Fernando (Antonio Nogueira)

Anouilh, Jean (Marie Lucien Pierre)
1910-1987 . . . . . . **CLC 1, 3, 8, 13, 40, 50;**
DAM DRAM
See also CA 17-20R; 123; CANR 32;
MTCW

Anthony, Florence
See Ai

Anthony, John
See Ciardi, John (Anthony)

Anthony, Peter
See Shaffer, Anthony (Joshua); Shaffer,
Peter (Levin)

Anthony, Piers 1934- . . **CLC 35; DAM POP**
See also AAYA 11; CA 21-24R; CANR 28,
56; DLB 8; MTCW; SAAS 22; SATA 84

Antoine, Marc
See Proust, (Valentin-Louis-George-Eugene-)
Marcel

Antoninus, Brother
See Everson, William (Oliver)

Antonioni, Michelangelo 1912- . . . . . **CLC 20**
See also CA 73-76; CANR 45

Antschel, Paul 1920-1970
See Celan, Paul
See also CA 85-88; CANR 33; MTCW

Anwar, Chairil 1922-1949 . . . . **TCLC 22**
See also CA 121

Apollinaire, Guillaume
1880-1918 . . . . **TCLC 3, 8, 51;**
DAM POET; PC 7
See also Kostrowitzki, Wilhelm Apollinaris
de
See also CA 152

Appelfeld, Aharon 1932- . . . . **CLC 23, 47**
See also CA 112; 133

Apple, Max (Isaac) 1941- . . . . **CLC 9, 33**
See also CA 81-84; CANR 19, 54; DLB 130

Appleman, Philip (Dean) 1926- . . . . . **CLC 51**
See also CA 13-16R; CAAS 18; CANR 6,
29, 56

Appleton, Lawrence
See Lovecraft, H(oward) P(hillips)

Apteryx
See Eliot, T(homas) S(tearns)

Apuleius, (Lucius Madaurensis)
125(?)-175(?) . . . . **CMLC 1**

Aquin, Hubert 1929-1977 . . . . **CLC 15**
See also CA 105; DLB 53

Aragon, Louis
1897-1982 . . . . . **CLC 3, 22; DAM NOV,**
POET
See also CA 69-72; 108; CANR 28;
DLB 72; MTCW

Arany, Janos 1817-1882 . . . . **NCLC 34**

Arbuthnot, John 1667-1735 . . . . **LC 1**
See also DLB 101

Archer, Herbert Winslow
See Mencken, H(enry) L(ouis)

Archer, Jeffrey (Howard)
1940- . . . . **CLC 28; DAM POP**
See also AAYA 16; BEST 89:3; CA 77-80;
CANR 22, 52; INT CANR-22

Archer, Jules 1915- . . . . **CLC 12**
See also CA 9-12R; CANR 6; SAAS 5;
SATA 4, 85

Archer, Lee
See Ellison, Harlan (Jay)

Arden, John
1930- . . . . . **CLC 6, 13, 15; DAM DRAM**
See also CA 13-16R; CAAS 4; CANR 31;
DLB 13; MTCW

Arenas, Reinaldo
1943-1990 . . . . . . **CLC 41; DAM MULT;**
HLC
See also CA 124; 128; 133; DLB 145; HW

Arendt, Hannah 1906-1975 . . . . . **CLC 66, 98**
See also CA 17-20R; 61-64; CANR 26;
MTCW

Aretino, Pietro 1492-1556 . . . . **LC 12**

Arghezi, Tudor . . . . **CLC 80**
See also Theodorescu, Ion N.

Arguedas, Jose Maria
1911-1969 . . . . **CLC 10, 18**
See also CA 89-92; DLB 113; HW

Argueta, Manlio 1936- . . . . **CLC 31**
See also CA 131; DLB 145; HW

Ariosto, Ludovico 1474-1533 . . . . **LC 6**

Aristides
See Epstein, Joseph

Aristophanes
450B.C.-385B.C. . . . . **CMLC 4; DA;**
DAB; DAC; DAM DRAM, MST; DC 2
See also DLB 176; YABC

Arlt, Roberto (Godofredo Christophersen)
1900-1942 . . . . . **TCLC 29; DAM MULT;**
HLC
See also CA 123; 131; HW

Armah, Ayi Kwei
1939- . . . . **CLC 5, 33; BLC;**
DAM MULT, POET
See also BW 1; CA 61-64; CANR 21;
DLB 117; MTCW

Armatrading, Joan 1950- . . . . **CLC 17**
See also CA 114

Arnette, Robert
See Silverberg, Robert

Arnim, Achim von (Ludwig Joachim von
Arnim) 1781-1831 . . . . **NCLC 5**
See also DLB 90

Arnim, Bettina von 1785-1859 . . . . **NCLC 38**
See also DLB 90

Arnold, Matthew
1822-1888 . . . . . **NCLC 6, 29; DA; DAB;**
DAC; DAM MST, POET; PC 5; WLC
See also CDBLB 1832-1890; DLB 32, 57

Arnold, Thomas 1795-1842 . . . . . . **NCLC 18**
See also DLB 55

Arnow, Harriette (Louisa) Simpson
1908-1986 . . . . **CLC 2, 7, 18**
See also CA 9-12R; 118; CANR 14; DLB 6;
MTCW; SATA 42; SATA-Obit 47

Arp, Hans
See Arp, Jean

Arp, Jean 1887-1966 . . . . **CLC 5**
See also CA 81-84; 25-28R; CANR 42

Arrabal
See Arrabal, Fernando

Arrabal, Fernando 1932- . . . **CLC 2, 9, 18, 58**
See also CA 9-12R; CANR 15

Arrick, Fran . . . . **CLC 30**
See also Gaberman, Judie Angell

Artaud, Antonin (Marie Joseph)
1896-1948 . . . **TCLC 3, 36; DAM DRAM**
See also CA 104; 149

Arthur, Ruth M(abel) 1905-1979 . . . . **CLC 12**
See also CA 9-12R; 85-88; CANR 4;
SATA 7, 26

Artsybashev, Mikhail (Petrovich)
1878-1927 . . . . **TCLC 31**

Belloc, (Joseph) Hilaire (Pierre Sebastien Rene Swanton)
1870-1953 . . . **TCLC 7, 18; DAM POET**
See also CA 106; 152; DLB 19, 100, 141, 174; 1

Belloc, Joseph Peter Rene Hilaire
See Belloc, (Joseph) Hilaire (Pierre Sebastien Rene Swanton)

Belloc, Joseph Pierre Hilaire
See Belloc, (Joseph) Hilaire (Pierre Sebastien Rene Swanton)

Belloc, M. A.
See Lowndes, Marie Adelaide (Belloc)

Bellow, Saul
1915- . . . . . . **CLC 1, 2, 3, 6, 8, 10, 13, 15, 25, 33, 34, 63, 79; DA; DAB; DAC; DAM MST, NOV, POP; SSC 14; WLC**
See also AITN 2; BEST 89:3; CA 5-8R; CABS 1; CANR 29, 53; CDALB 1941-1968; DLB 2, 28; DLBD 3; DLBY 82; MTCW

Belser, Reimond Karel Maria de 1929-
See Ruyslinck, Ward
See also CA 152

Bely, Andrey . . . . **TCLC 7; PC 11**
See also Bugayev, Boris Nikolayevich

Benary, Margot
See Benary-Isbert, Margot

Benary-Isbert, Margot 1889-1979 . . . **CLC 12**
See also CA 5-8R; 89-92; CANR 4; CLR 12; MAICYA; SATA 2; SATA-Obit 21

Benavente (y Martinez), Jacinto
1866-1954 . . . . . **TCLC 3; DAM DRAM, MULT**
See also CA 106; 131; HW; MTCW

Benchley, Peter (Bradford)
1940- . . . . **CLC 4, 8; DAM NOV, POP**
See also AAYA 14; AITN 2; CA 17-20R; CANR 12, 35; MTCW; SATA 3, 89

Benchley, Robert (Charles)
1889-1945 . . . . **TCLC 1, 55**
See also CA 105; 153; DLB 11

Benda, Julien 1867-1956 . . . . **TCLC 60**
See also CA 120; 154

Benedict, Ruth (Fulton)
1887-1948 . . . . **TCLC 60**
See also CA 158

Benedikt, Michael 1935- . . . . **CLC 4, 14**
See also CA 13-16R; CANR 7; DLB 5

Benet, Juan 1927- . . . . **CLC 28**
See also CA 143

Benet, Stephen Vincent
1898-1943 . . . . . . **TCLC 7; DAM POET; SSC 10**
See also CA 104; 152; DLB 4, 48, 102; 1

Benet, William Rose
1886-1950 . . . . . . **TCLC 28; DAM POET**
See also CA 118; 152; DLB 45

Benford, Gregory (Albert) 1941- . . . . **CLC 52**
See also CA 69-72; CAAS 27; CANR 12, 24, 49; DLBY 82

Bengtsson, Frans (Gunnar)
1894-1954 . . . . **TCLC 48**

Benjamin, David
See Slavitt, David R(ytman)

Benjamin, Lois
See Gould, Lois

Benjamin, Walter 1892-1940 . . . . . **TCLC 39**

Benn, Gottfried 1886-1956 . . . . **TCLC 3**
See also CA 106; 153; DLB 56

Bennett, Alan
1934- . . . **CLC 45, 77; DAB; DAM MST**
See also CA 103; CANR 35, 55; MTCW

Bennett, (Enoch) Arnold
1867-1931 . . . . **TCLC 5, 20**
See also CA 106; 155; CDBLB 1890-1914; DLB 10, 34, 98, 135

Bennett, Elizabeth
See Mitchell, Margaret (Munnerlyn)

Bennett, George Harold 1930-
See Bennett, Hal
See also BW 1; CA 97-100

Bennett, Hal . . . . **CLC 5**
See also Bennett, George Harold
See also DLB 33

Bennett, Jay 1912- . . . . **CLC 35**
See also AAYA 10; CA 69-72; CANR 11, 42; JRDA; SAAS 4; SATA 41, 87; SATA-Brief 27

Bennett, Louise (Simone)
1919- . . . . . **CLC 28; BLC; DAM MULT**
See also BW 2; CA 151; DLB 117

Benson, E(dward) F(rederic)
1867-1940 . . . . **TCLC 27**
See also CA 114; 157; DLB 135, 153

Benson, Jackson J. 1930- . . . . **CLC 34**
See also CA 25-28R; DLB 111

Benson, Sally 1900-1972 . . . . **CLC 17**
See also CA 19-20; 37-40R; CAP 1; SATA 1, 35; SATA-Obit 27

Benson, Stella 1892-1933 . . . . **TCLC 17**
See also CA 117; 155; DLB 36, 162

Bentham, Jeremy 1748-1832 . . . . . **NCLC 38**
See also DLB 107, 158

Bentley, E(dmund) C(lerihew)
1875-1956 . . . . **TCLC 12**
See also CA 108; DLB 70

Bentley, Eric (Russell) 1916- . . . . . . **CLC 24**
See also CA 5-8R; CANR 6; INT CANR-6

Beranger, Pierre Jean de
1780-1857 . . . . **NCLC 34**

Berdyaev, Nicolas
See Berdyaev, Nikolai (Aleksandrovich)

Berdyaev, Nikolai (Aleksandrovich)
1874-1948 . . . . **TCLC 67**
See also CA 120; 157

Berdyayev, Nikolai (Aleksandrovich)
See Berdyaev, Nikolai (Aleksandrovich)

Berendt, John (Lawrence) 1939- . . . . **CLC 86**
See also CA 146

Berger, Colonel
See Malraux, (Georges-)Andre

Berger, John (Peter) 1926- . . . . . . **CLC 2, 19**
See also CA 81-84; CANR 51; DLB 14

Berger, Melvin H. 1927- . . . . **CLC 12**
See also CA 5-8R; CANR 4; CLR 32; SAAS 2; SATA 5, 88

Berger, Thomas (Louis)
1924- . . . . **CLC 3, 5, 8, 11, 18, 38; DAM NOV**
See also CA 1-4R; CANR 5, 28, 51; DLB 2; DLBY 80; INT CANR-28; MTCW

Bergman, (Ernst) Ingmar
1918- . . . . **CLC 16, 72**
See also CA 81-84; CANR 33

Bergson, Henri 1859-1941 . . . . **TCLC 32**

Bergstein, Eleanor 1938- . . . . **CLC 4**
See also CA 53-56; CANR 5

Berkoff, Steven 1937- . . . . **CLC 56**
See also CA 104

Bermant, Chaim (Icyk) 1929- . . . . . . **CLC 40**
See also CA 57-60; CANR 6, 31, 57

Bern, Victoria
See Fisher, M(ary) F(rances) K(ennedy)

Bernanos, (Paul Louis) Georges
1888-1948 . . . . **TCLC 3**
See also CA 104; 130; DLB 72

Bernard, April 1956- . . . . **CLC 59**
See also CA 131

Berne, Victoria
See Fisher, M(ary) F(rances) K(ennedy)

Bernhard, Thomas
1931-1989 . . . . **CLC 3, 32, 61**
See also CA 85-88; 127; CANR 32, 57; DLB 85, 124; MTCW

Berriault, Gina 1926- . . . . **CLC 54**
See also CA 116; 129; DLB 130

Berrigan, Daniel 1921- . . . . **CLC 4**
See also CA 33-36R; CAAS 1; CANR 11, 43; DLB 5

Berrigan, Edmund Joseph Michael, Jr.
1934-1983
See Berrigan, Ted
See also CA 61-64; 110; CANR 14

Berrigan, Ted . . . . **CLC 37**
See also Berrigan, Edmund Joseph Michael, Jr.
See also DLB 5, 169

Berry, Charles Edward Anderson 1931-
See Berry, Chuck
See also CA 115

Berry, Chuck . . . . **CLC 17**
See also Berry, Charles Edward Anderson

Berry, Jonas
See Ashbery, John (Lawrence)

Berry, Wendell (Erdman)
1934- . . . . **CLC 4, 6, 8, 27, 46; DAM POET**
See also AITN 1; CA 73-76; CANR 50; DLB 5, 6

Berryman, John
1914-1972 . . . . . . **CLC 1, 2, 3, 4, 6, 8, 10, 13, 25, 62; DAM POET**
See also CA 13-16; 33-36R; CABS 2; CANR 35; CAP 1; CDALB 1941-1968; DLB 48; MTCW

Bertolucci, Bernardo 1940- . . . . **CLC 16**
See also CA 106

Bertrand, Aloysius 1807-1841 . . . . **NCLC 31**

Bertran de Born c. 1140-1215 . . . . . **CMLC 5**

Besant, Annie (Wood) 1847-1933 . . . **TCLC 9**
See also CA 105

Bodker, Cecil 1927- . . . . **CLC 21**
See also CA 73-76; CANR 13, 44; CLR 23;
MAICYA; SATA 14

Boell, Heinrich (Theodor)
1917-1985 . . . . **CLC 2, 3, 6, 9, 11, 15, 27,
32, 72; DA; DAB; DAC; DAM MST,
NOV; SSC 23; WLC**
See also CA 21-24R; 116; CANR 24;
DLB 69; DLBY 85; MTCW

Boerne, Alfred
See Doeblin, Alfred

Boethius 480(?)-524(?) . . . . **CMLC 15**
See also DLB 115

Bogan, Louise
1897-1970 . . . . **CLC 4, 39, 46, 93;
DAM POET; PC 12**
See also CA 73-76; 25-28R; CANR 33;
DLB 45, 169; MTCW

Bogarde, Dirk . . . . **CLC 19**
See also Van Den Bogarde, Derek Jules
Gaspard Ulric Niven
See also DLB 14

Bogosian, Eric 1953- . . . . **CLC 45**
See also CA 138

Bograd, Larry 1953- . . . . **CLC 35**
See also CA 93-96; CANR 57; SAAS 21;
SATA 33, 89

Boiardo, Matteo Maria 1441-1494 . . . . **LC 6**

Boileau-Despreaux, Nicolas
1636-1711 . . . . **LC 3**

Bojer, Johan 1872-1959 . . . . **TCLC 64**

Boland, Eavan (Aisling)
1944- . . . . **CLC 40, 67; DAM POET**
See also CA 143; DLB 40

Bolt, Lee
See Faust, Frederick (Schiller)

Bolt, Robert (Oxton)
1924-1995 . . . . . . **CLC 14; DAM DRAM**
See also CA 17-20R; 147; CANR 35;
DLB 13; MTCW

Bombet, Louis-Alexandre-Cesar
See Stendhal

Bomkauf
See Kaufman, Bob (Garnell)

Bonaventura . . . . **NCLC 35**
See also DLB 90

Bond, Edward
1934- . . . **CLC 4, 6, 13, 23; DAM DRAM**
See also CA 25-28R; CANR 38; DLB 13;
MTCW

Bonham, Frank 1914-1989 . . . . **CLC 12**
See also AAYA 1; CA 9-12R; CANR 4, 36;
JRDA; MAICYA; SAAS 3; SATA 1, 49;
SATA-Obit 62

Bonnefoy, Yves
1923- . . . . . . **CLC 9, 15, 58; DAM MST,
POET**
See also CA 85-88; CANR 33; MTCW

Bontemps, Arna(ud Wendell)
1902-1973 . . . . **CLC 1, 18; BLC;
DAM MULT, NOV, POET**
See also BW 1; CA 1-4R; 41-44R; CANR 4,
35; CLR 6; DLB 48, 51; JRDA;
MAICYA; MTCW; SATA 2, 44;
SATA-Obit 24

Booth, Martin 1944- . . . . **CLC 13**
See also CA 93-96; CAAS 2

Booth, Philip 1925- . . . . **CLC 23**
See also CA 5-8R; CANR 5; DLBY 82

Booth, Wayne C(layson) 1921- . . . . . **CLC 24**
See also CA 1-4R; CAAS 5; CANR 3, 43;
DLB 67

Borchert, Wolfgang 1921-1947 . . . . . **TCLC 5**
See also CA 104; DLB 69, 124

Borel, Petrus 1809-1859 . . . . **NCLC 41**

Borges, Jorge Luis
1899-1986 . . . **CLC 1, 2, 3, 4, 6, 8, 9, 10,
13, 19, 44, 48, 83; DA; DAB; DAC;
DAM MST, MULT; HLC; SSC 4; WLC**
See also AAYA 19; CA 21-24R; CANR 19,
33; DLB 113; DLBY 86; HW; MTCW

Borowski, Tadeusz 1922-1951 . . . . . . **TCLC 9**
See also CA 106; 154

Borrow, George (Henry)
1803-1881 . . . . **NCLC 9**
See also DLB 21, 55, 166

Bosman, Herman Charles
1905-1951 . . . . **TCLC 49**

Bosschere, Jean de 1878(?)-1953 . . . **TCLC 19**
See also CA 115

Boswell, James
1740-1795 . . . . . . **LC 4; DA; DAB; DAC;
DAM MST; WLC**
See also CDBLB 1660-1789; DLB 104, 142

Bottoms, David 1949- . . . . **CLC 53**
See also CA 105; CANR 22; DLB 120;
DLBY 83

Boucicault, Dion 1820-1890 . . . . . **NCLC 41**

Boucolon, Maryse 1937(?)-
See Conde, Maryse
See also CA 110; CANR 30, 53

Bourget, Paul (Charles Joseph)
1852-1935 . . . . **TCLC 12**
See also CA 107; DLB 123

Bourjaily, Vance (Nye) 1922- . . . . **CLC 8, 62**
See also CA 1-4R; CAAS 1; CANR 2;
DLB 2, 143

Bourne, Randolph S(illiman)
1886-1918 . . . . **TCLC 16**
See also CA 117; 155; DLB 63

Bova, Ben(jamin William) 1932- . . . . **CLC 45**
See also AAYA 16; CA 5-8R; CAAS 18;
CANR 11, 56; CLR 3; DLBY 81;
INT CANR-11; MAICYA; MTCW;
SATA 6, 68

Bowen, Elizabeth (Dorothea Cole)
1899-1973 . . . . . . **CLC 1, 3, 6, 11, 15, 22;
DAM NOV; SSC 3**
See also CA 17-18; 41-44R; CANR 35;
CAP 2; CDBLB 1945-1960; DLB 15, 162;
MTCW

Bowering, George 1935- . . . . **CLC 15, 47**
See also CA 21-24R; CAAS 16; CANR 10;
DLB 53

Bowering, Marilyn R(uthe) 1949- . . . **CLC 32**
See also CA 101; CANR 49

Bowers, Edgar 1924- . . . . **CLC 9**
See also CA 5-8R; CANR 24; DLB 5

Bowie, David . . . . **CLC 17**
See also Jones, David Robert

Bowles, Jane (Sydney)
1917-1973 . . . . **CLC 3, 68**
See also CA 19-20; 41-44R; CAP 2

Bowles, Paul (Frederick)
1910- . . . . **CLC 1, 2, 19, 53; SSC 3**
See also CA 1-4R; CAAS 1; CANR 1, 19,
50; DLB 5, 6; MTCW

Box, Edgar
See Vidal, Gore

Boyd, Nancy
See Millay, Edna St. Vincent

Boyd, William 1952- . . . . **CLC 28, 53, 70**
See also CA 114; 120; CANR 51

Boyle, Kay
1902-1992 . . . . . **CLC 1, 5, 19, 58; SSC 5**
See also CA 13-16R; 140; CAAS 1;
CANR 29; DLB 4, 9, 48, 86; DLBY 93;
MTCW

Boyle, Mark
See Kienzle, William X(avier)

Boyle, Patrick 1905-1982 . . . . **CLC 19**
See also CA 127

Boyle, T. C. 1948-
See Boyle, T(homas) Coraghessan

Boyle, T(homas) Coraghessan
1948- . . . . . **CLC 36, 55, 90; DAM POP;
SSC 16**
See also BEST 90:4; CA 120; CANR 44;
DLBY 86

Boz
See Dickens, Charles (John Huffam)

Brackenridge, Hugh Henry
1748-1816 . . . . **NCLC 7**
See also DLB 11, 37

Bradbury, Edward P.
See Moorcock, Michael (John)

Bradbury, Malcolm (Stanley)
1932- . . . . **CLC 32, 61; DAM NOV**
See also CA 1-4R; CANR 1, 33; DLB 14;
MTCW

Bradbury, Ray (Douglas)
1920- . . . . . **CLC 1, 3, 10, 15, 42, 98; DA;
DAB; DAC; DAM MST, NOV, POP;
WLC**
See also AAYA 15; AITN 1, 2; CA 1-4R;
CANR 2, 30; CDALB 1968-1988; DLB 2,
8; INT CANR-30; MTCW; SATA 11, 64

Bradford, Gamaliel 1863-1932 . . . . . **TCLC 36**
See also DLB 17

Bradley, David (Henry, Jr.)
1950- . . . . . **CLC 23; BLC; DAM MULT**
See also BW 1; CA 104; CANR 26; DLB 33

Bradley, John Ed(mund, Jr.)
1958- . . . . **CLC 55**
See also CA 139

Bradley, Marion Zimmer
1930- . . . . **CLC 30; DAM POP**
See also AAYA 9; CA 57-60; CAAS 10;
CANR 7, 31, 51; DLB 8; MTCW;
SATA 90

Bradstreet, Anne
1612(?)-1672 . . . . . . **LC 4, 30; DA; DAC;
DAM MST, POET; PC 10**
See also CDALB 1640-1865; DLB 24

Brady, Joan 1939- . . . . **CLC 86**
See also CA 141

Campbell, Wilfred . . . . TCLC 9
See also Campbell, William

Campbell, William   1858(?)-1918
See Campbell, Wilfred
See also CA 106; DLB 92

Campion, Jane . . . . CLC 95
See also CA 138

Campos, Alvaro de
See Pessoa, Fernando (Antonio Nogueira)

Camus, Albert
1913-1960 . . . . CLC 1, 2, 4, 9, 11, 14, 32,
63, 69; DA; DAB; DAC; DAM DRAM,
MST, NOV; DC 2; SSC 9; WLC
See also CA 89-92; DLB 72; MTCW

Canby, Vincent   1924- . . . . CLC 13
See also CA 81-84

Cancale
See Desnos, Robert

Canetti, Elias
1905-1994 . . . . CLC 3, 14, 25, 75, 86
See also CA 21-24R; 146; CANR 23;
DLB 85, 124; MTCW

Canin, Ethan   1960- . . . . CLC 55
See also CA 131; 135

Cannon, Curt
See Hunter, Evan

Cape, Judith
See Page, P(atricia) K(athleen)

Capek, Karel
1890-1938 . . . . . . TCLC 6, 37; DA; DAB;
DAC; DAM DRAM, MST, NOV; DC 1;
WLC
See also CA 104; 140

Capote, Truman
1924-1984 . . . . . . CLC 1, 3, 8, 13, 19, 34,
38, 58; DA; DAB; DAC; DAM MST,
NOV, POP; SSC 2; WLC
See also CA 5-8R; 113; CANR 18;
CDALB 1941-1968; DLB 2; DLBY 80,
84; MTCW; SATA 91

Capra, Frank   1897-1991 . . . . CLC 16
See also CA 61-64; 135

Caputo, Philip   1941- . . . . CLC 32
See also CA 73-76; CANR 40

Card, Orson Scott
1951- . . . . . . CLC 44, 47, 50; DAM POP
See also AAYA 11; CA 102; CANR 27, 47;
INT CANR-27; MTCW; SATA 83

Cardenal, Ernesto
1925- . . . . CLC 31; DAM MULT,
POET; HLC
See also CA 49-52; CANR 2, 32; HW;
MTCW

Cardozo, Benjamin N(athan)
1870-1938 . . . . TCLC 65
See also CA 117

Carducci, Giosue   1835-1907 . . . . . . TCLC 32

Carew, Thomas   1595(?)-1640 . . . . LC 13
See also DLB 126

Carey, Ernestine Gilbreth   1908- . . . . CLC 17
See also CA 5-8R; SATA 2

Carey, Peter   1943- . . . . CLC 40, 55, 96
See also CA 123; 127; CANR 53; INT 127;
MTCW; SATA 94

Carleton, William   1794-1869 . . . . . . NCLC 3
See also DLB 159

Carlisle, Henry (Coffin)   1926- . . . . . . CLC 33
See also CA 13-16R; CANR 15

Carlsen, Chris
See Holdstock, Robert P.

Carlson, Ron(ald F.)   1947- . . . . CLC 54
See also CA 105; CANR 27

Carlyle, Thomas
1795-1881 . . . . NCLC 22; DA; DAB;
DAC; DAM MST
See also CDBLB 1789-1832; DLB 55; 144

Carman, (William) Bliss
1861-1929 . . . . TCLC 7; DAC
See also CA 104; 152; DLB 92

Carnegie, Dale   1888-1955 . . . . TCLC 53

Carossa, Hans   1878-1956 . . . . TCLC 48
See also DLB 66

Carpenter, Don(ald Richard)
1931-1995 . . . . CLC 41
See also CA 45-48; 149; CANR 1

Carpentier (y Valmont), Alejo
1904-1980 . . . . CLC 8, 11, 38;
DAM MULT; HLC
See also CA 65-68; 97-100; CANR 11;
DLB 113; HW

Carr, Caleb   1955(?)- . . . . CLC 86
See also CA 147

Carr, Emily   1871-1945 . . . . TCLC 32
See also DLB 68

Carr, John Dickson   1906-1977 . . . . . . CLC 3
See also CA 49-52; 69-72; CANR 3, 33;
MTCW

Carr, Philippa
See Hibbert, Eleanor Alice Burford

Carr, Virginia Spencer   1929- . . . . . . CLC 34
See also CA 61-64; DLB 111

Carrere, Emmanuel   1957- . . . . CLC 89

Carrier, Roch
1937- . . . CLC 13, 78; DAC; DAM MST
See also CA 130; DLB 53

Carroll, James P.   1943(?)- . . . . CLC 38
See also CA 81-84

Carroll, Jim   1951- . . . . CLC 35
See also AAYA 17; CA 45-48; CANR 42

Carroll, Lewis . . . . NCLC 2, 53; PC 18; WLC
See also Dodgson, Charles Lutwidge
See also CDBLB 1832-1890; CLR 2, 18;
DLB 18, 163, 178; JRDA

Carroll, Paul Vincent   1900-1968 . . . . CLC 10
See also CA 9-12R; 25-28R; DLB 10

Carruth, Hayden
1921- . . . . CLC 4, 7, 10, 18, 84; PC 10
See also CA 9-12R; CANR 4, 38; DLB 5,
165; INT CANR-4; MTCW; SATA 47

Carson, Rachel Louise
1907-1964 . . . . CLC 71; DAM POP
See also CA 77-80; CANR 35; MTCW;
SATA 23

Carter, Angela (Olive)
1940-1992 . . . . . . CLC 5, 41, 76; SSC 13
See also CA 53-56; 136; CANR 12, 36;
DLB 14; MTCW; SATA 66;
SATA-Obit 70

Carter, Nick
See Smith, Martin Cruz

Carver, Raymond
1938-1988 . . . . CLC 22, 36, 53, 55;
DAM NOV; SSC 8
See also CA 33-36R; 126; CANR 17, 34;
DLB 130; DLBY 84, 88; MTCW

Cary, Elizabeth, Lady Falkland
1585-1639 . . . . LC 30

Cary, (Arthur) Joyce (Lunel)
1888-1957 . . . . TCLC 1, 29
See also CA 104; CDBLB 1914-1945;
DLB 15, 100

Casanova de Seingalt, Giovanni Jacopo
1725-1798 . . . . LC 13

Casares, Adolfo Bioy
See Bioy Casares, Adolfo

Casely-Hayford, J(oseph) E(phraim)
1866-1930 . . . . TCLC 24; BLC;
DAM MULT
See also BW 2; CA 123; 152

Casey, John (Dudley)   1939- . . . . CLC 59
See also BEST 90:2; CA 69-72; CANR 23

Casey, Michael   1947- . . . . CLC 2
See also CA 65-68; DLB 5

Casey, Patrick
See Thurman, Wallace (Henry)

Casey, Warren (Peter)   1935-1988 . . . CLC 12
See also CA 101; 127; INT 101

Casona, Alejandro . . . . CLC 49
See also Alvarez, Alejandro Rodriguez

Cassavetes, John   1929-1989 . . . . CLC 20
See also CA 85-88; 127

Cassian, Nina   1924- . . . . PC 17

Cassill, R(onald) V(erlin)   1919- . . . CLC 4, 23
See also CA 9-12R; CAAS 1; CANR 7, 45;
DLB 6

Cassirer, Ernst   1874-1945 . . . . TCLC 61
See also CA 157

Cassity, (Allen) Turner   1929- . . . . CLC 6, 42
See also CA 17-20R; CAAS 8; CANR 11;
DLB 105

Castaneda, Carlos   1931(?)- . . . . CLC 12
See also CA 25-28R; CANR 32; HW;
MTCW

Castedo, Elena   1937- . . . . CLC 65
See also CA 132

Castedo-Ellerman, Elena
See Castedo, Elena

Castellanos, Rosario
1925-1974 . . . . . . CLC 66; DAM MULT;
HLC
See also CA 131; 53-56; CANR 58;
DLB 113; HW

Castelvetro, Lodovico   1505-1571 . . . . LC 12

Castiglione, Baldassare   1478-1529 . . . LC 12

Castle, Robert
See Hamilton, Edmond

Castro, Guillen de   1569-1631 . . . . LC 19

Castro, Rosalia de
1837-1885 . . . . . . NCLC 3; DAM MULT

Cather, Willa
See Cather, Willa Sibert

Cather, Willa Sibert
1873-1947 .... **TCLC 1, 11, 31; DA;**
DAB; DAC; DAM MST, NOV; SSC 2;
WLC
See also CA 104; 128; CDALB 1865-1917;
DLB 9, 54, 78; DLBD 1; MTCW;
SATA 30

Cato, Marcus Porcius
234B.C.-149B.C. .... **CMLC 21**

Catton, (Charles) Bruce
1899-1978 .... **CLC 35**
See also AITN 1; CA 5-8R; 81-84;
CANR 7; DLB 17; SATA 2;
SATA-Obit 24

Catullus c. 84B.C.-c. 54B.C. ..... **CMLC 18**

Cauldwell, Frank
See King, Francis (Henry)

Caunitz, William J. 1933-1996 ..... **CLC 34**
See also BEST 89:3; CA 125; 130; 152;
INT 130

Causley, Charles (Stanley) 1917-..... **CLC 7**
See also CA 9-12R; CANR 5, 35; CLR 30;
DLB 27; MTCW; SATA 3, 66

Caute, David 1936-.... **CLC 29; DAM NOV**
See also CA 1-4R; CAAS 4; CANR 1, 33;
DLB 14

Cavafy, C(onstantine) P(eter)
1863-1933 .... **TCLC 2, 7; DAM POET**
See also Kavafis, Konstantinos Petrou
See also CA 148

Cavallo, Evelyn
See Spark, Muriel (Sarah)

Cavanna, Betty .... **CLC 12**
See also Harrison, Elizabeth Cavanna
See also JRDA; MAICYA; SAAS 4;
SATA 1, 30

Cavendish, Margaret Lucas
1623-1673 .... **LC 30**
See also DLB 131

Caxton, William 1421(?)-1491(?)..... **LC 17**
See also DLB 170

Cayrol, Jean 1911-................ **CLC 11**
See also CA 89-92; DLB 83

Cela, Camilo Jose
1916-..... **CLC 4, 13, 59; DAM MULT;**
HLC
See also BEST 90:2; CA 21-24R; CAAS 10;
CANR 21, 32; DLBY 89; HW; MTCW

Celan, Paul ..... **CLC 10, 19, 53, 82; PC 10**
See also Antschel, Paul
See also DLB 69

Celine, Louis-Ferdinand
.... **CLC 1, 3, 4, 7, 9, 15, 47**
See also Destouches, Louis-Ferdinand
See also DLB 72

Cellini, Benvenuto 1500-1571 .... **LC 7**

Cendrars, Blaise .... **CLC 18**
See also Sauser-Hall, Frederic

Cernuda (y Bidon), Luis
1902-1963 .... **CLC 54; DAM POET**
See also CA 131; 89-92; DLB 134; HW

Cervantes (Saavedra), Miguel de
1547-1616 .... **LC 6, 23; DA; DAB;**
DAC; DAM MST, NOV; SSC 12; WLC

Cesaire, Aime (Fernand)
1913-.............. **CLC 19, 32; BLC;**
DAM MULT, POET
See also BW 2; CA 65-68; CANR 24, 43;
MTCW

Chabon, Michael 1963-........... **CLC 55**
See also CA 139; CANR 57

Chabrol, Claude 1930-............ **CLC 16**
See also CA 110

Challans, Mary 1905-1983
See Renault, Mary
See also CA 81-84; 111; SATA 23;
SATA-Obit 36

Challis, George
See Faust, Frederick (Schiller)

Chambers, Aidan 1934-........... **CLC 35**
See also CA 25-28R; CANR 12, 31, 58;
JRDA; MAICYA; SAAS 12; SATA 1, 69

Chambers, James 1948-
See Cliff, Jimmy
See also CA 124

Chambers, Jessie
See Lawrence, D(avid) H(erbert Richards)

Chambers, Robert W. 1865-1933... **TCLC 41**

Chandler, Raymond (Thornton)
1888-1959 .... **TCLC 1, 7; SSC 23**
See also CA 104; 129; CDALB 1929-1941;
DLBD 6; MTCW

Chang, Jung 1952-.............. **CLC 71**
See also CA 142

Channing, William Ellery
1780-1842 .... **NCLC 17**
See also DLB 1, 59

Chaplin, Charles Spencer
1889-1977 .... **CLC 16**
See also Chaplin, Charlie
See also CA 81-84; 73-76

Chaplin, Charlie
See Chaplin, Charles Spencer
See also DLB 44

Chapman, George
1559(?)-1634 ..... **LC 22; DAM DRAM**
See also DLB 62, 121

Chapman, Graham 1941-1989 ...... **CLC 21**
See also Monty Python
See also CA 116; 129; CANR 35

Chapman, John Jay 1862-1933 ..... **TCLC 7**
See also CA 104

Chapman, Lee
See Bradley, Marion Zimmer

Chapman, Walker
See Silverberg, Robert

Chappell, Fred (Davis) 1936-.... **CLC 40, 78**
See also CA 5-8R; CAAS 4; CANR 8, 33;
DLB 6, 105

Char, Rene(-Emile)
1907-1988 .... **CLC 9, 11, 14, 55;**
DAM POET
See also CA 13-16R; 124; CANR 32;
MTCW

Charby, Jay
See Ellison, Harlan (Jay)

Chardin, Pierre Teilhard de
See Teilhard de Chardin, (Marie Joseph)
Pierre

Charles I 1600-1649 .... **LC 13**

Charyn, Jerome 1937-........ **CLC 5, 8, 18**
See also CA 5-8R; CAAS 1; CANR 7;
DLBY 83; MTCW

Chase, Mary (Coyle) 1907-1981 ..... **DC 1**
See also CA 77-80; 105; SATA 17;
SATA-Obit 29

Chase, Mary Ellen 1887-1973....... **CLC 2**
See also CA 13-16; 41-44R; CAP 1;
SATA 10

Chase, Nicholas
See Hyde, Anthony

Chateaubriand, Francois Rene de
1768-1848 .... **NCLC 3**
See also DLB 119

Chatterje, Sarat Chandra 1876-1936(?)
See Chatterji, Saratchandra
See also CA 109

Chatterji, Bankim Chandra
1838-1894 .... **NCLC 19**

Chatterji, Saratchandra .... **TCLC 13**
See also Chatterje, Sarat Chandra

Chatterton, Thomas
1752-1770 .... **LC 3; DAM POET**
See also DLB 109

Chatwin, (Charles) Bruce
1940-1989 .. **CLC 28, 57, 59; DAM POP**
See also AAYA 4; BEST 90:1; CA 85-88;
127

Chaucer, Daniel
See Ford, Ford Madox

Chaucer, Geoffrey
1340(?)-1400 .... **LC 17; DA; DAB;**
DAC; DAM MST, POET; PC 19
See also CDBLB Before 1660; DLB 146;
YABC

Chaviaras, Strates 1935-
See Haviaras, Stratis
See also CA 105

Chayefsky, Paddy .... **CLC 23**
See also Chayefsky, Sidney
See also DLB 7, 44; DLBY 81

Chayefsky, Sidney 1923-1981
See Chayefsky, Paddy
See also CA 9-12R; 104; CANR 18;
DAM DRAM

Chedid, Andree 1920-............. **CLC 47**
See also CA 145

Cheever, John
1912-1982 ...... **CLC 3, 7, 8, 11, 15, 25,**
64; DA; DAB; DAC; DAM MST, NOV,
POP; SSC 1; WLC
See also CA 5-8R; 106; CABS 1; CANR 5,
27; CDALB 1941-1968; DLB 2, 102;
DLBY 80, 82; INT CANR-5; MTCW

Cheever, Susan 1943-........... **CLC 18, 48**
See also CA 103; CANR 27, 51; DLBY 82;
INT CANR-27

Chekhonte, Antosha
See Chekhov, Anton (Pavlovich)

Chekhov, Anton (Pavlovich)
1860-1904 ..... **TCLC 3, 10, 31, 55; DA;**
DAB; DAC; DAM DRAM, MST; SSC 2;
WLC
See also CA 104; 124; SATA 90

Chernyshevsky, Nikolay Gavrilovich
1828-1889 . . . . NCLC 1

Cherry, Carolyn Janice   1942-
See Cherryh, C. J.
See also CA 65-68; CANR 10

Cherryh, C. J. . . . . CLC 35
See Cherry, Carolyn Janice
See also DLBY 80; SATA 93

Chesnutt, Charles W(addell)
1858-1932 . . . . TCLC 5, 39; BLC;
DAM MULT; SSC 7
See also BW 1; CA 106; 125; DLB 12, 50,
78; MTCW

Chester, Alfred   1929(?)-1971. . . . . . . CLC 49
See also CA 33-36R; DLB 130

Chesterton, G(ilbert) K(eith)
1874-1936 . . . . TCLC 1, 6, 64;
DAM NOV, POET; SSC 1
See also CA 104; 132; CDBLB 1914-1945;
DLB 10, 19, 34, 70, 98, 149, 178; MTCW;
SATA 27

Chiang Pin-chin   1904-1986
See Ding Ling
See also CA 118

Ch'ien Chung-shu   1910- . . . . CLC 22
See also CA 130; MTCW

Child, L. Maria
See Child, Lydia Maria

Child, Lydia Maria   1802-1880 . . . . NCLC 6
See also DLB 1, 74; SATA 67

Child, Mrs.
See Child, Lydia Maria

Child, Philip   1898-1978 . . . . CLC 19, 68
See also CA 13-14; CAP 1; SATA 47

Childers, (Robert) Erskine
1870-1922 . . . . TCLC 65
See also CA 113; 153; DLB 70

Childress, Alice
1920-1994 . . . . CLC 12, 15, 86, 96; BLC;
DAM DRAM, MULT, NOV; DC 4
See also AAYA 8; BW 2; CA 45-48; 146;
CANR 3, 27, 50; CLR 14; DLB 7, 38;
JRDA; MAICYA; MTCW; SATA 7, 48,
81

Chin, Frank (Chew, Jr.)   1940- . . . . DC 7
See also CA 33-36R; DAM MULT

Chislett, (Margaret) Anne   1943- . . . . CLC 34
See also CA 151

Chitty, Thomas Willes   1926- . . . . CLC 11
See also Hinde, Thomas
See also CA 5-8R

Chivers, Thomas Holley
1809-1858 . . . . NCLC 49
See also DLB 3

Chomette, Rene Lucien   1898-1981
See Clair, Rene
See also CA 103

Chopin, Kate
. . . . TCLC 5, 14; DA; DAB; SSC 8
See also Chopin, Katherine
See also CDALB 1865-1917; DLB 12, 78;
YABC

Chopin, Katherine   1851-1904
See Chopin, Kate
See also CA 104; 122; DAC; DAM MST,
NOV

Chretien de Troyes
c. 12th cent. - . . . . CMLC 10

Christie
See Ichikawa, Kon

Christie, Agatha (Mary Clarissa)
1890-1976 . . . . . . CLC 1, 6, 8, 12, 39, 48;
DAB; DAC; DAM NOV
See also AAYA 9; AITN 1, 2; CA 17-20R;
61-64; CANR 10, 37; CDBLB 1914-1945;
DLB 13, 77; MTCW; SATA 36

Christie, (Ann) Philippa
See Pearce, Philippa
See also CA 5-8R; CANR 4

Christine de Pizan   1365(?)-1431(?) . . . . LC 9

Chubb, Elmer
See Masters, Edgar Lee

Chulkov, Mikhail Dmitrievich
1743-1792 . . . . LC 2
See also DLB 150

Churchill, Caryl   1938- . . . CLC 31, 55; DC 5
See also CA 102; CANR 22, 46; DLB 13;
MTCW

Churchill, Charles   1731-1764. . . . . LC 3
See also DLB 109

Chute, Carolyn   1947- . . . . CLC 39
See also CA 123

Ciardi, John (Anthony)
1916-1986 . . . . CLC 10, 40, 44;
DAM POET
See also CA 5-8R; 118; CAAS 2; CANR 5,
33; CLR 19; DLB 5; DLBY 86;
INT CANR-5; MAICYA; MTCW;
SATA 1, 65; SATA-Obit 46

Cicero, Marcus Tullius
106B.C.-43B.C. . . . . CMLC 3

Cimino, Michael   1943- . . . . CLC 16
See also CA 105

Cioran, E(mil) M.   1911-1995. . . . . . . CLC 64
See also CA 25-28R; 149

Cisneros, Sandra
1954- . . . . . CLC 69; DAM MULT; HLC
See also AAYA 9; CA 131; DLB 122, 152;
HW

Cixous, Helene   1937- . . . . CLC 92
See also CA 126; CANR 55; DLB 83;
MTCW

Clair, Rene. CLC 20
See also Chomette, Rene Lucien

Clampitt, Amy   1920-1994 . . . CLC 32; PC 19
See also CA 110; 146; CANR 29; DLB 105

Clancy, Thomas L., Jr.   1947-
See Clancy, Tom
See also CA 125; 131; INT 131; MTCW

Clancy, Tom. . . . . CLC 45; DAM NOV, POP
See also Clancy, Thomas L., Jr.
See also AAYA 9; BEST 89:1, 90:1

Clare, John
1793-1864 . . . . NCLC 9; DAB;
DAM POET
See also DLB 55, 96

Clarin
See Alas (y Urena), Leopoldo (Enrique
Garcia)

Clark, Al C.
See Goines, Donald

Clark, (Robert) Brian   1932-. . . . . . . CLC 29
See also CA 41-44R

Clark, Curt
See Westlake, Donald E(dwin)

Clark, Eleanor   1913-1996 . . . . CLC 5, 19
See also CA 9-12R; 151; CANR 41; DLB 6

Clark, J. P.
See Clark, John Pepper
See also DLB 117

Clark, John Pepper
1935- . . . . CLC 38; BLC; DAM DRAM,
MULT; DC 5
See also Clark, J. P.
See also BW 1; CA 65-68; CANR 16

Clark, M. R.
See Clark, Mavis Thorpe

Clark, Mavis Thorpe   1909- . . . . CLC 12
See also CA 57-60; CANR 8, 37; CLR 30;
MAICYA; SAAS 5; SATA 8, 74

Clark, Walter Van Tilburg
1909-1971 . . . . CLC 28
See also CA 9-12R; 33-36R; DLB 9;
SATA 8

Clarke, Arthur C(harles)
1917- . . . . CLC 1, 4, 13, 18, 35;
DAM POP; SSC 3
See also AAYA 4; CA 1-4R; CANR 2, 28,
55; JRDA; MAICYA; MTCW; SATA 13,
70

Clarke, Austin
1896-1974 . . . . . . CLC 6, 9; DAM POET
See also CA 29-32; 49-52; CAP 2; DLB 10,
20

Clarke, Austin C(hesterfield)
1934- . . . . CLC 8, 53; BLC; DAC;
DAM MULT
See also BW 1; CA 25-28R; CAAS 16;
CANR 14, 32; DLB 53, 125

Clarke, Gillian   1937- . . . . CLC 61
See also CA 106; DLB 40

Clarke, Marcus (Andrew Hislop)
1846-1881 . . . . NCLC 19

Clarke, Shirley   1925- . . . . CLC 16

Clash, The
See Headon, (Nicky) Topper; Jones, Mick;
Simonon, Paul; Strummer, Joe

Claudel, Paul (Louis Charles Marie)
1868-1955 . . . . TCLC 2, 10
See also CA 104

Clavell, James (duMaresq)
1925-1994 . . . . CLC 6, 25, 87;
DAM NOV, POP
See also CA 25-28R; 146; CANR 26, 48;
MTCW

Cleaver, (Leroy) Eldridge
1935- . . . . . CLC 30; BLC; DAM MULT
See also BW 1; CA 21-24R; CANR 16

Cleese, John (Marwood)   1939- . . . . . CLC 21
See also Monty Python
See also CA 112; 116; CANR 35; MTCW

Cleishbotham, Jebediah
See Scott, Walter

Cleland, John   1710-1789 . . . . LC 2
See also DLB 39

Constant (de Rebecque), (Henri) Benjamin
1767-1830 . . . . **NCLC 6**
See also DLB 119

Conybeare, Charles Augustus
See Eliot, T(homas) S(tearns)

Cook, Michael 1933- . . . . **CLC 58**
See also CA 93-96; DLB 53

Cook, Robin 1940- . . . . **CLC 14; DAM POP**
See also BEST 90:2; CA 108; 111;
CANR 41; INT 111

Cook, Roy
See Silverberg, Robert

Cooke, Elizabeth 1948- . . . . **CLC 55**
See also CA 129

Cooke, John Esten 1830-1886 . . . . . **NCLC 5**
See also DLB 3

Cooke, John Estes
See Baum, L(yman) Frank

Cooke, M. E.
See Creasey, John

Cooke, Margaret
See Creasey, John

Cook-Lynn, Elizabeth
1930- . . . . **CLC 93; DAM MULT**
See also CA 133; DLB 175; NNAL

Cooney, Ray . . . . **CLC 62**

Cooper, Douglas 1960- . . . . **CLC 86**

Cooper, Henry St. John
See Creasey, John

Cooper, J(oan) California
. . . . **CLC 56; DAM MULT**
See also AAYA 12; BW 1; CA 125;
CANR 55

Cooper, James Fenimore
1789-1851 . . . . **NCLC 1, 27, 54**
See also CDALB 1640-1865; DLB 3;
SATA 19

Coover, Robert (Lowell)
1932- . . . . **CLC 3, 7, 15, 32, 46, 87;**
DAM NOV; SSC 15
See also CA 45-48; CANR 3, 37, 58;
DLB 2; DLBY 81; MTCW

Copeland, Stewart (Armstrong)
1952- . . . . **CLC 26**

Coppard, A(lfred) E(dgar)
1878-1957 . . . . **TCLC 5; SSC 21**
See also CA 114; DLB 162; 1

Coppee, Francois 1842-1908 . . . . . . **TCLC 25**

Coppola, Francis Ford 1939- . . . . **CLC 16**
See also CA 77-80; CANR 40; DLB 44

Corbiere, Tristan 1845-1875 . . . . . **NCLC 43**

Corcoran, Barbara 1911- . . . . **CLC 17**
See also AAYA 14; CA 21-24R; CAAS 2;
CANR 11, 28, 48; DLB 52; JRDA;
SAAS 20; SATA 3, 77

Cordelier, Maurice
See Giraudoux, (Hippolyte) Jean

Corelli, Marie 1855-1924 . . . . **TCLC 51**
See also Mackay, Mary
See also DLB 34, 156

Corman, Cid . . . . **CLC 9**
See also Corman, Sidney
See also CAAS 2; DLB 5

Corman, Sidney 1924-
See Corman, Cid
See also CA 85-88; CANR 44; DAM POET

Cormier, Robert (Edmund)
1925- . . . . **CLC 12, 30; DA; DAB; DAC;**
DAM MST, NOV
See also AAYA 3, 19; CA 1-4R; CANR 5,
23; CDALB 1968-1988; CLR 12; DLB 52;
INT CANR-23; JRDA; MAICYA;
MTCW; SATA 10, 45, 83

Corn, Alfred (DeWitt III) 1943- . . . . **CLC 33**
See also CA 104; CAAS 25; CANR 44;
DLB 120; DLBY 80

Corneille, Pierre
1606-1684 . . . . **LC 28; DAB; DAM MST**

Cornwell, David (John Moore)
1931- . . . . **CLC 9, 15; DAM POP**
See also le Carre, John
See also CA 5-8R; CANR 13, 33; MTCW

Corso, (Nunzio) Gregory 1930- . . . **CLC 1, 11**
See also CA 5-8R; CANR 41; DLB 5, 16;
MTCW

Cortazar, Julio
1914-1984 . . . . . . **CLC 2, 3, 5, 10, 13, 15,**
33, 34, 92; DAM MULT, NOV; HLC;
SSC 7
See also CA 21-24R; CANR 12, 32;
DLB 113; HW; MTCW

CORTES, HERNAN 1484-1547 . . . . . **LC 31**

Corwin, Cecil
See Kornbluth, C(yril) M.

Cosic, Dobrica 1921- . . . . **CLC 14**
See also CA 122; 138

Costain, Thomas B(ertram)
1885-1965 . . . . **CLC 30**
See also CA 5-8R; 25-28R; DLB 9

Costantini, Humberto
1924(?)-1987 . . . . **CLC 49**
See also CA 131; 122; HW

Costello, Elvis 1955- . . . . **CLC 21**

Cotes, Cecil V.
See Duncan, Sara Jeannette

Cotter, Joseph Seamon Sr.
1861-1949 . . . . **TCLC 28; BLC;**
DAM MULT
See also BW 1; CA 124; DLB 50

Couch, Arthur Thomas Quiller
See Quiller-Couch, Arthur Thomas

Coulton, James
See Hansen, Joseph

Couperus, Louis (Marie Anne)
1863-1923 . . . . **TCLC 15**
See also CA 115

Coupland, Douglas
1961- . . . . **CLC 85; DAC; DAM POP**
See also CA 142; CANR 57

Court, Wesli
See Turco, Lewis (Putnam)

Courtenay, Bryce 1933- . . . . **CLC 59**
See also CA 138

Courtney, Robert
See Ellison, Harlan (Jay)

Cousteau, Jacques-Yves 1910- . . . . . . **CLC 30**
See also CA 65-68; CANR 15; MTCW;
SATA 38

Coward, Noel (Peirce)
1899-1973 . . . . **CLC 1, 9, 29, 51;**
DAM DRAM
See also AITN 1; CA 17-18; 41-44R;
CANR 35; CAP 2; CDBLB 1914-1945;
DLB 10; MTCW

Cowley, Malcolm 1898-1989 . . . . **CLC 39**
See also CA 5-8R; 128; CANR 3, 55;
DLB 4, 48; DLBY 81, 89; MTCW

Cowper, William
1731-1800 . . . . . . **NCLC 8; DAM POET**
See also DLB 104, 109

Cox, William Trevor
1928- . . . . **CLC 9, 14, 71; DAM NOV**
See also Trevor, William
See also CA 9-12R; CANR 4, 37, 55;
DLB 14; INT CANR-37; MTCW

Coyne, P. J.
See Masters, Hilary

Cozzens, James Gould
1903-1978 . . . . **CLC 1, 4, 11, 92**
See also CA 9-12R; 81-84; CANR 19;
CDALB 1941-1968; DLB 9; DLBD 2;
DLBY 84; MTCW

Crabbe, George 1754-1832 . . . . **NCLC 26**
See also DLB 93

Craddock, Charles Egbert
See Murfree, Mary Noailles

Craig, A. A.
See Anderson, Poul (William)

Craik, Dinah Maria (Mulock)
1826-1887 . . . . **NCLC 38**
See also DLB 35, 163; MAICYA; SATA 34

Cram, Ralph Adams 1863-1942 . . . . **TCLC 45**

Crane, (Harold) Hart
1899-1932 . . . . **TCLC 2, 5; DA; DAB;**
DAC; DAM MST, POET; PC 3; WLC
See also CA 104; 127; CDALB 1917-1929;
DLB 4, 48; MTCW

Crane, R(onald) S(almon)
1886-1967 . . . . **CLC 27**
See also CA 85-88; DLB 63

Crane, Stephen (Townley)
1871-1900 . . . . **TCLC 11, 17, 32; DA;**
DAB; DAC; DAM MST, NOV, POET;
SSC 7; WLC
See also AAYA 21; CA 109; 140;
CDALB 1865-1917; DLB 12, 54, 78; 2

Crase, Douglas 1944- . . . . **CLC 58**
See also CA 106

Crashaw, Richard 1612(?)-1649 . . . . . **LC 24**
See also DLB 126

Craven, Margaret
1901-1980 . . . . **CLC 17; DAC**
See also CA 103

Crawford, F(rancis) Marion
1854-1909 . . . . **TCLC 10**
See also CA 107; DLB 71

Crawford, Isabella Valancy
1850-1887 . . . . **NCLC 12**
See also DLB 92

Crayon, Geoffrey
See Irving, Washington

Creasey, John 1908-1973 . . . . **CLC 11**
See also CA 5-8R; 41-44R; CANR 8;
DLB 77; MTCW

Crebillon, Claude Prosper Jolyot de (fils)
1707-1777 . . . . **LC 28**

Credo
See Creasey, John

Creeley, Robert (White)
1926- . . . . . **CLC 1, 2, 4, 8, 11, 15, 36, 78;
DAM POET**
See also CA 1-4R; CAAS 10; CANR 23, 43;
DLB 5, 16, 169; MTCW

Crews, Harry (Eugene)
1935- . . . . **CLC 6, 23, 49**
See also AITN 1; CA 25-28R; CANR 20,
57; DLB 6, 143; MTCW

Crichton, (John) Michael
1942- . . . . **CLC 2, 6, 54, 90; DAM NOV,
POP**
See also AAYA 10; AITN 2; CA 25-28R;
CANR 13, 40, 54; DLBY 81;
INT CANR-13; JRDA; MTCW; SATA 9,
88

Crispin, Edmund . . . . **CLC 22**
See also Montgomery, (Robert) Bruce
See also DLB 87

Cristofer, Michael
1945(?)- . . . . **CLC 28; DAM DRAM**
See also CA 110; 152; DLB 7

Croce, Benedetto 1866-1952 . . . . . . **TCLC 37**
See also CA 120; 155

Crockett, David 1786-1836 . . . . **NCLC 8**
See also DLB 3, 11

Crockett, Davy
See Crockett, David

Crofts, Freeman Wills
1879-1957 . . . . **TCLC 55**
See also CA 115; DLB 77

Croker, John Wilson 1780-1857 . . **NCLC 10**
See also DLB 110

Crommelynck, Fernand 1885-1970 . . **CLC 75**
See also CA 89-92

Cronin, A(rchibald) J(oseph)
1896-1981 . . . . **CLC 32**
See also CA 1-4R; 102; CANR 5; SATA 47;
SATA-Obit 25

Cross, Amanda
See Heilbrun, Carolyn G(old)

Crothers, Rachel 1878(?)-1958 . . . . . **TCLC 19**
See also CA 113; DLB 7

Croves, Hal
See Traven, B.

Crow Dog, Mary (Ellen) (?)- . . . . **CLC 93**
See also Brave Bird, Mary
See also CA 154

Crowfield, Christopher
See Stowe, Harriet (Elizabeth) Beecher

Crowley, Aleister . . . . **TCLC 7**
See also Crowley, Edward Alexander

Crowley, Edward Alexander 1875-1947
See Crowley, Aleister
See also CA 104

Crowley, John 1942- . . . . **CLC 57**
See also CA 61-64; CANR 43; DLBY 82;
SATA 65

Crud
See Crumb, R(obert)

Crumarums
See Crumb, R(obert)

Crumb, R(obert) 1943- . . . . **CLC 17**
See also CA 106

Crumbum
See Crumb, R(obert)

Crumski
See Crumb, R(obert)

Crum the Bum
See Crumb, R(obert)

Crunk
See Crumb, R(obert)

Crustt
See Crumb, R(obert)

Cryer, Gretchen (Kiger) 1935- . . . . . **CLC 21**
See also CA 114; 123

Csath, Geza 1887-1919 . . . . **TCLC 13**
See also CA 111

Cudlip, David 1933- . . . . **CLC 34**

Cullen, Countee
1903-1946 . . . . . . **TCLC 4, 37; BLC; DA;
DAC; DAM MST, MULT, POET**
See also BW 1; CA 108; 124;
CDALB 1917-1929; DLB 4, 48, 51;
MTCW; SATA 18; YABC

Cum, R.
See Crumb, R(obert)

Cummings, Bruce F(rederick) 1889-1919
See Barbellion, W. N. P.
See also CA 123

Cummings, E(dward) E(stlin)
1894-1962 . . . . . . **CLC 1, 3, 8, 12, 15, 68;
DA; DAB; DAC; DAM MST, POET;
PC 5; WLC 2**
See also CA 73-76; CANR 31;
CDALB 1929-1941; DLB 4, 48; MTCW

Cunha, Euclides (Rodrigues Pimenta) da
1866-1909 . . . . **TCLC 24**
See also CA 123

Cunningham, E. V.
See Fast, Howard (Melvin)

Cunningham, J(ames) V(incent)
1911-1985 . . . . **CLC 3, 31**
See also CA 1-4R; 115; CANR 1; DLB 5

Cunningham, Julia (Woolfolk)
1916- . . . . **CLC 12**
See also CA 9-12R; CANR 4, 19, 36;
JRDA; MAICYA; SAAS 2; SATA 1, 26

Cunningham, Michael 1952- . . . . **CLC 34**
See also CA 136

Cunninghame Graham, R(obert) B(ontine)
1852-1936 . . . . **TCLC 19**
See also Graham, R(obert) B(ontine)
Cunninghame
See also CA 119; DLB 98

Currie, Ellen 19(?)- . . . . **CLC 44**

Curtin, Philip
See Lowndes, Marie Adelaide (Belloc)

Curtis, Price
See Ellison, Harlan (Jay)

Cutrate, Joe
See Spiegelman, Art

Czaczkes, Shmuel Yosef
See Agnon, S(hmuel) Y(osef Halevi)

Dabrowska, Maria (Szumska)
1889-1965 . . . . **CLC 15**
See also CA 106

Dabydeen, David 1955- . . . . **CLC 34**
See also BW 1; CA 125; CANR 56

Dacey, Philip 1939- . . . . **CLC 51**
See also CA 37-40R; CAAS 17; CANR 14,
32; DLB 105

Dagerman, Stig (Halvard)
1923-1954 . . . . **TCLC 17**
See also CA 117; 155

Dahl, Roald
1916-1990 . . . . . . **CLC 1, 6, 18, 79; DAB;
DAC; DAM MST, NOV, POP**
See also AAYA 15; CA 1-4R; 133;
CANR 6, 32, 37; CLR 1, 7, 41; DLB 139;
JRDA; MAICYA; MTCW; SATA 1, 26,
73; SATA-Obit 65

Dahlberg, Edward 1900-1977 . . . **CLC 1, 7, 14**
See also CA 9-12R; 69-72; CANR 31;
DLB 48; MTCW

Dale, Colin . . . . **TCLC 18**
See also Lawrence, T(homas) E(dward)

Dale, George E.
See Asimov, Isaac

Daly, Elizabeth 1878-1967 . . . . **CLC 52**
See also CA 23-24; 25-28R; CAP 2

Daly, Maureen 1921- . . . . **CLC 17**
See also AAYA 5; CANR 37; JRDA;
MAICYA; SAAS 1; SATA 2

Damas, Leon-Gontran 1912-1978 . . . **CLC 84**
See also BW 1; CA 125; 73-76

Dana, Richard Henry Sr.
1787-1879 . . . . **NCLC 53**

Daniel, Samuel 1562(?)-1619 . . . . **LC 24**
See also DLB 62

Daniels, Brett
See Adler, Renata

Dannay, Frederic
1905-1982 . . . . **CLC 11; DAM POP**
See also Queen, Ellery
See also CA 1-4R; 107; CANR 1, 39;
DLB 137; MTCW

D'Annunzio, Gabriele
1863-1938 . . . . **TCLC 6, 40**
See also CA 104; 155

Danois, N. le
See Gourmont, Remy (-Marie-Charles) de

d'Antibes, Germain
See Simenon, Georges (Jacques Christian)

Danticat, Edwidge 1969- . . . . **CLC 94**
See also CA 152

Danvers, Dennis 1947- . . . . **CLC 70**

Danziger, Paula 1944- . . . . **CLC 21**
See also AAYA 4; CA 112; 115; CANR 37;
CLR 20; JRDA; MAICYA; SATA 36,
63; SATA-Brief 30

Da Ponte, Lorenzo 1749-1838 . . . . **NCLC 50**

Dario, Ruben
1867-1916 . . . . . **TCLC 4; DAM MULT;
HLC; PC 15**
See also CA 131; HW; MTCW

Darley, George 1795-1846 . . . . **NCLC 2**
See also DLB 96

Dixon, Paige
See Corcoran, Barbara

Dixon, Stephen 1936- . . . . . **CLC 52; SSC 16**
See also CA 89-92; CANR 17, 40, 54;
DLB 130

Dobell, Sydney Thompson
1824-1874 . . . . **NCLC 43**
See also DLB 32

Doblin, Alfred . . . . **TCLC 13**
See also Doeblin, Alfred

Dobrolyubov, Nikolai Alexandrovich
1836-1861 . . . . **NCLC 5**

Dobyns, Stephen 1941- . . . . **CLC 37**
See also CA 45-48; CANR 2, 18

Doctorow, E(dgar) L(aurence)
1931- . . . . . **CLC 6, 11, 15, 18, 37, 44, 65;**
DAM NOV, POP
See also AITN 2; BEST 89:3; CA 45-48;
CANR 2, 33, 51; CDALB 1968-1988;
DLB 2, 28, 173; DLBY 80; MTCW

Dodgson, Charles Lutwidge 1832-1898
See Carroll, Lewis
See also CLR 2; DA; DAB; DAC;
DAM MST, NOV, POET; MAICYA; 2

Dodson, Owen (Vincent)
1914-1983 . . . . **CLC 79; BLC;**
DAM MULT
See also BW 1; CA 65-68; 110; CANR 24;
DLB 76

Doeblin, Alfred 1878-1957 . . . . **TCLC 13**
See also Doblin, Alfred
See also CA 110; 141; DLB 66

Doerr, Harriet 1910- . . . . **CLC 34**
See also CA 117; 122; CANR 47; INT 122

Domecq, H(onorio) Bustos
See Bioy Casares, Adolfo; Borges, Jorge
Luis

Domini, Rey
See Lorde, Audre (Geraldine)

Dominique
See Proust, (Valentin-Louis-George-Eugene-)
Marcel

Don, A
See Stephen, Leslie

Donaldson, Stephen R.
1947- . . . . **CLC 46; DAM POP**
See also CA 89-92; CANR 13, 55;
INT CANR-13

Donleavy, J(ames) P(atrick)
1926- . . . . **CLC 1, 4, 6, 10, 45**
See also AITN 2; CA 9-12R; CANR 24, 49;
DLB 6, 173; INT CANR-24; MTCW

Donne, John
1572-1631 . . . . **LC 10, 24; DA; DAB;**
DAC; DAM MST, POET; PC 1
See also CDBLB Before 1660; DLB 121,
151

Donnell, David 1939(?)- . . . . **CLC 34**

Donoghue, P. S.
See Hunt, E(verette) Howard, (Jr.)

Donoso (Yanez), Jose
1924-1996 . . . . **CLC 4, 8, 11, 32, 99;**
DAM MULT; HLC
See also CA 81-84; 155; CANR 32;
DLB 113; HW; MTCW

Donovan, John 1928-1992 . . . . **CLC 35**
See also AAYA 20; CA 97-100; 137;
CLR 3; MAICYA; SATA 72;
SATA-Brief 29

Don Roberto
See Cunninghame Graham, R(obert)
B(ontine)

Doolittle, Hilda
1886-1961 . . . . . **CLC 3, 8, 14, 31, 34, 73;**
DA; DAC; DAM MST, POET; PC 5;
WLC
See also H. D.
See also CA 97-100; CANR 35; DLB 4, 45;
MTCW

Dorfman, Ariel
1942- . . . . **CLC 48, 77; DAM MULT;**
HLC
See also CA 124; 130; HW; INT 130

Dorn, Edward (Merton) 1929- . . . **CLC 10, 18**
See also CA 93-96; CANR 42; DLB 5;
INT 93-96

Dorsan, Luc
See Simenon, Georges (Jacques Christian)

Dorsange, Jean
See Simenon, Georges (Jacques Christian)

Dos Passos, John (Roderigo)
1896-1970 . . . . . . **CLC 1, 4, 8, 11, 15, 25,**
34, 82; DA; DAB; DAC; DAM MST,
NOV; WLC
See also CA 1-4R; 29-32R; CANR 3;
CDALB 1929-1941; DLB 4, 9; DLBD 1;
DLBY 96; MTCW

Dossage, Jean
See Simenon, Georges (Jacques Christian)

Dostoevsky, Fedor Mikhailovich
1821-1881 . . . . . . **NCLC 2, 7, 21, 33, 43;**
DA; DAB; DAC; DAM MST, NOV;
SSC 2; WLC

Doughty, Charles M(ontagu)
1843-1926 . . . . **TCLC 27**
See also CA 115; DLB 19, 57, 174

Douglas, Ellen . . . . **CLC 73**
See also Haxton, Josephine Ayres;
Williamson, Ellen Douglas

Douglas, Gavin 1475(?)-1522 . . . . **LC 20**

Douglas, Keith 1920-1944 . . . . **TCLC 40**
See also DLB 27

Douglas, Leonard
See Bradbury, Ray (Douglas)

Douglas, Michael
See Crichton, (John) Michael

Douglas, Norman 1868-1952 . . . . . . **TCLC 68**

Douglass, Frederick
1817(?)-1895 . . . . **NCLC 7, 55; BLC; DA;**
DAC; DAM MST, MULT; WLC
See also CDALB 1640-1865; DLB 1, 43, 50,
79; SATA 29

Dourado, (Waldomiro Freitas) Autran
1926- . . . . **CLC 23, 60**
See also CA 25-28R; CANR 34

Dourado, Waldomiro Autran
See Dourado, (Waldomiro Freitas) Autran

Dove, Rita (Frances)
1952- . . . . **CLC 50, 81; DAM MULT,**
POET; PC 6
See also BW 2; CA 109; CAAS 19;
CANR 27, 42; DLB 120

Dowell, Coleman 1925-1985 . . . . **CLC 60**
See also CA 25-28R; 117; CANR 10;
DLB 130

Dowson, Ernest (Christopher)
1867-1900 . . . . **TCLC 4**
See also CA 105; 150; DLB 19, 135

Doyle, A. Conan
See Doyle, Arthur Conan

Doyle, Arthur Conan
1859-1930 . . . . **TCLC 7; DA; DAB;**
DAC; DAM MST, NOV; SSC 12; WLC
See also AAYA 14; CA 104; 122;
CDBLB 1890-1914; DLB 18, 70, 156, 178;
MTCW; SATA 24

Doyle, Conan
See Doyle, Arthur Conan

Doyle, John
See Graves, Robert (von Ranke)

Doyle, Roddy 1958(?)- . . . . **CLC 81**
See also AAYA 14; CA 143

Doyle, Sir A. Conan
See Doyle, Arthur Conan

Doyle, Sir Arthur Conan
See Doyle, Arthur Conan

Dr. A
See Asimov, Isaac; Silverstein, Alvin

Drabble, Margaret
1939- . . . . **CLC 2, 3, 5, 8, 10, 22, 53;**
DAB; DAC; DAM MST, NOV, POP
See also CA 13-16R; CANR 18, 35;
CDBLB 1960 to Present; DLB 14, 155;
MTCW; SATA 48

Drapier, M. B.
See Swift, Jonathan

Drayham, James
See Mencken, H(enry) L(ouis)

Drayton, Michael 1563-1631 . . . . **LC 8**

Dreadstone, Carl
See Campbell, (John) Ramsey

Dreiser, Theodore (Herman Albert)
1871-1945 . . . . **TCLC 10, 18, 35; DA;**
DAC; DAM MST, NOV; WLC
See also CA 106; 132; CDALB 1865-1917;
DLB 9, 12, 102, 137; DLBD 1; MTCW

Drexler, Rosalyn 1926- . . . . **CLC 2, 6**
See also CA 81-84

Dreyer, Carl Theodor 1889-1968 . . . . **CLC 16**
See also CA 116

Drieu la Rochelle, Pierre(-Eugene)
1893-1945 . . . . **TCLC 21**
See also CA 117; DLB 72

Drinkwater, John 1882-1937 . . . . . . **TCLC 57**
See also CA 109; 149; DLB 10, 19, 149

Drop Shot
See Cable, George Washington

Droste-Hulshoff, Annette Freiin von
1797-1848 . . . . **NCLC 3**
See also DLB 133

Drummond, Walter
See Silverberg, Robert

Eckert, Allan W. 1931- .... **CLC 17**
See also AAYA 18; CA 13-16R; CANR 14,
45; INT CANR-14; SAAS 21; SATA 29,
91; SATA-Brief 27

Eckhart, Meister 1260(?)-1328(?) .. **CMLC 9**
See also DLB 115

Eckmar, F. R.
See de Hartog, Jan

Eco, Umberto
1932- ... **CLC 28, 60; DAM NOV, POP**
See also BEST 90:1; CA 77-80; CANR 12,
33, 55; MTCW

Eddison, E(ric) R(ucker)
1882-1945 .... **TCLC 15**
See also CA 109; 156

Eddy, Mary (Morse) Baker
1821-1910 .... **TCLC 71**
See also CA 113

Edel, (Joseph) Leon 1907- ...... **CLC 29, 34**
See also CA 1-4R; CANR 1, 22; DLB 103;
INT CANR-22

Eden, Emily 1797-1869 .... **NCLC 10**

Edgar, David
1948- .... **CLC 42; DAM DRAM**
See also CA 57-60; CANR 12; DLB 13;
MTCW

Edgerton, Clyde (Carlyle) 1944- .... **CLC 39**
See also AAYA 17; CA 118; 134; INT 134

Edgeworth, Maria 1768-1849... **NCLC 1, 51**
See also DLB 116, 159, 163; SATA 21

Edmonds, Paul
See Kuttner, Henry

Edmonds, Walter D(umaux) 1903- .. **CLC 35**
See also CA 5-8R; CANR 2; DLB 9;
MAICYA; SAAS 4; SATA 1, 27

Edmondson, Wallace
See Ellison, Harlan (Jay)

Edson, Russell .... **CLC 13**
See also CA 33-36R

Edwards, Bronwen Elizabeth
See Rose, Wendy

Edwards, G(erald) B(asil)
1899-1976 .... **CLC 25**
See also CA 110

Edwards, Gus 1939- .... **CLC 43**
See also CA 108; INT 108

Edwards, Jonathan
1703-1758 .... **LC 7; DA; DAC;
DAM MST**
See also DLB 24

Efron, Marina Ivanovna Tsvetaeva
See Tsvetaeva (Efron), Marina (Ivanovna)

Ehle, John (Marsden, Jr.) 1925- .... **CLC 27**
See also CA 9-12R

Ehrenbourg, Ilya (Grigoryevich)
See Ehrenburg, Ilya (Grigoryevich)

Ehrenburg, Ilya (Grigoryevich)
1891-1967 .... **CLC 18, 34, 62**
See also CA 102; 25-28R

Ehrenburg, Ilyo (Grigoryevich)
See Ehrenburg, Ilya (Grigoryevich)

Eich, Guenter 1907-1972 .... **CLC 15**
See also CA 111; 93-96; DLB 69, 124

Eichendorff, Joseph Freiherr von
1788-1857 .... **NCLC 8**
See also DLB 90

Eigner, Larry .... **CLC 9**
See also Eigner, Laurence (Joel)
See also CAAS 23; DLB 5

Eigner, Laurence (Joel) 1927-1996
See Eigner, Larry
See also CA 9-12R; 151; CANR 6

Einstein, Albert 1879-1955 .... **TCLC 65**
See also CA 121; 133; MTCW

Eiseley, Loren Corey 1907-1977 ..... **CLC 7**
See also AAYA 5; CA 1-4R; 73-76;
CANR 6

Eisenstadt, Jill 1963- .... **CLC 50**
See also CA 140

Eisenstein, Sergei (Mikhailovich)
1898-1948 .... **TCLC 57**
See also CA 114; 149

Eisner, Simon
See Kornbluth, C(yril) M.

Ekeloef, (Bengt) Gunnar
1907-1968 .... **CLC 27; DAM POET**
See also CA 123; 25-28R

Ekelof, (Bengt) Gunnar
See Ekeloef, (Bengt) Gunnar

Ekwensi, C. O. D.
See Ekwensi, Cyprian (Odiatu Duaka)

Ekwensi, Cyprian (Odiatu Duaka)
1921- ...... **CLC 4; BLC; DAM MULT**
See also BW 2; CA 29-32R; CANR 18, 42;
DLB 117; MTCW; SATA 66

Elaine .... **TCLC 18**
See also Leverson, Ada

El Crummo
See Crumb, R(obert)

Elia
See Lamb, Charles

Eliade, Mircea 1907-1986 .... **CLC 19**
See also CA 65-68; 119; CANR 30; MTCW

Eliot, A. D.
See Jewett, (Theodora) Sarah Orne

Eliot, Alice
See Jewett, (Theodora) Sarah Orne

Eliot, Dan
See Silverberg, Robert

Eliot, George
1819-1880 ..... **NCLC 4, 13, 23, 41, 49;
DA; DAB; DAC; DAM MST, NOV;
WLC**
See also CDBLB 1832-1890; DLB 21, 35, 55

Eliot, John 1604-1690 .... **LC 5**
See also DLB 24

Eliot, T(homas) S(tearns)
1888-1965 ..... **CLC 1, 2, 3, 6, 9, 10, 13,
15, 24, 34, 41, 55, 57; DA; DAB; DAC;
DAM DRAM, MST, POET; PC 5;
WLC 2**
See also CA 5-8R; 25-28R; CANR 41;
CDALB 1929-1941; DLB 7, 10, 45, 63;
DLBY 88; MTCW

Elizabeth 1866-1941 .... **TCLC 41**

Elkin, Stanley L(awrence)
1930-1995 ...... **CLC 4, 6, 9, 14, 27, 51,
91; DAM NOV, POP; SSC 12**
See also CA 9-12R; 148; CANR 8, 46;
DLB 2, 28; DLBY 80; INT CANR-8;
MTCW

Elledge, Scott .... **CLC 34**

Elliot, Don
See Silverberg, Robert

Elliott, Don
See Silverberg, Robert

Elliott, George P(aul) 1918-1980..... **CLC 2**
See also CA 1-4R; 97-100; CANR 2

Elliott, Janice 1931- .... **CLC 47**
See also CA 13-16R; CANR 8, 29; DLB 14

Elliott, Sumner Locke 1917-1991 ... **CLC 38**
See also CA 5-8R; 134; CANR 2, 21

Elliott, William
See Bradbury, Ray (Douglas)

Ellis, A. E. .... **CLC 7**

Ellis, Alice Thomas .... **CLC 40**
See also Haycraft, Anna

Ellis, Bret Easton
1964- .... **CLC 39, 71; DAM POP**
See also AAYA 2; CA 118; 123; CANR 51;
INT 123

Ellis, (Henry) Havelock
1859-1939 .... **TCLC 14**
See also CA 109

Ellis, Landon
See Ellison, Harlan (Jay)

Ellis, Trey 1962- .... **CLC 55**
See also CA 146

Ellison, Harlan (Jay)
1934- ...... **CLC 1, 13, 42; DAM POP;
SSC 14**
See also CA 5-8R; CANR 5, 46; DLB 8;
INT CANR-5; MTCW

Ellison, Ralph (Waldo)
1914-1994 .... **CLC 1, 3, 11, 54, 86;
BLC; DA; DAB; DAC; DAM MST,
MULT, NOV; SSC 26; WLC**
See also AAYA 19; BW 1; CA 9-12R; 145;
CANR 24, 53; CDALB 1941-1968;
DLB 2, 76; DLBY 94; MTCW

Ellmann, Lucy (Elizabeth) 1956-.... **CLC 61**
See also CA 128

Ellmann, Richard (David)
1918-1987 .... **CLC 50**
See also BEST 89:2; CA 1-4R; 122;
CANR 2, 28; DLB 103; DLBY 87;
MTCW

Elman, Richard 1934-............. **CLC 19**
See also CA 17-20R; CAAS 3; CANR 47

Elron
See Hubbard, L(afayette) Ron(ald)

Eluard, Paul .... **TCLC 7, 41**
See also Grindel, Eugene

Elyot, Sir Thomas 1490(?)-1546 ..... **LC 11**

Elytis, Odysseus
1911-1996 .... **CLC 15, 49, 100;
DAM POET**
See also CA 102; 151; MTCW

Farley, Walter (Lorimer)
1915-1989 . . . . **CLC 17**
See also CA 17-20R; CANR 8, 29; DLB 22;
JRDA; MAICYA; SATA 2, 43

Farmer, Philip Jose 1918- . . . . **CLC 1, 19**
See also CA 1-4R; CANR 4, 35; DLB 8;
MTCW; SATA 93

Farquhar, George
1677-1707 . . . . **LC 21; DAM DRAM**
See also DLB 84

Farrell, J(ames) G(ordon)
1935-1979 . . . . **CLC 6**
See also CA 73-76; 89-92; CANR 36;
DLB 14; MTCW

Farrell, James T(homas)
1904-1979 . . . . **CLC 1, 4, 8, 11, 66**
See also CA 5-8R; 89-92; CANR 9; DLB 4,
9, 86; DLBD 2; MTCW

Farren, Richard J.
See Betjeman, John

Farren, Richard M.
See Betjeman, John

Fassbinder, Rainer Werner
1946-1982 . . . . **CLC 20**
See also CA 93-96; 106; CANR 31

Fast, Howard (Melvin)
1914- . . . . **CLC 23; DAM NOV**
See also AAYA 16; CA 1-4R; CAAS 18;
CANR 1, 33, 54; DLB 9; INT CANR-33;
SATA 7

Faulcon, Robert
See Holdstock, Robert P.

Faulkner, William (Cuthbert)
1897-1962 . . . . . **CLC 1, 3, 6, 8, 9, 11, 14,
18, 28, 52, 68; DA; DAB; DAC;
DAM MST, NOV; SSC 1; WLC**
See also AAYA 7; CA 81-84; CANR 33;
CDALB 1929-1941; DLB 9, 11, 44, 102;
DLBD 2; DLBY 86; MTCW

Fauset, Jessie Redmon
1884(?)-1961 . . . . **CLC 19, 54; BLC;
DAM MULT**
See also BW 1; CA 109; DLB 51

Faust, Frederick (Schiller)
1892-1944(?) . . . . . **TCLC 49; DAM POP**
See also CA 108; 152

Faust, Irvin 1924- . . . . **CLC 8**
See also CA 33-36R; CANR 28; DLB 2, 28;
DLBY 80

Fawkes, Guy
See Benchley, Robert (Charles)

Fearing, Kenneth (Flexner)
1902-1961 . . . . **CLC 51**
See also CA 93-96; DLB 9

Fecamps, Elise
See Creasey, John

Federman, Raymond 1928- . . . . . . **CLC 6, 47**
See also CA 17-20R; CAAS 8; CANR 10,
43; DLBY 80

Federspiel, J(uerg) F. 1931- . . . . **CLC 42**
See also CA 146

Feiffer, Jules (Ralph)
1929- . . . . . . **CLC 2, 8, 64; DAM DRAM**
See also AAYA 3; CA 17-20R; CANR 30;
DLB 7, 44; INT CANR-30; MTCW;
SATA 8, 61

Feige, Hermann Albert Otto Maximilian
See Traven, B.

Feinberg, David B. 1956-1994 . . . . . . **CLC 59**
See also CA 135; 147

Feinstein, Elaine 1930- . . . . **CLC 36**
See also CA 69-72; CAAS 1; CANR 31;
DLB 14, 40; MTCW

Feldman, Irving (Mordecai) 1928- . . . . **CLC 7**
See also CA 1-4R; CANR 1; DLB 169

Felix-Tchicaya, Gerald
See Tchicaya, Gerald Felix

Fellini, Federico 1920-1993 . . . . . **CLC 16, 85**
See also CA 65-68; 143; CANR 33

Felsen, Henry Gregor 1916- . . . . **CLC 17**
See also CA 1-4R; CANR 1; SAAS 2;
SATA 1

Fenton, James Martin 1949- . . . . **CLC 32**
See also CA 102; DLB 40

Ferber, Edna 1887-1968 . . . . **CLC 18, 93**
See also AITN 1; CA 5-8R; 25-28R; DLB 9,
28, 86; MTCW; SATA 7

Ferguson, Helen
See Kavan, Anna

Ferguson, Samuel 1810-1886 . . . . . **NCLC 33**
See also DLB 32

Fergusson, Robert 1750-1774 . . . . . . **LC 29**
See also DLB 109

Ferling, Lawrence
See Ferlinghetti, Lawrence (Monsanto)

Ferlinghetti, Lawrence (Monsanto)
1919(?)- . . . . **CLC 2, 6, 10, 27;
DAM POET; PC 1**
See also CA 5-8R; CANR 3, 41;
CDALB 1941-1968; DLB 5, 16; MTCW

Fernandez, Vicente Garcia Huidobro
See Huidobro Fernandez, Vicente Garcia

Ferrer, Gabriel (Francisco Victor) Miro
See Miro (Ferrer), Gabriel (Francisco
Victor)

Ferrier, Susan (Edmonstone)
1782-1854 . . . . **NCLC 8**
See also DLB 116

Ferrigno, Robert 1948(?)- . . . . **CLC 65**
See also CA 140

Ferron, Jacques 1921-1985 . . . **CLC 94; DAC**
See also CA 117; 129; DLB 60

Feuchtwanger, Lion 1884-1958 . . . . . **TCLC 3**
See also CA 104; DLB 66

Feuillet, Octave 1821-1890 . . . . . . **NCLC 45**

Feydeau, Georges (Leon Jules Marie)
1862-1921 . . . . . **TCLC 22; DAM DRAM**
See also CA 113; 152

Fichte, Johann Gottlieb
1762-1814 . . . . **NCLC 62**
See also DLB 90

Ficino, Marsilio 1433-1499 . . . . **LC 12**

Fiedeler, Hans
See Doeblin, Alfred

Fiedler, Leslie A(aron)
1917- . . . . **CLC 4, 13, 24**
See also CA 9-12R; CANR 7; DLB 28, 67;
MTCW

Field, Andrew 1938- . . . . **CLC 44**
See also CA 97-100; CANR 25

Field, Eugene 1850-1895 . . . . **NCLC 3**
See also DLB 23, 42, 140; DLBD 13;
MAICYA; SATA 16

Field, Gans T.
See Wellman, Manly Wade

Field, Michael . . . . **TCLC 43**

Field, Peter
See Hobson, Laura Z(ametkin)

Fielding, Henry
1707-1754 . . . . . . **LC 1; DA; DAB; DAC;
DAM DRAM, MST, NOV; WLC**
See also CDBLB 1660-1789; DLB 39, 84,
101

Fielding, Sarah 1710-1768 . . . . **LC 1**
See also DLB 39

Fierstein, Harvey (Forbes)
1954- . . . . . **CLC 33; DAM DRAM, POP**
See also CA 123; 129

Figes, Eva 1932- . . . . **CLC 31**
See also CA 53-56; CANR 4, 44; DLB 14

Finch, Robert (Duer Claydon)
1900- . . . . **CLC 18**
See also CA 57-60; CANR 9, 24, 49;
DLB 88

Findley, Timothy
1930- . . . . . . **CLC 27; DAC; DAM MST**
See also CA 25-28R; CANR 12, 42;
DLB 53

Fink, William
See Mencken, H(enry) L(ouis)

Firbank, Louis 1942-
See Reed, Lou
See also CA 117

Firbank, (Arthur Annesley) Ronald
1886-1926 . . . . **TCLC 1**
See also CA 104; DLB 36

Fisher, M(ary) F(rances) K(ennedy)
1908-1992 . . . . **CLC 76, 87**
See also CA 77-80; 138; CANR 44

Fisher, Roy 1930- . . . . **CLC 25**
See also CA 81-84; CAAS 10; CANR 16;
DLB 40

Fisher, Rudolph
1897-1934 . . . . **TCLC 11; BLC;
DAM MULT; SSC 25**
See also BW 1; CA 107; 124; DLB 51, 102

Fisher, Vardis (Alvero) 1895-1968 . . . . **CLC 7**
See also CA 5-8R; 25-28R; DLB 9

Fiske, Tarleton
See Bloch, Robert (Albert)

Fitch, Clarke
See Sinclair, Upton (Beall)

Fitch, John IV
See Cormier, Robert (Edmund)

Fitzgerald, Captain Hugh
See Baum, L(yman) Frank

FitzGerald, Edward 1809-1883 . . . . **NCLC 9**
See also DLB 32

Fitzgerald, F(rancis) Scott (Key)
1896-1940 . . . . **TCLC 1, 6, 14, 28, 55;
DA; DAB; DAC; DAM MST, NOV;
SSC 6; WLC**
See also AITN 1; CA 110; 123;
CDALB 1917-1929; DLB 4, 9, 86;
DLBD 1; DLBY 81, 96; MTCW

Fitzgerald, Penelope 1916-... **CLC 19, 51, 61**
See also CA 85-88; CAAS 10; CANR 56;
DLB 14

Fitzgerald, Robert (Stuart)
1910-1985 .... **CLC 39**
See also CA 1-4R; 114; CANR 1; DLBY 80

FitzGerald, Robert D(avid)
1902-1987 .... **CLC 19**
See also CA 17-20R

Fitzgerald, Zelda (Sayre)
1900-1948 .... **TCLC 52**
See also CA 117; 126; DLBY 84

Flanagan, Thomas (James Bonner)
1923- .... **CLC 25, 52**
See also CA 108; CANR 55; DLBY 80;
INT 108; MTCW

Flaubert, Gustave
1821-1880 .... **NCLC 2, 10, 19, 62; DA;
DAB; DAC; DAM MST, NOV; SSC 11;
WLC**
See also DLB 119

Flecker, Herman Elroy
See Flecker, (Herman) James Elroy

Flecker, (Herman) James Elroy
1884-1915 .... **TCLC 43**
See also CA 109; 150; DLB 10, 19

Fleming, Ian (Lancaster)
1908-1964 ..... **CLC 3, 30; DAM POP**
See also CA 5-8R; CDBLB 1945-1960;
DLB 87; MTCW; SATA 9

Fleming, Thomas (James) 1927- .... **CLC 37**
See also CA 5-8R; CANR 10;
INT CANR-10; SATA 8

Fletcher, John 1579-1625...... **LC 33; DC 6**
See also CDBLB Before 1660; DLB 58

Fletcher, John Gould 1886-1950 ... **TCLC 35**
See also CA 107; DLB 4, 45

Fleur, Paul
See Pohl, Frederik

Flooglebuckle, Al
See Spiegelman, Art

Flying Officer X
See Bates, H(erbert) E(rnest)

Fo, Dario 1926-..... **CLC 32; DAM DRAM**
See also CA 116; 128; MTCW

Fogarty, Jonathan Titulescu Esq.
See Farrell, James T(homas)

Folke, Will
See Bloch, Robert (Albert)

Follett, Ken(neth Martin)
1949- .... **CLC 18; DAM NOV, POP**
See also AAYA 6; BEST 89:4; CA 81-84;
CANR 13, 33, 54; DLB 87; DLBY 81;
INT CANR-33; MTCW

Fontane, Theodor 1819-1898 ..... **NCLC 26**
See also DLB 129

Foote, Horton
1916- .... **CLC 51, 91; DAM DRAM**
See also CA 73-76; CANR 34, 51; DLB 26;
INT CANR-34

Foote, Shelby
1916- ...... **CLC 75; DAM NOV, POP**
See also CA 5-8R; CANR 3, 45; DLB 2, 17

Forbes, Esther 1891-1967......... **CLC 12**
See also AAYA 17; CA 13-14; 25-28R;
CAP 1; CLR 27; DLB 22; JRDA;
MAICYA; SATA 2

Forche, Carolyn (Louise)
1950- .... **CLC 25, 83, 86; DAM POET;
PC 10**
See also CA 109; 117; CANR 50; DLB 5;
INT 117

Ford, Elbur
See Hibbert, Eleanor Alice Burford

Ford, Ford Madox
1873-1939 .... **TCLC 1, 15, 39, 57;
DAM NOV**
See also CA 104; 132; CDBLB 1914-1945;
DLB 162; MTCW

Ford, John 1895-1973............. **CLC 16**
See also CA 45-48

Ford, Richard .... **CLC 99**

Ford, Richard 1944-.............. **CLC 46**
See also CA 69-72; CANR 11, 47

Ford, Webster
See Masters, Edgar Lee

Foreman, Richard 1937-.......... **CLC 50**
See also CA 65-68; CANR 32

Forester, C(ecil) S(cott)
1899-1966 .... **CLC 35**
See also CA 73-76; 25-28R; SATA 13

Forez
See Mauriac, Francois (Charles)

Forman, James Douglas 1932-...... **CLC 21**
See also AAYA 17; CA 9-12R; CANR 4,
19, 42; JRDA; MAICYA; SATA 8, 70

Fornes, Maria Irene 1930-...... **CLC 39, 61**
See also CA 25-28R; CANR 28; DLB 7;
HW; INT CANR-28; MTCW

Forrest, Leon 1937- .... **CLC 4**
See also BW 2; CA 89-92; CAAS 7;
CANR 25, 52; DLB 33

Forster, E(dward) M(organ)
1879-1970 ..... **CLC 1, 2, 3, 4, 9, 10, 13,
15, 22, 45, 77; DA; DAB; DAC;
DAM MST, NOV; WLC**
See also AAYA 2; CA 13-14; 25-28R;
CANR 45; CAP 1; CDBLB 1914-1945;
DLB 34, 98, 162, 178; DLBD 10; MTCW;
SATA 57

Forster, John 1812-1876 .... **NCLC 11**
See also DLB 144

Forsyth, Frederick
1938- .. **CLC 2, 5, 36; DAM NOV, POP**
See also BEST 89:4; CA 85-88; CANR 38;
DLB 87; MTCW

Forten, Charlotte L. .... **TCLC 16; BLC**
See also Grimke, Charlotte L(ottie) Forten
See also DLB 50

Foscolo, Ugo 1778-1827.......... **NCLC 8**

Fosse, Bob .... **CLC 20**
See also Fosse, Robert Louis

Fosse, Robert Louis 1927-1987
See Fosse, Bob
See also CA 110; 123

Foster, Stephen Collins
1826-1864 .... **NCLC 26**

Foucault, Michel
1926-1984 .... **CLC 31, 34, 69**
See also CA 105; 113; CANR 34; MTCW

Fouque, Friedrich (Heinrich Karl) de la Motte
1777-1843 .... **NCLC 2**
See also DLB 90

Fourier, Charles 1772-1837 ..... **NCLC 51**

Fournier, Henri Alban 1886-1914
See Alain-Fournier
See also CA 104

Fournier, Pierre 1916-............ **CLC 11**
See also Gascar, Pierre
See also CA 89-92; CANR 16, 40

Fowles, John
1926- ...... **CLC 1, 2, 3, 4, 6, 9, 10, 15,
33, 87; DAB; DAC; DAM MST**
See also CA 5-8R; CANR 25; CDBLB 1960
to Present; DLB 14, 139; MTCW;
SATA 22

Fox, Paula 1923-............... **CLC 2, 8**
See also AAYA 3; CA 73-76; CANR 20,
36; CLR 1, 44; DLB 52; JRDA;
MAICYA; MTCW; SATA 17, 60

Fox, William Price (Jr.) 1926- ..... **CLC 22**
See also CA 17-20R; CAAS 19; CANR 11;
DLB 2; DLBY 81

Foxe, John 1516(?)-1587 .... **LC 14**

Frame, Janet
1924- .... **CLC 2, 3, 6, 22, 66, 96**
See also Clutha, Janet Paterson Frame

France, Anatole .... **TCLC 9**
See also Thibault, Jacques Anatole Francois
See also DLB 123

Francis, Claude 19(?)- .... **CLC 50**

Francis, Dick
1920- .... **CLC 2, 22, 42; DAM POP**
See also AAYA 5, 21; BEST 89:3; CA 5-8R;
CANR 9, 42; CDBLB 1960 to Present;
DLB 87; INT CANR-9; MTCW

Francis, Robert (Churchill)
1901-1987 .... **CLC 15**
See also CA 1-4R; 123; CANR 1

Frank, Anne(lies Marie)
1929-1945 .... **TCLC 17; DA; DAB;
DAC; DAM MST; WLC**
See also AAYA 12; CA 113; 133; MTCW;
SATA 87; SATA-Brief 42

Frank, Elizabeth 1945-.......... **CLC 39**
See also CA 121; 126; INT 126

Frankl, Viktor E(mil) 1905-........ **CLC 93**
See also CA 65-68

Franklin, Benjamin
See Hasek, Jaroslav (Matej Frantisek)

Franklin, Benjamin
1706-1790 ..... **LC 25; DA; DAB; DAC;
DAM MST**
See also CDALB 1640-1865; DLB 24, 43,
73; YABC

Franklin, (Stella Maraia Sarah) Miles
1879-1954 .... **TCLC 7**
See also CA 104

Fraser, (Lady) Antonia (Pakenham)
1932- .... **CLC 32**
See also CA 85-88; CANR 44; MTCW;
SATA-Brief 32

Fraser, George MacDonald 1925-.... **CLC 7**
See also CA 45-48; CANR 2, 48

Fraser, Sylvia 1935-............. **CLC 64**
See also CA 45-48; CANR 1, 16

Frayn, Michael
1933-............. **CLC 3, 7, 31, 47;**
DAM DRAM, NOV
See also CA 5-8R; CANR 30; DLB 13, 14;
MTCW

Fraze, Candida (Merrill) 1945-..... **CLC 50**
See also CA 126

Frazer, J(ames) G(eorge)
1854-1941 .... **TCLC 32**
See also CA 118

Frazer, Robert Caine
See Creasey, John

Frazer, Sir James George
See Frazer, J(ames) G(eorge)

Frazier, Ian 1951-............... **CLC 46**
See also CA 130; CANR 54

Frederic, Harold 1856-1898...... **NCLC 10**
See also DLB 12, 23; DLBD 13

Frederick, John
See Faust, Frederick (Schiller)

Frederick the Great 1712-1786 ...... **LC 14**

Fredro, Aleksander 1793-1876..... **NCLC 8**

Freeling, Nicolas 1927-........... **CLC 38**
See also CA 49-52; CAAS 12; CANR 1, 17,
50; DLB 87

Freeman, Douglas Southall
1886-1953 .... **TCLC 11**
See also CA 109; DLB 17

Freeman, Judith 1946-............ **CLC 55**
See also CA 148

Freeman, Mary Eleanor Wilkins
1852-1930 .... **TCLC 9; SSC 1**
See also CA 106; DLB 12, 78

Freeman, R(ichard) Austin
1862-1943 .... **TCLC 21**
See also CA 113; DLB 70

French, Albert 1943- .... **CLC 86**

French, Marilyn
1929-............... **CLC 10, 18, 60;**
DAM DRAM, NOV, POP
See also CA 69-72; CANR 3, 31;
INT CANR-31; MTCW

French, Paul
See Asimov, Isaac

Freneau, Philip Morin 1752-1832.. **NCLC 1**
See also DLB 37, 43

Freud, Sigmund 1856-1939 .... **TCLC 52**
See also CA 115; 133; MTCW

Friedan, Betty (Naomi) 1921-...... **CLC 74**
See also CA 65-68; CANR 18, 45; MTCW

Friedlander, Saul 1932-........... **CLC 90**
See also CA 117; 130

Friedman, B(ernard) H(arper)
1926-........................ **CLC 7**
See also CA 1-4R; CANR 3, 48

Friedman, Bruce Jay 1930-.... **CLC 3, 5, 56**
See also CA 9-12R; CANR 25, 52; DLB 2,
28; INT CANR-25

Friel, Brian 1929-.......... **CLC 5, 42, 59**
See also CA 21-24R; CANR 33; DLB 13;
MTCW

Friis-Baastad, Babbis Ellinor
1921-1970 .... **CLC 12**
See also CA 17-20R; 134; SATA 7

Frisch, Max (Rudolf)
1911-1991 ..... **CLC 3, 9, 14, 18, 32, 44;**
DAM DRAM, NOV
See also CA 85-88; 134; CANR 32;
DLB 69, 124; MTCW

Fromentin, Eugene (Samuel Auguste)
1820-1876 .... **NCLC 10**
See also DLB 123

Frost, Frederick
See Faust, Frederick (Schiller)

Frost, Robert (Lee)
1874-1963 .... **CLC 1, 3, 4, 9, 10, 13, 15,**
26, 34, 44; DA; DAB; DAC; DAM MST,
POET; PC 1; WLC
See also AAYA 21; CA 89-92; CANR 33;
CDALB 1917-1929; DLB 54; DLBD 7;
MTCW; SATA 14

Froude, James Anthony
1818-1894 .... **NCLC 43**
See also DLB 18, 57, 144

Froy, Herald
See Waterhouse, Keith (Spencer)

Fry, Christopher
1907-..... **CLC 2, 10, 14; DAM DRAM**
See also CA 17-20R; CAAS 23; CANR 9,
30; DLB 13; MTCW; SATA 66

Frye, (Herman) Northrop
1912-1991 .... **CLC 24, 70**
See also CA 5-8R; 133; CANR 8, 37;
DLB 67, 68; MTCW

Fuchs, Daniel 1909-1993 .... **CLC 8, 22**
See also CA 81-84; 142; CAAS 5;
CANR 40; DLB 9, 26, 28; DLBY 93

Fuchs, Daniel 1934-.............. **CLC 34**
See also CA 37-40R; CANR 14, 48

Fuentes, Carlos
1928-...... **CLC 3, 8, 10, 13, 22, 41, 60;**
DA; DAB; DAC; DAM MST, MULT,
NOV; HLC; SSC 24; WLC
See also AAYA 4; AITN 2; CA 69-72;
CANR 10, 32; DLB 113; HW; MTCW

Fuentes, Gregorio Lopez y
See Lopez y Fuentes, Gregorio

Fugard, (Harold) Athol
1932-......... **CLC 5, 9, 14, 25, 40, 80;**
DAM DRAM; DC 3
See also AAYA 17; CA 85-88; CANR 32,
54; MTCW

Fugard, Sheila 1932- .... **CLC 48**
See also CA 125

Fuller, Charles (H., Jr.)
1939- .... **CLC 25; BLC; DAM DRAM,**
MULT; DC 1
See also BW 2; CA 108; 112; DLB 38;
INT 112; MTCW

Fuller, John (Leopold) 1937-....... **CLC 62**
See also CA 21-24R; CANR 9, 44; DLB 40

Fuller, Margaret .... **NCLC 5, 50**
See also Ossoli, Sarah Margaret (Fuller
marchesa d')

Fuller, Roy (Broadbent)
1912-1991 .... **CLC 4, 28**
See also CA 5-8R; 135; CAAS 10;
CANR 53; DLB 15, 20; SATA 87

Fulton, Alice 1952-............. **CLC 52**
See also CA 116; CANR 57

Furphy, Joseph 1843-1912....... **TCLC 25**

Fussell, Paul 1924-............... **CLC 74**
See also BEST 90:1; CA 17-20R; CANR 8,
21, 35; INT CANR-21; MTCW

Futabatei, Shimei 1864-1909 ...... **TCLC 44**
See also DLB 180

Futrelle, Jacques 1875-1912 ...... **TCLC 19**
See also CA 113; 155

Gaboriau, Emile 1835-1873 ...... **NCLC 14**

Gadda, Carlo Emilio 1893-1973 .... **CLC 11**
See also CA 89-92; DLB 177

Gaddis, William
1922-..... **CLC 1, 3, 6, 8, 10, 19, 43, 86**
See also CA 17-20R; CANR 21, 48; DLB 2;
MTCW

Gage, Walter
See Inge, William (Motter)

Gaines, Ernest J(ames)
1933-......... **CLC 3, 11, 18, 86; BLC;**
DAM MULT
See also AAYA 18; AITN 1; BW 2;
CA 9-12R; CANR 6, 24, 42;
CDALB 1968-1988; DLB 2, 33, 152;
DLBY 80; MTCW; SATA 86

Gaitskill, Mary 1954-............. **CLC 69**
See also CA 128

Galdos, Benito Perez
See Perez Galdos, Benito

Gale, Zona
1874-1938 ...... **TCLC 7; DAM DRAM**
See also CA 105; 153; DLB 9, 78

Galeano, Eduardo (Hughes) 1940-... **CLC 72**
See also CA 29-32R; CANR 13, 32; HW

Galiano, Juan Valera y Alcala
See Valera y Alcala-Galiano, Juan

Gallagher, Tess
1943-.. **CLC 18, 63; DAM POET; PC 9**
See also CA 106; DLB 120

Gallant, Mavis
1922-............ **CLC 7, 18, 38; DAC;**
DAM MST; SSC 5
See also CA 69-72; CANR 29; DLB 53;
MTCW

Gallant, Roy A(rthur) 1924- .... **CLC 17**
See also CA 5-8R; CANR 4, 29, 54;
CLR 30; MAICYA; SATA 4, 68

Gallico, Paul (William) 1897-1976 ... **CLC 2**
See also AITN 1; CA 5-8R; 69-72;
CANR 23; DLB 9, 171; MAICYA;
SATA 13

Gallo, Max Louis 1932-........... **CLC 95**
See also CA 85-88

Gallois, Lucien
See Desnos, Robert

Gallup, Ralph
See Whitemore, Hugh (John)

Gibbon, Lewis Grassic . . . . TCLC 4
See also Mitchell, James Leslie

Gibbons, Kaye
1960- . . . . CLC 50, 88; DAM POP
See also CA 151

Gibran, Kahlil
1883-1931 . . . . TCLC 1, 9; DAM POET,
POP; PC 9
See also CA 104; 150

Gibran, Khalil
See Gibran, Kahlil

Gibson, William
1914- . . . . CLC 23; DA; DAB; DAC;
DAM DRAM, MST
See also CA 9-12R; CANR 9, 42; DLB 7;
SATA 66

Gibson, William (Ford)
1948- . . . . CLC 39, 63; DAM POP
See also AAYA 12; CA 126; 133; CANR 52

Gide, Andre (Paul Guillaume)
1869-1951 . . . . TCLC 5, 12, 36; DA;
DAB; DAC; DAM MST, NOV; SSC 13;
WLC
See also CA 104; 124; DLB 65; MTCW

Gifford, Barry (Colby) 1946- . . . . . . CLC 34
See also CA 65-68; CANR 9, 30, 40

Gilbert, W(illiam) S(chwenck)
1836-1911 . . . . . TCLC 3; DAM DRAM,
POET
See also CA 104; SATA 36

Gilbreth, Frank B., Jr. 1911- . . . . . . CLC 17
See also CA 9-12R; SATA 2

Gilchrist, Ellen
1935- . . . . CLC 34, 48; DAM POP;
SSC 14
See also CA 113; 116; CANR 41; DLB 130;
MTCW

Giles, Molly 1942- . . . . CLC 39
See also CA 126

Gill, Patrick
See Creasey, John

Gilliam, Terry (Vance) 1940- . . . . . . CLC 21
See also Monty Python
See also AAYA 19; CA 108; 113;
CANR 35; INT 113

Gillian, Jerry
See Gilliam, Terry (Vance)

Gilliatt, Penelope (Ann Douglass)
1932-1993 . . . . CLC 2, 10, 13, 53
See also AITN 2; CA 13-16R; 141;
CANR 49; DLB 14

Gilman, Charlotte (Anna) Perkins (Stetson)
1860-1935 . . . . TCLC 9, 37; SSC 13
See also CA 106; 150

Gilmour, David 1949- . . . . CLC 35
See also CA 138, 147

Gilpin, William 1724-1804 . . . . . . NCLC 30

Gilray, J. D.
See Mencken, H(enry) L(ouis)

Gilroy, Frank D(aniel) 1925- . . . . CLC 2
See also CA 81-84; CANR 32; DLB 7

Gilstrap, John 1957(?)- . . . . CLC 99

Ginsberg, Allen (Irwin)
1926-1997 . . . . . CLC 1, 2, 3, 4, 6, 13, 36,
69; DA; DAB; DAC; DAM MST, POET;
PC 4; WLC 3
See also AITN 1; CA 1-4R; 157; CANR 2,
41; CDALB 1941-1968; DLB 5, 16, 169;
MTCW

Ginzburg, Natalia
1916-1991 . . . . CLC 5, 11, 54, 70
See also CA 85-88; 135; CANR 33;
DLB 177; MTCW

Giono, Jean 1895-1970 . . . . CLC 4, 11
See also CA 45-48; 29-32R; CANR 2, 35;
DLB 72; MTCW

Giovanni, Nikki
1943- . . . . . . CLC 2, 4, 19, 64; BLC; DA;
DAB; DAC; DAM MST, MULT, POET;
PC 19
See also AITN 1; BW 2; CA 29-32R;
CAAS 6; CANR 18, 41; DLB 5,
41; INT CANR-18; MAICYA; MTCW;
SATA 24; YABC

Giovene, Andrea 1904- . . . . CLC 7
See also CA 85-88

Gippius, Zinaida (Nikolayevna) 1869-1945
See Hippius, Zinaida
See also CA 106

Giraudoux, (Hippolyte) Jean
1882-1944 . . . . TCLC 2, 7; DAM DRAM
See also CA 104; DLB 65

Gironella, Jose Maria 1917- . . . . CLC 11
See also CA 101

Gissing, George (Robert)
1857-1903 . . . . TCLC 3, 24, 47
See also CA 105; DLB 18, 135

Giurlani, Aldo
See Palazzeschi, Aldo

Gladkov, Fyodor (Vasilyevich)
1883-1958 . . . . TCLC 27

Glanville, Brian (Lester) 1931- . . . . . . CLC 6
See also CA 5-8R; CAAS 9; CANR 3;
DLB 15, 139; SATA 42

Glasgow, Ellen (Anderson Gholson)
1873(?)-1945 . . . . TCLC 2, 7
See also CA 104; DLB 9, 12

Glaspell, Susan 1882(?)-1948 . . . . . TCLC 55
See also CA 110; 154; DLB 7, 9, 78; 2

Glassco, John 1909-1981 . . . . CLC 9
See also CA 13-16R; 102; CANR 15;
DLB 68

Glasscock, Amnesia
See Steinbeck, John (Ernst)

Glasser, Ronald J. 1940(?)- . . . . CLC 37

Glassman, Joyce
See Johnson, Joyce

Glendinning, Victoria 1937- . . . . CLC 50
See also CA 120; 127; DLB 155

Glissant, Edouard
1928- . . . . CLC 10, 68; DAM MULT
See also CA 153

Gloag, Julian 1930- . . . . CLC 40
See also AITN 1; CA 65-68; CANR 10

Glowacki, Aleksander
See Prus, Boleslaw

Gluck, Louise (Elisabeth)
1943- . . . . CLC 7, 22, 44, 81;
DAM POET; PC 16
See also CA 33-36R; CANR 40; DLB 5

Glyn, Elinor 1864-1943 . . . . TCLC 72
See also DLB 153

Gobineau, Joseph Arthur (Comte) de
1816-1882 . . . . NCLC 17
See also DLB 123

Godard, Jean-Luc 1930- . . . . CLC 20
See also CA 93-96

Godden, (Margaret) Rumer 1907- . . . CLC 53
See also AAYA 6; CA 5-8R; CANR 4, 27,
36, 55; CLR 20; DLB 161; MAICYA;
SAAS 12; SATA 3, 36

Godoy Alcayaga, Lucila 1889-1957
See Mistral, Gabriela
See also BW 2; CA 104; 131; DAM MULT;
HW; MTCW

Godwin, Gail (Kathleen)
1937- . . . . CLC 5, 8, 22, 31, 69;
DAM POP
See also CA 29-32R; CANR 15, 43; DLB 6;
INT CANR-15; MTCW

Godwin, William 1756-1836 . . . . . . NCLC 14
See also CDBLB 1789-1832; DLB 39, 104,
142, 158, 163

Goebbels, Josef
See Goebbels, (Paul) Joseph

Goebbels, (Paul) Joseph
1897-1945 . . . . TCLC 68
See also CA 115; 148

Goebbels, Joseph Paul
See Goebbels, (Paul) Joseph

Goethe, Johann Wolfgang von
1749-1832 . . . . NCLC 4, 22, 34; DA;
DAB; DAC; DAM DRAM, MST,
POET; PC 5; WLC 3
See also DLB 94

Gogarty, Oliver St. John
1878-1957 . . . . TCLC 15
See also CA 109; 150; DLB 15, 19

Gogol, Nikolai (Vasilyevich)
1809-1852 . . . . NCLC 5, 15, 31; DA;
DAB; DAC; DAM DRAM, MST; DC 1;
SSC 4; WLC
See also Monty Python

Goines, Donald
1937(?)-1974 . . . . CLC 80; BLC;
DAM MULT, POP
See also AITN 1; BW 1; CA 124; 114;
DLB 33

Gold, Herbert 1924- . . . . . . CLC 4, 7, 14, 42
See also CA 9-12R; CANR 17, 45; DLB 2;
DLBY 81

Goldbarth, Albert 1948- . . . . CLC 5, 38
See also CA 53-56; CANR 6, 40; DLB 120

Goldberg, Anatol 1910-1982 . . . . CLC 34
See also CA 131; 117

Goldemberg, Isaac 1945- . . . . CLC 52
See also CA 69-72; CAAS 12; CANR 11,
32; HW

Golding, William (Gerald)
1911-1993 .... **CLC 1, 2, 3, 8, 10, 17, 27, 58, 81; DA; DAB; DAC; DAM MST, NOV; WLC**
See also AAYA 5; CA 5-8R; 141; CANR 13, 33, 54; CDBLB 1945-1960; DLB 15, 100; MTCW

Goldman, Emma 1869-1940 ...... **TCLC 13**
See also CA 110; 150

Goldman, Francisco 1955- .... **CLC 76**

Goldman, William (W.) 1931- .... **CLC 1, 48**
See also CA 9-12R; CANR 29; DLB 44

Goldmann, Lucien 1913-1970 ...... **CLC 24**
See also CA 25-28; CAP 2

Goldoni, Carlo
1707-1793 .... **LC 4; DAM DRAM**

Goldsberry, Steven 1949- .... **CLC 34**
See also CA 131

Goldsmith, Oliver
1728-1774 ...... **LC 2; DA; DAB; DAC; DAM DRAM, MST, NOV, POET; WLC**
See also CDBLB 1660-1789; DLB 39, 89, 104, 109, 142; SATA 26

Goldsmith, Peter
See Priestley, J(ohn) B(oynton)

Gombrowicz, Witold
1904-1969 .... **CLC 4, 7, 11, 49; DAM DRAM**
See also CA 19-20; 25-28R; CAP 2

Gomez de la Serna, Ramon
1888-1963 .... **CLC 9**
See also CA 153; 116; HW

Goncharov, Ivan Alexandrovich
1812-1891 .... **NCLC 1**

Goncourt, Edmond (Louis Antoine Huot) de
1822-1896 .... **NCLC 7**
See also DLB 123

Goncourt, Jules (Alfred Huot) de
1830-1870 .... **NCLC 7**
See also DLB 123

Gontier, Fernande 19(?)- .... **CLC 50**

Gonzalez Martinez, Enrique
1871-1952 .... **TCLC 72**
See also HW

Goodman, Paul 1911-1972 .... **CLC 1, 2, 4, 7**
See also CA 19-20; 37-40R; CANR 34; CAP 2; DLB 130; MTCW

Gordimer, Nadine
1923- .... **CLC 3, 5, 7, 10, 18, 33, 51, 70; DA; DAB; DAC; DAM MST, NOV; SSC 17**
See also CA 5-8R; CANR 3, 28, 56; INT CANR-28; MTCW; YABC

Gordon, Adam Lindsay
1833-1870 .... **NCLC 21**

Gordon, Caroline
1895-1981 ... **CLC 6, 13, 29, 83; SSC 15**
See also CA 11-12; 103; CANR 36; CAP 1; DLB 4, 9, 102; DLBY 81; MTCW

Gordon, Charles William 1860-1937
See Connor, Ralph
See also CA 109

Gordon, Mary (Catherine)
1949- .... **CLC 13, 22**
See also CA 102; CANR 44; DLB 6; DLBY 81; INT 102; MTCW

Gordon, Sol 1923- .... **CLC 26**
See also CA 53-56; CANR 4; SATA 11

Gordone, Charles
1925-1995 ..... **CLC 1, 4; DAM DRAM**
See also BW 1; CA 93-96; 150; CANR 55; DLB 7; INT 93-96; MTCW

Gorenko, Anna Andreevna
See Akhmatova, Anna

Gorky, Maxim .... **TCLC 8; DAB; WLC**
See also Peshkov, Alexei Maximovich

Goryan, Sirak
See Saroyan, William

Gosse, Edmund (William)
1849-1928 .... **TCLC 28**
See also CA 117; DLB 57, 144

Gotlieb, Phyllis Fay (Bloom)
1926- .... **CLC 18**
See also CA 13-16R; CANR 7; DLB 88

Gottesman, S. D.
See Kornbluth, C(yril) M.; Pohl, Frederik

Gottfried von Strassburg
fl. c. 1210- .... **CMLC 10**
See also DLB 138

Gould, Lois .... **CLC 4, 10**
See also CA 77-80; CANR 29; MTCW

Gourmont, Remy (-Marie-Charles) de
1858-1915 .... **TCLC 17**
See also CA 109; 150

Govier, Katherine 1948- .... **CLC 51**
See also CA 101; CANR 18, 40

Goyen, (Charles) William
1915-1983 .... **CLC 5, 8, 14, 40**
See also AITN 2; CA 5-8R; 110; CANR 6; DLB 2; DLBY 83; INT CANR-6

Goytisolo, Juan
1931- ..... **CLC 5, 10, 23; DAM MULT; HLC**
See also CA 85-88; CANR 32; HW; MTCW

Gozzano, Guido 1883-1916 .... **PC 10**
See also CA 154; DLB 114

Gozzi, (Conte) Carlo 1720-1806 .. **NCLC 23**

Grabbe, Christian Dietrich
1801-1836 .... **NCLC 2**
See also DLB 133

Grace, Patricia 1937- .... **CLC 56**

Gracian y Morales, Baltasar
1601-1658 .... **LC 15**

Gracq, Julien .... **CLC 11, 48**
See also Poirier, Louis
See also DLB 83

Grade, Chaim 1910-1982 .... **CLC 10**
See also CA 93-96; 107

Graduate of Oxford, A
See Ruskin, John

Grafton, Garth
See Duncan, Sara Jeannette

Graham, John
See Phillips, David Graham

Graham, Jorie 1951- .... **CLC 48**
See also CA 111; DLB 120

Graham, R(obert) B(ontine) Cunninghame
See Cunninghame Graham, R(obert) B(ontine)
See also DLB 98, 135, 174

Graham, Robert
See Haldeman, Joe (William)

Graham, Tom
See Lewis, (Harry) Sinclair

Graham, W(illiam) S(ydney)
1918-1986 .... **CLC 29**
See also CA 73-76; 118; DLB 20

Graham, Winston (Mawdsley)
1910- .... **CLC 23**
See also CA 49-52; CANR 2, 22, 45; DLB 77

Grahame, Kenneth
1859-1932 .... **TCLC 64; DAB**
See also CA 108; 136; CLR 5; DLB 34, 141, 178; MAICYA; 1

Grant, Skeeter
See Spiegelman, Art

Granville-Barker, Harley
1877-1946 ...... **TCLC 2; DAM DRAM**
See also Barker, Harley Granville
See also CA 104

Grass, Guenter (Wilhelm)
1927- ..... **CLC 1, 2, 4, 6, 11, 15, 22, 32, 49, 88; DA; DAB; DAC; DAM MST, NOV; WLC**
See also CA 13-16R; CANR 20; DLB 75, 124; MTCW

Gratton, Thomas
See Hulme, T(homas) E(rnest)

Grau, Shirley Ann
1929- .... **CLC 4, 9; SSC 15**
See also CA 89-92; CANR 22; DLB 2; INT CANR-22; MTCW

Gravel, Fern
See Hall, James Norman

Graver, Elizabeth 1964- .... **CLC 70**
See also CA 135

Graves, Richard Perceval 1945- .... **CLC 44**
See also CA 65-68; CANR 9, 26, 51

Graves, Robert (von Ranke)
1895-1985 ...... **CLC 1, 2, 6, 11, 39, 44, 45; DAB; DAC; DAM MST, POET; PC 6**
See also CA 5-8R; 117; CANR 5, 36; CDBLB 1914-1945; DLB 20, 100; DLBY 85; MTCW; SATA 45

Graves, Valerie
See Bradley, Marion Zimmer

Gray, Alasdair (James) 1934- ...... **CLC 41**
See also CA 126; CANR 47; INT 126; MTCW

Gray, Amlin 1946- .... **CLC 29**
See also CA 138

Gray, Francine du Plessix
1930- .... **CLC 22; DAM NOV**
See also BEST 90:3; CA 61-64; CAAS 2; CANR 11, 33; INT CANR-11; MTCW

Gray, John (Henry) 1866-1934 .... **TCLC 19**
See also CA 119

Guillois, Valentin
See Desnos, Robert

Guiney, Louise Imogen
1861-1920 . . . . TCLC 41
See also DLB 54

Guiraldes, Ricardo (Guillermo)
1886-1927 . . . . TCLC 39
See also CA 131; HW; MTCW

Gumilev, Nikolai Stephanovich
1886-1921 . . . . TCLC 60

Gunesekera, Romesh . . . . CLC 91

Gunn, Bill . . . . CLC 5
See also Gunn, William Harrison
See also DLB 38

Gunn, Thom(son William)
1929- . . . . CLC 3, 6, 18, 32, 81;
DAM POET
See also CA 17-20R; CANR 9, 33;
CDBLB 1960 to Present; DLB 27;
INT CANR-33; MTCW

Gunn, William Harrison 1934(?)-1989
See Gunn, Bill
See also AITN 1; BW 1; CA 13-16R; 128;
CANR 12, 25

Gunnars, Kristjana 1948- . . . . CLC 69
See also CA 113; DLB 60

Gurdjieff, G(eorgei) I(vanovich)
1877(?)-1949 . . . . TCLC 71
See also CA 157

Gurganus, Allan
1947- . . . . CLC 70; DAM POP
See also BEST 90:1; CA 135

Gurney, A(lbert) R(amsdell), Jr.
1930- . . . . CLC 32, 50, 54; DAM DRAM
See also CA 77-80; CANR 32

Gurney, Ivor (Bertie) 1890-1937 . . . TCLC 33

Gurney, Peter
See Gurney, A(lbert) R(amsdell), Jr.

Guro, Elena 1877-1913 . . . . TCLC 56

Gustafson, James M(oody) 1925- . . CLC 100
See also CA 25-28R; CANR 37

Gustafson, Ralph (Barker) 1909- . . . . CLC 36
See also CA 21-24R; CANR 8, 45; DLB 88

Gut, Gom
See Simenon, Georges (Jacques Christian)

Guterson, David 1956- . . . . CLC 91
See also CA 132

Guthrie, A(lfred) B(ertram), Jr.
1901-1991 . . . . CLC 23
See also CA 57-60; 134; CANR 24; DLB 6;
SATA 62; SATA-Obit 67

Guthrie, Isobel
See Grieve, C(hristopher) M(urray)

Guthrie, Woodrow Wilson 1912-1967
See Guthrie, Woody
See also CA 113; 93-96

Guthrie, Woody . . . . CLC 35
See also Guthrie, Woodrow Wilson

Guy, Rosa (Cuthbert) 1928- . . . . CLC 26
See also AAYA 4; BW 2; CA 17-20R;
CANR 14, 34; CLR 13; DLB 33; JRDA;
MAICYA; SATA 14, 62

Gwendolyn
See Bennett, (Enoch) Arnold

H. D. . . . . CLC 3, 8, 14, 31, 34, 73; PC 5
See also Doolittle, Hilda

H. de V.
See Buchan, John

Haavikko, Paavo Juhani
1931- . . . . CLC 18, 34
See also CA 106

Habbema, Koos
See Heijermans, Herman

Hacker, Marilyn
1942- . . . . CLC 5, 9, 23, 72, 91;
DAM POET
See also CA 77-80; DLB 120

Haggard, H(enry) Rider
1856-1925 . . . . TCLC 11
See also CA 108; 148; DLB 70, 156, 174,
178; SATA 16

Hagiosy, L.
See Larbaud, Valery (Nicolas)

Hagiwara Sakutaro
1886-1942 . . . . TCLC 60; PC 18

Haig, Fenil
See Ford, Ford Madox

Haig-Brown, Roderick (Langmere)
1908-1976 . . . . CLC 21
See also CA 5-8R; 69-72; CANR 4, 38;
CLR 31; DLB 88; MAICYA; SATA 12

Hailey, Arthur
1920- . . . . CLC 5; DAM NOV, POP
See also AITN 2; BEST 90:3; CA 1-4R;
CANR 2, 36; DLB 88; DLBY 82; MTCW

Hailey, Elizabeth Forsythe 1938- . . . CLC 40
See also CA 93-96; CAAS 1; CANR 15, 48;
INT CANR-15

Haines, John (Meade) 1924- . . . . CLC 58
See also CA 17-20R; CANR 13, 34; DLB 5

Hakluyt, Richard 1552-1616 . . . . LC 31

Haldeman, Joe (William) 1943- . . . . . CLC 61
See also CA 53-56; CAAS 25; CANR 6;
DLB 8; INT CANR-6

Haley, Alex(ander Murray Palmer)
1921-1992 . . . . CLC 8, 12, 76; BLC; DA;
DAB; DAC; DAM MST, MULT, POP
See also BW 2; CA 77-80; 136; DLB 38;
MTCW

Haliburton, Thomas Chandler
1796-1865 . . . . NCLC 15
See also DLB 11, 99

Hall, Donald (Andrew, Jr.)
1928- . . CLC 1, 13, 37, 59; DAM POET
See also CA 5-8R; CAAS 7; CANR 2, 44;
DLB 5; SATA 23

Hall, Frederic Sauser
See Sauser-Hall, Frederic

Hall, James
See Kuttner, Henry

Hall, James Norman 1887-1951 . . . TCLC 23
See also CA 123; SATA 21

Hall, (Marguerite) Radclyffe
1886-1943 . . . . TCLC 12
See also CA 110; 150

Hall, Rodney 1935- . . . . CLC 51
See also CA 109

Halleck, Fitz-Greene 1790-1867 . . NCLC 47
See also DLB 3

Halliday, Michael
See Creasey, John

Halpern, Daniel 1945- . . . . CLC 14
See also CA 33-36R

Hamburger, Michael (Peter Leopold)
1924- . . . . CLC 5, 14
See also CA 5-8R; CAAS 4; CANR 2, 47;
DLB 27

Hamill, Pete 1935- . . . . CLC 10
See also CA 25-28R; CANR 18

Hamilton, Alexander
1755(?)-1804 . . . . NCLC 49
See also DLB 37

Hamilton, Clive
See Lewis, C(live) S(taples)

Hamilton, Edmond 1904-1977 . . . . . . CLC 1
See also CA 1-4R; CANR 3; DLB 8

Hamilton, Eugene (Jacob) Lee
See Lee-Hamilton, Eugene (Jacob)

Hamilton, Franklin
See Silverberg, Robert

Hamilton, Gail
See Corcoran, Barbara

Hamilton, Mollie
See Kaye, M(ary) M(argaret)

Hamilton, (Anthony Walter) Patrick
1904-1962 . . . . CLC 51
See also CA 113; DLB 10

Hamilton, Virginia
1936- . . . . CLC 26; DAM MULT
See also AAYA 2, 21; BW 2; CA 25-28R;
CANR 20, 37; CLR 1, 11, 40; DLB 33,
52; INT CANR-20; JRDA; MAICYA;
MTCW; SATA 4, 56, 79

Hammett, (Samuel) Dashiell
1894-1961 . . . . CLC 3, 5, 10, 19, 47;
SSC 17
See also AITN 1; CA 81-84; CANR 42;
CDALB 1929-1941; DLBD 6; DLBY 96;
MTCW

Hammon, Jupiter
1711(?)-1800(?) . . . . NCLC 5; BLC;
DAM MULT, POET; PC 16
See also DLB 31, 50

Hammond, Keith
See Kuttner, Henry

Hamner, Earl (Henry), Jr. 1923- . . . CLC 12
See also AITN 2; CA 73-76; DLB 6

Hampton, Christopher (James)
1946- . . . . CLC 4
See also CA 25-28R; DLB 13; MTCW

Hamsun, Knut . . . . TCLC 2, 14, 49
See also Pedersen, Knut

Handke, Peter
1942- . . . . CLC 5, 8, 10, 15, 38;
DAM DRAM, NOV
See also CA 77-80; CANR 33; DLB 85,
124; MTCW

Hanley, James 1901-1985 . . . CLC 3, 5, 8, 13
See also CA 73-76; 117; CANR 36; MTCW

Hannah, Barry 1942- . . . . CLC 23, 38, 90
See also CA 108; 110; CANR 43; DLB 6;
INT 110; MTCW

Hannon, Ezra
See Hunter, Evan

Hersey, John (Richard)
1914-1993 .... **CLC 1, 2, 7, 9, 40, 81, 97;
DAM POP**
See also CA 17-20R; 140; CANR 33;
DLB 6; MTCW; SATA 25;
SATA-Obit 76

Herzen, Aleksandr Ivanovich
1812-1870 .... **NCLC 10, 61**

Herzl, Theodor 1860-1904 .... **TCLC 36**

Herzog, Werner 1942- .... **CLC 16**
See also CA 89-92

Hesiod c. 8th cent. B.C.- .... **CMLC 5**
See also DLB 176

Hesse, Hermann
1877-1962 .... **CLC 1, 2, 3, 6, 11, 17, 25,
69; DA; DAB; DAC; DAM MST, NOV;
SSC 9; WLC**
See also CA 17-18; CAP 2; DLB 66;
MTCW; SATA 50

Hewes, Cady
See De Voto, Bernard (Augustine)

Heyen, William 1940- .... **CLC 13, 18**
See also CA 33-36R; CAAS 9; DLB 5

Heyerdahl, Thor 1914- .... **CLC 26**
See also CA 5-8R; CANR 5, 22; MTCW;
SATA 2, 52

Heym, Georg (Theodor Franz Arthur)
1887-1912 .... **TCLC 9**
See also CA 106

Heym, Stefan 1913- .... **CLC 41**
See also CA 9-12R; CANR 4; DLB 69

Heyse, Paul (Johann Ludwig von)
1830-1914 .... **TCLC 8**
See also CA 104; DLB 129

Heyward, (Edwin) DuBose
1885-1940 .... **TCLC 59**
See also CA 108; 157; DLB 7, 9, 45;
SATA 21

Hibbert, Eleanor Alice Burford
1906-1993 .... **CLC 7; DAM POP**
See also BEST 90:4; CA 17-20R; 140;
CANR 9, 28; SATA 2; SATA-Obit 74

Hichens, Robert S. 1864-1950 ..... **TCLC 64**
See also DLB 153

Higgins, George V(incent)
1939- .... **CLC 4, 7, 10, 18**
See also CA 77-80; CAAS 5; CANR 17, 51;
DLB 2; DLBY 81; INT CANR-17;
MTCW

Higginson, Thomas Wentworth
1823-1911 .... **TCLC 36**
See also DLB 1, 64

Highet, Helen
See MacInnes, Helen (Clark)

Highsmith, (Mary) Patricia
1921-1995 .... **CLC 2, 4, 14, 42;
DAM NOV, POP**
See also CA 1-4R; 147; CANR 1, 20, 48;
MTCW

Highwater, Jamake (Mamake)
1942(?)- .... **CLC 12**
See also AAYA 7; CA 65-68; CAAS 7;
CANR 10, 34; CLR 17; DLB 52;
DLBY 85; JRDA; MAICYA; SATA 32,
69; SATA-Brief 30

Highway, Tomson
1951- ..... **CLC 92; DAC; DAM MULT**
See also CA 151; NNAL

Higuchi, Ichiyo 1872-1896 ...... **NCLC 49**

Hijuelos, Oscar
1951- .... **CLC 65; DAM MULT, POP;
HLC**
See also BEST 90:1; CA 123; CANR 50;
DLB 145; HW

Hikmet, Nazim 1902(?)-1963 ...... **CLC 40**
See also CA 141; 93-96

Hildegard von Bingen
1098-1179 .... **CMLC 20**
See also DLB 148

Hildesheimer, Wolfgang
1916-1991 .... **CLC 49**
See also CA 101; 135; DLB 69, 124

Hill, Geoffrey (William)
1932- ... **CLC 5, 8, 18, 45; DAM POET**
See also CA 81-84; CANR 21;
CDBLB 1960 to Present; DLB 40;
MTCW

Hill, George Roy 1921- .... **CLC 26**
See also CA 110; 122

Hill, John
See Koontz, Dean R(ay)

Hill, Susan (Elizabeth)
1942- .. **CLC 4; DAB; DAM MST, NOV**
See also CA 33-36R; CANR 29; DLB 14,
139; MTCW

Hillerman, Tony
1925- .... **CLC 62; DAM POP**
See also AAYA 6; BEST 89:1; CA 29-32R;
CANR 21, 42; SATA 6

Hillesum, Etty 1914-1943 .... **TCLC 49**
See also CA 137

Hilliard, Noel (Harvey) 1929- ...... **CLC 15**
See also CA 9-12R; CANR 7

Hillis, Rick 1956- .... **CLC 66**
See also CA 134

Hilton, James 1900-1954 .... **TCLC 21**
See also CA 108; DLB 34, 77; SATA 34

Himes, Chester (Bomar)
1909-1984 .... **CLC 2, 4, 7, 18, 58; BLC;
DAM MULT**
See also BW 2; CA 25-28R; 114; CANR 22;
DLB 2, 76, 143; MTCW

Hinde, Thomas .... **CLC 6, 11**
See also Chitty, Thomas Willes

Hindin, Nathan
See Bloch, Robert (Albert)

Hine, (William) Daryl 1936- .... **CLC 15**
See also CA 1-4R; CAAS 15; CANR 1, 20;
DLB 60

Hinkson, Katharine Tynan
See Tynan, Katharine

Hinton, S(usan) E(loise)
1950- .... **CLC 30; DA; DAB; DAC;
DAM MST, NOV**
See also AAYA 2; CA 81-84; CANR 32;
CLR 3, 23; JRDA; MAICYA; MTCW;
SATA 19, 58

Hippius, Zinaida .... **TCLC 9**
See also Gippius, Zinaida (Nikolayevna)

Hiraoka, Kimitake 1925-1970
See Mishima, Yukio
See also CA 97-100; 29-32R; DAM DRAM;
MTCW

Hirsch, E(ric) D(onald), Jr. 1928-... **CLC 79**
See also CA 25-28R; CANR 27, 51;
DLB 67; INT CANR-27; MTCW

Hirsch, Edward 1950- .... **CLC 31, 50**
See also CA 104; CANR 20, 42; DLB 120

Hitchcock, Alfred (Joseph)
1899-1980 .... **CLC 16**
See also CA 97-100; SATA 27;
SATA-Obit 24

Hitler, Adolf 1889-1945 .... **TCLC 53**
See also CA 117; 147

Hoagland, Edward 1932- .... **CLC 28**
See also CA 1-4R; CANR 2, 31, 57; DLB 6;
SATA 51

Hoban, Russell (Conwell)
1925- .... **CLC 7, 25; DAM NOV**
See also CA 5-8R; CANR 23, 37; CLR 3;
DLB 52; MAICYA; MTCW; SATA 1,
40, 78

Hobbes, Thomas 1588-1679 .... **LC 36**
See also DLB 151

Hobbs, Perry
See Blackmur, R(ichard) P(almer)

Hobson, Laura Z(ametkin)
1900-1986 .... **CLC 7, 25**
See also CA 17-20R; 118; CANR 55;
DLB 28; SATA 52

Hochhuth, Rolf
1931- ..... **CLC 4, 11, 18; DAM DRAM**
See also CA 5-8R; CANR 33; DLB 124;
MTCW

Hochman, Sandra 1936- .... **CLC 3, 8**
See also CA 5-8R; DLB 5

Hochwaelder, Fritz
1911-1986 ...... **CLC 36; DAM DRAM**
See also CA 29-32R; 120; CANR 42;
MTCW

Hochwalder, Fritz
See Hochwaelder, Fritz

Hocking, Mary (Eunice) 1921- ..... **CLC 13**
See also CA 101; CANR 18, 40

Hodgins, Jack 1938- .... **CLC 23**
See also CA 93-96; DLB 60

Hodgson, William Hope
1877(?)-1918 .... **TCLC 13**
See also CA 111; DLB 70, 153, 156, 178

Hoeg, Peter 1957- .... **CLC 95**
See also CA 151

Hoffman, Alice
1952- .... **CLC 51; DAM NOV**
See also CA 77-80; CANR 34; MTCW

Hoffman, Daniel (Gerard)
1923- .... **CLC 6, 13, 23**
See also CA 1-4R; CANR 4; DLB 5

Hoffman, Stanley 1944- .... **CLC 5**
See also CA 77-80

Hoffman, William M(oses) 1939- ... **CLC 40**
See also CA 57-60; CANR 11

Hoffmann, E(rnst) T(heodor) A(madeus)
1776-1822 .... **NCLC 2; SSC 13**
See also DLB 90; SATA 27

Hrabal, Bohumil 1914-1997..... **CLC 13, 67**
See also CA 106; 156; CAAS 12; CANR 57

Hsun, Lu
See Lu Hsun

Hubbard, L(afayette) Ron(ald)
1911-1986 .... **CLC 43; DAM POP**
See also CA 77-80; 118; CANR 52

Huch, Ricarda (Octavia)
1864-1947 .... **TCLC 13**
See also CA 111; DLB 66

Huddle, David 1942- .... **CLC 49**
See also CA 57-60; CAAS 20; DLB 130

Hudson, Jeffrey
See Crichton, (John) Michael

Hudson, W(illiam) H(enry)
1841-1922 .... **TCLC 29**
See also CA 115; DLB 98, 153, 174;
SATA 35

Hueffer, Ford Madox
See Ford, Ford Madox

Hughart, Barry 1934-............. **CLC 39**
See also CA 137

Hughes, Colin
See Creasey, John

Hughes, David (John) 1930- .... **CLC 48**
See also CA 116; 129; DLB 14

Hughes, Edward James
See Hughes, Ted
See also DAM MST, POET

Hughes, (James) Langston
1902-1967 ..... **CLC 1, 5, 10, 15, 35, 44;**
BLC; DA; DAB; DAC; DAM DRAM,
MST, MULT, POET; DC 3; PC 1;
SSC 6; WLC
See also AAYA 12; BW 1; CA 1-4R;
25-28R; CANR 1, 34; CDALB 1929-1941;
CLR 17; DLB 4, 7, 48, 51, 86; JRDA;
MAICYA; MTCW; SATA 4, 33

Hughes, Richard (Arthur Warren)
1900-1976 ...... **CLC 1, 11; DAM NOV**
See also CA 5-8R; 65-68; CANR 4;
DLB 15, 161; MTCW; SATA 8;
SATA-Obit 25

Hughes, Ted
1930- .... **CLC 2, 4, 9, 14, 37; DAB;**
DAC; PC 7
See also Hughes, Edward James
See also CA 1-4R; CANR 1, 33; CLR 3;
DLB 40, 161; MAICYA; MTCW;
SATA 49; SATA-Brief 27

Hugo, Richard F(ranklin)
1923-1982 .... **CLC 6, 18, 32;**
DAM POET
See also CA 49-52; 108; CANR 3; DLB 5

Hugo, Victor (Marie)
1802-1885 .... **NCLC 3, 10, 21; DA;**
DAB; DAC; DAM DRAM, MST, NOV,
POET; PC 17; WLC
See also DLB 119; SATA 47

Huidobro, Vicente
See Huidobro Fernandez, Vicente Garcia

Huidobro Fernandez, Vicente Garcia
1893-1948 .... **TCLC 31**
See also CA 131; HW

Hulme, Keri 1947- .... **CLC 39**
See also CA 125; INT 125

Hulme, T(homas) E(rnest)
1883-1917 .... **TCLC 21**
See also CA 117; DLB 19

Hume, David 1711-1776............ **LC 7**
See also DLB 104

Humphrey, William 1924-......... **CLC 45**
See also CA 77-80; DLB 6

Humphreys, Emyr Owen 1919-..... **CLC 47**
See also CA 5-8R; CANR 3, 24; DLB 15

Humphreys, Josephine 1945-.... **CLC 34, 57**
See also CA 121; 127; INT 127

Huneker, James Gibbons
1857-1921 .... **TCLC 65**
See also DLB 71

Hungerford, Pixie
See Brinsmead, H(esba) F(ay)

Hunt, E(verette) Howard, (Jr.)
1918- .... **CLC 3**
See also AITN 1; CA 45-48; CANR 2, 47

Hunt, Kyle
See Creasey, John

Hunt, (James Henry) Leigh
1784-1859 ...... **NCLC 1; DAM POET**

Hunt, Marsha 1946-............... **CLC 70**
See also BW 2; CA 143

Hunt, Violet 1866-1942 .... **TCLC 53**
See also DLB 162

Hunter, E. Waldo
See Sturgeon, Theodore (Hamilton)

Hunter, Evan
1926- .... **CLC 11, 31; DAM POP**
See also CA 5-8R; CANR 5, 38; DLBY 82;
INT CANR-5; MTCW; SATA 25

Hunter, Kristin (Eggleston) 1931-... **CLC 35**
See also AITN 1; BW 1; CA 13-16R;
CANR 13; CLR 3; DLB 33;
INT CANR-13; MAICYA; SAAS 10;
SATA 12

Hunter, Mollie 1922-............. **CLC 21**
See also McIlwraith, Maureen Mollie
Hunter
See also AAYA 13; CANR 37; CLR 25;
DLB 161; JRDA; MAICYA; SAAS 7;
SATA 54

Hunter, Robert (?)-1734............ **LC 7**

Hurston, Zora Neale
1903-1960 .... **CLC 7, 30, 61; BLC; DA;**
DAC; DAM MST, MULT, NOV; SSC 4
See also AAYA 15; BW 1; CA 85-88;
DLB 51, 86; MTCW; YABC

Huston, John (Marcellus)
1906-1987 .... **CLC 20**
See also CA 73-76; 123; CANR 34; DLB 26

Hustvedt, Siri 1955-.............. **CLC 76**
See also CA 137

Hutten, Ulrich von 1488-1523....... **LC 16**
See also DLB 179

Huxley, Aldous (Leonard)
1894-1963 ..... **CLC 1, 3, 4, 5, 8, 11, 18,**
35, 79; DA; DAB; DAC; DAM MST,
NOV; WLC
See also AAYA 11; CA 85-88; CANR 44;
CDBLB 1914-1945; DLB 36, 100, 162;
MTCW; SATA 63

Huysmans, Charles Marie Georges
1848-1907
See Huysmans, Joris-Karl
See also CA 104

Huysmans, Joris-Karl............ **TCLC 7, 69**
See Huysmans, Charles Marie Georges
See also DLB 123

Hwang, David Henry
1957- .... **CLC 55; DAM DRAM; DC 4**
See also CA 127; 132; INT 132

Hyde, Anthony 1946-............. **CLC 42**
See also CA 136

Hyde, Margaret O(ldroyd) 1917- ... **CLC 21**
See also CA 1-4R; CANR 1, 36; CLR 23;
JRDA; MAICYA; SAAS 8; SATA 1, 42,
76

Hynes, James 1956(?)-............ **CLC 65**

Ian, Janis 1951- .... **CLC 21**
See also CA 105

Ibanez, Vicente Blasco
See Blasco Ibanez, Vicente

Ibarguengoitia, Jorge 1928-1983.... **CLC 37**
See also CA 124; 113; HW

Ibsen, Henrik (Johan)
1828-1906 .... **TCLC 2, 8, 16, 37, 52;**
DA; DAB; DAC; DAM DRAM, MST;
DC 2; WLC
See also CA 104; 141

Ibuse Masuji 1898-1993.......... **CLC 22**
See also CA 127; 141; DLB 180

Ichikawa, Kon 1915-.............. **CLC 20**
See also CA 121

Idle, Eric 1943-.................. **CLC 21**
See also Monty Python
See also CA 116; CANR 35

Ignatow, David 1914-...... **CLC 4, 7, 14, 40**
See also CA 9-12R; CAAS 3; CANR 31, 57;
DLB 5

Ihimaera, Witi 1944- .... **CLC 46**
See also CA 77-80

Ilf, Ilya................ **TCLC 21**
See also Fainzilberg, Ilya Arnoldovich

Illyes, Gyula 1902-1983 .... **PC 16**
See also CA 114; 109

Immermann, Karl (Lebrecht)
1796-1840 .... **NCLC 4, 49**
See also DLB 133

Inchbald, Elizabeth 1753-1821 ... **NCLC 62**
See also DLB 39, 89

Inclan, Ramon (Maria) del Valle
See Valle-Inclan, Ramon (Maria) del

Infante, G(uillermo) Cabrera
See Cabrera Infante, G(uillermo)

Ingalls, Rachel (Holmes) 1940-..... **CLC 42**
See also CA 123; 127

Ingamells, Rex 1913-1955 .... **TCLC 35**

Inge, William (Motter)
1913-1973 .. **CLC 1, 8, 19; DAM DRAM**
See also CA 9-12R; CDALB 1941-1968;
DLB 7; MTCW

Ingelow, Jean 1820-1897 .... **NCLC 39**
See also DLB 35, 163; SATA 33

Ingram, Willis J.
See Harris, Mark

Jensen, Johannes V.   1873-1950.... **TCLC 41**

Jensen, Laura (Linnea)   1948- ...... **CLC 37**
See also CA 103

Jerome, Jerome K(lapka)
1859-1927 .... **TCLC 23**
See also CA 119; DLB 10, 34, 135

Jerrold, Douglas William
1803-1857 .... **NCLC 2**
See also DLB 158, 159

Jewett, (Theodora) Sarah Orne
1849-1909 .... **TCLC 1, 22; SSC 6**
See also CA 108; 127; DLB 12, 74;
SATA 15

Jewsbury, Geraldine (Endsor)
1812-1880 .... **NCLC 22**
See also DLB 21

Jhabvala, Ruth Prawer
1927- .... **CLC 4, 8, 29, 94; DAB;**
DAM NOV
See also CA 1-4R; CANR 2, 29, 51;
DLB 139; INT CANR-29; MTCW

Jibran, Kahlil
See Gibran, Kahlil

Jibran, Khalil
See Gibran, Kahlil

Jiles, Paulette   1943-.......... **CLC 13, 58**
See also CA 101

Jimenez (Mantecon), Juan Ramon
1881-1958 ..... **TCLC 4; DAM MULT,**
POET; HLC; PC 7
See also CA 104; 131; DLB 134; HW;
MTCW

Jimenez, Ramon
See Jimenez (Mantecon), Juan Ramon

Jimenez Mantecon, Juan
See Jimenez (Mantecon), Juan Ramon

Joel, Billy .... **CLC 26**
See also Joel, William Martin

Joel, William Martin   1949-
See Joel, Billy
See also CA 108

John of the Cross, St.   1542-1591 .... **LC 18**

Johnson, B(ryan) S(tanley William)
1933-1973 .... **CLC 6, 9**
See also CA 9-12R; 53-56; CANR 9;
DLB 14, 40

Johnson, Benj. F. of Boo
See Riley, James Whitcomb

Johnson, Benjamin F. of Boo
See Riley, James Whitcomb

Johnson, Charles (Richard)
1948- .... **CLC 7, 51, 65; BLC;**
DAM MULT
See also BW 2; CA 116; CAAS 18;
CANR 42; DLB 33

Johnson, Denis   1949-............ **CLC 52**
See also CA 117; 121; DLB 120

Johnson, Diane   1934-....... **CLC 5, 13, 48**
See also CA 41-44R; CANR 17, 40;
DLBY 80; INT CANR-17; MTCW

Johnson, Eyvind (Olof Verner)
1900-1976 .... **CLC 14**
See also CA 73-76; 69-72; CANR 34

Johnson, J. R.
See James, C(yril) L(ionel) R(obert)

Johnson, James Weldon
1871-1938 .... **TCLC 3, 19; BLC;**
DAM MULT, POET
See also BW 1; CA 104; 125;
CDALB 1917-1929; CLR 32; DLB 51;
MTCW; SATA 31

Johnson, Joyce   1935-............ **CLC 58**
See also CA 125; 129

Johnson, Lionel (Pigot)
1867-1902 .... **TCLC 19**
See also CA 117; DLB 19

Johnson, Mel
See Malzberg, Barry N(athaniel)

Johnson, Pamela Hansford
1912-1981 .... **CLC 1, 7, 27**
See also CA 1-4R; 104; CANR 2, 28;
DLB 15; MTCW

Johnson, Robert   1911(?)-1938..... **TCLC 69**

Johnson, Samuel
1709-1784 ..... **LC 15; DA; DAB; DAC;**
DAM MST; WLC
See also CDBLB 1660-1789; DLB 39, 95,
104, 142

Johnson, Uwe
1934-1984 .... **CLC 5, 10, 15, 40**
See also CA 1-4R; 112; CANR 1, 39;
DLB 75; MTCW

Johnston, George (Benson)   1913- ... **CLC 51**
See also CA 1-4R; CANR 5, 20; DLB 88

Johnston, Jennifer   1930-........... **CLC 7**
See also CA 85-88; DLB 14

Jolley, (Monica) Elizabeth
1923- .... **CLC 46; SSC 19**
See also CA 127; CAAS 13

Jones, Arthur Llewellyn   1863-1947
See Machen, Arthur
See also CA 104

Jones, D(ouglas) G(ordon)   1929-.... **CLC 10**
See also CA 29-32R; CANR 13; DLB 53

Jones, David (Michael)
1895-1974 .... **CLC 2, 4, 7, 13, 42**
See also CA 9-12R; 53-56; CANR 28;
CDBLB 1945-1960; DLB 20, 100; MTCW

Jones, David Robert   1947-
See Bowie, David
See also CA 103

Jones, Diana Wynne   1934- .... **CLC 26**
See also AAYA 12; CA 49-52; CANR 4,
26, 56; CLR 23; DLB 161; JRDA;
MAICYA; SAAS 7; SATA 9, 70

Jones, Edward P.   1950-........... **CLC 76**
See also BW 2; CA 142

Jones, Gayl
1949- .... **CLC 6, 9; BLC; DAM MULT**
See also BW 2; CA 77-80; CANR 27;
DLB 33; MTCW

Jones, James   1921-1977.... **CLC 1, 3, 10, 39**
See also AITN 1, 2; CA 1-4R; 69-72;
CANR 6; DLB 2, 143; MTCW

Jones, John J.
See Lovecraft, H(oward) P(hillips)

Jones, LeRoi .... **CLC 1, 2, 3, 5, 10, 14**
See also Baraka, Amiri

Jones, Louis B. .... **CLC 65**
See also CA 141

Jones, Madison (Percy, Jr.)   1925- ... **CLC 4**
See also CA 13-16R; CAAS 11; CANR 7,
54; DLB 152

Jones, Mervyn   1922- .... **CLC 10, 52**
See also CA 45-48; CAAS 5; CANR 1;
MTCW

Jones, Mick   1956(?)- .... **CLC 30**

Jones, Nettie (Pearl)   1941- .... **CLC 34**
See also BW 2; CA 137; CAAS 20

Jones, Preston   1936-1979 .... **CLC 10**
See also CA 73-76; 89-92; DLB 7

Jones, Robert F(rancis)   1934-....... **CLC 7**
See also CA 49-52; CANR 2

Jones, Rod   1953- .... **CLC 50**
See also CA 128

Jones, Terence Graham Parry
1942- .... **CLC 21**
See also Jones, Terry; Monty Python
See also CA 112; 116; CANR 35; INT 116

Jones, Terry
See Jones, Terence Graham Parry
See also SATA 67; SATA-Brief 51

Jones, Thom   1945(?)- .... **CLC 81**
See also CA 157

Jong, Erica
1942- .... **CLC 4, 6, 8, 18, 83;**
DAM NOV, POP
See also AITN 1; BEST 90:2; CA 73-76;
CANR 26, 52; DLB 2, 5, 28, 152;
INT CANR-26; MTCW

Jonson, Ben(jamin)
1572(?)-1637 ...... **LC 6, 33; DA; DAB;**
DAC; DAM DRAM, MST, POET;
DC 4; PC 17; WLC
See also CDBLB Before 1660; DLB 62, 121

Jordan, June
1936- ..... **CLC 5, 11, 23; DAM MULT,**
POET
See also AAYA 2; BW 2; CA 33-36R;
CANR 25; CLR 10; DLB 38; MAICYA;
MTCW; SATA 4

Jordan, Pat(rick M.)   1941- .... **CLC 37**
See also CA 33-36R

Jorgensen, Ivar
See Ellison, Harlan (Jay)

Jorgenson, Ivar
See Silverberg, Robert

Josephus, Flavius   c. 37-100 ...... **CMLC 13**

Josipovici, Gabriel   1940-........ **CLC 6, 43**
See also CA 37-40R; CAAS 8; CANR 47;
DLB 14

Joubert, Joseph   1754-1824 .... **NCLC 9**

Jouve, Pierre Jean   1887-1976...... **CLC 47**
See also CA 65-68

Joyce, James (Augustine Aloysius)
1882-1941 .... **TCLC 3, 8, 16, 35, 52;**
DA; DAB; DAC; DAM MST, NOV,
POET; SSC 26; WLC
See also CA 104; 126; CDBLB 1914-1945;
DLB 10, 19, 36, 162; MTCW

Jozsef, Attila   1905-1937......... **TCLC 22**
See also CA 116

Juana Ines de la Cruz   1651(?)-1695 ... **LC 5**

Judd, Cyril
See Kornbluth, C(yril) M.; Pohl, Frederik

Kennedy, Adrienne (Lita)
1931- . . . . . **CLC 66; BLC; DAM MULT;**
DC 5
See also BW 2; CA 103; CAAS 20; CABS 3;
CANR 26, 53; DLB 38

Kennedy, John Pendleton
1795-1870 . . . . **NCLC 2**
See also DLB 3

Kennedy, Joseph Charles 1929-
See Kennedy, X. J.
See also CA 1-4R; CANR 4, 30, 40;
SATA 14, 86

Kennedy, William
1928- . . . **CLC 6, 28, 34, 53; DAM NOV**
See also AAYA 1; CA 85-88; CANR 14,
31; DLB 143; DLBY 85; INT CANR-31;
MTCW; SATA 57

Kennedy, X. J. . . . . **CLC 8, 42**
See Kennedy, Joseph Charles
See also CAAS 9; CLR 27; DLB 5;
SAAS 22

Kenny, Maurice (Francis)
1929- . . . . **CLC 87; DAM MULT**
See also CA 144; CAAS 22; DLB 175;
NNAL

Kent, Kelvin
See Kuttner, Henry

Kenton, Maxwell
See Southern, Terry

Kenyon, Robert O.
See Kuttner, Henry

Kerouac, Jack . . . . . **CLC 1, 2, 3, 5, 14, 29, 61**
See also Kerouac, Jean-Louis Lebris de
See also CDALB 1941-1968; DLB 2, 16;
DLBD 3; DLBY 95

Kerouac, Jean-Louis Lebris de 1922-1969
See Kerouac, Jack
See also AITN 1; CA 5-8R; 25-28R;
CANR 26, 54; DA; DAB; DAC;
DAM MST, NOV, POET, POP; MTCW;
WLC

Kerr, Jean 1923- . . . . **CLC 22**
See also CA 5-8R; CANR 7; INT CANR-7

Kerr, M. E. . . . . **CLC 12, 35**
See also Meaker, Marijane (Agnes)
See also AAYA 2; CLR 29; SAAS 1

Kerr, Robert . . . . **CLC 55**

Kerrigan, (Thomas) Anthony
1918- . . . . **CLC 4, 6**
See also CA 49-52; CAAS 11; CANR 4

Kerry, Lois
See Duncan, Lois

Kesey, Ken (Elton)
1935- . . . . . . **CLC 1, 3, 6, 11, 46, 64; DA;**
DAB; DAC; DAM MST, NOV, POP;
WLC
See also CA 1-4R; CANR 22, 38;
CDALB 1968-1988; DLB 2, 16; MTCW;
SATA 66

Kesselring, Joseph (Otto)
1902-1967 . . . . . **CLC 45; DAM DRAM,**
MST
See also CA 150

Kessler, Jascha (Frederick) 1929- . . . . **CLC 4**
See also CA 17-20R; CANR 8, 48

Kettelkamp, Larry (Dale) 1933- . . . . **CLC 12**
See also CA 29-32R; CANR 16; SAAS 3;
SATA 2

Key, Ellen 1849-1926 . . . . **TCLC 65**

Keyber, Conny
See Fielding, Henry

Keyes, Daniel
1927- . . . . **CLC 80; DA; DAC;**
DAM MST, NOV
See also CA 17-20R; CANR 10, 26, 54;
SATA 37

Keynes, John Maynard
1883-1946 . . . . **TCLC 64**
See also CA 114; DLBD 10

Khanshendel, Chiron
See Rose, Wendy

Khayyam, Omar
1048-1131 . . . . **CMLC 11; DAM POET;**
PC 8

Kherdian, David 1931- . . . . **CLC 6, 9**
See also CA 21-24R; CAAS 2; CANR 39;
CLR 24; JRDA; MAICYA; SATA 16, 74

Khlebnikov, Velimir . . . . **TCLC 20**
See also Khlebnikov, Viktor Vladimirovich

Khlebnikov, Viktor Vladimirovich 1885-1922
See Khlebnikov, Velimir
See also CA 117

Khodasevich, Vladislav (Felitsianovich)
1886-1939 . . . . **TCLC 15**
See also CA 115

Kielland, Alexander Lange
1849-1906 . . . . **TCLC 5**
See also CA 104

Kiely, Benedict 1919- . . . . **CLC 23, 43**
See also CA 1-4R; CANR 2; DLB 15

Kienzle, William X(avier)
1928- . . . . **CLC 25; DAM POP**
See also CA 93-96; CAAS 1; CANR 9, 31;
INT CANR-31; MTCW

Kierkegaard, Soren 1813-1855 . . . . **NCLC 34**

Killens, John Oliver 1916-1987 . . . . . **CLC 10**
See also BW 2; CA 77-80; 123; CAAS 2;
CANR 26; DLB 33

Killigrew, Anne 1660-1685 . . . . **LC 4**
See also DLB 131

Kim
See Simenon, Georges (Jacques Christian)

Kincaid, Jamaica
1949- . . . . **CLC 43, 68; BLC;**
DAM MULT, NOV
See also AAYA 13; BW 2; CA 125;
CANR 47; DLB 157

King, Francis (Henry)
1923- . . . . **CLC 8, 53; DAM NOV**
See also CA 1-4R; CANR 1, 33; DLB 15,
139; MTCW

King, Martin Luther, Jr.
1929-1968 . . . . **CLC 83; BLC; DA; DAB;**
DAC; DAM MST, MULT
See also BW 2; CA 25-28; CANR 27, 44;
CAP 2; MTCW; SATA 14; YABC

King, Stephen (Edwin)
1947- . . . . **CLC 12, 26, 37, 61;**
DAM NOV, POP; SSC 17
See also AAYA 1, 17; BEST 90:1;
CA 61-64; CANR 1, 30, 52; DLB 143;
DLBY 80; JRDA; MTCW; SATA 9, 55

King, Steve
See King, Stephen (Edwin)

King, Thomas
1943- . . . . . **CLC 89; DAC; DAM MULT**
See also CA 144; DLB 175; NNAL

Kingman, Lee . . . . **CLC 17**
See also Natti, (Mary) Lee
See also SAAS 3; SATA 1, 67

Kingsley, Charles 1819-1875 . . . . . **NCLC 35**
See also DLB 21, 32, 163; 2

Kingsley, Sidney 1906-1995 . . . . **CLC 44**
See also CA 85-88; 147; DLB 7

Kingsolver, Barbara
1955- . . . . **CLC 55, 81; DAM POP**
See also AAYA 15; CA 129; 134; INT 134

Kingston, Maxine (Ting Ting) Hong
1940- . . . . **CLC 12, 19, 58; DAM MULT,**
NOV
See also AAYA 8; CA 69-72; CANR 13,
38; DLB 173; DLBY 80; INT CANR-13;
MTCW; SATA 53; YABC

Kinnell, Galway
1927- . . . . **CLC 1, 2, 3, 5, 13, 29**
See also CA 9-12R; CANR 10, 34; DLB 5;
DLBY 87; INT CANR-34; MTCW

Kinsella, Thomas 1928- . . . . **CLC 4, 19**
See also CA 17-20R; CANR 15; DLB 27;
MTCW

Kinsella, W(illiam) P(atrick)
1935- . . . . **CLC 27, 43; DAC;**
DAM NOV, POP
See also AAYA 7; CA 97-100; CAAS 7;
CANR 21, 35; INT CANR-21; MTCW

Kipling, (Joseph) Rudyard
1865-1936 . . . . . . **TCLC 8, 17; DA; DAB;**
DAC; DAM MST, POET; PC 3; SSC 5;
WLC
See also CA 105; 120; CANR 33;
CDBLB 1890-1914; CLR 39; DLB 19, 34,
141, 156; MAICYA; MTCW; 2

Kirkup, James 1918- . . . . **CLC 1**
See also CA 1-4R; CAAS 4; CANR 2;
DLB 27; SATA 12

Kirkwood, James 1930(?)-1989 . . . . . . **CLC 9**
See also AITN 2; CA 1-4R; 128; CANR 6,
40

Kirshner, Sidney
See Kingsley, Sidney

Kis, Danilo 1935-1989 . . . . **CLC 57**
See also CA 109; 118; 129; MTCW

Kivi, Aleksis 1834-1872 . . . . **NCLC 30**

Kizer, Carolyn (Ashley)
1925- . . . . . **CLC 15, 39, 80; DAM POET**
See also CA 65-68; CAAS 5; CANR 24;
DLB 5, 169

Klabund 1890-1928 . . . . **TCLC 44**
See also DLB 66

Klappert, Peter 1942- . . . . **CLC 57**
See also CA 33-36R; DLB 5

Klein, A(braham) M(oses)
1909-1972 . . . . CLC 19; DAB; DAC;
DAM MST
See also CA 101; 37-40R; DLB 68

Klein, Norma 1938-1989 . . . . CLC 30
See also AAYA 2; CA 41-44R; 128;
CANR 15, 37; CLR 2, 19;
INT CANR-15; JRDA; MAICYA;
SAAS 1; SATA 7, 57

Klein, T(heodore) E(ibon) D(onald)
1947- . . . . CLC 34
See also CA 119; CANR 44

Kleist, Heinrich von
1777-1811 . . . . NCLC 2, 37;
DAM DRAM; SSC 22
See also DLB 90

Klima, Ivan 1931- . . . . . CLC 56; DAM NOV
See also CA 25-28R; CANR 17, 50

Klimentov, Andrei Platonovich 1899-1951
See Platonov, Andrei
See also CA 108

Klinger, Friedrich Maximilian von
1752-1831 . . . . NCLC 1
See also DLB 94

Klopstock, Friedrich Gottlieb
1724-1803 . . . . NCLC 11
See also DLB 97

Knapp, Caroline 1959- . . . . CLC 99
See also CA 154

Knebel, Fletcher 1911-1993 . . . . CLC 14
See also AITN 1; CA 1-4R; 140; CAAS 3;
CANR 1, 36; SATA 36; SATA-Obit 75

Knickerbocker, Diedrich
See Irving, Washington

Knight, Etheridge
1931-1991 . . . . CLC 40; BLC;
DAM POET; PC 14
See also BW 1; CA 21-24R; 133; CANR 23;
DLB 41

Knight, Sarah Kemble 1666-1727 . . . . . LC 7
See also DLB 24

Knister, Raymond 1899-1932 . . . . . . TCLC 56
See also DLB 68

Knowles, John
1926- . . . . . . CLC 1, 4, 10, 26; DA; DAC;
DAM MST, NOV
See also AAYA 10; CA 17-20R; CANR 40;
CDALB 1968-1988; DLB 6; MTCW;
SATA 8, 89

Knox, Calvin M.
See Silverberg, Robert

Knox, John c. 1505-1572 . . . . LC 37
See also DLB 132

Knye, Cassandra
See Disch, Thomas M(ichael)

Koch, C(hristopher) J(ohn) 1932- . . . CLC 42
See also CA 127

Koch, Christopher
See Koch, C(hristopher) J(ohn)

Koch, Kenneth
1925- . . . . CLC 5, 8, 44; DAM POET
See also CA 1-4R; CANR 6, 36, 57; DLB 5;
INT CANR-36; SATA 65

Kochanowski, Jan 1530-1584 . . . . LC 10

Kock, Charles Paul de
1794-1871 . . . . NCLC 16

Koda Shigeyuki 1867-1947
See Rohan, Koda
See also CA 121

Koestler, Arthur
1905-1983 . . . . . . CLC 1, 3, 6, 8, 15, 33
See also CA 1-4R; 109; CANR 1, 33;
CDBLB 1945-1960; DLBY 83; MTCW

Kogawa, Joy Nozomi
1935- . . . . . . CLC 78; DAC; DAM MST,
MULT
See also CA 101; CANR 19

Kohout, Pavel 1928- . . . . CLC 13
See also CA 45-48; CANR 3

Koizumi, Yakumo
See Hearn, (Patricio) Lafcadio (Tessima
Carlos)

Kolmar, Gertrud 1894-1943 . . . . . . TCLC 40

Komunyakaa, Yusef 1947- . . . . . . CLC 86, 94
See also CA 147; DLB 120

Konrad, George
See Konrad, Gyoergy

Konrad, Gyoergy 1933- . . . . . . CLC 4, 10, 73
See also CA 85-88

Konwicki, Tadeusz 1926- . . . . . CLC 8, 28, 54
See also CA 101; CAAS 9; CANR 39;
MTCW

Koontz, Dean R(ay)
1945- . . . . . . CLC 78; DAM NOV, POP
See also AAYA 9; BEST 89:3, 90:2;
CA 108; CANR 19, 36, 52; MTCW;
SATA 92

Kopit, Arthur (Lee)
1937- . . . . . CLC 1, 18, 33; DAM DRAM
See also AITN 1; CA 81-84; CABS 3;
DLB 7; MTCW

Kops, Bernard 1926- . . . . CLC 4
See also CA 5-8R; DLB 13

Kornbluth, C(yril) M. 1923-1958 . . . . TCLC 8
See also CA 105; DLB 8

Korolenko, V. G.
See Korolenko, Vladimir Galaktionovich

Korolenko, Vladimir
See Korolenko, Vladimir Galaktionovich

Korolenko, Vladimir G.
See Korolenko, Vladimir Galaktionovich

Korolenko, Vladimir Galaktionovich
1853-1921 . . . . TCLC 22
See also CA 121

Korzybski, Alfred (Habdank Skarbek)
1879-1950 . . . . TCLC 61
See also CA 123

Kosinski, Jerzy (Nikodem)
1933-1991 . . . . CLC 1, 2, 3, 6, 10, 15, 53,
70; DAM NOV
See also CA 17-20R; 134; CANR 9, 46;
DLB 2; DLBY 82; MTCW

Kostelanetz, Richard (Cory) 1940- . . CLC 28
See also CA 13-16R; CAAS 8; CANR 38

Kostrowitzki, Wilhelm Apollinaris de
1880-1918
See Apollinaire, Guillaume
See also CA 104

Kotlowitz, Robert 1924- . . . . CLC 4
See also CA 33-36R; CANR 36

Kotzebue, August (Friedrich Ferdinand) von
1761-1819 . . . . NCLC 25
See also DLB 94

Kotzwinkle, William 1938- . . . CLC 5, 14, 35
See also CA 45-48; CANR 3, 44; CLR 6;
DLB 173; MAICYA; SATA 24, 70

Kowna, Stancy
See Szymborska, Wislawa

Kozol, Jonathan 1936- . . . . CLC 17
See also CA 61-64; CANR 16, 45

Kozoll, Michael 1940(?)- . . . . CLC 35

Kramer, Kathryn 19(?)- . . . . CLC 34

Kramer, Larry 1935- . . CLC 42; DAM POP
See also CA 124; 126

Krasicki, Ignacy 1735-1801 . . . . NCLC 8

Krasinski, Zygmunt 1812-1859 . . . . NCLC 4

Kraus, Karl 1874-1936 . . . . TCLC 5
See also CA 104; DLB 118

Kreve (Mickevicius), Vincas
1882-1954 . . . . TCLC 27

Kristeva, Julia 1941- . . . . CLC 77
See also CA 154

Kristofferson, Kris 1936- . . . . CLC 26
See also CA 104

Krizanc, John 1956- . . . . CLC 57

Krleza, Miroslav 1893-1981 . . . . CLC 8
See also CA 97-100; 105; CANR 50;
DLB 147

Kroetsch, Robert
1927- . . . . CLC 5, 23, 57; DAC;
DAM POET
See also CA 17-20R; CANR 8, 38; DLB 53;
MTCW

Kroetz, Franz
See Kroetz, Franz Xaver

Kroetz, Franz Xaver 1946- . . . . CLC 41
See also CA 130

Kroker, Arthur 1945- . . . . CLC 77

Kropotkin, Peter (Aleksieevich)
1842-1921 . . . . TCLC 36
See also CA 119

Krotkov, Yuri 1917- . . . . CLC 19
See also CA 102

Krumb
See Crumb, R(obert)

Krumgold, Joseph (Quincy)
1908-1980 . . . . CLC 12
See also CA 9-12R; 101; CANR 7;
MAICYA; SATA 1, 48; SATA-Obit 23

Krumwitz
See Crumb, R(obert)

Krutch, Joseph Wood 1893-1970 . . . . CLC 24
See also CA 1-4R; 25-28R; CANR 4;
DLB 63

Krutzch, Gus
See Eliot, T(homas) S(tearns)

Krylov, Ivan Andreevich
1768(?)-1844 . . . . NCLC 1
See also DLB 150

Kubin, Alfred (Leopold Isidor)
1877-1959 . . . . **TCLC 23**
See also CA 112; 149; DLB 81

Kubrick, Stanley 1928- . . . . **CLC 16**
See also CA 81-84; CANR 33; DLB 26

Kumin, Maxine (Winokur)
1925- . . . . . **CLC 5, 13, 28; DAM POET;**
PC 15
See also AITN 2; CA 1-4R; CAAS 8;
CANR 1, 21; DLB 5; MTCW; SATA 12

Kundera, Milan
1929- . . . . **CLC 4, 9, 19, 32, 68;**
DAM NOV; SSC 24
See also AAYA 2; CA 85-88; CANR 19,
52; MTCW

Kunene, Mazisi (Raymond) 1930- . . . **CLC 85**
See also BW 1; CA 125; DLB 117

Kunitz, Stanley (Jasspon)
1905- . . . . **CLC 6, 11, 14; PC 19**
See also CA 41-44R; CANR 26, 57;
DLB 48; INT CANR-26; MTCW

Kunze, Reiner 1933- . . . . **CLC 10**
See also CA 93-96; DLB 75

Kuprin, Aleksandr Ivanovich
1870-1938 . . . . **TCLC 5**
See also CA 104

Kureishi, Hanif 1954(?)- . . . . **CLC 64**
See also CA 139

Kurosawa, Akira
1910- . . . . **CLC 16; DAM MULT**
See also AAYA 11; CA 101; CANR 46

Kushner, Tony
1957(?)- . . . . **CLC 81; DAM DRAM**
See also CA 144

Kuttner, Henry 1915-1958 . . . . **TCLC 10**
See also Vance, Jack
See also CA 107; 157; DLB 8

Kuzma, Greg 1944- . . . . **CLC 7**
See also CA 33-36R

Kuzmin, Mikhail 1872(?)-1936 . . . . **TCLC 40**

Kyd, Thomas
1558-1594 . . . . **LC 22; DAM DRAM;**
DC 3
See also DLB 62

Kyprianos, Iossif
See Samarakis, Antonis

La Bruyere, Jean de 1645-1696 . . . . . . **LC 17**

Lacan, Jacques (Marie Emile)
1901-1981 . . . . **CLC 75**
See also CA 121; 104

Laclos, Pierre Ambroise Francois Choderlos
de 1741-1803 . . . . **NCLC 4**

Lacolere, Francois
See Aragon, Louis

La Colere, Francois
See Aragon, Louis

La Deshabilleuse
See Simenon, Georges (Jacques Christian)

Lady Gregory
See Gregory, Isabella Augusta (Persse)

Lady of Quality, A
See Bagnold, Enid

La Fayette, Marie (Madelaine Pioche de la
Vergne Comtes 1634-1693 . . . . **LC 2**

Lafayette, Rene
See Hubbard, L(afayette) Ron(ald)

Laforgue, Jules
1860-1887 . . . . **NCLC 5, 53; PC 14;**
SSC 20

Lagerkvist, Paer (Fabian)
1891-1974 . . . . **CLC 7, 10, 13, 54;**
DAM DRAM, NOV
See also CA 85-88; 49-52; MTCW

Lagerkvist, Par . . . . **SSC 12**
See also Lagerkvist, Paer (Fabian)

Lagerloef, Selma (Ottiliana Lovisa)
1858-1940 . . . . **TCLC 4, 36**
See also Lagerlof, Selma (Ottiliana Lovisa)
See also CA 108; SATA 15

Lagerlof, Selma (Ottiliana Lovisa)
See Lagerloef, Selma (Ottiliana Lovisa)
See also CLR 7; SATA 15

La Guma, (Justin) Alex(ander)
1925-1985 . . . . **CLC 19; DAM NOV**
See also BW 1; CA 49-52; 118; CANR 25;
DLB 117; MTCW

Laidlaw, A. K.
See Grieve, C(hristopher) M(urray)

Lainez, Manuel Mujica
See Mujica Lainez, Manuel
See also HW

Laing, R(onald) D(avid)
1927-1989 . . . . **CLC 95**
See also CA 107; 129; CANR 34; MTCW

Lamartine, Alphonse (Marie Louis Prat) de
1790-1869 . . . . . **NCLC 11; DAM POET;**
PC 16

Lamb, Charles
1775-1834 . . . . **NCLC 10; DA; DAB;**
DAC; DAM MST; WLC
See also CDBLB 1789-1832; DLB 93, 107,
163; SATA 17

Lamb, Lady Caroline 1785-1828 . . **NCLC 38**
See also DLB 116

Lamming, George (William)
1927- . . . . **CLC 2, 4, 66; BLC;**
DAM MULT
See also BW 2; CA 85-88; CANR 26;
DLB 125; MTCW

L'Amour, Louis (Dearborn)
1908-1988 . . . . **CLC 25, 55; DAM NOV,**
POP
See also AAYA 16; AITN 2; BEST 89:2;
CA 1-4R; 125; CANR 3, 25, 40;
DLBY 80; MTCW

Lampedusa, Giuseppe (Tomasi) di
1896-1957 . . . . **TCLC 13**
See also Tomasi di Lampedusa, Giuseppe
See also DLB 177

Lampman, Archibald 1861-1899 . . **NCLC 25**
See also DLB 92

Lancaster, Bruce 1896-1963 . . . . **CLC 36**
See also CA 9-10; CAP 1; SATA 9

Lanchester, John . . . . **CLC 99**

Landau, Mark Alexandrovich
See Aldanov, Mark (Alexandrovich)

Landau-Aldanov, Mark Alexandrovich
See Aldanov, Mark (Alexandrovich)

Landis, Jerry
See Simon, Paul (Frederick)

Landis, John 1950- . . . . **CLC 26**
See also CA 112; 122

Landolfi, Tommaso 1908-1979 . . . **CLC 11, 49**
See also CA 127; 117; DLB 177

Landon, Letitia Elizabeth
1802-1838 . . . . **NCLC 15**
See also DLB 96

Landor, Walter Savage
1775-1864 . . . . **NCLC 14**
See also DLB 93, 107

Landwirth, Heinz 1927-
See Lind, Jakov
See also CA 9-12R; CANR 7

Lane, Patrick
1939- . . . . **CLC 25; DAM POET**
See also CA 97-100; CANR 54; DLB 53;
INT 97-100

Lang, Andrew 1844-1912 . . . . **TCLC 16**
See also CA 114; 137; DLB 98, 141;
MAICYA; SATA 16

Lang, Fritz 1890-1976 . . . . **CLC 20**
See also CA 77-80; 69-72; CANR 30

Lange, John
See Crichton, (John) Michael

Langer, Elinor 1939- . . . . **CLC 34**
See also CA 121

Langland, William
1330(?)-1400(?) . . . . . . **LC 19; DA; DAB;**
DAC; DAM MST, POET
See also DLB 146

Langstaff, Launcelot
See Irving, Washington

Lanier, Sidney
1842-1881 . . . . . . **NCLC 6; DAM POET**
See also DLB 64; DLBD 13; MAICYA;
SATA 18

Lanyer, Aemilia 1569-1645 . . . . . . **LC 10, 30**
See also DLB 121

Lao Tzu . . . . **CMLC 7**

Lapine, James (Elliot) 1949- . . . . **CLC 39**
See also CA 123; 130; CANR 54; INT 130

Larbaud, Valery (Nicolas)
1881-1957 . . . . **TCLC 9**
See also CA 106; 152

Lardner, Ring
See Lardner, Ring(gold) W(ilmer)

Lardner, Ring W., Jr.
See Lardner, Ring(gold) W(ilmer)

Lardner, Ring(gold) W(ilmer)
1885-1933 . . . . **TCLC 2, 14**
See also CA 104; 131; CDALB 1917-1929;
DLB 11, 25, 86; MTCW

Laredo, Betty
See Codrescu, Andrei

Larkin, Maia
See Wojciechowska, Maia (Teresa)

Larkin, Philip (Arthur)
1922-1985 . . . . **CLC 3, 5, 8, 9, 13, 18, 33,**
39, 64; DAB; DAM MST, POET
See also CA 5-8R; 117; CANR 24;
CDBLB 1960 to Present; DLB 27;
MTCW

Masefield, John (Edward)
1878-1967 . . . . **CLC 11, 47; DAM POET**
See also CA 19-20; 25-28R; CANR 33;
CAP 2; CDBLB 1890-1914; DLB 10, 19,
153, 160; MTCW; SATA 19

Maso, Carole 19(?)- . . . . **CLC 44**

Mason, Bobbie Ann
1940- . . . . **CLC 28, 43, 82; SSC 4**
See also AAYA 5; CA 53-56; CANR 11,
31, 58; DLB 173; DLBY 87;
INT CANR-31; MTCW

Mason, Ernst
See Pohl, Frederik

Mason, Lee W.
See Malzberg, Barry N(athaniel)

Mason, Nick 1945- . . . . **CLC 35**

Mason, Tally
See Derleth, August (William)

Mass, William
See Gibson, William

Masters, Edgar Lee
1868-1950 . . . . . . **TCLC 2, 25; DA; DAC;**
DAM MST, POET; PC 1
See also CA 104; 133; CDALB 1865-1917;
DLB 54; MTCW; YABC

Masters, Hilary 1928- . . . . **CLC 48**
See also CA 25-28R; CANR 13, 47

Mastrosimone, William 19(?)- . . . . . . **CLC 36**

Mathe, Albert
See Camus, Albert

Mather, Cotton 1663-1728 . . . . **LC 38**
See also CDALB 1640-1865; DLB 24, 30,
140

Mather, Increase 1639-1723 . . . . **LC 38**
See also DLB 24

Matheson, Richard Burton 1926- . . . **CLC 37**
See also CA 97-100; DLB 8, 44; INT 97-100

Mathews, Harry 1930- . . . . **CLC 6, 52**
See also CA 21-24R; CAAS 6; CANR 18,
40

Mathews, John Joseph
1894-1979 . . . . . . **CLC 84; DAM MULT**
See also CA 19-20; 142; CANR 45; CAP 2;
DLB 175; NNAL

Mathias, Roland (Glyn) 1915- . . . . . . **CLC 45**
See also CA 97-100; CANR 19, 41; DLB 27

Matsuo Basho 1644-1694 . . . . **PC 3**
See also DAM POET

Mattheson, Rodney
See Creasey, John

Matthews, Greg 1949- . . . . **CLC 45**
See also CA 135

Matthews, William 1942- . . . . **CLC 40**
See also CA 29-32R; CAAS 18; CANR 12,
57; DLB 5

Matthias, John (Edward) 1941- . . . . . . **CLC 9**
See also CA 33-36R; CANR 56

Matthiessen, Peter
1927- . . . . **CLC 5, 7, 11, 32, 64;**
DAM NOV
See also AAYA 6; BEST 90:4; CA 9-12R;
CANR 21, 50; DLB 6, 173; MTCW;
SATA 27

Maturin, Charles Robert
1780(?)-1824 . . . . **NCLC 6**
See also DLB 178

Matute (Ausejo), Ana Maria
1925- . . . . **CLC 11**
See also CA 89-92; MTCW

Maugham, W. S.
See Maugham, W(illiam) Somerset

Maugham, W(illiam) Somerset
1874-1965 . . . . . . **CLC 1, 11, 15, 67, 93;**
DA; DAB; DAC; DAM DRAM, MST,
NOV; SSC 8; WLC
See also CA 5-8R; 25-28R; CANR 40;
CDBLB 1914-1945; DLB 10, 36, 77, 100,
162; MTCW; SATA 54

Maugham, William Somerset
See Maugham, W(illiam) Somerset

Maupassant, (Henri Rene Albert) Guy de
1850-1893 . . . . . **NCLC 1, 42; DA; DAB;**
DAC; DAM MST; SSC 1; WLC
See also DLB 123

Maupin, Armistead
1944- . . . . **CLC 95; DAM POP**
See also CA 125; 130; CANR 58; INT 130

Maurhut, Richard
See Traven, B.

Mauriac, Claude 1914-1996 . . . . **CLC 9**
See also CA 89-92; 152; DLB 83

Mauriac, Francois (Charles)
1885-1970 . . . . **CLC 4, 9, 56; SSC 24**
See also CA 25-28; CAP 2; DLB 65;
MTCW

Mavor, Osborne Henry 1888-1951
See Bridie, James
See also CA 104

Maxwell, William (Keepers, Jr.)
1908- . . . . **CLC 19**
See also CA 93-96; CANR 54; DLBY 80;
INT 93-96

May, Elaine 1932- . . . . **CLC 16**
See also CA 124; 142; DLB 44

Mayakovski, Vladimir (Vladimirovich)
1893-1930 . . . . **TCLC 4, 18**
See also CA 104; 158

Mayhew, Henry 1812-1887 . . . . . . **NCLC 31**
See also DLB 18, 55

Mayle, Peter 1939(?)- . . . . **CLC 89**
See also CA 139

Maynard, Joyce 1953- . . . . **CLC 23**
See also CA 111; 129

Mayne, William (James Carter)
1928- . . . . **CLC 12**
See also AAYA 20; CA 9-12R; CANR 37;
CLR 25; JRDA; MAICYA; SAAS 11;
SATA 6, 68

Mayo, Jim
See L'Amour, Louis (Dearborn)

Maysles, Albert 1926- . . . . **CLC 16**
See also CA 29-32R

Maysles, David 1932- . . . . **CLC 16**

Mazer, Norma Fox 1931- . . . . **CLC 26**
See also AAYA 5; CA 69-72; CANR 12,
32; CLR 23; JRDA; MAICYA; SAAS 1;
SATA 24, 67

Mazzini, Guiseppe 1805-1872 . . . . **NCLC 34**

McAuley, James Phillip
1917-1976 . . . . **CLC 45**
See also CA 97-100

McBain, Ed
See Hunter, Evan

McBrien, William Augustine
1930- . . . . **CLC 44**
See also CA 107

McCaffrey, Anne (Inez)
1926- . . . . **CLC 17; DAM NOV, POP**
See also AAYA 6; AITN 2; BEST 89:2;
CA 25-28R; CANR 15, 35, 55; DLB 8;
JRDA; MAICYA; MTCW; SAAS 11;
SATA 8, 70

McCall, Nathan 1955(?)- . . . . **CLC 86**
See also CA 146

McCann, Arthur
See Campbell, John W(ood, Jr.)

McCann, Edson
See Pohl, Frederik

McCarthy, Charles, Jr. 1933-
See McCarthy, Cormac
See also CANR 42; DAM POP

McCarthy, Cormac
1933- . . . . **CLC 4, 57, 59, 101**
See also McCarthy, Charles, Jr.
See also DLB 6, 143

McCarthy, Mary (Therese)
1912-1989 . . . . . . **CLC 1, 3, 5, 14, 24, 39,**
59; SSC 24
See also CA 5-8R; 129; CANR 16, 50;
DLB 2; DLBY 81; INT CANR-16;
MTCW

McCartney, (James) Paul
1942- . . . . **CLC 12, 35**
See also CA 146

McCauley, Stephen (D.) 1955- . . . . . **CLC 50**
See also CA 141

McClure, Michael (Thomas)
1932- . . . . **CLC 6, 10**
See also CA 21-24R; CANR 17, 46;
DLB 16

McCorkle, Jill (Collins) 1958- . . . . . . **CLC 51**
See also CA 121; DLBY 87

McCourt, James 1941- . . . . **CLC 5**
See also CA 57-60

McCoy, Horace (Stanley)
1897-1955 . . . . **TCLC 28**
See also CA 108; 155; DLB 9

McCrae, John 1872-1918 . . . . **TCLC 12**
See also CA 109; DLB 92

McCreigh, James
See Pohl, Frederik

McCullers, (Lula) Carson (Smith)
1917-1967 . . . . **CLC 1, 4, 10, 12, 48, 100;**
DA; DAB; DAC; DAM MST, NOV;
SSC 9, 24; WLC
See also AAYA 21; CA 5-8R; 25-28R;
CABS 1, 3; CANR 18;
CDALB 1941-1968; DLB 2, 7, 173;
MTCW; SATA 27

McCulloch, John Tyler
See Burroughs, Edgar Rice

McCullough, Colleen
1938(?)- . . . . **CLC 27; DAM NOV, POP**
See also CA 81-84; CANR 17, 46; MTCW

McDermott, Alice 1953- . . . . CLC 90
See also CA 109; CANR 40

McElroy, Joseph 1930- . . . . CLC 5, 47
See also CA 17-20R

McEwan, Ian (Russell)
1948- . . . . CLC 13, 66; DAM NOV
See also BEST 90:4; CA 61-64; CANR 14,
41; DLB 14; MTCW

McFadden, David 1940- . . . . CLC 48
See also CA 104; DLB 60; INT 104

McFarland, Dennis 1950- . . . . CLC 65

McGahern, John
1934- . . . . CLC 5, 9, 48; SSC 17
See also CA 17-20R; CANR 29; DLB 14;
MTCW

McGinley, Patrick (Anthony)
1937- . . . . CLC 41
See also CA 120; 127; CANR 56; INT 127

McGinley, Phyllis 1905-1978 . . . . . . CLC 14
See also CA 9-12R; 77-80; CANR 19;
DLB 11, 48; SATA 2, 44; SATA-Obit 24

McGinniss, Joe 1942- . . . . CLC 32
See also AITN 2; BEST 89:2; CA 25-28R;
CANR 26; INT CANR-26

McGivern, Maureen Daly
See Daly, Maureen

McGrath, Patrick 1950- . . . . CLC 55
See also CA 136

McGrath, Thomas (Matthew)
1916-1990 . . . . CLC 28, 59; DAM POET
See also CA 9-12R; 132; CANR 6, 33;
MTCW; SATA 41; SATA-Obit 66

McGuane, Thomas (Francis III)
1939- . . . . CLC 3, 7, 18, 45
See also AITN 2; CA 49-52; CANR 5, 24,
49; DLB 2; DLBY 80; INT CANR-24;
MTCW

McGuckian, Medbh
1950- . . . . CLC 48; DAM POET
See also CA 143; DLB 40

McHale, Tom 1942(?)-1982 . . . . . . CLC 3, 5
See also AITN 1; CA 77-80; 106

McIlvanney, William 1936- . . . . CLC 42
See also CA 25-28R; DLB 14

McIlwraith, Maureen Mollie Hunter
See Hunter, Mollie
See also SATA 2

McInerney, Jay
1955- . . . . CLC 34; DAM POP
See also AAYA 18; CA 116; 123;
CANR 45; INT 123

McIntyre, Vonda N(eel) 1948- . . . . . CLC 18
See also CA 81-84; CANR 17, 34; MTCW

McKay, Claude
. . . . TCLC 7, 41; BLC; DAB; PC 2
See also McKay, Festus Claudius
See also DLB 4, 45, 51, 117

McKay, Festus Claudius 1889-1948
See McKay, Claude
See also BW 1; CA 104; 124; DA; DAC;
DAM MST, MULT, NOV, POET;
MTCW; WLC

McKuen, Rod 1933- . . . . CLC 1, 3
See also AITN 1; CA 41-44R; CANR 40

McLoughlin, R. B.
See Mencken, H(enry) L(ouis)

McLuhan, (Herbert) Marshall
1911-1980 . . . . CLC 37, 83
See also CA 9-12R; 102; CANR 12, 34;
DLB 88; INT CANR-12; MTCW

McMillan, Terry (L.)
1951- . . . . CLC 50, 61; DAM MULT,
NOV, POP
See also AAYA 21; BW 2; CA 140

McMurtry, Larry (Jeff)
1936- . . . . CLC 2, 3, 7, 11, 27, 44;
DAM NOV, POP
See also AAYA 15; AITN 2; BEST 89:2;
CA 5-8R; CANR 19, 43;
CDALB 1968-1988; DLB 2, 143;
DLBY 80, 87; MTCW

McNally, T. M. 1961- . . . . CLC 82

McNally, Terrence
1939- . . . . CLC 4, 7, 41, 91; DAM DRAM
See also CA 45-48; CANR 2, 56; DLB 7

McNamer, Deirdre 1950- . . . . CLC 70

McNeile, Herman Cyril 1888-1937
See Sapper
See also DLB 77

McNickle, (William) D'Arcy
1904-1977 . . . . . . CLC 89; DAM MULT
See also CA 9-12R; 85-88; CANR 5, 45;
DLB 175; NNAL; SATA-Obit 22

McPhee, John (Angus) 1931- . . . . . . CLC 36
See also BEST 90:1; CA 65-68; CANR 20,
46; MTCW

McPherson, James Alan
1943- . . . . CLC 19, 77
See also BW 1; CA 25-28R; CAAS 17;
CANR 24; DLB 38; MTCW

McPherson, William (Alexander)
1933- . . . . CLC 34
See also CA 69-72; CANR 28;
INT CANR-28

Mead, Margaret 1901-1978 . . . . CLC 37
See also AITN 1; CA 1-4R; 81-84;
CANR 4; MTCW; SATA-Obit 20

Meaker, Marijane (Agnes) 1927-
See Kerr, M. E.
See also CA 107; CANR 37; INT 107;
JRDA; MAICYA; MTCW; SATA 20, 61

Medoff, Mark (Howard)
1940- . . . . CLC 6, 23; DAM DRAM
See also AITN 1; CA 53-56; CANR 5;
DLB 7; INT CANR-5

Medvedev, P. N.
See Bakhtin, Mikhail Mikhailovich

Meged, Aharon
See Megged, Aharon

Meged, Aron
See Megged, Aharon

Megged, Aharon 1920- . . . . CLC 9
See also CA 49-52; CAAS 13; CANR 1

Mehta, Ved (Parkash) 1934- . . . . CLC 37
See also CA 1-4R; CANR 2, 23; MTCW

Melanter
See Blackmore, R(ichard) D(oddridge)

Melikow, Loris
See Hofmannsthal, Hugo von

Melmoth, Sebastian
See Wilde, Oscar (Fingal O'Flahertie Wills)

Meltzer, Milton 1915- . . . . CLC 26
See also AAYA 8; CA 13-16R; CANR 38;
CLR 13; DLB 61; JRDA; MAICYA;
SAAS 1; SATA 1, 50, 80

Melville, Herman
1819-1891 . . . . . NCLC 3, 12, 29, 45, 49;
DA; DAB; DAC; DAM MST, NOV;
SSC 1, 17; WLC
See also CDALB 1640-1865; DLB 3, 74;
SATA 59

Menander
c. 342B.C.-c. 292B.C. . . . . CMLC 9;
DAM DRAM; DC 3
See also DLB 176

Mencken, H(enry) L(ouis)
1880-1956 . . . . TCLC 13
See also CA 105; 125; CDALB 1917-1929;
DLB 11, 29, 63, 137; MTCW

Mendelsohn, Jane 1965(?)- . . . . CLC 99
See also CA 154

Mercer, David
1928-1980 . . . . CLC 5; DAM DRAM
See also CA 9-12R; 102; CANR 23;
DLB 13; MTCW

Merchant, Paul
See Ellison, Harlan (Jay)

Meredith, George
1828-1909 . . TCLC 17, 43; DAM POET
See also CA 117; 153; CDBLB 1832-1890;
DLB 18, 35, 57, 159

Meredith, William (Morris)
1919- . . CLC 4, 13, 22, 55; DAM POET
See also CA 9-12R; CAAS 14; CANR 6, 40;
DLB 5

Merezhkovsky, Dmitry Sergeyevich
1865-1941 . . . . TCLC 29

Merimee, Prosper
1803-1870 . . . . NCLC 6; SSC 7
See also DLB 119

Merkin, Daphne 1954- . . . . CLC 44
See also CA 123

Merlin, Arthur
See Blish, James (Benjamin)

Merrill, James (Ingram)
1926-1995 . . . . CLC 2, 3, 6, 8, 13, 18, 34,
91; DAM POET
See also CA 13-16R; 147; CANR 10, 49;
DLB 5, 165; DLBY 85; INT CANR-10;
MTCW

Merriman, Alex
See Silverberg, Robert

Merritt, E. B.
See Waddington, Miriam

Merton, Thomas
1915-1968 . . CLC 1, 3, 11, 34, 83; PC 10
See also CA 5-8R; 25-28R; CANR 22, 53;
DLB 48; DLBY 81; MTCW

Merwin, W(illiam) S(tanley)
1927- . . . . . . CLC 1, 2, 3, 5, 8, 13, 18, 45,
88; DAM POET
See also CA 13-16R; CANR 15, 51; DLB 5,
169; INT CANR-15; MTCW

Metcalf, John 1938- . . . . CLC 37
See also CA 113; DLB 60

Mohr, Nicholasa
　　1935- . . . . . **CLC 12; DAM MULT; HLC**
　　See also AAYA 8; CA 49-52; CANR 1, 32;
　　CLR 22; DLB 145; HW; JRDA; SAAS 8;
　　SATA 8

Mojtabai, A(nn) G(race)
　　1938- . . . . **CLC 5, 9, 15, 29**
　　See also CA 85-88

Moliere
　　1622-1673 . . . . . **LC 28; DA; DAB; DAC;**
　　　　　　　　　　DAM DRAM, MST; WLC

Molin, Charles
　　See Mayne, William (James Carter)

Molnar, Ferenc
　　1878-1952 . . . . . **TCLC 20; DAM DRAM**
　　See also CA 109; 153

Momaday, N(avarre) Scott
　　1934- . . . . . **CLC 2, 19, 85, 95; DA; DAB;**
　　　　　　DAC; DAM MST, MULT, NOV, POP
　　See also AAYA 11; CA 25-28R; CANR 14,
　　34; DLB 143, 175; INT CANR-14;
　　MTCW; NNAL; SATA 48;
　　SATA-Brief 30; YABC

Monette, Paul 1945-1995. . . . . **CLC 82**
　　See also CA 139; 147

Monroe, Harriet 1860-1936. . . . . . . **TCLC 12**
　　See also CA 109; DLB 54, 91

Monroe, Lyle
　　See Heinlein, Robert A(nson)

Montagu, Elizabeth 1917- . . . . **NCLC 7**
　　See also CA 9-12R

Montagu, Mary (Pierrepont) Wortley
　　1689-1762 . . . . **LC 9; PC 16**
　　See also DLB 95, 101

Montagu, W. H.
　　See Coleridge, Samuel Taylor

Montague, John (Patrick)
　　1929- . . . . **CLC 13, 46**
　　See also CA 9-12R; CANR 9; DLB 40;
　　MTCW

Montaigne, Michel (Eyquem) de
　　1533-1592 . . . . . . **LC 8; DA; DAB; DAC;**
　　　　　　　　　　　　DAM MST; WLC

Montale, Eugenio
　　1896-1981 . . . . **CLC 7, 9, 18; PC 13**
　　See also CA 17-20R; 104; CANR 30;
　　DLB 114; MTCW

Montesquieu, Charles-Louis de Secondat
　　1689-1755 . . . . **LC 7**

Montgomery, (Robert) Bruce 1921-1978
　　See Crispin, Edmund
　　See also CA 104

Montgomery, L(ucy) M(aud)
　　1874-1942 . . . . **TCLC 51; DAC;**
　　　　　　　　　　　　　　　　DAM MST
　　See also AAYA 12; CA 108; 137; CLR 8;
　　DLB 92; DLBD 14; JRDA; MAICYA; 1

Montgomery, Marion H., Jr. 1925- . . **CLC 7**
　　See also AITN 1; CA 1-4R; CANR 3, 48;
　　DLB 6

Montgomery, Max
　　See Davenport, Guy (Mattison, Jr.)

Montherlant, Henry (Milon) de
　　1896-1972 . . . . **CLC 8, 19; DAM DRAM**
　　See also CA 85-88; 37-40R; DLB 72;
　　MTCW

Monty Python
　　See Chapman, Graham; Cleese, John
　　(Marwood); Gilliam, Terry (Vance); Idle,
　　Eric; Jones, Terence Graham Parry; Palin,
　　Michael (Edward)
　　See also AAYA 7

Moodie, Susanna (Strickland)
　　1803-1885 . . . . **NCLC 14**
　　See also DLB 99

Mooney, Edward 1951-
　　See Mooney, Ted
　　See also CA 130

Mooney, Ted . . . . **CLC 25**
　　See also Mooney, Edward

Moorcock, Michael (John)
　　1939- . . . . **CLC 5, 27, 58**
　　See also CA 45-48; CAAS 5; CANR 2, 17,
　　38; DLB 14; MTCW; SATA 93

Moore, Brian
　　1921- . . . . . . **CLC 1, 3, 5, 7, 8, 19, 32, 90;**
　　　　　　　　　　DAB; DAC; DAM MST
　　See also CA 1-4R; CANR 1, 25, 42; MTCW

Moore, Edward
　　See Muir, Edwin

Moore, George Augustus
　　1852-1933 . . . . **TCLC 7; SSC 19**
　　See also CA 104; DLB 10, 18, 57, 135

Moore, Lorrie . . . . **CLC 39, 45, 68**
　　See also Moore, Marie Lorena

Moore, Marianne (Craig)
　　1887-1972 . . . . **CLC 1, 2, 4, 8, 10, 13, 19,**
　　　　47; DA; DAB; DAC; DAM MST, POET;
　　　　　　　　　　　　　　　　　　　PC 4
　　See also CA 1-4R; 33-36R; CANR 3;
　　CDALB 1929-1941; DLB 45; DLBD 7;
　　MTCW; SATA 20; YABC

Moore, Marie Lorena 1957-
　　See Moore, Lorrie
　　See also CA 116; CANR 39

Moore, Thomas 1779-1852. . . . . **NCLC 6**
　　See also DLB 96, 144

Morand, Paul 1888-1976 . . **CLC 41; SSC 22**
　　See also CA 69-72; DLB 65

Morante, Elsa 1918-1985. . . . . **CLC 8, 47**
　　See also CA 85-88; 117; CANR 35;
　　DLB 177; MTCW

Moravia, Alberto
　　1907-1990 . . . . **CLC 2, 7, 11, 27, 46;**
　　　　　　　　　　　　　　　　　SSC 26
　　See also Pincherle, Alberto
　　See also DLB 177

More, Hannah 1745-1833 . . . . **NCLC 27**
　　See also DLB 107, 109, 116, 158

More, Henry 1614-1687. . . . . **LC 9**
　　See also DLB 126

More, Sir Thomas 1478-1535 . . . . **LC 10, 32**

Moreas, Jean . . . . **TCLC 18**
　　See also Papadiamantopoulos, Johannes

Morgan, Berry 1919- . . . . **CLC 6**
　　See also CA 49-52; DLB 6

Morgan, Claire
　　See Highsmith, (Mary) Patricia

Morgan, Edwin (George) 1920- . . . . . **CLC 31**
　　See also CA 5-8R; CANR 3, 43; DLB 27

Morgan, (George) Frederick
　　1922- . . . . **CLC 23**
　　See also CA 17-20R; CANR 21

Morgan, Harriet
　　See Mencken, H(enry) L(ouis)

Morgan, Jane
　　See Cooper, James Fenimore

Morgan, Janet 1945- . . . . **CLC 39**
　　See also CA 65-68

Morgan, Lady 1776(?)-1859. . . . . . **NCLC 29**
　　See also DLB 116, 158

Morgan, Robin 1941- . . . . **CLC 2**
　　See also CA 69-72; CANR 29; MTCW;
　　SATA 80

Morgan, Scott
　　See Kuttner, Henry

Morgan, Seth 1949(?)-1990 . . . . **CLC 65**
　　See also CA 132

Morgenstern, Christian
　　1871-1914 . . . . **TCLC 8**
　　See also CA 105

Morgenstern, S.
　　See Goldman, William (W.)

Moricz, Zsigmond 1879-1942 . . . . . **TCLC 33**

Morike, Eduard (Friedrich)
　　1804-1875 . . . . **NCLC 10**
　　See also DLB 133

Mori Ogai . . . . **TCLC 14**
　　See also Mori Rintaro

Mori Rintaro 1862-1922
　　See Mori Ogai
　　See also CA 110

Moritz, Karl Philipp 1756-1793 . . . . . . **LC 2**
　　See also DLB 94

Morland, Peter Henry
　　See Faust, Frederick (Schiller)

Morren, Theophil
　　See Hofmannsthal, Hugo von

Morris, Bill 1952- . . . . **CLC 76**

Morris, Julian
　　See West, Morris L(anglo)

Morris, Steveland Judkins 1950(?)-
　　See Wonder, Stevie
　　See also CA 111

Morris, William 1834-1896 . . . . **NCLC 4**
　　See also CDBLB 1832-1890; DLB 18, 35,
　　57, 156, 178

Morris, Wright 1910- . . . **CLC 1, 3, 7, 18, 37**
　　See also CA 9-12R; CANR 21; DLB 2;
　　DLBY 81; MTCW

Morrison, Arthur 1863-1945 . . . . . . **TCLC 72**
　　See also CA 120; 157; DLB 70, 135

Morrison, Chloe Anthony Wofford
　　See Morrison, Toni

Morrison, James Douglas 1943-1971
　　See Morrison, Jim
　　See also CA 73-76; CANR 40

Morrison, Jim . . . . **CLC 17**
　　See also Morrison, James Douglas

Nakos, Lilika 1899(?)-. . . . . **CLC 29**

Narayan, R(asipuram) K(rishnaswami)
1906- . . . . . . **CLC 7, 28, 47; DAM NOV;**
SSC 25
See also CA 81-84; CANR 33; MTCW;
SATA 62

Nash, (Frediric) Ogden
1902-1971 . . . . **CLC 23; DAM POET**
See also CA 13-14; 29-32R; CANR 34;
CAP 1; DLB 11; MAICYA; MTCW;
SATA 2, 46

Nathan, Daniel
See Dannay, Frederic

Nathan, George Jean 1882-1958 . . . **TCLC 18**
See also Hatteras, Owen
See also CA 114; DLB 137

Natsume, Kinnosuke 1867-1916
See Natsume, Soseki
See also CA 104

Natsume, Soseki 1867-1916. . . . . **TCLC 2, 10**
See also Natsume, Kinnosuke
See also DLB 180

Natti, (Mary) Lee 1919-
See Kingman, Lee
See also CA 5-8R; CANR 2

Naylor, Gloria
1950- . . . . . **CLC 28, 52; BLC; DA; DAC;**
DAM MST, MULT, NOV, POP
See also AAYA 6; BW 2; CA 107;
CANR 27, 51; DLB 173; MTCW; YABC

Neihardt, John Gneisenau
1881-1973 . . . . **CLC 32**
See also CA 13-14; CAP 1; DLB 9, 54

Nekrasov, Nikolai Alekseevich
1821-1878 . . . . **NCLC 11**

Nelligan, Emile 1879-1941. . . . . . . **TCLC 14**
See also CA 114; DLB 92

Nelson, Willie 1933-. . . . . **CLC 17**
See also CA 107

Nemerov, Howard (Stanley)
1920-1991 . . . . **CLC 2, 6, 9, 36;**
DAM POET
See also CA 1-4R; 134; CABS 2; CANR 1,
27, 53; DLB 5, 6; DLBY 83;
INT CANR-27; MTCW

Neruda, Pablo
1904-1973 . . . . . **CLC 1, 2, 5, 7, 9, 28, 62;**
DA; DAB; DAC; DAM MST, MULT,
POET; HLC; PC 4; WLC
See also CA 19-20; 45-48; CAP 2; HW;
MTCW

Nerval, Gerard de
1808-1855 . . . . . **NCLC 1; PC 13; SSC 18**

Nervo, (Jose) Amado (Ruiz de)
1870-1919 . . . . **TCLC 11**
See also CA 109; 131; HW

Nessi, Pio Baroja y
See Baroja (y Nessi), Pio

Nestroy, Johann 1801-1862 . . . . . . **NCLC 42**
See also DLB 133

Netterville, Luke
See O'Grady, Standish (James)

Neufeld, John (Arthur) 1938- . . . . . . **CLC 17**
See also AAYA 11; CA 25-28R; CANR 11,
37, 56; MAICYA; SAAS 3; SATA 6, 81

Neville, Emily Cheney 1919-. . . . . . **CLC 12**
See also CA 5-8R; CANR 3, 37; JRDA;
MAICYA; SAAS 2; SATA 1

Newbound, Bernard Slade 1930-
See Slade, Bernard
See also CA 81-84; CANR 49;
DAM DRAM

Newby, P(ercy) H(oward)
1918- . . . . **CLC 2, 13; DAM NOV**
See also CA 5-8R; CANR 32; DLB 15;
MTCW

Newlove, Donald 1928- . . . . **CLC 6**
See also CA 29-32R; CANR 25

Newlove, John (Herbert) 1938-. . . . . **CLC 14**
See also CA 21-24R; CANR 9, 25

Newman, Charles 1938-. . . . . **CLC 2, 8**
See also CA 21-24R

Newman, Edwin (Harold) 1919- . . . . **CLC 14**
See also AITN 1; CA 69-72; CANR 5

Newman, John Henry
1801-1890 . . . . **NCLC 38**
See also DLB 18, 32, 55

Newton, Suzanne 1936-. . . . . **CLC 35**
See also CA 41-44R; CANR 14; JRDA;
SATA 5, 77

Nexo, Martin Andersen
1869-1954 . . . . **TCLC 43**

Nezval, Vitezslav 1900-1958 . . . . . **TCLC 44**
See also CA 123

Ng, Fae Myenne 1957(?)-. . . . . **CLC 81**
See also CA 146

Ngema, Mbongeni 1955- . . . . **CLC 57**
See also BW 2; CA 143

Ngugi, James T(hiong'o). . . . . . . **CLC 3, 7, 13**
See also Ngugi wa Thiong'o

Ngugi wa Thiong'o
1938- . . . . . **CLC 36; BLC; DAM MULT,**
NOV
See also Ngugi, James T(hiong'o)
See also BW 2; CA 81-84; CANR 27, 58;
DLB 125; MTCW

Nichol, B(arrie) P(hillip)
1944-1988 . . . . **CLC 18**
See also CA 53-56; DLB 53; SATA 66

Nichols, John (Treadwell) 1940-. . . . **CLC 38**
See also CA 9-12R; CAAS 2; CANR 6;
DLBY 82

Nichols, Leigh
See Koontz, Dean R(ay)

Nichols, Peter (Richard)
1927-. . . . . **CLC 5, 36, 65**
See also CA 104; CANR 33; DLB 13;
MTCW

Nicolas, F. R. E.
See Freeling, Nicolas

Niedecker, Lorine
1903-1970 . . . . **CLC 10, 42; DAM POET**
See also CA 25-28; CAP 2; DLB 48

Nietzsche, Friedrich (Wilhelm)
1844-1900 . . . . **TCLC 10, 18, 55**
See also CA 107; 121; DLB 129

Nievo, Ippolito 1831-1861 . . . . **NCLC 22**

Nightingale, Anne Redmon 1943-
See Redmon, Anne
See also CA 103

Nik. T. O.
See Annensky, Innokenty (Fyodorovich)

Nin, Anais
1903-1977 . . . . . . **CLC 1, 4, 8, 11, 14, 60;**
DAM NOV, POP; SSC 10
See also AITN 2; CA 13-16R; 69-72;
CANR 22, 53; DLB 2, 4, 152; MTCW

Nishiwaki, Junzaburo 1894-1982 . . . . **PC 15**
See also CA 107

Nissenson, Hugh 1933-. . . . . **CLC 4, 9**
See also CA 17-20R; CANR 27; DLB 28

Niven, Larry . . . . **CLC 8**
See also Niven, Laurence Van Cott
See also DLB 8

Niven, Laurence Van Cott 1938-
See Niven, Larry
See also CA 21-24R; CAAS 12; CANR 14,
44; DAM POP; MTCW

Nixon, Agnes Eckhardt 1927-. . . . . . **CLC 21**
See also CA 110

Nizan, Paul 1905-1940. . . . . **TCLC 40**
See also DLB 72

Nkosi, Lewis
1936- . . . . . **CLC 45; BLC; DAM MULT**
See also BW 1; CA 65-68; CANR 27;
DLB 157

Nodier, (Jean) Charles (Emmanuel)
1780-1844 . . . . **NCLC 19**
See also DLB 119

Nolan, Christopher 1965-. . . . . **CLC 58**
See also CA 111

Noon, Jeff 1957-. . . . . **CLC 91**
See also CA 148

Norden, Charles
See Durrell, Lawrence (George)

Nordhoff, Charles (Bernard)
1887-1947 . . . . **TCLC 23**
See also CA 108; DLB 9; SATA 23

Norfolk, Lawrence 1963-. . . . . **CLC 76**
See also CA 144

Norman, Marsha
1947-. . . . . **CLC 28; DAM DRAM**
See also CA 105; CABS 3; CANR 41;
DLBY 84

Norris, Benjamin Franklin, Jr.
1870-1902 . . . . **TCLC 24**
See also Norris, Frank
See also CA 110

Norris, Frank
See Norris, Benjamin Franklin, Jr.
See also CDALB 1865-1917; DLB 12, 71

Norris, Leslie 1921-. . . . . **CLC 14**
See also CA 11-12; CANR 14; CAP 1;
DLB 27

North, Andrew
See Norton, Andre

North, Anthony
See Koontz, Dean R(ay)

North, Captain George
See Stevenson, Robert Louis (Balfour)

North, Milou
See Erdrich, Louise

Northrup, B. A.
See Hubbard, L(afayette) Ron(ald)

Parkin, Frank 1940-.............. **CLC 43**
See also CA 147

Parkman, Francis, Jr.
1823-1893 .... **NCLC 12**
See also DLB 1, 30

Parks, Gordon (Alexander Buchanan)
1912- ... **CLC 1, 16; BLC; DAM MULT**
See also AITN 2; BW 2; CA 41-44R;
CANR 26; DLB 33; SATA 8

Parmenides
c. 515B.C.-c. 450B.C........ **CMLC 22**
See also DLB 176

Parnell, Thomas 1679-1718 .... **LC 3**
See also DLB 94

Parra, Nicanor
1914- ...... **CLC 2; DAM MULT; HLC**
See also CA 85-88; CANR 32; HW; MTCW

Parrish, Mary Frances
See Fisher, M(ary) F(rances) K(ennedy)

Parson
See Coleridge, Samuel Taylor

Parson Lot
See Kingsley, Charles

Partridge, Anthony
See Oppenheim, E(dward) Phillips

Pascal, Blaise 1623-1662 .... **LC 35**

Pascoli, Giovanni 1855-1912 ...... **TCLC 45**

Pasolini, Pier Paolo
1922-1975 .... **CLC 20, 37; PC 17**
See also CA 93-96; 61-64; DLB 128, 177;
MTCW

Pasquini
See Silone, Ignazio

Pastan, Linda (Olenik)
1932- .... **CLC 27; DAM POET**
See also CA 61-64; CANR 18, 40; DLB 5

Pasternak, Boris (Leonidovich)
1890-1960 ...... **CLC 7, 10, 18, 63; DA;
DAB; DAC; DAM MST, NOV, POET;
PC 6; WLC**
See also CA 127; 116; MTCW

Patchen, Kenneth
1911-1972 ... **CLC 1, 2, 18; DAM POET**
See also CA 1-4R; 33-36R; CANR 3, 35;
DLB 16, 48; MTCW

Pater, Walter (Horatio)
1839-1894 .... **NCLC 7**
See also CDBLB 1832-1890; DLB 57, 156

Paterson, A(ndrew) B(arton)
1864-1941 .... **TCLC 32**
See also CA 155

Paterson, Katherine (Womeldorf)
1932- .... **CLC 12, 30**
See also AAYA 1; CA 21-24R; CANR 28;
CLR 7; DLB 52; JRDA; MAICYA;
MTCW; SATA 13, 53, 92

Patmore, Coventry Kersey Dighton
1823-1896 .... **NCLC 9**
See also DLB 35, 98

Paton, Alan (Stewart)
1903-1988 ...... **CLC 4, 10, 25, 55; DA;
DAB; DAC; DAM MST, NOV; WLC**
See also CA 13-16; 125; CANR 22; CAP 1;
MTCW; SATA 11; SATA-Obit 56

Paton Walsh, Gillian 1937-
See Walsh, Jill Paton
See also CANR 38; JRDA; MAICYA;
SAAS 3; SATA 4, 72

Paulding, James Kirke 1778-1860.. **NCLC 2**
See also DLB 3, 59, 74

Paulin, Thomas Neilson 1949-
See Paulin, Tom
See also CA 123; 128

Paulin, Tom .... **CLC 37**
See also Paulin, Thomas Neilson
See also DLB 40

Paustovsky, Konstantin (Georgievich)
1892-1968 .... **CLC 40**
See also CA 93-96; 25-28R

Pavese, Cesare
1908-1950 ..... **TCLC 3; PC 13; SSC 19**
See also CA 104; DLB 128, 177

Pavic, Milorad 1929-............. **CLC 60**
See also CA 136

Payne, Alan
See Jakes, John (William)

Paz, Gil
See Lugones, Leopoldo

Paz, Octavio
1914- .... **CLC 3, 4, 6, 10, 19, 51, 65;
DA; DAB; DAC; DAM MST, MULT,
POET; HLC; PC 1; WLC**
See also CA 73-76; CANR 32; DLBY 90;
HW; MTCW

p'Bitek, Okot
1931-1982 .... **CLC 96; BLC;
DAM MULT**
See also BW 2; CA 124; 107; DLB 125;
MTCW

Peacock, Molly 1947-............. **CLC 60**
See also CA 103; CAAS 21; CANR 52;
DLB 120

Peacock, Thomas Love
1785-1866 .... **NCLC 22**
See also DLB 96, 116

Peake, Mervyn 1911-1968 .... **CLC 7, 54**
See also CA 5-8R; 25-28R; CANR 3;
DLB 15, 160; MTCW; SATA 23

Pearce, Philippa .... **CLC 21**
See also Christie, (Ann) Philippa
See also CLR 9; DLB 161; MAICYA;
SATA 1, 67

Pearl, Eric
See Elman, Richard

Pearson, T(homas) R(eid) 1956- .... **CLC 39**
See also CA 120; 130; INT 130

Peck, Dale 1967- .... **CLC 81**
See also CA 146

Peck, John 1941- .... **CLC 3**
See also CA 49-52; CANR 3

Peck, Richard (Wayne) 1934- ...... **CLC 21**
See also AAYA 1; CA 85-88; CANR 19,
38; CLR 15; INT CANR-19; JRDA;
MAICYA; SAAS 2; SATA 18, 55

Peck, Robert Newton
1928- .. **CLC 17; DA; DAC; DAM MST**
See also AAYA 3; CA 81-84; CANR 31;
CLR 45; JRDA; MAICYA; SAAS 1;
SATA 21, 62

Peckinpah, (David) Sam(uel)
1925-1984 .... **CLC 20**
See also CA 109; 114

Pedersen, Knut 1859-1952
See Hamsun, Knut
See also CA 104; 119; MTCW

Peeslake, Gaffer
See Durrell, Lawrence (George)

Peguy, Charles Pierre
1873-1914 .... **TCLC 10**
See also CA 107

Pena, Ramon del Valle y
See Valle-Inclan, Ramon (Maria) del

Pendennis, Arthur Esquir
See Thackeray, William Makepeace

Penn, William 1644-1718........... **LC 25**
See also DLB 24

Pepys, Samuel
1633-1703 ..... **LC 11; DA; DAB; DAC;
DAM MST; WLC**
See also CDBLB 1660-1789; DLB 101

Percy, Walker
1916-1990 .... **CLC 2, 3, 6, 8, 14, 18, 47,
65; DAM NOV, POP**
See also CA 1-4R; 131; CANR 1, 23;
DLB 2; DLBY 80, 90; MTCW

Perec, Georges 1936-1982 .... **CLC 56**
See also CA 141; DLB 83

Pereda (y Sanchez de Porrua), Jose Maria de
1833-1906 .... **TCLC 16**
See also CA 117

Pereda y Porrua, Jose Maria de
See Pereda (y Sanchez de Porrua), Jose
Maria de

Peregoy, George Weems
See Mencken, H(enry) L(ouis)

Perelman, S(idney) J(oseph)
1904-1979 ...... **CLC 3, 5, 9, 15, 23, 44,
49; DAM DRAM**
See also AITN 1, 2; CA 73-76; 89-92;
CANR 18; DLB 11, 44; MTCW

Peret, Benjamin 1899-1959 .... **TCLC 20**
See also CA 117

Peretz, Isaac Loeb
1851(?)-1915 .... **TCLC 16; SSC 26**
See also CA 109

Peretz, Yitzhok Leibush
See Peretz, Isaac Loeb

Perez Galdos, Benito 1843-1920... **TCLC 27**
See also CA 125; 153; HW

Perrault, Charles 1628-1703 .... **LC 2**
See also MAICYA; SATA 25

Perry, Brighton
See Sherwood, Robert E(mmet)

Perse, St.-John .... **CLC 4, 11, 46**
See also Leger, (Marie-Rene Auguste) Alexis
Saint-Leger

Perutz, Leo 1882-1957 .... **TCLC 60**
See also DLB 81

Peseenz, Tulio F.
See Lopez y Fuentes, Gregorio

Pesetsky, Bette 1932-............. **CLC 28**
See also CA 133; DLB 130

Pteleon
  See Grieve, C(hristopher) M(urray)
  See also DAM POET

Puckett, Lute
  See Masters, Edgar Lee

Puig, Manuel
  1932-1990 . . . . **CLC 3, 5, 10, 28, 65;
    DAM MULT; HLC**
  See also CA 45-48; CANR 2, 32; DLB 113;
    HW; MTCW

Purdy, Al(fred Wellington)
  1918- . . . . **CLC 3, 6, 14, 50; DAC;
    DAM MST, POET**
  See also CA 81-84; CAAS 17; CANR 42;
    DLB 88

Purdy, James (Amos)
  1923- . . . . **CLC 2, 4, 10, 28, 52**
  See also CA 33-36R; CAAS 1; CANR 19,
    51; DLB 2; INT CANR-19; MTCW

Pure, Simon
  See Swinnerton, Frank Arthur

Pushkin, Alexander (Sergeyevich)
  1799-1837 . . . . . **NCLC 3, 27; DA; DAB;
    DAC; DAM DRAM, MST, POET;
    PC 10; WLC**
  See also SATA 61

P'u Sung-ling 1640-1715 . . . . **LC 3**

Putnam, Arthur Lee
  See Alger, Horatio, Jr.

Puzo, Mario
  1920- . . . . . **CLC 1, 2, 6, 36; DAM NOV,
    POP**
  See also CA 65-68; CANR 4, 42; DLB 6;
    MTCW

Pygge, Edward
  See Barnes, Julian (Patrick)

Pym, Barbara (Mary Crampton)
  1913-1980 . . . . **CLC 13, 19, 37**
  See also CA 13-14; 97-100; CANR 13, 34;
    CAP 1; DLB 14; DLBY 87; MTCW

Pynchon, Thomas (Ruggles, Jr.)
  1937- . . . . . **CLC 2, 3, 6, 9, 11, 18, 33, 62,
    72; DA; DAB; DAC; DAM MST, NOV,
    POP; SSC 14; WLC**
  See also BEST 90:2; CA 17-20R; CANR 22,
    46; DLB 2, 173; MTCW

Pythagoras
  c. 570B.C.-c. 500B.C. . . . . **CMLC 22**
  See also DLB 176

Qian Zhongshu
  See Ch'ien Chung-shu

Qroll
  See Dagerman, Stig (Halvard)

Quarrington, Paul (Lewis) 1953- . . . . **CLC 65**
  See also CA 129

Quasimodo, Salvatore 1901-1968 . . . **CLC 10**
  See also CA 13-16; 25-28R; CAP 1;
    DLB 114; MTCW

Quay, Stephen 1947- . . . . **CLC 95**

Quay, The Brothers
  See Quay, Stephen; Quay, Timothy

Quay, Timothy 1947- . . . . **CLC 95**

Queen, Ellery . . . . **CLC 3, 11**
  See also Dannay, Frederic; Davidson,
    Avram; Lee, Manfred B(ennington);
    Marlowe, Stephen; Sturgeon, Theodore
    (Hamilton); Vance, John Holbrook

Queen, Ellery, Jr.
  See Dannay, Frederic; Lee, Manfred
    B(ennington)

Queneau, Raymond
  1903-1976 . . . . **CLC 2, 5, 10, 42**
  See also CA 77-80; 69-72; CANR 32;
    DLB 72; MTCW

Quevedo, Francisco de 1580-1645 . . . . **LC 23**

Quiller-Couch, Arthur Thomas
  1863-1944 . . . . **TCLC 53**
  See also CA 118; DLB 135, 153

Quin, Ann (Marie) 1936-1973 . . . . **CLC 6**
  See also CA 9-12R; 45-48; DLB 14

Quinn, Martin
  See Smith, Martin Cruz

Quinn, Peter 1947- . . . . **CLC 91**

Quinn, Simon
  See Smith, Martin Cruz

Quiroga, Horacio (Sylvestre)
  1878-1937 . . . . . **TCLC 20; DAM MULT;
    HLC**
  See also CA 117; 131; HW; MTCW

Quoirez, Francoise 1935- . . . . **CLC 9**
  See also Sagan, Francoise
  See also CA 49-52; CANR 6, 39; MTCW

Raabe, Wilhelm 1831-1910 . . . . **TCLC 45**
  See also DLB 129

Rabe, David (William)
  1940- . . . . . . **CLC 4, 8, 33; DAM DRAM**
  See also CA 85-88; CABS 3; DLB 7

Rabelais, Francois
  1483-1553 . . . . . . **LC 5; DA; DAB; DAC;
    DAM MST; WLC**

Rabinovitch, Sholem 1859-1916
  See Aleichem, Sholom
  See also CA 104

Rachilde 1860-1953 . . . . **TCLC 67**
  See also DLB 123

Racine, Jean
  1639-1699 . . . . **LC 28; DAB; DAM MST**

Radcliffe, Ann (Ward)
  1764-1823 . . . . **NCLC 6, 55**
  See also DLB 39, 178

Radiguet, Raymond 1903-1923 . . . . **TCLC 29**
  See also DLB 65

Radnoti, Miklos 1909-1944 . . . . **TCLC 16**
  See also CA 118

Rado, James 1939- . . . . **CLC 17**
  See also CA 105

Radvanyi, Netty 1900-1983
  See Seghers, Anna
  See also CA 85-88; 110

Rae, Ben
  See Griffiths, Trevor

Raeburn, John (Hay) 1941- . . . . **CLC 34**
  See also CA 57-60

Ragni, Gerome 1942-1991 . . . . **CLC 17**
  See also CA 105; 134

Rahv, Philip 1908-1973 . . . . **CLC 24**
  See also Greenberg, Ivan
  See also DLB 137

Raine, Craig 1944- . . . . **CLC 32**
  See also CA 108; CANR 29, 51; DLB 40

Raine, Kathleen (Jessie) 1908- . . . **CLC 7, 45**
  See also CA 85-88; CANR 46; DLB 20;
    MTCW

Rainis, Janis 1865-1929 . . . . **TCLC 29**

Rakosi, Carl . . . . **CLC 47**
  See also Rawley, Callman
  See also CAAS 5

Raleigh, Richard
  See Lovecraft, H(oward) P(hillips)

Raleigh, Sir Walter
  1554(?)-1618 . . . . **LC 31, 39**
  See also CDBLB Before 1660; DLB 172

Rallentando, H. P.
  See Sayers, Dorothy L(eigh)

Ramal, Walter
  See de la Mare, Walter (John)

Ramon, Juan
  See Jimenez (Mantecon), Juan Ramon

Ramos, Graciliano 1892-1953 . . . . . **TCLC 32**

Rampersad, Arnold 1941- . . . . **CLC 44**
  See also BW 2; CA 127; 133; DLB 111;
    INT 133

Rampling, Anne
  See Rice, Anne

Ramsay, Allan 1684(?)-1758 . . . . **LC 29**
  See also DLB 95

Ramuz, Charles-Ferdinand
  1878-1947 . . . . **TCLC 33**

Rand, Ayn
  1905-1982 . . . . . . **CLC 3, 30, 44, 79; DA;
    DAC; DAM MST, NOV, POP; WLC**
  See also AAYA 10; CA 13-16R; 105;
    CANR 27; MTCW

Randall, Dudley (Felker)
  1914- . . . . . . **CLC 1; BLC; DAM MULT**
  See also BW 1; CA 25-28R; CANR 23;
    DLB 41

Randall, Robert
  See Silverberg, Robert

Ranger, Ken
  See Creasey, John

Ransom, John Crowe
  1888-1974 . . . . **CLC 2, 4, 5, 11, 24;
    DAM POET**
  See also CA 5-8R; 49-52; CANR 6, 34;
    DLB 45, 63; MTCW

Rao, Raja 1909- . . . **CLC 25, 56; DAM NOV**
  See also CA 73-76; CANR 51; MTCW

Raphael, Frederic (Michael)
  1931- . . . . **CLC 2, 14**
  See also CA 1-4R; CANR 1; DLB 14

Ratcliffe, James P.
  See Mencken, H(enry) L(ouis)

Rathbone, Julian 1935- . . . . **CLC 41**
  See also CA 101; CANR 34

Rattigan, Terence (Mervyn)
  1911-1977 . . . . **CLC 7; DAM DRAM**
  See also CA 85-88; 73-76;
    CDBLB 1945-1960; DLB 13; MTCW

Richardson, John
1796-1852 . . . . **NCLC 55; DAC**
See also DLB 99

Richardson, Samuel
1689-1761 . . . . . . **LC 1; DA; DAB; DAC;**
DAM MST, NOV; WLC
See also CDBLB 1660-1789; DLB 39

Richler, Mordecai
1931- . . . . **CLC 3, 5, 9, 13, 18, 46, 70;**
DAC; DAM MST, NOV
See also AITN 1; CA 65-68; CANR 31;
CLR 17; DLB 53; MAICYA; MTCW;
SATA 44; SATA-Brief 27

Richter, Conrad (Michael)
1890-1968 . . . . **CLC 30**
See also AAYA 21; CA 5-8R; 25-28R;
CANR 23; DLB 9; MTCW; SATA 3

Ricostranza, Tom
See Ellis, Trey

Riddell, J. H. 1832-1906 . . . . **TCLC 40**

Riding, Laura . . . . **CLC 3, 7**
See also Jackson, Laura (Riding)

Riefenstahl, Berta Helene Amalia 1902-
See Riefenstahl, Leni
See also CA 108

Riefenstahl, Leni . . . . **CLC 16**
See also Riefenstahl, Berta Helene Amalia

Riffe, Ernest
See Bergman, (Ernst) Ingmar

Riggs, (Rolla) Lynn
1899-1954 . . . . . **TCLC 56; DAM MULT**
See also CA 144; DLB 175; NNAL

Riley, James Whitcomb
1849-1916 . . . . . . **TCLC 51; DAM POET**
See also CA 118; 137; MAICYA; SATA 17

Riley, Tex
See Creasey, John

Rilke, Rainer Maria
1875-1926 . . . . **TCLC 1, 6, 19;**
DAM POET; PC 2
See also CA 104; 132; DLB 81; MTCW

Rimbaud, (Jean Nicolas) Arthur
1854-1891 . . . . . **NCLC 4, 35; DA; DAB;**
DAC; DAM MST, POET; PC 3; WLC

Rinehart, Mary Roberts
1876-1958 . . . . **TCLC 52**
See also CA 108

Ringmaster, The
See Mencken, H(enry) L(ouis)

Ringwood, Gwen(dolyn Margaret) Pharis
1910-1984 . . . . **CLC 48**
See also CA 148; 112; DLB 88

Rio, Michel 19(?)- . . . . **CLC 43**

Ritsos, Giannes
See Ritsos, Yannis

Ritsos, Yannis 1909-1990 . . . . . **CLC 6, 13, 31**
See also CA 77-80; 133; CANR 39; MTCW

Ritter, Erika 1948(?)- . . . . **CLC 52**

Rivera, Jose Eustasio 1889-1928 . . . **TCLC 35**
See also HW

Rivers, Conrad Kent 1933-1968 . . . . . . **CLC 1**
See also BW 1; CA 85-88; DLB 41

Rivers, Elfrida
See Bradley, Marion Zimmer

Riverside, John
See Heinlein, Robert A(nson)

Rizal, Jose 1861-1896 . . . . **NCLC 27**

Roa Bastos, Augusto (Antonio)
1917- . . . . . **CLC 45; DAM MULT; HLC**
See also CA 131; DLB 113; HW

Robbe-Grillet, Alain
1922- . . . . . . **CLC 1, 2, 4, 6, 8, 10, 14, 43**
See also CA 9-12R; CANR 33; DLB 83;
MTCW

Robbins, Harold
1916- . . . . **CLC 5; DAM NOV**
See also CA 73-76; CANR 26, 54; MTCW

Robbins, Thomas Eugene 1936-
See Robbins, Tom
See also CA 81-84; CANR 29; DAM NOV,
POP; MTCW

Robbins, Tom . . . . **CLC 9, 32, 64**
See also Robbins, Thomas Eugene
See also BEST 90:3; DLBY 80

Robbins, Trina 1938- . . . . **CLC 21**
See also CA 128

Roberts, Charles G(eorge) D(ouglas)
1860-1943 . . . . **TCLC 8**
See also CA 105; CLR 33; DLB 92;
SATA 88; SATA-Brief 29

Roberts, Elizabeth Madox
1886-1941 . . . . **TCLC 68**
See also CA 111; DLB 9, 54, 102;
SATA 33; SATA-Brief 27

Roberts, Kate 1891-1985 . . . . **CLC 15**
See also CA 107; 116

Roberts, Keith (John Kingston)
1935- . . . . **CLC 14**
See also CA 25-28R; CANR 46

Roberts, Kenneth (Lewis)
1885-1957 . . . . **TCLC 23**
See also CA 109; DLB 9

Roberts, Michele (B.) 1949- . . . . **CLC 48**
See also CA 115; CANR 58

Robertson, Ellis
See Ellison, Harlan (Jay); Silverberg, Robert

Robertson, Thomas William
1829-1871 . . . . **NCLC 35; DAM DRAM**

Robeson, Kenneth
See Dent, Lester

Robinson, Edwin Arlington
1869-1935 . . . . **TCLC 5; DA; DAC;**
DAM MST, POET; PC 1
See also CA 104; 133; CDALB 1865-1917;
DLB 54; MTCW

Robinson, Henry Crabb
1775-1867 . . . . **NCLC 15**
See also DLB 107

Robinson, Jill 1936- . . . . **CLC 10**
See also CA 102; INT 102

Robinson, Kim Stanley 1952- . . . . . . **CLC 34**
See also CA 126

Robinson, Lloyd
See Silverberg, Robert

Robinson, Marilynne 1944- . . . . **CLC 25**
See also CA 116

Robinson, Smokey . . . . **CLC 21**
See also Robinson, William, Jr.

Robinson, William, Jr. 1940-
See Robinson, Smokey
See also CA 116

Robison, Mary 1949- . . . . **CLC 42, 98**
See also CA 113; 116; DLB 130; INT 116

Rod, Edouard 1857-1910 . . . . **TCLC 52**

Roddenberry, Eugene Wesley 1921-1991
See Roddenberry, Gene
See also CA 110; 135; CANR 37; SATA 45;
SATA-Obit 69

Roddenberry, Gene . . . . **CLC 17**
See also Roddenberry, Eugene Wesley
See also AAYA 5; SATA-Obit 69

Rodgers, Mary 1931- . . . . **CLC 12**
See also CA 49-52; CANR 8, 55; CLR 20;
INT CANR-8; JRDA; MAICYA;
SATA 8

Rodgers, W(illiam) R(obert)
1909-1969 . . . . **CLC 7**
See also CA 85-88; DLB 20

Rodman, Eric
See Silverberg, Robert

Rodman, Howard 1920(?)-1985 . . . . . **CLC 65**
See also CA 118

Rodman, Maia
See Wojciechowska, Maia (Teresa)

Rodriguez, Claudio 1934- . . . . **CLC 10**
See also DLB 134

Roelvaag, O(le) E(dvart)
1876-1931 . . . . **TCLC 17**
See also CA 117; DLB 9

Roethke, Theodore (Huebner)
1908-1963 . . . . . . **CLC 1, 3, 8, 11, 19, 46,**
101; DAM POET; PC 15
See also CA 81-84; CABS 2;
CDALB 1941-1968; DLB 5; MTCW

Rogers, Thomas Hunton 1927- . . . . . **CLC 57**
See also CA 89-92; INT 89-92

Rogers, Will(iam Penn Adair)
1879-1935 . . . **TCLC 8, 71; DAM MULT**
See also CA 105; 144; DLB 11; NNAL

Rogin, Gilbert 1929- . . . . **CLC 18**
See also CA 65-68; CANR 15

Rohan, Koda . . . . **TCLC 22**
See also Koda Shigeyuki

Rohmer, Eric . . . . **CLC 16**
See also Scherer, Jean-Marie Maurice

Rohmer, Sax . . . . **TCLC 28**
See also Ward, Arthur Henry Sarsfield
See also DLB 70

Roiphe, Anne (Richardson)
1935- . . . . **CLC 3, 9**
See also CA 89-92; CANR 45; DLBY 80;
INT 89-92

Rojas, Fernando de 1465-1541 . . . . . . **LC 23**

Rolfe, Frederick (William Serafino Austin
Lewis Mary) 1860-1913 . . . . . . **TCLC 12**
See also CA 107; DLB 34, 156

Rolland, Romain 1866-1944 . . . . **TCLC 23**
See also CA 118; DLB 65

Rolle, Richard c. 1300-c. 1349 . . . **CMLC 21**
See also DLB 146

Rolvaag, O(le) E(dvart)
See Roelvaag, O(le) E(dvart)

Romain Arnaud, Saint
See Aragon, Louis

Romains, Jules 1885-1972 . . . . **CLC 7**
See also CA 85-88; CANR 34; DLB 65;
MTCW

Romero, Jose Ruben 1890-1952 . . . **TCLC 14**
See also CA 114; 131; HW

Ronsard, Pierre de
1524-1585 . . . . **LC 6; PC 11**

Rooke, Leon
1934- . . . . **CLC 25, 34; DAM POP**
See also CA 25-28R; CANR 23, 53

Roosevelt, Theodore 1858-1919 . . . . **TCLC 69**
See also CA 115; DLB 47

Roper, William 1498-1578 . . . . **LC 10**

Roquelaure, A. N.
See Rice, Anne

Rosa, Joao Guimaraes 1908-1967 . . . **CLC 23**
See also CA 89-92; DLB 113

Rose, Wendy
1948- . . . . **CLC 85; DAM MULT; PC 13**
See also CA 53-56; CANR 5, 51; DLB 175;
NNAL; SATA 12

Rosen, Richard (Dean) 1949- . . . . **CLC 39**
See also CA 77-80; INT CANR-30

Rosenberg, Isaac 1890-1918 . . . . . . **TCLC 12**
See also CA 107; DLB 20

Rosenblatt, Joe . . . . **CLC 15**
See also Rosenblatt, Joseph

Rosenblatt, Joseph 1933-
See Rosenblatt, Joe
See also CA 89-92; INT 89-92

Rosenfeld, Samuel 1896-1963
See Tzara, Tristan
See also CA 89-92

Rosenstock, Sami
See Tzara, Tristan

Rosenstock, Samuel
See Tzara, Tristan

Rosenthal, M(acha) L(ouis)
1917-1996 . . . . **CLC 28**
See also CA 1-4R; 152; CAAS 6; CANR 4,
51; DLB 5; SATA 59

Ross, Barnaby
See Dannay, Frederic

Ross, Bernard L.
See Follett, Ken(neth Martin)

Ross, J. H.
See Lawrence, T(homas) E(dward)

Ross, Martin
See Martin, Violet Florence
See also DLB 135

Ross, (James) Sinclair
1908- . . . . . . **CLC 13; DAC; DAM MST;**
SSC 24
See also CA 73-76; DLB 88

Rossetti, Christina (Georgina)
1830-1894 . . . . . **NCLC 2, 50; DA; DAB;**
DAC; DAM MST, POET; PC 7; WLC
See also DLB 35, 163; MAICYA; SATA 20

Rossetti, Dante Gabriel
1828-1882 . . . . **NCLC 4; DA; DAB;**
DAC; DAM MST, POET; WLC
See also CDBLB 1832-1890; DLB 35

Rossner, Judith (Perelman)
1935- . . . . **CLC 6, 9, 29**
See also AITN 2; BEST 90:3; CA 17-20R;
CANR 18, 51; DLB 6; INT CANR-18;
MTCW

Rostand, Edmond (Eugene Alexis)
1868-1918 . . . . . . **TCLC 6, 37; DA; DAB;**
DAC; DAM DRAM, MST
See also CA 104; 126; MTCW

Roth, Henry 1906-1995 . . . . **CLC 2, 6, 11**
See also CA 11-12; 149; CANR 38; CAP 1;
DLB 28; MTCW

Roth, Joseph 1894-1939 . . . . **TCLC 33**
See also DLB 85

Roth, Philip (Milton)
1933- . . . . . **CLC 1, 2, 3, 4, 6, 9, 15, 22,**
31, 47, 66, 86; DA; DAB; DAC;
DAM MST, NOV, POP; SSC 26; WLC
See also BEST 90:3; CA 1-4R; CANR 1, 22,
36, 55; CDALB 1968-1988; DLB 2, 28,
173; DLBY 82; MTCW

Rothenberg, Jerome 1931- . . . . **CLC 6, 57**
See also CA 45-48; CANR 1; DLB 5

Roumain, Jacques (Jean Baptiste)
1907-1944 . . . . **TCLC 19; BLC;**
DAM MULT
See also BW 1; CA 117; 125

Rourke, Constance (Mayfield)
1885-1941 . . . . **TCLC 12**
See also CA 107; 1

Rousseau, Jean-Baptiste 1671-1741 . . . **LC 9**

Rousseau, Jean-Jacques
1712-1778 . . . . **LC 14, 36; DA; DAB;**
DAC; DAM MST; WLC

Roussel, Raymond 1877-1933 . . . . . **TCLC 20**
See also CA 117

Rovit, Earl (Herbert) 1927- . . . . **CLC 7**
See also CA 5-8R; CANR 12

Rowe, Nicholas 1674-1718 . . . . **LC 8**
See also DLB 84

Rowley, Ames Dorrance
See Lovecraft, H(oward) P(hillips)

Rowson, Susanna Haswell
1762(?)-1824 . . . . **NCLC 5**
See also DLB 37

Roy, Gabrielle
1909-1983 . . . . **CLC 10, 14; DAB; DAC;**
DAM MST
See also CA 53-56; 110; CANR 5; DLB 68;
MTCW

Rozewicz, Tadeusz
1921- . . . . **CLC 9, 23; DAM POET**
See also CA 108; CANR 36; MTCW

Ruark, Gibbons 1941- . . . . **CLC 3**
See also CA 33-36R; CAAS 23; CANR 14,
31, 57; DLB 120

Rubens, Bernice (Ruth) 1923- . . . **CLC 19, 31**
See also CA 25-28R; CANR 33; DLB 14;
MTCW

Rubin, Harold
See Robbins, Harold

Rudkin, (James) David 1936- . . . . . . **CLC 14**
See also CA 89-92; DLB 13

Rudnik, Raphael 1933- . . . . **CLC 7**
See also CA 29-32R

Ruffian, M.
See Hasek, Jaroslav (Matej Frantisek)

Ruiz, Jose Martinez . . . . **CLC 11**
See also Martinez Ruiz, Jose

Rukeyser, Muriel
1913-1980 . . . . **CLC 6, 10, 15, 27;**
DAM POET; PC 12
See also CA 5-8R; 93-96; CANR 26;
DLB 48; MTCW; SATA-Obit 22

Rule, Jane (Vance) 1931- . . . . **CLC 27**
See also CA 25-28R; CAAS 18; CANR 12;
DLB 60

Rulfo, Juan
1918-1986 . . . . **CLC 8, 80; DAM MULT;**
HLC; SSC 25
See also CA 85-88; 118; CANR 26;
DLB 113; HW; MTCW

Rumi, Jalal al-Din 1297-1373 . . . . **CMLC 20**

Runeberg, Johan 1804-1877 . . . . . . **NCLC 41**

Runyon, (Alfred) Damon
1884(?)-1946 . . . . **TCLC 10**
See also CA 107; DLB 11, 86, 171

Rush, Norman 1933- . . . . **CLC 44**
See also CA 121; 126; INT 126

Rushdie, (Ahmed) Salman
1947- . . . . **CLC 23, 31, 55, 100; DAB;**
DAC; DAM MST, NOV, POP
See also BEST 89:3; CA 108; 111;
CANR 33, 56; INT 111; MTCW; YABC

Rushforth, Peter (Scott) 1945- . . . . . **CLC 19**
See also CA 101

Ruskin, John 1819-1900 . . . . **TCLC 63**
See also CA 114; 129; CDBLB 1832-1890;
DLB 55, 163; SATA 24

Russ, Joanna 1937- . . . . **CLC 15**
See also CA 25-28R; CANR 11, 31; DLB 8;
MTCW

Russell, George William 1867-1935
See Baker, Jean H.
See also CA 104; 153; CDBLB 1890-1914;
DAM POET

Russell, (Henry) Ken(neth Alfred)
1927- . . . . **CLC 16**
See also CA 105

Russell, Willy 1947- . . . . **CLC 60**

Rutherford, Mark . . . . **TCLC 25**
See also White, William Hale
See also DLB 18

Ruyslinck, Ward 1929- . . . . **CLC 14**
See also Belser, Reimond Karel Maria de

Ryan, Cornelius (John) 1920-1974 . . . **CLC 7**
See also CA 69-72; 53-56; CANR 38

Ryan, Michael 1946- . . . . **CLC 65**
See also CA 49-52; DLBY 82

Ryan, Tim
See Dent, Lester

Rybakov, Anatoli (Naumovich)
1911- . . . . **CLC 23, 53**
See also CA 126; 135; SATA 79

Ryder, Jonathan
See Ludlum, Robert

Ryga, George
1932-1987 . . **CLC 14; DAC; DAM MST**
See also CA 101; 124; CANR 43; DLB 60

S. S.
See Sassoon, Siegfried (Lorraine)

Saba, Umberto 1883-1957 .... **TCLC 33**
See also CA 144; DLB 114

Sabatini, Rafael 1875-1950 ...... **TCLC 47**

Sabato, Ernesto (R.)
1911- .... **CLC 10, 23; DAM MULT;**
HLC
See also CA 97-100; CANR 32; DLB 145;
HW; MTCW

Sacastru, Martin
See Bioy Casares, Adolfo

Sacher-Masoch, Leopold von
1836(?)-1895 .... **NCLC 31**

Sachs, Marilyn (Stickle) 1927- ..... **CLC 35**
See also AAYA 2; CA 17-20R; CANR 13,
47; CLR 2; JRDA; MAICYA; SAAS 2;
SATA 3, 68

Sachs, Nelly 1891-1970 .... **CLC 14, 98**
See also CA 17-18; 25-28R; CAP 2

Sackler, Howard (Oliver)
1929-1982 .... **CLC 14**
See also CA 61-64; 108; CANR 30; DLB 7

Sacks, Oliver (Wolf) 1933- .... **CLC 67**
See also CA 53-56; CANR 28, 50;
INT CANR-28; MTCW

Sade, Donatien Alphonse Francois Comte
1740-1814 .... **NCLC 47**

Sadoff, Ira 1945- .... **CLC 9**
See also CA 53-56; CANR 5, 21; DLB 120

Saetone
See Camus, Albert

Safire, William 1929- .... **CLC 10**
See also CA 17-20R; CANR 31, 54

Sagan, Carl (Edward) 1934-1996 .... **CLC 30**
See also AAYA 2; CA 25-28R; 155;
CANR 11, 36; MTCW; SATA 58;
SATA-Obit 94

Sagan, Francoise .... **CLC 3, 6, 9, 17, 36**
See also Quoirez, Francoise
See also DLB 83

Sahgal, Nayantara (Pandit) 1927-... **CLC 41**
See also CA 9-12R; CANR 11

Saint, H(arry) F. 1941- .... **CLC 50**
See also CA 127

St. Aubin de Teran, Lisa 1953-
See Teran, Lisa St. Aubin de
See also CA 118; 126; INT 126

Sainte-Beuve, Charles Augustin
1804-1869 .... **NCLC 5**

Saint-Exupery, Antoine (Jean Baptiste Marie
Roger) de
1900-1944 .... **TCLC 2, 56; DAM NOV;**
WLC
See also CA 108; 132; CLR 10; DLB 72;
MAICYA; MTCW; SATA 20

St. John, David
See Hunt, E(verette) Howard, (Jr.)

Saint-John Perse
See Leger, (Marie-Rene Auguste) Alexis
Saint-Leger

Saintsbury, George (Edward Bateman)
1845-1933 .... **TCLC 31**
See also DLB 57, 149

Sait Faik .... **TCLC 23**
See also Abasiyanik, Sait Faik

Saki .... **TCLC 3; SSC 12**
See also Munro, H(ector) H(ugh)

Sala, George Augustus .... **NCLC 46**

Salama, Hannu 1936- .... **CLC 18**

Salamanca, J(ack) R(ichard)
1922- .... **CLC 4, 15**
See also CA 25-28R

Sale, J. Kirkpatrick
See Sale, Kirkpatrick

Sale, Kirkpatrick 1937- .... **CLC 68**
See also CA 13-16R; CANR 10

Salinas, Luis Omar
1937- ..... **CLC 90; DAM MULT; HLC**
See also CA 131; DLB 82; HW

Salinas (y Serrano), Pedro
1891(?)-1951 .... **TCLC 17**
See also CA 117; DLB 134

Salinger, J(erome) D(avid)
1919- ..... **CLC 1, 3, 8, 12, 55, 56; DA;**
DAB; DAC; DAM MST, NOV, POP;
SSC 2; WLC
See also AAYA 2; CA 5-8R; CANR 39;
CDALB 1941-1968; CLR 18; DLB 2, 102,
173; MAICYA; MTCW; SATA 67

Salisbury, John
See Caute, David

Salter, James 1925- .... **CLC 7, 52, 59**
See also CA 73-76; DLB 130

Saltus, Edgar (Everton)
1855-1921 .... **TCLC 8**
See also CA 105

Saltykov, Mikhail Evgrafovich
1826-1889 .... **NCLC 16**

Samarakis, Antonis 1919- .... **CLC 5**
See also CA 25-28R; CAAS 16; CANR 36

Sanchez, Florencio 1875-1910 ..... **TCLC 37**
See also CA 153; HW

Sanchez, Luis Rafael 1936- .... **CLC 23**
See also CA 128; DLB 145; HW

Sanchez, Sonia
1934- ...... **CLC 5; BLC; DAM MULT;**
PC 9
See also BW 2; CA 33-36R; CANR 24, 49;
CLR 18; DLB 41; DLBD 8; MAICYA;
MTCW; SATA 22

Sand, George
1804-1876 .... **NCLC 2, 42, 57; DA;**
DAB; DAC; DAM MST, NOV; WLC
See also DLB 119

Sandburg, Carl (August)
1878-1967 .... **CLC 1, 4, 10, 15, 35; DA;**
DAB; DAC; DAM MST, POET; PC 2;
WLC
See also CA 5-8R; 25-28R; CANR 35;
CDALB 1865-1917; DLB 17, 54;
MAICYA; MTCW; SATA 8

Sandburg, Charles
See Sandburg, Carl (August)

Sandburg, Charles A.
See Sandburg, Carl (August)

Sanders, (James) Ed(ward) 1939- ... **CLC 53**
See also CA 13-16R; CAAS 21; CANR 13,
44; DLB 16

Sanders, Lawrence
1920- .... **CLC 41; DAM POP**
See also BEST 89:4; CA 81-84; CANR 33;
MTCW

Sanders, Noah
See Blount, Roy (Alton), Jr.

Sanders, Winston P.
See Anderson, Poul (William)

Sandoz, Mari(e Susette)
1896-1966 .... **CLC 28**
See also CA 1-4R; 25-28R; CANR 17;
DLB 9; MTCW; SATA 5

Saner, Reg(inald Anthony) 1931- .... **CLC 9**
See also CA 65-68

Sannazaro, Jacopo 1456(?)-1530...... **LC 8**

Sansom, William
1912-1976 ...... **CLC 2, 6; DAM NOV;**
SSC 21
See also CA 5-8R; 65-68; CANR 42;
DLB 139; MTCW

Santayana, George 1863-1952 ..... **TCLC 40**
See also CA 115; DLB 54, 71; DLBD 13

Santiago, Danny .... **CLC 33**
See also James, Daniel (Lewis)
See also DLB 122

Santmyer, Helen Hoover
1895-1986 .... **CLC 33**
See also CA 1-4R; 118; CANR 15, 33;
DLBY 84; MTCW

Santoka, Taneda 1882-1940....... **TCLC 72**

Santos, Bienvenido N(uqui)
1911-1996 ...... **CLC 22; DAM MULT**
See also CA 101; 151; CANR 19, 46

Sapper .... **TCLC 44**
See also McNeile, Herman Cyril

Sapphire 1950- .... **CLC 99**

Sappho
fl. 6th cent. B.C.- .... **CMLC 3;**
DAM POET; PC 5
See also DLB 176

Sarduy, Severo 1937-1993 .... **CLC 6, 97**
See also CA 89-92; 142; CANR 58;
DLB 113; HW

Sargeson, Frank 1903-1982 .... **CLC 31**
See also CA 25-28R; 106; CANR 38

Sarmiento, Felix Ruben Garcia
See Dario, Ruben

Saroyan, William
1908-1981 ..... **CLC 1, 8, 10, 29, 34, 56;**
DA; DAB; DAC; DAM DRAM, MST,
NOV; SSC 21; WLC
See also CA 5-8R; 103; CANR 30; DLB 7,
9, 86; DLBY 81; MTCW; SATA 23;
SATA-Obit 24

Sarraute, Nathalie
1900- .... **CLC 1, 2, 4, 8, 10, 31, 80**
See also CA 9-12R; CANR 23; DLB 83;
MTCW

Sarton, (Eleanor) May
1912-1995 .... **CLC 4, 14, 49, 91;**
DAM POET
See also CA 1-4R; 149; CANR 1, 34, 55;
DLB 48; DLBY 81; INT CANR-34;
MTCW; SATA 36; SATA-Obit 86

Sartre, Jean-Paul
1905-1980 .... **CLC 1, 4, 7, 9, 13, 18, 24,
44, 50, 52; DA; DAB; DAC;
DAM DRAM, MST, NOV; DC 3; WLC**
See also CA 9-12R; 97-100; CANR 21;
DLB 72; MTCW

Sassoon, Siegfried (Lorraine)
1886-1967 .... **CLC 36; DAB;
DAM MST, NOV, POET; PC 12**
See also CA 104; 25-28R; CANR 36;
DLB 20; MTCW

Satterfield, Charles
See Pohl, Frederik

Saul, John (W. III)
1942- ...... **CLC 46; DAM NOV, POP**
See also AAYA 10; BEST 90:4; CA 81-84;
CANR 16, 40

Saunders, Caleb
See Heinlein, Robert A(nson)

Saura (Atares), Carlos 1932- ...... **CLC 20**
See also CA 114; 131; HW

Sauser-Hall, Frederic 1887-1961.... **CLC 18**
See also Cendrars, Blaise
See also CA 102; 93-96; CANR 36; MTCW

Saussure, Ferdinand de
1857-1913 .... **TCLC 49**

Savage, Catharine
See Brosman, Catharine Savage

Savage, Thomas 1915- .... **CLC 40**
See also CA 126; 132; CAAS 15; INT 132

Savan, Glenn 19(?)- .... **CLC 50**

Sayers, Dorothy L(eigh)
1893-1957 ..... **TCLC 2, 15; DAM POP**
See also CA 104; 119; CDBLB 1914-1945;
DLB 10, 36, 77, 100; MTCW

Sayers, Valerie 1952- .... **CLC 50**
See also CA 134

Sayles, John (Thomas)
1950- .... **CLC 7, 10, 14**
See also CA 57-60; CANR 41; DLB 44

Scammell, Michael 1935- .... **CLC 34**
See also CA 156

Scannell, Vernon 1922- .... **CLC 49**
See also CA 5-8R; CANR 8, 24, 57;
DLB 27; SATA 59

Scarlett, Susan
See Streatfeild, (Mary) Noel

Schaeffer, Susan Fromberg
1941- .... **CLC 6, 11, 22**
See also CA 49-52; CANR 18; DLB 28;
MTCW; SATA 22

Schary, Jill
See Robinson, Jill

Schell, Jonathan 1943- .... **CLC 35**
See also CA 73-76; CANR 12

Schelling, Friedrich Wilhelm Joseph von
1775-1854 .... **NCLC 30**
See also DLB 90

Schendel, Arthur van 1874-1946 ... **TCLC 56**

Scherer, Jean-Marie Maurice 1920-
See Rohmer, Eric
See also CA 110

Schevill, James (Erwin) 1920- .... **CLC 7**
See also CA 5-8R; CAAS 12

Schiller, Friedrich
1759-1805 .... **NCLC 39; DAM DRAM**
See also DLB 94

Schisgal, Murray (Joseph) 1926- ..... **CLC 6**
See also CA 21-24R; CANR 48

Schlee, Ann 1934- .... **CLC 35**
See also CA 101; CANR 29; SATA 44;
SATA-Brief 36

Schlegel, August Wilhelm von
1767-1845 .... **NCLC 15**
See also DLB 94

Schlegel, Friedrich 1772-1829 .... **NCLC 45**
See also DLB 90

Schlegel, Johann Elias (von)
1719(?)-1749 .... **LC 5**

Schlesinger, Arthur M(eier), Jr.
1917- .... **CLC 84**
See also AITN 1; CA 1-4R; CANR 1, 28,
58; DLB 17; INT CANR-28; MTCW;
SATA 61

Schmidt, Arno (Otto) 1914-1979.... **CLC 56**
See also CA 128; 109; DLB 69

Schmitz, Aron Hector 1861-1928
See Svevo, Italo
See also CA 104; 122; MTCW

Schnackenberg, Gjertrud 1953-..... **CLC 40**
See also CA 116; DLB 120

Schneider, Leonard Alfred 1925-1966
See Bruce, Lenny
See also CA 89-92

Schnitzler, Arthur
1862-1931 .... **TCLC 4; SSC 15**
See also CA 104; DLB 81, 118

Schopenhauer, Arthur
1788-1860 .... **NCLC 51**
See also DLB 90

Schor, Sandra (M.) 1932(?)-1990 ... **CLC 65**
See also CA 132

Schorer, Mark 1908-1977 .... **CLC 9**
See also CA 5-8R; 73-76; CANR 7;
DLB 103

Schrader, Paul (Joseph) 1946-...... **CLC 26**
See also CA 37-40R; CANR 41; DLB 44

Schreiner, Olive (Emilie Albertina)
1855-1920 .... **TCLC 9**
See also CA 105; DLB 18, 156

Schulberg, Budd (Wilson)
1914- .... **CLC 7, 48**
See also CA 25-28R; CANR 19; DLB 6, 26,
28; DLBY 81

Schulz, Bruno
1892-1942 .... **TCLC 5, 51; SSC 13**
See also CA 115; 123

Schulz, Charles M(onroe) 1922- .... **CLC 12**
See also CA 9-12R; CANR 6;
INT CANR-6; SATA 10

Schumacher, E(rnst) F(riedrich)
1911-1977 .... **CLC 80**
See also CA 81-84; 73-76; CANR 34

Schuyler, James Marcus
1923-1991 ..... **CLC 5, 23; DAM POET**
See also CA 101; 134; DLB 5, 169; INT 101

Schwartz, Delmore (David)
1913-1966 ... **CLC 2, 4, 10, 45, 87; PC 8**
See also CA 17-18; 25-28R; CANR 35;
CAP 2; DLB 28, 48; MTCW

Schwartz, Ernst
See Ozu, Yasujiro

Schwartz, John Burnham 1965- .... **CLC 59**
See also CA 132

Schwartz, Lynne Sharon 1939-..... **CLC 31**
See also CA 103; CANR 44

Schwartz, Muriel A.
See Eliot, T(homas) S(tearns)

Schwarz-Bart, Andre 1928-....... **CLC 2, 4**
See also CA 89-92

Schwarz-Bart, Simone 1938-........ **CLC 7**
See also BW 2; CA 97-100

Schwob, (Mayer Andre) Marcel
1867-1905 .... **TCLC 20**
See also CA 117; DLB 123

Sciascia, Leonardo
1921-1989 .... **CLC 8, 9, 41**
See also CA 85-88; 130; CANR 35;
DLB 177; MTCW

Scoppettone, Sandra 1936-........ **CLC 26**
See also AAYA 11; CA 5-8R; CANR 41;
SATA 9, 92

Scorsese, Martin 1942- .... **CLC 20, 89**
See also CA 110; 114; CANR 46

Scotland, Jay
See Jakes, John (William)

Scott, Duncan Campbell
1862-1947 .... **TCLC 6; DAC**
See also CA 104; 153; DLB 92

Scott, Evelyn 1893-1963........... **CLC 43**
See also CA 104; 112; DLB 9, 48

Scott, F(rancis) R(eginald)
1899-1985 .... **CLC 22**
See also CA 101; 114; DLB 88; INT 101

Scott, Frank
See Scott, F(rancis) R(eginald)

Scott, Joanna 1960- .... **CLC 50**
See also CA 126; CANR 53

Scott, Paul (Mark) 1920-1978.... **CLC 9, 60**
See also CA 81-84; 77-80; CANR 33;
DLB 14; MTCW

Scott, Walter
1771-1832 .... **NCLC 15; DA; DAB;
DAC; DAM MST, NOV, POET; PC 13;
WLC**
See also CDBLB 1789-1832; DLB 93, 107,
116, 144, 159; 2

Scribe, (Augustin) Eugene
1791-1861 .... **NCLC 16; DAM DRAM;
DC 5**

Scrum, R.
See Crumb, R(obert)

Scudery, Madeleine de 1607-1701..... **LC 2**

Scum
See Crumb, R(obert)

Scumbag, Little Bobby
See Crumb, R(obert)

Seabrook, John
See Hubbard, L(afayette) Ron(ald)

Sealy, I. Allan 1951- .... **CLC 55**

Search, Alexander
See Pessoa, Fernando (Antonio Nogueira)

Sebastian, Lee
See Silverberg, Robert

Sebastian Owl
See Thompson, Hunter S(tockton)

Sebestyen, Ouida 1924- .... **CLC 30**
See also AAYA 8; CA 107; CANR 40;
CLR 17; JRDA; MAICYA; SAAS 10;
SATA 39

Secundus, H. Scriblerus
See Fielding, Henry

Sedges, John
See Buck, Pearl S(ydenstricker)

Sedgwick, Catharine Maria
1789-1867 .... **NCLC 19**
See also DLB 1, 74

Seelye, John 1931- .... **CLC 7**

Seferiades, Giorgos Stylianou 1900-1971
See Seferis, George
See also CA 5-8R; 33-36R; CANR 5, 36;
MTCW

Seferis, George .... **CLC 5, 11**
See also Seferiades, Giorgos Stylianou

Segal, Erich (Wolf)
1937- .... **CLC 3, 10; DAM POP**
See also BEST 89:1; CA 25-28R; CANR 20,
36; DLBY 86; INT CANR-20; MTCW

Seger, Bob 1945-................ **CLC 35**

Seghers, Anna .... **CLC 7**
See also Radvanyi, Netty
See also DLB 69

Seidel, Frederick (Lewis) 1936-..... **CLC 18**
See also CA 13-16R; CANR 8; DLBY 84

Seifert, Jaroslav
1901-1986 .... **CLC 34, 44, 93**
See also CA 127; MTCW

Sei Shonagon c. 966-1017(?) ...... **CMLC 6**

Selby, Hubert, Jr.
1928- .... **CLC 1, 2, 4, 8; SSC 20**
See also CA 13-16R; CANR 33; DLB 2

Selzer, Richard 1928-............. **CLC 74**
See also CA 65-68; CANR 14

Sembene, Ousmane
See Ousmane, Sembene

Senancour, Etienne Pivert de
1770-1846 .... **NCLC 16**
See also DLB 119

Sender, Ramon (Jose)
1902-1982 .. **CLC 8; DAM MULT; HLC**
See also CA 5-8R; 105; CANR 8; HW;
MTCW

Seneca, Lucius Annaeus
4B.C.-65...... **CMLC 6; DAM DRAM;
DC 5**

Senghor, Leopold Sedar
1906- ..... **CLC 54; BLC; DAM MULT,
POET**
See also BW 2; CA 116; 125; CANR 47;
MTCW

Serling, (Edward) Rod(man)
1924-1975 .... **CLC 30**
See also AAYA 14; AITN 1; CA 65-68;
57-60; DLB 26

Serna, Ramon Gomez de la
See Gomez de la Serna, Ramon

Serpieres
See Guillevic, (Eugene)

Service, Robert
See Service, Robert W(illiam)
See also DAB; DLB 92

Service, Robert W(illiam)
1874(?)-1958 ...... **TCLC 15; DA; DAC;
DAM MST, POET; WLC**
See also Service, Robert
See also CA 115; 140; SATA 20

Seth, Vikram
1952- .... **CLC 43, 90; DAM MULT**
See also CA 121; 127; CANR 50; DLB 120;
INT 127

Seton, Cynthia Propper
1926-1982 .... **CLC 27**
See also CA 5-8R; 108; CANR 7

Seton, Ernest (Evan) Thompson
1860-1946 .... **TCLC 31**
See also CA 109; DLB 92; DLBD 13;
JRDA; SATA 18

Seton-Thompson, Ernest
See Seton, Ernest (Evan) Thompson

Settle, Mary Lee 1918- .... **CLC 19, 61**
See also CA 89-92; CAAS 1; CANR 44;
DLB 6; INT 89-92

Seuphor, Michel
See Arp, Jean

**Sevigne, Marie (de Rabutin-Chantal) Marquise
de** 1626-1696 .... **LC 11**

Sewall, Samuel 1652-1730 .... **LC 38**
See also DLB 24

Sexton, Anne (Harvey)
1928-1974 .... **CLC 2, 4, 6, 8, 10, 15, 53;
DA; DAB; DAC; DAM MST, POET;
PC 2; WLC**
See also CA 1-4R; 53-56; CABS 2;
CANR 3, 36; CDALB 1941-1968; DLB 5,
169; MTCW; SATA 10

Shaara, Michael (Joseph, Jr.)
1929-1988 .... **CLC 15; DAM POP**
See also AITN 1; CA 102; 125; CANR 52;
DLBY 83

Shackleton, C. C.
See Aldiss, Brian W(ilson)

Shacochis, Bob .... **CLC 39**
See also Shacochis, Robert G.

Shacochis, Robert G. 1951-
See Shacochis, Bob
See also CA 119; 124; INT 124

Shaffer, Anthony (Joshua)
1926- .... **CLC 19; DAM DRAM**
See also CA 110; 116; DLB 13

Shaffer, Peter (Levin)
1926- ...... **CLC 5, 14, 18, 37, 60; DAB;
DAM DRAM, MST; DC 7**
See also CA 25-28R; CANR 25, 47;
CDBLB 1960 to Present; DLB 13;
MTCW

Shakey, Bernard
See Young, Neil

Shalamov, Varlam (Tikhonovich)
1907(?)-1982 .... **CLC 18**
See also CA 129; 105

Shamlu, Ahmad 1925- .... **CLC 10**

Shammas, Anton 1951-............ **CLC 55**

Shange, Ntozake
1948- .... **CLC 8, 25, 38, 74; BLC;
DAM DRAM, MULT; DC 3**
See also AAYA 9; BW 2; CA 85-88;
CABS 3; CANR 27, 48; DLB 38; MTCW

Shanley, John Patrick 1950-....... **CLC 75**
See also CA 128; 133

Shapcott, Thomas W(illiam) 1935-.. **CLC 38**
See also CA 69-72; CANR 49

Shapiro, Jane.................... **CLC 76**

Shapiro, Karl (Jay) 1913- .. **CLC 4, 8, 15, 53**
See also CA 1-4R; CAAS 6; CANR 1, 36;
DLB 48; MTCW

Sharp, William 1855-1905 .... **TCLC 39**
See also DLB 156

Sharpe, Thomas Ridley 1928-
See Sharpe, Tom
See also CA 114; 122; INT 122

Sharpe, Tom.................... **CLC 36**
See also Sharpe, Thomas Ridley
See also DLB 14

Shaw, Bernard................. **TCLC 45**
See also Shaw, George Bernard
See also BW 1

Shaw, G. Bernard
See Shaw, George Bernard

Shaw, George Bernard
1856-1950 ... **TCLC 3, 9, 21; DA; DAB;
DAC; DAM DRAM, MST; WLC**
See also Shaw, Bernard
See also CA 104; 128; CDBLB 1914-1945;
DLB 10, 57; MTCW

Shaw, Henry Wheeler
1818-1885 .... **NCLC 15**
See also DLB 11

Shaw, Irwin
1913-1984 .... **CLC 7, 23, 34;
DAM DRAM, POP**
See also AITN 1; CA 13-16R; 112;
CANR 21; CDALB 1941-1968; DLB 6,
102; DLBY 84; MTCW

Shaw, Robert 1927-1978 .... **CLC 5**
See also AITN 1; CA 1-4R; 81-84;
CANR 4; DLB 13, 14

Shaw, T. E.
See Lawrence, T(homas) E(dward)

Shawn, Wallace 1943- .... **CLC 41**
See also CA 112

Shea, Lisa 1953-................. **CLC 86**
See also CA 147

Sheed, Wilfrid (John Joseph)
1930- .... **CLC 2, 4, 10, 53**
See also CA 65-68; CANR 30; DLB 6;
MTCW

Sheldon, Alice Hastings Bradley
1915(?)-1987
See Tiptree, James, Jr.
See also CA 108; 122; CANR 34; INT 108;
MTCW

Sheldon, John
See Bloch, Robert (Albert)

Simpson, N(orman) F(rederick)
1919- . . . . **CLC 29**
See also CA 13-16R; DLB 13

Sinclair, Andrew (Annandale)
1935- . . . . **CLC 2, 14**
See also CA 9-12R; CAAS 5; CANR 14, 38;
DLB 14; MTCW

Sinclair, Emil
See Hesse, Hermann

Sinclair, Iain 1943-. . . . . **CLC 76**
See also CA 132

Sinclair, Iain MacGregor
See Sinclair, Iain

Sinclair, Irene
See Griffith, D(avid Lewelyn) W(ark)

Sinclair, Mary Amelia St. Clair 1865(?)-1946
See Sinclair, May
See also CA 104

Sinclair, May. . . . . **TCLC 3, 11**
See also Sinclair, Mary Amelia St. Clair
See also DLB 36, 135

Sinclair, Roy
See Griffith, D(avid Lewelyn) W(ark)

Sinclair, Upton (Beall)
1878-1968 . . . . . . **CLC 1, 11, 15, 63; DA;**
DAB; DAC; DAM MST, NOV; WLC
See also CA 5-8R; 25-28R; CANR 7;
CDALB 1929-1941; DLB 9;
INT CANR-7; MTCW; SATA 9

Singer, Isaac
See Singer, Isaac Bashevis

Singer, Isaac Bashevis
1904-1991 . . . . **CLC 1, 3, 6, 9, 11, 15, 23,**
38, 69; DA; DAB; DAC; DAM MST,
NOV; SSC 3; WLC
See also AITN 1, 2; CA 1-4R; 134;
CANR 1, 39; CDALB 1941-1968; CLR 1;
DLB 6, 28, 52; DLBY 91; JRDA;
MAICYA; MTCW; SATA 3, 27;
SATA-Obit 68

Singer, Israel Joshua 1893-1944 . . . **TCLC 33**

Singh, Khushwant 1915-. . . . . **CLC 11**
See also CA 9-12R; CAAS 9; CANR 6

Sinjohn, John
See Galsworthy, John

Sinyavsky, Andrei (Donatevich)
1925- . . . . **CLC 8**
See also CA 85-88

Sirin, V.
See Nabokov, Vladimir (Vladimirovich)

Sissman, L(ouis) E(dward)
1928-1976 . . . . **CLC 9, 18**
See also CA 21-24R; 65-68; CANR 13;
DLB 5

Sisson, C(harles) H(ubert) 1914-. . . . . **CLC 8**
See also CA 1-4R; CAAS 3; CANR 3, 48;
DLB 27

Sitwell, Dame Edith
1887-1964 . . . . **CLC 2, 9, 67;**
DAM POET; PC 3
See also CA 9-12R; CANR 35;
CDBLB 1945-1960; DLB 20; MTCW

Sjoewall, Maj 1935-. . . . . **CLC 7**
See also CA 65-68

Sjowall, Maj
See Sjoewall, Maj

Skelton, Robin 1925-. . . . . **CLC 13**
See also AITN 2; CA 5-8R; CAAS 5;
CANR 28; DLB 27, 53

Skolimowski, Jerzy 1938- . . . . **CLC 20**
See also CA 128

Skram, Amalie (Bertha)
1847-1905 . . . . **TCLC 25**

Skvorecky, Josef (Vaclav)
1924- . . . . **CLC 15, 39, 69; DAC;**
DAM NOV
See also CA 61-64; CAAS 1; CANR 10, 34;
MTCW

Slade, Bernard. . . . . **CLC 11, 46**
See also Newbound, Bernard Slade
See also CAAS 9; DLB 53

Slaughter, Carolyn 1946-. . . . . **CLC 56**
See also CA 85-88

Slaughter, Frank G(ill) 1908- . . . . . . **CLC 29**
See also AITN 2; CA 5-8R; CANR 5;
INT CANR-5

Slavitt, David R(ytman) 1935-. . . . **CLC 5, 14**
See also CA 21-24R; CAAS 3; CANR 41;
DLB 5, 6

Slesinger, Tess 1905-1945 . . . . **TCLC 10**
See also CA 107; DLB 102

Slessor, Kenneth 1901-1971. . . . . . . **CLC 14**
See also CA 102; 89-92

Slowacki, Juliusz 1809-1849 . . . . . **NCLC 15**

Smart, Christopher
1722-1771 . . . **LC 3; DAM POET; PC 13**
See also DLB 109

Smart, Elizabeth 1913-1986. . . . . **CLC 54**
See also CA 81-84; 118; DLB 88

Smiley, Jane (Graves)
1949- . . . . **CLC 53, 76; DAM POP**
See also CA 104; CANR 30, 50;
INT CANR-30

Smith, A(rthur) J(ames) M(arshall)
1902-1980 . . . . **CLC 15; DAC**
See also CA 1-4R; 102; CANR 4; DLB 88

Smith, Adam 1723-1790. . . . . **LC 36**
See also DLB 104

Smith, Alexander 1829-1867 . . . . . **NCLC 59**
See also DLB 32, 55

Smith, Anna Deavere 1950-. . . . . . . **CLC 86**
See also CA 133

Smith, Betty (Wehner) 1896-1972. . . **CLC 19**
See also CA 5-8R; 33-36R; DLBY 82;
SATA 6

Smith, Charlotte (Turner)
1749-1806 . . . . **NCLC 23**
See also DLB 39, 109

Smith, Clark Ashton 1893-1961 . . . . **CLC 43**
See also CA 143

Smith, Dave. . . . . **CLC 22, 42**
See also Smith, David (Jeddie)
See also CAAS 7; DLB 5

Smith, David (Jeddie) 1942-
See Smith, Dave
See also CA 49-52; CANR 1; DAM POET

Smith, Florence Margaret 1902-1971
See Smith, Stevie
See also CA 17-18; 29-32R; CANR 35;
CAP 2; DAM POET; MTCW

Smith, Iain Crichton 1928- . . . . **CLC 64**
See also CA 21-24R; DLB 40, 139

Smith, John 1580(?)-1631 . . . . **LC 9**

Smith, Johnston
See Crane, Stephen (Townley)

Smith, Joseph, Jr. 1805-1844 . . . . **NCLC 53**

Smith, Lee 1944-. . . . . **CLC 25, 73**
See also CA 114; 119; CANR 46; DLB 143;
DLBY 83; INT 119

Smith, Martin
See Smith, Martin Cruz

Smith, Martin Cruz
1942- . . . . . **CLC 25; DAM MULT, POP**
See also BEST 89:4; CA 85-88; CANR 6,
23, 43; INT CANR-23; NNAL

Smith, Mary-Ann Tirone 1944-. . . . . **CLC 39**
See also CA 118; 136

Smith, Patti 1946- . . . . **CLC 12**
See also CA 93-96

Smith, Pauline (Urmson)
1882-1959 . . . . **TCLC 25**

Smith, Rosamond
See Oates, Joyce Carol

Smith, Sheila Kaye
See Kaye-Smith, Sheila

Smith, Stevie . . . . **CLC 3, 8, 25, 44; PC 12**
See also Smith, Florence Margaret
See also DLB 20

Smith, Wilbur (Addison) 1933-. . . . . **CLC 33**
See also CA 13-16R; CANR 7, 46; MTCW

Smith, William Jay 1918- . . . . **CLC 6**
See also CA 5-8R; CANR 44; DLB 5;
MAICYA; SAAS 22; SATA 2, 68

Smith, Woodrow Wilson
See Kuttner, Henry

Smolenskin, Peretz 1842-1885. . . . **NCLC 30**

Smollett, Tobias (George) 1721-1771 . . **LC 2**
See also CDBLB 1660-1789; DLB 39, 104

Snodgrass, W(illiam) D(e Witt)
1926- . . . . **CLC 2, 6, 10, 18, 68;**
DAM POET
See also CA 1-4R; CANR 6, 36; DLB 5;
MTCW

Snow, C(harles) P(ercy)
1905-1980 . . . . **CLC 1, 4, 6, 9, 13, 19;**
DAM NOV
See also CA 5-8R; 101; CANR 28;
CDBLB 1945-1960; DLB 15, 77; MTCW

Snow, Frances Compton
See Adams, Henry (Brooks)

Snyder, Gary (Sherman)
1930- . . **CLC 1, 2, 5, 9, 32; DAM POET**
See also CA 17-20R; CANR 30; DLB 5, 16,
165

Snyder, Zilpha Keatley 1927-. . . . . . . **CLC 17**
See also AAYA 15; CA 9-12R; CANR 38;
CLR 31; JRDA; MAICYA; SAAS 2;
SATA 1, 28, 75

Soares, Bernardo
See Pessoa, Fernando (Antonio Nogueira)

Stapledon, (William) Olaf
1886-1950 . . . . **TCLC 22**
See also CA 111; DLB 15

Starbuck, George (Edwin)
1931-1996 . . . . **CLC 53; DAM POET**
See also CA 21-24R; 153; CANR 23

Stark, Richard
See Westlake, Donald E(dwin)

Staunton, Schuyler
See Baum, L(yman) Frank

Stead, Christina (Ellen)
1902-1983 . . . . **CLC 2, 5, 8, 32, 80**
See also CA 13-16R; 109; CANR 33, 40;
MTCW

Stead, William Thomas
1849-1912 . . . . **TCLC 48**

Steele, Richard 1672-1729 . . . . **LC 18**
See also CDBLB 1660-1789; DLB 84, 101

Steele, Timothy (Reid) 1948- . . . . **CLC 45**
See also CA 93-96; CANR 16, 50; DLB 120

Steffens, (Joseph) Lincoln
1866-1936 . . . . **TCLC 20**
See also CA 117

Stegner, Wallace (Earle)
1909-1993 . . . **CLC 9, 49, 81; DAM NOV**
See also AITN 1; BEST 90:3; CA 1-4R;
141; CAAS 9; CANR 1, 21, 46; DLB 9;
DLBY 93; MTCW

Stein, Gertrude
1874-1946 . . . . . . **TCLC 1, 6, 28, 48; DA;**
DAB; DAC; DAM MST, NOV, POET;
PC 18; WLC
See also CA 104; 132; CDALB 1917-1929;
DLB 4, 54, 86; MTCW

Steinbeck, John (Ernst)
1902-1968 . . . . . . **CLC 1, 5, 9, 13, 21, 34,**
45, 75; DA; DAB; DAC; DAM DRAM,
MST, NOV; SSC 11; WLC
See also AAYA 12; CA 1-4R; 25-28R;
CANR 1, 35; CDALB 1929-1941; DLB 7,
9; DLBD 2; MTCW; SATA 9

Steinem, Gloria 1934- . . . . **CLC 63**
See also CA 53-56; CANR 28, 51; MTCW

Steiner, George
1929- . . . . **CLC 24; DAM NOV**
See also CA 73-76; CANR 31; DLB 67;
MTCW; SATA 62

Steiner, K. Leslie
See Delany, Samuel R(ay, Jr.)

Steiner, Rudolf 1861-1925 . . . . **TCLC 13**
See also CA 107

Stendhal
1783-1842 . . . . **NCLC 23, 46; DA; DAB;**
DAC; DAM MST, NOV; WLC
See also DLB 119

Stephen, Leslie 1832-1904 . . . . **TCLC 23**
See also CA 123; DLB 57, 144

Stephen, Sir Leslie
See Stephen, Leslie

Stephen, Virginia
See Woolf, (Adeline) Virginia

Stephens, James 1882(?)-1950 . . . . . . **TCLC 4**
See also CA 104; DLB 19, 153, 162

Stephens, Reed
See Donaldson, Stephen R.

Steptoe, Lydia
See Barnes, Djuna

Sterchi, Beat 1949- . . . . **CLC 65**

Sterling, Brett
See Bradbury, Ray (Douglas); Hamilton,
Edmond

Sterling, Bruce 1954- . . . . **CLC 72**
See also CA 119; CANR 44

Sterling, George 1869-1926 . . . . **TCLC 20**
See also CA 117; DLB 54

Stern, Gerald 1925- . . . . **CLC 40, 100**
See also CA 81-84; CANR 28; DLB 105

Stern, Richard (Gustave) 1928- . . . **CLC 4, 39**
See also CA 1-4R; CANR 1, 25, 52;
DLBY 87; INT CANR-25

Sternberg, Josef von 1894-1969 . . . . . **CLC 20**
See also CA 81-84

Sterne, Laurence
1713-1768 . . . . . . **LC 2; DA; DAB; DAC;**
DAM MST, NOV; WLC
See also CDBLB 1660-1789; DLB 39

Sternheim, (William Adolf) Carl
1878-1942 . . . . **TCLC 8**
See also CA 105; DLB 56, 118

Stevens, Mark 1951- . . . . **CLC 34**
See also CA 122

Stevens, Wallace
1879-1955 . . . . **TCLC 3, 12, 45; DA;**
DAB; DAC; DAM MST, POET; PC 6;
WLC
See also CA 104; 124; CDALB 1929-1941;
DLB 54; MTCW

Stevenson, Anne (Katharine)
1933- . . . . **CLC 7, 33**
See also CA 17-20R; CAAS 9; CANR 9, 33;
DLB 40; MTCW

Stevenson, Robert Louis (Balfour)
1850-1894 . . . . . **NCLC 5, 14; DA; DAB;**
DAC; DAM MST, NOV; SSC 11; WLC
See also CDBLB 1890-1914; CLR 10, 11;
DLB 18, 57, 141, 156, 174; DLBD 13;
JRDA; MAICYA; 2

Stewart, J(ohn) I(nnes) M(ackintosh)
1906-1994 . . . . **CLC 7, 14, 32**
See also CA 85-88; 147; CAAS 3;
CANR 47; MTCW

Stewart, Mary (Florence Elinor)
1916- . . . . **CLC 7, 35; DAB**
See also CA 1-4R; CANR 1; SATA 12

Stewart, Mary Rainbow
See Stewart, Mary (Florence Elinor)

Stifle, June
See Campbell, Maria

Stifter, Adalbert 1805-1868 . . . . . . **NCLC 41**
See also DLB 133

Still, James 1906- . . . . **CLC 49**
See also CA 65-68; CAAS 17; CANR 10,
26; DLB 9; SATA 29

Sting
See Sumner, Gordon Matthew

Stirling, Arthur
See Sinclair, Upton (Beall)

Stitt, Milan 1941- . . . . **CLC 29**
See also CA 69-72

Stockton, Francis Richard 1834-1902
See Stockton, Frank R.
See also CA 108; 137; MAICYA; SATA 44

Stockton, Frank R. . . . . **TCLC 47**
See also Stockton, Francis Richard
See also DLB 42, 74; DLBD 13;
SATA-Brief 32

Stoddard, Charles
See Kuttner, Henry

Stoker, Abraham 1847-1912
See Stoker, Bram
See also CA 105; DA; DAC; DAM MST,
NOV; SATA 29

Stoker, Bram
1847-1912 . . . . **TCLC 8; DAB; WLC**
See also Stoker, Abraham
See also CA 150; CDBLB 1890-1914;
DLB 36, 70, 178

Stolz, Mary (Slattery) 1920- . . . . **CLC 12**
See also AAYA 8; AITN 1; CA 5-8R;
CANR 13, 41; JRDA; MAICYA;
SAAS 3; SATA 10, 71

Stone, Irving
1903-1989 . . . . **CLC 7; DAM POP**
See also AITN 1; CA 1-4R; 129; CAAS 3;
CANR 1, 23; INT CANR-23; MTCW;
SATA 3; SATA-Obit 64

Stone, Oliver (William) 1946- . . . . . . **CLC 73**
See also AAYA 15; CA 110; CANR 55

Stone, Robert (Anthony)
1937- . . . . **CLC 5, 23, 42**
See also CA 85-88; CANR 23; DLB 152;
INT CANR-23; MTCW

Stone, Zachary
See Follett, Ken(neth Martin)

Stoppard, Tom
1937- . . . . . **CLC 1, 3, 4, 5, 8, 15, 29, 34,**
63, 91; DA; DAB; DAC; DAM DRAM,
MST; DC 6; WLC
See also CA 81-84; CANR 39;
CDBLB 1960 to Present; DLB 13;
DLBY 85; MTCW

Storey, David (Malcolm)
1933- . . . . . . **CLC 2, 4, 5, 8; DAM DRAM**
See also CA 81-84; CANR 36; DLB 13, 14;
MTCW

Storm, Hyemeyohsts
1935- . . . . **CLC 3; DAM MULT**
See also CA 81-84; CANR 45; NNAL

Storm, (Hans) Theodor (Woldsen)
1817-1888 . . . . **NCLC 1**

Storni, Alfonsina
1892-1938 . . . . . **TCLC 5; DAM MULT;**
HLC
See also CA 104; 131; HW

Stoughton, William 1631-1701 . . . . . . **LC 38**
See also DLB 24

Stout, Rex (Todhunter) 1886-1975 . . . **CLC 3**
See also AITN 2; CA 61-64

Stow, (Julian) Randolph 1935- . . **CLC 23, 48**
See also CA 13-16R; CANR 33; MTCW

Stowe, Harriet (Elizabeth) Beecher
1811-1896 . . . . . . **NCLC 3, 50; DA; DAB;**
DAC; DAM MST, NOV; WLC
See also CDALB 1865-1917; DLB 1, 12, 42,
74; JRDA; MAICYA; 1

Tallent, Elizabeth (Ann) 1954- ..... **CLC 45**
See also CA 117; DLB 130

Tally, Ted 1952- .... **CLC 42**
See also CA 120; 124; INT 124

Tamayo y Baus, Manuel
1829-1898 .... **NCLC 1**

Tammsaare, A(nton) H(ansen)
1878-1940 .... **TCLC 27**

Tam'si, Tchicaya U
See Tchicaya, Gerald Felix

Tan, Amy (Ruth)
1952- .... **CLC 59; DAM MULT, NOV,
POP**
See also AAYA 9; BEST 89:3; CA 136;
CANR 54; DLB 173; SATA 75

Tandem, Felix
See Spitteler, Carl (Friedrich Georg)

Tanizaki, Jun'ichiro
1886-1965 ...... **CLC 8, 14, 28; SSC 21**
See also CA 93-96; 25-28R; DLB 180

Tanner, William
See Amis, Kingsley (William)

Tao Lao
See Storni, Alfonsina

Tarassoff, Lev
See Troyat, Henri

Tarbell, Ida M(inerva)
1857-1944 .... **TCLC 40**
See also CA 122; DLB 47

Tarkington, (Newton) Booth
1869-1946 .... **TCLC 9**
See also CA 110; 143; DLB 9, 102;
SATA 17

Tarkovsky, Andrei (Arsenyevich)
1932-1986 .... **CLC 75**
See also CA 127

Tartt, Donna 1964(?)- .... **CLC 76**
See also CA 142

Tasso, Torquato 1544-1595 .... **LC 5**

Tate, (John Orley) Allen
1899-1979 .... **CLC 2, 4, 6, 9, 11, 14, 24**
See also CA 5-8R; 85-88; CANR 32;
DLB 4, 45, 63; MTCW

Tate, Ellalice
See Hibbert, Eleanor Alice Burford

Tate, James (Vincent) 1943- ... **CLC 2, 6, 25**
See also CA 21-24R; CANR 29, 57; DLB 5,
169

Tavel, Ronald 1940- .... **CLC 6**
See also CA 21-24R; CANR 33

Taylor, C(ecil) P(hilip) 1929-1981... **CLC 27**
See also CA 25-28R; 105; CANR 47

Taylor, Edward
1642(?)-1729 .... **LC 11; DA; DAB;
DAC; DAM MST, POET**
See also DLB 24

Taylor, Eleanor Ross 1920- .... **CLC 5**
See also CA 81-84

Taylor, Elizabeth 1912-1975 ... **CLC 2, 4, 29**
See also CA 13-16R; CANR 9; DLB 139;
MTCW; SATA 13

Taylor, Henry (Splawn) 1942- ..... **CLC 44**
See also CA 33-36R; CAAS 7; CANR 31;
DLB 5

Taylor, Kamala (Purnaiya) 1924-
See Markandaya, Kamala
See also CA 77-80

Taylor, Mildred D. .... **CLC 21**
See also AAYA 10; BW 1; CA 85-88;
CANR 25; CLR 9; DLB 52; JRDA;
MAICYA; SAAS 5; SATA 15, 70

Taylor, Peter (Hillsman)
1917-1994 ..... **CLC 1, 4, 18, 37, 44, 50,
71; SSC 10**
See also CA 13-16R; 147; CANR 9, 50;
DLBY 81, 94; INT CANR-9; MTCW

Taylor, Robert Lewis 1912- .... **CLC 14**
See also CA 1-4R; CANR 3; SATA 10

Tchekhov, Anton
See Chekhov, Anton (Pavlovich)

Tchicaya, Gerald Felix
1931-1988 .... **CLC 101**
See also CA 129; 125

Tchicaya U Tam'si
See Tchicaya, Gerald Felix

Teasdale, Sara 1884-1933 .... **TCLC 4**
See also CA 104; DLB 45; SATA 32

Tegner, Esaias 1782-1846 .... **NCLC 2**

Teilhard de Chardin, (Marie Joseph) Pierre
1881-1955 .... **TCLC 9**
See also CA 105

Temple, Ann
See Mortimer, Penelope (Ruth)

Tennant, Emma (Christina)
1937- .... **CLC 13, 52**
See also CA 65-68; CAAS 9; CANR 10, 38;
DLB 14

Tenneshaw, S. M.
See Silverberg, Robert

Tennyson, Alfred
1809-1892 .... **NCLC 30; DA; DAB;
DAC; DAM MST, POET; PC 6; WLC**
See also CDBLB 1832-1890; DLB 32

Teran, Lisa St. Aubin de .... **CLC 36**
See also St. Aubin de Teran, Lisa

Terence
195(?)B.C.-159B.C..... **CMLC 14; DC 7**

Teresa de Jesus, St. 1515-1582 ...... **LC 18**

Terkel, Louis 1912-
See Terkel, Studs
See also CA 57-60; CANR 18, 45; MTCW

Terkel, Studs .... **CLC 38**
See also Terkel, Louis
See also AITN 1

Terry, C. V.
See Slaughter, Frank G(ill)

Terry, Megan 1932- .... **CLC 19**
See also CA 77-80; CABS 3; CANR 43;
DLB 7

Tertz, Abram
See Sinyavsky, Andrei (Donatevich)

Tesich, Steve 1943(?)-1996...... **CLC 40, 69**
See also CA 105; 152; DLBY 83

Teternikov, Fyodor Kuzmich 1863-1927
See Sologub, Fyodor
See also CA 104

Tevis, Walter 1928-1984 .... **CLC 42**
See also CA 113

Tey, Josephine .... **TCLC 14**
See Mackintosh, Elizabeth
See also DLB 77

Thackeray, William Makepeace
1811-1863 .... **NCLC 5, 14, 22, 43; DA;
DAB; DAC; DAM MST, NOV; WLC**
See also CDBLB 1832-1890; DLB 21, 55,
159, 163; SATA 23

Thakura, Ravindranatha
See Tagore, Rabindranath

Tharoor, Shashi 1956- .... **CLC 70**
See also CA 141

Thelwell, Michael Miles 1939- ..... **CLC 22**
See also BW 2; CA 101

Theobald, Lewis, Jr.
See Lovecraft, H(oward) P(hillips)

Theodorescu, Ion N. 1880-1967
See Arghezi, Tudor
See also CA 116

Theriault, Yves
1915-1983 .. **CLC 79; DAC; DAM MST**
See also CA 102; DLB 88

Theroux, Alexander (Louis)
1939- .... **CLC 2, 25**
See also CA 85-88; CANR 20

Theroux, Paul (Edward)
1941- .... **CLC 5, 8, 11, 15, 28, 46;
DAM POP**
See also BEST 89:4; CA 33-36R; CANR 20,
45; DLB 2; MTCW; SATA 44

Thesen, Sharon 1946- .... **CLC 56**

Thevenin, Denis
See Duhamel, Georges

Thibault, Jacques Anatole Francois
1844-1924
See France, Anatole
See also CA 106; 127; DAM NOV; MTCW

Thiele, Colin (Milton) 1920- .... **CLC 17**
See also CA 29-32R; CANR 12, 28, 53;
CLR 27; MAICYA; SAAS 2; SATA 14,
72

Thomas, Audrey (Callahan)
1935- .... **CLC 7, 13, 37; SSC 20**
See also AITN 2; CA 21-24R; CAAS 19;
CANR 36, 58; DLB 60; MTCW

Thomas, D(onald) M(ichael)
1935- .... **CLC 13, 22, 31**
See also CA 61-64; CAAS 11; CANR 17,
45; CDBLB 1960 to Present; DLB 40;
INT CANR-17; MTCW

Thomas, Dylan (Marlais)
1914-1953 ... **TCLC 1, 8, 45; DA; DAB;
DAC; DAM DRAM, MST, POET;
PC 2; SSC 3; WLC**
See also CA 104; 120; CDBLB 1945-1960;
DLB 13, 20, 139; MTCW; SATA 60

Thomas, (Philip) Edward
1878-1917 ...... **TCLC 10; DAM POET**
See also CA 106; 153; DLB 19

Thomas, Joyce Carol 1938- .... **CLC 35**
See also AAYA 12; BW 2; CA 113; 116;
CANR 48; CLR 19; DLB 33; INT 116;
JRDA; MAICYA; MTCW; SAAS 7;
SATA 40, 78

Thomas, Lewis 1913-1993 .... **CLC 35**
See also CA 85-88; 143; CANR 38; MTCW

Thomas, Paul
See Mann, (Paul) Thomas

Thomas, Piri 1928-............. **CLC 17**
See also CA 73-76; HW

Thomas, R(onald) S(tuart)
1913- .... **CLC 6, 13, 48; DAB;**
DAM POET
See also CA 89-92; CAAS 4; CANR 30;
CDBLB 1960 to Present; DLB 27;
MTCW

Thomas, Ross (Elmore) 1926-1995 .. **CLC 39**
See also CA 33-36R; 150; CANR 22

Thompson, Francis Clegg
See Mencken, H(enry) L(ouis)

Thompson, Francis Joseph
1859-1907 .... **TCLC 4**
See also CA 104; CDBLB 1890-1914;
DLB 19

Thompson, Hunter S(tockton)
1939- ...... **CLC 9, 17, 40; DAM POP**
See also BEST 89:1; CA 17-20R; CANR 23,
46; MTCW

Thompson, James Myers
See Thompson, Jim (Myers)

Thompson, Jim (Myers)
1906-1977(?) .... **CLC 69**
See also CA 140

Thompson, Judith .... **CLC 39**

Thomson, James
1700-1748 ..... **LC 16, 29; DAM POET**
See also DLB 95

Thomson, James
1834-1882 ..... **NCLC 18; DAM POET**
See also DLB 35

Thoreau, Henry David
1817-1862 .... **NCLC 7, 21, 61; DA;**
DAB; DAC; DAM MST; WLC
See also CDALB 1640-1865; DLB 1

Thornton, Hall
See Silverberg, Robert

Thucydides c. 455B.C.-399B.C.... **CMLC 17**
See also DLB 176

Thurber, James (Grover)
1894-1961 .... **CLC 5, 11, 25; DA; DAB;**
DAC; DAM DRAM, MST, NOV; SSC 1
See also CA 73-76; CANR 17, 39;
CDALB 1929-1941; DLB 4, 11, 22, 102;
MAICYA; MTCW; SATA 13

Thurman, Wallace (Henry)
1902-1934 .... **TCLC 6; BLC;**
DAM MULT
See also BW 1; CA 104; 124; DLB 51

Ticheburn, Cheviot
See Ainsworth, William Harrison

Tieck, (Johann) Ludwig
1773-1853 .... **NCLC 5, 46**
See also DLB 90

Tiger, Derry
See Ellison, Harlan (Jay)

Tilghman, Christopher 1948(?)-..... **CLC 65**

Tillinghast, Richard (Williford)
1940- .... **CLC 29**
See also CA 29-32R; CAAS 23; CANR 26,
51

Timrod, Henry 1828-1867 .... **NCLC 25**
See also DLB 3

Tindall, Gillian 1938-............. **CLC 7**
See also CA 21-24R; CANR 11

Tiptree, James, Jr. .... **CLC 48, 50**
See also Sheldon, Alice Hastings Bradley
See also DLB 8

Titmarsh, Michael Angelo
See Thackeray, William Makepeace

Tocqueville, Alexis (Charles Henri Maurice
Clerel Comte) 1805-1859..... **NCLC 7**

Tolkien, J(ohn) R(onald) R(euel)
1892-1973 .... **CLC 1, 2, 3, 8, 12, 38;**
DA; DAB; DAC; DAM MST, NOV,
POP; WLC
See also AAYA 10; AITN 1; CA 17-18;
45-48; CANR 36; CAP 2;
CDBLB 1914-1945; DLB 15, 160; JRDA;
MAICYA; MTCW; SATA 2, 32;
SATA-Obit 24

Toller, Ernst 1893-1939 .... **TCLC 10**
See also CA 107; DLB 124

Tolson, M. B.
See Tolson, Melvin B(eaunorus)

Tolson, Melvin B(eaunorus)
1898(?)-1966 .... **CLC 36; BLC;**
DAM MULT, POET
See also BW 1; CA 124; 89-92; DLB 48, 76

Tolstoi, Aleksei Nikolaevich
See Tolstoy, Alexey Nikolaevich

Tolstoy, Alexey Nikolaevich
1882-1945 .... **TCLC 18**
See also CA 107; 158

Tolstoy, Count Leo
See Tolstoy, Leo (Nikolaevich)

Tolstoy, Leo (Nikolaevich)
1828-1910 ...... **TCLC 4, 11, 17, 28, 44;**
DA; DAB; DAC; DAM MST, NOV;
SSC 9; WLC
See also CA 104; 123; SATA 26

Tomasi di Lampedusa, Giuseppe 1896-1957
See Lampedusa, Giuseppe (Tomasi) di
See also CA 111

Tomlin, Lily..................... **CLC 17**
See also Tomlin, Mary Jean

Tomlin, Mary Jean 1939(?)-
See Tomlin, Lily
See also CA 117

Tomlinson, (Alfred) Charles
1927- .... **CLC 2, 4, 6, 13, 45;**
DAM POET; PC 17
See also CA 5-8R; CANR 33; DLB 40

Tomlinson, H(enry) M(ajor)
1873-1958 .... **TCLC 71**
See also CA 118; DLB 36, 100

Tonson, Jacob
See Bennett, (Enoch) Arnold

Toole, John Kennedy
1937-1969 .... **CLC 19, 64**
See also CA 104; DLBY 81

Toomer, Jean
1894-1967 ...... **CLC 1, 4, 13, 22; BLC;**
DAM MULT; PC 7; SSC 1
See also BW 1; CA 85-88;
CDALB 1917-1929; DLB 45, 51; MTCW;
YABC

Torley, Luke
See Blish, James (Benjamin)

Tornimparte, Alessandra
See Ginzburg, Natalia

Torre, Raoul della
See Mencken, H(enry) L(ouis)

Torrey, E(dwin) Fuller 1937-....... **CLC 34**
See also CA 119

Torsvan, Ben Traven
See Traven, B.

Torsvan, Benno Traven
See Traven, B.

Torsvan, Berick Traven
See Traven, B.

Torsvan, Berwick Traven
See Traven, B.

Torsvan, Bruno Traven
See Traven, B.

Torsvan, Traven
See Traven, B.

Tournier, Michel (Edouard)
1924- .... **CLC 6, 23, 36, 95**
See also CA 49-52; CANR 3, 36; DLB 83;
MTCW; SATA 23

Tournimparte, Alessandra
See Ginzburg, Natalia

Towers, Ivar
See Kornbluth, C(yril) M.

Towne, Robert (Burton) 1936(?)-.... **CLC 87**
See also CA 108; DLB 44

Townsend, Sue 1946-.. **CLC 61; DAB; DAC**
See also CA 119; 127; INT 127; MTCW;
SATA 55, 93; SATA-Brief 48

Townshend, Peter (Dennis Blandford)
1945- .... **CLC 17, 42**
See also CA 107

Tozzi, Federigo 1883-1920....... **TCLC 31**

Traill, Catharine Parr
1802-1899 .... **NCLC 31**
See also DLB 99

Trakl, Georg 1887-1914........... **TCLC 5**
See also CA 104

Transtroemer, Tomas (Goesta)
1931-........ **CLC 52, 65; DAM POET**
See also CA 117; 129; CAAS 17

Transtromer, Tomas Gosta
See Transtroemer, Tomas (Goesta)

Traven, B. (?)-1969............. **CLC 8, 11**
See also CA 19-20; 25-28R; CAP 2; DLB 9,
56; MTCW

Treitel, Jonathan 1959- .... **CLC 70**

Tremain, Rose 1943-............... **CLC 42**
See also CA 97-100; CANR 44; DLB 14

Tremblay, Michel
1942- ...... **CLC 29; DAC; DAM MST**
See also CA 116; 128; DLB 60; MTCW

Trevanian....................... **CLC 29**
See also Whitaker, Rod(ney)

Trevor, Glen
See Hilton, James

Trevor, William
1928- ..... **CLC 7, 9, 14, 25, 71; SSC 21**
See also Cox, William Trevor
See also DLB 14, 139

Trifonov, Yuri (Valentinovich)
1925-1981 .... **CLC 45**
See also CA 126; 103; MTCW

Trilling, Lionel 1905-1975 .... **CLC 9, 11, 24**
See also CA 9-12R; 61-64; CANR 10;
DLB 28, 63; INT CANR-10; MTCW

Trimball, W. H.
See Mencken, H(enry) L(ouis)

Tristan
See Gomez de la Serna, Ramon

Tristram
See Housman, A(lfred) E(dward)

Trogdon, William (Lewis) 1939-
See Heat-Moon, William Least
See also CA 115; 119; CANR 47; INT 119

Trollope, Anthony
1815-1882 ..... **NCLC 6, 33; DA; DAB;**
DAC; DAM MST, NOV; WLC
See also CDBLB 1832-1890; DLB 21, 57,
159; SATA 22

Trollope, Frances 1779-1863 ..... **NCLC 30**
See also DLB 21, 166

Trotsky, Leon 1879-1940 .... **TCLC 22**
See also CA 118

Trotter (Cockburn), Catharine
1679-1749 .... **LC 8**
See also DLB 84

Trout, Kilgore
See Farmer, Philip Jose

Trow, George W. S. 1943- .... **CLC 52**
See also CA 126

Troyat, Henri 1911- .... **CLC 23**
See also CA 45-48; CANR 2, 33; MTCW

Trudeau, G(arretson) B(eekman) 1948-
See Trudeau, Garry B.
See also CA 81-84; CANR 31; SATA 35

Trudeau, Garry B. .... **CLC 12**
See also Trudeau, G(arretson) B(eekman)
See also AAYA 10; AITN 2

Truffaut, Francois 1932-1984... **CLC 20, 101**
See also CA 81-84; 113; CANR 34

Trumbo, Dalton 1905-1976 .... **CLC 19**
See also CA 21-24R; 69-72; CANR 10;
DLB 26

Trumbull, John 1750-1831 ...... **NCLC 30**
See also DLB 31

Trundlett, Helen B.
See Eliot, T(homas) S(tearns)

Tryon, Thomas
1926-1991 ..... **CLC 3, 11; DAM POP**
See also AITN 1; CA 29-32R; 135;
CANR 32; MTCW

Tryon, Tom
See Tryon, Thomas

Ts'ao Hsueh-ch'in 1715(?)-1763 ...... **LC 1**

Tsushima, Shuji 1909-1948
See Dazai, Osamu
See also CA 107

Tsvetaeva (Efron), Marina (Ivanovna)
1892-1941 .... **TCLC 7, 35; PC 14**
See also CA 104; 128; MTCW

Tuck, Lily 1938- .... **CLC 70**
See also CA 139

Tu Fu 712-770 .... **PC 9**
See also DAM MULT

Tunis, John R(oberts) 1889-1975 ... **CLC 12**
See also CA 61-64; DLB 22, 171; JRDA;
MAICYA; SATA 37; SATA-Brief 30

Tuohy, Frank .... **CLC 37**
See also Tuohy, John Francis
See also DLB 14, 139

Tuohy, John Francis 1925-
See Tuohy, Frank
See also CA 5-8R; CANR 3, 47

Turco, Lewis (Putnam) 1934- ... **CLC 11, 63**
See also CA 13-16R; CAAS 22; CANR 24,
51; DLBY 84

Turgenev, Ivan
1818-1883 .... **NCLC 21; DA; DAB;**
DAC; DAM MST, NOV; DC 7; SSC 7;
WLC

Turgot, Anne-Robert-Jacques
1727-1781 .... **LC 26**

Turner, Frederick 1943- .... **CLC 48**
See also CA 73-76; CAAS 10; CANR 12,
30, 56; DLB 40

Tutu, Desmond M(pilo)
1931- ..... **CLC 80; BLC; DAM MULT**
See also BW 1; CA 125

Tutuola, Amos
1920- .... **CLC 5, 14, 29; BLC;**
DAM MULT
See also BW 2; CA 9-12R; CANR 27;
DLB 125; MTCW

Twain, Mark
.... **TCLC 6, 12, 19, 36, 48, 59; SSC 26;**
WLC
See also Clemens, Samuel Langhorne
See also AAYA 20; DLB 11, 12, 23, 64, 74

Tyler, Anne
1941- .... **CLC 7, 11, 18, 28, 44, 59;**
DAM NOV, POP
See also AAYA 18; BEST 89:1; CA 9-12R;
CANR 11, 33, 53; DLB 6, 143; DLBY 82;
MTCW; SATA 7, 90

Tyler, Royall 1757-1826 .... **NCLC 3**
See also DLB 37

Tynan, Katharine 1861-1931 .... **TCLC 3**
See also CA 104; DLB 153

Tyutchev, Fyodor 1803-1873 ..... **NCLC 34**

Tzara, Tristan
1896-1963 .... **CLC 47; DAM POET**
See also Rosenfeld, Samuel; Rosenstock,
Sami; Rosenstock, Samuel
See also CA 153

Uhry, Alfred
1936- ..... **CLC 55; DAM DRAM, POP**
See also CA 127; 133; INT 133

Ulf, Haerved
See Strindberg, (Johan) August

Ulf, Harved
See Strindberg, (Johan) August

Ulibarri, Sabine R(eyes)
1919- .... **CLC 83; DAM MULT**
See also CA 131; DLB 82; HW

Unamuno (y Jugo), Miguel de
1864-1936 ... **TCLC 2, 9; DAM MULT,**
NOV; HLC; SSC 11
See also CA 104; 131; DLB 108; HW;
MTCW

Undercliffe, Errol
See Campbell, (John) Ramsey

Underwood, Miles
See Glassco, John

Undset, Sigrid
1882-1949 .... **TCLC 3; DA; DAB;**
DAC; DAM MST, NOV; WLC
See also CA 104; 129; MTCW

Ungaretti, Giuseppe
1888-1970 .... **CLC 7, 11, 15**
See also CA 19-20; 25-28R; CAP 2;
DLB 114

Unger, Douglas 1952- .... **CLC 34**
See also CA 130

Unsworth, Barry (Forster) 1930-.... **CLC 76**
See also CA 25-28R; CANR 30, 54

Updike, John (Hoyer)
1932- ...... **CLC 1, 2, 3, 5, 7, 9, 13, 15,**
23, 34, 43, 70; DA; DAB; DAC;
DAM MST, NOV, POET, POP;
SSC 13; WLC
See also CA 1-4R; CABS 1; CANR 4, 33,
51; CDALB 1968-1988; DLB 2, 5, 143;
DLBD 3; DLBY 80, 82; MTCW

Upshaw, Margaret Mitchell
See Mitchell, Margaret (Munnerlyn)

Upton, Mark
See Sanders, Lawrence

Urdang, Constance (Henriette)
1922- .... **CLC 47**
See also CA 21-24R; CANR 9, 24

Uriel, Henry
See Faust, Frederick (Schiller)

Uris, Leon (Marcus)
1924- .... **CLC 7, 32; DAM NOV, POP**
See also AITN 1, 2; BEST 89:2; CA 1-4R;
CANR 1, 40; MTCW; SATA 49

Urmuz
See Codrescu, Andrei

Urquhart, Jane 1949- .... **CLC 90; DAC**
See also CA 113; CANR 32

Ustinov, Peter (Alexander) 1921- .... **CLC 1**
See also AITN 1; CA 13-16R; CANR 25,
51; DLB 13

U Tam'si, Gerald Felix Tchicaya
See Tchicaya, Gerald Felix

U Tam'si, Tchicaya
See Tchicaya, Gerald Felix

Vaculik, Ludvik 1926- .... **CLC 7**
See also CA 53-56

Vaihinger, Hans 1852-1933 .... **TCLC 71**
See also CA 116

Valdez, Luis (Miguel)
1940- ..... **CLC 84; DAM MULT; HLC**
See also CA 101; CANR 32; DLB 122; HW

Voinovich, Vladimir (Nikolaevich)
1932- .... **CLC 10, 49**
See also CA 81-84; CAAS 12; CANR 33;
MTCW

Vollmann, William T.
1959- ...... **CLC 89; DAM NOV, POP**
See also CA 134

Voloshinov, V. N.
See Bakhtin, Mikhail Mikhailovich

Voltaire
1694-1778 ..... **LC 14; DA; DAB; DAC;
DAM DRAM, MST; SSC 12; WLC**

von Daeniken, Erich 1935- .... **CLC 30**
See also AITN 1; CA 37-40R; CANR 17,
44

von Daniken, Erich
See von Daeniken, Erich

von Heidenstam, (Carl Gustaf) Verner
See Heidenstam, (Carl Gustaf) Verner von

von Heyse, Paul (Johann Ludwig)
See Heyse, Paul (Johann Ludwig von)

von Hofmannsthal, Hugo
See Hofmannsthal, Hugo von

von Horvath, Odon
See Horvath, Oedoen von

von Horvath, Oedoen
See Horvath, Oedoen von

von Liliencron, (Friedrich Adolf Axel) Detlev
See Liliencron, (Friedrich Adolf Axel)
Detlev von

Vonnegut, Kurt, Jr.
1922- ...... **CLC 1, 2, 3, 4, 5, 8, 12, 22,
40, 60; DA; DAB; DAC; DAM MST,
NOV, POP; SSC 8; WLC**
See also AAYA 6; AITN 1; BEST 90:4;
CA 1-4R; CANR 1, 25, 49;
CDALB 1968-1988; DLB 2, 8, 152;
DLBD 3; DLBY 80; MTCW

Von Rachen, Kurt
See Hubbard, L(afayette) Ron(ald)

von Rezzori (d'Arezzo), Gregor
See Rezzori (d'Arezzo), Gregor von

von Sternberg, Josef
See Sternberg, Josef von

Vorster, Gordon 1924- .... **CLC 34**
See also CA 133

Vosce, Trudie
See Ozick, Cynthia

Voznesensky, Andrei (Andreievich)
1933- ...... **CLC 1, 15, 57; DAM POET**
See also CA 89-92; CANR 37; MTCW

Waddington, Miriam 1917- .... **CLC 28**
See also CA 21-24R; CANR 12, 30;
DLB 68

Wagman, Fredrica 1937- .... **CLC 7**
See also CA 97-100; INT 97-100

Wagner, Richard 1813-1883....... **NCLC 9**
See also DLB 129

Wagner-Martin, Linda 1936-....... **CLC 50**

Wagoner, David (Russell)
1926- .... **CLC 3, 5, 15**
See also CA 1-4R; CAAS 3; CANR 2;
DLB 5; SATA 14

Wah, Fred(erick James) 1939-...... **CLC 44**
See also CA 107; 141; DLB 60

Wahloo, Per 1926-1975 .... **CLC 7**
See also CA 61-64

Wahloo, Peter
See Wahloo, Per

Wain, John (Barrington)
1925-1994 .... **CLC 2, 11, 15, 46**
See also CA 5-8R; 145; CAAS 4; CANR 23,
54; CDBLB 1960 to Present; DLB 15, 27,
139, 155; MTCW

Wajda, Andrzej 1926-............ **CLC 16**
See also CA 102

Wakefield, Dan 1932-............. **CLC 7**
See also CA 21-24R; CAAS 7

Wakoski, Diane
1937- .... **CLC 2, 4, 7, 9, 11, 40;
DAM POET; PC 15**
See also CA 13-16R; CAAS 1; CANR 9;
DLB 5; INT CANR-9

Wakoski-Sherbell, Diane
See Wakoski, Diane

Walcott, Derek (Alton)
1930- .... **CLC 2, 4, 9, 14, 25, 42, 67, 76;
BLC; DAB; DAC; DAM MST, MULT,
POET; DC 7**
See also BW 2; CA 89-92; CANR 26, 47;
DLB 117; DLBY 81; MTCW

Waldman, Anne 1945- .... **CLC 7**
See also CA 37-40R; CAAS 17; CANR 34;
DLB 16

Waldo, E. Hunter
See Sturgeon, Theodore (Hamilton)

Waldo, Edward Hamilton
See Sturgeon, Theodore (Hamilton)

Walker, Alice (Malsenior)
1944- .... **CLC 5, 6, 9, 19, 27, 46, 58;
BLC; DA; DAB; DAC; DAM MST,
MULT, NOV, POET, POP; SSC 5**
See also AAYA 3; BEST 89:4; BW 2;
CA 37-40R; CANR 9, 27, 49;
CDALB 1968-1988; DLB 6, 33, 143;
INT CANR-27; MTCW; SATA 31;
YABC

Walker, David Harry 1911-1992.... **CLC 14**
See also CA 1-4R; 137; CANR 1; SATA 8;
SATA-Obit 71

Walker, Edward Joseph 1934-
See Walker, Ted
See also CA 21-24R; CANR 12, 28, 53

Walker, George F.
1947- .... **CLC 44, 61; DAB; DAC;
DAM MST**
See also CA 103; CANR 21, 43; DLB 60

Walker, Joseph A.
1935- .... **CLC 19; DAM DRAM, MST**
See also BW 1; CA 89-92; CANR 26;
DLB 38

Walker, Margaret (Abigail)
1915- .... **CLC 1, 6; BLC; DAM MULT**
See also BW 2; CA 73-76; CANR 26, 54;
DLB 76, 152; MTCW

Walker, Ted .... **CLC 13**
See also Walker, Edward Joseph
See also DLB 40

Wallace, David Foster 1962-....... **CLC 50**
See also CA 132

Wallace, Dexter
See Masters, Edgar Lee

Wallace, (Richard Horatio) Edgar
1875-1932 .... **TCLC 57**
See also CA 115; DLB 70

Wallace, Irving
1916-1990 ..... **CLC 7, 13; DAM NOV,
POP**
See also AITN 1; CA 1-4R; 132; CAAS 1;
CANR 1, 27; INT CANR-27; MTCW

Wallant, Edward Lewis
1926-1962 .... **CLC 5, 10**
See also CA 1-4R; CANR 22; DLB 2, 28,
143; MTCW

Walley, Byron
See Card, Orson Scott

Walpole, Horace 1717-1797......... **LC 2**
See also DLB 39, 104

Walpole, Hugh (Seymour)
1884-1941 .... **TCLC 5**
See also CA 104; DLB 34

Walser, Martin 1927-............. **CLC 27**
See also CA 57-60; CANR 8, 46; DLB 75,
124

Walser, Robert
1878-1956 .... **TCLC 18; SSC 20**
See also CA 118; DLB 66

Walsh, Jill Paton................. **CLC 35**
See also Paton Walsh, Gillian
See also AAYA 11; CLR 2; DLB 161;
SAAS 3

Walter, Villiam Christian
See Andersen, Hans Christian

Wambaugh, Joseph (Aloysius, Jr.)
1937- ...... **CLC 3, 18; DAM NOV, POP**
See also AITN 1; BEST 89:3; CA 33-36R;
CANR 42; DLB 6; DLBY 83; MTCW

Wang Wei 699(?)-761(?)........... **PC 18**

Ward, Arthur Henry Sarsfield 1883-1959
See Rohmer, Sax
See also CA 108

Ward, Douglas Turner 1930-....... **CLC 19**
See also BW 1; CA 81-84; CANR 27;
DLB 7, 38

Ward, Mary Augusta
See Ward, Mrs. Humphry

Ward, Mrs. Humphry
1851-1920 .... **TCLC 55**
See also DLB 18

Ward, Peter
See Faust, Frederick (Schiller)

Warhol, Andy 1928(?)-1987....... **CLC 20**
See also AAYA 12; BEST 89:4; CA 89-92;
121; CANR 34

Warner, Francis (Robert le Plastrier)
1937- .... **CLC 14**
See also CA 53-56; CANR 11

Warner, Marina 1946-............ **CLC 59**
See also CA 65-68; CANR 21, 55

Warner, Rex (Ernest) 1905-1986.... **CLC 45**
See also CA 89-92; 119; DLB 15

Wentworth, Robert
See Hamilton, Edmond

Werfel, Franz (V.) 1890-1945 ...... **TCLC 8**
See also CA 104; DLB 81, 124

Wergeland, Henrik Arnold
1808-1845 .... **NCLC 5**

Wersba, Barbara 1932- .... **CLC 30**
See also AAYA 2; CA 29-32R; CANR 16,
38; CLR 3; DLB 52; JRDA; MAICYA;
SAAS 2; SATA 1, 58

Wertmueller, Lina 1928- .... **CLC 16**
See also CA 97-100; CANR 39

Wescott, Glenway 1901-1987 ...... **CLC 13**
See also CA 13-16R; 121; CANR 23;
DLB 4, 9, 102

Wesker, Arnold
1932- .... **CLC 3, 5, 42; DAB;
DAM DRAM**
See also CA 1-4R; CAAS 7; CANR 1, 33;
CDBLB 1960 to Present; DLB 13;
MTCW

Wesley, Richard (Errol) 1945- ...... **CLC 7**
See also BW 1; CA 57-60; CANR 27;
DLB 38

Wessel, Johan Herman 1742-1785 .... **LC 7**

West, Anthony (Panther)
1914-1987 .... **CLC 50**
See also CA 45-48; 124; CANR 3, 19;
DLB 15

West, C. P.
See Wodehouse, P(elham) G(renville)

West, (Mary) Jessamyn
1902-1984 .... **CLC 7, 17**
See also CA 9-12R; 112; CANR 27; DLB 6;
DLBY 84; MTCW; SATA-Obit 37

West, Morris L(anglo) 1916- ..... **CLC 6, 33**
See also CA 5-8R; CANR 24, 49; MTCW

West, Nathanael
1903-1940 ..... **TCLC 1, 14, 44; SSC 16**
See also CA 104; 125; CDALB 1929-1941;
DLB 4, 9, 28; MTCW

West, Owen
See Koontz, Dean R(ay)

West, Paul 1930- .... **CLC 7, 14, 96**
See also CA 13-16R; CAAS 7; CANR 22,
53; DLB 14; INT CANR-22

West, Rebecca 1892-1983 .. **CLC 7, 9, 31, 50**
See also CA 5-8R; 109; CANR 19; DLB 36;
DLBY 83; MTCW

Westall, Robert (Atkinson)
1929-1993 .... **CLC 17**
See also AAYA 12; CA 69-72; 141;
CANR 18; CLR 13; JRDA; MAICYA;
SAAS 2; SATA 23, 69; SATA-Obit 75

Westlake, Donald E(dwin)
1933- .... **CLC 7, 33; DAM POP**
See also CA 17-20R; CAAS 13; CANR 16,
44; INT CANR-16

Westmacott, Mary
See Christie, Agatha (Mary Clarissa)

Weston, Allen
See Norton, Andre

Wetcheek, J. L.
See Feuchtwanger, Lion

Wetering, Janwillem van de
See van de Wetering, Janwillem

Wetherell, Elizabeth
See Warner, Susan (Bogert)

Whale, James 1889-1957 .... **TCLC 63**

Whalen, Philip 1923- .... **CLC 6, 29**
See also CA 9-12R; CANR 5, 39; DLB 16

Wharton, Edith (Newbold Jones)
1862-1937 ...... **TCLC 3, 9, 27, 53; DA;
DAB; DAC; DAM MST, NOV; SSC 6;
WLC**
See also CA 104; 132; CDALB 1865-1917;
DLB 4, 9, 12, 78; DLBD 13; MTCW

Wharton, James
See Mencken, H(enry) L(ouis)

Wharton, William (a pseudonym)
.... **CLC 18, 37**
See also CA 93-96; DLBY 80; INT 93-96

Wheatley (Peters), Phillis
1754(?)-1784 .... **LC 3; BLC; DA; DAC;
DAM MST, MULT, POET; PC 3; WLC**
See also CDALB 1640-1865; DLB 31, 50

Wheelock, John Hall 1886-1978 .... **CLC 14**
See also CA 13-16R; 77-80; CANR 14;
DLB 45

White, E(lwyn) B(rooks)
1899-1985 .. **CLC 10, 34, 39; DAM POP**
See also AITN 2; CA 13-16R; 116;
CANR 16, 37; CLR 1, 21; DLB 11, 22;
MAICYA; MTCW; SATA 2, 29;
SATA-Obit 44

White, Edmund (Valentine III)
1940- .... **CLC 27; DAM POP**
See also AAYA 7; CA 45-48; CANR 3, 19,
36; MTCW

White, Patrick (Victor Martindale)
1912-1990 .. **CLC 3, 4, 5, 7, 9, 18, 65, 69**
See also CA 81-84; 132; CANR 43; MTCW

White, Phyllis Dorothy James 1920-
See James, P. D.
See also CA 21-24R; CANR 17, 43;
DAM POP; MTCW

White, T(erence) H(anbury)
1906-1964 .... **CLC 30**
See also CA 73-76; CANR 37; DLB 160;
JRDA; MAICYA; SATA 12

White, Terence de Vere
1912-1994 .... **CLC 49**
See also CA 49-52; 145; CANR 3

White, Walter F(rancis)
1893-1955 .... **TCLC 15**
See also White, Walter
See also BW 1; CA 115; 124; DLB 51

White, William Hale 1831-1913
See Rutherford, Mark
See also CA 121

Whitehead, E(dward) A(nthony)
1933- .... **CLC 5**
See also CA 65-68; CANR 58

Whitemore, Hugh (John) 1936- ..... **CLC 37**
See also CA 132; INT 132

Whitman, Sarah Helen (Power)
1803-1878 .... **NCLC 19**
See also DLB 1

Whitman, Walt(er)
1819-1892 ..... **NCLC 4, 31; DA; DAB;
DAC; DAM MST, POET; PC 3; WLC**
See also CDALB 1640-1865; DLB 3, 64;
SATA 20

Whitney, Phyllis A(yame)
1903- .... **CLC 42; DAM POP**
See also AITN 2; BEST 90:3; CA 1-4R;
CANR 3, 25, 38; JRDA; MAICYA;
SATA 1, 30

Whittemore, (Edward) Reed (Jr.)
1919- .... **CLC 4**
See also CA 9-12R; CAAS 8; CANR 4;
DLB 5

Whittier, John Greenleaf
1807-1892 .... **NCLC 8, 59**
See also DLB 1

Whittlebot, Hernia
See Coward, Noel (Peirce)

Wicker, Thomas Grey 1926-
See Wicker, Tom
See also CA 65-68; CANR 21, 46

Wicker, Tom .... **CLC 7**
See also Wicker, Thomas Grey

Wideman, John Edgar
1941- .... **CLC 5, 34, 36, 67; BLC;
DAM MULT**
See also BW 2; CA 85-88; CANR 14, 42;
DLB 33, 143

Wiebe, Rudy (Henry)
1934- .... **CLC 6, 11, 14; DAC;
DAM MST**
See also CA 37-40R; CANR 42; DLB 60

Wieland, Christoph Martin
1733-1813 .... **NCLC 17**
See also DLB 97

Wiene, Robert 1881-1938 .... **TCLC 56**

Wieners, John 1934- .... **CLC 7**
See also CA 13-16R; DLB 16

Wiesel, Elie(zer)
1928- ...... **CLC 3, 5, 11, 37; DA; DAB;
DAC; DAM MST, NOV**
See also AAYA 7; AITN 1; CA 5-8R;
CAAS 4; CANR 8, 40; DLB 83;
DLBY 87; INT CANR-8; MTCW;
SATA 56; YABC

Wiggins, Marianne 1947- .... **CLC 57**
See also BEST 89:3; CA 130

Wight, James Alfred 1916-
See Herriot, James
See also CA 77-80; SATA 55;
SATA-Brief 44

Wilbur, Richard (Purdy)
1921- ... **CLC 3, 6, 9, 14, 53; DA; DAB;
DAC; DAM MST, POET**
See also CA 1-4R; CABS 2; CANR 2, 29;
DLB 5, 169; INT CANR-29; MTCW;
SATA 9

Wild, Peter 1940- .... **CLC 14**
See also CA 37-40R; DLB 5

Wilde, Oscar (Fingal O'Flahertie Wills)
1854(?)-1900 .... **TCLC 1, 8, 23, 41; DA;
DAB; DAC; DAM DRAM, MST, NOV;
SSC 11; WLC**
See also CA 104; 119; CDBLB 1890-1914;
DLB 10, 19, 34, 57, 141, 156; SATA 24

Wilder, Billy . . . . **CLC 20**
See also Wilder, Samuel
See also DLB 26

Wilder, Samuel 1906-
See Wilder, Billy
See also CA 89-92

Wilder, Thornton (Niven)
1897-1975 . . . . . . **CLC 1, 5, 6, 10, 15, 35,**
82; DA; DAB; DAC; DAM DRAM,
MST, NOV; DC 1; WLC
See also AITN 2; CA 13-16R; 61-64;
CANR 40; DLB 4, 7, 9; MTCW

Wilding, Michael 1942- . . . . **CLC 73**
See also CA 104; CANR 24, 49

Wiley, Richard 1944- . . . . **CLC 44**
See also CA 121; 129

Wilhelm, Kate . . . . **CLC 7**
See also Wilhelm, Katie Gertrude
See also AAYA 20; CAAS 5; DLB 8;
INT CANR-17

Wilhelm, Katie Gertrude 1928-
See Wilhelm, Kate
See also CA 37-40R; CANR 17, 36; MTCW

Wilkins, Mary
See Freeman, Mary Eleanor Wilkins

Willard, Nancy 1936- . . . . **CLC 7, 37**
See also CA 89-92; CANR 10, 39; CLR 5;
DLB 5, 52; MAICYA; MTCW;
SATA 37, 71; SATA-Brief 30

Williams, C(harles) K(enneth)
1936- . . . . **CLC 33, 56; DAM POET**
See also CA 37-40R; CAAS 26; CANR 57;
DLB 5

Williams, Charles
See Collier, James L(incoln)

Williams, Charles (Walter Stansby)
1886-1945 . . . . **TCLC 1, 11**
See also CA 104; DLB 100, 153

Williams, (George) Emlyn
1905-1987 . . . . . . **CLC 15; DAM DRAM**
See also CA 104; 123; CANR 36; DLB 10,
77; MTCW

Williams, Hugo 1942- . . . . **CLC 42**
See also CA 17-20R; CANR 45; DLB 40

Williams, J. Walker
See Wodehouse, P(elham) G(renville)

Williams, John A(lfred)
1925- . . . **CLC 5, 13; BLC; DAM MULT**
See also BW 2; CA 53-56; CAAS 3;
CANR 6, 26, 51; DLB 2, 33;
INT CANR-6

Williams, Jonathan (Chamberlain)
1929- . . . . **CLC 13**
See also CA 9-12R; CAAS 12; CANR 8;
DLB 5

Williams, Joy 1944- . . . . **CLC 31**
See also CA 41-44R; CANR 22, 48

Williams, Norman 1952- . . . . **CLC 39**
See also CA 118

Williams, Sherley Anne
1944- . . . . . **CLC 89; BLC; DAM MULT,**
POET
See also BW 2; CA 73-76; CANR 25;
DLB 41; INT CANR-25; SATA 78

Williams, Shirley
See Williams, Sherley Anne

Williams, Tennessee
1911-1983 . . . . . **CLC 1, 2, 5, 7, 8, 11, 15,**
19, 30, 39, 45, 71; DA; DAB; DAC;
DAM DRAM, MST; DC 4; WLC
See also AITN 1, 2; CA 5-8R; 108;
CABS 3; CANR 31; CDALB 1941-1968;
DLB 7; DLBD 4; DLBY 83; MTCW

Williams, Thomas (Alonzo)
1926-1990 . . . . **CLC 14**
See also CA 1-4R; 132; CANR 2

Williams, William C.
See Williams, William Carlos

Williams, William Carlos
1883-1963 . . . . **CLC 1, 2, 5, 9, 13, 22, 42,**
67; DA; DAB; DAC; DAM MST, POET;
PC 7
See also CA 89-92; CANR 34;
CDALB 1917-1929; DLB 4, 16, 54, 86;
MTCW

Williamson, David (Keith) 1942- . . . . **CLC 56**
See also CA 103; CANR 41

Williamson, Ellen Douglas 1905-1984
See Douglas, Ellen
See also CA 17-20R; 114; CANR 39

Williamson, Jack . . . . **CLC 29**
See also Williamson, John Stewart
See also CAAS 8; DLB 8

Williamson, John Stewart 1908-
See Williamson, Jack
See also CA 17-20R; CANR 23

Willie, Frederick
See Lovecraft, H(oward) P(hillips)

Willingham, Calder (Baynard, Jr.)
1922-1995 . . . . **CLC 5, 51**
See also CA 5-8R; 147; CANR 3; DLB 2,
44; MTCW

Willis, Charles
See Clarke, Arthur C(harles)

Willy
See Colette, (Sidonie-Gabrielle)

Willy, Colette
See Colette, (Sidonie-Gabrielle)

Wilson, A(ndrew) N(orman) 1950- . . **CLC 33**
See also CA 112; 122; DLB 14, 155

Wilson, Angus (Frank Johnstone)
1913-1991 . . **CLC 2, 3, 5, 25, 34; SSC 21**
See also CA 5-8R; 134; CANR 21; DLB 15,
139, 155; MTCW

Wilson, August
1945- . . . . **CLC 39, 50, 63; BLC; DA;**
DAB; DAC; DAM DRAM, MST,
MULT; DC 2
See also AAYA 16; BW 2; CA 115; 122;
CANR 42, 54; MTCW; YABC

Wilson, Brian 1942- . . . . **CLC 12**

Wilson, Colin 1931- . . . . **CLC 3, 14**
See also CA 1-4R; CAAS 5; CANR 1, 22,
33; DLB 14; MTCW

Wilson, Dirk
See Pohl, Frederik

Wilson, Edmund
1895-1972 . . . . **CLC 1, 2, 3, 8, 24**
See also CA 1-4R; 37-40R; CANR 1, 46;
DLB 63; MTCW

Wilson, Ethel Davis (Bryant)
1888(?)-1980 . . . . **CLC 13; DAC;**
DAM POET
See also CA 102; DLB 68; MTCW

Wilson, John 1785-1854 . . . . **NCLC 5**

Wilson, John (Anthony) Burgess 1917-1993
See Burgess, Anthony
See also CA 1-4R; 143; CANR 2, 46; DAC;
DAM NOV; MTCW

Wilson, Lanford
1937- . . . . . **CLC 7, 14, 36; DAM DRAM**
See also CA 17-20R; CABS 3; CANR 45;
DLB 7

Wilson, Robert M. 1944- . . . . **CLC 7, 9**
See also CA 49-52; CANR 2, 41; MTCW

Wilson, Robert McLiam 1964- . . . . . **CLC 59**
See also CA 132

Wilson, Sloan 1920- . . . . **CLC 32**
See also CA 1-4R; CANR 1, 44

Wilson, Snoo 1948- . . . . **CLC 33**
See also CA 69-72

Wilson, William S(mith) 1932- . . . . . **CLC 49**
See also CA 81-84

Winchilsea, Anne (Kingsmill) Finch Counte
1661-1720 . . . . **LC 3**

Windham, Basil
See Wodehouse, P(elham) G(renville)

Wingrove, David (John) 1954- . . . . . **CLC 68**
See also CA 133

Wintergreen, Jane
See Duncan, Sara Jeannette

Winters, Janet Lewis . . . . **CLC 41**
See also Lewis, Janet
See also DLBY 87

Winters, (Arthur) Yvor
1900-1968 . . . . **CLC 4, 8, 32**
See also CA 11-12; 25-28R; CAP 1;
DLB 48; MTCW

Winterson, Jeanette
1959- . . . . **CLC 64; DAM POP**
See also CA 136; CANR 58

Winthrop, John 1588-1649 . . . . **LC 31**
See also DLB 24, 30

Wiseman, Frederick 1930- . . . . **CLC 20**

Wister, Owen 1860-1938 . . . . **TCLC 21**
See also CA 108; DLB 9, 78; SATA 62

Witkacy
See Witkiewicz, Stanislaw Ignacy

Witkiewicz, Stanislaw Ignacy
1885-1939 . . . . **TCLC 8**
See also CA 105

Wittgenstein, Ludwig (Josef Johann)
1889-1951 . . . . **TCLC 59**
See also CA 113

Wittig, Monique 1935(?)- . . . . **CLC 22**
See also CA 116; 135; DLB 83

Wittlin, Jozef 1896-1976 . . . . **CLC 25**
See also CA 49-52; 65-68; CANR 3

Wodehouse, P(elham) G(renville)
1881-1975 . . . **CLC 1, 2, 5, 10, 22; DAB;**
DAC; DAM NOV; SSC 2
See also AITN 2; CA 45-48; 57-60;
CANR 3, 33; CDBLB 1914-1945;
DLB 34, 162; MTCW; SATA 22

Yonge, Charlotte (Mary)
    1823-1901 .... TCLC 48
    See also CA 109; DLB 18, 163; SATA 17

York, Jeremy
    See Creasey, John

York, Simon
    See Heinlein, Robert A(nson)

Yorke, Henry Vincent   1905-1974 ... CLC 13
    See also Green, Henry
    See also CA 85-88; 49-52

Yosano Akiko   1878-1942 .. TCLC 59; PC 11

Yoshimoto, Banana .... CLC 84
    See also Yoshimoto, Mahoko

Yoshimoto, Mahoko   1964-
    See Yoshimoto, Banana
    See also CA 144

Young, Al(bert James)
    1939- ..... CLC 19; BLC; DAM MULT
    See also BW 2; CA 29-32R; CANR 26;
    DLB 33

Young, Andrew (John)   1885-1971 .... CLC 5
    See also CA 5-8R; CANR 7, 29

Young, Collier
    See Bloch, Robert (Albert)

Young, Edward   1683-1765 .... LC 3
    See also DLB 95

Young, Marguerite (Vivian)
    1909-1995 .... CLC 82
    See also CA 13-16; 150; CAP 1

Young, Neil   1945- .... CLC 17
    See also CA 110

Young Bear, Ray A.
    1950- .... CLC 94; DAM MULT
    See also CA 146; DLB 175; NNAL

Yourcenar, Marguerite
    1903-1987 .... CLC 19, 38, 50, 87;
                                 DAM NOV
    See also CA 69-72; CANR 23; DLB 72;
    DLBY 88; MTCW

Yurick, Sol   1925- .... CLC 6
    See also CA 13-16R; CANR 25

Zabolotskii, Nikolai Alekseevich
    1903-1958 .... TCLC 52
    See also CA 116

Zamiatin, Yevgenii
    See Zamyatin, Evgeny Ivanovich

Zamora, Bernice (B. Ortiz)
    1938- ..... CLC 89; DAM MULT; HLC
    See also CA 151; DLB 82; HW

Zamyatin, Evgeny Ivanovich
    1884-1937 .... TCLC 8, 37
    See also CA 105

Zangwill, Israel   1864-1926 .... TCLC 16
    See also CA 109; DLB 10, 135

Zappa, Francis Vincent, Jr.   1940-1993
    See Zappa, Frank
    See also CA 108; 143; CANR 57

Zappa, Frank .... CLC 17
    See also Zappa, Francis Vincent, Jr.

Zaturenska, Marya   1902-1982 .... CLC 6, 11
    See also CA 13-16R; 105; CANR 22

Zeami   1363-1443 .... DC 7

Zelazny, Roger (Joseph)
    1937-1995 .... CLC 21
    See also AAYA 7; CA 21-24R; 148;
    CANR 26; DLB 8; MTCW; SATA 57;
    SATA-Brief 39

Zhdanov, Andrei A(lexandrovich)
    1896-1948 .... TCLC 18
    See also CA 117

Zhukovsky, Vasily   1783-1852 .... NCLC 35

Ziegenhagen, Eric .... CLC 55

Zimmer, Jill Schary
    See Robinson, Jill

Zimmerman, Robert
    See Dylan, Bob

Zindel, Paul
    1936- ..... CLC 6, 26; DA; DAB; DAC;
                DAM DRAM, MST, NOV; DC 5
    See also AAYA 2; CA 73-76; CANR 31;
    CLR 3, 45; DLB 7, 52; JRDA; MAICYA;
    MTCW; SATA 16, 58

Zinov'Ev, A. A.
    See Zinoviev, Alexander (Aleksandrovich)

Zinoviev, Alexander (Aleksandrovich)
    1922- .... CLC 19
    See also CA 116; 133; CAAS 10

Zoilus
    See Lovecraft, H(oward) P(hillips)

Zola, Emile (Edouard Charles Antoine)
    1840-1902 ...... TCLC 1, 6, 21, 41; DA;
                DAB; DAC; DAM MST, NOV; WLC
    See also CA 104; 138; DLB 123

Zoline, Pamela   1941- .... CLC 62

Zorrilla y Moral, Jose   1817-1893 .. NCLC 6

Zoshchenko, Mikhail (Mikhailovich)
    1895-1958 .... TCLC 15; SSC 15
    See also CA 115

Zuckmayer, Carl   1896-1977 .... CLC 18
    See also CA 69-72; DLB 56, 124

Zuk, Georges
    See Skelton, Robin

Zukofsky, Louis
    1904-1978 .... CLC 1, 2, 4, 7, 11, 18;
                            DAM POET; PC 11
    See also CA 9-12R; 77-80; CANR 39;
    DLB 5, 165; MTCW

Zweig, Paul   1935-1984 .... CLC 34, 42
    See also CA 85-88; 113

Zweig, Stefan   1881-1942 .... TCLC 17
    See also CA 112; DLB 81, 118

Zwingli, Huldreich   1484-1531 .... LC 37
    See also DLB 179

Literary Criticism Series
Cumulative Topic Index

This index lists all topic entries in Gale's *Classical and Medieval Literature Criticism, Contemporary Literary Criticism, Literature Criticism from 1400 to 1800, Nineteenth-Century Literature Criticism,* and *Twentieth-Century Literary Criticism.*

Wyndham Lewis and Vorticism, 330-8
characteristics and principles of
    Vorticism, 338-65
Lewis and Pound, 365-82
Vorticist writing, 382-416
Vorticist painting, 416-26

Women's Diaries, Nineteenth-Century
NCLC 48: 308-
54
    overview, 308-13
    diary as history, 314-25
    sociology of diaries, 325-34
    diaries as psychological scholarship, 334-
        43
    diary as autobiography, 343-8
    diary as literature, 348-53

Women Writers, Seventeenth-Century
LC 30: 2-58
    overview, 2-15
    women and education, 15-9
    women and autobiography, 19-31
    women's diaries, 31-9
    early feminists, 39-58

World War I Literature TCLC 34: 392-486
    overview, 393-403
    English, 403-27
    German, 427-50
    American, 450-66
    French, 466-74
    and modern history, 474-82

Yellow Journalism NCLC 36: 383-456
    overviews, 384-96
    major figures, 396-413

Young Playwrights Festival
    1988—CLC 55: 376-81
    1989—CLC 59: 398-403
    1990—CLC 65: 444-8

Twentieth-Century Literary Criticism
Cumulative Nationality Index

AMERICAN

Adams, Andy **56**
Adams, Henry (Brooks) **4, 52**
Agee, James (Rufus) **1, 19**
Anderson, Maxwell **2**
Anderson, Sherwood **1, 10, 24**
Atherton, Gertrude (Franklin Horn) **2**
Austin, Mary (Hunter) **25**
Baker, Ray Stannard **47**
Barry, Philip **11**
Baum, L(yman) Frank **7**
Beard, Charles A(ustin) **15**
Becker, Carl (Lotus) **63**
Belasco, David **3**
Bell, James Madison **43**
Benchley, Robert (Charles) **1, 55**
Benedict, Ruth (Fulton) **60**
Benet, Stephen Vincent **7**
Benet, William Rose **28**
Bierce, Ambrose (Gwinett) **1, 7, 44**
Biggers, Earl Derr **65**
Black Elk **33**
Boas, Franz **56**
Bodenheim, Maxwell **44**
Bourne, Randolph S(illiman) **16**
Bradford, Gamaliel **36**
Brennan, Christopher John **17**
Bromfield, Louis (Brucker) **11**
Burroughs, Edgar Rice **2, 32**
Cabell, James Branch **6**
Cable, George Washington **4**
Cahan, Abraham **71**
Cardozo, Benjamin N(athan) **65**
Carnegie, Dale **53**
Cather, Willa Sibert **1, 11, 31**
Chambers, Robert W. **41**
Chandler, Raymond (Thornton) **1, 7**
Chapman, John Jay **7**
Chesnutt, Charles W(addell) **5, 39**
Chopin, Kate **5, 14**
Cohan, George M. **60**
Comstock, Anthony **13**
Cotter, Joseph Seamon Sr. **28**
Cram, Ralph Adams **45**
Crane, (Harold) Hart **2, 5**
Crane, Stephen (Townley) **11, 17, 32**
Crawford, F(rancis) Marion **10**
Crothers, Rachel **19**
Cullen, Countee **4, 37**
Davis, Rebecca (Blaine) Harding **6**
Davis, Richard Harding **24**
Day, Clarence (Shepard Jr.) **25**
Dent, Lester **72**
De Voto, Bernard (Augustine) **29**
Dreiser, Theodore (Herman Albert) **10, 18, 35**
Dulles, John Foster **72**
Dunbar, Paul Laurence **2, 12**
Duncan, Isadora **68**
Dunne, Finley Peter **28**

Eastman, Charles A(lexander) **55**
Eddy, Mary (Morse) Baker **71**
Einstein, Albert **65**
Faust, Frederick (Schiller) **49**
Fisher, Rudolph **11**
Fitzgerald, F(rancis) Scott (Key) **1, 6, 14, 28, 55**
Fitzgerald, Zelda (Sayre) **52**
Flecker, (Herman) James Elroy **43**
Fletcher, John Gould **35**
Forten, Charlotte L. **16**
Freeman, Douglas Southall **11**
Freeman, Mary Eleanor Wilkins **9**
Futrelle, Jacques **19**
Gale, Zona **7**
Garland, (Hannibal) Hamlin **3**
Gilman, Charlotte (Anna) Perkins (Stetson) **9, 37**
Glasgow, Ellen (Anderson Gholson) **2, 7**
Glaspell, Susan **55**
Goldman, Emma **13**
Green, Anna Katharine **63**
Grey, Zane **6**
Griffith, D(avid Lewelyn) W(ark) **68**
Guiney, Louise Imogen **41**
Hall, James Norman **23**
Harper, Frances Ellen Watkins **14**
Harris, Joel Chandler **2**
Harte, (Francis) Bret(t) **1, 25**
Hatteras, Owen **18**
Hawthorne, Julian **25**
Hearn, (Patricio) Lafcadio (Tessima Carlos) **9**
Henry, O. **1, 19**
Hergesheimer, Joseph **11**
Higginson, Thomas Wentworth **36**
Holly, Buddy **65**
Hopkins, Pauline Elizabeth **28**
Horney, Karen (Clementine Theodore Danielsen) **71**
Howard, Robert E(rvin) **8**
Howe, Julia Ward **21**
Howells, William Dean **7, 17, 41**
Huneker, James Gibbons **65**
James, Henry **2, 11, 24, 40, 47, 64**
James, William **15, 32**
Jewett, (Theodora) Sarah Orne **1, 22**
Johnson, James Weldon **3, 19**
Johnson, Robert **69**
Kornbluth, C(yril) M. **8**
Korzybski, Alfred (Habdank Skarbek) **61**
Kuttner, Henry **10**
Lardner, Ring(gold) W(ilmer) **2, 14**
Lewis, (Harry) Sinclair **4, 13, 23, 39**
Lewisohn, Ludwig **19**
Lindsay, (Nicholas) Vachel **17**
Locke, Alain (Le Roy) **43**
London, Jack **9, 15, 39**
Lovecraft, H(oward) P(hillips) **4, 22**
Lowell, Amy **1, 8**

Markham, Edwin **47**
Marquis, Don(ald Robert Perry) **7**
Masters, Edgar Lee **2, 25**
McCoy, Horace (Stanley) **28**
McKay, Claude **7, 41**
Mencken, H(enry) L(ouis) **13**
Millay, Edna St. Vincent· **4, 49**
Mitchell, Margaret (Munnerlyn) **11**
Mitchell, S(ilas) Weir **36**
Monroe, Harriet **12**
Muir, John **28**
Nathan, George Jean **18**
Nordhoff, Charles (Bernard) **23**
Norris, Benjamin Franklin Jr. **24**
O'Neill, Eugene (Gladstone) **1, 6, 27, 49**
Oskison, John Milton **35**
Phillips, David Graham **44**
Porter, Gene(va Grace) Stratton **21**
Post, Melville Davisson **39**
Rawlings, Marjorie Kinnan **4**
Reed, John (Silas) **9**
Reich, Wilhelm **57**
Rhodes, Eugene Manlove **53**
Riggs, (Rolla) Lynn **56**
Riley, James Whitcomb **51**
Rinehart, Mary Roberts **52**
Roberts, Elizabeth Madox **68**
Roberts, Kenneth (Lewis) **23**
Robinson, Edwin Arlington **5**
Roelvaag, O(le) E(dvart) **17**
Rogers, Will(iam Penn Adair) **8, 71**
Roosevelt, Theodore **69**
Rourke, Constance (Mayfield) **12**
Runyon, (Alfred) Damon **10**
Saltus, Edgar (Everton) **8**
Santayana, George **40**
Sherwood, Robert E(mmet) **3**
Slesinger, Tess **10**
Steffens, (Joseph) Lincoln **20**
Stein, Gertrude **1, 6, 28, 48**
Sterling, George **20**
Stevens, Wallace **3, 12, 45**
Stockton, Frank R. **47**
Stroheim, Erich von **71**
Sturges, Preston **48**
Tarbell, Ida M(inerva) **40**
Tarkington, (Newton) Booth **9**
Teasdale, Sara **4**
Thurman, Wallace (Henry) **6**
Twain, Mark **6, 12, 19, 36, 48, 59**
Van Dine, S. S. **23**
Van Doren, Carl (Clinton) **18**
Veblen, Thorstein (Bunde) **31**
Washington, Booker T(aliaferro) **10**
Wells, Carolyn **35**
West, Nathanael **1, 14, 44**
Whale, James **63**
Wharton, Edith (Newbold Jones) **3, 9, 27, 53**
White, Walter F(rancis) **15**

Salinas (y Serrano), Pedro **17**
Unamuno (y Jugo), Miguel de **2, 9**
Valera y Alcala-Galiano, Juan **10**
Valle-Inclan, Ramon (Maria) del **5**

SWEDISH
Bengtsson, Frans (Gunnar) **48**
Dagerman, Stig (Halvard) **17**
Heidenstam, (Carl Gustaf) Verner von **5**
Key, Ellen **65**
Lagerloef, Selma (Ottiliana Lovisa) **4, 36**
Soderberg, Hjalmar **39**
Strindberg, (Johan) August **1, 8, 21, 47**

SWISS
Ramuz, Charles-Ferdinand **33**
Rod, Edouard **52**
Saussure, Ferdinand de **49**
Spitteler, Carl (Friedrich Georg) **12**
Walser, Robert **18**

SYRIAN
Gibran, Kahlil **1, 9**

TURKISH
Sait Faik **23**

UKRAINIAN
Aleichem, Sholom **1, 35**
Bialik, Chaim Nachman **25**

URUGUAYAN
Quiroga, Horacio (Sylvestre) **20**
Sanchez, Florencio **37**

WELSH
Davies, W(illiam) H(enry) **5**
Lewis, Alun **3**
Machen, Arthur **4**
Thomas, Dylan (Marlais) **1, 8, 45**

Nationality Index

ISBN 0-7876-1172-7

90000